MW01687179

Children with Exceptionalities in Canadian Classrooms

fourth edition

MARGRET WINZER

UNIVERSITY OF LETHBRIDGE

Allyn & Bacon Canada

Scarborough, Ontario

Canadian Cataloguing in Publication Data

Winzer, Margret,
Children with exceptionalities in Canadian classrooms

4th ed.
Third ed. published under title: Children with exceptionalities:
a Canadian perspective.
ISBN 0-205-19636-5

1. Special education — Canada. 2. Exceptional children — Canada.
I. Title. II. Title: Children with exceptionalities: a Canadian perspective.

LC3984.W56 1995 371.9'0971 C95-932657-X

A Division of the Simon & Schuster Publishing Higher Education Group
1870 Birchmount Road
Scarborough, Ontario, M1P 2J7

ISBN 0–205–19636–5

Executive Editor: Clifford J. Newman
Managing Editor: Marta Tomins
Production Editor: Imogen Brian
Copy Editor: Jocelyn Smyth
Production Coordinator: Anita Boyle-Evans
Cover Design: Monica Kompter
Cover Image: Helen D'Souza
Page Layout: Heather Brunton/ArtPlus Limited

3 4 5 00 99 98 97

Printed and bound in the United States

Table of Contents

SECTION 7: Parents and Families 541

Preface

Children with Exceptionalities is designed to serve as a comprehensive introduction to children with exceptionalities in Canada and to Canadian special education. It is intended to be a practical and readily understandable guide for those who are studying the problems of these children for the first time as well as a resource for more advanced students. The text is useful for both education and psychology courses. It should interest students who are involved in special education, regular education, early childhood education and early childhood special education, rehabilitation, nursing, social work, and allied child-care disciplines such as audiology, speech therapy, and language pathology.

The text is essentially designed to present portraits of children with exceptionalities within Canadian special education. Although Canadian special education shares much with that of other countries in both its historical development and contemporary practice, there is also much that is unique and special to the Canadian situation. This text sets out to capture the flavour of the Canadian services, to provide recognition of considerable Canadian achievements in the field, and to detail the exciting new advances that are occurring.

All of those involved in any way with children and education require knowledge of the philosophies, practices, and policies that determine the care and education of children with special needs in this country. This book aims to open a window on the Canadian experience through which students may discover the depth of the concern and care for children with exceptionalities being manifested in Canada. Right across this vast country, the needs of special children are being served in innovative and creative ways.

Efforts are being made to serve all children, regardless of the degree and type of their exceptional condition, in regular neighbourhood schools and regular classrooms. This is happening in small rural districts as well as in large urban centres, enabling children with disabilities to remain with their families in their home communities. While this text is founded on the proposition that no two children are alike and that individualization is the essence of special education, it also promotes the inclusion of all children into regular education milieus.

This text is devoted to the portrayal of children with exceptionalities as learners with special needs rather than to generic or specific teaching and instructional practices. Those hoping to intervene with children with exceptionalities must understand the unique difficulties faced by such children, the developmental consequences of various disabilities, and the multiple types of intervention necessary to accommodate them effectively in local schools. With a strong base of understanding and knowledge, teachers and others can build specific educational and therapeutic interventions suited to the unique needs of each particular child.

Throughout this text a categorical approach is adopted. Not only is this the most practical and logical manner in which to organize such a huge body of information, but it allows a focus on the specific needs of diverse groups of children who require additional educational, medical, and therapeutic services.

A number of improvements and revisions distinguish the fourth edition. Even as the stress remains on the children, much more has been added about schooling, curriculum, and individualization. This aligns with emerging philosophies regarding inclusion and the need for every classroom teacher to be aware of methods, approaches, and techniques that enhance the learning of all students. Because of the new emphasis in special education on preschool special education, transition, and the adult experience of disabled persons, two new chapters focusing on these areas have been added. Different types of special education for children from diverse cultural backgrounds are also an emerging and exciting area in contemporary special education, and we have revised the chapter on cultural diversity to reflect new trends.

While contemporary special education is replete with new movements and trends, all designed to serve children more effectively, many of these trends remain controversial and even contentious. In this age of greater teacher accountability and increased teacher decision making it is vital that those within the profession and those aspiring to join it fully understand the debates circulating in the field so that they can justify their own practice and explain it to others. New sections that are designed to present both sides of certain relevant debates have been added to this edition. Given the research base and their own readings and dicussions, we hope that teachers and students will arrive at their own reasoned decisions on these issues.

A multidisciplinary approach is maintained throughout the text; particular attention is paid to the medical, psychological, sociological, and educational aspects of the various categories of exceptionality. Within each chapter, the reader will find material dealing with etiology; developmental consequences; definitions and classification; prevalence; identification and measurement; and educational, medical, and technical interventions for each type of condition.

Each chapter includes developmental profiles as concrete illustrations of issues covered in the text. Individual programs for specific children as well as tips for teachers add to the profiles. Glossary terms are marked for ease of reference. Chapters also feature research notes that present the newest research and findings in relevant areas.

Supplemental Teaching and Learning Aids

A Student Workbook accompanies the text. This workbook, completely rewritten to accompany the fourth edition, is designed as a study guide for students and contains key terms, concepts and names, and summaries of each chapter. Review questions assist students in studying the material. Application questions and activities allow students to pursue areas of interest and research arising from the material presented. Additional supplements are an Instructor's Manual, a Test Item File and a Computerized Test Item File.

Acknowledgments

Many people contributed to the preparation of this text. I would like to acknowledge all the students who contributed in different ways. The students at the University of Lethbridge were generous in discussing, criticizing, and offering suggestions for improvements to the text and the student workbook. I am particularly indebted to Helen Taylor, whose assistance was invaluable. Her graciousness, humour, and organizational skills are deeply appreciated.

Marta Tomins of Allyn & Bacon Canada and Jocelyn Smith similarly deserve my gratitude, Jocelyn for her excellent editorial work and Marta for her patience and kindness throughout this enterprise. As well, many people from across the country have written to me over the past few years with valuable advice that I deeply appreciate.

This book is written for my mother

SECTION 1

Introduction and Overview

In a philosophical and humanitarian sense, all children are special. All children have certain strengths and weaknesses, their own particular pattern of inter- and intra-individual differences. In most children, however, the strengths outweigh the weaknesses. In this text, we are concerned with the other children, those for whom the balance of strengths and weaknesses may tip a different way.

This book is about **children with exceptionalities**, those who have difficulty in realizing their full human potential. Their intellectual, emotional, physical, or social performance falls below or rises above that of other children. The differences may be related to physical, psychological, cognitive, emotional, or social factors, or a combination of these.

In the past few decades, the prospects for children who are exceptional have altered dramatically. We have made major gains in our ability to provide sophisticated services for individuals who are exceptional. In medicine, great strides have been made in the prevention of handicapping conditions, in intervention to ameliorate them, and in the care of children who must live with them. Closely linked to medicine, technological advances have provided a variety of adaptive devices and aids to help individuals with disabilities. In education, significant philosophical changes are occurring in the areas of school responsibility, program delivery, and program implementation for special education. For students with special needs, the most fundamental social change of recent decades has been the clear and unequivocal statement of the responsibility of educational authorities to provide all children equal access to an education in the manner most appropriate to their needs. As the concept of equal educational opportunities for children with special needs has become a dominant ideology, provincial governments and local school boards are increasingly obliged to develop appropriate programs for the entire school-aged population in the province. Outside the field of education, exceptional individuals are coming to be seen in a more positive light. Throughout Canada, public policies are changing as the authorities increasingly seek to develop the potential of individuals who are disabled and to make better use of their aptitudes.

This section of the text is designed to introduce children with exceptionalities, special education, and some general principles and practices that are germane to the care and education of individuals who are exceptional. The first chapter introduces the topic of exceptionality and children and adolescents who are seen to be exceptional within the school system. We consider the recognized exceptionalities and the ways in which students with special needs are educated.

Research attests that teachers and others who hold a clear understanding of exceptional conditions tend to be more tolerant and accepting than those who know little about etiologies and developmental consequences. In Chapter 2 we discuss why children manifest certain conditions that hinder their learning and development, and detail causes (etiologies) of certain conditions.

Educational services and the ideas that stimulate and direct their growth are never static. Changing needs lead to the formulation of new policies, legislation, and other administrative arrangements and practices. Nowhere is this more true than in the field of special education. In areas such as legislation, school placements, assessment, and teaching methodologies and approaches, today's special education is in a state of flux. Nearly all advocates for students with disabilities want "appropriate education in the least restrictive environment; public education that accommodates students with special problems; labels that carry the least possible social stigma; parental participation in decisions to provide special services; and collaboration among all service providers" (Kauffman, 1993). How these ends are to be achieved remains the subject of debate, and special education is grappling with innovative approaches and new forms of collaboration. Chapter 3 explores some of the major issues, trends, and movements that surround special education and exceptionality, with particular emphasis on the trend toward inclusive schooling and what it means to classroom teachers.

CHAPTER 1

Introduction to Children Who Are Exceptional

Historical Notes

Society's attitude toward persons with disabilities has always been complex, fashioned at any given time by the prevailing culture, religion, government, and economic conditions. The care and training of exceptional individuals has followed historical trends, rather than creating them.

The history of disability extends far back in time. Disabled persons were mentioned by the ancient Egyptians, Greeks, and Romans, and in the Bible. The greatest attention was directed toward those considered mad or insane, although this population included persons with mental retardation and those with epilepsy. Hippocrates and the Roman physicians Galen and Celsus also intervened in cases of people with deafness, blindness, and overt physical disabilities. The history of special education has a far briefer life span. Although the first documented reports of intervention with special students comes from late-sixteenth-century Spain, it was not until the middle decades of the eighteenth century that Britain and Europe turned their attention to the education of their disabled populations.

Until the mid-1700s, handicapped individuals were rarely looked upon with humane concern. Although the historical record is murky, it seems that from humanity's earliest beginnings, disabled persons have been grossly mistreated. Through many ages, their conditions were considered hopeless, and in most cultures, they were scorned as degraded and inferior beings.

Beginning in the fourth century, the Church assumed some responsibility for exceptional people. Hospices for the blind were established and the clergy began systematically to provide asylums for the less fortunate members of society. Like monasteries, these asylums followed a cloistered routine and offered protection from the cruelty of the outside world. However, asylums cared for only a few of the handicapped; the rest led degraded lives as beggars and outcasts.

The Renaissance concern with observation and scientific enquiry was accompanied by a new interest in education and humanitarianism, which ushered in a newer and marginally brighter era for handicapped persons. At the same time, there was a growing recognition of childhood as a special and distinct stage of development. Although there were advances during this period, education was still within the reach of only a favoured few. Most disabled individuals were abandoned to their age-old condition of wretchedness and degradation, while the majority of the public continued to take a moralistic view of the conditions as punishment for sin.

In the mid-1700s, Europeans turned for the first time to the systematic care and education of their handicapped populations. In France, a new social philosophy, ushered in by Enlightenment thought, brought about major educational advances. The social philosophers of France, the *philosophes*, took as their major source the empirical philosophy of the English physician and thinker John Locke (1632-1708).

Locke abandoned the notion that children were born with innate characteristics, imprinted on the soul before birth by God, nature, or the devil. Rather, he saw the child as a blank slate, a *tabula rasa* on which all experiences and sensations systematically made impressions. This empirical philosophy was enthusiastically embraced in France by the major thinkers of the Enlightenment — Rousseau, Diderot, Condillac, Voltaire — and many others, and precipitated much of the thought of the broad intellectual movement known as the French Enlightenment (Seigel, 1969). The pioneer French educators adopted the concepts of sensationalism, the psychology of language, and alternate sensory stimuli, and joined them to the new concepts of social equality and individual rights. These French educators took seriously the special needs of the handicapped and emerged as the founders of special education as we know it today.

With advances in schooling, the history of disability and the history of special education tended to merge. Schooling brought the special needs and the unique potentialities of disabled persons more into the public view and demonstrated that such people could learn and become productive citizens. This is not to imply that rapid advances occurred in the general status of people with disabilities in society. What it does say is that it was the nascent beginnings of a new humanitarian impulse that is only reaching fruition today. Throughout this text, we briefly explore the ways in which social attitudes slowly changed to provide more equal and normal lifestyles for persons with disabilities.

All children differ from one another to varying degrees. The colour of their eyes, hair, and skin differs; the way they dress and speak differs; and their physical, cognitive, social, and emotional development and skills differ. Every child possesses a unique combination of abilities and problems, interests and fears, successes and failures. These individual differences fall along a continuum and are characteristic of all humans.

We all have certain strengths, we all have some limitations on our mental and physical ability, and we all have some disabilities, however minor, when it comes to learning. Most of these problems fall into common areas — a tendency to be easily bored, distractibility, poor study habits, poor memory, inadequate motor control, family interference, and so on. Some of us have problems learning a foreign language, others forget directions or people's faces. For most of us, a perfect backhand is an unreachable goal.

Good teachers always adapt to learning differences and minor learning difficulties.

For the majority of people, the problems are not extreme. In classroom situations, teachers do not expect every student to learn the same things at the same pace, with the same materials, in the same time, and with the same amount of instruction. Good teachers always adapt to learning differences and minor learning difficulties.

In some students, the learning disabilities are more serious and the children deviate more significantly in one way or another. These are youngsters who are exceptional, those whose learning and behaviour deviates significantly from the norm. They may show differences in the physical, intellectual, communicative, social, or emotional domains, or in some combination of these.

Because the child with an exceptionality is different from the average in some or many areas of functioning, the study of children with exceptionalities is the study of differences. However, it would be quite wrong to focus the study of these children solely on differences. It is equally important that the similarities among children be given significant emphasis.

Children with exceptionalities do not differ in every way from their normally developing peers. They are children first and exceptional second. Individuals with exceptionalities share many attitudes, needs, and perceptions with everyone else. They desire acceptance, approval, and affection as much as do their non-exceptional peers. These similarities are important, and we must always be aware of the danger of seeing only the disability and losing sight of how much children with exceptional conditions resemble other children.

Differences, similarities, and diversity make the study of exceptionality a difficult undertaking. Many times, we are unable to make definitive statements about groups of children with the same exceptionality or even about a single child. Psychologists have not yet unravelled the mysteries of normal child development, so it is not surprising that many of the aspects of atypical child development remain unclear.

One commonality found in children and youth with exceptionalities is the need for skilled intervention and special care from trained professionals. Intervention may take many forms — medical, technical, therapeutic, and educational. In an educational context, children are considered exceptional only when their educational program must be altered to meet their unique needs. They must demonstrate a clear need for support to reach their full potential.

Special education means instruction that is specially designed to meet the unique needs of children and youth who are exceptional. Special education is provided for many students displaying disparate characteristics. It encompasses students who are having problems adjusting to the regular school curriculum and those who encounter difficulties in conforming to the social needs of the classroom. Some exceptional pupils may require specific physical adaptations in the classroom and the school environment. Gifted and talented children are recognized as exceptional because they too need specialized help from professionals to fully develop their gifts and talents.

The things that make special education special are done by good teachers every day.

Until quite recently, special education was chiefly identified with the school system and with school-age children and their teachers. This is no longer true. In the past two decades, special education has expanded dramatically. It now includes infants and preschoolers and reaches up to encompass adolescents and young adults. As well, recent demographic data suggest that public schools are faced with increasing linguistic and cultural diversity. One result of this change is that the special education system is increasingly serving students who are in the process of acquiring a second language or who come from home backgrounds where a language other than English is spoken. Today special education could be a mother using sign language with her deaf infant in the home, a caregiver in a nursery school modifying an activity for a preschooler, a classroom teacher using remedial techniques in the schoolroom, a counsellor setting up a work experience program for a young disabled adult, or a teacher assisting a child from a linguistic minority.

Special education is founded on the proposition that all children can reach their full potential given the opportunity, effective teaching, and proper resources. Both traditionally and currently, special education has been undertaken by different personnel in different settings. A few children may be placed in special schools or special classrooms with specially trained teachers. Others may be in the regular classroom with adapted or modified instruction and with special assistance in the resource room. Today, the majority of students with exceptionalities are in regular classrooms, with instruction generally presented by classroom teachers who are increasingly required to tailor classroom instruction to the individual, not the group.

Although the onus for direct instruction is increasingly being placed on teachers, these teachers are not alone in their efforts. Psychologists, speech therapists, physical and occupational therapists, counsellors, and other professionals consult and collaborate with teachers to help them to plan the best possible education for each student who is exceptional. These people form part of what is referred to as ancillary services, auxiliary services, the interdisciplinary team, or the inclusion team. We use the broad term **related services** to refer to those services that permit an exceptional child to benefit from special education. A sampling of the disciplines that may be involved is shown in Table 1-1.

Table 1-1

A sampling of disciplines involved with exceptional children

Medical	Paramedical	Educational	Psychological, social, behavioural
physician	audiologist	home-visiting teacher	intervenor
pediatrician	optometrist	infant stimulation therapist	social worker
neurologist	physical therapist	preschool teacher	school social worker
otolaryngologist	occupational therapist	regular classroom teacher	child care worker
ophthalmologist	public health nurse	special class teacher	guidance counsellor
dental surgeon	school nurse	remedial specialist	psychologist
psychiatrist		itinerant teacher	
nurse		learning assistant	
		school principal	
		speech therapist	
		language pathologist	
		aide	
		volunteer	

Development of the Field

In 1855, Harvey Peet, a special educator, wrote that "every child capable of instruction has a claim on the community for the best means of moral and mental cultivation" (Peet, 1855, p.22). When these words were written, special education in North America was little more than thirty years old. A few institutions to serve the special needs of the exceptional population were scattered across the country, but the enterprise was barely consolidated, and tenuous at best. Teachers were drawn chiefly from the ranks of the clergy and special education was viewed as a philanthropic undertaking, tangential to the major educational thrust.

Yet Peet, principal of the New York Institution for the Deaf and Dumb, expressed remarkably modern sentiments that would be echoed over and over again in the next hundred years. His call for universal education for all children, exceptionality notwithstanding, was perhaps not truly answered until 1975 and the passage of PL94-142, the Education of All Handicapped Children Act, in the United States and the adoption of similar legislation and policy in Canada.

In its development, special education has taken a fascinating journey, its route illuminated by many brilliant and often controversial pioneers. The advances toward today's propitious climate have been slow and halting, with many stops and detours along the route. Too often, the way was littered with divisiveness and confusion, overlapping services, some pseudo-scientific programs and projects, lack of proper co-ordination, inaccurate classification of children, and much literary licence concerning definitions (Frampton and Gall, 1955).

North American special education began in 1817 with the founding of an institution for deaf students at Hartford, Connecticut. The first Canadian special school, again for the deaf, opened near Montreal in 1831, but lack of funds forced it to close within five years and it was not until 1848 that permanent residential schools were established in British North America. At that period, exceptional persons were thought to differ qualitatively and quantitatively from other people; they were thought to have traits and characteristics of a degree and type that made them fundamentally different from the general run of humanity. Because of this, and for reasons of economy and convenience, exceptional students were chiefly educated in institutional settings.

Within the institutional complex, very few children were actually served. Differentiation among exceptional conditions was murky, and energies were directed to those with obvious and overt handicaps. Schooling was open to children with sensory handicaps (the deaf and the blind); to those with intellectual problems (known then as the idiotic and the feeble-minded); and to those considered to be socially at risk (vagrant, neglected and delinquent children). A concern for children with mild handicaps and the emergence of categories such as emotionally disturbed, childhood psychoses, physical and health handicaps, and learning disabilities, was largely a phenomenon of the twentieth century.

Students with mild handicaps came to the attention of educators when compulsory school laws were rigorously enforced in the opening decades of the twentieth century and the school system was challenged to find ways to accommodate students with behaviour and learning problems. Advances in medicine and psychology contributed to clearer differentiations among disabling conditions and led to new labels and to new categories of children seen as needing special services.

Special segregated classes within the public schools expanded rapidly in the first half of the twentieth century. However, the 1950s brought vexatious questioning of the value of special education and the 1960s saw a series of efficacy studies that further probed just what special education was achieving. By the 1970s, the dual philosophies of normalization and mainstreaming impelled many children with mild to severe disabilities into the orbit of the public schools.

Harvey Peet and his contemporaries who so vehemently extolled special education in the last century would surely have been pleased at the current propitious climate. Today, special education is an exciting professional area, alive with new ideas. It is no longer an unknown quantity, a poor cousin of regular education. In the past few years, special education has come of age as a vital component of the public education system. It has broadened its scope and drawn many more children into the orbit of the public schools. It has also faced teachers with new challenges and assigned them new roles.

Definitions of Students Who Are Exceptional

Children who have differences that substantially change the way they learn, respond, or behave have been described in many ways. In fact, you will find these children referred to as children with exceptionalities, children with exceptional conditions, children who are handicapped, children with special needs, and children with disabilities or disabling conditions. All of these terms are used more or less interchangeably, although the term *children with exceptionalities* tends to be the most encompassing.

Exceptionality can be defined and described in many ways that constantly change in attempts to make descriptors more socially useful and relevant. Today's terminology, both specific and general, is relatively non-stigmatizing. For example, we no longer use emotionally laden and essentially incorrect terms such as "deaf and dumb" or "feeble-minded." We know that deaf people are not dumb in any way and that people who are intellectually challenged in our society can learn and contribute.

Today we hold a more humanistic perception of the whole individual and see the handicap, disorder, or disability as only one part of the total person. We use terms that place the child first, the disability second. Hence, we speak of children with Down syndrome or children with intellectual disabilities rather than of "Down-syndrome children" and "mentally disabled children." Such flexibility in labelling leaves us free to develop systems that describe or profile children's behaviour patterns and moves the field closer to the development of systems in which the descriptions of children's needs, not etiological labels, drive intervention efforts (Bricker, 1993).

Both conceptual and operational definitions appear in the special education lexicon. A **conceptual definition** is a statement that describes a condition theoretically. Conceptual definitions are important because one must have a clear idea of what a condition is before one can identify the condition in individuals. Conceptual definitions are also the first step toward the development of **operational definitions** that can be used in everyday situations to identify students who have certain disabilities (Hammill, 1990) and to guide assessment of their eligibility for special education.

Precise definitions of individual handicapping conditions are the vital first step in providing solid rationales for generating theories, formulating hypotheses, classifying disorders, selecting subjects, communicating with others (Hammill, 1990), and obtaining accurate prevalence figures.

Nevertheless, the search for precise definitions is ongoing in the fields of exceptionality and special education. Children who are exceptional are constantly being reconceptualized, reconsidered, and renamed. In fact, the area of disability and handicap is characterized by conceptual chaos. Such chaos is perhaps inevitable, given the broad range of disciplines providing information and input, the various classification systems, the ongoing changes in terminology, and the continuing discovery of new etiologies.

Many disciplines contribute to research and intervention for exceptional children — education, social work, medicine, genetics, and psychology are only a few. The professionals allied with special education tend to have different ways of looking at exceptionalities, and therefore they tend to use a slightly different framework for classification. Some researchers assess differences according to how development deviates from the norm. Others classify differences in terms of some underlying organic or functional cause, while still others describe them in terms of educational functioning and achievement.

The educational use of the term *exceptional* differs from that used in biology, medicine, psychology, social work, and other disciplines. Educators use *exceptional* as an inclusive term that encompasses gifted children as well as those who function below the norm in some way. Within the school system, children are only considered exceptional if they require special education.

Nor is *exceptional* the only term used to describe these children. Together with a plethora of definitions, varied terminology has been spawned over the years. Other terms are used synonymously with *exceptional*, although the meanings are more restricted and slightly different. **Impairments** are concerned with abnormalities of body structure and system function resulting from any cause. **Disabilities** reflect the consequences of impairments in terms of functional performance and activity by the individual; a **disabled individual** suffers from a disability or impairment of function in one or more areas, such as vision, hearing, or mobility (World Health, 1980, p.14). In other words, a disability refers to the behaviour relevant to the completion of a task and obviously implies a limited aptitude in that task.

Handicaps are concerned with the disadvantages experienced by individuals as a result of impairments or disability and reflect an interaction of the individual with the environment (World Health, 1980). A **handicap**, then, refers to environmental or functional demands placed on a disabled person in a particular situation that are not met. A disability is always with a person, a handicap is not. A disability becomes a handicap when the disabled person is unable to meet environmental demands and achieve personal goals. For example, a bright child with spina bifida could function well in math class but would be handicapped on the ball field.

Atypical youngsters are those who do not reach the norm in some functional area or areas. **Special needs** is an educational term used to designate pupils who require special education.

The terms **high risk** or **at risk** are widely used in contemporary special education. Risk status is a mechanism for describing the likelihood that a particular individual will experience a specific outcome, given certain conditions (Planta, 1990). When the term *at risk* is used, children are seen to be vulnerable to some future condition. Some children are at risk for exceptional conditions that affect their functioning and achievement. Or a child may be at risk for learning and behavioural problems as a result of factors such as poverty or abuse, psychological disorders, or generally having an unproductive and unrewarding childhood. Older students may be at risk for dropping out of school or for delinquency.

Increasingly, and with varied levels of precision, the terms *developmental delay* and *developmental disability* are employed in special education. When the construct of developmental disability was introduced in 1970 with the passage of the United States Public Law 91-517, the original legislation included only individuals suffering mental retardation, epilepsy, and cerebral palsy. Amendments in 1978 broadened the concept. Today, a **developmental delay** is

> a condition which represents a significant delay in the process of development. It does not refer to a condition in which a child is slightly or momentarily lagging in development or is "at-risk" of a delay. The presence of a developmental delay is an indication that the process of development is significantly affected and that without special intervention, it is likely that educational performance at school age will be affected ("Developmental," 1991, p. 1).

Developmentally disabled individuals are those who suffer from chronic disabilities, attributable to mental and or physical impairments that are manifested before age twenty-two and that result in functional limitations in major life activities requiring special services and treatment that are of extended duration or are lifelong.

Children with developmental delays or disorders very often exhibit additional problems such as mental retardation, neurological impairments such as epilepsy, perceptual motor dysfunctions, and communication disorders. Because of the additional disabilities, many children with developmental delays have special health needs. Children with special health management needs are often referred to as **medically fragile children**. This category includes children who demonstrate a wide range of chronic and progressive illnesses and severe disabilities, such as cystic fibrosis, congenital malformations, neuromuscular diseases, and many others.

Major Categories of Exceptionality

Our current classification systems in special education evolved "gradually, haphazardly, and inconsistently" over the past century (Reschly, 1987, p. 37). The history of special education is replete with controversy over descriptive and functional definitions of acknowledged disabilities, and even today, the search for universal or specific features of various conditions is ongoing, futile, and frustrating. Classification systems remain imprecise; there is relatively little standardization in the study of children who are exceptional. There is not a single consistent and universally accepted method of describing different kinds of children.

In general, the special traits of children who are exceptional fall into the following categories:

- Intellectual differences, which include children who are intellectually superior and those who are intellectually disabled.
- Sensory handicaps, which include children with auditory impairments and those with visual problems.

- Communication disorders, which include children with speech difficulties and language problems. In this text, we group learning-disabled children in this category, although they could be placed in other areas, because so many of them manifest communication deficits. Similarly, we place children from different cultural backgrounds here as well in the belief that any academic difficulties are largely the result of delayed English language usage.
- Behaviour disorders, which include conduct disorders, social maladjustment, and juvenile delinquency.
- Physical handicaps and impaired health, which include children with neurological defects, orthopedic conditions, birth defects, and conditions that are a result of infection and disease.
- *Developmental disabilities* is an inclusive term. The category includes children with pervasive disorders such as severe retardation and infantile autism, and those with multiple handicaps such as such as cerebral palsy and mental retardation, or deafness and blindness.

Looking at Labels

A central theme of this book is that no two children are alike. Children who are exceptional should be viewed first as individuals, and then as people who differ from the norm in some way. A child's functional level and behaviour should be the critical components analyzed for intervention, and we should be wary of supplying labels that are arbitrary and that permanently assign a child to a specific category of exceptionality. Despite this, and despite the distrust of labels and categorization that permeates today's special education, discrete categories of exceptionality and specific labels for particular conditions still abound.

Labelling refers to the categorizing of children on the basis of their primary disability. The practice evolved gradually; no one really planned it. Labels are products of the human mind — in special education they grew from a psychomedical model which encompassed diagnosis, classification, and placement. The labels, and the influence they have, vary greatly. The variability depends upon the labeller's perspective which may be shaped by cultural and/or professional background.

The research on labels has been inconclusive (Brantlinger and Guskin, 1987), and child-based categorical systems retain their popularity. Many hold that some system for the identification and classification of children who are exceptional seems to be necessary and that there are advantages to the labelling process. Others look askance at the traditional groupings and labels. They contend that the labelling of exceptional children has one prominent objective: labels differentiate between normal and abnormal, or what a certain society calls normal and abnormal. Essentially, they say, categorical definitions of exceptional children maintain the purity of each population by focusing on discrepant attributes, the unique and elusive characteristics that distinguish one defined population from other categories in special education. Further, the practice offers few benefits to the labelled individual. In general, classification systems are too often unreliable and inconsistent, and labels seldom adequately reflect a child's educational and thereupetic needs. Some of the many pros and cons of the labelling dilemma are shown on the next few pages.

A Matter of Debate

Labels in special education

Arguments put forward by those who support the use of labels include

- A carefully considered classification can serve to simplify information for administrators, placement counsellors, educators, and parents.
- Labels may be helpful to parents, especially when a condition is initially diagnosed. For parents, the name of a handicap seems to give them some control over it (Akerley, 1975).
- Categories are necessary to ensure quality services. For example, the rehabilitation system cannot disregard the fact that the unique needs of the visually impaired require the services of specialized professionals (Gallagher, 1988).
- In England and Wales, where disability categories were completely abolished, there have been negative consequences (Feniak, 1988).
- Labels permit us to identify children whose learning and behavioural characteristics cause them to require differentiated instruction.
- Students with the same label may be assumed to share a common set of learning characteristics that may lead to efficient educational programming.
- Labels may be a necessary administrative lever within the school system to obtain funding for special services.
- Labels promote effective communication among agencies, services, and professionals that deal with individuals who are exceptional.
- Labels result in increased visibility for groups of people with special needs.
- Labels make others more tolerant of a disability. They may provide explanations for behaviour or appearance for which people may otherwise be blamed or stigmatized (Fiedler and Simpson, 1987).
- Teachers interact with children differently according to the child's classroom behaviour, not the label or handicap classification (Curci and Gottleib, 1990).
- The label "gifted" enhances a child's status in the family and affects the parents' perceptions of the child (Cornell 1983).

Those who disagree with labelling argue that

- The use of discrete categories for exceptional children tends to oversimplify the facts.
- Too often, a label describes only the lacks, problems, and deficiencies of a person. It picks out a single quality, calls attention to it, and stresses how this quality differs from the norm. When development is different from the norm, it is assumed that there is something wrong either in the family, the child, or the culture. An oversimplified label suggests that the child is an unhealthy, poorly functioning organism, deprived in some way. Strengths are obscured.

- Although children may share a common exceptionality, they do not form homogeneous groups. Each disability ranges from mild to severe. A subgroup of children with intellectual disabilities, for example, is extremely heterogeneous: children exhibit different behaviours and are affected by the disability in various ways. Also, a child who is mildly disabled functions quite differently than a child with a severe disability.
- Considerable overlap occurs in the classification of disabling conditions. Many exceptional children have more than one difficulty and because they do not fall easily into one specific category, they are difficult to classify.
- Labelling engenders unfortunate and often unanticipated consequences. In the past, many children were misclassified and shunted into unsuitable educational environments.
- Sometimes the labels are incorrect, as in making *dyslexia* synonymous with learning disabilities. Or labels may exaggerate the severity of a disability, as in the labelling of a hard-of-hearing child as deaf or a visually impaired youngster as blind.
- Children who have been traditionally classified and grouped as mildly handicapped — those described as learning disabled, mildly mentally retarded, and mildly emotionally disturbed — often exhibit similar behaviour. These children tend to share a variety of academic and behavioural characteristics that transcend traditional approaches to classification.
- Labels do not automatically result in better services for a child.
- A label suggests a permanent disorder requiring long-term professional treatment. Children must wear their labels everywhere and all the time, although they may not apply in all situations.
- People tend to view a labelled person differently from a non-labelled one. People are more likely to expect deviant behaviour from labelled individuals.
- Other students are sensitive to labels and to the differences between peers who attend different educational placements from their regular classroom. In one study (Bak et al., 1987) children responded to de facto labels of resource room and special classroom differently. They saw the students going to the resource room as significantly more capable than those in special classes.
- Labels may affect a teacher's interactions with students and may tend to absolve teachers of their responsibilities. If teachers are predisposed to expect behaviour consonant with a child's classification, it may negatively affect interactions with the child. For example, a teacher may not even try to help little Jimmy with arithmetic because Jimmy has been labelled as mildly disabled and the teacher does not believe that disabled children can learn to add and subtract.
- Labelling may filter down to affect perceptions of other children in a family. Richey and Ysseldyke (1983) conducted two investigations concerning teacher expectations of the younger siblings of learning-disabled students. In the first study, teachers who had previously taught an older learning-disabled sibling were asked to predict their student's future academic performance in the first week of school. In the second study, teachers were asked to predict the academic performance of hypothetical siblings for the following year when they had older learning-disabled students in the class. In both studies, the investigators found that teachers held low expectations for the siblings of learning-disabled children. Similarly, Sydney and Minner (1984) found

that teachers recommended placements in special programming for students with behaviour disorders more often for children with siblings identified as behaviourally disordered than for an identically described student with a non-disabled sibling.

- High expectations communicated through the labelling process for a gifted child may contribute to feelings of failure; the child never quite measures up to expectations (e.g. Buescher, 1991).
- Within the family, the presence of a child labelled as gifted has been found to have an ultimately negative impact on family dynamics and lead to adjustment difficulties among siblings. The gifted child may have a special position as family attention and resources are claimed for him or her, leading to increased competition in the family and sibling jealousy. (See Chapter 16.)
- The *Disability Rag*, a US disability activist publication, periodically editorializes against euphemisms created by non-disabled people. They point out that disabilities are real and present policies are needed to enable real choice, not euphemistic terms that gloss over the need for action (Sleeter and Grant, 1994).

Many of those opposed to the use of labels argue for generic or non-categorical approaches. Not only will such approaches encourage educators to emphasize the common characteristics that exist among children with learning difficulties, but they will do much to combat the stigmatization and stereotyping of individuals who are exceptional.

Non-categorical approaches focus on behaviours and learning patterns rather than on diagnostic categories. The stress is on the functional behaviour of a child as the most important factor in that child's educational program.

Generic approaches have been developed for students traditionally labelled as learning disabled, mildly mentally retarded, and mildly emotionally disturbed. In the past, these mildly disabled students were not thought to share common etiological factors and behavioural characteristics. Among the three groups, differences were said to exist in the level of cognitive ability, in academic achievement, in patterns of cognitive performance, in degree of underachievement, and in adaptiveness of social and emotional development.

Ongoing research, however, finds that in many respects, these students cannot be reliably distinguished from one another. The overlap occurs in a number of domains:

- Differential diagnosis. Children with mild problems are difficult to categorize through diagnostic methods such as diagnostic tests, WISC-111 profile analyses, or behavioural checklists. Researchers (Fensler, Rosenberg, and Rosenberg, 1991) continue to find a considerable degree of overlap between the diagnostic areas of learning disabilities and behavioural disorders.
- Learning. When children's actual performance in school is examined, there is considerable overlap. Behaviourally disordered children mirror the learning problems of those who are learning disabled (Kauffman, 1981); children with mild intellectual disabilities demonstrate similar deficits in memory, attention, and achievement.
- Instruction. Treatments and instructional methods often overlap. One study (Algozzine, Morsink, and Algozzine, 1988) found that instruction in forty classrooms serving groups of students designated as behaviourally disordered (emotionally disturbed), educable mentally retarded, or learning disabled did not differ to any degree.

- Behaviour. Research shows that both students with learning disabilities and those with intellectual disabilities exhibit behaviour disorders (e.g. Harris et al., 1984; Reiss, Levitan, and McNally, 1982).

Educators are also moving to adopt more generic categories for severe and profound disabilities. Developmental delay, which we explained earlier, is an inclusive, generic term. Students with severe handicaps are now generically defined as those who

> may possess severe language and/or perceptual/cognitive deprivations, and evidence abnormal behaviour such as i) failure to respond to pronounced social stimuli; ii) self-mutiliation; iii) self-stimulation; iv) manifestation of intense and prolonged temper tantrums and v) the absence of rudimentary forms of verbal contact. May also have extremely fragile physiological conditions (US Federal definition 20 USC 1401(7)).

Prevalence of Children Who Are Exceptional

An estimated 500 to 600 million people, approximately one-eighth of the world's population, can be regarded as disabled. Catastrophic as this figure seems, it may be conservative. The incidence of largely preventable diseases, such as water-borne blindness, tuberculosis, and leprosy, may be much greater than present figures suggest. Millions more suffer from the chronic debilitating conditions that stem from malnutrition, impure water, and inadequate sanitation. In all, the number of persons, world-wide, with severe disabilities is simply staggering (Mazurek and Winzer, 1994).

In the United States, approximately 35 million people are considered exceptional. In Canada, there are more than two million disabled persons (Wight-Felske and Hughson, 1986), a figure that represents about 9.8 percent of the Canadian population ("Directions", 1982). In 1986, there were an estimated 277 000 Canadian children with disabilities, representing 5 percent of all young people (Nessner, 1990). Among these children and adolescents, boys are more likely to be disabled than girls.

During the school years, approximately 15.5 percent of the Canadian school-age population is considered to be exceptional. The great majority of these students are mildly disabled; of the approximately 7 percent of children under the age of 15 with disabilities reported by Oderkirk (1993), 90 percent were mildly disabled, 8 percent moderately, and 3 percent severely.

Estimates of the numbers of exceptional individuals are generally reported as either incidence or prevalence rates. **Incidence** refers to the number of new cases of a particular condition identified over a given period of time, usually a year. **Prevalence** applies to the total number of existing cases, old and new. *Prevalence* is also used to refer to the percentage or proportion of the population that falls into a given category.

Any attempt to estimate the number of children and adolescents with exceptional conditions is fraught with hazards, and a precise determination of the incidence and prevalence rates for exceptional children and adolescents with specific conditions in Canada is very difficult. In general, estimates of the number of children with some identifiable special condition vary widely. Table 1-2 presents the proportions of children in Canada who belong to the major categories of exceptionality. Prevalence figures collected by the Canadian Council for Exceptional Children for particular conditions are embedded in the relevant chapters.

Approximately 15.5 percent of the Canadian school-age population is considered to be exceptional.

Table 1-2

Proportions of children belonging to major categories of exceptionality

Type of exceptionality	Number of students	Percentage of special education total	Percentage of school-age population
Mentally Handicapped	63 359	11.3%	1.75%
Learning Disabled	159 159	28.4%	4.41%
Behaviourally/ Emotionally Disabled	27 298	4.9%	0.78%
Speech Impaired	43 914	7.9%	1.22%
Sensorially Disabled Hearing	5 231	0.9%	0.14%
Physically Handicapped	2 971	0.5%	0.08%
Multiply Handicapped	11 369	2.0%	0.31%
Other	244 390	43.7%	6.77%
Total	559 717	100.0%	15.5%

Source: Canada, Council of Ministers, 1983.

Prevalence estimates are influenced by a complex set of interacting factors. Contributing to the difficulties in obtaining accurate figures are the varying definitions and descriptions of disabilities, the methods of data collection, and the interpretation of data. In addition, social factors related to stigmatization and public perception inhibit accurate prevalence estimates.

Definitional Problems

As noted earlier, we face serious definitional problems when we discuss children with exceptional conditions. These children require the services related to a range of professional disciplines, chiefly medical, therapeutic, and educational. Each discipline brings its own definitions and characterizations of what is exceptional.

In the educational system, students are only considered exceptional when their educational program must be altered to meet their unique needs. They must demonstrate a clear need for support services to reach their full human potential. Although heart disease is a serious condition, it may not impact on a student's learning in the way that a mental disability does, and therefore a child with a heart disorder may not be counted among the special education population. On the other hand, school systems tend to identify a greater number of students as special education recipients.

Not only do the disciplines allied to special education regard exceptional children in different ways, but special education itself uses many vague and inconsistent definitions. School systems tend to interpret a child's condition according to the services they provide. A child may be called learning disabled in one school district, and counted as a low achiever in another. Without clear definitions it is almost impossible to estimate prevalence.

Changing Diagnoses

The diagnosis of a disabling condition is not, nor should it be, immutable. A diagnosis that is correct today could easily be inappropriate tomorrow. Frequently, children who are handicapped by speech defects, behaviour disorders, or learning disabilities improve to such an extent that they are no longer considered disabled (Hallahan and Kauffman, 1991).

At the same time, there is much movement between the various categories, especially among those characterized as "mildly disabled." In the past, children labelled as mildly mentally retarded formed the major category of children requiring special education in Canadian schools. But in recent years, the whole field of mental retardation has altered so dramatically that some researchers (e.g., Polloway and Smith, 1983) have observed a decreasing interest in the field of mental retardation. At the same time, the growth of the field of learning disabilities has been little short of phenomenal.

Another factor that confounds efforts to estimate prevalence is ongoing research that brings new ways of looking at disabling conditions. For example, recent discoveries in neurology and genetics have altered traditional conceptions of the causes and nature of infantile autism; the condition is no longer classified as a severe emotional disturbance but as a neurological disability or a health handicap.

Multiple Diagnoses

Confusion arises about the classification of particular children. With congenital anomalies or malformations, there can be a number of diagnoses. Further, many children have more than one pertinent set of characteristics: a child might be mentally retarded and hearing-impaired, or speech handicapped and blind. Children with multiple handicaps are often classified according to their major handicap. For example, a deaf child with an emotional problem may be classified as hearing-impaired and receive services designed for deaf children, with the emotional problem presumed to be secondary. Or, the child may be numbered in both categories or simply as multiply handicapped. This makes rates unstable.

Early Identification

Low-incidence handicaps, such as severe retardation, serious physical impairment, or blindness, are usually identified early and involve more professional intervention than high-incidence conditions, such as mild intellectual disability. Mild intellectual disability, for example, may not be identified until the child has to confront the complexities of reading and writing in the classroom. Learning disabilities are most often identified in relation to academic functioning. As a result, low-incidence disabilities are more likely to be reported.

Changing Rates

Difficulties spring from different prevalence figures at different points in the life cycle. As we just pointed out, children with mild intellectual disabilities are often not identified until they reach school, where the deficits become most evident. Undoubtedly, problems occur in other situations, but the most pronounced difficulties clearly relate to the structured environment of formal schooling. During the school years, therefore, the prevalence of mild intellectual disability tends to show a sharp increase. And since most of the adults who function in this range achieve personal and vocational independence, the estimated prevalence of mild disability decreases substantially as these adults enter the working world and assume their places as productive citizens.

The Stigma of Identification

Some parents are reluctant to have their child identified as exceptional. They may not report a condition, or they may opt for a different category. Parents seem to see labels that specify a particular problem as less stigmatizing than those that imply a global, developmental impairment. For example, many parents find the term *learning disabilities* far preferable to *mild mental retardation.*

Survey Problems and Sampling Errors

Epidemiology refers to the study of the distribution and determinants of diseases and handicapping conditions in a population. Survey problems result when epidemiologists and other researchers use varied definitions of an exceptionality. Surveys can also be misleading when figures from a small area are extrapolated to the rest of the country. Newfoundland, for example, has a high rate of spina bifida, and to extrapolate Newfoundland figures to the rest of Canada would clearly be unwise.

Unidentified Populations

Any attempt to estimate the incidence rate of a relatively common disorder almost invariably fails to take into account some affected individuals. Many mildly handicapping conditions prove elusive and difficult to accurately pinpoint. And given the geographical vastness of Canada, it is not surprising that many exceptional children go unreported. For example, hearing loss is endemic in the North, especially in the Eastern Arctic (Watters, 1980). However, these prevalence figures are not generally known or included in estimates of disabling conditions.

Intervention with Children with Exceptionalities

Intervention is a general term that refers to the application of professional skills to maintain or improve a child's potential and functioning. **Early intervention**, a major trend in current special education practice, refers to the establishment of educational and support services for young children with or at risk for disabilities, and for their families. Although intervention is strongly associated with active educational programming, the term includes medical intervention and welfare provisions for the family and the child.

A number of processes are subsumed under the general rubric of intervention. The concept of habilitation comes from the Latin *habilitare*, to make skilled. In habilitation, people in medical, social, psychological, and educational fields support and assist children with disabilities in their development and daily lives. **Rehabilitation** is another therapeutic term that refers to procedures that endeavour to restore an individual to normal or optimal functioning. **Remediation** is an educational term that refers to helping a child to overcome, or compensate for, specific deficits in learning and development.

For the child who is exceptional, the major forms of intervention are medical, educational, and social. These are not all the forms of intervention, but they do represent the basic approaches to care and education. Each allied discipline has developed its own form of intervention, diagnosis, and terminology to reflect its professional orientation and traditions. We discuss some basic intervention techniques here; these are expanded upon in later chapters.

Medical Intervention

Medical intervention and treatment for exceptional children is a complex and highly sophisticated process that involves a variety of specialists with unique skills. Although medical treatment is extremely varied, the most common forms involve surgery; treatment that is life saving, such as insulin; the controlled use of medication; and supportive therapy.

Surgery

In recent decades, many forms of surgical treatment for children who are exceptional have emerged, leading to the development of subspecialities within the field of pediatric surgery. The most widely used surgical treatments currently include reconstructive surgery for repair of physical anomalies such as a cleft lip or palate; neurosurgery for disabling conditions of the brain and spinal cord; and orthopedic surgery for problems of the skeletal system that occur in youngsters with cerebral palsy or multiple

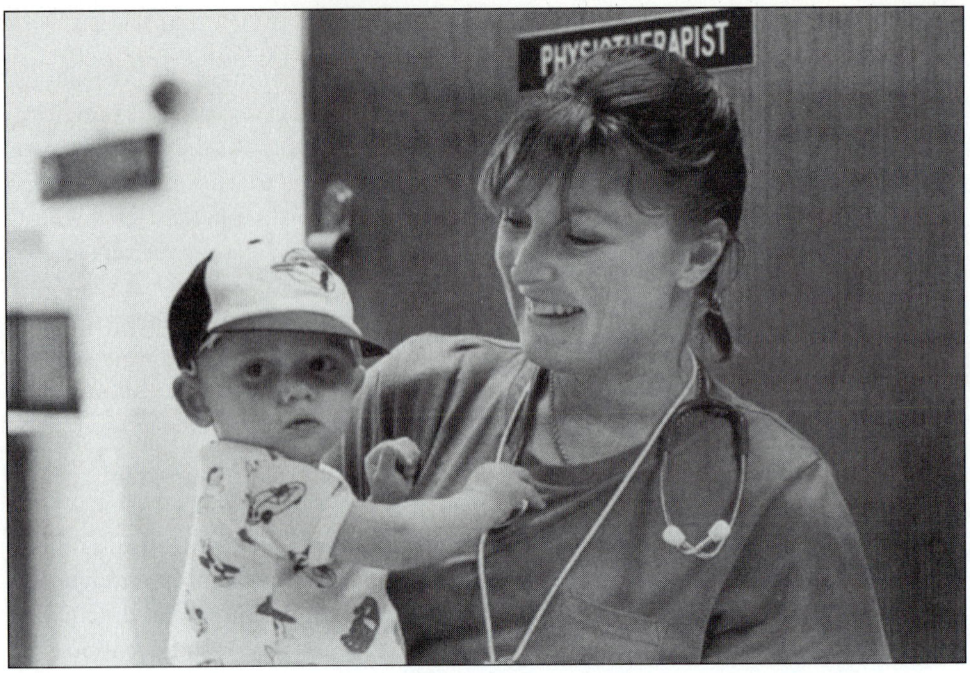

Intervention with exceptional children can involve a variety of specialists.

physical anomalies. Sophisticated techniques have also been developed, for example, to help Down syndrome children, to insert cochlea implants in deaf individuals, and to transplant organs in cystic fibrotic children.

Psychopharmacology

Of all the medical treatments for children with exceptional conditions, teachers are most likely to come into contact with psychopharmacology, or drug therapy. In 1937, Charles Bradley was the first to treat specific educational disabilities and hyperactive behaviour with a stimulant drug, Benzedrine. Bradley noticed an overall improvement in the children's moods, activity level, and educational achievement (Bradley, 1937). Since his seminal work, psychopharmacological approaches to treatment have increased dramatically.

Drugs administered to children vary widely in purpose and pharmacological action. Drug therapy is used extensively with children who demonstrate physical and neurological complications. In general, drugs are intended to manage problems of behaviour, activity level, emotion, or epilepsy. We discuss drug therapy fully in Chapter 11.

Therapy

Therapy is the treatment of an illness or disabling condition. It consists of a broad range of interventions to help children adapt to their particular disabilities. Physical, occupational, and speech/language therapists provide essential treatments for many handicapped children.

Physical and occupational therapy can help children to develop hand skills, body co-ordination, and other physical skills, and can aid in gross motor development, muscle relaxation, and fine motor control. Speech and language therapists are trained in the evaluation and remedial treatment of speech and language problems in children and adults, and they may develop appropriate augmentative communication for children who cannot talk. Speech and language therapy may also be used with children who have difficulty in controlling the fine motor muscles needed for eating.

There are different types of therapy. Direct therapy occurs when therapeutic techniques are used in a treatment that only the therapist can safely carry out. Monitoring, in which teachers are involved, occurs when therapists monitor treatment carried out by parents, teachers, or classroom aides (Dunn, 1989).

Educational Intervention

Most children with disabilities attend school. In 1986, 51 percent of children aged five to fourteen with disabilities were attending regular classes in regular schools. Another 30 percent were in regular schools in special classes, and 6 percent were attending special schools. About 6 percent of children living at home were not in school but had attended school at one time or another. Only about 3 percent of children with disabilities had never gone to school (Nessner, 1990).

Education for children who are exceptional may be provided through a variety of educational arrangements and instructional alternatives. Not all exceptional students will require the same type or intensity of special education over the same period. Table 1-3 illustrates how it is possible for different children to receive special assistance in different areas.

Educational Settings

When it comes to educational settings, the alternatives are determined by the unique needs of each child. Many different kinds and combinations of programs are required to accommodate the wide range of conditions that occur in varying degrees of severity and the need for different types and degrees of assistance at various age levels. In order to provide appropriate education for exceptional students a cascade, or continuum, of services, as represented in Figure 1-1, is necessary. The cascade model was first presented by Reynolds (1962) and expanded by Deno (1970). Settings on the cascade involve a series of options that move from contrived to more natural arrangements.

When a child who is exceptional is included in the regular classroom, the classroom teacher holds primary responsibility for that child.

Within a cascade of services, the wider the pyramid, the more children are encompassed; throughout are increasingly restrictive environments, with the point of the triangle generally considered to be the most restrictive because children on homebound instruction have little opportunity for social interaction with their peers.

Regular Classroom

It is the regular classroom that provides the child who is exceptional with the least restrictive environment and the opportunity for maximum integration with non-handicapped peers. When a child is included in the regular classroom, the classroom teacher holds primary responsibility for that child and must ensure that appropriate programs and curriculum modifications are made. The classroom teacher also works with a number of professionals to tailor education to the needs of the individual child.

Students in regular classrooms may be supported by itinerant teachers, specially trained educators who give individual assistance to a child for specific periods during the normal school schedule. The type and intensity of itinerant intervention depend on the needs of the child. Some children may simply need tutoring to keep up in regular school subjects; others may require a specific program in one area, such as speech and auditory training. Itinerant teachers may work with classroom teachers on program

Table 1-3

Areas of special assistance for different categories of exceptional children

Children with	IEP	Curriculum modifications (content, pacing, depth, etc.)	Special devices	Special classroom arrangements	Counselling services	Speech/ language therapy	Occupational physiotherapy	Other therapies	Medical services	Social services
Mild mental retardation	X	X			X					
Moderate mental retardation	X	X			X	X				
Speech and language difficulties	X	X			X	X				
Learning disabilities	X	X			X					
Hearing impairments	X	X	X	X	X	X				
Visual impairments	X	X	X	X	X					
Health disorders	X				X			X		
Physical disabilities	X	X	X	X	X	X	X		X	
Behavioural difficulties	X	X			X			X		X
Psychoses	X	X			X	X		X		
Severe and multiple handicaps	X	X	X	X	X	X	X	X	X	
Giftedness	X	X			X					

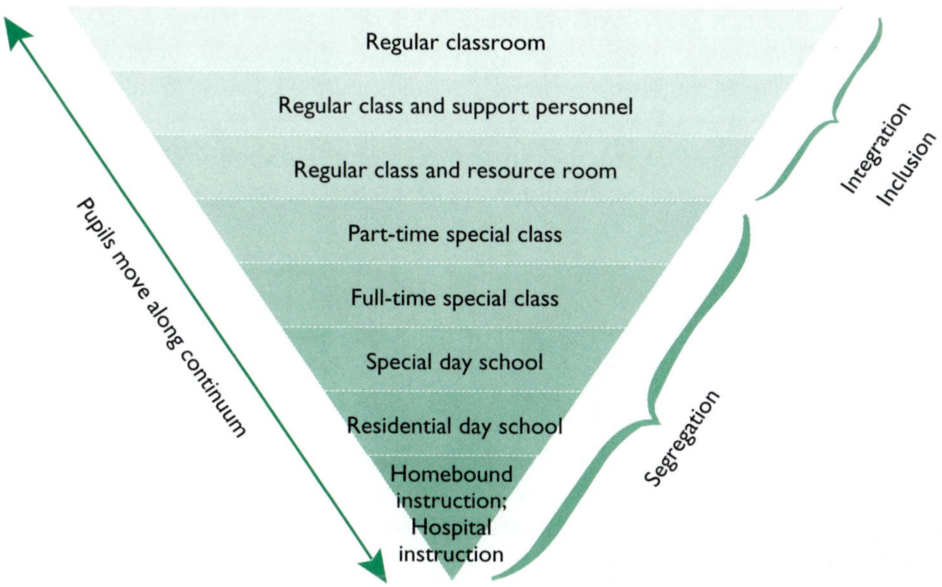

Figure 1-1
A diagrammatic model of a cascade of services

preparation and offer in-service training. They may also help prepare the exceptional child's classmates by explaining the child's disabling condition. In some instances, the itinerant teacher serves as an advocate to ensure that the special child receives the best education possible in the most appropriate environment.

In general, an educational consultant has no teaching responsibilities. The consultant assists classroom teachers throughout a school district to maintain exceptional children in their regular school programs. As an indirect servicer of exceptional children, the consultant may function as a diagnostician, a materials specialist, an administrator of various services, and as an advocate.

The paraprofessional (variously referred to as a teacher aide, teaching assistant, classroom assistant, child care worker, and so on) is an important part of the instructional team who shares responsibility in the area of learning facilitation. The aide must be able to develop and/or select daily elements of the curriculum as defined in an individualized educational plan, deliver instruction, provide for remedial experiences, and monitor a child's progress (Goodman, 1990). Aides are also used for individual educational assessments and the recording of behaviour.

Resource Rooms

The resource room helps children to make the transition between self-contained classrooms and regular classrooms. Before the advent of resource rooms, children with mild learning difficulties floundered in the regular classroom, were placed in special classes, or were sent to special schools. Resource rooms support integration, while removing the stigma of segregation.

For the child with special needs, resource rooms provide "an island of learning opportunities" (Vergason and Anderegg, 1993, p. 475). The resource room is a facility run by a teacher who deals directly with specific learning problems. Resource room teachers design, alter, and present instruction across a number of curriculum areas, and address elements that facilitate students' success in the mainstream environment. They may provide support in academic learning of both the core and remedial curricula, and training in social and communication skills that will help the student to interact better in the regular classroom.

Integrated exceptional pupils receive part of their education in the regular classroom and part of it in the resource room. This allows some learning to take place in a less distracting, less intense, and less competitive environment than the regular classroom. The regular classroom teacher still carries primary responsibility for program design but works in close co-ordination with resource room personnel.

Special Classes

The full-time special class has traditionally been the most popular vehicle for serving students with exceptional conditions. During the late 1960s, the notion of special classes was critically examined, and the resulting debates and evidence added impetus to the movement toward mainstreaming. Nevertheless, special classes remain a setting for some exceptional students. In special classrooms, which are staffed by specially trained teachers and are located within the regular school, children with similar disabilities are brought together for instruction and social interplay. Children follow the regular program closely enough to allow for partial integration when feasible.

Special Schools

During the late 1950s it was felt that a logical extension of the special class was the special school. Schools were designed and equipped to meet the needs of discrete populations of exceptional students. A few special day schools still provide special education services, usually to specific groups of exceptional children and often at the preschool level. Day schools allow a core of specially trained teachers and professionals to guide the child's education while the child continues to live at home.

Residential Schools

Special education in Canada began with residential institutions designed to serve the special needs of blind, deaf, and mentally retarded students. Provincially funded residential schools for hearing impaired, visually handicapped, emotionally disturbed, and mentally retarded children still function across Canada. In these settings, children live and are instructed with other youngsters who have the same exceptional conditions. One of the problems with residential schools is that they separate the child from the home. However, the concept of full-time residential placement has changed substantially in recent years and many of these schools could more correctly be termed residential/day as more students have been encouraged to commute.

Home Instruction

Homebound and hospital instruction is provided by local school boards for children who are confined because of illness, physical injury, or other problems. Intervention is initiated if the student's school absences begin to seriously affect progress.

In the Classroom

There exists no universal conviction about how to teach exceptional children. There is no such thing as a panacea. Behaviour modification, individualized programming, and task analysis, along with children's own motivations and needs, cannot be administered through a generalized curriculum and set of techniques that are appropriate to all students and to all teachers at all times. Among educators, common ground is only reached concerning the necessity for a more detailed assessment of strengths and needs, greater individualization of instruction and curriculum, and more careful and systematic monitoring of performance (Winzer, 1989).

The things that make special education special are done by good teachers every day. Good teachers recognize that all students have individual needs. They adapt materials, teaching techniques and activities to the particular needs of their students. They build curriculum, use concrete techniques, generalize skills, apply learning at the appropriate level, and begin instruction at children's tolerance level. They provide individual and small group instruction, evaluate progress carefully by means of various evaluation techniques, and keep careful records (Winzer, 1989).

There is no question that integrating students with exceptional conditions involves a wider range of organizational and instructional materials and alternatives than does regular teaching. Teachers are challenged to find innovative ways to enhance the learning environment in order to accommodate the learning differences and behavioural difficulties of exceptional pupils. Children may need special attention because of limited ability, poor motivation, sensory or physical impairements, or specific learning disabilities. Frequently their learning difficulties are related to a combination or interaction of a number of factors.

Teachers must provide supportive learning environments; they need to adapt and modify the physical, instructional, and psychosocial environments. In Table 1-4 we present some examples of very general adaptations that can be made to assist exceptional pupils. Throughout this text, readers will find featured tips for teachers and extracts from Individual Education Plans (IEPs) that provide further examples of modifications.

When educators adjust the nature of student programs in response to individualization, their students learn reliably and learn dramatically more.

Specialized adaptations are how teachers modify planned instruction beyond their routine adaptations in light of specific student difficulty (Fuchs et al., 1995). The array of modifications from which a teacher may choose is enormous. Strategies such as precision teaching, cognitive strategy training, co-operative learning, monitoring of children's on-task behaviour, appropriate pacing of instruction, and peer tutoring have been shown to be effective in integrated classes. The problem is matching appropriate modifications to student learning problems. This is facilitated when planning is individualized and documented in an IEP.

The essence of special education is individualization. When educators specifically adjust the nature of student programs in response to individualization, their students learn reliably and learn dramatically more (see Fuchs et al., 1995). Some people think that individualizing programs for exceptional pupils means that the teacher must work with that child on a one-to-one basis at all times. This is patently untrue. Individualization is not a teaching method but a plan for instructional organization that may incorporate many methods (Winzer, 1995).

Individual Education Plans

The process of modifying the regular curriculum and adapting the classroom environment is often begun with an Individual Education Plan. Each student's IEP is a broad statement that assists teachers by prespecifying the goals and objectives of instruction and ensuring that the educational program is appropriate to the child's specific needs. The plan of action outlines the short-term objectives and long-term goals, describes the methods and techniques that will be used to achieve them, and details the responsibilities of various people, such as the classroom teacher, the resource room teacher, or the speech therapist, who will help the child along the way.

Table 1-4

Supportive learning environments

Environment	Example of adaptation
Physical	FM system for a child with a hearing impairment.
	Seating close to the teacher for the child with a behaviour disorder.
	Increased lighting, but no glare, for the child with a visual disability.
	Extra space between desks for the child with a physical disability.
	A special notice board detailing homework, assignment dates, and so on for the learning-disabled adolescent.
Instructional	Slower pace with many redundant questions and much drill and practice for children with learning difficulties.
	Many diagrams, visual materials, media for students who must grasp ideas without depending solely on language.
	Maps, graphs, and so on in string, pasta, or raised glue for students with visual impairments.
	Work sheets with only one type of activity or question for students with disabilities.
	Self-tests and checklists so older students can monitor themselves.
	Practice questions before an examination for older students.
	Co-operative learning strategies for average and below average students; independent studies for gifted learners.
Psychosocial	Much reinforcement and many incentives for all students in the classroom.
	Provision for successful accomplishments daily.
	Structure in the classroom with routines and procedures carefully followed.
	Social skills training and reinforcement.

Although IEPs differ markedly, most contain certain components. These are:

1. IEP data. Many plans contain information about the preparation of the IEP. It may state the names and positions of those attending the team meeting when the IEP was drawn up and whether the IEP is an initial document, a second IEP, or an evaluation document.
2. Placement. This is a statement of the educational setting considered most appropriate for the student with special needs.

3. A summary of the student's present level of performance across a range of domains. Each individual plan is founded on an assessment designed to discover the child's strengths and weaknesses in the areas of cognitive development, physical and motor development, socio-emotional development, and adaptive behaviour. With a record of a child's performance based on information derived from an assessment or assessments, those preparing the IEP can pinpoint a child's present levels of performance and then determine the skills the child needs to acquire. That is, assessment data should tell us where a child is functioning and how that compares to normal developmental levels.
4. The long-term, or annual goals. A **goal** may be defined as a stated outcome desired as the result of some action. On an IEP, goals are broad general statements that help to focus on the general areas for which individualized programming is to be provided. They indicate the priorities for intervention — the major learning experiences the child will have and the broad range of skills that he or she can be expected to attain. Long-range goals are usually written for one year except in the case of children with significant handicaps, who may have long-range goals over a greater period, up to five years.

   Taking assessment results, translating them into present levels of performance, and then using them in planning and individualized programming is not as straightforward as it may seem at first. In fact, the process is quite complicated and takes much careful thought. In using assessment information for IEPs, there are three basic steps. The present levels of functioning should provide a list of a child's strengths and weaknesses. These are divided into skills that need remediation, skills that are delayed, and skills within the normal ranges. Once this is done, skills are targeted for intervention (long-term goals). These are then written as short-term objectives. Typically, five to ten goals are identified in the domains of functioning where the child is showing the greatest lags. When they are written down, the goals should represent a specific expectation or skill (as opposed to a vague generic statement). For example, "Learn to read" is not specific enough, whereas "Will read books at grade 1 level" is.
5. Short-term objectives for each annual goal. An **objective** is a clear statement of exactly what a teacher wants a child to be able to do as a result of instruction. Objectives refer to increments in the progress of learning from the present level of functioning to the child's annual goals. Objectives, the steps towards achieving the goals, direct instruction and learning on a day-to-day basis. Short-term objectives are provided for each annual goal. There is no rule, but generally three or four objectives are provided for each long-range goal.

   The way to turn long-range goals into short-term objectives is through **task analysis**, breaking skills down into their component parts. All of the small tasks that make up the larger skill are listed. The number of subskills depends on the task and the individual needs of the child.

   Good behavioural objectives are written as brief action statements that use verbs that lend themselves to observation and measurement. Appropriate verbs include apply, describe, recognize, repeat, copy, reproduce, choose, draw, classify, match, identify, or select.
6. The specific educational and support services needed to attain each educational objective. Once goals and objectives are identified, the next step is to select and

sequence the most appropriate learning experiences to achieve those aims and objectives. However, in a sense an IEP represents a philosophy of what should be taught rather than illustrations of how it should happen. Examples of how to accomplish an objective may appear but every approach, activity, or group interaction will not.

7. The personnel who will hold primary responsibility for specific long-range goals and short-term objectives. The program outlines the responsibilities of various people, such as teachers or therapists who will assist the child. It shows the kinds of services required (such as speech therapy), the type of instruction (individual or group), and the time to be spent in each activity (half an hour a day).
8. The date for the beginning of special education services.
9. The anticipated duration of the services.
10. Objective evaluation procedures for each objective. These are the specific criteria for determining whether the objectives have been attained.
11. Procedures for re-evaluating the total IEP document.

The IEP is a personalized program that is prepared annually, usually at an early point in the year. It is filled in before programming begins, and therefore writing the first Individual Education Plan for a child with a disability is largely guesswork. The goals and objectives are hypotheses about what a child can and cannot do and about a child's critical needs. Moreover, the process of programming for needs is a dynamic one. An IEP is not a static document or a performance contract. Nor is it written in stone. The IEP is a communication document which is constantly modified and changed to match a child's progress and needs. A child who is visually impaired, for example, may in fact be visually impaired for life, but that child's needs will change — not merely each year, but perhaps each week or even each day.

The major problem confronting teachers is determining and prioritizing the skills that are important to teach. Skill determination is easier for children with mild disabilities, who generally follow the curriculum designed for their normally developing peers. The most complex IEPs are for children with communication disorders because language is composed of so many interdependent functions.

Educational Teams

When teachers have exceptional students assigned to their classrooms, they accept assistance from a wide variety of support services; members of several disciplines pool their expertise in order to assist classroom teachers. The teacher may work on a school-based team with the principal, a psychologist, itinerant teachers, a speech therapist, a language therapist, and such allied child care personnel as audiologists and school nurses.

Before a child is assigned to special education, a team decides on both placement and program. Educational teams tend to be multidisciplinary in nature, with the major duties of planning, implementation, and evaluation of educational programs for special students. The team considers students' special difficulties in school and determines if these students are elegible for special education. It also provides a forum for regular and special educators to share ideas and concerns.

The organization of a team is largely determined by the needs of a child and school policy (see Bachor and Crealock, 1986; Winzer, 1989). It is crucial that school-based teams include all those involved with a special child. While participation in meetings can be time-consuming on one level, the eventual benefits accruing to both child and teacher outweigh the inconvenience.

Social Intervention

Social intervention covers a spectrum of services that can be grouped under the general category of child welfare. A primary concern is the care and treatment of the child within the family environment. A wide range of personnel are involved in service delivery — giving assistance to people who need it. They include social workers, family counsellors, foster parents, child advocates, child care workers, probation officers, and so on, who try to ensure that the child develops under the care of the family or surrogate family.

Child Advocacy

Child advocacy can be defined as any social, political, or legal action that is intended to achieve a better life for children from infancy to late adolescence (Lourie, 1975). A child advocate is anyone who pleads a child's cause or defends a particular child-related cause.

Child advocacy is a wide-ranging movement that functions at several levels. It involves a spectrum of activities that identify the needs of children and try to rectify unsatisfactory practices. A major goal of advocacy is to stimulate public and professional response to the child's needs and problems.

Increasingly, advocates are playing an integral part in the education of children who are exceptional. Largely because of inadequate public and professional response to their children's educational and other needs, and as a result of their own need for emotional support, parents began to organize on a local level in the 1940s and 1950s and on a national level in the 1960s. Parents and parent associations became advocates to obtain better support for their exceptional children. Parent organizations have initiated services in education, residential living (most specifically group homes), and vocational alternatives. Some parent groups have started and operated services while others have been cataylsts and now work with community organizations. (See Chapter 16.)

The efforts of parents have been supported and supplemented by professional and educational groups. For example, the Canadian Association for Community Living (formerly the Association for the Mentally Retarded) and the Canadian Learning Disabilities Association (formerly the Association for Children with Learning Disabilities) also view advocacy as one of their primary functions.

Summary

1. Children who are exceptional are those who deviate in some way from what society calls normal. However, the norm itself encompasses a wide range of behaviours from which everyone deviates to some degree.
2. It is only very recently that an emphasis on the dignity and worth of each person has brought wider acceptance of all exceptional individuals in school and society. In recent decades, special education and society's treatment of exceptional people have changed dramatically. Special education has come to be seen as a means of providing better educational opportunities for exceptional children.
3. Over the years, the way that professionals and society in general have described persons with exceptionalities has changed in a positive way. In the past, the terms used to describe people who were exceptional were value laden and tended to emphasize the person's handicap, disorder, or disability. Today's terms are non-stigmatizing and as clear and unambiguous as possible.

4. In spite of the proliferation of labels in the health and education fields, many professionals see the traditional system of labelling children by their primary disability as not always useful, and the classification and labelling process as fraught with hazards. Labels may broadly define categories of exceptionality, but no one classification can adequately describe the social, psychological, and physical qualities of an exceptional individual. Administrators and professionals will likely continue to use categories of exceptionality. However, in the classroom, alternative approaches may serve exceptional children better.
5. Children requiring special education may be taught in settings that range from the regular classroom to the residential school and hospital programs.
6. To fully accomplish the aim of individualizing instruction for children with exceptionalities, special education teachers and those involved in educationally integrating these students combine their resources with a wide range of personnel.
7. Many children with special needs require various types of therapy. A child with poor articulation may require help from a speech therapist; a child who has lost a limb will need physical therapy; an adolescent with cerebral palsy may benefit from occupational therapy.
8. When a statement that details the individual program for a child with a disability is prepared, the document is called an Individual Education Plan (IEP). The IEP is a written planning document that outlines educational services and learning objectives to meet the specific needs of a child. It aims to co-ordinate plans and services, personalize and individualize a child's program, and integrate the individual plan with the overall plans for the classroom group.
9. By individualizing the program for exceptional students, we attempt to fit the curriculum and the program to the child, rather than vice versa. The individualization is in the planning, not necessarily in the instruction.

CHAPTER 2

Etiology of Disabling Conditions

Historical Notes

People with disabilities have probably been in society since its beginnings. Responses to individuals who were different or deviant were influenced by many factors — culture, religion, government, and economics — and have included extermination, conversion, restraint, and cure. Educational and social intervention was little heeded until the middle of the eighteenth century.

The historical record is murky and existing data is scattered, but it does seem that earlier societies demonstrated much tolerance for individuals with disabilities. Certainly, history records some early attempts to ameliorate their condition, first by physicians and philosophers and then by the Church, but these were sparse. Given the rudimentary state of medical, technological, and educational skills, it would have been difficult for a handicapped person to survive and difficult for society to assist that person.

In Greece, handicapped children often did not survive infancy. In Sparta, newborn children were routinely brought before the elders to be examined for their fitness for citizenship. Under the laws of Lycurgus, imperfect children were exposed in a gorge in the Taygetus mountains or left in the wilderness. In the time of Solon and later, similar events occurred in Athens. Weak children were placed in clay vessels and left to die by the wayside (French, 1932).

Rome readily adopted the Greek attitude toward handicapped infants. Any child under three who might someday become a burden on society was thrown into the Tiber. Those who survived infancy or suffered from acquired handicaps were generally treated with aversion.

To physicians, philosophers, and legislators, handicapped persons, even in ancient times, became objects of attention. Fragments remaining from the writings of the great jurists, physicians, and philosophers of the ancient world offer confirmation that the handicapped received much careful consideration. It was the legal minds of the Romans that introduced the first legislation regarding persons with handicaps. With the sixth century legal Code of Justinian, persons with disabilities were classified with an infinity of detail. The type and intensity of disability determined a person's right to citizenship and accompanying rights.

Even in those early times, disability was bounded by medical paradigms. Conditions requiring medical treatment were the first to be addressed; the recognition and care of subnormal and sensorially deprived persons had to wait for more enlightened attitudes regarding social care, which historically tended to lag behind purely medical concerns. Most societies were content to simply impose legal, religious, and social strictures designed to control or eliminate the bulk of the handicapped population. The medical stress largely determined societal attitudes and legal mandates for persons with disabilities.

Disabilities were viewed as innate to a person, imprinted on the soul before birth and unamenable to social or educational intervention. Physicians treated a number of disorders; those that did not respond were then further attributed to God, the devil, witchcraft, the influence of the moon, and a host of other factors.

Physical and mental deviance was equated with sin, with immorality, and with madness. These attitudes persisted right up to the mid-eighteenth century when a group of French philosophers and physicians looked askance at such notions; they held that some conditions were the result of environment and that all were in some way amenable to educational intervention.

With the nineteenth century and the enormous interest in human genetics and heredity stimulated by Darwin's work, medical models again surfaced. Disabilities were attributed almost solely to "bad stock," and disabled persons were locked away, forbidden to marry and procreate, and viewed as pariahs in society. For children in the schools, medical models meant that a condition within a child could be diagnosed, the child could be labelled, and then placed in a class consonant with that label.

Medical models still remain important in special education. Today, however, educators focus on the learning styles and behaviours of a child rather than the presumed underlying etiology.

As increasing numbers of children with exceptional conditions move into regular educational milieus, teachers will encounter far more students with such medical problems as epilepsy, visual and auditory impairment, and orthopedic and urologic difficulty. The child's physical condition is, of course, the proper concern of the medical profession. However, many physical problems have obvious implications for education.

For children with disabling conditions, the educational process may be hindered or disrupted. A recent Canadian study found that 6 percent of school age children with disabilities have begun school later than most children and 17 percent have had their schooling interrupted for long periods. In total, almost one-third (32 percent) of school age children with disabilities have taken longer than other children to achieve their current level of education (Nessner, 1990). Once in school, a disability may place a child at risk for a host of learning and behavioural problems.

The psychological, social, and educational factors related to a disability cannot easily be separated from the biomedical causes. Knowledge of the pathophysiology, symptomology, and treatment of exceptional conditions is important for educational professionals because it leads to a better appreciation of the psychological, social, and educational implications. Effective treatment requires an appropriate theoretical understanding of a problem (Weiner and Harris, 1989). If professionals are to successfully identify, diagnose, prescribe treatment for, teach, remediate, motivate, or generally improve the life of a child with an exceptional condition, they first require an accurate and clear idea of the nature of the disability — its causes, developmental consequences, and prognosis.

Teachers require a basic understanding of **etiology**, the process of finding causes to explain how a particular problem came into existence. Etiological considerations concern symptoms, the overt reactions or manifestations of the body to a certain condition and **symptomology**, the study of symptoms and characteristics. Etiology likewise involves **teratology**, generally thought of as the study of the agents involved in major congenital malformations (Kalter and Warkany, 1983). The concept has recently been broadened to include more minor malformations and behavioural difficulties, and now involves the causes of malformations and looking at outcomes of long-term importance in the medical and psychological functioning of a child.

As well, teachers should have an understanding of **developmental risk factors**, the wide range of biological and environmental conditions that are associated with increased probability of cognitive, social, affective, and physical problems. Risk factors may be intrinsic or extrinsic, although to some extent this is an arbitrary distinction as variables under these two classifications often interact. *Extrinsic* refers to the environment that elevates risk — physical, cultural, and social. *Intrinsic* refers to aspects of an individual's make-up.

Teachers' understanding of medical conditions aids them in becoming sensitized to the social, emotional, and educational problems resulting from a child's disabilities. Such knowledge imparts confidence in the ability to cope, enhances an understanding relationship with the child, and creates an atmosphere of acceptance among classmates and others involved with the exceptional child.

Teachers' understanding of medical conditions aids them in becoming sensitized to the social, emotional, and educational problems resulting from a child's disabilities.

In order to adequately assist children with exceptionalities in the classroom, teachers must also be willing to provide necessary assistance beyond that of an educational nature. A child with spina bifida, for example, often requires an artificial bladder for urine drainage. The clinical manifestations of the child's urologic difficulties (incontinence) and the need for medical management (the bag worn on the stomach or flank) may create practical and psychological problems for the child. If the teacher is unable to assist and reassure the child, then the child's medical problems may create learning difficulties (Freund, Casey, and Bradley, 1982).

Some children with disabilities require medication on a regular basis. In 1986, 31 percent of Canadian children aged 5 to 14 with disabilities were taking medication at least once a week for their condition or health problem (Nessner, 1990). Depending on school board policy, the teacher may be involved in the monitoring of drug dosages.

As well, some children with disabilities have difficulty participating in certain physical activities. In 1986, for example, 30 percent of children aged 10 to 14 with disabilities were prevented by their condition or health problems from leisure-time participation in physical activities (Nessner, 1990). The teacher must be aware when certain activities are limited for an exceptional child, when to restrict the duration of an activity, and when to recommend an alternative learning experience.

A general knowledge of the types of treatment that may be given children with disabilities is helpful. In general terms, treatment can be classified into five categories:

1. Treatment that is necessary and lifesaving, such as insulin for diabetes.
2. Treatment that is ameliorative and avoids secondary complications, such as surgery for contractures in children with cerebral palsy.
3. Treatment that is adaptive and facilitates development, such as total communication for deaf individuals.
4. Treatment that is unproven but potentially useful, such as drug therapy.
5. Treatment that is controversial, such as special diets in the control of hyperactivity (Kessler, 1977).

In this chapter we will discuss some of the major and general causes of handicapping conditions that can occur. Etiological considerations relevant to specific handicapping conditions are briefly re-addressed in following chapters. Damage to, or deterioration of, the spinal cord and the brain are the most common causes of physical disabilities in children. Because serious brain insults produce such drastic reductions in children's development and functioning, we include a brief discussion of the human central nervous system.

The New Morbidity

Before the advent of antibiotics in the 1940s, diseases such as whooping cough, measles, smallpox, enteric fever, meningitis, and scarlet fever seriously impaired, even destroyed, the vision and hearing of many children, and left a range of other disabling conditions. Scarlet fever and other such conditions are virtually eliminated, but a new group of disorders related to new etiologies has emerged. These new disorders have been characterized as "the new morbidity," referring to the fact that they are the results of new etiologies.

Special education may be facing the emergence of what some are now calling a "bio-underclass," due in particular to pediatric AIDS and the use of drugs by pregnant women. AIDS is a "devastating epidemic disorder of extraordinary morbidity and mortality" (Church, Allen, and Stiehen, 1986, p. 423). Some researchers (e.g., Dokecki, Baumeister, and Kupstas, 1989) predict that **pediatric AIDS** — AIDS contracted by children under thirteen years of age — is destined to become a major cause of developmental and physical disabilities and death among infants and children in North America. In addition to children affected by pediatric AIDS, a frightening proportion of the next generation of school children will have impairments based on the physical and chemical damage done to fetal brains by drug-abusing mothers (Greer, 1990a).

Another group of children included in this category are those whom medical technology helps survive. Even twenty years ago, many of these children would not have lived. Extremely premature babies, rescued by aggressive medical treatments, are at high risk for a number of neurological and physical impairments. In addition, many severely and profoundly handicapped children and those with severe chronic illnesses can today expect a normal life span (Batshaw and Perret, 1986). The lowered mortality rate means that more severely impaired children are surviving and attending school (Korabek and Cuvo, 1986).

The Central Nervous System

Structurally, the human nervous system consists of the brain, spinal cord, and all associated nerves and sense organs. Structures are the fixed anatomical and physiological features of the central nervous system and are similar across the healthy brains of most individuals. How these structures respond to, organize, analyze, and synthesize incoming information varies with individuals and with the task involved. The way information is processed represents the problem-solving strategies of each person (Owens, 1988).

The spinal cord and the brain, the two major components of the central nervous system, are each composed of *neurons* and *glial cells* (the latter name is derived from the Greek *glia*, meaning glue). The number of glial cells is probably ten times the number of neurons (Groves and Rebec, 1988). Glial cells serve in a supportive role for the neurons — they transmit food (glucose and amino acids) from the blood supply to the neurons; some probably serve as scaffolding, and others manufacture a substance called *myelin.* The glial cells develop later than the neurons. They start to form at about thirteen weeks after conception, reach their peak of cell division from eighteen weeks after conception to four months after birth, and cease to form new cells by fifteen to twenty-four months after birth.

Neurons (nerve cells) are the basic units of neurological function; they undoubtedly hold the secrets of how the brain works. Researchers know their role in the transmission of nerve impulses and they know how the neural circuits work, but they are just beginning to unravel their more complex functioning in memory, emotion, and thought.

Neurons differ markedly in size and appearance, but they do possess some common characteristics. In common with nearly all cells, neurons have a cell body, a cell membrane, a nucleus, and a cytoplasm. Each neuron consists of three parts — the cell body, a simple long *axon* that transmits impulses away from the cell body, and several branching *dendrites* that receive impulses from other cells and transmit them toward the cell body. Neurons do not actually touch each other but are close enough to enable chemical electrical impulses to jump the miniscule space (synapse) between the axon of one neuron and the dendrites of the next. In short, the electrical charge of the neuron is changed by the release of neurotransmitters at its axon, which in turn effects the release of other neurotransmitters at the dendrite end of the second neuron.

There are approximately twelve billion neurons in the human nervous system. According to Cowan (1979), during the time the brain is growing in utero it must be generating neurons at a rate of more than 250 000 neurons per minute. Once the neurons are generated in germinal sites, they migrate to terminal locations where they are differentiated into appropriate neuron types. They are myelinated, form synapses with other neurons, and undergo some selective attrition (Rose, 1980). Unlike other cells, mature neurons do not reproduce. When they are destroyed, their loss is permanent.

What makes the nervous system work is a process in which the nerve fibres become sheathed with myelin in a process called myelinization. The myelin sheaths around individual nerves insulate them from one another and make it easier for messages to pass along the nerve pathways; they help speed up neural transmission and make the brain more efficient.

In one sense, the nervous system is complete at birth. That is, all the structures are present and the number of nerve cells does not increase, although the size of these cells does. At birth the parts of the brain most fully developed are those contained in what is usually called the midbrain. The cortex, the sophisticated part of the brain, is present at birth but considerably less developed than it will be later.

The central nervous system of newborn children contains the full complement of neurons, but comparatively few of the axons are covered with myelin. New connections continue to be built up by the process of myelinization, which occurs in different parts of the brain at different times and parallels brain development. For example, the part of the brain that controls gross motor skills is myelinated long before the parts that control fine motor skills. Four-year-olds can run, jump, and skip, but they must work endlessly to tie a bow or spread butter with a knife.

The Spinal Cord

The spinal cord is a pencil-thin, segmented collection of neurons that are related to specific parts of the body. Each segment contains both sensory and motor neurons. As damage to a particular portion of the brain will result in disability in the area of the body controlled by that part of the brain, so damage to the sensory cells in the spinal cord results in loss of sensation to the parts of the body affected by those cells.

The Brain

It is something of a paradox that the human brain is so complex that many scientists believe it is beyond its own ability to comprehend. The brain is a densely packed, incredibly complex organ that weighs about 1.4 kilograms and contains billions of neurons.

Figure 2-1
Human brain

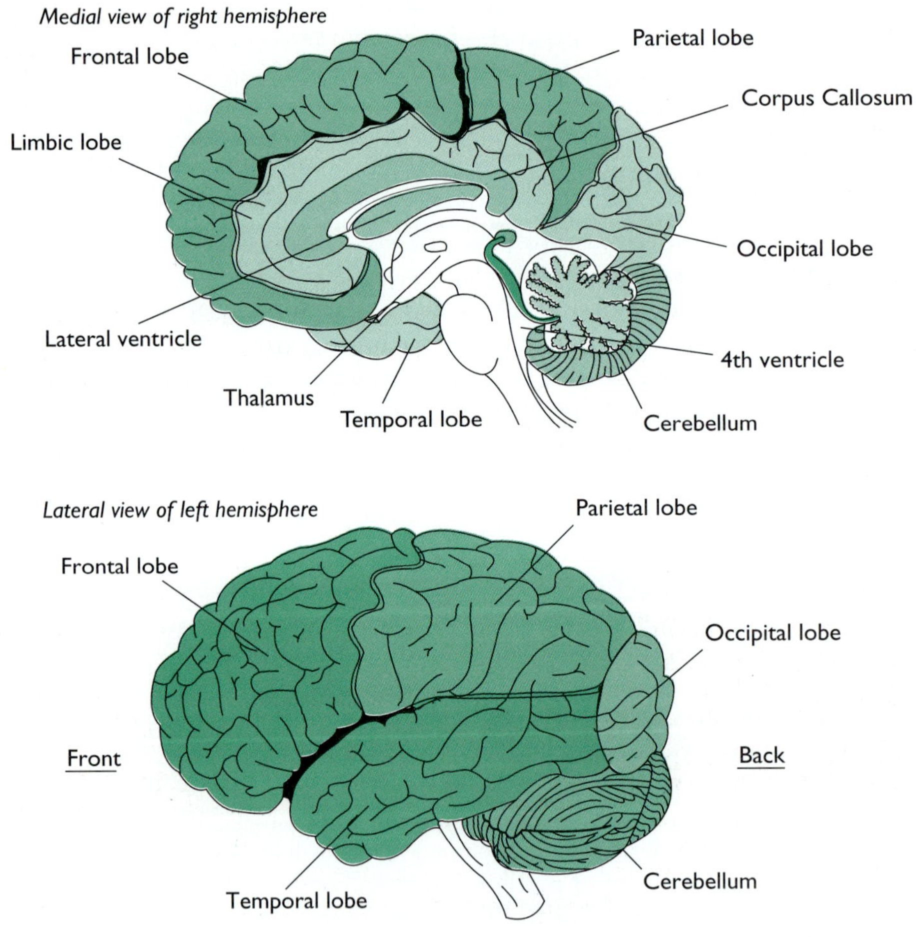

The cerebrum of the human brain — the grey matter that controls higher level intellectual functioning — is subdivided into two hemispheres. Joining the two cerebral hemispheres is the *corpus callosum*, a thick, boomerang-shaped band of fibres. The corpus callosum contains approximately 200 million neurons and is the massive midline conduit for processing and relaying information between the two hemispheres (Phillips, 1990).

Each hemisphere is divided into four lobes — frontal, parietal, occipital, and temporal. The occipital lobe is associated with vision, and the parietal lobe is involved in spatial orientation. The frontal lobe appears to be necessary in anticipatory activity; the temporal lobe has an auditory function. A fifth lobe, which is apparent only in a medial view of the brain, appears to be associated with sexual and emotional functions. The lobes may also perform other functions besides these primary ones. Indeed, researchers are finding that many parts of the brain contribute to functions hitherto associated with only one specific area.

The brain also contains four ventricles. At these sites, cerebrospinal fluid, the fluid that circulates around the brain and the spinal cord, is manufactured.

One of the wonders of human development is the manner in which the human brain, which consists of over 100 billion neurons, can develop so quickly from just a few initial neural cells. Cell differentiation within the brain of the fetus begins during the sixteenth week of gestation. Brain cells begin to multiply most rapidly after the first two months of fetal development, and progressively more slowly after birth. The last three months of fetal life and the first two months after birth are characterized by a spurt in brain growth.

Hemispheric Dominance

On casual examination, the two halves of the human brain look like mirror images of each other. However, there are both structural and functional differences. The left half is almost always larger. The right hemisphere contains many long neural fibres that connect widely separated areas of the brain, whereas the left hemisphere contains many shorter fibres that provide rich interconnections within a limited area (Geschwund and Galaburda, 1987).

Hemispheric specialization — cerebral lateralization — is evident from infancy (Kinsbourne and Hiscock, 1978). **Hemisphericity** refers to a person's tendency to rely more on one cerebral hemisphere to process certain types of information. Lateralization of the brain is not unique to humans, although the human brain may be the most asymmetrical. In humans, the right hemisphere is specialized for holistic processing through the simultaneous integration of information. It primarily houses, and is therefore dominant in, areas such as visio-spatial organization, orientation in space, perception, and recognition of faces, pictures, and photographs. The left hemisphere controls verbal function and the linear logical thinking associated with verbalization.

A hemisphere is said to be dominant if one process is primarily housed there. Yet overall, neither hemisphere is dominant over the other since each possesses specialized talents and brings different skills to a given task — neither hemisphere is competent to analyze data and program a response alone. Although they are responsible for specialized separate functions, the two hemispheres of the human brain are complementary and information passes readily between them through the corpus callosum and other subcortical bodies.

Etiology of Disabling Conditions

A huge variety of factors account for handicapping or potentially handicapping conditions in children. There are, for example, more than 200 known causes of mental retardation and perhaps nearly 2000 inborn errors of metabolism (Berlin, 1983); in total, more than 3500 genetic diseases have been identified. However, the etiology of a particular child's problem all too frequently remains obscure. Despite all that is known, nearly half of all childhood exceptionalities are attributable to unknown causes.

It is usually possible to identify infants with serious genetic or biological problems as disabled during the neonatal period, but it is impossible to predict with complete accuracy how severe the disabilities will be eventually. Early identification of infants with less severe problems or problems that do not become apparent in the neonatal period is more difficult. Children who are later classified as having cerebral palsy, developmental delays, or learning disabilities may exhibit only subtle symptoms in the early years (Dunlap, 1989).

Risk Factors

Risk factors are the causes of potential disabilities. When children are considered to be high risk or at risk, they are seen to be more prone to developing some form of disabling condition. Causes of high risk can be either biological or environmental. Within the causes exist thousands upon thousands of risk factors that can be slotted into three major categories — established risk, biological risk, and environmental risk (Tjossem, 1976). Much overlap exists between the categories.

Not all children who fall within these categories of increased vulnerability become disabled. In fact, the majority of children deemed to be within the traditionally accepted categories of biological and environmental risk, such as those who were born prematurely and those who are raised by young unmarried mothers with low incomes, will develop normally (Shonkoff and Meisels, 1991). Nevertheless, when compared to the general population, a greater proportion of children who are exposed to risk factors will develop significant developmental difficulties. Present estimates indicate that between 30 and 70 percent of infants classified at birth as at risk eventually develop problems that require some form of intervention.

Biological Risk

The established-risk category refers to medical conditions and anomalies that invariably result in a disability or developmental delay. **Established risk** is defined as a diagnosed medical disorder with a known etiology that bears "relatively well known" expectancies for developmental outcomes within varying ranges of developmental disabilities (Tjossem, 1976). This means that certain causes are known to relate to certain conditions and that there is a **continuum of reproductive casualty**, that is, the problems may range from relatively minor through to major difficulties. Established risk is most often related to genetic and chromosomal problems. Established risk includes conditions such as Down syndrome, fragile X syndrome, and infantile autism.

Biological risk relates to infants and toddlers with a history of prenatal, perinatal, neonatal, or early developmental events resulting in biological insults to the developing nervous system. Documented biological risk includes children whose pediatric history or current circumstances reveal significant biological conditions that do not lead inevitably to developmental delay or disorder but carry a greater probability of delay or disability than that found in the general population (Shonkoff and Meisels, 1991).

For purposes of discussion, it is useful to group biological causes of exceptionality into some major categories and then discuss them in specific developmental periods: the prenatal or gestation period; the perinatal, which extends from the seventh month of pregnancy and includes the delivery and birth period as well as the neonatal period, or first two weeks after birth; and the postnatal period.

Throughout the discussion, it should be kept in mind that a number of problems can occur at any time during the cycle. Moreover, a given teratological agent may have different effects depending on timing, severity, genotype, and unknown factors, while similar problems can be the result of various causes. Deafness, for example, can have pre-, peri-, or postnatal time of onset, and can be caused by agents such as rubella, syphilis, meningitis or, in the past, drugs such as streptomycin.

Some of the conditions that are discussed in this chapter and in the following pages are outlined in Table 2-1.

Table 2-1

Sample of disabling conditions and sequelae

Condition	Classification	Timing	Major sequelae
CMV	infection	birth	mental retardation; can be fatal
cystic fibrosis	hereditary anamoly	conception	involvement of digestive and respiratory systems
Down syndrome	chromosomal aberration	nondisjunction at conception or soon after	mental and physical anomalies
Fetal Alcohol Syndrome	intoxication	throughout pregnancy	mental and physical anomalies
fragile X syndrome	chromosomal aberration	conception	mental and physical anomalies
galactosemia	hereditary anomaly	conception	untreated, will result in mental retardation
herpes	infection	birth	mental retardation; often fatal
muscular dystrophy	X-linked genetic anomaly	conception	muscle degeneration

continued on next page

Condition	Classification	Timing	Major sequelae
phenylketonuria (PKU)	autosomal metabolic disorder	conception	untreated will lead to mental retardation
Rh factor	genetic problem	conception	jaundice, mental retardation, deafness
rubella	infection	first trimester	deafness, blindness, mental retardation, multiple handicaps
spina bifida	perhaps multifactorial inheritance		neurological impairments of varying degrees
syphilis	infection	second and third trimester	physical handicaps, mental retardation, sensory disabilities
Tay-Sachs disease	autosomal hereditary anomaly	conception	lethal
Turner's syndrome	chromosomal aberration	conception	mental and physical differences

Prenatal Period

Life begins not at birth, but at conception. At the beginning of life, a human being is smaller than the period at the end of this sentence. The individual is a single cell, barely visible to the naked eye, a tiny drop of fluid made up mainly of non-living material surrounding a miniscule nucleus of living matter. By the time of birth, some thirty-eight weeks later, the individual weights about 3.5 kilograms and contains 200 billion specialized cells (Montagu, 1977).

The prenatal period encompasses three stages. The first two weeks are known as the period of the ovum, or zygote. Next, the period of the embryo lasts until the beginning of the third month. The remaining gestation time is known as the period of the fetus. The change of labels charts the organism's growth from a simple cell to a recognizable human creature. Specific changes occur to the developing human at specific times. Every cell, every tissue, and every organ has its own timetable for coming into existence, for developing, and for beginning to carry out its functions. So consistent are these functions that embryologists can determine them with great accuracy.

From the moment of conception until delivery nine months later, the human being is more susceptible to environment than at any other time. The opening third of pregnancy, the **first trimester**, is the most important to development. Here the die is cast, so to speak, in that the organism is immutably effected. During this time, major organs and basic tissues take shape and develop into their finished forms; after this stage, it is difficult to affect their growth in any fundamental way (Montagu, 1977).

Genetic and Chromosomal Differences

All individuals are born with a unique combination of genes that are theirs alone from the moment of conception. Nothing will ever change. Individuals will die with the same number and set of genes and share these same genes with their offspring. Almost every human cell contains a complete package of hereditary instructions for the characteristics that comprise the individual. These instructions are located in forty-six chromosomes, arranged in twenty-three pairs. Each pair carries one chromosome from each parent.

The first twenty-two chromosomal pairs are **autosomal** (identical) and determine the thousands of traits that make up a human being, whether male of female. The twenty-third pair determines the sex of the individual. Each chromosome consists of thousands of genes, and each gene is made up of deoxyribonucleic acid (DNA) which in turn consists of thousands of combinations of four chemical subunits. The order in which these subunits are joined together spells out the gene's message in the genetic code. Whether a particular cell will become facial skin or ankle bone depends on which genes are "switched on" — a process that is still a mystery (Montagu, 1977).

Many human traits such as skin and hair colour, height and general body build, are controlled by the action of many genes operating together. Such interaction of numerous genes is known as **polygenic inheritance**. Genes are responsible for more than just physical traits: genetics is involved in intellectual factors, including IQ; specific cognitive abilities; academic achievement; reading disability and mental retardation; personality factors, including extroversion and neuroticism, temperament in childhood, and attitudes and beliefs; and psychopathology, including schizophrenia, affective disorders, delinquent and criminal behaviour, and alcoholism (Plomin, 1989).

About 3 to 5 percent of babies are born with a chromosomal abnormality, a clearly defined genetic disease, or a genetically influenced defect, such as malformation of the spine. Among these children, about 3 percent of newborns have some genetic birth defects and about one newborn in 200 has a chromosomal abnormality (Plomin, DeFries, and McClearn, 1990).

In recent decades, massive research has been undertaken in the field of cytogenetics, the study of the location and organization of genetic material from chromosomes. Research into genetic and chromosomal abnormalities has focused on the location, organization, and regulation of the genetic materials of the chromosomes, and on detecting a marker or unusual DNA sequence that is associated with a disease-causing gene (Nelkin and Tancredi, 1989).

Science tells us that just one misspelling in the DNA code throws off the entire process. But, even though a single gene has a dramatic effect on the development of an individual, it now seems that genetics involves far more complicated mathematics than the simple arithmetic of genetic transfer we associate with Gregor Mendel and his pea plants. Cystic fibrosis, for example, is no longer attributed to the action of one deviant gene; there may be as many as sixty different genetic differences that finally manifest as cystic fibrosis.

Genetic Disorders

As the embryo develops, DNA directs the chemical process within its cells. Scientists and researchers have looked for ways to locate and map defective genes to identify potential handicapping conditions before birth. Much of the chromosomal territory is still unknown, but here and there are little pockets of well-covered ground. More than 800 of the estimated

50 000 to 100 000 individual genes have been mapped, and 200 of the 3000 disorders known to be caused by a single gene have been diagnosed (Menolascino and Stark, 1988). The X chromosome is the most explored, with about 115, or 10 percent, of its genes now mapped.

One tiny flaw in the genetic structure can have tragic results. A change in DNA may repair itself or lead to spontaneous abortion (miscarriage). The flaw may also create abnormalities present at birth, called congenital abnormalities or **hereditary anomalies**. Because hereditary anomalies are in the genes, they may be passed on to subsequent generations, the rate depending on the type of inheritance. With dominant inheritance, a child usually has a parent with the same disorder. Dominant conditions tend to show marked variability, with different individuals having different degrees of symptoms, from none to severe.

The March of Dimes Birth Defects Foundation (1987) has catalogued about 2000 confirmed or suspected dominant genetic disorders that can result in mental retardation and other disabilities. These include achondroplasia, a form of dwarfism; Huntington's disease, progressive nervous system degeneration; and polydactyly, extra fingers or toes.

There are about 1000 confirmed or suspected recessive disorders, which include cystic fibrosis, galactosemia, and Tay-Sachs disease. With recessive inheritance, the child must inherit a gene from both parents. Under simple Mendelian inheritance, each child runs a four-to-one risk of manifesting the disorder.

Some disorders are linked to the genes on the twenty-third pair of chromosomes. In X-linked inheritance, the sons have a fifty-fifty chance of inheriting the condition though the mother. Of the more than 250 types of X-linked inheritance identified, colour blindness, hemophilia, and muscular dystrophy are probably the best known. **Multifactorial inheritance** results from the interaction of many genes with other genes and/or environmental factors. Patterns of transmission are poorly defined; some conditions thought to be multifactorial are spina bifida, clubfoot, and cleft lip or palate.

In some cases, various types of transmission can account for a condition. For example, retinitis pigmentosa is a condition that affects the retina, the film-like layer in the back of the eye, and causes progressive visual loss. Retinitis pigmentosa is an inherited disease, transmitted through generations by a gene which may be recessive, dominant, or sex-linked. An estimated one person in eighty carries the gene for recessive retinitis pigmentosa. At present, however, it is rarely possible to detect the carriers ("Children should see," 1980).

Rh (Rhesus) Factor A potential cause of childhood handicapping conditions is mother-child blood incompatibility called Rh factor. While the problem of Rh is rare among many groups — in Eastern Asia and the Pacific, for example — the factor for Rh is missing in about 15 percent of Caucasian and 5 percent of Black women in North America. Since about 1968, when researchers discovered that administration of Rho-gam to Rhesus-negative women after a birth, miscarriage, or abortion would prevent Rhesus incompatability in subsequent offspring, affected babies have been on the decline. Commonly associated sequelae include jaundice, retardation, and deafness.

Inborn Errors of Metabolism While metabolic problems due to hereditary defects account for only a small percentage of disabilities, the study of these disorders has provided valuable knowledge for the prevention and treatment of handicapping conditions due to other organic causes.

Most inborn errors of metabolism are the result of the action of a single pair of genes. Many result in missing or defective enzymes, which are the proteins that help the body convert one substance into another as, for example, in the transformation of nutrients to chemicals usable by the cells. The absence of, or defect in, one of the enzymes means that the normal chemistry of the cell is altered by the inability to provide or dispose of a critical chemical or protein, leading to unusual levels of particular chemicals in the body. Many of these conditions, such as phenylketonuria (PKU) and diabetes, can be treated or controlled; others, such as Tay-Sachs disease — a fatal deterioration of brain function — are untreatable.

Tay-Sachs disease is named after its discovers, Warren Tay, an English physician, and Bernard Sachs, an American physician who identified the condition in 1877. Tay-Sachs results from an enzyme deficiency caused by a single autosomal recessive gene. Infants appear normal at birth, but the nervous system is gradually destroyed because of the missing enzyme, hexosamidose A. The lack of this enzyme allows various fatty substances to build up in the body cells, including those of the brain. The excessive glycolipid in the cells of the nervous system cause the cells to swell, rupture, and finally die.

As the nerve cells die, the child becomes retarded, loses motor ability, and becomes deaf and blind. Effects of the condition can be seen at three to six months after birth. Death is inevitable, usually between four and six years of age.

About one in thirty Jews carries the defective gene. Tay-Sachs is also found in non-Jewish persons, but is a hundred times less frequent. The parents, who are heterozygous carriers, each have only about half of the regular amount of the enzyme, but this is sufficient for normal development.

Phenylketonuria (PKU), a relatively rare genetically transmitted metabolic disorder, was discovered in 1934 by a physician and biochemist, Dr. Ashborn Folling of Norway. (Henderson, 1989). PKU is carried on a double recessive gene by about one in every 600 people, so the chance of two carriers marrying is statistically one in every 3600. The condition affects about one child in every 14 000 and accounts for approximately one percent of all institutionalized mentally retarded individuals. Phenylketonuria is primarily a condition that affects whites, with the highest incidence in the United States and Europe. It is rare in African, Jewish, or Japanese populations.

Some genes act on other genes. These modifier genes then determine how the other genes express themselves. This happens in PKU. The condition is marked by an inability to oxidize normally the amino acid phenylalanine, which is found in fish, dairy products, and most protein sources. The excessive build-up of phenylalanine in the infant's system produces brain damage that can result in severe mental retardation.

The effects of PKU are eliminated or diminished by early screening and a special diet. The screening procedure includes urinalysis and blood tests shortly after birth. The most reliable test is the Guthrie blood test, developed by Dr. Robert Guthrie in 1961. It is performed between the third and sixth day after birth, with retesting after two weeks. Early detection of PKU is vital, because the infant must immediately be restricted to a diet low in phenylalanine. Although phenylalanine cannot be completely eliminated from the child's diet, it can be severely restricted with a phenylalanine-deficient formula, Lofenalac, a prepared milk substitute. Low phenylalanine foods include vegetables, fruits, juices, some cereals, breads, and starches. Milk and dairy foods are restricted and meat is eliminated from the child's daily intake.

Although the effects of phenylketonuria can be almost eliminated, some recent research has demonstrated mild problems even in children on strict diets. One group of researchers, for example, found that some treated children showed neurophysiological dysfunctions that interfered with academic functioning. Others discovered that in treated PKU children, the IQs are within normal limits but they tend to be lower than those of parents, siblings, and non-sibling control subjects (see Ozanne, Kaimmer, and Murdoch, 1990).

Another metabolic disorder that can result in mental retardation is *galactosemia.* In this case, the child lacks the ability to metabolize galactose. As with PKU, successful treatment depends upon early detection and a special diet.

Chromosomal Factors

Chromosomal problems result from chromosomal nondisjunction, which reflects a malfunction in cell division. Problems occur when there is an extra chromosome, or when pieces or parts of chromosomes attach themselves to other chromosomes.

There are many different chromosomal disorders that affect children. Some reveal themselves in newborns through intra-uterine growth retardation, anomalies of the face and hands, or hypotonia which is present at birth even when normal tone or spasticity develops later (Fenichel, 1980). The effects of the damage vary greatly. Wide variations occur in the onset of symptoms, the parts of the body involved, the nature of the symptoms, the degree of severity, and the possible multiplicity of impairments.

Down Syndrome

The most common chromosomal aberration is Down syndrome, which occurs in approximately one in every 1000 live births (Plomin, De Fries, and McClearn, 1990). Down syndrome is an equal opportunity disability: it can occur in any family, regardless of race, socio-economic class, or the education of the parents. It usually happens only once in a family, and strikes most often when the mother is approaching the end of her child-bearing days.

The condition was first identified in 1866 by John Langton Down, a physician at the Earlswood Asylum in Surrey, England. The facial features of children with the condition prompted Down to refer to it as "Mongolian idiocy." He assumed that the condition represented a re-emergence of a more primitive evolutionary status, which he erroneously believed to also be that of the Mongolian race (Blanton, 1976). The Mongolian resemblance, however, is due simply to the development of a fold in the upper eyelid, which is caused not by inheritance but by the failure of the root of the nose to develop normally (Montagu, 1977). Today we have discarded the term "mongoloid" as demeaning and developmentally inappropriate.

Down syndrome was one of the first conditions to be linked to a genetic abnormality. The major breakthrough came in 1959 when Swedish geneticists determined that the correct number of chromosomes in humans was forty-six. When they discovered the extra chromosome in Down, the link between Down syndrome and nondisjunction was confirmed.

There are three major types of Down syndrome — Trisomy 21, translocation, and mosaicism. In each type, the mental and physical problems of the child are caused by extra chromosomal material which somehow disturbs the orderly development of both body and brain.

Down syndrome is the most common chromosomal aberration.

Chromosome 21 is the smallest human chromosome; it contains only about 1.5 percent of the total genetic material (Patterson, 1987). Yet cases of Down syndrome are somehow linked to this tiny chromosome. There are no individuals with the clinical symptoms of Down syndrome who do not have at least partial Trisomy 21.

Trisomy 21 accounts for the great majority of children afflicted with Down syndrome (about 93 percent). There are actually fourteen different types of Trisomy 21, but all are basically problems of dysfunction. In each case, the twenty-first pair of chromosomes contains three chromosomes instead of two. This may result from a mistake in chromosomal distribution in the egg or sperm, or because the chromosomes were distributed unequally when the fertilized egg began to divide.

Of the rest of the population with Down syndrome, 5 percent have translocation, in which only part of chromosome 21 is present in triplicate. In this condition, the extra chromosomal material most often attaches to chromosome 14, 15, 21, or 22 (Patterson, 1987). Although the actual chromosome count is forty-six, the affected child suffers from the same overdose of chromosome 21 as the child with standard Trisomy. There may be hereditary components in translocation.

Mosaicism accounts for about 2 percent of Down syndrome cases. This condition results when there is a faulty distribution of chromosomes in later cell divisions. The child possesses some normal cells and some with a Trisomy condition. Any resulting physical and mental anomalies depend on the number of affected cells.

More than fifty physical signs are listed as characteristic of Down syndrome. Some are apparent at birth, some appear much later, and some disappear with age. The number of physical features that a child displays bears no relationship to the degree of retardation. Few children have all the characteristics typical of the syndrome. Table 2-2 outlines the most common.

Table 2-2

Some observable physical characteristics associated with Down syndrome

Head	**Hair**	**Face**
distinctive shape; skull rounded and small	sparse, fine and soft	flat profile
Nose	**Eyes**	**Ears**
small and "pug"; flat bridge; undeveloped or absent nasal cartilige; mucous discharge common	epicanthic fold; speckling of iris (Brushfield's spots); strabismus or nystagmus common	small and low-set; overlapping upper letices
Mouth	**Teeth**	**Tongue**
high arched; thick, fissured lips; narrow palate	small, irregularly aligned; late erupting	coarse, protruding
Hands	**Muscles**	**Feet**
broad, stumpy, with short fingers; palmar crease (simian line) on one or both hands; incurved little finger (clindactly)	general hypotonia; flexible joints	broad and short; excessive space between first and second toes
Skin	**Abdomen**	**Stature**
thick, dry, rough; mottled or flushed	prominent umbilical hernia common	short; average height: male – 152.4 cm female – 139.7 cm

The chances of having a child with Down syndrome increase dramatically with the age of the parents, particularly the mother. (Very young mothers are an exception to this rule: they are more likely to have a Down syndrome baby than women in their twenties or thirties.) For the woman over forty, the chances of bearing a Down infant are approximately one in 80. For women over forty-five, the chances increase to one in 60 (Hansen, 1978).

Many authorities believe that Down syndrome may result from a combination of two factors — chemical changes in the egg cells due to the mother's aging ovaries, and a reduction in the secretion of various hormones in older women (Montagu, 1977). The mother's age may not be the only factor, however. Researchers are discovering possible links between Down syndrome and the amount of the mother's exposure to radiation and certain viruses. They are also exploring the role of the aging father, who contributes the extra chromosome in 20 to 25 percent of the cases (Abroms and Bennett, 1983). For men aged forty-one and up, there is an increased risk of fathering children with Trisomy 21, regardless of the age of the mother.

Fragile X Syndrome

Fragile X syndrome is a relatively recent addition to the catalogue of causes of retardation. The fragile X chromosome was first reported in 1969, but the syndrome was not consistently diagnosed until the 1980s (Hagerman, 1988). Identification uses a karyotype with a special culture medium low in folic acid.

Today fragile X syndrome is second only to Down syndrome among cytogenetic abnormalities associated with mental retardation (Simen and Rogers, 1989). The prevalence of individuals affected by the fragile X syndrome is approximatelty one in 1000. The incidence among live male births is about one in 1350; among female births, about one in 2033 (Webb et al., 1986). The prevalence of carriers is higher. Reports of the prevalence of fragile X syndrome (those affected and carriers) in the general population ranges from 1.9 to 5.9 percent (Blomquist et al., 1983; Jacobs, Mayer, and Abruzzo, 1986).

Fragile X is a marker on the X chromosome at position 927. The syndrome is caused by an abnormal gene(s) at the lower end of the long arm of the X chromosome. The chromosome is brittle in places and may even be separated into two or more pieces. Chromosomal analysis will demonstrate a fragile site (a narrowing of the chromosome in this region) in some cells of all affected males and in most females who are carriers.

The genetics involved in fragile X seem to be unlike those of most typical X-linked recessive conditions. Santos (1992) notes that fragile X runs through a family tree in a multi-step process, resulting two or three generations later in full activation of the mutation. During this time many people can be affected to various degrees (physically, cognitively, and behaviourally) before a complete diagnosis is made. If this current theory proves true, says Santos, then physicians will have an increased ability to diagnose fragile X and this may have a significant impact on prevalence estimates. The number of people affected, either mildly or more severely, may be higher than originally thought (Santos, 1992).

Clinicians familar with fragile X syndrome utilize physical findings to aid in diagnosis of affected males (see Table 2-3). Fragile X patients undergo changes in appearance from childhood through the adult years. During the growth period in males, testicular volume increases, the face grows in an elongated pattern, the forehead becomes more prominent, and the ears enlarge. The adult male patient typically has a long face, large ears, a prominent forehead, midface hypoplasia, and a prominent jaw. The most common feature seen in the postpubescent male is macro-orchidism (large testicles). However, among prepubertal males macro-orchidism is only reported in approximately 50 percent of the population (Simen and Rogers, 1989).

Figure 2-2
Diagram of fragile X.

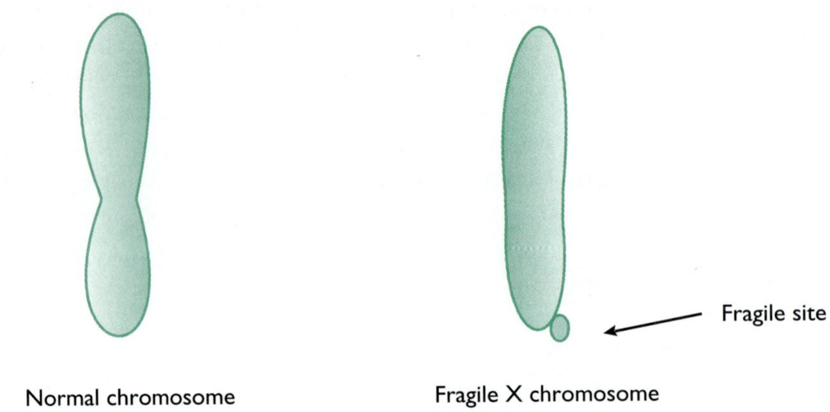

Some of the physical features typical of fragile X males can also be seen in female carriers, such as mildly prominent ears, a long face, and hyperextensible finger joints. Female carriers who are affected cognitively are more likely to show these physical features (Hagerman, 1988). Among fragile X positive females, however, facial features are exceedingly variable and do not serve as an aid in diagnosis.

Table 2-3

Features of the fragile X syndrome

Physical	Non-physical
large head size	developmental delay
large flat ears	mental retardation
long narrow face	learning disabilities
prominent forehead	hyperactivity
broad nose	short attention span
high palate	autistic behaviours
large testicles	fearfulness, shyness
large hands; non-tapering fingers	rapid, repetitive speech
mitral valve prolapse (heart murmur)	talkativeness
increased birth-weight	difficulty adjusting to change
repeated ear infections	

Source: Finucane, 1988

Turner's Syndrome

Turner's syndrome (TUS) is a condition affecting offspring in one of approximately 2000 live female births. Diagnosis is made by karyotype. Women with TUS either lack an X chromosome or have a structural abnormality in one of the X chromosomes.

The syndrome is characterized by short stature, growth failure, or gonadal dysgenesis (unformed reproductive systems) that inhibits spontaneous pubertal onset and fertility. Some women with TUS have abnormal appearances and/or medical problems such as problems of the aorta, hypertension, and renal abnormalities. Individuals with TUS also have a characteristic pattern of cognitive abilities consisting of normal verbal IQ and relatively lower performance IQ due to difficulty with space forms and number concepts (Downey et al., 1991).

Infections and Intoxications

During pregnancy, the mother's health and adequate nutrition are vital to the development of the fetus. Any maternal condition that impairs the transport of oxygen and nutrients to the fetus or the exchange of metabolic waste products has the potential to act deleteriously on fetal development.

Etiologically, environmental agents that may harm the developing infant are known as **teratogens**, from the Greek *teros*, meaning monster. Teratogens that can cause damage include prescription drugs, hard drugs, nicotine, and alcohol.

Rubella

Rubella (German measles) is a major cause of handicapping conditions in children. The potential damage caused by rubella was first identified in 1941 by Australian physician McAllister Gregg.

Rubella provides an example of a critical period when exposure to a certain teratogen is most harmful to the fetus. A **critical period** is a part of the life cycle during which the developing organism is particularly sensitive or responsive to specific environmental forces. Outside this period, the same event or influences are thought to have little if any lasting effects.

The rubella virus crosses the placenta and affects the developing fetus. The fetal organs likely to be affected by rubella are those whose development is underway when the mother contracts the virus. The eye, ear, nervous system, and heart are especially vulnerable at early periods of fetal development. In cases where the mother contracts rubella during the first trimester of pregnancy, it is estimated that 50 percent of fetuses are damaged if the disease is contracted in the first month, while 20 percent of embryos affected in the second month are born with defects (Rosenblith and Sims-Knight, 1985).

Severe sensorineural hearing loss is the major effect of maternal rubella (Hardy and Bordley, 1973); other major permanent features include cataracts, glaucoma, mental retardation, congenital heart disease, and cerebral palsy. As well, a number of reports (e.g., Menser, Forrest, and Bransky, 1978; Preece, Kearney, and Marshall, 1977) have documented a significant occurrence of late onset defects of rubella (conditions that are not apparent at birth but occur later), including vascular disease, growth hormone deficency, thryroid dysfunction, and diabetes mellitus.

Rubella is often seen in epidemics that are estimated to occur in twenty-five-year cycles. In 1964, the last major rubella epidemic created a phenomenal spike in the charts measuring the numbers of special children who were left deaf and blind or with other multiple handicaps as a result of the disease. Vaccines developed in 1969 make a rubella baby rare today, however.

Syphilis

Syphilis, one of the venereal diseases, is produced by the bacterium *Treponema pallidum* (also called *Spirocheta pallida*). It does not affect the developing organs as does rubella but produces destructive lesions (abnormal changes in structure) in already developed organs.

While rubella is most critical during the first trimester of pregnancy, syphilis affects the fetus after the sixteenth or eighteenth week of gestation. If the disease is controlled by penicillin before that time, only about 2 percent of fetuses will contract it. After the fifth month, uncontrolled syphilis will affect about 40 percent of fetuses. Twenty-five percent of affected babies die before birth; 33 percent of those who survive die in early childhood.

Infants who survive may suffer many handicaps, including mental retardation, blindness, and deafness. Other affected infants show liver problems, peritonitis, central nervous system disorders, and pegged teeth (Montagu, 1977; Rosenblith and Sims-Knight, 1985).

Drugs

When we talk about drugs, we are referring to a wide assortment of potentially harmful agents that range from hard drugs such as heroin, through prescription and over-the-counter drugs, to drugs widely used in Canadian society — nicotine and alcohol. The problem is significant, and it is growing. Some studies report that as many as 15 percent of pregnant women admit to using illegal drugs or alcohol; experts fear that the real rate may be double that (Greer, 1990a). Because cocaine, for example, is illegal, only selected samples of children have been tested. The numbers of affected children could therefore be far higher than current estimates.

Chemicals can cause a wide range of congenital abnormalities, said to account for about 10 percent of birth defects (Schwartz and Yaffe, 1980). Dr. Harold Nickens of the American Society of Addiction Medicine has observed that the growing number of infants born to addicted mothers may require the medical community "to define an entirely new, organic brain syndrome" (Greer, 1990a). These children suffer from what Nickens calls "a well of yet to be determined birth defects" (Greer, 1990a). Experts anticipate that these children will form part of what has been characterized as a "bio-underclass" and will be prominent among the next generation of special education students. Many of the problems will arise because they are likely to experience the same dysphoria and thought and mood disorders as a recovering addict, which is what the child is (Greer, 1990a).

Keep in mind throughout this discussion on drug use and abuse that it is extremely difficult to attribute specific characteristics to certain drugs, since abuse of multiple drugs is common. Mothers who are multi-drug users (cocaine plus other drugs) have children with the most adverse outcomes (Van Dyke and Fox, 1990). Infants of multi-drug users fare worse than infants exposed to single drugs in regard to birth-weight, gestational age, withdrawal responses, and length of hospital stay (Kaye et al., 1989). In addition, prenatal exposure is often compounded by the presence of social factors such as poverty, neglect, or drug use by others in the home.

Prescription Drugs Prescription drugs have been shown to have an adverse effect on fetal development. Research has linked some antibiotic, anticonvulsant, and anti-cancer medications to fetal malformations (Batshaw and Perret, 1986). There is also evidence that pain-relieving drugs administered during labour and delivery can result in behavioural differences in infants (Rosenblith and Sims-Knight, 1985).

Cocaine The 1980s saw an increase in the use of cocaine for all socio-economic classes, races, ages, and sexes. Cocaine now surpasses heroin as America's leading street drug (Tarr and Macklin, 1987). In the United States, the president's National Drug Cohort Strategy Report estimated that 100 000 babies are born to cocaine-using women each year (Kusserow, 1990). With the increased use of cocaine, there is growing concern about the long-term effects of this drug on the fetus and the neonate (Van Dyke and Fox, 1990). However, researchers point out that "there is no typical profile of children prenatally exposed to drugs, though there seems to be a developmental continuum of vulnerabilities that persist into the preschool years" (Cole, Jones, and Sadofsky, 1990, p. 1).

The use of drugs — both illegal and legal — during pregnancy can result in serious birth defects.

Some neurochemical studies on cocaine in utero suggest that if it is present during gestation, it may affect developing fetal neuromotor systems, which could have a significant impact on the developing nervous system (Van Dyke and Fox, 1990). In the fetus, cocaine affects the vascular system causing the blood vessels to constrict in a state known as vasoconstriction (Chasnoff, 1987). This in turn puts increasing pressure on the heart and the blood vessels, increases blood pressure and restricts the flow of oxygen (Schneider and Chasnoff, 1987). Babies are therefore more prone to intercranial hemorrhages.

Cocaine use during the last trimester may cause fetal hyperactivity, increased fetal blood pressure, or premature placental detachment from the uterus, which endangers both mother and child. Other research (Bingol et al., 1987) has concluded that cocaine use in humans significantly reduces the weight of the fetus, increases the stillbirth rate related to abruptio placentae, and is associated with a higher malformation rate. Infants are likely to die before birth, to be born prematurely, and to be abnormally small for their ages (Brody, 1988; Rest, 1990).

Case histories of congenital abormalities among cocaine-exposed children show missing fingers and forearm bones, cardiac anomalies, and microcephaly (Hoyme et al., 1990). Newborns may be born with deformed heads, lungs, digestive systems, or limbs. Researchers also describe children experiencing convulsions and stoppage of breathing (Chasnoff, Chisum, and Kaplan, 1988; Chasnoff et al., 1988). Other reports of afflicted infants point to poor baby state, which includes tremors, chronic irritability, and poor visual orientation.

Later, in learning situations, these children demonstrate poor abstract reasoning and memory, poor judgment, inability to concentrate, inability to deal with stress, frequent tantrums, a wide variety of behaviour disorders, and violent acting out.

In the late 1980s, crack, a relatively pure and inexpensive form of cocaine, emerged on the drug scene. As with cocaine, there is no single profile of an infant born to a crack-using mother. Some appear healthy; some are adversely affected.

Some crack-using mothers are giving birth to addicted babies who are having strokes and seizures, who are born with small heads, missing bowels, and malformed genitals. Crack babies are irritable, tremelous, and difficult to soothe for at least three months. They have a significantly higher rate of Sudden Infant Death Syndrome (SIDS) than babies who are not prenatally exposed. Many suffer neurological damage from prenatal drug exposure (Rest, 1990).

Too often, the infant's environment simply compounds the problems. Children born exposed to crack leave the hospital and enter homes often headed by poor, drug-addicted young mothers who are not able to cope with the demands of their own care, let alone the needs of a high-strung, difficult to soothe, unhealthy infant (Paciorek and Munro, 1995).

Heroin Heroin passes the placenta so that infants of addicted women are born addicted. Withdrawal symptoms can prove fatal to the tiny infant. Survivors suffer a number of difficulties, but it is not known whether these extend beyond infancy. Methodone, the substitute that is used to withdraw heroin addicts, may cause even more physiological damage to the fetus. Children are small and subject to high mortality (Finnegan, Reeser, and Connaughton, 1977). They suffer more seizures and central nervous system damage, and seem to have altered breathing responses that persist twenty to forty days after methodone is no longer detected in their systems (Rosenblith and Sims-Knight, 1985).

Fetal Alcohol Syndrome Together with nicotine, alcohol is the drug most likely to be used and abused by Canadians. Alcohol in moderate amounts used to be thought safe during pregnancy. We now realize that even small amounts can cross the placenta and damage the developing fetus. Alcohol ingestion by pregnant women has been found to be the culprit in a number of abnormalities in children.

A small proportion of children of drinking mothers are born with a **syndrome** — a constellation of findings similar from patient to patient — known as Fetal Alcohol Syndrome (FAS), first described in 1973 by Kenneth Jones and his colleagues. FAS exists on a continuum ranging from the full-blown syndrome to minor developmental defects. Children may have the full-blown syndrome or Fetal Alcohol Effect (FAE). General estimates of the incidence of full-blown FAS are one to two per 1000 live births. Children who exhibit only FAE effects are thought to number three to five per 1000 (Sandor, 1981).

In children affected by FAS, mental retardation is a major characteristic. As the condition varies in intensity, there are also differences in outward expression and in the degree of mental retardation involved. Full-blown FAS affects the whole body system, causing malformations and anomalies in the nervous system, the musculoskeletal structure, and the internal organs, especially the heart and urinogenital tracts. Examples of anomalies are shown in Table 2-4. Other problems that may be associated with alcohol consumption on the part of the pregnant woman include spontaneous abortions and miscarriages.

Table 2-4

Specific sequelae associated with FAS

Neurological	Craniofacial
mental retardation	low-set ears
microcephalus	short low-bridged nose
seizures	epicanthic folds
tremors	short lower jaw
irritability	long upper lip
poor fine co-ordination	droopy eyelids
hyperactivity	high-arched palate
Skeletal	**Other**
club foot	cardiac defects
spinal fusion	kidney defects
growth deficiency	genital problems
abnormal palmar creases	poor weight gain

Physical and mental anomalies occur because alcohol hinders fetal growth and produces small babies with small brains. Damage to the fetus is caused when the ethanol in the alcohol takes fluid from the developing brain, causing the death of brain cells. Children with FAS may have specific physical stigmata, such as small eyes, a flat bridge of the nose, retarded growth, and a small head circumference, known as microcephaly. The more physical handicaps evident, the more severe the retardation is likely to be (Montagu, 1977).

In the third trimester of pregnancy, the unborn child is gaining most of its eventual birth weight and the brain cells are rapidly multiplying and increasing in size. Some evidence indicates that the toxic effects of alcohol inhibit the development of major tissues, which may explain the presence of delays in growth and such conditions as congenital cardiac and kidney defects (McLeod, 1981). Iber (1980) postulated that craniofacial abnormalities occur because particular parts of the face are dependent upon a brain of normal size to fill out the face. The critical period for the development of the facial features associated with FAS seems to be the third or fourth week of prenatal development when the head is starting to take shape.

Much is still unknown about FAS; the connection between alcohol consumption and reproductive risk is not clear. The medical profession has not yet determined a safe level of alcohol for the pregnant woman, and the influence of moderate drinking is unknown. Certainly, infants of mothers who drink heavily are at greater risk, but even in moderate drinkers there is evidence that the amount of alcohol consumed is related to infant's arousal levels and central nervous system functioning (Streissguth, Barr, and Martin, 1983).

It has been suggested that heavy drinking implies an intake of ninety millitres of alcohol a day during pregnancy (Landesman-Dwyer et al. 1980). One study found that two ounces of alcohol in the first trimester (one six-pack of beer) led to 12 percent of the sample having infants with malformations, similar to children of chronic alcoholics ("Crisis," [1986]). However, given the metabolic variations between individuals, there is no correlation between the quantity and frequency of the ingestion of alcohol and the number of defects in a child.

Maternal Smoking When the mother smokes a cigarette, the fetus smokes it too. After the first few puffs its heart begins to beat faster, it feels a drop in oxygen (hypoxia) and an increase in carbon dioxide. It stops moving and increases its fetal breathing to try to make up for the hypoxia. All these responses have a severe enough cumulative effect in heavy smokers to contribute to spontaneous abortions, bleeding during pregnancy, premature rupture of the amniotic sac, fetal deaths, and deaths of newborns (Salkind, 1990). Smokers are twice as likely as nonsmokers to have low-birth-weight babies. The infants of smokers weigh an average of 200 grams less than infants of nonsmokers (Vorhees and Mollnow, 1987).

Coffee has also been implicated. One large-scale study (Linn et al., 1982) that analyzed the medical records of 12 205 women who gave birth over a three-year period found that birth problems were more common among heavy coffee drinkers (three or more cups a day). Problems, however, could not be attributed to coffee alone since it was often accompanied by cigarette smoking.

Maternal Nutrition

A mother's diet and nutrition play a significant role in the growth and development of her fetus. The importance of nutrition is suggested by the relationship between the mother's diet, the newborn's weight, and the child's eventual learning ability (see Salt, Galler, and Ramsey, 1988).

The period of intrauterine development and the first eighteen months after birth are crucial to the physiological development of every organ system. This is especially true for the brain. Inadequate prenatal nutrition can affect the relationship between the body's biochemistry and the functioning of the brain. Severe malnutrition can stunt brain growth and produce a significant lowering of intellectual ability. Nutrition in the mother seems to be particularly important in the third trimester when the fetus should be making rapid gains in weight.

Postnatal malnutrition, especially during the first six months of an infant's life, is also a critical factor in brain development. Various important neural structures and interconnections between the brain cells develop during this period. In the postnatal period, research indicates that severe chronic deprivation of either general nutrition or certain special diet substances can cause behaviour disorders as well as physical disorders and mental retardation (Lahey and Ciminero, 1980). When prenatal and postnatal malnutrition both exist, problems are likely to be much more severe.

Maternal nutritional deficiency covers a wide range of problems and developmental consequences. In general, malnourished women are much more likely to produce low-birth-weight babies although it may be that low birth-weight per se is not so much a problem as that maternal malnutrition increases the fetus's vulnerability to other risk factors. Severe malnutrition increases the risk of congenital defects, prolonged labour, stillbirth, and infant mortality during the first year. **Toxemia**, which refers to several common disorders of pregnancy, may well be related to maternal nutrition (Montagu, 1977).

Toxemias appear in the first trimester of pregnancy and are characterized by edema (water retention), hypertension, and protein in the urine. Toxemias are not passed on to the child but alter the intrauterine environment in which the child is developing. Severe cases lead to extreme blood pressure and convulsions, known as eclampsia. Toxemias may impair normal fetal growth, and the drugs used to treat them may also harm the fetus (Berlin, 1983).

Unknown Prenatal Influence

There are a number of conditions present at or before birth for which there is no known cause. One such condition is **microcephaly**, a rare phenonomon in which brain development is impaired by an abnormally small cranium. Another is **macrocephaly**, which refers to an enlargement of the head, most frequently caused by **hydrocephalus**, a build-up of cerebrospinal fluid in the brain. Retardation may follow, but its severity can be reduced or eliminated by early diagnosis and treatment. To treat hydrocephalus, a shunt is surgically implanted to drain excess fluid away from the brain and into a vein behind the ear or in the neck. (See also Chapter 13).

Birth and Neonatal Development

Birth is neither a beginning nor an ending, but a bridge between two stages of life. Birth takes place in three stages: labour, delivery, and afterbirth. It is a long process. An average first labour takes fourteen hours; the average for later labours is eight hours. In many areas, too much or too little is not a good thing. This is true of labour — labours that are too long or too short produce a greater likelihood of problems.

Birth can be dangerous for the child and/or the mother. The fetus may be in an unusual position, such as breech or transverse presentations. The membranes may rupture too early, leading to infection. An incorrectly placed placenta may mean excessive bleeding. Drugs and forceps used during delivery may cause harm to the fetus.

Before the child is born, there is no contact with the atmosphere. The oxygen that is necessary for fetal survival and to the orderly development of the body reaches the fetus by way of the mother's bloodstream. However, when the time of birth draws near, the oxygen level in the placenta and in the child's circulatory system drops sharply. During the birth process, the human fetus is squeezed through the birth canal for several hours, during which time the head sustains considerable pressure and the infant is intermittently deprived of oxygen. Most infants tolerate this without difficulty; in spite of surface appearances, the stresses of normal delivery are usually not harmful (Lagercrantz and Slotkin, 1986).

Sometimes, however inadequate uterine environments pose additional risks, and the infant cannot tolerate the normal changes of labour. If the child is overly deprived of oxygen, the condition is called **anoxia**. Most birth injuries result in deprivation of oxygen to the immature brain, which leads to abridgment of nervous system function. Pathologically and clinically, deprivation of oxygen in the infant brain is similar to cases of stroke in the adult brain (Fenichel, 1980). If supplies of oxygen to the nerve cells of the brain are too greatly reduced, brain damage or death can result.

When a portion of the brain is damaged, the part of the individual that is controlled by that portion of the brain is also damaged. Anoxia may be a villain in cerebral palsy, some types of epilepsy, and some mental retardation. Mild anoxia can also produce other subtle forms of childhood disability, such as irritability, muscular tension, rigidity, learning disabilities, and motor defects.

Neurological Impairments

Neurological impairments can occur before, during or after birth. Any factor that leads to hormonal, chemical, or blood-flow imbalances can cause central nervous system problems.

While pre- and perinatal causes are crucial, the incidence of infant and preschool brain injury is increasing. Causes include household and auto accidents, meningitis and encephalitis; anoxia caused through such events as near-drowning, inhalatation of toxic fumes, and choking; and periventricular hemorrhage (Ewing-Cobbs, Fletcher, and Levin, 1985). Table 2-5 outlines some of the causes of damage to the central nervous system.

Table 2-5

Some causes of damage to the central nervous system, with examples

Causes	Examples
neoplasms	brain tumour
oxygen deprivation	carbon monoxide poisoning, anoxia
maternal infection	rubella, syphilis
maternal intoxication	Fetal Alcohol Syndrome
child intoxication	lead poisoning
child infection	encephalitis
malnutrition	inadequate protein to fetus or young child
vascular accidents	brain hemorrhage
radiation	excessive x-rays
genetic defects	errors of metabolism
developmental errors	absence of brain substance
trauma	automobile accidents resulting in direct head injury
chromosomal abnormalities	Down syndrome
gestational problems	prematurity

Damage to the brain may be so mild as to be undetectable or so profound as to reduce the child to a very low level of functioning. There may be focal brain damage that involves a very specific and delimited area of the brain, or diffuse brain damage involving a large or poorly defined area. Depending of the degree and location of the damage, the child's behaviour will be affected. For example, one of the traditional etiologies of learning disabilities is minimal brain dysfunction. On the other hand, generalized and diffuse brain damage results in mental retardation; damage to the motor areas causes cerebral palsy.

Pre-Term and Low-Birth-Weight Infants

Pre-term or **premature babies** are generally defined as those born before the completion of thirty-seven weeks, a full week short of the full thirty-eight week term. About 7 percent of children are born pre-term or of low birth-weight. Prematurity occurs in ten or twelve births per hundred (Berlin, 1983) and is is more likely to occur in multiple births. Premature babies generally weigh 2500 grams or less, as compared to the usual birth weight of 3000 to 3500 grams. Because of possible difficulties with placental nutrition, babies may be of low birth-weight but not premature.

The earliest stage possible for survival outside the womb is generally considered to be about twenty-seven weeks. Fetuses born before this have little chance of survival, primarily because of lung immaturity. A pre-term baby has vey little surfactin, a substance that normally coats the lungs during the last three or four weeks of pregnancy to prevent them from collapsing. The most critical problem for pre-term babies is obtaining enough oxygen. Respiratory distress syndrome is responsible for about half of all newborn deaths in North America.

More than half the premature infants who weight less than 1000 grams die at birth or shortly afterwards. Children born after twenty-seven weeks of gestation have a survival rate of 60 percent, and those born at twenty-eight weeks have an 85 to 90 percent chance of survival (Musgrove, 1984).

Research has clearly established that pre-term infants have a higher incidence of developmental problems in childhood than full-term infants. Studies show that those infants classified as at risk more often develop problems than those classified neonatally as well babies. Yet current efforts to predict which individual infants will develop subsequent disabilities using perinatal medical factors are not very successful. Thus, in populations of four-month-olds, it is often impossible to distinguish those who will be functioning normally at age two from those who will display serious developmental delays (Bricker and Squires, 1989).

Full-term but low-birth-weight infants are also prone to a range of potentially dangerous conditions. In Ontario, Sagal (1982) studied the developmental progress of 294 low-birth-weight infants. Of the 179 children who survived, 30 showed neurological impairments, including microcephaly, blindness, deafness, mental retardation, and retrolental fibroplasia. As they grow, small-for-date babies as a group tend to remain shorter and lighter than their age mates while pre-term babies who survive are more likely to achieve normal heights and weights.

Additional risk factors can compound the original probems of pre-term or small-for-term infants. For premature infants, the risk is a function of both gestational age and birth weight. Premature and low-birth-weight infants may experience central nervous system (CNS) difficulties that inhibit their ability to develop normally. Such CNS difficulties may be overcome in a stable family environment; in unstable low-income families lacking decent housing and enough money, the difficulties present at birth may result in developmental delays and learning problems (see Sameroff et al., 1987). (Parent interactions with pre-term infants are discussed in Chapter 16.)

An overly long pregnancy can also be problematic. Infants born two weeks or more beyond the expected due date are said to be **postmature**. These children are in somewhat greater danger from anoxia and cerebral hemorrhage than children born at the normal 266 to 270 days. They also have a higher death rate and suffer more frequently from severe congenital abnormalities (Montagu, 1977).

CMV and Herpes

Some conditions are transmitted to the baby right at the time of delivery. Two potentially harmful or fatal conditions of this nature are cytomegalovirus (CMV) and herpes.

CMV, a form of herpes, is the most frequently occurring congenital virus among newborns. It affects about 3 percent of pregnant women (Kurant and Sever, 1977). The condition can cause a range of devastating problems in children, including deafness and mental retardation. When babies are born to mothers who have infections in the active stages, the mortality rate is about 50 percent. Of children that survive, about half suffer from conditions such as microcephaly, spasticity, paralysis, seizures, deafness, or blindness (McIntosh, 1984). It is difficult to know how many cases of each are caused by CMV because it is often difficult to diagnose (Schildroth, Rawlings, and Allen, 1989).

Herpes (HVH) is actually less prevalent than CMV, but it is potentially as damaging and can be fatal. Although it is a rare occurrence, babies are infected as they pass through the cervix or vagina. Affected infants are treated with an antiviral drug, but survivors are still at considerable risk for permanent damage (Hetherington and Parke, 1986).

Pediatric AIDS

Acquired Immuno-Deficiency Syndrome (AIDS) was first reported in 1981 as a mysterious ailment that seemed only to afflict particular groups in society. However, within a few years AIDS was recognized as a condition resulting from a viral infection that can afflict anyone of any class, any age, or either sex.

The T-cell lymphotropic virus, Type 111, is commonly called the human immunodeficiency virus (HIV). HIV is the cause of the deadly AIDS. The virus attacks and seriously disrupts the body's immune system, its defence against disease. Without the protection of the immune system, AIDS sufferers are prone to fatal infections and cancers. HIV is taking many forms and, contrary to the usual evolution of infectious agents, it appears to develop within an infected individual toward more rather than less virulent strains (Cheng-Meyer et al., 1988). This finding suggests that HIV is an even more threatening virus than originally believed (Dokecki, Baumeister, and Kupstas, 1989).

AIDS in children may be the result of tainted blood transfusions or, rarely, it may be contracted through the mother's milk. The vast majority of children with pediatric AIDS have obtained their infection during birth from the mother, who used intravenous drugs or was sexually active with infected men (Baumeister, Kupstas, and Klindworth, 1990). Placental passage in utero and newborn contact with the mother's blood or vaginal fluids during the process of labour and delivery are the two major routes of perinatal HIV infection (Dokecki, Baumeister, and Kupstas, 1989).

Children infected with HIV will likely develop symptoms of AIDS; between 30 and 60 percent of children born to HIV mothers will contract AIDS (Dokecki, Baumeister, and Kupstas, 1989). Pediatric AIDS is fully discussed in Chapter 13.

Postnatal Development

Postnatally, accidents are the most common cause of handicapping conditions in children, followed by cancer in its various forms. As well, a variety of childhood diseases and infections can hinder children's progress.

Infections

Meningitis and encephalitis can cause devastating childhood handicaps. Both can result in mental retardation, visual impairment, deafness, cerebral palsy, and other disabling conditions. **Meningitis** attacks the meninges, or coverings of the brain and spinal cord; it is accompanied by a high fever. Spinal meningitis has a mortality rate of about 10 percent in young children and is often an offshoot of influenza B. Recently a new vaccine became available to protect children from spinal meningitis.

Encephalitis can be caused by viral, bacterial, or parasitic infections. More encephalitic children suffer retardation than do meningitic children.

Environmental Factors

It is almost impossible to determine the relative influences of heredity and environment on human behaviour, for every human life is a complex interplay of heredity and environment. The genes alone cannot produce a human being; an environment must also exist to provide nourishment, warmth, stimulation, and protection. Both heredity and environmental factors are crucial to child development. A child's growth will be seriously hampered by restricted sensory stimulation, deprivation, and impoverishment.

We are increasingly able to identify the environmental conditions that increase the likelihood that a child will have a learning or a behaviour problem (Werner, 1986). Documented environmental risk includes children whose pediatric histories, caregiving circumstances, and current family situation contain risk factors that do not lead invariably to developmental delay but that carry a greater probability of delay or disability than that found in the general population (Shonkoff and Meisels, 1990). In this sense, **environmental risk** applies to infants and toddlers who are considered biologically sound but whose early life experiences (including maternal and family care, health care, nutrition, opportunities for expression of language, adaptive behaviour, and patterns of physical and social stimulation) are limited to an extent that creates a high probability of delayed development (Tjossem, 1976).

The two environmental problems that have been studied most are the lack of early psychological stimulation and the effects of severe malnutrition. These two factors are not always independent: in many cases, malnutrition and lack of early stimulation operate in the same child.

Prevention

The prevention of handicapping and potentially handicapping conditions is usually classified as primary, secondary, and tertiary. **Primary prevention** is concerned with removing the causative factors that account for the initial occurrence of the disorder or strengthening the well-being of individuals in the population as a form of innoculation against the causes of subsequent problems. The focus is on the establishment of medical and social programs to reduce the occurrence of diseases and conditions that cause disabilities. The interventions are made available to the entire population and are targeted specifically toward groups and individuals who have not yet been identified as having the problem to be prevented (Planta, 1990). For example, providing medical care and fluoridated water to all children prevents childhood diseases and tooth decay (Planta, 1990). Other examples of primary prevention include measures to counteract poor nutrition, poverty, and prematurity (MacGregor, 1980).

Genetic counselling and educational programs on conditions such as Down syndrome are also part of primary prevention. **Genetic counselling** deals with the human and medical problems associated with the occurrence of risk or recurrence of a genetic disorder in the family. Counselling provides and interprets medical information based on our expanding knowledge of human genetics. The major goal is to convey an understanding of birth defects and genetic mechanisms to affected families and enable prospective parents to make informed decisions about child-bearing.

Secondary prevention refers to ascertaining, as early as possible, the evidence of disorders that may cause disabilities, as well as to allied attempts to reduce, remove, or reverse substantially complex aspects of disabilities. Successful secondary prevention programs provide services to high-risk groups to keep problems from becoming debilitating and to diminish the effects of dysfunctions that are identified early. There are two ways in which individuals are identified for secondary prevention. They manifest signs of potential dysfunction, or they are members of a high-risk group that has an elevated likelihood of having the problem but show no signs of problems as of yet (Planta, 1990).

In many cases, secondary prevention has proven very successful. For example, Tay-Sachs carriers are detected through a simple blood test. As a result of extensive testing and counselling, far fewer Tay-Sachs babies are conceived and born. In North America, the rate of Tay-Sachs among Jewish infants decreased by 95 percent in the 20 years from 1970 to 1990. As a result of prenatal testing, the incidence of Down syndrome has dropped from one in 600 twenty years ago to one in 1000 today (Plomin, de Fries, and McClearn, 1990).

Many types of prenatal assessment of the developing fetus fall into this category. Currently, about 200 diseases can be detected prenatally. The major method used in the prenatal diagnosis of Down syndrome and other genetic disorders is amniocentesis, usually performed between the tenth and nineteenth week of gestation. Amniocentesis can be used to detect about forty conditions, including abnormalities of the spinal cord such as spina bifida (Pre-natal [1987]; Rosenblith and Sims-Knight, 1985). In this procedure, a needle is inserted through the mother's abdominal wall to extract ten to twenty millilitres of amniotic fluid. A chromosomal analysis then checks whether free-floating fetal cells have karyotypes (genetic patterns) typical of specific handicapping conditions. The procedure is relatively safe, with a total 2.5 to 3 percent risk of miscarriage, of which 0.5 percent is due to the amniocentesis itself (Prenatal [1987]).

Chorionic villi sampling (CVS) is a newer procedure with a risk factor of about 4 to 5 percent, but the portion of this risk due to the CVS itself is not known (Prenatal, [1987]). CVS is performed between the ninth and twelfth week of pregnancy by removing a small amount of the tissue around the fetal sac that eventually becomes the placenta. The sample is removed using a catheter inserted through the vagina into the uterus under ultrasound guidance.

Other screening procedures include the new percutaneous umbilical blood sampling, ultrasonography, and fetoscopy. Ultrasound, which generates a picture (a sonogram), is used successfully in the prenatal diagnosis of hydrocephaly, anencephaly, and other multiple congenital deformities. Fetoscopy is a procedure used to evaluate fetuses that are at risk for certain genetic conditions. A fetoscope, equipped with a fibre-optic lens for viewing the fetus, is inserted into the amniotic sac. This process can be useful in determining whether a fetus has a congenital malformation that may be associated with mental retardation (Vitello and Soskin, 1985).

Secondary prevention also encompasses the management of conditions in order to ameliorate their impact. For example, certain organic conditions that cause mental retardation can be successfully managed when identified early. The effect of PKU can be prevented or diminished if a low phenylalanine diet is introduced in infancy. Hydrocephalus can be surgically treated, even in the fetus, by the insertion of a shunt to remove excess cerebrospinal fluid (Henig, 1982). Examples of secondary prevention in the schools include dropout prevention programs.

Tertiary prevention consists of intervention strategies after a negative outcome has occurred. The object of tertiary prevention is to minimize residual handicapping conditions and maximize potential. Amelioration efforts seek to reduce the residual effects or adverse consequences of a disorder or failed outcome (Cowen, 1980). Methods of intervention may be medical, psychological, social, or educational.

Summary

1. Medical research is bringing a more complete understanding of the ways in which a child's psychological, social and educational environments are related to learning. Teachers' understanding of the etiology, developmental consequences, treatments, and prognoses of exceptional conditions will serve to increase their interactions with and understanding of children with disabilities.
2. A huge range of handicapping conditions affect children, the result of multiple etiologies. Disorders and diseases may arise from chromosomal or genetic aberrations, infections and intoxications, malnutrition, deprivation of oxygen, and environmental hazards.
3. At-risk children are those not currently identified as disabled but more likely to develop some type of problem. Studies show that infants classified as at risk more often develop problems than those classified neonatally as well babies.
4. The causes of childhood disabling conditions are changing; with the rapid advances in medical science, certain conditions have disappeared but others have filled their places. Premature babies are surviving, but a wide range of insults to the nervous and organic systems that can lead to mental retardation and other disabilities are possible with prematurity. As well, a frightening proportion of the next generation will be impaired by preventable causes, in particular pediatric AIDS and the use of drugs by pregnant women.

CHAPTER 3

Issues and Trends in Canadian Special Education

Historical Notes

When special education began in North America, exceptional individuals were believed to differ from the rest of the population in almost every domain. Because of this, and for reasons of economy and convenience, exceptional children were educated chiefly in institutional settings designed to protect the rest of society from the deviant child as much as to protect the children from an intolerant and prejudiced world.

Residential schools — variously referred to as asylums, institutions, colonies, or training schools — were first established in Canada in the 1860s to serve children described in the parlance of the day as deaf and dumb, blind, and idiotic or feeble-minded. In the United States and Canada these special schools were divorced from the general educational system and administered along with prisons, asylums, and public charities. Not until the early 1900s were special schools in most parts of Canada placed under provinicial departments of education.

By the early 1900s, schooling had become the social norm for most children in Canada. As the public schools assumed responsibility for socializing and educating huge numbers of children, they were faced with an unforeseen problem. How could schools best provide for children who could not be handled in the regular classes? These difficult students, labelled as truant, delinquent, incorrigible, and feeble-minded, were those with mild handicaps to behaviour and learning. More seriously handicapped children were still relegated to institutional settings or excluded from education altogether.

To keep order in the schools and to protect the education of other students and the time of teachers, special segregated classes seemed the ideal solution. Special classes were first introduced in the 1880s with the formation of unruly classes for incorrigible and delinquent students, ungraded classes for slow learners, and "steamer classes" for immigrant children. Although these special classes had a slow and halting beginning, by 1910 they were a feature of most urban education systems. Rapid expansion in the 1920s saw special classes handle a wider range of students — there were classes for deaf children, blind children, and gifted children, as well as lip-reading and sight-saving classes (Winzer, 1993).

In Canada the first special day classes were started in 1906 for children with physical problems — those who were described as crippled, sickly, and malnourished. These were followed by provisions for mentally retarded pupils, sight-saving classes, home instruction, speech correction, and lip-reading classes. There were also orthopedic classes, vocational and advancement classes, and remedial reading programs. In 1910, Ontario's Special Classes Act permitted boards of education to legalize existing classes. Teacher training began soon afterwards; in 1916, the first course for teachers of special classes was given at Wellesley School in Toronto (McIntosh, 1977).

Institutions, special classes, and special schools remained important in the education of students with disabilities into the 1960s. Children remained in these classes for their entire school careers; few graduated to regular classrooms. Segregation was rationalized on the grounds that the public school system could not provide for grossly deviant children and the low incidence of certain disabilities in the population made it difficult to group affected children locally for educational purposes. Teachers needed very specialized training, and specialized equipment such as Braillers and hearing aids could not easily be provided by the regular school system (Roberts and Lazure, 1970). Educators also believed that segregated classes could offer handicapped students the most benefits. A low student-teacher ratio could afford more individualized instruction for each child, while homogeneous groupings could enable the teacher to concentrate on fewer teaching strategies. Because the academic environment would be less competitive, the students' self-esteem would be improved. Segregated classes could also provide a remedial program to send some children back into the regular classroom.

In the 1960s, parents, advocates, legislators, and educational systems began to reject the notion that exceptional students should be educated separately from their peers or that mentally handicapped people should be herded into large institutional settings. Some claimed that special classes were too often used as dumping grounds. Gallagher (1972) pointed out that special education was often exclusionary rather than remedial and did not appear to be returning a significant number of children to the regular classroom. Educators also argued that special education classes cast a stigma on exceptional children, provided low quality education, and were often allotted inferior facilities and untrained teachers. Children from special classes, moreover, were barely tolerated by regular classroom teachers and administrators.

Grave dissatisfaction with special classes was bolstered by numerous efficacy studies that compared the progress of exceptional children in segregated and regular classes. These studies found that children performed no better in special classes than in regular classrooms (e.g. Dunn, 1968; Gallagher, 1972; Myers, 1976; Reynolds and Birch, 1977).

In the 1970s, discontent with special classes continued to mount. Agitation by parent and professional groups led to new legislation and many of the changes that are apparent in special education today. In Canada, the philosophical underpinnings of desegregation appeared in the Hall-Dennis Report (1968); the Report of the Commission on Emotional and Learning Disorders in Children (Roberts and Lazure, 1970); the 1971 Report on Standards for Education of Exceptional Children in Canada (Hardy et al., 1971); and the 1976 report on Canadian education prepared by the Organization for Economic Co-operation and Development (Csapo, 1984). The late seventies and early eighties were the period in which the practice of special education came of age and the true movement toward integration got under way.

Social attitudes toward the education, care, and training of individuals who are exceptional usually reflect more general cultural attitudes toward the obligations of a society to its individual citizens. It is only recently that the creation of societies where exceptional persons can live productive and fulfilling lives has become an imperative, not just a dream. As a newly evolving social philosophy has emphasized the value of the individual and the rights of every citizen, the prospects for individuals who are exceptional have altered dramatically. There has been a significant increase in public awareness and understanding of exceptional individuals. Current social philosophy aims to provide individuals who are exceptional with an education and a lifestyle as close to normal as possible.

In Canada, special education has emerged as a key priority. Policies related to the rights of exceptional individuals are formulated at the federal, provincial, and local levels of government. The federal government is involved through Indian Affairs, National Defence, Manpower, Penitentiary Services, and Health and Welfare (Goguen, 1980).

Special education describes an extremely complex social and conceptual system that is designed to assist all children in reaching their full potential. A field as diverse as special education is bound to reveal controversial issues and to reflect major trends and movements. Some issues arise from the history of the field. The roots of special education lie deeply embedded in medical models of treatment, and many of our current philosophies, legislation, techniques, and approaches spring from the attitudes and activities of the last century (Winzer, 1993). In addition, special education has traditionally placed heavy reliance on knowledge and theories from a number of core disciplines. As an integrative professional area, special education cuts across a spectrum of services, makes use of many different fields of knowledge, and depends upon the techniques, the concepts, and the practices of several allied disciplines.

Since its inception, one issue has been paramount in special education. The location of special education — where students should sit — has received more attention, undergone more modifications, and generated more controversy than have discussions about what students are taught (Jenkins and Heinen, 1989). At least since the 1950s, efficacy studies have tended to focus on physical placement to the exclusion of how a teacher manages the class and what happens to the peer group. In doing this, studies have tended to overstress the setting and the extent to which setting affects students' learning and social development (Bickel and Bickel, 1986). This is just as true in the 1990s as it ever was.

Today's most hotly debated issue concerns inclusion, or inclusive schooling. In a broad sense, inclusion applies to cultural, social, linguistic, racial, gender, and physical and mental differences. But within special education, inclusion revolves around the question of how thoroughly children with mental and physical disabilities should be integrated into the regular school system and how school districts can go about incorporating children with special needs into regular classrooms. While most parents, teachers, and school administrators agree that the days of total segregation and institutionalization are long over, the manner in which the inclusion of students with exceptionalities can be most effectively attained has still not been worked out in practice.

A broad spectrum of other trends and movements, all related in some way to inclusion, are germane to contemporary special education as educators continue their efforts to reform, revamp, and generally improve services for students with special needs. These include, but are not restricted to, teacher competencies, curriculum planning and delivery, individualization, consultation and collaboration, the use of paraprofessionals, assessment practices and procedures, early identification and intervention, transition services for adolescents, and legislation.

To do justice to these issues would take an entire book. We can only discuss some of the major issues quite briefly in this chapter in an attempt to alert readers to the movements and trends and to lay the groundwork for later chapters in this text. We direct the greatest attention to issues and trends that directly impact on the teacher in the classroom. Throughout the discussion, it should be kept in mind that reforms in education are continuous and reflect a society's views of what is important at a given time. In this sense, reform in education is an open-ended social issue and a definitive solution is illusory. As well, this text is a document written in a particular place at a particular time. It represents only a snapshot of special education and cannot faithfully reproduce the dynamic shifts that are occurring in the field.

Development of the Field

In the past thirty years, interest and involvement in special education has increased dramatically. Both as a phrase and a service program, special education has taken on new and expanded meaning. It has moved from educating children in institutional settings, to specialized separate classes, to the integration of many students into regular programs and regular classes. Today sees continuing efforts by boards of education and other agencies to increase the universality of special education services.

The late 1940s saw a huge expansion of special education due to simple demographics. The postwar baby boom increased the number of disabled children; advances in medical technology kept more children alive and limited degrees of impairment. The polio epidemic of the 1950s and the rubella epidemic of the 1960s generated still more demand for special education.

At the same time, there were advances that resulted from changing social conceptions regarding the rights of disabled persons and their role in the community. In the 1960s, the civil rights movement brought about new conceptions and the principles of normalization and deinstitutionalization were articulated.

Normalization refers to the philosophical belief that all exceptional individuals, no matter what their level and type of disability, should be provided with an education and living environment as close to normal as possible. Bank-Mikkleson (1969) introduced the concept of normalization that was later defined by Benge Nirje as "making available to all mentally retarded people patterns of life and conditions of everyday living which are as close as possible to the regular circumstances of society" (Nirje, 1979, p.173).

Normalization principles provide guidelines for the treatment of people with disabilities, as well as concrete suggestions for action. Its adherents want society to regard disabled persons as individuals and to treat them fairly and humanely. The major goal is a normal family and community life for all individuals. Under a normalization philosophy, the traditional boundaries raised by disabling conditions are broached as people who are exceptional fill a variety of roles in general society. Those with disabilities are offered the chance of a normal life routine, normal developmental experiences, independent choices, and the right to live, work, and play in normal surroundings. Ultimately, normalization will have occurred when exceptional individuals live with members of the cultural group in a normal domicile within the community and have access to all the privileges and services that are available to others.

An obvious outgrowth of the philosophy of normalization is the process of deinstitutionalization. In the physical sense, deinstitutionalization is the movement of individuals from large institutions into community-based living arrangements such as group homes and half-way houses. In the broader social context, deinstitutionalization addresses a return to the community, maintenance in the community, the respect of other citizens, and acceptance by peers and others in the culture.

An institution is defined as a publicly supported, professionally managed facility housing fifteen or more people with similar disabilities. In 1982 there were 1.4 million disabled Canadians of working age, of whom 45 000 were in institutions, 20 000 in sheltered workshops, and 1.37 million in the community (Directions, 1982). By 1991, about 16 000 people with intellectual disabilities were living in institutions in Canada (Fine, 1991). Any building of new institutions is being strongly resisted by citizens' groups who are demanding community supports and services instead. Today the residential institution is rarely considered an option for disabled children. In fact, most provinces now adhere to a "no new admittances" policy.

The educational arena saw mounting dissatisfaction with segregated classes from the sixties on. A series of efficacy studies demonstrated that children in special education classes were achieving no better than special needs students in regular classes. Legal arguments were joined to the whole civil rights movement of the 1960s. Critics of special education held that persons with disabilities had a civil right to live, attend school, and work in the same environment as others. They pointed to the inherent discrimination they saw in providing separate schooling for children based on presumed mental, physical, or behavioural incapacities. Still others castigated special education for the disproportionate number of ethnic and minority group children found in special segregated classrooms. Ethically, critics deplored labelling children and separating them from their normally developing peers.

Prompted by these changes in public and educational perceptions, attitudes toward people with disabilities began to alter dramatically. The ideological shift during the 1960s and the 1970s held that community settings were superior in their effects on social, vocational, and academic learning. By the mid-1970s, the treatment of persons with disabilities in non-restrictive, normalized settings gained priority.

Mainstreaming became the dominant ideology in the 1970s. In the 1980s, educators proposed the Regular Education Initiative (REI) which stressed that special education must redefine its relationship with general education. In the 1990s, inclusion is among the hottest topics in education.

Reforms in Special Education

In the past ten years, reform has become a major objective in North American education. Some believe that education is tottering on the brink of chaos and failure and that educational reform must be a top political priority (Greer, 1992). Parents, legislators, the general public, and educators themselves point to the gaps and deficiencies in the current educational system. The current literature is flooded with a rash of new terms and phrases associated with a growing concern over the quality and delivery of education in today's schools (Treffinger, 1991). We find terms such as *educational reform*, *accountability*, *parent participation*, *collaborative schools*, *back to the basics*, and the *Regular Education Initiative.*

The outcomes of education became a key concern of educational reform during the 1980s. Many different initiatives designed to improve education can be grouped under the rubric of school reform. Ideas ranging from administrative practices such as lengthening the school day to full-scale restructuring of education systems (for example, providing open enrollment options) have been proposed (Ysseldyke, Algozzine, and Thurlow, 1992).

Every time a report is published on the deficiencies of public education, there is a call to go back to the basics. Reform efforts call for greater accountability from schools and teachers; advanced academic achievement from our students, especially in mathematics and science; ways to improve literacy skills; ways to halt the dropout rates; ways to incoprorate multi-ethnic and multicultural perspectives into classrooms and schoools; ways to promote bilingualism and to teach students with limited English proficiency; and ways to ensure educational equality and opportunity for all students.

The reform movement has not passed special education by. On the contrary. In the 1990s, special education is deeply embroiled in reform efforts and "is being subjected to enormous pressures for change" (Kauffman, 1993, p. 6). Rhetoric calls for us to "break the mould," for "revolution," a "paradigm shift," a "fundamental reconceptualization," and "radical restructuring" (Kauffman, 1993, p. 10). *Inclusive schooling* is another of the phrases from the rash of terms associated with a growing concern over the quality and delivery of special education in contemporary schools.

While many people say that contemporary special education is at a crossroads and in a state of flux, we must keep in mind that educational services and the ideas that stimulate and direct their growth are never static; changing needs lead to the formulation of new policies and the adoption of new legislation and other administrative arrangements. Prevailing social values define what is exceptional, different, or a problem, and how it should be dealt with. Therefore, reforms in education are continuous and reflect a society's views of what is important in education at a given time.

The notion of reform embraces the idea of a need for change and is as old as the special educational system itself. A reading of the Historical Notes throughout this text clearly indicates that special education has never been a quiescent enterprise. Major changes occurred at the opening of this century with the establishment of segregated classes in the public schools. In the 1940s, parents began to form advocacy groups and often opened schools for children with moderate and severe disabilities. The civil rights movement of the 1960s spilled over to affect special education and saw efficacy studies on special classes, exposés of institutions, calls for educational equity, and the development of ameliorative programs for very young children, such as Head Start. The 1970s witnessed enormous changes as large numbers of students with exceptional conditions moved into regular schools and regular classrooms as a result of enabling legislation in both the United States and Canada. In the 1980s, we saw a major reform movement that called for the merging of special education and regular education, and that advocated the integration of students with low-incidence and severe disabilities into the general educational system and the retention of students with mild and moderate disabilities in general classrooms. In 1986 a new discipline, early childhood special education, was born. Throughout the eighties, there were dramatic increases in the number of students mainstreamed into regular classrooms so that by 1991 only 26 percent of students with disabilities in Canada attended a special school or a special class in a regular school (Oderkirk, 1993).

The phrase *progressive inclusion* is used to describe the history of special education and the gradual but unremitting progress toward assuring equal educational opportunity (Reynolds and Birch, 1988). Over the past four decades, there has been a gradual increase in the numbers and proportions of children with disabilities who receive their special education while enrolled in general education classes and schools.

Table 3-1

The progression of settings for special education

1817	Institutions for deaf, blind, and mentally retarded persons.	Special people were seen as largely deviant.
1910	Segregated classes	Segregated classes remained the most important vehicle to serve students with disabilities right into the 1960s.
1960s	Integration	A movement away from special classes, based on civil rights, various exposés, and efficacy studies.
1975	Mainstreaming	The social context of the 1970s added impetus to the advocacy on mainstreaming while legislative action accelerated integration. The least restrictive environment and a continuum of services were put into place.
1980s	Regular Education Initiative	An intensive effort to mainstream students with mild disabilities, to merge regular and special education, and to restructure education.
1990s	Inclusion	The goal is to create a community in which all children work and learn together and develop mutually supportive repertoires of peer support while remaining aware of individual differences.

Changing Views of Exceptionality

Traditionally, North American society has not demonstrated a high tolerance for exceptional persons. In the past, individuals were stigmatized and stereotyped by prevailing attitudes toward their disabilities. Special education was a service delivery system that adhered to contemporary social attitudes toward deviance. When the old adage "out of sight, out of mind" held sway, exceptional persons were placed in institutions for their care and training.

Recent decades have witnessed significant increases in public awareness and understanding of exceptional individuals. In general, our society has shifted from qualitative to quantitative conceptions of exceptionality. The qualitative model held that persons with disabilities were different and deviant — they learned, perceived, and thought in ways that were unlike the normal. Conversely, the quantitative model views differences as a matter of degree, not kind — exceptional people develop and function much as others do, but their progress may be slower and their achievements more restricted. Exceptionalities are no longer viewed as solely within the individual; a complex interplay of innate characteristics and environmental variables is instead considered.

Supporters of normalization argue that all exceptional people deserve an educational and living environment as close to normal as possible.

Many of the changes in attitudes and perceptions can be dated to the 1960s and the birth of the normalization movement. Today's efforts to provide surroundings, opportunities, and programs much like those provided for non-disabled persons stem from programs originally undertaken in the Scandinavian countries, specifically the ideas of normalization and deinstitutionalization. (See Development of the Field, p. 65.) A newly evolved social philosophy has emphasized the value of the individual and the rights of every citizen. Overcoming barriers to allow Canadians with disabilities to fully participate in social and economic life has become a major policy concern in Canada over the past three decades.

Educational Changes

For children with special needs, the most fundamental social change of the past decade has been the clear and unequivocal statement of the responsibility of educational authorities to provide equal access to an education in a manner most appropriate to their needs. This statement of responsibility, embedded in legislation and supported by ethical and philosophical precepts, has meant that exceptional students are increasingly drawn within the orbit of the public schools. Parents, teachers, and advocacy groups have supported the development of integrated classrooms on the presumption that primary placement in general education in proximity to normal peers is preferable to removal to segregated settings (York and Vandercook, 1990).

Changes in the way that schools conceptualize the needs of students with exceptionalities and attend to those needs show a movement from isolation to full inclusion that spans almost two centuries. Students with special needs were first educated in large institutions. In 1910, segregated classes in public schools accompanied the rigorous enforcement of compulsory education laws. The normalization and civil rights movements of the 1960s affected education and brought about the trend toward mainstreaming. In the 1990s, we are witnessing a movement toward inclusive schooling.

Many people use the terms *integration, mainstreaming,* and *inclusion* as though they mean the same thing. But although inclusion is a logical step after mainstreaming, the terms do not mean the same thing at all and there are fundamental differences between mainstreaming and inclusion.

Mainstreaming

In the 1950s and 1960s, *integration* was the common term used to refer to the education of students with exceptionalities in regular classrooms. The term is still widely used along with *mainstreaming,* which emerged in special education in the 1970s. The basic goal of mainstreaming is the provision of free, appropriate education in the most suitable setting for all youngsters who are exceptional. Mainstreaming is

> the physical, intellectual, social, and emotional integration of exceptional children and youth into the regular educational milieu. It demands individual programming, co-operative planning, and a range of educational options and support services (Winzer, 1989).

Mainstreaming is both a philosophy and a process. Philosophically, it sees the regular educational system as the most suitable learning and social environment for students who are exceptional; the focus is on the integration of children who are exceptional with their non-handicapped peers within the context of the regular neighbourhood school.

As a process, mainstreaming provides services along a continuum so that a range of available services allow pupils who are exceptional to be integrated in the manner best suited to their individual needs. Further, mainstreaming is a learning experience that is ongoing — a process through which children who are exceptional will be prepared for life and for work. To work effectively, the process needs a co-operative effort between regular and special educators. Students with mild disabilities are frequently the responsibility of both regular and special educators. They function in the regular classroom for most of their academic work but with additional support or individual work within a resource room for areas of weakness.

The Regular Education Initiative (REI)

Traditionally, regular education and special education functioned as parallel rather than integrated enterprises. By the 1980s, many educators contended that special education and regular education could no longer exist as separate entities; they must join forces to provide the most appropriate education for every child, exceptional or not.

The solution was called the Regular Education Initiative (REI). Essentially, the REI required a merger of general and special education resources that would bring about a system of education in which children with quite diverse, heterogeneous needs were educated in the same classroom (York et al., 1992). The REI proposed "that the general education system assure unequivocal, primary responsibility for all students" (Braaten et al., 1988, p. 21).

The REI was proposed in the context of reform in general education. One of the primary hypotheses was that students with disabilities can be best served by the improvement of education for all students. Because all students are seen to be more alike than different, and because the basic principles of learning apply to all children, special education becomes redundant. When students of every type and description are integrated into regular classrooms, special designations and labels disappear, costs are lowered through the elimination of special budgets, and the focus becomes excellence for all (Kauffman, 1989b).

The REI, which had as its primary goal changing the place of instruction from special to regular classrooms, was based on a number of premises. Supporters cited a complex of historical and contemporary problems within special education as justification for their approach (see Kauffman, 1989b). They pointed out that the question of how to make special education classes more effective had not been solved (Vergason and Anderegg, 1989). Few students were exiting the special education system, suggesting both a failure of the interventions offered to exceptional children and the presence of a stable and increasing population of students who might be the educational equivalent of a permanent underclass (Walker et al., 1988).

Many questioned the necessity for a dual system of education, and particularly for the high proportion of educational funding directed toward special education. They were critical of the fragmentary nature of so much of special education's service delivery, saw segregated classes as inherently discriminatory and unequal, and expressed concerns about the stigmatization of children identified as handicapped.

Inclusive Schooling

The current movement to educate all children in general education is variously termed *inclusion*, *inclusive schooling*, and *inclusive education*. Inclusive education, an attempt to create a unified educational system, is a natural outgrowth of the REI. While the concepts have been evolving for decades, the terms are new. They were rarely seen before 1990 and seem to have popped up out of nowhere. Inclusion, as a merger of regular and special education, was mentioned in the mid-1980s (e.g., Stainback and Stainback, 1984, 1985; Will, 1986). In 1987 writers (Reynolds, Wang, and Walberg, 1987) called for "the joining of demonstrably effective practices from special, compensatory, and general education to establish a general educational system that is more *inclusive*, and better serves all students, particularly those who require greater-than-usual educational support" (p. 394, italics added).

Inclusive schooling defies easy interpretation. There is no single model of inclusive education and it is not a fully developed structure with paradigms and a data base. Proponents of the various kinds of inclusion do not agree on definitions. Inclusion means different things to different people who want different things from it. This is because inclusion can be seen in different ways. First of all, it is part of the reform movement that is permeating all of education in Canada and the United States. Inclusion can also be seen as a reflection of civil rights and as a philosophy about our treatment of students with special needs.

Inclusive learning is a process that is geared to improving schools from within (Barth, 1990). Teachers, students, parents, and administrators define the school and classroom culture as including children with diverse backgrounds, abilities, and contributions (Salisbury, 1991). Inclusive schools begin with a philosophy and vision that all these children belong and can learn in the mainstream of school and community life. The classroom is seen as a community where all children work, talk, co-operate, and share. Diversity is valued and celebrated. It is believed that this diversity strengthens the class and offers all of its members greater opportunities for learning. An inclusive school is one that is "structured to serve a wide range of students; the environment is flexible and organized to meet the unique needs of all students. In an inclusive school, everyone belongs, is accepted, supports and is supported while having individual education needs met" (Barnes and Lehr, 1993, p. 82). Classrooms are designed to welcome diversity and to address the individual needs of all students, disabled or not. The ultimate goal of inclusion is the creation of a collaborative school.

The civil rights argument for inclusion rejects pull-out programs and segregated classes. It sees segregated classes as indefensible (e.g. Wang, Reynolds, and Walberg, 1989), as discriminatory and unequal, and in violation of the democratic ethos that allows equal access to education for all students.

Philosophically, inclusion becomes a value that is manifested in the way we promote and conceptualize the education and development of children. Inclusive programs are not an end in themselves but a condition under which children with disabilities derive great benefits that aren't possible in segregated settings.

"In an inclusive school, everyone belongs, is accepted, supports and is supported while having individual education needs met."

Inclusion or inclusive schooling implies subtle but real differences from mainstreaming, the "least restrictive environment," and integration. Advocates of inclusive schooling argue that the social-cultural realities of mainstreaming and integration are that one group is viewed as the "mainstream" and one group is not; hence, one group must "push in" to the activities and settings occupied by the other (Salisbury, 1991). Under the principles of inclusion, children do not push into the mainstream because the underlying supposition in inclusive programs is that all children will be based in the classrooms they would attend if they did not have a disability.

Some advocates of inclusive schooling hold that "All children with learning problems, whether they be 'special education' students, 'at-risk' students, or otherwise regarded as disadvantaged in schooling, belong in regular classroom environments" (Laski, 1991, p. 412). Full inclusion means the education of students with identified disabilities in the schools and classrooms they would attend if not disabled, via collaboration by general and special educators to bring support and services to the student (Rogers, 1993).

Others agree that wider access to regular classrooms is desirable for the great majority of students with disabilities. But while most contend that students ought not to be segregated from their classmates, there are also caveats. Special class placement may be necessary for students who "can be reliably classified as needing distinctive instruction" and where "superior results can be shown for such segregation" (Wang, Reynolds, and Walberg, 1989, p. 64).

The two groups of children who present the greatest challenges to inclusion are those with significant disabilities and those with serious behaviour disorders. Some argue that it is deleterious to the child with behaviour disorders, the teacher, and other students to retain children in regular classes who cannot conform to the basic expectations of the classroom.

There is even more disagreement within the field as to whether students with intensive educational needs belong in general education classrooms. In fact, the major placement issue of the day is whether students with severe intellectual disabilities should be based in regular or special education classrooms in home schools.

Historically, students presenting intensive educational challenges to our schools have been served outside the regular classroom and, in many cases, outside the community school (Thousand et al., 1986). At the moment, a growing number of parents and educators are calling for the inclusion of all students within the mainstream of

- Social integration. Through peer contact, children with disabilities observe more appropriate models for social behaviour, have access to responsive social partners, and engage in normalized social experiences. For many children, however, spontaneous improvement in social behaviour does not result from merely being placed in a setting. Integration of moderately and severely impaired children is unlikely to result in social interactions without additional structure and teacher input. Without implementing planned interventions in integrated programs, teachers cannot be sure that social interactions between disabled and non-disabled students will occur.

  There are both formal and informal ways of meeting the needs of students who require properly orchestrated, multiple interactions daily in the classroom. One key to successful integration is the development of informal peer supports and friendships for isolated students. Teachers can foster proximity through peer tutoring, co-operative learning, buddy systems, and involvement in extra-curricular activities. They can encourage support and friendships by teaching peer support and friendship skills, by fostering respect for individual differences, and by providing a positive model (Stainback, Stainback, and Wilkinson, 1992).

Teachers can foster social interactions through peer tutoring, co-operative learning, buddy systems, and involvement in extra-curricular activities.

- Collaboration and co-operation. Procedures such as collaborative teaming and teaching and shared planning underlie the success of inclusion. **Collaboration** refers to any mutual effort to plan, implement, or evaluate educational programs for a student or students (Morsink, Thomas, and Correa, 1991). With collaboration, "multidisciplinary planning support is given to classroom teachers to improve the quality of instruction provided to learning disabled and other low achieving students presently receiving educational services in general education settings" (Bauwens, Hourcade, and Friend, 1989, p. 17).
- Team approaches. Effective inclusion depends on the development of innovative and efficient ways of working with support disciplines involved with students with special needs. **Teaming** is the process in which two or more persons share information and expertise in order to meet a common goal (Morsink, Thomas, and Correa., 1991). "Teamwork among regular educators, special education teachers, support personnel, parents and peers is critical to the success of integrated education programs" (York and Vandercook, 1991, p. 22). Teaming will mean new forms of collaboration between parents, administrators, teachers, and others. (See Chapter 15.)
- Classroom adaptations. These include adapting the learning environment; for example, a child may be seated closer to the board, or group work may be stressed to facilitate social interactions. They also include adapting materials, books, tests, grading practices, and instructional strategies. Other adaptations involve specific devices or equipment such as braillers for students with visual impairments, an FM system for a deaf child, or a walker for a child with an orthopedic disability.
- Administrators who promote and support inclusion.
- A developed research base. There is an inadequate research base to support the drastic change in system design that inclusion would mean. Anecdotal reports of successful inclusion are emerging in the literature. A few studies (e.g., Giangreco et al., 1993; Janney et al., 1995; Kozleski and Jackson, 1993; Salisbury, Palambaro, and Hollowood, 1993) have found increases in positive teacher attitudes following the experience of including children with severe disabilities. However, there is very little empirical data on inclusion. For example, there is a paucity of research on the effectiveness of teaching children in mainstreamed classes (Brady et al., 1992). And,

while paraprofessionals are crucial to the success of inclusion, their use is not founded on a solid research base. Jones and Bender (1993) found only thirteen experimental or quasi-experimental studies on the effects of paraprofessionals on student outcomes in special education from 1957 to 1993. To provide guidelines to successful practice, an empirical base is also necessary.

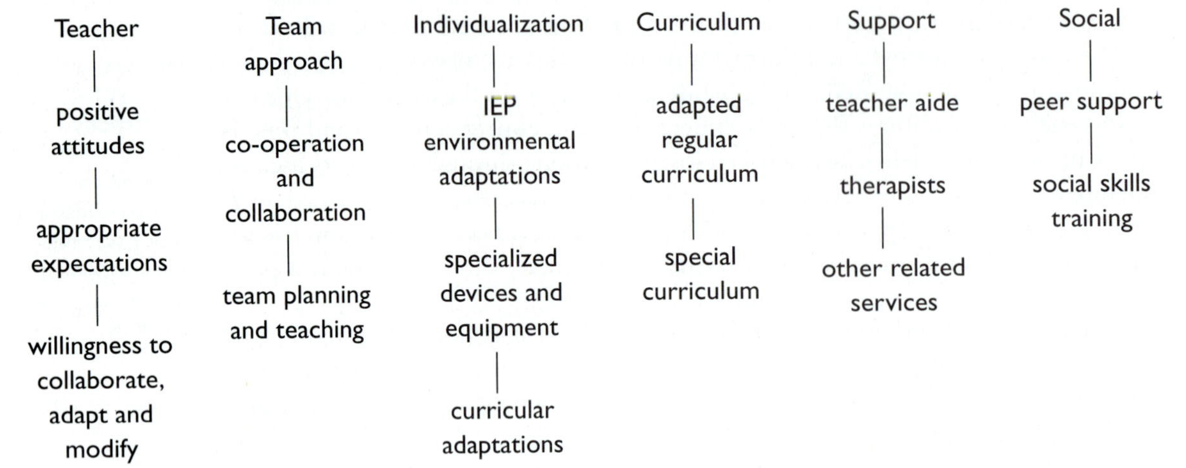

Figure 3-1
Elements for Successful Inclusion

Typical Services in the 1990s

In Canada, there is no legal mandate on, or consistent definition of, inclusion. Most Canadian legislation speaks to the idea of inclusion but not to the practice. All provincial and territorial education ministries and departments, based on a philosophy of integration, offer a continuum of services and all promote the integration of students with special needs into the most appropriate and least restrictive learning environment. Only two ministry of education policies — those in Saskatchewan and the Northwest Territories — explicitly refer to inclusion.

Across Canada, the amount of integration into the regular classroom depends on provincial policy and the individual school district. Although the tide is flowing toward inclusion, the norm within most North American schools is still for intensively challenged students to be educated in schools or classrooms other than those of their neighbours' children. In both Canada and the United States, the full integration of students with severe disabilities has not been realized in many school districts. Two major barriers are a lack of trained classroom teachers and physical barriers in the schools.

Some Canadian school jurisdictions have adopted policies of full inclusion where all students, regardless of the severity of handicaps, are educated in regular classrooms with their age peers (Flynn and Kowalczyk-McPhee, 1989). New Brunswick and Nova Scotia have adopted integration as have many boards in large urban centres in British Columbia and Alberta. In Ontario, the majority of students with special needs in the public school system are not integrated; in the Catholic system, the majority are. In Quebec, most students with physical disabilities are integrated; those with intellectual disabilities are not.

Profile

Classroom Modifications

a. A co-operative group lesson adapted for an adolescent with multiple handicaps.

Thirteen-year-old Bob is in seventh grade at his local junior high school. In a biology class, students were arranged in groups of three or four students to dissect a frog. Instead of using lab tables to do their dissection work, Bob's group used the laptray attached to the wheel chair.

For the grade seven students, the general objective of the dissection was to identify body parts. Bob's objectives centred on a structured communication program (a two-choice discrimination task between real objects randomly placed on either side of his laptray). His peers implemented this along with their dissection activities at points throughout the class period. A second objective was to increase the frequency of Bob's vocalizations. Teammates were instructed to regularly use his name as they worked.

b. A co-operative group lesson adapted for a student with multiple handicaps.

John is eight years old in a combined first/second grade classroom in his local school. He occasionally vocalizes loudly, but does not yet use vocal behaviour to communicate. One long-range goal for John is to develop his use of various switches as a first step in developing an augmentative communication system. Other goals are remaining with a group throughout an activity, keeping his hands off others' materials, and refraining from making loud vocalizations in a group.

In this lesson, students were assigned to groups of five. All group members, John included, were expected to sit in a circle, stay with their group, and use an "indoor" voice level. Each group had a copy of a story tape, a tape recorder, and an illustrated book. They were to listen to the story and follow along with the illustrations in the book. Each child in a group was assigned a specific job or role to perform during the lesson. One job was to turn the pages of the story book to correspond with the tape recording; another was to operate the tape recorder.

John was assigned the role of tape recorder operator in his group and provided with an adapted tape recorder that he could activate by pushing on a panel switch. This addressed two of his IEP goals. It allowed for assessing the switch's potential for use in a meaningful real-life situation and it inhibited John's grabbing behaviour.

c. An adapted reading lesson for a child with significant disabilities.

Stacy is in grade three in her local school. Long-term goals include co-operating with others, following classroom directions, and adhering to the rules and routines of the classroom.

In this lesson, the teacher read a book, Hot Fudge Pickles, to the class. Stacy's objective was to sit on the floor in an assigned spot and direct her attention to the teacher. The second part of the lesson was to colour a cut-out pickle. While the other children chose their colours for their pickles, a peer handed Stacy a green marker and instructed her to colour one side of the pickle. The other children then wrote a story about their pickles. Stacy generated two sentences orally that were recorded by the teacher. Later, when the children read their stories in groups, Stacy was prompted by the teacher to point to the words in her story.

(After Hamre-Nietupski, McDonald, and Nietupski, 1994; Thousand and Villa, 1990).

A large number of school districts in Canada have chosen to maintain a continuum of services that includes segregated options and typically approach inclusion on a one-to-one basis. This may be because teachers remain cautious about welcoming severely and profoundly disabled children into regular classrooms. They feel they have limited resources, are not properly trained, and may not believe that these students really belong in regular classrooms (see ATA, 1993; Dahl, 1986; Winzer, 1995). Even the placement of older students with disabilities is not settled. Wayne Nesbit (1990) points out that for senior students with special needs, a case can be made for special programming. "Some of the necessary curricular elements are simply not present in the educational mainstream," says Nesbit. He goes on to say that it is the special aspects of the senior program that will do much to facilitate long-term normalization.

It is also held that case-by-case decisions are consistent with the essence of special education. Rather than a blanket policy, the special needs of each pupil must be carefully assessed and the most appropriate educational placement for that child judged. In order to provide the highest level of individualized programming within the most normal social environment, a cascade of services is required, together with a full range of associated related services.

Throughout the rest of this text, readers will find many discussions of educational setting and curricula. These stress a continuum of educational services and the most appropriate placement for each individual child. We see inclusion as a philosophy that values and nurtures diversity, that accepts all children, and that promotes a school as a community. However, special education is founded on the proposition that children with certain developmental characteristics require education matched to their individual needs. The essence of special education is individualization, and addressing diversity is a matter of attitude, not location. Of course, for many children the regular classroom is the least restrictive environment in that children interact with their peers in normalized settings. It may not always be the most enabling environment when children with significant disabilities need training in functional skills, when gifted children need opportunities to interact with similarly gifted peers, when children with limited English proficiency need English as a Second Language instruction, or when a child with serious behaviour disorders needs assistance to learn more effective and positive ways of interacting.

Legislation

The function of schools is to help individuals meet their needs. Schools must be accessible to all children and provide programs that give a reasonable assurance of benefiting the child.

In Canada, except for the Declaration of Human Rights, there is no federal law to outline or guarantee the rights of exceptional children; the right of every child to education is not entrenched by any constitutional provision. The 1867 British North America Act (Sec. 93) was chiefly concerned with protecting the educational rights of linguistic and religious minorities. In the absence of constitutional provisions, the responsibility for education rests entirely with provincial legislation. Canadian jurisdictions have been slow to enact positive legislation guaranteeing educational rights. Only two provincial human rights codes (Saskatchewan and Quebec) list education as a right (MacKay, 1987a).

Each of the ten provinces and two territories has its own school system based upon provincial (or territorial) education legislation. Only a few schools and institutions are controlled by the provincial governments directly, such as provincial resource centres for the deaf. The rest are administered through local school boards, each of which is responsible for a geographical school district. Funding stems from a combination of property taxes and provincial government grants, according to formulae that vary from province to province (Clarke and Kendall, 1976). Each provincial government can develop its own legislation, regulations, policies, and procedures to ensure that all children receive a free and appropriate education.

Law may be defined as a sytem of rules and regulations relating to the behaviour of individuals and society as a whole (Warren, 1988). **School law** is the legislation, regulations, by-laws, and judicial decisions that apply primarily to all or part of the public school system (Nicholls and Martin, 1983). It springs from diverse sources — federal and provincial constitutional provisions, federal and provincial statutory law, administrative rules and regulations, and case law. As well, each province establishes its own educational goals and priorities in policy documents, the most relevant of which are issued by the ministries of education.

There are four main approaches to the development of legal rights in Canadian education. Some depend upon law decisions, others rely on statutory statements (Cruickshank, 1983). The four approaches are

1. Case law, which emerges from customs and legal precedents of earlier court decisions in which there were similar factual situations. Some legislation therefore arises from interpretations of existing statements in provincial education acts.
2. An express legislated statement on the right to education in provincial education acts.
3. An expressly legislated right to education in provincial human rights acts.
4. A right to education developed under the equality rights of the Canadian Charter of Rights and Freedoms.

The function of the law should be to encourage new sensitivity to the needs of disabled persons; to guard against unwarranted discrimination; to facilitate the provision of services, especially in education, housing, and access; and to reinforce work with people with disabilities themselves and those who help them. Legislation in this sense can be viewed as an effective means by which to provide improved status, facilities, and education for individuals who are exceptional.

Legislation for special education occurs because school boards fail to develop thorough and systematic policies on their own initiative. Varying practices mean that some boards go well beyond official mandates in assessment and placement but others do not establish policies and procedures and do not systematically identify, assess, and place exceptional children. Legislation makes school boards implement fair and equitable provisions for special education assessment, placement, and programming.

The relationship between legislation and litigation and the quality of services is not a direct correlation. Attitudes cannot be legislated, nor can responsibility. In the final analysis, the measure of responsible education will not be the number and length of laws, court cases, and interpretative regulations. The quality of education will be determined by the nature of the direction provided by educational leaders and the commitment to quality by teachers and others as they attempt to implement the intent of the directions provided. Legislation therefore may not reshape special education but it reflects the efforts that special educators have been working for years to achieve.

Legislation in the United States

In Canada, special education has tended to follow the American model. Canadian educational issues, legislative, administrative, and curricular, are directly influenced by events, philosophies, and pedagogy from the United States. As a result, Canadians have a touchstone against which to critically assess their progress and greater freedom to meld practices and philosophies to Canada's unique educational system.

The United States has a long history of relying on legislative and judicial remedies for social issues, including special education. In recent years, a number of important pieces of legislation related to children with disabilities of both school age and preschool age have been passed and then amended in various ways.

In the early seventies, reports in the United States indicated that four million of a total seven million disabled youngsters were being inappropriately or inadequately served (Meadow, 1980). Such reports, together with the empirical evidence of studies on segregated classes, parent activism, and professional pressure, stimulated the passage of mandatory special education legislation.

The philosophy and practice of educational integration was institutionalized with the 1975 passage of Public Law 94-142 signed into law in November, 1975 by President Ford. This law, the Education for All Handicapped Children Act, was the 142nd Bill in the 94th Congress of the United States.

As a legislative remedy to some of the past failures of schools in providing appropriate education, Public Law 94-142 had a tremendous impact on the provision of services to children who were in some way exceptional. It represented official recognition by the Congress of the United States of the growing dissatisfaction with placing handicapped students in special classes away from regular classrooms. The Act and its amendments legitimized the notion of placing students with exceptional conditions in the public schools and in regular classroom settings. The legislation led to the institutionalization of individualized instruction, increased the role of parents in the instruction of their disabled children, and made education possible for previously unserved seriously handicapped children (Will, 1986).

PL94-142 was the broadest and most complex education law passed by the American government. Its terms are both specific and mandatory. Essentially, PL 94-142 has four major purposes:

1. To guarantee free and public special education programming to children who need it.
2. To assure fairness in decisions made about providing special education to handicapped children and youth.
3. To establish management and auditing requirements and procedures regarding special education at all levels of government.
4. To help local and state governments implement the law by providing federal funds. Pl94-142 is a grant-in-aid law, which means that having established the right to an appropriate education, it provides funds to state and local educational agencies for the purpose of education. To be elegible for federal funds, state and local agencies must comply with the requirements of the law.

PL94-142 mandates that children with special needs must be educated in the least restrictive environment with an Individual Education Plan (IEP) developed, maintained, and evaluated for each child. States must assume non-discriminatory testing, confidentiality, and ensure due process procedures for all children with disabilities and their parents or guardians. As well, the states must actively attempt to identify children in need of special services and must provide a complete system of personnel development.

Although deeply significant, PL94-142 is not model legislation and some of the promises have yet to be fulfilled. The prescriptive nature of the legislation has engendered its own special set of problems. One of the major areas of concern is the meaning of the "least restrictive environment." The original 1975 law was never intended to force schools to educate all exceptional children in the regular classroom. It was meant to ensure the most effective education in the most appropriate environment for each child based on that child's unique needs.

Particularly problematic is the requirement concerning Individual Education Plans, the accountability attached to these documents, and the amount of teacher time needed for preparation of the plans. The Individualized Education Plan (IEP) is the sine qua non of PL94-142, the necessary component to monitor and enforce the law (Smith, 1990). For special education, there is no document more significant to students, agencies, parents, teachers, and administrators. Because of the legal basis for the IEP, every American teacher with an exceptional student in the classroom must have an IEP for that child.

However, the whole area of IEPs has become contentious and proven extremely difficult for the American system. Studies indicate that even with research and practice, the intent of the legislation of IEPs is not being met. Concerns about IEPs include increased work load, excessive paperwork, insufficient support, and lack of adequate training (Dudley-Marling, 1985).

Some teachers have complained that the law requires them to spend too much time giving tests and filling out forms. This interferes with teaching because so much time must be spent meeting detailed technical requirements (Katzen, 1980). One study found that, on average, a teacher spends about eleven hours formulating and writing each IEP (Safer et al., 1978). Plans for hearing-impaired students take the longest time; those for children labelled as trainable mentally retarded, the least.

Moreover, IEPs may not be adequately fulfilling the intention of providing an individual program for every exceptional student. For example, Dudley-Marling (1985) assessed teachers' responses on accountability of IEPs and their utility in planning daily instruction. Half of the teachers surveyed reported that the IEP assisted their planning of daily instruction less than half of the time. Fewer than one-quarter indicated that the IEP helped them plan more than 75 percent of the time. Of the teachers, 86 percent reported that the IEP was kept in a locked filing cabinet; the remaining 14 percent reported that the IEP was kept either on or in their desks. They did not refer to the IEP often: 55 percent referred to it less than monthly; 36 percent less than weekly, and only 9 percent referred to the IEP at least once a week.

Amendments

Like other comprehensive federal laws in the United States, PL94-142 periodically undergoes re-authorization and amendments in response to changing circumstances. Under the original legislation, all states were mandated to serve children between the ages of six and eighteen. Ongoing amendments have extended the rights to preschool exceptional children and initiated transition programs for adolescents. PL99-457 (1986) amended PL94-142 to give full services for three-year-olds by 1992 and dramatically increased funding for preschool programs. PL99-457 divided the preschool population into two groups — infants and toddlers (birth to three years) and preschoolers (three to six years). Part H of PL99-457 refers to infants; Part B to preschoolers. The area of early intervention is further addressed in Chapter 16.

In 1990, the Individuals with Disabilities Education Act (IDEA) (PL101-476) amended PL94-142. IDEA retained all the basic provisions of the original legislation but included autism and traumatic brain injury as categories of exceptionality. The title of the law was also changed to stress people-first terminology; that is, to say "a child with a disability," rather than "a handicapped child." In 1990, the Americans with Disabilities Act (ADA), which guaranteed equal opportunity and access, was also passed.

Legislation in Canada

Across Canada it cannot be said that the law clearly and unequivocally obliges the publicly supported school system to provide appropriate forms of education for all students, exceptionality notwithstanding. In fact, since the late 1960s, studies of special education have drawn attention to the shortcomings of Canadian legislation and the provision of special education services (Csapo, 1981c; Hall and Dennis, 1968; Poirier and Goguen, 1986; Poirier, Goguen, and Leslie, 1988; Roberts and Lazure, 1970). Repeatedly authors contrast the progress made in American special education, particularly with reference to PL94-142, with the lack of progress in Canada (Carter and Rogers, 1989). Rapid advances are apparent on the Canadian horizon, but the gap in the assumption of universal responsibility is not yet fully closed.

The major catalysts for change in the 1960s and 1970s included the legislative and court systems. In addition, the fundamental rights of Canadians are guaranteed by the Canadian Charter of Rights and Freedoms, which promotes equal opportunities for all and promises protection against discrimination on the grounds of race, national or ethnic origin, colour, religion, sex, age, or mental and physical disability.

Law and public policy have had a profound effect on the type and quality of education offered to exceptional children and youth. In some cases, they decide whether exceptional students are educated at all; in others, they determine how such children are educated. In recent years, all of the provinces and territories have elevated the concept of equal educational opportunity for all students to the status of the dominant educational ideology. Nevertheless, differences in provincial responses to exceptional youngsters are readily observed. Canadian provinces have recognized the right to an education for all children in different ways which can be broadly categorized as mandatory and permissive. Within legislation resides the concept of **zero reject**, a process that prevents a child from being totally or functionally excluded. Total exclusion keeps children out of school because of disability; functional exclusion occurs when a child receives inappropriate services.

Legislative activity has tended to focus on students with disabilities. Although gifted youngsters are considered to be exceptional in their need for special education, they have not fared as well in the legislative arena, perhaps because legal arguments for gifted students are different from those for children suffering handicapping conditions; they are not fought on denial of access but denial of appropriate programs.

In the United States, PL94-142 did not apply specifically to gifted and talented students. Their needs for financial assistance and programs were originally addressed in PL 95-561, the Gifted and Talented Children's Education Act of 1978. In Canada, both territories and eight of the ten provinces include gifted students in some definition of exceptional pupil, either at the legislative, regulatory, or administrative policy level. The two provinces without a mention are Nova Scotia and Prince Edward Island (Ritchey, 1993).

The tempo of legislative activity with respect to children with exceptional conditions in Canadian society accelerated during the late 1970s. To the occasional stick wielded by private litigation and parent militancy was added the formidable carrot of PL 94-142, the American landmark special education legislation. Currently, legislation governing the rights of Canadian exceptional children to education and the responsibility of school boards to provide suitable programs has been enacted in some provinces and contemplated in others. The current legislation in each province and territory is summarized in Table 3-2.

Litigation

Legislation refers to laws or bills enacted by lawmakers. Litigation, a process that occurs through the court system, also plays a part in altering public policy and the functioning of the school system. Litigious influence has affected architectural barriers, assessment and classification, residential facilities, mainstreaming, custody of children, life management and sterilization, and appropriate educational practices.

Judicial decisions are one of the principal means by which society exerts pressure over, and provides direction to, public schools (Nicholls and Martin, 1983). Litigation involves an individual or a small group of people filing a suit against another group. The suit represents a complaint against the status quo. For example, a parent of an intellectually disabled child may sue a school board on behalf of the child or as a class action for all children who are intellectually disabled.

In the United States, court actions have confirmed the rights of exceptional children to an appropriate education and have mandated public schools to provide that education. In Canada, the emphasis on using the power of the courts to settle disputes of an educational nature is less pronounced but nevertheless does occur with some regularity.

Much litigation is initiated by parents. Sometimes, parents ask that a school district provide special educational services to a child or extend the amount of special education. In other cases, parents view the regular school as the most appropriate educational setting for the special child and disagree with the decisions regarding their child's placement in a particular program or exclusion from a program.

For example, in Alberta the landmark Shelley Carrier case saw the parents of a child with cerebral palsy challenge her rejection by educational authorities. The Supreme Court ruled that Lamont County was responsible for the child's education. In his judgment, Chief Justice O'Byrne found that the County had a duty, that the duty was refused, and that the performance of the duty "must be done and done immediately" (Cameron, 1979, p.2). In *McMillan vs. Commission Scolaire de Ste. Foy* in 1981 an autistic child in an anglophone kindergarten was asked to move to either a special class for francophone autistic children or an anglophone class in Montreal. However, the judge ruled that the local school board was under an obligation to provide education.

Table 3-2

Canadian special education legislation and policies

Province/Territory	Type	Policy
Newfoundland	Mandates boards to provide special education	"All students are entitled to programs designed to respond to their individual strengths and needs which are provided in the most enhancing environments. The policy promotes the idea of a continuum of supports."
Nova Scotia	Mandatory legislation; zero-reject policy. Education Act (consolidated, 1990)	"The issue is no longer whether students with exceptional needs should or should not be integrated, but what support is needed for integration to be successful."
Prince Edward Island	Mandatory, non-categorical, zero-reject	
New Brunswick	Mandatory legislation introduced 1986; inclusion	Legislation to improve "educational programs for exceptional students and emphasized placement of students with exceptionalities into regular classrooms."
Quebec	Mandatory; human rights approach with zero-reject and regulations	Amendments in 1979
Ontario	Mandatory legislation	Education Amendment Act (1980)
Manitoba	Mandatory legislation; all-inclusive policy	Amendment to the Public School Act of 1975; under revision
Saskatchewan	Mandatory	"Education in Saskatechewan is based on the belief of the innate value and dignity of all people and the understanding that the inclusion of people with exceptional needs into every aspect of community life benefits all ... in society."
Alberta	Permissive. Mandatory legislation proposed under C26, the Amended School Act (1988). School Act amended September, 1990. Zero-reject. Policy formalized September, 1993	"There is a need for a variety of partners to work together as a team to meet each student's needs." Regular classroom is the first in a range of options.

Province/Territory	Type	Policy
British Columbia	Permissive; inclusive, non-categorical	"A board shall ensure that an administrative officer offers to consult with a parent of a student [with disabilities] regarding ... placement."
Yukon	Mandatory legislation; non-categorical School Act has sections based on least restrictive environment and most enabling environment.	"The Education Act 1990 requires that all students with exceptionalities be provided with an IEP implemented in the least restrictive and most enabling environment."
Northwest Territories	Mandatory legislation; zero-reject inclusion.	"Inclusive schooling shall be (a) characterized by equal access, (b) builds on student strengths and needs, (c) community based, and (d) shall promote the involvement of parents ... in their child's education."

Source: Canadian CEC (1993).

Other Canadian litigation has involved the rights of handicapped people, sometimes brought by individuals or sometimes brought on their behalf. In 1982 the Adult Mental Incompetency Act came under close scrutiny in the case of *Clark vs. Clark* heard in County Court, Lanark, Ontario (Baker, 1983). In this case, Justin Clark, a youngster with cerebral palsy won his rights. In British Columbia, the Stephen Dawson case involving sustaining life support was brought forward on Stephen's account (Savage, 1983).

It is very likely that the growth of judicial activity in Canada may be stimulated by the courts' interpretation of the Charter of Rights. The Charter allows for judicial intervention into governmental action, including educational decision making, where traditionally only experts held sway (MacKay, 1987a). Wayne MacKay (1987a) observes that "the courts are a new partner in educational decision making" and that "special education is on the front line of educational rights and will likely blaze a judicial trail in respect to constitutional rights to education" (p. 120).

The Charter is the federal and supreme law of Canada. Section 15 of the Charter, which came into effect in April, 1985, states that

> every individual is equal before and under the law and has the right to equal protection of the law without discrimination and in particular, without discrimination based on ... mental or physical disability (s.15 (1)).

While it is still unclear how the courts will interpret the Charter as it pertains to school governance in general and student rights in particular, there is consensus that the courts are entering into a period of complex and difficult decision making in which they will have a unique opportunity to significantly influence educational policy and practice in the context of Canada's new "rights reality" (Manley-Casimir,

1987). Educators are understandably reluctant to have lawyers too heavily involved in shaping education in Canada, and they "regard the Charter generally and the equality provisions in particular, with considerable alarm" (MacKay, 1986, pp. 293-294).

One of the earliest and most controversial Charter of Rights challenges to the existing educational structure came from the parents of an intellectually disabled lad, Luke Elwood, in the case of *Elwood vs. Halifax County — Bedford School District.* In October, 1986, the Board insisted on a special placement for Luke and rejected the parents' requests for integration into the local school. The Elwoods went to court in 1987 in quest of the right of students with mental handicaps to be integrated into regular classrooms. When challenged on the grounds of discrimination on the basis of mental disability, the Board reversed its decision and negotiated under clauses of the Charter. A pre-trial agreement signed between the Board and the family resulted in the child being integrated in the local regular public school classroom (MacKay, 1987b). MacKay (1987b) described the use of the Charter of Rights in this case as an "important negotiating tool for students and parents" (p. 110) and suggested that the Elwood case may protect children with special needs from "unreasonable parents and educators" (Hill, 1988).

More recently, Ontario has seen *Rowett vs. Board of Education of the Region of York* (Taylor, 1990) and the Eaton case against the Brant County Board of Education. The Eaton case involved a student with cerebral palsy who had no communication system and the educational placement of the child. The child was first placed in regular ECS and grade one with supports. However, a recommendation was made by the school in consultation with the parents for a more specialized and segregated placement. After a number of appeals to educational tribunals, the parents appealed to the Ontario Court of Appeals. The Court ruled that under Section 15 of the Charter of Rights and Freedoms, placement cannot be made without parental consent as placement without consent is discriminatory. The ruling was made on this, not on the educational merits of regular placement or a more specialized setting (see Smith, 1995).

Trends and Movements

As we pointed out in the introduction to this chapter, there are a number of issues germane to current special education. Most of them either directly or peripherally revolve around the notion of inclusion for students who are exceptional. The following section outlines some of the most important and influential general trends.

Expansion of Services

As educational programming is provided for all youngsters, whatever the type and degree of their disability, there have been increasing pressures on special education to assume responsibility for the education of a greater proportion of the school population and a concomitant expansion of services. Programs are reaching down to encompass infants and preschoolers and up to provide transition programs and post-secondary education for exceptional students.

Early Intervention

Early identification and early intervention are two of the most promising areas of contemporary special education. In the 1990s, intervention for infants, toddlers, and pre-

The early detection of a child's problems may prevent the development of more complex learning difficulties later in life.

schoolers with disabilities is a vibrant and rapidly expanding field, one that is characterized by innovation and creativity and a range of program models and options.

Early identification is used to identify children with established disabilities, those who are at risk for problems, and those experiencing lags and delays. **Early intervention** refers to the establishment of educational and support services for preschool children and infants who are at risk for disabilities, and their families. Both early intervention and its natural corollary, early identification, rest on the belief that children with disabilities can make positive gains if their problems are identified and diagnosed as early as possible and if they receive educational and therapeutic services attuned to their special needs.

The late 1960s saw the beginning of what was essentially a melding of early childhood education, special education, and ameliorative programs — that is, programs designed to assist children who are at risk for learning or behavioural difficulties, such as Head Start in the United States. By the mid-1980s, research, anecdotal reports, and successful experience demonstrated that effectiveness of the amalgamation and a new term and discipline, *early childhood special education*, emerged.

The clearest direction in early childhood special education programs today is toward family-centred models and the involvement of parents. There are three major principes of family-centred practice: establishing the family as the focus of services; supporting and respecting family decision making; and providing intervention services designed to strengthen family functioning (McBride et al., 1993).

Today's early intervention programs serve a broad range of children from birth to school age. They serve children with all types of disabilities, children whose disabilities vary in severity and degree, as well as children considered to be biologically or environmentally at risk for the development of conditions that can hinder learning and behaviour. Early intervention is fully dicussed in Chapter 16.

Transition

Many adults with disabilities are not faring well once they leave school. Increasingly, educators are becoming concerned with job placements, acquisition of a job, and maintenance of the job for young adults with disabilities. To ease the passage fom school to work, transition programs are becoming more apparent in secondary special education.

Transition programs rest on the premise that the quality of life and the extent to which disabled youth achieve the desired goals of employment, community living, and social and leisure opportunities are dependent upon the effectiveness and appropriateness of secondary school experiences as well as on co-operative service planning and the availability of needed adult services (Johnson, Bruininks, and Thurlow, 1987).

With high national unemployment figures for disabled Canadians, the importance of intervention that can ease the transition from school to work is underscored. The area of secondary programming and transitions is discussed in Chapter 17.

Technological Advances

Computers are perhaps the technology that most obviously affects the lives of disabled people (Brody, 1989). As educational tools, computers are found in increasing numbers in classrooms. Perhaps more important for the population of persons with disabilities is the computer technology that brings to them a huge and varied range of assistive devices.

In the classroom, computers are an effective supplement to classroom instruction — a tool that helps students learn more and have fun doing so. In special education, Computer Assisted Instruction has proven effective in influencing the educational outcomes of students of all ages. Computers seem to promote academic achievement and more positive attitudes about learning, particularly for disadvantaged students and other low achievers (Lepper and Gurtner, 1989). They are efficient and patient teachers that can repeatedly present material to those students requiring additional drill and practice. Children can work independently at their own pace and receive rewards and corrections as the program progresses.

Computer Assisted Instruction (CAI) has proven to be particularly effective for children with intellectual disabilities, for example, and use can start before formal schooling. When researchers (Fazio and Rieth, 1986) investigated computer use with mildly to moderately handicapped children in two preschool classrooms, they found the children to be enthused about computers. In fact, the children chose them during free time choice periods and tended to stay for their allotted time.

For other children with special needs who are not often interested in other people or comfortable with them, a computer may serve as a catalyst for social interaction. If children work in pairs, studies show that they spontaneously teach, help, and praise one another in computer environments, asking more questions of one another than of their teachers (Borgh and Dickson, 1986). McCormick (1987) used computers with socially and language delayed preschoolers, mixing disabled and non-disabled pairs. He found higher levels of social interaction and social play from the delayed children. Others (Villarruel, Martin, and Dickson, 1985) found that three preschoolers identified as socially delayed demonstrated significantly more turn taking, pro-social behaviour and cognitively complex and imaginative verbalizations during a computer activity than during lunch or free play periods.

Nevertheless, computers as instructional tools have been somewhat disappointing. In the early 1980s, the microcomputer was lauded as the device to provide the greatest amount of assistance in the widest variety of areas to the maximum number of students. Much of the early optimism has evaporated. Raymond Kurzweil (1990) notes that "the content and process of education remains unchanged and the computer revolution, which is radically transforming the office and factory, has not yet made its mark in the schools." Similarly, in the early 1980s, Richard Stoker claimed: "It is not an exaggeration to suggest that the microcomputer chip will be remembered as the technological product that changed the course of history for the hearing impaired population" (1983, p. 364). In a meta-analysis of the literature, however, Braden and Shaw (1987) found a lack of evidence supporting the superiority of CAI over other instructional methods. They concluded that "there is no reason to believe that CAI is a panacea for deaf children, and in fact, there is no evidence to suggest that it is anything except an instructional placebo" (p. 191).

As technology to improve lifestyles, computers provide sensory input, enhance mobility, develop cognitive and language skills, strengthen motor and perceptual functioning, and facilitate communication (Clements, 1985). Computer technology can provide reading for blind students, language for those who are deaf, and speech for students deprived by serious handicaps. Children can use computerized word synthesizers to help with reading and writing (Bertin, 1988). An ultrasonic head position interface for wheelchair control has enabled significantly impaired people to interact with others and their environment in unprecedented ways.

Assessment Practices

The primary goal of assessment is to gather and analyze enough pertinent information to teach the child effectively.

Diagnosis is a term derived from the Greek root *dia* (apart) and *gignoskien* (to know). By definition, diagnosis is the art of identifying disease from its symptoms. **Differential diagnosis** implies the precise specification that a given set of symptoms is indicative of one disorder rather than another.

The word *assessment* rather than *diagnosis* is used in education because it is more relevant to instruction by stressing the current level of developmental functioning. In special education, assessment consists of measurement, judgment, and decision making (Wilson and Rees, 1990). **Assessment** refers to the process of gathering "valid evidence to guide decisions about curriculum and instruction, and to evaluate the outcomes of instruction" (Calfee, 1987, p. 738). Assessment is undertaken with normally developing children and with those who appear to be making an inadequate adjustment in some aspect of their development whether it be behavioural, social, emotional, or communicative, or some combination of these.

Assessment is not intended to label a child or to propel him or her toward special education. The basic purposes of assessment are to collect information, to clarify the "why's" of a child's performance and behaviour, and to make a decision. Assessment is designed to target behaviours — social, communication, motor, or self-care — that will result in a child's being able to function more adequately. We need to determine how the child learns best, the behavioural characteristics that will affect learning, and whether there are any sensory or motor impairments relevant to achievement and performance.

In special education, assessment is the bridge between teaching and the psychological principle that every child is unique. If an educational program is truly to meet a child's needs, it must be based on assessment. Moreover, there is no clear line between assessment and intervention. Assessment activities should interface with the curriculum and be allied with preventative programs or intervention programming. The effectiveness of programs depends upon the continuity between assessment and intervention: we cannot devise a program for a child without a diagnosis, and we cannot arrive at a diagnosis without an assessment.

Over the years, the responsibility for assessing students with disabilities has come to be viewed as substantially different from assessment in general education. This is not correct: assessment in special education is best viewed as an extension of the measurement and evaluation techniques used by all teachers to assess student learning. However, the process in special education is more varied and complex. In special education, a single test, person, or occasion is not a sufficient source of information. We gather data from several sources, instruments, settings, and occasions to produce a valid description of a child's status. Assessment should occur on multiple occasions with various types of tools and measures employed and different strategies undertaken.

In recent years, practices in assessment for learning problems have progressed considerably. A great deal of interest has been generated around developing alternative methods that are relevant to the primary purposes of learning and that can be used to enhance teachers' instructional planning (Fuchs and Deno, 1994). The main changes that can be seen currently are in the types of tools and measures preferred, the environment used for assessment, the flexibility of the procedures, and the greater involvement of regular and special education personnel in the procedures. Increasingly, teachers are recognizing the importance of assessing student performance and learning outcomes in the context of the classroom and home environment.

In this short section, we could not possibly detail all the new developments, which include authentic assessment, the use of portfolios, performance assessment, curriculum-based measurement, and so on. We can only point out some procedures; assessment for special populations is further embedded in each chapter of the text.

The actual assessment process can be conceptualized as three inter-related stages — survey, or screening; specific, or diagnostic; and intensive, or medical and paraprofessional. Each of these stages involves different strategies and is undertaken by different professionals. All, however, focus on developing efficient treatment and educational programs for an individual child. The primary goal is to gather and analyze enough pertinent information to teach the child effectively. Assessment addresses both diagnostic evaluations and the ongoing monitoring that is critical if the progress of a child's program is to be determined.

Medical Assessment

A huge variety of medical procedures are used with children with disabilities, often starting at birth or even before. Professionals involved at the medical level of assessment include the school nurse, the family doctor, the pediatrician, the neurologist, the audiologist, and the ophthalmoligist, to mention only a few. The medical community uses a combination of testing devices, including clinical history, physical examinations, and laboratory tests to arrive at a diagnosis.

A complete look at the child's health history and current medical status must form part of the child's total assessment. Suppose, for example, that a grade one child, who appears bright and outgoing, cannot seem to comprehend such sound-symbol associations as "S is for snake." Before any specific psycho-educational diagnosis is undertaken, the child should be referred to an audiologist for a complete assessment of hearing acuity.

Screening

Screening is a term used in medicine and education to refer to developmental and health activities that are intended to identify those children who have a high probability of exhibiting delayed or abnormal development. Screening devices originated in the medical literature but are becoming more prevelant in the behavioural sciences (Fineman and Carran, 1986).

Medically, screening may begin as early as the prenatal period with the use of amniocentesis to determine the presence of certain genetic disorders. Immediately following birth, screening occurs as physicians check for obvious handicapping conditions or genetic and metabolic disorders. Later, a public health nurse using a sweep test to check hearing or a Snellen chart for visual acuity is screening for physical problems.

When we talk about screening in education, we are referring to a classroom activity that generally occurs prior to direct testing. Screening looks at large groups of children and begins to identify those who may have difficulties in behaviour and learning. Screening is a first step in determining whether children may need intervention or special services for a condition that could prove disabling or whether children might profit from a modified or individualized educational program due to disabilities or giftedness. Screening measures are not valid for diagnostics and should only be used to assist in referring a child for future in-depth assessment — that is, for direct testing.

In the classroom, procedures to screen in the intellectual and behavioural domains may include first-hand observations, child and parent interviews, past records, developmental checklists, behaviour rating scales, inventories, teacher-made tests, criterion-referenced tests, group achievement tests, and error analysis (see Winzer, 1989).

Child interviews are one of many screening procedures used to identify students who might profit from a modified or individualized education program.

Standardized screening tests typically employ cut-off scores, If a child's performance falls below the cut-off for his or her chronological age, further testing is warranted. On average, most educational screening identifies about 85 percent of exceptional children (Lerner, Mardell-Czudnowski, and Goldenberg, 1981). However, some non-exceptional children may be identified (false positives) and some exceptional children may be missed (false negatives). It should be noted that many students with severe or multiple disabilities do not pass through a screening evaluation, as they are obviously disabled, and the assessment process for them begins with psycho-educational testing (Gaylord-Ross and Holvoet, 1985).

Specific Assessment

Psycho-educational assessment refers to testing children across a variety of domains relevant to social and eduational performance. Psycho-educational assessment provides further information on children who were identified as at-risk intellectually or behaviourally using primary screening measures. The process confirms or discounts the existence of a problem and helps determine what treatment and intervention are needed.

The primary purpose of some measures is to indicate a child's developmental level in relation to that of other children. When an individual child's performance is compared to the normative group consisting of other children of the same age, the instrument is referred to as **norm-referenced**.

When explicit criteria for performance are established in advance, we are said to be testing. **Tests** are defined as controlled and structured procedures that attempt to elicit particular responses that the child might not demonstrate spontaneously (Bailey and Brochin, 1989).

IQ tests (measures of mental ability), which assess a child's performance and intelligence levels against norms of other children of the same age, are probably the best-known and the most controversial of the norm-referenced measures. They provide an **intelligence quotient** (IQ), which is the relationship between a child's mental age (MA) and chronological age (CA). IQ reflects the difference between the child's performance on the tests and the normative performance for the child's age level.

Certain assumptions underlie the definition of IQ. The most crucial is the notion that intelligence, as measured on standardized tests of mental ability, is normally distributed. A **normal distribution** is a continuum of scores that vary from the average score by predictable amounts. Figure 3-2 shows the normal curve of intelligence, based on the scores of the Wechsler Intelligence Scale for Children-Revised (WISC-R) (Wechsler, 1974). This widely used test of intelligence has an average score of 100 and a standard deviation of 15. In 1991 a revised scale, the Wechsler Intelligence Scale for Children (3rd. edition) (WISC-111) appeared. It shares most features with the WISC-R but has an additional subtest.

The subtests of the Wechsler scales are divided into two parts, a Performance scale and a Verbal scale. Subtests involve tasks such as mental arithmetic, word meanings, puzzles, tracing through mazes, showing what is missing in a picture, and reproducing a geometric design with blocks.

Teachers' involvement in assessing intelligence and cognitive functioning is usually limited to observation, screening measures, and determining instructional targets. Referrals are made to the appropriate services if deeper assessment is needed (Bailey and Wolery, 1984). Because IQ tests are delicate instruments and need careful interpretation, their use is restricted to psychologists and others who have received special training.

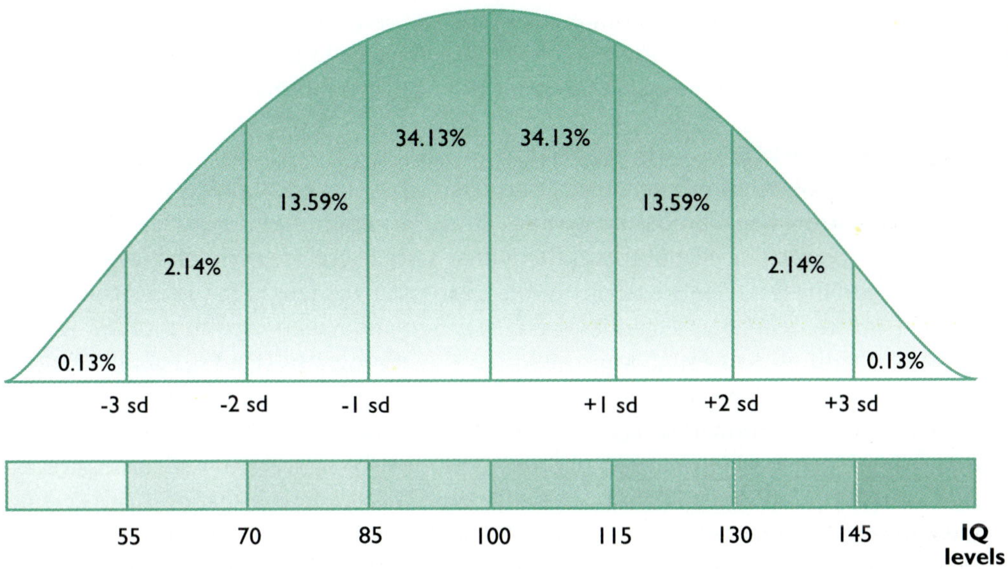

Figure 3-2
The normal curve of intelligence based on the WISC-R

Many educators query the need for psychological services. Cullen and Pratt (1992) addressed the issue of measuring and reporting success in Canadian schools. They consider large-scale norm-referenced testing and grading systems to be of limited value in determining the needs and styles of inclusive classrooms. Nevertheless, psychometric assessment is still widely used. Advocates stress that an assessment of a child's cognitive skills is essential to a complete understanding of his or her development because cognitive skills are closely intertwined with skills in other domains, especially language, social functioning, and behaviour.

Although it should be recognized that testing is but one of several strategies for gathering information about children, when properly used and interpreted, tests perform important functions. The greatest advantage of standardized tests is their potential for comparing a child's performance to that of other children (the norm group), and they are still used with considerable success to predict academic achievement. As well, some school districts demand intellectual assessment as a major source of data in the designation and placement of students in special classes (Wilson and Humphries, 1986).

However, these measures are more important for defining delays than for program planning. Standardized measures tap isolated intellectual and language abilities but do not yield intervention-relevant information on functional skills that can be included in an individual child's program and easily integrated with daily activities.

Criterion-Referenced Measures

Criterion-referenced tests are particularly valuable because they do not assess a child against some group norm but against the child's own individual progress toward preset criteria. Criterion-referenced tests may be commercially produced; many are designed by the classroom teacher to assess the progress of an individual child.

Criterion-referenced testing is particularly easy to integrate with a child's individual educational program. The testing is performed simply to determine what needs to be taught. The teacher sets instructional objectives, or criteria, for the child to work toward. For example, if a short-term objective is for a child to learn the addition facts to nine, then the test would assess how that child achieved in that particular objective.

Curriculum-Referenced Measures

A special form of criterion-referenced test is referred to as curriculum-referenced testing or **curriculum-based assessment** (CBA). Curriculum-referenced tools are similar to criterion-referenced, but they differ in that a predetermined criterion is not necessarily set and the test is always explicitly related to what was taught in the classroom.

CBA can be defined as a standardized measurement system used to monitor a student's academic growth and to improve instructional programs (Fuchs et al., 1992). It is a methodology for indexing student proficiency in the curriculum and can be used for screening, referral, individual education planning, progress monitoring, and program evaluation (Fuchs and Deno, 1992). CBA measures performance in a particular curriculum area and compares children's progress and performance with that of their peers in the same school or school division (Deno, 1985). The goal is to give the teacher information on the progress a child is making in the curriculum in use. The fundamental question of CBA is "How is the student progressing in the curriculum of his or her school?"

There are a variety of models of CBA. All are guided by the premise that curricula should serve as the basis for assessment, and all emphasize measurement that is brief, frequent, based on the student's classroom curriculum, and that can be used to monitor instructional programs and effectiveness (Potter and Wamre, 1990). To prepare CBA, teachers determine the annual curriculum goals for a student; devise and present short tests from the curriculum; and use this information to monitor student progress and to adjust programs.

CBA has been found to be an accurate screening measure for referral to special education, less influenced than other measures by teacher variables (Overton, 1992). In addition, the measurement of progress by using actual curriculum-based items and by direct daily measurement has also been found to have a noticeable effect on academic achievement when the results are used to modify instructional planning (Overton, 1992).

Developmental Assessment

Development-referenced assessment is concerned with the location of a learner's skills within a specified hierarchy of skills (developmental milestones). Under a developmental model, the skills of a child are compared to the normal developmental sequence. The developmental approach to assessment is founded on the assumption that children progress through specific patterns and that these patterns can be used in the detection of qualitative and quantitative differences between children.

The use of developmental scales to establish lags or problems in one or more areas of growth is the basis of the developmental approach to assessment. Developmental assessment often uses norm-referenced tests to determine the extent of deviation from the norm. Sometimes teachers devise their own simple scales of developmental milestones that are compilations of developmental information taken from various developmental scales and charts. Developmental scales provide guidelines that give a baseline against which evaluation statements are made.

Developmental screening provides an assessment of a child's developmental status in order to determine if the child has a high probability of experiencing delays in development (Meisels, 1988, 1989). Comprehensive screening ensures that all aspects of a child's growth and development are checked so that comparisons can be made within and across domains.

The goal of the developmental model is to assist progress through the normal sequences of development. Teachers compare the skills of a student to the normal developmental sequence. If the student fails an item, it is rewritten as an instructional objective, based on the assumption that skills must be taught in the same order as they are acquired by non-handicapped children.

Functional Approaches

The functional approach stresses the assessment of specific observable behaviours that form the mode of the current and future existence of the child. It is based on the direct collection of performance data; the identification of factors that affect performance, such as those under teacher control; the presentation and examination of repeated teaching trials; and close assessment to assess the success of teaching (Sugai and Maheady, 1988). It looks at elements of the child's behavioural repertoire that interfere with instructional objectives; appropriate steps to reduce the skill-inhibiting elements of behaviour; conditions that motivate the child to attend or those that elicit a response; and the level of assistance that is required for a child to complete a task not accomplished spontaneously (Strain, Sainato, and Maheady, 1984). (See Chapter 4.)

In dynamic assessment some teaching is allowed during the process so that effective instructional techniques can be identified.

Dynamic Assessment

Dynamic assessment refers to an interventionalist approach to assessment. In this way, it is in direct opposition to the one-tester, one-child norm-referenced approaches.

The term *dynamic assessment* was coined by Feuerstein in 1980 (Feuerstein, 1985). Today, many models of dynamic assessment are described in the research literature. The salient feature that characterizes all dynamic assessment is the use of guided learning to determine a learner's potential for change (Campione, 1989). Dynamic assessment approaches share the philosophy that a student's learning will be maximally aided by assessing how much help the student needs to facilitate learning.

In dynamic assessment, some teaching is allowed during the assessment process. A "test, teach, test" format is used in order to measure the amount of change that can be produced in a guided teaching and learning situation. The purpose is to try to determine the amount and type of intervention that brings about change in a child. During assessment, examiners attempt to identify obstacles that may be hindering a child's performance and specify the conditions under which learning and performance may be improved. The observations and results obtained during the assessment may lead directly to instructional suggestions since these techniques have been shown, in the assessment, to enhance the learning efficiency of the child.

A number of rationales support the use of dynamic assessment. Advocates argue that traditional assessment is concerned with the products rather than the processes of learning and fails to address the responsiveness of an individual to instruction because it is based on the premise that prior learning adequately predicts future performance. Further, traditional assessment does not provide prescriptive information for designing potentially effective interventions (Bransford et al., 1987). In dynamic assessment, however, motivational and instructional factors are considered in the analysis of performance.

Arena Assessment

In the past, assessment procedures devolved chiefly on taking the child out of the setting and comparing his or her abilities with those of a relatively broad population of children of the same age. There is a trend today away from assessment in clinical settings to assessment in more naturalistic contexts, especially for children with severe and multiple disabilities. Arena assessment is an observational assessment approach in which people from several disciplines focus on their particular domains such as motor skills or language within the context of play.

Summary

1. Special education today is a vibrant and exciting area of education, alive with the pulse of new ideas. Issues, trends and movements apparent in the field are all designed to ultimately improve conditions of living and learning for all persons who are exceptional.
2. Changing social philosophies and public perceptions have brought massive changes to the field of special education. Helping children with exceptionalities to fit into the mainstream of school, society and community life has become a major goal of special education during the past decades. Special education is no longer a sanctu-

ary for a few children, separate from the mainstream of education. Instead, it is everybody's concern, from the specialist to the regular classroom teacher.

3. Special education is deeply involved in reforming the system at various structural and theoretical levels. However, there is nothing new about reform in special education. In fact, since its inception in North America in 1817, special education has been constantly subjected to changes in educational settings, student eligibility, curriculum considerations, and so on.
4. Probably no question has occupied special education professionals more in past decades than the effects, real and potential, of integrating children with disabilities and children developing normally. While current reform efforts point in various directions and to various groups, the issues most germane to current special education still revolve around how thoroughly children with mental and physical handicaps should be integrated into the regular school system and how school districts can go about incorporating children with special needs into regular classrooms.
5. The most encompassing reform is within the paradigms and principles of what is referred to as inclusion, inclusive education, or inclusive schooling. While the concepts of inclusive schooling apply to all students, and include children with diverse backgrounds, abilities, and contributions, the issue most pressing is those students presenting intensive educational challenges to our schools who have historically been served outside the regular classroom and, in many cases, outside the community school.
6. Litigation and legislation underlie much of the process of educational integration witnessed today. Parent groups, court decisions, escalating educational costs, and the example set by Pl94-142 have all exerted pressure on governments. Movement has been toward giving schools boards the duty, not the discretion, to provide appropriate programs for all students within their jurisdiction.
7. Recent trends in special education include the extension of programming to encompass children at the post-secondary and pre-school and infant levels, new approaches to assessment, and transition programs for adolescents.
8. Computer technology is important in terms of both educational tools and prosthetic and assistive devices. Computers and Computer Assisted Instruction help students with disabilities to gain the learning necessary to enable them to function in regular classrooms.
9. During the past twenty years, interest in beginning intervention as early as possible has increased dramatically. Vastly increased interest is manifest in the rapid expansion of programs, new and innovative initiatives in personnel training, and the wider population of children served.
10. Before we can help children who are exceptional, we must accurately pinpoint their problems. For each child, we need a detailed picture of strengths and weaknesses in a variety of domains. Only then can we develop an effective educational program. Failure to incorporate diagnostic assessment results into program planning denies a child specially designed instruction and, without this, there can be no special education.
11. Assessment serves little purpose if the process is undertaken merely to collect data. Data from screening and psycho-educational diagnosis are only useful when used to initiate more effective services and programming for children.
12. A medical examination should be a routine part of the diagnostic process.

13. With norm-referenced measures, the concern is how a child performs in comparison to a same-age reference group. The concern with criterion-referenced and curriculum- referenced tests is how the child performs related to a predetermined set of tasks or activities. The latter are more appropriate in targeting skills. CBA provides information about a child's status in regard to a prespecified curriculum sequence because assessment covers the same materials as those presented during instruction. Dynamic assessment provides information about the responsiveness of a learner to intervention. Developmental measures assess children in relation to normal milestones.

SECTION 2
Intellectual Differences

Intellectual differences is a category that includes two very different groups of children. Children who are intellectually disabled are markedly slower than their age mates in using memory effectively, associating and classifying information, reasoning, and making judgments. Gifted children are exactly the opposite. They learn more, faster, and more thoroughly than their peers. Yet both these groups are considered exceptional and require special education and related services to develop their full potential.

In the past thirty years, education for gifted children and youth and for students with intellectual disabilities has advanced considerably. Positive changes have occurred in public perception, terminology, identification and assessment, educational administrative arrangements, and service delivery. However, a broad range of issues and problems remain to be solved. Some of these problems are due to the lack of any universally accepted definition of either giftedness or intellectual disability. Others are more complex and lie at the heart of our societal and personal values. In the field of intellectual disabilities, issues revolve around normalization and deinstitutionalization and the manner in which individuals can be most effectively integrated into schools, communities, and work places. The major issue in the education of gifted students is whether an egalitarian school system should provide special services for children already well endowed. This single issue will determine the fate of education for students with special gifts and talents.

CHAPTER 4

Children with Intellectual Disabilities

Historical Notes

History offers many examples of individuals who were seen to differ noticeably in their intellectual capacity. As a human condition, mental retardation has been acknowledged in literature for 2500 years. Aspects of retardation, such as cretinism, were recognized and studied by some of the great names in medicine (Mahendra, 1985). Hippocrates, for example, described several forms of mental retardation involving cranial anomolies. Confucius wrote about society's responsibility for the "weak minded" (Scheerenberger, 1964).

Nevertheless, throughout history and right into the twentieth century, mental retardation was misunderstood. Part of the reason for the enduring confusion arose from ignorance concerning the characteristics, needs, and capabilities of people with intellectual disabilities. For many centuries, they were generally viewed as part of the mentally ill population, a characterization that was challenged only very late in the 1700s. Furthermore, training and education for persons with mental retardation occurred only after treatment for the mentally ill population was in place.

Information about attitudes to persons with mental retardation before the seventeenth century is sparse and scattered. In this long period, nature (heredity) conceptions about many forms of exceptionality held sway. It was generally believed that exceptional conditions such as deafness, blindness, and mental retardation were imprinted on the soul by God, nature, or the devil before birth and were therefore unamenable to amelioration through education, religion, or medicine. The physician Paracelsus (1493-1541), for example, provided a clinical description of cretinism, but was led to observe that "to restore fools, nothing has been found. From its nature it is not possible" (Mahendra, 1985, p.392).

Little was done for those in society who appeared different or deviant. Generally, superstition and myths surrounded persons with mental retardation. Often they were treated cruelly, sometimes as buffoons, and sometimes as special conversants with higher powers. In Rome, for instance, mentally retarded dwarfs provided entertainment in some households. Later, fifteenth-century Hamburg placed an "idiot's cage" within the city walls. Martin Luther held that the mutterings of persons with mental retardation were conversations with the devil and suggested that one mentally retarded individual be thrown in the river and drowned. In other places, village folk protected their handicapped citizens, believing that the divine retribution intended for all of them had been heaped on the exceptional person. Others regarded idiots superstitiously as blessed "infants of the good God" and allowed them to roam unmolested (Kanner, 1964).

Beginning in about the fourth century, Europe saw a major movement toward monasticism, and a small chain of hospices arose to protect disabled people from the rigours of the world. For example, Saint Nicholas Thaumaturgos, Bishop of Wyre in present-day southern Turkey, opened a hospice for handicapped individuals in the fourth century. For this, Nicholas earned a reputation as protector of the "feeble-minded." (As Leo Kanner (1964) points out, Nicholas was also the patron saint of children, sailors, and pawn brokers, as well as the prototype of Santa Claus.)

By the fifteenth century, large institutional lunatic hospitals had sprung up across Europe. These housed all manner of persons considered different or deviant. Individuals with intellectual or physical differences or mental illness, epileptics, paupers, deflowered daughters, and political dissenters all found their way into the madhouses.

In the seventeenth century, John Locke (1632-1704) challenged the notion that disabling conditions were imprinted on the soul before birth and therefore not open to amelioration. Locke's belief that handicaps were not innate led to an assumption that they could be at least partly overcome through education. This optimistic view underlay the thought and work of pioneer educators and practitioners who, in the second half of the eighteenth century, directed their attention to the special needs of persons with disabilities. France led the way: there, in the brief fifty years between 1750 and 1800, the education of deaf, blind and mentally retarded students was established as a viable enterprise and exceptional persons were proven worthy of educational intervention.

The special education that began in France soon spread to the New World. Special facilities were established in Boston in 1848 and Ontario in 1873. Throughout this early period, optimism characterized the enterprise. Mental retardation was understood as a state in which the faculties lay dormant and underused; educational intervention was seen as reawakening the individual to a sense of his or her potential and responsibility.

Throughout the nineteenth century, physicians slowly established different criteria for mental retardation and mental illness. Beginning with John Langdon Down in 1866, they also identified specific sub-categories of retardation. Such advances in etiological understanding and classification brought greater understanding of the developmental consequences of mental retardation.

By about 1880, however, biological theories of degeneracy and repressive theories of heredity had crushed the early optimism and were ushering in a period of cruel and callous treatment. Eugenics, essentially founded on the idea that the future good of society depended on allowing only the average or superior to marry and procreate, developed as an important and influential theory. It determined to a large extent the treatment of persons with mental retardation until the 1930s.

Eugenic beliefs, bolstered by IQ tests, caused the public to direct a general attitude of fear and alarm toward individuals seen as mentally retarded. Proponents of the heredity theory of exceptionality lent little credence to the value of education. Rather, they believed that handicapped individuals, especially those labelled by that elastic term, *feeble-minded*, should be segregated in institutions, not only to protect them but to protect society.

Eugenics as a cause and the "threat of the feeble-minded" faded in the 1930s. Enlightened educators saw the disabled population as a pool of potentially productive citizens, whose problems most often stemmed from neglect, mistreatment, inadequate economic support, and inappropriate schooling. Nevertheless, it was not until the 1960s that humanitarian movements and concerns about civil and social rights wrought real changes in the care and treatment of individuals with intellectual disabilities.

Legislation, litigation, civil rights, and parent pressure brought about normalization and deinstitutionalization, and changed the location of education for students with mild disabilities in the 1970s. Under mainstreaming, the regular classroom became the most common option for the education of these children. At the same time, interest in learning disabilities increased dramatically, and there was a decline in attention to mental retardation. "It is ironic", observed Edgar (1987), "that it was the mildly retarded who once generated the most research in special education but now seem to be ignored" (p. 558).

An intellectual disability is not an illness, nor is it a disease. Essentially, the term refers to delayed intellectual growth which is manifested in immature reactions to environmental stimuli and below average social and academic performance.

As with many areas of special education, the field of intellectual disabilities is characterized by constant change, evolution, and growth in attitudes, in research, in expectations, and in education and training. Compared to even thirty years ago, present attitudes toward individuals who are intellectually disabled are strikingly positive. As a result of new research, professionals now entertain rising, but realistic, expectations for their intellectually disabled clients.

Development of the Field

In France in the second half of the eighteenth century, the intellectual movement known as the French Enlightenment and the philosophies it spawned underlay designs for the education of many groups with disabilities. In a progression that characterized the historical development of special education, deaf children were the first to receive special assistance, followed by those suffering visual impairments. Intervention with mentally ill persons preceded the development of training and education for those designated as mentally retarded.

One of the earliest attempts to educate a child presumed to be mentally retarded was undertaken by Jean Marc Itard (1775-1858), a French physician who worked at the National Deaf Mute Institute in Paris. Itard's work wielded profound influence in the later development of the field of mental retardation, specifically in the use of sense training as an instructional technique. The full story of Itard and Victor is found in Chapter 6.

Édouard Séguin, (1812-1880) carried on Itard's work. Séguin believed that mental retardation, except in cases of brain damage, was caused by sensory isolation or deprivation and viewed the mentally retarded brain as dormant but capable of arousal by powerful motor and tactual stimuli. By interpreting and expanding Itard's methods of sense training, Séguin created a structured and systematic program of education called the physiological method.

In 1837, Séguin opened the first school for mentally retarded children in France. Many physicians at that period declared categorically that educational efforts for idiots were useless (Kanner, 1964). Séguin persevered and in 1842 a Commission of the French Academy declared that he had definitely solved the problem of idiot education (Kanner, 1964). In 1848, distrustful of the new French regime, Séguin emigrated to the United States where he opened a school for "feebleminded" children in Syracuse, New York, in 1854.

When Séguin arrived in the United States, he found that Samuel Gridley Howe, a Massachusetts physician, had opened an experimental school for "idiotic and feeble-minded" children in 1848. Howe had convinced Massachusetts legislators that the training and education of such children was a public responsibility and that they could, in some cases at least, learn enough to become productive citizens.

In 1876, the first Canadian institution for mentally retarded persons opened in Orillia, Ontario, and a proper school was organized there twelve years later. Training involved a kindergarten program (one of the first in Canada), sense training as prescribed by Séguin, physical training, singing, and some academic schoolwork for the less retarded students (Hackett, 1969).

In the early 1900s, special classes developed in the public schools to extend schooling to larger numbers and a more varied clientele of students for longer periods. Right into the 1960s, segregated classes, euphemistically titled "opportunity classes" or "auxiliary classes" or "classes for slow learners," remained the most important vehicle to serve the needs of children who were mentally retarded. In that decade a matrix of factors persuaded the educational system to embark on a search for more appropriate ways to educate children with mental retardation. Parent pressure, legislation, litigation, a panel on mental retardation called by President John F. Kennedy, and exposés of the deplorable conditions in institutions for mentally retarded persons and for juvenile delinquents created a climate for change. As well, a series of efficacy studies indicated that children in special classes were doing no better than they would have in the regular classroom.

With the 1975 passage of Public Law 94-142 in the United States, the notion of educating all students in the least restrictive environment emerged. The advent of mainstreaming philosophies and practices proved particularly advantageous for children classified as intellectually disabled, and "yesterday's orthodoxy has become today's heretical view" (Zigler, Hoddap, and Edison, 1990). Now, virtually all children called mildly intellectually disabled are educated in regular classrooms.

In the 1980s, the Regular Education Initiative stressed the needs of children with mild disabilities in regular classrooms and called for a merger of regular education and special education. The 1990s are witnessing the inclusion movement, which seeks regular education advantages for all children with disabilities.

In the past, children with moderate and severe intellectual disabilities attended special schools. Although these schools provided an appropriate curriculum, a controlled learning environment, and a suitable daily schedule, they had the drawback of segregation. Today students who need special education arrangements may be in the regular classroom with assistance or perhaps placed in small, self-contained special classes in the regular school. Under inclusion, all children in regular classrooms are supported by individualization, and paraprofessionals and teachers may collaborate and co-ordinate with special education personnel.

Definitions of Intellectual Disabilities

Intellectual disabilities have long been recognized as an exceptional condition, and numerous attempts have been made to define retardation within various disciplines, including medicine, psychology, social work, and education. These definitions have not yet been standardized, however, and no universally accepted definition exists.

Definitions are not static: as more information becomes available, their meaning begins to shift. Past definitions of intellectual disability assumed a condition intrinsic to the individual; they emphasized the endogeneous, or internal, determination of defective intelligence. Mental retardation was seen as a condition that existed at birth; only a passing nod was given to negative environmental factors. Alfred Binet, for example, characterized idiots as being unable to talk or to understand language (Peterson, 1925). Tredgold (1908) defined mental retardation as "a state of incomplete mental development of such a kind and degree that the individual is incapable of adapting himself to the normal environment of his fellows in such a way as to maintain existence independent of supervision, external control, or support." In the 1940s, Edgar Doll presented six criteria defining persons with intellectual disabilities: social and occupational incompetency; inability to manage affairs at an adult level; mental subnormality; intellectual retardation from an early age; intellectual retardation during maturity; and incurable (Doll, 1941).

Recent definitions are much more flexible. To reflect the heterogeneity of the population adequately, they are also more precise in describing subgroups. The emphasis has shifted from innate incurable levels of intelligence, as judged by IQ tests, to a stress on the interplay between the individual and the environment. In current definitions, the concept of adaptive behaviour is a key criterion because it is recognized that a person can score in the low range on an intelligence test but still function adequately in society.

Today's primary definition of mental retardation is that first adopted in 1959 by the interdisciplinary American Association on Mental Deficiency (AAMD) (today known as the American Association on Mental Retardation (AAMR)). The criterion for adaptive behaviour, not in the 1959 version, was added later. Under this widely accepted definition, **mental retardation** refers to

> substantial limitations in personal functioning, characterized by significant subaverage intellectual functioning, existing concurrently with related limitations in two or more of the following adaptive skills: communication, self-care, home living, social skills, community use, self-direction, health and safety, functional academics, leisure, and work. Mental retardation is manifested before age eighteen (AAMR, 1993).

The three important points in the definition are those that refer to subaverage intellectual functioning, deficits in adaptive behaviour, and manifestation during the developmental period.

Subaverage General Intellectual Functioning

Individuals are not considered intellectually disabled unless they score below 70 IQ on a standardized test of mental ability; that is, two or more standard deviations below the mean. These are relatively recent cut-off points — before the 1970s children who fell between one and two standard deviations below the norm (IQ 85 and below) were included in the mentally retarded category. The definition adopted by the American Association on Mental Deficiency in 1973 limited the category of mental retardation to those with an IQ of 70 or less (Moores, 1987). With this change, 80 percent of the mentally retarded population was eliminated (Zetlin and Murtaugh, 1990). Today, students whose IQ scores fall between 85 and 70 are considered borderline or slow learners, not mentally retarded.

Adaptive Behaviour

Since the 1950s, changing definitions of mental retardation have given increasing prominence to the concept of adaptive behaviour. The construct was first delineated as a component of mental retardation by Edgar Doll in the early 1940s and formally added as a criterion in 1961 (Heber, 1961). The phenomenon of adaptive behaviour was expanded by Mercer (1973), who described the "six hour retarded child;" that is, the one who cannot cope with the methods, pace, and materials of the regular educational classroom but functions quite adequately in other environments. Nicholas, the child profiled below, has an abundance of "street smarts" but demonstrates little knowledge of reading and writing in his grade 2 classroom.

Profile

Nicholas

In his grade 2 classroom, Nicholas is far behind his peers in reading and math. He has a short attention span, poor on-task behaviour, low motivation, and generally seems to find school very trying and difficult. His teacher has attempted a number of adaptations such as peer tutoring in reading and a token economy to improve on-task behaviour, but to little avail. He eventually referred Nicholas to the school principal, asking for an assessment and some assistance in developing an appropriate program.

A school psychologist administered a number of measures to Nicholas, including the WISC-111, a measure of receptive language (Peabody Picture Vocabulary Test, PPVT), a test of language usage (Test of Language Development, Primary TOLD-P), a reading test (Test of Early Reading Ability, TERA), and a measure of math readiness (Test of Early Mathematical Ability, TEMA). She also carefully noted Nicholas's presenting behaviour — the way he approached the situation and the measures, and the way he interacted with her.

In some ways, the test results confirmed the teacher's suspicions. Nicholas showed a Full scale IQ score of 86 with very little difference between the Verbal and the Performance scale and very little scatter between the subtests. The raw scores on the other measures were all reported as percentiles, and the psychologist found that Nicholas scored in the 41st percentile on the PPVT, the 44th on the TOLD-P, the 4th on the TERA, and the 22nd on the TEMA.

What surprised the psychologist was Nicholas's interactions during the testing sessions. Although he seems to dislike classroom work, he really enjoyed the one-to-one situation with the psychologist and readily attempted everything presented him. And he talked throughout. He demonstrated (quite surprisingly, given the teacher's referral) adequate vocabulary, acceptable syntax, and good logic and sequencing in his stories. He particularly wanted to tell the psychologist about his hockey and how the night before his team "had just killed those guys from Medicine Hat," and gone on to win the trophy.

When the psychologist, the classroom teacher, and the parents met to discuss Nicholas's program, the psychologist stressed this area. She asked the parents many questions about Nicholas's activities outside the classroom and how he performed in the home and the neighbourhood. His competence outside school did not match his obvious lacks in classroom learning. The psychologist later noted that he showed the profile of what is described as a "six hour retarded child."

The program developed for Nicholas focuses very heavily on functional skills and uses materials from his own experiences and interests. An extract from Nicholas's IEP is found later in this chapter.

With the addition of the adaptive behaviour construct, the conception of mental retardation broadened. Adaptive behaviour is crucial to today's definitions. Individuals must demonstrate poor adaptive behaviour as well as subaverage intellectual functioning before they can be classified as retarded. Students who manifest deficits in adaptive behaviour but score within the normal range on IQ tests are usually labelled emotionally disturbed or learning disabled (Reis, Levitan, and McNally, 1982).

Nearly all conceptions of adaptive behaviour use the basic definition formulated by the AAMD, in which adaptive behaviour is seen as the degree and efficiency with which an individual meets "the standards of personal independence and social responsibility of his age or cultural group" (Grossman, 1977, p.11). In other words, **adaptive behaviour** refers to how well a person is able to adapt to environmental demands and differs according to the individual's age group and particular situation.

Adaptive behaviour is a dynamic construct influenced by cultural norms and age-related expectations. The preschooler, for example, needs sensorimotor skills, communication, self-help skills, and socialization to adapt to the environment. We do not expect the preschooler to be interested in vocational prospects and an expanded peer group; these are the adaptive concerns of the adolescent.

The dynamic nature of adaptive behaviour implies that, over time and with experience, adaptive behaviour can change. Specific adaptive limitations often co-exist with strengths and other personal capabilities; with appropriate supports over a sustained period, the life functioning of the person with intellectual disabilities will generally improve.

Adaptive behaviour is a broad concept. Some interpretations include academic and more cognitively oriented skills; others intentionally omit these types of behaviour. Generally, adaptive behaviour includes social functioning and interpersonal relationships, functional academic competencies, and vocational/occupational competencies. Competencies related to functional independence are perhaps the most widely accepted component of adaptive behaviour. Skills involved relate to toileting, dressing, feeding, avoiding danger, and maintenance of a minimal level of health and safety (Reschley, 1989).

For more than forty years, adaptive behaviour has been critical in the identification of mental retardation. Even so, lively debate about and criticism of the construct are common. Some researchers want to disregard adaptive behaviour and focus solely on subaverage intellectual functioning (e.g. Zigler, Balla, and Hodapp, 1984); others (e.g. Barnett, 1986) stress adaptive behaviour and see the interaction between individual characteristics and societal demands as absolutely vital. Other recent issues concerning adaptive behaviour revolve around a definition, the integration of the construct with broader models of personal competence, empirical investigations of the nature of the construct, and the assessment of adaptive behaviour (see McGrew, Bruininks, and Thurlow, 1992).

Developmental Period

Under the AAMR definition, the developmental period refers to the time between the child's conception and eighteenth birthday.

Terminology

If you have been reading this chapter carefully, you will have noticed that we use the term intellectual disabilities and only refer to mental retardation when explicitly discussing information that comes from the AAMR. This usage reflects new trends in labelling.

Over the centuries, persons with intellectual disabilities have been described by a plethora of labels, many of them offensive. In 1910, Henry Goddard, an American psychologist, divided retardation into the categories of *feeble-minded, moron, idiot*, and *imbecile*. These terms lingered until the 1950s when the term *mental retardation* became generally accepted. Today, however, that term suffers its own problems. Because it is used for individuals with the most severe disabilities, it evokes in many people the impression of a condition that is always a permanent and comprehensive incapacity. However, especially in the ease of mild conditions, mental retardation does not include the expectation of biologically based, permanent, and comprehensive incompetence (Harry, 1992). The new AAMR definition sees mild mental retardation as a condition that can improve as a result of changes in either the individual or the environment.

As well, the term *retardation* suggests a deficit within the individual (Harry, 1992). Some people today prefer *intellectually challenged*, which reflects the social aspects of the disability; that is, people find difficulties in meeting the challenges of our highly industrialized, technologically oriented, and fast-paced society. Others in the field prefer to use the more inclusive term, *developmental disability*.

Classification of Intellectual Disabilities

Most professionals agree that the most useful system to classify retardation is that proposed by the American Association on Mental Retardation (AAMR), which considers the condition along a continuum, or scale, of severity. The AAMR's categories — mild, moderate, severe, and profound retardation — describe the individual's functioning clearly. The AAMR system carries no negative stereotyping and little stigma. As adjectives, the words *mild, moderate, severe*, and *profound* apply to many other things besides retardation (Hallahan and Kauffman, 1991).

When severity classifications are employed, it is important to remember that there will probably be as much variability within any one group as there is between the groups and between or within groups of normally developing individuals. As well, the cut-off scores leave room for clinical judgment. An IQ of 54 may be judged as moderate or mild mental retardation. Table 4-1 indicates, in broad terms, the educational expectations at each severity level.

While many educators prefer the AAMR classification system, we still occasionally hear the rather traditional terms *educable* and *trainable* which educators have used over the years to try to describe the educational needs of children who are intellectually disabled. This terminology reflects the ability of educable mentally retarded (EMR) children to benefit from academic instruction, whereas trainable mentally retarded (TMR) children are presented with a more non-academic program that focuses on training in skills related to taking care of their basic needs.

Prevalence of Intellectual Disabilities

It is extremely difficult to obtain true and accurate prevalence figures for intellectual disabilities. There are several reasons for this:

Table 4-1

Degrees of intellectual disability and expected developmental and academic outcomes

IQ level	Expectations
70-90	Not classified as intellectually disabled. Capable of competing in school in many areas.
55-70 mild	Capable of basic academic subjects up to advanced elementary levels; will achieve about half to two-thirds of what normally developing peers do. General achievement ranges from second to fifth grade. Gap widens in secondary school.
40-55 moderate	Capable of attaining self-help skills, communication skills, and social adjustment. Limited academic achievement, but can attain many functional skills and basic functional academics. Can achieve economic usefulness later in routine jobs under supervision or perhaps in sheltered workshops.
25-40 severe	Can attain basic communication and self-help skills. May or may not be ambulatory. Additional handicapping conditions hinder attainments.
below 25 profound	With intensive training, may learn basic self-help and communication skills. Often not ambulatory; may be medically fragile and/or technology dependent.

- Different IQ cut-off points are used. Whereas the AAMR uses an IQ of 70 as the beginning of the designation of mild mental retardation, a school system may use an IQ of 75.
- Methods of gathering data for prevalence studies differ.
- Different definitions of adaptive behaviour are used.
- Different regions and social classes show different prevalence. Because the majority of children labelled as intellectually disabled come from a lower socio-economic bracket, large urban areas with a high lower-class population show a higher proportion of mental retardation. Children from lower socio-economic strata have a greater risk of incurring brain damage because of factors such as malnutrition, poor prenatal and postnatal care, and environmental hazards during infancy (Baumeister, Kupstas, and Klindworth, 1991; Dunlap, 1989).
- There are gender differences within prevalence estimates. A higher percentage of boys than girls are found among the population considered to be mildly intellectually disabled, somewhere between five to ten times as many boys as girls. This may result from a higher probability of adverse biological factors affecting male children. It may also result from the fact that expectations tend to be higher for males, or it may be that the more aggressive behaviour usually found among males can lead to the label of mental retardation.
- Different age groups show different prevalence figures, especially among the group classified as mildly mentally retarded. Prevalence is low in the preschool years and

high among school-age children, no doubt a reflection of the environmental demands of the school. As a social system, the school has a certain set of expectations which some of these children fail to meet, and this leads some researchers to contend that high-functioning mentally retarded children do not officially become retarded until they enter school and encounter reading, writing, and math. They pass through the school system labelled as intellectually disabled but then go on to occupy normal roles in society. This means that the reported prevalence of mild mental retardation declines rapidly during late adolescence and young adulthood.

- With the continuing movement among categories, especially in the milder levels of handicap, and with the strong surge toward non-categorical approaches, prevalence figures for mild mental retardation are muddied.

Given a normal curve, a theoretical 2.27 percent of the population might be expected to fall two or more standard deviations below the mean. In reality, this does not happen. Only about 1 to 1.5 percent of the population meets the AAMR definition of retarded in both intellectual functioning and adaptive behaviour. For example, the U.S. Department of Education (1989) reported that for 1987-88, 1.21 percent of the population aged six to seventeen was identified as mentally retarded. Of these, more than 75 percent were mildly retarded.

Table 4-2 shows prevalence figures from Canadian provinces that group students categorically.

Table 4-2

Prevalence of intellectual disabilities

	Total school population	Exceptional population	Mentally retarded population	Percentage of total school population	Percentage of exceptional population
Nfld.	136 228	10 165	800 TMR	0.59	7.87
Nova Scotia	169 581	18 822	452 TMR	0.27	2.40
			1 599 EMR	0.94	8.49
Quebec	943 652	126 417	2 404 TMR	0.25	1.90
			4 955 EMR	0.52	3.91
Ontario	1 796 244	136 356	7 600 TMR	0.42	5.57
			23 559 EMR	1.31	17.28
Saskatchewan	204 097	6 016	728 TMR	0.35	12.10
B.C.	504 464	60 623	1 254 TMR	0.24	2.06
			4 108 EMR	0.81	6.77

Source: Canadian Council for Exceptional Children, 1989

Figure 4-1
Prevalence and severity

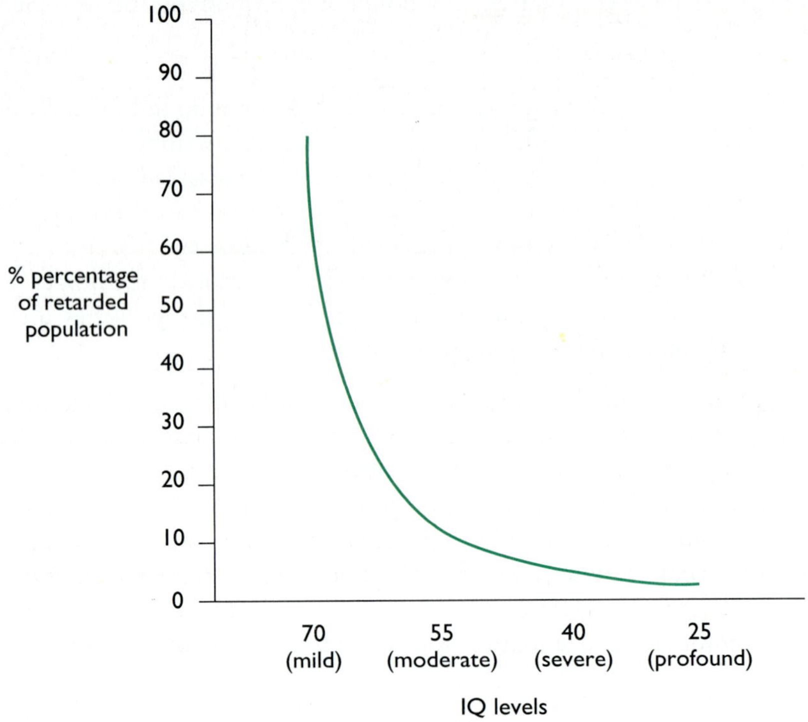

As can be seen in Table 4-2 and Figure 4-1, the great majority of students labelled as intellectually disabled fall into the mild level, with far fewer classified as moderately disabled. Severe and profound intellectual disabilities are extremely low-incidence conditions. For the moderate, severe, and profound levels, a review of twenty studies using an IQ of 50 or below found 3 or 4 persons per 1000 (McLaren and Bryson, 1987).

At the moment, mental retardation is a shrinking category, both in the number of children identified and labelled and in the amount of research directed toward it (see Edgar, 1987). Reduction in the rate of mental retardation has not resulted from any significant change in rates for severe and profound — and perhaps moderate — retardation, but from dramatic changes in the way we now define and label the condition.

Three major reasons account for this:

- There is a movement toward non-categorical approaches for mildly disabling conditions. As we discussed in Chapter 1, non-categorical approaches are founded on the contention that disabilities are not mutually exclusive but overlap, and that children have special needs that extend across several categories of behaviour — physical, intellectual, linguistic, perceptual, social, and emotional. Under non-categorical approaches, educators dispense with traditional labelling, categorization, and etiological considerations; instead, they focus on the behaviours and the most appropriate forms of intervention for each individual child.
- There has been a redistribution among categories that is a direct result of the birth of the field of learning disabilities in 1963 and the redefinition of retardation ten years later. This led to a kind of hydraulic relationship among the mild categories of exceptionality, with the most significant movement occurring between learning disabilities and mild mental retardation.

Today, many youngsters who previously wore the label of mild mental retardation are being propelled into the classification of learning disabilities. In the United States, federal data for the period 1976 to 1982 showed a decrease of 17 percent in children classified as mentally retarded and a 104 percent increase in those termed learning disabled (Forness, 1985). By 1985, it was reported that the number of individuals in all handicapped categories had increased 16 percent since 1976-77, but the number in the learning disabilities category showed a massive 119 percent increase (Edgar and Hayden, 1984-85). In Canada in 1986, 9 percent of all children with disabilities were reported to have a mental handicap, such as a developmental delay or mental retardation. Those with a learning disability made up the largest single group of disabled learners — 26 percent (Nessner, 1990).

- The concept of mild mental retardation is particularly controversial since children in this category are drawn almost exclusively from poor families, often of minority origin. Although gender and racial imbalance (more males and ethnic children) continue (Polloway et al., 1986), there is also a greater hesitancy to label children as EMR. The greater social desirability of the term *learning disabilities* reflects the notion of an impairment that is specific rather than global in nature and that is therefore less stigmatizing to the child and the family. Parents are more accepting of terms such as *learning disabled* and *slow learner* than of retardation-related labels.

What all this means is that the current population of children considered to be mild mentally retarded or educable mentally retarded (EMR) has changed quite dramatically. Today, we find that pupils identified as mildly mentally retarded tend to have greater disabilities than those of previous years (Epstein et al., 1989; MacMillan, 1988; Polloway, 1985). The average ability level of children in EMR programs is lower than before. Today, EMR classes serve Down syndrome children and those classified before as trainable mentally retarded (TMR) (Robinson et al., 1989).

Etiology of Intellectual Disabilities

In both historical and contemporary contexts, etiological considerations have been prominent in the field of mental retardation. Accurate diagnosis of the etiology of mental retardation is basic to understanding and treating the disorder. It is important in defining high- and low-risk children, in determining a possible course of treatment, and in deciding on long-term measures necessary for prevention (Chaney and Eyman, 1982). However, causes of intellectual disability remain highly controversial. Even though our knowledge has increased a hundredfold, we are still unable to answer some of the most fundamental questions and are frequently powerless to explain the condition of a specific child.

The agents that cause intellectual disabilities are legion and include genetic and chromosomal differences, infections such as maternal rubella, intoxicants such as drugs, postnatal diseases such as meningitis, and childhood accidents. However, as few as 20 to 25 percent of all persons with intellectual disabilities suffer from medical abnormalities caused by clear-cut organic conditions (Garrard and Richmond, 1975). Only in a small percentage of cases can the cause of retardation actually be specified, and these cases are almost exclusively in the moderate to profound severity levels, where organic causes are far more common. As etiology is more easily determined for children who suffer from moderate, severe, or profound retardation, the condition of these children is more readily apparent and is frequently diagnosed before school entrance. Sometimes diagnosis occurs shortly after birth, as is often the case with Down syndrome.

Generally, the etiology of moderate to severe mental retardation related to organic causes is classed into two very broad categories — genetic factors and brain damage (MacMillan, 1982). When no clear-cut evidence of an organic cause can be found, the condition is referred to as non-specific mental retardation. Most children with mild intellectual disabilities fall into this category.

In all, more than two hundred causes of mental retardation are known. Some of the etiologies are also the villains in other handicapping conditions. Rubella, for example, can leave a child with a range of handicapping conditions that affect almost every organ. Table 4-3 presents a sample of etiologies, some common and some rare, that can lead to mental retardation. Note that some conditions occur within more than one classification.

Table 4-3

Some causes of mental retardation

Infections and intoxicants	*Infections:* rubella, syphilis, toxoplasmosis, herpes simplex, bacterial infections, viral infections, parasitic infections *Intoxicants:* drugs, poisons, smoking, caffeine, alcohol, lead.
Trauma or physical agents	anoxia, irradiation, trauma
Metabolism or nutrition	*Lipid storage diseases:* Tay-Sachs disease, Hurler's, Hunter's. *Carbohydrate disorders:* galactosemia, hypoglycemia *Endocrine disorders:* hypothyroidism *Amino acid disorders:* phenylketonuria *Other:* Prader-Willi syndrome, malnutrition
Gross brain disease	neurofibromatosis (von Recklinghausen's disease), Sturge-Weber syndrome, tuberous sclerosis (epiloia), Huntington's chorea
Unknown prenatal influence	anencephaly, microcephaly, Apert's syndrome, myelomeningocele, hydrocephalus
Chromosomal abnormality	*Chromosomal aberration:* Down syndrome, Klinefelter's syndrome, cri-du-chat. *Autosomal dominant gene disorders:* neurofibromatisis, tuberous sclerosis, Sturge-Weber syndrome. *Autosomal recessive gene disorders:* phenylketonuria, congenital hypothyroidism, maple syrup urine disease, Tay-Sachs disease, Smith-Lemli-Optiz syndrome. *X-linked disorders:* Lesch-Nyhan syndrome, fragile X syndrome.
Gestational disorders	prematurity, postmaturity, low birth-weight
Psychiatric disorders	psychoses
Environmental influences	psychosocial disadvantage, sensory deprivation

Sources: Aase, 1979; Grossman, 1977; Vitello and Soskin, 1985.

The following brief discussion on the etiologies of intellectual disabilities supplements the information presented in Chapter 2.

Genetic Defects

Problems due to heredity account for only a small percentage of mental retardation. The study of these disorders, however, provides valuable knowledge that can lead to the prevention and treatment of retardation due to other causes. Phenylketonuria (PKU) and galactosemia, two genetic disorders that are potential causes of mental retardation, result from the body's inability to metabolize essential proteins. Children with untreated PKU have intellectual levels below 50 IQ and may also be subject to noisy and destructive psychotic episodes (Robinson and Robinson, 1976).

Chromosomal Problems

Chromosomal abnormalities include too many chromosomes, too few chromosomes, and chromosomes that are attached to one another. Abnormalities in the structure and number of chromosomes can be caused by natural mutation of genes, by radiation, and by a host of other factors that are only partly understood. Apart from Down syndrome, the number of children with intellectual disabilities due to chromosomal abnormality is quite small.

Down syndrome is by far the most common and widely known form of chromosomal aberration. Worldwide, Down is the most common clinical cause of mental retardation (Manfredini, 1988). Intellectually, the Down child can fall anywhere in the retardation spectrum, but most tend to be classed as moderately retarded. Down syndrome accounts for approximately 10 percent of all cases of moderate and severe mental retardation (Hallahan and Kauffman, 1991). Down individuals with normal intellectual development are almost exclusively those with the mosaic form of the condition.

The fragile X (Fra (X)) syndrome has attracted the interest of health, education, and human service professionals because it is common, its inheritance pattern is unique, and it presents a wide variety of disabilities. Frequency estimates indicate that Fra (X) may be second only to Down syndrome as an etiology of mental retardation in males. Among males with fragile X, approximately 30 percent may be severely or profoundly retarded; the majority are moderately or mildly retarded, and 10 percent have borderline or low-normal IQs (Dykens et al., 1988; Hagerman and Sobesky, 1989). Lesser degrees of impairment are found in fragile X females. Research indicates that they are usually less cognitively affected than males, although one-third have mental retardation, usually in the mild range (Reiss and Freund, 1990). A controversial finding relates to the possibility of a decline in cognitive skills with age. Various studies have reported significant drops in IQ over time. The reason may involve progressive neurological degeneration (Simen and Rogers, 1989).

Infections and Intoxications

Infections and intoxications that lead to mental retardation can occur in the pregnant mother, the infant, or the young child. Rubella is particularly dangerous. The virus can cross the placenta and damage the developing fetus during the first trimester of pregnancy.

Syphilis in the mother is another infection that can cross the placental barrier and damage the fetus. Unlike rubella, syphilis is most dangerous after the fifth month of pregnancy.

Pediatric AIDS is the fastest-growing infectious cause of mental retardation and brain damage in children (Gray, 1989). Of infants born with HIV infection, 78 to 93 percent become developmentally disabled through central nervous system involvement (Gray, 1989).

Intoxicants and poisons, in the pregnant mother or the child, can also cause mental retardation. One of the most important outcomes in this category is Fetal Alcohol Syndrome (FAS), which joins Down syndrome, fragile X syndrome, and spina bifida as the most common known causes of mental retardation. Of these conditions, FAS is the most directly preventable, at least in principle. Mental retardation appears to be associated with the more severe cases of FAS. One study of twenty patients found that 60 percent had IQs more than two standard deviations below the mean (Streissguth, Herman, and Smith, 1978). Other researchers have reported an average IQ of 65, with a range from 16 to 106 (Landesman-Dwyer et al., 1980). Still others note that although the structural deformities caused by a mother's drinking during pregnancy are permanent, the behavioural problems of alcohol-exposed children seem to increase with age (Vorhees and Mollnow, 1987).

In the developing child, meningitis and encephalitis can lead to mental retardation and other anomalies. More encephalitic children than meningitic children suffer retardation. Childhood accidents involving cerebral assault or prolonged loss of consciousness can also cause brain damage that leads to retardation. Child abuse is increasingly being cited as another cause of brain damage (see Chapter 12).

Environmental Influences

As we observed earlier, most children with intellectual disabilities are categorized as mildly retarded with the etiology "causes unknown." These children often come from deprived backgrounds and many of their problems spring from psychosocial disadvantage, poverty, inadequate nutrition, family instability, lack of educational opportunity, or an unstimulating infant environment.

Subtle genetic factors may interweave with socio-economic deprivation to further affect a child's development. In the case of mildly retarded children from deprived backgrounds, the relative influence of genetic factors and environmental ones is unknown.

Identification of Intellectual Disabilities

The identification and assessment of intellectual disabilities fulfills several major needs. Medical diagnosis leads directly to necessary treatment regimes. A full pediatric medical evaluation of the child is vital to pinpoint secondary conditions and allow the physician to recognize and identify the child's strengths. The physician searches for whatever potentialities will help the child achieve more efficient functioning. These include all the sensory and motor strengths that can be used for later training and development.

Within the educational milieu, identification must determine if the child's mental ability and adaptive behaviour fulfill the definitional criteria. However, the most important use of assessment data is the provision of an appropriate program and/or treatment plan, and the establishment of objectives and remedial strategies.

But even with the thousands of tests, measures, inventories, and scales available, identification and assessment remain problematic. Diagnosticians still encounter grave difficulties in arriving at an accurate assessment of the learning potential and adaptive behaviour of many children who are intellectually disabled.

Formal diagnosis is not a one-shot affair. The assessment of children with intellectual disabilities necessarily incorporates a range of medical, formal, and informal processes using a variety of assessment instruments, different types of procedures, and different personnel. In an extreme case, as an example, a child with a severe disability and additional handicaps may be seen by a physician for physiological assessment, an audiologist for hearing acuity, an ophthalmologist for visual efficiency, a physical therapist for gross motor functioning, an occupational therapist for fine motor skills, a psychologist for intellectual ability, and a teacher for educational achievement.

Procedures may include direct testing, ecological assessment, arena assessment, or some other assessment procedure. The tools selected depend on the strengths and needs of the child. A test that is eminently suitable for a mildly disabled child, for example, will likely be inappropriate for one with severe retardation.

Educational Screening

In the school system, educational screening often precedes psycho-educational diagnosis. For children suffering moderate to profound intellectual handicaps, screening may not take place simply because many of these children will have overt and obvious problems that were diagnosed well before school entrance. The clear-cut organic or psychological signs that accompany most severe disabilities make it possible to identify these in infancy. Children with Down syndrome are frequently identified in the delivery room, or shortly afterwards. In infants with no physical anomalies, a low Apgar score may be an indication of damage.

On the other hand, many cases of mild intellectual disability are not suspected until children enter school. Teachers hold a crucial position in identification of these youngsters. Not only can teachers observe students over a period of time and note academic performance in the classroom and social behaviour in and out of the classroom, but they also have access to pertinent school records and to the observations and comments of other teachers who may have encountered the child in earlier grades. They may therefore be the first to recognize that these children have problems and be at the forefront in identifying their needs and referring them for further assessment.

Teachers may be the first to recognize that children with mild intellectual disabilities have problems and be at the forefront in identifying their needs.

Assessment of Intelligence

In the formal assessment of intellectual disabilities, the first major areas of concern are IQ and adaptive behaviour. Of the two, IQ has been around longer, and there are a range of measures to assess this domain of functioning. Since Alfred Binet devised the first real tests of mental ability in 1905, IQ tests have been the primary instruments in the measurement of intelligence. Although we no longer place uncritical faith in intelligence tests, they are still used with considerable success to predict academic achievement.

With children suspected of intellectual disability, an assessment of intelligence is important in order to meet the definitional criteria of an IQ level two or more standard deviations below the norm. Children in the more severe ranges of intellectual disability are often untestable through the usual standardized IQ tests, such as the

WISC-111. In cases where organic brain pathology and physical handicaps are present, IQ levels are estimated through the use of developmental scales, measures of adaptive behaviour, observations, and other tools. (See Chapters 14 and 15.)

Assessment of Adaptive Behaviour

The inclusion of adaptive behaviour in the definitions and assessment of intellectual disabilities has led to the development of numerous adaptive behaviour scales. However, no single, quantifiable, and reliable assessment procedure exists. One problem is the rather murky definition of adaptive behaviour; another relates to the relative newness of the concept. As well, there exists no simple relationship between adaptive behaviour and chronological age in children who are intellectually disabled (Volkmar, et al., 1987).

Many adaptive skills are very visible — using the toilet or feeding oneself, for example. Adaptive behaviour scales generally consist of lists or inventories of behaviour which are completed by someone close to the child — a parent, teacher, or primary caregiver. Scales in common use include the Balthazar Scales of Adaptive Behavior (Balthazar, 1973, 1976), the Adaptive Behavior Checklist (Allen, Cortazzo, and Adams, 1970), the Cain-Levine Social Competence Scale (Cain, Levine, and Elzey, 1963), the AAMD Adaptive Behavior Scales (Lambert and Windmiller, 1981; Nihira et al., 1974), the Vineland Adaptive Behaviour Scale-Revised (Sparrow, Balla, and Cicchetti, 1984) and the Battelle Developmental Inventory (Newborg, Stock, and Wnek, 1984). Most of these scales assess children in all severity ranges by examining critical developmental skills, such as eating, dressing, and peer relations, as well as areas of maladaptive behaviour.

When adaptive behaviour is the primary focus of assessment, the procedure may be referred to as functional assessment, which leads into a functional educational approach that we discuss later in this chapter.

Functionality refers to the characteristics of skills needed for effective and individual coping within the daily environment. There are two criteria of functionality. The first is that the skill will increase a child's ability to interact with people and objects in the daily environment. The second concerns whether the skill will have to be performed by someone else if the child has not been taught to do it.

The functional approach stresses the assessment of specific observable behaviours that form the mode of the current and future existence of the child. It is based on the direct collection of performance data; the identification of factors that affect performance, such as those under teacher control; the presentation and examination of repeated teaching trials; and close assessment to evaluate the success of teaching (Suigai and Maheady, 1988). It looks at elements of the child's behavioural repertoire that interfere with instructional objectives; appropriate steps to reduce the skill-inhibiting elements of behaviour; conditions that motivate the child to attend or those that elicit a response; and the level of assistance that is required for a child to complete a task not accomplished spontaneously (Strain, Sainato, and Maheady, 1984).

Prevention of Intellectual Disabilities

Research suggests that for the moderate, severe, and profound levels of retardation, postnatal causes account for about 5 percent, perinatal causes for about 15 percent, and prenatal causes for about 80 percent (Milunsky, 1975). Various estimates claim that about 20 to 30 percent of cases could be prevented with the intensive application of current knowledge (National Prevention Committee, 1982).

Great strides have been made in identifying contributing causes and developing preventative measures. Genetic counselling is now available, and more than forty genetic conditions are detectable through amniocentesis. Conditions such as FAS are preventable and some, such as PKU, are controllable by diet.

Developmental Consequences of Intellectual Disabilities

Intellectual disabilities include a variety of physical, intellectual, academic, and behavioural characteristics. Individuals who are described as intellectually disabled vary widely in almost every aspect of human behaviour, human personality, and human temperament. Despite their intellectual limitations, youngsters who are intellectually disabled show more similarities to other children than they do differences. They feel, think, hope, play, have fun, and find mischief, just like everyone else. While they will have difficulties with complex academic material, many children who are intellectually disabled develop into productive and self-sufficient adults. They marry, have children, assume mortgages, hold down jobs, and participate in social activities. Of course, the amount and degree of the retardation is of prime importance; within the various levels of disability is found a wide range of behaviours and abilities. Viewing intellectual disability on a continuum, we can place mildly disabled children who are having trouble with academic subjects at one end and profoundly retarded youngsters who may be non-ambulatory and non-responsive to their surroundings at the other. However, when discussing the population of persons with intellectual disabilities, we must keep in mind that categories of severity often overlap and are subject to change. Very early intervention allows teachers and parents to reduce the handicap's impact on child development.

The possibility of changing IQ is an example of *trait plasticity.* Experts say that IQ is malleable by about 20 points. Early intervention with Down syndrome children, for example, has shown that the condition need not always cause moderate to severe mental retardation. The psychological profile of Down babies shows that they seem to develop normally in early infancy. The rate of development slows after six months of age, and by ten months these infants receive lower scores than normally developing infants on measures of intellectual development (Kopp, 1983). For children with Down syndrome, early and sustained intervention halts the decline in cognitive development (see Guralnick and Bricker, 1987). It also appears to prevent further decreases throughout the remaining early childhood years.

Physical Development

Individuals who are mildly intellectually disabled present few if any divergent physical symptoms that differentiate them from their peers. Minor differences may be seen in measures of health and of physical and motor performance. In early childhood, children with intellectual disabilities reach developmental milestones later; they may take up to nine months longer to learn to walk, talk, eat, and use the toilet. These children are also likely to be somewhat below the comparative standards for height, weight, and skeletal maturity. In motor areas, they perform below the standards of non-disabled children (Bruininks, 1977; Bruininks and Warfield, 1978).

Physical impairments become more complex in children with moderate retardation. These children tend to be markedly less able physically and more unco-ordinated.

Traditionally, researchers and practitioners have tended to group people with severe and profound intellectual disabilities together, but the two groups differ in several ways. Of course, the categories do overlap, as do severe and moderate disabilities. Common to both groups are the presence of additional handicapping conditions. Blindness, deafness, cerebral palsy, epilepsy, and other physical anomalies are the rule rather than the exception.

There exists a strong negative correlation between IQ level and the presence of organic brain pathology, central nervous system impairment, and other handicapping conditions. In other words, as one proceeds down the scale, the incidence of additional handicaps increases, which then serves to compound the original retardation. A British Columbia study of non-specific retardation (Herbst and Baird, 1983) found that 27 percent of people with mild intellectual disabilities had additional handicapping conditions. In contrast, 73.1 percent of profoundly retarded individuals suffered additional handicaps.

Severely retarded individuals may show poor speech, inadequate social skills, poor motor development or non-ambulation, incontinence, sensory impairments, seizures, and cerebral palsy. The population of profoundly retarded persons can be divided functionally into two groups (Miller, 1976). "Relative" profoundly retarded persons have less organic damage and are capable of some degree of ambulation, communication, and self-help skills. "Absolute" profoundly retarded individuals are some of the most seriously impaired of all disabled people. The nature and degree of their handicap is so great that without various forms of intensive training and therapy, they exhibit virtually no adaptive behaviour. As well, many of these people exist in what is referred to as a medically fragile state.

Survival rates vary with the level of retardation. Herbst and Baird (1983) found that the death rate among people with mild intellectual disabilities was twice as high as that of the general population. It was seven times higher among those severely retarded, and thirty-one times higher among those profoundly disabled. Moreover, the mortality rate among profoundly retarded people is almost 50 percent higher than among those with severe retardation. Mortality rates for non-ambulant persons are significantly higher than for those who are ambulant (Balakrishnan and Wolf, 1976).

Down Syndrome

Apart from their physical stigmata, children with Down syndrome are prone to a range of sensory impairments and very serious health problems. Only within recent years has their life span begun to approach that of the general population. In 1929, individuals with Down syndrome had a life expectancy of nine years; by 1980, it had advanced to more than thirty years; now 25 percent live to the age of fifty (Patterson, 1987). The mortality rate is still high, however, especially perinatally and in the first years of life, largely because of congenital heart conditions and increased susceptibility to infections (Burgio, Fraccaro, and Tiepolo, 1981). After age one, mortality is considerably reduced. Between ages five and ten, life expectancy is only 6 percent below normal.

Down syndrome is a cause of mental retardation, ranging from mild to profound.

About 40 percent of children with Down syndrome have congenital heart defects. Gastrointestinal malformations and reduced resistance to respiratory infections are common. Down syndrome children are especially suspectible to otitis media and the resultant conductive hearing loss (Whitman, Simpson, and Compton, 1986). As many as 75 percent of Down children may have significant hearing losses (Northern and Lemme, 1982), and the detrimental effects of hearing loss are believed to be greater for them than for non-retarded youngsters (Yarter, 1980).

Children with Down syndrome have biochemical differences as well. Recent research on chromosome 21 has shown that its genes are linked not only to Down, but also to susceptibility among normal individuals to cancer, Alzheimer's, congenital heart defects, and vision problems.

If individuals with Down syndrome survive to middle age, they are more likely to develop cataracts, leukemia, and Alzheimer's (Patterson, 1987). There is a twenty- to fiftyfold increase in the risk of developing leukemia, probably because of a gene on chromosome 21 that is known to cause leukemia if improperly activated (Patterson, 1987; Siwolop and Mohs, 1985). Middle-aged people with Down almost invariably suffer from Alzheimer's (Allore et al., 1988; Patterson, 1987).

Cognitive Development

Cognition is the the process of recognizing, identifying, associating, and inferring meaning beyond the figural information provided by the environment that allows an understanding of a concept and application to new conditions (DeRuiter and Warsarl, 1982). **Cognitive development** implies orderly changes that occur in the way children understand and cope with their world.

By definition, intellectual disability equates with deficiencies in cognitive development. Nevertheless, an intellectual disability only means slowing down, not stopping. Individuals with intellectual disabilities demonstrate impaired or incomplete mental development; their problems are specifically a retardation in the development of intellectual and adaptive behaviour. Their ability to learn and their capacity for putting learning to use is limited but certainly not non-existent.

More and more research evidence indicates that retardation is quantitative rather than qualitative. That is, children who are intellectually disabled pass through the same cognitive development stages in the same order and manner as non-disabled children. In studies of Down syndrome children compared with non-disabled children of the same developmental level and socio-economic status, for example, investigators have found no differences in the sequence of sensorimotor development (Rogers, 1988a). But children with intellectual disabilities pass through the stages more slowly and attain lower levels of achievement. In terms of Piaget's periods, those mildly intellectually disabled function no higher than concrete operations; the moderately disabled do not surpass preoperational stages, and those with severe and profound disabilities remain at the sensorimotor stage (Robinson and Robinson, 1976).

Learning and Memory

The most specific consequences of intellectual disability involve its effects on an individual's potential to learn and to progress academically. Although intellectually disabled youngsters basically learn in the same fashion as others, students have difficulties in all aspects of intellectual functioning, including concept learning, attention, and language. Children with intellectual disabilities have particular trouble with memory, a key aspect of learning. Memory efficiency decreases as the level of retardation increases.

Memory is often explained through the constructs of **information processing**, which holds that we process information in different ways and at various levels of analysis. Essentially, information processing recognizes the sensory register, where information is perceived and attended to; short-term memory, where information that has been passed through the sensory register is held for about 5 seconds; and long-term memory, where retained information is stored, probably permanently. We could use the example of a young child hearing a catchy jingle on TV. The child attends to the jingle (sensory register), takes it into short-term memory, then sings along, repeating the jingle over and over (rehearsal and elaboration), and in this way passes it to long-term memory where it is stored for retrieval later when the child, perhaps, wants to sing it for daddy.

For information to move from short-term to long-term memory, we must, like that child, do something to help us retain the information. Memory strategies include such things as rehearsal, sub-vocalization, and mnemonics. For individuals with disabilities, the greatest difficulty seems to be with short-term memory and may result from not using memory strategies efficiently. In addition, students often do not understand why they are memorizing certain information, in what context the information is meaningful, or how to internalize the structure provided by teachers (Gerber, 1988).

Students with intellectual disabilities can be taught to use strategies successfully and thereby improve their memory functioning. (See Chapter 7). And once they have thoroughly learned information, their long-term memory is comparable to that of non-disabled learners (Ellis, 1983).

Difficulties with memory are compounded by problems with observational learning, organization, selective attention, generalization, and motivation. Students with intellectual disabilities find it very hard to select learning tasks and attend to all their relevant dimensions. They also have difficulty paying attention and keeping on task. In the classroom, they tend to be less attentive, spend less time on academic tasks, and spend more time out of their seats than non-disabled children (Finkelstein, Gallagher, and Farran, 1980; McGee and Richgels, 1990). As well, they are less able to apply the knowledge or the skills they have learned to new tasks, problems, or stimulus situations; they have problems in generalizing and transferring skills.

Motivation, a key factor in all learning and achievement, refers to a student's affect, or emotional response, to a problem situation, which then influences how the problem will be viewed and solved. Children with intellectual disabilities appear less motivated to succeed. They don't seem to take the pleasure that their non-disabled peers do in manipulating and mastering their environments. Lack of motivation seems to accompany an expectation of failure; because children with intellectual disabilities tend to experience failure more often than other children, they learn to expect it. This process creates a self-defeating cycle: as children picture themselves as underachieving or non-achieving, they become passive and lose their initiative. They grow overly dependent on others to tell them what to do, surrendering control to an outward locus.

Rewarding effort rather than ability is likely to serve as a motivator for children with intellectual disabilities, and indeed for all children.

Concepts are the building blocks of human knowledge, but children with intellectual disabilities show difficulties in concept development, especially at abstract levels. For example, children with mild disabilities have significant deficits in the understanding of basic concepts such as "above," "always," "other," and "different."

As the degree of retardation increases, problems with learning and memory become more severe. However, learning is both possible and common for children with moderate to profound mental retardation. Using classical and operant conditioning procedures, educators have taught many skills in the domains of adaptive behaviour, simple academics, and vocational skill formation to severely retarded, and some profoundly retarded, individuals.

Academic Achievement

Pupils categorized as mildly intellectually disabled form the largest group of retarded learners and possess the widest range of skills and needs. In general, these students are slower than non-retarded children in developing motor and social skills. They acquire speech and language skills more slowly and tend to have a higher rate of deviations. In the classroom, they tend to underachieve in all academic areas — that is, they do not achieve at a level commensurate with their intellectual potential.

Students who are mildly retarded achieve about two-thirds of what other children will accomplish in an academic year. Most of them will be above the 2.5 level in reading, language arts, and math, and they will possess the oral language and listening skills sufficient to give and follow instructions. Depending on the degree of retardation, the maximum level of achievement for mildly mentally retarded youngsters is generally believed to fall somewhere between third and seventh grades in most academic areas.

However, as they proceed through the school, the lags between them and their non-handicapped peers widen, as is shown in Figure 4-2. This lag presents challenges to secondary level educators as we discuss in Chapter 17.

Figure 4-2
Differences in functioning of mildly retarded and non-retarded children in school

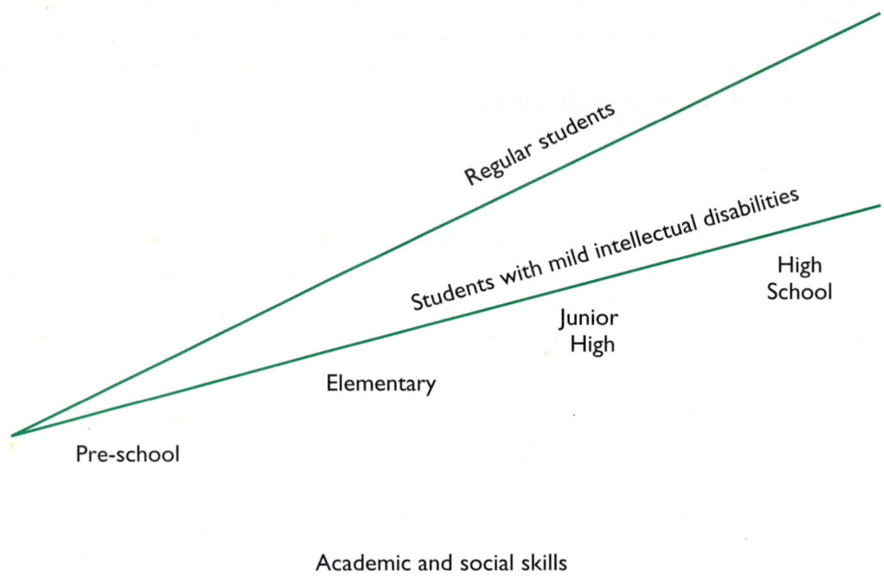

Apart from limited cognitive ability, the reasons why students underachieve are legion. We have already mentioned poor motivation, problems with short-term memory, lowered ability to generalize and transfer skills, and failure to use the strategies needed for successful learning. These students also have short attention spans and quickly become frustrated by academic tasks. They cannot gain insight easily or reason as well as non-disabled children, and they find it more difficult to remember abstract ideas than concrete information. They often require more time than their normally achieving peers to attain accuracy and speed of performance.

The problems faced by pupils with intellectual disabilities in academic areas may be specific to one subject or generalized. Most often, pupils will encounter problems across academic domains, with the most severe difficulties in the area of reading. Because mental age is one of the few measures that have some reliable relationship to reading achievement, reading retardation is prevalent among intellectually disabled learners. At the same time, many youngsters are below their actual mental age in reading achievement; this underachievement is most pronounced in reading comprehension.

Not that math and arithmetic are easy for students with mild disabilities. They often have difficulty with such basic skills as counting, writing numerals, and learning basic associations, and may not be competent even in the basic addition and subtraction facts. Students will meet particular difficulties in comprehending arithmetic concepts that involve abstract notions and symbols, and are unlikely to follow systematic strategies for solving word problems.

Individuals who are moderately retarded have limited intellectual ability, difficulties in working with abstract ideas, and problems in generalizing learning to new situations. They are not ready for much academic work until their early teens. Children and young adults who are severely or profoundly retarded experience major challenges to successful adaptation. Their intensive instructional and technological needs must be met if they are to overcome the intellectual and adaptive demands of their homes, schools, and communities. Many individuals suffer such serious problems that they will likely require life care and supervision. Severely retarded individuals can acquire basic skills; they may learn to regulate toilet habits, to eat with a spoon or fork, to throw a ball at a target, to understand simple verbal directions, and to participate in simple play and games (Anderson and Greer, 1976).

Students learn more easily if good demonstrations and visual aids provide them with a concrete model to watch and imitate.

Communication Development

Youngsters with intellectual disabilities acquire language more slowly. Typically, their language levels remain below those of non-handicapped children and are often below their general mental age.

Children who are intellectually disabled demonstrate delays in sentence length, sentence complexity, and speech sound discrimination. Their expressive language tends to be less complex, and some have trouble generalizing the rules of grammar (Cramer, 1978). They do not gain as much information from verbal or non-verbal receptive language. Both children and adults who are mentally retarded are less able to decipher affective facial expressions than their peers (Adams and Markham, 1991; Maurer and Newbrough, 1987).

Language problems are not related to the etiology of the retardation, but to its severity. Youngsters who are mildly intellectually disabled may be delayed in talking, but mutism is rare. Moderately mentally retarded individuals use stereotypical language, rarely free of defects. Among persons who are profoundly retarded, expressive speech and language skills are extremely limited. Mutism is common among severely and profoundly retarded individuals, as are primitive levels of speech, such as babbling and jabbering (Jordan, 1976).

In children with Down syndrome, speech and language acquisition is often significantly delayed (Pruess, Vadasy, and Fewell, 1989). Down babies vocalize less frequently. Many of these children do not acquire two-word phrases until three or four years of age; some do not acquire functional speech until eight years (Drash et al., 1989).

It is estimated that speech disorders affect about 55 percent of the total population of persons with intellectual disabilities. For example, intellectually disabled persons are more likely to be labelled as stutterers (Chapman and Cooper, 1973). Some speech problems are the result of structural differences or malformations. For example, children with Down syndrome often have oral problems that affect articulation — an overly large tongue, over which they have less muscle control than other children, or an inability to close the passage from the nose to the mouth, resulting in hypernasal speech.

Social and Emotional Development

Children with intellectual disabilities often have special personal and social problems and exhibit atypical development patterns in socialization. The more severe the handicap, the lower the amount of social interaction with non-disabled peers (Guralnick, 1981).

These children initiate far fewer social exchanges and tend to engage in shorter sequences of reciprocal interaction than do their normally developing counterparts. They may fail to respond readily to initial overtures from others; this lack of response further isolates them as it serves to discourage interaction.

In general, students with intellectual disabilities are not well accepted by their non-disabled peers and often have trouble making friends (Luftig, 1988; Zetlin and Murtaugh, 1988). They are frequently the subject of teasing, which serves to diminish their self-concept and further compound the problems in self-esteem that accompany low achievement. Children may be rejected because they look different or show unusual behaviour and then give up trying because of low motivation.

Moderately retarded students have rather clear-cut deficits in adaptive behaviour; they have problems with interpersonal relationships, social concepts, emotional instability, and communication. As children with moderate intellectual disabilities grow older, the progressive widening of their developmental lag tends to make their retardation more obvious. This is in contrast to persons who are mildly retarded, whose condition becomes less obvious in adulthood.

Behavioural Development

There exists a significant correlation between the level of retardation and psychiatric processes. Estimates of the prevalence of mental illness among the retarded population range from 14 to 64 percent (see Galligan, 1990). One of the most serious disorders is schizophrenia.

Especially in children, it is extremely difficult, if not impossible, to determine whether the emotional disturbance caused the mental retardation or vice versa. Children who are emotionally disturbed in early childhood may be deprived of the normal sources of intellectual and social development. A low IQ (especially if below 50) increases the probability that an infant will have problems in perceiving, understanding, and responding to the environment, and is therefore found associated with the pathology of psychoses (Bhatara, 1980; Fish and Ritvko, 1979). Conversely, the retarded child may withdraw and display the behaviours characteristic of emotionally disturbed children.

Maladaptive behaviour, which includes both inappropriate and self-injurious behaviours, is found across the spectrum of the intellectually disabled population but more commonly in severely and profoundly retarded persons. As with skill development, the frequency of maladaptive behaviours is extremely variable.

Inappropriate behaviours include aggression toward other people and objects, tantrums, and such stereotypic behaviour as meaningless repetitive movements, rocking, and hand waving. Hand mouthing (finger and hand sucking) is common. Less prevalent behaviours include vomiting and rumination, disrobing, pica and coprophagy (eating inedible objects, including feces), stealing, and material hoarding (Whitman and Scibak, 1979).

Self-injurious behaviour, defined as any self-inflicted, repetitive action that leads to laceration, bruising, or abrasions of the person's own body, is common. Severely and profoundly retarded persons may engage in head banging, eye gouging, biting, scratching, self-pinching and hitting, and rectal digging. The prevalence of self-injurious behaviour ranges from 8 to 19 percent (Gedye, 1989). Higher frequencies are found among those severely retarded (49 percent) and profoundly retarded (40 percent) as compared to mildly retarded persons (12 percent).

Intervention with Children Who Are Intellectually Disabled

Many different types of intervention are used with individuals with intellectual disabilities. Medical and pharmacological interventions are important, especially for individuals with organic etiologies. Social and early intervention is crucial for infants and preschoolers and their families (see Chapter 16). Various therapists may intervene to improve motor, language, and speech functioning. It is in the schools, however, that the major focus occurs. Most students with mild disabilities are placed in regular classrooms, and there has been a shift in recent years to greater placement in the public schools for students with moderate to profound mental retardation.

There is often much more intervention at the elementary than the secondary level. Although services for a majority of students with intellectual disabilities have significantly improved and expanded in the years since the passage of Public Law 94-142 in the United States, the provision of appropriate educational services remains problematic for many secondary-aged students with disabilities (Edgar, 1987; Zetlin and Hosseini, 1989). Recently, the process of transition from school to the adult community and work place has piqued the interest of educators because of the many difficulties students find in negotiating the transition successfully. The practice of transition and other educational arrangements for older students and adults with intellectual disabilities are discussed in Chapter 17.

Medical Intervention

No surgical procedures or miracle drugs are known to actually improve intellectual ability or adaptive behaviour. In general, medical intervention attempts to prevent or correct the organic causes of retardation, rather than to alleviate the condition itself. We have already discussed the values of screening in cases such as phenylketonuria.

Surgical intervention has been used with Down syndrome children in an effort to alleviate speech and eating problems and render their appearance more normal. Increasing numbers of families are seeking this option, especially for tongue reduction to improve speech and looks.

Technical Aids

Technological advances have resulted in the development of devices designed specifically for persons with intellectual disabilities. A range of instructional technology is employed in classrooms; independent functioning is supplemented with aids for self-help skills and environmental control. These include a device that produces a signal for a non-toilet-trained child to go to the bathroom, a self-feeding tray for multiply disabled persons, and special bathing devices. Adaptive equipment is discussed in Chapter 13. Instructional technology primarily involves microcomputers and innovative software. (See Chapter 3.)

Educational Intervention

Intellectual disabilities are related to delayed intellectual development in areas considered important for school success. Students classified as intellectually disabled achieve below grade level and usually experience difficulties throughout their school careers.

Within the school system, the current trend is to include students with intellectual disabilities in the regular classroom, especially those with mild disabilities. A student's success in the classroom depends on a number of additional factors that include support services, curriculum modifications, acceptance by the other students, the classroom teacher's experience with and exposure to exceptional children, the availability of community resources, and the age of the student. Depending on the nature of inclusion, some students may have resource room assistance.

Research Notes

Resource rooms

The resource room was an innovation in education brought to the field by special education. The model developed in the 1960s for two reasons. One was the need to serve more children directly, and the other was to provide support services to teachers who were instructing children with special needs (Winzer, 1989).

Resource rooms were designed to help children make the transition from self-contained classrooms to regular classrooms. At the same time, the model of the resource room serves to support the principle of normalization and removes the stigma of segregation. Programs attempt to overcome various problems associated with special classes while preserving quality service for exceptional pupils. In addition, resource rooms provide a place to assess behaviour precisely and allow for the rapid acceleration of those children who can function for most of the day in the regular classroom.

After 1975, the most common way of educating students with special needs was through a combination of regular classroom instruction and special assistance in the resource room. Despite the popularity of resource room (pull-out) programs, however, research indicates that these arrangements have not been an unqualified success. Resource rooms have been charged with often failing to increase academic learning time (Haynes and Jenkins, 1986) and failing to produce transfer to the regular program (Anderson-Inman, 1986). Resource room assistance, therefore, does not result in direct improvement of regular class performance, and this becomes increasingly apparent in the upper grades (Anderson-Inman, 1986). Critics note that resource room programs disrupt classroom instruction (Wang, Reynolds, and Walberg, 1987) and absolve classroom teachers of responsibility for the instruction of low-performing students (Pugach and Lilly, 1984). Instruction is different in content and focus; instructional materials are often different (Anderson-Inman, 1986); and resource rooms fail to co-ordinate their instruction with that of the regular classroom (Johnston, Allington, and Afflerbach, 1985; Haynes and Jenkins, 1986). What is more, resource rooms cost more than other alternatives (Affleck et al., 1988) and are ineffective (Gallagher, 1984).

Some opponents argue that pull-out programs attach stigmas to children who are pulled out (Will, 1986). However, one study (Bak et al., 1987) found that children responded to de facto labels of resource room and special classroom differently. They saw the students going to resource room as significantly more capable than those in special classes. Another study of student preferences for pull-out and in-class instruction (Jenkins and Heinen, 1989) found that students were influenced by both the types of programs in which they were currently serviced and their grade levels. The majority of students who were in a resource room preferred it, while those in regular classrooms were split evenly between in-class and pull-out services. Older students receiving in-class services preferred pull-out programs.

Successful accommodation of students with intellectual disabilities relies on the teacher's willingness to make curriculum modifications, to promote social interactions, and to use adaptive equipment if necessary. A broad overview of curriculum components is shown in Figure 4-3.

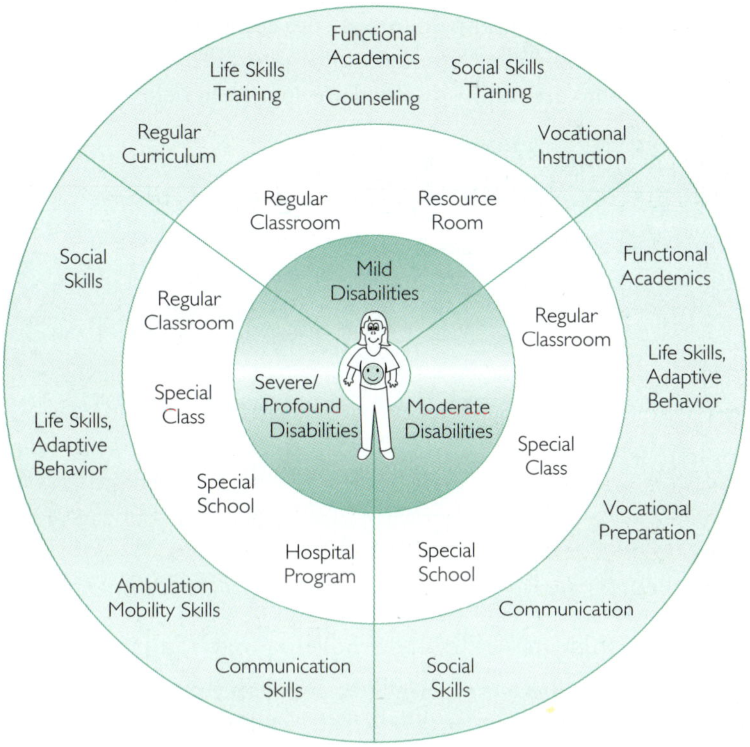

Figure 4-3
Curriculum components

Educational Approaches

There are three major goals in the education of students with intellectual disabilities: productivity, independence, and participation. To accomplish these goals, students are presented with instruction in the areas of academic, social, self-help, community living, and vocational skills. Depending on the extent and severity of the disability, the major goals are not always fully achievable; success may be only fractional for children functioning at the low end of the continuum.

Approaches for Students with Mild Intellectual Disabilities

The actual curriculum objectives are the same for students with mild intellectual disabilities as for their peers. Students require instruction in basic academic skills, particularly basic literacy and numeracy. Teachers must also stress the cognitive, language, and social domains. Each program will be individualized, based on a student's unique set of strengths and weaknesses.

In the early grades, children who are mildly disabled are taught readiness skills in such areas as math and reading. At the intermediate levels, educational emphasis may be placed on activities related to everyday life. These may include functional reading, writing, and math, as well as areas such as transportation, budgeting, peer relationships, and personal hygiene. At the secondary level, students with mild disabilities are taught personal-social adjustment and occupational skills, along with basic academics.

While various curriculum modifications and adaptations can be incorporated in order to accommodate students with disabilities in the regular classroom, changes in teaching methods are not that obvious or major. Specialized competencies and teaching methods are extensions and refinements of core competencies rather than new sets of teaching behaviours and skills (Ysseldyke and Algozzine (1990). Various strategies for teaching children who are mildly disabled are suggested below.

Tips for Teachers

Tips for teachers of children with mild intellectual disabilities

Classroom climate

- Promote an atmosphere of success.
- Motivation increases as competitiveness decreases. Rewarding effort rather than ability is likely to serve as a motivator for all students.
- Motivation also involves allowing students opportunities to control and monitor their own learning and behaviour. Allow some degree of freedom in selecting tasks or assignments.
- Feelings of personal competence and self-esteem are closely tied to experiences of success. Through individualization, provide for success in academic domains.
- As these students are more limited in their learning, they require more reinforcement.

Instruction

- Present tasks in an uncomplicated, brief, and sequential fashion. Sequence from the simple to the more complex.
- Ensure mastery of new material through repetition and overlearning. Provide many opportunities for *drill* (repeating a task) and *practice* (applying the task to similar situations). In math, for example, students may be drilled on number facts through rote repetition, work sheets, and games. They may then practise the skills through the actual performance of a task, such as applying the number facts to addition problems.
- Students learn more easily if good demonstrations and visual aids provide them with a concrete model to watch and imitate.
- Promote transfer of learning by applying learning to other situations, objects, and problems in the learner's environment.
- As a general rule, the more abstract the learning experience, the less these students will be able to experience success. Emphasize concrete, meaningful content, especially in initial instructional presentations.
- Students with memory problems tend to be passive learners, another reason to use many concrete materials and manipulatives.
- Use a variety of alternative approaches to instruction, that is, many methods to present material and reinforce learning.
- Use co-operative learning strategies.
- Use peer tutoring in the classroom. Arrange for these students to peer tutor younger children.

Behaviour

- Use positive reinforcement carefully but often.
- Teach social skills if necessary.

Including students with special needs demands some modifications in three major areas — lesson content, specific knowledge, and the learning environment. Elementary teachers report that the instructional modifications used most frequently include shortened assignments, oral tests, study buddies, lower level worksheets, and preferential seating (Bacon and Schulz, 1991).

In presenting instruction, teachers should alter the stress and pacing of lessons, the type and amount of seatwork, and grading practices. Changes must often be made in the content of the lesson, which may be modified to make it more concrete and relevant to children's recent experiences.

One hallmark of an effective learning environment for students with mild disabilities is the degree to which the environment is constructively active. In an effective learning environment, the teacher engages in active teaching and the student is actively engaged in successfully completing academically relevant tasks. The teacher monitors student performance and provides informed feedback (Ysseldyke and Christenson, 1987). This approach is referred to as conventional teaching (Walberg, 1991), or direct instruction.

Direct instruction refers to activity-focused, teacher-directed classroom procedures that are systematic and usually conducted according to an individual plan. Direct instruction procedures include prompting, shaping, and reinforcing that are implemented in a precise and consistent fashion. Learning is achieved by identifying the specific objective to be attained, arranging appropriate stimuli to elicit the responses, programming learning sequences in small steps, and reinforcing desired behaviours.

Walberg (1991) argues that such a direct didactic approach has the best track record. He describes the teacher doing certain things:

- daily review, homework check, and if necessary, reteaching;
- rapid presentation of new content and skills in small steps;
- guided student practice under close teacher monitoring;
- corrective feedback and reinforcement;
- independent practice in seatwork and homework;
- weekly and monthly review (p. 44).

Approaches for Children with Moderate Intellectual Disabilities

For students with moderate disabilities, the curriculum is less academically oriented than it is for the mildly disabled child. In general, children who are moderately disabled do not learn to read beyond the first grade level. They are taught to read names, directions, labels, and to write relevant names and words. They are also introduced to numbers, time, and simple money exchange.

The ultimate goal of education is functional independence. Recent trends in public school curricula for moderately and severely handicapped students and young adults has seen a movement away from the specification of curricular goals based on developmental age; teachers now direct instruction toward chronologically age-appropriate skills that students need to meet the demands of their community environments (Wiggins and Behrmann, 1988).

When functionality is the core of the curriculum, the approach is referred to as life-skills instruction. Adaptive behaviour, self-help skills, life skills, and social skills are the important components of this approach.

Individual Education Plan iep

Extract from Nicholas's IEP

Name: Nicholas
Teacher: Mr. McPhee
C.A.: 8-2
Grade: 2
School: St. Basil

Present levels of functioning

Nicholas was referred by his classroom teacher for psycho-educational assessment as he is falling further and further behind his classmates, especially in the core areas of reading and math.

Cognitive: on the WISC-111, Nicholas showed a Full scale score of 86 (+/- 5). While within the average range, this is almost one standard deviation below the norm.

Language: Nicholas appears to have average language ability based on results of the PPVT-R and the TOLD-P. The psychologist noted his strong use of appropriate language when talking about things that really interested him.

Reading: Nicholas has barely made a start in formal reading. He is at a beginning grade 1 level.

Math: all math concepts seem to be difficult for Nicholas. He does not seem to understand place value. However, he knows the names of coins and seemed further advanced and far more interested when using real money.

Long-range goals

- Stimulate interest in school activities by building on relatively strong language based on his own experiences.
- Develop a sight word vocabulary.
- Read very short paragraphs and books (Sports Illustrated for Kids) about sports.
- Use coins as the major manipulative to teach rational counting, place value, addition and subtraction facts, and basic computation.

Short-term objectives

- Learn ten sight words related to sports with the teacher, in a small group, or with a peer tutor.
- Read and discuss short paragraphs about sports in a small group.
- Use written exercises (fill-the-blank, draw, underline the word) to stress sight words and to teach reading directions.
- Use pennies for rational counting to 99 forward and backwards.
- Use coins for simple equations.

Functional skills are those that help children to get along in their current and future environments. The skills are displayed throughout a lifetime and tend to be practised in progressively more complex and varied forms as children grow (Wolery, 1991). Along with such fundamental things as dressing and eating, functional skills include those needed for participation in routine home and community activities such as playing with siblings, helping with simple chores, and eating at a fast food restaurant.

Self-help skills are functional. They include the ability to care for oneself, which is fundamental in achieving independence and self-sufficiency. The collected self-help skills are divided into those related to eating, dressing, bathing, grooming, and toileting. Training is undertaken in such skills as independent eating, dressing, using the toilet, washing, combing hair, brushing teeth, and using a handkerchief. Students also learn simple homemaking skills, such as dusting, sweeping, setting and clearing a table, washing and drying dishes, washing and ironing, sewing, using simple tools, and telephoning. They are taught the safety rules and how to use public transportation.

For all children, the functional approach becomes more important as they grow older. Life skills essentially include all the components a student requires to successfully negotiate life as an adult. Programming identifies the myriad demands of adulthood, relates the demands to specific skills, and bases the curriculum on teaching these skills (Robinson et al., 1989). A variety of job-related skills are presented. Deficits in student performance during the school years and beyond suggest that skill instruction is best conducted in real-world settings in the presence of non-handicapped people and using naturally occurring situations and materials (Hamre-Nietupski et al., 1982). Natural environments include grocery stores, restaurants, public transportation, banks, and drug stores. Secondary education programs are more explicitly vocationally oriented and directed toward securing employment upon graduation. In some cases, such programs are operated in conjunction with sheltered workshops. (See Chapter 17.)

Communication training is designed to help the child develop the skills necessary for everyday communication. Personal and social skills include consideration for others, common courtesy, obedience, and self-judgment. Students also learn perceptual-motor and physical skills, which include sense training in the visual, auditory and tactile modalities; eye-hand co-ordination; balance; and gross and fine motor movement.

Profile

Jane

Jane L. is seven years and ten months old. She was diagnosed as having Down syndrome at birth. When she was six months old, she and her mother began to attend an infant stimulation program for developmentally disabled children and their families. At age three, Jane was enrolled in a nursery school for developmentally disabled children. During these preschool years, her mother spent a great deal of time with her, carrying out the suggestions of the infant therapist and then the preschool teachers.

A recent psychological testing of Jane indicated that, both cognitively and socially, she is functioning in the high end of the moderately retarded scale. While Jane's verbal and non-verbal intelligence scores were similar, her social age was somewhat higher, as measured by the Vineland Social Maturity Scale. Her use of receptive language, measured by the Peabody Picture Vocabulary Test, was more advanced than her expressive language. Jane's language problems are compounded by speech problems associated with the physical anomalies of Down syndrome.

Janes loves school. She attends the local public school in a self-contained classroom. Her teacher is using a language experience method to expand her receptive language vocabulary. Jane enjoys this approach, and also finds integrated activities great fun — simple non-cooked recipes, dusting, sweeping, and "playing house." Jane is less enthusiastic about her sessions on articulation with the speech therapist. However, she is always eager to attempt any of the motor tasks suggested by the physical therapist to improve the quality of her movements.

Jane's social aptitude serves her well. She is well liked by the other children in the class and could be considered the class leader. At first, on the playground, she was very shy of other children in the school. Recently, however, she has begun to join the games of some of the kindergarten children, who accept her quite readily.

Within a functional approach, targets for instruction are selected by analyzing the child's environment. Teachers identify specific skills that will immediately improve the child's ability to interact with the environment and that will increase the probability that the child will perform functional critical behaviours for success and survival in future environments. Important skills are then broken down into small, building steps in a task analysis. Skills are taught for generalization as well as for functional usefulness. Teaching a child to grasp a toy may, for example, generalize to grasping a hair brush or a tooth brush, both necessary self-help skills. Or if the objective is to teach students to operate a musical device during their leisure time, it is more functional for a fifteen-year-old to use a cassette player rather than a gaily coloured Fisher Price music box.

Training in life skills is essential for students with mental handicaps.

Approaches for Students Who Are Severely and Profoundly Disabled

While almost all students with mild intellectual disabilities will be educated in regular classrooms and most trainable students will be in regular classes or schools, the placement of severely and profoundly disabled students is more controversial. For these youngsters, there exist conflicting and extreme ideologies that revolve around the issue of inclusive schooling. This was fully discussed in Chapter 3.

There is no question that for children who are severely and profoundly disabled, we must redefine the term education beyond its traditional academic limits. The goals are different from those for non-disabled students and those with milder disabilities, and many more personnel are involved. These children often require a range of other services that involve such professionals as doctors, speech therapists, social workers, and psychologists.

The major educational goals for individuals who are severely and profoundly retarded are to decrease dependence on others, increase awareness of environmental stimulation, teach basic communication and self-help skills, and push achievement levels higher. The training of these students begins with basic survival and self-help skills, along with the elimination of undesirable behaviour. Repetition and simple conditioning are primary teaching strategies. At first, teachers focus on obtaining responses to environmental stimulation; these responses include head and trunk balance, sucking, swallowing, chewing, grasping, movement of body parts, and vocalization. Later training includes imitation, language acquisition, self-feeding, ambulation, dressing skills, toilet training, social and recreational behaviour, and functional academic skills (Stainback and Stainback, 1976).

Although behaviour modification is used with virtually every type of handicapping condition, it is particularly useful in the education and training of children with severe and profound disabilities. Behavioural methods seem to succeed where others fail, and the behavioural emphasis on specific task analysis is particularly well suited to the problems of individuals who are severely disabled. Behaviour modification has been successfully used to teach a diverse array of skills, ranging from the self-help skills to socializiation and language acquisition. As well, a variety of behaviour modification techniques have been employed in the elimination of maladaptive behaviours.

Further discussions on the education of persons with severe delays are found in Chapters 14 and 15.

Social Intervention

Advocacy groups of parents and professionals exist for the sole purpose of improving life conditions for the population of intellectually disabled persons. The Canadian Association for Community Living (CACL) (formerly the CAMR) promotes the welfare and protects the rights of intellectually disabled persons and their families. Essentially, the CCCL performs the following functions:

- Encourages the acceptance of all intellectually disabled people into the life of the community.
- Promotes the enactment and implementation of legislation to improve the welfare of intellectually disabled people.
- Promotes improved educational and vocational training for intellectually disabled people.
- Furthers the education and training of personnel for work in the field of intellectual disabilities.
- Provides centres for the gathering and distribution of information about intellectual disabilities.
- Fosters research concerning all aspects of intellectual disability.
- Develops better public understanding of people who are intellectually disabled and their needs (CAMR, 1980).

Summary

1. As a human condition, mental retardation has been identified since ancient times, and always it has been misunderstood.
2. In the nineteenth century, institutions were the common mode of placement for students with mental retardation. Then, right into the 1960s, segregated classrooms formed the most common vehicle for service delivery to these students. When normalization, with its corollaries of deinstitutionalization and mainstreaming, became the dominant ideology in the education and treatment of intellectual disability, educational intervention altered drastically. Major changes have taken place in definitions, terminology, program options, and program delivery.
3. Under the AAMR definition, three factors must be present for an individual to be considered within the category of mental retardation — subaverage general intellectual functioning, deficits in adaptive behaviour, and manifestation during the developmental period.
4. Adaptive behaviour is a difficult construct to operationalize, define, and measure. In the broadest sense, adaptive behaviour refers to an individual's ability to cope or deal effectively with personal and social demands. Limitations in adaptive skills exist within the context of community environments typical of the individual's age peers and are indexed to the person's individualized needs for support.
5. Today's definitions of mental retardation, especially mild disability, do not see it as a permanent condition but as one that improves with sustained intervention and also one linked to the demands of formal schooling. There is a higher incidence of retardation during the school years, with lower incidence figures during the preschool years and adulthood.
6. Under non-categorical aproaches, children with mild disabilities are grouped with the learning disabled and behaviourally disordered populations for instruction, and the entire notion of mild mental retardation has changed. The redefining of children labelled as mentally retarded in 1973 to omit those functioning between one and two standard deviations below the mean resulted in increasing numbers of students being categorized as learning disabled. The latter category is today the largest focus of special education in many school districts, and mental retardation per se seems to be a category of declining importance.
7. The agents that cause mental retardation are legion. They include genetic and chromosomal differences, infections such as maternal rubella, intoxicants such as drugs, postnatal diseases such as meningitis, and childhood accidents.
8. Although Down syndrome can cause disabilities that fall anywhere in the spectrum from mild to profound retardation, Down individuals with normal intellectual development are almost exclusively those with the mosaic form of the condition. Within the field of education, students with fragile X syndrome are entering a variety of special education classrooms and bringing with them a complex genetic history as well as diverse educational needs.
9. In trying to pinpoint the existence and severity of intellectual disabilities, clinicians are challenged to find a range of observations and measures that are appropriate for individual children. Data on a child's levels of cognitive functioning are employed as one measure used to determine the educational program.

10. Although youngsters with mild intellectual disabilities may consistently lag in academic areas such as reading, math, science, and social studies, they learn in the same way as other pupils. Studies on the learning characteristics of mildly disabled children show that even if their rate of learning is slower and the level reached is not as high, their learning curves approximate those of non-disabled pupils.

11. Severely and profoundly retarded individuals must often struggle to achieve ambulation and simple physical activities. For individuals in these two levels of severity, physical development is often impaired and multiple handicapping conditions are common.

12. Children labelled as mildly intellectually disabled form the greatest proportion of the retarded population. Today, the majority of these students are educated in regular classrooms, sometimes with additional resource room assistance. Following graduation, many mildly disabled individuals blend into the social fabric of their neighbourhoods, holding jobs, marrying, and having families. Once that adjustment is made, they are no longer, according to the AAMR definition, retarded.

13. There is much documentation of the successful accomplishment of specific academic objectives through direct instruction.

14. Children with moderate levels of intellectual disability are being educated in regular schools, either in the regular classroom or in special self-contained classrooms. Teachers present limited academic curricula with a stress on functional skills in all domains.

15. The inclusion of students who are severely or profoundly retarded is beset by controversy. These children have grave barriers to learning, often demonstrate maladaptive behaviour, and are often multiply handicapped. Although structured behavioural programs can impart useful skills, argument rages about the most appropriate placement in which to present these skills.

CHAPTER 5

Children Who Are Gifted, Creative, and Talented

Historical Notes

Cultural values have always determined the attitudes of society towards its outstanding members. Different cultural eras have valued achievement in different fields of endeavour. Ancient Greece admired the philosopher, Rome the soldier and orator, and Renaissance Italy the artist. Nonetheless, throughout recorded history, two threads are consistently discernable in the perceptions most people have had of those who were gifted. On the one hand, much honour was paid to individuals who made significant contributions to their own or succeeding cultures. On the other, even as honour was paid to gifted persons, the notion of precocity was shrouded in myth and mysticism, and genius was often misunderstood. Even in the late 1800s, genius was still popularly viewed as directly related to insanity.

Remarkable early development, or precocity, was characteristic of many major historical figures. Beethoven performed in public at age seven. Thomas Jefferson began serious study at five, and Pablo Picasso drew before he could walk. John Stuart Mill's father, an outstanding intellectual himself, began tutoring his son at the age of three. By the time the boy was eight, he had read many Greek authors and was starting to learn Latin, geometry, algebra, and calculus (Laycock, 1979). Mill's childhood precocity yielded remarkable contributions in maturity; he exerted powerful influence upon nineteenth century social thought.

Other major contributors to our culture and society, such as Winston Churchill, Thomas Edison, and Auguste Rodin, bloomed later and only after surviving hardships or overcoming disabilities. Winston Churchill was a sickly child with a speech impediment; Edison's teachers described him as "addled"; and Rodin suffered from a learning disability. Vincent van Gogh suffered crippling bouts of depression that eventually led to his suicide. Mozart suffered the indignity of being exhibited as a child prodigy; as early as age seven, he was forced by his father to perform for the amusement of the nobility and the furthering of the family's finances. Throughout his life, Mozart endured constant pressure from his father and lived mainly in penury. Charles Dickens also struggled with childhood poverty.

Little systematic research has been conducted into the characteristics of, and developmental influences on, these people (Callahan, 1981). Before the mid-nineteenth century, giftedness was a visible, yet poorly defined and understood phenomenon. Studies of gifted individuals and the precursors of giftedness arose largely out of the eugenics movement and, in fact, contributed to the spread of the philosophy. Francis Galton, an English scientist and eugenics advocate, was one of the first to research and write about giftedness. For his 1869 work, *Hereditary genius*, Galton took as subjects eminent British statesmen, soldiers, scientists, writers, poets, artists, and ministers who lived between 1768 and 1868. He found that many of his group of 977 men had close relatives as eminent as themselves and, on the basis of these data, determined that genius was largely a hereditary factor. Galton proposed that motivation to achieve was innate and inborn and claimed that genius would actualize itself despite external circumstances (Galton, 1869), a position that led to the enduring and dangerous myth that "the cream will rise to the top" regardless of difficulties or lack of environmental support.

In the same time frame, the Italian scientist Cesare Lombroso (1835-1909), interested in aspects of individual differences that were much broader than intellectual functions, investigated the popular notion that genius is closely related to insanity. In *The man of genius* (1891), Lombroso concluded that genius is a marked aberration from the norm and akin to other mental aberrations. In 1926 Catherine Cox, one of Terman's co-workers, published a work on genius that, like Galton's, used accounts of the lives of eminent men as sources of data. Cox estimated the IQs of the men and concluded that youthful genius had a superior hereditary and environmental advantage; that it was manifested at an early age; and that later eminence was a function of high IQ and persistence, motivation, effort, self-confidence, and great strength and force of character (Cox, 1926).

As a descriptive term for a specific group of individuals who are highly intelligent and strong academic achievers, *gifted* was first used in the literature by Guy M. Henry in 1920. In the following years, behavioural scientists used *gifted* as the sole designation to describe people with high intelligence. As a wider conception of the array of human potential developed, the constructs *talented* and *creative* came into use in the 1960s.

Current researchers contend that intellectual giftedness, creativity, and talent interact with one another to a greater or lesser degree. Some individuals soar to great heights in the talent domain, others in intellectual ability, and still others in creative endeavours. A few individuals achieve remarkably high levels across several domains.

Giftedness is a somewhat abstract term applied to people who, by virtue of outstanding abilities, are capable of high performance (Clark, 1988). Gifted individuals have greater ability in some areas than most of us. Generally, we admire such people, but occasionally we are a little envious of their talents and achievements. We seem to have to work much harder than they do to achieve only mediocre results.

Special education attempts to provide for any child markedly different from the average, even if this difference is a positive one. Gifted, creative, and talented students have special educational needs — they may learn in ways different from other students; they are more curious; and they think more abstractly. At the same time, gifted students are vulnerable to the same forces that affect other children and youth and can become frustrated and bored in unstimulating learning environments.

To reach their full potential, gifted, creative, and talented children must be confronted with suitable challenges and stimulating educational experiences. However, the provision of special services to this population has always been a complex and difficult undertaking that poses many complex issues and problems for educators. A great deal of professional skill and sensitivity is required to identify the special needs of gifted students, while the development of appropriate programs taxes the skill, resourcefulness, and empathy of teachers.

The restrictions placed on programs for gifted students are both academic and attitudinal. All are associated, to a greater or lesser extent, with the notion that "the cream will rise to the top." Many people still believe that gifted children are smart enough to make it on their own. They see gifted students typically doing well in school, easily meeting age and grade levels for achievement, and tending to be well behaved. They therefore rationalize that gifted pupils will develop their abilities even if not provided with special education. If students don't do well, then they're not gifted, anyway.

Myths about gifted students being able to do well regardless of environment and the amount of stimulation and opportunity are compounded by the fact that most gifted children demonstrate no immediate problems that can serve as a basis for an emotional appeal for special services. Traditionally, special education has been viewed as a way to help children who perform poorly in school, and children with outstanding abilities rarely arouse the same level of concern as do handicapped youngsters. Gifted and talented children are not perceived as suffering from social stigma or unhappiness; rather, giftedness is considered highly desirable and a boon to social status.

Many educators feel that although we are morally obliged to help children with disabilities, there is no moral necessity to assist those children who are already advantaged. They question the ethics of a society that labels a select few, that provides special opportunities for the elite, and that attends "to the exclusive needs of only a small segment of learners" (Sapon-Shivin, 1984, p. 79).

The underlying concern is that special education for the gifted might subvert our commitment to egalitarianism and jeopardize the principle of democratic education by creating an over-advantaged elite or meritocracy within the school population. Because of this attitude, we direct our special education programs, and the taxes that support them, largely into programs for students who are disabled. Our regular education programs serve the needs of average children. The gifted we leave to fend for themselves, even when this involves a waste of their potential.

Yet an increasing number of educators, administrators, legislators, parents, and researchers support the idea that giftedness needs to be fostered and nurtured. They argue that gifted children have the same right as other children to develop to their full potential and therefore require special education and appropriate related services. Without educational opportunities and challenges, gifted children may hide their abilities or bury them in underachievement. In fact, probably half of the gifted population do not match their tested ability with comparable achievement in school.

Most thinking individuals would agree that Canada's gifted and talented youth form one of its greatest undeveloped resources. Many of the leaders, scientists, and artists of the next generation are likely to emerge from the current crop of gifted and talented children. Nevertheless, debates surrounding the issue of egalitarianism versus special programs for gifted students continue and are germane to today's education of these students. Educators are challenged by the philosophical and practical problems of how to educate gifted children adequately in a public education system that is philosophically and administratively egalitarian in nature. But if education for the gifted is to survive, this issue will have to be resolved.

Development of the Field

In one sense, schools have always accommodated gifted students; early schools were populated by the rich, the bright, and the very ambitious. In the late nineteenth century, the introduction of mass education and the needs of an industrializing society dictated that children be educated in groups of similar age levels and pass through school and enter the job market at prespecified ages. With the passage of compulsory school laws, gifted students, along with their average and below average counterparts, flowed into the newly created free public schools. Teachers were then faced with the unpromising task of providing adequately for classes of children of the same age level but of vastly differing abilities. While attempting to follow a course adapted to the main group of students — the average — teachers found that their time was taken up with the below average students who required extra help. Meanwhile, the above average were left to themselves. True, they could master the work in a much shorter time, but if they finished early they were only given more of the same to keep them busy. Often, children became bored, resentful, or demanding, or behaved in ways that disrupted the class and exhausted the teacher.

Special day classes for gifted pupils emerged in the United States during the 1890s, but the movement was small and the classes scattered. By the mid-1930s, there were still only 75 classrooms in the country with 1834 children in programs for the gifted. Canada rapidly followed in establishing classes, but again the movement, compared to that for children with disabilities, was small.

Community-based gifted education was founded in London, Ontario, in the late 1920s, when concerned teachers and parents worked together to design an enrichment program for the elementary grades (Bain, 1980). On the Prairies, the Enterprise Method developed and trained students in learning and community-oriented group activities. The Major Work Program, first adopted in Alberta, flourished briefly across the country. It offered selected children greater intellectual stimulation, along with training in advanced creativity and problem solving (Bain, 1980).

Over the decades, other programs have developed in Canada, many of them based on the philosophy of Samuel Laycock of Saskatchewan. From the 1930s to the late 1960s, Laycock championed the cause of those exceptional children who were capable of creativity and leadership, but were too often ignored by society. Saskatchewan, in fact, has had a continuous program since the 1930s for very gifted learners (Lipp, 1988).

In the 1970s, concern for the special needs of gifted children was reawakened in large measure by the evidence that many of these youngsters were bored with the lock step of mass education and were turning into chronic underachievers and dropouts. Another major spur was the mounting pessimism of North American educators as they saw their educational standards drop far below those of the Japanese and the Europeans. Another was an offshoot of the women's movement that began to open avenues for females to enter less traditional roles.

But even today, attempts to provide appropriate programs are undermined by popularly held stereotypes and myths. Galton's myth that "the cream will rise to the top" has been perpetuated as educators have persistently argued about whether special programming for individuals already well endowed violates the ethics of a democratic school system. Funding, willingly ceded to children functioning below the norm, has been only grudgingly allowed to those with superior abilities. Compared to that for disabled children, education provided for the gifted and talented has been a very small-scale enterprise.

Definitions

To be gifted is to be superior in some way to the average. But beyond this almost meaningless statement, no definition of gifted children has been agreed upon. In fact, the importance of adequately defining giftedness as a precursor to identification and as an indicator of prevalence has led to a multiplicity of definitions. In one quite recent publication, seventeen different conceptions of giftedness were identified (Sternberg and Davidson, 1986).

Many factors underlie the definitional problems found in the field. These can be summarized as follows:

- There is no such thing as a typical gifted child; particular talents and social environments give rise to varying personality patterns.
- Although many different gifts and talents have been identified and creativity can be, at least partly, explained and measured, gifted, talented, and creative individuals are typically lumped together as a single category.
- Definitions of giftedness have changed. When the roots of the field of gifted education were laid down by pioneers such as Francis Galton and Lewis Terman, high IQ was viewed as the critical dimension of giftedness. Because children with high IQs were the most deeply investigated, early definitions tended to be narrow and restricted. They relied on psychometric measures and limited giftedness to specific performance on an intelligence test. Over time, definitions have become much more liberal in terms of both the types of behaviours attributed to gifted individuals and the degree of behaviour that must be elicited before the label *gifted* is applied.
- There is no consensus on how to measure superiority or how to recognize potential giftedness.
- There are two quite different views about the definitions of giftedness. One looks at giftedness as potential; the other looks at it as the actual production of outstanding work. The giftedness-as-potential view often uses an IQ cut-off between 120 and 140 or restricts giftedness to a percentage of the population, ranging from the top 1 to 20 percent. When giftedness-as-product is used, definitions dismiss the idea that IQ alone determines giftedness; they focus on the attributes of identified gifted individuals and their potential value to society. This is because "school-house giftedness," connoted by high test scores and good grades, is only weakly associated with adult eminence or creative contribution (Siegler and Kotovsky, 1985; Sternberg, 1987). Product definitions therefore base giftedness on an individual's consistently remarkable performance in some socially useful area and only assign the term *gifted* to people who have attained outstanding achievements.
- There is no agreement about the relationship of giftedness, creativity, and talent. Some definitions describe giftedness partly or completely in terms of an individual's creativity; others are more traditional but comprehensive enough to include talent and creativity.

A widely employed definition, originally adopted by the United States Office of Education in 1977 and revised in 1981, states that gifted children are those

> who give evidence of high performance capability in areas such as intellectual, creative, artistic, leadership capacity, or specific academic fields, and who require

> services or activities not ordinarily provided by the school in order to develop such capabilities (PL 97-35, sec 572).

This definition manages to be inclusive, specific, and practical. It encompasses a wide range of gifts, talents, and creative aptitudes; stresses the necessity for special education provisions for students identified as gifted; and ties identification to the necessity for programming.

Newfoundland has adopted this definition; Alberta's 1983 Minister's Task Force on Gifted and Talented Pupils recommended a similar definition. Ontario has quite a specific definition that includes characteristics and programming (Ontario, Ministry of Education, 1981). British Columbia has adopted an official definition, and the Yukon has adopted the model proposed by Renzulli (1978).

Joseph Renzulli, who believes in defining giftedness largely as product, holds that in the end, giftedness is determined by the contributions an individual makes to humanity. Renzulli studied adults known to be gifted and concluded that three characteristics were required for remarkable achievement: high intellectual ability, high creativity, and the ability to carry tasks through to completion. The interaction is shown in Figure 5-1. It is not enough to possess only one of these traits; as the figure shows, it is only where the circles intersect that the three traits come together and that, according to Renzulli, true giftedness is found (Renzulli and Reis, 1991). Renzulli (1978) feels that gifted and talented children "are those possessing or capable of developing this composite of traits and applying them to any potentially valuable area of human performance" (p. 261).

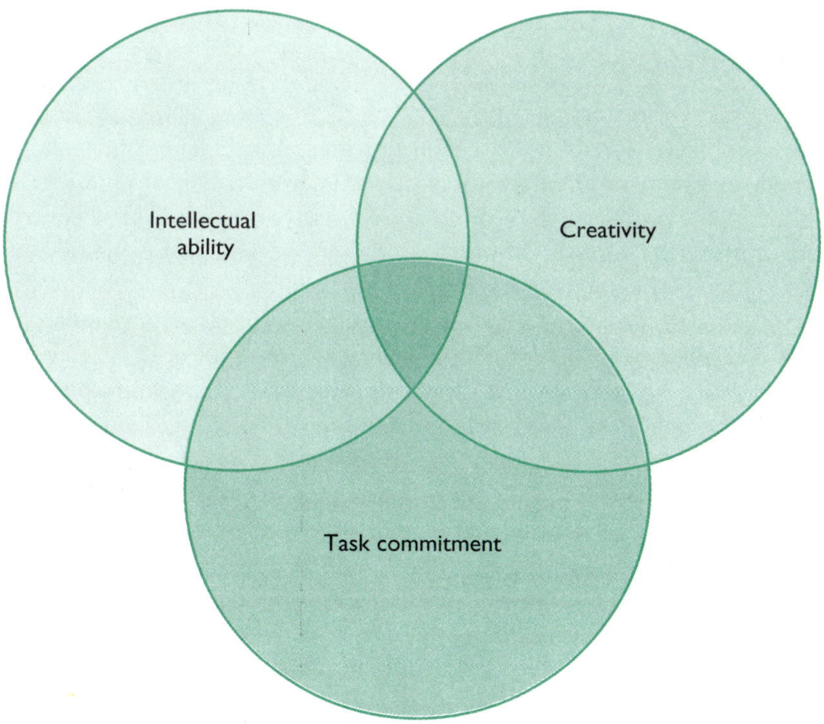

Figure 5-1 *Interaction of Renzulli's characteristics*

Terminology

To compound definitional problems, a host of other terms are used to describe gifted individuals. Words such as *precocious, talented, creative,* and *genius* are all used, and the terms *gifted* and *talented* are frequently used interchangeably.

Genius was the original term used to indicate a particular aptitude or capacity. Today, we reserve the use of the word for those persons who demonstrate extremely rare intellectual powers. In the early 1920s, the term *gifted* evolved to describe high-achieving students. It may be defined as a combination of above average general ability, a high level of creativity, and a high level of task commitment (Renzulli and Reis, 1991).

During the 1960s, definitions began to add components of creativity. Barbara Clark (1988) observes that "creativity is a very special condition, attitude, or state of being that nearly defies decription" (p. 46). Creativity may be seen as the "activities and products invented in the interest of solving a problem" (Cole and Sarnoff, 1980, p. 6).

Sometimes, young gifted children are said to be precocious. This word comes from the Latin *preacox,* meaning to precook or to boil beforehand. **Precocity** refers to remarkable early development. Many highly gifted children show precocity in particular areas of development, such as language, music, or mathematical ability.

If giftedness is above average competence, then talent is above average performance. **Talent** refers to a specific dimension of a skill in areas such as music, visual arts, drama, athletics, and particular academic domains. Canadian psychologist François Gagné calls talent "the developmental product of an interaction between aptitudes and intrapersonal and environmental catalysts" (1991, p. 66).

Classification

Classification systems do not appear in relation to giftedness as they do in fields such as intellectual ability. Severity levels would not make much sense. We could perhaps call a person mildly or moderately gifted but not severely or profoundly gifted. Any classification, therefore, revolves around the varied components that contribute to giftedness. It is closely aligned with the terminology we have just explained and takes into account that people may possess many components.

The term *gifted* implies the possession of special abilities in diverse areas; however, it is most often used to refer to students with above average academic endowment. This happens because, educationally speaking, the most important components of giftedness are those defined relative to the school in which an individual finds himself or herself. *Academic ability* refers to intellectual ability measured by performance on IQ and standardized tests of academic achievement (Marland, 1972). Academically talented students are generally considered to be those scoring at the 95th percentile or higher on these measures.

Essentially **creativity** refers to the process of bringing unusual and unexpected responses to bear on given situations; it is a capacity to restructure the world in unusual or useful conceptual terms. Creative thinking includes fluency of ideas, or producing a number of responses to a given stimulus; flexibility, or shifts in thinking from one category to another; originality, or unusual and clever responses; and elaboration, or the addition of details to basic ideas or thoughts (Torrance, 1969).

Divergent thinking, a type of thinking in which considerable searching about is done and a number of answers are produced, is part of creativity. Divergent thinking is the basis of creative problem solving and is in some ways the opposite of convergent thinking, which focuses on one right answer, or toward a relatively determined answer. This is diagrammed in Figure 5-2.

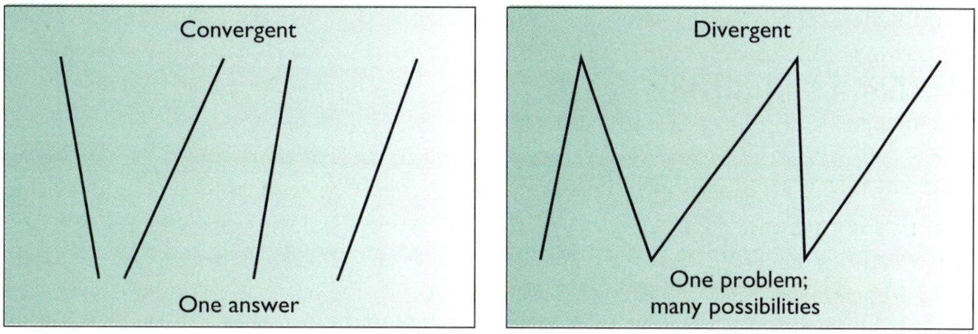

Figure 5-2 *Convergent and divergent thinking*

The link between intelligence and creativity remains difficult to pinpoint. Above a threshold score of about 120 IQ, the correlation between giftedness and creativity disappears. A Canadian study (Kershner and Ledger, 1985) found that highly intelligent boys and girls aged nine to eleven were, as a group, more creative than less intelligent children. Not all the gifted children were more creative than their peers, however, and girls were significantly more creative than boys, especially on verbal tasks.

Creativity may very well be an innate trait that can be stimulated or quashed. Creativity seems generally to decrease as children get older, a tendency that may be accounted for by both age and culture. As well, creativity tends to occur in spurts. During the first three years of school, most children increase their creativity, perhaps because teachers in these grades allow much freedom of expression. After grade three, a sharp drop in creativity occurs, followed by a gradual decrease during the remaining elementary and middle school years (Bernard, 1973). To stimulate creative students, teachers should allow learning by exploring, testing the limits, searching, manipulating, and playing.

To stimulate creative students, teachers should allow learning by exploring, testing the limits, searching, manipulating, and playing.

Research has not yet shown the relationship of talent to giftedness. We can say that giftedness is a prerequisite for talent, but a gifted individual is not necessarily talented (Gagné, 1985). Some children have unusual talents in one field and limited abilities in other areas. The direction of an individual's talent depends on many factors, such as experience, motivation, interest, emotional stability, hero worship, parental urging, and even chance.

Talented children begin to nurture their special traits early. Children are usually encouraged by their parents and extensively tutored or coached by experts. There seem to be three phases in talent development. First there is playful exploration that entices the learner into further involvement. Then there is acquisition of skills and attention to detail, with rigorous practice. Finally, a commitment to excellence is made (Bloom, 1985).

Leadership can be defined as the ability to effect positive and productive changes that are self-enhancing or group-enhancing. Plowman (1981) described leadership in these terms: charismatic, intuitive, generative, analytical, evaluative, and synergistic.

Those with high leadership abilities demonstrate empathy and sensitivity, personality and proficiency, and possess charisma, the ability to actualize values to the extent that dynamic group change is effected (Lindsay, 1978). Children who display early leadership qualities will interact easily with a variety of people; be sought out by others; possess confidence; establish the mood of the group; be sensitive to the feelings of others; show others how to improve on a task; and generate many ideas and solutions (Karnes and Strong, 1978).

Prevalence of Giftedness

The lack of a universally accepted definition of giftedness makes it very difficult to estimate its prevalence in the population at large and in school-aged children. However, we can reasonably assume that only a small percentage of a school population will require special programming for the gifted. In this general sense, giftedness is said to occur in 2 to 5 percent of school-aged children.

Only Ontario specifically includes gifted students in its special education legislation. Of school-aged children, about 1.3 percent are educated in the gifted category. British Columbia, the only other province for which the Canadian Council for Exceptional Children (1989) reported, identified 1.9 percent of school-aged students as gifted.

Factors Contributing to Giftedness

Gifted and talented children are found at every economic level and in every stratum of society, throughout all ethnic, cultural, and racial groups. However, we do not yet understand what contributes most to giftedness, or why some gifted people achieve eminence and others fade into obscurity. As Jospeph Renzulli (1980) stated, "We simply don't know what factors cause only a minuscule number of Thomas Edisons and Langston Hugheses or Isadora Duncans to emerge, while millions with equal 'equipment' and educational advantages (or disadvantages) never rise above mediocrity."

The relative contribution of genetic and environmental factors with respect to giftedness is not clearly understood.

The effects of heredity and environment are both important in the development of gifted and talented children, but the relative contribution of genetic and environmental factors is not clearly understood. Genes carry potential for various characteristics from parent to child down through the generations, but the genes alone cannot produce a human being. Each of us is born in a unique environment in which conditions act and react with one another. The individual human being is the total expression of all these complex and constantly interacting forces.

Genetic Factors

The proposition that intelligence and abilities are inherited is not popular in our egalitarian society. Francis Galton and other early researchers maintained that most human traits were passed down through the generations on 'germ plasm.' When the dangers of a purely genetic view of development became obvious, the pendulum swung toward a strong emphasis on environmental conditions, especially after the 1930s.

Nevertheless, it is now abundantly clear from the field of behavioural genetics that there is a significant role played by genetic transmission in the development of intelligence (Gallagher, 1991). Most authorities in the area of behavioural genetics hold that genetic factors are at least as important as environmental factors in determining intelligence (e.g., Bouchard and McGue, 1981; Scarr-Salapatek, 1975). Among Caucasian children in North America and Europe, it is estimated that half to three-quarters of intelligence variation is due to genetic factors (Eysenck, 1979; Scarr-Salapatek, 1975). There is no doubt that some of us have more inborn capabilities in music or visual perception or linguistic ability than others (Plomin, 1989).

Environmental Factors

The complex study of genetics has not yet revealed how genes influence giftedness. Moreover, even the strongest hereditarians acknowledge the great influence of environment on the development of intelligence. Genetic capabilities must be nurtured in order to reach their full development. The unique development of gifted traits can only occur through specific interactions within family units and later with appropriate training and education.

The importance of nurturing has been clearly evidenced by many deprivational studies that have demonstrated the negative effects of malnutrition and lack of stimulation on infant functioning. The high proportion of first-borns among the gifted population also suggests the importance of environment to the full development of intellectual potential (Laycock, 1979). Unlike younger siblings, first-borns receive full attention and much stimulation from their parents, even if only for a short time.

No race, ethnic group, or culture holds a monopoly on giftedness. However, the statistical probability of giftedness increases when a child's parents have higher than average intelligence and provide a better than average home environment. Bright children are more likely to be born to bright parents, although some gifted children are born to slow learners. Gifted children are also more likely to have parents of above average income.

Other factors in the environment that seem most clearly to affect the development of giftedness are the values and expectations of the culture; the socio-economic level of the family, with accompanying nutritional and other health variables, attitudes, and values; the position of the child in birth order and the number of children in the family; and the presence of environmental stimulation (Eysenck, 1979; Laycock, 1979).

Numerous studies have attempted to identify the specific family characteristics associated with gifted-level abilities in children (e.g., Colangelo and Dettman, 1983; Cornell, 1983, 1984). Results have emphasized the many favourable qualities of these families, particularly the importance of parental interest in child-rearing and strong commitment to the development of the child's talents and abilities (Bloom, 1982, 1985). When Benjamin Bloom and his colleagues (Bloom, 1985; Bloom and Sosniak, 1981) examined the home environments and the early training of exceptional people in the arts, in athletics, and in cognitive skill areas, they found that the home environment and the person's parents were almost entirely responsible for nurturing the children's early interests and the development of their skills.

Highly educated parents are more likely to produce gifted children and to provide them with enriching environments. On the Stanford-Binet Individual Intelligence Test, the average score for children of college graduates is more than 10 points above the mean, whereas for children of parents with less than high school education it is about 6 points below the mean (Kaplan and Saccuzzo, 1993). In a Canadian study of gifted kindergarten children, Perks (1984) found that 59.5 percent of their fathers and 50 percent of their mothers had post-secondary education. This compared to 30.9 percent of fathers and 27 percent of mothers for non-gifted children. Perks compared the reading material available in the children's homes and found that 61.9 percent of the families of gifted children had more than 300 books, as compared to 18.4 percent of families of non-gifted children. Certainly, bright children come from lower socio-economic homes, but not as often as we would expect. Intervening factors may include lack of motivation, family expectations, neighbourhood aspirations, and financial pressures.

Identification and Assessment of Giftedness

Much of the success of programs for students who are gifted is contingent upon sound identification procedures. At first glance, the identification of gifted and talented children and youth may seem to be a relatively simple task. Nothing could be further from the truth. From the outset, one of the major concerns in gifted education has been the problem of identification and its measurement correlates. Even today there is much confusion, and the issue of identification and assessment remains highly problematic for our population of gifted, creative, and talented students. The heterogeneity of the population, the plethora of available definitions, and the administrative problems make identification particularly difficult and uncertain. Problems can and do occur at various points in the process. This led Borland (1989) to suggest that the process of selecting students and placing them in appropriate programs is the most difficult, controversial, and thankless of all the tasks in developing and implementing programs for the gifted.

Part of the difficulty lies in the wide range of areas to be assessed. Outstanding ability comes in a number of different forms and requires a variety of ongoing identification procedures as well as a variety of special educational programs. There exists no single adequate identification procedure or combination of procedures that addresses all important areas and therefore effectively taps a high proportion of gifted students.

Another problem with all forms of identification systems is that they are less than perfect. The younger the child, the less confidence can be placed in the reliability and validity of the measures. So when the term *gifted* is used to describe young children, it essentially applies to potential rather than accomplishment and is making guesses about the future with limited information (Colangelo and Fleuridas, 1986).

In addition, the selection of students for gifted programs should be a recurring activity, not a one-shot affair. Both IQ and interests can change and specific abilities can emerge. The correlation of the IQ of a child at age six or seven with the same person's IQ at age seventeen is approximately +0.7 (Bloom, 1964).

The process of identifying gifted and talented learners is becoming more diversified, especially in terms of the instruments used. In the past, giftedness was viewed as a univariate construct, basically consisting of those traits that were measured by IQ tests. Children with high IQ scores formed the bulk of the population identified as gifted. Conceptions of giftedness as IQ were established by Lewis Terman who conducted an important longitudinal study into giftedness.

Research Notes

The Terman studies

Lewis Terman, an American educator and psychologist, expanded the concepts and procedures related to IQ developed by Alfred Binet in France at the beginning of this century. Terman believed the Binet scale assessed a wide range of performance and could be adapted for use with high-functioning children. In 1916, he published the Stanford-Binet Individual Intelligence Test in conjunction with Stanford University.

Terman held that intelligence was manifested essentially in the ability to acquire and manipulate concepts. He defined the gifted as those who scored in the top one percent of general intellectual ability as measured by the Stanford-Binet Scale or a comparable instrument (Terman, 1926). Terman carefully distinguished giftedness from talent and creativity. He viewed talent as the potential for unusual achievement, but only when combined with high IQ scores. Creativity, he believed, was a personality factor, and thus differed from both giftedness and talent (Wolf and Stephens, 1982).

In 1922, armed with the Stanford-Binet tests and a single measure concept of intelligence, Terman embarked on a massive study of giftedness among California school children. This study, which included 1528 children, "was designed to discover what physical, mental, and personality traits are characteristic of gifted children as a class, and what sort of adult the typical gifted child becomes" (Terman and Oden, 1951, p. 21).

To determine his population, Terman relied on teacher nominations and group intelligence tests. He then identified his gifted children from those scoring at or above 140 points on the Stanford-Binet Individual Intelligence Test.

Although Terman died in 1956, the study continues today. The remaining "Terman kids" are now in their early eighties. The longitudinal research found the following:

- Most students in the sample came from a middle or higher socio-economic group, with a low incidence of broken homes.
- Nearly half of the children could read before entering kindergarten.
- One in five children skipped part or all of the first grade.
- On average, the children finished school 14 percent faster than normal students.
- The children averaged 40 percent higher than their age mates on achievement tests.
- They preferred abstract subjects, such as literary debate and ancient history, and were less interested in such practical concerns as penmanship and manual training.

- They read more and better books, made numerous collections, and had many hobbies.
- When retested as adults, they were found to have retained their intellectual superiority.
- As adults, they were ahead in terms of occupational status, incomes, publications, and patents. They earned more money, had more managerial jobs, and made more literary and scientific contributions than the average adult (Terman and Oden, 1959). When checked in 1959, Terman's group had published over 2000 scientific papers and 33 novels and taken out 230 patents (Sprinthall and Sprinthall, 1990).
- Middle-aged people in Terman's sample maintained their superior physical characteristics (Terman and Oden, 1959). They were far above their age mates in general health, physique, mental health, and emotional adjustment. Fewer than 5 percent of Terman's population were rated as seriously maladjusted, and the incidence of problems such as ill health, psychiatric disturbance, alcoholism, and delinquent behaviour was but a fraction of that normally observed in the general population.
- Although reaching college age just before the Great Depression, when college attendance was not common for women, over 67 percent of the Terman women earned at least a bachelor's degree.
- The female sample contained more childless women than normative samples of similar ages and as a group had relatively higher incomes and levels of employment than women of comparable ages (Holahan, 1991).

Terman's study represented the first full-scale longitudinal study of the nature of giftedness; it legitimized the field, and the serious inception of a gifted movement can therefore be said to have begun with Terman. On the other hand, Terman's work established for three decades the superiority of IQ tests as the sole measure of giftedness. Nonetheless, many of Terman's findings remain remarkably relevant; so far, his study is unsurpassed in the field of giftedness.

Psychologists are no longer satisfied with intelligence defined simply as what IQ tests measure. Today's researchers are finding evidence of multiple intelligences rather than a single general intelligence. Psychologist J.P. Guilford of the University of Southern California was one of the first to contribute to multidimensional theories regarding intelligence. Guilford's Structure of Intellect analyzes intelligence in terms of its specific skills and divides intellectual performance into three dimensions: operations, contents, and products. Each of these dimensions encompasses several abilities. The first, operations, stresses the methods people use to process information. Guilford's second dimension, contents, has to do with how a learner classifies processed information. The third, products, refers to the forms and structures that people use to organize information.

Within the psychological field, Guilford's distinctive approach prompted researchers to reconsider intelligence as a diverse range of intellectual and creative abilities. Within gifted education, Guilford inspired interest in the characteristics of creative thought processes and creativity tests. However, Guilford's is not the only theory of multiple intelligence. Howard Gardner (1983) sees capabilities as falling into seven areas — linguistic, logical-mathematical, spatial, bodily, kinesthetic, musical, and interpersonal-intrapersonal.

Given these expanded conceptions of giftedness, those involved today in the identification and assessment of gifted children are strongly persuaded to look not only for children with high IQs but also for those who are gifted in other dimensions as well.

Assessment Measures

In the field of gifted education, "the ideal identification system has not been developed" (Feldhusen, Hoover, and Sayler, 1990). When educators define giftedness in terms of potential, they use identification procedures that emphasize IQ tests and other predictive measures such as academic achievement, creative products, and critical thinking. When giftedness is seen as current achievements, identification procedures stress observations and nominations, performance in academic subjects, performance assessment, or a review of a portfolio. Diagnosticians may incorporate information from many sources: nominations (teacher, parent, peer, self); previously demonstrated achievement; school grades; family histories and interviews; case studies; tests of creativity; and observations of physical, personality, and social traits. Whichever focus is taken, a co-ordinated effort is made to pool the information derived from these sources in order to determine the most appropriate placement and program for a particular child. The process is shown in Figure 5-3.

Figure 5-3 *Identification of gifted students*

	Screening			Formal	
Intelligence	**Nominations**	**Creativity**	**Other**	**Intelligence**	**Achievement**
Group IQ tests	teacher parent peer self Gifted Screening Form rating scales	tests of creativity and divergent thinking e.g. Torrance Tests, Creativity Assessment Package	school grades case history interviews observations performance tests portfolios exhibitions auditions	IQ tests e.g. Structure of Intellect–Learning Abilities, WISC-III, Stanford-Binet	Achievement tests e.g. Canadian Test of Basic Skills

There is little to indicate that any one identification procedure is better than another. For example, researchers (Shore and Tsiamis, 1986) compared two groups of children either on the basis of traditional measures of achievement or on that of parent and teacher identification. They found that the groups were not distinguishable and concluded that formal selection by testing was not necessary for a substantial number of gifted students.

Observation

Screening involves a broad range of procedures that may use different instruments and procedures. Especially for young children, observation is one of the most potent ways to identify those who are potentially gifted. A three-year-old may be observed to tackle mathematical problems that are taught in grade three. A four-year-old may be able to read and draw maps as well as most adults (Robinson, Roedell, and Jackson, 1979).

High verbal ability is a good indicator of IQ; children may show early and extensive vocabulary development. An eighteen-month-old child may use language like most children at thirty months. Older children ask many questions and have good memories. Many children with advanced vocabularies have an intense interest in books. They learn to read relatively early and easily and carry out the task fluently. One-half to three-quarters of verbally talented children are reading by the age of five (Piirto, 1994). (Parenthetically, very advanced reading in the early grades does not guarantee that students will still be outstanding years later [Mills and Jackson, 1990].)

Parents and teachers should not expect very young children to be gifted in everything. Especially in preschool children who are potentially gifted, we see dyssynchrony, that is, uneven development. This applies particularly to motor skills. Some children learn their letters from some combination of teaching by parents, older siblings, and preschool teachers and try to write early. But even if children know the letters, they probably do not possess the fine motor skills to form them well.

Group Tests

Because giftedness has traditionally been defined on the basis of intelligence, identification procedures have typically involved some measures of intellectual ability. Some schools begin by screening students with standardized group intelligence tests. However, all currently available group intelligence tests have a high prevalence of underidentification and overidentification of exceptional children, particularly with reference to creative divergent thinkers and very young children (Roedell, Jackson, and Robinson, 1980). It is not unusual for scores on group intelligence tests and individual IQ tests to vary as much as thirty points (Martinson, 1975). In addition, group intelligence tests may identify proficient tests takers at the expense of those who may score somewhat lower, but who are highly creative and original thinkers (Renzulli, 1979). Group intelligence tests also appear to penalize children from lower socio-economic and minority groups.

Teacher Nominations

Teacher nomination has traditionally been, and remains today, a major method for identifying gifted, talented, and creative youngsters. It is an inexpensive screening method founded on the premise that teachers know their students well enough to spot gifted and talented children.

But even as teacher nominations are appreciated for their apparent relevance to children's educational experiences and functioning, they are criticized for their ineffectiveness in accurately identifying gifted children. "In many instances, teacher nominations are suspect and invalid" (Davis and Rimm, 1994) and may result in the correct identification of as few as one in five gifted children (Martinson, 1975). Teachers, who are fairly efficient in identifying students requiring special help, are relatively poor in identifying gifted, talented, and creative youngsters (Perks, 1984), and teacher nomination proves no better than conventional group screening. One study (Renzulli, 1979) found that teachers who were in close contact with gifted students were only 50 percent successful when requested to identify those students whom they considered to be gifted and talented. Others (Haywood Gear, 1976; Perks, 1984) discovered effectiveness rates of between 10 and 57 percent with effectiveness measured as the number of pupils correctly identified as gifted.

Why are teachers, who know their children well, so poor in identification procedures? Teachers may look for the wrong things. Some tend to choose one sex over the other; others tend to choose conformist high achievers and overlook creative or divergent thinkers (Martinson, 1975). Teachers fail to recognize gifted and talented children most frequently at the primary level, where early identification is of the utmost importance (Khoury and Appel, 1979).

Teacher accuracy in the identification of gifted and talented children can be improved up to 40 percent if they are asked to identify children on the basis of clearly defined characteristics (Haywood Gear, 1976; Perks, 1984). Training programs, questionnaires, and rating scales can all increase effectiveness. Rating scales are particularly helpful in objectifying teacher judgment. Measures such as the Scale for Rating Behavioral Characteristics of Superior Students (Renzulli, Hartman, and Callahan, 1975) are designed to obtain teachers' estimates of student traits in specific areas. The teacher is asked to rate each pupil on a series of four-point scales related to areas of learning, motivation, creativity, leadership, communication, and the arts.

Parent Nomination

Parent nomination questionnaires are another economical means of identifying gifted and talented children. Parents see their children make up games and stories, invent and build things, solve problems, and create all sorts of products. From these observations, parents may identify high performance. One study found that parents' implicit beliefs about their child's ability levels closely related to children's actual tested IQ. Parents were especially accurate in their assessment of creative thinking, abstract thinking, and memory abilities (Louis and Lewis, 1992). In another survey in the United States of 1039 parents of gifted children, 70 percent of the children were identified accurately by age three. Of all the characteristics that caused parents to suspect giftedness, "early verbal expression" was mentioned most frequently (Gogel, McCumsey, and Hewitt, 1985).

Studies have shown that parent accuracy varies from 11 to 76 percent (Khoury and Appel, 1979), which still tends to be better than teacher nomination. Nonetheless, problems do exist. Parents from lower socio-economic neighbourhoods are more likely to report their child as gifted than parents from higher socio-economic locales, partly because well-educated parents tend to set higher intellectual standards for their children (Roedell, Jackson, and Robinson, 1980). Other parents may be unaware of their child's outstanding abilities, especially if they have little chance to compare his or her accomplishments with those of other children of a similar age (Vernon, Adamson, and Vernon, 1977).

Peer Nominations

Peer nomination forms have been judged very favourably by experts in the field and are growing in popularity as a screening technique for giftedness (Gagné, 1989). One survey (Cox, Daniel, and Boston, 1985) found that 25 percent of school boards surveyed in the United States used peer nominations.

Davis and Rimm (1985) wrote that "peers are extraordinarily good at nominating gifted and talented students" (p. 78) while others (Richert, Alvino, and McDonnell, 1972), have judged peer nominations to be the most adequate technique for screening leaders and creative individuals. Peer nomination may be especially helpful in identifying minority children, as well as disadvantaged, handicapped, and rural gifted students (Banbury and Wellington, 1989).

Self-Nominations

Self-nomination forms have been used with students who have strong artistic, creative, scientific, or other interests and talents. Davis and Rimm (1994) especially recommend self-nominations at the junior and senior high school levels where peer pressure may cause youths to mask special talents.

Tests of Mental Ability

Following screening, promising students are administered individual intelligence tests. In the identification of potentially gifted students, the Stanford-Binet Individual Intelligence Test and the Wechsler Intelligence Scale for Children (3rd. ed.) (WISC-111) are the two most commonly used measures.

In many ways, individual IQ tests appear to be the best single method for identification of children with superior cognitive abilities. They possess high validity as predictors of success in academic settings and their scores are relatively stable over time. Assuming that motivation remains constant, these tests can reveal not only a child's present abilities, but those that will develop in the future. IQ tests can also identify those gifted children who are underachieving.

Even with these finer points, the tests are not a panacea and a number of problems exist. In the identification of gifted students, IQ measures may reflect a racial or a socio-economic bias and reinforce existing inequalities in selection of these children for special programs. As well, giftedness seems to be characterized by qualitative differences in thinking and insightfulness, which may not be clearly reflected by performance or intelligence tests (Reis, 1989). The tests may fail to measure some traits, behaviours, and potentials that are significant indicators of giftedness and thereby fail to identify some of our most promising and potentially capable students.

Achievement Tests

Achievement tests can be employed systematically to identify gifted and talented children who are already achieving at a high level academically. These tests have been used very successfully to identify school children performing extremely well in specific fields, such as mathematics (Stanley, 1979). However, tests of educational achievement do not detect the gifted child who is not achieving above the average. As a result, the use of achievement tests in the identification of gifted children remains a contentious issue.

Measuring Creativity

Gifted children may be identified by their high levels of achievement, creativity, and motivation. Achievement is fairly easy to measure; creativity is not. Even as attempts to define creativity beyond the traditional IQ parameters helped broaden notions of giftedness, they generated a new set of problems — how to assess and define creativity.

Perhaps the greatest fallacy in gifted education is the notion that there should be an instrument that will yield a single score or index of children's creativity or creative giftedness so that they can be more effectively included in or excluded from gifted programs (Treffinger, 1986). This is a fallacy because there is still no unifying theory of creativity which is embraced by all researchers and practitioners. Given the complexity of the construct of creativity and the variety of its manifestations in daily life, it seems unlikely that a general theory will ever emerge.

Despite these difficulties, more than 60 instruments for measuring or assessing creativity exist (Treffinger, 1986). Many measures of creativity are based on Guilford's work. For example, Torrance used Guilford's assumption that the most important factors in creativity are fluency, flexibility, and originality in his Torrance Tests of Creative Thinking (Torrance, 1966) Designed to measure divergent thinking, not creativity per se, the Torrance has two subtests — "Thinking creatively with words" and "Thinking creatively with pictures."

The Group Inventory for Finding Creative Talent (GIFT) and its update (Rimm and Davis, 1976) contain a five-level inventory with items to measure perseverance, interests, biography, independence, and curiosity. For example, on the perseverance measure, a child responds to the statement, "Easy puzzles are the most fun." Those who agree are considered to be less creative than those who disagree (Rimm and Davis, 1976).

The Creativity Assessment Package (CAP)(Williams, 1980) consists of two group tests for children: a Test of Divergent Thinking and a Test of Divergent Feeling. A third instrument, the Williams Scale, is a rating measure for parents and teachers. All three instruments can be used to screen, identify, and evaluate the most important factors of creativity among all children.

For many years, J.P. Guilford has been involved in developing a battery of tests based on the 120 factors of the Structure of Intellect. While the test, the Structure of Intellect–Learning Abilities (SOI-LA), is classified as an intelligence test, there is a Gifted Screening Form (GSF) which consists of ten areas that Guilford determined to be most related to the characteristics of gifted individuals (Meeker, 1979). The SOI Gifted Screening Form is used in many districts as an instrument for screening students for special programs and as an approach to individualizing curriculum for the gifted (O'Tuel, 1983).

Portfolios

Portfolios, a type of performance test made up of continuous collections of a student's work, are emerging as a promising measure in the assessment of gifted learners. A portfolio (sometimes called a process folio) is a folder of representative work that meets certain criteria or purposes. Portfolios are joint projects between the teacher and a student. They include information selected by the student under the guidance of the teacher as well as a series of statements that reflect a student's thoughts about the contents (Wolf, Bixby, and Gardiner, 1991). The portfolio will include work samples and projects, and may include the results of tests. As the portfolio is a continuous collection of a student's work, developmental growth is evidenced through the work presented (reports, artwork, poetry, and video, for example). In using portfolios, students are expected to participate fully in assessment and are provided with access to the results of such evaluation (Nixon, 1990).

Leadership

Leadership does not describe inborn characteristics, but cumulative capabilities that result from an intermix of the child's innate abilities and experience. To assess leadership, observation of performance together with some rating checklist is most appropriate.

Visual and Performing Arts

In this field, talent is still most often assessed by expert judges in an audition setting. Experts in the arts are not enthusiastic about the use of tests to determine artistic ability and prefer exhibitions, performances, auditions, and interviews. Nevertheless, a range of measures are available to assess potential and aptitude, especially in the areas of music and visual art (Khatena, 1982).

Special Problems in Identification

The identification and assessment of gifted children and youth is beset by difficulties. Whatever method, or combination of methods, is employed, some special populations of children are often overlooked and these gifted children pass through school unidentified, their talents uncultivated.

Conventional methods of identification have been criticized as inappropriate for atypical gifted children, a population that includes children who are disabled, those from minority backgrounds, children who are culturally different from the majority population, and children with learning disabilities (Minner, 1990). This led Paul Torrance (1980) to observe that the scenario for giftedness has, in general, "been too passive, too white, and too middle class" (p. 43). Also overlooked are gifted underachievers and gifted females.

Gifted Underachievers

Intellectually gifted students, in contrast to those gifted in athletics, arts, or leadership, may be at risk for learning difficulties in school (Whitmore, 1988). Many gifted and talented children do not develop to their full potential. Sadly, about 50 percent of gifted children become non-active learners by age ten (Nolte, 1976). At the secondary level, about 30 percent of the top 10 percent in intellectual capacity drop out of school, a rate that is about three times higher than the average (Banks, 1979; Gowan, 1968).

Teachers can provide for individual differences and stimulate an interest in learning if they understand the techniques that enhance motivation and provide for personal development.

Academic underachievers are those about whom we can make a reasonable prediction of academic potential that is not fulfilled. These are children who are gifted on IQ tests but whose academic achievement is grade level or less on standardized tests (Yewchuk, 1984). For underachieving gifted students, this does not necessarily equate with failure or underproduction. Children may indeed perform at an average level which is, however, not commensurate with their ability. Others, of course, do not even attain average levels.

A complex of factors contribute to the high proportion of underachievers among the gifted population. Joanne Whitmore (1988) points out that pervasive misunderstandings of the nature of giftedness have created conditions in homes, schools, and communities that exacerbate the natural vulnerability of gifted children to underachievement. Those misunderstandings result in inappropriate expectations for gifted students and consequent adult responses that place students even more at risk. For example, when parents and teachers believe that learning and school achievement are easy for all gifted students, they tend to demand more effort and tolerate little error or imperfection. Or when adults believe that gifted children are more mature than their peers developmentally, they tend to expect more mature behaviour than is reasonable and forget the childishness that is necessarily present in gifted children.

Impossible expectations may bring on underachievement; so may the conflict between giftedness and creativity and the typically rigid classroom. Gifted children are turned off by conformity to precise directions, excessive repetition, memorization and drill, uniformity of assignments, and the lack of opportunity to pursue interests and work independently. In a classroom that requires a high degree of conformity and achievement on schedule with a restricted and often dull curriculum, these children may feel stifled and frustrated, and in not conforming to classroom mores, they may gradually sink into underachievement. They may feel that there is nothing to learn that is interesting and challenging.

In some cases, underachievement may begin with learning not to learn. In the early years, the student may need to make little, if any, effort to make good grades. Consequently, when academic demands become greater, the student does not know how to apply effort. Underachievers may lack confidence, have poor study habits, do inconsistent work, and may not have learned to make the effort to perform well.

Social and emotional factors can also enter into play. Some students may underachieve because it is socially safe. Students may feel that peer relationships are jeopardized by expectations of superior performance and may not want to be singled out as different. Other students may have unfavourable self-concepts that distort their perceptions of the world and undermine their motivation and goal orientation.

One father described his underachieving son as "an emperor and a Renaissance man at age four, dethroned by age six, and a behavior problem and underachiever thereafter," (in Rimm and Lowe, 1988, p. 358). We can see the same pattern in William, a student with high potential who became an underachiever by early adolescence.

Profile

William

William was identified during fourth grade as a gifted child. On the WISC-R he scored 162 on the Verbal Scale and 108 on the Performance Scale for a Full Scale of 134. Achievement testing showed his reading to be at grade level, although his math was only at grade four. During the testing sessions, William was resentful and manipulative, and stated that he "did not appreciate having his brain examined." He eventually complied with the examiner's requests and finally confided that "When I was five I was an optimist; at seven a pessimist. Now I'm a cynicist."

Although William revealed outstanding abilities in verbal tasks and abstract thinking, he showed a severe deficit in visual-motor dexterity functioning. He had an aversion to written classroom assignments, which had begun to significantly lower his achievement. William also had a tendency toward acting-out behaviours and poor peer relations, chiefly attributable to his bossy and directive attitude. This was compounded by his inability or unwillingness to comply with expected school behaviour in matters of dress and personal hygiene.

William was accelerated and skipped grade six. At the same time, he was given special help to compensate for his visual-motor deficits. However, William increasingly failed to achieve at levels commensurate with his potential. By grade nine, he was functioning in a slow-moving junior high school stream. When William was sixteen, he dropped out of school. Currently, he is unemployed with few prospects for work in the future.

Gifted Females

Both in school and in the working world, more males than females are considered gifted and talented. By an overwhelming margin, men achieve high status and recognition more frequently than women of the same age. There is no conclusive evidence that this disparity is the result of biological differences; rather, available research points far more clearly to social and cultural expectations as an explanation for the disproportionate number of males recognized as gifted.

Society encourages narrow role definitions and behaviour options for women and broader ones for men. It is considered neither proper nor advantageous for girls to be too superior. Girls who insist on their giftedness are encouraged to become musicians or artists, rather than physicists or engineers. Females have not been encouraged to enter those academic disciplines and careers historically dominated by males. Certainly, more women are entering such non-traditional professions as chemistry, engineering, dentistry, and physics, but the numbers are still very small.

Gifted females should be encouraged to participate in traditionally male-dominated activities.

Fewer than one-quarter of senior male and female high school students take math and science (International Association, 1988), and talented girls are even less likely than talented boys to pursue a career in the sciences. In fact, young women's interest in the sciences has actually declined in the past two decades, despite the women's movement and a range of efforts to encourage young women to pursue careers in these fields (Astin, Green, and Korn, 1989). Women tend not to pursue math to the same extent as mathematically gifted males. Kerr (1988) contends that gifted girls are rewarded for intellectual achievement at early ages but by adolescence they are rewarded for social conformity which may include seeing math as masculine.

Even in careers traditionally assigned to women, men tend to achieve high status and recognition more frequently than women of the same age by an overwhelming margin. For example, men are disproportionately represented in positions of power and influence in education. The 1970 Royal Commission on the Status of Women in Alberta found that "a man was 7.5 times more likely to become a principal, although he was only 2.5 times as likely to have higher qualifications than a woman" (Nixon, 1989). Twenty-five years later, educational leaders are still male.

The reasons put forward to account for the smaller proportion of girls identified as gifted are legion. Barriers may come from the protection of a feminine self-image (Meece et al., 1982), non-assertiveness (Hollinger and Fleming, 1984), fear of success (Lavach and Lanier, 1975), conflicts arising from achievement versus self-concept (Fox, 1977), or fear of loss of social acceptance (Casserly, 1979). Gifted girls find it difficult to reconcile their academic interests with the areas of excellence traditionally seen by society as sex-role appropriate for women (Schwartz, 1980). As high achievers, gifted girls are expected to be active, assertive, and exploratory; as females, they are encouraged to be nurturant, passive, and dependent (Handel, 1983).

Gifted and talented girls need early entry into stimulating and challenging programs and models that contradict sex-role stereotypes.

It is during early adolescence, the age when sex roles are heavily reinforced by parents and peers, that girls generally begin to encounter problems that obscure their giftedness (Dishart, 1981). Often parents of gifted girls are more concerned about their daughters' social adjustment than their academic boredom. Teachers tend to reinforce quiet, non-aggressive and uncompetitive behaviour among girls.

Gifted Students Who Are Disabled

A gifted disabled child may be described as one who demonstrates at least one attribute of educational, emotional, or physical/sensory impairment. When measured by objective testing procedures, such individuals may deviate substantially both above and below the norm (Meisgeier, Meisgeier, and Werble, 1978). In other words, a gifted disabled person has both strengths and weaknesses that are very pronounced (Maker, 1977).

The prevalence of giftedness is the same in the disabled population as in the total population (Maker, 1977). However, gifted children who also suffer disabilities are in the overlap between categories; they form a minority within a minority. A number of factors may militate against their receiving appropriate programs designed to stimulate their creative and gifted behaviour.

For one thing, gifted children who are also disabled exhibit many contradictions; they fail to meet our stereotyped expectations of the gifted. They may exhibit developmental delays, or they may lack the opportunity to reveal superior mental or creative ability (Whitmore, 1981). Many teachers, administrators, students, and parents have trouble accepting that a child with a disability may also have outstanding abilities: they focus entirely on the child's disability to the exclusion of his or her individual potential and capabilities.

Gifted children with disabilities frequently exhibit secondary emotional problems. They may have very low self-concepts that spring from their inability to understand fully the inconsistencies between the level of comprehension and data processing of which they are aware within themselves and the less than acceptable performance that they may give. It is highly likely that the gifted child tends to be more adept at perceiving the unconscious cues as well as the conscious responses of teachers and others to his or her poor performance in problem areas (Meisgeier, Meisgeier, and Werble, 1978).

The abilities of non-handicapped gifted children are usually readily observable by their classroom teachers, parents, and peers. However, the abilities of gifted children who are blind, hearing impaired, or cerebral palsied may not be so easily apparent. No one instrument or checklist is capable of identifying the range of characteristics and conditions that may be present in a gifted child with a disability. Observations of the child's behaviour must be made over time rather than in isolation (Pledgie, 1982). This is true for all children, but even more so when identifying those who are both gifted and disabled.

Children who are handicapped in one way may be exceptionally gifted in another area.

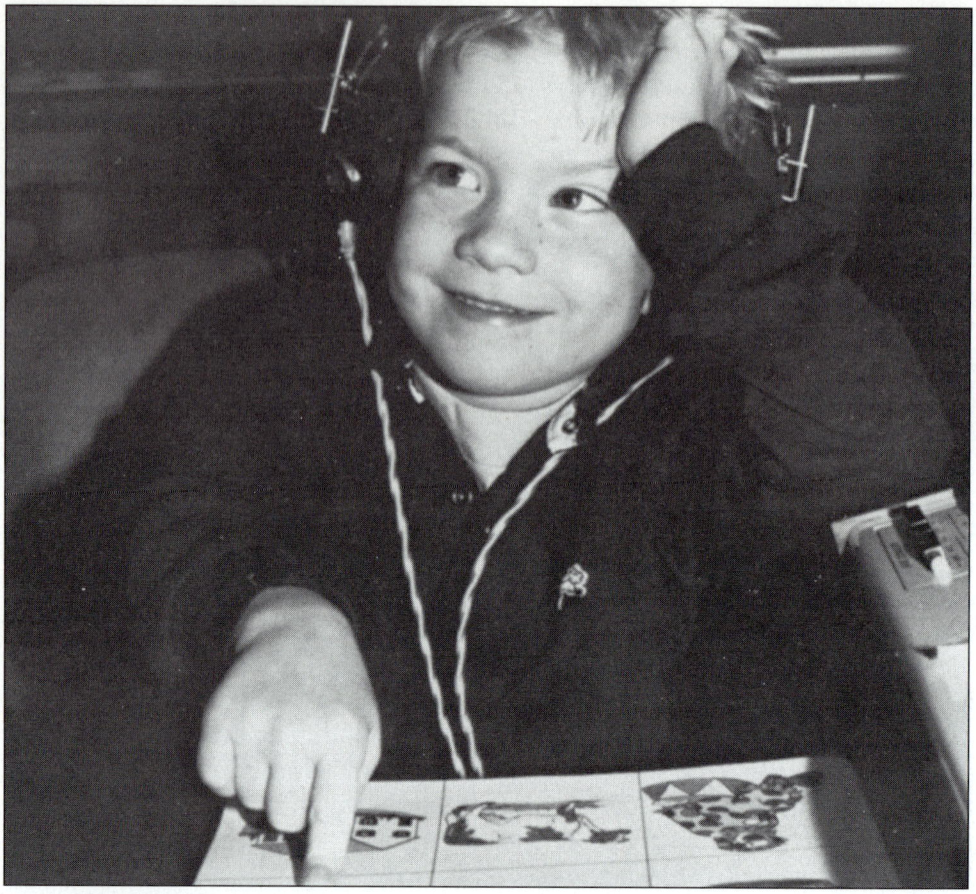

Gifted Students with Learning Disabilities

Children who are both gifted and learning disabled are often not identified (Gyndereson, Maesch, and Rees, 1987). These students exhibit talents and strengths in some areas and disabling weaknesses in others (Baum, 1995).

For gifted students with disabilities, teachers should provide a nurturing environment that values individual differences and encourage strategies that help to compensate for the disability.

Sometimes, when the two exceptionalities exist, they tend to mask one another so that neither the giftedness nor the disability is immediately evident (Silverman, 1989). In other words, the disability may depress the IQ and achievement scores so that these students are not eligible for gifted programs, yet their giftedness allows them to compensate well enough for their weaknesses to maintain grade level expectations, which prevents detection of their learning difficulty (Silverman, 1989). The result is that they frequently do not qualify for special education services. This is clearly illustrated in the case of Richard, profiled below. An extract from Richards' IEP as related to the gifted component appears later in this chapter.

As we observed earlier, gifted children with disabilities may display many contradictions in their performances. Gifted students with learning disabilities, for example, often have excellent reasoning ability but difficulties in memorizing, paying attention, or following several directions at once. Solving math story problems is often easier for them than remembering multiplication facts. They can frequently talk astutely about complex ideas but may write slowly and illegibly. While they are often creative, they have difficulty managing time and are slow in processing information (Cordell and Cannon, 1985).

Profile

Richard

The school that Richard attends has a small pull-out program for children identified as gifted beginning at the grade three level. The teacher of this program is very popular with all the students, and because she insists on always presenting the products of the gifted class, the whole school is aware of her program and many children are eager to enter it.

Eight-year-old Richard, however, seemed an unlikely candidate. He was identified in grade two as suffering from a learning disability that affected his ability in reading and written language. He attends the resource room daily for additional assistance in these areas. When the teacher of the gifted students asked classroom teachers to nominate children for her program, Richard was not mentioned. However, the teacher used a group of rating scales — parent, teacher, peer, and self-nomination.

While the teacher's nomination scale gave no indications of gifted potential in Richard, the teacher was puzzled by the peaks and valleys in performance indicated by the parents. They agreed, for example, that Richard suffered serious lags in reading but judged him highly in his oral language abilities, his commitment to projects once started, and his interest in a range of hobbies and collections. Richard did not rate himself highly, but his peers did. In the peer nominations, they agreed overwhelmingly that Richard was the child who could think up unusual and interesting stories and games.

With such contradictory evidence, the teacher of the gifted decided to have the school psychologist present Richard with a WISC-R. On this, he was above average on both the Verbal and the Performance scales for a Full Scale score of 141. To Richard's delight, he was admitted to the gifted program while still attending the resource room daily.

Today, all three teachers speak well of his progress. The resource room teacher reports that Richard is really applying himself to improving his reading and written language skills, and the classroom teacher is pleased that incipient behavioural problems have muted. Richard now wears his glasses without prompting, for example. In the gifted program, Richard achieved on a level with the other students.

The Culturally Different Gifted Child

Many non-white, non-middle-class children and children from language minority groups are not identified and taught as gifted learners. When children are stereotyped by ethnicity, language differences, or social status, we are likely to overlook giftedness and tend to overrate or underrate them on any characteristic because they do not conform to our expectations.

Children who have limited English proficiency, if they are identified as gifted at all, are typically identified after they have mastered English and can receive instruction in an all-English classroom. An obvious point is that a child does not have to be fluent in English to be intelligent. There is no inherent need to delay the education of gifted children who are not fully proficient in English if bilingually competent teachers of the gifted are available (Barkan and Bernal, 1991).

Children from other cultures are shaped by value systems that may be at odds with that of the dominant society. Certain traits that define giftedness in the dominant culture may not even be allowed to appear because culturally different children show different interests and attitudes. For example, white, middle-class gifted children tend to display a high level of verbal ability. In contrast, Native children raised on reservations are normally very quiet, in accordance with the norms of their band. As a result, verbal ability would not be an indicator for Native gifted children (Haugen, 1981). What is clever and creative for the child on the reservation, where different value systems are in operation, will not be the same as for the child growing up in the suburbs.

Culturally different children should not be expected to demonstrate the same strengths as white, middle-class children. To assess giftedness in culturally different children, the examiner should look for certain traits. The gifted child should be able to meaningfully manipulate a symbol system held valuable in the culture; think logically when given appropriate data; use stored knowledge to solve problems; reason by analogy; and extend or extrapolate knowledge to new situations or unique applications (Clark, 1988).

Developmental Consequences of Giftedness

Like every population, the gifted are a heterogeneous group. Individual differences run the gamut of possibilities; among the gifted will be found the active, the lethargic, the healthy, the infirm, high achievers, low achievers, the painstakingly patient, and the lightning quick. The one thing that gifted students have in common "is the ability to absorb abstract concepts, to organize them more effectively, and to apply them more appropriately than the average youngster" (Gallagher, 1975, p, 19).

Table 5-1 outlines some of the common characteristics of gifted, talented, and creative students. View this list with caution; probably no child displays all these traits. Rather, each child possesses a unique subset of descriptors, which come from, but do not include, all the behaviours of the larger set. As well, attach no credence to the notion that these are *wunderkind*, adept in all areas of functioning. Like everyone else, gifted children have their warts, and teachers must accommodate problems as well as potentials. Also be aware of the great variance in the gifted population that renders many other characteristics possible. The true extent of that variance is not even known because of our inability to identify all gifted children.

Physical Development

Throughout history, there has been a persistent stereotype of the gifted individual as an "egghead." The gifted person was viewed as physically weak, homely, socially inept, narrow in interests, and prone to emotional instability. Such stereotypes were shattered by Lewis Terman who found that as a group, gifted individuals exhibit superior physical traits. The children in Terman's study were larger at birth, walked sooner, went through puberty earlier, had fewer diseases and operations, and reported less nervousness than average persons (Terman and Oden, 1959). However, although gifted children tend to physically outstrip their age mates later on, their superiority is seldom detectable at birth or even during the first year.

Academic Development

Three general characteristics seem typical of the learning behaviour of gifted students — an internal locus of control, independence, and self-motivation. In fact, one of the most ubiquitous traits of productive gifted students and eminent adults is high motivation and persistence.

Table 5-1

Some common characteristics of gifted, creative, and talented children

Traits common in gifted children
• Wide range of ability
• High academic achievement
• Insatiable curiosity
• Good observational skills, with a willingness to observe both the usual and the unusual
• Verbal fluency and a large vocabulary; may talk a lot and have many ideas; often use metaphors and abstract ideas and enjoy debating issues
• Ask a lot of questions; inquisitive about the world and want to know the why and how as well as the what
• Committed to finding out what happens if something is done, as in a science experiment
• High motivation with persistent goal-directed behaviour and high task commitment; stick to a topic to completion
• Long attention span; become absorbed in self-selected tasks
• High energy level, with an intense concentration of activity
• Organizational and planning skills
• Innovative, creative, divergent responses
• Ability to synthesize large amounts of diverse information; ability to think and perform in an interdisciplinary manner
• Superior reading ability
• Ability to grasp and retain knowledge
• Ability to convey ideas effectively
• Ability to work independently, with little or no need for adult monitoring
• Ability to assume and discharge responsibility; possess decision-making capabilities and leadership qualities
• Avid collectors and hobbyists; join many clubs
• Easy adjustment to new situations
• Mature sense of humour
• Appreciation of social values; show advanced ethical thinking; often prize integrity, independent judgment and social values and ideals; are interested in political and social issues
• Tend to be task- and contribution-oriented more than recognition-oriented
• Superior in height, weight, health, energy, and vitality
• Establishment of favourable relationships

Continued on next page

Traits common in creative children

- Tendency to ask many questions, which may be embarrassing, advanced, or controversial, often challenging the teacher and the textbook
- Production of work that is off the beaten track, with much humour and playfulness
- Boredom with recitation and memorization of facts; preference for talking about ideas and problems
- Good problem-solving ability with new and unusual ways of solving problems; show a variety of approaches to problem solving; are resourceful and can solve problems through ingenious methods
- Keen sense of humour and a fine sense of the absurd; reputation among teachers and students for wild and silly ideas
- Skill in abstract thinking
- Use a wide variety of resources
- Considerable energy
- Unexpected answers on examinations
- Pleasure in working alone
- Apparent lack of hard work, coupled with good performance in examinations
- Unusual capacity for originality, concentration, and hard work on special projects
- Imagination and inventiveness; show playfulness in experimentation.
- Versatility and diversity of interests
- See associations and innovations

Traits common in talented children

- Persistent goal-directed behaviour and high task commitment
- Imaginative and inventive; acute observational skills
- Perceptive and imaginative in the interpretation of stimuli
- Pronounced intuitive sense combined with a high degree of artistic integrity
- Ability to interpret and interconnect to a refined degree
- Attack drawing, painting or sculpting in non-prescribed ways, often not taught by the teacher
- Use of technical ability as a foundation for reinterpretation, refocussing, and retranslating, chiefly for personal satisfaction
- Ability to detach oneself from the surroundings and focus intently on the task at hand. This is especially true of auditory attention in musicians.

Gifted children learn more, faster, and more easily than do their age mates. They learn to read sooner and continue to read at a consistently more advanced level. Gifted students can master the curriculum content of a grade two or three times faster than the average child. In elementary mathematics, a good rule of thumb for gifted students is that two years of standard content can be covered in one year (Van Tassel-Baska, Landau, and Olszewski, 1985).

Students who are gifted like learning, enjoy difficult subjects, and are willing to spend extra time on projects that stimulate their interest. Gifted children are also more adept at critically evaluating facts and arguments. Because they more readily recognize relationships and comprehend meanings, they can reason out problems more effectively. In a recent study of the problem-solving skills of three groups of elementary students — those classified as normal, mentally retarded, and gifted — it was found that intellectually disabled students had the poorest problem-solving skills. Researchers concluded that "the sophistication of children's scientific problem-solving strategies is related to intelligence" (Ferretti and Butterfield, 1989, p. 431).

All these factors place gifted children far ahead in academic achievement. They tend to be more advanced in reading than in areas that require manual dexterity, such as writing and art.

Research has not found significant differences in the attitudes of gifted and non-gifted students toward school (Schneider et al., 1992). However, gifted students are often impatient with the routines in a regular classroom and dislike programmed instruction. Chalk and talk, endless drill and practice and repetition, along with a concomitant lack of stimulation and challenge, can bore and frustrate gifted learners. Bored children may daydream in school; others may pace themselves so as to finish with the rest of the class. By the age of thirteen or fourteen, some of these youngsters have a motivation to avoid failure at any cost rather than a motivation to succeed. These children are often too critical of others and of themselves and need help in accepting failure.

Gifted students require programming that allows them to delve deeper into the curriculum and to pursue topics of their own interest.

Social and Emotional Development

One common and persistent myth regarding gifted individuals, especially those in the arts, is that they are prone to mental disease. The question of whether gifted individuals are more emotionally stable, self-sufficient, and less prone to neurotic and psychotic disorders than average people has been the subject of intense research which offers modest support for the superior adjustment of the gifted (Grossberg and Cornell, 1988). In a study of gifted grade five, eight, and ten students, Ottawa researchers (Schneider et al., 1992) found that the gifted children were relatively well-adjusted individuals. However, extremely precocious students may be at greater risk for social problems than modestly gifted children (Dauber and Benbow, 1990).

Gifted children tend to be well liked by their peers, although popularity may taper off in secondary settings. Sometimes they alienate peers simply by the discrepancy between them or by their eagerness to demonstrate their unusual talents. Tannenbaum (1962) reported that bright students most favoured by peers were intelligent, athletic, and non-studious. The least-favoured gifted students were intelligent, studious, and non-athletic. In the Tannenbaum studies, boys rated more highly than girls. A later study (Cramond and Martin, 1987) of teachers and preservice teachers found much the same. Respondents did not value academic brilliance but athleticism as a critical determinant in a person's likability. Males were rated more highly than females.

Modestly gifted students seem to have the most favourable profiles in terms of personality and peer acceptance and interaction. Exceptionally gifted students may be disadvantaged. Students with very high IQs are less popular and have more difficulty with peer relations than age mates. Possibly their unusually high intelligence makes it difficult for their age mates to relate to them intellectually or socially. One study (Dauber and Benbow, 1990) discovered that extremely gifted students viewed themselves as more introverted, less socially adept, and more inhibited. The extremely gifted adolescents also reported that their peers saw them as much less popular, less socially active, less athletic, and less active in the crowd.

Behaviour

Like other children, gifted students are not always well behaved. They may interrupt others, fail to listen, be argumentative, refuse to comply with requests they view as trivial, be excessively critical, teasing or bossy, or display a high energy level that results in perpetual motion and disorganized work habits (Whitmore, 1979).

Creativity leads to a set of personality traits characterized by a strong self-concept that gives little credence to outside academic and social sanctions. Creative children tend to have high independence and be less conforming than their peers. This is especially true of boys. In junior high school classrooms of gifted students, creative boys are eight times as likely to quarrel with the opinions of peers and teachers as creative girls.

Ethical Development

Students who are gifted develop steadfast values quite early, with strong concerns for right and wrong (Piechowski, 1991). They wrestle with problems that we often associate with adults. When Derevensky and Coleman (1989) asked 70 gifted children aged 7 to 13 in a Toronto school for the gifted, "What are the things to be afraid of?" the students gave fears generally expressed by chronologically older students, such as death and nuclear war. Nicholas Colangelo (1989) asked 125 gifted children to define problems that were important to them. More than 50 percent chose typical teenage dilemmas of friendships and love relationships. However, they also identified 36 issues dealing with more adult themes such as public welfare and life and death scenarios.

Intervention with Gifted, Creative, and Talented Students

The basic educational goals for gifted and talented children are the same as for all other students: to develop their abilities in ways that are consistent with their personal needs and the best interests of society. At the same time, schools must develop mechanisms to identify gifted children and provide them with appropriate educational programs. Gifted and talented children cannot just fend for themselves; they possess no magical ability to help them overcome the obstacles to their growth. Like other exceptional children, these youngsters need special assistance to fulfill their potential for achievement.

Technical Aids

For most gifted children, technical aids, in the sense of hearing aids and wheelchairs, are not relevant. Gifted children should, however, be able to take advantage of the new advances in information and communication technology, specifically as related to computers. For gifted students computers can become idea engines, their tool to discovery, exploration, and collaboration. They can do research and apply thinking skills by working with real problems and computer simulations.

Profile

Dear Gerry,

Sorry that I haven't written for a while but you know how it is; have been busy with the boys, especially Gerry the Younger. In fact, it's because of Gerry that I'm writing to you tonight. The boys got your package today. John really liked the whip. Made of elephant hair, eh? The African headgear that you sent Gerry, though! Now that was really something else. The interesting thing was that he knows all about the thing, how it was made, history, symbolism, the works. I gather he saw a picture of one of them in one of those books you left at the house and read up on it.

It's downright disturbing what that kid knows. After all, he's only eight years old and in grade three but he reads better than John who's two years older. Now, I'm not saying that the kid can read a university book on Africa and extract all the information, but he did read some of it and understood a whole lot more. He remembers all of it, too. And he never shuts up about it. Question, question, question, talk, talk, talk!

The kid is really something special. I know that all parents say that but in this case it's true. He's a ball of energy, always poking into things, always doing or saying something weird. Always asking "Why?" Makes me feel like a jerk sometimes. Most of the stuff he asks I don't know "why."

You know what the young Mr. Spock's latest interest is? My computer. He and John are playing games on it. I've had the thing for three years and I can't get it to do that. Gerry said he learned how to do it in school. He's in grade three. I was in grade eleven before I learned to use a slide rule. I take that back — I never learned how to use a slide rule.

Mixed feeling time, old buddy. I feel kind of not up to the job of raising the kid. I know he'll be more on the ball than his old man ever was. But on the other hand, I'm proud of him. Another thing is that I sometimes think I'm spending too much time and money on Gerry at the expense of Number One Son. I know John sometimes resents his kid brother, but then again he won't let anyone kick sand in the kid's face.

So long, buddy,

John

Educational Intervention

Inevitably, educational models and approaches are a function of definition, be they implicit or explicit. Reflecting the difficulties in pinpointing the most effective definition of giftedness and gifted individuals is the wide variety of practices and programs that have been devised to cater to gifted children over the years. In 1985 a nationwide survey of gifted programming in the United States found sixteen different types, from simple enrichment programs within the regular classroom to full-time special schools (Greer, 1990b).

Another factor affecting programming is the attitudes of classroom teachers. In a review of the literature, researchers (Cramond and Martin, 1987) found that teachers had conflicting attitudes toward gifted students. Some studies found that teachers view gifted students positively and give them preferential treatment; others found teacher discomfort and resentment that could lead to apathy toward gifted education. In a sample of 98 parents of gifted children, Kaufman and Sexton (1983) found that 45 percent had encountered a teacher who they felt was unsympathetic to the special needs of the gifted child.

Some teachers disagree with special programming on both philosophical and pragmatic grounds. Bransky (1987) found negative attitudes among classroom teachers which she attributed to a poor foundation of knowledge about the pull-out programs for gifted students. Others realize that teachers of gifted students need special traits, but are unaware of the traits or have little confidence in their ability to develop them. (See Research Notes). Archambault and Hallmark (1992) found that 42 to 62 percent of 7000 teachers in their studies had absolutely no exposure to methods for teaching the gifted.

Some teachers argue that the classroom that loses gifted children is robbed of leadership. Others express concern about the fragmentation of their programs or the need to reschedule lessons (Meyers, 1984). Occasionally, teachers are adverse to designing programs for gifted learners.

Nobody is sure of the best way to educate gifted students, and it is true to say that there is a lack of systematically developed models and systematic experimental evaluation of programs and program models with explicit goals, objectives, and specified outcomes (Busse and Mansfield, 1986; Renzulli, 1980). Numerous programs have been attempted, all intended to come to grips with three major problems: the balance between the quest for excellence and a zeal for equality; the wide range of abilities among the gifted population; and teachers' lack of special instructional methods.

Educational Settings

The education of gifted students is replete with curriculum models that can be offered in various settings (see Davis and Rimm, 1994). Typically, more program options are available in urban and suburban areas and in the elementary schools. The three most common types of educational provisions are enrichment, ability grouping, and acceleration. All three models are used in Canada.

Studies unanimously support acceleration for academic excellence. The research does not provide clear evidence for or against ability grouping. Similarly, research on the results of enrichment programs does not yield clear evidence that they adequately stimulate gifted children.

Research Notes

Teachers of gifted, creative, and talented students

Should gifted children be taught by gifted teachers? This is one of the controversial questions that exist in the field of education of gifted students. If it is decided that gifted children should be taught by gifted teachers, then what exactly is a gifted teacher? Is it the teacher who possesses gifted traits? Or is it the teacher who is gifted at the profession of teaching?

Research on gifted teachers has generally looked at three areas: the personal characteristics of outstanding teachers of the gifted; their competencies; and those behaviours that set outstanding teachers apart (Whitlock and Du Cette, 1989).

An early study (Bishop, 1968) found that gifted students opt for teachers who are older and experienced and well above average in intellectual pursuits, who enjoy their profession and are respectful to students and other teachers. Later research has bolstered these findings, showing that gifted students preferred teachers with creative and positive personalities and high intelligence (e.g. Webb, Meckstroth, and Tolan, 1982). The characteristic most often described as desirable is that of being a facilitator of learning. Additionally, traits such as flexibility, creativity, good self-concept, depth and breadth of knowledge, sense of humour, counselling ability, maturity, teaching experience, and resourcefulness were deemed important (Story, 1985). These characteristics, of course, are the mark of any good teacher.

Certainly, the teacher of gifted children should possess all the traits common to good teachers. But they should also possess knowledge, understanding, and sympathy for the gifted population. The teacher should have a high level of creativity and energy to meet the special demands of gifted children. As well, teachers of gifted students need to be lifelong learners; to possess superior mental abilities; to be divergent thinkers; to be well educated in the liberal arts; to demonstrate competence in effectively individualizing instruction; to demonstrate skills in teaching science and arts; to have excellent skills in communication; and to have a healthy self-concept (Bell, 1986; Whitmore, 1985). Teachers also need knowledge of subject areas, an eagerness to be with bright children and dedication to students, and they must believe in the importance of enhancing pupils' self-image and maturity (Whitlock and Du Cette, 1989).

It is only recently that teacher-training programs have presented more than a cursory overview of the education of gifted students. Across the country, special education faculties are increasingly offering special courses and diploma programs related to the education of gifted and talented students. Richert (1990) recommends that all education students should have a three-hour course in gifted education as a bare minimum.

Acceleration

Acceleration means moving faster through academic content. Students speed up their progress through the existing curriculum to complete a prescribed program in a shorter time period. Included within acceleration models are early school beginning, grade skipping, ungraded classes, high school courses for credit, extra load, seminars for college credit, early admittance to post-secondary programs, and honours programs.

Acceleration is one of the most time-honoured options in gifted education. However, there is probably no area in the education of gifted students more controversial. In general, "[R]esearch studies are unanimous in their support of the benefit of accelerative alternatives, both academically and socio-emotionally" (Keating, 1980, p. 56). But even though the literature on academic acceleration of gifted students consistently demonstrates a lack of harmful effects, many educators and administrators resist the implementation of the model in their schools (Feldhusen, 1989; Southern, Jones, and Fiscus, 1989).

Many view the practice of allowing gifted students to progress through the educational system at their own rate as potentially hazardous to the social and emotional adjustment of students. These opponents of acceleration have marshalled an impressive array of arguments that focus on psychosocial rather than academic reasons (Swiatek and Benbow, 1991). The controversy continues, and the major arguments from both sides of the debate are presented below.

A Matter of Debate

Acceleration for gifted students

There is no argument more contentious in gifted education that that revolving around acceleration. Opponents of acceleration have marshalled an impressive array of arguments. The psychosocial reasons for hesitation in implementing acceleration programs are more numerous than the academic reasons (Swiatek and Benbow, 1991). On the other hand, advocates cite eighty years of positive research findings.

Arguments in Favour	Arguments Against
Acceleration programs reduce the time that students need to complete the curriculum; by accelerating, students can maximize their intellectual potential and maintain their interest and motivation.	Students may burn out if they are placed in classes that are advanced for their chronological ages.
Students can enter high school, college, and graduate studies earlier, and get a faster start on their careers.	Acceleration may lead to gaps in knowledge of the participants or poor retention of material learned at an accelerated pace (Van Tassel-Baska, 1989).
A meta-analysis of the results of 314 studies of the academic, social, and psychological effects of acceleration at the elementary and secondary levels (Rogers, 1990) found that "no form of acceleration led to a decrease in any area of performance — academic, social, or emotional," and that "There appears to be generally positive effects from most forms of acceleration."	Children cannot escape the physical and emotional limits imposed by chronology. Gifted children may show deficient or retarded psychosocial development.
Literature reviews (Swiatek and Benbow, 1991) show that no studies yield evidence that accelerated students exhibit deficits in knowledge or achievement.	Children will not fit with more mature classmates.
Most gifted children are psychosocially mature. Little research evidence links forms of acceleration to socio-emotional adjustment problems (Cornell, Callahan, and Loyd, 1991).	Special education opportunities lead gifted students to become conceited and self-centred; children will become contemptuous of their age peers and may suffer negative emotional and social consequences (Southern, Jones, and Fiscus, 1989).

Arguments in Favour	**Arguments Against**
Empirical research indicates that acceleration provides academic settings that are well suited to the needs of high ability students (Benbow, 1991). Gifted youth may have self-concepts which clearly relate to and recognize giftedness, and their self-concepts may be influenced positively by participation in a gifted program (Feldhusen and Hoover, 1986). A body of literature spanning five decades has consistently associated the acceleration of precocious children with positive change in their academic achievement and a lack of negative effects on social and emotional growth. Studies do not indicate that acceleration is harmful, and many indicate that it is beneficial (Southern, Jones, and Fiscus, 1989). Academically, acceleration promotes intellectual achievement. It allows gifted students to learn more efficiently (Feldhusen, Proctor, and Black, 1986) and increases effectiveness (Davis and Rimm, 1994). Accelerated students perform as well as older students with whom they are placed and exceed the achievement of non-accelerated students of the same age and ability by almost a year (Kulik and Kulik, 1984). "[F]ailure to advance a precocious child may result in poor study habits, apathy, lack of motivation, and maladjustment" (Feldhusen, Proctor, and Black, 1986, p. 27). With acceleration, "boredom, restlessness, frustration, underachievement, and disruptiveness can be replaced by enhanced motivation, improved self-concepts, and improved study habits and productivity" (Davis and Rimm, 1994). Both early admission and later acceleration have been extensively studied and no reliable research exists that documents harm (Daurio, 1979; Kulik and Kulik, 1984; Pollins, 1983; Proctor, Black, and Feldhusen, 1984). Acceleration is supported by an analysis of costs (Weiss and Gallagher, 1982). It costs little to implement and may actually save school systems money if students spend fewer years in the system (e.g., Stanley and Benbow, 1982).	Acceleration programs emphasize the differences between gifted and average students, thereby jeopardizing the social acceptance of gifted students; those enrolled in special classes will lose the ability to function in the larger world of average people (Swiatek and Benbow, 1991). The self-concepts of gifted students will suffer if they are set apart from their average counterparts. Accelerated pupils will not socialize with older children, will have fewer friends, will not be happy, and will miss important social interactions (Southern, Jones, and Fiscus, 1989). Research knowledge only sporadically finds its way into educational practice, even when the research has produced substantial knowledge related to problems of real-world importance (see Malouf and Schiller, 1995, p. 414). Acceleration conflicts with the school's perceived role to socialize students and make them good workers.

Ability Grouping

Gifted students need interaction with peers who share their interests and concerns. The general tenor of research indicates that they require social and emotional support from a group of true peers in order to maintain positive self-concept and intellectual interaction and to transform abilities into productive reality. True peers are simultaneously the student's intellectual and chronological equals.

As the name suggests, ability groupings (pull-out programs) refer to changing the environment to bring gifted students into contact with each other. They are removed from heterogeneous settings and placed in special groups. In some cases, children go to special classrooms. In others, independent groups of students progress at different rates within the same classroom.

Special groups may meet full-time or only part-time. They may be made up of students from a single school or from several schools within a district. Groups may meet during regular school hours or on an extra-curricular basis. For example, programs of the Roman Catholic school board in St. John's pull out students for one day a week and they meet in a central location. A day's activities include such things as boundary breakers, computer skills training, philosophy for children, creative/critical thinking skills, creative problem solving, special units of study such as archeology or the stock market, and open learning experiences such as futuristics or story telling (Craig, 1988).

Certain criteria ensure the success of pull-out programs. These include integration with the regular curriculum; daily program experience; placement with intellectual peers; pace of program matched with the students' learning rate; complex and higher level curriculum; and excellent teachers (Belcostas, 1987).

In special programs, competition may be important, especially for older students. Some educators disagree with competition in the classroom and many have moved toward a greater emphasis on co-operative learning strategies. However, co-operative learning may not be appropriate for gifted students. A study of the preferred learning styles of 169 gifted high school students showed that both males and females preferred individualistic learning styles over co-operative learning for all subjects (Li and Adamson, 1992). The research dealing with the gifted child's self-esteem in pull-out programs is inconclusive. In one study carried out in Calgary (Bourque and Li, 1987), the researchers assessed sixty gifted students between the ages of nine and eleven placed in regular and segregated settings to see if they differed in perceived competence, social adjustment, and peer relations. Educational setting did not appear to have any differential impact on social adjustment as rated by teachers, on peer relations, or on sociometric nominations. The investigators concluded that educational setting, per se, is not an important factor for self-esteem, social adjustment, or peer relations.

As with acceleration, pull-out programs are far from universally accepted. Opponents claim that the practice is undemocratic and that it fosters intellectual elitism and limits contacts between gifted and normal children. Pragmatically, they contend that pull-out programs are often frivolous. Programs often diverge from the regular school curriculum; do not give grades, do not have instruction in traditional subject matter, focus on the affective rather than the academic, and do not have written curricula (Van Tassel-Baska, 1987).

Proponents of ability grouping argue that only when gifted children are grouped together can they be provided with truly effective instruction. Davis and Rimm (1994) are quite adamant that "gifted education and gifted students are in deep trouble without grouping practices" (p. 10). Others (Kulik, 1992; Kulik and Kulik, 1991) have shown that children of medium and low ability are either not affected or are negatively affected by ability grouping, but that the achievement of high-ability students is positively affected by ability grouping that includes curriculum modifications directed to their learning characteristics. As far as curriculum is concerned, some educators believe that since separate gifted programs provide for students who differ from the norm, the programs also should differ in their adherence to the conventional structures associated with education.

Mentor Programs

Mentor programs are designed to allow students to work, at a specified time, with adults in the community with whom they share a special interest. Usually, the teacher, the mentor, and the student set up a project with the final results to be presented to the class in some form.

Many advantages accrue to mentor programs. Not only are they particularly cost-effective, but they serve as a liaison between the school and the community while allowing students to pursue special interests. Other benefits for involved students include career and interest advancement; increase in knowledge and skills; development of talent; enhancement of self-esteem and self-confidence; development of a personal ethic or set of standards; establishment of long-term friendships; and enhancement of creativity (Edlind and Heansly, 1985)

Enrichment

In many situations it is impossible and perhaps unnecessary to take gifted children from their assigned classrooms. Enrichment programs provided by regular classroom teachers, often in consultation and co-operation with resource room personnel, may be one answer.

Enrichment involves providing special activities in the regular classroom setting. These activities, which involve a broader range of skills and deeper understanding than the regular curriculum, are designed to challenge and interest children while focusing on their unique patterns of strengths and weaknesses. Of course, enrichment activities are good for all students, and it must be kept in mind that for gifted students there have to be higher order objectives outlined within enrichment.

The enrichment unit presented as an example examines seeds and plants and is loosely based on Benjamin Bloom's taxonomy of educational objectives (1956). This type of unit can be used effectively with gifted students as a group assignment or as independent study.

Advocates of enrichment programs maintain that they allow a child to remain in the regular classroom with age level peers. Detractors point out the difficulty of meeting individual needs with a few extra activities in a generally inadequate learning environment. They contend that enrichment often promotes the false impression that something substantial is being done for the gifted. In fact, enrichment has been referred to as "busywork and irrelevant" (Stanley and Benbow, 1986).

Enrichment activities include a number of recognized instructional models. Three important models are the Enrichment Triad, the Revolving Door, and the Autonomous Learner Model.

The Enrichment Triad delineates three types of enrichment activities for students. Type I, General Exploratory Activities, are appropriate for all students. Type I activities expose pupils to exciting topics, ideas, and fields of knowledge not ordinarily covered by the regular curriculum, and include visiting speakers, field trips, demonstrations, interest development centres, and the use of many different kinds of audio-visual materials. Type II, Group Training Activities, are also appropriate for all children. They consist of methods, materials, and instructional techniques designed to develop thinking processes, research and reference skills, and personal and social skills. Type III activities, Small Group Investigations, are very rigorous and challenging. Students self-select areas of study and take responsibility for initiating, conceptualizing, and planning the activity or project. They investigate real problems and topics using appropriate methods of enquiry (Reis and O'Shea, 1984).

The Revolving Door model (Renzulli and Smith, 1984) is designed to identify giftedness, to provide enrichment activities, and to overcome many of the problems related to student selection, motivation, and interests. The model is essentially a resource room adjunct program. Students participate as their interest and motivation dictate; they are not permanently in or out of the program, but can apply for special consideration to work on projects of their own choosing. Renzulli claims that this approach teaches students they must earn the right to participate.

The Autonomous Learner Model (ALM) (Betts, 1985) is designed for secondary special classrooms but can also be used at elementary levels. It is usually presented during one period at specified times throughout the week. While not a total program, ALM meets the socio-emotional needs of gifted learners and encourages independence in the learning setting.

In a three-year sequence, students move through five major dimensions:

- orientation, which includes understanding giftedness and group building activities
- individual development, which includes learning skills and career involvement
- enrichment activities, which involve exploration and investigation
- seminars, which include general interest and advanced knowledge
- in-depth study, which includes independent projects and mentorships

Educational Approaches

The differences between the regular program and the program for gifted students is one of degree. Some classroom practices currently being studied include independent projects, creative writing on self-selected topics, teaching thinking skills, encouraging discovery, and using classroom questioning that encourages reasoning and logical thinking (Gubbins, 1991).

To educate gifted students a school can make changes in the learning environment, in the content of lessons, and in the skills taught (B.C., 1995; Gallagher, 1985). Environmental changes include acceleration and ability grouping, which we have already discussed.

Content includes both what students study and the rate at which they study it. Gifted students don't need more work but different work that is challenging and interesting. As well, since pace is one of the most important variables in teaching, and these students may learn fifteen times faster than others, teachers must present material more rapidly and with less practice than for average learners. Skills relate both to process — how the students work with information — and to products — how they represent what they know.

Gifted students require structured and systematic programming that allows them not only to delve deeper into the regular curriculum but also to pursue topics of their own interest. A deeper examination of the regular curriculum cannot be achieved by adding a few tasks. Rather, it needs a consistent and structured curriculum expansion founded on broad goals directed at their specific needs. Curriculum should be designed to allow gifted children to master important conceptual systems that are at the level of their abilities in various content fields.

Enrichment Unit

Plants and seeds

Knowledge

- List all the parts of a seed plant you can find.
- Define the following terms (related to seed plants): bulb germination, dormancy, dicotyledon, dissemule, root hair.
- List the many methods of seed dispersal.
- Name the conditions necessary for germination and development in a plant.
- List the enemies of plants (as many as you can find).
- Look at several beauty magazines to see how plants are used in make-up and other beauty aids.

Comprehension

- Why do leaves change colour in the fall?
- Explain how a plant takes water from the earth and uses it in its living processes.
- Explain the difference between *coniferous* and *deciduous.*
- Describe how a plant grows, from fertilization through to maturity. If you like, you can use an example to help you.
- Describe the role of chlorophyll in photosynthesis, explaining why green plants turn yellow and die if they do not get enough sunlight.
- Describe the role of a seed plant in the ability for life to exist on earth.

Application

- Using a microscope, diagram the cell structure of a leaf.
- Diagram the different parts of a seed plant.
- Show how you can tell how old, and tall, a tree is.
- Make your own perfume, using the leaves of flowers.
- Show how a seed plant takes root and begins to grow.

Analysis

- Conduct an experiment to see how far seeds can travel.
- Compare and contrast coniferous and deciduous trees, and the way they grow.
- Conduct an experiment to see what happens when seeds are crowded too close together.
- Compare past and present uses of plants in the field of medicine. Are there any similarities?
- Conduct an experiment to see what will happen to a leaf when it is coated with Vaseline. Why does this happen?
- Conduct an experiment to determine the lengths to which plants will go so that they can get sunlight?

Synthesis

- Design an environment possessing ideal conditions for the growth of seed plants.
- Choose two plants and, using your knowledge about genetics and plant breeding, predict the outcome of a cross between them. Describe the new creation. What are its strength and weaknesses, if any?
- Grow several bean seeds, controlling different environmental conditions in each instance. Predict the outcome in each case, and compare it with the actual results.

Evaluation

- Decide whether or not the commercial use of greenhouses can be beneficial to people in the long run.
- Acid rain has a great effect on plants. What exactly is that effect, and what can we do about it? Are we doing all we can right now?
- Assess the value of gardens in space. Are they worth the trouble?

Source: Hicks, 1987

Figure 5-4
Curriculum components

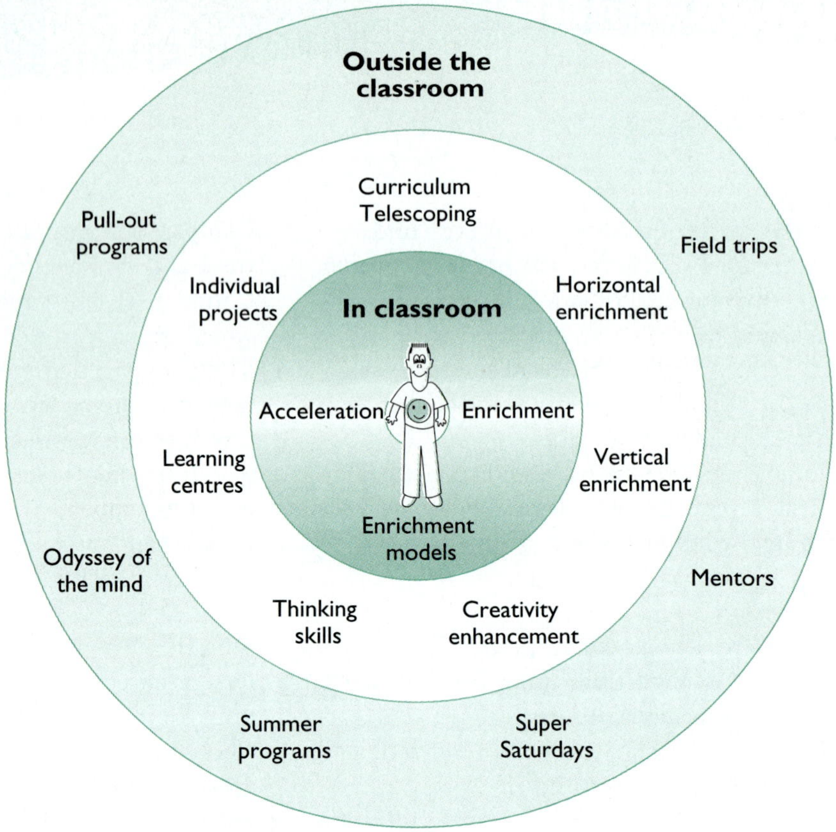

Various terms describe these processes. *Curriculum telescoping* refers to moving through the curriculum far more rapidly. *Horizontal enrichment* involves examining a certain curriculum area in greater depth. *Vertical enrichment* refers to students doing additional independent work of their own choosing in the classroom.

At the same time, students must be assisted in developing skills and strategies that enable them to become more independent, creative, and self-sufficient seekers after knowledge. This means that we need to add a fourth R — research skills — to the curriculum. Lacking research skills, students cannot undertake self-directed learning (also called autonomous learning, self-teaching, individualized education, independent learning, and personalized teaching).

There are almost as many conceptualizations of self-directed learning as there are researchers and theorists. Essentially, self-directed learning means that students are given autonomous control of their own instruction (Sellin and Birch, 1980). Included are library research projects, scientific research projects, and independent study in art, music, and drama, learning centres, and field trips.

Teachers can provide for individual differences and stimulate an interest in learning if they understand the techniques that enhance motivation and provide for personal development. Some very general tips for teachers focusing on academic skills and affective development of gifted students follow.

Tips for Teachers

Classroom Climate
- Try to find mentors.
- Individualize as much as possible.
- In the classroom, the degree of conformity should be reasonable and flexible. The young child, for example, may not listen intently when you read to the class, but neither should that child be permitted to divert the attention of others.

Instruction
- Design curriculum that facilitates the movement from teacher-directed to self-directed learning styles.
- Do not work in a qualitatively different way than for other children; just present more advanced material.
- First teach the basic structure of a discipline but then try to have the students approach it as the specialist approaches it.
- Introduce important ideas as early as possible.
- Teach to the highest cognitive level possible.
- Teach gifted students to utilize all of their thinking processes.
- Use individual reading assignments with self-selection of materials.
- Use written expression for a variety of purposes — informative and persuasive as well as narrative.
- Stress technical writing. For example, teach children how to phrase research questions.
- Teach methods by which the children can discover knowledge for themselves.
- Teach students how to write proposals and how to present primary research data in graph, table, diagram, and statistical form.
- Stress the processes of problem solving as well as the products of work.
- Let students teach each other through small-group work and co-operative learning activities.

Psychosocial
- Provide time for students to do their own work at school.
- Have gifted students regularly share with the class what they are doing.
- Make assignments that allow some choice.
- Encourage career explorations.

A number of interesting out-of-school programs have developed for gifted learners. Some centres offer special summer programs. Odyssey of the Mind is a North American program in which interested schools can participate. Super Saturdays are programs organized to give children a day of special programming.

Approaches for Special Populations

The life patterns of underachievers are set by age fourteen or fifteen and cannot be changed by a pep talk. Rather, the students need support and respect for their efforts. Teachers need to establish standards and provide instruction, guidance, and support, with encouragement and co-operation rather than competition (Whitmore, 1980). Gifted underachievers may need an extensive period of self-discovery, the creation of the proper atmosphere, and changes in the educational environment.

Joanne Whitmore (1980) reported a positive result for gifted primary grade underachievers emerging from an intensive special class experience in which the teacher focused on building self-concept, fostering motivation, and learning to take risks. Whitmore believes it is important to begin in the early grades before the patterns of resistance in underachievers become too ingrained.

Individual Education Plan iep

Extract from Richard's IEP

Name: Richard
Date: November 12, 1994
School: Ourtown Elementary
Teacher: Jim Brown
Grade: 3

Results from formal assessment

Test	Date administered	Results
WISC-111		
Full scale	21 Sept., 1994	93rd %tile
Performance		91st %tile
Verbal		95th %tile

Results from other assessment

Test	Date	Results
Gates-MacGinitie	September	Vocabulary 2-1 GE
Reading Test		Comprehension 1-8 GE
Woodcock Reading	September	21st %tile
Test of Early Reading Ability	October	23rd %tile
Key Math Diagnostic Arithmetic Test	October	41st %tile
Test of Language Development	November	78th %tile

Strengths
Works well alone
Strong oral language
Improvements in math
Very popular
Independent

Weaknesses
Serious lags in reading
Poor spelling
Minimal written language
Misaligned, misformed printing

Major needs
Opportunities to make use of oral skills.
Activities that build on logical and thinking skills.
Remediation in all areas of language arts.
Encouragement to continue improvement in math.

Setting
Regular classroom/resource room/pull-out gifted program

Long-range goals in pull-out program
Learn basic research skills
Explore a topic of own choosing in depth
Communicate findings to grade 3 class
Adhere to a contract for an independent project prepared with the teacher.
Start to develop better time management skills

Gifted adolescent girls have little opportunity to explore their true interests. They are placed under more pressure to conform and are less likely than males to find learning opportunities with a supportive teacher (Dishart, 1981). The key to helping a gifted female fulfill her potential lies in better assessment, counselling, and career development. Callahan (1979) suggests that gifted and talented girls need early entry into stimulating and challenging programs, models that contradict sex-role stereotypes, and information about scholastic requirements for career alternatives to stereotypical disciplines.

It is not often that youngsters with learning disabilities are identified as gifted. Difficulties in learning can create a smoke screen that masks their talents. For students who are learning disabled or who have other disabilities, the first step to programming for giftedness is ongoing and comprehensive identification. Individualized programs should then be structured to focus on the child's strengths and to stimulate creativity and problem-solving abilities. Teachers should provide a nurturing environment that values individual differences and encourage strategies such as advance organizers, the development of test-taking skills, and special notes that help to compensate for the disability.

Children from diverse cultural backgrounds require additional planning. For example, Cambridge Bay is a community of approximately 850 people of whom about 80 percent are Inuit. When an enrichment program was established there, parents were reluctant to lend it support. This was attributed mainly to their lack of initial involvement in program planning (Mulcahy et al., 1984). Educators need to gain parental involvement and support and develop program models, goals, and objectives that are meaningful for the local culture.

Summary

1. There is not another category in special education as fraught with political, emotional, and educational issues as that of giftedness. Difficulties revolve around just who is gifted, how to identify gifts and talents, how to offer special programming, and how to balance the needs of gifted students within the parameters of an egalitarian school system.
2. Giftedness is considered to be a component of special education because gifted students require appropriate educational opportunities and challenges if they are to develop their full potential.

3. Not the least of the problems that plague the field of gifted edcuation is the lack of a universally accepted definition. It is very difficult to find a definition that encompasses gifted, talented, and creative children and youth because these students demonstrate such a broad array of characteristics and behaviours. This lack of definition distorts prevalence figures and renders identification more difficult.
4. No consensus has been reached on whether to define giftedness as performance or potential.
5. Although we no longer claim that giftedness springs entirely from the genes, it is only reasonable to assume that genetics have some effect. Environment is important, but beyond the obvious general advantages, it is not known what specific factors in upper- and middle-class homes encourage giftedness.
6. For a long time after IQ tests were made viable in 1905, the study of giftedness was dominated by the single variable IQ. This complete reliance on IQ tests continued into the 1960s. Today, the most prevalent identification models used call for multiple means of identification. When nominations are used, the process is guided by effectiveness and efficiency. Assessing creativity presents the challenging problem of how to devise a standardized means of identifying non-standard behaviour.
7. Within identification procedures, many gifted children go undiscovered, particularly those who are culturally, ethnically, linguistically, socially, or economically different from the norm. Better identification measures are needed to identify gifted females and gifted children within minority groups, such as those who are gifted and disabled and gifted children from other cultures.
8. Children who are disabled in one way may be exceptionally gifted in another. When the child has a learning disability, his or her superior intellectual ability is working overtime to compensate for the weaknesses caused by the disability.
9. The provision of programs for gifted students is one of the most controversial issues in special education. Research on the efficacy of any particular administrative model is somewhat inconclusive, but acceleration appears to have a strong edge. However, practitioners seem to regard acceleration in general and early entrance in particular as risky approaches in serving the needs of gifted children.
10. There is strong support in the literature favouring segregated settings on academic and intellectual grounds. The special classroom provides opportunities for acceleration and for horizontal expansion of the curriculum.
11. Enrichment in the classroom implies more than tacking on a few activities to the existing curriculum. To assist teachers in planning and presenting classroom enrichment, a number of models have been successfully used.
12. Self-directed learning, very important for gifted students, is claimed to be very effective.

SECTION 3

Children with Communication Disorders

In all the enormous repertoire of human skills and abilities, communication is one of the most critical tools. Communication is the essence of human socialization, the link that provides reciprocal interaction between the individual and the environment. Humans use communication to meet needs and desires, control environmental events, establish social relationships, and learn new skills and concepts. Communication includes written language and speech as well as a variety of non-speech forms such as sign language and many non-verbal forms such as gesture and body language.

Human language is incredibly complex, bound by structured rules and characteristic patterns of usage that change in different settings — intrapersonal, interpersonal, group, and societal (Levine, 1981). Yet for most children, the ready acquisition of their culture's language and speech is a natural part of early maturation. Small children learn language long before school age and do so with vivacity and playfulness.

All children show great variability in the age at which they will demonstrate a particular level of speech and language performance (Bernstein and Tiegerman, 1989). However, for children with communication exceptionalities, the variability falls outside what could be considered normal. These youngsters encounter serious difficulties in the acquisition and use of speech and language. For many school-aged children, inferior communication skills inhibit learning and contribute to feelings of failure (Wesanko, 1990).

The use of language is closely tied to cognitive development and self-concept. Problems can impair a child's functioning in play and with peers and can result in the development of secondary behavioural problems. As well, unresolved difficulties will hinder a child's future progress. Competence with language has a direct influence on a child's ability to learn to read and write (Polloway and Smith, 1982), and young children with speech and language difficulties are more likely to meet problems in learning to read later on.

About 8 to 10 percent of school-aged children have some type of speech or language disorder. For some children, this is a short-term delay in acquiring articulation proficiency. Other children have chronic, recurrent speech and language difficulties, such as stuttering. For others, speech and language difficulties are part of a more complex constellation of disorders that may limit their lifetime options (Ilott, 1990).

Problems in speech and language not only constitute a field of exceptionality by themselves, but they cut across other areas. For many young children with disabilities, learning to communicate is not a simple or a naturally occurring task. Communication demands so much of the human organism that language learning is vulnerable to all the problems which can and do affect children. Among children with disabilities, lacks in speech and language development are probably the most apparent deficits that teachers will see.

Many children diagnosed as learning disabled also suffer problems in the areas of speech and language. The term "language learning disabilities" refers to the language disorder syndrome associated with learning disabilities.

Studies suggest that language is the primary deficit for 60 percent of students with learning disabilities (LD), while for all LD students language is one component of their disorder (Wesanko, 1990). Children who come from different cultural backgrounds may encounter difficulties in acquiring the rules of English in a sufficiently sophisticated form to enable them to function in academic settings. Children from other cultural backgrounds who suffer specific handicapping conditions are doubly disadvantaged.

Teachers look for strategies to teach communication to all young children, including those with disabilities, those from non-English-speaking families, those who are lagging in development, and those who are preverbal. However, research has not indicated which strategy for teaching communication is the most effective. Skilled teachers use descriptive feedback, directing, telling and explaining, question asking, modelling, and prompt and coaching statements. When necessary, they use teacher-mediated and peer-mediated strategies and direct teaching.

In this section, we first introduce the subject of speech and language disorders and illustrate how they affect children who suffer these as their sole disabilities. We then discuss the very special problems of children diagnosed as learning disabled, with particular emphasis on aspects of speech and language. The final chapter in this section concerns children from different cultural backgrounds. We look particularly at children who are at risk because of poor language and speech acquisition as well as those who suffer other disabling conditions.

CHAPTER 6

Children with Speech and Language Differences

Historical Notes

For centuries, parents, scholars, and teachers have been fascinated by the way children acquire and use language. Virtually all the major philosophers since Plato and Aristotle have considered the problems of the origin and role of human language. Debates centred on the role of language in the progressive differentiation of humans from other creatures and the way in which reason, if an original endowment of humans, manifested itself in language.

Eighteenth-century empiricists were particularly intrigued by language development in humans. John Locke speculated on language and its place in human development. Pointing to the arbitrary nature of language, he asserted that words derive their meaning from a culture that accepts certain relationships and certain designations: "[W]ords in their primary or immediate signification stand for nothing but the ideas in the mind of him that uses them" (Locke, 1690/1894, p.9).

With Locke as a touchstone, the French *philosophes* embarked on a rigorous analysis of the structures and functions of language. The origin of speech and language was seen as the key to the history of thought (Knowlson, 1965), while the use of language was viewed as the mode through which people would be taught to think rationally, clearly and, above all, scientifically (Seigel, 1969). The interest throughout was in language as a system of communication somehow able to explain reflective thought, not in language as a system of syntactic and semantic structures.

In the nineteenth century, the study of speech and language was known as philology; most of the research was in the form of diary studies. These soon gave way to an examination of children's vocabulary, which is perhaps the most traditional approach to the study of language acquisition.

In the early twentieth century, the study of language development emphasized language form. Much of the data was anecdotal; data collection was inconsistent, and many important aspects of development were overlooked. In general, language forms were identified and classified into categories related to sentence types, parts of speech, and so on (Owens, 1988). By the 1930s and 1940s, data collection had become more formalized.

Today, the study of how children learn language is like many other academic pursuits in that different theories that attempt to explain the phenomenon compete for acceptance. Every theory advanced to explain language development has been criticized. The question is fiercely debated and there are champions of every conceivable position. Occasionally one theory predominates, but generally portions of each are used to explain different aspects. Part of the problem in designing an overall theory is the complexity of both language and communication behaviours (Owens, 1988).

Behaviourists consider language a subset of other learned behaviours and stress reinforcement in language acquisition. A social learning view of language incorporates many of the elements of the behavioural position but also includes the processes of imitation. Children are believed to learn to speak one language rather than another, and to speak it with particular vocabularies and idioms, because they imitate and are reinforced for imitating the language spoken in their homes and neighbourhoods.

Because children of all cultures learn language at about the same age and tend to learn it in similar ways, others question whether humans are born with a natural innate tendency to acquire language. Piaget believed that language acquisition is a direct result of cognitive development, that language is the handmaiden of thought. To Piaget, we cannot develop language skills until at least the last stage of sensorimotor development because it is not until then that a child's mental apparatus allows him or her to represent symbolically an object that is no longer present.

Noam Chomsky (1965), also holding a cognitive-biological position, believes that a sense of grammar is innate, or native, to the human brain. Chomsky postulates an innate language acquisition device unique to and present in all humans that enables us to learn language simply by being exposed to it.

Enormously complex and comprehensive research into the nature and acquisition of language continues apace. The more that is discovered about language and language impairments, the greater the number of questions that emerge. Studies throughout the 1980s included all the traditional topics: phonology, morphology, syntax, pragmatics, and semantics. Stress was placed on the acquisition of pragmatics — an individual's ability to use language appropriately in social situations.

Recently, the functional definition of language has been expanded in important ways. First, communicative behaviour is seen as any behaviour that conveys a social message from one person to another. Spoken language, sign language, and the use of communication boards are considered diverse but legitimate modes of language. This accompanies the realization that formal language is only one of several forms of communicative behaviour. Gestures and actions (reaching, directed eye movements, use of objects) are other forms of communicative behaviour, which is defined by its function in a social interaction rather than by its form (Rogers-Warren and Warren, 1984).

The common thread in these new assumptions about language is that social interaction is integral to the development of communication (Rogers-Warren and Warren, 1984). In other words, a primary social relationship is critical to language learning. Researchers stress that:

- language includes both verbal and non-verbal forms;
- all language should be viewed in the broader context of social communication;
- language is a social behaviour based in social interaction and arises from the child's early non-verbal, communicative interchanges with a primary caregiver;
- language as a formal and functional system is learned;
- elaborated forms of communication are built on simpler forms. The progression of communication moves from signals (cries, for example), to the use of sign (systematic, consistent gesturing to indicate wants, for example), to the use of increasingly complex linguistic forms, to the metalinguistic uses of language;
- language learning occurs in an ecosystem. Because language is a social behaviour learned in social contexts, it is part of a reciprocal influence pattern between child and caregiver, learner and teacher (Rogers-Warren and Warren, 1984).

Of all the achievements of early childhood, the acquisition and development of speech and language is one of the most remarkable. Tiny infants, initially able to produce only vegetative sounds and reflexive cries, rapidly acquire language and speech through exposure and experience. As children listen and respond to the language in their environments, they typically make enormous progress in speech and language development and quite unconsciously learn to produce an infinite variety of intelligible utterances. Without formal instruction, most children in their first two years develop a lexicon of spoken words and learn to form simple multilevel utterances. By the age of five, most children have acquired such mastery over language that they have a firm linguistic base on which teachers can formally build reading and writing. As children develop speech and language, they are also developing **communicative competence** — they know how to interact, how to communicate appropriately in various situations, and how to make sense of what others say and do in communicative interactions.

Although small children accomplish this monumental task with ease, linguists, psychologists, anthropologists, and many others either directly or peripherally involved in language research remain unsure of how the process actually progresses. It only attests to the complexity of language acquisition that no technique has yet been devised to teach any language satisfactorily and no scientist has yet developed a satisfactory description of any language.

The first three years are the crucial period for the development of speech and language: about twice as much language growth occurs between the first and third years as between the third and fifth years (Cratty, 1986). The language explosion that occurs in the preschool years is most apparent in the growth of vocabulary — from about 50 words at eighteen months to 200 words at age two, to between 8000 and 14 000 words at age six (Carey, 1978). This means that, from age two to age six, the average child learns between six and ten words a day.

Sometimes teachers of older students ignore this early development and focus only on what a child does in the formal school setting. We cannot do this with speech and language; what happens in the developmental stages is reflected in the child's performance in the classroom later on.

A basic understanding of the normal development of language and speech underlies an appreciation of the nature of communication disorders. We therefore begin this chapter with a brief overview of normal speech and language development.

Overview of Speech and Language

Communication may be seen as the process of exchanging information and ideas between participants. It is said that all living things communicate in some way, and in this sense, communication includes the entire spectrum of acts performed by living creatures in order to pass on and respond to messages. Speech and language are the typically human activities in communication. **Language** is a system of symbols organized into conventional patterns to communicate meaning. Speech is essentially a mechanical production of language. Other methods than speech may be appropriately employed to express language — sign language and writing, for example. However, while it is possible to possess language and lack the ability to speak, it is not possible to have speech without language.

Development of the Field

In the past, investigators from a variety of disciplines, including philosophy, history, physiology, psychology, and linguistics, turned their skills toward children's language acquisition. As a discrete discipline, psycholinguistics emerged in the early 1950s and from then on language became a favourite research area.

The schools became involved in children's speech and language problems early on. In the 1880s, classes were developed in the public schools for children who were hard of hearing. There were also "steamer classes," special reception classes designed to rapidly teach English to new arrivals.

As special classes expanded in the first decades of the twentieth century, children with speech and language problems as their sole area of dysfunction were accommodated. For example, by 1910 schools in Chicago were employing specialists to work with children with communication disorders.

Special teaching was boosted by the formation of the American Speech and Hearing Society (ASHA) at a meeting in Iowa City in 1925. In 1978, the group became the American Speech, Language, and Hearing Society (ASLHA).

As for most types of deviancy from the norm, special classes remained the prime instructional vehicle for children with speech and language disorders well into the 1960s. Much new research in language acquisition came from the development of the discipline of psycholinguistics in the 1950s. Much of this stressed the social context of language acquisition, and educators were slowly persuaded against separate and clinic settings.

Today, natural environments are used for almost all children with speech and language difficulties. Several reasons are given for adopting the natural environment as a setting for language assessment and training:

- Much language is learned in a social context. Language production is necessarily the result of an interaction between the skills of the speaker and events in the environment, and language is best taught through social interaction and naturally occurring events.
- The problems of generalizing skills are circumvented. A major problem in language training concerns the transfer of learned language from the training setting to the natural environment. The generalization of language skills appears to be more restricted in children with language disorders, and it is uncertain whether language learned in clinical settings will generalize to other environments (Spradlin and Siegel, 1982).
- Persons in the child's natural environment can be the chief intervenors. Teachers and peers facilitate strategies.
- Because training occurs in natural settings, it is bound to be functional, and this enhances the likelihood that new language will be maintained and generalized.

As children acquire speech and language they typically pass through certain stages. These should not be viewed as a set of discrete milestones through which children pass on the way to mastering adult communication; rather, language should be seen as a process that is generative, systematic, and rule-governed. Language learning begins in infancy and continues throughout life. Formal language use is one point on a continuum of communication behaviour that begins in non-verbal social exchanges during infancy and extends through the use of written language.

Another important aspect of language is the creativity involved. Children are not passive organisms into which language is poured; rather, they are catalytic agents. In other words, it is not so much that language develops but that language is acquired. The process is clearly marked by open-endedness and productivity. It is clear quite early that children do not put words together only if they have heard those words together in combination before; rather, they produce utterances they have never heard. As children develop vocabulary and internalize a knowledge of the rules of their native language, they can potentially create an infinite number of unique utterances.

A further remarkable finding about language acquisition is that children acquiring language do so in essentially the same order. In English, children learn *in* and *on* before other prepositions such as *under*, and they learn the progressive form using *ing* before other verb endings such as *ed*. After they learn regular plurals and past tenses as in *horses* and *skated* they create some forms of their own, like *mouses* and *eated* (Gleason, 1985).

Elements of Language

Language consists of interrelated and intertwined components, all of which must be present or developing for appropriate usage. Children must simultaneously learn the sound structure of the language (the phonology), the rules that govern the ordering of words within sentences (the syntax or grammar), and the meaning of words and phrases (semantics). If their usage is to attain appropriate meaning, children must employ pragmatics — the use of language in its social context.

Syntax is the network of organizational principles underlying linguistic expression. Without syntax, language would become an incoherent jumble of vocabulary and sound (Crystal, Fletcher, and Garman, 1976). Syntactic rules govern what we call the grammar of language. **Grammar** may be defined as the sum total of conventions that govern the communication of meaning of a particular language. It comprises those procedures employed by a speaker to build up a functionally satisfying symbol sequence.

Children do not learn syntax all at one time but progress through distinct stages. For example, as children learn to express questions, a definite sequence of acquisition can be observed. In the first stage, the question is expressed by a slight rising of the voice. The second stage involves the use of an interrogative word, such as *who, what, where, which,* and *why.* These words are placed in front of a word, phrase, or complete sentence, resulting in such questions as "Who that?" "What this?" and "Why you cry?" (Byrne and Shervanian, 1977). The third stage involves the principle of inversion. The child places the verb before the subject of the sentence to ask "Is Daddy home?" and "Does it belong here?" Some children rely on the ubiquitious "Eh?" Tag questions, such as "You have one, don't you?" appear a little later (de Villiers and de Villiers, 1978).

Semantics is concerned specifically with meaning. The acquisition of words, their meanings, and the links between them does not usually happpen at once. Words are clearly comprehended before they are spoken, and the number of words comprehended continues to be greater all through language development and in later life. Comprehension of the first word is about three months ahead of production of the first word, and the gap grows; comprehension of fifty words appears to occur five months before production of fifty words (Benedict, 1979). Moreover, children learn to produce fifty words before they string them together into sentences. Vocabularly growth begins slowly, but there is a great spurt in word learning between twenty-four and thirty months (Reich, 1986).

Morphology is the system of word building in the language. Morphemes may be words or significant elements, such as prefixes and suffixes. Sound units that are not words by themselves are called **bound morphemes** because they are units of meaning only when combined with words. For example, the suffix *ness* can be added to many words in English.

Phonology is the sound system of language; the smallest sound units are called phonemes. Phonology encompasses the rules for using the sounds of language, for combining phonemes in particular ways to form identifiable language units such as the /s/ that we add to make words plural. People who speak American or Canadian English recognize about 40 different phonemes. Other languages recognize different sounds.

Phonetics is the description of the speech sounds of a language. There are only twenty-six letters — vowels and consonants — in the English alphabet, but they are pronounced in different ways. For example, *s* may be pronounced /sh/ as in *sugar* or /z/ as in *rose.*

Pragmatics is concerned with the ways in which we use language, the role of context in communicative interactions. Pragmatics develops from the early stages as children use their language to query, request, deny, and declare. How they use language — the content of their interactions — changes with the interaction and the situation. They can talk baby talk to infants, tell jokes and riddles, be rude to their friends and, usually, polite to their teachers and parents.

The Speech Mechanism

The act of speech is enormously complicated. English speakers talk at an average rate of 150 words a minute. A speaker produces 14 phonemes per second, using about 100 muscles that require 100 motor units apiece (Shames and Wiig, 1990).

The anatomical structures involved in the comprehension and production of language and speech include the nervous system, the respiratory system, the oral part of the digestive tract, and the auditory sense receptors. These structures are all involved in biological adaptations through breathing, sucking, chewing, swallowing, and alertness to danger signals (Byrne and Shervanian, 1977).

The physical structures involved in the production of speech function in a highly organized and integrated fashion. Each part is synchronized with other parts to produce a meaningful sequence of accurate speech sounds while maintaining proper levels of loudness, pitch, and a pleasing voice quality (Byrne and Shervanian, 1977).

Speech is produced in an airstream that is shaped and resonated by the lips, tongue, teeth, jaw, nasal cavity, larynx and pharynx. Figure 6-1 shows the organs and musculature of speech.

Simply stated, the physiological process of speech involves three stages — vocalization, articulation, and modulation (Byrne and Shervanian, 1977). **Vocalization** is the ability to produce sound. **Articulation** involves the generation of speech sounds by modifications of the vocal tract, which consists basically of the mouth and nasal and pharyngeal cavities. Changes in placement and manner of articulators (lips, teeth, tongue, palate, pharynx) cause changes in speech sounds (Moores, 1987). For example, /t/ and /d/ are formed by closing the lips and then opening them to allow air to escape. The only difference between /t/ and/d/ or /p/ and /b/ is that /d/ and /b/ are voiced, while /t/ and /p/ are voiceless. **Modulation** is the ability to control the loudness of the sounds produced. Within these major processes, respiration, phonation, and resonance are the main components of the speech process.

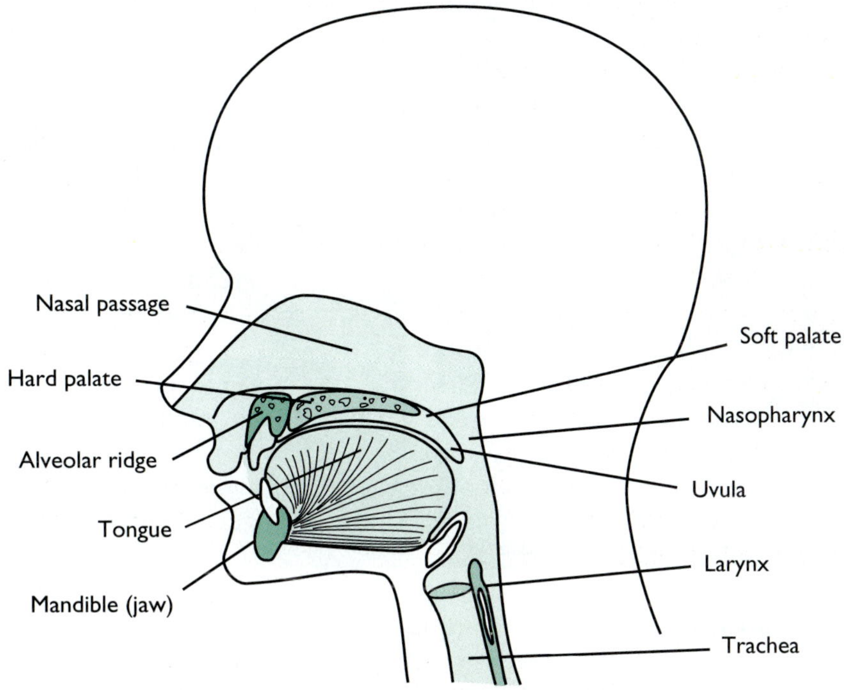

Figure 6-1
The sound-producing mechanism in humans

Respiration provides the air stream from which speech is developed; it depends on the lungs and various muscular and skeletal elements. Phonation, or vocal tone production, depends on the larynx, which produces a vibrating air stream (Moores, 1987). The larynx produces sound, and the pharynx modifies it, providing resonance. (In addition to voice production, the larynx functions in crying, in keeping foreign objects out of the lungs, in coughing, and as a regulator of the exchange of oxygen and carbon dioxide in breathing (Leonard, 1982). The pharynx changes its shape, size, and tension, and combines with the nose or mouth to form the resonating chambers for speech. As the larynx and resonating cavities develop, the voice becomes louder, the pitch becomes lower, and the vocal tone increases in variety and range of inflectional patterns.

Speech and Language Development

Language acquisition overlaps and relies upon social and cognitive growth. These aspects of development are closely intertwined, and really cannot be considered separately. Further, it is extremely difficult to separate speech and language development in the early years because language usage is expressed so cogently in speech forms in most children.

Language is first and foremost a social behaviour. At the outset, the quality of adult-child interactions is the single most important influence on the child's language development. Comprehensive studies of early language development clearly demonstrate the importance of mother's talk to infants (Stern, 1977). Child-adult communicative interaction is sometimes called **motherese**, which is characterized by rather unique alterations in speech, meaning, form, and even language usage. When interacting with infants, both adults and children tend to use what are called register changes — a

Early stimulation from parents and siblings aids in an infant's language acquisition.

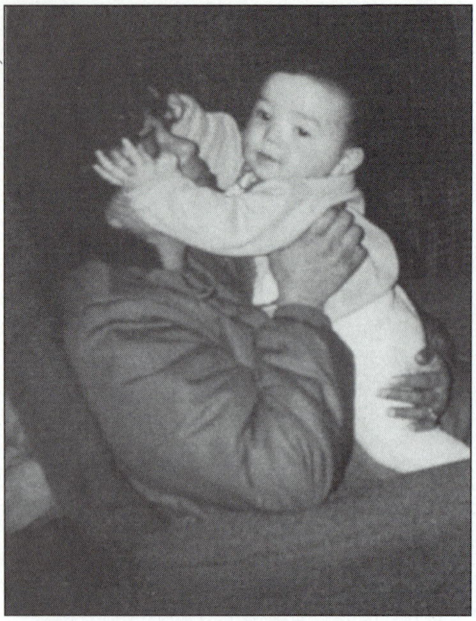

higher pitch, exaggerated intonation, clear enunciation, a slower rate with more pauses between utterances, simplified speech sounds, repeated syllables, and simplified syntax.

Without social interaction, language acquisition will be hindered or halted. Two children in quite different eras who were deprived of early stimulation are described in the profiles that follow.

Profile

Genie

The story of Genie illustrates the severe effects of emotional and social deprivation on language and speech development. Genie's father believed her to be hopelessly retarded, and from the time she was twenty months old, he confined her to a small room. The room was barren, completely unfurnished save for a small crib entirely covered with wire mesh, and an infant potty. During the day, the child was strapped in the crib or tied to the potty chair. At night she was stuffed into a sleeping bag specially made to restrain her.

Genie's father never spoke to her and beat her if she made any noise. Sometimes, he pretended he was a dog, barking and growling and sometimes scratching the child with his fingernails. Genie's mother could only visit her for a few minutes each day to feed her. There was no radio or television in the house.

When Genie was thirteen and a half, the parents had an especially violent fight and the mother left. At about this time, in November 1970, Genie was discovered by the California authorities. Her father committed suicide on the day he was to be brought to trial.

When she was found, Genie weighed a mere 27 kg and was 137 cm tall. She could not chew solid food, was not toilet trained, was unable to stand erect, and could only shuffle, not walk. Genie was mute and could only understand a few simple commands. She appeared to have no comprehension of grammmar. However, when tested at the hospital, Genie was found to have normal hearing, vision, and eye-hand co-ordination.

Genie was placed with a foster family who treated her much as they would a normal child. She began to develop speech, following a normal course of language development but with marked differences. After seven years of language acquisition, Genie continued to have articulation problems. She used two hundred words before she began making two-word combinations. She did not ask questions spontaneously and she demonstrated inconsistencies in word order.

After many years of working with Genie, language therapists concluded that failure to acquire language during the normal period makes development laborious and incomplete, but that the similarities between delayed and normal acquisition outweigh the differences (de Villiers and de Villiers, 1978).

Victor

Jean Marc Gaspard Itard (1755-1838), a French physician, is remembered for his intervention with Victor, the so-called wild boy of Aveyron. The boy was caught in the woods, and was reported to have been raised by wolves. When the lad finally reached Paris on Bastille Day, 1800, he was placed in the school for the deaf because of his muteness. Itard called him Victor, perhaps in anticipation of the victory that education would achieve (Seguin, 1864).

Victor was stunted in growth, with a light complexion and scarred, pockmarked skin — probably the result of the smallpox he had caught in captivity. A huge scar ran across his larynx, suggesting that his throat had been cut before he was abandoned in the forest (Lane and Pillard, 1978). Instead of resembling Rousseau's "noble savage," the boy was dirty, incapable of focusing attention, and insensitive to the basic sensations of heat and cold. He lapped his food, uttered inarticulate sounds, fixated on empty space, bit people who came too close, and spent most of his time sleeping or rocking back and forth. Observers concluded that Victor's constitution was defective; the boy was not an idiot because he had been left in the wilds, but had been left in the wilds because he was an idiot.

Itard could not accept that Victor was irreversibly idiotic. Instead, he believed that the child was mentally arrested due to social and educational neglect; Victor had acquired idiocy through isolation, suffering a sort of mental atrophy from disuse of his senses. Despite Victor's appearance and lack of responsiveness, Itard believed that appropriate environmental conditions could humanize the boy and decided to try to educate him rather than sending him to a lunatic hospital.

Itard began his work with little concept of the complexities involved in working with a severely handicapped child. Using crude diagnostic methods, he determined that Victor's sense organs were intact, though "dull" or insensitive. Victor would not, for example, respond to loud noises, not even to the sound of a pistol shot. On the other hand, he would react to such subtle signals as the cracking of a walnut.

Itard used a variety of means to make Victor aware of sensation — hot baths, massages, tickling, emotional excitement, even electric shock. Along with sensory stimulation and discipline, Itard presented Victor with a systematic series of specific sense training activities designed to improve his visual, auditory, and motor skills. He taught the activities in order and at a variable rate tailored to fit Victor's progress. Especially, Itard tried to teach the boy to communicate through speech and sign language.

In time, Victor became moderately socialized but not, as Itard had naively hoped, normal. Victor's ability to communicate continued to increase, and he learned the basic skills of eating and dressing. Nevertheless, after five years, Itard concluded that his work had been a failure and left Victor in the care of a friendly housekeeper.

Speech development begins with the first sound following the birth cry and ends with full articulatory control. Infants begin to experiment with sound in the early months of life and increase their sound-making capacity in conjunction with other aspects of development, specifically neural, motor, and social. In the very early stages, speech and motor development are seen as occurring in a synchronous fashion so that acquisition follows an orderly progression, with advances in speech and motor skills intertwined to a considerable extent.

Newborns have a limited range of vocalizations. They cry, burp, cough, and make a few other sounds. For the later development of language, cooing is the most important. Cooing is the production of clear vowels, often in isolation. By their eighth week, infants can usually produce various vowel and consonant sounds. As the infant approaches the six-month mark, the nature of cooing changes and consonant-vowel patterns begin to appear.

This incorporation of vowel and consonant sounds is known as babbling — random sound play of almost infinite variety. Babbling is an almost universal response during infancy and does not seem to require exposure to language or other environmental auditory input. Even deaf infants babble although they do not babble in the same way; their babbling is substantially delayed (Oller and Eilers, 1988; Stoel-Gammon and Otomo, 1986) and these sounds usually stop around one year of age (Pettito and Marenette, 1991). The exceptions to the universal nature of babbling behaviour are autistic and neurologically damaged children who may not babble at all.

There is considerable controversy over the relationship between babbling and later speech. Most researchers now believe that babbling and early speech are one continuous phenomenon (Gleason, 1985; Vihman, 1986) and that the babbling stage is a period of "tuning up" and establishing the necessary integrations between hearing/listening and sound production. Even if the sounds of babbling don't approximate speech, the intonation of babbling does. Babbling also helps to develop the musculature of the lips and the mouth necessary for the later articulation of speech sounds (Mysak, 1982).

At the same time that infants begin to babble, they also show the first indications of comprehension. Babies at about six months of age begin to associate certain sounds with people, events, and objects in the environment. Infant signals also take on a relatively consistent form and are produced in the expectation that they will promote a consistent response (see Roug, Lundberg, and Lundberg, 1989).

Because they require finer motor control of the tongue and lips, consonant sounds are more difficult to produce than vowel sounds. Once infants are using consonants in their babbling, they attempt to imitate adult sounds. At about eight months of age, infants begin to use echolalic speech, or **echolalia** — speech that is an immediate imitation of that of some other speaker. Soon infants move into the jargon stage; they begin to imitate adults consistently and are able to reproduce the intonation patterns or melodies of the language they hear.

At around one year of age, two new developments occur — expressive intonation in babbling and first words. By ten or eleven months children are babbling in sentences, combining several incomprehensible "words" and uttering them with correct inflections (Reich, 1986). At the same time, children are having a great many experiences with listening to language, and they rapidly become adept at discerning meaning from contextual as well as voice clues. Children show comprehension of words; they learn to follow simple directions and associate many environmental clues with speech that they have heard and with gestures (Acredolo and Goodwyn, 1988).

After months of coaxing and prompting the meaningless babble of their babies, parents are rewarded by the emergence of the first word. First words emerge when there is sufficient mastery of articulatory mechanisms to produce clusters of phonemes (Mysak, 1976), usually at the end of the first year, when the infant's motor system for speech production has become co-ordinated with breath control and the movements of lips and tongue. The age for first words ranges from nine to nineteen months for normal children. As children move into using single words, there is a corresponding decrease in babbling.

Children's first single-word utterances are remarkably efficient and maximally communicative. The speech has been called **holophrasic**, because a single word is used to express a more complex idea. Although the first words may differ markedly from adult pronunication, they are likely to be simplifications of adult usage involving the omission of final consonants, the reduction of consonant clusters, the omission of unstressed syllables, or the reduplication of syllables (Lindfors, 1987). Single words are used for naming favourite toys or foods, family members, or pets, and to make requests, comments, and enquiries. Children also incorporate single-word approximations of frequently used adult phrases such as "all gone" or "bad boy."

Several weeks after the first word, vocabulary begins to grow quite rapidly as new words are learned daily. Children learn to produce about fifty words before they string them together. Between eighteen and twenty-four months of age, they begin to combine words. These early phrases (presentences) are the precusors of true sentences. For example, the child may express phrases such as: "Me fall," "Bump table," "Daddy no," "Car now," or "No more milk." Children show a wide range of variation in the number of presentences they use. Some children use only a few; others as many as a thousand (Byrne and Shervanian, 1977).

The sentence is the key landmark in language acquisition. The first true sentences used by small children are described as **telegraphic speech** because they resemble a telegram in that only the essential aspects of the message, those possessing meaning, are included. In these utterances, children begin to use syntax and morphology. They also use inflections to signify plurality, possession, verb tense, subject-verb agreement, and comparative and superlative forms of adjectives. Children at this stage also use function words such as *in* and *on*, and the articles, *a*, *an*, and *the*.

By the time they are using simple sentences at about two years of age, children are about 70 to 80 percent intelligible in their speech. However, the full development of all of the sounds of English is a slow process. It is not until they are about eight years old that children are able to produce all the speech sounds: vowels, consonants, dipthongs, and blends.

By three years of age, most children demonstrate the construction of simple affirmative-declarative sentences. They put together a noun phrase for a subject and a verb phrase for a predicate (Elliot, 1981). As syntax develops, the child learns how to change word order and add and replace words to express more complex grammatical relationships. These changes are called transformations; as syntax becomes more complex, many transformations are used within the same utterances.

In first using language, young children tend to regularize the language because they have not yet learned the exceptions. A small child is likely to say, "He runned," or "He hurt hisself." As well, small children often reach beyond the borders of word meaning and overextend their word usage, as in the little boy who calls every animal a doggie.

Between the third and fourth year, language is established in all its main forms. Children at this age are able to describe the events of the past and expectations of the future as well as present experiences. Increasingly, too, they become aware of their listener's needs for information and are soon able to communicate with people outside their immediate families.

By the age of four, most children have achieved a great deal of language maturity. They have usually mastered the basic structures of their language and have developed an array of conversational skills that enable them to engage in extensive social and play interactions with their peers and others in the environment.

Pronunciation improves as children gain greater control over the speech mechanisms. Speech is now more than 90 percent intelligible. Children still have have difficulty with /r/, /s/, /j/, and /z/, and blends such as /ch/ and /sh/. The last English sound that most children acquire is the /zh/ as in *leisure* and *measure*.

By the time they arrive at school at about five years of age, children have a firm linguistic base, with a sophisticated grasp of semantic and syntactic rules, and an ever-expanding vocabulary. Six-year-olds are sophisticated language users. They can not only talk better, but they have become aware of how language is used. They can recognize its nuances, and begin to take delight in jokes and riddles that rely on ambiguity (de Villiers and de Villiers, 1978).

Compared to language during the preschool years, language during the school years is complex and sophisticated. In school-aged children, the developmental emphasis moves from semantics and syntax to metalinguistics and pragmatics. Once in school, children require a variety of language functions, a greater variety of discourse styles and organization, more abstract vocabulary, more complex syntax, and the ability to reflect on all the aspects of language (metalinguistics) (Westby, 1992). They need to recognize instructional discourse — the language that gives them information about the curriculum and feedback on their efforts in mastering it.

During middle childhood, children correct many of their syntactical errors and begin to use a number of complex grammatical forms that did not appear in their earlier speech, such as personal pronouns and passive voice. They develop metalinguistic skills, the ability to think about language. For example, nine-year-olds are more likely than five-year-olds to recognize grammatical errors in sentences and to be able to correct them.

Speech and Language Difficulties

Learning to communicate and understand the communication of others is one of the biggest challenges young children face. It is little surprise, then, that delays and disorders in speech and language are the most common and varied disabilities that teachers of young children will encounter. Teachers may see children with phonological or articulation disorders or with voice problems, children who stutter, some who have delayed or deviant language, and some who have difficulties in expressive or receptive modes. Most often, there is a combination of these problems. Speech and language difficulties often spill over to affect other areas of a child's functioning. Children with speech problems may talk only when absolutely necessary because of the negative feedback they have received in the past; they would rather respond with a shake of the head or a shrug. As well, children who are not successful in communication often demonstrate negative, resistant, or attention-getting behaviour (Owens, 1991).

Communication disorders encompass a wide range of problems in speech, language, and hearing. Within this generic classification, we find speech disorders and language delays and disorders. Speech problems include delayed onset of speech, speech usage below age-level expectations, oddities in articulation, peculiar usage of grammar, stuttering, unusual intonations or voice quality, paucity of speech, inability to recall familiar words, poor self-expression, or total absence of speech (Chess and Rosenberg, 1974). Language disorders include delayed language, different language, deviant language, or even no language. Typically, language disorders are more complex in identification, diagnosis, and remediation than are speech problems.

The overlap between speech and language is considerable. For clarity, however, we describe speech and language disorders separately.

Table 6-1

Signs and effects of communication disorders

Disorder	Signs	Effects
Language delay	More than six months behind norm in reaching language milestones	Slower in the all elements of language acquisition and usage
Language disorders	May show impaired comprehension and poor verbal expression	Failure to understand instructions; withdrawal from group situations
Aphasia	Impaired reception or production of oral language	Failure to understand speech or to produce meaningful sentences
Apraxia	Inability to sequence the muscle movements needed for speech	Failure to produce meaningful speech
Articulation disorders	Abnormal production of speech sounds; speech not typical of chronological age	May be ridiculed by peers; may have decoding and comprehension problems with respect to specific words
Dysfluency	Impaired fluency and rhythm	Peer ridicule, oral difficulties
Voice disorders	Abnormal vocal quality, pitch, loudness, or duration	Self-confidence may suffer; withdrawal
Orofacial defects	Variety of clefts, such as cleft lip or cleft palate	May have problems in feeding, speech, or respiration
Dysarthria	Paralysis of the muscles associated with speech	Distorted speech

Definitions of Language Problems

Language problems encompass a range of difficulties with the linguistic code, or with the rules for linking the symbols and the symbol sequences. Children who demonstrate significant lags but whose language is still progressing according to the stages of normal language development are said to have **language delays**.

Language disorders are more complex. As defined by the American Speech and Hearing Association (1982), **language disorders** refer to impairment or deviant development of comprehension or of the use of a spoken, written, or other symbol system. These disorders may involve form, content, function, or any combination of these. *Form* refers to phonological, morphological, and syntactical elements. *Content* is semantics, and *function* refers to pragmatics.

Prevalence of Language Problems

Researchers and practitioners are no more adept at estimating the number of students with language delays and disorders than they are at pinpointing numbers for other forms of disability. The prevalance issue is particularly confused for language problems because:

- Researchers disagree on the definition and classification of language problems. Many types of speech and language disorders remain ambiguous and controversial; no consensus has been reached concerning the patterns of subtypes of language impairments or the criteria for classification.
- Many other terms are used to describe language disorders. These include *aphasia, dysphasia, communicatively impaired*, and *language learning disabled*. Some clinicians prefer the terms *aphasia* or *dysphasia* because they suggest fairly specific conditions. Others prefer the use of the general term *language disabled*.
- Surveys of language problems are often based on interviews of questionable validity, and there is likely a tendency to under-report the presence of communication disorders.
- Some researchers (e.g. Shames and Wiig, 1982) define a language disorder as a form of speech disorder. Of children with speech disorders, they claim that 3 to 5 percent have language disabilities. Others (e.g. de Villiers and de Villiers, 1978) define language problems as separate from speech disorders. They estimate that 12 percent of children with communication problems have language delays or disorders.
- Children in other categories of exceptionality often have language problems. For example, learning-disabled students more often than not demonstrate deviations or delays in language; children who are intellectually disabled do not develop language commensurate with their intellectual ability; language problems are the chief difficulty of hearing-impaired children.

As far as prevalence is concerned, the most we can say is that the overall number for communication disorders of all types may be as high as 12 to 15 percent, and speech and language disorders are estimated at about 5 percent of school-aged children ("Children with communication," 1995). On most measures of language production, girls are more proficient than boys, middle-class children more proficient than lower-income children, first-borns more proficient than later-borns, single-borns more proficient than twins. Of all language-disabled students, about two-thirds are boys (Silva, 1980).

Classification of Language Problems

In general, language problems relate to disorders in the recognition and understanding of spoken language or in the ability to formulate well-organized grammatical sentences. As we noted, children may be characterized as having delayed or disordered language, a distinction that depends on the type, intensity, and duration of the difficulties.

Language disorders may also be classified as receptive or expressive. **Receptive disorders** are those that interfere with the comprehension of spoken language; **expressive disorders** are those that affect the formulation of grammatic utterances. Language disorders in children frequently combine both receptive and expressive problems. They range in severity from mild language learning difficulties to profoundly debilitating disorders.

Delayed Language Development

A child with delayed language development learns language in an orderly progression but more slowly and less proficiently than normal age peers. Minor delays in language development may be caused by generalized immaturity rather than a pervasive language problem. Clinicians sometimes use the "rule of six" in defining language delays; that is, if a child's language development lags six months behind what is considered to be normal, the child is said to have a delay. Many young children who show minor delays catch up with their peers by the time they are five or six. Other children with language delays may not close the gap in functioning.

Delays and disorders in speech and language are the most common and varied disabilities that teachers of young children will encounter.

Language Deviations (Disorders)

Some children show such difficulties in developing language in a normal progression that they may never attain adult levels. Some language-disordered children may demonstrate bizzare language behaviour. The great majority meet such difficulties with acquisition that they require structured and systematic intervention. Many children show deviant language as part of other disabling conditions.

Aphasia

Aphasia is a condition in which a child's primary impairment is the inability to communicate effectively with verbal language because of comprehension and/or production difficulties. Aphasia may be developmental (often referred to as dysphasia) or acquired.

Children with developmental aphasia show severe delays in the development of receptive and expressive language but do not suffer from any apparent additional disabling conditions (Eisenson and Ingram, 1972). **Acquired aphasia** refers to conditions (trauma) that occur after language has been developed. Acquired aphasia is a loss in linguistic ability that usually results from brain damage arising from serious illness, trauma to the head, or stroke. Verbal output and understanding are diminished but not always altogether absent (Leonard, 1982).

Aphasia is also classified as receptive or expressive. Receptive aphasia, the inability to understand speech symbols, is usually accompanied by some expressive difficulty. Children with receptive aphasia appear to talk in a free-flowing manner, but their words are incomprehensible. Expressive aphasia manifests itself as trouble remembering words (dysnomia), blocking on a word, and hesitating often when speaking. Severe global aphasia (both expressive and receptive present) refers to a condition where individuals experience a variety of other perceptual problems, even though they have normal physical sight and hearing (Byrne and Shervanian, 1977; Mysak, 1976).

Etiology of Language Problems

Many factors account for language problems. The most prominent are brain dysfunction, psychological problems, and dialect. The latter are discussed in Chapter 14 on developmentally disabled children and Chapter 8 on children from diverse cultural backgrounds.

There are at least three well-established major language areas in the left hemisphere of the brain. The major sites for language and speech, Wernicke's area and Broca's area, are connected by a thick band of fibres. The standard model for language holds that language making and comprehension arise in Wernicke's area and then travel via the pathway to Broca's, where they call up the program that causes the phrases to be spoken (Phillips, 1990).

Neurological dysfunction underlies the most severe types of speech and language disorders. Damage to the speech/language centres of the brain can lead to aphasia or generalized communication disorders with varying characteristics depending on the site of the lesion.

In acquired aphasia, the age of onset is a critical factor. In children as young as four, evidence exists that the hemispheres of the brain process symbolic communication differently, with left hemisphere dominance in speech and language. With age, the brain becomes fixed and the various functions cannot be easily assumed by the other related segment of the brain. It is assumed that by about school age the brain has lost much of the organic plasticity found in young children. In adults functional locational phenomena are even more pronounced and adults are less able to recover functions lost through brain injury than are children. Nevertheless, many adults recover completely when they suffer serious brain damage of the left hemisphere (Snow, 1987).

Children who sustain injuries before the age of three may become temporarily mute and show a general inability to respond to the speech of others. However, very young children often make rapid improvement. They seem to relearn language in the same sequence as children acquiring language for the first time. In children over three years, symptoms of aphasia are usually different. These children may find it hard to retrieve words they have used only moments earlier. Recovery is slower and residual problems are likely to remain.

Disruptions in early social interactions may contribute to the particular difficulties experienced by some children. Language disorders may be exacerbated by the child's interactions with the family. Children who are neglected, for example, show delays in language development (Allen and Wasserman, 1985). Children with other disabilities are doubly disadvantaged because the original disability may lead to secondary language problems. Disabled children may have fewer opportunities to learn the social, play, and communication skills that are unique to and emerge from child-child social interchange (Guralnick, 1986) and from adult-child interaction. They may hear less language than other children; adults tend to speak less to non-verbal or low-verbal children but to talk more *for* them. Parents of children with language disorders also engage in fewer play and language activities. Mothers claim their children do not enjoy these games, but reluctance to interact seems reciprocal (Leonard, 1982).

Studies of Down syndrome children suggest that their language acquisition and development is essentially similar to the language development of non-retarded children (Tager-Flusberg et al., 1990). They follow the same general path in acquiring language as do normally developing children, but their language lags behind their non-verbal cognitive abilities and may proceed at a slower rate. In social interactions with their mothers, Down syndrome infants show atypical interactive behaviours when compared with normal infants matched for mental age (Coggins and Morrison, 1981), and this may contribute to the language delays seen in these children. Other studies have found that mothers of three-month-old infants with minor facial anomalies (cleft lip and palate) were less active during interactions with their infants than were mothers of normal infants (Barden et al., 1989).

Speech Disorders

There are a huge variety of **speech disorders**, problems encountered in the oral production of language. All speech disorders, however, have one thing in common — an impairment of verbal communication such that the intelligibility of spoken language is reduced. "Speech is abnormal when it deviates so far from the speech of other people that it calls attention to itself, interferes with communication, or causes the speaker or his listeners to be distressed" (Van Riper and Emerick, 1990, p. 34).

Speech disorders should not be confused with the speech errors that all young children make when learning to talk. In small children, mispronunciations and dysfluencies are common; children are about eight years of age before they are stable in all the sounds of the English language. Mispronunciations and dysfluencies only become disorders when they persist as characteristics in the speech of children who should have acquired certain sounds. We would worry more, for example, about the seven-year-old who talks about his "Wittle wellow wabbit" than the child of the same age who could not get her tongue around the /zh/ in *leisure* and *measure* (Winzer, 1995).

Prevalence of Speech Disorders

In concert with language problems, reliable figures on the prevalence of speech disorders among children are difficult to obtain. This happens for several reasons:

- Criteria and definitions of communication disorders vary.
- Many speech problems, such as articulation problems, simply disappear as children mature. When minor delays are due to general immaturity, most children catch up with their peers without special intervention.
- Prevalence varies according to age. Milisen (1971) estimates that 12 to 15 percent of children in kindergarten to grade four suffer speech problems. In grades five to eight, the proportion drops to 4 to 5 percent and this remains constant after grade eight unless treatment intervenes.
- Estimates of the prevalence of voice disorders similarly depend on the age group surveyed and the criteria used to define abnormalities (Eisenson and Ogilvie, 1983). However, children in the lower grades of school are likely to present more voice disorders (Moore, 1986).
- Speech problems are more common among boys than girls, especially in the early grades (Eisenson, 1971) and this is particularly true in the case of stuttering.

In 1986, 17 percent of Canadian children aged 5 to 14 with disabilities were reported to have a speech disorder (Nessner, 1990). Articulation problems are the most usual type of communication disorder; approximately 75 percent of speech disorders are articulation disorders. Clefts occur in approximately one in every 750 live births (Moran and Pintz, 1995). Incidence rates are higher among Native Americans and Asians, lower among Blacks (McWilliams, Morris, and Shelton, 1990). Among Black babies, the ratio is one in every 1000 to 1500. Usually more males than females are affected, except in the rare condition of a cleft palate only, in which case more females are affected. Clear prevalence figures are also available for stutterers, who make up about 1 percent of the entire population.

Classification of Speech Disorders

There are many ways to classify speech disorders. For the sake of clarity and simplicity, we focus on specific major areas — articulation problems, voice disorders, problems with speech flow, orofacial defects, and problems associated with muscle control.

Articulation Disorders

The terms *articulation disorder* and *phonological disorder* are often used synonymously although they refer to slightly different problems. Phonological difficulties are present if a person does not understand how to use speech sounds according to linguistic rules and to communicate meaning accurately. When a child has a sound and pronounces it correctly in some contexts but not in others, the child has a phonological problem. Children with phonological impairments are aware of the effect of their errors on a listener's comprehension and will make adjustments to enhance verbal comprehension (Owens 1991).

Articulation problems are present if an individual cannot or does not understand how to actually make speech sounds. With an articulation disorder, the child cannot produce the sound. Children with articulation disorders, particularly those with multiple sound errors, also have difficulties with comprehension, syntax, and vocabulary (Bernthal and Bankson, 1981). Disorders result from changes in the placement and manner of articulators that cause changes in speech sounds. These may have started as errors in sound production that were the result of inadequate co-ordination of oral and facial muscles and that became habitual. Some articulation errors result from problems such as cleft palate, but in the large majority of cases, such defects are not present and the disorders appear to result from deficiencies in learning (Winitz, 1975).

Articulation disorders are characterized by omissions, substitutions, distortions, and additions of speech sounds which may occur in the initial, medial, or final position in a word. The most commonly misarticulated sounds are /s/, /z/, voiceless /th/ as in *bath*, /r/, /l/, /sh/, and /j/ as in *judge* (Gearheart, Mullen, and Gearheart, 1993).

Omission errors are those in which one or more sounds are left out of words — *pay* for *play* or *kool* for *school*, for example. Omissions of speech sounds occur most frequently with blended sounds, such as /bl/,/pl/, /pr/, and /tr/. When words begin with a double consonant such as /st/, /dr/, or /sm/, children may drop one sound so that *smell* becomes *mell* or *break* become *reak*.

Substitutions of speech sounds occur when one consonant is replaced by another — /b/ for /v/, /w/ for /r/, or /w/ for /l/. A lisp is a substitution where /th/ is used for /s/ or /z/. Some children may substitute sounds in some words but not in others. A child may be able to say the word *yes* correctly, but substitute /l/ for /y/ in the word *yellow*.

Distortions involve deviations from normal speech sounds, often caused by placing the tongue or lips in the wrong position for the production of a particular sound. Addition of sounds refers to the adding of a sound to a word. The extra sounds are usually added between blended sounds such as *terain* for *train*.

Voice Disorders

Voice disorders are probably the least understood of all the various communication disorders. A voice that lacks power, is unpleasant, or abuses the vocal mechanism is likely to be considered defective (Perkins, 1978). The child who 'talks through the nose' has hypernasal speech. This may result from a cleft palate, or from partial paralysis of the soft palate rendering the necessary closure of the nasal passages impossible.

Voice disorders include hoarseness (too nasal or rough), breathiness, loudness (too loud or too soft), pitch (too high or too low), and sudden breaks in pitch. They are frequently combined with other speech problems to form a complex communication disorder. Deviations may impair both speaking and singing.

The most common deviations in pitch seen by speech and language clinicians are levels that are too high or low and levels that are monotonous with little variation of pitch (Moore, 1982). Children who do nor speak loudly enough for their needs may suffer from hearing loss, an organic disorder, or reticence about speaking. Some children do not know how to use a "big" voice without abusing the vocal mechanism (Moore, 1982).

For some people, pitch problems are caused by too small a larynx (too high) or too large a larynx (too low). Some may result from overall slow maturation. In children, however, most voice disorders are functional, related to poor learning of voice control. Children who scream or talk loudly are in danger of abusing their vocal cords (Perkins, 1978). Vocal abuse can lead to vocal nodules or polyps that may have to be removed surgically.

Dysfluency

Fluency is the smooothness with which sounds, syllables, words, and phrases flow together; the opposite, dysfluency, describes conditions in which the flow of speech is interrupted with blocking, repetitions, or prolongations of sounds, words, phrases, or syllables.

Stuttering, the major subcategory of dysfluency (speech flow) disorder, affects approximately one percent of the entire population. Two to ten times more males than females stutter. The condition is not related to social class or cognitive functioning; stuttering is found among all ethnic and socio-economic groups. Many famous people were stutterers, including Aesop, Aristotle, Demosthenes, Charles I, Winston Churchill, Charles Darwin, and George VI (Taylor, 1976).

The earliest age of onset of stuttering is generally around eighteen months, the time children begin to speak in short phrases. However, a child may begin to stutter at any time; the mean age of onset is 3.6 years and the incidence of onset declines each year from 18 months on (Bloodstein, 1975). In some cases, stuttering may progress from a sporadic to a chronic problem. In others, it may spontaneously disappear by adolescence. In another group, stuttering may disappear, only to resurface later.

"Stuttering is a complicated, multidimensional communication problem" (Shames and Wiig, 1990, p. 307). Most researchers agree that stuttering is best explained in terms of a continuum, rather than a limited set of behaviours. At one end is normal dysfluency, which is not stuttering but a part of speech development in young children at about three years of age. The progression is then to primary stuttering, which is characterized by breaks in speech caused by repetitions of syllables and sounds, and sometimes prolongations, but which is not usually accompanied by physical signs. The final stage is secondary stuttering, which is terse, non-fluent speech in which the rate and rhythm are severely affected. Secondary stutterers show symptoms such as eye blinking, head jerking, facial grimaces and tension, other types of body distortions, muscular tension, and forcing when they try to speak. Secondary stuttering is much harder to overcome than primary stuttering.

Cluttering

Cluttered speech should not be confused with stuttering. Cluttering involves rapid, jerky, stumbling speech with marked omissions. Speakers may chip off speech sounds, omit sounds, and have rapid fire bursts of speech.

Cluttered speech shows excessive speed combined with disorganized sentence structure and articulation problems. It lacks appropriate phrasing or grouping of words within an utterance and is difficult to understand. In severe cases, the speech is confused, disorganized, and even chaotic (Van Riper and Emerick, 1990).

Muscle Control

Dysarthria refers to a group of speech disorders resulting from disturbed muscular control over the speech mechanisms (La Pointe, 1982). The articulation of speech sounds is disturbed when there is a partial or complete paralysis of the muscles associated with speech. When a child with dysarthria tries to talk, consonant sounds are distorted and efforts at speech may not be successful. Indeed, the harder the child tries to speak, the more difficult speech becomes.

Apraxia is the inability to program, position, and sequence the muscle movements involved in speech. The child with apraxia can produce the movements involved in articulation, but often fails to combine these movements into meaningful speech (Byrne and Shervanian, 1977).

Orofacial Defects

Clefts are known as midline defects. They are only one of the wide variety of craniofacial anomalies, but they are also one of the most common and generally least severe. There are several patterns of clefting — for example, cleft mandible, double mouth, cleft tongue, cleft uvula, undeveloped tongue, cleft lip, cleft palate, and cleft lip and palate (Shah, 1985). Clefts also vary in severity. A cleft lip can range from a slight notch in the vermillion (coloured portion of the lip) to a complete separation of the lip extending up and into the nose. When there is a cleft lip, the alveolar ridge (upper gum ridge) may also be separated. Lip clefts can occur on one or both sides. Clefts may also be part of a disorder such as Crouzon's disease or Treacher Collins syndrome, both of which are accompanied by facial anomalies.

The palate separates the respiratory and the digestive systems. Many children with clefts are born with a gap in the roof of the mouth (palate) which opens into the nasal cavity. Because of this, children with clefts have problems with swallowing, mastication, and correct respiration. In addition, there may be malocclusion of the teeth. Between 25 and 60 percent of children with cleft palates also suffer from a degree of hearing loss due to intermittent occurrence of middle ear disease (Harrison and Philips, 1971).

Children with clefts may exhibit delayed language development and are more likely to have language-based learning disabilities (Moran and Pintz, 1995). As well, delayed articulation is not uncommon in children with clefts. Children may have difficulty building and sustaining enough air pressure in the mouth to make pressure consonants such as /p/, /b/, /s/, /z/, and /ch/.

Mutism

The condition where there is no voice is known a aphonia. This is different from **mutism**, the total absence of speech.

Mutism is a rare condition, related to severe emotional, neurological, or sensory deficit. The term **elective mutism** describes emotionally disturbed children who do not speak or who speak only in certain circumstances. Elective mutism may be associated with a traumatic event and is always symptomatic of a deep disturbance of psychological functioning.

Etiology of Speech Disorders

Most often, children with articulation and voice disorders do not differ from others in anatomical variables, auditory variables, intelligence, or personality. Nor is there any clear evidence that stutterers are biologically different from non-stutterers. (See Research Notes).

Structural inadequacies are a major cause of speech disorders in children. These may be structural inadequacies in the vocal folds (larynx), tongue, teeth, lips, palate, and resonating cavities. Most defects of this type are of a developmental nature, although they can result from physical injury or disease.

Another cause of speech disorders is damage or maldevelopment of the central and/or peripheral nervous system. Dysarthria, for example, results from a fundamental disturbance in the movement or motoric function brought about by damage to the nervous system. Children with cerebral palsy often suffer from dysarthria. The motor impairment that affects the lips, tongue, jaw, and soft palate hinders the intelligibility of their speech (La Pointe, 1982). Inadequacy of the hearing mechanism, causing hearing impairment, is a third major cause of speech disorders.

The causes of clefts are not known, but it is generally agreed that most result from an interaction of genetic and environmental influences (Moran and Pintz, 1995). Numerous villains have been suggested, including alcohol, aspirin, certain foods, and an excess or lack of vitamin A (Shah, 1985).

Identification and Assessment of Speech and Language Problems

We must identify delays and disorders in speech and language as early as possible because such disorders affect other areas of development, impact negatively on social integration, and hinder educational and personal achievement. Because language and speech are so intimately connected, assessment usually includes both areas. However, language is far more complex both in assessment and remediation.

Robert Owens Jr. (1991) describes the evaluation of language as "part science and part art" (p. 290). This statement reflects the multiple contexts in which communication assessment should be implemented, the variability in children's functioning, the vast range of areas to be assessed, and a relative shortage of appropriate tools. Moreover, the types of measures used, the domains sampled, and the targeted skills are quite different for children with mild delays and for those with severe disabilities of which language is only one component. Students with severe or multiple disabilities may be functioning at prelinguistic or minimally linguistic levels. (See Chapter 15).

Research Notes

Stuttering

One of the most difficult things about stuttering is the inability to confidently point to a precise cause. The search for causes is long-standing and the assumptions underlying the research, theories, and therapies related to stuttering range from obvious to obscure.

Reich (1986) points out that twentieth-century explantions include lack of cerebral dominance, neurotic symptom arising out of psychodynamic conflicts developed in early childhood, biochemical causes, perseveration, lateral auditory dominance, laryngeal dysfunction, and auditory feedback dysfunction. Genetic predisposition has been a popular explanation, but whether there is a predisposition to stuttering behaviour or whether it is learned is debatable. For example, Farber (1981) studied ninety-five sets of identical twins raised apart. A genetic predisposition would find pairs of stutterers, but only five individuals in the group stuttered, and in each case only one member of the pair stuttered. On the other hand, stuttering is found in families. For men who stutter, the chances of their children having the condition is 9 percent for daughters and 22 percent for sons. For stuttering women, the figures are 17 percent for daughters and 36 percent for sons (Andrews et al., 1983).

The current situation in stuttering research is such that "no one can be confident in the measures that form the foundation of current research in and treatment of this disorder" (Ingham, 1990). Probably the most useful approach for understanding stuttering is to view it as a result of multiple causative factors including potential constitutional vulnerability, cumulative results of faulty learning, and resultant apprehension and anxiety related to speech (Perkins, 1990).

Current practices tend to focus on three broad groupings. Some speech pathologists regard stuttering as a symptom of physical impairment or instability; others look at it as a symptom of personal maladjustment or emotional instability; still others are of the opinion that it is symptomatic of neither but simply a form of learned behaviour found in normal individuals.

When stuttering is regarded as a symptom of an underlying emotional problem, psychotherapeutic intervention is in order. The objective of treatment is to eliminate stuttering or decrease its effect. Other treatments include air flow techniques — breathing manoeuvres that release the laryngeal spasm (a locking of the vocal cords as speaking begins), together with stress reduction — and procedures that build confidence and develop self-motivation (Schwartz, 1988). Biofeedback, counselling, and speech therapy are also widely used. Free-token response-cost programs have been used successfully to modify stuttering during speech therapy (Salend and Andress, 1984).

Whatever the intervention, the trend is to attempt to remediate the condition early. Clinicians stress the elimination of stuttered speech at the time it first appears (Onslow, Costa, and Rue, 1990). Many hold that "optimal intervention involves early detection and prevention" and that "less risk is involved in overdiagnosis than underdiagnosis of stuttering" (Moore and Perkins, 1990).

Assessing Language Problems

Language problems are generally assessed by a team comprising a psychologist, a speech clinician, a physician, and possibly an educator or a neurologist. All physical and psychological disturbances to normal language development, such as hearing loss or low IQ, must first be ruled out. Assessment should involve both linguistic and cognitive skills, since both are inherent in language processes.

A comprehensive assessment consists of:

- An interview with the family to gather all pertinent developmental and behavioural data.
- Formal tests to evaluate areas of the child's language abilities and disabilities. Speech pathologists rely heavily on standardized tests to determine the presence or absence of communication disorders (Shames and Wiig, 1990). Standardized language tests are available for both screening and diagnosis. These tests usually include normative data which indicate how children of various ages might be expected to perform. Those children who perform below a certain score on a screening tests are given further testing.
- Informal assessments, including a sample of the child's language. A spontaneous or elicited language sample should consist of at least fifty and preferably a hundred utterances.
- Criterion-referenced tests.
- Observations of children's performances in spontaneous discourse. This includes receptive language comprehension to determine if the child responds appropriately to gestures, words, and short and complex sentences, as well as expressive language and vocabulary to check whether the child uses gestures, noises, jargon, baby talk, and concrete and abstract words.

Assessing Speech Disorders

Assessment of articulatory, voice, and fluency disorders is undertaken by a speech/language therapist in the school or in a clinic setting.

Articulation assessment is a rapid and effective way of obtaining a sample of a child's speech. In its crudest form, the articulation test is a test of the child's ability to pronounce correctly, in the view of the investigator, a certain number of words. Children under age four are usually tested on their ability to echo or imitate the clinician's model. Children over four are usually asked to name either objects or pictures. Older children may be asked to read words or sentences or to describe objects (Byrne and Shervanian, 1977).

During the assessment, the clinician may test the child's production of phonemes in isolation and in the initial, medial, and final position in words. The clinician also tries to determine whether there is a consistency in the child's error patterns. The profile of Benny provides an example of a testing situation and follow-up.

Developmental Consequences

Language is inextricably intertwined with our mental life — our perceiving, remembering, attending, comprehending, and thinking — in short, all of our attempts to make sense of our experiences with the world. All types of speech and language disorders affect the ease with which children can communicate with their world. Children who communicate poorly, whether because of speech problems or language disorders, may be hindered in their academic performance and in almost every aspect of functioning.

Profile

Bennie

Bennie is seven and a half years old with normal hearing and no deviations in his speech mechanisms. When Bennie is nervous or in a hurry, his speech becomes difficult to understand. He is easier to understand when his sentences or replies are short. Bennie is the baby of the family, the youngest of four children. His parents both work outside the home and are away all day. Bennie knows he does not speak clearly. He has told the clinician that he tries hard, but he is bashful about speaking because the children at school make fun of him.

During the assessment, the clinican asked Bennie to name the objects in a series of pictures. Bennie correctly produced all the phonemes in the initial, medial, and final word positions up to approximately the developmental level of a five-year-old. He produced substitutions and distortions of certain sounds, such as /ts/, /s/, and /z/ in all positions. He could not correctly pronounce /th/ and usually substituted an /f/ sound. He also had problems with /r/ sounds and sometimes substituted /w/ for /l/.

Bennie's clinician was not able to detect a clear /s/ in his conversational speech. She tested Bennie more thoroughly for the sounds that were consistently missing or mispronounced, using the Peabody Picture Vocabulary Test, the Illinois Test of Psycholinguistic Abilities, and an Articulation Test of Single Phonemes.

Bennie does not have enough chances to talk at home, and his self-consciousness at school further deprives him of necessary practice. This speech clinician and teacher have decided that he needs individual speech training. They have arranged an hour of speech therapy for him every day at school. Fortunately, Bennie's school has a full-time speech therapist to work with children with speech and language problems.

Bennie's problems are caused by a combination of immaturity, lack of opportunity to practise speaking, and self-consciousness. His clinician has found that he consistently mispronounces the sounds /s/, /th/, /l/ and blended sounds such as /tr/, /pr/, and /cl/. Now she must determine whether he fails to perceive these sounds, or simply mispronounces them. Then she can teach Bennie how to correctly produce the misarticulated sounds and give him a great deal of speaking practice.

Cognitive Development

Children with language disorders often perform within normal limits on non-verbal intelligence tests (Leonard, 1981). Even children with aphasia, dysphasia, and apraxia, caused by a disturbance of brain function, are often near or within normal range in most other respects (Mysak, 1980).

However, many cognitive abilities are clearly language-dependent and children with language problems tend to be more rigid and literal in their thinking. They lack the flexibility required for pretending, for playing word games, for laughing at riddles and jokes, and for effective social interaction.

Language-disabled children may continue to overextend words into inappropriate contexts. For instance, a child may call all liquids that can be poured into a glass "juice" as opposed to milk, water, or soda. Or the child may learn to call all articles of clothing that have sleeves "sleeves" rather than shirts, sweaters, and coats because something about the sleeve is meaningful to the him or her.

Teachers will notice that the vocabulary used by language-impaired children tends to be small, superficial, and reflective of reductions in the development of underlying concepts. Language-impaired children have a tendency to deal with objects or events in wholes rather than parts. When children are asked a question, their replies rarely provide new information related to the topic.

Semantic difficulties are demonstrated in a narrow use of semantic cases, failure to understand verbal directions, failure to fully comprehend conversations, and an inability to synthesize auditorily received information. Students with syntax difficulties use ungrammatical forms, overuse short basic sentences, and have a limited variety of sentence forms. They may lack appropriate pronoun use, misapply articles, and show an inability to sequence information. Problems in the social use of language — pragmatics — are seen in students who fail to communicate intent, show an inability to take turns in conversation, and fail to cue their listeners to the topic of discussion (see Hasenstab, 1985). We discuss language learning disabilities further in Chapter 7.

One of the most potent methods teachers can use to foster language is to ask questions meaningful to the child in a way that activates the child's thinking and promotes problem-solving.

Academic Achievement

As one would expect, children with language problems perform poorly in those aspects of learning that rely on language. Literacy skills suffer because children with problems in language acquisition and use invariably have difficulties learning to read. The abstract and symbolic material that becomes important by about grade four makes it increasingly difficult for children with language disorders to cope with academic subjects (Wiig, 1982).

Neurological disorders such as aphasia have more severe effects. Aphasia in children negatively impacts on comprehension, the formation of grammatic utterances, word usage, and the expression of meaning (Byrne and Shervanian, 1977).

Children with speech disorders are usually painfully aware of the fact. They may react by withdrawing from social contact or by using physical means to gain others' attention. Many children find it so difficult to communicate that they become frustrated, withdrawn, and depressed. Others learn to rely on gesture and body language.

Social and Emotional Development

Any degree of disturbance in our communication with others in the environment has an impact on social adjustment. It is not surprising, then, that there is a relationship between communication disorders, emotional disorders, and behavioural disorders in children and adolescents (Audet et al., 1990).

The research literature "strongly suggests that children with delays or disorders of development in speech or language are "at risk" for both psychiatric and learning disorders" (Baker and Cantwell 1987, p. 546). Immaturity, short attention span, excitability, tantrums and solitary behaviour seem to be characteristic of children with speech and language disorders (Baker, Cantwell, and Mathison, 1980). Children with articulation problems and those with language problems tend to demonstrate a higher prevalence of behaviour problems (Baker and Cantwell, 1982).

More serious psychiatric problems also emerge. When investigators (Gualtieri et al., 1983) surveyed forty consecutive admissions to a child psychiatric inpatient facility, they found — after in-depth speech, language, and intelligence testing — that twenty of the forty had moderate to severe language disorders. "There appears to be a strong association between developmental language deficits and severe psychiatric disorders," they observed, (p. 168) and concluded that "disorders of the development of language are likely to be central to the development of human personality" (p. 169).

Stuttering can lead to serious social and educational problems. Moreover, the longer people stutter, the more likely they are to have associated emotional problems (Shames and Florance, 1982). In general, stutterers tend to be more anxious, less self-confident, and more socially withdrawn than non-stutterers. (Block and Goodstein, 1971). Young stutterers become rapidly aware of listeners' reactions and often feel embarrassed, guilty, frustrated, and angry. Older students may respond to their difficulties with aggression or by denying that they have a problem (Shames and Florance, 1982). Others may avoid situations where talking is expected.

Some children with clefts may meet social discrimination from peers and teachers (Moran and Pinz, 1995). Parents of children with clefts often worry about the physical manifestations and social stigma. Of particular concern to them are the child's appearance; the need for immediate surgery; speech development; feeding; reaction of the spouse, siblings, family and friends; intellectual development; financial considerations; and a recurrence of the defect in future children.

Intervention for Children with Speech and Language Disorders

The goal of any language intervention effort is to enhance a child's ability to use language as an effective means of communication in everyday life.

Language specialists and educators have developed many new forms of treatment for children with speech and language disorders, both for the classroom and for the clinic. Nevertheless, as we observed in the introduction to this chapter, a guaranteed method to correct speech and language difficulties simply does not exist, and diversity in remediation programs characterizes the status quo.

A range of methods are used depending on the needs of the child, the severity of the disability, the setting for intervention, the targeted skills, and the expertise of the teacher. In this section, we provide only an overview of approaches used with children with mild and moderate disabilities. We return to the topic of intervention for children with severe disorders in Chapter 15.

Medical Intervention

Some forms of speech disorders result from structural defects or inadequacies. For these, medical intervention is an important element and often the first step in habilitation. Surgery is used for speech disabilities that result directly from defects of the respiratory, oral, and facial musculature involved in speech production.

Corrective and plastic surgery can largely prevent the wide-ranging speech problems associated with cleft palate and other orofacial defects. Clefts of the primary and secondary palates and velopharyngae (lip and palate) inefficiency require special examinations and treatments by a number of different professionals over many years (Paynter, Jordan, and French, 1990). The lip is typically repaired early in the first year of life. The time for surgical repair of the cleft palate is more variable, but is most commonly performed before the child is two years of age (Moran and Pintz, 1995).

When other facial-skeletal anomalies accompany the cleft palate, prostheses designed to facilitate speech are prescribed. Dental surgery may also be necessary for children with cleft palates.

Therapy

Speech/language pathologists or therapists are concerned with communication, its normal development, and its disorders. They are trained in the evaluation and remedial treatment of speech and language problems in children and adults. In most provinces, a qualified clinician requires a master's degree in speech pathology and a year of closely supervised clinical work. Speech pathologists work as consultants to schools and special education programs; they are also employed in hospitals and rehabilitation centres.

The speech/language pathologist works with teachers to identify potential communication disorders, assesses and diagnoses problems, and plans and recommends intervention activities. The pathologist works with children to teach them how to speak and listen effectively and how to overcome the effects of communication disorders.

To treat articulation disorders, therapists teach children to listen, recognize, and discriminate consonant sounds; to produce articulated speech sounds; and to retain the memory of speech sounds (Winitz, 1975). Major emphases in voice therapy include listening and articulatory adjustments and breath-control training. Breath control includes training to relax and reduce laryngeal tension as well as other specialized techniques (Van Osdol and Shane, 1982).

Although the many studies of the symptoms and treatment of stuttering have not revealed all the possible underlying causes, many effective therapeutic methods have been developed to treat the problem. Psychotherapy, behaviour modification, and biofeedback are used to reduce the intensity of stuttering or eliminate it (Perkins, 1990). Some therapists combine a variety of techniques, including new therapies such as desensitization, parent-child verbal interaction, and fluency shaping (Shames and Florance, 1982). The Research Notes on stuttering outline some of the major treatments.

Technical Intervention

Technology is a boon for individuals unable to use speech. Elaborate computer-driven devices enable disordered children and adults to communicate more complex and subtle messages. These devices offer multiple outputs, such as print-out, screen, or speech synthesized voice. They are easily activated by a variety of volitional movements, including eye control, finger contact, or sipping and puffing on a blow stick. One technique uses a light-sensitive scanner that is interfaced with the computer and detects light from the whites of the eyes of the disabled person. This enables the computer to analyze eye movements that indicate the position of the desired word (Cartwright, Cartwright, and Ward, 1984). Further technical devices are described in the section on augmentative communication in Chapter 15.

Educational Intervention

In many ways, efficient speech and language underlie academic success. The goal of any language intervention effort is to enhance a child's ability to use language as an effective means of communication in everyday life. As well, various communication skills have been found to predict social acceptance in middle childhood (Dodge et al., 1986), and training in communicative skills is used as a means of bolstering peer acceptance in school-aged children. Moreover, "Understanding and correcting deficiencies of language can improve behaviour and help a child resolve at least some of his emotional dilemmas" (Gualtieri et al., 1983, p. 169).

Children with minor speech and language disorders can often receive adequate assistance within the school from a learning-assistance teacher or speech-and-language clinician.

The goal of training for children with mild or moderate delays is not absolutely correct grammar or pronunciation. Training should accelerate general communicative development and help children communicate in a way that is understood by others and that seems comfortable for the child.

Educational Settings

Language develops in the framework of family associations, social interactions, and interpersonal relationships. The key word in recent language intervention trends is *natural.* Natural procedures take place in naturally occurring situations and pay attention to functional communication and conversational skills. As much as possible, settings should be natural environments and all those close to the child — parents, peers, and teacher — should be involved (Bernstein and Tiegerman, 1989; Lahey, 1988). This means that the regular classroom is the most appropriate setting for almost all children with speech and language difficulties as their sole impairment. Special setting considerations may be given to children whose problems arise from hearing disorders (see Chapter 9), neurological dysfunction such as aphasia, or problems so severe that functioning is at prelinguistic or minimally linguistic levels (see Chapter 15).

In most cases, children with minor disorders are in regular classrooms and may have extra support from a speech clinician, a school counsellor, an experienced aide, or volunteers. Very occasionally, a language centre/class managed by a specially trained language teacher may be in operation within a regular school. This environment allows for individualized programming and therapy, and small group experiences. The curriculum includes a range of oral and written language activities and academic subjects at the child's level (MacDonald, 1985).

Educational Approaches

All educational approaches attempt to improve a child's linguistic competence. Although some approaches are designed for special classes or clinics, contemporary intervention, as we have just seen, focuses on natural interaction in natural settings — that is, intervention from the teacher in the regular classroom. The major approaches can be grouped as diagnostic-prescriptive, syntax-based, performance-oriented, or interpersonal-interactive.

The regular classroom is the most appropriate setting for almost all children with speech and language difficulties as their only impairment.

- *Diagnostic-prescriptive approaches* are designed for specialized settings. There are two forms of the diagnostic-prescriptive approach — the process or ability model and the task analysis model (Wiig, 1982).

  In the process or ability model, intervention focuses on all the abilities involved in perceiving and discriminating speech, interpreting spoken language, and formulating language and speech. Intervention may also encompass short- and long-term memory, verbal reasoning, word retrieval, and the visual and motor processes involved in speaking, reading, and writing (Wiig, 1982). In the task analysis model, every task involved in speech, language, and communication becomes the focus of intervention. The task analysis approach is often derived from the child's performance on criterion-referenced tests, such as the Clinical Evaluation of Language Functions (CELF) (Semel and Wiig, 1980).
- *Syntax-based programs* may be taught in regular classrooms or special settings. Syntactic disorders seem to respond best to direct teaching, and direct language instruction might be initially used to introduce a new structure that can then be generalized through the use of more interactive techniques.

  Programs based on syntax teach the child specific language structures, such as subject, verb, and object, and word order relationships, such as question forms. Studies have shown that these structured language programs are effective with linguistically delayed children (Illebrun and Leong, 1981).

  A number of commercial tests and programs support syntax-based programs. For example, the Language Assessment, Remediation and Screening Procedures (LARSP) (Crystal, Fletcher, and Garman, 1976) provides a systematic methodology for the description and treatment of syntactical problems. The Fokes Sentence Builder (1976) is another example of a syntax-based remedial language program. SOS — Sound, Order, Sense (Semel, 1970) is designed to help children to develop listening skills in order to better comprehend spoken language. Stress is on perception, order, and the sense of what is being said.
- *Performance-oriented approaches*, which attempt to modify, decrease, or increase language behaviours, are designed for regular classrooms. Intervention is aimed at overt, measurable disordered communication behaviours. Since much language is learned by imitation, imitation and modelling of correct communication behaviours are stressed. The teacher may say "Show me —," or "You say this now." Teachers also use expansions to promote language development. For example, the child

may say "Car go," and the teacher expands it to "Yes, the car goes." When teachers or parents use expansions, the complexity of children's language increases more rapidly over time (e.g. Hoff-Ginsberg, 1986).

In paraphrasing, the adult repeats a statement or question to elicit a reply — responding, for example, to "Want ball," with "Do you want the ball?" Extension follows the child's statement with different words. For example, if a child says "I miss the bus," the teacher may respond with, "You missed the bus. Were you late for the dentist?" Using recast sentences involves repeating or restating of a child's words in the correct form.

Experiential units are part of the performance approach. The teacher may modify instruction to focus on tasks such as building things, setting up household tasks, or preparing food. This gives a child constant repetition of specific language.

- *Interpersonal-interactive approaches,* also used in regular classrooms, aim to strengthen a child's ability to use language and to develop communicative competence. Children learn what language is by learning what language can do. Specific objectives include helping the child to interpret contextual clues, strengthening role-taking and role-playing abilities, and increasing the range of verbal and nonverbal communication styles (Wiig, 1982).

Curricula

Figure 6-2
Curriculum components

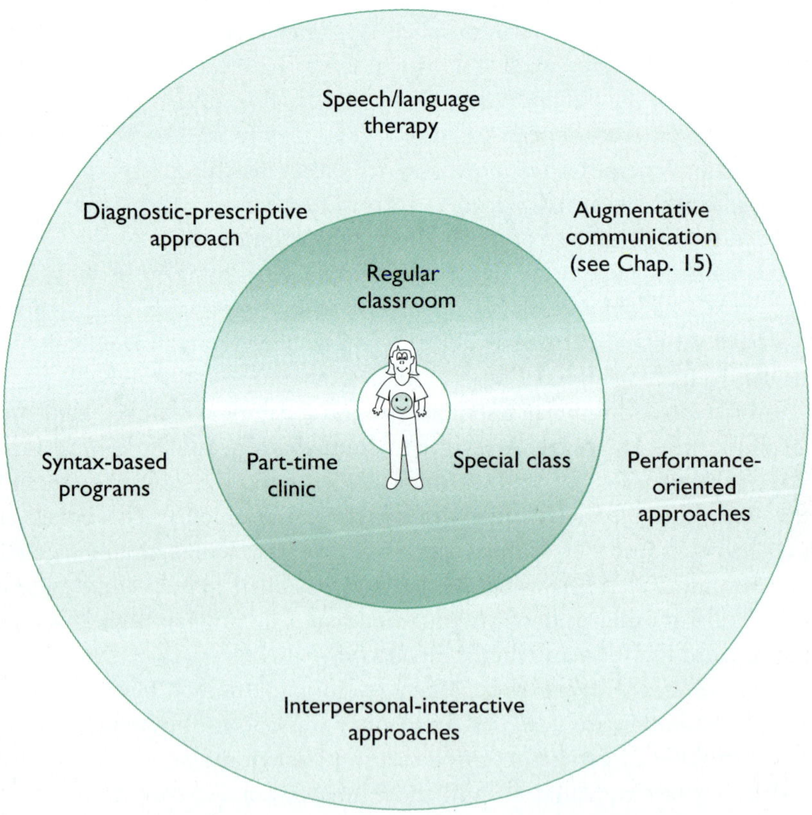

No special curriculum apart from the above models exists for children with speech and language disorders. Generally, language teaching for delayed children should be based on normal language acquisition processes. Teachers provide the motivation to communicate, many opportunities for teacher-child and child-child interactions, and much peer and adult modelling. They create realistic conversational atmospheres, focus on children's interests, and help them to use language to promote or regulate social interaction, and to develop skills that refine listening, attention, and memory. They also stress the language arts curriculum of listening, expressive language, and reading.

Tips for Teachers

Tips for Teachers of Children with Speech and Language Disorders

Classroom Climate

- Don't place pressures on the child to use oral language.
- Don't speak for the child.
- Focus on making language a part of children's routines.
- Provide access to interesting materials and activities.
- Create realistic conversational atmospheres where speech is valued.
- Focus on the interests of children.
- Follow the child's lead and reply to the child's initiations or comments. Communication is maintained by conversational responses, not "Good talking." For example, "I saw monkeys" is related to "Monkeys are funny," not "Good talking" (Owens, 1991).
- When asking questions, wait patiently for an answer. For children with language problems, teachers should respond to the content rather than the correctness of the language. That is, stress the content of the answer, not the grammar.
- The function of language depends on its effects on the environment. Classrooms should be arranged so that there are materials and activities of interest to children. Teachers must set the scene, provide materials, and prompt dialogues that children can use with each other.

Instruction

- Give directives as explictly as possible. Avoid using unnecessary words. After giving a direction, have the child repeat it to show comprehension.
- Speak clearly and at a moderate speed to be more easily understood. However, research confirms that rapid sound changes cause dysphasic children problems that impair their ability to identify and discriminate consonants. For these children, speak at a slower rate to improve their comprehension.
- Repeat and reword if the child seems confused.
- Don't overenunciate. Speak at normal pace and loudness.
- In a lesson, stress important points with "Watch now," or "Listen carefully."
- Use much modelling, imitation, and expansion of the child's utterances as well as paraphrasing, extensions, and recast sentences.
- Use indirect commands such as "Tell Tommy what you want."
- One of the most potent methods teachers can use to foster language is to ask questions in a way that activates children's thinking and promotes problem solving. Questions should be meaningful to the child and be designed to extend thinking, introduce and extend concept development, stress new vocabulary, and improve language abilities.

Summary

1. Human communication is incredibly complex. As a component of communication, language is a typically human activity. Language is a complex system of symbols and rules for using these symbols. It is the product of all aspects of development — physical, sensory, social, and neurological. Speech is essentially a mechanical production of language.
2. Language, one of the most distinctive features of humans, is still very poorly understood.
3. Speech and language disabilities interfere with the ease with which a child interacts with the world. Speech disorders are problems in the articulation of language sounds, voice production, and fluency. Language disorders are problems in the acquisition, comprehension, and formulation of language. Youngsters with language disorders may have the rudiments of a language code but show large gaps in linguistic development and display little consistency in their various deficits.
4. Speech and language problems cut across other categories of exceptionality but they also constitute a category of exceptionality by themselves. Many, if not most, children with other disabling conditions also manifest speech and language problems that further hinder their optimal development. Children with hearing handicaps, learning disabilities, intellectual disabilities, and severe emotional disturbance often have speech and language problems.
5. With language, all the major developmental milestones are reached in infancy or early childhood.
6. A linguistic environment, an intact cognitive/perceptual system, and normal social interaction all underlie the development of language. If the child does not hear language, has some impairment of the cognitive/perceptual mechanism, or has a troubled family background, then the child's development of language will reflect these problems.
7. Speech development depends on having something to say (language) and the opportunity to say it (social interaction). It also depends on the development of the speech mechanisms and articulators — the pharynx and larynx, the tongue, the palate, the lips, and the teeth. The production and modulation of breath flow is also important to speech production.
8. Many types of speech and language disorders remain ambiguous and controversial. They are manifested in a staggering array of distinct forms. Language disorders may manifest themselves in speech and writing, either at the phonological or grammatical level, or both; in the comprehension of specific concepts, or of language structures; or in some combination of these areas. Speech is defective when it is conspicuous, unintelligible, or unpleasant.
9. Dysarthria and aphasia are related to brain dysfunction. Children with clefts may show delayed language and speech development. While the search for definitive causes of stuttering has been extensive, the results have been largely negative.

10. Communication disorders can have painful consequences for all aspects of a child's development. Disorders of speech and language socially isolate the those who suffer from them and impoverish their lives. There is a fairly large body of literature that suggests that when communicatively disordered children are considered as a group, they have an increased prevalence of learning problems and psychiatric disorders.

11. There is a growing body of knowledge addressing communication skills and their impact on school success.

12. Many speech problems are developmental rather than physiological and respond well to remedial instruction. Most children are integrated into regular classrooms.

CHAPTER 7

Children with Learning Disabilities

Historical Notes

It is probably true to say that there have always been people with learning disabilities if by that we refer to persons of average intelligence who suffer some dysfunction that hinders their learning by traditional methods. By definition, however, learning disabilities are tied to academic achievement. Therefore, when pushing a plough was more important than pushing a pen, and when schooling was not a social norm for all children, the unique problems of individuals with learning disabilities would simply not have existed.

By the opening decades of the twentieth century, compulsory school laws had propelled all children into some form of education. It was then that the particular difficulties of students with learning disabilities came to the fore. The earliest research was undertaken in the British public (private) schools; investigators searched for reasons other than mental retardation or emotional disturbance to explain the learning deficits of middle- and upper-class school children. For poorer and immigrant children, labels such as *feeble-minded*, *moron*, or even *moral imbecile* were freely applied to deficient learners (see Winzer, 1993).

Many different disciplines contributed to the field of learning disabilities. Physicians, neurologists, ophthalmologists, speech therapists, psychologists, and educators all brought their own professional orientation and focus. Early research into learning disabilities, conducted by physicians and psychologists who emphasized clinical investigation rather than practical application in the schools, focused primarily on three disorders — spoken language, written language, and motor and perceptual problems. In 1877, for example, Kaussmaul first described congenital word-blindness. In 1896 James Kerr, a British physician, and W.P. Morgan, an ophthalmologist, also reported cases of "word-blindness." Eye surgeon James Hinshelwood investigated cases of word-blindness, word-deafness, and mind blindness. He published *Congenital word-blindness* (1917), the first true monograph on the unique problems of children we now refer to as learning disabled.

Much of the pioneering research concerned children with reading problems. Hinshelwood held that reading disabilities were due to the destruction or improper development of the memory centres of the left cerebral hemisphere of the brain (Park and Linden, 1968). In the early 1920s, Samuel Orton, an American psychiatrist, noted that children with learning problems often displayed mixed laterality and suggested that the failure of one hemisphere of the brain to become dominant caused the disorder. Orton invented the term "strephosymbolia" to designate individuals who saw "mixed symbols" when they tried to read (Orton, 1927).

Although these early researchers made some provocative and relevant findings, it was the work of Alfred Strauss and Heinz Werner that established the conceptual base and the research and theories in the field. Strauss, a neurologist, and Werner, a developmental psychologist, left Nazi Germany in the early 1930s and eventually arrived in the United States. They joined the staff of the Wayne County Training School in Northville, Michigan, where they began a program of training and research for brain damaged children who were also mentally retarded.

As Strauss and Werner studied the impact of brain damage on children's behaviour and psychological development, they drew a distinction between the exogenous (largely brain damaged) and the endogenous (largely genetic) mentally retarded population. When they began to study children of normal ability who were nevertheless experiencing learning difficulties, Strauss and Werner were able to delineate a group of common behaviours — a behavioural syndrome — that they believed characterized children suffering from minimal brain damage. The Strauss Syndrome, as this is now called, has five principal components: hyperactivity, hyperemotionalism, impulsiveness, distractibility, and perseveration. While these components have been expanded, subdivided, and made more specific over the years, they still describe the core behavioural characteristics of children with learning disabilities.

When the disabilities were attributed to various types of brain damage, terminology generally reflected a medical orientation. Common terms included *minimal brain dysfunction*, *brain crippled*, *cerebral disordered*, *neurologically impaired*, *dyslexic*, and *dysphasic*.

Orton, Werner, Strauss, and other pioneers in the field who studied brain-damaged children often looked for perceptual disturbances in their subjects and identified a number of perceptual abnormalities, sometimes in children with no overt evidence of brain damage. After Strauss and Werner, the focus of research continued to be seemingly normal children who were achieving poorly in school. Researchers popularized the notion that learning-disabled children have perceptual and perceptual-motor problems and that perception and neurological problems are key factors in learning disabilities. In recent years, the emphasis on perceptual problems has diminished.

Language problems have a long history in the field of learning disabilities dating from Orton in the 1920s. There is today renewed interest in language disorders as opposed to perceptual dysfunctions. As well, metacognitive strategy training (also known as learning-thinking instructional programs, cognitive training, and cognitive behaviour modification) has piqued the interest of those working with learning-disabled students. Many different types of educational procedures fit under this rubric including self-instruction, academic strategy training, and metacomprehension training. Essentially, the procedures are designed to improve learning effectiveness and social performance in school settings. The basic idea is to teach students to become independent learners.

Perhaps more than any other field of exceptionality, learning disabilities have generated controversy, confusion, misconceptions, and polarization among concerned professionals. While some categories in special education can be easily identified by a common trait, such as hearing loss, visual impairment, or speech dysfunction, the area of learning disabilities does not concern a single, easily identifiable handicap and children with learning disabilities do not form a unified homogeneous group. On the contrary. Learning disabilities constitute a syndrome, a group of related and overlapping conditions, and include vastly different populations who reveal a wide variety of behavioural, learning, social, and interpersonal problems.

Although individuals who are learning disabled may differ from one another in many critical ways, they do share some common problems. First of all, they show a marked discrepancy between their potential and their performance. These students have average or above average intelligence, but they seem unable to learn through regular channels and cannot reach their full potential when taught through traditional instructional methods. Second, students with learning disabilities show academic lags; they may also show hyperactivity, inconsistent performances, memory and attention problems, and perceptual deficits that place them at severe disadvantage for learning.

Even while many of these students appear bright and receptive in all sorts of ways, they still fail in school. They earn report cards larded with comments such as "Could try harder," or "Should apply herself," or "He is not working up to his potential." But many of these young people are applying themselves, and the more they try and fail, the more unhappy and frustrated they become. Eventually they are caught up in a cycle of frustration and failure that threatens their entire educational careers and engenders lack of motivation, social problems, increasingly unacceptable classroom behaviours, and dropping out, or even being subtly pushed out, of a school system that can't accommodate to their unique needs. The following profile offers a particularly poignant example of a child whose learning disability was not identified. The letter was written many years after he had left school.

Profile

Dear Teacher,

You will not, I am sure, remember me. I am the child you failed in the second grade many years ago. That failure had profound effects on my life. It was my first, but not my last, bitter taste of defeat. I never found out from my mother why I failed that year. I was told only that "it was thought best."

The full implication of repeating a grade did not dawn on me until the day school started that next autumn. I had once felt like my younger sister's smart older brother, but now I felt like her slow, retarded brother. From that day onward, she and I were both in the same grade until we parted company in high school.

I hated school after that first day of my second go round in grade two. Teacher, I hated you. I hated being the same mental age as my younger sister. I hated authority. I had done my best to please you the year before and my best was not good enough. I quit trying to please anyone in school.

You never asked me why I was hyperactive and could not sit still. You never wondered how it felt to be in the Blue Birds slow reading group. You never asked how I felt about math which I just could not do. I wanted to be good at numbers, but I could just not cope with the anger that math provoked in me. To some people, numbers are friendly little creatures that love you. To me, numbers were mean ugly biters that bullied me every chance they got. Hell, I thought, must be having to do numbers forever by working them out in your head. Spelling was also a painful subject. I used to avoid your eyes, and prayed that you would not call on me.

As a young teenager, I thought I had found the answer to all my problems in the power of alcohol. I relied on alcohol to change my fear into temporary courage, and to turn my feelings of low self-worth into superman-like confidence. At first my answer worked. But in time it became a one-way ticket to training school, jail, and personal defeat. Only by luck did I meet a counsellor who understood my learning problems and helped to set me on the right path.

In closing, I'd just like to say that today you have other children like me in your classroom. They may be the shy wallflower types or the loud performers that get on your nerves and disturb the rest of the class. They may be the ones with hidden secrets who daydream all day long. One thing is certain — they are already awake and the nightmare will not go away.

Thank you for listening teacher,

Brian

In the past, children with learning disabilities have been described as hyperactive, distractible, inattentive, brain damaged, slow learning, dyslexic, perceptually disabled, aggressive, and emotionally labile. More unsavoury terms have included *dull, lazy, inept,* and *disturbed.* Because of difficulties in identification, youngsters with learning disabilities were often been shunted into classes for mentally retarded or emotionally disturbed children. Others were placed in non-stimulating settings where their problems and progress were improperly evaluated.

Students with learning disabilities are neither emotionally disturbed nor intellectually disabled. They stand in good company with similarly afflicted historical figures. Thomas Edison's teacher, for example, described him as "addled." Auguste Rodin's father complained that he had "an idiot for a son." Woodrow Wilson had severe problems with reading and writing (Thompson, 1971). Albert Einstein did not speak until age three; he found school so difficult that one teacher predicted that "nothing good" would come of him (Patten, 1973). Nelson Rockefeller, who became vice-president of the United States, encountered great difficulties with reading. Rockefeller later wrote that he "just struggled to understand words that seemed to garble before my eyes, numbers that came out backward, sentences that were hard to grasp" (Rockefeller, 1976).

Definitions of Learning Disabilities

Learning disabilities remain a puzzling condition — one of the least understood and the most difficult with which to deal. This is partly the result of the field's evolution, its accelerated growth, and its interdisciplinary nature. More importantly, the extremely heterogeneous nature of the learning-disabled population defies easy categorization or description.

Development of the Field

The field of learning disabilities is the most recent category in special education. The term *learning disabilities* came into use in 1963 to describe students who experienced continual school failure yet did not fit into the traditional categories of exceptionality. It was first used as a standard description for children of normal intelligence with learning problems by Samuel Kirk, one of the pioneers in the field, at a Chicago parent's meeting in 1963. Kirk defined his term carefully:

> Recently, I have used the term *learning disabilities* to describe a group of children who have disorders in development in language, speech, reading, and associated communication skills needed for social interaction. In this group, I do not include children who have sensory handicaps, such as blindness and deafness, because we have methods of managing and training the deaf and the blind. I also exclude from this group children who have generalized mental retardation (Kirk, 1963, p.3).

Kirk's speech had three major effects. First, it isolated the general characteristics of the population to be subsumed under the label of learning disabilities. The new term implied an educational rather than a medical orientation. Because it was also relatively non-stigmatizing, it appealed greatly to parents and educators. Second, it precipitated a vote to reorganize diverse groups into the Association for Children with Learning Disabilities (ACLD), renamed the Learning Disabilities Association (LDA) in 1989. Primarily a forum for parents of learning-disabled children, the ACLD expanded rapidly and became a powerful lobby group in both Canada and the United States.

Third, the creation of a new term served as a catalyst to stimulate interest in the field. Kirk's conception created an entirely new area of special education and set it on the road to an astonishing expansion. Such growth has never been experienced by any other area in special education in such a short time. The growth of interest in the area, the number of students identified and served as learning disabled, the development of parent and professional organizations, and the contributions of allied disciplines has been little short of phenomenal. Today, learning disabilities are the largest single focus of special education in many Canadian school districts.

As it expanded, the field of learning disabilities brought changes and innovations to the entire area of special education. Novel instructional approaches, new materials, and different types of tests and assessment measures have all been spawned. Then too, new ways have evolved of conceptualizing special education, especially as it applies to students who are mildly handicapped. Probably the most important new construct is that of non-categorical or generic approaches to the education of mildly handicapped students, as we discussed in Chapter 1.

Over the years, a range of settings developed to serve this extremely heterogeneous group. Today, as in the past, more options are available at elementary than at secondary levels. This reflects the traditional emphasis placed on the remediation of learning disabilities in the early grades. Almost all students with learning disabilities are served adequately in the regular classroom with some modification of approach. More severely disabled students may attend a special class or school for a time, although these placements are never permanent and all have the ultimate goal of placing the student back in the regular milieu as quickly as possible.

Since its beginnings, the most challenging issue in the field of learning disabilities has been the search for an appropriate definition. Perhaps in no other area of special education has so much effort been expended to define the field. One study (Ysseldyke et al., 1983) found more than forty-two definitional criteria in the literature. Yet a universally acceptable definition has remained elusive. Lack of a clear definition in turn creates confusion in estimates of prevalence and considerations of etiology, and presents major difficulties in the design and use of tools and tests for assessment.

There are many reasons for the difficulties that face parents and professionals when they attempt to identify and define a child's learning disabilities. Chief among them:

- The disparate characteristics of the learning-disabled population make a general definition of the category extremely tenuous. As Ysseldyke (1987) observed, "There are no characteristics of behaviour specific to learning disabilities, there are no characteristics that students labeled as learning disabled evidence that are not demonstrated with equal frequency by low-achieving students who are not learning disabled."
- Learning disabilities cannot be simply measured by a numerical designation, such as an IQ score or a decibel loss.
- Learning disabilities are ill-defined in the minds of many educators, psychologists, and parents; their implications are neither fully understood nor adequately conceptualized.
- Some people think that there is no such thing as a learning disability; others use the term to label every learning problem.
- While "learning disabilities" implies a distinct syndrome of behaviours, the components of the syndrome are varied and confused. This means that the term is often applied to students who could more accurately be described as slow learners, as children who are naughty in class, as those who are absent often or move from school to school, or as average learners in an above average school district (Shepard, Smith, and Vojir, 1983).
- The movement among categories that we described in Chapter 4 has many more children moving under the learning disabilities umbrella although the term may not accurately apply to them.
- The acceptability of the term *learning disabilities* as compared to *slow learner* or *intellectually disabled* means that many children are categorized as learning disabled even though their problems are of a different nature. The greater social desirability of the term generally reflects the notion of an impairment that is specific rather than global in nature and is therefore less stigmatizing to the image of the child as a whole person (Harry, 1992).

As you can see, most of the problems revolve around accurately pinpointing the characteristics of learning disabilities. Despite the problems, many definitions of learning disabilities have emerged and all have their advocates and their opponents. Most modern definitions echo Kirk's original model, quoted earlier in this chapter. Among the current plethora of definitions, the one proposed by the National Joint Committee on Learning Disabilities (NJCLD) seems to have the best chance of becoming the consensus definition (Hammill, 1990). It defines the syndrome of learning disabilities, outlines some proposed etiologies, and explains the developmental consequences. According to the NJCLD,

> *Learning disabilities* is a general term that refers to a heterogeneous group of disorders manifested by significant difficulties in the acquisition and use of listening, speaking, reading, writing, reasoning, or mathematical abilities. These disorders are intrinsic to the individual, presumed to be due to central nervous system dysfunction, and may occur across the life span. Problems in self-regulatory behaviour, social perception, and social interaction may exist with learning disabilities but do not by themselves constitute a learning disability. Although learning disabilities may occur concomitantly with other handicapping conditions (for example, sensory impairment, mental retardation, severe emotional disturbance) or with extrinsic influences (such as cultural differences, insufficient or inappropriate instruction), they are not the result of these conditions or influences (National Joint Committee on Learning Disabilities, 1988).

This definition stresses that learning disabilities are a syndrome of behaviours that manifest differently in different individuals. The disabilities are intrinsic to the individual, affect learning and behaviour, and are directly related to problems in school learning. Social, emotional, and motor difficulties may accompany the learning disability but do not constitute disabilities by themselves.

Even though the NJCLD definition has much credibility, it is not universally accepted and there is continuing debate on the matter. It is therefore perhaps more relevant to examine common elements that are found in most definitions of learning disabilities.

Neurological Dysfunction

Much of the theoretical understanding of learning disabilities grew out of work with children described as brain damaged in the 1930s and 1940s. Alfred Strauss argued that children with brain injuries are subject to major disorders in perception, thinking, and behaviour that reduce their ability to read, write, spell, and calculate.

Many theorists still attribute learning disabilities to some type of brain impairment or central nervous system (CNS) dysfunction. This pathological emphasis is particularly evident among medical professionals; in educational circles, the tendency over the years has been to de-emphasize pathological aspects of the problems and stress behavioural ones. Many educators today would like to see the concept of presumed neurological impairment dropped entirely. They prefer to focus on each child's particular perceptual, cognitive, learning, and motor problems and skills so that appropriate educational programming can be developed.

Uneven Growth Pattern

Students with learning disabilities are presumed to have irregular or uneven development of the various components of mental ability. While some of the components mature quickly, other areas of development lag behind. Uneven development manifests as peaks and valleys in the performance of children with learning disabilities. For example, some children are precocious verbally but far behind in motor and hand skills. These children, ahead of their age group in the use of oral language, may nevertheless find it hard to hold a pencil or crayon, make shapes, or learn to print.

Difficulty in Academic Tasks

Academic problems are perhaps the clearest indication of a learning disability. A child may encounter difficulties with a wide range of learning tasks. Specific problems may occur in the acquisition of speech and oral language, in reading, in written language, in handwriting, in spelling, or in arithmetic. Depending on the definition, thinking, motor skills, perceptual skills, and psychosocial skills could be added.

Academic difficulties are the hallmark of the learning-disabled population.

Discrepancy Between Potential and Performance

Children with learning disabilities are perhaps best described as those who manifest educationally significant discrepancies between their tested potential for academic tasks and their performance in academic and social domains. The discrepancy between a child's potential and performance refers to the gap between what a child is capable of learning and what the child actually achieves. Such a conception allows educators to distinguish learning-disabled children from those who fail because of low intelligence, behaviour disorders, or other disabling conditions. The child's potential is judged by the mental age obtained on standardized tests of mental ability, which is then compared to the child's performance on achievement tests. A difference of two years between the estimated potential and the performance is frequently used as an indicator of academic retardation.

Exclusion of Other Causes

Most definitions of learning disabilities exclude children whose exceptionality is primarily the result of other causes. Learning-disabled children are not intellectually disabled, behaviourally disordered, visually or hearing impaired, or socially or economically disadvantaged. This is not to say that children with other disabilities cannot also be learning disabled. However, by excluding other disabilities, the field of learning disabilities gains clarity regarding its special population of learners.

Nevertheless, the exclusionary clauses tend to add more confusion. Too often we simply define learning disabilities by another type of exclusion — if you don't have any other problems, then you must be learning disabled. This means that today "learning disabilities" is somewhat a residual category that includes many students who would have been classified differently in the past. For example, the category of learning disabilities has come to include minority language children who are not necessarily handicapped at all (see Jacobs, 1991).

Average or Above Average Intelligence

Inherent in the whole concept of learning disabilities, and closely associated with the exclusionary clause, is the notion that the learning-disabled child is of average or above average intelligence.

Changing Terminology

The roots of the field of learning disabilities are embedded in the medical areas of neurology, ophthalmology, and other medical specialities. Although the terminology drawn from neurology is used less often today, some terms are still in general use and warrant explanation. In the following terms, the prefix *a* means an absence of and *dys* means a disturbance of:

- *Agnosia* is a lack of knowledge, an inability to recognize the significance of sensory stimuli.
- *Dysgraphia* means a disturbance in the ability to express thoughts in writing.
- *Dyscalculia* is a disturbance in the ability to use and remember numbers and do arithmetic.
- *Dyslexia* is a disturbance in the ability to read, despite conventional instruction, adequate intelligence, and socio-cultural opportunity (Tansley and Panckhurst, 1981).

Of all these terms, *dyslexia* is the one that has become part of the common language. Precise definitions vary but generally, "dyslexia refers to a severe difficulty in learning to read" (Mercer, 1987, p. 374). It is "an inability to read normally as a result of damage to the brain" (Myers and Hammill, 1990, p. 63).

The terms *dyslexia* and *learning disabilities* should not be used synonymously. Many children with reading problems are not categorically identified as learning disabled. And, while up to 85 percent of learning-disabled children have reading difficulties, it is best to view learning disabilities as a syndrome comprising a number of behaviours.

Although the general public still clings to the term *dyslexia*, most educators are dispensing with it in favour of *reading disability.* As early as 1968, the National Advisory Committee on Dyslexia and Related Reading Disorders in the United States set out to examine its terminology. The next year, the Committee stated: "In view of ... divergencies of opinion, the Committee believes that the use of the term dyslexia serves no useful purpose" (p.38).

Prevalence of Learning Disabilities

Estimates of the prevalence of learning-disabled children are so high (but vary to such a great degree) that it seems that the school system has fallen in love with the notion. Since 1963, the numbers of students identified and categorized as learning disabled has risen phenomenally. In the United States, according to the Twelfth Report to Congress, the number of students labelled as learning disabled has more than doubled during the past ten years (CEC, 1990; Fox and Forbing, 1991). In Canada, students with learning disabilities make up the largest single group of children with disabilities. In 1986, 26 percent of all disabled children had a learning disability (Nessner, 1990). Some Canadian estimates of prevalence from provinces that adhere to categorical definitions are are shown in Table 7-1.

Table 7-1

Prevalence of learning disabilities

	Total school population	Exceptional children	Learning disabilities	Percentage of total school population	Percentage of exceptional children
Nfld.	136 228	10 165	8 700	6.38	85.60
Nova Scotia	169 581	18 822	12 106	7.14	64.32
Quebec	943 652	126 417	96 585	10.23	76.40
Ontario	1 796 244	136 356	55 768	3.10	40.90
Saskatchewan	204 097	6 016	3 665	2.95	60.92
B.C.	514 464	60 623	6 637	1.29	10.95

Source: CEC (1989)

Because figures depend upon the definition and the procedures used, definitional problems and inconsistent identification procedures render exact proportions impossible. As shown in Table 7-1, prevalence figures vary quite dramatically across Canada, ranging from 1.2 to 10.2 percent of the total school-aged population.

By definition, however, learning-disabled students are atypical, so numbers could not be in very high ranges. Generally, the best Canadian estimates place the number of students with disabilities serious enough to hamper their educational progress at from 2 to 4 percent of the school-aged population.

Within the population of students with learning disabilities, boys outnumber girls about four to one (MacGregor, Rosenbaum, and Skoutajan, 1982). The reasons for this are somewhat unclear. It may be that boys tend to indulge in more overt, acting-out behaviour, and are therefore more likely to be referred for in-depth diagnosis.

Classification of Learning Disabilities

Efforts to classify specific subtypes of learning disabilities may be traced back almost as far as the concept itself. But even after years of intense research, no consensus has been reached about how to define or how to classify learning disabilities. Affected children and youth do not fit into any of the traditional categories of disabling conditions. Moreover, the concept of learning disabilities is not a unitary one; it represents a group of students displaying disparate characteristics who fail to learn appropriately for diverse reasons. Because learning disabilities encompass a complex constellation of behaviours and conditions, they can be classified and categorized in many ways, with some support for each classification scheme (Samuels and Miller, 1985).

In Canada, the severity classifications of mild, moderate, and serious learning disabilities are widely employed. Severity classifications are founded on the belief that learning disabilities are less a question of kind than of degree, and consequences can occur on a continuum from severely learning disabled to subtle differences in attention and performance (Little, 1980).

Learning disabilities are also classified as general or specific. With general learning disabilities, a student's academic progress lags behind that of normal peers in most areas. Specific learning disabilities may imply that the student has difficulties in particular areas but performs adequately in others. The term is also used to refer to students who have very serious and deep-seated disabilities.

Etiology of Learning Disabilities

The causes of learning disabilities are complex and varied. Experts do not agree and therefore many etiologies have been proposed. Some say that learning disabilities result primarily from physiological factors. Others stress that the school tasks we expect students to accomplish contribute to learning disabilities by making demands on their maturity levels or learning styles that they are unable to meet. Still others blame environmental factors such as inadequate nutrition, inappropriate diet, or allergies. Moreover, various suspected causes interact in subtle ways, rendering etiology even more difficult to determine. In most cases, the cause of a child's learning disability remains unknown.

Minimal Brain Dysfunction

In the 1940s, Alfred Strauss and other pioneer researchers examined and classified children with discernable brain damage. They then worked with children who showed no apparent brain damage but displayed syndromes of behaviour typical of child with brain damage.

A presumption of some type of brain injury is still found in many of today's definitions. The term **minimal brain dysfunction** (MBD) is used as a diagnostic classification for children who present a variety of mildly disabling symptoms. The term suggests that slight damage to the brain hinders its most efficient functioning and points to disruption of neural cell development during early fetal development (Hynd and Semrud-Clikeman, 1989).

Some researchers believe that minimal brain dysfunction is the root cause of all learning disabilities. But it is seldom possible to prove that a learning-disabled child has suffered actual damage to the brain (Sandoval and Haapmanen, 1981). Because of this lack of evidence, some professionals are willing to diagnose minimal brain dysfunction on the basis of a variety of signs (Gaddes, 1981). These behavioural signs are called "soft" signs because, unlike the "hard" signs of classical neurology, they offer only borderline indications of brain dysfunction. Examples of soft signs include an awkward gait, clumsiness, and mixed hand dominance (Kneedler, 1984).

Biochemical Disturbances

Some researchers believe learning-disabled children may suffer from physiological problems or biochemical disturbances. Commonly mentioned sources of these disturbances are diet- or environment-related allergies that adversely affect learning.

Food allergies were theoretically linked to hyperactivity by Benjamin Feingold (1975, 1976). Dr. Feingold noted that artificial flavours, artificial preservatives, and artificial dyes were consumed in increasing quantities by North American children. He argued that approximately 50 percent of hyperactive children can be helped by eliminating from their diet artificial food colourings, dyes, and foods (such as apples, oranges, tomatoes, and strawberries) that contain certain natural salicylates, aspirin-like compounds occurring in some fruits and vegetables.

Genetic Factors

Learning disabilities tend to run in families. For example, Yule and Rutter (1976) reported that slow-reading children were three times more likely to reveal a family history of reading failure. A large-scale study (Decker and Defries, 1980, 1981) that compared the families of 125 children with reading disorders to a control group of average readers found common reading problems in the families of the poor readers, especially among the male members, which led the investigators to argue that learning problems were familial in nature. Studies of twins generally show that when one twin has a reading disability, the other twin probably does as well if the twins are monozygotic rather than dizygotic.

Whether familial reading problems are due to hereditary factors or to similar learning environments is still a matter of speculation. Writing, spelling and reading problems are not biological features that can be inherited. Rather, they stem from some underlying cognitive or neurological defect.

Research only indicates that some reading problems seem to be inherited and suggests that the influence of the genes on learning disabilities operates at several levels. Certain genes may have an influence in producing a specific disability. For example, a gene influencing dyslexia is found on chromosome 15 (Smith and Pennington, 1987). As well, the B2 microglobulin gene which is thought to influence the immune system and male sexual development is also found on chromosome 15, which may help to explain the high prevalence of males among the learning-disabled population (Smith and Pennington, 1987).

Maturational Lags

A child with a **maturational lag** is slow to reach some developmental milestones. Professionals estimate that between 5 and 40 percent of kindergarten children with average or above average intelligence experience developmental lags or perceptual handicaps (Bradley, 1975).

Such a developmental lag does not necessarily imply a structural deficiency or limited potential. Some children may simply be progressing at a slower rate in language, motor, cognitive, or socio-emotional development. Most of these children overcome their behaviour and learning problems as they grow older, although some may continue to lag behind their age-mates. It has been demonstrated, for example, that developmentally young children who appeared to be reading disabled at grade three responded by grade five and were low average readers by grade eight (Badian, 1988).

It may be that the effects of schooling on children with developmental lags create the appearance of mild handicaps (Shank, 1990). Children become penalized when they are drawn in by procedures intended to find potential problems (Beers and Beers, 1980) and are labelled as learning disabled. Although the child who is developmentally young will manifest characteristics of a child with learning disabilities, such as behaviour, reading, and attention span problems, special education services are "both unnecessary and inappropriate" (Senior, 1986, p. 161).

Environmental Factors

Children do not catch a disability when they enter school. In most cases they bring with them as yet unspecified cognitive, behavioural, linguistic, and affective characteristics developed over time, which interact with the academic and social ecology (Cooper and Speece, 1990). However, some researchers propose that children may indeed "catch" learning disabilities when they enter school, primarily because of a mismatch between their learning styles and readiness and classroom expectations.

Lloyd (1975), who describes this phenomenon as **dyspedagogia** (maleducation), suggests that children in this category do not have learning problems, but their schools do. Coles (1978) went so far as to assert that learning disabilities are a way to blame a group of students for the failure of the schools. In the same vein, Englemann (1977) argues that "perhaps 90 percent or more of the children who are labelled 'learning disabled' exhibit a disability not because of anything wrong with their perception, synapses or memory, but because they have been seriously mistaught. Learning disabilities are made, not born" (pp.46-47).

Proponents of the maleducation point of view believe that if teachers were better prepared to handle the special learning problems of children in the early school years, many learning disabilities could be avoided. They point to inappropriate teaching settings, narrow bands of acceptable behaviour, inflexible grouping practices, and narrow curricula. Studies (e.g., Cole et al., 1993; Mills et al., 1995; Yoder, Kaiser, and Alpert, 1991) suggest that one curriculum may not be best for all children and that programs should match the individual needs of the child.

Dyspedagogia implies more than poor teaching and a mismatch between instruction and child needs. It also includes poor curricula, poor health in the child, and poor attendance at school. Poor parental and professional attitudes may also function to weaken a child's motivation.

Prevention of Learning Disabilities

The prevention of many learning problems has already been discussed in Chapter 2 and in the section on the prevention of intellectual disabilities in Chapter 4. The reader should review these sections, bearing in mind their relevance to the prevention of learning disabilities. More specifically, one way to prevent learning disabilities is through the prevention of neurological damage. In addition, dyspedagogia can to some extent be eliminated through efficient early identification, early intervention, and appropriate program delivery designed to meet the unique needs of individual students.

Identification and Assessment of Learning Disabilities

While there is little agreement on definition, prevalence, or remedial procedures in the field of learning disabilities, there is almost universal agreement on the need for the efficient diagnosis of this population. Before setting up remedial programs and deciding on the most appropriate educational placement, it is incumbent on educators to conduct a thorough evaluation of the student in order to pinpoint the kind and degree of specific disabilities present as well as the strengths and weaknesses in each developmental domain.

The identification and assessment of children with possible learning disabilities is anything but easy. Assessment practices are fraught with problems. An acceptable assessment framework is lacking, appropriate instruments are not available, and many of the assumptions that have traditionally underlain assessment practices are under attack. Often, too, the process suffers from lack of co-ordination. Many professionals within and outside the school system become involved and each of these may hold very different views regarding the nature of learning disabilities. The pediatrician may stress minimal brain dysfunction, the psychiatrist behavioural disorders, and the psychologist intellectual inadequacy. Even within the school system, identification and assessment are often a rather hit-and-miss process. There is currently no single procedure to identify learning disabilities. Clinicians use a variety of tests and rely heavily on personal diagnostic judgment. As well, there is little consensus regarding when children should be tested, by whom, and to what purpose.

Children with learning disabilities may show deficits and lags in specific developmental tasks in several or all of the following functions: sensorimotor abilities, language, perception, thought processes, emotions, and social behaviour. A comprehensive and detailed examination of a child's physical and psychological make-up depends upon a battery of psychological and educational tests. Measures are supplemented by observations of the child, a physical examination, an evaluation of hearing and vision, interviews with the child and the parents, and information gathered from other sources. School records and the comments of earlier teachers are potent sources of data.

Generally, identification involves two processes — screening and psycho-educational diagnosis, as shown in Figure 7-1. **Screening** procedures examine large groups of children in order to identify those who fall below or rise above specified levels of behaviour and attainment. Diagnosis follows screening and investigates selected children to determine the precise nature of their difficulties.

Figure 7-1
An overview of the assessment process

Medical	Informal screening	Formal/psycho-educational
observations	observations	IQ measures, e.g. WISC-111
physical examination	interviews	achievement tests
hearing assessment	school records	visual, auditory, motor, sensorimotor functioning
vision assessment	case histories	diagnostic tests
	inventories	language measures
	rating scales	
	teacher-made measures	
	portfolios	

By definition, a learning disability involves a discrepancy between a student's potential and performance. Therefore, one of the first steps in the formal diagnosis is an assessment of intellectual potential to rule out the possibility of mental retardation and simultaneously to establish the fact of normal mental ability.

Broad coverage tests such as the Wechsler Intelligence Scale for Children-111 (WISC-111) are usually given first. The Wechsler scales have proven both valid and reliable in the assessment of children with learning disabilities. Once intelligence is judged to be normal, clinicians use more specific measures in a range of areas — auditory, visual, and motor processing; achievement, most particularly in language arts and mathematics; diagnostic tests to pinpoint specific areas of weakness; and perhaps vocational skills and adaptive behaviour.

Achievement tests are used to measure a spectrum of tasks such as oral reading, reading comprehension, language, spelling, math, and general knowledge. In addition, tests are often administered to identify the specific psychological processes in which a child is deficient. For example, a child's reading problems may be the result of a processing problem in auditory discrimination or visual figure-ground processing.

Psychological processing refers to how an individual processes sensory information and puts it to meaningful intellectual use. Theories about learning disabilities have long taken into account the possibility of processing deficiencies; indeed, this has been the major position in the field for the past thirty years.

The use of tests to diagnose underlying processing deficits was introduced at the same time that learning disabilities developed as a category of exceptionality. These measures have generated much concern and controversy. Opponents argue that because psychological processes are not directly observable and must be inferred from a child's performance, it is almost impossible to accurately assess underlying psychological processes. Nevertheless, a wide variety of measures that purport to assess such areas as auditory and visual processing, motor sub-skills, and kinesthetic functions are available. Table 7-2 shows the auditory and visual sub-skills upon which many of these tools focus.

Table 7-2

Examples of visual and auditory processes

Process	Ability	Implications and problems
visual perception	the ability to make visual stimuli meaningful	The child may have problems attending to and interpreting visual stimuli.
visual discrimination	the ability to perceive dominant features in different objects or symbols	The child may confuse letters and words that look alike.
		The child may not see the internal detail, as in *rid/red*, or may fail to see the general configuration as in *ship/snip*.
visual closure	the ability to identify a common object from an incomplete visual presentation	The child may have difficulty assembling puzzles and objects, identifying missing parts, or completing words by closing spaces between letters, as in *rab-bit*.
visual figure-ground	the ability to focus on the foreground and ignore the background visual stimuli	The child may not be able to distinguish words; for example, the child may be unable to point to the first word of the second paragraph.
visual memory	the ability to recall the dominant features of the stimulus item	The child may not be able to copy patterns or arrange blocks in a series.
visual sequential memory	the ability to recollect the sequence of a number of items presented visually	The child fails to recognize visually familiar words and forgets the arrangement of letters in a word.
auditory perception	the ability to recognize and interpret stimuli that are heard	The child may have problems attending to and interpreting auditory stimuli.
auditory discrimination	the ability to recognize differences between sounds and to identify similarities and differences between words	The child may not hear the similarities in initial or final sounds in words or be able to discriminate short vowels such as *pin, pan, pen*.
auditory closure	the ability to identify sounds and words from an incomplete auditory presentation	The child may have problems in sound-symbol association and especially in blending sounds.
auditory figure-ground	the ability to focus on the foreground sound and ignore other sounds	The child may not focus on the dominant sound; the fan on the overhead projector may be more important than the teacher's voice.
auditory memory	the ability to recognize and recall previously presented auditory stimuli	The child may have problems retaining and recalling auditory experiences.
auditory sequential memory	the ability to reproduce from memory sequences presented auditorily	The child may forget or confuse oral directions, the sequence of events, the sequence of letters in a word, and the sequence of words in a sentence.

As language problems assume greater importance in learning disabilities, there is a concomitant emphasis on assessing language competencies. Teachers use both process and product assessment. In process assessment, they administer measures to see why a discrepancy exists, the "why" of the disability. Children who score one standard deviation or more below the mean on a process measure are seen to be at risk, whereas children who score in the lowest 5 percent may be seen as having a learning disability (Berninger and Rutberg, 1992). In product assessment, teachers administer measures such as the Test of Written Language (Hammill and Larsen, 1983) to see exactly what a child can achieve.

Developmental Consequences of Learning Disabilities

Individuals who are learning disabled simply do not seem to learn in the same way everyone else does — they sometimes do complicated things very well and then amaze and puzzle us with their lack of competence in areas that seem elementary. Sometimes these youngsters seem to remember incongruous items — they know all the words of TV jingles but forget simple spelling words from one day to the next. Their performance is inconsistent; they show great variability in areas of functioning — large differences between skill areas. Often, the energy level of these students frustrates teachers; they may spend more time out of their seats than in them and have a higher rate of motor activity than other class members.

Learning disabilities represent a constellation of widely varied behaviours and conditions. The problems take a different course in each individual. In some students, the effects may be global; in others, they may only impinge on specific areas of functioning.

Some common characteristics are shown in the Research Notes on page 234. This list certainly does not cover all the behaviours that have been attributed to learning-disabled students and it should be regarded with extreme caution. No child with learning disabilities will display all the behaviours, while the disparate characteristics of the learning-disabled population means that additional behaviours may exist in some children. Most importantly, one attribute or behaviour does not a learning disability make; we probably all have at least one or two of the listed behaviours. As we have said, learning disabilities should be viewed as a syndrome, as a group of behaviours that adversely affect a child's academic and/or social and emotional functioning.

Cognitive Development

Cognitive delays are associated with intellectual disabilities. Learning disability is not a cognitive delay. By definition, students with learning disabilities possess average or above average intelligence. Also by definition, students with learning disabilities do not acquire academic skills at grade expectancy or at a normal rate and will lag in some or all academic areas. They show a marked discrepancy between potential and performance.

Thinking requires the ability to conceptualize and solve problems. Because learning-disabled children are of normal intelligence, they are clearly able to think. However, significant numbers of them suffer memory and thinking disorders: they have problems remembering information over long or short periods of time and demonstrate memory deficits for both auditory and visual stimuli (Swanson, 1987; Torgensen, 1988). They have trouble recalling what things sounded like or looked like and forget math

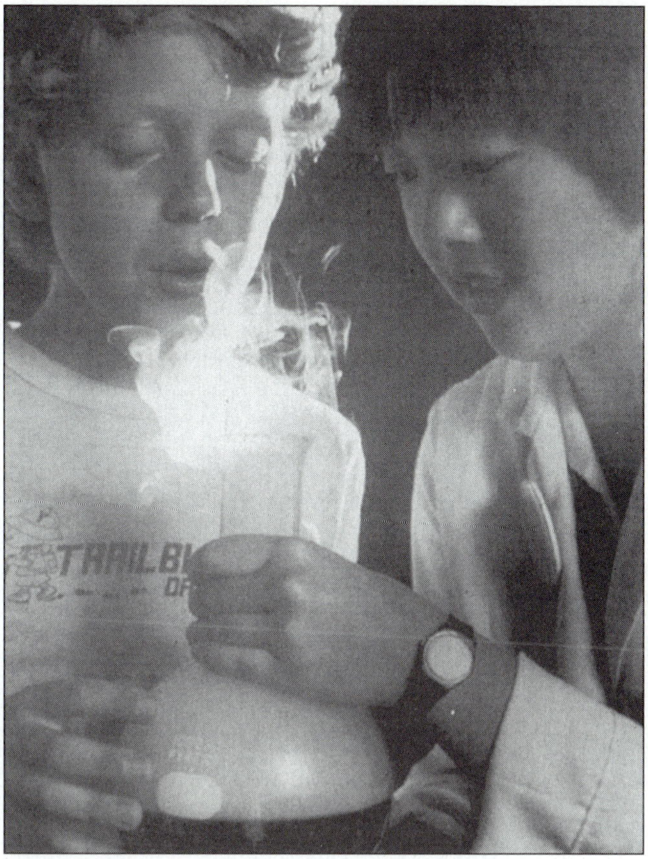

Peer tutoring is usually helpful to students with learning disabilities.

facts, spelling words learned only the day before, and directions. These children forget basic personal information, such as their telephone numbers and their addresses.

Many researchers consider the development of memory to be synonymous with the development of memory strategies (Howe and O'Sullivan, 1990), which include strategies for learning and for problem solving. Self-regulated learners are flexible problem solvers who plan, select, correct, and monitor effective strategies for learning (Corno and Mandinach, 1983). They anticipate problems and reflect on tasks when they are finished (Paris and Cross, 1983). When students monitor and orchestrate their own learning strategies, the processes form part of a cognitive procedure referred to as **metacognition**, the awareness of basic learning strategies.

In most cases, students with learning disabilities do not have deficits in the actual ability to learn. They seem to have performance deficits rather than ability deficits; that is, they are weak in the development of learning and problem-solving strategies and have deficiencies in metacognitive skills. Their learning strategies — or lack of them — prevent them from using their basic abilities to the best advantage.

Students who organize information poorly tend to be impulsive when solving problems, miss a logical train of thought, and fail to consider appropriate alternatives before embarking on a course of action. Their responses to problem situations indicate an inability to generalize and apply what they have learned in other situations. Lacking the skills to direct and monitor their learning and behaviour, learning-disabled students flounder in traditional classrooms.

Research Notes

Some common characteristics seen in learning-disabled children

Attitudes and Behaviour

- Intelligent but fails at school.
- May be reluctant to try anything new, be frightened by change.
- Lacks flexibility and is upset when the routine is different or the schedule changed.
- Has difficulty in changing from one task to another.
- Says "I don't care" or "I won't" and really means "I can't"; would rather be called bad than dumb.
- Impulsive — says what first comes to mind; calls out in class.
- Forgets assignments and homework as well as books, coats, and pencils.

Language

- Hears the dog barking, a truck honking, the scratching of pencils, the sound of the air conditioner, and footsteps outside, but barely hears mother calling and does not hear what the teacher says.
- Forgets names of people, places, things, own address and telephone number, but does remember the ads on television.
- May be an expert strategist in checkers or chess but cannot understand a riddle or joke.
- Many hesitations and repetitions in oral language; blurred pronunciations in speech.
- Poor verbal expression; language is jumbled and shows poor usage of syntax and semantics. Stops and starts in the middle of a sentence or idea, talks about hospitals, animals, and enemies all at once. Has trouble in relating a story or incident.
- Difficulty in concept formation. Calls breakfast lunch and is confused by yesterday, today and tomorrow.
- Asks the same thing over and over; asks constant questions but does not seem interested in the answers.

Academic performance

- Rushes headlong into work; is the first one finished, and has done all the problems wrong.
- May read *on* for *no*, write 41 for 14, *p* for *d*, or *q* for *b*, and cannot remember the sequence of letters that make up a word.
- May be able to add and multiply but not subtract or divide; or can do math mentally but cannot write it down.
- Skips words, omits them, or adds them when reading aloud.
- Frequently confuses directions, both oral and written.
- Needs instructions explained for each assignment.
- Can't plan studies and assignments.
- Sloppy and disorganized book work.
- Has difficulty beginning or completing tasks.
- Doesn't complete lengthy assignments.

Co-ordination

- May hug the cat too tightly but can't hold a pencil, get frostbite in the snow and not feel the hot water until it burns.
- May be a good swimmer but stumbles up the stairs.
- Does not look before walking, bumps into the door, swings lunch boxes into the nearest legs, and trips easily.
- Has trouble lining up, cannot help bothering the child ahead in the line.

Social

- Relates poorly to peers; may be socially inept and always on the fringe of a group.
- Has poor self-esteem and self-concept.
- Lacks judgment.
- Does not seem to understand the affective status of others from facial expressions, body movements, and tone of voice.
- Cannot keep a friend and prefers to play with younger children.

Source: See MacGregor, Rosenbaum and Skoutajan, 1982

Communication

Language disabilities appear to be closely connected with learning disabilities of all types. So apparent is the connection that some researchers use the term *language learning disabilities* to refer to students with language disorders that adversely affect academic performance. In the classroom, these may be the students who sit at the back and hope that the teacher won't call on them. They rarely volunteer answers, and when they are asked to speak they may be hesitant, stumble over words, and use a sparse vocabulary.

Students with learning disabilities tend to reach a plateau of language abilities in the areas of semantics, syntax, memory, and pragmatics at levels expected of children between eight and ten years old (Wesanko, 1990). Although they have problems with both expressive and receptive language, they seem to have greater difficulty using expressive language (Hessler and Kitchen, 1980; Noel, 1980). With expressive language, these youngsters may demonstrate particular problems with semantics and with pragmatics. Along with expressive and receptive problems, students with learning disabilities tend to be seriously affected in the areas of generalization, conceptualization, and abstraction, difficulties that may stem from limited vocabulary or the inability to absorb the full significance of words.

All the elements of language overlap and must develop in tandem if students are to be communicatively competent. Deficits in one area therefore affect the others. In language, students with learning disabilities show deficits in:

- Listening. The teaching/learning process proceeds on the assumption that participants listen to each other. When instructing, teachers use an initiation-reply-evaluate mode. They ask questions, listen, and then judge whether the reply indicates that the children have mastered the task.

  Listening (and therefore responding accurately) is a problematic area for learning-disabled children. When listening, they tend to misperceive phonemes requiring very fine discrimination, such as /m/ and /n/. They also confuse voiced and unvoiced consonants, such as /f/ and /v/ (Wiig and Semel, 1976).
- Phonology. Children with learning disabilities often have difficulties with articulation (Montgomary, 1981). They may show immature speech patterns, mild speech irregularities, general unintelligibility, and cluttered speech. They may substitute inappropriate words, repeat the same phrase over and over, or use a monotonous voice.
- Semantics. The vocabulary used by language-impaired children tends to be small, superficial, and reflective of reductions in the development of underlying concepts. Normally developing children of eight or nine years of age recognize the multiple meanings of frequently used words; learning-disabled adolescents may not perceive multiple meanings and may misinterpret when they read or listen. They often take things very literally, missing the subtle nuances of the language. For example, one adolescent went to the laundromat for the first time with a small load of washing. On a towel, he read the instruction, "Wash colours separately." He proceeded to do exactly that, using a separate washing machine for each colour. He spent nine dollars and infuriated the other patrons. Another student was handed a tape by a frazzled teacher and asked to "Put it on the video." The boy set it neatly on top of the machine.

Other children cannot remember the meanings of new words, whether the words are identified by the teacher as necessary for general vocabulary acquisition or discovered by the students when attempting to read English literature, social studies, science, and so on. Research indicates that 43 percent of learning-disabled students have word finding problems (Wesanko, 1990).

- Syntax. Students with learning disabilities may have problems organizing phrases and words into sentences and are more likely to make syntactical and grammatical errors (Bryan and Pflaum, 1978). They may talk about things out of order, produce rambling and repetitive utterances, and make unrelated statements.
- Pragmatics. Problems in the social use of language are seen in students who fail to communicate intent, show an inability in turn-taking in conversation, and fail to cue their listeners to the topic of discussion (Hasenstab, 1985).

Academic Development

Academic underachievement is the hallmark of the learning-disabled population. Some children suffer deficits in all areas; for others, only a few specific academic skills may be affected. Reading, writing, and mathematics, are three of the major areas in which difficulties occur.

Students with learning disabilities appear to reach a plateau at about a fourth or fifth grade achievement level (matching their achievement in language). This is about the point at which basic skill instruction generally ceases and students move on to apply their skills to reading comprehension, math applications, expository writing, and greater use of textbooks in science and social studies (Sheinker, Sheinker, and Stevens, 1984). Moreover, the gap between achievement scores and grade expectancy level seems to widen as students with learning disabilities progress through high school. Even when placed in secondary school resource programs, students do not seem to recoup basic skills. Despite intensive instruction, many adolescents with learning disabilities do not master the higher-level skills involved in reading and written expression.

In 1989, 2.7 million Canadian adults, 15 percent of the population aged 16 to 69 with reported abilities in either English or French, had limited reading skills such that they could not deal with the majority of written material that they encountered (Montigny, 1990). Among all children, reading problems are the major cause of poor school performance, affecting 10 to 15 percent of the school-aged population (Harris and Sipay, 1980). Reading disorders rank high on the list of academic problems of students who are learning disabled; the figure could be as high as 85 percent (Kaluger and Kolson, 1978). One sample of 200 elementary students with learning disabilities found that 54.5 percent had deficits in reading (Rivers, 1986). Using the Wide Range Achievement Test (WRAT), another study (Weiner, Harris, and Shirer, 1990) found learning-disabled elementary students to have a mean percentile of 7.74. At the secondary level, the primary reading disability of learning-disabled students is in the area of reading comprehension.

Students with hard-core reading difficulties manifest a variety of problems. Comprehension is the main purpose of reading, but comprehension is not possible unless a reader can translate the printed words into the language they represent (decode). Word attack skills are often deficient; students may be unable to deal with symbols, unable to synthesize parts of a word into a whole, or unable to organize words into meaningful clusters. As well, reading-disabled students often miss or confuse important details, such as *and* or *but,* resulting in confused interpretation of meanings. When these students read aloud, their reading may be stilted and full of substitutions, omissions, and additions. Individuals with learning disabilities also seem to lack sensitivity to various patterns of textual organization and to the relative importance of major and minor ideas (Vallecorsa and Garriss, 1990).

Many of these students show marked impairments in all forms of written expression. Spelling for learning-disabled students has been described as a "seemingly impossible task" (Leuenberger and Morris, 1990) and their spelling achievement usually lags far behind their grade placement. On the spelling subtest of the WRAT one study found a mean percentile of 7.52 (Weiner, Harris, and Shirer, 1990). Poor spelling correlates with reading difficulties; good readers can be deplorable spellers, but poor readers are certain to be bad spellers.

Some children who are learning disabled can speak well yet cannot write a simple sentence. Students with a writing disability tend to write little or laboriously, using incorrect grammar, syntax, and punctuation. They produce confused or truncated sentences, with an incorrect sequence of tenses, pronoun reference, and word order. Figure 7-2 shows the written work of an eleven-year-old student with obvious difficulties in written expression and handwriting.

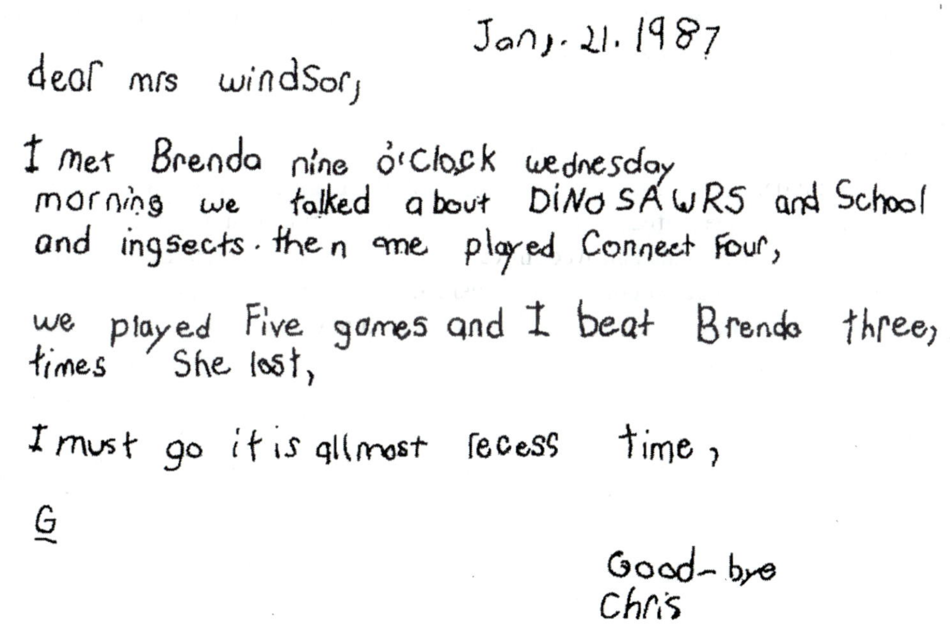

Jan,. 21. 1987

dear mrs windsor,

I met Brenda nine o'clock wednesday morning we talked about DINOSAWRS and School and ingsects. then me played Connect Four,

we played Five games and I beat Brenda three, times She lost,

I must go it is allmost recess time,

G

Good-bye
Chris

Figure 7-2
Work of an 11-year-old with difficulties in written expression.

At the secondary level, a student's linguistic age in writing may lag six to eight years behind the linguistic age in speaking. In one study (Linn et al., 1987) using standardized competency tests, learning-disabled adolescents in general performed poorly, specifically on communication items requiring identification of an irrelevant statement in a selection, use of apostrophes, and use of *s* to show possessives.

Many writing problems are characterized by shorter and lower quality stories that those written by normal students. While students with learning disabilities may have a basic understanding of story structure, their stories often lack organization and coherence, and contain relatively few story elements over all (see Montague and Graves, 1993). Students generally include basic story elements such as setting, plot, and resolution, but they frequently omit the critical elements of good stories such as the internal responses or plans of the characters (Leavitt and Ioannides, 1993; Montague, Maddux and Dereshiwsky, 1988).

To improve writing, teachers must first build the motivation to write and the student's confidence that his or her thoughts are worthy of communication.

Many problems in written expression stem from a lack of understanding of linguistic rules. Some students with learning disabilities may be unable to classify and categorize information into coherent sentences; others are unable to produce sentences displaying correct syntactic and grammatical order (Wallace and McLoughlin, 1979).

Students with a handwriting disability tend to write laboriously and as little as possible. They may produce clearly deviant writing, manifested by scrawling letter formations, reversals, transformations, uneven slant, and inability to keep the lines on the paper. Unco-ordinated motor movements and difficulty in judging the writing space are the most common causes of penmanship problems (Gerard and Junkala, 1980).

Math for learning-disabled students is typically characterized by high failure (Carpenter, 1985). Numerous investigations have found that many students with identified learning disabilities experience much greater difficulty in most aspects of math performance than their non-disabled peers (see O'Melia and Rosenberg, 1994). Children meet difficulty with such basic skills as counting, writing numerals, and learning basic associations. In fact, few of these children are competent even in the basic addition and subtraction facts (Connor, 1983).

Academic problems are exacerbated by the significant problems students with learning disabilities experience in social perceptions, self-concept, and motivation (Schrader and Valus, 1990). Compared to their peers, these students tend to hold lower self-concepts about academic performance, even in areas in which they have had little experience or instruction.

Students with learning disabilities tend to develop an **external locus of control** — that is, they view themselves as controlled by outer rather than inner forces. They are less likely than their peers to attribute success to their own ability and failure to their own lack of effort. They hold lower expectations for success, credit any successes to luck or the ease of the task rather than to their own abilities or efforts, and view failure as further verification of their own persistent lack of ability (Licht and Kistner, 1986). They have less optimism about improving their performance in the future, even when they receive special education services. Such pessimistic appraisals will almost certainly lead to reduced levels of effort and negative affect.

Students who retain an outward locus of control may revert to learned helplessness, a situation in which they attribute failure to external causes rather than effort and tend to show decreases in performance following failure (Licht and Dweck, 1984). Learned helplessness is an important individual difference that appears to affect children's performance in a variety of settings (Fencham, Hokada, and Sandus, 1989). Children who display learned helplessness have no faith that their efforts will result in desired outcomes. Because they expect to fail, they lose their motivation.

With all of this, it seems little wonder that students often develop secondary emotional problems. Learning-disabled children may develop an **emotional overlay**, an adverse reaction to learning problems and academic failure. In many cases it is extremely difficult to determine whether the learning or the adjustment problem came first, and the exact interaction of these in the child's functioning.

Perceptual Development

Perceptual and processing difficulties in the auditory and visual modes together with problems in co-ordination and motor skills are part of the traditional conception of learning disabilities. Also included are haptic disorders, which concern the information transmitted through touch, body movement, and position.

Perception involves the use of the senses to recognize, discriminate, and interpret stimuli. Students unable to recognize, interpret, and discriminate stimuli are said to have perceptual disorders, which are classed as psychological processing deficits.

Visual perception problems are those most commonly associated with learning disabilities. Many studies (e.g., Calfee, 1977; Satz et al., 1978) indicate that visual perception problems are common among reading/learning-disabled children and that as a group, children with learning disabilities perform poorly on tasks designed to assess visual perceptual abilities (Hallahan, 1975). Visual perceptual problems lead to difficulties with oculomotor co-ordination, with spatial relations, with figure-ground perception, with the discrimination of differences, and with the recognition of likenesses.

Several studies (e.g., Flynn and Byrnre, 1970; Harber, 1980; Henry, 1975) also show that auditory disorders occur with greater than normal frequency among children who are learning disabled. These children are often recognized when they attempt to spell words. Their poor spelling results from their inability to discriminate sounds, to blend sounds, and to encode (spell) or decode (read) words. The child with an auditory dysfunction may have difficulty synthesizing sounds into words, analyzing words into word parts, and associating sounds with symbols.

Behaviour

Various observational studies have demonstrated that children with learning disabilities behave in a less appropriate fashion in mainstream and special classes than non-learning-disabled children. They often display maladaptive styles of responses during instructional activities, possibly as a result of their poor cognitive performance (Cosden et al., 1987).

Teacher ratings indicate that students with learning disabilities demonstrate more problem behaviours than non-handicapped students in mainstream classes (Bender and Smith, 1990).

Specifically, students with learning disabilities demonstrate less task-oriented behaviour during instruction and more non-constructive off-task behaviour. Also, they spend more time engaged in socially off-task behaviour in regular classes than they do in special education environments (Crealock, 1989). In one classroom, observers found that all students were on task for most of the time, but learning-handicapped students tended to demonstrate significantly more off-task behaviour (Cosden et al., 1987). Similar research found a learning-disabled sample to be on task only 57 percent of the time, as compared to 70 percent for the non-disabled sample (McKinney, McLure, and Feagans, 1982). Others (Roberts, Pratt, and Leach, 1991) reported that a group of students with mild disabilities were off-task twice as often as were non-disabled students.

One controversial theory links learning disabilities with juvenile delinquency. Research finds that students with learning disabilities are more at risk for adjudication regardless of race or socio-economic level (Keilitz and Dunivant, 1986).

Research Notes

Suggested link with juvenile delinquency

A theoretical linkage between learning disabilities and juvenile delinquency is logical (Trapani, 1990) based on a significantly greater prevalence of learning disabilities reported in delinquent youth populations than in non-delinquent populations (Keilitz and Miller, 1980; Prout, 1981).

In Canada, a review of the prevalence of learning disabilities among adolescents in trouble with the law indicates a range of 4 to 36 percent, with the lower incidence figure reflecting strict identification criteria and the higher one reflecting relatively lenient levels of discrepancy between ability and achievement (Murphy, 1986). Other Canadian studies have found that 20 to 30 percent or more of young offenders have academic problems (Crealock, 1986), and that learning problems may sometimes be a predisposing factor in delinquency (Pihl and McLarnon, 1984).

The nature of the relationship between the constructs of learning disabilities and juvenile delinquency is not clear (Larson and Gerber, 1987). The notion of a link arises, at least in part, from the continual school failure that characterizes both conditions. The academic careers of juvenile delinquents follow a common pattern. Many experience school failure, frustration, acting out, truancy, apprehension by the authorities, more frustration, the development of a poor self-image, and alienation. Eventually, they are expelled or drop out of school in response to an overwhelming sense of defeat. The experiences of learning-disabled students show many parallels to this cycle. By the time learning-disabled children reach adolescence, they may be deeply enmeshed in a web of failure and unhappiness. According to Seigel (1974), adolescents who are learning disabled are prone to impulsiveness, a low frustration threshold, irritability, low self-esteem, and suggestibility. Seigel claims that, under certain conditions, these behaviours may result in antisocial or criminal acts.

Learning-disabled and non-disabled youth are apprehended by the authorities in approximately the same numbers for the same misdemeanours and offences (Zimmerman et al., 1978). However, learning-disabled youth are more likely to be brought before the courts and are adjudicated more frequently than non-learning-disabled adolescents (Broder et al., 1981; Zimmerman et al., 1981). Higher rates of adjudication could be due to the language and communication problems of students with learning disabilities or to subtle personality problems. In addition, the courts may hold a somewhat negative predisposition toward learning-disabled students based on their poor school records (Lane, 1980).

Motor Development and Co-ordination

Haptic problems, which encompass touch, body movement, and position in space, are thought to be relatively uncommon (Mercer, 1979). Haptic problems may be important in handwriting, because tactile information dictates the grasp of the pen or pencil. As well, many researchers have suggested a relationship between visual-motor and haptic abilities, and body image and laterality (Hallahan, Kauffman, and Lloyd, 1985).

Laterality refers to an internal knowledge of the differences between left and right while **directionality** is an awareness of left and right in the environment outside the body. Out of an infinite number of motor experiments, children learn the differences between an activity on the right side of the body and the same activity on the left. The pattern thus becomes a skill, and the skill becomes a habit. Laterality is the motor basis for spatial concepts. When children have developed laterality, they can project this to directionality concepts in external space such as up and down, and in front and behind. **Body image** refers to a person's awareness of the body, its capabilities, the interrelationship of body parts, and the relationship of the body to the environment.

At approximately five or six years of age, most children establish complete cerebral dominance and consistently prefer to use one side of their bodies in dealing with the world. The laterality theory maintains that learning is adversely affected if the child does not establish a tendency to perform most functions with one side of the body. Incomplete or mixed dominance has been associated with specific learning disorders.

In the past, many left-handed children were considered to be at high risk for learning disabilities. While it is true that among the learning-disabled population (and indeed among nearly all populations of problem learners) there is a far higher proportion of left-handers than in the general population, the hand dominance in itself does not seem to be the problem. The difficulties arise when mixed dominance translates into confusion in directionality, or right and left discrimination (Belmont and Birch, 1973).

The failure to establish laterality, directionality, and dominance may account for many reversals and similar confusions seen in children's reading and writing. When mixed dominance is encountered with other signs, such as enuresis (bed-wetting), preference for play with younger children, or infantile speech patterns, it may suggest a maturational lag or developmental immaturity which can interfere with a child's abilities to function in academic work (Murray, 1981).

Children with body image problems may not be able to organize themselves within their environment. They may be clumsy, slow in dressing and undressing, have difficulty in putting on a sweater, show problems in walking across the classroom without knocking down chairs and desks, or with drawing figures.

General inco-ordination refers to a lack of muscular control. Motorically disordered children may walk with an awkward gait, be unco-ordinated in physical activities, and have difficulties in running, skipping, or throwing and catching a ball. Children may demonstrate balance problems or spatial disorganization manifested by poorly developed concepts of space and a distorted body image. Overflow movements, which occur when the child wants to perform a movement with one hand and the other hand involuntarily follows in a shadow movement, may be present.

Children with perceptual-motor impairments have problems identifying or reproducing information they receive through their senses. They have difficulty discriminating symbols, and may reverse letters and shapes in their printing and drawing. They do poorly in accurately reproducing or copying information received visually or auditorily. Examples of perceptual-motor problems include difficulties in identifying the letters of the alphabet, reading the printed page from left to right, drawing basic shapes, and staying on the line when printing or writing.

Perceptual-motor disabilities tend to improve with age. However, studies show that some disabilities persist as significant during adolescence — in particular, fine and gross motor co-ordination problems and handwriting difficulties involving illegibility, poor spacing, cramping, and laboriousness in writing (Whyte, 1984).

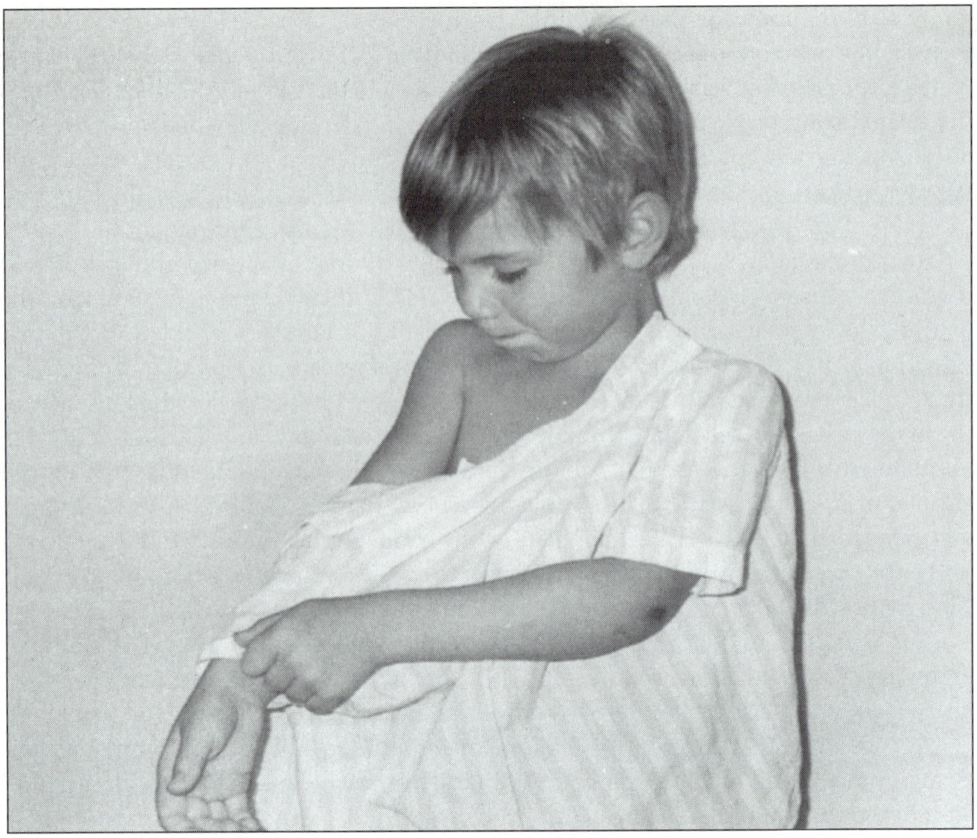

Children with body image problems often have difficulty with tasks such as dressing.

Attention Disorders

Attention problems are endemic among youngsters with exceptional conditions, and those with learning disabilities are no exception. It has been suggested that students with learning disabilities exhibit a developmental lag in their selective attention abilities relative to their normal peers. Studies that demonstrate the presence of attention problems and hyperactivity in children designated as learning disabled present estimates ranging from 33 to 80 percent (Shaywitz and Shaywitz, 1987). Students with learning disabilities have been found to be less attentive in a variety of school subjects. We discuss attention, distractibility, and impulsivity in Chapter 11.

Social and Emotional Development

Some definitions define learning disabilities strictly in terms of intellect and achievement; others include emotional and social complications that may adversely affect school learning and achievement. A body of research since the early 1970s has documented the social difficulties encountered by many students with learning disabilities. It suggests that the social interaction and social acceptance of children with learning disabilities remains deficient in comparision with other children's. This seems to be true regardless of whether the judgment of the child's social competence is based on teacher perceptions, parent perceptions, peer perceptions, or the actual behaviour of the child observed in social interaction (Coleman and Minnett, 1992).

Profile

John

John is seven years old and in a grade two class. His teacher describes him as fidgety, as boundlessly energetic, as an excessive talker to the point of perseveration. According to the teacher, John only attends to tasks for a very short period and often fails to complete work at all. He draws attention to himself in the classroom by being awkward and clumsy and acts out his anger rather than verbalizing it. John also has trouble making and keeping friends. He seldom engages in constructive play, alone or with classmates.

John's mother found similar behaviour in the home. John could never seem to sit still. He talked from morning to night, wandering aimlessly from one topic to another. In the social domain, he showed extreme frustration when corrected and often embarrassed his family in public. He was also very hard on his personal possessions.

Because John was an only child, his parents had no other children with whom to compare his behaviour. However, they were deeply concerned about it and were reaching the point of exhaustion. They readily agreed when school personnel suggested an in-depth diagnostic work-up.

A psycho-educational assessment confirmed the observations of John's teacher and parents. Although the psychologist found him inattentive, distractible, and unbable to control his continuous activity, John did manage to complete a WISC-R and a number of other tests. The psychologist concluded that John displayed normal intelligence. His severe learning deficits, such as his inability to learn to read, were due to his disturbing classroom behaviours. The psychologist found that John had not yet developed laterality and experienced left-right confusion. John performed poorly on auditory tasks involving discrimination, sequence, and memory. This may have accounted for his anomalies in articulation and syntax as well as his failure to learn basic reading skills through a phonics approach. The psychologist suggested that further medical evaluation of John's hyperactive behaviour be undertaken (Adapted from Darnforth, 1984).

Learning-disabled students are less likely to be accepted by their peers than non-learning disabled children (Weiner, 1987). One study (Weiner, Harris, and Shirer, 1990) found that approximately 50 percent of a sample of 90 learning-disabled children in suburban schools had peer relationship problems, with about 35 percent being neglected and 15 percent rejected.

The reasons why individuals with learning disabilities inspire negative responses are not clear. However, inadequacies in social cognition, specifically in skills employing empathy and making social inferences, have consistently been found in individuals with learning disabilities. *Social cognition* refers to the knowledge and cognitive activities employed by people in dealing with their social world (Pearl, 1987).

Studies suggest that inadequate skills in social perception are distinct contributors to the difficulties crucial to relationships experienced by children with learning disabilities (Holder and Kirkpatrick, 1991). These children are less adept at role taking and at interpersonal tasks that require taking an alternative viewpoint (Horowitz, 1981). They tend to ignore interpersonal signals from their peers, have trouble perceiving the moods of others, and are less accurate than non-disabled children in interpreting the non-verbal behaviour of others. An inability to interpret facial expressions is probably central to the problem (Holder and Kirkpatrick, 1991). It has also been suggested that learning-disabled students possess the necessary social skills but lack the motivation and cognition to apply them when necessary (Perlmutter, 1986).

Intervention with Children with Learning Disabilities

Learning disabilities are found in children who do not have any marked cognitive deficits or emotional problems, and do not come from home environments that could provide a reason for their behaviour (Henker and Whalen, 1989). Students with learning disabilities exhibit an entire syndrome, or collection of symptoms. Their problems lie well outside the normal range for their age level and persist despite repeated efforts to correct them. They are handicapped by their disabilities and prevented from realizing their full potential.

Since a learning disability can be highly deleterious to a child's academic and social functioning, as well as to future success in life, treatment becomes a critical issue. The prime time for intervention is before the end of grade three. Young children learn inappropriate strategies that soon become habitual and that can present an almost insurmountable obstacle to remediation. Teachers are well aware, for example, of how difficult it is to change the way children form letters once they have internalized incorrect formations.

Achievement levels in third grade seem to have particular predictive value. If reading is still poor at the end of the third grade, then the prognosis for subsequent rapid gains is bleak (Badian, 1988). Indeed, it has been estimated that only 10 to 15 percent of children who first receive remediation in grades five to seven can be brought up to regular classroom work (Strag, 1972).

Children with learning disabilities may enter into a cycle of frustration and failure. Their production deficiencies, the learned helplessness syndrome, and the inactive characteristics of these children all interact to produce learners who are passive, incapacitated by feelings of self-defeat, and fearful of learning. By the time they reach adolescence, students have developed ineffective coping mechanisms that limit their academic success and thwart their emotional development. Ineffective coping skills include not asking questions, resisting making choices, exhibiting discomfort when given a compliment, having poor eye contact, being poor risk takers, failing to use effective study skills, and failing to use self-monitoring strategies (Kay, 1986).

A wide variety of intervention approaches have been employed with children with learning disabilities, but none has proven effective with the entire learning-disabled population. Some approaches are controversial; others contradictory. For example, some early studies supported training for visual perceptual functions (Brod and Hamilton, 1973; Meikle and Kilpatrick, 1971) while other research suggested that such training was not in the least helpful (Camp, 1973; Chapman and Wedell, 1972). Special education is particularly open to fraudulent treatment claims, and controversy surrounds interventions such as psycholinguistic training and various therapies and techniques. Although not as controversial, stimulant drugs and diets cause concern.

Much of the controversy surrounding intervention springs from the disparate characteristics of students who are learning disabled. Because of the extremely heterogeneous nature of the population, no single approach, method, or technique can offer a solution to every problem. Today, however, it is academic deficits that drive intervention.

Medical Intervention

Historically, medicine and learning disabilities have been closely linked, particularly in the area of diagnosis. Until quite recently, learning disabilities were conceptualized in relation to biophysical disorders — specifically some form of minimal brain dysfunction. Today, the field has moved away from a medical model to a diagnostic and educational model for remediation. However, the medical profession continues its active interest in learning disabilities. The current foci of medical interest are drug therapy and diet management.

Psychopharmacological Management

Natural sources of behaviour-changing drugs have long been known. Among the institutionalized population of retarded persons, the emphasis on pharmacology in behaviour management began with the development of sedatives and hypnotics in the nineteenth century (Sprague and Baxley, 1978). Drugs were first used in the treatment of hyperactive children in 1937 (Lall, 1977). However, only in the last few decades have synthetic compounds rendered the effects of drugs more predictable. Today, psychopharmacological treatment for children diagnosed as hyperactive and/or with attention deficits is the most frequently used method of management. A comprehensive discussion of drug therapy with children designated variously as affected with learning disabilities, behaviour disorders, and Attention Deficit Hyperactivity Disorder is found in Chapter 11.

Diets

One theoretical source of biochemical disturbance is allergy to foods, food dyes, artificial flavours, and preservatives. For example, Kittler (1970) reported studies in which the behaviour of some children improved when foods such as chocolate and milk were excluded from their diet.

Benjamin Feingold (1975) popularized the notion that some substances in foods could be linked to hyperactivity. Feingold hypothesized that artificial colourings and flavourings were pharmacologically active substances that produced or aggravated hyperactive symptoms in children. He proposed a diet (the K-P Diet) to restrict the intake of artificial food colours, flavours, preservatives, and foods with natural salicylates. After a stabilization period, foods would be gradually reintroduced to identify the particular items that affected the child.

Informal clinical evaluations and parent testimony suggested that Feingold's diet relieved hyperactivity in 30 to 40 percent of the children who tried it (Swanson and Kinsbourne, 1980). Results of controlled studies have shown equivocal results (Spring and Sandoval, 1976). Findings of a few well-conducted studies indicate that Feingold's diet may help only a small percentage of hyperactive children (Spring and Sandoval, 1976). A few studies also suggest that claims for the importance of food allergies in causing learning disabilities are exaggerated (Henker and Whalen, 1980).

But while skepticism concerning Feingold's hypothesis persists, concerns about the diet's adverse effects seem unwarranted. Rimland (1983) warned that we must be wary of abandoning something with few, if any, ill effects and the potential for some good results.

Technical

Computer technology has much to offer students with learning disabilities. When, for example, researchers (Trifiletti, Frith, and Armstrong, 1984) used a math program with twelve learning-disabled students for forty minutes a day over a school year and compared the results with those of learning-disabled students taught in regular resource room instruction for the same time and period, they found that the students in the computer instruction group learned almost twice the number of new math skills.

The computer has infinite patience for daily review. There are program learning packages, voice printers, programs to teach logic, and programs to develop self-concept. Some programs have been designed to provide supplementary drill and practice in academic skills. Other programs attempt to overcome passivity and help the child take a more active part in the learning process. These programs develop active learning styles and problem-solving strategies, focusing on discovery learning rather than drill.

Some computer programs have been designed to provide practice in academic skills for learning-disabled children.

Educational Intervention

The problems for those involved with students who are learning disabled revolve around how to prevent learning failure, how to individualize education for particular children, and how to provide special education programs for students who are not responding to traditional instructional approaches. Educators must be deeply concerned about how and what to teach pupils who have demonstrated that they learn differently and not very readily the things that education is charged with teaching them.

Within the public school system, almost all students with learning disabilities are educated in regular classrooms. In the United States in 1989/1990, for example, 98.5 percent of children with learning disabilities were in regular settings (McLeskey and Pacchiano, 1994).

The regular classroom-resource room combination is a common method of program delivery. However, intervention in educational settings varies, largely determined by how learning disabilities are defined and understood in a particular school. Approaches, program delivery, procedures, and teaching tactics also vary from situation to situation and from teacher to teacher according to personal preference and training.

Educational Approaches to Learning Disabilities

In a field as important as learning disabilities, one would think that the way to teach these children most effectively would have been the subject of intense investigation and practice. Such is not the case. Issues of definition, etiology, referral, and identification seem to have taken precedence over the pragmatics of actual classroom practice, and educational intervention has been somewhat ignored. In a survey of eight major special education journals between 1978 and 1987, for example, researchers (Lessen et al. 1989) found only 119 of 3106 articles (4 percent) that addressed academic intervention for learning-disabled students.

A wide range of general and specific approaches exists in educational intervention for students with learning disabilities. General approaches refer to techniques such as adapting curriculum and modifying grading requirements in the regular classroom or providing resource room assistance in areas of academic lag. Specific approaches refer to a great deal more program adaptation and direction such as teaching to sub-skill deficits or metacognitive training.

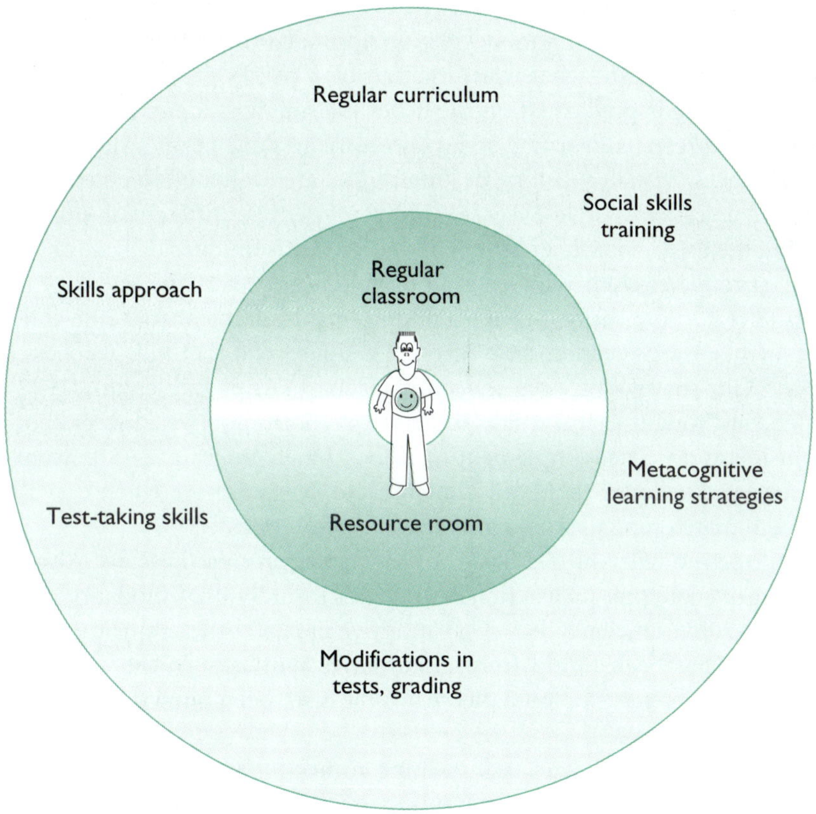

Figure 7-3
Curriculum components

In instructional terms, learning disabilities may be seen in three ways. Programs focus on underlying problems (processing), observable problems (skills), and strategy problems. However, the techniques used by teachers to assist affected students have altered quite dramatically since the birth of the field in 1963. Educators have moved away from process-training approaches that focused on the remediation of a developmental (processing) disability toward behavioural (skills) or cognitive (strategy training) approaches. These techniques that stress careful instruction in the academic areas and the cognitive approach tend to be more successful than the earlier indirect approaches that attempted to train students in the dysfunctional process that was interfering with learning (LLoyd, 1988).

Traditional Approaches

The ability-training model was based on the premise that learning disabilities are caused by impaired processes within the child. Proponents of ability training held that impaired perceptual processes can be measured and then reduced or eliminated through training procedures designed to improve specific perceptual problems, such as attention, language, discrimination, thinking, memory, and so forth.

Studies indicated that ability training succeeded in only about 24 percent of cases. More often than not, even when perceptual processes improved, academic performance and reading achievement did not. Moreover, for children older than nine years of age, remediation is unlikely to be effective for perceptual problems of discrimination, memory, sequence, closure, and spatial organization. By this age, basic processing ability seems to be as developed as it will ever be (Wepman et al., 1975).

Allied to the ability-training model was an approach that stressed skill acquisition but directed instruction to what is assumed to be a child's prime learning modality. Modality processing is predicated on the belief that many students with learning disabilities develop preferred learning styles and come to depend on a specific modality. Modal preferences (visual, auditory, or kinesthetic) are evaluated to determine particular individual learning styles. These are then used in differential programming emphasizing the use of visual, auditory, or kinesthetic techniques (Kavale and Forness, 1987). For example, a child with a visual dysfunction prefers the auditory modality and learns to read more easily through a phonics method. In contrast, the child with a visual preference learns reading best through a sight word method. Teachers hold to these beliefs. One survey of special education teachers (Arter and Jenkins, 1977) found that 99 percent thought that a child's modality strengths and weaknesses should be a major consideration when implementing educational programs; 93 percent of the teachers surveyed believed that their students had learned more when they modified instruction to match modality strengths (Kavale and Forness, 1987).

However, the modality model has not yielded the promised results. Although the presumption of matching instructional strategies to individual modality preferences to enhance learning efficiency has great intuitive appeal, little empirical support for the proposition has been found from quantitative syntheses of the extant research. Neither modality testing nor modality teaching have been shown to be efficacious (Kavale and Forness , 1987).

The combination ability- and task-training approach encourages teachers to work with academic materials while still attempting to improve perceptual processes. Sometimes the term VAKT — visual, auditory, kinesthetic and tactile — is applied here in order to stress that all modalities are employed in learning.

Behavioural Approaches

Behavioural approaches, also referred to as a skill model or task-based perspective, assume that a child's problems are external and result from some gap in instruction. The skills model focuses on the mismatch between school tasks and the unique ability patterns and learning styles of students with learning disabilities. Teachers provide direct instruction in weak academic areas and focus on the skills needed for academic success, such as word decoding and basic number facts.

Within each skill subject, a hierarchy of skills is defined. Briefly, teachers would follow these steps:

1. Determine the student's current repertoire of skills and information through informal and formal testing, school records, and medical data.
2. Determine the student's skills and informational deficits.
3. Specify the long- and short-term goals of the instructional program for the student.
4. Break these down into small, measurable, and more immediate objectives.
5. Select instructional procedures and techniques.

Task analysis — analyzing the behavioural components and prerequisite skills of a task — plays an integral role. When a teacher "task analyzes" an objective, the elements of the task that a child must master are clearly identified. For example, reading skills are broken down into the smallest possible steps and taught one step at a time. Instruction begins at the level of the simplest skill not mastered by the child.

As in any teaching approach, the skills model should be tailored to the needs of the individual child. The teacher may need to adjust the materials, change the timing, alter the lesson format, or adjust evaluation techniques to help an individual child achieve success. We see this in the case of Danny.

Not everyone agrees with such a structured approach based on specific building steps. While content areas such as math and handwriting lend themselves quite nicely to such a developmental approach, the language arts are more problematic. Indeed, a skills approach in reading and written language, which comes from a behavioural orientation, is in direct opposition to the precepts and approaches that arise from the context of emergent literacy and the more humanistic philosophy of whole language (Winzer, 1995). We discuss this later in the chapter.

Cognitive Approaches

Advances in cognitive psychology have resulted in the development of programs that concentrate on learning and thinking skills. They focus on metacognition — individuals' awareness of their own cognitive performance and the use of this awareness in altering their own behaviour. Metacognitive strategies "are used to plan how to solve a problem, to monitor one's solution strategy as it is being executed, and to validate the results of this strategy once it has been implemented" (Sternberg and Spear, 1985, p. 303). The efficient use of metacognitive processes enables individuals to better control their thinking and thereby become more effective and flexible learners (Shore and Dover, 1987).

Two types of behaviour are commonly characterized as comprising metacognition: knowledge and skill (Shore and Dover, 1987), sometimes referred to as learning strategies and cognitive strategies (control executive strategies). A strategy is an individual's approach to a task; it includes how the person thinks and acts when planning, executing, and evaluating performance on a task and its outcomes (Deshler and Lenz, 1989). Strategies are the regulatory mechanisms used by an active learner during an ongoing attempt to solve problems.

Individual Education Plan iep

Extract from IEP with a skill approach to intervention

Name: Danny CA 8-1
Grade: 3

Present Levels

In arithmetic, Danny exhibits a marked discrepancy between his potential and his performance. He functions more than two years below his grade level in this area. He is also retarded in his reading, though not as severely. By using his extensive sight word vocabulary, he is able to partly camouflage his deficit in word attack skills. Danny's academic problems seriously frustrate him and he is increasingly resorting to overt, acting-out behaviour.

Suggested Program

Danny requires an individual math program that will help him learn the basic skills in which he is deficient. He must master the number facts to nineteen and develop a concept of place value before he can learn the four arithmetic processes. To master the number facts he needs daily oral and written drill as well as many opportunities to generalize these facts to other solutions. Place value should be taught with many concrete materials, such as popsicle sticks, Cuisenaire rods, and a calculator. Danny will need much practice to translate concrete sums into numerical notation.

Improvements in reading may be accomplished by a word family approach. This will build on Danny's strong sight word vocabulary while strengthening his weak phonic skills. Rather than focusing on sound symbol association, Danny may benefit from much work in structural analysis of such items as prefixes, suffixes, and compound words. Although Danny should try to remain in the same reading program as the rest of his class, his success and attitudes to reading might improve with a special set of high interest, low vocabulary readers.

Danny's social problems appear to rise directly from his academic frustration. Learning tasks should be structured to allow him much success. He must demonstrate mastery of each step before progressing onward. To build his self-esteem, praise should be realistic and consistent. Danny's progress should be charted with some type of graphic display.

Long-range Goals

Danny will improve decoding skills in reading.
Danny will improve math skills by learning basic facts.
Danny will learn about days and months, time, and simple money exchange.

Short-term Objectives

Using a listening station, Danny will decode 15 to 20 selected words.
Danny will use the words in his own stories.
Danny will read the decoded words in short paragraphs.
In a paragraph, he will capitalize and use periods.
Using a software program on calendar skills, Danny will recognize the days of the week and say them in order.
Using concrete objects, he will say and write numbers to 100.
With a peer tutor, Danny will practise number facts to 19 to 100 percent accuracy.
When given short addition and subtraction problems, Danny will align them on the page correctly and solve to 100 percent accuracy using concrete objects.

Learning strategies (knowledge) are the general processes used in accomplishing a learning goal — the single and specific skills used in executing the goal (Derry, 1990). They are the self-regulating mechanisms for successful completion of a task and include planning, setting goals for studying, skimming information, locating information, generating questions, and in general deciding how to attack a learning task. Some strategies are generic; others are domain specific. General strategies are problem-solving skills such as note taking and test writing that apply across many areas of the curriculum. Specific strategies are those used in a specific situation such as remembering a /sh/ combination in reading or a principle in geometry.

Cognitive strategies (skills) are the regulation and control processes, the mental operations used to facilitate the learning process (Glatthorn, 1993). Skills encompass an awareness of the strategies and resources needed to perform the task effectively; these self-regulating mechanisms relate to tracking attention to task, asking questions such as, "Am I understanding this?" monitoring speed, and assessing the amount of time it takes to learn and understand certain material. They include motivation strategies such as self-coping and affirmation statements, establishing goals, and self-reinforcement.

Cognitive functions, including such concepts as operations, principles, attitudes, and work habits, are largely acquired (Mulcahy et al., 1986). But while some pupils seem to spontaneously develop the use of metacognitive strategies, others do not. Poor learners fail to develop these strategies; they simply do not understand the relation between strategic learning and successful performance.

Many students with learning disabilities have deficits in using metacognitive processes; they do not lack the processes entirely, but they seem to use them inefficiently and ineffectively. They often do not understand or recognize situations when efficient strategies such as verbal rehearsal and chunking are called for and so do not apply them spontaneously (deBettencourt, 1987). Research findings indicate that children with learning disabilities in general lack comprehension monitoring skills (Chan, 1988) and efficient task strategies (Baker, 1982), and fail to maintain and generalize learned strategies (Brown and Palinscar, 1982).

Individuals with learning disabilities show significant improvement following training in the application of various strategies. For example, when Lorna Chan and Peter Cole (1986) trained learning-disabled students to use self-questioning and underlining strategies while reading and then examined the effects of the training on comprehension, recall, and transfer, they found their subjects to demonstrate a higher level of performance in reading comprehension than a control group. Later Chan (1988) specifically taught students with learning disabilities to compare one proposition with another in a passage; she found that explicit instruction and strategies improved reading comprehension.

Strategy training stresses the strategies needed for acquiring information from written material, techniques for remembering information, and methods for improving written expression. There are three main areas — teaching students to consider the many variables involved in problem solving; teaching students to regulate the processes involved in problem solving, such as planning, checking, testing, revising and evaluating; and increasing student effectiveness in the use of specific cognitive skills employed in problem solving (Palinscar, 1986).

Some researchers characterize strategy training as little more than telling children what to do and expecting them to memorize and reproduce the steps of a strategy procedure exactly. Cognitive strategy instruction involves far more than that (see Harris and Pressley, 1991). True strategy training is geared to developing students' sensitivity to learning and to enhancing their awareness of the factors affecting their learning. Presumably, the more knowledge students have about their abilities and learning strategies, the more apt they are to acquire new knowledge and skills.

Strategy instruction is not a quick fix but it does work if integrated with the rest of the curriculum. For training in the use of learning strategies to have a significant impact on student success, the instruction must be intensive and extensive (Pressley, Levin, and McDonald, 1987; Slavin, 1989). The ultimate aim is to provide students with tools that will enable them to become autonomous learners and devise their own strategies.

Typically, a cognitive strategy provides the learner with a set of self-instructional steps which increase student effectiveness in acquisition, organization, and expression of information. Students must analyze the task at hand; identify the steps necessary to complete the task; identify the effective strategies; delineate the necessary steps; and decide how to go about implementing the strategies. The process may be outlined as follows:

In addition to being taught how to use metacognitive strategies, students must be taught when strategies can be appropriately used and how to tell if the strategy is working.

- Students reflect on what they already know.
- They devise a plan for attacking the new problem.
- They monitor their progress.
- They evaluate the outcome of the plan (Lowenthal, 1986).

One way to initiate the procedures is to have an adult first perform the specified task while verbalizing aloud, covering questions about the task, self-guiding instruction on how to do the task, and a self-evaluation of the performance of the task. The student then performs the task while the adult instructs aloud; following this the pupil performs the task while verbalizing aloud. The student can now perform the task while using self-verbalization in a whisper and, finally, perform the task using merely subvocalizations. Throughout, the student should be provided with feedback about the utility of the self-instructions for performance. To increase the efficacy of the procedures, teachers can explicitly point out other tasks and settings in which self-instruction can be used and use a variety of trainers, settings and tasks to increase the chances that the student will learn to use self-instruction successfully outside of the training session.

Students should be trained in the techniques until a reasonable criterion for performance has been reached, then followed-up with booster sessions in order to give a better chance that the trained skills will be maintained. In the early stages of strategy acquisition, students may require considerable help, direct explanation about the benefits of the strategies, and demonstrations of how and when to use them. Extensive instruction may be necessary to foster the use and transfer of appropriate strategies.

Simply telling students about effective strategies is not enough. In addition to being taught how to use metacognitive strategies, students must be taught when strategies can be appropriately used and how to tell if the strategy is working (Levin, 1986; Pressley, 1986). For example, mnemonic devices can be extremely valuable in aiding student recall of important information because they strengthen the relationship between what is known and what is to be learned (Levin and Levin, 1990). When Scruggs and Mastropieri (1989) taught adolescents with mild disabilities information about the First World War using a variety of mnemonic strategies or the more traditional drill and practice, students who learned though mnemonics recalled substantially more content than the traditionally taught group and retained the information for a longer period. While mnemonic strategies have emerged as one of the most powerful instructional techniques in special education for promoting the acquisition of academic content (Scruggs and Mastropieri, 1990), students must know when mnemonics are suitable. They may help with science content but may not be as applicable to learning a passage of Shakespeare.

Instrumental Enrichment

Mention should be made of the innovative approach devised by Feuerstein, whose work began with intervention with children from postwar Israeli refugee camps. Over the past forty years, Feurstein has been working toward the development of procedures to facilitate active-modification programs for exceptional students. He has been concerned with assessing the untapped cognitive potential of deprived children in order to remedy their deficiencies through an active intervention program which attempts to build a more effective cognitive structure. The acquisition of such a structure will enable a person of low mental ability to become more adaptable and flexible and therefore more capable of comprehending, planning, and solving problems (Lewis and Samuda, 1989).

Feuerstein calls his program Instrumental Enrichment and describes it as "active modification" because he sees children's performances as modifiable under appropriate social, cultural, and educational policies (Harth, 1988). The aim of instrumental enrichment is to "change the overall cognitive structures of the retarded performer by transforming his passive and dependent cognitive style into the characteristic of an autonomous and independent thinker" (Feurstein, 1980, p. 1).

Instrumental Enrichment is a paper-and-pencil curriculum administered three to five times a week over a two- to three-year-period. Each lesson takes about one hour and is typically used as part of a school program. The program is taught to a whole class in a specific sequence (Harth, 1988). The more than 500 pages of exercises are divided into fifteen instruments. Each instrument primarily focuses on one deficient cognitive function although it addresses other cognitive functions as well. Each of the instruments is content free; it does not address any specific curriculum skill or content area but rather focuses on the processes of learning directly (Harth, 1988).

Curriculum Modifications

A major characteristic of pupils with learning disabilities is an inability to learn adequately in the regular classroom through traditional teaching techniques. Because of the heterogenous nature of the learning-disabled population, schools must provide different administrative arrangements and varied approaches. In addition, they must be willing to permit modifications to the regular curriculum and assessment procedures.

Modifications include differentiated assignments, focused questions, intermittent tutoring, grouping, and supplementary instruction. If possible, curriculum modifications should stress changing the format rather than watering down the curriculum. Some general tips for teachers of students with learning disabilities follow.

Not only is language ability critical to learning in general, but a majority of individuals with reading disorders have weakness in receiving, processing, or expressing language as well (Smith, 1991). Until recently, however, professionals have tended to overlook language in favour of perceptual problems even though a sizable proportion of children with learning disabilities suffer language dysfunctions. Students may require specialized help with speech production and oral language, especially syntax and pragmatics. (See Chapter 6.)

Tips for Teachers

Tips for teachers of students with learning disabilities

Classroom Climate

- Maintain a warm and supportive emotional climate.
- Be organized and consistent. Disorganized and chaotic classrooms can elevate hyperactivity in children as can unpredictable classroom schedules.
- Be honest but liberal with praise. Use consistent reinforcement and provide continuous and immediate feedback. Students are led to persist longer if they are given attribution feedback on effort ("You've been working hard.") or ability ("You're good at this.") or some blend of the two, particularly ability feedback combined with teaching particular strategies in math and reading comprehension (Dohrn and Bryan, 1994).
- Emphasize co-operation rather than competition; effort over achievement.
- Be specific, consistent, and sytematic in expectations and actions.

Adaptations

- Seat students near to the front of the room so that distractions are behind them, or use carrels to cut down distractions.
- Have students keep an assignment notebook.
- Provide alternative assignments.
- Allow manipulatives.
- Highlight textbooks.
- On worksheets, use lot of spacing; provide ample space for writing or drawing; avoid crowding and extraneous print; limit the type of questions; provide clear and concise directions; provide examples; use typing or printing in place of handwriting:
- If homework is important to your program, keep in mind that too much can overwhelm the learning-disabled student.
- Modify grades and report cards to reflect the individual student's level of improvement.
- Teach students how to do the test. Students are at a great disadvantage if they do not understand the format or the instructions of a test.
- Allow students to use different strategies in test taking. For example, a youngster may respond more easily if allowed to tape record test answers.
- Administer practice tests before the real thing.
- Use many organizational devices to assist student learning such as dates for assignments written on the board, reminders about homework.
- Provide supplementary content written to a lower level than the textbook.
- Provide outlines of textbook chapters and outlines of lecture presentations for older students.
- Teach strategies to improve memory.
- Divide teaching into small modules; teach in small building steps.
- Use visual and auditory cues and prompts to enhance students' ability to discriminate between various stimuli (Polloway et al, 1989).
- Have students explain concepts and skills in their own words.

Instruction

- Allow short answers to questions.
- In order to provide pacing and ensure better understanding, read orally to the class.
- Preteach and preview major concepts.
- State a purpose for reading such as looking for specifics.
- Provide for much repetition in instruction.

The debate about how to teach reading efficiently to students experiencing difficulties has remained unresolved for almost a century. Experts disagree about the best way to teach reading and almost every method used has failed with a significant number of people. The debate first concerned the relative merits of phonics and whole-word approaches. Today the philosophies of optimal reading instruction split between special education (skills) and general education (whole language) and often seem to be in stark contrast. Key concepts in special education such as direct instruction, teaching to mastery, curriculum-based assessment, and the use of explicit reinforcement procedures, clash with the whole language or literature-based approaches to reading (see Gersten and Dimino, 1993).

Whole language advocates often vehemently attack the orientation of many remedial and compensatory instructional programs in discrete comprehension and word attack skills. Opponents of the whole language approach for students with special needs argue that there appear to be far too many instances of low achieving students floundering in whole language contexts (Reyes, 1991).

In comparison to good writers, poor writers have difficulty in generating ideas, in understanding cause and effect relationships, and in using sequential thought processes. Writing problems are prevalent and difficult to remediate because proficiency in this area relies on an expanded experiential and knowledge base and the development of adequate listening, speaking, and reading skills (Smith, 1991). To improve writing, teachers must first build the motivation to write and the student's confidence that his or her thoughts are worthy of communication. A writing program should include daily writing, sustained writing, and peer collaboration in the writing process (Englert et al., 1988). "[W]hen young children collaborate on writing tasks, they use talk to elaborate their writing and to become more familiar with words, ideas, and composing procedures" (Daiute, 1989, p. 457).

Some handwriting difficulties are due to basic problems such as poor co-ordination or perceptual motor difficulties. The left-handed child may need special help to orient paper and pencil, while other children may need assistance to overcome letter reversals and misorientations. Still other children need help to keep between the lines, form letters, and maintain spacing.

Two general procedures directly helpful to students with learning disabilities are co-operative learning and peer tutoring.

The study and remediation of math deficiencies among students with learning disabilities has not received the same level of attention as other areas, such as reading and language (Bender, 1992). Remediation of arithmetic problems requires step-by-step instruction, beginning at the child's level of performance and advancing at the child's own rate. In teaching math, teachers must always provide learning-disabled children with practical associations. For example, decimals should be taught as related to money and integers with the temperatures on the thermometer. Whenever possible, concrete materials should be used.

Two general procedures directly helpful to students with learning disabilities are co-operative learning (see Chapter 8) and peer tutoring. Peer tutoring is defined as "a more able child helping a less able child in a co-operative working pair carefully organized by a teacher" (Topping, 1989, p. 489). For students with learning disabilities, peer tutoring is an effective instructional alternative, especially when the tutoring program emphasizes repetition and incorporates review and when the child being tutored reaches mastery level before advancing to the next tasks (see Bierne-Smith, 1991).

A Matter of Debate

Reading instruction

The philosophy of whole language has become an important reform movement in today's public education. Although the term was scarcely known in the early 1980s, the idea of whole language has taken off in most Canadian provinces in the last decade. In classrooms right across the country, teachers are being encouraged to break away from skills dominated instruction in favour of a whole language approach to teaching reading and writing (McConagh, 1988). In Quebec and Nova Scotia, whole language programs have become official policy.

Whole language is representative of a re-understanding of the way in which humans learn. It implies that we learn in real and purposeful contexts, that we learn by restructuring knowledge, and that we learn by becoming engaged in authentic activities (Sumara, 1991). Reading should develop in a natural, developmental fashion, much as language developed when children were younger.

Pragmatically, whole language approaches have meant a shift from a basal skills approach to a literature-based language approach. Whole language classrooms are student centred, literature centred, rich in the variety of printed matter they contain, and often organized to support small group work. Within these classrooms, language learning extends across the curriculum and teachers do not rely on basal reading programs for direction in teaching reading and writing (McConagh, 1988).

While there is much that is positive about a whole language philosophy, controversy surrounds it and criticism of whole language has steadily emerged in the literature. Skills, it is argued, are not being taught, and teachers are accused of sacrificing learning to a laissez-faire style of teaching and learning. Stakeholders in education are mounting a counter movement against whole language because of deficiencies that they see in the implementation of the theory (Sumara, 1991). They point out that evidence accumulated over decades opposes at least some of the principles of a whole language philosophy. Specifically, research shows that teachers of beginning reading should present well-designed phonics instruction (Anderson et al., 1985). The Canadian Psychological Association has called for more phonics instruction as has the Reading and Literacy Institute of Alberta (Simner, 1995). They call for a balance in instruction between a top down whole language approach and a bottom up code emphasis approach.

Against whole language	In favour of whole language
A meta-analysis of research on holistic approaches to reading instruction in the primary grades (both whole language and language experience approach) (Stahl and Miller, 1989) found that overall, holistic approaches were no more effective than conventional basal reading approaches. This was judged on standardized measures of reading as well as far more naturalistic measures (such as oral miscue analysis and attitude measures).	Contemporary research on emergent literacy (Teale and Sulzby, 1989) and the early stages of reading, writing, and speaking among 2- to 4-year-old children suggests that language acquisition is a holistic, cognitive process linked to the experiences of children.

Against whole language	In favour of whole language
Stahl and Miller (1989) essentially concluded that whole language does not make sense as a comprehensive reading approach for students with potential reading difficulties.	A true whole language program is one that integrates language across the curriculum, surrounds children with print, and stresses the communicative and social functions of language.
Chall (1989) says that whole language "puts at even greater risk those children who need the instruction most — low income, minority, and learning disabled children" (p. 532).	Whole language provides both functional and enriched language experiences for children and explores them through a variety of meaningful experiences and materials.
Mastery does not materialize from osmosis, brief encounters, or casual meetings. Students need direct instruction. But whole language does not tolerate modelling, error correction, or task sequencing.	The underlying premise of the whole language approach is that reading and writing are learned in much the same fashion as speaking and listening (Newman, 1985).
The incidental nature of whole language threatens to leave gaps in learners' basic skill repertoire.	Children are invited to learn to read and write, by reading and writing rather than by mastering sub-skills (Goodman, 1986).
Students with disabilities typically meet problems in many aspects of language and speech development, so whole language seeks to build on a weakness.	There are concerns about direct instruction as a means of helping students read independently and enjoy the reading experience in other contexts than the classroom.
Much research strongly supports an early emphasis on letter-sound correpsondences, especially for children at risk for reading failure (O'Connor et al., 1993).	
Reading methods that include explicit, synthetic phonics instruction result in better first grade achievement in word recognition and spelling, and these effects spread in second grade to comprehension, reading rate, and vocabulary (O'Connor et al, 1993).	

Summary

1. Controversies continue to plague the field of learning disabilities. These chiefly revolve around the formulation of a universally acceptable definition. Although the term *learning disabilities* has gained wide recognition among educators and the general public, a precise definition has not yet surfaced. Current definitions fail to reflect any consistency and this spills over to influence such critical areas as classification, identification, prevalence, and instructional approaches.

2. Many terms have been used to describe learning-disabled children and youth and a range of behaviours have been attributed to them.
3. Learning disabilities should be viewed as a syndrome, a group of behaviours that adversely affect a child's functioning across domains. The common thread is the inability of these students to learn adequately in regular classrooms under traditional teaching approaches and methods. Learning-disabled youngsters cannot conform to normal educational demands — there is a marked gap between capability and performance on academic tasks. These children are sound in mind and body but still cannot seem to get the hang of reading, writing, and arithmetic, and therefore lag noticeably in school. Students who have difficulty learning often have problems adjusting to the school, classroom routines, the pressures of daily life, peer groups, and a succession of different teachers.
4. Their difficulties in dealing with various types of information may cause learning-disabled children to be less task oriented, less verbally facile, and less responsive than non-learning-disabled students. They are likely to have attention problems, be more distractible, show poor self-esteem, an external locus of control, poor motivation, and learned helplessness. They are often disorganized, unco-operative, slow to adapt to change, and overly active. Many children with learning disabilities experience negative social relations with significant people in their lives — parents, teachers, peers — and with strangers as well.
5. The reasons why students with learning disabilities fail are not easily discerned. Numerous etiological factors have been proposed.
6. Arithmetic problems occur with less frequency than reading disabilities and have traditionally received less attention. Problems in visual perception and visual processing include difficulties with oculomotor co-ordination, spatial relations, figure-ground perception, the discrimination of differences, and the recognition of likenesses.
7. Recently educators have begun to reconceptualize learning-disabled students as those who have not developed effective learning strategies. They see a need for strategy training to teach affected students how to use metacognitive skills. Metacognitive skills involve self-monitoring, practising, reality testing, and co-ordinating the processes of studying and learning. These thinking strategies, which serve to support, guide, and extend the thinking processes of their users, are internal to the individual.
8. Cognitive instructional programs stress information processing, organizational skills, study skills, application of information, and problem solving. Good cognitive strategy instruction encourages learners to construct powerful cognitive strategies.
9. There is clear evidence that children with learning and behaviour problems benefit from peer tutoring and co-operative learning.

CHAPTER 8

Children from Diverse Cultural Backgrounds

Historical Notes

Canada is a country of immigrants. Almost since its beginnings, it has witnessed an influx of peoples from every corner of the earth. Before 1901 the pace of immigration to Canada was relatively stable; the vast tide from Eastern and Central Europe came in the early 1900s. The Yukon gold rush, the completion of the first transcontinental railway, the building of other lines, the closing of the American frontier, the new developments in dry-land farming, and the Canadian government's first concentrated policy to promote immigration, all contributed to attract more than three million immigrants to Canada between 1896 and 1914 (Palmer, 1975). Restrictive immigration policies after 1924 saw a huge dip in the number and type of newcomers. When these policies were reversed after the Second World War, nearly all of the new immigrants were of European origin.

In 1951 less than 2 percent of the population represented racial minorities (Ramcharan, 1988). By 1981, Census of Canada data indicated 105 ethnic origins in the population, of which persons of non-British or non-French origin accounted for 33.1 percent of the total Canadian population (Statistics Canada, 1985)

From 1983 to 1988 more than 100 000 school-age children — most of whom did not speak a word of English — flooded the schools under a federal government policy of increased immigration (McLaren, 1988). Today, more children from Asia and the Caribbean are entering our school systems. Chinese and other Asian students are especially highly represented in Vancouver and Toronto; one in nine residents of British Columbia is of Asian ancestry (Renaud and Badets, 1993).

If immigration proceeds according to Canada's five-year immigration plan, an increase in the number of children under fifteen can be expected. More than 300 000 children from diverse countries with unique linguistic and cultural backgrounds were expected to arrive in Canada from 1990 to 1995 (Burke, 1992). It is estimated that by the year 2001 some 15 percent of the population will be members of a visible minority group (Ramcharan, 1988)

Canada is a country of ethnic and linguistic differences. The number of immigrants who have come to Canada since Confederation has dramatically changed the composition of the country. Whereas in 1867, Canada was basically a bicultural society — British and French — it is now a multicultural society. So much so that the United Nations recognizes Toronto as the most culturally and ethnically diverse city in the world (Lewington and Orpwood, 1993).

In 1991, 31 percent of the population reported an ethnic background other than English or French, up from 25 percent in 1986. Just over one million people reported aboriginal origins. Ethnic diversity brings language diversity, although this tends to be an urban phenomenon. According to the 1991 census, almost 15 percent of Canada's 27 million people speak neither English or French as their mother tongue. Almost half the students in Toronto and Vancouver speak a first language other than English. In Vancouver, for instance, 47.9 percent of school students speak English as a second language (Early, 1990). A Canadian secondary school reported that it enrolled students with fifty-four first languages other than English.

Figure 8-1
Ethnic composition of Canada

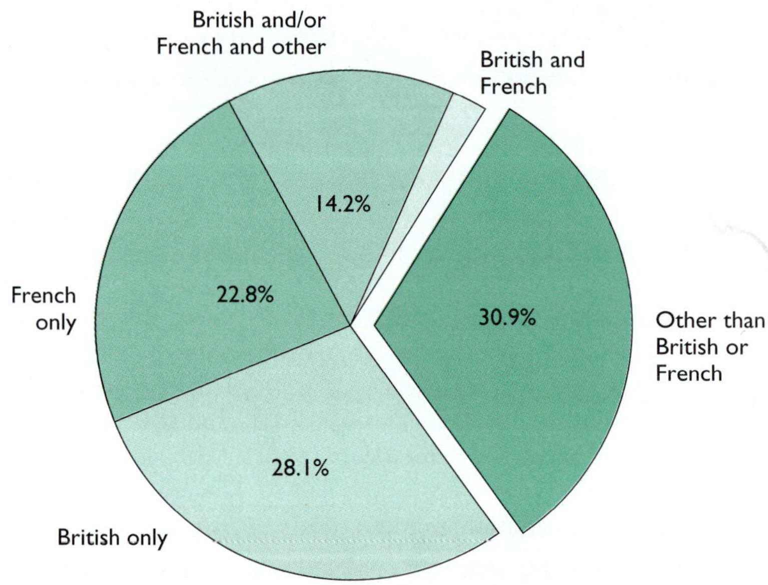

The dominant Canadian culture is made up of several subgroups that formed as a result of different geographic, economic, educational, and ethnic influences. Consider, for example, the difference between an outporter from Newfoundland, a prairie child, and a Torontonian. To the dominant Canadian culture, New Canadians add a further diversity of cultural and linguistic roots.

Every aspect of human life is profoundly related to cultural expectations and norms. Although individuals may transfer into another society, they do not leave behind the influences of their culture — the social value systems, traditions, and symbolic communication patterns of their native environments. Culture, as it relates to children, can strongly affect many aspects of learning. Some students from other cultures do extremely well in Canadian schools; others do not. However, identifying the factors that account for the academic perfomance of cultural minorities is complex. Social scientists are still trying to determine the attitudes, beliefs, behavioural styles, and opportunities that foster the success of a particular group (Jacob and Jordan, 1987).

There are many students whose daily living experiences are influenced by cultural beliefs that differ from the thought patterns of the majority. These students must learn to live and negotiate in at least two different social and linguistic systems that often dictate conflicting expectations for normal behaviour and appropriate development (Luce and Smith, 1986). Patterns of eye contact, physical contact, use of language, and ways of responding to persons in positions of authority may vary greatly from one group to another. For example, the Native child who won't look at the teacher may appear to that teacher to be rude and insubordinate, when actually the child is conforming to the customs and standards of his or her society.

To live and develop successfully in two cultural systems is sufficiently challenging for students with no exceptional conditions; the difficulties multiply for students who have special problems in communication, mobility, or development. Disabled children from different cultural backgrounds encounter a double-edged sword — the lack of the majority language combined with a disabling condition.

In this chapter, we discuss two broad groups of children. The first are those who may encounter difficulties in the school system because of different cultural values and differences in language. This includes children of Native heritage and refugee children who may have experienced war, famine, or other forms of suffering in their native lands or in internment camps. Our intention here is to alert readers to a special group, not to create a new category of special education. Although we stress the language difficulties faced by children from diverse cultures, children are not at risk unless the lack of English means that they are unable to participate effectively in the social and educational processes that enable them to grow and benefit from the opportunities available in the mainstream.

As well, we delve into a new area of concern in special education, the very special problems of children from diverse cultural backgrounds who also have conditions that hinder their learning or behaviour. For special educators, this is a new field. Up to now, special education has not been noted for its responsiveness to cultural differences; it has tended to view the disability as taking precedence over minority group membership and assigned secondary importance to any minority value system or cultural values (see McNeil, 1990). There has existed little recognition or understanding of the cultural and linguistic variables that occur among culturally different populations (Erickson and Walker, 1983).

In many ways, approaches and methodologies for children from diverse cultures who are also disabled extend the procedures used with other culturally different children. Children with exceptional conditions will need additional language training while receiving special education directed to their unique pattern of exceptionalities. Generally, the special education approaches offered will not differ from those we present in this text for specific exceptionalities. While the goals and procedures are similar to those for dominant-culture disabled peers, however, there are important differences in the teacher competencies needed to achieve these goals and some differences in teaching strategies.

One important component in today's Canadian classroom is a multicultural perspective. While multicultural education means many different things and can be implemented in many ways, a major objective is ensuring that all students are instructed in ways that do not penalize them because of their cultural differences and that in fact capitalize on their cultural heritage (Hallahan and Kauffman, 1991).

When language is mentioned in the context of a multicultural perspective, the first thing that comes to mind for many people is the child who speaks little or no English. While we cannot reduce a multicultural perspective to a remedial exercise that focuses on teaching a child English or the use of standard dialect, the increasing numbers of students coming to school who do not speak English as their primary language make language an important issue for teachers. They must decide what language is best suited to instructing students and how best to promote academic growth as well as English language acquisition.

Earlier in this book, we pointed out that Canadian and American special education show more parallels than differences. In most areas, research findings are relevant to both nations. This is not the case with children from diverse cultural backgrounds. Far from it. Canadian ideas about multiculturalism, multicultural education, bilingualism, and other language programs not only differ from American practices, they are sometimes in direct opposition to them. Canada, for example, has a Multiculturalism Act; the Americans fiercely debate whether or not multiculturalism is a valid route for schools to follow. Similarly, Canadian researchers lead the way in second language programs. Many Americans treat bilingualism with deep suspicion, if not actual distaste.

Development of the Field

Multiculturalism depends upon the desire of ethnic groups to maintain their own distinctive culture and the commitment of the majority group to provide support (Young, 1979). Although Canada is the first country in the world to pass a Multicultural Act (Mazurek, 1991), an official policy of multiculturalism is quite new here.

As policy, multiculturalism was first introduced during the Trudeau years. It emerged as a by-product of the Federal Comission on Bilingualism and Biculturalism. As the Commission endorsed English and French as Canada's official languages, it was forced to confront the fact that Canada was a mosaic of many cultures and ethnic groups. This led to an official federal policy of multiculturalism. In July, 1988, the policy, which had been accepted by all political parties in 1977, became statute law when Bill C-93 was passed by the Parliament of Canada.

The introduction of the Canadian Multiculturalism Act was a move directed toward the vigorous implementation of an egalitarian, culture-retentionist policy that reflects the character of Canada today. The Act provides a legislative basis and firm foundation for governmental initiatives for multicultural purposes. According to Kas Mazurek (1991), "the inaugration of multiculturalism as official state policy ... represents one of the most elevating and enlightened moments in Canadian history." It showed that Canada is officially and politically committed to the preservation and enhancement of the multicultural character of the country, to equality of both majority and minority ethnocultural groups, and to the promotion of cultural interaction and sharing ("President's," 1988).

The original policy set itself three major focused goals. The first was to materially improve the socio-economic conditions of disadvantaged ethnic groups. A second goal sought to increase equality of opportunity for ethnic groups in areas such as schooling and employment. Third, the policy sought to nurture and perpetuate the social acceptance of diverse cultures (Mazurek, 1991).

Multiculturalism has many faces; there are varied perceptions of the concept, and so far only broad typologies have been established (Mazurek, 1987). One way to promote tolerance and respect is to incorporate multicultural perspectives in the schools. Under multiculturalism, schools must not only embrace cultural pluralism and promote tolerance for differences but also remove ethnocentric biases from curriculum, pedagogy, testing, and placement (see Mazurek, 1991). All children will be seen to possess equal cultural capital.

However, the type of multicultural education that may be legitimately implemented in Canadian schools has been a matter of contention because it remains unclear how we can find a conception that consistently and fully corresponds to Canadian multiculturalism. Moreover, there are a number of ways to approach multicultural education. It can be viewed as the education of culturally different students; education about cultural differences; education for cultural pluralism; and bicultural education.

In the past, multicultural issues were often relegated to social studies curricula. Increasingly, however, more attention is being focused on other curriculum areas as it is realized that social science perspectives form only one part of a comprehensive picture of our diversity and that other curriculum areas must abandon a unicultural perspective in light of our school's multicultural student population (Wood, 1985).

Definitions of Children from Diverse Cultural Backgrounds

A great many cultures are represented in Canadian classrooms. Culturally different children come from subgroups within our society that differ on a variety of factors, including racial, geographic, economic, educational, and ethnic background. Although we prefer the term *diverse cultural backgrounds*, children and groups may be described in other ways. *Minority group, ethnic group, culturally different, New Canadian*, and *immigrant* are also widely used terms.

Conventional definitions of exceptionalities do not apply to exceptional children from diverse cultural backgrounds, particularly those for whom English is not a first language. Many special factors must be considered when defining a culturally different disabled child. These include the role of language, the family's expectations, cultural attitudes toward disabilities, and the relationship between the child's cultural community and the larger society. Given these factors, **disabled children from different cultures** can best be described as children who have diagnosable handicapping conditions that are recognized as such by their cultural community.

Terminology

Many of the terms and definitions that relate to cultural differences do not come from the field of education but from sociology, anthropology, and other disciplines. A number of terms are important in the understanding of children from diverse cultures. These are:

- *Culture.* Most contemporary social scientists view culture as consisting primarily of "the symbolic, ideational, and intangible aspects of human societies" (Banks, 1988, p. 73). In other words, **culture** means the distinctive creativity of a particular group of people (Hilliard, 1980).
- *Race* is a socially determined category that is related to physical characteristics in a complex way.
- *Ethnicity* is used to refer to "groups that are characterized in terms of a common nationality, culture, or language" (Betancourt and Lopez, 1993). However, race and ethnicity are not synonymous with culture. Culture is not a fixed entity, transmitted through the genes.
- *Culturally diverse population* refers to individuals from populations other than the majority population of Canada.
- *Language proficiency* refers to the degree to which students exhibit control over the use of language.
- *Language minority children* have "been exposed to two languages in natural speaking contexts [and] come from homes where they have made functional use of a language other than that of the dominant culture during interactions with one or more family members" (Mattes and Omark, 1984, p. 2).
- *Limited English proficient students* are those for whom English is a second language and who are, to some degree, unable to benefit from English language instruction in the classroom. Some authors feel that *potential English proficiency* (PEP) is a more positive and acceptable term (Hamayan and Domico, 1991).
- *Cultural pluralism* is a concept that reflects the belief that the contributions of many groups strengthen and enrich our society.
- *Acculturation* is the process of incorporating aspects of the new culture while maintaining one's native cultural identity (Baca and Harris, 1988).
- *Value systems* refer to the set of beliefs and values that guide the members of a culture in social interactions. What is accepted as desirable conduct in one culture may be considered inappropriate in another. For example, there exist many discrepancies between the values of the dominant culture and that of our Native people.
- *Culture shock* occurs as people adjust to a culture that is significiantly different from their own. They often become confused, anxious, and frustrated because they do not know what is expected of them in different situations. The disorientation or confusion is called culture shock.
- *Culture conflict* is the clash between a family's cultural values and those of the dominant society caused by disparities in social conventions, values, and expectations. The more different the culture from the Canadian norm, the greater the likelihood of conflict.
- *Culturally deprived* is an old term that was used to describe students who had "experiences in homes which do not transmit the cultural patterns necessary for the type of learning characteristic of the schools and the larger society" (Bloom, 1965, p. 4). Since the 1960s, the term has undergone some changes, first from *culturally deprived* to *culturally disadvantaged.* Today, the preferred term is *educationally disadvantaged.*
- *Socialization* is the general process by which a child acquires the beliefs, skills, values, behavioural patterns, and other characteristics considered appropriate for a particular society.

A great many cultures are represented in Canadian classrooms.

Prevalence of Children from Diverse Cultural Backgrounds

The fact that our student population is made up of ever increasing numbers of cultural groups is a given. Many Canadian school children come from homes in which English is not the first language, and many metropolitan areas are educating large numbers of bilingual students. Thirty percent of the students enrolled in Toronto schools were born outside Canada, and almost 50 percent have a first language other than English (Cummins, 1987).

Large numbers of children were expected to come to Canada between 1990 and 1995. Of the more than 300 000 children arriving in those five years, it was predicted that about 73 percent would be aged five to fourteen; the rest would be under the age of five. Most immigrants were expected to settle in Ontario (55 percent), Quebec (18 percent), and British Columbia (12 percent). By far the largest proportion of children would be those born in Asia (47 percent), followed by Europe (27 percent). A huge 66 percent of the Asian-born children were expected to settle in British Columbia, while European immigrants were expected to be highest among the Atlantic provinces. Most of these children would be unfamiliar with either English or French (Burke, 1992).

Culturally different children are represented in all categories of exceptionality. It has been estimated that the incidence of exceptionality among culturally different children is as high as that for the general population, if not higher. The incidence of physical handicaps in some minority groups is related to conditions associated with poverty (Erickson and Walker, 1983), so any additional incidence may be due to problems with health and nutrition.

Classification

Classification schemes as we use them in the rest of this text are not relevant to children from different cultures. Trying to determine any commonalities between children from diverse cultural backgrounds is an impossible undertaking. All children, regardless of ethnicity, become socialized within a cultural context. Moreover, these children are, by definition, an extremely heterogeneous population. Cultural factors vary widely from group to group. Economic background, parental education levels, and residential settings also vary widely, just as they do among the entire Canadian population. However, we can group children within some very broad parameters.

Bilingual Children

Bilingual is a term used to describe individuals who speak two languages. Those who speak three languages are trilingual, and so on. The ideal bilingual person can read, speak, write, and think in two languages with native-like control over each. The prevalence of bilingualism reflects the cultural mix of a country. Canada has a bilingualism rate of about 24 percent (Walker, 1990).

For many years, educators viewed early bilingualism as a hazard to school learning. They feared that two languages could lead to confusion and language handicaps or could impair intelligence and cripple creativity. Research in the 1950s indicated that bilingual children did poorly in school and suffered retarded language development in both languages (Segalowitz, 1981). Parents were advised not to teach more than one language at home and educators did not introduce a second language until the late elementary grades.

The long-held assumption that children are at a disadvantage when learning two languages and that their progress in both languages is delayed has not been supported by recent research. Today most linguists consider it advantageous for children to be bilingual. Research literature indicates that, far from hurting children, bilingualism helps thinking and does not interfere with performance in either language. Bilingual children show better performance on verbal and non-verbal IQ tests. They show earlier development and enhanced performance in metalinguistic abilities as well as increased achievement in areas other than language studies (Galambos and Goldwin-Meadow, 1990; Hakuta, 1989).

Children with Limited English Proficiency

Linguistically diverse children may represent any number of different groups: children who have immigrated from another country, children living in Canada who are learning two or more languges concurrently, and second generation children who prefer not to speak English at home. Children who are still learning the dominant language will be at an obvious disadvantage in a linguistically oriented, English-speaking classroom. Education for these children stresses rapid acquisition of the mainstream language, often while retaining and improving the heritage language.

Refugee Children

Many new Canadians are refugees who have lived in camps for several years. During this period, it is unlikely that schooling was provided. Some children who come to school have never sat at a desk, used an exercise book, or written with a pen or pencil. These students may have great difficulty adjusting to school after never attending an educational institution or not attending one for a long period.

At-risk Children

The term *at risk* is used to describe a number of different categories of children. It refers to those who are physically, medically, or psychologically in danger of failing to thrive as well as those adversely affected by economic, environmental, or geographic factors. Other children designated at risk include those from low socio-economic level families, not attending or participating regularly in school, not achieving, and disruptive and delinquent. Among these children are many for whom English is not a first language and many who are educationally disadvantaged as a result of coming from environments which hinder growth and have a restricted use of language. When these disadvantages are coupled with poor family attitudes, poor motivation, and poor facilities, it is easy to see the formidable problems. Readers are urged to re-address the sections on mild intellectual disabilities for information on disadvantaged children; this chapter focuses on those from varied cultural backgrounds only.

Native Children

Native children may attend federal, provincial, territorial, parochial, or band-controlled schools (More, 1984). Native people are becoming increasingly aware of the extent to which language and culture are inextricably mixed. At the present time, more and more bands are developing on-reserve schools.

In general, Native programs include areas such as traditional crafts, life skills, Native studies, learning assistance, English as a Second Language, language arts, alternative programs, counselling, tutoring, academic skill development, home and school co-ordination, work experience, and Native language instruction (Csapo and Clarke, 1984).

Exceptional Children from Diverse Cultural Backgrounds

Disabilities of the same type and prevalence affect children from diverse cultural backgrounds just as they do those in the dominant culture. A few conditions tend to be geographically or racially particular — for example, cleft palate among Asians, sickle cell anemia among Blacks, cystic fibrosis in Caucasians, and Tay-Sachs disease among Jews.

Disabled children from different cultures present a unique challenge to the educational system not only because of the obvious difficulties in language systems but also because of disparities in cultural values. Communication problems may be related to structural dissimilarities in the language as well as to differences in basic understandings and values.

Identification and Assessment

As a broad generalization, we can say that culturally different children are less homogeneous as a group than children of the dominant Anglo-Canadian culture. There are wider linguistic, educational, and social differences within ethnic minority groups. As a result, there seems to be more variance in test scores among minority group members.

Issues surrounding how, when, what, and who should assess children from diverse cultural backgrounds form some of the major areas of concern within this field of education. For a variety of reasons, widely used measures and procedures are inappropriate with minority group children. IQ tests, for example, are standardized on a representative sample of the general population and none of the tests commonly used in this country have been normed on Canadian children or our Native population (Bachor and Crealock, 1986).

Under most circumstances, typical IQ tests are biased against many minority children (Cummins, 1987). While the Wechsler scales are clearly the tests of choice for the assessment of the intellectual functioning of individual children, there is increasing concern as to whether using an American-normed psychometric instrument results in significant cultural bias against Canadian majority or ethnic and racial minority children (Mueller et al., 1986). In a survey of a Western Canadian city, Cummins (1987) found that minority students performed very much below norms on the WISC-R; scores were significantly more depressed on the verbal parts of the test compared with the non-verbal parts (Cummins, 1987). Similarly, studies on Canadian Native students have tended to report average or better performance scores and below average verbal scores for the WISC and the WISC-R (Mueller et al., 1986; Seyfort, Spreen, and Lahmer, 1980).

Another problem in using standardized tests is that many children from other cultures have never had the opportunity to develop test-taking skills. Some have never seen the puzzles and games that the tests use and often children must be first trained in how to take the test (Omark and Watson, 1983). As well, they must understand the purpose of the procedure if they are to be motivated to perform their best.

Furthermore, the elaborate, stylized English commonly used in standardized tests may prevent them from accurately measuring the achievement, ability, or skills of students with limited English (see Hoover, Politzer, and Taylor, 1987). For Native children, for example, most commonly used tests stress verbal responses which place children at a disadvantage both because of culture and because of language. On the reserve, orientation toward speech and verbal fluency play a minor role in the culture.

Any form of measurement and evaluation must place priority on the child's language. A major problem arises when a student's fluency in conversational English is mistaken for full language competence. The disparity between superficial and substantial competency leads psychologists and teachers to administer English-language intelligence and achievement tests and to interpret the findings as they would for children whose first langage is English. Inappropriate data generation leads to incorrect conclusions about a child's ability and ultimately to inappropriate educational placements. This is discussed in the Research Notes that follow.

The cultural heterogeneity as well as the socio-economic inequalities of North American society make it impossible for responsible professionals to rely solely on information from current standardized assessment approaches (Cummins, 1989; Ginsberg, 1986). A number of researchers have proposed multidisciplinary approaches. Zappia (1989) proposed a case study approach that includes observation, interviews, formal tests, informal measures, and a review of cumulative records.

An alternative procedure is to adopt a functional approach to testing which examines a child's performance within the context of naturalistic environments (see Chapter 4). The functional approach is based on the direct collection of performance data, the identification of factors that affect performance, such as those under teacher control, the presentation and examination of repeated teaching trials, and close assessment to determine the success of teaching (Sugai and Maheady, 1988).

Research Notes

Ethnicity and exceptionality are distinctly different concepts. In some ways, however, the difficulties in accommodating newcomers into the schools and special education are intertwined. Both fit within the broad rubric of what may be referred to as the question of providing equal access to educational services for all students in the Canadian school system.

In both a historical and contemporary sense, much research attests that students from visible ethnic minority groups have been discriminated against by school personnel as well as by school policies. A disproportionate representation of culturally different students in certain programs for exceptional children is a recurring concern in special education (Brosnan, 1983; Chinn and Hughes, 1987; Reschly, 1988; Tucker, 1980). The numbers of culturally different students referred for psychological services is out of proportion to their presence in the schools. They are more likely to be referred for special education and are at greater risk for being inappropriately placed in special classes. Immigrant and minority group children have been over-represented in such classifications as slow learner, educably mentally retarded, and learning disabled (e.g., Cummins, 1986; Gelb and Mikokawa, 1986; Sleeter 1986).

Fine (1985), for example, outlined the concerns that exist in the Black community in Toronto. Statistics from the North York Board of Education point to the fact that Black students are over-represented in the basic and vocational courses, and under-represented in the advanced courses leading to post-secondary education. Reasons include the absence of role models in the schools and the curriculum; lack of understanding of a child's culture and language; biased expectations on the part of teachers and counsellors; insufficient and inappropriate remedial assistance; and biased testing, assessment, and placement procedures.

A mix of factors account for the over-representation of minority children in special education (and their under-representation in programs for the gifted). First of all, members of minority or ethnic groups are more apt to be identified as disabled because their differences are not well understood or valued by others. This may happen when the majority group is viewed as setting the standard for all others (Hallahan and Kauffman, 1991). Members of that group fail to realize that what they see as deviant and unacceptable in their own group may be normal or adaptive in another. In this way, ethnicity and exceptionality overlap, and we have a socially constructed category of special education: exceptionality does not stem from actual disability but from a perceived difference between the individual and the majority group.

Second, teachers may unwittingly contribute to the problem. When confronted with struggling students from a language minority group, many teachers are baffled by their seemingly unpredictable rate of academic progress. Often teachers turn to special education as they are unsure how to adapt the curriculum or what level of English to use.

The third factor, unfair and discriminatory assessment practices, is the one one that has generated the most data and concern. Especially in the United States, the assessment of the intellectual functioning of minority children has been the focus of a storm of criticism. Since the 1970s, there has been growing controversy over the mislabelling of disadvantaged and bilingual children and inappropriate placement in special education classes. Many contend that the common assessment measures used by teachers and psychologists may reflect a racial or socio-economic bias and reinforce existing inequalities in the selection of these children for special programs (Bailey and Harbin, 1980).

As early as 1970 the board of the National Association for Retarded Citizens (NARC) in the United States asserted that psychological evaluation "should always include the use of individual test procedures which measure a range of skills and which are appropriate to a child's cultural and linguistic background" (Cegelka, 1978, p.29). Today, the AAMD definition of mental retardation insists that valid assessment consider cultural and linguistic diversity, as well as differences in communication and behavioural factors.

Recognition of the discriminatory nature of tests, especially IQ tests used for educational placement, was prompted by litigation in the United States. The most famous case was that of *Larry P. vs. Riles*, in which a California court ruled that IQ test scores could not be used as a primary criterion for recommending children for special class placement.

Canadian jurisdictions have recently moved toward the adoption of non-discriminatory measures. The Ontario Ministry of Education Consultative Committee for Student Assessment and Program Placement for Equal Educational Opportunity has proposed a number of recommendations and guidelines concerning non-discriminatory assessment.

When the child has an exceptional condition, assessment challenges the ingenuity of educators. Clinicians often seek assistance from speakers of the child's language or dialect. For disabled children from diverse cultures, the predictive ability of most standardized tests is poor. Therefore, data should be chiefly used for diagnosis of strengths and weaknesses rather than prediction of future functioning. The diagnostic validity is excellent if the tests are used along with informal data and demographic information (De Blassie and Franco, 1983).

An eclectic approach is recommended; a battery of measures should be employed with assessment seen as an ongoing process rather than a single event. A comprehensive individual assessment should include observations of the child in various settings and situations; informal measures such as rating scales, interviews, and case studies; educational assessments; sensorimotor functioning assessment; adaptive behaviour scales; intellectual assessment; and developmental and medical data.

Language assessment is particularly important. Language disorders can exist in the context of language differences and must not be overlooked (Langdon, 1989). Because language performance is so intimately linked to academic success, the question of differentiating a language disorder from a bilingual, cross-cultural difference in a student with limited English proficiency is a crucial one for all specialists involved (Langdon, 1989).

Assessment Measures

One of the major criticisms of standardized tests is that they are normed on certain groups and are loaded with cultural items directed toward that group. To give an idea of the impact of culturally loaded tests, we present items drawn from a measure designed, somewhat tongue-in-cheek, for use with Newfoundland students. As Nesbit (1988) observes, the difficulties can be seen if we imagine a student in Calgary puzzling over the meaning of the word *dwoi* (a snow shower). On the other hand, this may not be too far removed from the Newfoundland child attempting to match the word *bronco* with one of the four graphic presentations on the Peabody Picture Vocabulary Test. Further examples are drawn from other measures based on Black English. The final items come from a measure devised in 1917 and one specific to Hawaiian culture.

Research Notes

Examples of bias in tests

Newfoundland

1. A *dwoi* (pronounced *dwy*) is
a) a short snow shower *
b) a dried-up mud hole
c) the back sitting room in a boat
d) a Boethuck Indian word meaning 'a small creek.'

2. The term *ballycaters* means
a) saltwater spray frozen to the beach rocks *
b) a rowdy, ignorant person
c) fat-bellied people
d) a flock of saltwater ducks

Black English

1. "Hully Gully" comes from
a) East Oakland
b) Fillmore
c) Watts *
d) Harlem
e) Motor City

2. T-bone Walker got famous for playing what?
a) trombone
b) piano
c) T-flute
d) guitar
e) hambone *

3. Which word is most out of place here
a) splib
b) blood
c) gray *
d) spook
e) black

4. The most succesful method for catching catfish is
a) gigging
b) setting a hot line
c) dynamiting *
d) creating an electric shock with two pokers and a car battery

1917 Army Alpha Test

1. Alfred Noyes is famous as a
a) painter
b) poet *
c) musician
d) sculptor

2. An aspen is a
a) machine
b) fabric
c) tree *
d) drink

3. The number of a Kaffir's legs are
a) two *
b) four
c) six
d) eight

Hawaii

1. If someone wanted to say dinner was delicious, he would say it was
a) papas
b) kukui
c) ewa *
d) lola
e) ono

Figure 8-2
The assessment process

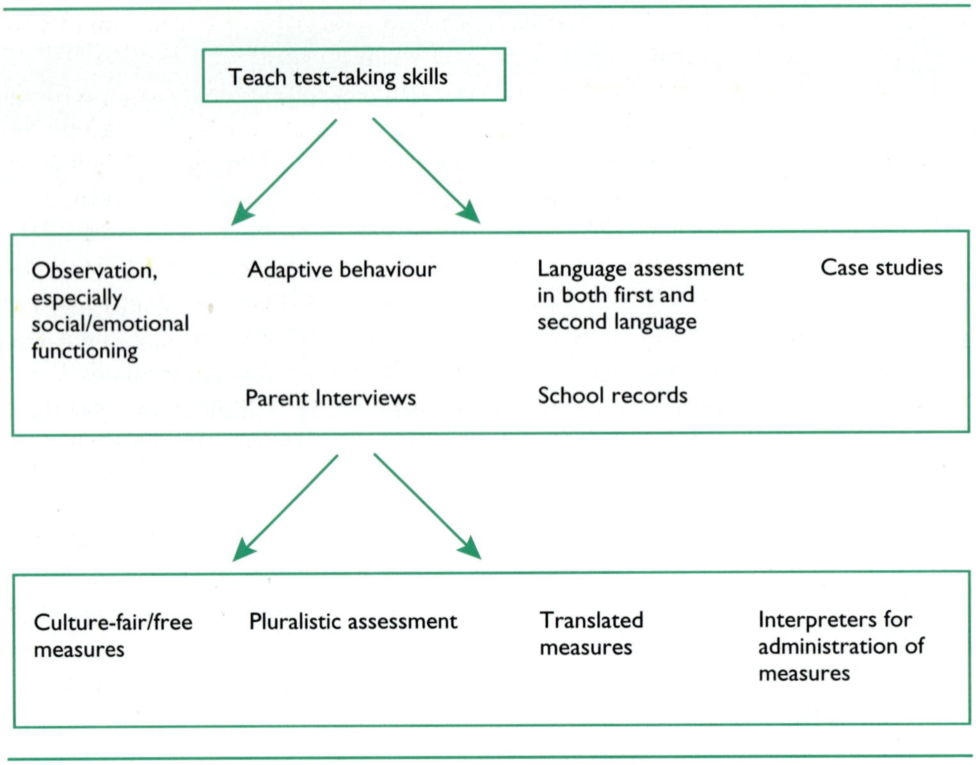

Attempts have been made to improve assessment in order to reduce the misprepresentation of minority group children in special programs. These include the creation of culture-free (culture-fair) and culture-specific tests; the development of separate local or ethnic norms; the translation of test protocols into the primary language of the student; the development of criterion-referenced tests; and engagement in pluralistic testing (Sugai and Maheady, 1988).

Culture-free measures purport to be free from culturally loaded content. These tests contain items that are common to all cultures so that children will not be disadvantaged by the nature of the measure. To be culture-fair, a test

- should make it possible to make the same predictions from the results across cultures;
- should keep language and reading to a minimum;
- must use pictures or symbols in items that are familiar to all cultures;
- should not penalize subjects by timed items;
- must contain item content that is either familiar or unfamiliar to the majority of cultures;
- should contain items or tasks that equally motivate (appeal to) all cultures (Gonzales, 1989, p. 391).

Although the idea of culture-free tests sounds logical and reasonable, results have been generally disappointing. Since knowledge and language are culture bound, there is no reason to believe that a culture-free test can actually be constructed. There is no way to measure aptitudes such as memory, learning, perceiving, and problem solving except through content, and content is always culturally related.

Culture-specific measures are those that are written from the perspective of a particular minority culture or subculture. Culture-specific tests were developed to counter inappropriate testing of culturally and linguistically different populations. Validation occurs in terms of the accuracy of the measures in predicting educational, vocational, and social competence within those specific cultures or subcultures.

Pluralistic testing includes the System of Multi-Pluralistic Assessment (SOMPA) (Mercer and Lewis, 1981). This is a battery of tests that measure a student's adaptive behaviour, collects data on health history, includes scales for measuring the socio-cultural background of the family, and retains the Wechsler Intelligence Scale for Children-Revised (Mercer, 1989). Although the SOMPA uses a traditional measure of intelligence, it treats the WISC-R as an individually administered achievement test, not as a measure of intelligence. When a student's performance is compared to the norms for the test, the score is interpreted simply as a measure of what the student has learned about the dominant Anglo core culture and the student's level of functioning in that culture (Mercer, 1989). Results are weighed according to the social and family characteristics of the child. Thus, a child with an IQ score of 111 can, when compared with children from similar socio-cultural backgrounds, obtain an estimated learning potential score of 134, placing in the top one percent of children in that socio-cultural group (Day, 1986).

Similarly, the Kaufman Assessment Battery for Children (K-ABC)(Kaufman and Kaufman, 1983) was partly aimed at reducing the "potential 'community gap' with preschool, minority group, and exceptional children" (Kaufman and Kaufman 1983, p. 8).

Developmental Consequences

Cultural differences per se present no pedagogical problems. During the late 1960s and early 1970s, several studies examined academic achievement among different ethnic groups. These studies indicated that, given equal opportunity, culturally different students would perform as well academically as their classmates.

Many children first encounter the dominant society at school and, for some of them, school can be a frightening and alienating experience. They must struggle with a strange language and somehow make sense of the confusing attitudes and expectations of teachers and peers. Two major problems emerge in school situations — children are at a cultural and linguistic disadvantage, and there is conflict between traditional and Canadian values.

The age of immigrant children entering the Canadian school system may determine their future success. Older children may have missed school work, and the time that they must spend learning English causes them to fall further behind their English-speaking peers. They may grow discouraged and eventually become early school leavers (Caccia, 1975).

When considering a child from a different cultural background with a disability, the developmental consequences of a condition are related to the consequences of limited

English, to the consequences of the specific disability condition, and to the additive nature of language deficiency and a handicapping condition. An important element is the impact of the condition on the child's family, the family's acceptance, and the acceptance within that wider cultural group.

Language

Language is much more than a set of words and grammar rules. It is the most important aspect of culture — a forceful instrument that gives individuals their identity and interaction. Linguistic distinctness is a basic component of personal identity for many of Canada's ethnic minorities. For many children from different cultures, however, language acquisition and use are the primary problems in school.

There are two aspects to language acquisition and use. First, there is the acquisition of conversational English skills. Second are those skills required for academic success in school. Very different time periods are required for minority students to achieve appropriate levels in these two aspects of second language proficiency.

While most culturally different children acquire fairly fluent peer-appropriate face-to-face communication skills within the first two years of their arrival in Canada, these skills develop more quickly than academic language skills. In a longitudinal study of the achievement of immigrant children in a large Canadian city, Cummins (1984), found that while most students had superficial language competence after three years of English as a Second Language (ESL) training, it was not until they had been functioning in English for at least five years that they demonstrated comprehension of concepts at the level that is normally required for academic work. This means that students may be able to carry on a conversation about the latest video but still not have the sophisticated language to master subject matter lessons or the language competence to grasp complex verbal and semantic relationships. Monique, whom we meet in the following Profile, is an example of a child skilled only in one area.

It is important that teachers understand the different rules for the social use of language that students from diverse cultures may have learned.

Even when children acquire English as a second language, they may still remain different from the students in the dominant culture. They may speak with an accent caused by the non-equivalence of sounds between languages. For example, many speakers of Japanese have trouble pronouncing the phoneme /r/.

Communication is embedded in cultural systems. Cultural values and assumptions directly affect the nature of communication which in turn affects cognition and transmission. Individual languages and cultures have many rules governing language behaviour, and these differ from language to language and culture to culture. Culture affects language use in such variables as turn-taking behaviour, greeting behaviour, proximity, and rules of conversation.

When children come to school with different rules for the social use of language, these may contrast sharply with the behaviours expected of them in the classroom and can lead to serious misunderstandings between child and teacher. Many children from different cultural groups, for instance, are taught to restrain their expressive behaviour in the presence of adults and strangers. But in Canadian schools, children are continually required to express themselves in front of adults and strangers despite cultural norms to the contrary.

Profile

Monique

Eleven-year-old Monique attends the regular grade five class of her local school. However, in the past few months the teacher has become increasingly concerned about her lack of academic progress, especially in the language arts. Monique was reading below grade level when she entered grade five, and now that she must apply reading skills in order to gain information in other subject areas, she is falling further and further behind. Poor reading skills spill over to influence her spelling and, most specifically, her creative writing. In this last area, Monique seems to have many ideas but she can't get them onto paper and is functioning at least three years below grade level.

Monique has been in Canada for a little more than three years. Although the family came from French-speaking Mauritius, they chose to settle in a large English-speaking urban area. Monique's father has acquired fairly fluent English skills but her mother has only a few words. The younger brother speaks and reads English fluently. Monique is in the middle. She has fluent conversational skills, certainly good enough to play and communicate with peers and to negotiate through the community. To a large extent, though, she has rejected the French of the home and uses her English at all times, thereby closing off much communication with her mother.

In the context of the demands of the classroom, Monique's peer-appropriate communication skills are not adequate. Moreover, as she tends to lag further and further behind the other children, she is losing friends and becoming a butt of jokes and mild ridicule. Monique reacts poorly to this teasing and is beginning to withdraw into herself. So serious is the situation that the teacher has made a referral for a full psycho-educational assessment and is beginning to feel that a special education placement may be more suitable for Monique at this point in her school career.

Language is often a problem for the Native child because of the many different languages and dialects spoken. There are fifty-three distinct Native languages spoken in Canada, belonging to eleven different language families, and for many Native children English is a second language. In the Canadian North, the language spoken before the coming of the Europeans is still the first language of the people. Elsewhere, many Native students come to school speaking a non-standard English dialect, made up of elements of standard English, with some pronunciations, grammar, and idioms transferred from the Native language (Barth, 1979).

Dialects

The most noticeable and lasting effect that parents have on their children's language is on their sound structures. The way that children pronounce vowels, the cadence of their questions, and the rate of the speech stream itself are influenced by parents and are very difficult to change in later life.

Language variations, if systematic and associated with a specific geographic, cultural, or socio-economic group, are called **dialects**. Conditioned as they are by linguistic, social, educational, and geographic experiences, dialects are variations in language content and form. Some dialect differences are in the pronunciation of words;

Language and dialect variations can result in academic problems for Native children.

others will be in the words and the word combinations used. The prosody of the language refers to the way that the phonemes of a particular language are arranged in patterns of stress, rhythm, and pitch. There are often subtle differences in the prosodic patterns of speakers who do not have English as their native language.

A standard dialect is a variety of a language system. Standard American or Canadian English is an idealized version of English that occurs rarely in conversation although many Canadians are classified as users. It is the form of English used on newscasts and in textbooks.

All systems of language use some dialect of the idealized standard language; that is, we all speak a dialect. Nevertheless, there is controversy as to whether some dialects that differ considerably from standard English are acceptable forms of the language. In fact, some uses of the word *dialect* make it synonymous with good/bad or standard/non-standard or standard/substandard. The preferred, or standard, English is often seen as superior in some way and somehow better suited for communication than the disfavoured non-standard English or vernacular varieties.

There is no such thing, however, as a right or wrong language, only language that is appropriate or inappropriate in certain contexts. Each dialect within a language is just as logical, complex, and rule-governed as the standard form of the language. Furthermore, dialect is a product of a child's background and culture. One of the things that conversational participants must be able to do is to structure their sentences according to the language rules of the community (Lindfors, 1987), and children who speak a dialect usually communicate effectively with others in their culture. As dialects used by groups are systematic and used for communication among members of a particular segment of society, they should not be considered ungrammatical or substandard, only different and less valued in some situations.

The problem therefore is not one of communication but rather of social acceptance (Otto and Smith, 1980). Because of this, educators in the past, were led to disregard dialects and try to teach children standard English. For example, in a Newfoundland school, a child was heard to ask the teacher how to spell *glutch*. The teacher responded with "swallow, s-w-a-l-l-o-w" (Brown, 1988). Today many researchers and educators deplore the elimination of dialects. They say that in our schools we force children to abandon vernaculars which are lovely, fluent, and various. They feel that by abandoning children's dialects we not only reduce their ability to communicate, but we also reduce their self-esteem by attacking the speech which is so intimately identified with family, social class, and community (Paddock, 1988).

Teachers should accept a child's non-standard dialect as a valid and correct language system but also teach the standard dialect.

Academic Achievement

Children from diverse cultural backgrounds often encounter problems in school. For many students, the tasks of simultaneously learning a new language and mastering the core academic curriculum is daunting.

Children who do not speak English will have the most trouble in content subjects. Language arts, especially reading, present the greatest academic difficulties to culturally different children. An estimated 50 percent of West Indian children in Toronto, for example, have severe difficulties in the language arts (D'Oyley, 1976). Further, a study of 106 North York schools in Ontario listed the main reasons for reading problems; in 69 percent of the schools, another language spoken at home was the main reason given (Wancyzki, 1983). Math presents less of a problem.

Many experts contend that it is not necessary for students to speak standard English in order to write standard English. However, children who grow up speaking regional dialects may experience difficulties in some classroom activities. Studies of Black American and Native Canadian children have revealed considerable problems in English usage and comprehension. When Laurie Walker (1979) examined the impact of dialect on the spelling performance of grade four students in Nova Scotia and Newfoundland, he found that the Newfoundland sample experienced more spelling difficulties than the Nova Scotia sample. Interferences that were dialect-based were not limited to spelling isolated words in a controlled exercise but were also found in a free writing exercise, so that dialect represented an extra impediment in the students' writing.

Native children's achievement is often one or more years below expected grade level standards and the gap increases as pupils proceed through the grades. One study found that Native students in grade eight were about two grade levels behind in almost all core skill areas (Report, 1981). The average Native student fails about half of all school courses (More, 1985). In Canada, aboriginal students complete fewer grades; that is, grade retention occurs more often for aboriginal than for Caucasian students. Among Native students, the high school completion rate is about a third the rate for non-Native students.

The average dropout rate in Canada is 30 percent but studies have shown that the rate is higher among Native students than among students from other groups (Neufeld and Stevens, 1992). Estimates of aboriginal student dropout rates range from 80 to 90 percent in some areas. However, aboriginal and Caucasian students typically drop out of school at about the same age.

The causes of underachievement among Native students are complex. Factors include dialect differences, lack of home support for education, poor home-school relations, lack of motivation, insufficient school financing, and lack of stimulation and experiences. A recent study of aboriginal children living in villages and cities in British Columbia found that experiential background, not ethnicity, was a major determinant of information-processing ability and the development of reading skills (Williams, 1988).

The educational attainments of Native students have improved considerably over the past decade. Recent improvements are attributed to more appropriate curricula, more Native-run schools, and the use of Native people as teachers and teachers' aides (More, 1985).

Social and Emotional Development

If social and emotional problems arise, they are likely to occur as children and families interact with the wider dominant society. The conflict often makes it difficult for newly arrived children to adjust to Canadian schools. Students may be torn between getting along in the home environment, which has its own expectations, and assimilating into the school system, which also has embedded cultural codes for thought and conduct.

Culture conflict may occur between the child and the family or between the family and the school. For example, a child who is rewarded for maintaining silence at home may find it very difficult to speak aloud in the classroom. As well, many immigrant parents do not approve of what they perceive as the permissiveness of Canadian schools. Some believe that their children are neglected or not sufficiently encouraged to intermingle with school peers. Often torn in different directions by the teacher and the immigrant parent, children are at a pivotal point in the acculturation process and this alone can cause great stress.

Within the family, different attitudes toward discipline may lead to value conflicts. When discipline problems do arise, however, they tend to derive from the same sources as disciplinary problems among Canadian-born children (Ashworth, 1975).

Culture conflict between home and school obliges youth to choose either one or the other. This causes conflicts in personality and other personal variables. Having to act one way at school and another way in the home, and use different sets of rules and different languages can be extremely difficult (Grossman, 1984). Children who suffer the effects of culture conflict often become anxious and defensive; their sense of alienation and isolation may lead to frustration, anger, antisocial behaviour, and difficulties both at home and at school (Head, 1984).

Culturally different children who fail to get along in society seem to share some characteristics. These are an experiential background that does not fit the expectations of the middle-class-oriented curriculum; economic impoverishment; poor self-concept; a feeling of rejection by society; and a poor attention span in school (Cohen and Manion, 1983).

In the school setting, culture influences behaviour. Culturally different children may have distinctive work styles, views, values, and language. They bring different standards and expectations to the classroom, and their backgrounds may affect their reactions to the classroom climate, the classroom structure and routine, and the classroom discipline. The regimented school day typical of an urban, industrial society is often foreign to Native children. An emphasis on individual self-expression and original thought for young children is not common in some Asian cultures. Our academic requirements are often seen as "soft" by some Europeans and Asians (Wood, 1986). All of this leads to a frequent mismatch between the culture of education and that of the children and their communities.

Intervention

The diversity of cultures places increasing challenges before the school system. Students show four major categories of educational difficulties:

- different learning styles and classroom interaction;
- changes in the student-teacher relationship;
- language barriers;
- difficulties due to physical, intellectual, language, social, or behavioural differences.

Recognition of the impact of culture and linguistic differences on learning problems is a relatively recent phenomenon in special education (Rueda, 1989). Today's educators understand that at-risk culturally diverse children with exceptionalities have a variety of basic educational needs that must be addressed. These include their native language development and instruction in ESL, bilingual education, self-concept enhancement, enculturation enhancement, and family and community involvement. Because most special educators are not equipped to provide all of these services to exceptional children, a variety of service providers must collaborate to present a co-ordinated program in the most appropriate educational setting (Baca and Harris, 1988).

Often regular classroom teachers do not have specific strategies to assist students with limited English proficiency or those with limited English and disabilities. Teachers are typically not bilingual and do not have training and experience working with students who have little English competency. Nevertheless, there are bridges that join the original culture to the mainstream culture and language of the classroom. These do not mean eliminating the original culture but seeing diversity as a resource.

Bridges include

- Teacher attitudes and knowledge. Teacher expectations and student behaviour interact in subtle and complicated ways. Many factors influence teachers' expectations — socio-economic level, gender, race, test scores, comments from other teachers, student appearance, behaviour, and non-standard English patterns are only a few. While we live in a culturally pluralistic society, most of us have difficulty in perceiving behaviours other than those we were taught as having validity. Teachers are continually making decisions based on how people behave without having any real knowledge of their cultural background. Educators need to understand the lifestyles, value systems, family structures, and programmatic priorities of these children from diverse cultural backgrounds and their families.
- Bilingual education. Bilingual education involves teaching students in some combination of their first and second language.
- English as a Second Language (ESL) and other language programs.

- Multicultural curriculum.
- Adaptations to the classroom environment that stress methods such as co-operative learning. Co-operative learning is not a patent medicine to solve all classroom ills, but it does improve language. It also increases cross-race friendships, and the newly formed friendships are mutual rather than unreciprocated (see Lehr, 1984).
- Materials and resources.

Additional bridges exist for students with exceptionalities:

- Bilingual special education. Students in bilingual special education not only have limited Engish proficiency but also specific learning problems and disabling conditions that interfere with the acquisition of English and retention of skills or content material (Baca and Cervantes, 1984). Bilingual education is not, however, an alternative to special education. Just teaching a child in the native language cannot compensate for other disabilities or deficits.

Handicapped children from different cultural backgrounds are doubly challenged.

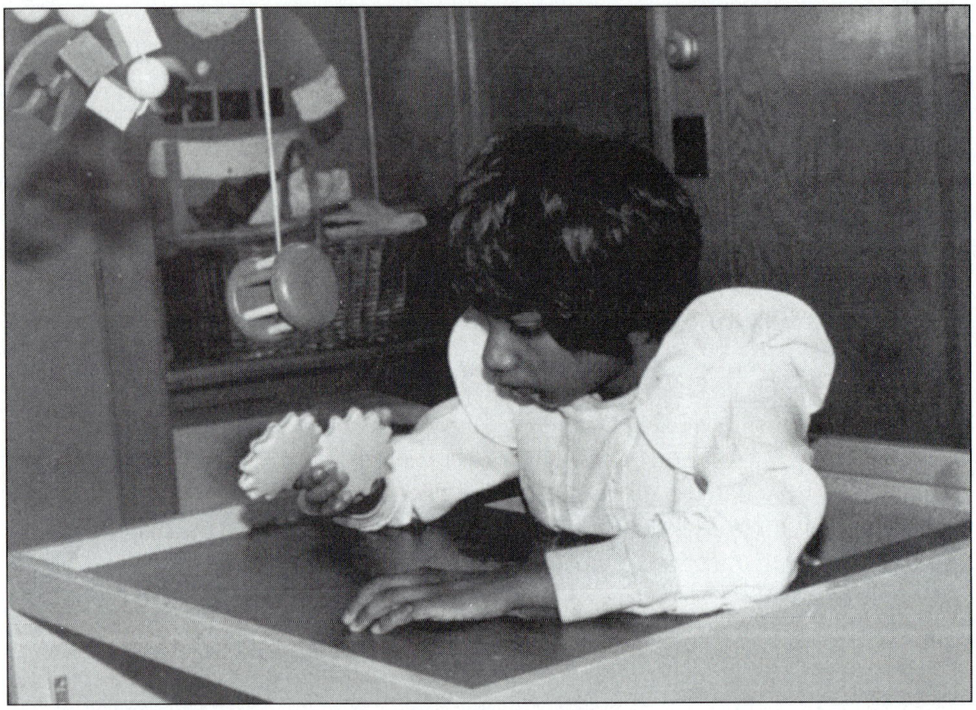

- Specific techniques for students who are exceptional. For specific conditions, intervention is related to the implications of the particular disability for learning and behaviour. A child with cerebral palsy, for example, requires handling and positioning regardless of background.
- Bilingual aides. These paraprofessionals should have a high level of competence in the first language and the ability to develop the first language in children; a level of English competency sufficient to understand and participate in the planning and implementation of bilingual programs; and willingness to work as a member of a team.
- Parent participation. For those intervening with disabled children fron diverse cultures, more than just knowledge of the etiology of the condition is essential. Cul-

tural and social perspectives are important in undertanding how the condition impinges on the development of the child and the family climate.

Educational Settings

During the past fifteen years the number of students in Canadian urban schools systems whose home language is different from that of the schools has increased dramatically. Within the school system, rapid acquisition of English and a successful language shift are the major aims, since inadequate English results in poor academic achievement and denial of social mobility (Paulston, 1980).

In teaching language, teachers need to take an eclectic approach, stressing usage, providing ample opportunities for students to talk to each other and to adults, and creating situations where speech is necessary.

The school placement of culturally different children stresses English language development. To accommodate the language needs of culturally different children, a huge range of programs are in place. Some are administered and presented within the school system; others are the bailiwick of community and ethnic groups. Some attempt to teach English, others to retain the child's first language together with learning English. Across Canada, the range of options for language development include

- Regular classes. Some educators who promote integration stress placing newly arrived children straight into regular classrooms. However, if children are placed at the level of their English language development, older students may find themselves with much younger children. Ten-years-olds placed in a grade one class are likely to become very discouraged.
- Withdrawal classes. Withdrawal classes attempt to provide children with the opportunity to learn English but still be a part of the school. There are three major types of withdrawal programs: half-day classes, itinerant ESL classes, and school-based ESL instruction. Children spend part of the day in an integrated setting and the rest of the time receiving intensive language training from an ESL teacher.
- Reception classes (sometimes referred to as Sheltered English). These special withdrawal classes are reserved for children with little or no English. Children spend all of the time with a qualfied ESL teacher. Language learning is the prime objective.
- Transition programs. These programs use the minority language to help children keep up with academic content while acquiring proficiency in English. Some transition programs are not committed to long-term fluency or literacy in the native language. While the programs are bilingual, the goal is often monolingualism. Other transition programs stress maintenance; that is, retaining the first language as well as learning English.

  Large numbers of transition programs have been established in Canada since the 1960s. Cummins (1993) mentions the Edmonton Public School Board's English-Ukrainian program, the English-Ukrainian programs in Manitoba, the Montreal Hebrew-English programs, the Italian Kindergarten transition program in Toronto, the English-Italian kindergarten program in Ottawa, the Vancouver Punjabi-English program, and the Toronto English-Portuguese programs.
- Heritage language. The home language is called the heritage language. Heritage language programs strive for culture maintenance and educational enrichment (Yu, 1988). They help ethnic groups retain knowledge of their mother tongue and a continuing appreciation of their cultural background as well as providing opportunities for new language learning. Several provinces provide support for cultural preserva-

tion through heritage language programs. In Ontario, the heritage language program supports the teaching of home languages in schools, but usually outside the regular school day.

- Minority language programs. In Ontario, minority language education refers to the education of French-speaking pupils in their own language. In Ontario approximately 5 percent of all pupils are in French-language schools.
- Adjunct schools. Adjunct schools teach in English but use the ethnic language and culture as subjects of instruction (Csapo, 1983).
- Ethnic schools. Ethnic schools serve as substitute schools and use the ethnic language as the medium of instruction for teaching accredited and non-accredited subjects (Csapo, 1983). Curriculum is based on the social goals and aspirations of a particular community. The German Language School in St. John's, for example, was set up in 1974 by parents of German background and is today financially supported by the Federal Republic of Germany, the Secretary of State, and student fees. For some students, the school introduces the language, but in most cases the children already speak German and the parents hope that the school will help them with the reading and writing of the language.
- After-school language classes. After-school language classes are offered to children in their first language.
- Immersion programs. In these programs, a child learns the second language not as a subject but through being exposed to it as the language of instruction and interaction. Immersion requires the exclusive use of the target language as the medium of instruction at the early grade levels. The major thrust is the re-creation in school of an environment that approximates as far as possible the natural environment in which the first language was acquired (Safty, 1988).

Educational Approaches

Education does not mean seeking to melt away cultural differences or that teachers should merely tolerate cultural pluralism. To acknowledge childrens' heritage without accommodating their instructional needs does little to enhance their performance on school-related tasks. Curriculum for culturally different students should be based on a school's knowledge and understanding of the specific minority culture and the students' attitudes about school and themselves.

Multicultural Education

Within both society and our schools, multiculturalism is becoming a dominant ideology. The responsibility for preparing all children to live in Canada's multicultural society has significant implications in terms of general approaches for education, as well as in the provisions for special populations.

Cultural diversity in our society brings new challenges and perspectives to the schools. In a democracy, schools are expected to provide citizens with much of the knowledge and skills they need to meet the challenges of life and to profit from the opportunities that it presents them. To be truly democratic, a society should assure all students the same opportunity to succeed in school regardless of their country of origin, English-language proficiency, ethnic background, socio-economic class, the geographic area where they live and study, their gender, or their disability.

Tips for Teachers

Classroom climate

- Be familiar with the home and community.
- Know the child as an individual.
- Be aware of differences in order to understand the behaviours of students from diverse cultures.
- Become familiar with features of students' dialects so as to understand better and distinguish miscues from errors.
- Assign students classroom roles that capitalize on their strengths and do not make unrealistic demands on English skills.
- For children with exceptionalities, try to get trained aides who speak the child's language.

Instruction

- Use much oral language work. Garcia (1988) found that students learn math and literacy skills most effectively when student-student discussions take up to at least 50 percent of instructional time.
- Stress oral language and conversational skills before moving to reading and written language.
- Adapt English instruction to make it highly contextualized and multisensory so that it is more easily understood by the students.
- Use puppets; young children tend to be braver in their use of language when they are protected by the puppet.
- Relate learning to the child's environment.
- Provide language instruction around real life situations.
- Use reciprocal interactive teacher models such as co-operative learning and whole language which promote empowerment and learning via verbal and written dialogue between students as well as between students and teachers (Figueroa, Fradd, and Correa, 1989; Ortiz and Yates, 1989)
- Use general materials such as catalogues from Sears or Canadian Tire.
- Incorporate materials from a variety of cultures.

This, of course, is the underlying philosophy of inclusive schooling. It is also the dominant theme that guides multicultural education. That is, "The concept of multicultural education is not based on the premise that there are ethnic minorities in the classroom, but that there are differences in students within any classroom and that all of those students live in a pluralistic society" (Rodriguez, 1982, p. 227). The presence of children of different backgrounds and ability is seen as a strength, not a weakness.

A multicultural perspective is a state of mind, a way of learning and teaching that is shaped by beliefs in the way that our society should function. The concept of multicultural education rejects assimilation and values cultural pluralism. Multicultural education does not attempt to eliminate differences; rather, the idea is to build on cultural diversity as a strength of our society.

The multicultural curriculum should provide and promote values, attitudes, and behaviours that support ethnic pluralism. An important component of multicultural education is the use of culturally responsive instruction in which educators employ instructional strategies and curriculum adaptations that are consistent with students' experiences, perspectives, and developmental ages (Collier and Kalk, 1989; Irvine, 1990).

Multicultural content should be integrated into all subject areas. Walsh (in Morris, 1983) suggests one method for doing this: "After listing the subjects or activities which normally comprise the daily program, the teacher describes at least two activities for each through which a multicultural dimension could be integrated" (p. 81).

A multicultural curriculum generally includes aspects such as,

- Multicultural perspectives. Students need many opportunities to develop an appreciation of varied cultures. They should be encouraged in the sharing of aesthetic traditions from various ethnic groups (Cohen and Manion, 1983).
- Demonstration of the racial and cultural diversity of Canada.
- The study and sharing of cultures. In multicultural education, the curriculum should reflect the culture of various groups as well as the shared national culture. All students should have access to materials that provide accurate information about cultural groups (Banks, 1988). It is necessary to provide culturally relevant materials and resources such as readers with pictures of culturally different children and kits designed to teach about specific cultures. Good multicultural materials should have accurate content; cultural relevancy and significance to the child; and accurate representations of current attitudes and customs. They should be historically accurate and interrelated with the curriculum.

Multicultural education is for all students. At the moment, emphasis is being placed on exposing students enrolled in special education classes to carefully planned multicultural awareness activities (Mack, 1988). These activities are designed to help students better appreciate cultural similarities and differences and develop a more positive understanding of their own cultural heritage.

Figure 8-3 *Goals of multicultural education*

Bilingual Education

Historically, two assumptions have guided the education of students from language minorities. The first is that English is the only legitimate medium for learning and instruction. The second is that linguistic minority students must be immersed in English as quickly as possible if they are to succeed in school and society.

Considerable research data, however, suggests that for minority groups who experience disproportionate levels of academic failure, the extent to which a student's language and culture are incorporated into the school program constitutes a significant prediction of academic success (e.g., Campos and Keating, 1988; Willig, 1985). In programs in which minority students' first language skills are strongly reinforced, their school success appears to reflect both the more solid cognitive and academic foundation derived through first language instruction and also the reinforcement of their cultural identity (Cummins, 1989).

Instruction and services provided through the use of two languages is generally referred to as bilingual education. Stern (in Swain and Barik, 1978) defines **bilingual education** as "schooling provided fully or partly in the second language with the object of making students proficient in the second language while at the same time maintaining and developing their proficiency in the first language and fully guaranteeing their educational development" (p. 22).

Proponents of bilingual education believe that all children have the right to maintain and develop their first language as well as to become proficient in English. They present many arguments in favour of the process. Among them:

- A person's language is as much a part of his or her cultural heritage as is religion or feelings of nationalism. But when a high-prestige, socially powerful language such as English is introduced as the exclusive language of instruction, children are being exposed to what has been called "subtractive bilingualism." That is, they are forced to lose their native language in the process of learning the majority language (Cummins, 1979). Keeping their ethnic identity and promoting their language as valuable is additive bilingualism, which gives children a sense of belonging and group pride and provides them with a framework for acquiring self-esteem and self-worth.
- Bilingual education first reinforces the native language and culture so that children are able to master reading and writing in the first language as well as feel proud of themselves and their heritage. At the same time, children learn to speak the second language.
- All bilingual education programs assume that the language and culture a child learns at home can promote normal and healthy psychological development and communicative competence (Sleeter and Grant, 1994).

Support for native language instruction does not mean that students should not learn to speak, read, and write English. The aim is to use the native language to expand the linguistic repertoire of students while they become proficient in English. In bilingual programs, students learn English but receive basic academic instruction in their first language so that they do not fall behind academically.

Bilingual Special Education

Bilingual special education is "designed to meet the academic, socio-cultural, and psychological needs of non-English-speaking handicapped pupils who cannot meet performance standards normally expected of a comparable group of English-speaking handicapped pupils" (Plata and Santos, 1981, p. 98). Bilingual special education is more than just the sum of the two fields joined. It is defined as "use of the home language and the home culture along with English in an individually designed program of special instruction" (Baca and Cervantes, 1984, p. 18).

Bilingual special education is "an emerging discipline with a brief history" (Baca and Amato, 1989, p. 168). It was not until the early 1970s that the first references to bilingual special education were made in the educational literature. The field of bilingual special education is so new that a body of effective practices has yet to be established (Yates and Ortiz, 1991). There are few reports of empirical research with exceptional children which have attempted to examine the issue of bilingualism. Some recent research indicates that bilingual intervention programs are successful in producing lasting gains in the academic and second language proficiency development of children in bilingual special education and mainstream placements (see Arreaga-Mayer, Carta, and Tapia, 1994).

When the educational needs of students with both limited English and disabilities are considered, the use of the child's non-English language becomes a central issue (Fradd and Vega, 1987). The major concerns are:

- When bilingualism is not imposed by the living conditions of the family, is it advisable to engage children with disabilities in second language learning?
- Can children with disabilities benefit from prolonged bilingual exposure?
- In situations where bilingualism is a fact of life, how does one start with the disabled child?
- When should one start?
- How much of a second language can a disabled child be expected to learn?
- What are the implications of second language learning?

Many educators hold that the language of instruction should be the language through which the child learns more effectively. If that language is other than English, placement must be with a teacher who is fluent in that language, knowledgeable about the child's cultural background and values, and well versed in the process of instructing in a second language. If bilingual personnel are not available, then the child should be provided with an ESL program.

There are others who point out that while the retention of the first language is only to be encouraged, children who are already at risk with severe language difficulties may find the use of two systems simply too confusing. We can see this in the case of Johann.

ESL Programs

The first approach to teaching new arrivals English is the pull-out English as a Second Language (ESL) program. ESL programs are an integral component of transitional, maintenance, and two-way bilingual education. However, ESL is not by itself a form of bilingual instruction. Both ESL and bilingual programs share the common goal of promoting English proficiency, but bilingual education is more comprehensive in nature.

Profile

Johann

Johann came to the attention of preschool educators when a special clinic at a large hospital discovered that he had a profound bilateral sensorineural hearing loss. The sudden deafness arose from an attack of meningitis; no other disabling conditions resulted. Although the parents had been warned that serious handicaps could ensue from meningitis, they were were devastated by the diagnosis; Johann was an only child and they had great plans for him.

Twenty-month-old Johann had been born in Canada just a few months after his parents arrived. They had come from a small village in southern Germany and settled in a similar small rural Canadian community. Both parents quickly learned basic English but always spoke German at home.

When a special home-visiting service for hearing-impaired infants and preschoolers was first offered, the mother was somewhat reticent. She had not yet internalized the diagnosis of the clinic and did not understand the profound implications of hearing loss on a child's speech and language development. However, she agreed that the teacher could come for one visit.

Johann's mother relaxed when she found that the teacher spoke fluent German, and was relieved when the teacher demonstrated how to manage the hearing aid, insert the ear moulds, and help Johann to accept the instrument. But as the visits continued, the mother was not as willing to involve herself and Johann with other agencies such as parent self-help groups and preschool programs, or with home training programs. She did not feel that her language was adequate for associating with English-speaking people or for reading in English.

Research points out that opposite expectations at home and at school create additional communication problems for hearing-impaired children who are involved in negotiating their environment without the incidental learning available to normally hearing children. When the child learns English at school, he or she will then miss much of the communication between other family members speaking the first language. The child then is at risk for developing psychological adjustment problems because the missing information leads to a wide gap in understanding and clarifying rules between the two cultures (Yacobacci-Tam, 1987).

This happened with Johann as serious dissension arose on the issue of language. The teacher felt that Johann was unable to master two languages and needed a consistent language system; English at school and German in the home would be too confusing. She asked the mother to speak English at all times, at least until Johann demonstrated some understanding of language. The mother felt that the child would lose his German heritage and that the teacher did not understand her culture. She was also convinced that the Canadian school system for deaf children would not train Johann for the career that she envisioned for him. Ultimately Johann's mother returned to Germany with the boy, leaving the father in Canada.

ESL programs concentrate on the linguistic requirements of new arrivals who need a second language as a means of survival in the new culture. ESL instruction includes English taught from a second language point of view and aimed at the students' level of English proficiency (Ovanso and Collier, 1985). Students who cannot yet adequately express themselves in English spend no time studying grammar but are "bathed" in communication. By providing enough opportunities for practice and review, the teacher helps the child acquire and internalize the language. For students with disabilities, ESL training can help prevent special educators from setting impossible goals, such as requiring them to master academic content in a language they neither speak nor understand (Ortiz and Wilkinson, 1989).

Standard English

Because it is unrealistic to expect the child to master both standard and community codes, questions have been raised about the feasibility of teaching children in their restricted code rather than the standard one. Regardless of children's oral language usage, however, they must have the opportunity to achieve mastery of standard English if their educational opportunities are to be equal to those of other children. We need to teach children the rules for effective communication in the dominant culture while understanding and accepting the effectiveness of their home language in its cultural context (Delpit, 1988; Foster, 1986).

Teachers should accept a child's non-standard dialect as a valid and correct language system but also teach the standard dialect. When children are shown the difference between their speech and standard English and this is done without criticism, they show no resentment (Cooper and Stewart, 1987). Teachers may encourage students to use regular dialect in school but to retain their own patterns outside (Risko, 1981).

Co-operative learning is a powerful strategy for accomplishing many multicultural goals.

Co-operative Learning

Children from some minority groups are less willing to compete and more willing to cooperate with their peers than children from the dominant culture (e.g. Kagan, 1983). Because of the mismatch between the co-operative orientation of some children and the competitive orientation of some classrooms, Kagan (1983) has argued that there is a structural bias in those classrooms that may actually work against these children.

Shared learning experiences are known as co-operative learning, collaborative learning, or small group learning. Ad hoc groups are temporary groups formed in response to directives such as "Turn to your partner and discuss this question." Co-operative learning is a structured form of shared learning. The term *co-operative learning* is defined as "a generic term for the instructional organization of children into small, mixed-ability study groups in which participants co-operate with one another to achieve academic goals" (Rich, 1986, p. 339).

Research data document a plethora of advantages to using co-operative learning strategies. Among the many positive aspects for students from diverse cultures, the data suggest that the procedures reduce the importance of differences and suppress any that do exist. In this way, co-operative learning is a powerful cross-content, cross-grade-level strategy for accomplishing many multicultural goals, including educational equity, intergroup understanding and harmony, and the establishment of positive collaborative relationships among students.

The results of co-operative learning strategies seem to be an improved ability to see the world from another person's point of view. As well, there are more interpersonal relationships characterized by mutual liking, positive attitudes toward each other, mutual concern, friendliness, attentiveness, and a respect for other students. Therefore, says Rich (1986), an especially significant arena for the application of co-operative approaches is the mixed-ethnic, mixed-ability classroom in schools where the interpersonal goals of schooling are of prime, immediate importance.

An atmosphere constricted by silence is a deterrent, not an aid, to learning.

Co-operative learning means changes in the form of instructional organization, not the content. There is a large repertoire of co-operative learning strategies, methods, models, structures, and procedures (see Winzer, 1995). The essence of all co-operative learning is assigning a group goal, such as producing a single product or achieving as high a group average on a test as possible, and rewarding every group member on the basis of the quality or quantity of the group product according to a fixed set of standards (Johnson and Johnson, 1978). Co-operative learning is built on the premise that when teachers systematically and positively reinforce students for group accomplishments and prosocial co-operative behaviour while holding individuals accountable for their own behaviour, individual and group achievement is often higher than it is when teachers record only individual achievement (Margolies, McCabe, and Schwartz, 1990).

Teachers in traditional classrooms engage in lecturing, presenting information, disciplining, and giving instructions. They want a quiet classroom, which for years has been perceived as the productive classroom. Noise level is an informal index of behaviour management, classroom climate, and on-task behaviour. Students sit in straight rows at assigned seats with little or no opportunity for interaction. The lecture method predominates, especially in middle- and secondary-level classrooms.

An atmosphere constricted by silence is a deterrent, not an aid, to learning (Wood, 1987). Classrooms that use co-operative learning are more active and indubitably noisier. Teachers who use co-operative learning become different types of communicators; they facilitate communication among students by encouraging and giving feedback. For students, co-operative groups accommodate different learning styles and modalities. Students talk, discuss, share information, plan together and, especially at the outset, argue.

There are three special concerns of co-operative learning with students with language difficulties and special needs: students' fear and anxiety, worries of normal children that their grades may be affected; and the passive attitude of some children. To overcome these, procedures should be carefully structured and explained, each team member assigned a role, and students with special needs closely monitored to ensure that they don't become "hitchhikers."

Curricula

To develop and implement a comprehensive curriculum for exceptional children with limited English, teachers should

1. Plan, convert, and adapt the curriculum to each child's cultural and linguistic background. The content, scope and sequence, pace of learning, and the utility of materials should be considered.
2. Become familiar with each child's background, culture, and language.
3. Become familiar with each child's learning styles and educational needs.
4. Plan the IEP.

Recent research on effective teaching strategies for bilingual students with disabilities supports the adoption of interactive or experiential models of pedagogy (Swedo, 1987; Willig, Swedo, and Ortiz, 1987). Instruction is best carried through with the use of integrated instruction organized around units. Thematic instruction helps students to make connections, and the same concepts can be reinforced over and over using different methods and different situations.

A central tenet of the interactive or experiential model is that talking and writing are means to learning. In teaching language, teachers need to take an eclectic approach, stressing usage. Teacher behaviours that have significant positive associations with second language achievement include requiring students to manipulate objects or aids so that the teacher can check comprehension; asking students questions based on previously presented information in order to reduce ambiguity; and clarifying the meanings of new words using antonyms and synonyms (Ramirez and Stromquist, 1978). Teachers can provide students with ample opportunities to talk to each other and to adults and create situations where speech is necessary. They should use high levels of functional speech themselves — verifying assignments, checking for understanding, and encouraging task-related skills (Garcia, 1991).

Teachers should design reading programs that are consistent with the basic style of the child. For children learning English, teachers need to give plenty of oral practice in a meaningful context and tailor the reading so that children are not asked to read language with which they are not familiar. When second language learners read texts congruent with their background knowledge, they read them faster, they recall both the gist and the details better, and they summarize and read the story better (Ruiz, 1989). One study found that when children were provided with an abundance of high-interest storybooks in English, their progress in reading and listening comprehension increased at almost twice the normal rate (Ellery and Mangubshai, 1983).

Interacting with Families

Today our classrooms are serving increasing numbers of children with exceptionalities who come from diverse cultural backgrounds. This means, notes Beth Harry (1992), that "the special education system is faced with the challenge of explaining its services and practices to people who may hold radically different types of cultural understandings, assumptions, and expectations regarding education."

Part of the challenge is that parents possess a variety of culturally based perspectives concerning the etiology of their child's disabilities. Studies focusing on special education find that culturally different parents often have no parallel in their home countries (Lynch and Stein, 1987), and the cultural meanings attached to concepts of disability may be very different from those in the North America (Correa, 1989; Figler, 1981).

For any family, the process by which it discovers, adjusts to, and eventually accepts a handicapping condition in a member is complex and difficult; it varies greatly among families. The wide range of responses relate to psychological, socio-economic, educational, and religious differences. Most importantly, culturally based beliefs affect the manner in which families adapt to the child with a disability. The responses of families with different cultural backgrounds to their disabled child have much in common with those from the dominant culture. Yet for minority families, the process may be even more stressful. Problems may arise because of culturally determined attitudes toward handicaps. This area is further discussed in Chapter 16.

When educators involve parents as partners in their children's education, parents appear to develop a sense of efficacy that communicates itself to children with positive academic consequences.

As well, ethnic and minority families may not respond to traditional methods for establishing family-school relationships. In fact, "the literature on the participation of low-income families from racial minorities groups in special education paints a dismal picture of numerous barriers to effective professional-parent communication" (Harry et al., 1993, p. 48). Many parents who are new arrivals are unfamiliar with the role of active, collaborative parents who visit the school.

One telling factor is that attitudes toward professionals vary across cultures. Some parents may not wish to answer personal questions. Some may view the educational system as a bureaucracy that is controlled by educators, monocultural and monolingual individuals whom they have little right to question (Nicolau and Ramos, 1990). Or, out of respect, parents may be reluctant to disagree with professionals; discuss controversial issues or share their emotions; ask questions and seek clarification; question test results and the recommendations of professionals; or make eye contact (see Salend and Taylor, 1993).

Other parents may find it difficult to participate simply because of logistical problems such as transportation and child care requirements. Still others may not come to school because of language difficulties that impede communication.

Still, parent involvement has been recognized as important for a child's progress. When educators involve parents as partners in their children's education, parents appear to develop a sense of efficacy that communicates itself to children with positive academic consequences (Cummins, 1989). Henderson (1987) reported on research that showed parent involvement resulting in higher academic achievement for the student. As a result of being taught how to assist their children, parents have been able to ensure appropriate programming in the least restrictive environment; facilitate successful vocational/special education programs through collaborative consultation with the schools; and improve the mathematical ability of students with disabilities.

Clearly, effective culturally sensitive communication can lead to greater co-operation and collaboration between parents, students, and teachers — a development that can, in turn, promote equity by creating more access to learning for students. Schools must find ways to encourage these families to participate to a much greater extent. Such efforts should involve various cultural groups and organizations in the community (Ramirez, 1988).

Summary

1. As Canada prepares to enter the twenty-first century, it faces many challenges. One of the most profound is to be found in the changed demographic composition of our society.
2. Cultural diversity is a reality in Canadian education. In the classroom, students need to learn about the amount of attention they can expect, when and how to speak, and about verbal communication. For many children from different cultures, language acquisition and use will present problems.
3. There is little argument that most tests are designed for and validated against the values and lifestyles of the middle class and that they therefore often discriminate against other socio-economic groups and non-dominant cultural groups. Recently, culture-fair (culture-free) and culture-specific tests have emerged.
4. Communication problems arise not only when people do not share a language but also when variations exist within a single language.
5. More minority children will need special instruction than children whose homes and cultural environments share most features with the school culture. For most children, this will take the form of language instruction presented through a wide variety of educational options.
6. Canadian education, with the student population it serves, is increasingly multicultural and multiracial in nature. Multicultural education was not conceived in a vacuum. Like other educational innovations, it originated in a socio-political milieu and was, to a large extent, a product of its times.
7. Societal institutions, particularly schools, are expected to make their contributions to Canadian multiculturalism. School curricula that incorporate multicultural principles and practices not only broaden the perspectives of all children, but also build acceptance of newcomers through respect for their culture. Multicultural education means that teachers should be oriented toward the cultural environment of all students.
8. Bilingual education involves the use of two languages for instruction for some or all classroom activities. English is taught as a second language. Bilingual special education is a rapidly developing field.
9. ESL is offered as part of the regular day program for school-aged children who require additional language training in order to take advantage of regular instruction in the schools. ESL programs are a systematic process to help students acquire English conversational skills and to master the academic language required for subject and content area instruction.
10. A curriculum for children from diverse cultures who have conditions that impair their learning stresses language along with the special procedures that are necessary to accommodate a particular condition.
11. Educators must remain acutely sensitive to the special language and cultural needs of families.
12. Co-operative learning has been shown to improve intergroup relationships.

SECTION 4

Children with Sensory Impairments

Hearing and vision are known as the distant senses, because they connect us so profoundly with our environment. The loss of hearing or vision isolates the individual from family, friends, the community, and the physical environment. Hearing and visual handicaps can damage a person psychologically, socially, emotionally, and educationally.

Few children of school age are completely blind or deaf. Far more common are children who see poorly or who are hard-of-hearing. Many hearing and vision problems go undetected until children reach school age. Some children's problems are never identified. These children may be mislabelled as learning disabled, or dismissed as dull, stupid, or lazy.

In rural or remote areas, children with vision or hearing problems are especially likely to go undetected. These areas suffer from a lack of efficient identification procedures and appropriate services. Hearing and visual impairments are very widespread, for example, among the Native population. They are endemic throughout the Northwest Territories, and most prevalent in the Eastern and Central Arctic. Despite these wide-ranging problems, however, many hearing and visual disorders go undetected and untreated (Watters, 1980). Moreover, incidence and prevalence rates in these areas are extremely difficult to determine.

Like much special education, the teaching of blind and deaf children has moved from segregated institutions and schools to integrated programs within public schools. Today hearing- and visually-impaired children in North America attend schools in their home communities. Resource-room and itinerant-teacher programs have been established, and residential schools have become more community-oriented.

CHAPTER 9

Children with Hearing Impairments

Historical Notes

Throughout most of history, exceptional conditions have been attributed to mystical and supernatural causes. This was especially true of deafness, which had no physical manifestations but placed limitations on many aspects of development.

In ancient Greece, Aristotle directed considerable philosophical enquiry toward sensory deprivation. He viewed blindness as more serious, but less debilitating intellectually, than deafness. This led him to characterize deaf persons as "senseless and incapable of reason," and as "no better than the animals of the forest and unteachable" (McGann, 1888). In Rome, deaf persons who could not speak were given guardians and deprived of the rights and responsibilities of citizenship. The early Christian Church also imposed sanctions. Because deaf individuals could not "hear the Word" they were, until about the twelfth century, banned from Church membership and unable to marry without the express dispensation of the Pope.

Although society treated them poorly, deaf persons were the first to receive eduational intervention. Authenticated evidence of successful teaching comes from Spain in 1578 where a monk, Pedro Ponce de Leon, successfully taught the deaf children of some of Spain's wealthiest families. Following Ponce de Leon, successful attempts were made to teach individual deaf persons using oral (speech and speech reading) and manual (sign language and finger-spelling) methods.

The principle that deaf persons were the first to be educated was continued in France. As well, the irreconcilable controversy concerning the most appropriate communication modes to be used in instruction crystallized. In the short period between 1750 and 1780 Jacob Perière in France, Samuel Heinicke in Prussia, and Thomas Braidwood in Edinburgh all taught deaf individuals using oral methods. At the same time, the Abbé Michel Charles de l'Épée in France systematized a sign language specifically for the use of deaf persons.

Michel de l'Épée (1712-1789) became interested in handicapped children when he met a parishoner with two deaf daughters. In 1760, he opened a school in his own home in Paris where he taught chiefly the children of the poor, arguing that the rich could afford other educational means.

At the outset, the abbé knew little about deaf people, their education, their language, or the impact of deafness. He turned to the philosophy of John Locke, who had argued that language was arbitrary — that the words we use to signify a thing have no intrinsic connection with the thing itself. With this in mind, the abbé decided that a sign would signify language as adequately as a spoken word.

The abbé studied his pupils closely and soon noticed that without any teaching or guidance, they evolved a language of simple signs by which to communicate. Building on these basic signs, he developed a system of what he called "natural signs." To teach his students metaphysical and abstract concepts, as well as the grammar of French, the abbé also created a system of "methodological signs" (de l'Épée, 1860). In devising a structured system, he provided deaf persons their own systematic and documented language of signs, the first use of an alternative method of sensory input to provide deaf children with information.

De l'Épée's influence was widespread and pervasive. His successes encouraged Valentin Haüy to establish the first school for blind pupils. De l'Épée also attempted to educate deaf-blind persons and it was at his school, renamed the National Deaf Mute Institute, that Jean Itard worked with Victor, the wild boy of Aveyron. Further, the first American teacher of deaf students, Thomas Hopkins Gallaudet, trained at the National Deaf Mute Institute in Paris in 1816. Gallaudet returned to the United States with the sign language and with a teacher from the Institute, Laurent Clerc. Under the influence of Gallaudet and Clerc, the education of deaf students in North America was almost exclusively through manual modes until the 1860s.

Hearing loss is silent, painless, and invisible, one of the least recognized and most misunderstood ailments. Deafness is a low-incidence condition; however, milder forms of hearing impairment are widely prevalent. Hearing loss can be acquired at any age, although the likelihood of developing it increases with age. Men are more likely to suffer hearing losses. In Canada, the male proportion is 56.7 percent; in the United States, 61.4 (Schein, 1994). This happens, in part, because of men's disproportionate participation in war, high-risk occupations, and sports (McLoughlin, 1982). For example, Edmonds (1985) found that more than 70 percent of professional divers had evidence of sensorineural high-frequency deafness.

Most people think of deafness as simply a lack of sound, but this is one of the least of the problems. The greatest single handicap of serious hearing impairment revolves around the development of communication skills. Hearing loss, as a physical ailment, spills over to affect the development of speech and language, the most important components of interpersonal communication. As Helen Keller (1933) pointed out, deafness also means "the loss of the most vital stimulus — the sound of the voice that brings language, sets thoughts astir, and keeps us in the intellectual company of men" (p.68). The greater the hearing loss, the greater the potential isolation from the environment for the affected individual.

For children, hearing impairment poses a serious threat because hearing is so crucial to learning. In normal child development, speech and language are acquired spontaneously and almost effortlessly. From their earliest days, normally hearing infants process language, preparing to become competent communicators. They have intact auditory processes on which to build an early mastery of the sound, shape, and sense of language. Babies do not merely listen passively to the language around them; they take in, process, and organize the language they hear, and like miniature linguists, they recreate for themselves the language of their culture. For deaf babies, life is devoid of sound effects and spoken script. Hearing-impaired children do not hear the sounds made by themselves and others. They are isolated from the human voice, and this inevitably hinders or halts their acquisition of speech and language.

In the past, few children with serious hearing impairments were admitted to regular classrooms. However, the vigorous advocacy of the past twenty years on behalf of all children who are exceptional has wrought profound and fundamental changes in the particular area of the education of students with hearing handicaps. Although provincially funded schools remain an important instructional vehicle, the current emphasis on appropriate integration with support services has meant shifts in program locations, student placements, and greater possibilities for regular class participation for youngsters who are hearing impaired.

Nevertheless, educational integration is an issue (only one of many) that remains beset with controversy. When inclusion or mainstreaming is discussed, many deaf people and some professionals working with deaf students reject the practice (see Rodda, Grove, and Finch, 1986). They see little benefit for deaf students within the present inclusive practices. The issue is intertwined with the continuing viability of deaf culture and the deaf community as well as with the mode of communication and bilingual education for young children who are deaf.

Development of the Field

Permanent education and intervention for the disabled population began in North America in 1817 when Thomas Hopkins Gallaudet (1787-1851) and Laurent Clerc established the American Asylum for the Education and Instruction of Deaf and Dumb Persons in Hartford, Connecticut. In 1857, Gallaudet's youngest son, Edward, became president of the National Deaf Mute College in Washington, D.C. In 1864, the college, with Abraham Lincoln as patron, became a degree-granting institution, and in 1893, its name was changed to Gallaudet College in memory of Thomas Hopkins Gallaudet. Now Gallaudet University, the facility remains the world's foremost degree-granting institution for hearing-impaired students.

As in Europe and the United States, the education of deaf students was the first form of special education to be undertaken in Canada. In 1829, Ronald McDonald, a reporter with the Montreal Gazette, was sent by the government of Lower Canada to train with Gallaudet in Hartford. In 1831, McDonald opened a school for deaf children in Champlain, Quebec, but lack of funds closed the establishment after only five years. McDonald returned to reporting, but continued his advocacy for deaf persons. His pleas bore fruit when the Catholic Church in Quebec opened schools for deaf boys in 1848 and deaf girls in 1851 (Clarke and Winzer, 1983).

The most prominent pioneer in the early history of Canadian special education was John Barrett McGann (1810-1880), who arrived in Toronto from Ireland, via New York, in 1855. McGann had developed an interest in deafness when he worked for Harvey Peet at the New York Institution for the Deaf and Dumb and was hopeful of initiating education for the deaf in Toronto. McGann soon discovered that there were three hundred dcaf people in the city, and many more scattered throughout the province (McGann, 1888). In 1858, McGann persuaded the City Council, the government, and various social leaders to donate money for a school for deaf and blind children. His first school opened in a spare classroom of the Phoebe Street School in Toronto in the same year.

Between 1858 and 1869, McGann taught his deaf students while his daughter taught those who were blind. With support from Egerton Ryerson, he also persuaded the Ontario government to found permanent institutions for the deaf and for the blind. The Ontario Institution for the Education and Instruction of the Deaf and Dumb was established at Belleville in 1870 and the Ontario

Institution for the Education and Instruction of the Blind at Brantford in 1872.

McGann lent his influence to the establishment of other Canadian special schools. He helped J. Scott Hutton to promote the Halifax School for the Deaf and assisted Thomas Widd in fund-raising at the MacKay Institution for the Deaf in Montreal. McGann was also active with the deaf community and was influential in initiating the Ontario Deaf-Mute Association and the Ontario Mission of the Deaf.

In all, twelve members of McGann's family became involved in special education in Canada and the United States. One daughter taught deaf and blind children in Ontario, a second taught deaf children in Michigan, and a third became principal of the MacKay School for the Deaf in Montreal. A son-in-law founded the Manitoba School for the Deaf in 1886, as well as a similar institution in Washington State. Another son-in-law established a short-lived school for the deaf in Vancouver in 1888 (Winzer, 1993).

The Human Ear

The human ear is a truly marvellous instrument. It is one of the most complex organs in the body, a triumph of miniaturization, fitting into a space not much larger than a hazelnut. It can detect sounds much softer than the dropping of a pin but still filter sounds a million times louder.

The ear collects sound, processes it, and transmits it to be decoded in the brain. Hearing impairment can be caused by interference with any part of the ear's transmission system. Impairment may take the form of restriction in the range of frequencies received, distortions along the frequency spectrum, or a failure to perceive sounds.

The ear's anatomy is usually discussed in terms of the external, the middle, and the inner ear. Figure 9-1 illustrates the major parts of the human hearing mechanism.

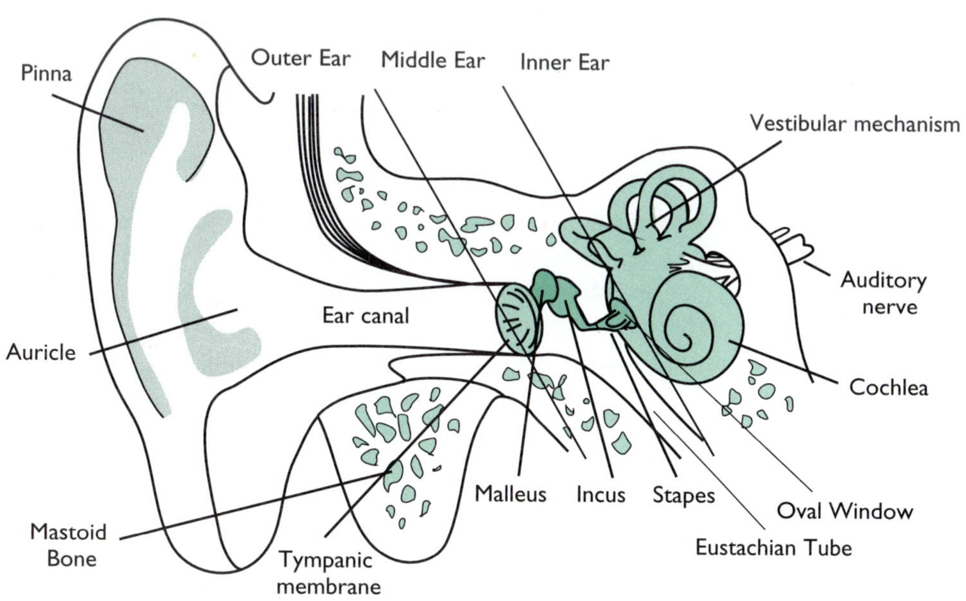

Figure 9-1
Anatomy of the human ear

The External Ear

The outer ear is the visible cartilage structure on the side of the head, referred to as the **pinna**. This is the least complex part of the hearing mechanism and the least important for hearing. An external canal, or **meatus**, runs obliquely from the pinna to the ear drum. The ear drum, or **tympanic membrane**, is a tough, tightly stretched tissue that separates the outer from the middle ear. At the ear drum, hearing really begins.

The pinna serves to collect sound waves and filter them into the meatus. The external canal is lined with coarse hairs and four thousand wax glands that secrete cerumen. The wax traps insects, dust, and other irritants, guards against infection, and lubricates the canal and the ear drum. The ear drum is a concave mechanism that vibrates freely when struck by sound waves. Even the faint vibrations of a whisper cause it to vibrate, but perhaps only a millionth of a centimetre.

The Middle Ear

The inner surfarce of the ear drum is located in the air-filled cavity of the middle ear. The middle ear drum surface holds three small bones, the **malleus**, the **incus**, and the **stapes**, also called the hammer, the anvil, and the stirrup. These tiny bones, the smallest in the human body, form a bridge, the ossicular chain, between the ear drum and the inner ear entrance at another drum called the **oval window**. There are two muscles in the middle ear, one joined to the stapes and the other to the ear drum. The **Eustachian tube** connects the middle ear to the nasopharynx.

In the middle ear, the transmission of sound becomes more sophisticated. When sound waves strike the ear drum, it vibrates and moves the three small bones. These bones transmit the vibrations across the middle ear cavity to the inner ear through the oval window. The middle ear amplifies the sound about twenty-two times, and also protects the inner ear from very loud noise. The Eustachian tube serves to equalize the pressure on both sides of the ear drum. You may have experienced the discomfort of unequal pressure in an airplane descent. To clear the Eustachian tube, and to make the ears "pop," passengers yawn deeply, suck on hard candy, blow their noses, or swallow.

The Inner Ear

The inner ear, the real organ of hearing, is located in a cavern of the skull. It is about the size of a pea, an intricate mechanism with thousands of moving parts. Because it looks like a complex maze of passages, the inner ear is called the **labyrinth**. It contains the cochlea and the vestibular mechanism, which are independent in their functioning.

The **cochlea** is a tiny, snail-shaped structure filled with a fluid similar to cerebrospinal fluid. Its twisting interior is studded with thousands of microscopic hair cells, each one tuned to a particular vibration which responds to a particular fragment of sound. Within the cochlea are highly specialized structures, such as the organ of Corti and Reissner's membrane. The auditory nerve, which is about the diameter of a pencil lead and consists of more than 31 000 nerve fibres, relays messages to the brain (Clark and Tong, 1985).

Behind the cochlea lies the **vestibular mechanism**, composed of three fluid-filled semi-circular canals. These loops of tubing are the organs of balance. Information regarding movement and balance is fed to the brain through the vestibular mechanism. Other nerve endings in the body also contribute to the sense of balance — those in the eyes, feet, muscles, and joints.

The intricacy of the inner ear structure is matched by the complexity of its function. When air-carried (conducted) sound pushes on the ear drum, it causes the stapes to vibrate on the oval window leading to the inner ear, which makes the fluid in the cochlea begin to move. A low-pitched sound pushes at the top of the cochlea and a high-pitched sound at the base. For example, if middle C is sounded, then the cochlea's middle C hair cells vibrate, waving in the fluid. The waving produces a wisp of electricity that feeds into the auditory nerve and is transmitted to the brain. There the signal is unscrambled and converted into meaningful sound. The sequence is overviewed in Table 9-1.

Table 9-1

The sequence of hearing

1. Sound waves enter the ear, travel through the external canal, and vibrate the ear drum.
2. The vibrations of the ear drum move the bones of the middle ear.
3. The footplate of the stapes moves the oval window and sets the cochlear fluid in motion.
4. The movement causes the hairs immersed in the cochlear fluid to move. This stimulates the attached cells to send a tiny electrical impulse along the fibres of the auditory nerve to the brain.
5. In the brain, impulses are translated into meaningful sound.

We hear our own voices not by air conduction but by the the bone conduction of sound. Sound travels directly through the jawbone and the mastoid bone to the inner ear fluid. Thus, we hear ourselves quite differently from how our listeners hear us and often have trouble recognizing our own voices on a tape recorder.

Definitions of Hearing Impairment

The broad category of hearing impairment stretches from marginal hearing losses that may only be a real concern in noisy situations to profound deafness where individuals cannot hear voiced sounds, even with amplification (hearing aids), and must resort to speech reading and, often, sign language. A number of definition and classification systems are used in the field of hearing impairment.

A general definition states that:

- **Hearing impairment** is a generic term indicating a hearing disability that may range in severity from mild to profound. It includes the subsets of deaf and hard-of-hearing.
- A **deaf person** is one whose hearing disability precludes successful processing of linguistic information through audition, with or without a hearing aid.

- A **hard-of-hearing person** is one who, generally with the use of a hearing aid, has residual hearing sufficient to enable succesful processing of linguistic information through audition.

Classification of Hearing Impairment

The distinction between deaf and hard-of-hearing is not as clear-cut as the above definition implies. Both groups are heterogeneous, and sub-categories of each are often used.

The classifier's orientation often determines the system of classification. Those with a strictly physiological perspective are interested primarily in the measurable degree of hearing loss. On the other hand, educators want to know how hearing impairment will affect a child's functioning. Because hearing loss is closely linked to language delay, educators tend to categorize chiefly on the basis of language ability.

Four major, though closely interrelated, classification systems for hearing impairment are in use. These are founded on the degree of hearing impairment, the cause, the site of the deficit, and the age at which the impairment developed.

Table 9-2

Classification of hearing impairment

Severity	Time of onset	Etiology	Site
mild	prelingual	congenital	conductive
moderate	post-lingual	adventitious (deafened)	sensorineural
severe			
profound			

Classification by Severity Levels

Hearing loss is classified according to the amount of hearing in a person's better ear. The acuity is measured by the subject's response to loudness across a range of frequencies. Decibels and hertz are used to measure the loudness and the frequency. Individuals are classed as deaf or hard-of-hearing, depending on whether they hear sounds at certain intensities of loudness across a range of frequencies. This classification is further structured by designation as mild, moderate, severe, or profound hearing loss. Table 9-3 illustrates the levels of hearing impairment.

A bel, named after Alexander Graham Bell, is the unit of loudness intensity. Each bel is broken down into ten parts, known as decibels (dB). A **decibel** represents the smallest difference in loudness intensity that can be perceived.

Hearing loss is measured on a decibel scale, beginning with 0 dB, a figure that designates the point at which people with normal hearing can detect the faintest sound. Inability to hear sounds of 25 to 30 dB or more is considered to be a hearing loss. However, a loss of 60 dB is not merely six times greater than a loss of 10 dB. The figures are logarithmetic, not arithmetic, so that 60dB is 10^6 times louder than 10dB. Figure 9-2 shows the decibel (dB) level of some common sounds on an audiogram, a chart on which hearing is recorded.

Table 9-3

Levels of hearing impairment

Range	Severity	Implications
0-25 dB	insignificant	
25-40 dB	mild hearing loss; hard-of-hearing	May have difficulty with faint or distant sounds. May have problems in conversations, groups, or settings with much ambient noise.
40-60 dB	moderate hearing loss; hard-of-hearing	Frequent difficulty with normal speech, especially in conversations, groups, and class discussions.
60-90 dB	severe hearing loss; hard-of-hearing	Great difficulty with even loud or amplified speech, which seems faint and distorted. Requires amplification and intense speech and language training.
90dB+	profound hearing loss; deaf	May be aware of loud sounds and vibrations, but generally cannot understand even amplified speech.

Sound waves are produced by the to- and- fro waving movement of molecules. One complete to- and fro- movement makes a cycle, and the number of cycles per second determines the frequency of a sound. Cycles per second are measured in hertz (Hz) — a frequency of 1000 Hz indicates 1000 cycles per second. As the frequency increases, the pitch of the sound becomes higher.

Although the human ear is sensitive to frequencies between 50 Hz and 20 000 Hz, most human speech falls between 500 and 2000 Hz. This range of pitch is known as the **speech range**. Middle C on a piano is about 500 Hz.

Classification by Site of Loss

Hearing impairment is also classified according to the part of the hearing mechanism that is affected. Problems in the mechanical transmission of sound waves through the outer and middle ear are called **conductive hearing losses** because something

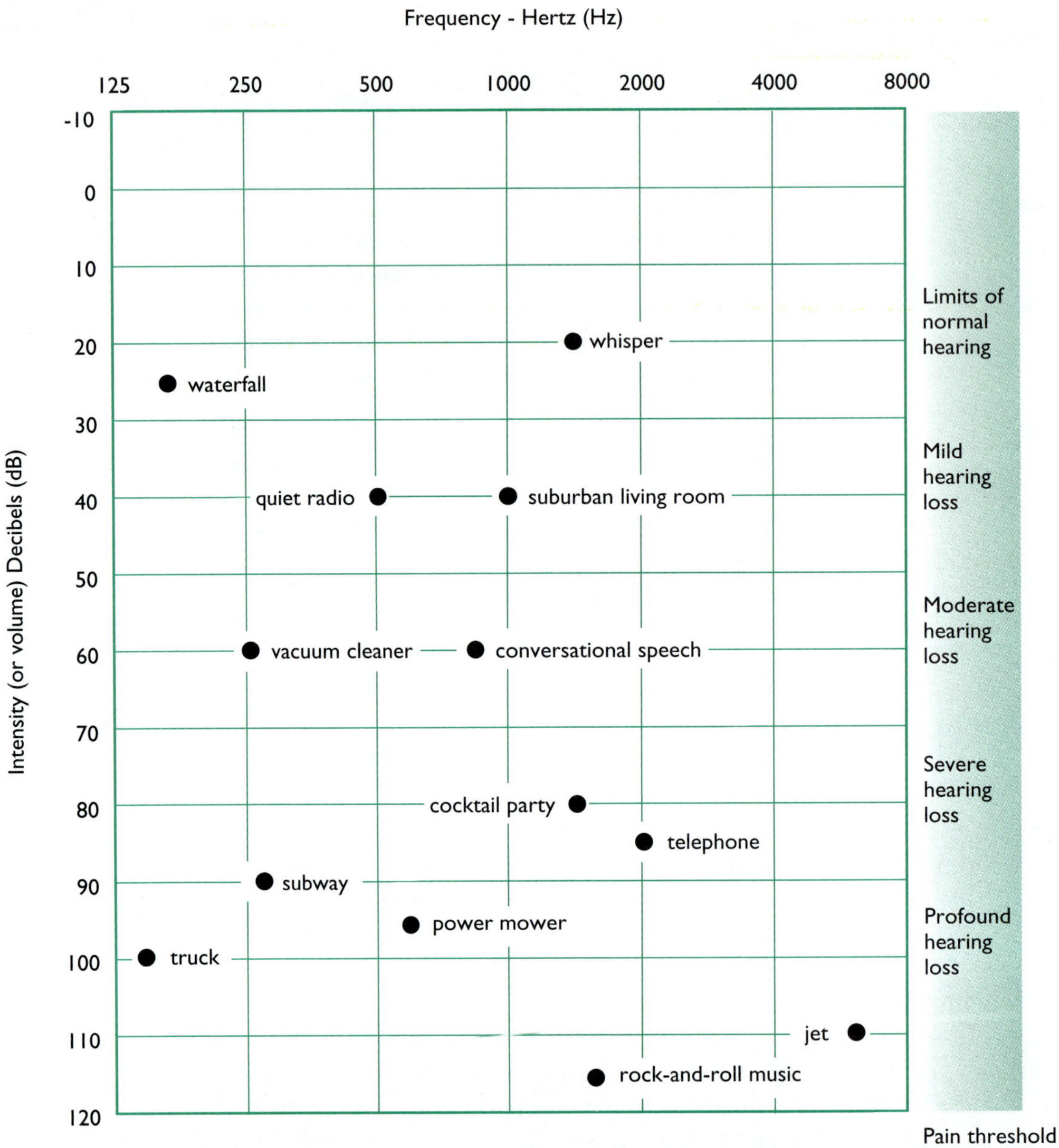

Figure 9-2 *Chart showing the hearing level of some common sounds*

stops the air conduction of sound. Conductive losses generally affect the intensity of sound reception but do not distort the sound. Most conductive losses, affecting the outer and middle ear only, usually respond favourably to medical or surgical intervention.

Impairment in the inner ear is caused by abnormal sense organs or defective auditory nerves. These **sensorineural** hearing impairments interfere with the conversion of sound waves into neural impulses for the brain. Not only is sound intensity hampered, but any sound received may also be distorted. Sensorineural hearing loss is the most common among seriously impaired children.

Classification by Etiology

A **congenital hearing impairment** is one that is present at birth; an **adventitious hearing impairment** is acquired some time after birth, through accident or disease. People with adventitious hearing losses are sometimes described as deafened.

Classification by Age of Onset

Closely connected to the classification of adventitious and congenital hearing impairment is that concerned with age of onset. Because hearing impairment and language delay are closely connected, educators tend to focus upon the age of onset classification.

Children with **prelingual deafness** are those who were deaf prior to the development of speech and language. Children with **post-lingual deafness** became deaf after the development of speech and language. The cut-off point is often set at two years of age (Meadow, 1980). Fewer than one child in ten who are deaf loses hearing after the age of two.

Children with prelingual (congenital) hearing losses do not have the opportunity to practise the listening skills essential to developing speech and language. Inevitably, prelingual impairment affects every aspect of communication development from birth onwards. Children who acquire hearing impairments after they develop speech and language usually find it easier to develop communication skills. The later in life an impairment occurs, the greater the child's linguistic capabilities are likely to be.

Prevalence of Hearing Impairment

Approximately one in ten Canadians, or about two million people, have some form of hearing impairment. Perhaps one in forty has an impairment serious enough to affect daily life and communication, and one in four hundred, or about fifty thousand, suffers from profound deafness. Hearing loss among the aged is especially common. Serious hearing problems affect one in ten people over sixty-five years of age, and four out of every ten over seventy-five (Ontario, Ministry of Health, 1978).

Hearing loss is most tragic when it strikes the very young. Its incidence at birth is quite low, however — in Canada, hearing loss affects one baby in every 1500 (Canadian Hearing Society, 1976). Hearing impairment occurs at similar rates within various ethnic, genetic and socio-economic groups (Greenberg and Calderon, 1984). Approximately one-third of all hearing-impaired children suffer from additional handicapping conditions (Meadow, 1980).

Estimates of hearing impairment vary considerably. One widely accepted estimate holds that 5 percent of school-aged children have hearing outside the normal limits. Of this number, 10 to 20 percent require some type of special education ("Children with communication," 1995). Recent figures collected by the Canadian CEC for students identified and taught as hearing-impaired are shown in Table 9-4.

It is extremely difficult to arrive at a true determination of the prevalence of hearing impairment. Of the many factors that hinder researchers from arriving at accurate prevalence and incidence figures, the most important are

- Inconsistent definitional data.
- Confusion regarding identification and reporting.

- Methodological problems in surveys. For example, after comparing surveys in Canada and the United States, Jerome Schein (1994) found that hearing impairment in the United States has a prevalence rate of 86 per 1000 as compared to 41 per 1000 in Canada, which reflects the younger overall age of the Canadian population. Schein also found that rates vary considerably across the Canadian provinces from a low of 34 per 1000 in the Northwest Territories to 61 per 1000 in Prince Edward Island and Manitoba.
- Difficulties in accurate early identification of hearing loss.
- Increasing prevalence of hearing impairment with age.
- Difficulties in estimating hearing impairments among individuals with multiple handicaps, who are often reported according to their primary disability.
- A shortage of research in some areas. An extensive body of research deals with deafness; much less exists in relation to hard-of-hearing individuals. While hard-of-hearing children are much more common, their true numbers are unknown as many cases are misdiagnosed or simply overlooked.

Table 9-4

Prevalence of serious hearing impairment

Province	Percentage of total school age population	Percentage of exceptional population
Newfoundland	0.14	1.9
Nova Scotia	0.1	0.9
Quebec		
Ontario	0.08	1.15
Saskatchewan	0.12	4.18
B.C.	0.15	1.31

Source: Canadian CEC, 1989

Etiology of Hearing Impairment

Etiological and diagnostic considerations in hearing impairment are the venue of medical and paramedical personnel. Audiologists are chiefly involved in the assessment of hearing and in recommending and fitting amplification equipment. Otolaryngologists are medical personnel who are concerned with problems of the ear, nose, and throat that affect hearing and speech. They also handle voice disorders through medication and surgery.

Impairments of the Outer Ear

External otitis, or swimmer's ear, is an infection of the skin of the external auditory canal. Also in the canal, an excessive build-up of wax can result in lessened hearing acuity. Infrequently, a child is born with missing or undeveloped auditory canals. This condition, known as **auditory atresia**, interferes with the air conduction of sound and requires medical or surgical intervention before it impedes a child's education. Microtia refers to a misshapen or extremely small pinna. Perforation of the ear drum, resulting from any number of causes, can also produce hearing impairments.

Impairments of the Middle Ear

Middle ear hearing impairments are more serious than those affecting the outer ear, but most are surgically correctable. The great majority of middle ear conditions are conductive hearing losses, meaning that the conduction of sound by air is hindered. The result is a loss of intensity of sound, though not usually a distorted pattern. Conductive losses do not exceed 65 dB.

The most common form of ear infection in children is **otitis media**, a condition in which the mucosal lining of the middle ear becomes inflamed and the cavity filled with fluid. When this happens, air conduction of sound is hindered.

Otitis media is most extreme in infancy, when the Eustachian tube is shorter, wider, and in a more horizontal position. The condition may affect two-thirds of children in the first years of life (Wallace et al., 1988). The peak prevalence for otitis media is between six and thirty-six months (Bluestone, 1982). After six years of age, the incidence steadily decreases. However, in the normal school environment, 20 to 30 percent of children between the ages of five and twelve will have at least one bout of middle ear effusion. Of these, 10 to 20 percent will probably develop chronic middle ear problems (Brooks, 1977).

With otitis media, there is a higher incidence in summer than in winter (Canada, Health and Welfare, 1984). The prevalence is higher among lower socio-economic groups, children with cleft palates and other cranio-facial anomalies, and more common in males than in females. Down syndrome children are especially susceptible to otitis media and its resulting conductive hearing loss (Whitman, Simpson, and Compton, 1986).

There is a higher prevalence among Native children (Scaldwell and Frame, 1985) but a lower prevalence among Blacks (Robinson, Allen, and Root, 1988). When Scaldwell and Frame (1985) examined children in six Ontario Native communities, they found a higher incidence of otitis media among school-aged children. The reasons for the higher prevalence among Natives is unclear but it may be a combination of genetic, socio-cultural, environmental, and economic factors (McShane, 1982).

Otitis media causes temporary to chronic mild conductive hearing losses. Because of the nature of the condition, the degree of hearing loss may fluctuate. Under certain conditions, such as when the child has a heavy cold, the loss may be much greater. As well, certain environments, such as a noisy classroom, can compound the effects of a mild conductive hearing loss.

Otosclerosis is a hereditary condition that affects 2 percent of the population and is clinically active in more than 0.5 percent ("Hearing loss," 1982). The condition is characterized by the destruction of the capsular bone in the middle ear and the growth of a weblike bone that attaches to and restricts the stapes. The condition is rare in children and is not usually noticed until adolescence or the early twenties. Resultant hearing losses can be at the 50 or 60 dB level, necessitating the use of a hearing aid or corrective surgery. Otosclerosis is twice as common in females as in males.

Other middle ear problems can be caused by blows to the head or a fall. They can also result from congenital defects.

Impairments of the Inner Ear

The most devastating hearing impairments are caused by sensorineural problems of the inner ear. A great many childhood sensorineural impairments are attributed to "causes unknown." However, Donald Moores (1982) documented five major causes of sensorineural deafness: heredity, maternal rubella, meningitis, mother-child blood incompatibility (Rh factor), and prematurity. The most profound losses stem from meningitis, maternal rubella, and hereditary factors.

Estimates of the number of children with hearing loss due to hereditary factors range from 30 to 60 percent (Moores, 1982). Marriages between hearing-impaired people is a factor in the high incidence of hereditary hearing loss. Many schools for the deaf cater to children whose parents and grandparents were also students there. One Canadian study traced a family with a genetic trait of deafness from 1865 to 1978. Of 154 descendants, nearly 10 percent (15 persons) were born deaf (Winzer, 1993).

There are about sixty-five types of hereditary deafness. Hearing problems may be inherited on a dominant trait (14 percent), a recessive trait (44 percent), or as a sex-linked disorder (2 percent) (Lowenbraun and Thompson, 1982). Hearing loss can be inherited alone or in combination with other abnormalities in a syndrome. Hearing loss accompanies skeletal deformities in Treacher-Collins syndrome and abnormal skin pigmentation in Waardenburg's syndrome, and it is sometimes part of the multiple disabilities of Down syndrome. Approximately 4 to 5 percent of congenitally hearing-impaired individuals suffer from Usher's syndrome, which results in hearing impairment and a progressive deterioration in the visual field through retinitis pigmentosa (Bond, 1981). Pendred's syndrome and Jervell and Lang-Neilson syndrome are also associated with hearing impairment.

Maternal rubella is the most common identifiable cause of deafness from an external source. Rubella (German measles) is acquired by pregnant women via an airborne virus. The infection may cause the child to be born with hearing loss, defective vision, heart irregularities, and disorders of the nervous system. Children whose hearing impairment is due to rubella may show progressively more severe hearing loss as they grow. (Anvar, Mencher, and Keet, 1984). There may also be a late onset of other disabilities, such as strabismus.

Meningitis is a major cause of acquired sensorineural hearing loss because the high fever that accompanies the disease is very dangerous to the inner ear. Incompatibility of blood type between mother and infant may also cause hearing impairment, along with several other disorders.

Prematurity of itself does not cause deafness. However, premature and low-birth-weight babies are at higher risk for hearing disorders. A problem such as undetected rubella may be the cause of early delivery. Deafness can also result from birth complications such as prolonged labour, abrupt birth, or the use of obsterical instruments. Failure to breathe immediately after birth — apnea — is another commonly reported cause of hearing problems.

Among adults, progressive nerve deterioration, known as presbycusis, is the most common cause of auditory defect. The older one gets, the more one is prone to presbycusis. As well, inner ear fistula (a build-up of inner ear fluid), acoustic neuroma (tumour on the auditory nerve), and viral infections and vascular spasms in the inner ear can cause permanent or temporary Sudden Hearing Loss Syndrome. Intracranial tumours, cerebral hemorrhages, and prolonged exposure to tones of high intensity are also increasingly recognized as causes of sensorineural hearing loss. Ménière's disease, a condition characterized by nausea, vertigo, and tinnitus, is a particularly devastating problem for adults.

Both deaf and hearing individuals can suffer from tinnitus. The word derives from the Latin, meaning to "tinkle or ring like a bell." For some sufferers it may be a ringing or a hiss, but for others it is living constantly with the noise of a squeaking door hinge, the squealing of an unoiled metal bearing, or the sound of fingernails being dragged across a blackboard (Agnew, 1986). The chronic nature of the condition causes great distress and becomes the central issue in the lives of some affected people.

Tinnitus is not an audiological phenonomen but a medical condition. The actual mechanism of tinnitus is not known. It does not have a specific site of origin; it can be produced anywhere along the auditory mechanism, or it may not be generated by the auditory system at all. Anything that can go wrong with the ear has tinnitus associated with it as a symptom — wax against the drum, tumours on the nerve, otosclerosis, Ménière's disease, and exposure to excessively loud sounds (Agnew, 1986).

Prevention of Hearing Impairments

In North America we pay less attention to hearing loss than to almost any other medical condition (Hopper, 1975). While not all hearing loss can be prevented, increased awareness can serve to prevent many problems.

In the prevention of acquired deafness, problems associated with mother-child blood imcompatibility have descreased since the 1968 advent of anti-Rh gamma globulin (RhoGam). If injected into the mother within seventy-two hours of birth, she will not produce the harmful antibodies that can harm later infants. A rubella vaccine, developed in 1968, is given to preschool children. As well, a vaccine to prevent some forms of meningitis in children has been developed.

High-Risk Registers

A child termed "high risk" is more likely than most children to develop some specific disability. High-risk factors for hearing impairment include complications during the mother's pregnancy, certain postnatal conditions, the medical or genetic history of the family, and the socio-economic background of the family. Most hospitals document these factors in high-risk registers that aid in identifying infants at risk for hearing loss. A high-risk register for hearing impairment might list the following:

- the family history of childhood hearing impairment;
- perinatal complications, such as prolonged labour, prematurity, complications during delivery, the use of obsteric instruments, or severe anoxia;
- neonatal complications, such as low birth-weight or very high birth-weight;
- anatomic malformations involving the head or neck.

Genetic Counselling

The genetics specialist is primarily concerned with prevention. Counselling is offered to couples to inform them of genetic risks. Once armed with this knowledge, the couple can plan their family accordingly.

In the past few decades, the fertility of deaf adults has rapidly approached that of the general population. Moreover, a deaf person typically marries someone else with a hearing handicap. Today, in-group marriages are estimated at between 86 and 90 percent of all marriages involving deaf people (see Reagan, 1988). As a result, genetic transmission of deafness has become increasingly common. Empirical evidence gathered since the 1870s indicates that the risk of deaf offspring for a deaf couple is approximately 10 percent (Fay, 1898; Fraser, 1976). This average figure includes couples at very high risk and others for whom the risk is minimal.

Environmental Factors

Noise levels sufficient to cause hearing damage are a growing problem in society. For example, a power mower emits 100 dB, a subway train 90, a riveting gun 130, and a jet take-off 105 or more. Muscles in the middle ear protect the inner ear from excessively loud low-pitched sounds, but no such action protects the ear from the new high-pitched sounds.

Modern music may also be causing hearing impairments. Rock bands often reach 115 dB. One expert argues that tickets to shows should be labelled: "Warning — this concert may be hazardous to your ears" (Hopper, 1975).

The problem of foreign objects in the ear has always existed and probably always will. Nature designed the ear to clean itself. An old saying claims that if a finger were intended to go in the ear, it would have been made small enough to fit. Unfortunately, many other things do fit — the ends of pencils, beads, carrots, peanuts, and bobby pins. Even cotton swabs can do enormous damage, either by puncturing the paper thin ear drum or pushing accumulations of wax further into the ear.

Identification and Measurement

Measuring a hearing impairment is quite complicated because measurement must incorporate the physical, psychological, and educational aspects as well as the impact on speech and language acquisition and development. To assess the various domains, a number of professionals and paraprofessionals may need to be involved — physicians, audiologists, psychologists, educators, and speech and language therapists.

Measurement of Hearing Loss

Audiology is the science of detecting and correcting hearing impairment. The major purposes of audiology are

- to assist in medical diagnosis;
- to provide an overall assessment of hearing in order to ascertain the need for supportive services;
- to screen large populations for individuals who require more in-depth assessment;
- to detect changes in hearing that may have resulted from exposure to hazard (Davis, 1978).

Audiologists use many sophisticated methods to assess hearing. They use three general types of hearing tests — pure tone audiometry, speech audiometry, and specialized tests for very young and difficult-to-assess children.

Screening

It is during infancy that children who are born deaf most closely resemble their hearing peers. Deaf infants follow the normal patterns of visual exploration and motor development. They also cry and coo and vocalize like other children during the first few months of life. Not until they reach the babbling stage at about six months do their sound patterns become differentiated from those of hearing infants. By the age of ten months, deaf infants show a significant decrease in babbling behaviour. This happens because deaf infants cannot hear their own babbling and do not receive reinforcement from the speech of adults.

Deafness is often suspected when children are about twelve months of age and expected to say their first words. Ross (1990b) found that many mothers, especially of profoundly deaf children, suspected a loss before the child was one year old. For children with milder losses, the problems may not be identified until they undergo a routine school screening.

Teachers should be alert for behaviours that suggest mild hearing loss and send children with suspected problems for audiological evaluation.

The most common screening instrument is the **sweep test**, which uses a portable audiometer to present tones at 20 to 25 dB across a range of frequencies. Children who reveal problems at the screening level are then referred for in-depth audiological testing.

Screening may not identify all children requiring in-depth assessment. School screening has been known to fail to identify at least half of children with otitis media (Gdowski, Sanger, and Decker, 1986), and especially children who suffer a recurrent "on-again, off-again" otitis media and therefore present inconsistent responses. Screening may also fail to detect students with high frequency losses.

Table 9-5 outlines some of the behaviours that suggest mild hearing loss. Teachers and parents should be alert for these behaviours and send children with suspected problems for in-depth audiological evaluation.

Table 9-5

Possible signs of mild hearing loss in children

- There appears to be a physical problem associated with the ears, such as buzzing, earaches, discharge, or frequent colds and sore throats.
- The child has poor articulation, particularly missing some of the consonant sounds.
- The child cocks the head or turns the body toward the speaker in an obvious effort to hear more accurately.
- The child has more than usual trouble in following directions.
- The child frequently asks for information to be repeated.
- The child appears to be inattentive when spoken to in a normal voice.
- The child speaks or sings too loudly or too softly.
- The child talks too much and appears not to want to relinquish control of the conversation.
- The child is withdrawn and unwilling to mingle with classmates or neighbours.
- The child gives incorrect answers to simple questions.
- The child is functioning below potential ability in school.
- The child is becoming a behaviour problem at school or at home.

Pure Tone Audiometry

An individual's degree of hearing loss, measured in decibel and hertz units, can be ascertained through pure tone audiometry administered in an environment relatively free of external noise. Pure tone audiometry is designed to establish an individual's threshold of hearing at a variety of different frequencies. A **threshold of hearing** is the level at which a person can first detect a sound.

The procedure for pure tone testing is relatively simple. The audiologist presents a variety of tones at levels from 0 to 110 dB across a range of frequencies, usually 125 Hz to 8000 Hz, testing each ear individually. The person being tested responds by raising a hand when a sound is detected, and the data for each ear are plotted on a chart of hearing called an **audiogram**. Figure 9-3 shows an audiogram on which is plotted the average loss (both ears) of three individuals.

Figure 9-3
Audiogram

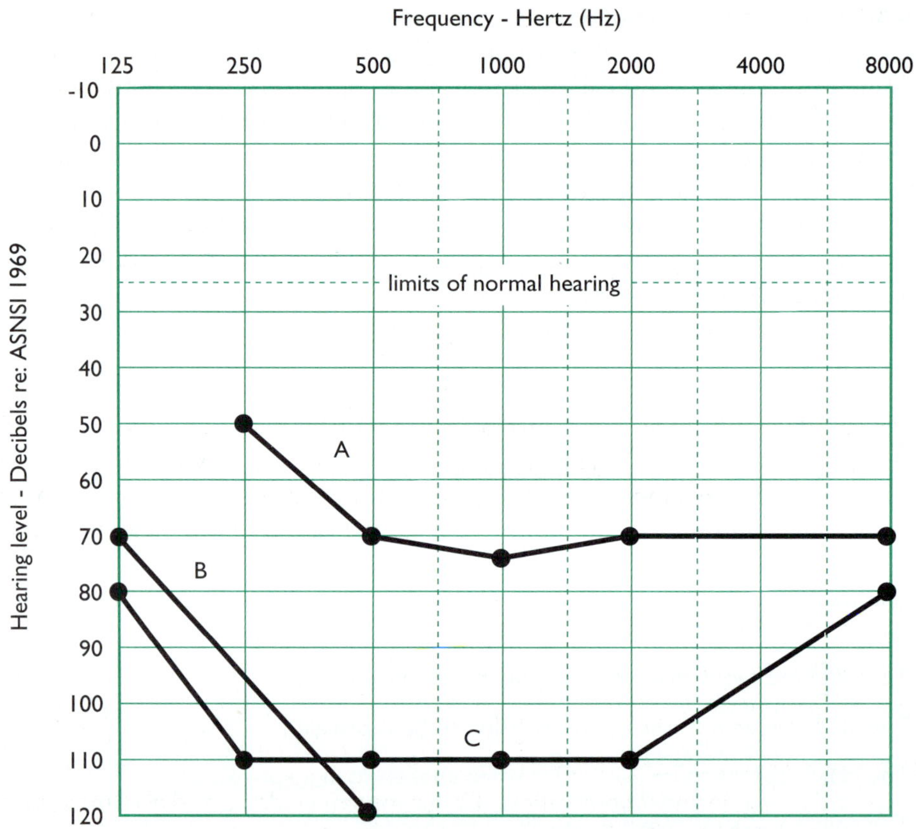

Person A has a flat loss of about 70 dB. In other words, Person A only begins to detect sounds at the level of 70 dB and would be regarded as moderately hearing impaired. Because of the amount of residual hearing, especially across the speech range (500 to 2000 Hz), a hearing aid would probably help this individual.

Person B suffers a hearing loss described as a ski slope loss because of its shape. This person, with little usable hearing above 90 dB and none across the speech range, would be categorized as profoundly deaf. Person C displays a saucer-shaped audiological pattern which a number of researchers (e.g. Anderson, Barr, and Wedenberg, 1970) have found common in children with hearing loss due to rubella.

omit

Speech Audiometry

Speech audiometry is designed to assess an individual's ability to detect and understand speech. The speech detection threshold refers to the intensity level at which a person can hear, but not necessarily understand, speech. Much more important is the **speech reception threshold** (SRT), which is the level at which an individual actually understands speech.

To ascertain the speech reception threshold, the tester presents the person with a list of two-syllable words (called spondees) that have equal stress on each syllable — *baseball* or *ice cream*, for example. Each ear is tested separately, and the level at which half of the words are understood is considered to be the speech reception threshold.

Tests for Young Children

Pure tone audiometry can only be used with people who understand what is expected of them. The diagnostic process requires a person to discriminate among sounds of different intensity and tone and then communicate their discriminations. For a child under the age of about four, the process is too complicated. So that hearing impairment can be identified as early as possible, a number of special tests have been devised for very young children. Special tests have also been developed for those whose handicaps do not suit standard pure tone audiometric testing. The two most common forms of specialized hearing tests are electrophysiological and behavioural assessments. (Other specialized tests are discussed in Chapter 15.)

Electrophysiological Assessment

Electrophysiological procedures include electroencephalography-evoked (EEG) response audiometry and impedance audiometry. EEG assessment measures responses to auditory stimuli but requires no active participation on the part of the child. Electrodes are attached to the scalp and reveal changes in the brain's electrical activity when the subject hears a sound (Wiley, 1980).

Acoustic impedance audiometry assesses conductive hearing losses by measuring the movement of the ear drum and middle ear muscles and bones in response to auditory stimulation (Northern, 1980). The audiologist can detect fluid in the middle ear, a sign of otitis media, for example.

Behavioural Assessment

Behavioural testing includes observation of behaviour and reflexes, and play audiometry. Infants show an orienting response by turning their heads toward the source of a sound. Diagnosticians can therefore gain a crude measure of hearing status by observing infants' reactions to loud sounds. Under the age of five or six months, infants also display reflexive behaviours that are useful for testing hearing. A startle movement, a reflex that affects face, arms, trunk, legs, and eyes, is present at birth and elicited by loud sound.

Play audiometry is used with children over two years of age. It involves an audiometer and a game in which the child performs an activity in response to the sound. The child may respond by building a stacking toy, dropping blocks into a box, or putting pieces into a puzzle.

Psycho-Educational Assessment

A range of measures are needed to assess the psychological and educational functioning of students with hearing impairments. The one commonality among measures is that they circumvent the effects of the hearing loss and match the linguistic deficits of the child.

Non-verbal tests are the most appropriate for deaf children. The most widely used IQ test is the Performance Scale of the Wechsler Intelligence Scale for Children (WISC-111), which is believed to yield fairly valid IQ scores for deaf children aged nine to sixteeen. The Verbal Scale is usually omitted from the battery, and an IQ score is calculated on the basis of the Performance Scale alone. The Performance Scale of the WISC-R was standardized using a hearing-impaired sample (Anderson and Sisco, 1977).

Other popular measures include the Goodenough Harris Drawing Test (Harris, 1963) and Raven's Progressive Matrices (Raven, 1948) for children nine years of age and older. The Leiter International Performance Scale (Leiter, 1948) has remained popular for young children because it can be administered by pantomime and needs no verbal cues or responses.

Students with hearing impairments have special needs in the classroom.

Developmental Consequences of Hearing Impairment

The major handicap of hearing impairment is its impact on the development of speech and language. This may spill over to adversely affect other developmental domains.

Cognitive Development

The cognitive development of individuals who are hearing impaired is a provocative and challenging area of research. Studies dating back to the nineteenth century have considered IQ levels, the relationship between language and thought, concept acquisition and development, perceptual processes, and memory function. As 150 years of research findings accumulated, ideas about the cognitive development of individuals with hearing impairments changed, sometimes quite dramatically.

For example, studies before 1950 showed deaf school children to be three or four years behind hearing children and about ten IQ points below the norm (Meadow 1980). However, the reason for past perceptions of poorer intellectual development lay not within the child but in the testing procedures used. When testing procedures are matched to their linguistic capabilities, deaf students score within the normal range of the performance scales on tests of mental ability. In general, the hearing-impaired population fits on the same curve for intelligence as does the rest of the population (Quinsland and Vanginkel, 1990).

The relationship between language and thought has fascinated psychologists for decades, and different views have emerged. Benjamin Whorf (1956) took an extreme view, holding that thought could not really exist without language. Jean Piaget characterized language as "the handmaiden of thought," but Jerome Bruner gives it a central place in cognitive development (see Winzer, 1995).

If cognitive development is not dependent on language, then one would expect hearing-impaired children, despite their linguistic deficits, to develop the same abilities in much the same manner as hearing children. Some researchers have found that deaf children consistently demonstrate the same thinking processes as hearing children when the tasks involved are not dependent on language (Furth, 1966, 1971). In a study using Paigetian tasks with preschoolers, Bond (1987) found the hearing-impaired children to lag slightly but not significantly behind hearing children. Others have found that deaf children who have acquired some language consistently outperform those with less language ability (Schlesinger and Meadow, 1972; Silverman, 1967).

Studies of the performance of deaf children on memory tasks show conflicting results. For example, deaf children are more likely to retain words that have a sign equivalent than words that do not, and they are more likely than hearing children to remember geometric forms better than digits.

Early researchers (e.g. Mykelbust, 1960) argued that the perceptual and conceptual processes of congenitally deaf children failed to develop normally. Deaf persons were said to lack abstract thinking capacity and to function normally only if restricted to concrete activities. While recent comparisons of concept formation and abstract thinking skills between hearing-impaired and normally hearing children yield somewhat inconsistent results, many educators and researchers now accept that deaf children can think logically without a linguistic system. Braden (1987), however, asserts that all deaf children suffer metacognitive deficits. These may result in part from the memorization, drill and rote learning so characteristic of programs for the education of deaf students.

Communication Development

Speech and language are the areas of development most severely affected by a hearing impairment. Problems in this area vary considerably as a result of many factors. These include the degree of hearing loss, the training and use of residual hearing, the child's age at the impairment's onset, the etiology of the impairment, the family climate, the early mode of communication, and the educational setting.

For children with mild or moderate hearing losses, the effect on speech and language may be minimal. Communication for the hard-of-hearing child has more in common with that of the normally hearing child than with that the deaf child because both hearing and hard-of-hearing individuals use audition rather than vision as the primary mode for speech and language development (Berg, 1986). Hard-of-hearing children can use their residual hearing to develop speech and language, and so they can use spoken language adequately to transmit and receive information although they may speech read as a supplement to auditory skills.

Because the education of hearing impaired children is complex and difficult, it is essential that classroom teachers acquire an understanding of hearing loss and its educational and social implications.

Even so, hard-of-hearing children may still be at risk for educational failure. Some research suggests that a mild to moderate hearing loss (10 to 40 dB) impairs the listening performance of a young child to the extent of becoming an auditory handicap (Gdwoski, Sanger, and Decker, 1986). Moreover, many environmental variables such as extraneous noise, the distance from the speaker, and even the child's language capacity, can adversely affect a child's auditory comprehension.

Children who have suffered mild losses, especially from otitis media, often demonstrate language and learning difficulties in the preschool years (Wallace et al., 1988), and otitis media may be implicated in later speech disorders (Roberts et al., 1988). Children with recurrent middle ear disease are at considerable risk for losing high frequency auditory sensitivity, and recent psycho-acoustic studies have observed that intensity discrimination is adversely affected by the presence of high frequency hearing losses (Fausti, [1987]). Children with early onset otitis media may be left with permanent effects, such as inefficient listening skills, that persist in later life. These children may demonstrate sporadic misunderstandings in speech; they may, for example, confuse the markers *ed* and *ing* and misunderstand small words in connected speech such as *are, to,* and *in.*

For deaf children, most loud speech is inaudible, even with the most sophisticated hearing aids. Children who are deaf have significant problems in learning language, as well as significant articulation, voice quality, and tone discrimination problems. Because deaf children cannot hear the words of people around them, they have no language models. Even with optimal intervention, the language levels of most deaf children are seriously retarded.

Every element of language is affected — semantics, syntax, morphology, pragmatics, and phonology. As well, constructions such as phrasal verbs (*turn off, run in*) pose great difficulties.

Figurative language (idioms, similes, metaphors, proverbs, and so on) involves every area of comprehension and semantics and is beyond most deaf students (see Arnold and Hornett, 1990). An idiom such as "hit the road" transgresses the laws of logic and is almost impossible to justify for a literal-thinking deaf person. One teacher tells how a young deaf child looked bewildered when she signed to him, "Your nose is running." To the child, running was something done on the playground and not something that noses did.

Speech is another area of great difficulty. In one study (Jensema, Karchmer, and Trybus, 1978) teachers rated the intelligibility of the speech of their hearing-impaired students; more than 42 percent of the children were rated as unintelligible or barely intelligible. According to the survey, approximately 13 percent of the children would not even try to use their voices for speech.

Lip reading or **speech reading** is the skill of understanding speech through watching the lips and face. The latter term is more accurate because facial expressions impart to spoken words a whole spectrum of feelings, attitudes, and visual clues.

It is a commonly held myth that deaf individuals are endowed with a compensatory speech reading ability that atones for their loss of hearing. Yet deaf school leavers can speech read no better than hearing peers (Conrad, 1979). In fact, hearing persons may be better at speech reading simply because they possess a strong linguistic base to fill in missing information.

Speech reading is a difficult skill to acquire because only about 30 percent of English sounds are visible on the lips (Stewart, 1984). For example, the colour words *red, white,* and *green* all look pretty much the same on the lips, as do *bat* and *mat, manic* and *panic,* and *measure* and *pleasure.* The difficulties with such look-alike words are almost insurmountable. Imagine a child trying to distinguish between "a red bat" and "a green mat." When words look the same, speech readers must anticipate them and fill them in, but this takes sophisticated language knowledge — an area of deficit for most deaf people. To add to the problems, the average speaker makes about thirteen articulatory movements a second during normal conversation. The average observer, however, can only visually record eight or nine movements a second (Sanders, 1971).

Academic Achievement

In the past, incorrect assumptions about the cognitive abilities of persons who were hearing-impaired led researchers to conclude that educational programming should concentrate on developing motor and mechanical skills rather than intellectual abilities (Pintner, 1941). Today, the curriculum matches that presented to hearing students, but with a far greater emphasis on speech and language development.

The academic achievement of students with hearing disabilities is closely aligned to their acquisition of language. With the difficulties that most of these students meet in acquiring language, it is perhaps not surprising that their academic performance compares poorly with documented potential. Hard-of-hearing pupils who rely primarily on residual hearing and speech for communication have well-documented language deficiencies that limit their reading comprehension as well as their oral communication skills (Gearheart, Weishahn, and Gearheart, 1988). Deaf students uniformly appear to lag educationally by three to five years.

Numerous studies of reading achievement have shown that the mean reading scores of deaf children are well below those of hearing children; there is a lag of two to eight years. According to data published by the Center for Assessment and Demographic Studies at Gallaudet University (1991), the average eighteen-year-old with a severe to profound hearing loss reads with the comprehension of a normally hearing child in the early months of third grade. This is below or barely at literacy level. Only 3 percent of deaf eighteen-year-olds read at the same level as the average hearing reader of the same age.

There is some evidence that deaf readers use many of the same metacognitive strategies to comprehend print as do hearing readers (Andrews and Mason, 1991). Case studies of deaf children involved in the reading process show that they use contextual information to reconstruct the text using their semantic knowledge. But many deaf students show restricted vocabulary (LaSasso and Davey, 1987); most can't comprehend even the most commonly used words. Children with limited vocabularies are likely to experience great difficulties in language and reading. These will be especially noticeable if reading words are removed from context, creating an unnaturally difficult situation. To add to the language and semantic difficulties, many deaf readers lack background knowledge or prior experience of many of the topics found in commercial texts.

Deaf children are less educationally behind in more mechanical skills such as arithmetic and spelling. But while they seem to achieve well in mathematical computation, they are less successful at mathematical problem solving, which is predicated on a language base.

Deaf students tend to leave school earlier than their hearing counterparts. In Canada, 22.7 percent of deaf adults had 13 or more years of education, compared to 24.3 percent for hard-of-hearing persons and 42.4 percent for those with normal hearing (Schein, 1994). Only 3 percent of deaf Canadians attend university.

Social and Emotional Development

Hearing impairment may lead to adjustment problems in children. This is not to say that the hearing-impaired child lacks the potential for normalcy. However, hearing impairment often results in impairments with language and communication and may produce barriers to normal social interaction that appear impossible to overcome (Warren and Hasenstab, 1986). The severity of social maladjustment patterns often depends on the severity of the hearing loss and the type of impairment. Severe hearing losses are more likely to result in social isolation.

In the case of hard-of-hearing students, the hearing impairment may be misdiagnosed and a child's inappropriate responses may be erroneously seen as behaviour problems or learning disorders. When this happens, the child's self-sufficiency, social maturity, and personality development are placed at risk, as we see in the profile of Ramon, a lad with an unidentified hearing loss. An extract from Ramon's IEP is shown later in this chapter.

In very young hearing-impaired children, communication deficits interfere with normal play development (Higginbotham, Baker, and Neill, 1980). Hearing-impaired children tend to engage in less complex and less social play than do normally hearing children (Esposito and Koorland, 1989). One study (Higginbotham and Baker, 1981) found that hearing-impaired preschoolers between 47 and 66 months of age preferred solitary constructive play, whereas hearing children of the same age preferred co-operative dramatic play.

Deaf children show a higher degree of emotional instability, neurosis, and maladjustment than hearing children. Estimates of the rates of emotional disturbance among hearing-impaired students range from 8 to 22 percent (Adams and Tidwell, 1989; Meadow, 1980). Although the range is broad, there is sufficient evidence to conclude that the frequency of behaviour disorders is higher than for the general population of school-age children (Adams and Tidwell, 1989).

Profile

Ramon

At seven and a half, Ramon already had a reputation for being disruptive in the classroom and difficult to manage. He was inattentive and restless, aggressive with other children, and poor in academic work. His speech was slurred and he had a lisp.

In kindergarten and grade one, Ramon's teachers had considered him immature and somewhat slow to learn. As he approached his eighth birthday, however, his learning problems were increasing. He was having particular trouble with language arts. Although Ramon had a small vocabulary of sight words, he was defeated by their use in context and any comprehension or sequencing exercises that were presented.

After a teacher initiated referral for in-depth psycho-educational diagnosis, Ramon was labelled as learning disabled. However, even in a one-to-one situation in a resource room, he made little progress, and his parents blamed the school for his increasing frustration and unhappiness.

When Ramon saw the speech/language pathologist, the root of his learning difficulties was finally discovered. The pathologist found that Ramon had trouble recognizing and enunciating high-pitched speech sounds, and this inevitably led her to suspect hearing impairment.

Audiological assessment diagnosed Ramon as suffering a 55 dB bilateral hearing loss. Because this loss occurred in the high frequencies between 4000 and 8000 Hz, it had been missed in regular school screening tests. Ramon's audiologist did not suggest amplification for him. However, the classroom environment and curriculum have been modified. Ramon has been moved to a seat at the front of the room. His teacher is concentrating on building a strong sight word vocabulary and using a whole word family approach to improve his reading skills. Most importantly, Ramon now understands his problem and his sense of frustration and alienation is beginning to fade.

Abnormal social development in hearing-impaired children is often manifested by impulsive, irresponsible, and dependent behaviour. Frequently, deaf children seem to disregard the feelings and misunderstand the actions of others. They typically exhibit a high degree of egocentricity and a low frustration threshold. These traits cause them to make inordinate demands and to act out their frustrations if demands are not met (Meadow, 1980).

Additional Disabling Conditions

With the multiple etiologies that can lead to hearing impairment, it is little wonder that many children suffer additional disabilities. It is estimated that 33 percent of children with hearing impairments suffer additional handicapping conditions, of which emotional disorders, mental retardation, and learning disabilities are the most common. All studies on vision screening also indicate a higher incidence of visual deficits than among normally hearing children (Silberman, 1981).

A 1989 Alberta study found that teachers believed that 14 percent of their hearing-impaired students suffered vision problems and that 11.4 percent had physical disabilities; 9.1 percent were seen to have a mental handicap and 12.8 percent to have behavioural or emotional problems. Almost one in five of the students (19.4 percent) was seen as learning disabled (Alberta Response, 1989).

Family Variables

The way in which the parents and the family react to and accept a disabling condition profoundly influences the development of the child with the disability. This is even more true in the area of hearing impairment, where the hearing status of the parents is a significant variable and where parental child-rearing attitudes appear to be the best predictors of the self-concept of severely to profoundly hearing-impaired children (Warren and Hasenstab, 1986).

Approximately 10 percent of hearing impaired babies are born to deaf parents. These children form a distinct sub-group within the hearing-impaired population. Children deafened by genetic factors tend to have far more positive outcomes than do deaf children born to hearing parents.

Emotional and behavioural disturbance is about half as prevalent among deaf children with deaf parents as among deaf children with hearing parents (Stokoe and Battiston, 1975). Deaf children of deaf parents outperform deaf children of hearing parents on measures of language skills. In school, these youngsters consistently perform at a higher level on tests of academic achievement than do deaf children of hearing parents, achieving at about two-thirds the rate of hearing students (Vernon, 1969).

The reasons that underlie the differences between deaf children of hearing parents and those of deaf parents are not difficult to pinpoint. First of all, deaf children of deaf parents are born into families that already have experience with deafness. Deaf parents understand the child's condition and seem better able to cope with any negative feelings that accompany diagnosis. Second, deaf parents are fluent in sign language, so their children usually experience language acquisition and family interaction earlier and at a greater rate than other deaf children. This prevents frustration for both parents and children, and assists the children's emotional development. As well, deaf children with deaf parents have closer exposure to other deaf people and to the discrete culture of the deaf community. (See Profile 9-2). Finally, deaf children of deaf parents rarely suffer additional injuries to the nervous system before birth. As a result, their incidence of secondary handicaps is no greater than for the population at large.

Hearing Children of Deaf Parents

We cannot close this section without a passing glance at another sub-group with potential language, speech, and social and emotional difficulties. Although not actually hearing-impaired, the hearing children of deaf parents often develop problems.

Research in this area is fairly scattered. One study (Schiff and Ventry, 1976) of fifty-two hearing children of deaf parents found that only twenty-three had developed normal language. The other twenty-nine developed speech and language problems, including defective articulation, deviant stress and intonational patterns, and fluency disorders, problems that did not disappear after the children entered school. In another study, Murphy and Slorach (1983) found that, of six preschool hearing children of deaf parents, three showed delayed and deviant language development and three had other language problems. Finally, a British study (Flaxbeard and Toomey, 1987) of ten hearing children of deaf parents found that the children exhibited conversational difficulties, memory problems, reasoning difficulties, and poor language comprehension.

Profile

Christopher

Increasingly, the teachers are beginning to complain about the behaviour and attitudes of thirteen-year-old Christopher. In his home room and in the other classes, Chris shows acting-out behaviour and, if reprimanded, sulks and will not participate in the lesson at all. When the teacher speaks to him, he reaches up and turns off his aid and closes his eyes. At first, Chris's peers seemed to admire his audacious defiance of the teachers, but now they seem to be bored with his constant disruptions of the class.

Christopher's parents are both deaf, and a younger sibling has a profound hearing impairment. Chris himself has been diagnosed as severely hard of hearing. He has a flat loss in both ears of 80 dB. He wears aids in both ears and has an interpreter in some classes (English, math, science, and social studies) to translate the teacher's message into sign language and to translate back the comments that Chris makes and questions he answers. At the moment, the interpreter is rather at a loss; she never knows how many of Chris's "off the cuff" and rude remarks to interpret for the teacher and is therefore playing the role of mediator.

This is only the second year that Chris has been integrated into a classroom with normally hearing peers. For all of elementary school, he was in a residential school for deaf students. His parents agreed, with some trepidation, when the residential school suggested that Chris could be integrated.

Chris uses sign as his main mode of communication but has developed quite acceptable speech. Both his language and reading are well below grade level, however, and he has great difficulty in keeping up with the work of the classroom.

As Chris's behaviour became worse and worse, team meetings were called with the classroom teachers, the special education teacher, the principal of the school for the deaf, Chris's parents, and a psychologist. Although most people in the room believed that integration is the most effective educational setting for hearing-impaired students, they considered whether Chris should return to the residential school.

Before the next meeting, both the school counsellor and the psychologist met with Chris at different times. They later reported that the residential setting was indeed where Chris wanted to be. He found the competition with his peers too difficult, did not feel that he was accepted in the class, often could not understand what was going on, even with an interpreter, and missed his deaf friends. Most especially, Chris stressed that he was a "deaf boy" and wanted to use sign, not speech, and to identify more closely with the deaf community. If his parents wanted him to go to university, then he would choose Gallaudet.

Intervention with Children Who Are Hearing Impaired

Children and youth who are deaf or hard-of-hearing require considerable intervention to provide health care, rehabilitation, therapy, and education. Generally, intervention involves two major components. The first is medical intervention to try to correct the physical causes of hearing loss and to provide amplification. The second form of intervention focuses on minimizing the educational and psychological consequences of hearing loss through counselling, special education, and related services.

Medical Intervention

Many conductive hearing losses can be corrected medically. Chronic otitis media can be alleviated by antibiotics in the early stages and by a **myringotomy**, or puncturing of the ear drum to drain off fluid. Microsurgery now permits an operation to free the stapes in the case of otosclerosis.

Today's otological surgeon can surgically reconstruct the middle ear (tympanoplasty), rebuild the three tiny bones of the ossicular chain, and repair, shift, or rebuild an ear drum. Surgeons can construct new membranous windows into the inner ear. When infants are born with an atresia, surgeons can make a bony canal into the middle ear ("Hearing loss," 1982).

Cochlear Implants

Although at the moment no prosthetic devices are capable of fully restoring normal hearing, the possibility does exist of replacing some lost function of the cochlea through the use of a prosthesis called a cochlear implant. These devices are designed for persons over age two with a profound loss in both ears, who receive little or no benefit from hearing aids or vibrotactile devices, and who are motivated to persevere through the necessary auditory training (Clark, Tong and Patrick, 1990). Not all deaf people are suitable recipients for implants; those with tinnitus, for example, may actually suffer an increase of head noises with the devices. Nevertheless, for many hearing-impaired people, cochlear implants bring sound into a world that was previously silent.

The term **cochlear implant** is somewhat misleading as it implies surgical reconstruction of the cochlea by repair or transplant. In actual fact, the implant is any one of a number of devices available that convert sound into mild electrical currents to stimulate the cochlea and allow for some recognition of speech.

Since they first appeared in the 1970s, cochlear implants have improved dramatically and an enormous range of rehabilitative devices are now available. There are intra-and extra-cochlear implants, and single and multichannel systems used with pre- and post-lingually deafened individuals. Added sophistication may eventually lead to entire speech perception without dependence on any speech reading (Iadorola and Kerrigan, 1986).

All cochlear implants consist of basically the same components and work essentially the same way. Each implant has a microphone to receive sound; an encoder (speech processor) which is a tiny computer that changes the sound to electrical impulses; an electrode driver that transmits the signal to the electrode either across the skin or by direct connection; and an electrode that transmits the impulses to the nerve through the cochlea (Burgio, 1986). The entire process takes milliseconds; there is virtually no delay between the presence of sound and its coding by the processor and interpretation by the brain.

Cochlear implants simulate cochlea function as closely as possible and selectively transmit the most important elements of language. Implants provide more and better sound cues to the person than do hearing aids (Cunningham et al., 1986). Individuals who, prior to the implantation, relied entirely on speech reading, can carry on a conversation more adequately because they can hear at least some of their own voice and are able to recognize the words of others. Cochlear implants are now considered viable alternatives to hearing aids for some children; these children show improvement in speech perception abilities (Moog and Greer, 1991).

Technical Aids

In the classroom, it is seldom necessary to find special materials or equipment for the child with a hearing impairment other than their particular prosthetic equipment. Such equipment involves amplification or tactile methods to improve auditory comprehension. In addition, computer technology may hold promise for the education of hearing-impaired children. (See Chapter 3.)

Amplification

Once a child's medical and audiological data have been gathered, he or she should receive and wear a personal hearing aid as soon as possible. All hearing-impaired infants, children, and adults can benefit from an aid.

Hearing aids are primarily sound amplifiers. As such, they can help children to develop residual hearing, to improve the audition of their own voices, to use speech in a purposeful way, and to expand their vocabulary and language abilities. Even for those who are profoundly deaf, the few distorted fragments of amplified sound that reach them may assist in the development of speech and language.

Aids differ in size, cost, and efficiency. While the various types can provide equivalent amounts of amplification (technically called *gain*), certain aids are designed to provide more amplification than others. This means that there can be a close match between the type of aid and the user's unique needs.

Despite the proven effectiveness of hearing aids, only one person in three or four actually owns and uses one (see Schein, 1994). A review of the literature (Stone and Adam, 1986) indicates that most hearing-impaired children are wearing inadequate aids. Of the many reasons for non-use and incorrect use, the most important are

- Many children resist wearing a hearing aid because the awkwardness of the strange appliance outweighs their awareness of any benefits. After children are fitted with hear-

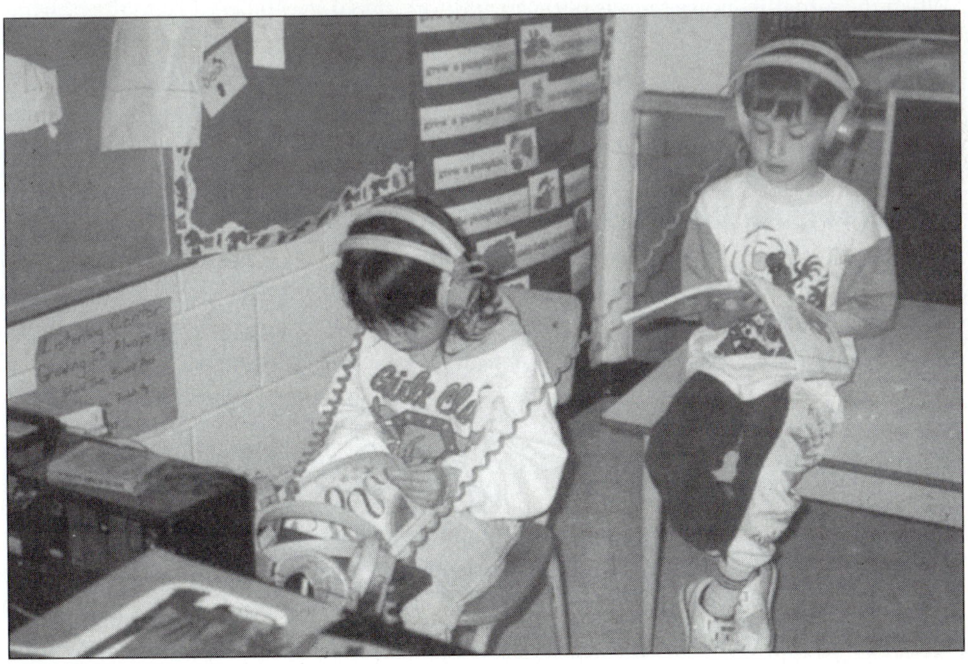

With sufficient amplification, reading a story while listening to it on headphones can help hearing-impaired students associate vocalizations with written language.

ing aids, they still have much work to do before they can use or understand speech. They must learn to interpret the sounds they hear and to duplicate the sounds of speech.

- There is a widespread belief that persons with sensorineural hearing losses cannot benefit at all from an aid. One deaf adult, with a loss of 100 dB in both ears, showed that this is not always true. With amplification in both ears, he enjoys reading the text of a story while listening to it on tape. By listening while reading, he can associate the vocalizations with the corresponding words and phrases in the text (Pottharst, 1983).
- Another belief holds that hearing aids are not appropriate for persons with mild hearing losses. However, some mild losses can be alleviated successfully with amplification.
- A particularly misleading fallacy claims that high frequency losses cannot be corrected with a hearing aid. This may be true of body aids that rub against clothing and drown out the high frequencies with low frequency sounds (Sanders, 1971). However, behind-the-ear models create no such problems. Hearing aids can also be programmed to amplify certain frequencies more than others.
- Some people cannot get used to the noise of the hearing aid. Amplification is indiscriminate, and hearing aids pick up extraneous reverberations (Blair, 1990). This can distort what is heard and may flood the individual with disconcerting auditory stimulation.
- Some people refuse to wear a hearing aid out of vanity or self-consciousness.
- Economic factors may also prevent people from wearing hearing aids. Not only are the aids expensive, but batteries, ear moulds, and receivers need to be replaced periodically.

In classroom situations, group amplification systems may be used. The FM (frequency modulation) system is the most popular. With a classroom FM system, the carrier wave is transmitted through the air via frequency modulation from a teacher-worn microphone to a student-worn FM receiver. FM transmission allows hearing-impaired students to hear the teacher clearly from any location in the classroom, whereas an individual hearing aid has a restricted range.

One of the biggest difficulties facing all hearing aid users is background noise. When the signal-to-noise ratio is poor, an auditory signal may be audible to the hearing-impaired child but may not be intelligible. With **direct audio input systems**, an FM system is joined to the child's individual aid. This means that the hearing aid can be adapted for a wide variety of difficult listening situations and can cut out at least some extraneous classroom noise.

Vibrotactile Devices

Vibrotactile devices are tactile aids that help individuals to feel sound using the tactile/kinesthetic senses. They aid in speech development by vibrating to sounds so that users can feel and imitate the differences in duration, intensity, rhythmic pattern, pitch, and voice control. They also differentiate look-alike consonants, such as *p/b/m, t/d/n/l/* and *sh/ch*. Children hold the device in their hands or strap it to an arm.

Telephone Devices

The telecommunication device (TTD), sometimes called the TTY (tele-typewriter), offers deaf persons direct telephone access to each other and to community services. Instead of listening to a message and responding orally, the deaf person with a TTD communicates by reading and typing. Typed messages are changed to electrical signals and then translated back to print on a TTD at the other end of the telephone connection.

Household Devices

To aid deaf adults in the home, a number of tools have been developed. These devices visually signal through flashing lights when, for example, the baby is crying, the telephone or door bell is ringing, or a wake-up alarm, smoke alarm, or fire alarm has sounded.

Captioned Films

Captioned television shows have been a boon to the hearing-impaired population. The closed captioning process translates dialogue into captions or subtitles. These captions are then converted to electronic codes that can be inserted into the television picture on specially adapted sets. (All TV sets made in the United States after July 1993 have a built-in caption decoder chip that makes separate decoders unnecessary).

Educators of hearing-impaired children make extensive use of captioned films in the classroom. Unfortunately, not all films are suitable for captioning. Some soundtracks cannot be duplicated through subtitles because of the rate or inflection of speech, the use of ambient noise or sound effects, or the speed of quick-cut editing and rapid scene changes (Parlatto, 1977).

Educational Intervention

Seriously hearing-impaired students may require extensive curricular modifications to compensate for the educational handicaps that accompany severe and profound hearing impairments. Modification of educational objectives may also be necessary to address the child's actual functional level rather than chronological age or grade placement.

Educational Settings

Various educational settings are available for students with hearing impairments. Setting is more than a matter of location. For deaf students, setting makes differences in the communication mode used, the type and amount of support services, the stress of the curriculum, and the possibility of identification with the deaf community and deaf culture.

Approximately one-third of students who are deaf attend residential schools and an estimated two-thirds attend programs in schools for students who are deaf or day classes located in regular schools. A small number are mainstreamed into regular classrooms ("Children with communication," 1995). These percentages and the interaction of the variables mentioned, are shown in Figure 9-4.

Within the major settings, there are six educational programs for students with hearing impairments:

- Residential schools are the most traditional setting for the education of deaf students. Many children in these schools now return daily to their own homes. Canada has seven large residential schools, all of which offer day programs. Because deaf parents often prefer to send their children to residential schools, these facilities have helped foster the concept of a deaf community and a deaf culture (Meadow, 1980; Winzer, 1993).
- Day schools are similar to residential schools except that all students live at home.
- Self-contained special classes, located within regular elementary or secondary schools, offer separate programs for hearing-impaired students.

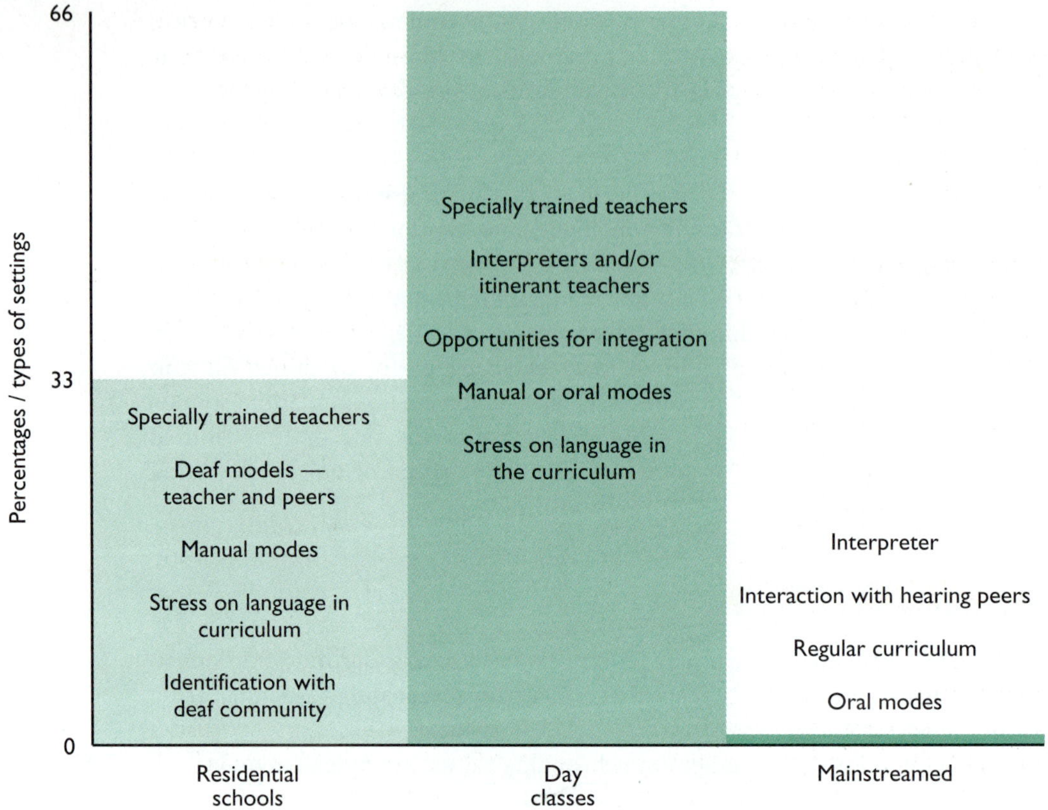

Figure 9-4 *Educational settings*

- Part-time integration programs encourage hearing-impaired students from special classes to spend part of their day with normally hearing students. Hearing-impaired students may attend regular classes for physical education and art, or for subjects such as mathematics and social studies. In the regular classroom, an interpreter may be available for them.
- Resource rooms offer hearing-impaired students from regular classes a chance to obtain tutorial assistance in a special class from a trained teacher of the deaf. Again, an interpreter may be available for the students when in the regular classroom.
- Itinerant programs provide specialist teachers who offer tutorial assistance to hearing-impaired students who are mainstreamed into regular classrooms. The itinerant teacher assists the child and the regular classroom teacher, and also acts as a facilitator or liaison with other support personnel, parents, and school administrators.

Inclusion

Many people disagree with schools for the deaf and special class placements; they tend to equate them with settings for mainstreaming failures, not as appropriate settings catering to the individual needs of many deaf students. On the other hand, many deaf people and professionals working with deaf students do not accept educational integration as it is now conceptualized. They describe the integration of deaf students as "forced assimilation" — an unnatural attempt to make deaf persons hearing (Elliott, 1993, p. 11).

Those in favour of integration argue that regular classroom placement exposes students to excellent language models and that there they must learn to use speech in order to interact with teachers and peers. In the psycho-social domain, students' perceptions of themselves are based on comparisons with hearing peers, preparing them to cope in an integrated society. Some studies have found that integrated hearing-impaired students are more successful academically than those not integrated (Kluwin and Moores, 1985).

Those opposed to integration marshall arguments that centre on deafness defined as a distinct culture — a deaf community. They argue that deaf persons "constitute a legitimate cultural and linguistic group and that they are entitled to educational programs which take this into account" (Reagan, 1988, p. 1). Viewing themselves in this fashion, deaf people tend to see the residential schools as a cultural component vital in creating group solidarity.

In academic terms, Michael Rodda and his colleagues (1986) found that only about 10 to 15 percent of all deaf children can be successfully mainstreamed. Others hold that students with severe disabilities may be unable to bear the stress of daily competition with hearing peers, especially if their families are not supportive. Lacking adequate communication skills, hearing-impaired children may feel lonely or socially rejected.

The findings on whether or not inadequate communication affects peer interaction are equivocal. Aplin (1987), who studied forty-two children aged seven to sixteen with sensorineural losses attending ordinary schools, found them significantly better adjusted than their peers in special schools. Others, however, have found that many deaf students are permanent "outsiders" and never really become an integral part of their mainstream classes (Jaussi, 1991). Hearing-impaired students demonstrate only minimal self-initiated interaction with normally hearing teachers and peers (Raimondo and Maxwell, (1987). Graduates of residential high school programs have described their social experiences more positively than graduates of mainstream programs.

For older hearing-impaired students in particular, techniques such as co-operative learning can be used to promote peer interaction and communication skills.

Social mainstreaming may be more difficult to achieve than academic mainstreaming since deaf students are frequently on their own when trying to initiate or sustain friendships with peers (Foster, 1988). An Alberta survey (Alberta Response, 1989), showed that 79.3 percent of schools had only one or two students with hearing impairments. For secondary level hearing-impaired students, at least, acceptance may be an evolving thing. One study (Ladd, Munson, and Miller, 1984) discovered that over a two-year-period, social interactions became more frequent, more reciprocal with respect to interactive roles, and more social in orientation.

When discussing the education of deaf students and their possible integration, we cannot overlook another key group — the teachers who will be responsible for the success of the venture. The education of hearing-impaired children is complex, difficult, and often frustrating, and it is not unusual for teachers to express anxiety about working with a hearing-impaired student in a regular setting (Chorost, 1988). One thing that classroom teachers require is an understanding of hearing loss and its educational and social implications. However, many regular classroom teachers are not very knowledgeable about hearing impairment and related considerations (Martin, Daly, and Cody, 1988). Rittenhouse (1987), for example, found that only about 25 percent of the high school teachers he sampled felt that the information made available to them equipped them adequately for the task of developing IEPs. In Nova Scotia and New Brunswick, surveys reveal that the primary areas of concern for teachers are information on hearing loss in general, techniques for attaining comprehension, expectation levels for hearing-impaired students, effective techniques for teaching and managing behaviour, and the effective use of amplification (French and MacDonnell, 1985).

Although teachers may feel daunted by the task of integrating and educating hearing-impaired children in their classrooms, Chorost (1988) found that many teachers became more positive after having worked with a child during the school year. Teachers who did not express positive feelings had two major concerns — the hearing-impaired child took too much time away from other students and the hearing-impaired child was academically too far below the other students to be truly mainstreamed. Another study in the United States (Martin, Daly, and Cody, 1988) found that while regular classroom teachers did not reject the notion of accepting hearing impaired students, they would prefer substantial support and in-service training.

Educational Approaches

Today's most contentious and controversial debates in special education revolve around the philosophy and practice of inclusive schooling. But regardless of how heated the debate becomes, it is unlikely that the inclusion issue for deaf students will supercede the longest-standing argument in all of special education — that of the most appropriate communication modes to employ in the education of deaf children and youth. **Communication mode** refers to "the form in which the content of a message is expressed" (Sailor et al., 1980, p. 72).

Authenticated evidence of the education of deaf students can be traced back to the late sixteenth century. Almost since that time, teachers have divided themselves into two irreconcilable camps. The "oralists" have viewed deafness as a human handicap to be overcome through the development of speech and speech reading. The "manualists" have argued that deafness is a human difference that requires its own language, the language of signs.

Rampant conflicts in expert opinion about the use of sense modalities in the education of hearing-impaired children still exist. The stances are not as irreconcilable as they once were, but educators still hold quite different philosophies about the most effective means to impart language. Many modes are possible, the most important of which are described below, moving from unisensory to multi-sensory approaches.

- *Acoupedic methods.* The acoupedic or unisensory approach is an oral method that aims to develop intelligible speech through the maximum development of listening skills (Pollack, 1970). It is founded on the belief that children in the first year of life have hearing abilities that, if activated sufficiently, play a functional role in determining speech development. On the other hand, auditory deprivation during this time diminishes these abilities and obstructs speech development. Evidence suggests that the process is irreversible (Brokx, 1987).

  The acoupedic approach requires early intervention, early amplification, unisensory stimulation, a normal listening environment, the use of auditory feedback mechanisms, and the preparation of parents to act as first models of communication (Pollack, 1980). This method excludes all visual clues, such as speech reading, and encourages the child to use residual hearing to the greatest extent possible. With major advances in hearing aid technology, acoupedic approaches have gained in popularity (see Gregory, 1986).
- *The oral/aural method.* Like other processes in special education, the oral/aural method used with deaf children today evolved through a number of stages. Beginning about 1867, teachers employed a pure oral method that placed stress on speech

reading and writing but forbade the natural gestures that we all use as part of our communication. The pure oral method evolved into the oral method of speech and speech reading along with amplification through hearing aids, which were invented in the 1920s. This method downplayed the importance of writing and permitted natural gestures. From this grew the current oral method, more correctly called the oral/aural approach. It places stress on speech and speech reading and uses amplification and auditory training as integral components of speech and language development.

- *Cued Speech.* Originated by Orin Cornett at Gallaudet University, cued speech is another primarily oral method of communication, more widely used in the United States and Australia than in Canada. The system uses eight hand configurations and four hand positions to supplement the visible manifestations of speech (Cornett, 1984). The hand cues add information to the speech reading process so that all single sounds can be identified by the hearing-impaired child.
- *The Rochester Method.* This method was named after the Rochester School for the Deaf in New York where it was first used in 1877. It employs finger spelling in conjunction with speech, speech reading, and amplification. Finger spelling adds a visible supplement to oral/aural language to provide deaf children with more complete visible language patterns. Ontario schools experimented with this method in the 1980s but today there are no programs that use finger spelling alone (Luetke-Stahlman and Luckner, 1991).
- *Total communication.* By the early 1970s the benefits of using some manual components in the education of hearing-impaired children was apparent, and many educators turned from an oral emphasis to one that stresses a combination of methods. **Total communication** uses speech, speech reading, and amplification, along with a school-based manual system. Allegiance to the total communication philosophy means communicating with a totality of parameters that range from the most visible and most audible speech, to the most legible finger spelling, to non-verbal expressions and gestures, to proficiently signed utterances (see Seal, 1986).

  The school-based manual systems of Total Communication are a marriage of necessity between American Sign Language (ASL) and English. The systems, such as Signing Essential English or Manual English, incorporate the necessity of English and the utility of sign. Signs are presented in the order of English with correct morphological structures.
- *American Sign Language.* Unlike school-based manual systems, American Sign Language (ASL or Ameslan) does not follow the semantic and syntactic structure of spoken language. ASL has its own rule-governed syntactic system, a rich system of morphological processes, and a large lexicon of vocabulary.

ASL is recognized by linguists as a true language in itself. It is not related to or in any way derived from spoken English but is more accurately viewed as a distinct and genetically unrelated language (Reagan, 1988). Deaf people see ASL as their natural mode of expression and show great attachment to their "beloved language" (Schein, 1989, p. 29). In 1988 Manitoba recognized ASL as a heritage language of the deaf; Alberta followed in 1990.

ASL is founded on a combination of symbolic gestures produced by the shape, the location, and the movement of the hands. Many of the signs symbolize concepts rather than individual words. Most have an arbitrary tie to the referrent. Some are

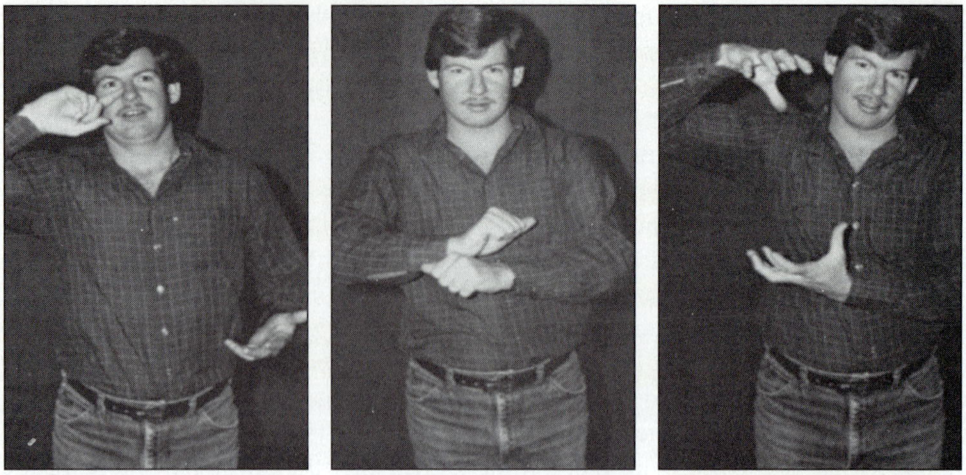

ASL has its own semantic and syntactic structure. This deaf sign-language user is talking about his work. Literally, the signs translate as (a) boring, (b) work, (c) a lot.

iconic in that they represent an object or action for which they stand; some are metonymic — they take a relatively small aspect or feature of the referrent and use that as the basis of the sign. For example, the sign for dog is snapping the fingers. ASL has no signs for the grammatical markers, such as *ed* or *ing* endings, that express verb tense and condition. Rather, users depend on facial expressions and body language to replace voice intonation and enhance meaning (Meadow, 1980; Odgen and Lipsett, 1982).

Sign systems around the world essentially evolved from the sign language systemized by de l'Épée in France in the mid-1700s. However, these systems are no longer universal. They were quickly adapted to local needs and, like spoken language, each country has its own unique version. In North America ASL is used as an almost generic term. There is also CSL (Canadian Sign Language) and LSQ (Langue de Signes Québécoise).

Bilingual Programs in Deaf Education

Many deaf parents and educators support the idea of bilingual education for deaf students. In other words, very young children would first learn sign language, which many people consider to be the natural language of deaf persons, and then build English onto this linguistic base.

On May 14, 1993, Ontario became the first province (and the first place) to authorize the use of ASL and a LSQ as the languages of instruction for deaf students (Carbin, 1993/94). Ontario schools for the deaf now use ASL and written English and allow students opportunities to develop their auditory and speech potential.

There are six key principles to Ontario's bilingual/bicultural policy. These are child-centred education, development of literacy skills in ASL, development of literacy skills in English, understanding and appreciation of deaf culture, appreciation of cultural diversity, and the development of a positive self-image ("Statement," 1993, p. 1).

Bilingual education for deaf students is founded as much on philosophical arguments as it is on educational considerations, and the idea is far from universally accepted. Some of the arguments for and against bilingual education for deaf students are outlined on the following pages.

A Matter of Debate

Bilingual education for deaf students

Language is commonly taken as central to group identity, as its most important marker. The deaf community stresses the role of deaf persons in determining their own destiny and denotes sign language as essential to their identity. Deaf adults favour bilingualism that includes ASL for all deaf children. But, as to be expected, bilingual education for young deaf children has generated heated debate. Some of the arguments presented are

- ASL is the natural language of the deaf community throughout Anglophone North America.
- Adult communication is bilingual in that ASL is the common language of discourse, and English is the written language and the means of access to the hearing world.
- It seems that communication in humans is a resistant phenomenon: when prevented from emanating from the mouth, it comes almost irrepressibly from the hands.
- The similarities between the development of spoken language and sign suggest a biological foundation for language learning. Deaf children are "preprogrammed" to learn sign. Those without any contact with sign language invent their own "home sign," a kind of communication through pantomime. However, home signs progress from simple single signs to real "sentences" (see Mayberry et al., 1987).
- As well, accumulating research evidence indicates that children taught by oral methods use sign language with their peers even when punished for doing so.
- Teaching speech "is a matter in which human ingenuity has simply not been able to triumph over human biology" (Lane, cited by Elliott, 1993).
- Only about 17 percent of students taught by oral methods ever become orally fluent, but nearly 75 percent of deaf children become fluent manually.
- School-based systems are unpopular with deaf adults and the claim that they improve English remains unproven (Reagan, 1988).
- Educationally, deaf parents prefer to see their children intellectually challenged rather than constantly taught language.
- Deaf children rarely develop functional oral communication skills anyway, so little is lost by the absence of spoken language in their environments.
- It now seems that early manual communication helps rather than hinders the development of oral language.
- Young deaf children who are taught a conventional sign system, such as ASL or signed English, develop language in sign that is comparable in both content and form to the child language that young hearing children develop in speech (Goldwin- Meadow, and Morford, 1985).
- A strong base in one language facilitates learning another language. With ASL, deaf children come to school with a firm linguistic base.
- The mastery of a language system is of enormous benefit in problem solving and academic performance.

- The absence of meaningful, satisfying communication between young deaf children and their parents may result in disturbed and fragmented communication, isolation from the family, poor school achievement later, and higher rates of psychiatric disturbance (Greenberg and Calderon, 1984).
- The deaf child is a member of a unique linguistic and cultural group. "Forcing deaf children to be part of the hearing world denies them the right to themselves" (Elliott, 1993, p. 11).
- Canadians are extremely sensitive to language issues, and acceptance of sign language will assist them in relating to a small group of people with very special language needs.
- Deaf people point to a vast array of meaningful research that clearly shows ASL to be a viable, rich language, and to bilingual education programs in Canada and around the world as evidence that this approach can be feasible and beneficial to students (MacDougall, 1988).

Those who hold reservations or who are entirely against bilingual education for deaf students argue that

- Children who use signs will not be motivated to learn to speak, use their residual hearing, or speech read.
- Sign may be more natural for deaf children, but a sign system does not have to be ASL — it can be an English-based system.
- English is crucial for functioning in our society.
- English should be signed as it is spoken so that the linguistic input results in mastery of English.
- The needs of deaf children to learn English must be carefully balanced with their need to develop intellectually (Erting, 1985).
- Speech is important to deaf students in their efforts to negotiate the hearing world.
- Under bilingualism, only some children may benefit from auditory and speech training.
- Whatever aptitude the child may have to develop speech might be jeopardized by a practice that fosters ASL to the exclusion of speech.
- Speech proficiency is of undeniable value to the deaf individual (see Stuckless, 1991).
- The language of the majority culture is English, not ASL.
- Deaf children are often learning to read at the same time they are learning English.
- Sign language use may impact on reading. Forms of sign language are structurally different from English and deaf readers must recode print into their own language (Andrews and Mason, 1991).
- Ninety percent of deaf children are born to hearing parents who are not part of the deaf community.
- Hearing parents use spoken language as their primary mode of communication.
- Hearing parents must learn some form of sign (Sacks, 1990).

A number of fascinating and provocative studies support the use of signed systems with deaf children. In acquiring language, for example, deaf infants pass through the same stages as hearing children. That is, deaf babies usually begin by babbling in sign — forming rough approximations of the signs that their parents use. They then proceed to one-word signs and the kinds of signs that they first use are virtually identical to the categories of words that hearing children first acquire. They then use a type of telegraphic sign (Bonvillian, Orlansky and Novack, 1983).

Children exposed to ASL show an earlier onset of the first sign than would normally be expected for a child's first spoken word, and they typically acquire a sign language vocabulary more rapidly than a hearing child does spoken one (Bonvillian, Orlansky, and Novack, 1983). First signs tend to emerge earlier than first words because human infants, whether deaf or hearing, typically initiate their symbolic communication in the gestural mode rather than the vocal mode because control of the hands matures more rapidly than the speech areas of the brain. According to Bay (1975), the visual cortex matures prior to the auditory cortex, facilitating the onset of a visual language system before an oral/aural system.

Curricula

In the education of students with hearing impairments, the content is similar to that presented to hearing children. Differences are chiefly a matter of degree. For hearing students, teachers build a mastery of reading and written language upon a child's intact linguistic base of listening and speaking. In contrast, schools and classes for the hearing-impaired must teach an entire language system. For example, to learn the single word *mother*, a deaf child must:

- Learn the concept.
- Learn to say the word.
- Learn to speech read the word.
- Learn the sound of the word through the hearing aid.
- Learn to recognize the printed word.
- Learn to recognize the written word.
- Learn to spell the word.
- Learn to print or write the word.
- Learn to sign the word.
- Learn to read the sign.
- Learn to finger spell the word.
- Learn to read the finger-spelled word.
- Learn to use the word in context.
- Learn to use the word in different contexts.

(After Levine, 1981, p. 100.)

As you can see, the process of developing language skills is long, arduous, and often tedious. Two major strategies for the teaching of language have evolved — the formal or grammatical approach and the informal or natural approach. All other methods essentially hark back to these two traditional approaches.

The grammatical approach focuses the students' attention on the structural aspects of language. (In Chapter 6, variations of this approach were described as diagnostic-prescriptive and syntax-based). Armed with structural information, students learn to generate language deductively. The natural approach (performance) attempts to parallel the ways in which hearing children acquire language. The content and sequence of instruction are determined by the needs of individual children. Ramon, whom we met earlier in this chapter, is in a regular classroom where the teacher is implementing a natural approach. The extract from Ramon's IEP indicates the long-range goals and some objectives.

Individual Education Plan — iep

Extract from Ramon's IEP

CHILD: Ramon **SCHOOL:** Central

DOB: 12 June, 1987 **TEACHER:** Ms Smith

GRADE: 2

MEDICAL INFORMATION	ADAPTIVE EQUIPMENT
Audiological assessment showed Ramon to have a high frequency bilateral hearing loss that places just into the moderate range.	None recommended at this time. Special seating in the classroom — middle row, front.
AREAS OF NEED	**AREAS OF STRENGTH**
Speech training, auditory training, language and reading skills.	Normal cognitive functioning, good motivation.

ASSESSMENT/PERFORMANCE INFORMATION

Date	Test	Result
14-10-94	Informal observations	Poor receptive and expressive language; small vocabulary; many speech deviations, especially high frequency consonants such as *s*, *sh*, *t*, and *th*.
16-10-94	Test of Language Development (TOLD-Primary)	Well below normal levels in language; numbers of serious speech problems.
16-10-94	Test of Early Reading Ability (TERA)	Developing literacy skills in that he understands the use of print. About a year below grade level, which means barely a start on formal reading. Only a small sight vocabulary; poor comprehension even of orally related material.
20-10-94	Articulation tests	Poor articulation on initial and final consonants.
24-10-94	WISC-111 Performance scale only	Normal cognitive functioning

PERSONS RESPONSIBLE		
Teacher	Ms Smith	Stress oral skills; work proactively with therapist; model speech taught in individual lessons.
Resource room teacher	Ms Brown	Improve reading skills to grade 2 level.
Speech therapist	Mr. Jones	Correct articulation errors. One hour weekly.

LONG-RANGE GOALS

Ramon's program will target speech and language development within the regular curriculum and with specialized assistance from a speech/language therapist. Speech skills (and motivation) will improve through individual lessons with the therapist. In the classroom, the teacher will stimulate language and communication skills through promoting interaction with other children, modelling, specific language intervention, and co-operative learning.

A second long-term goal is to improve Ramon's reading skills. This will be done in the resource room with follow-up in the regular classroom. Teacher will use a word-recognition approach initially to circumvent the problems caused by the hearing loss. Once Ramon has a reliable sight vocabulary, the teacher will use a more holistic, experience-based method.

SHORT-TERM OBJECTIVES

1. When presented with words on flashcards, Ramon will say the word, say it in a sentence, and write the word.
2. Ramon will read short paragraphs containing new words and short stories at level.
3. Ramon will write in his journal daily with encouragement to use new reading words.
4. Ramon will be placed in a co-operative learning group for a social studies module.
5. To further promote peer interaction, peer tutoring (10 minutes daily) will be arranged for oral reading.

Interpreters

The great majority of classroom teachers do not have proficiency in sign language and finger spelling. Enabling students to attend mainstream classes requires special assistance (Ross, 1990a), and teachers may have to work with an interpreter in the classroom (Rittenhouse, Rahn, and Morreau, 1989). McGee (1990) observes that "The inestimable importance of classroom interpreters ... is obvious if students are to have access to the mainstream curriculum afforded hearing students" (p. 205).

The interpreter, sometimes called a transliterator, is a normally hearing person who facilitates the transmission of information between individuals who do not communicate with a common language or code. Educational interpreters assist the academic performance of a student with a hearing impairment in a regular classroom by translating directions, content, and assignments presented orally by teachers and the comments of peers, and by sharing the student's responses and questions with teachers and peers (Salend and Longo, 1994).

There are different types of interpreters. A signed system interpreter makes speech visible and, in turn, converts manual communication to speech. The interpreter translates spoken language directed toward a student with a hearing impairment into a signed system such as ASL or a school-based system. An oral interpreter facilitates the student's understanding of verbal messages by subtly mouthing the complete verbal message or its paraphrased equivalent (Castle, 1988).

The interpreter should be seated in a glare-free, well-lit location with a solid coloured background free of visual and auditory distractions. Interpreters should sit in front of the student without blocking the view of the chalkboard, overhead projector, or the teacher.

Teachers must also make some general accommodations if they are to provide adequately for the children's education. Some general tips for teachers of hearing impaired students are presented below.

Tips for Teachers

Tips for teachers of hearing-impaired children

Environment and classroom climate

- Allow hearing-impaired students to make full use of the visual clues they rely on so heavily. Seat them near the front of the room and a little to one side. The second seat from the front allows an optimal distance of about two metres for speech reading and the detection of visual clues.
- Ensure good lighting, especially on the speaker's face. The teacher should face the light source.
- Natural light is better than fluorescent lighting.
- Provide an environment as quiet as possible so the child can listen to the best auditory message.

Adaptive devices

- Keep the auditory and visual distractions in the classroom to a minimum. Environmental noises are a problem for children with hearing aids because all sounds are amplified.
- Check daily that hearing aids are working. Try to keep a supply of extra batteries.
- Be in close proximity when speaking. Speech reading is best at about two metres, and aids function best within the same distance.

Instruction

- Allow children to turn in their seats when other students are talking or to move their seats when they need a better view.
- Point or move your head to cue children in to the person who is talking or the object under discussion.
- Speak naturally. Do not overenunciate, as this makes speech reading more difficult. Try not to smile or whisper while speaking, as this distorts the shape of the lips.
- Try to stand still while talking. Remember that children cannot speech read if you talk to the chalkboard or speak in the dark during a movie or film strip.
- Use many visual aids. These are helpful for hearing children as well.
- Keep your book low while reading aloud to allow children a good view of your face.
- Repeat and rephrase information and directions.
- Encourage children to ask questions if they are not sure.
- Especially for older students, use techniques such as co-operative learning to promote peer interaction and communication skills.

The Deaf Community

The deaf population is extremely heterogeneous, comprising people of varying levels of auditory capabilities, linguistic skills, cognitive abilities, social skills, and emotional development (Bullis and Reiman, 1992) as well as varying ethnicity, socio-economic status, geographic location, and so on. People in this heterogeneous population who use sign language find that their lives are defined by unique experiences and communication modalities that differ from those of an English-based hearing society. This leads inevitably to the strength of the deaf community.

Although the deaf community in Canada can be traced back to the formation of the first residential schools, it is only in recent decades that political and social activism has characterized the community. This development paralleled the increased acceptance of ASL as a discrete language.

Today, many deaf adults describe themselves as a cultural or minority group and use the term *deaf* to designate cultural group membership (Dolnick, 1993). "The cultural view of the deaf community ... views deaf people as a group that shares a common language and a common means of communication" (Stewart and Ahamatsu, 1988, p. 238).

Summary

1. Hearing loss or hearing impairment is a generic term that encompasses two major groups — those who are deaf and those who are hard-of-hearing. The difference lies in the intensity of the hearing loss and the amount of auditory input that the individual can use. People who are deaf cannot, even with the use of a hearing aid, hear speech. On the other hand, people who are hard-of-hearing can hear speech with or without amplification (hearing aids).
2. A hearing impairment is not the deprivation of sound but the deprivation of language. Because hearing loss interferes with both the reception and the production of language, the greatest single handicap of defective hearing is its effect on the development of communication skills. Hearing-impaired children are isolated from the human voice and therefore isolated from language. As teaching is essentially a linguistic activity, hearing impairment poses a serious threat to children's learning.
3. Deaf children are likely to be identified during the preschool years. In contrast, the auditory problems of hard-of-hearing children may not be detected until they undergo a routine school screening, and perhaps not even then.
4. As long of the sounds of conversational speech remain audible, effective communication skills are possible. However, even mild losses can be educationally devastating.
5. Hearing-impaired individuals are usually deficient in the language of the majority culture even when expert in the language of signs. Although they possess the same intellectual potential as the rest of the population, their deprivation in language can cause problems in every aspect of functioning. Academically, most deaf graduates today can barely read the daily newspaper. Emotionally, deaf students are prone to a greater number of emotional and psychological problems. Socially, many deaf persons turn for acceptance to the deaf community where sign language is the accepted mode of communication.

6. Many of the etiologies responsible for hearing losses — rubella, meningitis, and Rh factor in particular — affect many domains of development and cause multiple handicapping conditions.
7. In recent decades, the education of deaf students has undergone major changes. There has been a widespread movement toward educational integration, a widespread adoption of total communication, and the initiation of bilingual education.
8. Over the years, many approaches have evolved. Today, any communication mode attempts to overcome the spoken language communication barrier with hearing aids, auditory trainers, and the like.
9. In the past, children who persisted in using ASL outside the classroom were made to feel that their language was not appropriate. Today, the deaf community wants children to use what they see as their natural language and wants educators to accept bilingual education that includes ASL.
10. One essential service that many students with hearing impairments attending regular classes may need is an educational interpreter.

CHAPTER 10

Children with Visual Impairments

Historical Notes

Over the centuries, the history of visual impairment has been surrounded by fear, myth, and superstition, all interwoven into two contradictory themes. One common thread has blindness associated with darkness, despair, loneliness, and punishment — "one of those instruments by which a mysterious Providence has chosen to afflict man" (Address, 1836). The opposing theme held that blind persons were compensated for their lack of sight by both psychological and physical factors. Their condition was associated with superhuman and spiritual powers, uncanny memory ability, and musicality (Koestler, 1976).

In ancient Egypt, blind persons became priests, seers, and musicians. Greece produced Homer and Aesop and tales of blind kings and others who achieved eminence. In pragmatic Rome, blind boys were often trained to become beggars or sold as rowers; blind girls became prostitutes (French, 1932).

Perhaps because blindness is such an obvious handicap and so feared by most people, blind persons were early granted special privileges, albeit ones that confirmed their deviant and different status in society. In Rome, only those who were blind were allowed to beg on the steps of the temples, and throughout the centuries this privilege extended to the steps of churches in many places. Other meagre advantages added to their usual occupation as beggars. In Spain from 1340 until the eighteenth century, for example, blind persons held the sole privilege of singing in public places. In Portugal they held exclusive rights to sell newspapers on the streets.

Beginning in the fourth century, the Catholic Church assumed some responsibility for exceptional people. Hospices for the blind were the first to be established. In the thirteenth century, one of the first hospitals was founded in Paris for blinded soldiers returning from the crusades. However, asylums cared for only a few of the blind and other handicapped persons; the rest led degraded lives as beggars and outcasts.

Formal schooling for blind persons began in Paris in 1784, in Boston in 1832, and in Halifax in 1870. Nevertheless, even in the mid-1800s, very few, if any, blind persons had remunerative employment. The great majority were locked in asylums or begged in the streets. The general public was apathetic and indifferent to their fate (MacDonald, 1925). Changes in attitudes toward blind persons and the opportunities open to them arose from slowly changing perceptions that accompanied educational intervention. "Of all the defective classes," workers averred, "the blind give the largest and most hopeful returns for the efforts made on their behalf" (Willis, 1897, p. 11).

Many positive changes were wrought by dedicated schoolmen such as Samuel Gridley Howe, by slowly evolving legislation, and by advocacy groups such as the Canadian National Institute for the Blind (CNIB), which was formed by blinded veterans after the First World War. Since its inception, The CNIB has championed the cause of blind persons in Canada in many areas.

Many blind individuals overcame their disabilities to forward the cause of the blind population or to make remarkable contributions in diverse areas, thereby demonstrating that blind individuals were worthy of the same rights and responsibilities as their sighted counterparts. The blind poet Edward Rushton established the first school for blind children in Great Britain. Louis Braille was a blind teacher who made blind literacy possible by inventing an embossed system of writing. Fanny Crosby, who was born in 1820 and blinded at six weeks of age, became a poet and hymn writer. She worked for the New York Institute for the Blind and addressed Congress in order to improve attitudes. Helen Keller, both deaf and blind, spent much of her adult life advocating the cause of persons with disabilities. Sir Frederick Fraser, the founding principal of the Halifax School for the Blind, was a pioneer in education and social intervention for blind persons in Canada.

It is difficult for most of us to imagine life without sight. Vision and hearing are the senses that most connect us with our world. Well over half of the information our brains receive about the world comes through our eyes (Immen, 1995). In fact, the visual system is so dominant that many of us close our eyes to think more clearly and concentrate. To many people, a world without images would seem bleak, frightening, and virtually impossible to navigate. It would seem socially cold; through expression and eye contact, our eyes play a crucial role in social interaction. Sight also affects our other senses; seeing something good to eat, for example, can trigger hunger pangs.

Most of us have a special fear of blindness (Conant and Budoff, 1982). A 1988 survey found that blindness was the most feared disability for 42 percent of the 1072 adults surveyed. In the same survey, blindness was listed the fourth most feared disease, after AIDS, cancer, and Alzheimer's disease (Augusto and McGraw, 1990).

Despite these common perceptions, visual handicaps are not as daunting as they first seem. Many blind persons have contributed significantly to our culture and many other thousands who did not achieve fame lived normal and successful lives in spite of their disability. This is not to deny that visual impairments can be among the most severe of all physical handicaps.

In any individual, severe visual impairment can interfere with learning, social growth, adjustment, and mobility. In children, visual impairments cause complex developmental problems that make special education a necessity. Unique education needs include, but are not restricted to, early intervention; concept development; listening, study, and research skills; alternative methods for reading, writing, and mathematical computation; sensory training; daily living, socialization, and recreational skills; sexuality, career, and vocational training; utilization of low vision; accessibility to technology; orientation and mobility training; and meaningful transition programs (Huebner, 1985).

Many individuals overcome visual impairments.

In recent years, many changes have occurred in the education of students who are visually impaired. Among the most dramatic is the integration of many of these children into public school classes. As well, greater attention is directed toward the functional rather than the legal definitions of sight handicaps, which has broadened the category of students who can benefit from special education. Children with borderline problems now qualify for special education services, as do visually impaired children with multiple handicaps. Educators have also learned a great deal more about the effects of visual handicaps on learning, and there is increased emphasis on the development of residual vision. It is now realized that residual sight is enhanced, rather than diminished, with use, and children who were formerly classified as blind are now classified as "low vision" or "visually impaired" (Barraga, 1976). At the same time, braille literacy is being reaffirmed by many in the field as an educational priority for children with severely limited vision (Schroeder, 1989; Stephens, 1989). The ability to read and write braille maximizes students' chances of educational and vocational success and lays the foundation they need to benefit from many new technological advances (Stephens, 1989). New advances have also occurred in the diagnosis and treatment of visual disorders, particularly in the fields of ophthalmology and optometry. Vastly improved optical aids have been developed to enable children with severe sight impairments to read print materials. Advanced computer technology means many sophisticated devices to compensate for the lack of vision.

Development of the Field

In the early part of the eighteenth century a faint interest in the education of the blind was to be discerned, but it was little more than speculation. It was not until 1784 that Valentin Haüy (1745-1822) founded the first school for the blind in Paris.

Haüy was a member of the clergy, an abbé, (although he appears to have married twice) from an upper-class Parisian family. He was well steeped in the philosophical speculations arising from the thinkers of the French Enlightenment and familiar with Denis Diderot's theoretical "Letter on the blind" that carefully analyzed the thought processes of the blind and dropped hints concerning their education (French, 1932). Haüy was also impressed with the application of philosophical principles to the education of deaf individuals as undertaken by the Abbé de l'Épée.

Haüy opened his school after witnessing the heartless exploitation of the blind on the streets of Paris. In this school, he taught his blind students to read using raised character print. In his quest to provide blind persons opportunities for remunerative employment, Haüy stressed vocational training; he taught weaving, basket and mat making, chair caning, and the rope trade (Guillie, 1817). Haüy's success prompted the government to establish the National Institute for the Blind. Later, in 1800, he displeased Napoleon and hastily left France. He then founded an institution for the blind in Russia, and laid the groundwork for a school in Berlin ("Address," 1836; French, 1932).

As the ideas of the French pioneers influenced the early American educators of deaf students, so the notions of Haüy soon crossed the Atlantic. In Boston, Samuel Gridley Howe (1801-1876), a physician, promoted education for blind individuals. Howe was a major educational reformer involved in a wide range of humanitarian, social, and educational movements. He deplored the prejudices that labelled the blind as helpless and dependent. He believed that instead of pity, blind persons should be enabled to achieve dignity and usefulness through appropriate education ("Address," 1836).

Howe first undertook a census to determine the number of blind people in New England; he then sent a teacher to France to learn the methods of teaching blind children. At the same time, he persuaded the legislature of Massachusetts of the viability of a special institution. In 1832, Howe became founding principal of the first North American school for the visually impaired, afterwards named the Perkins School for the Blind.

Many who applauded the formation of special institutions saw them as removing from society "so many dead weights" and preventing these people from becoming "taxes on the community" (Dunscombe, 1836, p. 97). In contrast, Howe argued that "the original capacity of the intellect is precisely the same in the blind as in seeing children" (Perkins Inst., 1837, p. 5). Howe set three educational criteria for his students: each child was considered an individual and trained for personal ability; the curriculum of the school followed that of the public schools, but with greater stress on music and crafts; and blind children were helped to become contributing members of society (Perkins Inst., 1834).

John Barrett McGann was the first person in Canada to undertake the education of the blind. Beginning in 1861, he admitted blind children to his Toronto school where they were taught by his fifteen-year-old daughter, Effie. In 1866, the Grey Nuns founded the Nazareth Institution in Montreal. Publicly supported institutions for the blind opened in Halifax in 1870 and Ontario in 1872. Frederick Fraser became founding principal of the Halifax School for the Blind. (Winzer, 1993) Like McGann, Fraser worked to change public prejudices. He urged upon legislators the unassailable right of blind children to an education (MacDonald, 1925).

By 1875 there were three institutions in Canada which gathered pupils from all across the Dominion. It was common practice, for example, for Alberta students with visual disabilities to be sent to the Ontario institution as late as the 1970s (Conn-Blowers and McLeod, 1989).

Founded with the best of intentions, these institutions were isolated and served to segregate students from the mainstream. Samuel Gridley Howe was one of the first to promote educational integration for handicapped students. As early as 1839, he argued that blind children deserved "an equal participation in the blessing of education with seeing children" (Perkins, 1839, p. 80). But although Howe and others hammered at this theme, it was not until the opening of the twentieth century that classes for blind children were established in the public schools.

Chicago in 1900 witnessed the establishment of the first special class for blind students. After that, classes for blind children and sight-saving classes for those with visual impairments who were able to read print opened in most urban school districts. In sight-saving classes, children with poor sight were encouraged to "save" or reduce demands on their vision.

Segregation was not as prominent for students with visual impairments as it was for students with mental retardation or other disabilities. As early as 1911 there are reports of blind children integrated into regular classrooms, and some educators were wont to argue that children with visual impairments were easily assimilated and taught in regular classrooms. In 1949, the year that the first children with retrolental fibroplasia reached school, the total number of visually impaired students in the public schools began to increase, and their population grew faster than that of the residential schools. By 1956, 25 percent of visually impaired children attended regular schools; by 1980, the numbers had risen to 95 percent. With the advent of mainstreaming practices, these students were the first to be integrated into regular classes.

The Visual System

The visual system consists of the eye, which receives the light image; the nerve pathways, which transmit the image to the optical centres of the brain; and the brain itself, which interprets the image. Visual impairments can result from any interference with the passage of light as it travels from the outer surface of the eye along the nerve pathways to the brain.

The Eye

The eye is probably the most precious square inch in the human body. It is only 2.5 centimetres in diameter but its functions are extraordinarily complex and precise. It is composed of the eyeball and the accessory structures, such as the eyelids and muscles, that protect and move it. The eyeball is held in place by connective tissue in the orbit and is protected in front by the upper and lower eyelids. Figure 10-1 shows the structure of the eyeball.

The eyeball is a sphere wrapped in three layers of tissue. The outermost layer consists of the sclera and the cornea. The middle layer contains the iris and the lens, the muscles that support them, and the fluids that fill the eye's two chambers. The inner layer is the retina, the actual seeing part of the eye (Havener, 1979).

Figure 10-1
Anatomy of the eye

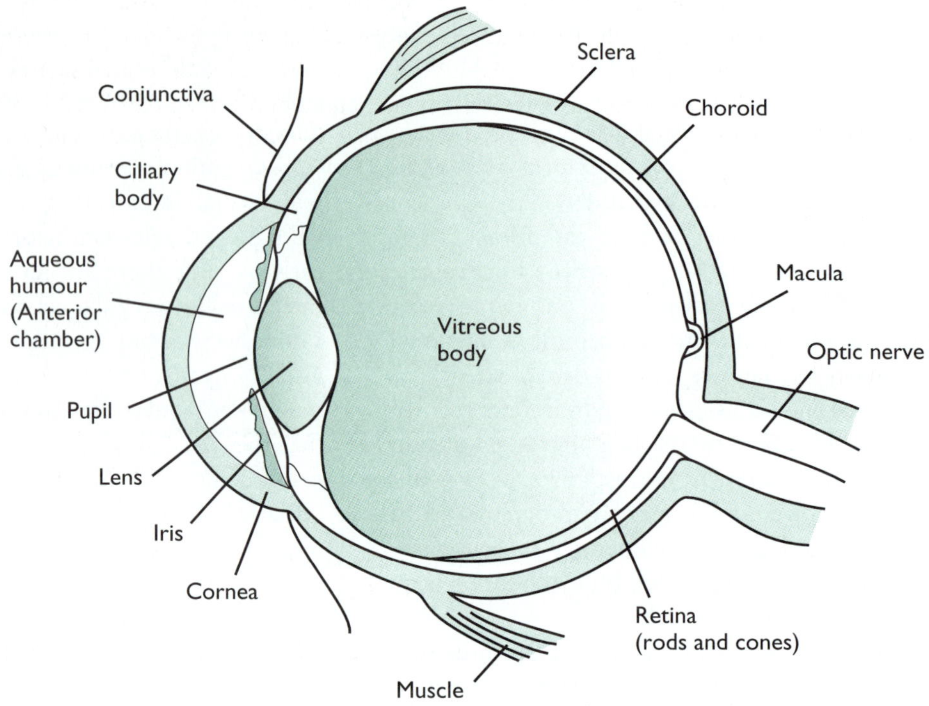

Light is essential for sight. A close look at the eye reveals that behind the black pupil and coloured iris there is a clear lens that is responsible for focusing light gathered from the environment onto the retina. On reaching the cornea, the rays of light are refracted to pass through the anterior chamber of the eye. As the rays pass through the crystalline lens, they are further refracted. The lens is capable of changing its shape to accommodate light from objects at various distances. From the lens, the light makes its way through the vitreous humour and comes to focus on the **fovea**, the most sensitive spot of the retina. Images received by the fovea are here inverted, making the bottom appear like the top and vice versa (Abang 1980). The refraction and inversion of an object are illustrated in Figure 10-2.

Figure 10-2
Refraction and inversion of an object

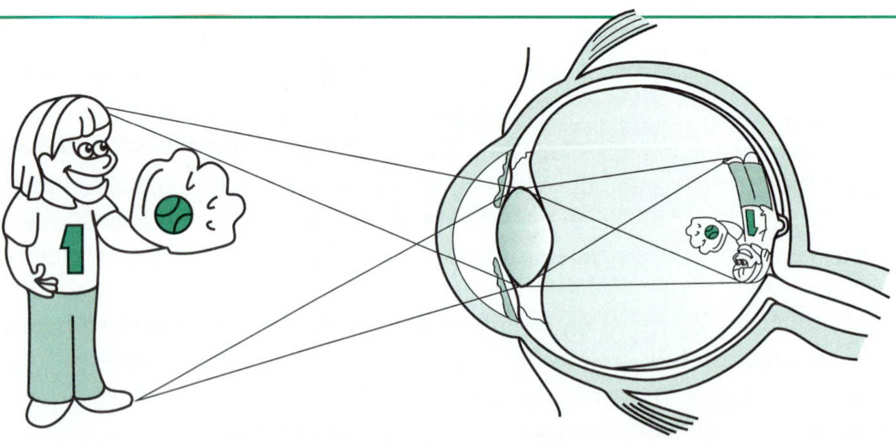

The fovea possesses a rich supply of light-sensitive nerve cells, the rods and cones, which convert the light into electrochemical impulses. These impulses are transmitted to the brain from the back of the eye through the bundles of nerve fibres that form the optic nerve. Immen (1995) describes the nerves that connect the eye to the brain as the original information highway. The data are sent digitally, in a steady stream of electrical impulses, along a chain of nerve endings. Images are received and interpreted in the occipital lobe of the brain. Hence, vision is a function of the brain, not the eye. Table 10-1 outlines the important parts of the eye. The sequence of vision is shown in Table 10-2.

Table 10-1

Parts of the eye

Sclera	Tough, flexible, white outer covering of the posterior portion of the eye. Its front part is commonly recognized as the white of the eye.
Cornea	A transparent window covering the front of the eye, continuous with the sclera.
Lacrimal apparatus	Glands that provide the tear film essential to the health of the cornea.
Iris	A circle of muscles that gives the eye its colour and adapts the size of the pupil aperture in response to light intensity.
Lens	A crystalline lens held in suspension by the iris.
Choroid	A vascular layer in which the blood supply to the retina is embedded.
Retina	A tissue-thin, intricate, and sensitive layer that consists of up to a quarter of a billion photo receptors and other nerve cells. Lines the back of the eye.
Ocular muscles	The six muscles connected to the outside of the eyeball that allow the eye to focus on an object, follow a moving target, and rotate. The muscles of one eye work in perfect synchrony with one another and with those of the other eye to enable the two eyes to co-ordinate. They are among the most rapidly responding muscles in the body.
Fovea	The most sensitive spot on the retina.
Macula	A crater-shaped yellow area of the retina in the centre of our focus. The point of clearest vision even though it represents only one-thousanth of our field of vision.
Cones	Photoreceptors that collect bright light.
Rods	Photoreceptors that work in teams to collect low light.

Table 10-2

The Sequence of vision

1. When light reflected from an object hits our eye, the light rays pass through the cornea where they are refracted.

2. From the cornea, the light rays pass through the acqueous humour and proceed on their journey to the lens and the vitreous humour.

3. The rays are there directed to the central part of the retina. This contains rods and cones which are light receptor cells. These are then stimulated by the light rays and consequently converted to electro-chemical energy.

4. The energy is further transmitted through the optic nerve to the visual centre of the brain where the visual information is interpreted (Abang, 1980).

Definitions of Visual Impairment

People categorized as visually impaired range from individuals with mild visual losses to those with low vision to those who are totally blind. Given this wide range, a number of terms and definitions are in use.

The most generic term is *visual impairment*, which may be mild, moderate, or severe. Many people reading this text will have mild or even moderate impairments that are correctable through prescription glasses. People with severe visual impairments would be unable to read the print. *Severe visual impairment* refers to serious visual problems ranging from an inability to read newsprint with the use of ordinary glasses to total blindness.

Apart from the generic *visual impairment*, two different types of definitions are used — legal definitions and educational definitions. Medical-legal definitions are not as appropriate for educational purposes because they do not adequately describe a child's visual functioning. Moreover, definitions of legal blindness vary considerably around the world (Colenbrander, 1976). In Canada and the United States, the legal definition of blindness includes many people who in other countries would not be entitled to social, educational, or other services (Rogow, 1987b).

Legal Definitions

In Canada, **legal blindness** is defined as an acuity measure of 20/200 (6/600) or less in the better eye with the best correction; or visual acuity of more than 20/200 if the widest diameter of the field of vision subtends an angle of no greater than 20 degrees (CNIB, 1980). Legal definitions are founded on **visual acuity**, the measure of the smallest image distinguishable by the eye. Visual acuity of 20/200 means that a normally sighted person can see at 200 feet (approximately 60 metres) what the visually impaired person can see at 20 feet (6 metres). The visual field, reported in degrees, is the entire area that can be seen when staring straight ahead. Normal individuals can see 180 degrees.

Acuity measures may vary with age, lighting conditions, the effects of movement, and other factors. They cannot predict how effectively children who are visually impaired will utilize their remaining vision (Barraga, 1976) or how they will vary in their experience of sight. And, although the term is *legally blind,* the majority of individuals in this category have some usable vision; that is, they can read large print or regular print books (Willis, 1976).

The legal definition of partial sight includes those who have a visual acuity greater than 20/200 but not greater than 20/70 in the better eye after correction (CNIB, 1980).

Educational Definitions

Visual functioning or **visual efficiency** refers to what the impaired person does with his or her residual vision. There is no correlation between the amount of residual vision children have and the way in which the vision is used. Two children with the same etiology and visual acuity may be very different in the way they use their residual vision. As well, fatigue, lighting, and emotions may affect the manner in which residual vision is utilized.

For these reasons, functional definitions that indicate how well the child can use vision for learning are more useful than legal ones for educational purposes. Under a functional definition, a child with a visual impairment would be described as one "whose visual impairment interferes with his optimal learning and achievement, unless adaptations are made in the methods of presenting learning experiences, the nature of the materials used and/or in the learning environment" (Barraga, 1977).

Classification of Visual Impairment

There are many kinds of visual handicaps and they are attributable to diverse causes. As a result, there are a number of ways to classify the conditions. One classification system is not necessarily better than another; they just describe different things and are used for different purposes.

Classification by Degree

Individuals with visual impairments may be classified in terms of the type and degree of disability as follows:

- *Near normal vision.* Individuals so categorized are able to function without special training whatever the strength of corrective lenses or reading aids they may need.
- *Moderate functional impairment.* People in this group have a moderate reduction of acuity and no significant field loss; they require specialized aids and lighting.
- *Reduction in central vision.* These people have a moderate field loss and a possible inability to cope physically or psychologically with impaired vision. They may qualify for special services as legally blind individuals.
- *Low vision.* Most visually disabled persons have low vision — their corrected vision is lower than normal. According to Corn (1980), a person with low vision is "one who is still severely visually impaired after correction, but who may increase visual functioning through the use of optical aids, non-optical aids, environmental modi-

fications and/or techniques" (p.3). That is, a person with low vision can read with special aids such as magnifying glasses or large-print books.

- *Poor functional vision and possible poor central vision.* These people show marked field loss and psychological or physical adaptation problems. For them, standard refraction is of little or no benefit; they usually require strong reading aids.
- *Blindness.* Individuals in this group are the most visually impaired; they require education, habilitation, or rehabilitation to function at an independent level (Faye, 1976).

Barraga (1976) uses severity levels:

- *Moderate visual disability.* Comparable to normal vision with correction.
- *Severe visual disability.* Less accurate than normal with special aids.
- *Profound visual disability.* No useful vision for detailed tasks and great difficulty with gross visual tasks.

Classification by Age of Onset

Children with visual impairments are often classified by age of onset of the problems. **Congenital low vision** refers to conditions that are diagnosable at birth or shortly thereafter. **Adventitious low vision** refers to conditions caused by accident or disease some time after birth.

Because many eye conditions change over time, age of onset can be critical in adjustment and learning, particularly in the development of concepts such as colour. Teresa Abang (1980) tells of a congenitally blind man who, when asked what he saw, said, "I see nothing." An adventitiously blind man responded to the same question with "I see darkness all around me." While the first man did not realize that he was experiencing darkness, the other had a memory of light and darkness.

Prevalence of Visual Impairments

Severe visual impairment, including total blindness, is a low-incidence condition. Moreover, visual impairment is primarily an adult disability, probably one-tenth as prevalent in children as in adults (Hallahan and Kauffman, 1991). Only about one in 1000 children have visual impairments so severe that special education is necessary.

People with low vision (including some designated as legally blind) far outnumber totally or functionally blind people who have no usable sight at all. Low-vision students comprise between 75 and 80 percent of the school-aged visually impaired population (Bryan and Jeffrey, 1982).

In 1986, Statistics Canada conducted a special post-census disability survey. While this provided only estimates of disability, it did indicate that the prevalence of visual impairment in the general population was 2.6 percent. Among the disabled population, the prevalence of visual impairment was 15.9 percent (Naeyaert and Grace, 1990). Table 10-3 shows some of the numbers and percentages from across Canada as collected by the Candian CEC.

Although severe visual impairment is a low-incidence condition in the western world, it is of particularly high prevalence in many countries of the Third World,

Table 10-3

Prevalence of visual impairment

	Total school-age population	Exceptional population	Visually impaired	Percent of total	Percent of exceptional
Newfoundland	136 228	10 165	200	0.15	1.97
Nova Scotia	169 581	18 822	147	0.08	0.78
Ontario	1 792 244	136 356	512	0.03	0.37
Saskatchewan	204 097	6 016	80	0.039	1.33
B.C.	514 464	60 623	402	0.08	0.66

Source: Canadian CEC (1989)

where blindness affects millions of children and adults. In Asia, Africa, and South America, poverty and lack of sanitation create conditions in which severe visual impairment thrives. There are probably ten million blind people living in the world today (Mazurek and Winzer, 1994).

Etiology of Visual Impairment

Visual problems arise from any interference with the formation of images on the retina or the transmission of retinal images to the brain. Optical errors, defects of the eyes, diseases, syndromes, and associated conditions all affect vision to a greater or lesser extent. An outline of some conditions, their consequences, and their etiologies is shown in Table 10-4.

In the last century, the major causes of visual impairment included such things as ophthalmia neonatorum (inflammation of the eyes of the newborn); syphilis and smallpox; and massive epidemics of meningitis and scarlet fever. Measures such as washing the eyes of the newborn, vaccinations, and vastly improved sanitary conditions have eliminated most of these causes. Today, intrauterine infections, such as rubella and toxoplasmosis, together with malformations of the developing visual apparatus of the fetus are the most common causes of congenital visual impairment in children. In recent years, blindness from other prenatal factors, such as ingestion of drugs by the mother, has been increasing. In 77 percent of these cases, babies became blind at less than one year of age. A third of these lost all useful vision (Harley and Lawrence, 1977).

Heredity is another leading cause of blindness in children under one year of age (Harley and Lawrence, 1977), with cataracts and retinoblastoma the most significant causes in terms of the number of children affected (Suran and Rizzo, 1983). Metabolic and vascular diseases, which include diabetes in the mother and disturbances in the metabolism of the infant, are another major cause of visual impairments.

Table 10-4

Examples of types of visual impairment and their etiologies

Category	Example	Manifestation	Etiology
Refractive errors	myopia	near-sightedness	
	hyperopia	long-sightedness	
	astigmatism	distorted or blurred vision	
	cataracts	growth over lens	aging, heredity, disease, and infection.
Eye pathologies	glaucoma	impaired outflow of vitreous fluid causes pressure on eyeball	congenital heredity aging
	retinopathy of prematurity	fibrous mass that destroys the retina	results from prematurity; oxygen in incubator
	retinoblastoma	malignant tumour on the retina	genetic
	albinism	lack of skin pigmentation	genetic, error of metabolism
	optic nerve atrophy	nerve degeneration	damage to the optic nerve
	retinitis pigmentosa	narrowing of field of vision	hereditary condition
Ocular-motor problems	strabismus	see double	
	nystagmus	rapidly moving eyeballs	
	amblyopia	lazy-eye blindness; lack of depth perception	arises from strabismus
Other problems	colour blindness	deficient in colour vision	genetic
	photophobia	extreme sensitivity to light	

Prematurity has been implicated in severe visual defects, as have birth traumas, hydrocephaly, infections of the nervous system acquired after birth, oxygen deprivation, and brain hemorrhage. Abnormalities of the central nervous system may result in disruption of eye muscle co-ordination. Children with cerebral palsy caused by brain damage, for example, often have impaired vision as a result of loss of control of ocular muscles. Encephalitis, meningitis, and brain tumours may also produce disturbances of ocular motor function. Children with these conditions frequently have impaired eye movements all their lives or may fail to develop stereoscopic vision.

In general, the etiologies and consequent conditions in visual impairments may be grouped as follows:

- Refractive errors, caused by irregularities in the shape or size of the eyeball, the cornea, or the lens. Errors of refraction may also occur in association with diseases of the eye or with oculomotor disturbances.
- Oculomotor problems, caused by disturbances in eye movement.
- Eye pathologies, caused by damage or disease before or after birth to one or more of the structures of the eye.
- Additional causes.

Refractive Errors

There are four common types of refractive errors that cause visual impairment — myopia, hyperopia, astigmatism, and presbyopia. **Myopia** (nearsightedness) is the greatest single cause of defective vision in children and young adults. The myopic eye is unable to focus the image precisely on the retina; the length of the eye or the shape of the cornea cause light rays to focus in front of the retina. In most cases, myopia can be corrected with concave optical lenses. **Hyperopia** (farsightedness) is caused by too short an eye or too flat a corneal surface. The image is focused behind the retina. Corrective lenses aid hyperopic people. **Astigmatism** is the result of an irregularity in the curvature of the cornea or lens of the eye. The rays of light are refracted unevenly so that horizontal and vertical rays are focused at different points on the retina. In most cases, astigmatism is correctable (Harley and Lawrence, 1977).

With advancing age, numerous body changes occur. Some of these natural developments relate to changes in the eye's muscle tone and other tissues. **Presbyopia**, from the Greek word meaning "sight of age," is a condition in which the lens of the eye loses its ability to accommodate to near objects. In the eye, the lens changes shape and lets us concentrate on a particular spot. To focus on distant objects, it flattens somewhat. When moving in close, it gets rounder. As we get older, the lens loses some of its adaptability and up-close focus becomes more difficult. In addition to blurring and difficulty with reading at normal distances, persons with presbyopia will usually experience "tired eyes" or headaches while doing close work. Most people at the age of forty or thereabouts develop some degree of presbyopia and need glasses for close work.

Disturbance of Ocular Motility

Normal vision requires the co-ordinated use of two eyes. Images from each eye are fused in the vision centres of the brain so that only one image is perceived. To achieve a synchronized image, each ocular muscle must work in perfect harmony with the other muscles in the two eyes.

The most common oculomotor disturbances prevent the eye from controlling its direction of focus. **Strabismus** results from inefficient ocular motor mobility and can affect one or both eyes. Strabismus may be evident at birth or may not appear until the child begins to look at objects close up. Divergent strabismus causes what is called a "wall eye." **Amblyopia**, sometimes called lazy-eye blindness, results from strabismus. The brain will not tolerate double vision and eventually supresses the image coming from the weaker eye.

Surgery, eye exercises, patches, or prescription lenses are used for strabismus. Treatment becomes less effective the longer it is postponed, and the longer supression goes untreated, the more difficult it becomes to restore normal visual functioning.

Diplopia, or double vision, may result from lack of co-ordination between the two eyes. **Nystagmus**, a rhythmic involuntary movement of the eyes, is often found in conjunction with other handicapping conditions, such as Down syndrome. Abnormalities of the central nervous system can also result in faulty eye-muscle co-ordination. Ocular motility problems are common in children with cerebral palsy and other neurological disorders.

Diseases of the Eye

The most common eye diseases found in children cause clouding of the cornea and lens and dysfunctions of the retina and optic nerves. These diseases may be congenital or acquired some time after birth.

A **cataract** is an opacity of the lens or its capsule which restricts the eye's ability to receive light and interferes with central and peripheral visual acuity. If the lens becomes cloudy, the light rays are blocked or distorted when they reach the retina, making things look hazy or dull, or dazzlingly bright.

Cataracts are caused by a chemical change in the lens itself. The exact reasons for the change are not understood, although there may be a hereditary tendency to develop cataracts. For the most part, cataracts are associated with aging and almost half the population over the age of sixty-five will suffer some degree of cataract formation ("Cataracts," 1990). Younger people may be affected in association with conditions such as diabetes. Some babies are born with cataracts, often the result of maternal rubella. In rare cases, cataracts result from a blow to the eye or from exposure to radiation, toxic chemicals, or intense heat ("Cataracts," 1990).

Glaucoma, a condition responsible for 12 percent of the blindness in Canada and the United States, has been called "the sneak-thief of sight" because its onset can be slow and insidious. Glaucoma is caused by the increased intra-ocular pressure that occurs when the eye fluid that should be continually drained backs up along the outflow route. The increased pressure destroys intricate, sensitive structures in the retina, which then loses its ability to transmit pictures to the brain. Congenital glaucoma is a baffling and mysterious hereditary condition that is a major cause of severe visual defects in children. Untreated glaucoma can cause total blindness in both children and adults.

Retinopathy of prematurity (ROP), until recently called retrolental fibroplasia (RLF), describes a condition affecting the retina and the vitreous humour. The problem begins as a distortion and outgrowth of the blood vessels of the retina. This is followed by the separation of the retina and the formation of an opaque mass behind the lens composed of detached retina, blood vessels, and fibrous tissue.

ROP was first described in 1942. It was seen in low-birth-weight (under 1.5 kg) babies and was soon attributed to high levels of oxygen in incubators. After its cause was discovered, there was a drop in the incidence of ROP. Since the mid-sixties, the incidence of milder ROP has been rising, and the 1980s saw a further resurgence of ROP as babies with even lower birth-weights survived (Trief et al., 1989). Today, ROP primarily affects babies with a birth-weight of less than 1000 grams. About 20 percent of infants born weighing less than 1500 grams also show evidence of ROP (Trief et al., 1989).

Bleeding, scarring, and detachment of the retina are still considered characteristic of the condition; the extent of visual impairment depends on the amount of scarring. However, current research indicates that oxygen alone does not account for all cases of ROP. Birth-weight, gestation age, and duration of administration of oxygen are the most important factors in the development of ROP (Trief et al., 1989).

Retinitis pigmentosa is a hereditary condition that causes degeneration of retinal tissues and loss of peripheral vision. The age of onset of retinitis pigmentosa may vary from childhood to early adulthood. Other abnormalities, such as cataracts and glaucoma, may also be present. When deafness is associated with retinitis pigmentosa, the condition is known as Usher's syndrome, named after the British ophthalmologist who in 1918 stressed the link between visual and auditory impairments. Usher's syndrome is a leading cause of deaf-blindness.

Damage to the blood vessels that supply the retina can cause macular retinal degeneration. The macula is the small area in the central portion of the retina that is responsible for fine or distinct vision, such as is required for reading. Macular degeneration may be inherited, but it is also associated with injuries such as contusions and concussions (Harley and Lawrence, 1977). The condition results in extremely poor central vision and may be undetected in young children. Another type of retinal degeneration is associated with a high degree of myopia. Abnormal growth in the length of the eye causes a thinning of the retina and destruction of the retinal cells.

Diabetes is a major cause of retinal disease in young adults. **Diabetic retinopathy** is a disease of the retina's blood vessels. Not all diabetics develop retinopathy; generally, however, the longer the disease has been present, the more likely that changes in the retina will occur. People who have had diabetes for more than fifteen years are at greatest risk, and as medical technology and synthetic insulin prolong the life expectancies of diabetics, retinopathy is becoming more common. The type of diabetes a person has does not seem to determine whether he or she will be affected; some people with mild diabetes that is completely controlled by diet lose their sight, while others with severe forms of the disease do not experience any visual loss ("Diabetic," 1990).

In the early stages of retinopathy, the blood vessels in the retina start to weaken and break. The leaked fluid distorts the light rays entering the eyes, and the person's vision blurs and fluctuates; or the person may see floating spots and a reddish haze. In the later stages, the blood vessels may shut down completely. When this happens, the retinal nerves that transmit sight images to the brain die from loss of nourishment. This kind of vision loss is gradual but permanent. New abnormal blood vessels may replace the old ones but they are unable to nourish the retina properly. They may start to grow into the normally transparent inner chamber of the eye, further interfering with the person's vision. If scar tissue forms, it can pull on the retina, tearing or detaching it completely, and the result is total blindness ("Diabetic," 1990).

Retinal detachment occurs when a hole or rip in the retina allows the inner retina layer to separate from the back portion. Eye fluid can then enter through the break, seep between the layers and further pressure the inner layer to peel or detach. Total blindness may result if the detached retina is not promptly reattached (Harley and Lawrence, 1977).

Optic nerve atrophy occurs when there has been damage to the fibres of the optic nerve. Degeneration of the nerve may be partial or complete, and its onset may be gradual or abrupt. Optic nerve atrophy may result from inadequate blood supply to the nerve or from optical diseases such as glaucoma or retinal degeneration.

Retinoblastoma results from a malignant tumour on the retina that may spread to the optic nerve and other areas. The condition usually arises in infancy or early childhood. It can be inherited as a Mendelian dominant trait with incomplete penetrance, which means that the person carrying the condition may not manifest the lesion but can still pass it on to offspring. In the past, surgical removal of the eyes was necessary for persons suffering from retinoblastoma. Today, the malignancy can be arrested without removal of the eyes. Still, blindness inevitably ensues and even a cured patient can transmit the condition to offspring.

Other Defects

Colour blindness is a rare, sex-linked, hereditary disorder found almost always in males. Defects of colour vision arise from the absence or malfunctioning of the cone cells of the retina. Cones come in three varieties, sensitive to the wavelengths of either blue, green, or red light. In some people, one of the three types of cones is missing, making them colour blind for that range of the spectrum (Immen, 1995). Persons with colour defects are likely to confuse colours, most commonly red and green. True colour blindness (seeing everything in shades of grey) is very rare. Although colour blindness is common among those with central vision problems, the condition is not necessarily associated with visual impairments.

Albinism is a condition carried as an inherited autosomal recessive trait. It is not sex-linked and the gene must be inherited from both parents, each of whom either has albinism or is a carrier of the trait. Albinism affects the metabolism of melanin, the pigment contained in hair and skin. It causes pigment deficiency in the retina, iris, and choroid, causing the pupil to take on a deep reddish colour and the iris to appear grey-ish, light blue, or pink. When the eyes are affected, albinism is characterized by decreased acuity, astigmatism, nystagmus, and **photophobia**, a condition in which very bright light blinds the individual and thus decreases acuity (Abang, 1980; Vander Kolk and Bright, 1983).

Some central nervous system disorders may manifest themselves by a lack of response to light stimulus in the cortex. **Cortical blindness** sometimes refers to blindness caused by swelling in the brain tissue due to trauma or congenital malformations (Hammer, 1984). At other times, the term describes blindness that cannot be medically explained. Most often, children who are congenitally cortically blind have other problems that are serious enough to affect several body systems.

Prevention of Visual Impairment

In many instances, visual impairment is of unknown origin. Prenatal care, which includes genetic counselling, proper nutrition, and avoidance of alcohol and other drugs, is the most important form of prevention.

Immediately after birth, the eyes of newborns are routinely washed with a one-percent silver nitrate solution to prevent infection. Later, children are given innoculations to prevent diseases that may result in visual impairments. Total blindness in older children can often be prevented with immediate medical and surgical intervention in cases of retinal detachment, cataracts, and other forms of treatable eye diseases.

Identification and Measurement of Visual Impairments

Studies reveal that most children with visual impairments either are born with the disability or acquire it at an early age. It is therefore very important that children be assessed early so that intervention can ensue. If detected early enough, at least some visual impairments can be corrected through the use of lenses, medication, and surgery.

A comprehensive assessment of a child with a visual impairment must take into account the medical diagnosis and treatment of the problem as well as psycho-educational assessment that will lead to efficient educational planning.

Screening

Screening procedures assess large numbers of children in order to identify those needing additional diagnosis. In Manitoba, Rathegerber (1981) reported on screening procedures that identified 21 to 34 percent of children on the first screening and 11 to 24 percent on the second. When the identified children were sent for professional examinations, more than two-thirds required some care, either as an immediate prescription or for some incipient condition noted by the eye practitioner.

The most common screening procedure used in the measurement of central vision acuity is the Snellen Chart, developed in 1862 by Herman Snellen, a Dutch ophthalmologist. The chart consists of a series of letters, numbers, or symbols that must be read from a distance of twenty feet. Each line is a different size that corresponds to a standard distance at which it can be distinguished by a person with normal vision. This gives the measure 20/20 vision, which should not be read as a fraction. Snellen's equation was $V = d/D$ when V is visual acuity, d is distance, and D is distance at which letters are clearly read.

The standard letter chart found on almost every doctor's door may be used for children; the symbol E chart is especially suitable for young children and those who cannot read. In this measure, only E's pointing in different directions are used. Screening tests that supplement the Snellen Chart include further measurements of visual fields and muscle-balance tests. One of the most common screening tests used with very young children is the Flash-Card Vision Test, which uses three symbols (apple, house, umbrella) that can be either verbally or manually matched.

Many children with visual problems are not identified until after they are enrolled in school and expected to read. In the identification of milder visual disorders, teachers may be on the front line in screening. Often children who have no outward appearance of anything wrong with the eyes exhibit abnormal behaviour such as frequent rubbing of the eyes, excessive blinking, crossing one eye when reading, or holding the book abnormally close or far away. Children who are suspected of having a visual problem should be referred for comprehensive eye examinations. Signs of visual problems that teachers can observe are presented below.

Some signs of visual problems

One eye turns in or out.
In near work, the child squints, closes, or covers one eye.
The child rubs the eyes, squints, or shakes the head while looking at near or far objects.
The child tilts the head or closes one eye.
The child is fearful of walking down stairs or running freely.
The child frequently falls or bumps into objects.
The child holds objects very close to — or far away from — the eyes.
The child appears to have abnormal eye movements.
The child complains of fuzzy vision.
The child has frequent eye infections, swollen eyelids, watery eyes, or reddened eyes or lids.
The eyes tear excessively.
The child has encrusted eyelids or frequent styes on the lids.
The child is poor or slow in reading.
The child is inattentive during reading class.
The child often loses the place when reading or persistently skips lines and confuses letters.
The child often stops to rest after brief periods of reading.
The head turns when the child is reading.
Pages in notebooks are poorly organized.
The child misaligns both horizontal and vertical series of numbers.
The child has difficulty in focusing on the blackboard.
The child can't remember things he or she has seen.

Diagnosis

Diagnosis in infants relies on observations of the child's responses to visual stimuli. Sometimes simple observation enables parents to identify a problem by the way the child responds to various stimuli, such as light or a moving object. Clinical observation includes reactions of the pupils of the eyes to light, blinking in response to light presentation, eye movements in response to objects moving in the visual field, and eye fixation on stationary objects (Rogow, 1987b).

Eye examinations are used with older children. Ophthalmologists look carefully for a wide range of visual impairments and the degree of the impairments as they affect the individual. The eye examination should determine a child's maximum potential for achieving acuity as well as the type of optical aids the child needs to reach the maximum acuity level (Abang, 1980).

Medical diagnosis of visual impairments considers both physical and functional aspects. The physical aspect involves measuring visual ability, which includes visual acuity, visual field, oculomotor control, and the effects of specific diseases or injuries and prenatal factors (Abang, 1980).

Profile

Abu

Abu's parents were very excited about their first child. They talked and planned and organized as they got ready for the arrival. When Abu was born, his handicapping condition was almost immediately noticeable to the attending physicians. Within twenty-four hours the parents were informed that their new baby was severely visually impaired. The grandparents did not live in Canada, so mother and father had almost no one to turn to for support.

The infant years were particularly difficult for Abu's mother. Many of her expectations for the child did not materialize. Certainly, he seemed to reach developmental milestones almost on target and by two years of age was developing language and some intelligible speech. Mother tried to hide her fears and played and talked with the child as much as possible. When he was three, she asked, with little optimism, if he could attend the local nursery school. To her surprise, the school personnel willingly accepted Abu and were pleased to allow her to work as a volunteer on condition that she intervene with all the children, not just Abu.

The nursery school experience has proved an enormous success for Abu and for his mother. The teachers modify activities where necessary for Abu. For example, they add sand to the finger paints so that he has greater tactile experiences. An extract from Abu's IEP is shown later in this chapter.

Abu's mother knows that his inability to perceive through the use of his eyes changes the way he learns, understands, and relates to the world, and that he will require additional assistance to overcome the deficits imposed by severe visual impairment. But she now realizes that Abu can learn and interact, and that he may achieve some of the goals his parents so hopefully set for him.

Visual functioning refers to the ways in which a child uses vision for purposeful behaviour in the various activities of daily life (Hall, Orel-Bixler, and Haegerstom-Portnoy, 1991). In diagnosis, functional aspects include the extent to which residual vision is being utilized and whether the child has opportunity, incentive, or optical aids to enable him or her to use residual vision (Abang, 1980). Additional procedures used with children with multiple disabilities are discussed in Chapter 15.

Psycho-Educational Assessment

When a child is deficient in a sense modality, assessment is fraught with problems. Diverse factors contribute to these difficulties.

- Perhaps more than any other group, those with visual and/or reading impairments are at a diasadvantage in relation to psychological testing techniques, since most existing tests depend to a large extent on printed stimuli (Johnson, 1989).
- The intelligence levels of blind and sighted children cannot be easily compared (Warren, 1984).
- Many critics maintain that IQ tests for blind individuals do not evaluate them in a way comparable to the evaluation of sighted children (Warren, 1984).
- Few measures have been developed exclusively for children who are visually impaired.
- No intelligence tests have been devised that are equally meaningful for both sighted and visually impaired children.

- A number of test instruments have been developed or adapted for use with visually impaired students, but there exists no viable effective or standardized procedure for testing both the totally and partially blind populations (Johnson, 1989).
- Normative data based on blind subjects is inappropriate for the whole visually impaired population.
- Because of the scarcity of predictive studies with blind children, extreme caution should be used when interpreting test results for predictive purposes (Coveny, 1976).

Tests for sighted children rely heavily on visual content and administration. To circumvent the visual disabilities, much IQ testing of blind children has been conducted using the non-visual verbal portions of common IQ tests. For blind children, tests use tactile or auditory modes; for those partially sighted, aural modes, large type, or magnified materials are used.

Samuel Hayes, a psychologist involved with the Perkins School for the Blind, reasoned that blind children would be disadvantaged in using tests developed for sighted children. His modification of the Stanford-Binet Individual Intelligence Test, the Interim Hayes Stanford-Binet, eliminated items requiring sight. Following Hayes, various versions of the Binet tests, such as the Perkins-Binet, and the verbal scales of the WISC-R have been commonly used with blind children (Warren, 1984).

Because it is inappropriate to rely solely, or even primarily, on psychometric measures, most psychologists testing visually impaired children use a variety of tests or combine the subtests of different instruments (Barraga, 1976). Several tools have been designed for visually impaired populations or specially adapted from other measures. The Piagetian Approach to Visually Handicapped Education (PAVE) is designed to evaluate a congenitally blind child's reasoning abilities and provide reasoning-oriented intervention activities (Stephens, Grube, and Fitzgerald, 1977). The Stanford Achievement Tests have been adapted and are available in both braille and large print from second grade to college. The Maxfield-Buchholz Social Maturity Scale, an adaptation of the original Vineland Social Maturity Scale (Doll, 1941), screens the social maturity of blind children from birth to seventy-two months in the areas of general motor development, dressing, eating, locomotion, and occupation. Checklists or developmental scales such as the Developmental Activities Screening Inventory (Dubose and Langley, 1977) are useful indicators of social, physical, and communicative development.

Developmental Consequences of Visual Impairment

Obviously, the developmental consequences of total blindness differ in some respects from those related to low vision. Reading, other academic areas, socialization, life skills, and orientation and mobility will all be affected by the severity of the visual loss. The correlation is certainly not clear-cut, but as a broad generalization, we can say that the greater the degree of visual impairment, the more sharply reduced will be the range and variety of a child's experiences and the greater will be the restrictions placed on the child's ability to move freely within an environment.

Motor Development

Social, exploratory, and manipulative experiences lay the foundation for competence in communication, concept development, motor development, and self-reliance.

Vision plays a leading role in the infant's first efforts to independently expore the environment. As the infant's new world comes into sharper visual focus, the developing neuromuscular system sparks a push toward motor exploration and the infant reaches out to touch, feel, taste, and probe. Without vision, infants find it more difficult to explore their environment, to reach out into space, and to become aware of their bodies in space. Very young blind children have no natural motivation to lift their heads or roll, and they are less able to orient themselves to the external environment through such skills as reaching, crawling, and walking (Warren, 1984).

Restricted experiences mean that congenitally blind children may be delayed in motor development. While blind infants acquire early motor skills such as sitting and standing at about the same time as other children, they may be slower in crawling and walking. Delays in walking until sixteen to nineteen months are common in blind children, and even children with sufficient vision for orientation and mobility purposes may show a lack of confidence and a delay in ambulation.

Early play behaviour differs from that of sighted children. Of all handicapping conditions, infantile autism and blindness seem to be the ones that affect the development of sensorimotor and symbolic play the most significantly. Visually impaired children may be substantially delayed in sensorimotor play and exhibit delays or deficiencies in symbolic and social play. Abnormalities in symbolic play seem to be related to the limitations imposed by visual impairments.

Cognitive Development

The intelligence levels of persons who are visually impaired parallel those of the general population. How children learn and whether lags in learning are attributable to visual impairment is, however, a subject of intense debate.

Researchers debate whether or not blind children do more poorly on tasks involving abstract thinking and whether they are much more likely to deal with their environment in concrete terms. Because blind children rely far more on non-visual perceptions, the notions they form may differ from the notions of sighted children. However, many current researchers argue that the assumption that blind children experience problems of sensory reference has little basis in truth (Landau, 1983).

Another arnts lag sig

nificantly behind their sighted peers in the development of Piagetian tasks such as classification and conservation. Research is equivocal because much traditional testing of classification and conservation is based on visual information, and even when traditional visual tasks are adapted into a tactual mode, they cannot be considered comparable.

Perceptual Development

Hearing is the only distance sense available to blind individuals, and they must build their knowledge from auditory experiences joined to those that are olfactory, tactile, and kinesthetic. For blind children, the world is one of smells, sounds, and textures uninformed by the visual information that offers such a rich variety of colour, shape, and size detail to sighted persons.

It takes effort and concentration to learn to use the touch and auditory senses to compensate for lack of sight. There is no magical sensory compensation of the remaining senses; blind persons must learn to pay more attention to auditory and tactual clues that sighted people can afford to ignore.

For the person who is blind, texture, weight, temperature, shape, and size merge into a sequence of touch sensations to permit identification of an object (Scott, 1969). Blind persons use synthetic touch — the tactual exploration of objects small enough to be enclosed by one or both hands. For larger objects, the blind person employs analytic touch, exploring the various parts of an object and then mentally reconstructing the parts (Hallahan and Kauffman, 1991).

Communication

In the classroom, language arts, conversational practice, social skills instruction, and role playing are some of the ways that the communication skills of visually impaired students can be enhanced.

Verbal language serves many important social and information-gathering functions for blind children. Even before they develop speech, blind children use vocalizations to achieve and maintain social contact. They also learn a great deal about people in their environment from voices. They learn to measure personal attention by the nearness of the speaker and the touch gestures that accompany speech, and they become adept at interpreting meaning from nuance or variations in voice tone.

Studies of the speech and language development of children who are visually impaired have provoked controversy in the research literature. Whether language development parallels that of sighted children or whether it is delayed or different is not certain (Elstner, 1983; Matsuda, 1984). Bigelow (1987) found that very young blind children acquire vocabulary in the same way as sighted children, although some differences emerged in the percentage of words in each classification. Others have studied verbalisms where a child uses words inappropriately and without an experiential base. For example, "a shirt as red as an apple" is a verbalism. Others have looked at the increased numbers of questions that visually impaired children tend to ask as part of their information gathering. As sight increases, so questions decrease (Erin, 1986).

It may very well be that any speech and language difficulties in children who are visually impaired are more closely related to social and emotional factors than to low vision or blindness. Delays in speech and language development may be the result of little or no interaction with the people around them. As Teresa Abang (1980) states, "Unless blind children are encouraged, they do not learn to speak early. This may very well be because of the fact that, not being able to see, they have nothing to talk about unless they are helped." In other words, blind children who have been encouraged to explore their environments and interact with other people do not suffer delays in language acquisition.

Academic Achievement

The educational achievements of children who are visually impaired are as variable as the population itself. Academic success is more closely related to social, cultural, and familial factors than to the degree of visual impairment (Rogow, 1987b).

Students who are visually impaired tend to achieve more highly in some areas than others. In a review of studies, Weiss and Weiss (1981) found that blind students do not perform as well in arithmetic: they tend to be from 8 to 27 percent below average sighted children in basic arithmetic performance. On the other hand, the work of blind students in literary subjects was about the same as that of their sighted peers. Reading may be a problem, one prime reason being the slower rate of reading large print or braille. Students who use braille often encounter difficulties in spelling because the contractions in braille do not conform to English spelling usage.

Social and Emotional Development

Blind children often have special needs in relation to self-awareness, self-esteem, and social skills. Visual impairment causes unique differences in the emergence of a healthy self-image. In his classic work, Cutsforth (1951) maintained that internal psychological factors, such as distorted attitudes about self, are a much more serious problem than the visual impairment per se or even than the obstacles presented by society.

It is important that teachers try to emphasize blind children's strengths without denying their special needs.

Severe visual impairments tend to interfere with spontaneous social activity and with social interaction and communication. Blind children face obstacles in obtaining the full benefits of peer interaction; students who are visually impaired may have trouble in acquiring an adequate repertoire of interpersonal skills (Farkas et al., 1981), and they often behave in ways that decrease their effective interaction with peers. Problems may be attributed to the visually impaired child's inability to utilize visual clues which are needed for the modelling and feedback that underlie social skill acquisition.

Because of their visual limitations, these children miss many important non-verbal cues given by their teachers and peers through facial expressions, gestures, and body language (Scott, 1982). Children with severe visual impairments may fail to make expected eye contact with peers and typically will not smile. Their failure to look at people may be interpreted as disinterest rather than as a manifestation of the handicap itself. These children also possess no built-in feedback for appropriate head and facial movements once they are engaged in conversation.

During the adolescent period, many students who are visually impaired encounter difficulties in establishing relationships with peers. Even in integrated settings, they often do not interact (Hoben et al., 1979). Visually handicapped students often add to their problems by internalizing the role of a handicapped person, often as a result of the attitudes of those around them. Competition with sighted peers can cause difficulty, even with training and education.

Additional Handicapping Conditions

About one-third of visually impaired students have one additional handicap (Scholl, 1986). Emotional disorders, mental retardation, and learning disabilities are common additional handicapping conditions seen in children who are visually impaired. Much of the existing literature points to a relatively high incidence of autism among congenitally blind children.

Intervention with Students Who Are Visually Impaired

Intervention with the population of students who are visually impaired serves different purposes, depending on the nature and degree of the visual loss, as well as the unique goals of differing professional disciplines. Generally, the major areas of intervention are habilitation, education, learning to use alternate modalities, orientation and mobility training, and reading and optical enhancement.

A range of sophisticated technical aids and devices exist for reading, mobility and orientation, and magnification. We explain some of them later in this chapter under the relevant headings.

Medical Intervention

Medical intervention is provided by an opthalmologist who is a medical doctor; an optometrist who is a specialist in vision problems; and an optician who makes lenses. Medical intervention takes the form of medication, surgery, technical aids, and prescriptive lenses to control and maximize visual function. In the surgical area, laser beam techniques are used to reattach damaged retinas and there are sophisticated techniques for corneal transplants, artificial lens transplants, and the removal of cataracts. Drug therapies reduce the risk of blindness from glaucoma and diabetes.

Therapy

The occupational therapist evaluates the effect of a child's visual impairment on daily living, play, and readiness for preschool and school programs. Children need attention to gross motor skills for mobility and fine motor skills for independent functioning.

An important aspect of therapy is teaching children with severe visual impairments the efficient use of residual vision and compensatory hand skills. These children tend to use their hands in broad, sweeping motions and fail to acquire precise search and grasp skills. They therefore have weak hands and fingers and need manipulation of clay and plasticine, squeeze toys, pegboards, and puzzles.

clay material

Educational Intervention

Teachers should expect the same quality of work from students who are visually impaired as from other class members, and behavioural expectations should be the same.

Given the many types of visual impairment, the range of severity levels, and the unique ways that individuals use residual vision, it is not surprising that children with visual impairments form an extremely heterogeneous population. In a classroom, teachers may meet students with restricted vision who cannot see at a distance; those who are unable to see near images clearly; and those who need special lighting and optical aids to learn visually.

Although residential schools still play a role in Canada, the emphasis on mainstreaming has meant a shift from segregated residential school education for students with severe visual handicaps to education in neighbourhood schools. Today, totally blind and other visually impaired students are enrolled in regular schools in all grades from kindergarten to secondary school.

Early intervention is important for very young children with visual impairments and their families (see Chapter 16). From infancy on, children may be trained in motor skills, locomotion and mobility, self-help skills, and communication. When they are integrated into nursery schools or day-care centres, adaptations to the environment and modifications to the program enhance their progress. For example, the teachers at the Daycrest Centre prepared an individual program for Abu, the young child we met earlier in this chapter. An extract from Abu's IEP is shown on the next page.

Individual Education Plan

iep

Extract from Abu's IEP

Name: Abu
Age: 4-7
Centre: Daycrest
Supervisor: Ms Teacher
Report number: 2

Abu has been in the centre for almost a year. During this time, he has been working on individual goals and objectives embedded within the daily routines and activities of the centre. A specialist teacher assists with orientation and mobility training (white cane) on a bi-weekly basis.

Adaptations

No particular environmental adaptations are necessary. Additional lighting is provided in the reading corner. Some special materials are provided. For example, large and sturdy toys. There are books that provide alternative sensory information and pictures that are clear and uncluttered. Some toys are adapted. For example, some have bases covered in textures such as sandpaper.

Abu wears his glasses quite readily.

Assessment

At the outset, an assessment of Abu's potential and progress was undertaken. The full assessment included a psychological report as well as observations and informal checklists used by the teachers.

Present levels of functioning

Cognitive: the report of the psychologist confirms the observations of the teachers that Abu is a child functioning at the norm. His language, problem-solving skills, and the activities he undertakes in the centre are normal for a child of his chronological age, taking into account the visual disability. Play behaviour lags somewhat. Abu is still into the stage of constructive activities and is not yet involved in symbolic play alone or with peers.

Language: Abu shows good language skills although he requires more experience in some areas. He asks many questions and shows a natural curiosity.

Behaviour: At first Abu was very shy with his peers. As he becomes more confident, he is increasingly accepted by the other children. He is beginning to participate in group work.

Motor: Abu's gross motor skills are developing. Fine motor skills are lagging a little, probably the result of the visual impairment.

Long-range goals

- To develop security in the environment and in moving about in it.
- To strengthen the other sense modalities, especially audition and touch.
- To stimulate peer interactions.

Objectives

- Improve auditory skills through identification and localization of sound.
- Improve tactile discrimination.
- Improve taste and smell awareness.
- Encourage the use of residual vision.
- Improve social interaction through teaching appropriate smiling behaviour.

A variety of technical aids have been developed to assist children with visual impairments.

Successful integration of visually impaired students depends on five components—the availability of specialist teachers; access to special equipment and optical aids; a braille transcription service; co-operation among principals, regular teachers, and special education teachers; and access to alternative programs for students who need them. Classroom needs include a flexible teacher and peer acceptance and interaction. Personal student characteristics include social skills, a positive self-image, independence, family acceptance, and inner motivation (Bishop, 1986).

In providing educational options for students who are visually impaired, school districts often make available a continuum of placement options. The resource room functions as a part-time classroom staffed by a specialist teacher who provides individual instruction as required, administers special tests, and adapts regular classroom materials. Itinerant programs make it possible for most children with visual handicaps to be integrated into regular classes. On itinerant programs, the specialist teacher travels from school to school within a district. Itinerant teachers offer special instruction to children in all school levels, including those in special programs. Specialist teachers work closely with school personnel who are involved with visually impaired students. Self-contained programs are designed mainly for younger children or students with special learning difficulties. The special class permits intensive individualization of instruction and concentrated attention to a child's problems (see Winzer, 1989).

Teachers with specialized training in visual impairment increasingly collaborate with classroom teachers in assessing and developing instructional programs for visually impaired children and those with additional handicaps. They design and provide instructional programs in braille reading, braille math, and other academic subjects, and work with teachers to adapt learning materials and interpret the medical, educational, and social implications of visual impairments to others involved with the child. With students, specialists may assess braille-reading readiness, visual perception, mobility, and social development. They also teach the use of visual aids and electronic reading devices, and design and provide instruction in self-help skills.

Educational Approaches

Education for students who are visually impaired can be clustered into seven major areas for curriculum: regular curriculum; personal competence, such as self-help skills and daily living skills; orientation and mobility; communication skills; vocational guidance and career education; use of special aids and equipment; and visual stimulation.

Curriculum

Students who are visually impaired can participate in practically all aspects of school activities. Curriculum content for students with visual impairments combines the general curriculum goals of the child's grade level with specialized instruction. Teachers should expect the same quality of work from students who are visually impaired as from other class members, and behavioural expectations should be the same. Children should care for their own materials: they should be allowed a particular place for them that provides secure and safe storage.

Tips for Teachers

Tips for teachers of students who are visually impaired

Classroom environment and climate

- Point out classroom rules to which the student must adhere.
- Expect the same quality of work.
- If necessary, use a buddy at first but do not allow the student to grow too dependent.
- Don't move furniture in the classroom without informing the student.
- Cut down glare on glass, desks, and chalkboards in the classroom.
- Provide tilt-top desks.
- Try to have classroom displays on the eye level of the student.
- Try to emphasize blind children's strengths without denying their special needs.

Adaptive equipment

- Check the lighting needs of the child. In children who are sensitive to light, for example, acuity increases with decreasing illumination.
- Provide adequate storage space for materials while still keeping the student physically integrated.
- If glasses are worn, be sure that they are clean.
- Know how, when, and under what circumstances students can use their vision most effectively. Students with central field defects may benefit from eccentric viewing techniques. Those who have nystagmus need to discover the best posture for reading. Those with poor peripheral vision can turn their heads, rather than move their eyes for scanning.
- Become familiar with the optical aids, large print, and reading aids. Some students may need extra space for their equipment, but this does not imply that the child should be physically separated from other students.
- For older students, use graphs made of sandpaper, yarn, spaghetti, and other materials.

Instruction

- Provide direct learning experiences through a multi-sensory approach. Especially in the elementary years, students need concrete experiences, unifying experiences, and to learn by doing.
- Explain, using concrete terms.
- Use words such as "look" and "see" but avoid "this," "that" and other intangibles.
- Allow longer time for tasks that require reading.
- In teaching reading, a phonics approach may prove helpful for students who cannot see whole words.
- Tapes or records can be helpful teaching devices, giving the student a break from visual fatigue.
- Low vision students write in a size compatible with their own visual capacity. Stress legibility, not size.
- On application work sheets, blacken the print.
- Use buff rather than white paper.
- Never use purple spirit master copies.
- Assign the student a variety of types of seatwork.
- A low vision student works under extra pressure and will be tired at the end of the day. Large amounts of homework should not be assigned.

Evaluation

- Scores on standardized achievement tests may be depressed by slow responses due to a slower reading or writing rate, or even to the fear of making errors. Allow more time for tests.

Reading can be an area of difficulty for visually impaired students, often because of their slower reading speeds. For students who use braille, extra attention must be paid to English spelling forms. Mathematics is another subject in which these students may encounter difficulties. To master mathematical concepts, students with visual impairments need to explore the dimensions of shape and build up a vocabulary of meaningful mathematical terms.

Adequate development of communication skills is important for students who are visually impaired. Language arts, conversational practice, social skill instruction, and role playing are only some of the ways that communication skills can be enhanced. Physical education and creative activities are of particular importance to a well-rounded curriculum. Visually impaired students need daily opportunities for vigorous exercise. Older children may need to correct body posture and movement. They may hold their heads down, droop their shoulders forward, or walk with a shuffling gait.

Learning braille is complex and time-consuming.

Historical Notes

Braille

Braille originally arose from the work of Charles Barbier, engineer, inventor, philanthropist, and officer in Napoleon's army, who devised a code which he called *écriture nocturne* — night writing. These were not tracings of the ordinary alphabet but a secret code based on a twelve-dot unit, or cell, two dots wide and six high. Each dot or combination of dots stood for a letter or a phonetic sound. In 1808, when Barbier's system was presented to the French Academy of Sciences, it was hailed as a brilliant invention. Various adaptations of the system were undertaken by Barbier and duly submitted to the Academy. One report found its way to the school for the blind in Paris where the twelve-dot system was tried but rejected in 1820 as impractical: the cells were simply too large to be read by a single finger tip (Winzer, 1993).

Louis Braille (1809-1852), the son of a harness maker, was born in Coupvray, a French town about forty-five kilometres from Paris. He slit an eye at age three while playing with a sharp knife in his father's workshop and the resulting infection destroyed the vision in his other eye. Louis first attended the village school where he did very well even without the advantage of school books. Then, in 1819 his father sent him to the Paris Institute for the Blind. Louis proved an outstanding student and eventually became a teacher at the school.

Frustrated with the raised print method of teaching reading to blind pupils, Braille embarked on a search for a more efficient means and soon discovered Barbier's military code. When Braille undertook the adaptation of the Barbier system, he first solved the problem of the size of the cell by cutting the number of dots in half. He then devised a new code, alphabetic rather than phonetic, employing combinations of six dots. Because the new code was arbitrary, the symbols could stand for anything the users wanted to code. With his new system, Braille taught his students to read with more efficiency that was possible with embossed letters.

Braille's alphabetic code was published in 1834, his music notations in 1839. The braille system for reading and writing was officially adopted at the Paris School for the Blind in 1854. Dr. Simon Pollak, one of the founders of the Missouri School for the Blind, brought braille from Europe in the 1850s, but the braille code failed for many decades to find a niche in North America (Winzer, 1993).

In North America, educators preferred systems closer to regular written language. Schools for the blind used type faces such as Moon print, New York print, and raised print. It was not until 1892 that resistance to braille was finally overcome. Once accepted as a system to assist blind persons with reading and writing, braille evolved into a well-established system that employs many abbreviated signs and symbols.

Reading Aids

For the majority of students classified as severely visually impaired, large print materials will form the major reading medium. In large print, 18-point is one of the most popular types. Large print readers will generally use normal handwriting in their work; the size of the writing is likely to conform to their type-size preference.

Braille is the medium of literacy for blind persons. The braille alphabet uses six dots arranged in two rows of three dots each. Each dot is numbered. Figure 10-3 shows the braille alphabet. Numbers and punctuation signs are also represented in braille; numbers use dots 3 to 6, and the use of dot 6 just before a letter indicates a capital. Braille has been adapted to many written languages, including those that do not use Roman letters. As well, a scientific and mathematical code has been developed.

Figure 10-3
The Roman alphabet in braille

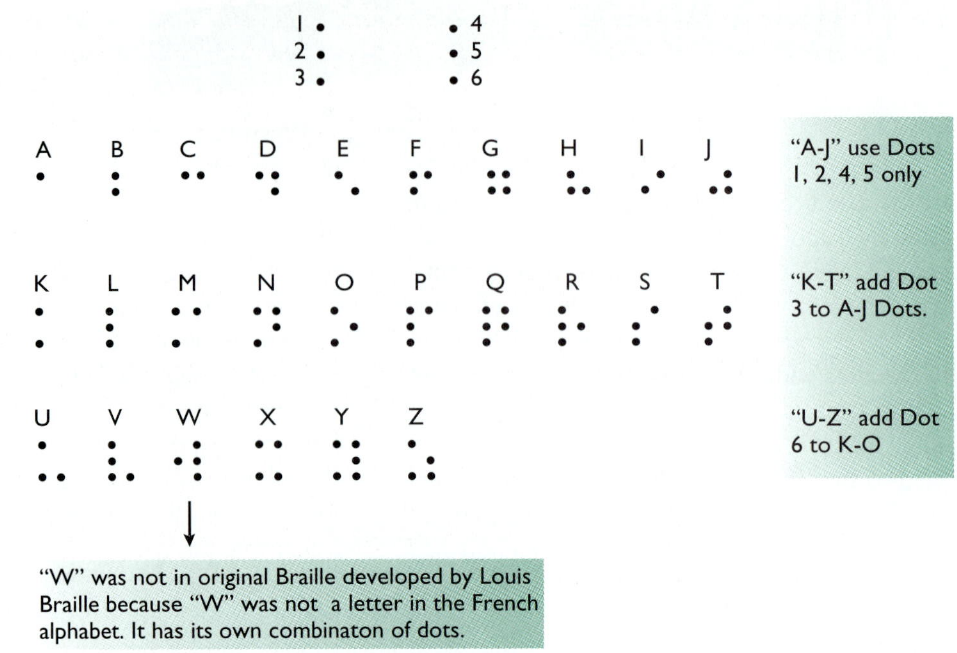

Because of the complex rules underlying braille structure and the many accepted abbreviations, the teaching of braille reading is more complex and time-consuming than that of print reading. For the reader, the process is slower than reading print because the reading range of the fingers is much narrower than that of the eye. Reading efficiency is more difficult to achieve: readers must develop tactile tracking skills, a light touch, good reading posture, and smooth co-ordination of both hands (Mangold, 1982).

A skilled two-handed reader begins by placing both hands at the beginning of a line. When the middle of the line is reached, the right hand continues across the line while the left hand locates the beginning of the next line. The left hand begins to read the first several words of the new line while the right hand moves to its new reading position (Mangold, 1982).

Blind braille-reading students require braille textbooks. Traditional braille transcription was expensive and facilities were sparse. Computerized braille has almost superseded the slow and tedious manual versions and made the process both rapid and compact. Today, computer braille transcription centres are available in both Canada and the United States (Cox, 1984).

The Optacon (Optic to Tactile Converter), which converts printed material to braille, is the most widely used reading device. By passing a scanning device over the printed material, the microprocessor converts the words to braille via a small electronic braille-writing device that permits a blind person to "read along" as the viewer passes over the written words. Young children as well as adults can use the Optacon to gain immediate access to print materials.

Reading with the Optacon is not analogous to reading with braille. With the Optacon, the user holds a small camera in one hand to read printed material and convert it into impulses. With the index finger of the other hand, the user can feel the letters and numbers through a tactile array of 144 small vibrating rods contained in a portable battery-operated electronic section about the size and weight of a portable cassette tape recorder. For example, if the camera moves across the letter H, the user of the Optacon feels two vertical lines and one horizontal line moving beneath his or her fingers and tries to recognize the letter shape (Abang, 1980). Recognition of letter shapes requires a great deal of skill and practice.

Raymond Kurzweil's reading machine, first introduced in 1976 (Kurzweil, 1990), is designed to convert printed materials to an audio output. Its camera picks up printed letters which are then converted into synthesized speech.

For writing, the slate and stylus are the braille version of pen and paper. The user presses the stylus through openings in the slate that holds the paper. Since the material must be read from the underside of the paper, it must be written in reverse by starting at the right margin and moving toward the left.

In the first decade of this century, Frank Hall invented a machine, the brailler, that allowed the visually impaired person to "type" braille. Although less portable than a slate and stylus, the brailler is easier to use. Paperless braillers, such as the Cranmer Modified Perkins Brailler, allow students to feed information into a computer and receive a braille printout. The user can also write in braille, store material, and correct or amend material as on a standard computer (Mellor, 1981).

Closed circuit television reading aids resemble regular television sets. They have a camera that scans reading material and conveys it to a monitor for enlargement. Users can regulate the size of the image to their own needs. Some machines are powerful enough to use with microfiche. Variable speech tape recorders are the most commonly used speech compressors (Rogow, 1987b).

Visual Stimulation

Until quite recently it was believed that children should conserve their vision so as not to "wear it out." Today's educators believe that if residual sight is used rather than saved, most visually handicapped children can actually improve their visual functioning. The more children use their vision, particularly at close range, the more they stimulate the pathways to the brain. The brain accumulates a variety of visual images and stores them as memories. This process enables children with visual handicaps to function as visual learners (Barraga, 1976).

Some children require consistent vision stimulation. Visual skills include attention to lights and objects; tracing and scanning; and figure-ground discrimination. Visual perception encompasses object discrimination, the use of pictures, sorting and classification, and sequencing.

Vision is stimulated with the use of prescription devices and low-vision aids. These can considerably increase a child's ability to maximize near-vision potential. However, visually impaired and blind students need additional training in the use of special aids and equipment, including aids for magnification.

In recent years, great strides have been made in the development of optic aids. There are three main types of magnification and telescopic aids: hand-held magnifiers and telescopes; stand magnifiers, fixed focus or focusable; and headband aids — spectacles, clip-on loupes, and telescopes (Kelleher, 1979).

Personal Competence

Very young visually impaired students may need help in acquiring self-help skills such as dressing, feeding, and toileting. In older children, personal competence revolves around social skills. Students often need assistance to balance their interests and tackle new areas of learning. They may need more support and encouragement to take risks and overcome a fear of failure.

Orientation and Mobility

Persons who are visually impaired must be able to move at a reasonable rate and with grace, comfort, and safety along existing routes between an origin and a destination. Orientation and mobility training can enable blind children to move with confidence and independence within their environment. Orientation refers to an individual's knowledge of his or her position in space; mobility refers to negotiating that space.

The prescription cane is the most commonly used travel aid for blind children and adults.

To move freely and confidently, individuals who are visually impaired must know where they want to go, how, and in what direction. Independent travel is accomplished through the use of auditory, tactual, and kinesthetic senses together with any residual vision. Visually impaired persons must also learn to correctly use a travel aid, such as a cane or a dog.

Orientation (cognitive mapping) involves knowing the spatial relations among objects or landmarks and one's own position in relation to the relevant objects or landmarks (Bigelow, 1991). Sighted persons use their visual system for orientation. Vision provides information as to where a seen object is in relation to the body, stimulating other senses so that they can determine whether or not the object is moving.

Vision also maintains accurate functioning and position in space in spite of changes in the position of the eyes, head, and body, and judges relative direction (Howard and Templeton, 1966). These orientation tasks involve the retina, eye movements, visual direction, kinesthetic judgments, the vestibular apparatus, and auditory location.

Those who are blind have little or no access to the visual information needed to construct cognitive maps. They acquire knowledge of the spatial relations among objects through tactile, proprioceptive, or auditory modes (Bigelow, 1991). Whereas a sighted person relies on visual representation, a blind individual may rely on sound distance to judge relationship to an object. For example, to indicate the spatial relationship between the pupil and the teacher, the teacher may have to clap his or her hands (Abang, 1980).

Blind children also learn to gauge distance and direction from variations in sound. They perceive direction through sound localization, not visual angle of perspective. When they develop an obstacle sense, they are able to detect subtle changes in the pitch of high frequency echoes as they move toward objects. They use the Doppler effect, a physical principle that says the pitch of a sound rises as a person moves toward the source (Hallahan and Kauffman, 1991).

Most blind children learn to travel safely and independently. When guides are used, human guides are probably the most efficient. But human guides are not always available and a constant human guide would inevitably lead to a decrease in independence.

Teaming a properly trained dog with a blind person helps in the achievement of independent mobility. Only a small proportion of the blind population actually use a dog guide. To qualify, the individual must be over sixteen, emotionally mature, and responsible. Children do not use guide dogs. The most usual breeds used for guiding are German shepherds, Labradors, retrievers and sometimes setters, and these are too big for young children to handle. As well, the dogs are not pets and need constant grooming and care, and children are not mature enough to refrain from playing with the animal or to competently care for its needs.

Ideally, all guide dogs are placid, steady, precise animals of constant concentration, ignorant of people around them as they work with their blind owner to whom their responses are exclusively directed. But such dogs are rare, and all have idiosyncracies that must be taken into account when matching a dog with a master. Some dogs are too fast for the owner; others are too slow. The profile of Pete tells of one man's difficulties with his dogs.

The prescription cane, also called the long cane, the white cane, and the Hoover cane, is the most common travel aid used by children and adults. It essentially came from the long staff that has been the symbol of blindness at least since Roman times. The cane is made of aluminum or fibreglass and its length is determined by the user's height and comfort level. The traveller holds the cane in front, swinging it in small arcs to detect obstacles.

A wide variety of other travel aids exist. Many work on a radar principle sending out beams of ultrasound which cannot be heard by the human ear. If the beam hits an object, some of the ultrasound is reflected back to the device and converted into audible tones. For example, the Sonicguide supplies three kinds of information about an object — direction, distance, and general characteristics. The Sonicguide may be used with a long cane or a dog guide, and can be fitted into eyeglass frames. Another device is the laser cane, which transmits invisible infrared light. When it detects an obstacle, some of the light beam is reflected back to the cane, vibrating a pin beneath the user's index finger. The Mowat Sensor is a small hand-held device, light enough to be carried in the pocket or purse. It can be used to locate fallen objects, doorways, or even mailboxes (Mellor, 1981).

Profile

Pete

Pete is now twenty-seven years old. He lost his vision as the result of an accident when he was only three years of age. Pete was sent to a residential school for the elementary years but attended the local high school near his home. He is now taking his Master's degree at the university.

At school, Pete was taught to use the Hoover cane and developed excellent mobility and orientation skills. But he wanted a guide dog and as soon as he was old enough applied for one to a centre in the United States. When Pete's application was accepted, he went to the centre and worked for nearly a month with the dog selected for him, under the guidance of a highly qualified trainer. Not only did Pete learn about how the dog could assist his own mobility, but he learned how to care for the dog — to feed it properly, to groom it regularly, and to provide it with lots of exercise. After Pete brought his dog home, workers checked on both his progress and the dog's care and health.

Pete's first dog eventually grew too old to work and Pete keeps him as a beloved pet. He now has a second dog, a young Irish setter. He is, however, finding this experience a little different. The dog is young and more skittish than the first one. When people, not realizing that the dog is working, play and pet it, the dog responds. It also moves very fast and Pete has had a couple of falls. Pete is not sure he can overcome these problems and is thinking that the white cane may be more suitable for him at the moment.

The age of onset of a visual impairment does not predict the individual's ability with mobility skills (McLinden, 1988). Canes are used with young blind children to increase mobility, early exploration of the environment, and self-confidence, and to decrease dependence on others (Pogrund and Rosen, 1988). Young blind children can also be taught to use specially adapted sensing devices. These can improve the locomotion and mobility of children as young as one year (Harris et al., 1985). The infant's Sonicguide uses a headband mounting and permits obstacle detection as close as fifty centimetres. The Canterbury Child's Aid is a binaural spatial sensor that reflects objects sensed from two receiving trandsductors mounted a small distance apart on an adjustable headband. Echoes are transduced into audible sounds that are presented to the ears through small speakers or earphones. The distance of an object is coded primarily in frequency — high frequencies signify far away objects. The lower the frequency, the nearer the object (Harris et al., 1985).

A tactual map is a raised map that is used by blind persons as a supplemental aid for travel and navigation. Maps portray immediate indoor and outdoor environments, providing just enough information to support the specific movement requirements of the visually impaired person (Golledge, 1991).

Social

The care and training of blind persons made rapid advances with the return of blinded soldiers from Europe after the First World War. In 1917, a representative group of blinded soldiers and civilians met with women's organizations and businessmen and set about forming the Canadian National Institute for the Blind (CNIB) ("Canadian war blinded," 1942). Since that time, the CNIB has developed as a national voluntary service that serves more than 39 000 blind and visually impaired Canadians. The CNIB has two major objectives: to foster the integration of visually impaired Canadians into the mainstream of society and to prevent visual handicaps.

The Canadian Council of the Blind is a national organization made up of and run entirely by blind people. It is concerned with the welfare of blind individuals and maintains active committees on legislation, recreation, employment and other matters of concern to blind Canadians. The Council works in close liaison with the CNIB.

Summary

1. Visual handicaps vary widely in both degree and type. At one end of the spectrum are people who are totally blind and have no sight at all. At the other end are those with near normal vision.
2. Mild visual impairments are a high-incidence condition, while the incidence of severe visual impairment and blindness is very low. Severe visual impairment accounts for only about one percent of all disabled children.
3. At the simplest level, the human eye can be seen as consisting of three parts — the eye itself, which picks up visual messages; the optic nerve, which transfers the messages; and the brain, which interprets the messages. Images are passed through the eye and along the optic nerve to the brain by light. If anything stops or hinders the correct passage of the light, visual problems occur.
4. A huge range of causes account for visual impairment. Some impairments are the result of the villains, such as rubella, that cause many childhood handicapping conditions, while others are unique to the etiology of visual impairment.
5. All children should be screened and observed in the classroom for behavioural and physical symptoms of visual impairment. Complete eye examinations are necessary to diagnose visual acuity and functioning and to determine optical needs. In psychoeducational assessment, children with severe visual impairments are particularly difficult to assess using standard measures and procedures.
6. A severe impairment in one of the most important of the human senses affects many other areas of a child's functioning, most particularly motor and mobility skills.
7. Surgery and correction are the most common forms of medical intervention.
8. The majority of visually impaired and blind children are educated in the regular school system, often integrated into regular classrooms. For special curriculum such as mobility and orientation, they may receive additional assistance in a resource room, from an intinerant teacher, or in a segregated classroom.

SECTION 5

Behaviour Disorders

Just about every parent has, at some time or another, been frustrated and annoyed with the behaviour of his or her child. In the classroom, on an almost daily basis, every teacher confronts minor misdemeanours and unacceptable behaviours. In most cases, poor behaviours are passing and easily controlled by parent or teacher.

More intimidating are students who persistently demonstrate unacceptable classroom behaviours. These students seem intent on satisfying impulses that are incompatible with the kinds of classroom control and academic activities that the teacher has in mind. When the behaviours become chronic, excessive, and far beyond the norm expected at a certain age, they are known as behaviour disorders and the children demonstrating them are often referred to as behaviourally disordered.

The category of behaviourally disordered is of great concern to researchers, educators, and parents. That concern is reflected in a number of fundamental questions that seem to be asked more frequently today by parents, educators, the public, and the media — questions such as:

- How are behaviour disorders precisely defined?
- How many young people show behavioural disturbances?
- How do we best understand and treat behaviour problems?
- Is the prevalence of behaviour disorders on the rise?
- How likely is it that the disorders will persist in later life?

One of the most fundamental and pressing of these questions revolves around finding a precise definition of behaviour disorders. Abnormal behaviour has an obvious referrent in normal behaviour, but there is a continuum that runs from mental health to mental illness. Therefore, behaviour disorders constitute an open-ended area of deviance rather than an entity, and problems in identification occur when we try to pinpoint just where on the continuum behaviour becomes aberrant. Lack of a precise and universally accepted definition of just what a behaviour disorder is has created problems in estimating prevalence, in identifying characteristics, in assessment, in etiology, in devising treatments, and in educational approaches.

Yet it would seem that the overt behaviour disorders of children and youth would be easy to identify and define. Most of us have had some experience with children and youth that we would characterize as behaviourally disordered. These troubled children create problems for almost everyone with whom they interact. They exhibit, to a marked and prolonged extent, behaviour that is clearly undesirable, inappropriate, and maladaptive in its social context. Some behaviourally disordered children withdraw; the great majority strike out with hostility and aggression. Their behaviour affects their own learning and social interactions as well as the equilibrium of those in their environments.

Teachers are particularly concerned with children and youth displaying behaviour disorders. One of the major tasks of teaching is to establish and maintain order in the classroom, and discipline is usually the number one issue facing individuals who are responsible for any classroom, particularly if they are new teachers. In fact, research has repeatedly found that new teachers list maintaining classroom discipline and motivating students as among their greatest concerns (Veenman, 1984). In one survey (Feitler and Tokar, 1982), chronic student misbehaviour was noted as the main source of job stress by 50 percent of the respondents.

Because of this, classroom behaviour problems are the most common reason children are referred to special education; in one study (Phipps, 1982), 82 percent of the boys referred for special education were referred primarily because of their behaviour. Students with behaviour disorders have been found to be among those least preferred by regular classroom teachers, who often feel that such students should be segregated in special classes (Johnson, 1987).

Nevertheless, most students with behaviour disorders can function in regular classroom settings. Once educators understand the behavioural difficulties likely to be seen in children and youth, they may better appreciate that children with behaviour disorders are not in direct control of their deviant behaviours. Among the diversity of symptoms seen in these children runs an undercurrent of anxiety, inhibition, apprehension, depression, and overcontrol (Edelbrock, 1979). Understanding of the problems can also help teachers to formulate expectations, plan assessment strategies, and develop programs for behaviour and learning.

In this section, we address behaviour disorders that include conduct disorders, anxiety and withdrawal, delinquency, and Attention Deficit Hyperactivity Disorder. The more profound disorders of behaviour, such as childhood schizophrenia, are discussed in the chapter on pervasive developmental disorders (Chapter 14).

CHAPTER 11

Children with Behaviour Disorders

Historical Notes

Traditionally, the field of emotional disturbance (behaviour disorders) has encompassed two groups of children — those with mild and moderate conditions and those with severe and profound disabilities. When they received attention, children with severe and profound emotional handicaps were joined with the population suffering from intellectual disabilities (see Chapter 14).

Children and youth with milder behavioural disabilities gained the attention of reformers and educators in the middle decades of the nineteenth century, becoming a part of what was referred to as the child rescue movement. Child rescue advanced in tandem with the stress on free and compulsory education for all students that began in Canada in the late 1840s and became law in the 1870s. At the same time, legislation was gradually passed in the areas of child labour, family courts, juvenile courts, and children's aid societies.

The term *emotional disturbance* did not appear until 1910. Nevertheless, a plethora of terms emerged to describe children who in some way, whether intentionally or not, violated social norms. They were labelled as neglected, vagrant, delinquent, or incorrigible. In the 1880s, the term *moral imbecile* emerged to describe individuals of normal intelligence who seemed unable to conform to society's norms.

Some of the earliest care for neglected and vagrant children took the form of orphanages. From 1830 to 1860, orphanages to care for orphaned and dependent children were opened in Montreal, Kingston, Toronto, and Halifax. Other neglected, vagrant, and delinquent children roamed the streets of the larger cities, sometimes resorting to petty crimes. When apprehended, these children were routinely committed to penitentiaries and common jails along with adult offenders. Between 1835 and 1857, some 683 persons between the ages of ten and twenty were sentenced to the penitentiary (Canada, *Journals*, 1858).

By mid-century, reformers were arguing the dangers of associating children with hardened criminals. These efforts led to the establishment of reformatories in Canada East (Quebec) in 1858, Canada West (Ontario) in 1859, and Nova Scotia in 1864. In the 1870s, alternative institutions to serve neglected children were developed. In 1886, the Victoria Industrial School for Boys opened in Mimico, near Toronto. This residential institution accepted children between eight and fourteen on the principle that a change in the environment might redeem a potentially criminal personality. Across Canada, the industrial school became an important way to handle potentially delinquent youth. By the turn of the century, alternative dispositions, such as foster care, were added to industrial schools and reformatories.

In 1893 new legislation led to the formation of the first children's aid societies. At the same time, compulsory education laws meant that schooling became a social norm for all children and that the schools were forced to find ways to accommodate students who were unruly, recalcitrant, or truant.

The solution was the establishment of segregated classrooms within the public schools where children could obtain special instruction and where they would not disrupt other pupils or take a teacher's time. The first segregated classes in the public schools, called unruly classes, opened in the 1880s to handle students with what are now called behaviour disorders. By 1920, segregated special classes were a permanent feature of most urban school systems. These classes remained the most important vehicle for providing services to children and youth with behaviour disorders into the 1960s. But as time passed, more of these children were placed in classes for the mentally retarded, the brain injured, or the severely and profoundly disturbed. With segregated classes, placements in reformatories, industrial (training) schools, and institutions remained important.

Very often, school exclusion, expulsion, or suspension was the last solution to a behaviourally disordered pupil. Into the first half of the twentieth century, the courts typically found that disruptive and mentally retarded children could be excluded from the schools for the sake of preserving order, protecting the teacher's time from excessive demands, and sparing children the pain of seeing others who were disabled.

Segregated settings persisted until the late 1960s and early 1970s when a number of provincial and national reports on education stressed the need for expanded and more effective educational services for behaviourally disordered children. Some of these reports — the Commission on Emotional and Learning Disorders in Children (Roberts and Lazure, 1970); the Standards for Education of Exceptional Children in Canada (Hardy et al., 1971); and Children in Canada Residential Care (Csapo, 1981a, b) — urged the federal and provincial governments to assume responsibility for the education of all behaviourally disordered children. They also asked local education authorities to provide educational services for all children within their jurisdictions (Csapo, 1981 a).

The provision of service for students with behaviour disorders developed rapidly. In 1969, for example, a survey of British Columbia schools (Laycock and Findlay, 1969) found that 65 percent of school districts had no definite policy concerning the education of behaviourally disordered children. By 1981, 17 percent of districts provided classes for autistic children, 75 percent had rehabilitation classes, 49 percent had classes for the severely handicapped, and 14 percent had classes for mildly disturbed children (Csapo, 1981b). Currently, the intensity and breadth of services for behaviourally disordered students varies, with each province clearly attempting to arrive at its own individual solutions. But despite the increasing focus on their special problems, Kauffman (1987) still feels that behaviourally disordered children are the most underserved within all of special education.

Children and adolescents with behaviour disorders are not rare, and most of us have come into contact with or observed such young people. These disturbing, different, and disapproving individuals test the limits of our society in ways that challenge the wisdom of convention. They are often harmful and destructive in their actions, and they never permit us to rest comfortably in our routines (Wood, 1982). These students are some of the most difficult to handle, and they lack the appeal that others have. They frequently withdraw from proferred help or reject it outright.

Special education for students with behaviour disorders is a fairly modern development. Not until the 1950s did special education for mildly and moderately disturbed children and youth really emerge, and even today it is, in many ways, both confused and confusing. Terminology is inconsistent and much dissatisfaction exists with current definitions (Hallahan and Kauffman, 1991). Treatment regimes and interventions vary. The majority of current intervention practices, administrative arrangements, and teacher training programs have been developed with younger children in mind, and most special programs for behaviourally disordered children are found in elementary schools. Fewer provisions have been made for disturbed students at secondary levels.

The two most common behaviours exhibited by behaviourally disordered students are aggressive acting-out behaviour and social withdrawal (Heward and Orlansky, 1992). In the classroom, aggressive, acting-out, and disruptive children are unlikely to escape attention. Such youngsters challenge and frustrate teachers, disrupt classrooms and hinder the achievement of everyone in the environment. Behavioural excesses include physical and verbal aggression, defiance, temper tantrums, lying, swearing, stealing and disrupting the classroom. Anxious and withdrawn children are more likely to be overlooked at the outset, but most teachers will quickly respond to their unusual patterns of behaviour.

No single approach suits each child with a behaviour disorder, and the approach that works today may not work tomorrow. Teachers employ various methods of discipline and management. They combine these with teaching children specific prosocial behaviours through methods such as modelling, shaping, coaching, and cognitive problem-solving skill development (Gresham, 1986; Hollinger, 1987), and prompt children to engage in interactions and role playing. Teachers also attempt to change the attitudes of normally developing children toward their disabled peers through role playing, peer tutoring, and reinforcement.

Development of the Field

Although a specific category of emotionally disturbed or behaviourally disordered did not appear in the lexicon of the nineteenth century, much interest was directed toward children labelled as deviant, dependent, delinquent, neglected, vagrant, incorrigible, and so on. Generally, this came from legal, correctional, and social welfare systems, rather than from the education or medical establishments.

During the early 1900s, Freud and others promoted the idea that deviant behaviour could be explained in terms of subconscious phenomena and inner turmoil. Until the 1960s, students with behaviour disorders were chiefly the concern of psychiatrists. During the 1960s, a radically different approach to treatment was developed by the behaviourist school of psychology. It postulated that disordered behaviour has no innate or underlying cause but is specific to situations and can be learned. Further supplementing studies of behavioural disorders in children was research into organic and genetic causes, the development of the humanistic model in psychology, and research into social psychology, with its emphasis on cultural influences on behaviour (Newcomer, 1980).

Today, special education for behaviour disorders includes a broad range of intervention practices. The central role played by psychoanalytic theory and behavioural principles in offering hypotheses and prescribing treatment has been replaced by social learning and cognitive theory. Some theorists stress ecological approaches and attribute disturbed behaviour to poor interactions between the child and the environment.

Definitions of Behaviour Disorders

The original term for behaviour disorders, *emotionally disturbed*, first appeared in the literature about eighty years ago without being defined (Reinert, 1980). Although numerous definitions of this complex condition have emerged in the intervening years, no universally accepted definition of behaviour disorders currently exists. Deviant behaviour is defined and conceptualized in many ways, and definitions proposed come from a variety of perspectives and disciplines.

The study and treatment of behaviour disorders has historically been the domain of clinical psychologists, researchers specializing in abnormal psychology, and psychiatrists. From a psychological perspective, the field of behaviour disorders is known as *developmental psychopathology*, defined as "the study of clinical dysfunction in the context of maturational and developmental processes" (Kazdin, 1989, p. 180). *Clinical dysfunction* refers to psychological problems that have a serious impact on everyday functioning.

Clinical researchers have attempted to define disturbed child populations; others have focused on defining the disturbed behaviour; to still others, "behaviour disorders" is not a condition but a label, a subjective appraisal by the beholder. Even among educators, we find definitional confusion. Definitions may variously reflect administrative arrangements, describe observed in-class behaviour, describe the child as disabled, specify deficiencies in certain areas of behaviour, or focus on the interaction between pupil and teacher (Csapo, 1981c).

Many factors contribute to the difficulties in defining behaviour disorders:

- There is not a single symptom that is common to all pupils who are behaviourally disordered, or even to a subgroup of these children, because there is no such thing as a typical behaviourally disordered student.
- Behavioural deviance necessarily has a referrent in normal behaviour. But human emotions and behaviour are so varied that a precise notion of normalcy is difficult to derive. Lack of an adequate definition of mental health makes behaviour disorders an open-ended category of deviance.
- If we cannot define normalcy, then it is difficult to define behaviour disorders. All behaviour disorders are abnormal in the sense that abnormal means away from the norm and behaviour disorders are deviations from average or standard behaviour. Any deviation in behaviour should, however, be viewed along a continuum from normal to markedly abnormal. But it is very hard to draw a line between serious behaviour disorders and problematic behaviour that is fairly common in childhood.
- Behaviour disorders cannot be measured quantitatively. We have no instruments to determine a mental health quotient analogous to the IQ test.
- Varying behaviours are exhibited by all children. Deviant and unusual behaviours may exist in the repertoires of normal children, usually as transient outlets for tension. At the same time, disturbed children may sometimes behave quite normally. Distinctions between normal and disturbed behaviour are generally in the amount or degree rather than in kind. Children with behaviour disorders perform certain behaviours too often or too intensely, or not often or intensely enough, but specifying this amount and degree is difficult.
- The patterns of behaviour exhibited by disordered children are often unpredictable and subtle, rendering their conditions even harder to define. Children with behav-

iour disorders are likely to display a wide variety of inappropriate behaviours which may or may not be associated with particular situations. In some children, for example, a certain subject in school or a specific object will trigger an anxiety attack.

- The behaviour problems change as children grow older. Four-year-olds may disobey their parents; as teenagers, they may engage in vandalism and delinquency.
- Varying professional perspectives exist. Many disciplines work with behaviourally disordered children, each with its own theories concerning the causes, definitions, and treatment of the disabilities.
- Legal and educational terms differ, and while the educational and the legal system are not at odds, their perspectives and their solutions may be different. *Delinquency* is a legal term applied by the criminal justice system to indicate that a youth has been adjudicated by the courts and found guilty of criminal behaviour. The educational term, *antisocial behaviour*, is less restrictive than *delinquency* because it includes behaviours that are norm violating but not necessarily delinquent (Nelson et al., 1991).
- Social and cultural expectations differ. Behaviour disorders occur among the rich, the poor, the gifted, the intellectually disabled, and members of all racial and ethnic groups. There are, however, varying reactions to certain behaviours. Deviance is defined by social groups that recognize some behaviours as infractions of the rules and label as deviant persons who do not conform to these socially defined rules. Minority group children, for example, may bring to school different skills, different expectations, and different competencies than those valued by the dominant culture. Behaviour considered normal and adaptive in a subculture may be looked upon as deviant or inadequate by members of the dominant group (Hallahan and Kauffman, 1991).

The expectations of teachers play a key role in defining behaviour disorders.

- Children rarely decide for themselves that they are behaviourally disordered; that determination is made by teachers and parents. But to some degree at least, behaviour disorders correlate with teacher tolerance levels, and varying teacher tolerance levels of special behaviours result in a high degree of variability in the teacher decision-making process (Shinn, Tindel, and Spera, 1987).
- There is often a relationship between behaviour disorders and other disabling conditions. For example, some children with intellectual disabilities also manifest behaviour disorders. In an early study of hearing-impaired children (Schlesinger and Meadow, 1972), researchers found five times as many children with severe emotional disturbance and three times as many with moderate disturbance as they found among hearing students. As discussed in Chapter 7, many learning-disabled students develop an overlay of emotional problems that compound their learning difficulties and conceal their primary disorder.

Of the many definitions of behaviour disorders currently available, the one proposed by James M. Kauffman (1991a) is particularly relevant from an educational point of view. Kauffman notes that

> children with behaviour disorders are those who chronically and markedly respond to their environments in socially unacceptable and/or personally unsatisfying ways but who can be taught more socially acceptable and personally gratifying behaviour. Children with mild and moderate behaviour disorders can be taught effectively with their normal peers (if their teachers receive appropriate consultative help) or in special resource or self-contained classes with reasonable hope of quick reintegration with their normal peers.

This definition focuses on behaviours that are inconsistent with current societal standards and ones that are personally unsatisfactory. Kauffman recommends specific educational settings and maintains a positive outlook for the children's success through appropriate educational intervention. In addition, the definition pinpoints elements that are important in identifying behaviourally disordered children and that are shared by many current definitions. Generally, we can say that the behaviour of students with behaviour disorders exhibits the following characteristics:

- It deviates in an extreme way from the norm.
- It recurs chronically. The chronic nature of the behaviour is one differentiating factor. In children with behaviour disorders, the behaviours are not transient and episodic; rather, they last six months or longer, and interfere with expected age-appropriate functioning (Paul, 1987).

  In normally developing children, behaviour problems fluctuate and decline as children get older and are not necessarily signs of clinical deviance. Lying in children, for example, is reported to be a problem for the majority (53 percent) of six-year-old boys; by the age of ten, lying decreases to 10 percent of boys. In girls, the pattern is more dramatic with a high rate (about 48 percent) at age six and no lying reported as a problem at age eleven (see Kazdin, 1989). In children with behavioural disorders, the problems do not decline and problem behaviours are demonstrated far more often or far more intensely, or not age appropriately.
- It violates social or cultural expectations. This is an important criterion. Too often, a student's linguistic and cultural background is perceived as a handicap and he or she is then diagnosed and treated as learning disabled or behaviourally disordered.
- It affects a child's self-esteem, interpersonal relationships, and probably school achievements.
- It requires special education intervention.

Terminology

Many areas of special education have seen evolving terminology over the years. Traditionally, children and youth with behaviour disorders were described by a variety of names, largely arising from a psychiatric base, that included neurotic, psychotic, obsessive, and emotionally disturbed. While current educators prefer to dispense with psychiatric terms, they still debate whether to call these children emotionally disturbed, behaviourally disordered, socially maladjusted, deviant, psychologically impaired, educationally handicapped, character disordered, or delinquent.

In the past, the general category of behaviour disorders was referred to as emotional disturbance, with two severity levels differentiated. Children with milder conditions were referred to as mildly emotionally disturbed; those with serious problems, such as infantile autism and childhood schizophrenia, as seriously or profoundly emotionally disturbed. For those with milder disorders, professionals today opt for behaviour disorders because this focuses on the most obvious problems of this population (Huntze, 1985). Some suggest that the term *children in conflict* is more appropriate (Reinert and Huang, 1987).

Classification of Behaviour Disorders

Meaningful classifications of children's behavioural problems have only recently begun to emerge from research (Hallahan and Kauffman, 1991). Still, no consensus exists regarding the classification of these disorders into types and degrees of deviance. Problems in classification concern not only how and what to classify but the value of any classification system at all. Critics argue that present classification systems do not include enough relevant data about a child's personality components for the selection of appropriate treatment strategies and that current systems also fail to offer comparable information about different patients on a common set of components (Cummings and Finger, 1980).

Clinical Classification

The principal modern clinical classification scheme is that provided by the American Psychiatric Association (APA) in its *Diagnostic and Statistical Manual of Mental Disorders* (*DSM 111-R*, 1987, *DSM 1V*, 1992). DSM is a clinical manual that describes behavioural symptoms of all disorders currently recognized by the APA and defines the symptoms and signs required for the diagnosis of each disorder. The problem with the DSM classification is that disorders are judged as either present or absent, not evaluated on a continuum.

Classification by Severity

The major alternatives to the DSM model are based on two principles. First, individual differences can be defined as deviations from the norm. Classification is not an either-or proposition; rather it is based on how much behaviour differs from what is considered normal. Second, behaviours overlap to form a syndrome or cluster that contributes to a specific condition. For example, Attention Deficit Hyperactivity Disorder is characterized by clusters of behaviours that fall into three groupings — inattention, impulsivity, and hyperactivity. When behaviours are defined as deviations from the norm, they are classified in terms of the severity of their condition — mild, moderate, severe, or profound.

Dimensional Classification

When groupings or clusters of specific behaviours are used, we have a dimensional classification system. It is usually derived from observer descriptions of deviant behaviour, which are then clustered into groupings using the statistical procedure of factor analysis.

Perhaps the most widely used dimensional system is that of Quay and his colleagues (1972, 1986), who used behaviour ratings by teachers and parents, children's life history characteristics, and children's questionnnaire responses to statistically derive six behavioural dimensions, starting with conduct disorders, anxiety and withdrawal, socialized aggression, and immaturity/attention problems. Quay's fifth category of motor excess refers to states where a child is restless, unable to sit still, tense, unable to relax, and overtalkative. The sixth dimension includes those children who display psychotic behaviour — those who express far-fetched ideas, have repetitive speech, and show bizarre behaviour.

Dimensions similar to those of Quay have been found with remarkable consistency in many samples of children. For example, McDermott (1980, 1981) used the Bristol Social Adjustment Guides (Stott, 1979) which provide ratings on a hundred statements about children's behaviour. When the data from more than 900 teachers who observed and rated the behaviour of 2527 Canadian school children were analyzed, major dimensions similar to those discovered by Quay and other researchers were found.

The dimensional classification provides a relatively reliable basis for description. We discuss the behavioural components later in this chapter when we look at the characteristics of children with behaviour disorders (excepting psychotic behaviour, which is discussed in Chapter 14).

Prevalence of Behaviour Disorders

In ever increasing numbers, children are being identified as behaviourally disordered. Recent data (Schwaen-Kowalchuk and Roadhouse, 1990) suggest that the incidence of hyperaggressive, undercontrolled behaviour has increased dramatically during the past few decades. However, estimates of the prevalence of behaviour disorders vary tremendously, chiefly because of the lack of a clear and precise definitional construct. Table 11-1 presents numbers from provinces that adhere to a categorical approach as well as the percentages of the total school age population and the population of exceptional students. The variance is obvious. It does not mean that more children in Quebec suffer behaviour disorders but does mean that different definitions are used across the country. Moreover, these numbers are low. The best available research data indicate that 6 to 10 percent of the school-aged population exhibit serious and persistent behaviour problems (Kauffman, 1989; Kazdin, 1989). As well, disruptive behaviour is

Table 11-1

Prevalence of behaviour disorders

	School population	Exceptional population	Behaviourally disordered	Percentage of total	Percentage of exceptional population
Nova Scotia	169 581	18 822	747	.044	3.96
Quebec	943 652	126 417	13 722	1.45	10.85
Ontario	1 796 244	136 356	8 104	.045	5.94
Saskatchewan	204 097	6 016	548	.026	9.10
BC	514 464	606 624	2 578	.50	0.42

Source: Canadian CEC (1989)

often in the eye of the beholder, and any individual's interpretation of a situation is precariously subjective. Teachers place different demands on students depending on their own behaviour standards and the degree to which they are accepting of specific maladaptive behaviours. Students regarded as disruptive by one teacher may be ignored by another; rules might be enforced by one teacher but not by another.

Parents and teachers tend to describe 20 to 30 percent of children at any given age as "having problems" (e.g., Rich, 1982); they see 10 to 15 percent of children as in need of professional assistance for behavioural problems (Wood, 1982). Mothers typically report high frequencies of behaviour problems in their children. In one early study (Lapouse and Monk, 1958), mothers of a representative sample of children aged six to twelve in Buffalo, New York, reported that 49 percent of their children were overactive, 48 percent lost their tempers twice weekly, 28 percent experienced nightmares, and 10 percent wet their beds. Among school children, a longitudinal study of a large sample (see Balow, 1979) found that the individuals identified as "having problems" varied from year to year. After six years of schooling, almost 60 percent of the sampled children had been identified as a problem by at least one teacher. Other surveys have indicated that anywhere from 0.10 to 40 percent of children may be considered behaviourally disordered, depending on the age of the children, the criteria used (Balow, 1979; Morse, 1975), and the level of severity focused upon.

The vast majority of children identified as behaviourally disordered fall into the mild and moderate categories. Boys exhibit more behavioural deviance than girls, including learning difficulties, hyperactivity, bed wetting, and antisocial behaviour (Wicks-Nelson and Israel, 1991); they outnumber girls by at least two to one in every classification from mild through profound (Kelly, Bullock, and Dykes, 1977; Reinert, 1976). First-born males are more likely than later-borns to exhibit behaviour disorders and to be rated by teachers as anxious and aggressive toward their peers (Lahey et al.,1980).

Many children with behaviour disorders come to the attention of professionals in the middle childhood and early teen years (Kneedler, 1984). The prevalence of behaviour disorders is low in the beginning grades, reaches a peak in the middle grades, and begins to fall off in junior high.

Children from lower socio-economic levels are also more likely to be regarded as problems. There is a higher prevalence of aggressive behaviours among lower-class children as opposed to those from the middle and upper classes (Hallahan and Kauffman, 1991), and a higher proportion of those identified as behaviourally disordered are from minority groups (Rich, 1982).

Etiology of Behaviour Disorders

Psychiatrists, psychologists, and educators have traditionally placed great emphasis on identifying the causes of behavioural disorders in children, hoping that an understanding of the origins of the disorders would lead directly to their treatment and cure. Despite a vast amount of research, investigators still do not fully understand the causes of any type of psychopathology, and there exists no empirical evidence linking behavioural disorders to any specific causes. Deviant behaviour usually involves the interaction of several factors rather than a single cause. Each additional variable increases the risk of behaviour disorders, and the risk is greater when several factors combine (Rutter, 1990).

Most major developmental theories have been used to explain behaviour dysfunctions, and etiology is closely linked to the conceptual models that have emerged. As conceptual models tend to represent the different theoretical orientations of different disciplines, they differ considerably in the importance they attach to finding the causes of disturbance. The psychodynamic model, for example, focuses almost exclusively on causation while the behavioural model is concerned with the outward manifestations of deviancy. Table 11-2 presents an overview of the models.

Table 11-2

Conceptual models in the area of behaviour disorders

Approach	Assumption
Biophysical	Behavioural difficulties arise directly from constitutional, genetic, neurological, or biochemical problems. Disease, malnutrition, and substance abuse are included here.
Psychodynamic	Deviant behaviour is determined by past experiences; students with behaviour disorders are suffering inner turmoil; they can be helped by being made aware of their feelings and how to deal with them.
Psycho-educational	An eclectic approach that sees behaviour as having various causes. Focuses on academic achievement with therapy and counselling to seek the roots of the problems.
Behavioural	Emotional or behavioural deviance is the definable consequence of either mislearning or restricted learning. Normal, healthy and desirable behaviours may be acquired to supplement or replace undesirable behaviours by consistently applying established behavioural principles of learning.
Ecological	Behaviour disorders are a function of the reciprocity between the child and the environment; that is, problems are the result of agitated transactions between the child and those in the environment.
Psychosocial	Can be seen as part of an ecological model although the focus is on the child's relationship to family, peers, and others in the environment.
Holistic	Behaviour disorders have diverse etiologies that interact with each other.

Biophysical Model

A biophysical approach holds that behaviour disorders can be traced to biological causes. Some evidence suggests that certain biological factors — genetic conditions, constitutional conditions, prenatal and birth factors, and environmental hazards — increase the risk of behaviour disorders. However, information about the relationship between biophysical factors and behaviour disorders is scarce.

Geneticists maintain that no genes directly determine behaviour. Nevertheless, some genes do determine enzymatic and biochemical functions that, in turn, can have both major and subtle behavioural effects. Some very specific genetic defects may cause dramatically disturbed behavioural functioning. Children with untreated PKU, for example, often show deviant behaviour along with mental retardation.

From another line of genetic research, we know that temperaments are inherited, and temperamentally difficult children are more likely to become antisocial adolescents and adults (Baum, 1989). Boys and girls who were moody and ill-tempered at age ten tend to be ill-tempered young adults whose relations with their spouses and children are generally unpleasant and conflictual (Caspi, Elder, and Bern, 1987). Twin studies further suggest that heredity is involved in behaviour disorders, but little is known about the mechanisms.

Further, mounting evidence suggests the possibility of a relationship between behaviour disorders and neurological disturbances. The exact relationship between brain damage and behaviour disorders, however, continues to baffle researchers, who point out that "the evidence linking behavioural characteristics to brain dysfunction is circumstantial, speculative, and in most cases clearly not documentable" (Smith and Robinson, 1986, p. 223). Neurological causes are generally more evident among severely and profoundly disturbed children than among children with mild and moderate disorders. Even though there appears to be a link in some cases, most behaviour disorders are not caused by brain dysfunction and many children with brain disorders do not show behavioural disturbances (Werry, 1979).

As well as genetic problems and neurological disturbances, disease, malnutrition, and brain trauma may predispose children to develop emotional problems (Baumeister, Kupstas, and Klindworth, 1990; Lozoff, 1989). Substance abuse can also lead to serious emotional and behavioural problems (Newcomb and Bentler, 1989).

Despite accumulating evidence of some biophysical correlates of behaviour disorders, researchers remain wary. For one thing, it is rarely possible to demonstrate a relationship between a behaviour disorder and a specific biological factor. For another, medical models assume a qualitative difference between normal and abnormal. When clinicians apply a medical model to psychological disorders, they assume that the disorders have distinct patterns of symptoms and signs, that they result from different disease entities and causes, and that they respond to different treatments (Kovaks, 1989). But biology is hardly destiny, and social influences combine with biological predispositions to shape behaviour. When a biophysical condition does exist, environmental factors probably combine with it to trigger behavioural disorders.

Psychodynamic Model

The psychodynamic model and approaches originated with Sigmund Freud in the early 1900s and continue to exert a strong and persuasive influence on the terminology, definitions, and taxonomies of behaviour disorders.

While it is an extremely complex theory, essentially a psychodynamic approach is concerned with the development of and interaction among the intrapsychic (mental) processes believed to underlie human behaviour. It attempts to locate the origins of behaviour within the context of psychological developments. According to this model, behaviour disorders are observable symptoms reflecting inner turmoil created by abnormal intrapsychic processes.

Psycho-Educational Model

Advocates of the psycho-educational model agree that children with behaviour disorders may have dealt unsucessfully with developmental problems. While efforts are made to discover why children demonstrate deviant behaviour, a psycho-educational model simultaneously lays stress on the acquisition of academic and daily living skills.

Behavioural Model

Early twentieth-century investigations of reflexive and voluntary behaviour, arising particularly from the work of Ivan Pavlov and J. B. Watson, laid the groundwork for modern behavioural psychology. Bolstered by B.F. Skinner's principles of operant conditioning, the behavioural model has exerted a profound influence on psychotherapy, counselling, education, and special education (Cullinan and Epstein, 1982).

While the behavioural model includes a number of theories and points of view about human behaviour, two points most clearly define it. First is the assumption that behaviour — including deviant behaviour — is acquired and is regulated by certain experimentally identified principles of learning. Secondly, the behavioural model has a commitment to scientific methods of studying behaviour and behaviour change (Powers and Franks, 1988).

Behaviourists believe that all behaviour is learned and that behaviour disorders represent inappropriate learning. In general, behaviourists do not define and classify behaviour disorders; instead, they try to understand their origins by observing the relationship among the complex environmental factors that elicit and support deviant behaviour. They describe and measure deviant behaviour and note the conditions under which it occurs. By changing these conditions, they attempt to extinguish the undesirable behaviours and shape appropriate responses.

Ecological Model

Ecology refers to the overall pattern of relationships involving an organism and its environment (ecosystem) (Cullinan, Epstein, and Lloyd, 1991). Recently, educators of students with behaviour disorders have begun to examine the ecological concepts used in anthropology, ethnology, psychology, sociology, and other disciplines.

From an ecological point of view, problem behaviour does not simply reflect inappropriate action by the student; rather it is influenced by undesirable interactions and transactions between the student and others. That is, the behaviour disorders of children and youth arise when there are disturbances in the "goodness-of-fit" between a child and the ecosystem (Cullinan, Epstein, and Lloyd, 1991). Some characteristics of a child (usually the behaviour) agitate the ecosystem and the ecosystem responds in ways that lead the child to provoke further agitation. For example, a student's temper tantrums in school might be the problem of concern, but from an ecological perspective, the behaviour of the student's teachers, peers, and parents — their expectations, demands, and reactions to the tantrums — must also be taken into consideration (Kauffman, 1985).

The ecological approach reduces the danger of assuming that behavioural problems reside wholly within the child. It may be that the environment is not providing the necessary supports to enable the child to progress in adaptive development. In order to overcome the disturbance in the interaction between child and environment, changes may need to be made in both.

Psychosocial Model

The psychosocial model focuses both on the family and on extra-familial influences, those agencies outside the family that influence a child's cognitive, social, and emotional development. Three important extra-familial agents of socialization are schools, peer groups, and television. While the effect is not very large, critics have concluded that there is a significant cause-and-effect relationship between television violence and aggressive behaviour (Friedrich-Cofer and Huston, 1986).

Research Notes

The influence of television

In this electronic age, children face external influences as great as school has ever been — probably greater. Of all extra-familial influences on young children, television may be the most vital.

Television was introduced in 1939 when President F.D. Roosevelt broadcast the first transmission at the New York World's Fair. In the 1950s, TV permeated the market. Since then, researchers, parents, teachers, and legislators have debated the effects of television on children. Concerns centre on the impact of television on children's reading skills and attention levels and, most importantly, on the influence of media violence on the development of aggression.

Eighty percent of all prime time television programs contain at least one incident of physical violence. On average, prime time programs portray 7.5 violent acts an hour (Gerbner et al., 1980). With the high rate of violence that characterizes so much contemporary programming, child viewers are consistently exposed to examples of antisocial behaviour. "It would be absurd," wrote Howe (1977) "to deny that television does provide children and adults with the information and ideas that can affect the form and content of activities of an anti-social or criminal nature. Any medium by which information about the world is communicated can have this function" (p. 72).

Until quite recently, researchers would not state a definite connection between television violence and aggressive behaviour in children. However, a growing body of empirical data supports a relationship between aggression and violence viewing (Rule and Ferguson, 1986). Studies report that the viewing of violent programs, even cartoons, can lead to an increase in aggressive behaviour (Murray, 1984). Children who initially tend to be high in agggression seek out violent programming and respond to it with greater aggression.

In most homes, youngsters begin watching television at approximately one and a half to two years of age (Hapkewitz, 1979). Between the ages of three and eleven, Canadian children watch about three to four hours of television a day. The time increases gradually until about age twelve, then declines somewhat during adolescence (Murray, 1980). While the amount of viewing varies among households, Canadian children watch an average of twenty hours of television a week. This means that from kindergarten to grade twelve, the typical student will spend about 12 000 hours in front of the television set (Gage and Berliner, 1984).

The age of children at the time of viewing is crucial in developing aggressive attitudes. Leonard Eron (1982) suggests that children increase their viewing of violence up to the third grade, and then start to decrease it. However, the strongest relations between television violence and both simultaneous and later aggression have been reported for children in the eight- to twelve-year-old range (Eron, 1982). Eron (1982) speculates that because aggressive children tend to be unpopular they spend more time watching television. The violence they see then serves to reassure them of the appropriateness of their behaviour while teaching them new coercive techniques. A steady diet of violent programming may convince a child that the outside world is a violent place inhabited by people who rely on aggressive strategies to solve conflicts. One research team (Eron et al., 1983) looked at seven- to nine-year-old boys and girls who were judged to be highly aggressive by their peers. These children not only preferred violent programming but believed that violent shows were an accurate portrayal of everyday life.

Television programs also tend to maximize violent incidents and stress the impersonal nature of crime. Viewing violence may not only arouse emotions associated with aggressive thoughts, but at the same time may reduce emotional reactions to the negative consequences of aggression for the victim (Rule and Ferguson, 1986).

Not only is television a likely cause of aggressive behaviours in children, but the effects are long-lasting (Eron, 1982). Leonard Eron and Rowell Huesmann (1987) conducted a longitudinal study that followed subjects for twenty-two years. They found that television viewing habits measured in children related to aggressive behaviour in adulthood, probably because continued viewing of aggressive programs contributes to the development of certain attitudes and norms of behaviour and teaches youngsters ways of solving interpersonal problems that stay with them over the years. Moreover, continued exposure to television violence encourages children to become aggressive and to choose more aggressive programs. In the study it was found that the more violent the programs the children watched at age eight, the more aggressive they were at age nineteen, the more serious were the crimes for which they were convicted at age thirty, the more aggressive was their behaviour while under the influence of alcohol, and the harsher was the punishment of their own children (Eron and Huesmann, 1987).

The family is universally recognized as a fundamental influence on child behaviour. The family structure establishes the norms of behaviour and teaches, explicitly and implicitly, social, moral and psychological lessons to the developing child.

Research and theory that focus on family patterns as possible sources of behaviour disorders find that family conditions may predispose a child to develop behaviour disorders or precipitate maladaptive behaviours. Predisposing conditions include maladaptive families characterized by harsh discipline, little parental involvement with the child, and poor monitoring and supervision of the child's activities. Precipitating factors are an immediate stress or incident such as divorce, separation, or the chronic illness of one or both parents.

Parental attitudes and child-rearing techniques are often critical in the development of aggressive behaviour, and there seems to be a high degree of intergenerational similarity for antisocial behaviour (Farrington, 1987). Children in aggressive families are more likely to be aggressive and, in turn, their children are more likely to be aggressive (Huessman et al., 1984). As a predictor of an antisocial adult personality, having an antisocial parent places the child at significant risk for antisocial behaviour; having two antisocial parents puts the child at even greater risk (Robins and Earls, 1985). Patterson and Banks (1989), who investigated the paths that children at risk follow in their acquisition of delinquency, argue that a sequence of aggressive behaviour begins with incompetent and harsh parenting. This leads to an antisocial behaviour pattern that, in turn, is associated with school failure, peer rejection, membership in a deviant peer group, and ultimate socialization into a delinquency subculture.

Holistic Model

The holistic approach attempts to encompass many of the others. In a holistic view, the behaviour disorder is perceived as essentially an indivisible phenomenon that is more than just the sum of its separate parts (Cullinan, Epstein, and Lloyd, 1991). This approach recognizes that the etiology of inappropriate behaviours may be illness, childhood traumas, poor relations with others, inappropriate learning, problems in socialization, or any combination of these.

Characteristics of Children with Behaviour Disorders

Children with behaviour disorders exhibit a spectrum of behaviours ranging from disruptive and cantankerous outbursts to severe withdrawal from social interaction. Over a hundred different characteristics have been attributed to behaviourally disordered children and youth. Table 11-3 lists the most common characteristics and behaviours of disordered children, grouped within the dimensional classification system. Keep in mind that all children demonstrate some of these traits at one time or another; they only become problems when they occur chronically, acutely, and in tandem. It should also be noted that even though these children are categorized on different dimensions there is considerable overlap between groupings, especially between conduct disorders and socialized aggression and between immaturity and anxious and withdrawn. In addition, the problems of attention deficits may be seen in a number of populations of disabled learners.

Regardless of dimensional distinctions, children with behaviour disorders tend to demonstrate some common characteristics. In general terms, it can be said that they exhibit poor socialization, poor social competence, and poor social skills.

While temper tantrums in preschoolers are expected, the same type of behaviour in an older child may indicate a conduct disorder.

Table 11-3

Some behaviours seen in children and youth with behaviour disorders

Conduct disordered

- Fighting, hitting, assaults
- Destructive behaviour
- Impertinence and impudence
- Attention seeking
- Unco-operative and negative behaviour
- Hyperactivity
- Poor relationships with others
- Distractible, short attention span, and less task oriented than other children
- Lags in all academic areas, especially reading

Socialized aggressive

- Assaultive
- Delinquent activity
- Gang vandalism
- Destructive, disobedient, hostile, truant
- Lying
- Substance abuse
- Verbally abusive
- Sexually precocious

Anxious and withdrawn

- Anxious, fearful, shy, timid, tense and withdrawn
- Depressed and sad
- Self-conscious and hypersensitive
- Cries frequently
- Short attention span
- Poor self-esteem that affects interpersonsal relationships and academic achievement

Immature

- Clumsy
- Easily frustrated
- Poor in initiative
- Passive
- Messy
- Short attention span
- Socially inadequate

Motor excess

- Overtalkative
- Unable to relax
- Accelerated rates of motor movement
- Short attention span
- Impulsivity
- Distractibility

Socialization is the means by which individuals become reasonably acceptable and competent members of their society. Through socialization, children acquire the discipline and the skills, the knowledge, the ambitions, and the empathy for those around them that allow them to participate in the life of the family and later the school and the community (Winzer, 1995). **Social competence**, "the ability of children to successfully and appropriately select and carry out their interpersonal goals" (Guralnick, 1990, p. 4), includes the development of meaningful and productive relationships with peers, social and communication development, degrees of independence, and other factors that may contribute to becoming socially acceptable. Socially competent individuals perform behaviours that they believe will effect rewarding outcomes and avoid acting in ways that might cause negative outcomes (Schunk, 1987). **Social skills** are "those responses which within a given situation prove effective; or ... maximize the probability of producing, maintaining, or enhancing the positive effects for the interactor" (Foster and Richey, 1979, p. 626).

In more specific terms, children with behaviour disorders

- show an inability to learn that cannot be explained by intellectual, sensory, or health problems;
- demonstrate behaviours that do not compare favourably with those manifested by normal children;
- exhibit inappropriate types of behaviours or feelings under normal conditions;
- exhibit behaviours that are generally unacceptable to the child, to normal peers, and to adults;
- exhibit a comparatively high number of problem behaviours;
- show behaviours that interfere with their expected performance relative to chronological age;
- continue and even increase the behaviours unless structured and systematic intervention occurs;
- show an inability to build or maintain satisfactory interpersonal relationships with peers and teachers;
- show a tendency to develop physical symptoms, pains, or fears associated with personal or school problems.

Conduct Disorders

Conduct disorders is the term used to describe hyperaggressive and highly disruptive children, who form the major portion of those identified in the schools as behaviourally disordered. These students exhibit **antisocial behaviour**, which refers to overt, aggressive, disruptive behaviour, or to covert antisocial acts that are repeated infractions of socially prescribed behaviour patterns and that violate social norms and the rights of others (Kauffman, 1989; Loeber, 1985).

Teachers of behaviourally disordered children must be able to tolerate unpleasantness and rejection without being counteraggressive and reciprocally unpleasant.

Students with conduct disorders refuse to comply with requests, school rules, and the conventional limits of behaviour. They display problem behaviours that are acute, chronic, and characterized by various forms of aggression such as hitting, biting, and kicking. These students frequently suffer low self-esteem and poor self-concept which may manifest in numerous other deviant behaviours, including dependency, crying, and whining (Walker, 1983).

Children with conduct disorders have failed to develop reliable internal inner controls; their behaviour is impulsive, distractible, hyperactive, and disruptive. They have short attention spans and sometimes seem not to know right from wrong. Their behaviour is not age-appropriate. For example, temper tantrums are common among two- and three-year-olds as these young children strive toward independence. Among normal children, unfocused temper tantrums diminish during the pre-school period and are uncommon after age four (Hartup, 1974). In behaviourally disordered children, tantrums are more likely to continue; a twelve-year-old throwing a temper tantrum is demonstrating clearly inappropriate behaviour.

Aggression is one of the most overt manifestations of conduct disorders. **Aggression**, which may be defined as any form of behaviour designed to harm or injure another living being who is motivated to avoid such treatment (Baron and Byrne, 1981), is of more concern to teachers than any other behaviour disorder. The precursors, development, and outcomes of childhood aggression are discussed in the Research Notes below.

Most children become more aggressive as they develop. They use aggressive behaviour to overcome resistance. But for some children, aggression becomes a dominant theme in their social interactions. To be aggressive, children must know that they can get others to do what they want by causing them distress. At an early age, these children learn patterns of attack and counter-attack so well that they become blind to alternative ways of solving conflicts. Some of these children seem totally unresponsive to external pressure, whether it is in the form of a reward or of punishment. In fact, it seems the more they are rewarded, the worse they behave and the less they learn. Likewise, the more they are punished, the worse they behave and the less they learn.

Research Notes

Childhood aggression

Among all human emotions, aggression is probably the most studied. Aggression has been a favourite topic for psychologists for all of this century.

Aggression is "behaviour aimed at harming another person" (Perry, Perry, and Boldezar, 1990, p. 135). Aggressive behaviour seems to be one of the true differences between the sexes, and is found more strongly in males (Cummings, Ionatti, and Zahn-Waxler, 1989). It is also more tolerated in boys.

Arguments for aggression have come from evolution (no group in the animal kingdom is free of aggression), social learning (aggressive behaviour is learned and often rewarded), and modelling (children do what they see). All agree that although aggression in moderation is a useful survival tool, it becomes a problem when it is prolonged, frequent, and severe.

Psychologists distinguish two major types of aggression, hostile and instrumental (Feshbach, 1970). **Hostile aggression** seems to occur for its own sake and is its own goal. The bully who steals from a smaller child or calls the child names is exhibiting hostile aggression. Rewards for hostile aggression often come from other children or may come through vicarious means, such as identification with a bullying parent. **Instrumental aggression** is directed toward achievement of a non-aggressive goal. A child or adolescent may want something another student has and first tries a series of non-aggressive tactics, such as asking or offering to trade, to attain the object. Finally, he or she resorts to aggression — grabbing, punching, and using verbal abuse or other antisocial behaviours. If the child obtains the object, then the reward increases the probability that instrumental aggression will occur again.

Aggression shows a developmental progression in children. The early part of life is a particularly critical time for learning about aggression, and techniques for controlling others by aggressive means are rapidly acquired (Maccoby, 1980). Patterns of aggressive behaviour in children frequently seem to be well established before age nine (Patterson, 1982).

The temperamental traits that make infants "difficult" may be related to behaviour problems of aggression and anxiety (Bates, 1987), but infancy is at best a modest predictor of later problems. The knowledge that other people can serve as obstacles that block one's intended course of action probably comes very early, and it is between the ages of one and two that this knowledge seems to be extended (Maccoby, 1980). Anger in two-year-olds is distinctive and intense; children usually express their anger through undirected temper tantrums, hitting, and angry cries. After age three, when many children have their first social encounters, disputes with playmates rather than their parents are the primary cause of angry outbursts (Harris, 1986).

Children who are four years old and older know a variety of means to hurt others. Between the ages of three and five, children become more retaliatory and begin to express their anger verbally by scolding, insulting, or threatening others (Harris, 1986). However, children's conflicts are brief, usually lasting between 12 and 31 seconds (Eisenberg and Garvey, 1981; Houseman, 1972). Hay (1984) reported a median occurrence of five conflicts per hour among preschool children across twenty varying settings.

There is more overt aggressive behaviour in younger children, and younger children have more disputes over objects than do older children (see Peterson, 1992). Older children have more conflicts over behaviour and territory; they are in conflict over another child's actions or lack of action and factual disputes as to who's right or wrong (Shantz, 1987).

Aggression becomes more acceptable with age. Seven- to ten-year-olds who can easily discriminate accidental from deliberate harm-doing may react aggressively to almost any provocation, even one that they know is unintentional (Sancilio, Plumment, and Hartup, 1989). Older children (eighth graders) judge aggression to be less reprehensibe than do younger children.

Children, especially peers, seem to sanction aggression in each other. Children who tend to be aggressive may also pick on one child. When researchers (Perry, Perry, and Weiss, 1989; Perry, Williard, and Perry, 1990) studied patterns of aggresion in American elementary third grade children, they found that one child in ten was severely and repeatedly abused by highly aggressive classmates.

There is substantial stability of aggression over time (e.g., Cummings, Ionatti, and Zahn-Waxler, 1989). Antisocial behaviours such as aggression, truancy, and vandalism show relatively high continuity. Highly aggressive three-years-olds are likely to become aggressive five-year-olds (Cummings, Ionatti, and Zahn-Waxler, 1989). Children's level of physical and verbal aggression at ages six through twelve are fairly good predictors of their tendency to threaten, insult, tease, and compete with peers at ages ten to fourteen (Olweus, 1979). Antisocial or non-compliant behaviour is particularly likely to be stable over time when the first antisocial behaviour appears at a young age, is frequent, appears in more than one setting, and consists of several distinct forms of antisocial behaviour (Loeber, 1990).

Early forms of antisocial behaviour may be linked to the early onset of official juvenile offences. Dan Olweus (1987) found that children described as aggressive at thirteen and fifteen years of age were more likely at twenty-four to be engaged in criminal and antisocial activities. A Swedish study of more than 900 youths (Magnusson, 1988), found evidence that hyperactive/hyperaggressive behaviour in childhood predicts adult psychopathy. At the age of 13, teachers rated the boys on aggressiveness, motor restlessness, and lack of concentration. Of the 85 boys they rated as extremely aggressive, almost half were registered for criminal offences between ages eighteen and twenty-six. Of the 123 boys rated least aggressive, only 14 percent were registered, and then only a very small portion for serious crimes.

The major influences on aggression are the family, peers, temperament, and television. Investigations into the development of childhood aggression find that parents' attitudes and child-rearing strategies play an important role. In fact, one of the most reliable findings in the child-rearing literature maintains that cold and rejecting parents who apply physical punishment erratically and who permit their child to express frequent aggressive impulses are likely to raise hostile aggressive children (Eron, 1982; Olweus, 1980). Hostile and punitive parents resort to physical punishment, which provides both a model and a partial sanctioning of aggressive responses and which may also reinforce a child's aggressive behaviour toward others.

Children who live in highly coercive family settings may eventually become resistant to punishment. The use of arbitrary, high-intensity tactics elicits defiance from young children rather than the compliance that parents want (Crockenberg and Litman, 1990). Children learn to fight coercion with coercion, often defying their parents by repeating the very acts for which they are punished (Shaffer, 1985). If they are spanked, for example, the spanking serves as a model of the very aggressive behaviour that the parents are trying to suppress. Parents who rely on physical punishment to discipline aggression have children who are highly aggressive outside the home setting in which the punishment normally occurs (Eron, 1982).

The problems created by aggressive behaviour cannot be underestimated. Aggressive children are more likely to be disliked (Dodge et al., 1990). Childhood aggression is recognized as a strong predictor of behaviour difficulty in adolescence and early adulthood (Griffin, 1987). About half of antisocial children become adolescent delinquents and roughly half to three-quarters of the adult delinquents become adult offenders (Blumstein, Cohen and Farrington, 1988; Farrington, 1987).

It is not only the overt behavioural manifestations that contribute to conduct disorders. Most often, these youngsters lack social skills and possess unfortunate personality traits that elicit dislike and rejection from others. When high-risk students tend to be rejected by the group, they then turn toward others engaged in antisocial behaviour.

Socialized Aggression

Children and youth characterized as "socialized aggressive" are quickly spotted by teachers and families. They are chronic violators of broad cultural mores and social values. They are hostile, destructive, disobedient, and often verbally and physically abusive. They tend to lie, steal, and vandalize, sometimes assaulting people as well as property.

Unlike conduct-disordered children, those characterized as socialized aggressive are active in delinquent groups and loyal to delinquent friends. Delinquent behaviours are rewarded by peer attention at the same time as they attract some form of punishment from adult society. Thus a vicious circle is set in motion; more delinquent behaviour and more reward from the peer group, catalyzed by more punishment from the adult community and more anger on the part of the adolescent.

Socially aggressive children and youth are sometimes classed as socially maladjusted rather than emotionally disturbed or behaviourally disordered. This is because the United States Public Law 94-142 and its recent amendments (PL99-457) specifically exclude "children who are socially maladjusted, unless it is determined that they are seriously emotionally disturbed" (US Dept. of Health, Education and Welfare, 1977, p. 42478). The distinction is subtle and depends upon the effect of the condition on the child. It is felt that behaviour disorders are persistently distressing to the child while social maladjustment may not be. Within their gangs, socialized aggressive youths may enjoy considerable prestige as a result of their aggressive and norm-violating behaviours. Nevertheless, scholarly opinion holds this exclusionary clause in the US federal definition of emotional disturbance (behaviour disorders) to be ill-founded (Kauffman, 1989; Nelson et al., 1991). The ways of acting exhibited by these youths are clearly indicative of problems in socialization and ethic development that fall within the scope of the broader concept of behaviour disorders.

Socially maladjusted students take part in behaviours that include gang vandalism, stealing, fighting, truancy, sexual precocity, and substance abuse. Such behaviours are described under the rubric of **delinquent behaviour** which implies any illegal act by a juvenile, regardless of whether the perpetrators are apprehended (Nelson et al., 1991). For some students, these behaviours can rapidly lead to trouble with the law. Children and youth who come to the attention of the courts then gain a new label — juvenile delinquents or young offenders. **Delinquency** refers to a set of antisocial behaviours acquired over time. Historically, delinquency has been viewed as a social and a legal concern; hence, juvenile delinquency is a legal connotation, not an educational one.

Research Notes

Juvenile delinquency

Offences by juveniles are of grave concern to parents, the juvenile justice system, and law enforcement agencies. Teachers, too, must be deeply concerned about children and youth who fail to comply with the demands of the school and the classroom and who indulge in various forms of criminal and antisocial behaviour outside the school environment.

In our rapidly changing society, the elements of delinquency and delinquent behaviour have changed. Delinquency peaks during adolescence, but the age of children commiting delinquent acts is decreasing. Traditionally, the great majority of offenders have been boys, but delinquent behaviour is currently increasing among females. Once, delinquency was linked to low social class and socio-economic status, but these factors are becoming less important predictors as adolescent delinquent behaviour becomes distributed across all socio-economic levels (Braithwaite, 1981).

Along with accelerated rates of juvenile crime, there has been a striking increase in the rate of recidivism, a **recidivist** being anyone incarcerated for new charges within two years of release from prison. Current estimates of Canadian recidivism rates range from 48 to 60 percent. Seventy percent of recidivists return to jail within the first year; twice as many fifteen-year-olds as twenty-year-olds return to some form of confinement (Gendreau, Madden, and Leipeiger, 1977).

Few human behaviours have been subject to as many varied and contradictory explanations as juvenile delinquency. All the possible etiologies we have presented for behaviour disorders, plus quite a few more, have been proposed to account for juvenile delinqency. For example, Leyton (1979) views unfortunate family relationships as paramount in delinquency. Others see low self-confidence and fear of failure as characteristic of young offenders. Still others attribute at least some responsibility for delinquency to poor self-concept and school failure (Jacobson, 1974; Mann, Goodman, and Wiederholt, 1978). Schools may have played a part in the creation of delinquency. Such things as tracking, large school size, depersonalization, large classes, and poor communication between the school and the home may add to the problems (Gage and Berliner, 1986). In Chapter 7 we discussed the possible links betwen juvenile delinquency and learning disabilities.

Some researchers believe that delinquent youth have a character trait known as social anomie, a lack of entrenched societal norms and values. In other words, delinquent youth do not appear to internalize a coherent set of values and standards for regulating their own behaviour. Lawrence Kohlberg (1969) reported that juvenile delinquents display lower levels of moral judgment on moral problem-solving tasks than are found among law-abiding young people of the same age and intelligence. Other researchers adhere to the appealing theory of an innate criminal personality type. A survey of teachers in Canadian federal correction facilities indicated that 80 percent attributed criminal personalities to offenders (Doig, 1979). Similarly, over half the police officers in a mid-sized Canadian city agreed that most criminals have criminal personalities (Hylton and Matonovitch, 1979).

Delinquent youth are shaped through contact with a variety of social and emotional factors that increase the likelihood that they will become or continue to be adjudicated offenders. Loeber (1985) reported that the two best predictors of delinquency were composite measures of parental family management techniques and child problem behaviour. Expanding on this, a number of researchers (Patterson, 1982; Quay, 1986; Wahler and Dumas, 1986) observe that students at risk for juvenile delinquency are exposed to negative, harsh and incompetent parenting practices and, in some cases, have been aware of the commission of criminal acts by family members. They have well-developed patterns of antisocial and aggressive behaviour and are rejected by normal peers. In school, they have low academic performance, poor grades, and substandard achievement.

Boys starting their criminal careers in late childhood or early adolescence are at the greatest risk for becoming chronic offenders (Farrington, 1983; Loeber, 1982). Studies of prison populations have shown that recidivists are generally first arrested by age fourteen or fifteen, whereas one-time offenders are first arrested at a later age (Gendreau, Madden and Leipeiger, 1979). Farrington found that boys first arrested between ten and twelve years of age average twice as many convictions as later starters (Farrington et al., 1986); this comparison holds into early adulthood.

On the other hand, the late starter would be someone committing his or her first offence in middle to late adolescence. Lacking the early training for antisocial behaviours, this individual has not experienced the dual failure of rejection by normal peers and academic failure (Patterson, De Baryshe, and Ramsey, 1989).

In Canada, corrections are the responsibility of the federal government, which enacts legislation outlining juvenile offences, age limits, court procedures and penalties. Provincial governments administer the legislation, supply containment facilities, provide probation officers, and carry out court judgments.

Delinquent youth are provided for through a large network of child welfare and correctional resources. Canadian correctional programs extend along a continuum of levels of intervention, with diversion at one end and containment at the other. Programs may be open, residential, or community based, and are located wherever there is a substantial population of young people (see Reist, 1991). While a number of programs have been shown to be highly effective in preventing crime or reducing recidivism no one program has been found to work for all clients (Ross, 1982).

In the past, delinquent youth in Canada were subjected to treatment that, if applied to adults, would constitute clear violations of their rights. Canada's Bill C-61, the Young Offender's Act

(April, 1984), replaced the Juvenile Delinquent Act of 1908. Under the 1984 Act, a young offender is anyone between the ages of twelve and eighteen who commits a criminal act. Also established is a system of court procedures and dispositions for youths separate from those for adults.

In many ways, the 1984 Act provides more protection under the law for juvenile offenders. For example, an arresting officer must now inform accused youngsters of their right to contact a lawyer and their parents. Before juveniles are questioned by police, their rights and the nature of the charge must be explained in language they can understand. In addition, more emphasis is now placed on community work and helping the victims as methods of atonement (see Reist, 1991).

Anxiety and Withdrawal

Children with conduct disorders externalize their behaviour through such acts as disobedience, lying, stealing, fighting, sexual delinquency, and destructiveness. In contrast, anxious and withdrawn children internalize their behaviour. They may suffer from nausea, pains, headaches, phobias, fears, obsessions, shyness, nightmares, crying, depression, self-consciousness, and withdrawal.

Anxiety can be described as a fear with a future reference. Many people, for example, are anxious about entering a new situation and meeting new people. In fact, in a survey of high school and college students (Zimbordo, Pilkonis, and Norwood 1975), 40 percent reported that extreme shyness accompanied their interpersonal relations throughout their growing-up period. But while many of us are apprehensive of new situations, we are able to deal with them after some initial anxiety. Anxiety is considered abnormal when it happens in situations that most people can handle with little difficulty. Withdrawn and anxious children, for example, may be so shy they find it painful even to go to school.

A **phobia** is an anxiety reaction that is specific to one stimulus, an intense fear with no rational basis. Some of the most common phobias are fear of the dark, of animals, of vehicles, and of school. Among children, school phobia is one of the most common. It affects about 2 percent of the school-aged population and has the same incidence in boys and girls (Wolman, 1978).

School phobia seems to be more than simply an irrational fear of school. Children not only fear school but they suffer nausea, abdominal pain, and other physical difficulties asssociated with tension and extreme agitation. Children with severe school phobia may simply refuse to attend school. If forced, they may spend most of the time either mute or crying. Sadness and deep depression are not uncommon (Freedman and Doyle, 1974). Symptoms subside if the child is allowed stay at home and on weekends.

Anxious and withdrawn children do not necessarily suffer phobias. However, they do tend to develop a pattern of adjustment to cope with anxiety. In doing so, they forego assertive, independent behaviour and tend to become excessively withdrawn. They become fearful, secretive, and apathetic and often spend large amounts of time fantasizing and daydreaming instead of interacting with those around them. These children have low self-concept and little self-esteem; they are self-conscious, hypersensitive, and sad much of the time. Some withdrawn children regress to earlier stages of development and demand constant help and attention; others become depressed for no apparent reason (Klien and Last, 1989; Kovacs, 1989). Their depression is similar to that seen in adults (Hallahan and Kauffman, 1991).

In the classroom, both negative aggression and poor peer co-operation are outer-directed behaviours which can disrupt others. On the other hand, behaviours such as failure anxiety and the need for direction are inner-directed and typically not disruptive to other students (Safran and Safran, 1984). Teachers see failure anxiety, the need for direction, and confusion as the least disturbing or most tolerable behaviour problems. Therefore, unlike conduct-disordered children whose disruptive behaviours call attention to them, anxious and withdrawn children may be overlooked in the classroom.

Some anxious children become extremely withdrawn.

Also unlike conduct-disordered children, anxious and withdrawn children are greater threats to themselves than to those around them. These children have limited or ineffectual social relationships. The most extreme manifestation of their low self-image is suicide. Severe behavioural disorders are by far the most prevalent conditions associated with suicidal behaviour, and many studies have confirmed the link between suicidal behaviour and emotional instability (e.g., Pfeffer, 1986).

Immaturity

Not much is known about the special nature of immature children. Although similar to withdrawn children, immature children seem even less able to function in the regular classroom. They demonstrate many of the characteristics that we discussed in the chapter on learning disabilities in relation to maturational lags and attention deficits. They appear to be very clumsy, socially inadequate, passive, easily frustrated, messy, and lacking in initiative. They have a short attention span and frequently fail to finish assignments. Often they show a preference for younger playmates.

Attention Problems and Motor Excess

Attention-Deficit Hyperactivity Disorder (ADHD) is characterized as comprising developmentally inappropriate levels of sustained attention and impulse control and poor regulation of activity level to situational demands (Anastopoulos, Du Paul, and Barkley, 1991). In other words, ADHD is characterized by three primary features — inattention, impulsivity, and hyperactivity.

The disorder is frequently associated with other conditions, such as learning disabilities, conduct disorders, academic underachievement, and social skills deficits (Barkley, 1989). Across studies, for example, the prevalence of co-occurrence of ADHD and learning disabilities ranges from 9 to 63 percent (McKinney, Montague, and Hocutt, 1993).

ADHD is a medical diagnosis, seen with increasing frequency among school-aged children. In fact, when children in North America are referred for behavioural and emotional problems, more than 50 percent are diagnosed as hyperactive (Whalen, 1989). It's interesting that clinicians in Great Britain diagnose hyperactivity far less often than those in the United States and Canada.

Attention disorders are characterized by limited attention and difficulty in concentrating. Attention is the "process of tuning in to sensory information" (Bailey and Wolery, 1984, p.185) and involves engagement or active participation. The younger the child, the lower the rates of engagement. The parts of the brain that allow the child to sustain attention and screen out distractions become increasingly myelinated between the ages of about four and seven (Higgins and Turnure, 1984). Very young children are therefore likely to flit from activity to activity, show high rates of movement, and be easily distracted by visual and auditory stimuli. As children mature, their ability to control their attention, to discriminate between what is and what is not important, and to adapt their attention to details of the situation improves. They are able to maintain attention for longer periods because they are less easily distracted. However, students with attention disorders are unable to concentrate on a task because they have not learned to screen out irrelevant stimuli. They find it hard to focus their attention for appropriate lengths of time. They cannot sit still long enough to initiate and sustain the thought processes needed for school work and are repeatedly unable to concentrate on specific tasks long enough to complete them.

Teachers can hold the attention of ADHD students for longer periods by establishing eye contact, by using concrete aids, and by providing a lesson outline or glossary of key terms before the lesson.

Impulsivity represents a child's difficulty in withholding active responses such as blurting out statements or grabbing materials (Zentall, 1993). Impulsive students do things without thinking and do not learn from experience. They have difficulty organizing themselves, need much supervision, speak out of turn, and don't wait their turns in games or groups. They may show angry outbursts, be social isolates, blame others for their problems, fight with others quickly, and be very sensitive to criticism (Alderson, 1993). They are poorer at tasks requiring sustained attention and meet difficulties in problem solving and planning (see Reardon and Naglieri, 1992).

Impulsive students do not double-check their work. They ignore details, write before thinking and planning, leave off word endings, do not organize compositions, copy sloppily from the board, and do not self-correct. Students with ADHD may also **perseverate** — they purposelessly and sometimes disadvantageously repeat an activity. For example, a child may finish addition problems on page one and continue them on page two, even though the instructions clearly indicate a switch to subtraction.

Hyperactivity is defined as "a child's frequent failure to comply in an age-appropriate fashion with situational demands for restrained activity, sustained attention, resistance to distracting influences, and inhibition of impulsive responses" (Routh, 1980, p. 57). **Hyperactive children** display rates of motor behaviour that are too high for their age groups. They indulge in excessive, non-purposeful movement. Their accelerated rates of activity disturb others, worry teachers, and cause their families discomfort and even despair. Young hyperactive children are constantly on the move, pushing, poking, asking questions, but never waiting for answers. In the classroom, they are unable to sit still. When confined to a seat, they translate their need to be active into finger and foot tapping, as well as other disruptive activities. Hyperactive teenagers may drum their fingers, shuffle their feet, open and close their desks, and continually visit the pencil sharpener, other desks, and other areas of distraction. Even when asleep, the child shows excessive activity and other sleep problems (Alderson, 1993).

It is estimated that hyperactivity occurs in 3 to 20 percent of all elementary school children, with a sex ratio of three or more boys with the disorder to every girl (Wicks-Nelson and Israel, 1991). Girls with Attention Deficit Disorder are less likely to be hyperactive and also less likely to receive special education services for the condition (Berry, Shaywitz, and Shaywitz, 1985).

Longitudinal research shows that children with generalized hyperactivity have a very early onset of problems (Gillberg and Gillberg, 1988). Typically, signs are evident in early childhood, often by the age of three and even in infancy. There is a mean onset age of four years (Alderson, 1993; Barkley et al., 1988). A follow-up study of children who had been hyperactive in at least three different assessment settings at age seven revealed that 73 percent manifested pervasive hyperactivity at age eleven and 40 percent at age thirteen. All affected children in this study were noted to have been overactive by their parents before two years of age (Clarizio, 1990). Moreover, school achievement was problematic throughout the entire follow-up period. The vast majority of children (73 percent) with early onset of hyperactivity continued to have severe academic problems at age thirteen (Clarizio, 1990).

Research Notes

Attention Deficit Hyperactivity Disorder

Attention Deficit Disorder (ADD) has become one of the most popular conditions of the past decade. Writers observe that "not since the establishment of learning disabilities as a special education category has a condition so captivated both the professional community and general public as has attention deficit hyperactivity disorder (ADHD)" (Reid, Maag, and Vasa, 1993, p. 198). More children are being diagnosed, the term has entered educational parlance, and researchers are directing considerable attention to the condition.

Although the disorder was only given a specific name in 1980, children displaying symptoms now described as Attention Deficit Hyperactivity Disorder (ADHD) are not new to the fields of education, psychology, and pediatrics. In fact, ADHD has a long and rather confusing history. Hyperactivity was first described in 1845 by a German physician, Henrich Hoffman. In the intervening years, hyperactivity became one of the most deeply investigated and controversial disorders within the fields of pediatric medicine, clinical psychology, and education (Gadow, 1979). Hyperactivity has also been identified as the most common childhood behaviour disorder presented to doctors, psychiatrists, teachers, and other related professionals, not to mention parents (Weiss and Hechtman, 1979).

Children with the same clinical features have been given half a dozen or so different labels. In a review of the literature, Meents (1989) concluded that Attention Deficit Syndrome has at different times been referred to as neurological dysfunction, an anatomical dysfunction of the right cerebral hemisphere, and as a cognitive memory deficit. ADD children have been described as learning disabled, exhibiting soft neurological signs, and as having minimum brain dysfunction syndrome.

In 1968, DSM11 provided the first official diagnostic classification of hyperactivity. The term *Attention Deficit Disorder* was was first used in DSM111 in 1982. By 1987, DSM111-R used the term Attention Deficit Hyperactivity Disorder. And, since 1980, every new version of DSM has presented a revision of the ADD/ADHD criteria.

Following its introduction as a diagnostic category, research and interest in ADHD increased dramatically. Nevertheless, the procedures for identification, assessment, and treating ADHD have been embroiled in controversy (see Reid, Maag, and Vasa, 1993). There are numerous definitional and diagnostic problems, not the least being a lack of consensus about an exact name for the condition and the characteristics that accompany it.

Initial research defined two conditions — Attention Deficit Disorder (ADD) and Attention Deficit Hyperactivity Disorder (ADHD). More recent research indicates that Attention Deficit Disorder without hyperactivity is uncommon, and today there is more use of the composite syndrome, ADHD. Some research, however, suggests that ADD may occur more often with learning disabled students while ADHD may be more frequent among children with disruptive behaviour disorders (Barkley, Du Paul, and McMurray, 1990; Lahey and Carlson, 1991).

To be diagnosed as ADHD, a child must exhibit eight of fourteen symptoms appearing in DSM 111 that reflect attention difficulties, impulsivity, or motor hyperactivity, with onset before the age of seven. The three major criteria for ADHD are not situation specific; that is, they are displayed by affected children at all times.

ADHD is a medical diagnosis. The prevalent opinion of the cause is that ADHD is an invisible function with a basis in the central nervous system and that it involves a faulty regulation of a particular neurotransmitter, norepinephrine (Alderson, 1993). Some researchers have documented a genetic factor in ADHD; they report findings of similar characteristics for anywhere between 60 and 75 percent of the relatives of children with ADHD and for 30 to 50 percent of their siblings (Goodman and Sevenson, 1989).

Nevertheless, the efforts expended to find a biological etiology of ADHD have been generally inconclusive and often contradictory. As well, there are criticisms of the distinction between ADD and ADHD (see Stewart, 1994) and controversy over which version of DSM criteria is preferable (see McBurnett, Lahey, and Pfiffner, 1993).

Critics of the role of clinical diagnosis of ADHD have pointed out that it does not lead to special placement and does not predict response to instruction. They believe that adding ADHD as a disability category is unnecessary because students diagnosed as ADHD who manifest symptoms severe enough to impair educational performance currently are eligible for educational services under existing categories such as learning disabilities or behaviourally disordered (e.g. Ysseldyke, Algozzine, and Thurlow, 1992). Other educators object to ADHD because it may divert resources away from children with serious disabilities and it is difficult to define and identify (Aleman, 1991).

Identification and Assessment of Behaviour Disorders

Behaviour disorders are easier to identify than to define or classify. Children with conduct disorders attract attention with their overtly disruptive behaviours. Immature and withdrawn children are a little harder to identify but are still fairly recognizable. Nevertheless, when it comes to referral for diagnosis and additional assistance, teachers tend to over-refer children showing conduct disorders and under-refer those who are internalizing problems such as anxiety and withdrawn behaviour (Hallahan and Kauffman, 1991). Childhood aggression accounts for a disproportionate number of referrals to special education programs and to mental health and child guidance centres (Epanchin and Paul, 1987; Kauffman, 1989).

Table 11-4

Identification of behaviour disorders

Classroom screening, testing	Educational measures	Psychological measures
direct observation	achievement in reading, math, etc.	IQ tests
interviews	perceptual/motor functioning	personality measures
teacher ratings	auditory/visual processing	projective tests
peer ratings	language development	
self-ratings		
Q sorts		
social skills assessment		
sociometric measures		
rating scales on attitudes toward school, academics, and so on.		

As for all exceptional conditions, it is important to identify and intervene with behaviour disorders as early as possible. It is in the early years that long-term patterns of behaviour are established; research finds that students who developed serious behaviour problems in later years had difficulty in kindergarten (Koppitz, 1980). As well, very young children are more malleable, so early intervention may be more successful.

However, it is extremely difficult to identify behaviour disorders at an early age: all preschoolers display rapid and uneven development and wide variations in behaviour. Preschoolers with behaviour disorders may be somewhat more fussy and irritable than normal; they may exhibit irregular patterns of eating and sleeping and aggressive behaviour. Parents, however, have highly subjective expectations, values, and reactions to their children. One parent may view behaviour as too aggressive or active that another dismisses as normal. As parents bring their own temperaments and personal biases to bear on child-rearing attitudes, they may unwittingly neglect or exacerbate their child's developmental difficulties. In addition, some difficulties emerge only when a child is faced with a structured classroom situation and the complexities of reading and mathematics.

Within the educational system, children with behaviour disorders are so readily identified by school personnel that few schools bother to use systematic screening procedures (Hallahan and Kauffman, 1991). The identification of children with behaviour disorders often begins with a feeling in the mind of a parent or teacher that something is wrong, that the child is having real problems in meeting the classroom teacher's norms for acceptable behaviours. Teachers are fairly accurate in identifying behaviour disorders and their informal judgment has served as a fairly reliable means of screening these children (Edelbrock and Achenbach, 1984; Hallahan and Kauffman, 1991).

Once teachers have identified and referred a child, it is not a simple task to find out what is wrong, what is not connecting. Nor is it easy to determine whether a behaviour problem is serious enough to warrant further diagnosis. Many temporary behaviour disorders occur in normally developing children, and we do not want to identify a child incorrectly any more than we want to overlook a child who needs help.

The characteristics of children with behaviour disorders are so varied that no single measure or tool can pinpoint all of the symptoms or all of the causes of the behavioural and learning deficits. A range of additional measures are used to complement informal judgment and aid in quantifying data.

The approaches used by educators to identify and diagnose behaviourally disordered students are determined by both philosophical and pragmatic considerations — the conceptual model favoured and the availability of personnel for psycho-educational diagnosis. Measures for identification include behavioural observations, teacher ratings, peer ratings, and self-ratings by the target child. Formal and informal tools assess a child's mental ability, academic achievement, oral language development, perceptual-motor development, personality development, and auditory and visual acuity. The diagnostic process should also include interviews with the child and parents.

Some children who display severe overt disruptive behaviours will be referred directly for psycho-educational diagnosis; in other cases, teachers may use a variety of procedures devised to help identify youngsters who deviate significantly in intra- and interpersonal learning and social behaviours. Procedures should take into account a variety of settings and circumstances, such as different times and subject areas in the classroom, the playground, and other school activities.

Assessment may begin with a behavioural analysis technique such as direct observation. Teachers or observers record the instances of specific behaviours, which helps to establish the frequency, durability, and age-appropriateness of a behaviour.

Data recording may be as simple as a narrative system, or it may be more sophisticated with codes to score language skills, motor behaviour, and so on. There are limitations on the amount of behaviour that can be documented, however. We cannot observe all behaviour and must sometimes be content with a sample to make observations more manageable. With a sampling technique, systematic observations of a child are undertaken over a period of no less than a week, and preferably longer.

Event sampling is used to determine the frequency or length of a specific behaviour. Event sampling includes two types — frequency counts and duration recording. A frequency count is used for behaviour that is of relatively short duration such as the number of times a child hits another child. A duration measure (duration sampling) is an indication of how long something occurs and is used for behaviours that vary considerably in length, such as negative or positive peer interaction or self-stimulating behaviour.

Suppose, for example, that a teacher is particularly worried about the physically aggressive behaviours shown by James. In the course of a school day James slaps, punches, and generally annoys the other children in the room. In using direct observation techniques, the teacher would begin by measuring James's behaviour and comparing it to that of three other somewhat problematic children in the class. Over a period of at least five days, the teacher would enter a checkmark on a tally sheet each time James and the other three children exhibited physical aggression. The average number of aggressive behaviours in the five days provides a baseline. The teacher can profile James's baseline, compare it to those of the other children, and decide whether to refer him for intensive assessment. In addition, when a program is begun to improve James's behaviour, the teacher can quickly measure his progress by comparing his current status to the baseline. Figure 11-1 shows the baseline for James and the three other children.

Figure 11-1
Baseline graph for charting physical aggression in children

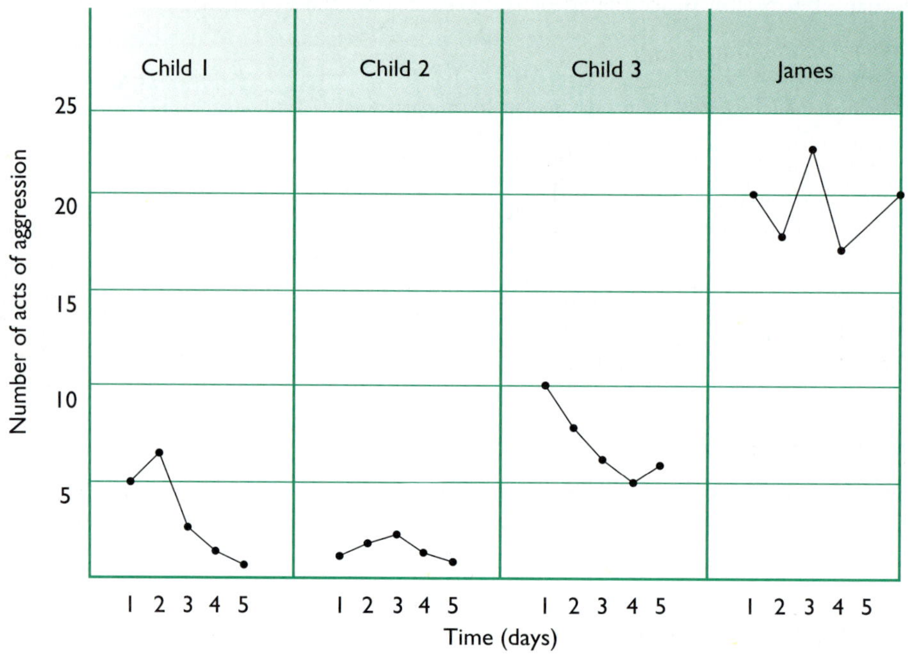

When more formal procedures are used, teacher judgment measures (teacher ratings of behaviour) are the most widely used tools for diagnosing conduct disorders in a classroom setting (Hoge and Andrews, 1992) and have been found to be quite accurate. Three commonly used measures are the Behavior Problem Checklist (Quay and Peterson, 1987), the Conners Teacher Rating Scale (Conners, 1969, 1973), and the Child Behavior Checklist (Achenbach and Edelbrook, 1983).

Following screening, a child may be referred for psycho-educational diagnosis. An estimation of potential based on an IQ test, assessment of communication skills, and pupil performance in academic, social, psychomotor, and self-help skills provides a basis for sound instructional decisions. Do be aware, however, that although a formal psycho-educational diagnosis will contain components that assess the child's potential and performance, the overall assessment remains subjective. No measure of behaviour disorders can parallel the IQ; emotions are simply not defined by objective parameters.

Ecological assessment, which comes from the social systems perspective, broadens the traditional view of assessment. The process views an individual's behaviour as a function of the values of the social system within which he or she is being evaluated, and includes the child's total ecological system (the various environments in which the child functions). Ecologic assessment includes an examination of the materials, methods, and curriculum, as well as teacher expectations, discipline, cultural and social factors, and so on.

Prevention of Behaviour Disorders

If the specific causes of behaviour disorders were known, then prevention would be greatly simplified. General preventative measures revolve around such broad areas as nutrition, the family climate, and the prevention of child abuse and neglect.

Developmental Consequences of Behaviour Disorders

Children and adolescents with behaviour disorders deviate significantly from their peers in the quantity, quality, and modes of their emotional expression. There is no symptom common to all behaviourally disordered pupils, or even to a subgroup of these children, because there is no such thing as a typical behaviourally disordered or disturbed student. Behavioural disorders may take one or many specific forms and can be manifested as pervasive adjustment difficulties. The severity of disturbance ranges from mild to serious and debilitating.

Cognitive Development

Compared to the normal distribution of intelligence, many children with behaviour disorders fall into the slow learner or mildly intellectually disabled category. Most have IQs in the dull-normal range — around ninety — and very few score above the bright normal range (Kauffman, 1985; Hallahan and Kauffman, 1991). Many are underachievers at school, as measured by standardized tests (Kauffman, 1989).

Academic Performance

One consistent finding is that antisocial children show poor academic achievement (Hawkins and Lishner, 1987; Wilson and Herrnstein, 1985). Only rarely is a disturbed child academically advanced; the few disturbed children who do seem competent academically are seldom able to apply their skills to everyday problems (Hallahan and Kauffman, 1991).

These students often experience difficulty with basic school skills (Lewis and Doorlag, 1991) and do not achieve academically at the expected level for their mental or chronological ages. Behaviourally disordered children are usually behind in reading, arithmetic, and spelling (Rose et al., 1981). Studies (e.g., Fehrmann, Keith, and Reimers, 1987) show a significant correlation between antisocial behaviour and failure to complete homework assignments.

Students tend to spend more time in off-task behaviour (Walker et al., 1987). Time variables such as time allocated and time engaged are positive measures of academic achievement (see Greenwood, 1991); it is estimated that 20 percent of student variance in achievement is accounted for by active participation in the learning process (Bloom, 1974). It is not surprising that students who spend their time being disruptive or inattentive lag in academic achievement.

Students with conduct disorders tend to be non-compliant and uncontrolled. The correlation between achievement and aggression is .39 for boys and .36 for girls (Feldhusen, 1979), which means that students may rapidly enter a pattern of severe academic failure that quickly becomes cyclical. When children do not learn the skills needed for coping with academic pressures, they react by withdrawing or lashing out in angry frustration. They soon learn to dislike the learning process and resent the school experience, and often resort to truancy.

At the same time, these students create problems in classroom management, often alienating teachers and other students in the process. Classroom teachers tend to instruct children with behaviour disorders with fewer academic questions, less extended feedback, and fewer dyadic work interactions. When teachers do this, the child's academic achievement falls still more and problems may become even more acute.

At first glance, anxiety may not seem as academically and socially debilitating as aggression. However, timid, passive behaviour, dependency, isolation, and withdrawal interfere with children's development of their potential (Conger and Keane, 1981). Anxious children develop a defeatist attitude along with feelings of worthlessness and excessive self-criticism which hamper their social relationships. Withdrawn children are fearful, secretive, and apathetic; they tend to spend large amounts of time fantasizing and daydreaming instead of interacting with those around them.

Inattention, distractibility, impulsivity, and hyperactivity are all characteristic of ADHD. They can cause or compound academic problems because children who are easily distracted from learning tasks learn less than those who pay attention. Children diagnosed as ADHD are easily distracted, don't stay on task, and have short attention spans. Attention is directly related to learning and language problems. The performance of ADHD students is worse when sustained attention is required to perform a repetitive task (Zentall, 1993).

More than 80 percent of eleven-year-old students with ADHD are reported to be at least two years behind in reading, spelling, math, or written language. Zentall (1993) reports that studies examining the academic achievement of ADHD students indicates that they are more likely to receive lower grades in academic subjects and lower scores on standard measures of reading and math. Zentall and colleagues (1993) also addressed the academic performance and behaviour of 121 non-disabled and 107 ADHD boys aged 7-4 years to 14-6 years. They found that the students with ADHD showed lower problem-solving scores in specific math concepts and slower computation performance than the non-disabled group.

Among hyperactive children, conduct disturbances and academic deficits are common. The short attention spans of hyperactive children elicit negative teacher responses. One study (Peter, Allen, and Horvath, 1983) found that hyperactive boys see greater teacher disapproval directed toward them. Misconduct is noted in as many as 70 percent of cases (Barkley, 1990).

Profile

As a preschooler in nursery school, Gary aggressively bit, fought, and scratched his way through the program. He threw terrible temper tantrums, and did not stop until he was about ten years old. He spent much of his time in elementary school ejected from the classroom or in the principal's office.

During Gary's first year in junior high school, his disruptive behaviour, fighting, and irrational conduct led to a number of suspensions. His achievement was at a very low level, hardly surprising given his behaviour problems, his apparent lack of academic interests, and his resentment of school and authority. Gary had large gaps in reading skills, both for word attack and comprehension. His spelling was poor and creative writing exercises were beyond him. Only in math did he show any interest or potential. Throughout his early school years, Gary worked at math and achieved at level. During math periods, his behaviour was also relatively serene.

By the middle of Gary's first year in junior high school, his behaviour had resulted in severe penalties. After he lit a fire on the school bus, he was transferred to a special class for children with problems. Even among this smaller group, Gary's behaviour continued to be outlandish. His achievement and academic interest were minimal, and he developed a more pronounced pattern of physical assault, swearing, truancy, and smoking.

Gary's teacher could see that his behaviour during math was calm, while his behaviour during reading or language was at its most violent. In light of this, the teacher mounted a two-pronged program to alter Gary's behaviour and improve his academic functioning.

Gary's classroom environment was changed so that students worked in cubicles on individual programs for the first half of the morning. At the same time, a token economy was established with the co-operation of all students in the class.

The teacher also decided to stress Gary's strengths in order to help his weaknesses. Reading, as a specific subject area, was eliminated from his timetable. Math became the fulcrum of Gary's education, and the starting point for integrated programming. For example, as Gary tackled math word problems, his reading comprehension improved; he later enjoyed writing math problems for the class. Math concepts, such as distance and scale, were extended to other areas, such as social studies.

By the end of the school year, Gary's reading tests showed an advance of almost two years in vocabulary, word attack skills, and comprehension. As Gary found success in reading, his other subject areas also showed progress. Most important, however, his behaviour improved dramatically. While aggressive episodes continued, they were more often directed toward inanimate objects. Verbal abuse decreased and truancy was eliminated as Gary, for probably the first time in his life, began to see value in the learning experience.

Despite this progress, Gary is not yet ready to be integrated back into a regular program. He still requires structured and consistent behavioural intervention in a supportive environment that offers much success. However, Gary's self-esteem is definitely on the rise. He is beginning to be accepted and even admired by other students.

Communication

Speech and language disorders cut across all areas of exceptionality and are likely to be found among children with behaviour disorders. In fact, a higher prevalence of behaviour disorders are found among seriously language-delayed children. On the other hand, teachers sometimes feel that behaviourally disordered children communicate too well. They interrupt in class, swear, use aggressive language, speak defiantly to adults, and indiscriminately vent their emotions. They often use language to disrupt and control social situations. This excessive use of language may not be a communication problem, but it is certainly a social problem.

Social Development

Children with excessive feelings of aggression and defiance develop intense and far-ranging interpersonal problems with teachers, peers, parents, and others in their environments. They meet trouble in the classroom with academics and in interactions with teachers and other students. By definition, those who are anxious and withdrawn fail to respond appropriately to those in their environments.

The teaching of social skills and adaptive interpersonal behaviours is a particularly important academic feature for children with behaviour disorders.

Sociability is a term that describes the child's willingness to engage others in social interaction and to seek their attention or approval. Rather than being sociable, behaviourally disordered children are disliked by most of their peers, especially highly aggressive children who are less likely to make friends and more likely to be attacked by peers. Studies of students with behaviour disorders at elementary and secondary levels indicate that they are seldom socially accepted; they are often actively rejected, not just neglected by their peers. Compared to samples of normally developing children, those with conduct disorders are usually less responsive to social reinforcement, less empathetic, and less sophisticated in their understanding of and responses to their peers' behaviour (Baum, 1989). When Walker and his colleagues conducted a series of longitudinal studies of the development of antisocial behaviour among middle school boys in school settings (Shinn et al., 1987; Walker et al., 1987; Walker, Steeber, and O'Neill, 1990) they found that pupils in the antisocial cohort exhibited significantly less academic engaged time in instructional settings, initiated and were involved in significantly more negative interactions with peers, and were rated by their teachers as substantially less socially competent and adjusted.

As aggressive children provoke a large number of fights, they are also more likely to become the targets of aggression. Non-aggressive children who are harmed under ambiguous circumstances are much more likely to retaliate if the harm doer has a reputation as an aggressive child (Dodge and Frame, 1982; Sancilio et al., 1989).

Prognosis

The problems created by the behaviour of aggressive children should not be underestimated, for children do not grow out of conduct disorders. Rejection and low levels of peer acceptance place a student at substantial risk for a wide variety of negative outcomes (Parker and Asher, 1987).

It is the conduct-disordered child or youth whose adulthood is most likely to be characterized by socially unacceptable behaviour (Hallahan and Kauffman, 1991). Antisocial behaviour in childhood generally leads to poor adjustment and mental health in later years, especially for boys. The continuation of antisocial behaviour in school is likely to lead to increased risk of school failure, membership in deviant peer groups, dropping out of school, and eventual delinquency (Robins, 1979; Walker et al., 1987).

Students whose anxiety disorders diminish in adolescence are not particularly likely to show serious maladjustment in adulthood. Children who are neurotic and withdrawn are more likely to later find and hold a job, overcome their emotional problems and stay out of jails and mental hospitals than are children with conduct problems (Hallahan and Kauffman, 1991). It is anxiety disorders in later adolescence that appear to predict adult maladjustment (Gersten et al., 1976). Over one-third of students with ADHD fail to finish high school (Weiss and Hechtman, 1986).

Intervention with Children with Behaviour Disorders

Methods of intervention for students with behaviour disorders have been largely developed according to various theoretical perspectives. No one method has proven effective for all behaviour disorders and a method that works one week may fail the next; those intervening with behaviourally disordered youngsters require a spectrum of different approaches and techniques. We only briefly outline some major interventions.

Medical Intervention

Medical intervention for students with behaviour disorders focuses almost entirely on psychopharmacology (drug therapy). In fact, faced with rambunctious, contrary, or unfocused children, some people leap to the conclusion that drugs can solve the problem, and in recent years, drugs have become the standard treatment regimen. In Alberta, for example, the use of Ritalin has increased tenfold since 1986. In 1992-1993, there was a 40 percent jump (Bell, Fisher, and Rodriguez, 1994).

Drugs administered to children vary widely in purpose and pharmacological action. Generally, the drugs fall into three major categories — stimulants, major tranquillizers, and anti-depressents. Stimulants are most often selected; stimulant medication is considered the first and least complicated of the possible medications and seems to produce the fewest side effects. Tranquillizers and anti-depressants are reserved for a smaller group of patients.

For most children, stimulants are the drugs of choice among physicians. Of those prescribed to control hyperactivity and inattentive behaviour, the most commonly recommended are the psychostimulants Ritilin (the trade name for methylphenidate hydrochloride) and dextroamphetamine (Dexedrine, Deanol, and Cylert). Of Ritalin, Dexedrine, and Cylert, Ritalin is the first choice of doctors, probably because it seems to produce fewer side effects. Ritalin is prescribed about ten times more than the other two combined (Gadow, 1986).

The major tranquillizers such as thioridazine (Mellaril), chloropromazine (Thorazine), and haloperidol (Haldol, Serenace) may also be prescribed for children with serious behaviour disorders. Antidepressants, such as imipramine (Tofranil) and amitriptyline (Taroxyle, Tryptant, Elevil) may be administered for problems such as enuresis and childhood depression.

About 1 to 2 percent of all elementary-aged school children receive medication for hyperactivity (Gadow, 1986). Perhaps 60 to 90 percent of children diagnosed with attention deficits and/or hyperactivity receive stimulant therapy for prolonged periods during their school careers (Copeland et al., 1987; Lambert et al. 1987; Safer and Krager, 1988).

Psychotropic drugs affect the neuron cells of the central nervous system either by increasing or decreasing their excitability (Ross and Ross, 1982). In the past, it was widely assumed that Ritalin affected children differently than it affected adults. It was seen to calm children instead of revving them up. However, the theory of "paradoxical effect," once widely accepted, has been discredited (Varley, 1984). It is now believed that Ritalin has the same focusing effects on children as it does on adults.

Psychotropic medications are prescribed to control hyperactive and inattentive behaviour in the hope that their effect will produce better peer relationships, improved self-image, and pleasure in acquiring competencies. Although clinical indications for the use of drug therapy remain controversial, there seem to be two conditions that respond well — poor selective attention and concentration, and impulsivity (Levine, 1982). Evidence attests that stimulants do facilitate academic functioning (Douglas et al., 1988) when used in carefully controlled dosages along with educational programs. The majority of youngsters show medication-related improvements, and there is little question that drugs are often successful in reducing hyperactive behaviour and increasing attention skills.

Nevertheless, there are major concerns about the ethics and advisability of wide drug use with children. On ethical grounds, the grave problems of contemporary society with psychoactive drugs makes it somewhat ironic that we have become accustomed to prescribing drugs to children.

Other concerns revolve around the short- and long-term effects of drug therapy. Long-term effects may include growth inhibition and sleep and diet disturbances. In the short term, drug therapy seems effective for many children. But because any beneficial effects dissipate rapidly upon discontinuation of the medication, researchers are concerned about what they refer to as "short-term efficacy." Given the short-lived effects, it can be argued that prescribing medication as the sole method of behaviour management seems inefficient. Medication is best viewed as one component of a comprehensive treatment program; an adjunct to other interventions such as special education and behaviour management.

The Canadian Pediatric Society (1988) outlined guidelines for helping children with Attention Deficit Disorder. They advocate a thorough interdisciplinary approach with teachers playing a major role in the entire process (Fishburne, 1989). In monitoring the effects of the therapy, the teacher has an essential role (Alderson, 1993).

Therapy and Counselling

Numerous therapies and counselling techniques are used with children with behaviour disorders. Many occur in a clinical setting although some are applicable to the classroom. However, only a loose connection exists between specific types of psychopathology and specific therapies.

Individual psychotherapy implies a transaction between the child and the therapist. In traditional psychoanalytic approaches, anxiety and its results are focal issues. But as techniques rely heavily on discussion and the probing of feelings and attitudes, traditional therapeutic approaches have not been entirely successful with children. Therapy is difficult because children may not realize that what they are experiencing is different from what other people experience. As well, children do not have adequate labels for internal experiences, and so they are unable to properly describe their feelings of anxiety, depression, or resentment.

Specialized therapies, devised to overcome these difficulties, employ music, art, pet therapy, or other approaches. Because young children communicate more easily through play than through words, various forms of play therapy have also evolved.

A Matter of Debate

Drug therapy

The use of psychotropic drugs to control behaviour and increase academic functioning is a matter of deep concern and considerable controversy.

Arguments in favour	Arguments against
The short-term efficacy of drug therapy with children is well established.	The welcome effects in the social sphere are often immediate and may even be dramatic, but they also tend to be short-lived (Whalen and Henker, 1991).
Stimulants decrease motor activity, diminish impulsive responding, and improve attention.	Stimulants are not helpful to all children.
Studies (Famularo and Fenton, 1987) report that academic performance during drug therapy is significantly superior to performance prior to drug therapy. In some cases, attention deficit and hyperactive children on stimulant medication have improved to the point of being indistinguishable from normal children (Fishburne, 1989).	It appears that methylphenidate does affect performance, but there is substantial evidence to suggest that stimulant medication has only a minimal effect on the improvement of academic learning (Ballinger, Varley, and Nolen, 1984).
Stimulants may help the child to focus attention, to think more clearly, to inhibit problem behaviours, to perform in a more controlled manner, and to engage in more goal directed pursuits (Guetzloe and Cline, 1979).	ADHD and hyperactivity are, in some cases at least, "in the eye of the beholder." Hyperactive behaviour cannot easily be medically determined. One person's energetic child may well be another's hyperactive child.
Stimulants enhance interpersonal harmony (Whalen and Henker, 1991). Many children exhibit signs of increased happiness, friendliness, and co-operation.	The use of drugs as a treatment may suggest that hyperactivity is a specific disease.
On rating scales, parents and teachers indicate large reductions in restlessness, crying, temper outbursts, distractibility, excitability, frustration, pouting, and other hyperkinetic symptoms.	Short-term side effects of drugs are common, although not all children are affected in the same way. The most frequent side effects seem to be a decrease in appetite and an increase in sleeplessness.
Once children can focus better in school, they stop viewing themselves as failures and begin seeing themselves as competent and successful.	Drugs may stimulate mood elevation and create a psychological dependence.
Anywhere from 60 to 90 percent of children improve to varying degres (Whalen and Henker, 1976).	Medications are poor substitutes for good educational programming.
	Drugs are palliative and do not cure the cognitive strategies or kinds of responses that children use and make. Stimulants only reduce a child's need to engage in stimulation-seeking activity so that the child is more amenable to education and social intervention (Zentall, 1983).

In play therapy, the therapist creates an atmosphere where the child can freely express feelings, concerns, and conflicts. He or she may assume the role of co-player, model, or observer. The therapist then interprets the child's play to find the source of fears and problems, or tries to reflect back the feelings expressed by the child.

In addition to different therapies, counselling has proven effective with behaviourally disordered children and their families. The major goal of counselling is to help the child eliminate unacceptable behaviours and learn more appropriate ways of responding to people and the environment.

Various types of counselling are possible — individual, group, family, guidance, and career and vocational. Although individual counselling is widely used, many counsellors suggest that **group therapy** — the simultaneous treatment of several children, usually in the same age range — is a more natural way to work with children. By treating children in a group, the therapist can use group processes and face-to-face peer interactions as primary vehicles for change (Suran and Rizzo, 1983).

Group therapy makes use of modelling, play, verbal interactions, peer influence, socialization, experience, and mutual support. Within the context of the group, children can unlearn inappropriate behaviours and learn new ways of relating more easily through the interaction and feedback in a safe practice situation with peers. At the same time, children learn to help other people, to accept help from others, and to talk openly about themselves and abandon facades. They take more risks and accept reponsibility for their growth and the growth of others (Ohlsen, 1977).

Educational Intervention

One of the most critical elements characterizing services for children and youth with behaviour disorders over the past thirty years has been the development of various conceptual models relating to the theory and practice of education for such students (Kauffman, 1989). While some components of some models are compatible, others are not. Many educators tend to draw ideas from a number of appproaches, arguing that no single method has proven adequate in the management of behaviourally disordered children. However, the incompatibility of models does limit the extent of teachers' selection from various models. Moreover, studies support the belief that programs with a solid philosophical base and with staff who believe in that philosophy are the most likely to be effective (Beare, 1991).

Nevertheless, no one intervention exists for every troubling behaviour that is manifested in the the classroom. No one cure-all strategy is out there waiting to be discovered. Teachers require a range of strategies and techniques and should be familiar with the components of all models.

Educational Settings

For most school-age children with behaviour disorders, the regular classroom is the common milieu. With support, appropriate programming, and individualization, regular teachers can teach and manage most students. However, when full inclusion is discussed, the two groups of students who force educators to consider carefully the most enabling environments are those with severe and multiple disabilities and those with serious behaviour disorders. Many writers assert that we may be glorifying the mainstream to the detriment of some children, especially those considered to be behaviourally disordered. Research, they say, clearly does not support the assertion that all students can be managed and taught effectively in regular classrooms (Hallahan et al., 1988; Lloyd et al., 1988).

Students with conduct disorders in particular are far from ideal classroom participants. They tend to invoke negative reactions and rejection. The majority of these youngsters are disruptive and defiant; they are deficient in social skills and they do not fit either the teacher's or the peers' expectations for classroom behaviour.

For students with conduct disorders, evidence does not suggest that general classrooms are always safe havens. These students are disliked by most of their peers. If a child's behaviour is so aggressive and disruptive that it entails active rejection and dislike for the child, then the regular classroom may be a more restrictive environment until the behaviour improves. Active rejection in a regular placement may only serve to further heighten the distress and lower the self-esteem of some students with behaviour disorders.

Teachers base their judgment of what is normal on environmental, cultural, and situational factors. Regular education teachers seem to be less tolerant of deviant behaviour than special education teachers (Safran and Safran, 1984, 1985). Studies of regular classroom teachers' behavioural standards and expectations have found them to be narrow, intense, and very demanding (Walker and Rankin, 1983). The most disturbing behaviour to elementary teachers seems to be negative aggression followed by poor peer co-operation (Safran and Safran, 1987).

Teachers' perceptions of and tolerance for behaviour problems have two major results. First, they suggest that accommodation for problem behaviour may be less feasible than accommodation for instructional needs (Ritter, 1989). Studies have consistently found that teachers tend to value affective and interpersonal aspects of instruction very highly in comparison with academic and cognitive aspects (Brookhart and Freeman, 1992). Teachers favour students with behaviour disorders less than they do learning-disabled students (Gottleib, Leyser, and Micheals, 1990) and teachers seem more prepared to alter a program for a child with learning needs than for one with behavioural needs. Teachers find the outbursts of children with behaviour disorders more disturbing than the behaviour of learning-disabled students (Mooney and Algozzine, 1978). Behaviourally disordered students are generally rated as more distractible and hostile and less task oriented and considerate than learning-disabled youngsters (McKinney and Forman, 1982).

Teacher tolerance also means that a high number of students exhibiting problem behaviour are referred to special education (Ritter, 1989). Students with behaviour disorders have much greater exposure to special education services or placement than other students (Nelson et al., 1991). They are the first to be removed from regular classrooms and among the last to be returned into integrated settings (Hersh and Walker, 1983).

The fact that students with behaviour disorders are viewed by many teachers as the most difficult to teach and the least likable, coupled with the fact that these students tend to be especially complex in their needs, suggests that effective teaching of behaviourally disordered students may require skills, attitudes, and beliefs different from those of teachers who work effectively with more ordinary students. Recent research on integration suggests that some teachers are more effective than others in working with difficult students (Kauffman and Wong, 1991). Teachers of behaviourally disordered children must be able to tolerate unpleasantness and rejection without being counteraggressive and reciprocally unpleasant.

All teachers have to devote some time to classroom control; typically about 10 percent of their time (Crealock, 1983). When a child raises classroom management from a chore to an obsession, disrupts the learning of other students, and demands too much teacher time, we must confront alternative programming for that child. Placement decisions must take into account the needs of the child as well as the boundary conditions — the classroom teacher and the other children in the class. Educators must determine the extent to which a student's learning or behaviour deviates from what is considered typical for age and grade; they must then address the teacher's tolerance and ability to deal with the child's difficulties.

No one intervention exists for every troubling behaviour in the classroom, and teachers should be familiar with a range of strategies and techniques.

Behaviourally disordered students should not be characterized out of hand as being unable to meet the academic and behavioural standards of the regular class environment. No student should be removed from the regular class until it is clear that effective programming cannot be provided there.

More restrictive placements include a regular classroom with a full-time or part-time aide; a regular classroom on a part-time basis with some special class placement; placement in a special classroom with some regular classroom integration; or full-time placement in a self-contained classroom. These should be considered temporary placements. The ultimate goal of segregation is rapid return to a regular classroom once the child has learned to behave more non-aggressively and non-disruptively.

Educational Models

A number of conceptual models from various disciplines have been used to explain and treat behaviour disorders. An outline of common interventions related to various conceptual models is shown in Table 11-5.

Psychotherapeutic Intervention (Psychodynamic Approach)

The psychothereupetic approach holds that the guiding principles of psychoanalysis should be employed in educational intervention with children with behaviour disorders. There are numerous theoretical orientations and practical approaches to psychotherapy, but all are essentially designed to relieve the child's distress and encourage development.

Proponents of the psychodynamic approach maintain that traditional psychoanalytic concepts can be used to find the underlying causes of behaviour disorders and emotional disturbance. They see little value in changing a person's overt behaviour and concentrate instead on altering the underlying psychopathology by helping the person remember unfortunate experiences from infancy and early childhood. These memories provide insight, allowing the patient to come to grips with the causes of disturbed behaviour.

Because disturbed behaviour is viewed as a pathological imbalance among the dynamic parts of the mind, psychodynamic intervention aims at removing the internal conflicts that are presumed to cause a child's unacceptable behaviour. Psychodynamic approaches emphasize the creation of a warm, supportive, and non-threatening atmosphere in which the child can continuously and consciously come to terms with repression, anxiety, conflict, and fear.

Educational intervention focuses on uncovering the underlying psychology to improve the child's psychological functioning. It is designed to reveal and relieve the

Table 11-5

Approaches to intervention with students with behaviour disorders

Approach	Treatment	Sample of methods
Biological	Alter the child's physiology.	Drug therapy, change in diet. The only intervention from this model of causation that has a research base is drug therapy.
Psychodynamic	Discover the underlying conflicts that cause problem behaviour.	Various therapies and counselling techniques. Verbalization and clarification of previously repressed thoughts; corrective emotional experiences resulting from the child's relationship with understanding adults; presentation of alternate modes of behaviour.
Psycho-educational	Create trust while helping the child to meet academic goals.	Therapies, crisis intervention, success in academic pursuits. Preventive classroom planning; permitting or sanctioning certain types of behaviour; tolerating behaviour beyond the child's control.
Behavioural	Rearrange environmental events. Focus on the behaviour, not the underlying causes.	Reinforcers, punishments, time-out, contracts, and so on. Selecting instructional programs on the basis of objectives to be achieved through practice with reinforcement and measurement until criterion performance is reached.
Ecological	Change the nature of the interaction between the child and the environment.	Counselling and a team approach. Crisis intervention; environmental modelling; curriculum planning. Identifying whatever norms happen to be used in the class setting; finding means for children to meet classroom goals.

child's unconscious psychic emotions and inner conflicts. The teacher's major concern is to help the child overcome inner turmoil rather than alter behaviours or focus specifically on academic skills.

Psycho-educational Approaches

When approaches are termed psycho-educational, the same supportive atmosphere, concern for underlying problems, and therapies are present as are seen in psychotherapeutic models. A far greater emphasis, however, is placed on educational success; teachers focus on academic skills and work closely with therapists to come to the root of a child's problems.

Teachers are trained to focus on their students' positive learning goals rather than on their defects and problems. This philosophical framework makes a psycho-educational approach to behavioural disorders a more positive, learning-directed approach than many other forms of mental health treatment.

Behavioural Approaches

It was in the 1960s that behaviourial psychology was systematically incorporated into work with students with behaviour disorders. Today behavioural approaches are the preferred intervention of many educators. Behaviourists do not concern themselves with the deep-rooted problems that psychodynamic theorists claim underlie behaviour problems. Nor do behaviourists categorize children's behaviour as abnormal, evil, mysterious, or deviant. Rather, they assume that the same principles that guide the development of normal behaviour are also involved in the development of inappropriate behaviour.

The behavioural approach maintains that all behaviour is caused and controlled by environmental events outside the child. All behaviour is therefore observable, measurable, and subject to change through a change in the environment. With this in mind, behaviourists attempt to use the principles of behaviour therapy (behaviour modification) to alter the inappropriate behaviour. Examples of behaviours that can be modified include hyperactivity, aggressiveness, distractibility, bed wetting, excessive fearfulness, and harmful anxiety.

There are three basic interrelated forms of treatment in the behavioural approach. The first uses teaching and training techniques to create behaviours that do not already exist. The second uses a number of techniques to maintain and generalize behaviours that are already established. The third uses other techniques to confine, reduce, or eliminate problem behaviour. Typically, all three modes of treament are undertaken simultaneously.

Behavioural techniques can be simply conceptualized on the ABC rule. In other words, the procedures attempt to change the events (antecedents) that precede problems (behaviours) as well as the events that follow (consequences). Compliance is not the sole goal of child socialization. Changing antecedents and consequences means bringing about more appropriate behaviours, not just eliminating poor behaviour. This is referred to as the "fair-pair" rule, which states that when a behaviour is decreased teachers should select a desirable behaviour to increase at the same time.

The fair-pair rule means that two questions need to be addressed in developing any behaviour change procedure. "What do I want the student to do instead?" and "What is the most effective and efficient means to help the student reach his or her goals?" Regardless of whether the student is withdrawn or aggressive, the first objective is to exhibit a positive response instead of the current behaviour; that is, give students a repertoire of appropriate responses rather than merely eliminating behaviours. For example, we may want a student to play with peers on the playground instead of playing alone and to play appropriately with groups instead of hitting peers during games. For both behaviour patterns, we have identified what we want the child to do instead of the current problem behaviour. Providing reinforcement for playing in a group may result in an increase in this behaviour along with a simultaneous and connected decrease in the inappropriate behaviour of hitting others.

Reinforcers or rewards are used to increase desirable behaviour and aversion techniques are used to decrease or extinguish undesirable behaviour. Reinforcement can be provided by anything that a child finds pleasurable. Reinforcers are usually divided into three types: primary reinforcers are candy and food; secondary reinforcers include objects that have no intrinsic value of their own, such as tokens and stars. Whether a child receives a primary or a secondary reinforcer, it is always accompanied by a social reinforcer such as a smile, a hug, or a pat on the back. Intervention is represented in Figure 11-2.

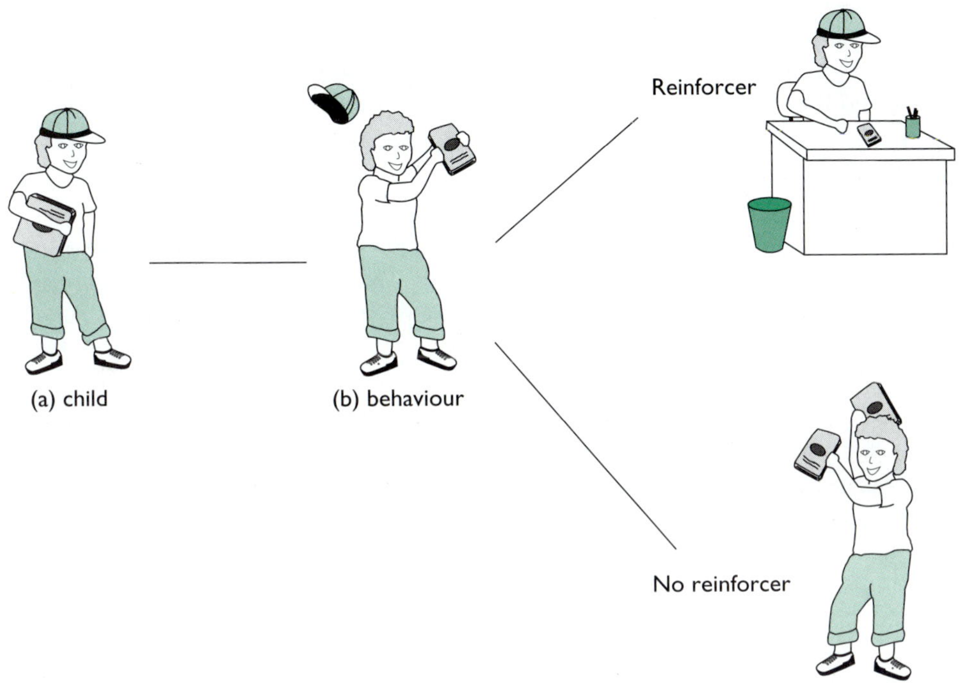

Figure 11-2 *How reinforcement works*

Positive reinforcement is far more effective than punishment, which is a poor deterrent to unwanted behaviour and should be used sparingly. Punishment generates students' anger, bringing greater conflict. Punishment does not answer the "why" of poor behaviour, does not teach appropriate behaviour, and does not suppress behaviour. In fact, it may lead to other unacceptable behaviours emerging, and may be used by children as a negative means of gaining attention from adults.

Some forms of behaviour modification are more suitable for general classrooms; others work better in self-contained settings. Token economies are widely used. Profile 11-2 presents a token ecomony system employed with an entire class. Such systems are equally applicable to individual class members (see Winzer, 1995).

Ecological Approaches

The usual positive aspects of life in school and community are not present for students with behaviour disorders. Ecological approaches focus on the match between the child and the environment. They use group processes such as dicussion groups, class meetings, and role playing. They may also include the teaching of the social skills and adaptive interpersonal behaviours. This is a particularly important academic feature for children with behaviour disorders because instruction helps children make and keep friends and get along with adults (Weissberg and Allen, 1986).

Profile

The grade seven class at the end of the hall was well known to all the students and teachers in the school. Any trouble, vandalism, or disruptive behaviour could generally be traced to that group of nine children. Although each child in the class was unique, they all behaved in ways that were unacceptable to the school and the community.

The children in this class had been punished so often that such disciplinary measures as detentions, time-out, and suspensions had little meaning for them. Indeed, such punishments usually resulted in increased resentment toward school personnel and an even more active dislike of learning. Rather than using further aversive measures, the grade seven teacher decided to institute a token-economy behavioural program.

Because of her students' age, the teacher invited and incorporated their suggestions for every step of the program. From some students, she won immediate co-operation. She decided to focus only on on-task behaviour because the students' problems were so diverse.

During the first weeks of the program, the children were told exactly how much seatwork would earn a token. For example, three math problems earned a poker chip. On Friday afternoon, students with ten chips could trade them in for a reinforcer, such as the viewing of a special film.

As the program continued, the teacher shaped her students' behaviour by making them work longer to earn tokens and by raising the token price of reinforcers. Wisely, she changed tokens and reinforcers often. She soon saw positive changes in behaviour, more on-task behaviour, increased learning, and a new sense of pride and achievement in the class.

Role playing involves both emotional and cognitive components. It is an activity in which participants assume a specific role in a demonstration or simulation. Some students may perform better with a script that shows the role played by the members, the sequence of activities, and the reward structure.

In the classroom, teachers may use bibliotherapy. Based on the concept that reading stories with positive role models can affect an individual's attitudes and behavioural responses, this approach is an important influence in shaping, moulding, and altering values (Lenkowsky, 1986).

TVDRP (TV or other media, discussion, rehearsal, and guided practice) is used to assist students with behaviour disorders. TVDRP stresses self-control, group participation, social awareness, social decision making, and problem solving (Elias and Taylor, 1995).

Social skills are specific behaviours that people perform when interacting with others. In the classroom, skills include communication skills, prosocial skills, collaborative skills, and group maintenance skills. These include listening, sharing and encouraging, and engaging in verbal and non-verbal interaction with others (Abrami et al., 1995). Further important social skills are:

- Greeting behaviours;
- Ways to extend and receive invitations;
- Positive listening skills;
- Conversational skills, such as asking about other people's interests, responding to others' questions, and maintaining an extended conversation by taking turns to comment on a topic;

- Giving verbal and non-verbal compliments and positive feedback;
- Positive methods of gaining teacher attention (for example, when asking about a work assignment);
- Acceptable habits of cleanliness, grooming, and health;
- The ability to inhibit reactions to stimuli to stem inappropriate outbursts;
- Self-management skills which enable children to select appropriate choices based on probable consequences.

Survey research indicates that virtually no difference exists between classroom and special education teachers' attitudes toward children's social behaviour, although both groups of teachers tend to be less tolerant of problem behaviour within the context of an already disruptive classroom (Kauffman and Wong, 1991). Research also shows that both classroom and special education teachers value academic-related social skills (Walker and McConnell, 1988). Teachers assign more importance to skills such as following rules and directions, volunteering answers, and interacting with teachers and peers about school work than skills involving conversation, initiating social contact with peers, and assertiveness.

The development of social skills has important implications for children's academic and vocational success as well as for long-term mental health adjustment. In a study of the factors that influence success in the mainstream (Bishop, 1986), interaction with peers ranked second and social skills ranked third among seventy variables that respondents thought to be associated with academic success.

The rationale for social skills intervention has found support in the peer acceptance literature, which has indicated that children with early peer difficulties are at risk for a number of negative outcomes, including dropping out of school (see Parker and Asher, 1987). The strategies employed and their rate of success are varied (Fox, 1989). Intervention to increase social acceptance has been attempted with low-status children in regular classrooms (Bierman, Miller, and Stabb, 1987); with children labelled as mentally retarded, learning disabled, and behaviourally disordered (Zaragoza, Vaughn, and McIntosh, 1991); and with mildly disabled children integrated into regular classrooms (Sasso and Rude, 1987).

The type of social skills that teachers perceive as critical for classroom success has implications for their selection of skills for intervention. The best way for teachers to determine which social skills to teach is to conduct informal natural observations (Cartledge and Kleefeld, 1989).

One way to promote social interaction is to introduce a social interaction program within the context of the entire classroom. Alternatively, training can be directed solely at children who show deficits, with the training taking place in settings where the social behaviour would most naturally occur. The lessons are best implemented in groups of three to five students and optimally should include socially competent peers to serve as models. The first group lesson should focus on three things: an explanation of why the group is meeting, a definition of what social skills are, and an explanation of what is expected of each student during the lesson. It may also be helpful to implement behaviour management procedures for the group, such as contingencies for compliance and non-compliance. It is important to prompt the students to use newly learned skills throughout the day and across settings to promote maintenance and generalization, and to reinforce the students when they use new skills (Lewis, Heflin, and DiGangi, 1991).

Anxious, withdrawn students need a supportive atmosphere that will help them to view themselves more positively.

Quite a number of commercial programs have been developed that incorporate effective methods of behaviour modification, modelling, role playing, feedback, and transfer of training. The techniques are applied to social skills for children and adolescents. Skills range from how to have a conversation to learning to resist peer pressure (e.g., Goldstein, et al., 1980).

The Early Childhood Social Skills Program (Odem, Kohler, and Strain, 1987) is a well-validated procedure that uses normal children and children with developmental delays in classroom implementation. The skills include making offers and requests to share, offering play suggestions, making offers and requests to give assistance, showing affection, and giving compliments. There are two phases in the program — formal teacher instruction and practice. For instruction, the teacher places children in groups during play and teaches a skill. Sharing is the first skill taught. To teach, the teacher demonstrates the strategy and then monitors as all children perform. For adolescents, the ASSET program (Hazel et al., 1981), developed at the Kansas Institute for Research in Learning Disabilities, provides a set of training procedures to help students gain social interaction skills.

Curriculum Adaptations

Managing children of any age, any grade, and any functional level can be a challenging and often frustrating task. No matter how well teachers manage their classrooms or centres, or how conscientious, consistent, and fair they are, there will inevitably be some children who fail to respond as positively as others and who consistently test the teacher's authority.

Controlling behaviour and teaching discipline and self-control are aspects of the broader construct referred to as classroom management. In general terms, **classroom management** refers to "the way in which teachers manipulate the classroom environment to minimize disruptions and give all children the optimum opportunity to engage in appropriate behaviour and reach learning and social goals" (Winzer, 1995, p. 627).

Classroom management includes curriculum planning, organizational procedures, resources, arranging the environment, maintaining child progress, and anticipating potential problems. Within the construct of classroom management, **behaviour management** refers to all the ways in which teachers control inappropriate and disruptive behaviour as well as ways in which children are taught discipline and to control their own behaviour.

The word *discipline* derives from *disciple*, a follower of the master's teaching. **Discipline** may be defined as helping children to learn to guide their own behaviour in a way that shows respect and caring for themselves, other people, and the physical environment. Self-discipline involves being able to consider an outcome and select the behaviour that will achieve it (Glenn and Nelson, 1987).

Discipline must be taught, learned, and internalized because discipline is necessary if the classroom and the children it contains are to function properly. The need for consistency is very high; most authorities agree that whatever system of classroom management is used, it can be successful only if it is implemented in a systematic and consistent fashion. Students need to know what to expect of the teacher, what is expected of them, and what the consequences are for success and failure.

The best way to handle inappropriate behaviours is to prevent them from happening in the first place. **Preventative discipline** refers to strategies and procedures that militate against any discipline problems arising. Good preventative discipline includes a warm and interesting environment, logical routines, clear rules, much positive reinforcement, children's knowledge of consequences for misdemeanours, and a curriculum matched to the needs of the child. When the curriculum is meaningful and well presented, students are less inclined to engage in disruptive behaviour.

The best way to handle inappropriate behaviours is to prevent them from happening in the first place.

Coherent, comprehensive descriptions of educational programs for students with behaviour disorders are relatively rare in the professional literature. Nevertheless, the curriculum for mildly behaviourally disordered students will generally parallel that for normal youngsters, although alternate methods for basic academic skill development may be required.

To the extent that the curriculum is not a powerful enough tool, the teacher needs to compensate with other methods. For students with behaviour disorders, academic curricula must come to terms with their affective needs. Affective development is rooted in an individual's self-concept. Besides academic success, disturbed children need a warm supportive atmosphere that promotes an increase in self-esteem and self-concept.

In the area of ADHD, only a handful of projects have contributed to more effective educational practices. Research into behaviour management for students with ADHD has focused on increasing on-task behaviour, task completion, compliance, impulse control, and social skills while reducing hyperactivity, off-task behaviour, and disruptive behaviour and aggression (Fiore, Becker, and Nero, 1993).

Children with intrinsic attention problems are difficult to handle in groups, and teachers may consider reducing the amount of time these students spend in group settings. Proximity control — seating the student near the teacher — may also help to sustain attention (Winzer, 1989).

Figure 11-3
Curriculum components

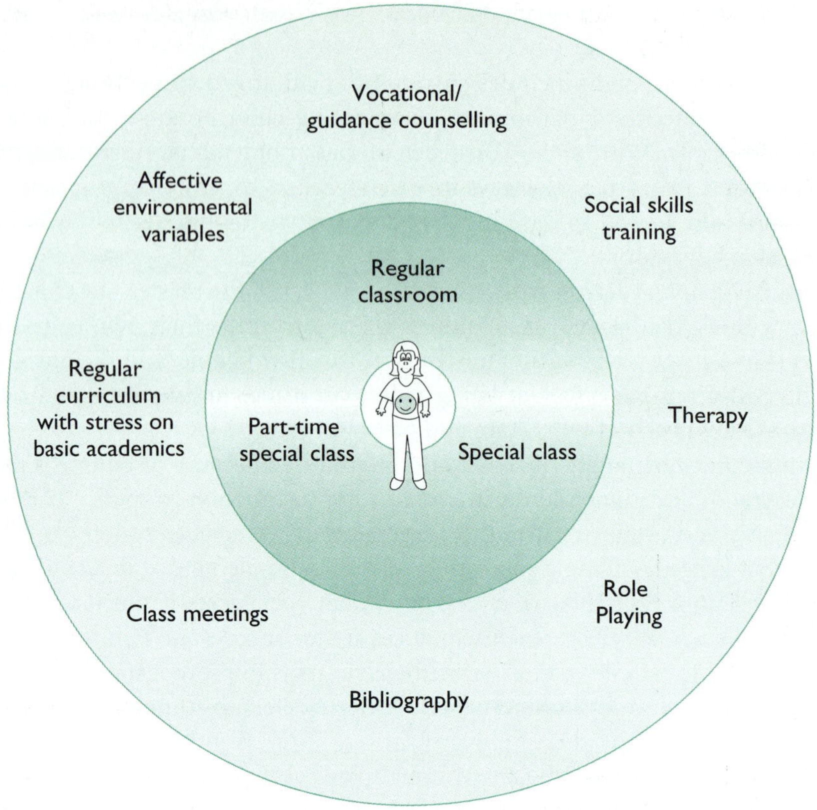

Tips for Teachers

Tips for teachers of students with behaviour disorders

Classroom climate

- Establish supportive interpersonal relationships with students.
- Try to create a warm atmosphere characterized by acceptance without permissiveness.
- Establish routines; set clear limits to behaviour.
- Make class rules sparingly. Often remind students of rules.
- Be consistent. When teachers are consistent in enforcing rules, children learn self-control.
- Bear in mind that each child is unique. Children must be treated as individuals regardless of their behaviour patterns.
- Focus on academic skills. Provide children with experiences in which they can succeed.
- Forgive and forget the past; do not allow past misdeeds to form the basis for present interactions.
- Convey the idea that you like the child even if you do not find the behaviour acceptable.
- Allow older students to be involved in setting up reinforcement systems.
- Provide models of non-aggressive responses to aggression-provoking behaviour.
- Provide reinforcement for non-aggressive behaviour; do not allow positive reinforcement for aggressive behaviour.

- If you step into an aggressive act, devote as much attention as possible to the victim and ignore the perpetrator as much as possible.

Adaptations

- Seat disruptive children among others who are well behaved.
- Consider the timetable: if a certain time or subject seems to cause disruption, alter the scheduling.
- Remove objects or toys that cause problems.
- Keep a careful eye on scissors, pencils, and other potentially dangerous objects.
- Immediately remove the results of poor behaviour.
- Keep rigorous documentation of behavioural interventions.

Instruction

- Break up long lessons by changing the pace and allowing some physical movement.
- Be consistent in demands and expectations.
- Teach social interaction skills.
- Ensure that students participate, as far as possible, in all aspects of school programs at the elementary and secondary levels.
- Help anxious, withdrawn and immature children to view themselves more positively.
- Do not call on withdrawn students to answer questions unless they volunteer.
- When an anxious student does answer and makes a mistake, be supportive with "That's a good try," or "You almost made it," and move onto another student immediately.
- For aggressive children, training must not only emphasize that the aggression is inappropriate but must also help them to generate non-aggressive solutions to conflict.
- To eliminate aggression, eliminate the payoff for aggression; model and coach, create non-aggressive environments, and teach social skills.
- For ADHD students, teachers can hold attention for longer periods by facing the student and establishing eye contact.
- Use concrete aids such as flow charts, flip charts, and overhead projectors. Students may also attend more closely if they are provided with a lesson outline or a glossary of key terms prior to the lesson (Winzer, 1989).

Social Intervention

Social intervention encompasses a variety of methods and services to help behaviourally disordered children and their families. Children's Mental Health Centres provide a spectrum of treatment programs. Foster care may also be used to remove a child from home for a period of time. This can be done if the family is unable to cope with the child's behaviour or if the home atmosphere is considered to be damaging for the child.

Summary

1. We use the term *behaviourally disordered* to describe children and youth meeting difficulties in adjusting to normal behavioural expectations.
2. In Canada special institutions such as reformatories, industrial schools, and refuges were founded in the middle decades of the last century to serve at least some of these children and youth. In the twentieth century, children with behaviour disorders became the concern of psychiatrists and psychologists, and the preferred treatment was psychiatric in nature. In many cases, education required changes in the child's total living environment, often placement in an institution or segregated

setting. With the recent movement of more and more students with behaviour disorders into regular schools and classrooms, educators are finding ways to cope with problem behaviours.

3. Children with behaviour disorders are not rare and most of us have come into contact with or observed such young people. These children are troubled, and they cause trouble for those with whom they interact. They exhibit, to a marked extent and over a long period of time, behaviour that is clearly undesirable, inappropriate, and maladaptive in the social context. Some disturbed children withdraw; the great majority strike out with hostility and aggression.
4. While deviant behaviour has been conceptualized in many ways and definitions have been proposed from a variety of perspectives and disciplines, no universally accepted definition of behaviour disorders exists. The expectations of teachers and other observers play a key role in defining behaviour disorders. In fact, in many instances, the importance of a behaviour is largely determined by the teacher's expectations.
5. Classification systems may use the the system proposed in the *Diagnostic and Statistical Manual*; however, it is most common today to establish clusters or dimensions of behaviour.
6. Of the many variables contributing to human experience, none has been conclusively shown to underlie emotional problems and many factors can lead young people to act out in ways that are unacceptable and reprehensible. The problems have a huge range of origins — genetic, biophysical, disturbed family climate, deleterious environment, academic difficulties, faulty learning and other school factors, to mention only a few. A combination of risks has far more negative effects on children than any single source of risk.
7. Behaviour can be seen as internalizing or externalizing. Children with conduct disorders attract attention with their overtly disruptive behaviours. Anxious and withdrawn children internalize their behaviour. They may suffer from nausea, pains, headaches, phobias, fears, obsessions, shyness, nightmares, crying, depression, self-consciousness, and withdrawal. Children with ADHD tend to be distractible and to spend more time in off-task behaviour than do their peers. Most researchers agree that attention deficits are pervasive disorders that appear early in life and persist into adult life. The problems associated with hyperactivity persist and affect academic and social functioning.
8. The character of childhood aggression changes dramatically with age as does children's perceptions of what is hostile.
9. Behaviour disorders are easier to identify than to define or classify. A major problem when evaluating behaviour centres on what is normal behaviour as opposed to what is abnormal in the classroom.
10. Stimulants and other drugs are often used in the management of children with behaviour disorders.
11. Most of these youngsters can be well served in regular classrooms provided teachers are given assistance regarding how to manage misbehaviour.

12. All psychotherapeutic approaches search for the child's inner conflicts and motivations while trying to explain current or past events. Behavioural approaches, using the principles of classical and operant conditioning first outlined by Ivan Pavlov, J.B. Watson, and B.F. Skinner, are more concerned with producing desirable behaviour. The ecological approach to behaviour disorders emphasizes the need to look at the total interaction of the child with the social environment in order to know how the youngster's ecological system functions and how his or her behaviours fit or do not fit these ecosystems.

13. Social acceptance is more than tolerance. The use of "skillstreaming" instruction can increase prosocial and positive behaviour.

SECTION 6
Children with Health Problems and Developmental Disabilities

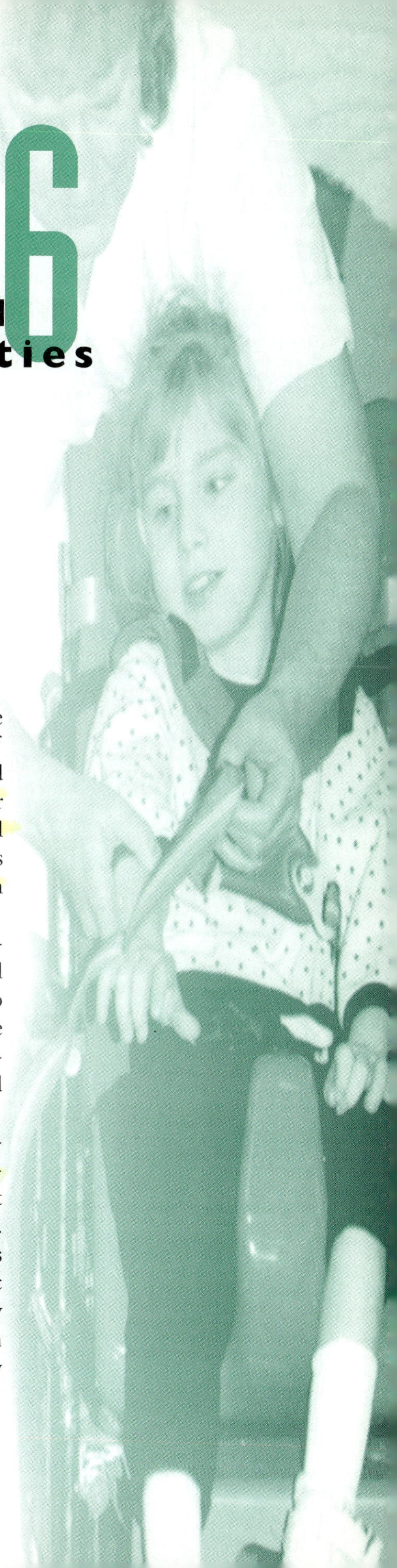

Nowhere in the study of exceptionality or special education is the spectrum of possible disorders more apparent than in the area of children with special health care needs, neurological disabilities, and orthopedic and physical handicaps. Of these youngsters, nearly half suffer from cerebral palsy. Children with asthma and allergies make up nearly all the remainder of the population. Children with other conditions, such as cystic fibrosis or spina bifida, form only a tiny percentage of those with physical and health disabilities.

Given such a diverse population, the medical, social, technical, and educational needs of these children vary dramatically. Some students will require intense intervention; others may need only minor adjustments to classroom physical layout or scheduling. Some children may use adaptive equipment, including orthotic and prosthetic devices, to assist their functioning. Much adaptive equipment is used for support, for mobility, and for positioning.

Although the range of physical and health disorders is vast, we are actually discussing low-incidence conditions. Pervasive developmental disorders and multiple handicaps are conditions of even lower incidence, but ones that have devastating effects on children's development and potential.

Pervasive developmental disorders are severe qualitative subnormalities that are not normal for any stage of development (American Psychiatric Association, 1980). They have been the subject of intense research activity and have spawned a variety of treatment approaches. These children present a tremendous challenge to the school system and test the ingenuity of teachers and diagnosticians.

Subsumed within the broad category of pervasive developmental disorders are childhood psychoses that affect many basic areas of psychological development at the same time and to a severe degree. Psychotic children display severe qualitative abnormalities and disturbances that are seen as distortions of development. Children with infantile autism differ markedly from those whose psychoses begin later, and most researchers today hold that autism is a developmental disorder that is distinct from childhood psychoses such as schizophrenia. Children who suffer from infantile autism present a shifting array of behaviours that seem to defy analysis; they indulge in repetitive, ritualistic, and solitary activities, responding to those in the environment with aloofness and indifference.

Children with multiple handicaps have a range of impairments. While innumerable combinations of handicaps are possible, some appear more often than others and some are more difficult to cope with than others. Within the multiply disabled population, deaf-blind children are among the most studied.

In discussing children with multiple impairments, it must be remembered that conditions are not additive. In other words, a child who is deaf and blind represents an entirely new category of exceptionality. The needs of these children are varied and complex; interventions involve a wide range of techniques and personnel.

Definitions in these areas are particularly untidy, and there are many ways of categorizing the conditions for purposes of discussion. We arbitrarily discuss children with specific health care needs in one chapter and then move on to children with neurological difficulties. Under pervasive developmental disorders, we discuss children with childhood schizophrenia and those with infantile autism. A chapter is reserved for children with multiply handicapping conditions. The reader must remain acutely aware that much overlap exists in all the conditions mentioned in this section. Many children with autism, for example, are actually multiply handicapped and many multiply handicapped children demonstrate autistic behaviours. Pediatric AIDS can be discussed as a health problem, as a neurological difficulty or, depending on the course of the disease, as a multiply handicapping condition.

CHAPTER 12

Children with Special Health Care Needs

Historical Notes

In this chapter we discuss a number of common diseases and conditions that affect the lives and functioning of children and adults. These health conditions, such as cancer, diabetes, asthma and allergies, and genetic problems such as cystic fibrosis and muscular dystrophy are essentially medical problems and are handled within medical parameters.

It is reasonable to assume that such health disorders, under these and different names, have plagued humanity from its beginnings. As we have pointed out, the Egyptian physicians, Hippocrates in Greece, and Galen and Celsus in Rome intervened with a wide variety of medical, sensory, and psychological conditions.

Hippocrates (circa. 460-377 B.C.), who founded one of the great medical schools on the island of Cos and probably worked in one of the temples of health, illuminated the path that later physicians would follow. In the treatment of illnesses and disabilities, Hippocrates adopted accounts of medical intervention from ancient Egypt. He intervened with a variety of conditions and largely discounted ancient conceptions of etiology — the gods, a malignant being, the moon, spells, and the like. Hippocrates assumed the mystical origins of mental and physical anomalies to be less important than causes explainable through observation and diagnosis based on contemporary knowledge of anatomy and physiology.

Hippocratic medicine was defined by butchering animals and examining battle wounds, not by examination of the human body. Fundamental to Hippocratic medicine were the four humours (fluids) — blood, lymph, yellow bile, and black bile — of which the ancients deemed blood the most important. Each humour was endowed with a basic quality, such as heat, cold, dryness, and moistness, from which arose certain traits and conditions. A sanguinous person, for example, was subject to inflammatory diseases but could sustain much blood letting; a choleric person was thought to be one who acted hastily and rashly. Disease developed when internal or external factors produced an excess of one of the humours or when an imbalance of these basic qualities acted as organs to produce deleterious effects (Winzer, 1993).

In the time of Augustus and Tiberias Caesar (the first half of the first century A.D.), the medical knowledge of the world was collected and probably amplified by Aulus Cornelius Celsus (25 B.C.-A.D. 50) in *De Medicina.* Celsus described how he followed the prescriptions of his great predecessors, especially Hippocrates. The most common cure from Celsus was hellebore which, given the numerous references in the non-medical literature, may have entered common usage in antiquity, much as aspirin has become a household word today.

Of all the physicians who thronged toward Rome, Galen (130-200) — anatomist, physiologist, and neurologist — was one of the most influential. He extended the humoural theory of Hippocrates into a body of medical writing that influenced medical progress until the Renaissance.

Medieval society was not a medical desert; it was replete with empirics, divines, parsons, and magicians, as well as responsible physicians. From the thirteenth century on, these physicians created a body of medical literature which contained descriptions and cures for a range of conditions. Medieval notions of anatomy, physiology, etiology, and treatment drew from Hippocrates, Celsus, and Galen. Neverthless, conceptions of anatomy and physiology were not exact, and treatments were often grafted on bizarre notions taken from religion and demonology so that cures lay in the realm of incantations, spells, witches' brews.

With the Renaissance arose a new interest in humanistic principles, individual learning, and the secular arts. Art led to an interest in the human body and so to the development of more sophisticated surgery and medical practices. The age-old fear of dissecting the human body dissolved, and a huge spurt in anatomy and physiology was witnessed.

In the following centuries, medical advances continued apace. Such advances as Franz Gall's discovery of the hemisperes of the brain and inklings of brain function, the discovery of vaccination and anaesthesia, and the first glimmerings of the hereditary aspects of certain conditions lent light to medical diagnosis and prognosis.

Regardless of major advances, however, the conditions we discuss in this chapter were often lethal — and indeed, still are. Before the very recent advent of sophisticated medical intervention and technical assistance and devices, afflicted individuals could anticipate only an abbreviated lifespan.

But causes, prevention, and cures are still, to a greater or lesser extent, baffling. While, for example, cystic fibrosis and muscular dystrophy are known to result from defective genes, cures are not yet available. Since the discovery of insulin in the early 1920s, diabetes is controlled, but not yet prevented or cured. Intense medical research has not yet established precise causes and cures for cancer and AIDS.

Special health care needs include a huge range of conditions and diseases. Many result from a variety of genetic and environmental causes, while others are associated with prenatal probems, prematurity, and problems of gestation. Some conditions are transient, others are lifelong; some occur more frequently in children than in adults. When found in children, the majority of chronic illnesses manifest themselves during the first three years of life.

Children with health care needs present educational challenges that differ in many ways from those presented by children with other disabilities. Medical concerns are one of the major factors affecting learning for these children; their medical needs and technological dependence must be met before they can benefit from the classroom experience.

Some of these children are technologically dependent; many need pharmacological management. Others may require supplemental assistance from support personnel such as physical and occupational therapists, nurses, and teacher aides. In addition, some conditions result in a roller coaster of changing needs as children are in remission or in acute periods or are recovering from surgery or serious bouts. This entails changing treatment and different side effects.

All educational personnel must be familiar not only with the appropriate medical procedures and interventions that are part of the regular care of students with special health care needs but also with those required in emergency situations. As well, educators must be aware of the factors that put students at risk for learning difficulties. These can include fatigue, limited vitality, short attention span, and limited mobility.

Regardless of the diagnostic category, children with special health care needs have the same wants as other youngsters. The basic goals of education are the same for these youngsters as they are for all other students. Children need to learn civic responsibilities, human relationships, self-realization, and economic efficiency, and they must be helped toward maximum self-sufficiency.

Not all, or even most, children with special health care needs will require special education, but most will need some type of additional monitoring by school personnel. In fact, almost all children with health difficulties will be placed in regular classrooms. Special education may be warranted only because the condition or illness resulted in loss of school time and the child is consequently falling behind in school work.

It is important to note that there may be psychological and emotional correlates of a number of physical and health problems. Serious questioning of the psychological and social development of children with special health needs has led to the emergence of the discipline of pediatric psychology.

While the number of health problems involving other body systems is staggering, in this chapter we restrict discussion to a few specific and sometimes life-threatening conditions and describe their impact on the lives of children and adolescents. We also discuss musculoskeletal impairments and child abuse or neglect.

Definitions

One of the major problems when discussing health care needs (and neurological disorders) is the diversity of the conditions and their sequelae. This leads to a range of overlapping descriptors. For example, orthopedic and neurologic impairments, while two distinct types of disabilities, may nevertheless cause similar limitations in movement (Shivers and Fait, 1985).

One child can be described in a number of ways. A child with muscular dystrophy, for example, can be said to have a health disorder, a musculoskeletal impairment, a physical disability, an orthopedic problem, or a motor impairment. Similarly, cerebral palsy can be categorized as a neurological impairment, a significant motor disability, a physical disability, and an orthopedic disability. The conditions discussed in this chapter and in Chapter 13 (excluding child abuse) are shown in Table 12-1 with their possible descriptors.

Commonly used descriptors include:

- ***chronic health problems*** occur when the presence of a disease or medical condition interferes with school attendance and learning and hinders the ability to lead a normal life. This category includes such conditions as sickle cell anemia, arthritis, cancer, and asthma.

Table 12-1

Conditions and possible descriptors

	Chronic health problems	Neurological dysfunction	Musculo-skeletal impairment	Orthopedic impairment	Physical/motor disability	Technology dependent/medically fragile
allergies	x					
arthritis	x		x		x	
asthma	x					
cancer	x					
cerebral palsy		x	x	x	x	
club foot			x	x	x	
cystic fibrosis	x					
diabetes	x					
epilepsy	x	x				
hydrocephelus						x
limb deficiencies			x	x	x	
multiple sclerosis	x	x		x	x	
muscular dystrophy			x	x	x	
pediatric AIDS	x	x				
scoliosis			x	x	x	x
sickle cell anemia	x					
spina bifida with myelomeningocele		x	x	x	x	
traumatic head injury		x				

- *infectious diseases* are conditions such as meningitis, which, though transient, can leave devastating sequelae.
- *physical disabilities* are those that affect body systems; they include health disorders and problems related to mobility and motor skills. Physical disabilities that have associated motor disabilities and deviations include cerebral palsy, muscular dystrophy, and spina bifida.
- *orthopedic conditions* are those that arise from any cause and affect mobility. Specifically, the term refers to

disabilities that relate primarily to disorders of the skeleton, joints, and muscles including clubfoot, the absence of some members, or other congenital anomalies; impairments caused by diseases such as poliomyelytis or bone tuberculosis; impairments caused by cerebral palsy; amputations; and contractures caused by fractures or burns (Federal Register, 1977).

- *musculoskeletal impairments* are specific disorders involving bones or muscles. **Musculoskeletal impairments** are those conditions that impede bodily movements in the absence of damage to the central nervous system. The causes of such conditions range from inherited diseases and congenital malformations to infections and accidents.
- *neurological dysfunctions* occur before, during, or after birth and include cerebral palsy and head traumas.
- *technology dependent* and/or *medically fragile* infants and children rely on technology in some way to mitigate health problems (CEC, 1988).
- *technology dependent* refers to conditions that require technological intervention. Children need "a medical device to compensate for the loss of vital bodily function and substantial ongoing nursing care to avert death or further disability" (OTA, 1987, p. 3). For example, a child may be ventilator dependent, oxygen dependent, or nutritional supplement dependent. The child may need heart monitoring, apnea monitoring, or kidney dialysis.
- *medically fragile* is a term that overlaps the above category. According to the Council for Exceptional Children (1988), "medically fragile children require specialized technological health care procedures for life support during the school day. These students may or may not require special education."

In this chapter we restrict our discussion to health problems and musculoskeletal impairments that do not have neurological involvement. Impairments directly related to damage of the central nervous system are discussed in Chapter 13.

Prevalence of Health Problems

The prevalence of chronic health problems is very difficult to determine, primarily because

- there is such a variety of conditions and there exist inconsistencies in defining various disabilities;
- different provinces use different methods for gathering data, producing very different results;
- nation-wide health statistics tend to rely on a limited number of categories, which means that many health problems go uncounted;
- in both provinicial and national surveys, individuals with multiple handicaps may be counted twice;
- there are reported increases in certain physical disabilities over the past two decades (Batshaw and Perrett, 1986), especially in allergies and asthma;
- physical disabilities are often found with other disabling conditions.

Although it is difficult to obtain exact prevalence and incidence figures for specific conditions, it can be said that most (though not all) are very low-incidence problems.

Of all Canadian children suffering from any form of disability in 1986, 9 percent had a heart problem or disease. Smaller percentages were affected by epilepsy (5 percent), cerebral palsy (4 percent), a kidney condition or disease (3 percent), or a lung condition or disease, excluding allergies, asthma, and bronchitis (Nessner, 1990).

Special Health Care Needs

Health disorders are essentially medical conditions requiring a complex and sophisticated range of interventions that include surgical procedures, prosthetic devices, drug therapy, diet management, and ongoing medical treatment. There is no necessary correlation between health disorders and impairments in other domains of functioning. Generally, children with health problems demonstrate normal development in cognitive, communication, and socio-emotional skills. However, there may be disruptions attributable to the condition, such as long periods of illness, hospitalization, and missing school and peer interactions. These mean that special accommodations and programs are sometimes required.

It is not unusual for a teacher to have a student in the classroom who has a terminal illness. With terminally ill children, teachers may need special training in managing their own and other students' attitudes toward death and dying (Shell, 1981). The inevitability of death has to be faced by the teacher and the other children on some level. When a child with AIDS is in the classroom, for example, children fare best when honest discussions about terminal illness occur right from the beginning (Weiner and Septimus, 1991). Children need to know they had no part in causing the illness and that it is not catching.

Cystic Fibrosis

Cystic fibrosis (CF) is is a genetically determined inborn error of metabolism characterized by pervasive dysfunction of the exocrine glands (glands in which secretions are passed through ducts). Cystic fibrosis is the most frequently occurring genetic disorder among Caucasians in North America and many European countries (Brinthaupt, 1991). However, the condition seems to be both ethnic and geographically variable — it is very rare among Swedes and among North American Blacks; it is virtually non-existent among Asians (Brinthaupt, 1991). One out of every 20 Caucasians is a carrier of the gene for cystic fibrosis, and approximately one birth in every 1600 to 2000 among North American Caucasians is affected (Brinthaupt, 1991). In a family with an affected child, two out of three siblings are likely to be carriers, and one out of five is likely to have the disease.

Cystic fibrosis is transmitted through an autosomal recessive gene, but it appears that more than one genetic defect can cause the disease. The main malformation in the CF gene's twisted double chain of DNA is the absence of a few chemicals. However, some 15 000 DNA samples taken from patients around the world with cystic fibrosis indicate that there are at least sixty and probably a good many more additional malformations that produce the symptoms that were classically lumped together as cystic fibrosis.

Cystic fibrosis is an extremely complex and involved disorder, quite variable in its manifestation. The condition primarily affects the respiratory and digestive systems, although there are varied degrees of system involvement. Fully manifested cases present a triad of chronic pulmonary disease, pancreatic enzyme deficiency, and inordinately high sweat electrolytes. Symptoms include high salt concentration in the sweat glands and the production of thick sticky mucus that clogs breathing and digestion. The mucus obstruction disrupts the functions of the lungs and other vital organs. In the lungs it creates pockets of infection and pulmonary dysfunction which frequently result in chronic episodes of pneumonia and bronchitis. With repeated infection, the lungs are gradually destroyed. As lung deterioration occurs, the heart is also burdened and heart failure is a common by-product of cystic fibrosis.

Excessive mucous secretions also interfere with or prevent digestion and other intestinal processes. Cystic fibrosis affects virtually every part of the digestive system. The pancreas, gall bladder, liver, and intestines often function abnormally and exhibit changes in the tissues. Children often fail to gain weight despite increased appetite. They grow very slowly and never appear to thrive (Holsclaw, 1978).

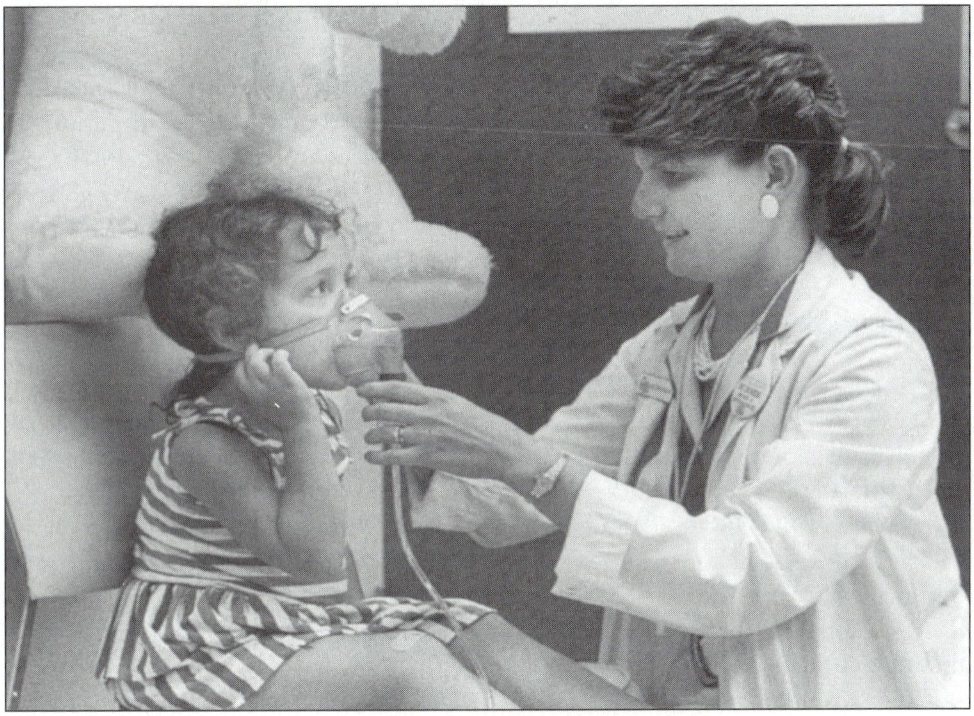

Treatment for cystic fibrosis is extensive. It involves diet management, respiratory disease management, and drug therapy.

Intervention for cystic fibrosis is as varied and complex as the disease, requiring diet management, therapy and management of respiratory disorders, and various regimes of drug therapy. Before antibiotics were available, approximately 75 percent of children with cystic fibrosis died before age ten. Life expectancy has been greatly extended and at present many older patients are being treated. Recently, surgical implants have become an option for cystic fibrotic patients.

The primary treatment procedures are medication and therapy. Antibiotics are prescribed for cystic fibrotic children when lung infections are present. With medication, percussion therapy serves to dislodge mucus as the chest is vigorously clapped and vibrated. In addition, diet can be quite effective in the management of disorders of the digestive system. The special diet is high in protein, high in calories, and low in fat. This is combined with dosages of an enzyme needed to compensate for the insufficiency of the pancreas.

Developmental Consequences

Children with cystic fibrosis do not suffer any form of intellectual impairment and should be educated in regular classrooms. However, they will probably miss many days of school because of respiratory infections or intestinal disorders. They may have a chronic cough and may need extra snacks during the day.

It is on the family that a child with cystic fibrosis seems to have the greatest impact. For many families, everyday activities are dependent on the current health status of the child with cystic fibrosis. Regimens of treatment, medication, feeding, positioning, and medical care can take up most of the day. Parents must learn the therapeutic techniques to assist in their child's treatment. This usually consists of twice daily half-hour sessions involving chest percussion and postural draining. The purpose of pounding the chest is to elicit coughing, which encourages the elimination of mucus. The changes in posture also aid in the draining process.

When the child is young, meal times can be a recurrent problem with hours spent feeding the child. As well, medical decisions become an ongoing part of family life. Parents spend much time searching out information and becoming fluent in the medical terms related to their child's illness. Moreover, illnesses such as cystic fibrosis are an affront to an assumed developmental order for the family life cycle; parents must confront the implications for development and life span.

Diabetes Mellitus

Diabetes mellitus is a disorder of sugar metabolism. It is caused by a pancreatic disorder in the production of insulin, a hormone needed to metabolize glucose. Unlike many chronic health disorders, diabetes is a high-incidence condition. In Canada, it affects one in every 600 children under the age of 10.

Diabetes is divided into two major types. Type I, or insulin-dependent diabetes, is usually associated with early onset (under twenty-five years of age) and includes juvenile diabetes. Type II, non-insulin-dependent diabetes, ordinarily occurs after age forty (Krupp and Chatton, 1983). Type II diabetics produce quantities of insulin but they do not use it efficiently.

Type I diabetes brews silently for several years. The onset of the disease is signalled by thirst, hunger, weight loss, fatigue or weakness, excessive urination, and sometimes blurred vision. Onset may occur several months after the outbreak of specific viruses (Rodger and Hunt, 1980). For example, there may be sequelae resulting from maternal rubella. One study of rubella-deafened children discovered that 2 percent had overt diabetes and a total of 20 percent had abnormalities of glucose metabolism (Shaver, Boughman, and Nance, 1985).

Young people stricken with insulin-dependent, or Type I, diabetes once faced certain death within a year of diagnosis. They died because the pancreas lost its ability to make insulin, which is required for normal metabolism. Without insulin, glucose accumulates in the blood stream and urine while the body draws on other sources of energy until it literally starves.

Isolation of the insulin hormone from animals in 1921 made it possible to control diabetes with daily insulin injections and has since meant survival for millions of diabetics. Neither animal insulin nor the more modern human form offers a cure. Injections must be taken once or more a day for life. Many diabetics eventually suffer from devastating complications. As the disease persists, blood vessels can be damaged, leading to heart disease, stroke, blindness, or kidney failure. Nerve damage is also common (Atkinson and MacLaren, 1990).

The symptoms of non-insulin-dependent diabetes, a disease caused by an entirely different mechanism that is not fully understood, are more subtle than Type I diabetes. Type II diabetics are usually older than forty and overweight; susceptibility may be genetically transmitted (Berkow, 1982). These patients produce various quantities of insulin but they typically use it inefficiently. Some of them are treated with insulin to control blood glucose levels, but they do not require the drug for day-to-day survival (Atkinson and Maclaren, 1990).

The treatment of diabetes involves a diet low in carbohydrates and fats, accompanied by regular injections of insulin. Food intake, insulin, and exercise must be carefully balanced and monitored throughout the diabetic's life.

Insulin intake, diet, and exercise can prevent immediate and long-term complications associated with hyperglycemia (high blood sugar) or hypoglycemia (low blood sugar). Hyperglycemia leads to ketoacidosis, a chemical imbalance that produces acute and serious illness, unconsciousness, coma, and ultimately death. Although moderate but chronic hyperglycemia is thought to cause the long-term complications associated with diabetes in adulthood (such as retinopathy and microvascular disease), the specific effects of a moderate elevation of blood glucose on children's brain functioning is not known. Severe hypoglycemia, caused by an excess of insulin intake, produces unconsciousness and seizures. Both hypoglycemic convulsions and ketoacidosis have been associated with abnormalities in brain functioning (Rovet, Erlich, and Hoppe, 1988).

Developmental Consequences

Diabetic children can participate in all school activities unless otherwise advised by a physician. In addition to regular education, diabetic children must be taught to manage their condition. Parents and medical personnel must teach older diabetic children to inject their own insulin, monitor their blood sugar and urine sugar levels, and maintain a balance among nutrition, exercise, and insulin levels.

For children, the balance of diet, exercise, and insulin is often difficult to maintain, particularly in the presence of illness or infection. School personnel must always be informed when a student is diabetic. Teachers should understand the child's condition and recognize signs of imbalance. Health personnel should provide appropriate guidelines regarding the timing of school meals and the timing of school exercise.

In the past, it was thought that diabetes caused no impediment to intellectual functioning. Recently, several investigators have reported that children and adolescents who develop their diabetes early in life are at risk for subsequent neuro-cognitive impairment. Researchers (Rovet, Erlich, and Hoppe, 1988) who explored the effects on children's cognitive development of insulin-dependent diabetes mellitus concluded that children who develop diabetes before the age of four are at greater risk for subsequent intellectual impairment. Particularly affected are skills in the visuo-spatial area of cognitive functioning and mathematical ability. These findings correlate with a poorer academic history and a greater need for special education. Girls appear to be somewhat more affected than boys.

An understanding and tactful teacher can minimize potentially uncomfortable situations and model accepting attitudes for students.

Diabetes is more than simply a matter of diet, insulin, and urine testing. It also involves an individual's emotional and physical development, which largely depend upon the reaction of others to the condition. The environment affects diabetic control, and diabetic control, in turn, affects the environment. This is particularly true of the school environment since children spend so much time in school. Diabetic students may experience embarrassment over their unusual diets, the urine testing, and any symptoms of diabetic shock that may be displayed. Peers may ridicule them and treat them differently. An understanding and tactful teacher can minimize any potentially uncomfortable situations and model accepting attitudes for other students. The teacher may also wish to explain diabetes so that the other children in the class can understand the condition.

The diabetic child often experiences feelings of being punished (injections and no sweets) and of being different and inadequate. The child is likely to lack in self-confidence and self-esteem and may avoid activities for fear of failure. Additional praise and encouragement for accomplishments may be necessary.

Profile

Bob

Bob is entering his first year of high school this year. While many students worry about the move to a large somewhat impersonal school plant with many teachers and different responsibilities, Bob's reactions are far beyond the usual. He has told his parents over and over that he does not wish to attend high school and that if they force him to go he'll run away from home. The parents, deeply concerned, nevertheless understand Bob's reluctance.

Two years ago Bob was stricken with juvenile diabetes. For a healthy, active, and outgoing child, the effects were devastating. Bob was old enough to understand the chronic nature of the disease and to realize the restraints it would place on his life in terms of insulin injections and diet. He abandoned many of his usual pursuits, ignored his friends, and began to fall seriously behind in school work. Although Bob is old enough to give himself insulin, monitor his urine, and adapt his diet, he tacitly refused to do any of these things. It took a psychologist many months to help Bob to realize the necessity of attending to his own health care needs.

Even though Bob now looks after his own needs, he is resentful of the disease and embarrassed about it in front of his friends. His reluctance to attend high school centres on his fear of acute embarrassment in the case of an insulin coma (of which he has suffered a few) as well as his dislike of anyone knowing of his condition. To help Bob, the parents have again contacted the psychologist and hope that counselling will help overcome some of his deep-seated resentment about the diabetes.

Cancer

Cancer is a general term used to describe about a hundred conditions characterized by abnormal and uncontrolled cell growth. Cancer is the chief cause of death by disease in children aged three to fourteen. The most common cancers in children are of the blood, bone, brain, nervous system, and kidney.

Approximately one-third of all cancers diagnosed in children are leukemias (Peckham, 1993). Leukemia is responsible for two-thirds of the deaths of children with cancer. However, survival rates for children with cancer have increased dramatically in the past two decades. Leukemia now has a survival rate of 70 percent or better.

Major treatments for cancer are surgery, chemotherapy, and/or radiation, which may result in short- and long-term effects. After diagnosis, a four-week treatment period begins with intensive therapy. When remission is confirmed, oral drugs are introduced.

important ✗

Developmental Consequences

Apart from the condition itself, one of the major outcomes of cancer is the physical and emotional problems arising from treatment. Each child will have a unique experience at the hospital and in the diagnosis and treatment of a particular kind of childhood cancer. For many children, chemotherapy drugs cause plumpness and hair loss. Other physical results include amputation, disturbances in normal growth patterns, mood swings, difficulties in concentration, muscle weakness, fatigue, nausea, and dramatic weight gain or weight loss.

School is a major part of each child's life and children with cancer gain special benefits from education at all stages of their illness. They need the satisfaction of being normal productive learners and should attend school even in the terminal stages of the illness, if possible. School attendance provides peer contact and opportunities for maintaining self-esteem and competence by completing short-term goals. School helps in distracting children from their physical concerns and in their long-term emotional and physical rehabilitation, and helps them reach their optimal social and psychological development.

One of the many ways teachers contribute to the total care of children with cancer is by helping them to interact with others.

It is important that teachers understand the illness and how it affects the child at each maturational stage. After a period of hospitalization, teachers must be aware that a youngster may be less energetic and very likely to hold deep concerns about the nature of the illness. Anger about forced dependency on parents and frustration at having to submit to the disruptions of therapy can cause withdrawal and regression. All this can result in decreased educational motivation, poor self-concept, social isolation, and an abnormally close relationship with one parent.

The teacher is a valuable link in the total care of the child. Teachers help by communicating with and supporting parents, by being a liasion between them and other professionals, and by helping the child to interact with others. Other class members should be prepared for physical changes — loss of hair, weight gain, and the like.

Acquired Immunodeficiency Syndrome (AIDS)

Acquired Immunodeficiency Syndrome (AIDS) is a new and frightening disease causing major concern around the world. The condition is caused by the virus HIV (human immunodeficiency virus) that attacks and seriously disrupts the body's immune system, its defence against disease. Without the protection of the immune system, AIDS sufferers are prone to fatal infections and cancers.

In our discussion on the etiology of pedriatric AIDS in Chapter 2, we said that the major cause is transmission from an affected mother, although some children may be infected by transfusions. For children who are affected before birth, the median incubation period is twelve months. Infants with HIV but without drug withdrawal are usually healthy; there are no signs of immunodeficiency for the first six to eight months of life (Hopkins, 1989). For children infected as a result of transfusion, the median incubation period is three to five years (Simonds and Rogers, 1992). This means that many young children with AIDS will be in the school system.

Some researchers predict that HIV infection promises to become the primary infectious cause of developmental disabilites and neurological impairment in children (Dokecki, Baumeister, and Kupstas, 1989). Symptomatic pediatric HIV cases involve central nervous system (CNS) damage in as many as 78 to 93 percent of cases (Diamond and Cohen, 1987).

Developmental Consequences of AIDS

Pediatric AIDS is a severe medical disability, an educational handicap, and a disease that carries a heavy weight of social and ethical concerns. Public ignorance and fear, coupled with sensationalist reporting, have combined to create an atmosphere of fear and misunderstanding. Because AIDS is fatal and incurable, and because it has been linked in the public consciousness to homosexuality and drug use, the disease evokes passionately held opinions and deep fears (Kirp and Epstein, 1989).

Schools have been among the key North American institutions in which the meaning of AIDS has been debated and deciphered. Schools are facing problems in trying to accommodate children with AIDS while coming to grips with the fears and misunderstandings circulating in the community. Scientists may have demonstrated that HIV is not transmitted by casual contact, but parents and teachers concerned about the devastating nature of AIDS are not going to give up the myths easily (Dodds, Volker, and Vivand, 1989). For parents, AIDS balances their interest in protecting the health and safety of their children against the public's interest in providing non-discriminatory schooling for all children. At the same time, AIDS poses a number of special challenges to teachers. Educators are being forced to confront the issues of risk, relationships, and education (Sloane and Sloane, 1990) and to deal with personal uncertainties, fear, and prejudices (Gilliss, 1990). Having a child who has AIDS in the classroom means facing many unknowns. Teachers ask, "How will the other students react?" "What will parents say?" "Can I handle it?" "What type of support can I expect?" and "What should I be concerned about?"

First and foremost, anyone working with or planning for children with AIDS must understand the nature and course of HIV infection in children. They should realize that affected children will have learning difficulties, a general loss of stamina, growth delays, repeated bacterial infections and progressive neurological defects, including speech, motor, and cognitive regressions. Children may also have to cope with social isolation, long-term hospitalization, parental illness and death, family problems, and lack of understanding.

The second challenge for teachers is to be consistently sympathetic and compassionate toward students and colleagues who may be infected with HIV. Excluding a child with AIDS teaches all children the wrong lessons about tolerance and about community.

Children with AIDS have periods of weakness and intermittent bouts of illness. They suffer chronic and frequent illnesses, failure to thrive, and a range of neurological and developmental problems. While children with pediatric AIDS are not necessarily special education candidates, many qualify because of limited strength and vitality and acute health problems. When they are placed in special education, the most successful programs for them parallel those for other special learners. Instruction should be designed for success, based on concrete experiences, and broken down into small, manageable steps.

Sickle Cell Anemia

The defective recessive gene involved in sickle cell anemia results in the production of defective hemoglobin. Affected individuals produce abnormal hemoglobin which then causes distortions in blood cells; under certain conditions, the red blood cells "sickle" (change shape). Sickle-shaped cells tend to clot together; the shape causes the cells to pile up and block small blood vessels, causing pain and tissue destruction (Pierce, 1990). However, the intensity of the effects vary widely.

Because the sickle cell trait protects against death from malaria, it is common in populations from malaria-prone parts of the world, which include areas of Africa and the Mediterranean countries. Sickle cell anemia is carried by about two million American Blacks (about one in ten). Among Hispanic Americans, about one in twenty is a carrier. Sickle cell is therefore thought to affect about 500 000 people in the United States. Of the 10 percent of Blacks with sickle cell, most are heterozygous (one normal and one abnormal gene). Only about 0.25 percent are homozygous (two defective genes).

Individuals who are homozygous often have long bouts of illness and die in childhood. Because sickle cell impairs circulation, sufferers experience severe pains in their abdomen, back, head, and limbs. The deformed blood cells rupture easily. The disease also causes the heart to enlarge and the brain cells to be deprived of blood. People with severe cases may suffer heart and kidney problems and pneumonia, which can be fatal. In fact, it is estimated that the condition causes 100 000 deaths a year.

Those who are heterozygous (carriers) suffer fewer effects, the intensity of which varies widely. Sickling occurs under certain conditions such as exposure to low oxygen levels. In carriers, 40 percent of the red blood cells may assume a sickle shape when the supply of oxygen to the blood is reduced. Treatment of a crisis usually involves rest, medication for pain, blood transfusions, and oxygen inhalation therapy.

In older children and adults, it appears that the sickle cell trait is generally benign and does not shorten life, although it may bring danger with exercise and increased altitude. The situation seems to be more serious for infants. In the United States, investigators have reported a mortality rate of 13 to 14 percent among sickle cell children under the age of two (Grover et al., 1983). The spleen, the most efficient blood filter in the body, is vulnerable (Eichner, 1986).

Sickle cell carriers can be detected by a simple blood test. Early medical screening can prevent early mortality by referring infants to programs structured for their care. Life-threatening complications of the disease can be diagnosed and treated early, while counselling can be provided to parents.

Allergies

Allergy, a term coined by Clemens von Pirquet in 1906, means "altered reaction" (Hay, 1990). The term is used interchangeably with *hypersensitivity*, and is defined as "an abnormal and varied reaction which occurs following a contact with substances or agents which normally do not cause symptoms in other individuals" (Kuzemko, 1978).

There are two major categories of allergies. Atopic allergies are associated with hereditary and/or familial factors. The risk to children when both parents have a positive history of allergy is 30 to 40 percent, while the risk to children when one parent has a positive history is 20 to 30 percent (Kuzemko, 1978). Non-atopic allergies do not have a hereditary component but result from antibodies produced in response to allergens in the environment.

Allergies are the most common chronic disease in pediatrics. Allergic conditions are estimated to occur in 6.6 percent to 33 percent of children and adolescents (Crawford, 1982). In Canada, recent studies have shown that one in every five school children has a major allergy (Alberta Response, 1989).

A huge range of substances can create allergic reactions in humans. Generally, substances that cause allergic responses are divided into four categories: inhalants, contactants, ingestants, and injectants. Inhalants include dust, pollen, mould, aerosol sprays, and strong odours. Contactants are substances that come into contact with the skin, including fabrics, metals, cosmetics, and chemicals. Ingestants are foods and drugs; injectants are agents or substances that enter the body through the skin, including insect bites, bee stings, and some drugs (Voignier and Bridgewater, 1980).

There are a number of types of allergic reaction. One of the most common is allergic rhinitis, which may be either seasonal or perennial. The seasonal type — hay fever — is induced by windborne pollens; the perennial form is present throughout the year. Both forms involve nasal congestion, itching of the nose, or repetitive sneezing. Allergic pulmonary disease is usually referred to as bronchial asthma. The major symptom is narrowing of the bronchial tubes resulting in diminished air flow. Urticaria and eczema are skin reactions resulting in rashes, itching, swelling, and seeping of body fluids through the skin. Physical allergy is a response to cold, heat, or sunlight. Allergic conjunctivitis involves itching of the eyes and excessive tears. Gastro-intestinal allergy is a response to specific foods or drugs.

Asthma

Asthma is defined as a "variable, reversible obstruction of the airwaves characterized by the narrowing of bronchial tubes, swelling of tissues, and clogging of mucus" (Smith, 1978, p.48). Asthma is a high-incidence condition in most developed nations. Estimates of prevalence range from 5 to 15 percent of children under fifteen years of age (Pituch and Bruggeman, 1982).

Asthma should never be considered anything less than a serious condition. There are, for example, 2000 to 4000 asthma-related deaths in the United States each year (Young, 1980). Asthma can occur at any age, but it is found most frequently in children. Many asthmatic children improve or go into remission in adolescence (Flenley, 1981). Boys are twice as likely as girls to exhibit the condition.

Asthmatic attacks are characterized by wheezing, paroxysmal coughing, and shortness of breath. A wide variety of stimuli are associated with bronchospasms. The first group, labelled as known factors, include allergens, drugs, exercise, industrial exposure, infections, and reflexes. A second category, probable causes, includes things such as air pollutants, chemical irritants, sinusitis, and vasculitis. A final group, classed as possible triggers, include emotions, hormonal imbalance, and weather (Young, 1980). Nevertheless, it is extremely difficult to pinpoint exactly which factor or factors trigger an individual asthma attack since the same factors are not always responsible for subsequent attacks (Howse, 1988).

An individual's asthma can be a continuous state of frequent attacks ranging in severity, or an intermittent state consisting of occasional attacks ranging from mild to severe (Howse, 1988). Various medications, of which drugs are the most common, are employed in the treatment of asthma. Since Adrenalin, the first drug treatment of asthma, was introduced, a wide number of drugs have emerged. These include drugs that act on the airways directly, drugs that halt the production of antigens, and corticosteroids which also hinder antigen production (Howse, 1988).

Bronchodilators are used to relieve obstruction of airflow. In severe cases, corticosteroids are useful. Both types of medication have side effects. Bronchodilators may overstimulate the child and cause hyperactive behaviour; excessive use of corticosteroids may result in abnormal hair growth, excessive appetite, and slowed growth. Common sense factors in treatment, other than medications, include rest, sufficient fluids, play and work to tolerance (Pilecka, 1995), and avoidance of the allergens that cause attacks. To further stave off asthma attacks, children can exercise regularly to improve postural drainage, strengthen the diaphragm muscles, and expand lung capacity (Butts, 1980).

Developmental Consequences of Asthma

Among asthmatic children, school absenteeism is a major problem, especially in the first three years of school. Asthma is estimated to account for as much as 20 to 25 percent of all school absences (Pituch and Bruggeman, 1982).

Despite the fact that asthmatic children tend to have IQs slightly higher than average, they are likely to be underachievers and have been found to be behind in school work, especially as adolescents. Asthmatic children suffer more emotional difficulties, but the nature of the relationship between psychological problems and asthmatic episodes is poorly understood (Pilecka, 1995).

Abused and Neglected Children

The history of humanity is rife with examples of cruelty to children, ranging from infanticide in early societies to child factory labour in the nineteenth century. (This is discussed in the Research Note on child abuse.) So although some researchers feel that child abuse is on the increase, it is more likely that abuse, under modern definitional constructs, is simply more open to identification and reporting.

It is not possible to assess the exact dimensions of child abuse and neglect because of widespread under-reporting. Many factors contribute to under-reporting, including the social stigma attached to child beating, cultural variations in expectations concerning the roles of parents and children, and the fact that only a portion of neglected and abused children are taken for medical intervention. As well, parents make up believable stories, children are too young or too frightened to disclose what actually happened, and some physicians would rather attribute the symptoms to an accident than confront the awful truth (Fontana and Besharov, 1979). Scientific studies of the prevalence of sexual abuse are rare, but there is a general consensus that the actual rate is underestimated by official reports because of the severe consequences of disclosure — public retribution, family disruption, unemployment and subsequent economic disaster, loss of friends, and incarceration (Csapo, 1988).

Research Notes

Child abuse

Child abuse is not a problem new to our modern Western society. As Lloyd de Mause points out, "The human track record of child raising is bloody, dirty and mean" (1975 p.85). For many centuries, maltreatment was justified in the belief that severe physical punishment was necessary to maintain discipline, to transmit educational ideas, to please certain gods, or to expel evil spirits (Radbill, 1974).

In tracing the history of child abuse, de Mause (1974) placed common societal reactions to children within six major, though overlapping and intertwined, stages: infanticidal, abandoning, ambivalent, intrusive, socializing, and helping. Infanticide existed in very early societies. It was not until the fourth century that the Church halted the practice. After that, many children were abandoned to wander, beg, or die by the wayside. The ambivalent mode appeared first in the late Middle Ages. Parents still displayed aggressive tendencies toward their children but generally kept them at home. Intrusive parenting, characterized by draconian authoritarianism, arose in the early eighteenth century.

The need for children to be socialized and helped paralleled the full blossoming of the notion of childhood as a discrete stage of development and children as separate beings, not miniature adults. Children were then provided with special environments, such as schools, and child labour laws brought them out of the mines and the factories.

Overt forms of child abuse prominent in earlier periods may have disappeared. Nevertheless, child abuse remains an endemic problem in modern society. In its modern garb, the problems of child abuse were first brought to the forefront by Caffey (1946), who suggested that ill treatment of children might be an intentional act on the part of parents. This caused a wave of concern, and throughout the 1950s research increased. In the early 1960s, a seminar on child abuse led to the identification of what became known as the Battered Child Syndrome (Kempe et al., 1962). Following this, there was a flurry of articles, books, and research papers reflecting a heightened interest on the part of educators, social workers, welfare agencies, and politicians. By the 1970s, policies were established and laws enacted that recognized and protected abused children.

Child abuse exists regardless of occupation, educational attainment, religion, marital status, or family configuration. Abuse occurs at every socio-economic level, though it is more frequently reported among poorer families (Harris, 1986); the frequency of child abuse appears to vary across cultures (Korbin, 1987).

The problem is caused by a complex combination of parent variables and child behaviours. Essentially, abuse is not a fixed single incident but an ongoing interaction between parents and children associated with dysfunctional parent/child relations (Youngblade and Bibby, 1989).

Definitions

There have been many thoughtful discussions about appropriate definitions of child abuse and neglect, psychological maltreatment of children, child sexual abuse and spouse abuse; however, no consensus has been reached (Emery, 1989). In a general sense, we can define child abuse as "any interaction or lack of interaction ... which results in non-accidental harm to the individual's physical and/or emotional state" (Helfer, 1987, p. 61).

Within the broad definition, sub-categories have been developed to describe specific aspects of abuse and neglect. Physical abuse is defined as non-accidental physical injury to a child. Physical abuse may be seen from overt and consistent signs. For example, it is always possible for children to acquire strange bruises in the course of normal activities; it is the frequency of such bruising that arouses the suspicion of abuse (Tower, 1984). Further indications of physical abuse include bald spots, burns from cigarettes or hot water, and marks from a strap or rope (Harrison, 1985). Behavioural indicators of physical abuse may include intolerance of physical contact and the wearing of inappropriate clothing that covers the body. Abused children may arrive at school early and stay late, suggesting a fear of going home.

Sexual abuse is one of the most studied areas. Sexual abuse may be defined as

> the sexual exploitation of a child who is not developmentally capable of understanding or resisting the contact, and a child or adolescent who may be psychologically and socially dependent upon the perpetrator (Csapo, 1988, p. 121).

Sexual involvement imposed upon a child by an adult includes pedophilia, rape, and all forms of incest. Incest, the most common type of sexual abuse, refers to any kind of sexual activity between a child and relatives, either blood or legal, including fathers, mothers, step-parents, siblings, and so on (Mouzakitis and Vachese, 1985). Victims of sexual abuse display a number of manifestations. Children may have difficulty walking or sitting, or may cry without provocation. They may show sudden drops in school performance or sudden non-participation in school activities accompanied by unusually infantile or withdrawn behaviour (Broadhurst, Edmunds, and MacDicker, 1979).

Neglect is the failure to provide adequate supervision, hygiene, nutrition, medical care, or the basic love and nurturing that children need to grow and develop. Emotional neglect refers to the failure of caretakers to provide the loving positive emotional atmosphere necessary to the development of self-esteem in a child.

Although instances of severe battering are the most visible forms of abuse, neglect has been cited as the most common form as well as the most destructive, causing more deaths, injuries, and long-term problems than other types of abuse. Physical neglect can be as damaging psychologically as overt physical or sexual abuse (Jurgrau, 1990), and experts now believe that strong and recurrent psychological abuse and neglect may prove to be even more harmful to children in the long run (Emery, 1989; Hart and Brassard, 1987).

Neglected children tend to be ill clothed and poorly fed. They may have untreated physical or medical problems and appear to be tired and listless. The possible behavioural responses include stealing food, falling asleep in class, frequent school absences, and pugnacious and destructive activity.

Indicators of emotional maltreatment are varied. Many children develop emotional or behavioural disorders for no apparent reason. Many of these cases could be the result of the caregiver failing to meet the child's basic emotional needs. In these children, observers may note delayed development, neurotic traits, or antisocial behaviour.

Prevalence of child abuse

Leavitt (1974) described child abuse as actually consisting of two problems — first, the abused child and secondly, the abusive parents. Studies that attempt to define the typical abusive family or parent present inconsistent results. Among parents, child abuse and neglect cannot be attributed to any single cause or to any particular class of people.

Abusive parents have been described as "immature, impulsive, self-centred, hypersensitive, and quick to react with poorly controlled aggression" (Leavitt, 1974, p. 209). Moreover, the maltreating caregiver tends to demonstrate extremely inconsistent patterns of interaction with the child (Steele, 1986). Abusive parents have little knowledge of good parenting and tend to hold unrealistic expectations; they ascribe adult functions to children and cannot understand that children possess limited control, capabilities, and comprehension. They expect children to be good, loving, and obedient at all times, and when their child's disobedience or inattention threatens their perceptions of themselves as good parents, they use excessive discipline because they see it as their duty to make children behave. Many abusing parents are unable to cope with the complex problems of life. They tend to be isolated or their lifestyle may be chaotic. Famularo and colleagues (1986) reported a significant over-representation of alcoholism in severe cases of child maltreatment.

Consistently, the literature points to a cycle of abuse theory. Some researchers feel that the assumptions are not supported by the available data and that the majority of abused parents do not abuse their own children (e.g. Benjamin, 1980; Widom, 1989). They argue that only about 30 percent of abused children become abusive parents (Kaufman and Zigler, 1989), and whether parents continue the cycle of abuse is influenced by many aspects of their developmental history, not just the abuse.

Others find that, in many cases, abusive parents were abused children themselves, and often patterns of maltreatment can be traced back three or four generations (Steele, 1986). Moreover, abused parents who abuse their own children tend to repeat the same types of abuse to which they were subjected, be it physical, sexual, or neglect (Steele, 1986). Children learn parenting techniques from their own experiences in the family. A loving, cared-for child learns to become a good parent. A child who is unloved, neglected, and abused learns poor parenting behaviours. If a parent who was abused has a healthy docile child, abusive tendencies may be held in check. However, if the child is ill or difficult to manage or if other stresses occur, the parent may well harm the child.

Abuse and neglect may occur from conception (alcoholic mothers) to adolescence. In some families, only one of several children in the family is abused. This child may be different by virtue of sex, by resembling a disliked family member, or by failing to meet the parent's expectations. There is a correlation between excessive crying and child abuse, although which is the cause and which is the effect is a matter of debate (Lamb, 1977). Children can be more open to abuse because of the mental, physical, and behavioural anomalies that increase their vulnerability to abuse or because they have developed characteristics that increase the likelihood of abuse (Frodi, 1981). Handicapped children, sick children, and premature and low-birth-weight children who require special attention or costly treatment and who fail to respond to the caregivers' efforts in ways the parents can appreciate appear to be at greater risk for abuse (Augoustinos, 1987; Frodi, 1981; Zirpoli, Snell, and Lloyd, 1987). Abuse seems very common among children with behaviour disorders (Zirpoli, 1990).

Developmental Consequences

There is sufficient empirical evidence to support the widely held assumption that child abuse and neglect have developmental effects on the physical, neurological, intellectual and emotional development of children (Augoustinos, 1987). The evidence strongly suggests that abused and neglected children display cognitive and behavioural deficits and may be at risk for psychological maladjustment. That is,

> Systematic abuse causes significant dysfunction in intellectual, emotional, developmental, and motoric ability. Systematic abuse creates substantial "at risk" conditions among adolescents for psychological, interpersonal, academic, medical, and legal problems. Self-image, motivation, personal satisfaction, and success in the workplace are negatively impacted (Fink and Janssen, 1992, p. 32).

Child abuse directly affects the amount of time children are in the classroom and their ability and interest in learning while in school. Intellectual development has been found to be delayed among some abused and neglected children with no evidence of neurological impairment (Augoustinos, 1987). One major study (Lynch and Roberts, 1982) found verbal scores to be more depressed than performance scores.

Teachers must know how to recognize the signs of abuse, how and where to report it, and what the school can do to offer support.

Abused children suffer a range of physical, psychological, and social problems. Abused toddlers, for example, often respond to age mates' distress with fear, anger, or physical attacks (Main and George, 1985). Older children tend to show more aggressive behaviour than their peers. Abused elementary-aged children tend to be highly aggressive and are often rejected by their peers (Downey and Walker, 1989). Adolescents frequently respond to abuse through depression, suicide attempts, explosive anger, alcohol, drug abuse, self-mutilation, running away, or prostitution (see Destad, 1987).

Child maltreatment is destructive to the child who experiences it, to the caregiver who commits it, and to the society that allows it. Teachers hold both a moral and a legal responsibility for reporting suspected cases of child abuse. They must know how to recognize the signs of abuse, how and where to report it, and what the school can do to offer support. When considering the significance of symptoms or behaviours, consultation with a public health nurse will prove to be very helpful.

Musculoskeletal Impairments

Musculoskeletal impairments are those that affect body movement and functioning but are not caused by neurological damage. These include a wide range of impairments; some are listed in Table 12-2 and a few are discussed in more detail below.

Depending on the type and severity of the conditions, physical and motor development is affected. Physical development refers to the acquisition of postural control and the necessary movement patterns to produce functional motor acts.

Motor is a term used to denote muscular movement and **motor development** is the process through which a child acquires movement patterns and skills. **Motor learning** involves using the body in such ways as to make the best use of what is perceived (Gibson, 1978). **Motor skills** are those related to the development and use of the muscles and limbs. **Gross motor skills** relate to large body movements such as running, climbing, and throwing. **Fine motor skills** are those that involve small body movements and refer to the muscles of the hand. Jumping is a gross motor skill; picking up a penny, fine motor.

Table 12-2
Some examples of orthopedic conditions that affect children

Club foot	Congenital malpositioning of one or both feet
Osteomyelitis	Bacterial infection of the bones
Osteogenesis imperfecta	Congenital abnormality of the bony cells resulting in frequent fractures causing deformities
Scoliosis	Congenital or acquired curvature of the spine, often caused by muscle weakness, dystrophy, or atrophy
Hip dislocation	Congenital misplacement of the thigh bone in the hip socket
Legg-Calvé-Perthes	Flattening of the head of a long bone, usually the thigh
Muscular atrophy	Degeneration of muscle tissue due to neural damage

Source: David, 1987

Limb Deficiencies

Limb deficiencies include the loss or absence of entire limbs or parts of limbs. A child born with such a condition is said to have a **congenital amputation**. Although congenital amputations have occurred throughout history, only recently have we begun to understand their causes.

There was a most dramatic occurrence of congenital amputations of unusually large proportions in the late 1950s and early 1960s. The culprit was found to be Thalidomide, an antinausea drug prescribed for morning sickness in pregnant women. In Canada, the United States, and Europe, thousands of children were born with missing or deformed limbs. This specific condition is called **phocomelia**, a congenital deformity in which parts of limbs or entire limbs are missing or very short.

Congenital amputations are much less prevalent than acquired amputations. Many children lose limbs in mishaps involving vehicles, contact with high voltage lines, burns, and other accidents. In some instances, surgical amputations may be performed to prevent the spread of bone cancer or massive infections. Defective limbs or parts of limbs may also be amputated to permit the use of **prostheses**, functional devices that substitute for missing body parts.

Abnormalities of the bony structures include a number of conditions other than limb deficiencies. Some are congenital, such as spina bifida, cleft palate, clubfoot, hip dislocation, and osteogenesis imperfecta. Others may result from a bacterial infection such as tuberculosis. Still others, such as curvature of the spine, may exist as secondary abnormalities associated with such primary disorders as atrophy, a form of muscle weakness caused by nerve degeneration (David, 1987)

Spinal Problems

There are three types of curvature of the spine — scoliosis, lordosis, and kyphosis. Lordosis is an anterior (forward) curvature when viewed from the side. Kyphosis is a posterior (backward) curvature when viewed from the side. Scoliosis, which refers to a lateral (side to side) curve in the spine that is absent in normal spines, is the most common form of curvature. It is associated with prominent shoulder blades, poor posture, uneven shoulders, and a flattening of the back (Bauer and Shea, 1989). Scoliosis can impair motor functions.

Muscular Dystrophy

A number of conditions are characterized by a weakening and wasting away of muscular tissue. If there has been neurological damage or if the muscles are weakened due to nerve degeneration, the condition is known as **atrophy**. Myopathy occurs when there is no evidence of neurological disease or impairment. When the myopathy is progressive and hereditary, the condition is referred to as dystrophy (Hallahan and Kauffman, 1991).

Muscular dystrophy refers to a group of inherited conditions characterized by degeneration of muscle fibres without neurological deficit. The condition occurs in different forms, all characterized by progressive muscle weakness. The different types differ with regard to age of onset, the site of initial muscle involvement, and the kinds of hereditary transmission.

The most common type of the disorder is Duchenne's muscular dystrophy, often called pseudohypertonic muscular dystrophy. The term *pseudohypertonic* means "false growth" and describes an enlargement of the calves and sometimes other muscles. This enlargement occurs as a result of fatty deposits in the muscle along with degeneration of the muscle fibres.

As Duchenne's muscular dystrophy is inherited through a sex-linked recessive gene, this form typically occurs in boys. At birth, the child appears normal. In the early stages, the condition is painless and the symptoms unnoticeable. But onset is early and may be evident when the boy is learning to walk. Gradually muscle fibres waste away to be replaced by fatty tissue. The child's pelvic area is affected first and then the shoulder girdle. By the age of four to seven years, the child exhibits a waddling gait and frequent falls, and has difficulty in climbing stairs and in standing up from a sitting position (Berkow, 1982). In the second stage of the condition, the child suffers difficulty in muscle movement; by the age of five, many affected children require ambulation aids. The condition worsens so that by the third stage, somewhere about eight years of age, the child is confined to a wheelchair. Finally, the individual is bedridden and totally dependent.

For children with Duchenne's muscular dystrophy, the progressive muscle weakness equates with an abbreviated life span. Before the advent of antibiotics, the life expectancy for children with Duchenne's was even shorter than today's twenty to thirty years. Death usually occurred in adolescence as a result of exhaustion, respiratory infection, heart failure, or most often, pneumonia. Although life expectancy has been extended and recent studies have located the gene for muscular dystrophy, no treatment has yet been found to halt muscle decline.

Another form of the condition is Landouzy-Dejerine muscular dystrophy, also known as facioscapulohumeral muscular dystrophy, reflecting the fact that the facial and shoulder girdle muscles are the areas first affected. The shoulder girdle is weakened but the forearms are spared. As well, the facial features of affected children show drooping of the eyelids and thickening of the lips.

Landouzy-Dejerine muscular dystrophy is inherited through dominant genes but is not sex-linked (Berkow, 1982) and is therefore found in both sexes. The condition commonly manifests itself in adolescence, although onset may occur any time between childhood and late adulthood. The progression of the condition alternates with prolonged periods of apparent arrest. Landouzy-Dejerine muscular dystrophy is not life threatening; life expectancy for affected individuals is normal (Krupp and Chatton, 1983).

Although these are the most common forms of muscular dystrophy, several others exist. All are characterized by progressive muscle weakness and tissue change but the predicted life span varies from one type to another.

There is some scattered evidence to indicate a decrease in intellectual function associated with muscular dystrophy. It has been found that about 50 percent of patients with Duchenne's have a lower IQ than genetic expectations would suggest (Berkow, 1982), and these children tend to have lower than average verbal IQs (Karagan and Zellweger, 1978).

Arthritis

Arthritis is a common term for a variety of chronic systemic conditions involving inflammation of the joints. Many people assume that arthritis is a condition exclusive to adults, especially the aged. In reality, it occurs frequently in children and is then called juvenile arthritis or Still's disease.

Juvenile arthritis is similar is some respects to the adult type. It affects the large joints, sometimes to the extent of interfering with growth in the bony structures. Joint pain is a common feature and destruction of the joints may ensue. Other complications of juvenile arthritis include eye and respiratory infections, enlarged spleen, and inflammation of the tissue covering the heart. The most severe form is juvenile rheumatoid arthritis, which affects the heart muscles and can be fatal. More girls than boys suffer from this condition.

Among children with disabilities, osteoarthritis is the most common form of arthritis. The cartilage around the joint is damaged, the space between the bones becomes smaller and loses its lubrication, and movement becomes painful or impossible. Osteoarthritis is especially likely to occur when the child has a condition in which a joint has been dislocated. Children with cerebral palsy, for example, may have recurring dislocation and suffer from painful arthritis (Hallahan and Kauffman, 1991).

The causes of both adult and juvenile arthritis are unknown and there is no cure. Aspirin seems to be the most effective medication. In children the prognosis is more favourable than it is for adults; about 75 percent of children with arthritis experience remission of the disease (Berkow, 1982).

Prevention of Physical and Health Disabilities

Although many physical and health handicaps are unpreventable, some precautions can be taken. Good prenatal health and appropriate nutrition reduce the risk to the developing fetus. Genetic counselling is valuable in cases of inherited conditions. With counselling, parents become aware of the risks and are able to make informed decisions.

Massive research continues to try to find means to identify cystic fibrosis and muscular dystrophy carriers and to alleviate the conditions in affected children. Recent medical discoveries in Canada and elsewhere have located the genes responsible for both conditions.

In Canada the awareness of child neglect and abuse has increased dramatically. A plethora of child protection laws have led to the development of policies and programs for intervention, education, and prevention. Law now requires the reporting of possible instances of abuse to the authorities. Teachers, neighbours, physicians, and anyone else who suspects child abuse are required to seek assistance for the child.

Identification and Assessment

Given the enormous range of conditions, malformations, and diseases encompassed in this category, it is well nigh impossible to make definitive statements regarding assessment. Generally, health handicaps and skeletal malformations do not impinge on cognitive and intellectual development, and diagnosticians can therefore use the same range of tools and tests as would be used with regular class children. With the chronic nature of these conditions, however, special attention must be directed toward social and emotional growth and adaptive behaviour. As well, adaptations in test materials and procedures may be necessary to circumvent a physical disability such as muscular dystrophy. (See Chapters 13 and 15.)

Profile

Ms Day

When Ms Day, a psychologist in private practice, was asked by the local school board to test Cheslov, she was somewhat reluctant. The school described the child as suffering from cystic fibrosis, a chronic and life-threatening disorder. Ms Day was unfamilar with the condition and its consequences and did not quite know what types of educational and psychological tests to use with such a child.

However, when Ms Day started into the testing session, she found that Cheslov performed well on the WISC-111. All his scores were within the average range and he presented a Full scale IQ score of 124. It was when Ms Day began to present some educational measures that problems emerged. Although this child obviously had good potential to learn in school, he was now nine years old and showed little progress beyond beginning-level in reading and the other language arts. Although he had developed some basic numeracy skills, his arithmetic was very poor in computation and in using basic addition, subtraction, and multiplication. Division problems were completely beyond him.

Ms Day could see the school's dilemma. Here was a child with good intellectual potential who was lagging far behind his peers simply because he had missed so many days of school due to illness. Yet the school was loath to designate the child as a special education candidate without some sort of classification that would assure funding.

Intervention for Children with Special Health Care Needs

Health disorders and physical disabilities impact on children's learning and progress in a number of ways. Learning will be hindered when a child has experienced a great many medical procedures which lead to long periods of recuperation as well as missed time in the classroom. Once in school, children may tire easily, have limited vitality, short attention spans, and limited mobility. A physical impairment can affect a child's range of motion, physical strength, communication, interaction with materials, independence, and daily living skills.

The children discussed in this chapter require a variety of medical, psychological, and educational interventions. Social service agencies frequently become involved with them and their families. As they grow older, students may require counselling and other support for independent living.

Medical management for health problems can be a significant part of a child's daily life.

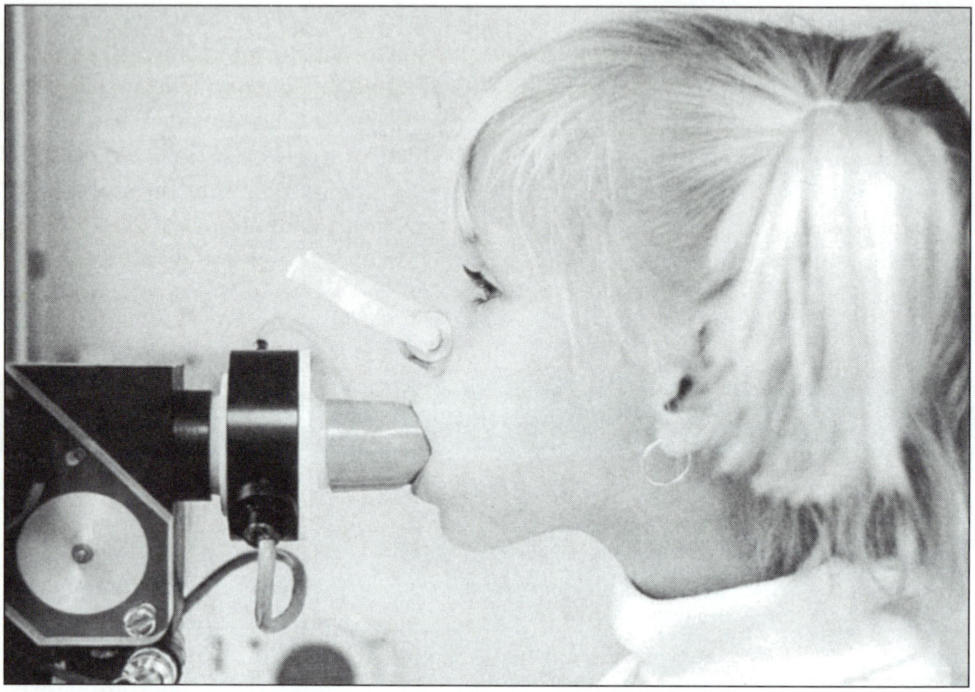

Medical

Health disabilities are essentially medical conditions requiring a complex and sophisticated range of interventions which include surgical procedures, prosthetic devices, drug therapy, diet management, and ongoing medical treatment. The medical management of these children is intensive, far beyond the scope of this text.

When a child with a health impairment is in the classroom, teachers should keep an emergency protocol that contains information on emergency practices and strategies developed by parents, school personnel, and medical personnel (Campbell, Cohen, and Rich, 1987). The protocol includes names, addresses, and telephone numbers of parents or guardians, emergency contacts, and family physicians.

Therapy

Students may need rehabilitation training and therapy from a range of therapists — physical, occupational, and speech and language. It is clear that age is related to the level of knowledge children have about their orthopedic handicaps (Dunn, McCartan, and Fugura, 1988). As they grow older, therefore, students may also need extra assistance from social workers and psychologists to help them understand and deal with the stresses of the disability and the treatment. By the time students reach adolescence, they will have gained a realistic appreciation of their health condition and the manner in which it affects their lives. Teenagers may require a variety of counselling interventions — personal, career, and therapeutic. (See Chapter 17.)

Technical

Many technical devices are designed to increase personal independence. Compensatory (assistive and adaptive) devices and equipment allow individuals to compensate for or mimimize the effects of a disability. These devices are fully discussed in Chapter 13.

Educational Intervention

Education is a social norm in the lives of children, and the presence of a physical or health problem should not be seen as a reason to halt schooling. Education and social contact are essential components of childhood, and educational intervention for children with special health care needs represents a critical aspect of the child's total health planning. Lacking school experiences, the child's psychosocial development would be seriously jeopardized. Special education assistance may be necessary simply because students are likely to be absent from school often. In most cases, children attend the regular public school and obtain special help from an itinerant teacher or in the resource room.

Ensuring that a child is accepted by peers is the teacher's task. A number of determinants of children's attitudes toward disability have been described. These include gender (females generally more accepting than males), parental attitudes, age, and the geographical layout of the school (see King et al., 1992). One way to increase positive attitudes is to answer accurately questions asked by other children about the differences in appearance and behaviour of the special child. This should be done at the time questions are asked, whether or not the special child is present.

The needs of children who are technology-dependent and/or medically fragile present greater challenges to the school system. They may be placed in a variety of educational settings, depending upon the type and severity of the condition, the related services available, and the prognosis of the disability. (See also Chapter 15.)

Hospital schools are found today in facilities that specialize in providing long-term care for chronically ill children. The classroom setting is designed to provide the children with familiar surroundings and continued interaction with other students. Academic involvement helps the child to keep abreast of school work and aids in self-development. Special education teachers provide regular organized instruction in a classroom setting where possible or on a tutorial basis.

For the child no longer hospitalized but still unready for school attendance, home-bound instruction is a valuable option. A home-visiting or itinerant teacher provides individual tutorials on a regular basis, following the curriculum of the child's classroom.

No special curricula exist or are really necessary for students with health problems. Some general, common-sense tips for teachers of children with special health care needs are given on the next page.

Tips for Teachers

Tips for teachers of children with special health care needs

Classroom environment and climate

- Learn as much as you can about the condition, including the etiology, developmental consequences, and the prognosis.
- Be aware of the treatment procedures being used, the potential side effects of certain medical treatments on appearance and behaviour, and the approximate schedule of upcoming treatments.
- Be sympathetic to the child's feelings about hospital and separation.
- Constantly be alert for crisis situations. For example, be aware of how to monitor the status of the diabetic child, know the symptoms of insulin reaction, and have a remedy immediately ready.
- Make children feel a part of the class even if illness keeps them absent for long periods.
- List and display special needs for substitute teachers.
- Adjust classroom schedules for students with limited vitality to create maximum on-task learning time.
- Encourage students to be as independent as possible in completing all self-help activities.
- Ensure a hygienically safe learning environment.

Adaptive equipment

- Keep an emergency list of personnel and telephone numbers close at hand.
- Be aware of the child's schedule for drug dosages and for special diet considerations.
- Check your school district's procedures for drug administration.
- Become familiar with any special equipment that the student might use in the classroom.

Summary

1. Special health care needs and physical impairments encompass an enormous variety of conditions and diseases. Some, such as cancer, are life threatening; others, such as muscular dystrophy, imply an abbreviated life span; still others mean that the child must carefully monitor activities, diet, or drugs.

2. Health disorders are so heterogeneous that no commonality can be found in students' behavioural, intellectual, and psychological functioning. Even with the same conditions, no two youngsters are affected in exactly the same way. The impact of a health or physical disorder depends upon a number of variables: the age of onset of the condition, the degree of disability, the visibility of the condition, family and social support, the attitudes toward the individual, and the individual's social status with peers.

3. Because the conditions are primarily medical, there is no reason that children should require special intervention. Nearly all children with health and musculoskeletal conditions will be educated within regular classrooms. Special education should be available to accommodate lags resulting from lost school time.

4. As increasing numbers of children are being infected with pediatric AIDS, schools must accommodate these special health and learning problems.

5. Child abuse occurs at every socio-ecomomic level. Parents often feel overwhelmed by stress, isolated, incapable of coping, and lacking in resources. More often than not, high stress is the common denominator in abusive families. Preschoolers, boys, handicapped children, sick children, and premature and low-birth-weight children appear to be at greater risk for abuse. There is sufficient empirical evidence to support the widely held assumption that child abuse and neglect have developmental effects on the physical, neurological, intellectual, and emotional development of children. Sexually abused children often carry emotional scars for life, while the experiential deprivation inherent in neglect affects every aspect of a child's development.

CHAPTER 13

Children with Neurological Disabilities

Historical Notes

When institutional settings for students with special needs were first established in the nineteenth century, they served discrete categories of students, specifically those who were deaf, blind, and mentally retarded. Children who were seriously crippled, not toilet-trained, or considered to be uneducable were not provided with schooling. Those with additional handicapping conditions, such as epilepsy, paralysis, or cerebral palsy, were seen as potential hindrances to programs because of the individual care they needed. When discussing the student population of his Massachusetts experimental school for feeble-minded and idiotic children, for example, Samuel Gridley Howe was quick to point out: "The institution is not intended for epileptic or insane children, nor for those who are incurably hydrocephalic or paralytic." Moreover, he asserted, "any such shall not be retained, to the exclusion of more improvable subjects" (cited in Wolfensberger, 1975, p. 25).

Probably no other nineteenth-century exceptional group was as misunderstood and inappropriately handled as those with epilepsy. In that period, no drugs to control the condition or technical devices to assess its etiology existed, and seizures engendered such fear in beholders that they retreated into the myth that epilepsy and insanity were inextricably joined (Winzer, 1993).

Institutionalization was imperative. Early in the century, epileptics were sent either to hospitals for the insane or to almshouses. With the expansion of institutions for the mentally retarded in the 1880s, many were institutionalized with retarded people, often in the custodial departments with "idiots" and the "juvenile insane." In some places, separate facilities for epileptics emerged. Physicians argued that "while the majority of cases are incurable so far as complete immunity from subsequent attacks is concerned, nearly all improve under enlightened treatment, cojoined with hygienic, dietetic and moral influences which, however, are possible only in properly constituted and wisely-managed institutions" (Vineland, 1896, p. 32).

Not only were epileptics confined with the insane or the retarded populations, but they were viewed as chronic, incurable invalids affected with a disease that was "hereditary in a high degree" (Vineland, 1896, p. 32). It was widely held that epileptics became temporarily deranged following seizures, or fell into an "insane furor" that could lead to crime or even homicide (Vineland, 1896, p. 34). Researchers pointed out that probably more than two-fifths of epileptics were insane at least part of the time, and that many lawless actions were perpetrated (Vineland, 1896, p.33). Even the sufferer in "fortunate circumstances" could not be prevented "from injurious brooding over his hopeless misery" nor stopped "from gratifying his often morbidly excessive appetite for injurious food or depraving himself by vicious practices" (Vineland, 1896, p. 32).

Normal development of the central nervous system is the outcome of a carefully timed and precisely regulated combination of structural and chemical events. Something amiss in these events can lead to damage to, or deterioration of, the central nervous system, which in turn is one of the most common causes of physical and neurological disabilities in children.

As in the case of health and musculoskeletal impairments, there exists a huge range of neurological disorders. Some are associated with impairments of the nervous system; others result from diseases and accidents. For many children, the decreased range of motion, the reduced strength of movement, or the addition of unwanted or uncontrolled movement can dramatically affect the way they perform. Many youngsters in this category also suffer additional handicapping conditions such as seizures or diabetes and can therefore be viewed as multiply handicapped.

Depending on the severity of the condition, the related services available, and the prognosis, students with neurological disabilities are served in regular classrooms, regular classroom and resource room combinations, or special classes. Because the conditions are not in themselves inherently intellectually handicapping, we should see almost all physically impaired children who do not suffer additional conditions integrated into regular classrooms in the future.

Children with physical disabilities can benefit from the same instructional practices as their non-disabled peers.

Definitions

Neurological impairments are one of the sub-categories of physical disabilities that we described in Chapter 12. Essentially, we can say that **neurological impairments** result from damage or dysfunction of the brain and/or the spinal cord. Such damage may occur before, during, or after birth. Potential risks include severe deprivation of oxygen before birth, especially during the first trimester when various important neural structures and interconnections between the brain cells are developing. Other risks are damage incurred during the birth process and damage directly caused by diseases, especially those that attack the central nervous system.

The effects of the damage vary greatly; wide variations occur in the onset of symptoms, the parts of the body involved, the nature of the symptoms, the degree of severity, and the possible multiplicity of impairments. Injury to the brain may result in a relatively limited specific disorder. For example, one of the traditional etiologies of learning disabilities is minimal brain dysfunction. On the other hand, generalized and diffuse brain damage may cause very wide-ranging effects, including motor disturbances, sensory loss, speech and language disorders, and emotional and behavioural disorders. Diffuse damage will result in mental retardation; damage to the motor areas will cause cerebral palsy.

Injury to the spinal cord alone tends to result in motor and sensory disabilities, without affecting intellectual function and special sensory functions (vision, hearing, and speech). Damage to the motor cells of the spinal cord results in **flaccid paralysis**, an inability to move the muscles because the neural impulses needed for muscle contractions are lacking.

The manner in which physical and neurological disabilities affect individuals varies widely. Some people are devastated by the condition and never achieve their optimal development. On the other hand, Canadians remember with special pride young people like Rick Hanson and Terry Fox who worked through their physical disabilities in efforts to help others.

Development of the Field

Schooling for children described as crippled was a very late development compared to that for deaf or blind children. There are reports of a class in Boston in 1866 for crippled children, but any facilities for these youngsters were generally not within the purview of the school system. In Montreal, the world's first organized movement on behalf of crippled children was started in 1906 by a group of educators at the Children's Memorial Hospital. Educational services for children with health impairments developed to address specific diseases such as polio and tuberculosis. In 1908 the Hospital for Sick Children in Toronto began an open air class on Toronto Island for children who were malnourished, sickly, or suffering from tuberculosis (McIntosh, 1977).

Once medications to control seizures were discovered, epileptic children were no longer excluded from the regular schools. On the other hand, children with physical disabilities were long taught in specialized facilities. In spite of the fact that these students presented a wide range of abilities, potential, and educational need, and that there is little or no difference between their classroom performance and that of non-disabled students, the majority of physically disabled pupils were restricted to special schools or special classes. Among other reasons, teachers felt that physically handicapped youngsters would be too difficult to handle and would take a disproportionate amount of time (Brulle et al., 1983). There has also existed a traditional predisposition to stereotype these children, to focus on their disabilities and ignore their strengths. Most terminology was based on medical anatomy or a medical evaluation, and there was a strict adherence to a medical model. In addition, many school plants were not equipped with the physical structures, the modifications, the technical equipment, and the support personnel to handle and teach physically handicapped students. It was seen as more economical to transport children to one central location and to bring the therapists, the teachers, and the other intervenors to the students. In addition, given the difficulties these children often have with mobility, it was more economical to construct one barrier-free building than to alter all the plants in a school district (Winzer, 1989).

The majority of chronic illnesses occur during the first three years of life. Many illnesses that are chronic were fatal in the past; with current medical intervention, they are no longer life-threatening. As these children enter the school system, they bring with them a range of challenges that extend from simply monitoring drug usage, to watching for fatigue, to classroom adaptations that accommodate neurological dysfunctions, to adaptive equipment for mobility and communication. Probably the greatest challenge for teachers is handling a terminally ill child in the classroom.

Prevalence of Neurological Disorders

While neurological conditions are extremely varied, they are low-incidence handicaps. The prevalence is only about 0.2 to 1.5 percent of the school-age population, although rates vary from locale to locale and from decade to decade. Recent figures from various Canadian provinces are shown in Table 13-1.

Table 13-1

Prevalence of physical and neurological disabilities

Province	Term	Number	Percentage of total school population	Percentage of exceptional population
Nova Scotia	Physically handicapped	174	0.10	0.92
Quebec	Physically handicapped	1458	0.15	1.15
Ontario	Orthopedically handicapped	1030	0.06	0.75
	Physically handicapped	1542	0.08	1.13
Saskatchewan	Orthopedically handicapped	173	0.08	2.87
B.C.	Physically handicapped	425	0.08	0.70

Source: CEC, 1989

Cerebral Palsy

Cerebral palsy is a condition characterized by damage to the brain before, during, or after birth. The condition is present at birth in more than two-thirds of cases (Verhaaren and Connor, 1981).

Cerebral palsy is chiefly a motor disorder, though it is often accompanied by other disabilities. It is one of the most common crippling conditions in children. The most commonly cited incidence figures range from 3 to 6 cerebral palsied children per 1000 live births (Apgar and Beck, 1974). Within the population of persons with cerebral palsy, there are more boys than girls. The condition occurs more often among children born to mothers in poor socio-economic circumstances (Hallahan and Kauffman, 1991). An extensive study of children with cerebral palsy (Nelson and Ellenberg, 1986) found that the factors most likely to be associated with it were mental retardation of the mother, premature birth, low birth-weight, and a delay of five minutes or more before the baby's first cry.

Cerebral palsy is sometimes referred to as Little's disease, after the surgeon who first described it. Another alternative label is "significant developmental motor disability."

Classification of Cerebral Palsy

Cerebral palsy may be classified by topography or by type. The topographical classification system, as shown in Table 13-2, refers to parts of the body and is not limited to cerebral palsy. In the topographical system, the suffix *plegia* refers to paralysis.

Table 13-2

Topographical classification of cerebral palsy

Monoplegia	One limb impaired.
Diplegia	Four limbs involved, with legs most impaired.
Hemiplegia	One side of the body impaired.
Paraplegia	Lower limbs of the body impaired.
Triplegia	Three limbs impaired.
Double hemiplegia	Both sides of the body impaired, with each side affected differently.
Quadriplegia	All four limbs impaired.

When classified by the type of brain damage and consequent motor disability, cerebral palsy can be differentiated according to specific motor patterns, as outlined in Table 13-3.

Spastic or **pyramidal cerebral palsy** affects approximately 50 percent of the cerebral palsied population. Individuals with this type of cerebral palsy have suffered damage to the motor cortex or to the pyramidal tracts of the brain (Batshaw and Perret, 1986). Pyramidal cerebral palsy results in problems with voluntary movements. *Spasticity*, therefore, refers to slow, laborious, poorly co-ordinated voluntary movements. Children with spastic cerebral palsy also demonstrate the continued presence of a number of primitive reflexes.

Table 13-3

Classification of cerebral palsy

Pyramidal cerebal palsy (Spasticity)	movement: slow and difficult co-ordination: poor muscle tone: weak, hypertonic
Extrapyramidal cerebral palsy Dyskinesia (five types)	
Athetosis	movement: consistent, involuntary, writhing co-ordination: poor muscle tone: fluctuating
Rigidity	movement: more severe than spasticity co-ordination: poor muscle tone: continuous tension
Hypotonia	movement: may develop into spastic or athetoid type co-ordination: varied muscle tone: low
Tremor	movement: involuntary, rhythmic co-ordination: depends upon affected limbs muscle tone: varied
Ataxia	movement: clumsy co-ordination: poor muscle tone: varied

Most of the primitive reflexes present in all newborns disappear by about six months of age (see Research Notes). If these reflexes persist, they act as impediments to the development of smooth, co-ordinated movement. Types of abnormal reflex movements seen in cerebral palsied children include the rooting reflex, startle reaction, stretch reflex, asymmetrical and symmetrical tonic neck reflex, protective extensive reactions, and righting reactions. In the presence of the stretch reflex, for example, a muscle contracts involuntarily when suddenly stretched. Thus, when the arm is bent suddenly, the biceps contract but the reflex causes contractions in the opposing triceps as well. A mini-war results, rendering movements impossible to control. This means that children with spastic cerebral palsy cannot move when and how they choose.

Extrapyramidal cerebral palsy includes athetosis, hypotonia, rigidity, and ataxia. In these cases, damage is outside the pyramidal tracts and results in abrupt involuntary movements and difficulty in maintaining posture (Batshaw and Perret, 1986). When there is damage to both the pyramidal and the extrapyramidal regions of the brain, the child may demonstrate mixed effects, such as spasticity of the legs and rigidity of the arms. About 25 percent of cases are classified as mixed cerebral palsy (Batshaw and Perret, 1986).

Athetoid cerebral palsy is found in approximately 25 percent of the cerebral palsied population. **Athetosis** is characterized by constant, involuntary writhing movements, especially in the hands and wrists. Contractions occur in successive groups of muscles, creating extraneous movement that interferes with purposive action. Children with athetoid cerebral palsy are unable to stop moving when they want to. Athetosis stops during sleep.

Rigidity occurs when there is a low level of motor stiffness that never relaxes. The condition is rare, as is **tremor**, an involuntary movement in one extremity, usually one hand or arm. In constant tremor, the movement is continuous; in intention tremor, the involuntary movement happens only when the child undertakes to do something.

Ataxic cerebral palsy occurs in approximately 15 percent of individuals with cerebral palsy. **Ataxia** is characterized by poor co-ordination of the movements associated with balance, posture, and spatial orientation. Children with ataxia tend to walk with a wide gait, their legs well apart to compensate for poor equilibrium. They also exhibit a generalized lack of co-ordination of both fine and gross motor movements.

Research Notes

Reflexes in infants

Reflexes are natural responses with which children are born. The presence of reflexes in infants and their eventual disappearance offers insights into the process of neurological development and organization, as well as information about the results of damage to discrete areas of the brain. Some reflexes are necessary for survival; others are interesting because they are controlled by the midbrain, that part of the brain that develops first. As the more advanced parts of the brain develop, these primitive reflexes disappear.

Newborns are unable to control their motor behaviour smoothly and voluntarily. Instead, behaviour consists of twitches, jerks, and random movements, most of which involve **reflexes** — automatic, involuntary motor patterns that are triggered by specific stimuli. The various feeding reflexes are necessary for survival. Infants come equipped with a rooting reflex. If babies are touched on the cheek anywhere near the mouth, they will turn their heads and root around to put their mouths on the object that touched them.

Among a second group of primitive reflexes is the Moro reflex, described by Ernst Moro in 1918. If a loud noise is made near an infant, or if the infant's position is changed suddenly, the baby will throw both arms outwards and then bring them into the body. This reflex disappears at about three months of age as the neurological system matures. With the Babinski reflex, babies splay out their toes and then curl them in if stroked on the bottom of the foot. In an adult or older child, only the curling occurs.

The reflex actions of babies allow them to react to things in their world as they are learning to control their own bodies (Braga and Braga, 1975). Reflexes also help to ensure survival by protecting vital systems. As well, a number of reactions appear to be the precursors of later development and can be used to diagnose certain kinds of brain damage.

Developmental Consequences

The consequences of cerebral palsy vary in relation to many factors. These relate chiefly to the type of cerebral palsy, the severity of the condition, and the presence or absence of additional handicapping conditions. While no two children with cerebral palsy develop in exactly the same way, the presence of extensive motor disorders alone is sufficient to interfere with normal development. Within twelve to fourteen weeks of birth, for example, normal children achieve control of head movements. Within six months, they pull to a sitting position. At about twelve months they begin to walk unaided. These milestones offer children increased opportunities to make better use of sensory experience, to gain greater perceptual awareness, and to learn to manipulate objects and their own bodies. Damage to the motor system impedes the course of normal development. Each stage of motor development causes a shift in the child's interaction with the environment. Children with cerebral palsy have little control of the musculature necessary to reach developmental milestones.

Cerebral palsy is generally not diagnosed right at birth because there are few abnormal neurological signs at this time. In fact, a brain-damaged neonate may appear to be perfectly normal for the first several weeks of life. Clues to neuromotor disturbance in infants include irritability, excessive listlessness, pallor, stiffening, arching, excessive startle, nystagmus, and jaundice (Cruickshank, 1976). In addition, cerebral palsied infants behave differently. They tend to sleep excessively, have a weak cry, a poor suck, and show little interest in their surroundings. They rest differently, lying in a floppy extended position instead of a semi-flexed one (Batshaw and Perret, 1986). Nevertheless, early diagnosis remains difficult. Not all of these signs are found in all cerebral palsied infants, and not all infants who manifest these signs have cerebral palsy.

As the child develops, predictions can be made on overall progress. If the child can sit by two years of age, for example, he or she will probably walk. About 80 percent of children with cerebral palsy are capable of learning to walk, although many need to use braces and other assistive devices (Bleck, 1979). If the child is able to utter recognizable sounds by age two, that child will probably learn to speak (Bleck and Nagel, 1982).

The brain damage that results in cerebral palsy is not always limited to motor areas. Indeed, cerebral palsy can generally be seen as a multi-handicapping condition. A high percentage of this population exhibits one or more additional impairments. These include mental rertardation, learning disabilities, sensory loss, epilepsy, and emotional and behavioural disorders. As well, disorders of posture, listening, breathing, voice, articulation, and language are all found in association with cerebral palsy.

Many people assume, given the external appearance of the condition, that children with cerebral palsy are concomitantly intellectually disabled. This is an incorrect assumption. However, it is true that the hypothetical intelligence curve for these children indicates that the incidence of intellectual disability is significantly higher than average. Estimates of the number of children who are cerebral palsied with some degree of intellectual impairment vary, ranging from 50 to 75 percent (Lefebrue, 1983; Nelson and Ellenberg, 1986). Little evidence exists to link the severity of intellectual impairment with any particular type of cerebral palsy. However, Batshaw and Perret (1986) point out that hemiplegia is associated with the best mental development.

The speech and language problems of children with cerebral palsy reflect the complexity of the condition. Estimates of the percentage of children with cerebral palsy who also have speech and language problems range from 50 to 83 percent (Cruickshank, 1976). In some cases damage, usually to certain areas of the left cerebral hemisphere, results in language delays and disorders. Nevertheless, language problems are less common than speech disorders.

Damage to the central nervous system can impair those centres in the brain involved with the regulation of breathing. Many children with cerebral palsy suffer breathing problems (Mysak, 1982) that may impair their ability to shift from vegetative breathing — breathing regulated by the autonomic nervous system — to speech breathing, a higher and more complex function. Children with cerebral palsy may also have weak thoracic and abdominal muscles, or airstream obstruction due to irregular movements of the vocal cords (Mysak, 1982).

Motor dysfunctions that affect the organs of speech may make intelligible speech impossible. The errors of articulation that accompany cerebral palsy are known as *dysarthria*, a condition we discussed in Chapter 6. The speech characteristics of children with spastic forms of cerebral palsy may include articulatory defects, laboured speech with distortions of sound, uncontrolled pitch changes, and husky voice quality.

Visual and auditory problems are the most prevalent and serious of the sensory difficulties associated with cerebral palsy. It is estimated that more than 50 percent of these children have visual defects of some type (Lefebrue, 1983). Children who have cerebral palsy secondary to brain damage often have impaired vision as a result of loss of control of the ocular muscles. There is also a high incidence of middle ear problems; approximately 25 to 30 percent of individuals with cerebral palsy have hearing defects (Jones, 1983). Other sensory problems include deficits in tactile sensation and the determination of pain, pressure, and temperature.

Children with cerebral palsy may show disorders such as short attention span and distractibility. Given these problems, it is estimated that from 15 to 20 percent are likely to have some type of specific learning disability (Telford and Sawrey, 1981).

An additional problem faced by children with cerebral palsy is some form of convulsive disorder. It is estimated that half of them suffer epileptic seizures. These are most common in hemiplegics and quadriplegics. As well, cerebral palsied children with normal IQs are three times more prone to psychiatric disorders (Seidel, Chadwick, and Rutter, 1975).

As the number of accompanying disorders indicates, cerebral palsy is a very complex multi-handicapping condition. However, not every affected child faces all or even most of these disorders. Usually children with limited and localized brain injuries face fewer limitations than children with diffuse, extensive brain damage.

Midline defects, often referred to as clefts, result from the failure of parts of the embryo to fuse completely. Such defects may occur in many parts of the body, including the lip, the palate, the eye, and the spine. **Spina bifida** is a congenital midline defect of the spinal column.

Technically, the term *spina bifida* refers to a defect in the bony arch of the vertebrae protecting the spinal cord (Mitchell, Fiewell, and Davy, 1983). In the early weeks of pregnancy, the neural tube of the embryo fails to develop normally. The bony arches of one or more spinal vertebrae do not fuse to protect the spinal cord, which leaves part of the nerve fibres of the cord exposed. The spinal defect may be found anywhere between the skull and the lowest segments of the vertebrae. Generally spina bifida is evident by the end of the fourth week of gestation and the severity of the problem is apparent at birth (Myers, Cerone, and Olson, 1981).

Profile

Kent

Kent suffers from a number of handicapping conditions that affect every aspect of his life and development. He has cerebral palsy and needs leg braces and a walker for mobility. Psycho-educational assessment has shown Kent to be functioning in the low area of the mildly retarded range, so he needs a modified school program based on his unique strengths and weaknesses. Kent also suffers from a moderate to severe bilateral hearing loss and the audiologist has fitted him with two hearing aids.

At eight years of age, Kent has developed very little communication. His special class teacher would like to integrate him into the regular classroom for short daily periods to stimulate his social functioning, but is concerned that he has no language.

In consultation with the language therapist, the teacher decided to introduce Kent to a language system. In the past, both Bliss symbolics and American Sign Language were tried, but these seemed to be too conceptually difficult for Kent. Because Kent's hand use is quite good, the therapist suggested that the teacher introduce some basic signs from the Amerind system and also teach these to the children in the proposed receiving class. Once Kent learns some simple signs and combinations, he may advance to American Sign Language.

Although the process is fairly well understood, the actual cause of spina bifida is unknown. Etiologically, it is believed that both heredity and the environment are interweaving factors. In Newfoundland, which has the highest rate of spina bifida in Canada, most affected children are conceived between May and August (Fraser, Frecker, and Allerdice, 1986).

Spina bifida can be initially detected prenatally by a test that looks at the level of alpha-fetoprotein in the mother's blood. Higher concentrations than usual indicate the necessity for ultrasound or fetoscopy.

The prevalence of spina bifida varies widely from country to country, from area to area, and even within the limits of a particular city. Worldwide, spina bifida occurs in from 0.1 to 4.13 live births per 1000 (Bleck and Nagel, 1982). The incidence in Ireland is about 4 or 5 children per 1000 live births, while in parts of Nigeria it is 0.2 per 1000 live births. In Canada, as mentioned, the highest rate of spina bifida is found in Newfoundland.

There is a slight tendency for the condition to run in families. If one baby is born with spina bifida, there is a 4 to 5 percent chance of siblings having the same defect (Myers, Cerone, and Olson, 1981). Spina bifida is found more often in lower socioeconomic groups and occurs more frequently in males (Bowley and Gardner, 1980).

Classification of Spina Bifida

Spina bifida refers to a group of defects ranging from those with few or no adverse effects to those with severely disabling consequences. Spina bifida is divided into two main forms: spina bifida occulta and spina bifida cystica. Of the affected population, about 40 percent suffer from spina bifida occulta and the remainder from cystica. This latter form is divided into two types — spina bifida with meningocele and spina bifida with myelomeningocele. The former accounts for 4 percent of individuals suffering the cystica form; the latter for 96 percent. (See Figure 13-1).

Figure 13-1
Types of spina bifida

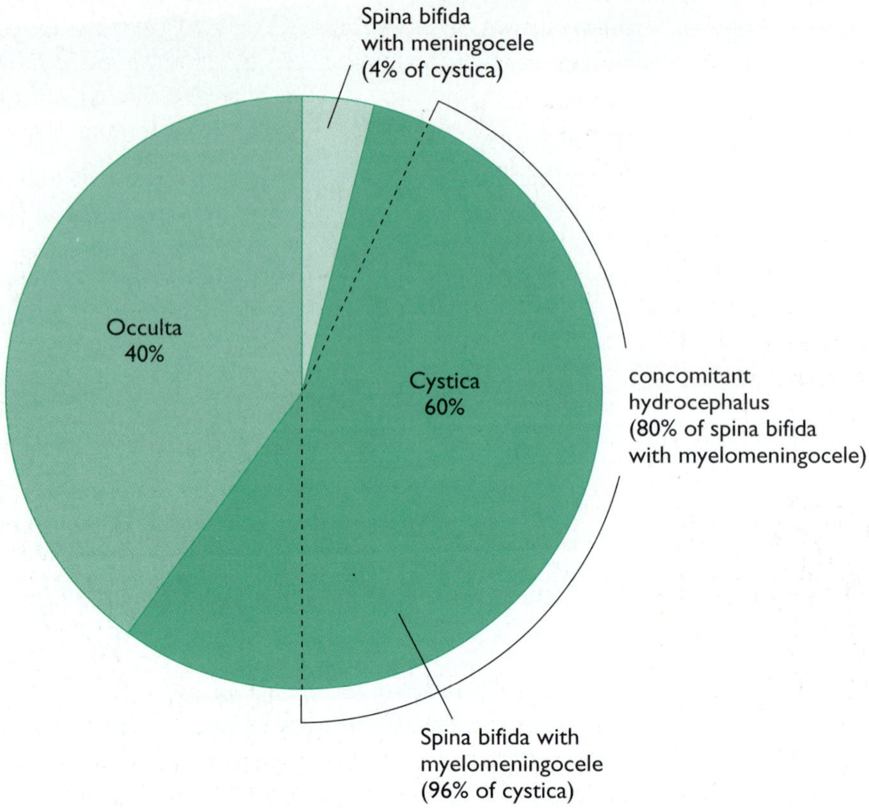

Spina bifida occulta is the mildest form of the condition and has few or no negative effects. The only visible sign of the condition, if any, is a clump of hair on the skin covering the area of the cleft.

The two forms of spina bifida cystica — with meningocele and with myelomeningocele — have different results. In **spina bifida with meningocele**, the meninges, the membranes surrounding the spinal cord, protrude from the plane of the spine and form a sac containing cerebrospinal fluid. Surgery is usually performed in the first days of life to restore the sac within the spinal column. Following treatment, this condition does not usually create any major difficulties, although children must be wary of being hit directly on the area.

Spina bifida with myelomeningocele, the most severe type, results in a protruding sac that contains parts of the spinal cord as well as cerebrospinal fluid. The spinal cord not only enters the sac but is itself abnormal. Surgical treatment is necessary to deal with the sac, but the neurological damage is irreversible.

The effects of myelomeningocele vary considerably depending on the location of the cleft. The higher the cleft, the greater the damage. Clefts in the lower part of the spine may result in incontinence without paralysis. Clefts in the higher spinal regions produce paralysis and loss of sensation in the lower limbs, incontinence, and kidney problems. In addition to the cleft of the vertebral arches associated with spina bifida, other vertebrae unusual in slope or connection can occur, resulting in an uneven growth of the spine (Myers, Cerone, and Olson, 1981).

In the past, babies born with severe forms of spina bifida rarely survived. They died from urinary infection or infection of the sac (Edgington, 1976). Improvements in medical intervention have led to an increase in the survival rate (Anderson and Spain, 1977).

Developmental Consequences of Spina Bifida

Children with spina bifida occulta or with meningocele are likely to develop normally. In the absence of additional handicapping conditions, spina bifida does not preclude adequate learning ability. Children with spina bifida occulta exhibit the normal range of intelligence. Those born with a meningocele are also likely to have normal intelligence, particularly if the meningocele is not accompanied by any hydrocephalus.

Children with myelomeningocele suffer neurological damage that interferes with growth and development. The most obvious neurological damage is the flaccid paralysis of the lower part of the body, which necessitates the use of braces, crutches, walkers, or wheelchairs. Problems occur in mobility and are compounded by extended school absences. Many children have difficulty moving from one place to another in the school. Affected children may miss numerous days in school for surgery, medical appointments, and therapy. If school time loss is extensive, students may be provided with hospital or home-bound instruction.

Children with myelomeningocele lack sensation and control of their bladders and bowel sphincters. Incontinence in itself does not create learning difficulties, but it may create social and psychological barriers for children in school. Non-disabled children usually view incontinence as a sign of immaturity or infantile behaviour and react accordingly. As incontinent children mature, they learn to cope with their condition. To drain the bladder, they are taught to catheterize themselves every three or four hours (Myers, Cerone, and Olson, 1981). Although it may not create problems, it has been found that spina bifida children experience very early puberty, with menstruation occurring as early as eight years of age (Allum, 1975). Researchers are uncertain of the cause of this phenomenon.

Children suffering from spina bifida with myelomenigocele generally have IQs in the low average to mildly retarded range (Calhoun and Hawisher, 1979). Perceptual and cognitive dysfunction is prevalent, especially in children with accompanying hydrocephalus (Anderson, 1973). Affected children show poorer general performance in reading, spelling, and arithmetic (Tew and Lawrence, 1975). However, most have good verbal ability, which may tend to mask the cognitive defects.

Although spina bifida may occur as a solitary condition, nearly 80 percent of children who have spina bifida with myelomeningocele suffer from hydrocephalus as well. The combination of the two conditions dramatically increases the number of disabilities. The damage to the brain from hydrocephalus and to the spinal cord from spina bifida is likely to produce a multiply disabled child.

Hydrocephalus

Hydrocephalus is a condition characterized by an excessive accumulation of cerebrospinal fluid in the brain due to an obstruction of its flow. Normally, cerebrospinal fluid is constantly manufactured in the ventricles of the brain, circulates through the the ventricles and the space between the two layers of meninges, and is absorbed into the circulatory system. Since fluids are largely non-compressible, a blockage of the flow results in the accumulation of cerebrospinal fluid in an enclosed area, placing pressure on the brain and the skull. The presssure against the skull creates thinning of the bone and separation of the sutures (the seams between the plates of the skull). The fluid also presses on the brain tissue, causing distortion of brain substance and damage and death to the neurons.

In some instances, hydrocephalus arrests itself spontaneously. In other cases, the condition progresses and creates increasing pressure on the skull. The progressive accumulation of cerebrospinal fluid may result in a range of disorders. Because mental retardation is a primary result, hydrocephalus is included among the clinical forms of mental retardation. Other sequelae include motor disorders, seizures, and even death.

Before the 1950s, no effective treatment existed for hydrocephalus. Children developed marked symptoms; by the age of three months, their heads became too large and heavy for them to lift, and their condition often ended in death. In 1952 an engineer named Holter developed an effective shunt (tube) to drain off excess cerebrospinal fluid and reduce the pressure on the brain. Since Holter's invention, many children with hydrocephalus have been spared extensive impairments.

Developmental Consequences of Hydrocephalus

In persons affected by hydrocephalus, develomental consequences vary with the degree of severity of the conditions, the presence or absence of additional handicapping conditions, and with the success or failure of treatment. Some individuals may attain average and above average intelligence scores; others may be severely impaired.

There exists contradictory evidence concerning cognitive functioning. Some researchers have found no correlation between the degree of severity of hydrocephalus and IQ levels (Soare and Raimondi, 1977); others have discovered that the average IQ of shunted children is 70 to 83 (Tew and Lawrence, 1975). Beyond the rather undescriptive intelligence scores, it has also been found that many hydrocephalic children have particular learning problems that result in uneven intellectual functioning. Some aspects of verbal ability, such as syntax and vocabulary, may be well developed, while comprehension and language usage are defective (Spain, 1972).

Epilepsy

The word *epilepsy* is derived from the Greek meaning "to be seized," and we still describe epilepsy in terms of seizures. During the 1800s Hughlings Jackson, a pioneer neurologist, defined epilepsy as a condition produced by a sudden violent electrical discharge of brain cells. Echoing Jackson's definition, epilepsy is today defined as

> a convulsive disorder [that] is the expression of a sudden, excessive, disorderly discharge of neurons in either a structurally normal or diseased cortex. The discharge results in an almost instantaneous disturbance of sensation, loss of consciousness, convulsive movement, or some combination thereof (Harrison, 1980, p. 131).

Implicit in this definition is the idea that epilepsy is not a disease but a symptom of a brain disorder which may be caused by any condition that results in damage to the brain. This does not imply that brain damage necessarily results in epileptic seizures, although it may. The definition further stresses the chronic and recurring nature of epilepsy. Chronicity is important because it is estimated that between 2 and 3 percent of the population have had, or will have, some form of epileptic seizure in their lifetime (B.C. Ministry of Health, 1978). However, such a symptom might reflect some transient event, such as a high fever, heat exhaustion, ingestion of certain chemicals, or interference with the normal supply of oxygen to the brain.

The causes of epilepsy are varied and often unclear. Perinatal conditions, early childhood infection, and head trauma are identified as known causative factors. In some cases, heredity may play an important role.

If an individual shows strong evidence of brain damage, the condition is known as **symptomatic epilepsy**. The most common causes are brain tumour and stroke; head trauma of any type; injury, infection, or systemic illness of the mother during pregnancy that affects fetal brain growth; brain injury to the infant during delivery; the aftermath of an infection such as meningitis; and poisoning from substance abuse or alcoholism (Epilepsy [1994]). In about 75 percent of cases, however, there is no known cause. When the causes of epilepsy cannot be found, the condition is referred to as **idiopathic epilepsy**, or epilepsy of unknown origin.

No one is immune; epilepsy can strike anyone at any age. However, from 70 to 80 percent of patients develop epilepsy before the age of 18. About 55 percent develop epilepsy before the age of 10, and 44 percent before the age of 5 (Epilepsy, [1994]). Idiopathic epilepsy usually begins between two and fourteen years of age.

Epilepsy affects more than one percent of the population — more than 280 000 Canadians. One of every 2000 people is diagnosed with epilepsy each year; about 14 000 new cases are reported annually (Epilepsy [1994]).

Classification of Epilepsy

Epilepsy is a term that describes both the conditions of seizure and the convulsions accompanying some types of seizures. Seizures occur as a result of a temporary breakdown in the brain's communication system caused by disorderly cell activity. There are many types of seizures, some fairly well understood and some still confusing to researchers. The type of seizure depends on the region of the brain where it originates. It also depends, to some extent, on the brain's maturation and its ability to spread the electrical discharge to other parts of the body (Robb, 1981).

The three main classifications of epilepsy are generalized seizures, partial seizures, and unclassified seizures. **Generalized seizures** are bilateral and symmetrical without local onset in the brain. They are often accompanied by loss of consciousness and most have motor components. Generalized seizures include petit mal (absence seizures), myoclonic seizures, grand mal (tonic-clonic seizures), and atonic seizures, which include infantile spasm convulsions. The most common forms of generalized seizures are grand mal and petit mal. Many individuals experience both these forms, and may be either idiopathic or symptomatic.

The grand mal seizure proceeds through relatively distinct stages. Some epileptics consistently experience an aura just before the seizure's onset. This aura may be a subjective sensory or memory experience, such as an odour that is not present in reality. It may take the form of an odd internal sensation, or even a memory phenomenon in which the person actually experiences a scene from the past (Krupp and Chatton, 1983). Shortly after the aura appears, the individual loses consciousness, falls, and develops generalized stiffness of the body. During this tonic phase, the arms are flexed (bent) and the legs extended. The trunk muscles are also in spasm so that breathing ceases. After a short but varying period of tonic activity, the clonic stage follows. In this phase, the person exhibits alternate relaxations and contractions of the skeletal musculature which produce what is often referred to as thrashing movements. In the throes of the clonic state, the person may lose bladder and bowel control, bite the tongue, and froth at the mouth. After two to five minutes, convulsive movements diminish and finally stop. This is followed by a gradual regaining of consciousness. During this time, the person may experience confusion, headache, or other symptoms. A period of deep sleep marks the end of the seizure. If a child suffers a grand mal seizure and then immediately passes into another seizure, the condition is known as status epilepticus. This is potentially life-threatening and medical aid should be sought immediately.

Grand mal seizures can occur at any time and in a school setting can be frightening for the beholders and distressing for the victim. Teachers can ease the situation by trying to provide privacy during and after a seizure. If a child begins to have a seizure, the teacher should allow or help the child to lie down, move away furniture, loosen restrictive clothing, and tilt the head to one side to drain saliva. Teachers should never try to hold the child, stop the seizure, or force anything into the mouth.

The **petit mal** or absence seizure is most frequently seen in children. Some children suffer up to two hundred absence seizures a day. These often occur when the child is sedentary, and infrequently during exercise (Berkow, 1982). In more than 70 percent of all cases, petit mal seizures cease altogether by age 18 (Nealis, 1983).

Petit mal is considerably less dramatic than grand mal; the classic absence seizure lasts only fifteen to thirty seconds and is so brief that it is often overlooked or misinterpreted. The child ceases all activity and appears to stare vacantly, as though daydreaming. During this period, there is a loss or clouding of consciousness. The return of consciousness is abrupt and the child immediately resumes interrupted activities.

There are other forms of petit mal seizures. During these, the child's eyes may blink or shift and the hands move aimlessly. On some occasions, the seizure may be prolonged, lasting for minutes or hours. During these long seizures, the child may simply appear confused and dazed.

Minor motor seizures, often called Lennox-Gastaug seizures, are similar to petit mal. They can be characterized by loss of muscle tone for a moment. Myoclonic seizures are so called because they are characterized by a single repetitive contracture of a muscle or group of muscles.

Partial seizures may be characterized as simple or complex. Partial seizures begin locally (in a specific area of the brain) and may or may not cause loss of consciousness. They occur in many forms but the common feature in all is the localized origin of brain irritability. Because they affect very local motor or sensory areas, partial seizures are sometimes referred to as focal seizures.

One form of partial seizure is the **Jacksonian seizure**, which only occurs in cases of symptomatic epilepsy. This type of seizure is characterized by motor symptoms without impaired consciousness. In a Jacksonian seizure, spasmodic (clonic) movements might start in the peripheral portion of a limb, such as the left thumb. These movements might then progress in an orderly fashion toward the central portion of the body and down into the left leg. Sometimes the violent electrical discharge that begins in one hemisphere of the brain spreads to the other. If this happens, the individual loses consciousness and undergoes a grand mal convulsion.

Another type of partial seizure is the **psychomotor seizure**, sometimes called the psychomotor equivalent or temporal lobe seizure because it is most characteristically associated with lesions of the temporal lobe of the brain. Psychomotor seizures are poorly understood. They often include a clouding of consciousness and amnesia (loss of memory of the event). Along with altered consciousness, other manifestations include a change of body position or limbs, confused activity, a dazed expression, nausea, vomiting, drooling, muttering, mumbling, wandering, pallor or flushing, incoherent or irrelevant speech and inappropriate emotional disturbances. Sometimes these symptoms are accompanied by relatively complex, well-organized movements, such as plucking clothing, or any other patterned activity.

The category of unclassified seizures includes all other types.

Developmental Consequences of Epilepsy

With epilepsy, the effects on learning can be chronic or relatively short-lived depending on factors such as the nature of the seizure disorders and the medications used (Huberty et al., 1992). Learning problems can range from brief transient disturbances in attention and short-term deficits in cognitive functioning to a more permanent impairment in the ability to process information (Binnie, Channon, and Marston, 1990).

Children with idiopathic epilepsy are more likely to develop normally than those with symptomatic epilepsy. Most children with idiopathic epilepsy function normally between attacks, and approximately 70 percent have normal or higher intelligence (Dikmen, Matthews, and Harley, 1975). Symptomatic epilepsy is often seen in children who experience seizures before age two. The early onset of seizures that are unremitting or persistent for several years are more likely to be related to learning problems than is later onset or lower seizure frequency (Rodin, 1989). These children are usually suffering the effects of developmental defects, birth injuries, or a metabolic disease affecting the brain, and are more likely to exhibit multiple disorders that can include mental retardation, sensory loss, or motor disability.

As well, generalized seizures are more likely than partial epilepsy to be associated with learning problems. Individuals with more generalized seizures are usually expected to suffer greater disability than those whose seizures are more focused and partial.

For epileptic children, the chronic nature of the disorder and the unpredictability of seizures can create problems. Individuals have to learn to live with the possibility of lifelong seizures. Although the majority of children with epilepsy are well controlled with medication, and although some may outgrow seizures, none can look forward to a cure. In addition, no one can predict when a seizure will occur; for this reason, there is little chance to adjust to epilepsy. Children may feel powerless at the prospect of losing control: the ambiguous nature of epilepsy can increase a child's apprehension at not knowing when and under what circumstances his or her behaviour will become visible to others (Knoblock, 1987).

However, the major handicap of epilepsy is not the condition itself, but society's reaction to it. Despite the success of modern treatment, confusion and misunderstanding still surround epilepsy. Some people continue to equate epilepsy with mental retardation or mental illness. Although some persons with symptomatic epilepsy may exhibit mental retardation, they are a minority in the epileptic population. Among persons with ideopathic epilepsy, mental illness or intellectual disability do not occur more frequently than in the general population.

Head Trauma

In the United States, injuries, usually accidents, are the leading cause of death among children aged one to fourteen; nearly half of these deaths occur among children aged one to four. Boys are involved in injuries twice as often as girls. Among injuries in general, head injuries are on the rise.

Traumatic brain injury (TBI) is defined as

> an insult to the brain, not of a degenerative or congenital nature but caused by an external physical force, that may produce a diminished or altered state of consciousness, which results in impairment of cognitive abilities or physical functioning. It can also result in the disturbance of behavior or emotional functioning. These impairments may be either temporary or cause potential or total functional disability or psychosocial maladjustment (Savage, 1988, p. 13).

While head injuries occur most often in the 15-24 age range, traumatic brain injury is becoming almost as frequent in children under age 15. In the United States, it is estimated that one out of every 500 school-aged children will be hospitalized for traumatic head injuries (Kraus, Fife, and Conroy, 1987).

In adolescents vehicle accidents, either pedestrian or passenger vehicle accidents, including automobile, motorcycle, and bicycle accidents, are the most common cause of head injuries. In young children, head injuries result from falls (the most frequent cause), bicycle accidents, other recreational activities, assaults, and child abuse.

TBI is not selective in its damage. It can cause diffuse cerebral swelling due to increased cerebral blood volume, and several areas of the brain can therefore be affected. Because of this, children and adolescents who suffer head injuries can be expected to present concomitant physical and perceptual-motor defects and organically based behaviour and emotional disorders (De Pompei and Blosser, 1987).

Each child with a traumatic brain injury progresses through the recovery process in a unique way. Recovery is influenced by the site and extent of the injuries to the brain, age, and other injuries or complications. Children are often in a coma and may at first show a state of confusion, as well as memory, attention, or speech and language impairments.

Children who have suffered a head injury may show chronic fatigue for up to a year. Whereas obvious motor problems may resolve relatively quickly, problems with the execution of refined and complex psychomotor movements, particularly when speed is involved, may persist. Children may show problems in attention, retention, and auditory and recent memory. These deficits have implications for the child in the classroom because they influence the degree to which the child can keep up with class procedures such as copying, organizing material, and producing significant amounts of work.

Continuing language problems may also influence how the child functions in the classroom. When deficits such as lack of speech, restricted expressive output, and problems of breath control are present right after a trauma, they may subside rapidly, but as part of a global disorganization process, more subtle and long-standing difficulties with language comprehension and expression may persist. These include problems of word finding, organization of sequenced utterances, and comprehension breakdown as instructional complexity increases (Mira and Tyler, 1991; Ylvisaker, 1986).

It is estimated that among children with mild head injuries, about 25 percent will require special classes; of children with serious injuries, about 50 percent will need special education (see Tyler and Mira, 1993). For special education intervention, however, there are no special tested techniques or educational modifications in place (Tyler and Mira, 1993).

Profile

Christopher

Christopher is now twenty-six years of age. He walks slowly, favouring his left side, writes painfully and slowly, slurs and stumbles over his speech when he is tired, and is subject to depression and sometimes violent temper outbursts.

Casual observers may think that Christopher suffers from some form of mental handicap. In reality, Christopher is suffering from permanent brain damage caused by an automobile accident when he was fifteen.

Christopher was out with a group of friends when their car hit some black ice and skidded into a lamp post. Even in his seat belt, Christopher was badly jarred and hit his head against the side window. He was in a coma for eleven days. When he finally awoke, he required intense physical and occupational therapy. The therapist began by helping him to walk with rails, to stop and roll a ball, and to move his tongue to produce articulate speech.

Recovery was slow. It was more than a year before Christopher could return to school. By then, he was far behind his peers, and his trouble with learning, processing, and retaining information presented him with almost unsurmountable problems. He finished school in a special class where he received additional help to overcome his learning difficulties.

Drug-Exposed Children

In Chapter 2 of this text, we pointed to the possible range of physical and behavioural difficulties that can affect a child exposed to drugs. It is important to keep in mind that there is a continuum of casualty risk. That is, the popular notion that all crack babies are severely affected is a myth; the effects vary dramatically and are moderated or exacerbated by other factors.

Teachers will find that children who do suffer effects are often overwhelmed by the ordinary experiences of a classroom — the classroom and environmental noises, the instructions, questions, interactions, and general business. Some children may show learning problems and have difficulty in dealing with the many different stimuli at once. Some children may withdraw; others may become wild and difficult to control (Rest, 1990).

These children need stability, routine, and sameness in the classroom to feel secure enough to learn (Walker, 1992/93). They should be given only one specific task at a time. As well as avoiding overload, teachers need to stress social skills, communication, and stable, consistent discipline.

Multiple Sclerosis

Multiple sclerosis is a progressive disease of the central nervous system characterized by patchy scarring or hardening of the myelin sheath of the nerve cells in the brain and the spinal cord. The cause is unknown, although it is believed that the body's immune system engages in a self-destructive attack against its own myelin. There is no specific treatment for multiple sclerosis at present.

Demyelination results in various neurological symptoms — sensory problems, tremors, muscle weakness, spasticity, speech difficulties, dizziness, mild emotional disturbance, difficulty in walking, and other problems (Hallahan and Kauffman, 1991). These difficulties intensify as the condition progresses. Sufferers have periods of remission of various lengths, followed by recurrence of symptoms.

Typically, multiple sclerosis does not affect young children. The destruction of the myelin sheath often begins in the young adult and lasts for the remainder of the patient's life (Haqq, 1985). Multiple sclerosis affects females more frequently than males and is more common in temperate climates than in the tropics. The incidence in temperate zones is approximately 1 per 1000 people, while the rate of occurrence in the tropics is 1 per 10 000 (Berkow, 1982).

Identification and Assessment

It is important for teachers to know and understand the precise nature of a child's problems.

Many of the conditions characterized as neurological disabilities require intensive medical diagnosis and management. Vision and hearing assessment are crucial; specific measures are discussed in Chapters 9, 10, and 15.

With psycho-educational assessment, no consensus exists as to the types of measures to use with children who are neurologically impaired. There is general agreement that testing for many of these children is fraught with difficulties that relate to the depth of physical and mental disabilities. Educators also agree that the information gathered in the screening and diagnostic processes must allow the formulation of a hypothesis that will take into account all the relevant factors and that will enable intelligent decisions to be made regarding placement and academic planning.

As means must be found to circumvent the disabilities in order to provide accurate assessment results, diagnosticians cannot rely on standardized tests. Instead, they must incorporate a battery of measures that range from developmental scales and ecological assessment, through communication and language tools, to tests of mental ability. They must also be willing to use different test procedures and must be flexible enough to incorporate various adaptations to tests and to responses.

The problems associated with the use of standardized tests with this population are well nigh insurmountable. Using standardized tests as the sole measure with children with physical disabilities places serious limitations on the child and may result in depressed scores that simply confirm the impairment without providing any functional information regarding the potential for achievement. If standardized tests are used at all, they must be used with a high degree of sophistication and form only one component of a test battery.

Norm-referenced tests are largely standardized on the physically normal population; measures have generally not been specifically developed for those with physical and neurological disabilities. Many of the tasks that are used in such tests must be eliminated because of motor difficulties, sensory impairments, and special problems. It is appropriate for testers to modify administrative procedures. For example, testers may eliminate verbal tests from a battery. Or they can adapt the way a test is presented, holding a picture closer to the child's eyes and so on. They can modify procedures, allowing more time for timed tasks, for example. Or they can alter the test stimuli by providing larger pictures or speaking more slowly. Or a physical or occupational therapist may be on hand to assist in handling and positioning techniques so as to maximize the child's performance.

When altering response requirements, there are three general techniques. First, a **support adaptation** is used when the child must be placed in a certain position or provided some general form of support before being able to pass an item. A **prosthetic adaptation** is provided for the child who needs a specific piece of equipment, such as braces or a hearing aid, to demonstrate a skill. A **general adaptation** is one that does not require support or a piece of equipment but that still represents a change in the basic requirements of the task or that changes the utility of the skill. For example, a hearing-impaired child may need to perform communication tasks with sign language. Or a child with a physical disability may be allowed to look toward the response rather than pointing manually.

As well as finding a measure of IQ, diagnosticians will attempt to assess achievement, social and emotional functioning, and language. For children with physical handicaps, data regarding communication skills, adaptive behaviour, and mobility are particularly important. Discussions about specific measures that can be used with this population are found in Chapters 4, 6, and 15.

For children with severe disabilities and motor impairments, regular and periodic assessment of development and motor movement provides data about how many skills a child has developed, what type of skills they are, and how they are used. Therapists have an in-depth knowledge of the neurobiological system which enables them to recognize the impact of specific impairments on movement and stability. Teachers should rely on the expertise of a physical or occupational therapist to conduct motor assessments. The therapist will conduct an assessment of the physical domains that considers physical status, mobility, and functional aspects, or how the child uses motor skills.

Developmental Consequences

Because of the diverse nature of physical handicaps and neurological disabilities, their varied severity, and associated handicapping conditions, it is impossible to draw a profile of a typical affected child.

For children with orthopedic and motor disabilities, the key factor is the extent to which the disability affects movement potential. Motor skills are integral to almost everything that a child does or wants to do in the environment, and physical and motor problems affect educational and social progress in other ways than mobility. Deficient motor skills can affect cognitive development because they hinder a child's manipulation and exploration. Children with motor impairments have different first-hand knowledge and experiences than their peers because they cannot explore the environment as other children can. At the sensorimotor stage, for example, children with cerebral palsy have been found to include more visual exploration and less tactile exploration of toys than is seen among children developing normally (see Rogers, 1988b).

Similarly, social skills may suffer because efficient motor skills are necessary for many forms of play with peers. Play depends on experience and opportunity, and this alone places restraints on children with severe physical handicaps. Children with motor disorders cannot manipulate toys and other objects, join in dramatic and pretend play or rough and tumble play, or engage in games in which children run or jump or skip.

Intervention with Students with Physical and Neurological Disabilities

Physical and neurological handicaps are primarily medical and therapeutic conditions, and intervention stretches far beyond the academic and educational. No single professional can effectively fill the multiple needs of physically and neurologically disabled children; they receive help from educators, physicians and medical specialists, occupational and physical therapists, speech and language pathologists, counsellors, and others. It is the secondary difficulties in such areas as communication, mobility, and cognitive functioning that are of most concern to educators in the classroom.

Medical Intervention

Medical interventions cover a broad spectrum of treatments. For example, the hip dislocations, contractures, spinal defects, fractures, and osteoporosis that are common among children with spina bifida require medical assistance.

Although cerebral palsy is neither progressive nor curable, various medical techniques improve functioning. Children with cerebral palsy (and spina bifida) often suffer from contractures — a permanent shortening of the muscles, tendons, and ligaments that results in postural distortion and decreased joint mobility. Surgery can ease contractures and correct dislocations, and may also involve repair of the joints to reduce the risk of arthritis (Batshaw and Perret, 1986). Another medical procedure — selective position rhizotomy — sees the surgeon cut selected nerve roots below the spinal cord that cause plasticity in the leg muscles to allow some spastic persons better control of certain muscles (Hallahan and Kauffman, 1991). The treatment allows some nonambulatory children to walk and helps others to move more normally.

Medical treatment for epilepsy focuses primarily on siezure control. Drug therapy can control about 50 percent of grand mal, 40 percent of petit mal, and 35 percent of psychomotor seizures. Drugs can also reduce the frequency of grand mal and petit mal seizures in 35 percent of cases, and of psychomotor attacks in 50 percent of cases (Berkow, 1982). The choice of drugs is related to the type of seizure pattern and the presence of side effects from other drugs. The primary goal of anticonvulsant therapy is to achieve maximum control with the fewest possible drugs and side effects.

In the case of head trauma injuries, immediate medical attention may help to reduce the extent of damage. Trauma medicine has made a great deal of progress in recent years; new brain scan techniques can pinpoint sites of injury in the brain.

Therapy

Physical, occupational, and speech and language therapies are indicated for many children with neurological and orthopedic disabilities. Spina bifida children with myelomeningocele, for example, frequently have other orthopedic complications and problems requiring extensive physical and occupational therapies. In children with cerebral palsy, physical therapy can ease contractures.

For children with orthopedic and neurologic impairments, therapies are most commonly associated with sensorimotor development, postural control, activities for daily living, and environmental adaptations. The need for occupational or physical therapy is determined by an absence of robust righting, protective extension, and equilibrium reactions; inefficient sitting and standing posture; limited ability to perform sensorimotor tasks; and inadequate physical fitness for daily living activities (Dunner, Connor-Kuntz, and Goodway, 1995).

Occupational therapists focus on motor development, attention to aspects of the sensory environment, and the achievement of functional daily tasks. They work to enhance a child's potential for learning and try to develop vestibular balance; tactile, kinesthetic, and perceptual motor co-ordination; and self-help skills.

Physical therapists work with children needing prosthetic management training, wheelchair mobility training, and gross-motor-skill exercises. Physical therapy is directed toward preventing disability; for example, developing, improving, or restoring more efficient muscular functioning and maintaining maximum motor functioning for each child. The physical therapist also provides information concerning positioning and handling of students and the use of adaptive equipment.

Promoting optimal postures and movement patterns for functional activities is an important objective for children with physical and motor disabilities. Areas of special concern are positioning and carrying. Carrying refers to the way that a child with a physical or motor disability is moved; **positioning** refers to how the child is seated or otherwise positioned.

Children with cerebral palsy have abnormal movement patterns — they show inefficient co-ordination movements and retention of primitive reflexes. Children with cerebral palsy and other physical disabilities must be handled in ways that normalize

Physically disabled children can participate in many activities with their non-disabled classmates.

muscle tone and prevent the development of secondary muscular and structural disorders. Proper positioning can facilitate normal muscle tone and symmetry, provide stable and aligned posture, inhibit primitive reflexes, facilitate normal movement patterns, stabilize head and trunk control, and compensate for the lack of sitting balance (Bailey and Wolery, 1984; Clark and Allen, 1985; Copeland and Kimmel, 1989). Individual positioning is prescribed for each child.

Technical Intervention

A range of equipment is now available for children with disabilities and is making a significant difference in the quality of their life by allowing them more control of events in their environment. Devices and equipment range from the very simple, such as adapted spoons and switch-adapted battery-operated toys to the very complex, such as computerized environmental control systems (Parette, Hofmann, and VanBiervliet, 1994).

Adaptive equipment is a general term for these devices. **Adaptive equipment** may be defined as any device designed or modified to lead individuals with disabilities to independence (Raschke, Dedrick, and Hanus, 1991, p. 25). Within the broad category of adaptive equipment are prosthetic, orthotic, and adaptive devices, chiefly used to assist children with physical and motor disabilities and those with sensory impairments. There is quite a lot of overlap in these categories.

Much adaptive equipment is individualized for a child. When individually adapted equipment is used, children demonstrate improved motor, self-care, and social skills (see Dunn, 1989).

In 1986, 26 percent of non-institutionalized children with disabilities used some form of assistive device, the majority of which assisted mobility and/or agility. That year, 8 percent of children with disabilities used medically prescribed footwear; 5 percent had some type of braces (other than teeth braces); 3 percent used a wheelchair; 2 percent had crutches or other types of walking aids. Fewer than 1 percent had an artificial limb (Nessner, 1990).

Prosthetic Devices

Prosthetic devices are used to replace lost functions and/or provide support. They duplicate normal body movements as nearly as possible while restraining normal functions as little as possible. For example, an artificial leg is a prosthesis for a child missing a leg.

Teachers must guard against a tendency to overprotect children with physical impairments.

Much special equipment is used for mobility. Equipment designed for mobility and to help children stand includes leg casts and braces, ankle-foot equipment, crutches, walkers, and wheelchairs. The most common mobility devices are braces, crutches, and wheelchairs.

Wheelchairs are designed for people who are unable to ambulate or whose ambulation is unsafe and unsteady, or for those for whom ambulation is too strenuous. Wheelchairs are almost as varied as the people who use them. A good wheelchair is tailored to the individual's needs. The main types are self-propelled wheelchairs, attendant-operated chairs, transit chairs, and electric or battery-powered chairs. An electronically controlled wheelchair can provide movement for a severely disabled person through voice activated commands; it is programmed to respond to the owner's voice and requires no muscle control (Cartwright, Cartwright, and Ward, 1984).

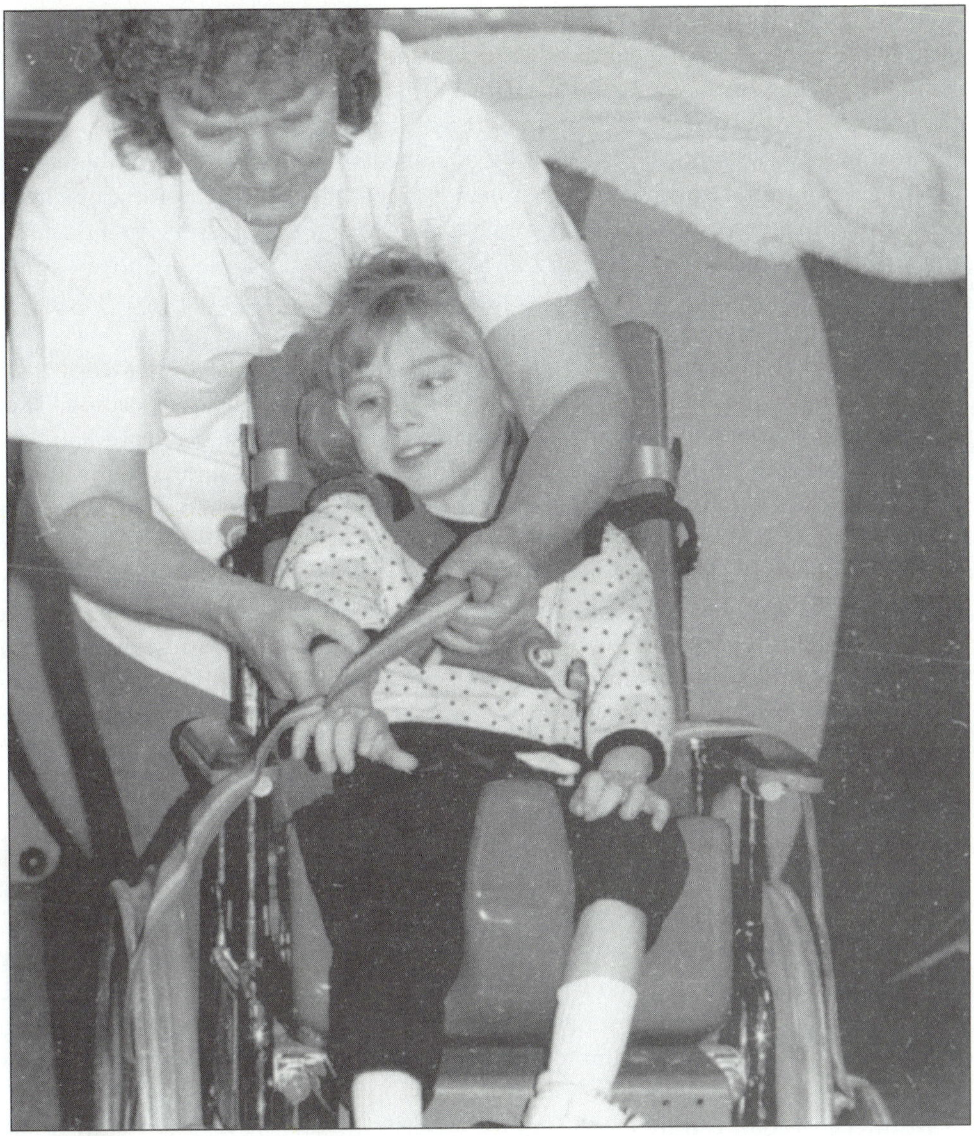

Teachers should know how to position children in wheelchairs.

Orthopedic braces are for the lower extremities. Braces do not prevent contractures or develop walking skills but serve the purpose of control and support. There are three main types — short leg braces, long leg braces, and hip braces. A short brace would be used on the ankle joint; a long leg brace from the knee to the ankle.

For children with cerebral palsy, braces are used chiefly for control. They help in ambulation, control involuntary movements, and serve to prevent or correct deformities. In spina bifida and muscular dystrophy, the braces are used chiefly for support. Support braces weigh less than control braces.

Crutches are used during periods of temporary disability to help with balance and locomotion, and to reduce weight on the lower extremities. When the disability is of long duration or permanent, crutches have to be designed to reduce the weight the legs must bear and provide stability and support. The surface on which the crutch may operate is important. If it is slippery, rubber tipped ends, spiked ends, or tripod legs should be provided.

Walkers are upright devices used to provide support and movement. Supported standing forces weight-bearing that is necessary for the normal formation of the hip joints. There are various types of walkers that can be modified in various ways to assist the individual. All provide standing support with forward inclined standing.

Prosthetic equipment may assist in the therapeutic techniques of positioning and carrying. Positioning equipment and strategies allow children with motor problems to achieve postures and movement that might otherwise be impossible or non-functional. Some children need support in a lying position and use adaptive boards, wedges, and bolsters. Positioning equipment is typically designed to place the child in one or more basic postures in as normal a body alignment a possible.

Sitting may be difficult for children with motor disorders. Because children spend a lot of time sitting, it is important that they sit in the most beneficial position. They need to find positions that allow the best hand use, that are easiest for eye-hand coordination, and that present the least difficulties for balance. Modified chairs are for children who have difficulty sitting well or those who have abnormal hip and leg patterns. A special chair aligns the body, limbs, and head; flexes the hips, knees, and ankles; and brings the head and shoulders slightly forward. Adapted chairs include corner chairs and bolster chairs. Both usually have removable trays. Dangling feet are harmful to children with motor problems, so an abduction block — a chunk of something that the child's legs can straddle — is usually used to prevent the child from sliding to the floor, while a footstool ensures that the child's feet reach a flat solid surface. Straps and other props are sometimes used to improve posture.

Orthotic Devices

Orthotic devices assist a limb's action. For example, special utensils (spoons, forks, and dishes) make eating and drinking easier for a child with a movement dysfunction.

A *spork* is a combination spoon and fork that many children use. Other eating implements have Velcro straps to make them easier for the child to handle and control. Adapted spoons have a built-up handle or swivel so that gravity can right the spoon and prevent spillage. A hand splint to support wrist extension can also be used to allow greater finger movements for manipulative tasks.

In the classroom, children may require specialized equipment. Page turners and book stands assist them in reading. Magnetized pencils and equipment are helpful for writing and drawing; there are specially adapted scissors for cutting.

Adaptive Devices

Much of the current technology requires pre-academic readiness skills, and most of today's technological devices operate through one dominant modality (for example, touch for keyboards, vision for monitors). However, devices are increasingly allowing for alternative modalities such as voice activated computers and television captioning (Sawyer and Zantal-Wiener, 1993), and the availability of instrumentation that permits handicapped persons whose cognitive level is less than two years old to control devices in their environment is also increasing. As well, many technologies are becoming more transparent (less noticeable and obtrusive). This is because of miniaturization, the use of lighter materials, and higher capacities for information processing.

Some children with physical disabilities have difficult or unintelligible speech. However, their receptive language is probably far ahead of their expressive language, and they may know and understand far more words than they can express. These students require devices that act as substitutes for speech (see Chapter 6). Teachers need to be aware of methods of communication such as Blissymbolics and other pictographic systems as a substitute for speech. Karen, the child profiled below, requires alternate forms of communication.

Educational Intervention

In 1986, slightly more than half of all non-institutionalized children with disabilities had a long-term condition or health problem that limited or prevented participation in many activities (Nessner, 1990). In the past, non-educational considerations would have taken priority and many students would have been placed in separate classrooms or special schools. Progress in medical science, improved technology, and changing attitudes have dramatically altered service delivery for these students, and today most are placed in regular classrooms. Educators realize that students with physical disabilities have the same educational needs as non-disabled children. They may need special help from some apparatus to make a response, but they can benefit from the same instructional practices and curriculum as their peers. Special class placement may still be provided for students who have additional problems with perception, cognition, or language.

Profile

Karen

Karen is nine years old, functioning in a regular grade three classroom at her local public school. She has cerebal palsy and walks with leg braces, but is more affected on the left than the right side. The motor impairment has affected her speech, and she has a constant drool. She also has a mild to moderate bilateral, sensorineural hearing loss. She uses amplification in both ears.

In most curriculum areas, Karen is an average student. She reads at level and her arithmetic skills are adequate. She prints with her right hand in a slow and laboured manner, and the school is planning to use a special large-print typewriter with her. Although her articulation is poor, she has good receptive language skills and supplements the auditory message with speech reading.

An itinerant teacher of the hearing impaired works with Karen individually for four hours weekly focusing primarily on enhancing the regular classroom curriculum. The itinerant teacher helps with homework and classroom assignments in order to maintain Karen's average grades. Some problems have also surfaced in the area of reading comprehension and social studies concepts, so an individual program has been devised in these areas. These gaps in Karen's learning are due to the expanded amount of auditory information she is expected to process. The itinerant teacher is therefore concentrating on the vocabulary and language structures inherent in reading and social studies.

Karen tries to use her voice at all times. In addition to her individual work with the itinerant teacher, she receives special help from a visiting speech therapist for her articulatory difficulties.

Individual Education Plan iep

Extract from Kent's IEP

Name: Kent
Age: 8

Present levels: Kent has cerebral palsy. There may be some language, but so far there is no speech development. Kent is in a special classroom but is moving into the regular setting for part of the day. The object is to expose him to language and social models.

Adaptive equipment: wheelchair, behind-the-ear aids in both ears; magnetized equipment for writing; large implements.

Additional assistance: physical therapy, speech therapy, individual aide in regular classroom.

Long-range Goals

During therapy, Kent will learn a simple manual communication system, Amerind. Signs will be used in the regular classroom by the aide.

Short-term objectives

- Within classroom activities, the aide will sign to Kent and prompt him to use known signs.
- When given a tape recorder, Kent will depress the special switch to turn the recorder on and off.
- Kent will join in small groups with assigned tasks to improve language and social skills.
- Kent will maintain a supported sitting position in the carpeted reading area.
- Kent will use page turners, with support.
- Kent will look at the book as a peer reads a story.
- Kent will use greeting behaviour — waving — when requested.

There is no special curriculum for students with physical and neurological disabilities. Program planning considers potential modes of communication; stamina levels; present levels of academic achievement; intellectual ability; independence in mobility and ambulation; and personal motivation (Gearheart, Weishahn, and Gearheart, 1992).

Additions to the regular curriculum may be necessary to provide ambulation training and to teach certain self-help skills, leisure skills, and articulation; as well, more emphasis may be placed on prevocational skills. Teachers may need to provide special help with a wheelchair, with toileting, and with dressing.

Tips for Teachers

Tips for teachers of children with neurological disabilities

Classroom environment and climate

- Know and understand the precise nature of the child's problems, including the characteristics and the limitations imposed.
- Lack of progress or deterioration of motor skills is a cause for concern. Observe children carefully.
- An unnecessary amount of experiential deprivation may accompany physical impairment, especially for pupils who are in wheelchairs. Parents and teachers, by overprotecting, can contribute to such deprivation. Teachers must guard against overprotection and against the child's developing a dependency upon the teacher or a non-handicapped peer.
- Children should be expected to learn what their peers do.
- They should be expected to join in all relevant classroom activities.

Adaptive equipment

- Learn about handling, which refers to how the child is picked up, carried, held, and assisted. Consult with parents and therapists.
- Be constantly aware of positioning. This refers to providing support for the child's body, changing the child's sitting position in the chair, and arranging instructional or play materials in certain ways.
- When moving a wheelchair, always ensure that the child's feet are on the footrest.
- Tell the child what you are going to do at all times, whether in positioning or moving.
- Wear rubber-soled shoes.
- Do not place the chair too close to heaters.
- Constantly check on sitting position; reposition the child at least every half hour.
- Do not pull by the arms; lift the child under the arms.
- At a desk, make sure that the child's heels touch the floor, knees are bent, and back is supported.
- When helping a child dress, put clothes on the more affected side first.
- To straighten a limb, push out at shoulder and elbow or hip and knee first.
- Don't try to pull a hand or foot through clothing — the limb will only bend tighter.
- Within the entire school, attention must be paid to modifications such as widened doorways.
- When children are wearing braces, teachers should be alert to circulation problems that may show up as swelling, coldness, change of colour, evidence of infection, or other skin problems.

Instructional

- Use magnetized rulers and instruments on the chair table.
- Use holders. To assist children with motor problems with grip, use a pencil grip made of a piece of clay or foam material wrapped around the pencil or pen.
- Make paintbrushes out of deodorant bottles by removing the tops, filling the bottle with tempera paint, and snapping the top back in place.
- Use large chunks of sponge for painting.
- Use marking pens for free flow.
- Anchor paper by taping it to the table or easel.

Summary

1. Children with physical disabilities encompass a broad range of youngsters. Although there are many physical handicaps, the conditions described in this chapter all stem from some form of neurological damage. In this sense, the conditions are not curable, although they can be ameliorated by medical intervention, therapy, drugs, and education.
2. The most common neurological difficulty seen in children is cerebral palsy, which takes a number of forms. Over half of cerebral palsied children have spasticity in which the muscles don't work in harmony — some muscles are too tight, some too loose. Athetoid children show jerky, uncontrolled, and writhing movements; those with ataxia show unco-ordinated movement and difficulties with positions in space. As well as the motor problems, cerebral palsy may include any number of intellectual, sensory, and behavioural disorders.
3. Spina bifida comes in a number of forms and may be the precursor of multiple handicaps. Damage to the developing nervous system may have left varying degrees of paralysis, sensory loss, bowel and bladder incontinence, and hydrocephalus.
4. *Epilepsy* is a term that describes both the conditions of seizure and the convulsions accompanying some types of seizures. Manifestations depend upon the location, severity and type of short circuit coming from the brain. The most frightening for the observer is the grand mal seizure, in which the child loses consciousness. Children may also suffer from petit mal — an extremely brief loss of consciousness. Other seizure types include Jacksonian and psychomotor. The developmental consequences of epilepsy are extremely varied and are largely determined by the number and types of additional disorders.
5. Traumatic head injury is an insult to the brain caused by an external physical force. Problems associated with traumatic head injury include cognitive problems and behavioural/psychological, sensory/motor, and language disorders.
6. Physical problems may limit mobility, socialization, independence, learning, and educational opportunities. Children may be further handicapped by their lack of ability to explore the environment adequately.
7. Depending on the extent and nature of a condition, a child may require the services of many disciplines, including psychology, physiotherapy, occupational therapy, speech pathology, audiology, and medicine.
8. Children with cerebral palsy have restricted movement and the retention of primitive reflexes. Occupational and physical therapists work in close collaboration with teachers and parents to assist the child in different functions.
9. Adaptive devices serve to make living easier. Students with physical disabilities require technical aids and adaptive equipment for mobility and ambulation, for seating, for classroom use, and for daily living.
10. For many children, special needs are not synonymous with a special education requirement. A physical or neurological disability, by itself, is no reason for special class placement.
11. Children with physical handicaps should be presented with the regular curriculum to the greatest extent possible. Sound teaching principles are the same for all children and there do not need to be differences in strategies and techniques for physically impaired children. However, whatever their educational placement, many children with physical disabilities will require additional assistance in areas of communication and mobility.

CHAPTER 14

Children with Pervasive Developmental Disorders

Historical Notes

Insanity and madness have long been a grave concern to humanity, and the historical and literary record abounds with tales of the insane. Cases of schizophrenia were recorded as early as 1400 B.C., and evidence remains of sophisticated discussions of mental illness by the Greek philosophers and educators, such as Hippocrates on epilepsy and Arataeus on mania and melancholy. However, the true etiology of psychotic disorders baffled investigators and observers. Apart from a few physicians, most people in early societies attributed severe behavioural deviance to demonic possession and treated it through exorcism and other religious rituals. Although the devil held sway for many more centuries, it was also believed that mentally ill persons were sinful or immoral, their madness due to possession by evil spirits, witchcraft, the effects of the moon, intemperance, or masturbation.

Right down to the end of the eighteenth century, the so-called insane population included those who were mentally retarded and those with epilepsy. Cruel and callous treatment was characteristic of the early lunatic hospitals. Often, inmates were chained naked in rat-infested cellars, fed on bread and soup, and restrained with whips, chains, and stocks.

Children were rarely included. In fact, it was held that "insane" children were extremely rare. Even in the nineteenth century, physicians were concerned with the effects of physical and neurotic ailments on adults, but only brief and fleeting descriptions of children exhibiting serious emotional problems surface in the literature. Most nineteenth-century practitioners disparaged the notion that emotional disturbance could affect children and stubbornly clung to the belief that "insanity is rare in childhood" (Vineland Inst., 1894, p. 37). They held that insanity was an adult disorder, while childhood manifestations were presumed to be mental deficiency. Generally, the recognition of insanity in children seems to have been delayed until the various early training centres for the mentally retarded were established.

When the condition was considered, nineteenth-century terminology and etiologies were varied, vague, confusing, and often contradictory. Sparse and scattered references to the disturbed child population included such terms as *ideational insanity*, *amentia*, Seguin's *incipient insanity*, and *juvenile insanity*. Samuel Gridley Howe understood the difficulties of separating emotionally disturbed children from those with mental retardation; he used the term *simulative idiocy* to describe the appearance of mental retardation in a non-retarded person (Winzer, 1993).

In 1868 Henry Maudsley (1835-1918), one of the few authoritative mid-century writers on the subject of the psychotic child, included a thirty-four-page chapter, "Insanity and early life," in his seminal work, *Physiology and pathology.* Maudsley attempted to relate the type of psychosis to the level of a child's development and described sensorimotor insanities such as epilepsies and choreic movements associated with hallucinations, and delusions that were related to the development of stable ideas (Hare, 1962). Still, it was not until the final decades of the nineteenth century that professionals finally confronted the notion that emotional disturbance constituted a childhood disability different from the adult form and separate from mental retardation. The psychotic child became an object of study as psychiatrists and others initiated careful efforts to observe, describe, and classify the disordered behaviours demonstrated by child patients. Attempts were made to collect and organize the existing material in monographs on psychic disorders, mental diseases, and insanity in children so that by 1900 there was an assortment of works announcing that children were known to display psychotic disorders (Kanner, 1962).

Kraepelin in 1912 devised a series of tests for evaluating emotionally disturbed persons. But it was Sante de Sanctus who in 1906 named the psychotic problems observed in youngsters *dementia praecoxissima.* Eugen Blueler (1857-1939), a Swiss psychiatrist, christened dementia praecox *schizophrenia* in 1911. To Blueler, schizophrenia was a reflection of an underlying integrative dysfunction — a splitting of the mind, a break in the synthesis of thought, feeling, and activity (Blueler, 1911). The work of de Sanctus, Blueler, and others contributed to the identification of a distinct condition known as childhood schizophrenia, and by 1935 schizophrenia in children was well documented (Howard, 1935).

Credit for first identifying autistic behaviours in children and adults also goes to Eugen Blueler, who isolated specific non-verbal and non-relating behaviours in 1906. Blueler used the word *autistic* as an adjective; it was not until Leo Kanner's major study in 1943 that an autistic syndrome, with *autism* as a noun, was identified in children.

Even after children were identified, serious confusion plagued the field. Until quite recently, parental affective behaviour was viewed as a major contributing factor to childhood psychoses and autism. Parents of autistic children were blamed for their children's condition; parental detachment and inability to relate were thought to foster the more severe isolation of autism. Today, investigators have largely abandoned the notion that parental behaviour is the sole cause of pervasive disorders, and so the onus of parental guilt has been lifted.

At the same time, many authorities viewed childhood psychoses as one inclusive category, ignoring distinctions among specific syndromes (Bomberg, Szurek, and Etemad, 1973). Others saw autism and childhood schizophrenia as one and the same; some claimed they were different (Miller, 1974). Still other researchers classified these disorders together, but distinguished them from other organic disorders (Ornitz, 1973). Another school of thought separated infantile autism from childhood schizophrenia but maintained that these two disorders constituted the major diagnostic divisions of childhood psychosis (Rimland, 1974; Rutter, 1974).

Lack of differentiation between autism and psychoses led to a confused classification system and a plethora of terms that were used interchangeably in the literature. Terms included *childhood psychoses, childhood schizophrenia, infantile autism, atypical child syndrome, symbiotic psychosis,* and *pervasive developmental disorder* (Cummings and Finger, 1980). It also meant that many investigators grouped these childhood disorders together into a broad category of severe and profound emotional disturbance. When children with infantile autism and those with childhood schizophrenia were discussed within the category of severe and profound emotional disturbance, much research was simply generalized from population to population. This became seriously evident in the disproportionate number of studies that focused on infantile autism and led to generalization of data that had little direct relevance to the schizophrenic group.

Today researchers clearly distinguish between childhood psychoses, which include childhood schizophrenia, and infantile autism. They note that although autistic and schizophrenic children share many common characteristics in terms of their overt observable behaviour, there are several important differences between them.

Pervasive developmental disorder is a general term used to describe children suffering from chronic and severe conditions that affect every aspect of their development. Different types of conditions, including childhood psychoses, childhood schizophrenia, and infantile autism, are found under the developmental disorder umbrella. As children with pervasive developmental disorders very often exhibit additional problems such as mental retardation, perceptual motor dysfunctions, and communication disorders, these conditions can also often be viewed as multiple disabilities.

Childhood psychoses and infantile autism represent the most extreme forms of emotional and behavioural disorders. Probably no other conditions are so hard to understand and so far removed from the range of normal experience. These disorders strike at the very essence of human relatedness and human communication and must therefore be considered the most devastating disorders that affect a child's learning and behaviour. Every aspect of functioning is affected.

Psychotic and autistic children frequently exhibit strange and inappropriate behaviour. Affected children may display bizarre body movements and they sometimes suffer inordinate fears. They may indulge in repetitive motor activity, self-stimulation, and self-mutilitation. Many are completely withdrawn; some never speak at all but pirouette in a silent internal dance, impervious to all around them. Their world may consist of touch sensations, of familiar routines, and rigidly obsessive behaviour. These children may fly into tantrums at the smallest change in their surroundings, from a parent's new hair style to a door left slightly ajar.

Autism is a rare, severely and permanently disabling developmental disorder with a suspected but poorly understood neurological basis. It reveals itself in fleeting eye contact, the failure to form attachments, and disrupted relationships. Autistic children have difficulty developing language skills, learning to communicate, and relating. Many function at pre-academic levels and fail to develop basic self-care skills and language. Schizophrenia is a condition characterized by qualitative changes in functioning such as association disturbances, delusions, hallucinations, attention deficits, and inappropriate social interaction.

Because childhood psychoses and infantile autism are so spectacular and bizarre, they have recently elicited an enormous amount of interest, concern, and research. The importance of the study of pervasive developmental disorders is not related to the incidence and prevalence of the conditions; childhood schizophrenia and autism are rare. However, researchers believe that if they can develop an understanding of psychoses and autism, they will have made a giant step in the direction of unravelling the triple helix of brain, behaviour, and environment.

A number of forms of psychoses, due to multiple etiologies, affect children. Heller's disease, for example, is due to disintegrative brain disease. Psychiatric disorders subsequent to brain injuries in older children have also been reported (Brink, Imbus, and Woo-Sam, 1980).

In this chapter we restrict our discussion of childhood psychoses to schizophrenia. We also delve into the complexities of infantile autism. The manifestations of autism are similar enough to those of childhood psychoses to discuss them together. Psychotic and autistic children show a pattern of behaviour characterized by a failure to recognize, understand, or respond appropriately to people in their environment. They demonstrate withdrawal and a high frequency of problematic and bizarre behaviour. Keep in mind, though, that etiology, treatment, and prognosis for autism and for schizophrenia differ quite radically.

Development of the Field

Even after recognition of psychoses in children and the formulation of methods for identification, diagnosis, and intervention, severe childhood emotional disturbance remained largely the bailiwick of psychiatrists and psychologists, and not the school system. Well into the twentieth century, children with severe and multiple handicaps were excluded from public school segregated classes and often not accepted into residential settings.

Very handicapped, however defined, was always a boundary condition that determined the success of any reform. Even if schools became relatively comfortable, or at least resigned, to children functioning below the norm in intellectual, physical, or social domains, they remained remarkably resistant to accepting students with severe and profound handicaps. Trained teachers, suitable facilities, and a range of support services were unavailable. Even when harassed parents could persuade school authorities to accept a severely handicapped child, it was usually on a trial basis. Often these children were abandoned to languish in institutional settings that only heightened their personal isolation.

During the 1930s, Despert, Potter, Leo Kanner, and others tried to clarify the characteristics of various categories of severe and profound emotional disturbance in children (Kauffman, 1989). Laura Bender of Bellevue Hospital in New York pioneered the development of education for schizophrenic children. There were further calls to educate these children, but they remained largely unheeded.

When treatment was given, institutionalization was the common mode. Many psychiatrists and other professionals believed that autistic and psychotic children could most effectively be treated away from their homes. Treatment was based on the development of a therapeutic relationship between therapist and child and typically took place in residential settings.

In the 1960s, interest in returning many previously institutionalized children to the community mounted and education began to assume responsibility for seriously emotionally disturbed children. This change resulted from strong attacks, both within and without psychiatry, on the legitimacy of a medical paradigm of illness as applied to children labelled severely emotionally disturbed (Paul and Warnock, 1980). As well, there was a lack of personnel resources in the mental health field, an emerging humanistic concern about the inadequacy of institutional psychiatric services for children, and the need to move youngsters out of adult wards.

By the 1970s, the education of developmentally disordered children was firmly entrenched and professionals began to encourage parents to keep their children at home. Today, many severely developmentally disabled children are taught in special day schools or residential settings; increasing numbers of these youngsters are attending classes in their neighbourhood schools.

Definitions of Pervasive Developmental Disorders

Children with pervasive developmental disorders suffer from conditions that affect every aspect of their present and probably future functioning. The adjective *pervasive* means that the conditions affect all developmental domains and will probably be extremely long-lasting, if not lifelong. To reiterate the definitions given in Chapter 1, a developmental delay (pervasive developmental disorder) is a condition that represents a significant delay in the process of development. As the process of development is significantly affected, the term does not refer to a maturational lag or an at-risk child. **Developmentally disabled** individuals are those who suffer from chronic disabilities, attributable to mental or physical impairments, or a combination of these, that are manifested before age twenty-two and that result in functional limitations in major life activities requiring special services and treatment that are of extended duration or are lifelong. Childhood psychoses and infantile autism fit under the broad category of pervasive developmental disorders.

Childhood Schizophrenia

In general terms, psychoses are serious mental disorders in which the behavioural and thought processes of an individual become so disturbed that the person is out of touch with reality. The more specific term, **childhood psychoses**, refers to

> a heterogeneous group of clinical syndromes characterized by any number of maladaptive behaviors or clusters of behaviors including severe disturbances in ego functioning. Such disturbances affect various aspects of adaptive behavior, including the perception and ordering of experience, the assessment of reality, the control and channeling of impulses, and the success of interpersonal relations (Cummings and Finger, 1980).

Childhood schizophrenia is one of the childhood psychoses. To many people, schizophrenia brings to mind the condition of split personalities depicted in movies such as *The Three Faces of Eve*. In reality, adult schizophrenia is not commensurate with split personality. Nor are adult schizophrenia and childhood schizophrenia parallel conditions with only developmentally determined variations in symptomology. Early findings that equated the childhood condition with the adult disorder have been replaced by research that sees childhood schizophrenia as a discrete, identifiable condition. Today, childhood schizophrenia is defined as

> a pervasive psychotic disorder involving a decline or arrest of ego development following a period of relatively normal development, occurring in children who demonstrate some degree of useful language and relatedness to others. Among children characterized as schizophrenic, there are wide variations in personality organization, clinical course, intellectual functioning, and identifiable etiological conditions (Cummings and Finger, 1980, p.510).

This definition points out that childhood schizophrenia occurs late in childhood, often around the beginning of puberty. Before its onset, the child has usually developed according to normal patterns. It stresses the wide range of behaviours seen in children characterized as schizophrenic and focuses on particular domains of deviation.

Infantile Autism

The word *autism* comes from the Greek *autos*, meaning "self." It is fitting, because the most prominent feature of children with infantile autism is their apparent self-absorption and socially withdrawn behaviour. However, a precise definition is difficult because the boundaries of autism remain vague and undifferentiated, and much remains to be known about the condition.

Autistic children demonstrate severe self-isolation.

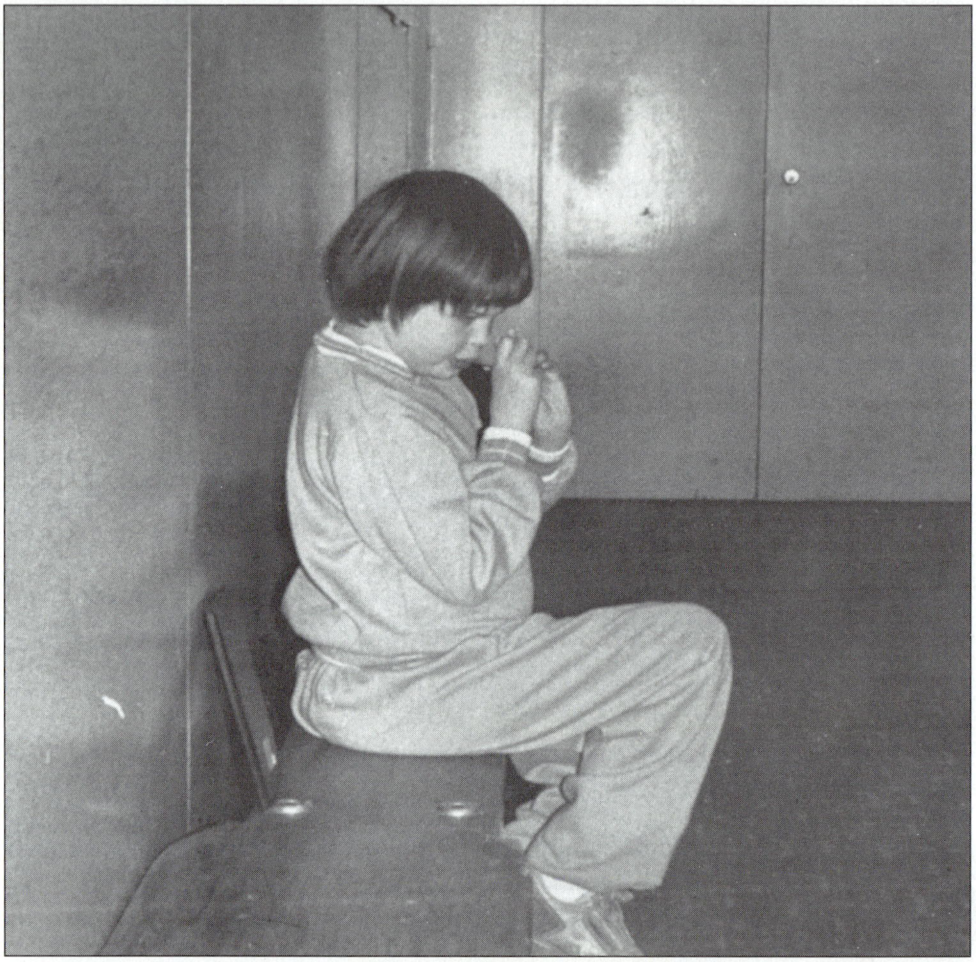

According to a recently proposed amendment to the Education for All Handicapped Children Act (PL94-142),

> Autism means a developmental disability significantly affecting verbal and nonverbal communication and social interaction, generally evident before age three, that adversely affects educational performance. Characteristics of autism include irregularities and impairments in communication, engagement in repetitive activities and stereotyped movements, resistance to environmental change or change in daily routines, and unusual responses to sensory experiences. The term does not include children with characteristics of the disability serious emotional disturbance (National Association, 1991, p. 2).

This definition is both inclusive and specific. It stresses that infantile autism is a developmental disability, not emotional disturbance. Manifestation is before age three, hence the common adjective *infantile*. Behaviours that affect educational performance are emphasized.

Classification of Pervasive Developmental Disorders

The purpose of most definitions of developmental disorders is to determine the locus of disturbance or disorder so that the definition can be extended to apply to the identification, measurement, and treatment of the condition. But dissension and controversy surround the classification of pervasive developmental disorders and the subcategories of psychoses and infantile autism. Many of these problems stem from the historical antecedents and the rapid alterations brought to the field by new genetic, psychological, and educational research.

Currently, the most commonly cited classification system is that appearing in the *Diagnostic and Statistical Manual of Mental Disorders* (DSM 111-R) (American Psychiatric Association, 1987) which identified several categories of adult, adolescent, and childhood severe and profound disorders. In DSM, the category of pervasive developmental disorders refers directly to childhood conditions and includes four sub-categories: infantile autism; disintegrative psychoses; other specific early childhood psychoses, including childhood schizophrenia; and unspecified psychoses.

Among these four groupings, infantile autism is clearly distinguishable from childhood schizophrenia on a number of variables. These include

- etiology, which we discuss later in this chapter.
- age of onset. This is one of the primary characteristics that distinguish autism from psychoses. Infantile autism occurs before thirty months of age and is usually preceded by markedly abnormal behaviour patterns. Childhood schizophrenia is of later onset; children show a normal early pattern of development, followed by severe regression as the condition takes hold.
- behavioural manifestations. Behavioural patterns in autism are pervasive; those in schizophrenia may be episodic. Children with schizophrenia exhibit a wide variety of symptoms and send very mixed messages to the outside world: their extremes of activity, sudden mood changes, and verbal disturbances bewilder observers. In this, schizophrenic children are unlike those affected with infantile autism, who tend to exhibit repetitive behaviour. As well, children with schizophrenia may develop delusions and experience hallucinations, whereas those with autism do not. One child with schizophrenia, for example, reported that a kitchen light said to do things and said to "shut up" (Russell, Bott, and Sammons, 1989).
- prognosis. Researchers in the area of childhood pervasive developmental disorders agree on only one thing — the dismal nature of prognosis for many of these children. However, in terms of prognosis, children affected by early infantile autism differ markedly from those whose difficulties begin later. Depending on the age of onset, the course of the condition, and the intensity of intervention, schizophrenic children may be returned to somewhat normal functioning.

Table 14-1 shows the major behavioural symptoms of infantile autism and childhood schizophrenia.

Table 14-1

Behavioural characteristics of psychotic and autistic children

Behavioural symptoms	Infantile autism	Childhood schizophrenia
Social development		
emotional responsiveness	-	x
lack of anticipatory response	+	-
social imitation	-	+
looks and walks through people	+	-
extreme aloneness	+	-
talks to, not with	+	-
strong attachment to inanimate objects	+	-
insistence on sameness	+	-
delusions and hallucinations	-	+
Motor and sensory functions		
not physically pliable	+	-
overly sensitive to stimuli	+	-
often graceful motor performance	+	x
unusual motor behaviours, such as repetitive movements	+	+
self-stimulation	+	+
self-mutilation	+	x
odd movements and grimaces	+	+
Language and communication		
delayed acquisition	+	-
deficient, deviant babble	+	-
sometimes thought to be deaf	+	-
overly sensitive to sound	+	-
non-verbal communication	-	+
echolalia	+	-
pronominal reversal	+	-
spontaneous speech	-	+
expressive-intonational features	-	+

\- seldom occurs   x may occur   + commonly occurs

Prevalence of Pervasive Developmental Disorders

Although pervasive developmental disorders are extremely low-incidence conditions, the changing terminology and classification make prevalence figures precarious. Most estimates allow five cases of pervasive developmental disorders per 10 000 children (Treffert, 1970). Infantile autism occurs less frequently than childhood schizophrenia, but prevalence figures for autism tend to vary more widely.

There are an estimated 3.1 cases of childhood schizophrenia per 10 000 children (Treffert, 1970). Among children, twice as many boys are schizophrenic. By adolescence, the condition is equally common in boys and girls (Wicks-Nelson and Israel, 1991).

Prevalence estimates for autism range from 0.7 per 10 000 to 4.8 per 10 000 school-aged children. Among the autistic population, boys are estimated to outnumber girls by ratios that range from two to one up to five to one (Csapo, 1979; Mullin, 1985).

Etiology of Pervasive Developmental Disorders

The etiology of pervasive developmental disorders is a broadly researched area. It is also widely disputed, and etiological data can best be described as inconclusive.

Many of the theories concerning the causes of developmental disorders can be categorized as either nature or nurture. Nature theories stress biological dysfunction; adherents of the nurture approach view the environment as the vital developmental factor. Until the late 1960s, theoretical constructs of childhood psychoses and autism focused on psychosocial (nurture) origins. Compelling recent research increasingly leans toward biological interpretations.

The best approach may be multifactorial, viewing these disorders not as a single entity but rather as the final common pathway of multiple etiologies: that is, attributing developmental disorders to a combination of biological and environmental factors. Infantile autism, for example, is probably a final expression of multiple determinants and may be the result of metabolic, infectious, developmental, environmental, and genetic insults.

Childhood Schizophrenia

If a multifactorial etiology is indeed the best approach to the etiology of childhood schizophrenia, then it is hardly surprising that its causes are the subject of considerable debate. Children who are schizophrenic display such a wide variety of symptom patterns and respond to so many different treatment modes that no one etiology seems sufficient to account for the disorder (Cummings and Finger, 1980).

Early investigations pinpointed environmental factors — maternal overprotection, maternal rejection, stimulus deprivation during infancy, inconsistent parenting, and severe and repeated emotional trauma (Cummings and Finger, 1980). However, many children exposed to these factors do not develop schizophrenia, and it is moot whether family forces alone are enough to produce such a devastating condition.

While the significance of environmental factors has not been completely discounted, the weight of accumulating evidence points toward biology as the primary factor in childhood schizophrenia. One consistent finding in support of biological factors is the high frequency of prenatal and perinatal complications among infants later diagnosed as schizophrenic (White, 1974). Pregnancy and birth complications include toxemias, vaginal bleeding, and maternal illness during pregnancy (Gittelman and Birch, 1967; Pollack and Woerner, 1966).

Investigators have also found a higher incidence of neurological symptoms in schizophrenic children, which leads to the suspicion that childhood schizophrenia may be a manifestation of subtle neurological damage, similar in origin to such disorders as minimal brain dysfunction (White, 1974). Moreover, neurological dysfunction is highly correlated with birth and pregnancy complications, further evidence that biological factors are responsible, at least to some degree, for childhood schizophrenia.

There is also convincing evidence that genetic factors contribute to schizophrenia (Plomin, 1989). Studies of monozygotic twins (e.g., Gottesman and Shields, 1976) have found that if one twin is affected, the other, regardless of environmental variables, is more prone to the condition. Because fraternal twins do not correlate nearly as highly, a genetic determinant is indicated. Yet while there seems to be a genetic component in schizophrenia, the evidence also indicates a strong environmental component. What appears to be transmitted is not the disorder itself but a predisposition to acquire the disorder.

Infantile Autism

In 1906, Eugen Blueler, a Swiss psychiatrist, used the term *autistic* to describe the withdrawn behaviours he observed among adult schizophrenics. As a discrete syndrome, autism was first identified by Leo Kanner in 1943. Kanner described a number of symptoms that he observed among a group of eleven children. In particular, he stressed the subjects' profound withdrawal from human contact and their obsessive desire for sameness in their environment. Kanner also identified similarities in the families of the eleven children. He found the parents to be highly intelligent and unusually high achievers, but also emotionally cold, aloof, and reserved in their interaction with their children.

Kanner himself did not reject biological factors as contributive causes of infantile autism. However, the researchers who followed him chose to focus almost exclusively on his psychogenic suppositions. They speculated that lack of adequate parenting was the primary factor in the onset of autism. Autistic infants were seen as withdrawing into isolation to escape a hostile world, deeply lacking in warmth, love, and nurturance. Bruno Bettelheim, who established the Sonja Shankman Orthogenic School for severely emotionally disturbed children in 1944, adopted this line of thought. He interpreted autistic behaviour as a defence against a world perceived as hostile and rejecting. Bettelheim argued that children become autistic when their parents reject them or fail to respond to their attempts to influence their environment. Because children feel unable to exert any control over the external world, they withdraw into a private fantasy world and try to impose some order and consistency through an obsessive insistence on sameness.

Bettelheim used the term "refrigerator mother" to charactertize the mothers of autistic children (Csapo, 1981c). An even more devastating term, "the schizophregenic mother" laid direct responsibility for the child's condition on the mother's failure to provide love and nurturance. All the same, Bettelheim did not deny the possibility that genetic or organic causes might also contribute to infantile autism. In fact, although researchers tended to agree that parents created a climate that encouraged autism, few investigators attributed the condition exclusively to parental behaviour. By the 1970s, researchers had largely abandoned environmental theories as emerging evidence indicated that children from emotionally deprived settings were not at higher risk for autism and that mothers of autistic children also had non-handicapped offspring. With little to support environmental theories, autism emerged as an ideal candidate for biological study.

Researchers turned their attention to investigating a range of biochemical, sensorimotor, neurological, and cognitive defects. Today the evidence for biological causes for autism is accumulating. A multifactorial neurobiological etiology has been posited (Goodman, 1987); however, this etiological diversity tends to cloud biological causes because so many have been suggested.

Neurobiological investigations indicate that factors critical to the normal development of the central nervous system seem to have gone awry in autism. Among autistic children, 83 percent have been found to have brain lesions or pathological enlargement of the left temporal horn (Hauser, De Long, and Rosman, 1975). Some investigators (e.g., Gillberg, Rosenhall, and Johansson, 1983) have attemped to account for autism on the basis of dysfunction in the vestibular area of the brain, the area thought to modulate the interaction of sensory and motor functions.

As in the case of childhood schizophrenia, there is solid evidence to connect obstetrical problems and subsequent autism in children. On average, autistic children experience more pre- and perinatal complications than their siblings (Links et al., 1980). In one study (Kolvin, Ounsted, and Roth, 1971), 54 percent of children with infantile autism had demonstrable neonatal and perinatal abnormalities when given neurological examinations.

It may be that both maternal and paternal age is a factor (Tsai and Stewart, 1983). In a small-sample study, Gillberg (1980) found the risk of having an autistic child to be nine times greater for mothers thirty-five or older than for mothers under thirty. Although Gillberg stresses that his small sample size makes generalizations difficult, the findings bolster earlier research on maternal age in the United States (Treffert, 1970), in Finland (Allanan, Arajar, and Vitamaki, 1964) and in Canada (Finnegan and Quarrington, 1979).

The importance of hereditary factors in the etiology of autism is well established (Folstein and Rutter, 1988). A number of researchers (e.g., Links et al., 1980) suggest a genetic factor in infantile autism; others point to the possibility of a genetic predisposition to autism (see Gerdtz and Bergman, 1990). Some support is lent to a genetic predisposition by the fact that autism is often accompanied by minor physical anomalies, such as fine hair, large head circumference, and malformed ears (Links et al., 1980).

Twin studies and the increasing number of reports on multiple incidence in siblings and second-degree relatives also lend credence to the genetic hypothesis. The prevalence of infantile autism is far higher in siblings and second-degree relatives of children with the disorder than in the general population (Folstein and Rutter, 1988; Ritvo, Ritvo, and Brothers, 1982).

In family studies (e.g., Folstein and Rutter, 1988), only about 2 percent of the siblings of autistic children display the condition, but this is 50 times greater than the expectation for the general population. The incidence of autism in the identical twin of an autistic child is around 50 percent (Folstein and Rutter, 1988). In one study (Steffenberg et al., 1989), nine of ten identical twin pairs were autistic as were all three children in a set of identical triplets.

Infantile autism has also been associated with various X-linked chromosomal abnormalities, and in particular with the genetic subtype fragile X, which has the highest incidence of autism of any documented syndrome or chromosomal abnormality. Of the entire population diagnosed with infantile autism, it is estimated that 10 to 14 percent have fragile X syndrome (Brown et al., 1986; Cohen, 1989). In studies of the fragile X population, autism has been reported in from 16 to 69 percent of fragile X males (Hagerman et al., 1986; Levitas, McBogg, and Hagerman, 1983).

This makes fragile X syndrome the most commonly known organic cause of autism (Hagerman, 1988).

Other investigators are attempting to correlate aspects of the autistic syndrome with neurochemical measures. Measurement of blood serotonin levels has been a source of both optimism and frustration in research on autism. Elevated platelet serotonin is the most consistently replicated biological abnormality found in subjects, occurring in roughly 30 percent of all cases (Piven et al., 1991), but its origin and significance are unclear. In addition, autism is associated with PKU, an example of aberrant biochemistry.

Identification and Assessment

Treatment programs for children with developmental disabilities relate to the accuracy and specificity with which problems and deficits are initially identified. Without clear and precise information about the nature of disabilities and a child's current level of functioning, an effective treatment strategy cannot be developed. But even when the conditions can be readily diagnosed, their causes often remain a mystery, and the most efficient identification may not lead directly to the most effective programming.

In the diagnosis of childhood psychoses and infantile autism, we find interwoven currents of research and investigation. We also find that diagnosis has provoked unresolved controversy. Clinicians vary in their theoretical conceptions of the conditions and emphasize different aspects as essential for specific diagnostic labels. The presence of additional handicapping conditions further muddies clear identification. Autistic children, for example, display a wide range of behaviours, many of them similar to those found in children with other disorders. Before they are correctly diagnosed, autistic children may be falsely labelled as blind or deaf. Mental retardation is often the initial diagnosis; however, this is not an either-or category, as a high percentage of autistic children are also retarded. As well, clinicians try to determine whether a child is classically autistic, mildly autistic, or shows autistic features (Eaves, 1988).

For students who are developmentally disabled, the actual assessment procedures are replete with difficulties. In the past, developmentally disabled children, especially those with infantile autism, were considered untestable by standardized intelligence tests. Their complex and varied handicaps make them exceptions to many of the rules by which psycho-educational tests are designed and administered. As a result, standardized tests were seldom administered; when tests were given, incomplete results were often interpreted on the basis of the examiner's intuitive sense of a child's peak skills.

Testing of psychotic and autistic students is particularly difficult because

- children often show a deficient ability to establish relationships;
- regular systems of reinforcement may be inadequate for these children;
- most of these children suffer impaired communication skills;
- sensory abnormalities may result in unusual responses to sensory stimuli;
- children have attention differences;
- children may show abnormal motor behaviour;
- clinicians must take into account the frequent co-existence of developmental disabilities, mental retardation, and neurological deficits;

- autistic children especially have a need for sameness and often demonstrate an inability to switch tasks;
- autistic children demonstrate marked variability on test performance. They may do poorly on tasks requiring abstract thought, symbolism, and sequential logic, but perform well on tasks that demand manual and visual spatial skills.

There is now a growing recognition that broad and thorough assessment of psychotic and autistic children is both possible and essential to provide the basis for educational and behavioural programming. Evaluation must be multidisciplinary and incorporate a variety of procedures, tools, and adaptations. Procedures require flexibility in administration, appropriate means of communication, alternation of free and structured time, motivation and reinforcers, predictable routines, and tools that limit the use of language to tasks that measure language skills.

Psychologists administer both formal and informal assessment measures to students who are developmentally disabled. Commonly used measures of mental ability include the Bayley Scales of Infant Development, the Hiskey Nebraska Test of Learning Aptitude, the McCarthy Scales, the Wechsler Pre-School and Primary Scale of Intelligence, and the Wechsler Intelligence Scale for Children-111. The Leiter International Performance Scale has been found useful for children who have poor verbal skills (Shah and Holmes, 1985).

Specially designed measures are also used to accommodate the variation typical of autistic children's profiles. For example, The Behavior Rating Scale for Autism and Atypical Children (Ruttenberg et al., 1977) observes children on eight scales that measure relationship to an adult, communication, drive for mastery, vocalization, expressive speech, sound and speech reception, social responsiveness, body movement, and psychobiological development. The Behavior Observation Scale for Autism (Freeman et al., 1978) has sixty-seven behaviours on a checklist. The Childhood Autism Scale (Schopler et al., 1980) has fifteen separate subscales on a seven-point continuum, ranging from normal to severely abnormal. Similarly, The Autism Screening Instrument for Educational Planning (Krug et al., 1979, 1980) has five components — sensory relating, body and object use, language, social skills, and self-help skills.

Specialized instruments are often needed to explore particular diagnostic and treatment questions. Tests used to determine receptive and expressive language skills, for example, include language questionnaires that are completed by parents and clinicians.

Developmental Consequences

Pervasive developmental disorders affect almost every domain of a child's development and seriously hinder all aspects of progress. Affected individuals exhibit a range of disordered behaviour and may appear to be severely retarded. As we observed earlier, much research has been directed toward autistic children and less toward those suffering from childhood schizophrenia. Many behaviours and developmental consequences are similar, although the prognosis for schizophrenic children is somewhat more optimistic.

Although psychotic and autistic children show extreme variability in intellectual functioning, many function at pre-academic levels. Especially in autistic children, language development is often so poor as to render verbal communication impossible;

language is either non-existent or bizarre in nature. Deficits range from phonological to syntactic and pragmatic defects. Many children do not speak at all, nor do they appear to comprehend language. Others show echolalia, parroting, meaningless jargon, and the incessant repetition of questions and statements.

Typically, these children live in their own isolated worlds, barely relating to others in the environment. Social development is minimal; even at their most developed, social interactions are limited in their quality and scope. Autistic children respond to other humans with aloofness and indifference, often becoming upset when interaction is demanded. Some severely disabled children throw massive temper tantrums, during which they bite, kick, scratch, and strike out at others.

Bizarre behaviour is characteristic of children with childhood psychoses and infantile autism.

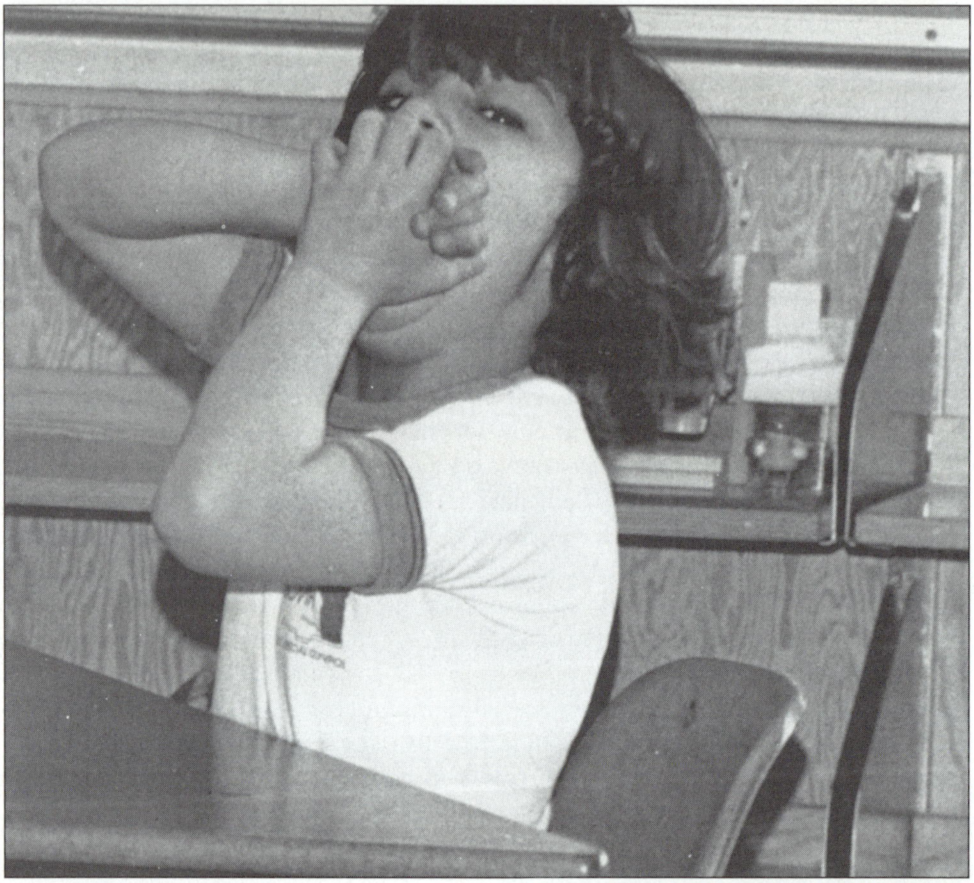

Children demonstrate maladaptive behaviours which fall largely within two classes. The first is aggressive behaviour, either self-directed (self-injurious behaviour) or directed toward others (Lovaas and Favell, 1987). Many children inflict serious injury upon themselves — they bang their heads against sharp corners, bite themselves, and gouge their own eyes. Some children hurt themselves so often they must be kept in restraints for their own safety. Aggressive behaviour can also sometimes cause serious physical harm to peers, parents, and teachers. Such aggressive behaviour may result in the child's being medicated and/or moved to a more restrictive environment (Lovaas and Favell, 1987).

The second class of maladaptive behaviour is self-stimulation. Self-stimulation is a persistent, stereotypic, repetitive mannerism. One of the defining characteristics of autism, it involves activities such as prolonged and repetitive body rocking, spinning, jumping, pacing, gazing at lights, twirling objects, excessive and repetitive vocalization, finger playing, flapping the hands, swishing saliva, patting the cheeks, and humming for hours on end. These behaviours do not possess the physical risks associated with aggressive behaviour, but they are socially stigmatizing and decrease the child's responsiveness to educational instruction (Lovaas, Newson, and Hickman, 1987).

Childhood Schizophrenia

Schizophrenia is a psychiatric illness characterized by serious loss of contact with reality and a marked deterioration in the ability to function. Children show delusions and hallucinations, emotional disturbance, apathy, and withdrawal.

Schizophrenia is extremely rare before the age of six, becomes more common in middle childhood, and is even more prevelant during adolescence. Because childhood schizophrenia typically does not take hold until early puberty, those affected escape early impairments of development in the realms of cognition, perception, and sensation. However, when the condition does take hold, affected children regress dramatically in their behaviour and demonstrate extreme withdrawal from the real world. Their close relationships are severely disrupted and they experience an overall deterioration in work, social relations, and self-care. They often lack or lose daily living skills, including such basic self-care skills as grooming, dressing, using the toilet, and feeding.

The behaviour of children with schizophrenia is extremely variable. However, Cantor (1989) listed four characteristics most often found in schizophrenic children:

- Sleep disturbance — a common symptom by the third year of life.
- Variable rather than short attention span. A schizophrenic child may attend for long periods of time to activities that are repetitive or perseverative.
- Variable behaviour — can vary from hyperactive to lethargic.
- Disturbances in thought processes.

Physical and Motor Development

Schizophrenic children tend to lag in physical and motor development. Individuals show serious deficits in gross motor areas but milder problems in the fine motor areas. As children with schizophrenia regress, acquired toilet and grooming skills may disappear.

Cognitive Development

Youngsters who are schizophrenic show great variability in cognitive functioning. On the Weschler scales, most individuals with schizophrenia achieve higher scores on the Performance than the Verbal subscales (Cantor, 1988).

Language is intimately related to cognition and to social development, and therefore the properties of language usage vary considerably as a function of the general level of language and cognitive development. As children with childhood schizophrenia regress, their speech becomes limited and may reveal incoherent thinking.

Social and Emotional Development

Schizophrenia in childhood has its most devastating effects on a child's ability to monitor and test reality (Foley, Johnson, and Raye, 1983) and on the ability to initiate and sustain interactions with others in the environment. Schizophrenia results in extreme withdrawal from the real world: affected children display a wide variety of disturbances in mood, thought, and behaviour. Schizophrenic children show a marked reduction in interests and human attachments. They appear to live in a fantasy world and show emotional apathy, indifference, and withdrawal. Apathy can quickly give way, however, to uncontrollable excitement or an enraged temper tantrum.

Social relationships are invariably disturbed. The profile of Mark describes a schizophrenic youngster who is demonstrating a marked increase in tantrum-throwing behaviour.

Profile

Mark

Mark had always been a difficult child. As a baby, he cried incessantly and was so afraid of strangers he would not let his mother out of his sight. During his preschool years, he was a whining, clinging child. By the time he was twelve, he had become totally withdrawn and seemed to survive in a fantasy world of his own making.

When Mark ventured out of his fantasy world, it was to kick, bite, scream, and throw tantrums. In Mark's special class in a large Toronto school, an incident occurred that illustrates his aberrant behaviour. Another child borrowed Mark's bottle of white-out fluid. Mark reacted by grabbing a nearby baseball bat, swinging it wildly, and threatening to kill the other child. When the teacher tried to restrain Mark by holding his arms, she was badly kicked, punched, and bitten.

Following his tirade, Mark sat for the rest of the day in his cubby. With his thumb in his mouth, he slowly rocked back and forth. All efforts to draw him out failed.

Mark has been diagnosed as suffering from childhood schizophrenia. He is in therapy and a special class, but he continues to withdraw more and more. His outbursts are becoming more violent and prolonged, and he treats other children with calculated cruelty. His parents find him almost impossible to handle at home and are seriously considering institutionalization.

Infantile Autism

Autism is found in a heterogeneous group of individuals who vary in terms of the nature and severity of inappropriate behaviour as well as in intellectual abilities. Children show a core group of symptoms. A further cluster of traits may not all be present in any given child. Autistic children demonstrate severe self-isolation, lack of appropriate use of language, stereotypical and inappropriate use of objects, a preoccupation with music, and abnormal motility patterns such as toe walking, body rocking, and bizarre choreoathetotic posturings. These and other behaviours that appear as the child develops are presented in Table 14-2.

Affected children never begin to establish normal human attachments. They are extremely alone from earliest infancy, and are unresponsive to other people. As infants, autistic children show far less mutual gaze and facial responsiveness than other children. Parents report that their autistic children do not respond in normal ways to being held. These children may be indifferent to physical contact, or may even show aversion to it. Infants fail to make the usual anticipatory movements prior to being picked up and fail to make the usual body adjustment to adapt to the person carrying or holding (Rimland, 1964).

Table 14-2

Symptoms of infantile autism in the preschool child

Birth to eighteen months

- No mutual gazing.
- Feeding problems, such as poor sucking.
- Lack of smiie response.
- Apathy and unresponsiveness.
- Rigidity and stiffness or limpness and hypotonia when held.
- Constant crying or an unusual absence of crying.
- Repetitive motor movements.
- Obsessive interest in certain objects.
- Great resistance to change.

Eighteen months to two years

- Continued poor eye contact.
- Withdrawal and isolation.
- Difficulties in toilet-training.
- Odd eating habits and food preferences.
- Feeding problems, such as refusal to hold food in mouth, refusal to chew or swallow, or gagging.
- Little or no development of speech.
- Little or no receptive language skills.
- Disinterest in toys, but obsessive play with some items.

After two years

- Continued withdrawal and isolation.
- No development of co-operative play.
- Continued problems with feeding, sleeping, and using the toilet.
- Slow or precocious motor development.
- Obsessive desire for sameness.
- Development of repetitive habits, gestures, and mannerisms.
- Tantrums at change or restriction of activities.

Between the fourteenth and eighteenth months, several disturbing symptoms begin to appear. These include prolonged rocking and head banging in the crib, apathy and disinterest in the surroundings, unusual fear of strangers, obsessive interest in certain toys or mechanical appliances, highly repetitive and ritualistic play, insistence on being left alone, demands that the physical environment remain unchanged, and very unusual language behaviour (Rimland, 1964).

In older children, autism reveals itself as fleeting eye contact, the failure to develop any relationships, and insistence on rituals and routines. These children fail to form attachments to other people. They seldom initiate contact and sometimes seem to look or walk through others. They appear distant, aloof, or in a shell, and are extremely alone. They have severely impaired communication skills and show an obsessive insistence on sameness. Their only strong attachments are toward inanimate objects. Children who are autistic, for example, are fascinated by things that spin. They can sit for hours with a toy car upside down, endlessly spinning the wheels. Unlike other children, they are virtually impossible to distract from this behaviour.

Physical and Motor Development

Children with infantile autism may show grace and normal motor skill development; however, it is not unusual to find ten-year-olds who are not yet toilet-trained or capable of dressing themselves. Children with autism tend to be healthier than other children with pervasive disorders (Schreibman and Charlop, 1989).

Cognitive Development

Although there is no common theoretical base, conceptions of autism share the assumption that it stems from some deficient cognitive structure. Poor cognitive development affects children's ability to learn, while behaviour problems interfere with attention and motivation.

Some degree of mental handicap is present in most individuals with infantile autism (Goodman, 1987); at least half of these children are mentally retarded (Sigelman and Shaffer, 1991), and they often display an extremely low level of cognitive functioning. Various estimates suggest that 60 to 80 percent of autistic persons are retarded with IQs below 50 (Kauffman, 1981; Koegel, Rincover, and Egel, 1982). In a British Columbia survey of 152 autistic children, Marg Csapo (1979) found 85 percent to have additional conditions which included mental retardation (51.1 percent), speech dysfunction and retardation (14 percent) and epilepsy and retardation (9.6 percent). Of children showing autistic symptoms before age six, 21 percent have been found to develop seizure disorders by age eighteen (Deykin and MacMahon, 1979). For one in three autistic children, problems worsen with the onset of puberty.

Cognitive development appears to differ from that observed in typical retardation; in autistic youngsters, IQ scores become stable over time, predictive of later functioning, and fail to rise with age-related improvements in clinical symptoms (Rutter, 1983). Some evidence suggests that, on average, autistic males have higher IQs than autistic females (Lord, Schopler, and Revicki, 1982).

Perceptual Development and Sensory Response

Children with pervasive developmental disorders, especially those diagnosed as autistic, may display abnormal responses to visual stimuli. They seem to suffer from constraints in attending to relevant cues and may exhibit a generalized over- or underresponsiveness to incoming stimuli. While fixating on an object or lights, they may flutter their hands, cross their eyes, glance to the side, or unfocus their eyes. They may try to smell new objects, or run their hands and tongues over rough and smooth surfaces. Sound may elicit indifference, distress, or intense fascination.

Faulty modulation of sensory input is an intrinsic feature of the pattern of autistic behaviour. To try to explain the disturbances of sensory input, a number of models have emerged. Some investigators believe that the child is overwhelmed by sensory input and unable to attend to pertinent environmental stimulation. Others see the child as fixated on relatively few stimuli and incapable of scanning the environment.

Language Development

Professionals have long been intrigued by autistic and psychotic children, especially their language patterns or, more often, lack of language. The central role of deficits in language and cognitive factors in autism are well documented.

Research data indicate fairly conclusively that autistic children have incurred some damage to the brain. This brain damage may particularly affect the language centres. One researcher (De Myer, 1977) holds that autistic children have a neurologically based language dysfunction that seriously interferes with their learning of expressive speech and abstract language. In addition, autistic children are thought to have a visual motor imitation deficiency akin to dyspraxia, which interferes with the learning of normal body language and the understanding of non-verbal communication, so important during the preverbal stage of development (Cummings and Finger, 1980).

It is the deviance in the quality and pattern of language usage, rather than language delay, that differentiates autism from other developmental disorders. Many children with autism seem to lack the awareness, intentionality, or competence to use language as a tool for conveying messages to others. From infancy, autistic children show little or no ability to analyze or make sense of sounds. As they mature, their language and communication skills remain impaired. Attempts to communicate are characterized by immaturity and abnormalities in grammatical constructions.

Many children fail to speak at all. Those who do speak demonstrate atypical language features — delayed echolalia, metaphorical language, pronoun reversals, and stereotypic utterances. Autistic children often use unusual words, with curious metaphors and odd expressions. They use neologisms, defined as "non-words" or words that are "obviously peculiar" (Le Couteur et al., 1989).

There are frequent pragmatic oddities, with language used in ways that are socially or contextually inappropriate (Hobson, 1988). Children typically perseverate on topics and fail to recognize turn-taking rules. Pronoun usage is unusual. A child may say "You want ride," when he means "I want to ride."

Facial and gestural expression of emotions can also be abnormal. Affected children fail to use gestures appropriately, and do not interpret such gestural clues as eye contact, body posture, tone of voice, and facial expression (Hobson, 1988).

If language is impaired, speech problems almost inevitably ensue. In their use of speech, children who are autistic are almost invariably delayed. Almost 50 percent of these children fail to develop speech (Cummings and Finger, 1980), especially those who are also mentally retarded. In the other 50 percent, speech is severely delayed and, if present, frequently consists of meaningless repetitive and stereotyped utterances.

When learning speech, the process is abnormal and different from that seen in, say, mentally retarded children. Acquisition of first words is often delayed; vocabulary often doesn't grow the way it does in other children; new words may appear but old ones are forgotten, resulting in a plateau (DeMyer, 1979). Some autistic children begin to speak and then lose all speech. Some then regain speech; others do not.

In children with speech, prosody is often peculiar (Rutter, 1985); for instance, everything may be said staccato or in a monotonous drone. In spontaneous speech usage, children with autism display a lack of expressive intonational features, such as stress and pitch, although echolalic children can repeat sentences and phrases with uncanny accuracy of intonation.

Echolalia is the most frequently cited language characteristic of individuals with autism who are verbal. It is estimated that 50 to 60 percent of persons with autism are verbal, and of this group, 75 percent are echolalic (Rydell and Mirenda, 1991). Echolalic children may repeat whole sentences in parrot-like fashion as if the sentence were unanalyzable into smaller components — as if they had learned the behaviour and stored it in memory ever since. Children who use echolalia seem able to attend to a linguistic string. They may even use a response to a consistent stimulus, but fail to relate it enough to the content to associate it with anything but a vague and general meaning.

Language problems weaken the capacity of children with autism for symbolic thought and abstract reasoning. In discussions of their behavioural deviations, for example, play disorders are consistently cited. Autistic children demonstrate significant delays in the development of all forms of play, especially symbolic play. Evidence indicates that their play is quite different from that of mentally retarded and other exceptional children. For children with autism, it is not delayed play, but play that differs in topography, pleasure, and complexity.

Even when intellectual level is allowed for, play is often obsessional, mechanical, and repetitive with a marked absence of both co-operative play and innovative pretend play. For autistic children, play as a vehicle for learning about objects and events and especially for engaging in make-believe does not appear to be intrinsically motivating (Lifter et al., 1993). Perhaps because of the language deficits that invariably characterize infantile autism, the play is striking in its lack of fantasy and its sterile, repetitive, ritualistic, and solitary nature.

These children do not seem to know how to use play forms. In a room full of toys, an autistic child is more likely to ignore the toys and engage in stereotypic self-stimulating body movements. If the child does play, toys are used in a deviant fashion. Unusual preoccupations (such a memorizing timetables) are characteristically pursued single-mindedly to the detriment of other activities (Rutter, 1985).

Social and Emotional Development

Impairments in social relatedness are increasingly considered to constitute some of the core symptoms of autism. Children with autism and other developmental disorders exhibit severe social interaction deficits. Autistic children have severely impaired relationships with parents, family members, and others in the environment. They do not attempt to gratify their needs through meaningful personal relationships; rather, they behave toward people as if they were inanimate objects. Children who are autistic often resent parents and others who try to show affection. They demonstrate both aggressive and stereotypic behaviours that further interfere with social interactions.

Prognosis

The outlook for children with infantile autism seems bleak. For many, there is little likelihood of attaining normal functioning within the context of currently available treatment and educational techniques. Even after years of the most effective treatment, many children are likely to remain at the retarded level, requiring close supervision and care.

Speech and language development is related to general prognosis; the outcome appears to depend on the child's intellectual functioning at diagnosis and communicative speech development prior to the age of six (Gillberg and Stiffenberg, 1987). Unless children achieve some use of spontaneous language by age five or six, the outlook is likely to be poor even for those with a relatively high level of non-verbal skills.

Profile

David

David is our third child. Although the pregnancy was uneventful, he was born nearly a month early after a prolonged and arduous labour. When we brought David home he was fussy and distractible, and he cried almost constantly. He had feeding problems with breast and bottle, and he could not be comforted by holding or rocking.

Even with his feeding problems, David gained weight and developed into a beautiful child. However, his crying continued and worried the entire family. By the time David was a year old, we were sure he had some problem or disorder.

Most of the time, David lay in his crib. He never seemed to notice when anyone walked into the room. He never smiled and never liked to be picked up and held. Except for crying, he made almost no sounds, especially not the babbling sounds his two older sisters had made.

At first, we suspected David was deaf. For nearly a year, we went from doctor to doctor seeking help. One doctor said David might be hearing-impaired, and told us to come back in six months. Another suggested he was severely mentally retarded, and another said he was simply slow in developing.

One evening, a friend who taught special children was visiting the house. He tried to play with David, but could garner no responses. We discussed our frustration and growing sense of hopelessness. The teacher suggested we get in touch with a local society that helped the parents of troubled children. At this time, the word *autism* had still never been mentioned.

Within a month of being directed to the right facilities, David had been diagnosed as autistic. In a way, the diagnosis was a relief. Although we had hoped that David was only slow to mature, we knew in our hearts that something was truly amiss. Professionals may rail against labels, but we badly needed a starting point, a direction in which to find help.

As soon as David was diagnosed, we contacted a local facility for autistic children. A therapist from the centre immediately began working with David in our home. When David was old enough, he attended a special preschool on a daily basis.

When he was nine years old, David moved from a special school into a special class in his local school and the team developed a number of integration strategies for him to give him more opportunities to interact with his peers. We have seen few changes in David's responsiveness and the prognosis still is not very good.

As a family, we now understand David's problems, although we sometimes find it very difficult to cope with them. He has developed only a few words of speech. His baby crying has given way to a high-pitched whine that goes on and on. David is extremely rigid in his attitudes. He has massive temper tantrums that frighten his sisters at home and embarrass us all in public. He is just beginning to be toilet-trained, and still has eating problems. He has great difficulty dressing himself, although he is better at taking his clothes off.

Another worry is the continuing effect of David's behaviour on his older sisters. Teenagers have their own wants and needs. We cannot let David disrupt their lives too seriously. Nor can we impose too heavily on them for babysitting.

Many children with autism require close supervision and care. About 50 percent are eventually placed in institutions and remain there into adulthood. Among the remaining 50 percent are some children who eventually achieve a degree independence and a large number who show moderate levels of disability (Lotter, 1978). One autistic child in six makes an adequate social adjustment to perform some kind of regular work in adulthood. Another one in six develops a modest degree of self-sufficiency.

Intervention with Pervasive Developmental Disorders

One of the major goals of any intervention with children with pervasive developmental disorders is to decrease the behavioural symptoms that interfere with the individual's functioning.

Children with pervasive developmental disorders present many challenging needs to those who attempt to help them develop more meaningful lives (Lovaas and Favell, 1987). At present, no specific treatment exists to help psychotic and autistic children reduce their anxiety and cope more effectively with reality. No one treatment method has proven notably effective with these children, and the prognosis remains poor. Nevertheless, some researchers exude an air of optimism. Lovaas and Favell (1987) write:

> Within the last thirty years, behavioral psychology and special education have contributed a great deal in helping developmentally disabled individuals acquire the kinds of behaviors that allow them to function in more normal and less restrictive environments. It is important to note that these developments are very recent and are occurring at a rapid rate. If we project the development within the last thirty years onto the next thirty, we will probably observe major psychological and educational growth in our clients, as well as major changes in many of the educational practices that are used in those individuals.

Medical Intervention

A wide variety of medications have proven useful in the treatment of schizophrenic youngsters. Of these, stimulants and tranquillizers are the most commonly administered. In contrast, drug therapy has shown inconclusive but unpromising results in the treatment of autism. There is little evidence that stimulants or tranquillizers significantly enhance the functioning of children who are autistic.

Therapy

Over the years, many different methods and approaches to therapy for psychotic and autistic children have been tried. These include psychotherapy, family therapy, speech therapy, residential treatment, psychiatric hospitalization, medication, megavitamin therapy, sensory stimulation, and sensory isolation. However, despite strong claims by individual researchers, no one method has been conclusively shown to substantially alleviate pervasive developmental disorders.

Increasing the depth and intensity of treatment may produce more encouraging results, however. Some recent research has indicated that if intensive treatment (forty hours or more of one-to-one treatment weekly) is begun before three and a half years of age, about 50 percent of autistic children may recover completely. They become indistinguishable from other children by the time they are in the first or second grade (Lovaas, 1982).

Educational Intervention

Although the precise causes of pervasive development disorders remain shrouded in confusion, various conceptual models have been used to treat them in various settings. Controversy still surrounds the placement of psychotic and autistic children in regular schools. Some argue for regular school placement; others hold that deviant behaviours such as resistance to change, an inability to generalize from one situation to another, and stereotypic and aggressive behaviour seriously jeopardize a child's functioning in a normalized environment.

Today, the majority of these children live in their own homes. If the strain on the family becomes too great, they may be placed in foster homes, groups homes, residential training centres, or institutions. Children are only enrolled in residential programs when they are seriously delayed in feeding, toilet use, or other self-help skills, when their families badly need relief; or when they must be placed under extensive observation for assessment purposes.

Educational Approaches

Regardless of setting, three major approaches tend to be applied in the education and training of developmentally disordered children. The psychodynamic and behavioural approaches are the most popular of these, but a psycho-educational approach is also widely employed.

Psychodynamic Approaches

Before the 1960s, almost all intervention with psychotic and autistic children was founded on psychodynamic principles; today, this approach is still widely used though not as popular. Psychodynamic treatment is usually conducted in a residential setting away from the parents. Typically, it lasts several years. Children are given individual therapy within a therapeutic setting designed to promote and sustain emotional growth. Treatment may also be given through outpatient clinics or day treatment centres.

The psychodynamic approach tries to help children understand the inner forces that guide their behaviour. By responding to the child in ways that are consistent, positive, and accepting, the therapist builds the child's confidence and trust. At the same time, the therapist helps the child to understand the sources of conflicting ambivalent emotions. Art, play, pet, and music therapy may be part of the psychodynamic approach. (See Chapter 11.)

While they prove very resistant to psychotherapy, autistic children do respond to behaviour modification techniques, and some success has been achieved with highly structured learning procedures.

Behavioural Approaches

Autism is extremely difficult to treat, and autistic children pose a variety of complex management problems. While they prove very resistant to psychotherapy, autistic children do respond to behaviour modification techniques, and some success has been achieved with highly structured learning procedures. In fact, the research literature has been flooded with positive reports of the use of behaviour therapy with psychotic and autistic children. Behavioural approaches have been used to teach autistic children to focus attention, to imitate actions, to develop basic speech skills such as vocalizing and word imitation, to label objects and pictures, and to extinguish temper tantrums (Block, Gersten, and Kromblum 1980. Forehand and Atkeson, 1981; Howlin, 1981; Lovaas, Schreibman, and Koegel, 1974).

Behaviour therapists do not claim to cure autism and give no promise of normalization or intellectual improvement for autistic children. Rather, they attempt to modify deficits and excesses in behaviour patterns. However, "the long-term effectiveness of behavioral therapy for autism remains much in question, at times sparking intense debate even among investigators using it" (Bower, 1989; p. 312).

Behaviourists claim that behaviour modification trains children who are autistic to lead a more useful existence. Critics respond that behavioural techniques program children to perform like robots, unable to generalize their training to other situations. These critics claim that the child's trained responses are much too closely linked to the original training situation. Light (1983) found that a child trained to answer "Fine, thank you," to one trainer's "How are you?" does not necessarily respond the same way to another trainer. Despite these criticisms, the general evaluation of behaviour therapy has been cautiously optimistic. But even with behaviour modification, most autistic children still need supervision.

Individual Education Plan iep

Extract from David's IEP

Name: David
School: John Brown
Grade: 4

Present levels of functioning: David has been diagnosed as autistic. No IQ levels have been estimated, but he is functioning at pre-academic levels. David has not developed any language or speech.

Placement: David is in a special class but there is to be increasing integration into the regular classroom for social purposes.

Annual goal: to increase interactions with others in the environment and awareness of environmental stimulation.

Long-range goals

- David will develop gaze-to-gaze behaviour.
- David will respond to others in the environment.
- David will use simple speech when it is modelled for him.
- David will participate in art classes with his peers on a daily basis.

Objectives

- When assisted to the correct hallway, David will locate and enter the art room independently.
- When given a visual cue by the teacher, he will sit in his assigned place.
- At the beginning of the class, he will respond to communication by waving or saying "Hi" to a peer.
- When presented with a choice of paints and a gestural cue for each option, David will select the colours he wishes to use.
- At the end of the class before clean-up, he will tap the arm of a peer at the table and will point to his own artwork to show it to the peer.
- When prompted by other students, he will look at their art work.
- When cued, David will place the finished work in his own folder.
- David will return to his own classroom with a peer.

Curriculum

The major goals of any intervention with children with pervasive developmental disorders is to decrease the behavioural symptoms that interfere with the individual's functioning and to promote the development of functions such as language, adaptive behaviour, and social and self-care skills. Many students need to be taught a wide range of basic daily living skills such as independent eating, dressing, and using the toilet. They must also learn how to relate effectively to others through training in social interaction and communication. Some students will need help to decrease inappropriate behaviours such as severe aggression or strong and persistent ritualistic and stereotyped behaviours (Lovaas and Favell, 1987). Because of their unresponsiveness and lack of communication skills, children with psychoses and infantile autism are very hard to train. Few receive academic training beyond basic levels.

Curriculum reflects all areas of development. Training often emphasizes early developmental skills usually thought of as too routine or too basic to be part of a regular instructional program. Training may begin with the sensorimotor levels. In this way, it clearly matches the curriculum we describe in Chapter 15 for children with multiple disabilities.

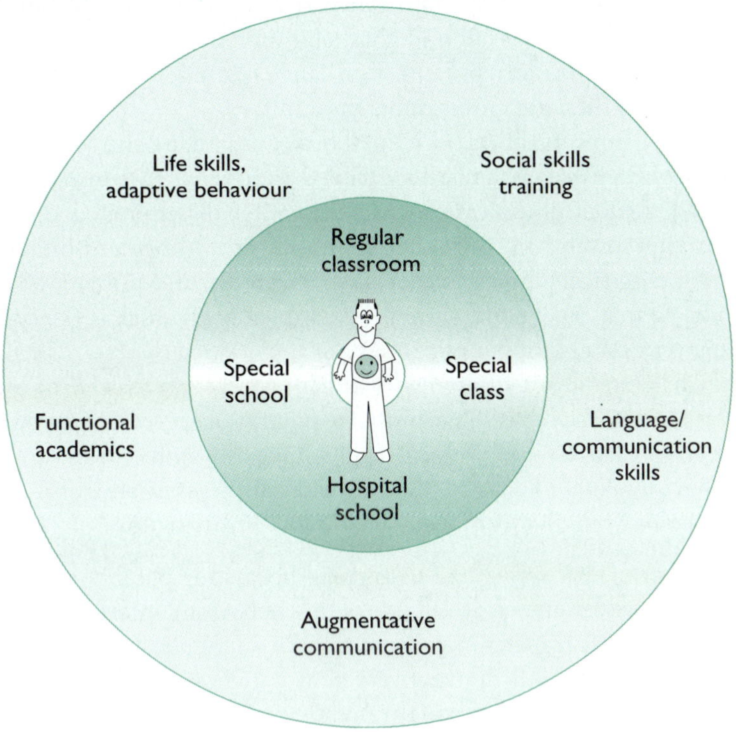

Figure 14-1 *Curriculum components*

The interrelated curriculum components are:

- Social skills training. A primary goal is to help children get in touch and keep in touch with their environments. Training begins with establishing self-concept; children must learn who, what, and where they are in order to realize that they are separate from others. Once they are aware of themselves as separate beings, they are ready to establish basic relationships. Their prognosis improves and they are ready to learn new tasks.
- Independent behaviour. Independent behaviour is behaviour performed without the assistance of others (Bailey, Harms, and Clifford, 1983). It includes self-help skills, those abilities needed for independent functioning in relation to such basic needs as food and warmth.

- Communication skills. Relatedness to others in the environment depends on some basic communication. For young children, language allows them to initiate contact and to act positively on the environment. For adolescents there are two primary goals in communication — participation in age-appropriate social relationships outside the family and development of the ability to use language to pursue one's interests (Lord, 1988).

  In some children, echolaliac speech is decreased by nonattention, and normal speech is gradually shaped by food rewards for imitation of the therapists's vocalizations (Lovaas and Smith, 1988). In the literature, however, doubts have been raised about the effectiveness of speech training with all autistic children. An alternative approach, relying on the simultaneous use of speech and sign language, has been attempted with some success (Konstantereas, Webster, and Oxman, 1979). One study (Konstantereas, 1984) found that sign and speech produced better results than speech alone, possibly because sign language relies primarily on visual and kinesthetic modalities and circumvents the auditory.

  Facilitated communication is a method of augmentative communication in which someone physically assists a disabled individual to communicate through typing. Facilitated communication has been widely disseminated and promoted as a breakthrough for autistic and other communication-impaired individuals. However, careful empirical studies (e.g., Mulick, Jacabson, and Kobe, 1993; Thompson, 1993) indicate that the facilitator, not the disabled individual, is the communicator in all but a very small number of cases.
- Appropriate behaviours. Children with autism and psychoses show both aggressive and stereotypic behaviours. The most frequently observed inappropriate behaviours are non-compliance, physical aggression, self-stimulation, and self-injury. Other behaviours include destruction of materials, temper tantrums, and a host of annoying actions ranging from teeth grinding to throwing toys.

Perhaps the most disruptive and disturbing behaviour pattern exhibited by these children is severe self-injury. Not only does this behaviour interfere with habilitative efforts, but it can be life threatening or lead to permanent physical damage. Lovaas and Smith (1987) found that self-destructive action is reduced by isolating the children. Very structured behavioural programs are often successful in ameliorating self-stimulating and self-destructive behaviours. With self-stimulation, for example, the adult can use reinforcers for an appropriate behaviour and ignore inappropriate responses.

Summary

1. Pervasive developmental disorders are exceedingly complex conditions. To many people, psychotic and autistic children are beyond comprehension. Their behaviour is bizarre, their emotions intense, and their isolation total. These children usually have difficulty developing language skills, learning to communicate, and learning to relate to others. They display unusual bodily movements, inordinate fears, and extreme resistance to change. Many children function at pre-academic levels and fail to develop, or lose, basic self-care skills or language.

2. Although infantile autism is generally considered the most devastating of developmental disorders, childhood schizophrenia is also extremely incapacitating. Schizophrenia is variously characterized by qualitative changes in functioning such as association disturbances, delusions, hallucinations, attention deficits, and inappropriate social interaction. Autism is a pervasive developmental disorder stemming from biophysical impairment.
3. The behaviour of psychotic children has traditionally placed them in the category of the uneducable. Even with structured intervention procedures, the prognosis is poor. Many psychotic children continue to exhibit disordered behaviour as adults. Instead of becoming self-sufficient, they require institutionalization or continuous care.
4. In 1906, Sante de Sanctus studied schizophrenic children for the first time. In 1911, the term *autism* came into use to refer to patients characterized by social withdrawal. In the years following Kanner's identification of the syndrome, most autistic children were institutionalized with minimal custodial care. In the 1950s, advocates began to argue that autistic and psychotic children could and should be educated. Today, children are placed in a range of settings.
5. Even after intense research efforts, the etiology of childhood psychoses and infantile autism remains vague, the symptoms severe and complex, the diagnosis difficult, the treatments unclear, and the prognosis uncertain at best. At the moment, the stress is on medical causality; serious biomedical research on autism is ongoing. While there is no irrefutable proof of causation, efforts have led to a much clearer understanding of the diagnosis of autism; today the condition is generally viewed not as a psychosis but as a developmental disability or a health problem.
6. Recent research suggests that autism and fragile X are associated and that fragile X has unique behaviourial characteristics.
7. A variety of informal measures, including rating scales and observation, are widely employed in assessment.
8. For children with autism, poverty of language is a major factor that interferes with adjustment, for it is through language that human beings make their impact upon the world and establish and maintain relationships.
9. Some autistic children fail to develop speech. Others have great difficulty following the conventions of conversation and interpreting linguistic and non-linguistic contextual rules.
10. Poor language development spills over to affect many other areas, such as play and imaginative skills. Instead of language, autistic children turn to less problematic, more predictable inanimate objects. They may sit for hours spinning or twirling an object, such as a shiny ashtray.
11. Psychotic and autistic children pose a variety of complex management problems. Of all the interventions that have been attempted, most children have responded best to behaviour modification techniques. Current educational treatments are unlikely to cure the disorders, but they can alleviate the symptoms. Children can learn to make small gains and develop basic skills.
12. The educational prognosis for children with pervasive developmental disorders improves as they learn social skills. Children must first learn basic social behaviours, such as communication, and be trained to refrain from socially unacceptable actions.

CHAPTER 15

Children with Multiple Disabilities

Historical Notes

History tells us very little about persons with multiple handicaps. Given the state of medical knowledge and the paucity of intervention and treatment regimes, it seems unlikely that many individuals with severe multiple disabilities would have easily survived.

An early mention of persons with multiple handicaps came from Blackstone, the oracle of English law, in the late seventeenth century. This was the time when law and medicine were beginning to differentiate between mental retardation and mental illness. When speaking of a person born deaf, dumb, and blind, Blackstone noted that such an individual was "in the same state as an idiot, by being supposed incapable of any understanding as wanting all the senses that furnish the human mind with ideas" (McGann, 1888).

Prior to the middle of the eighteenth century, little evidence exists of any social or educational interventions with persons with multiple handicaps. About that time, the Scots philosopher Dugald Stewart told of a deaf-blind lad named James Mitchell who responded to educational intervention. In Paris in the 1760s the Abbé de l'Epée, who devised a sign language for deaf persons, experimented with a system of raised print blocks to use with deaf-blind individuals.

It was not until the mid-1900s, however, that we find fully documented evidence of intervention with a multiply disabled individual. This came from the Perkins Institution for the Blind in Boston, where Samuel Gridley Howe undertook the education of Laura Bridgeman, a girl who had lost her sight, hearing, taste, and smell to scarlet fever at the age of two. In 1837 Howe was escorted to a New Hampshire farmhouse where he met seven-year-old Laura. He enrolled the child in the Perkins school and there embarked on a structured series of lessons and exercises. He first took common objects, attached labels to them that spelled the names in raised letters, and trained Laura to associate the name with the object touched. Once she knew that letters were single entities that could be rearranged into words, Laura advanced quickly. Howe then taught her the manual alphabet and eventually Laura read embossed books, did simple arithmetic, and mastered needlework and other kinds of handicrafts. She did not become fully independent and remained at Perkins until her death in 1889 (see Winzer, 1993).

Howe's extensive reports of Laura Bridgeman's education and development left an outstanding legacy to the entire field of special education, and to teachers of the deaf-blind in particular (Hallahan and Kauffman, 1991). His son-in-law, Michael Aganos, used Howe's directives when Helen Keller became a pupil at the Perkins Institution (Winzer, 1993).

Helen Keller, deafened and blinded by disease at the age of nineteen months was, until the age of seven, an untutored half-wild child, unable to perform the simplest tasks. Captain Keller took six-year-old Helen to see Alexander Graham Bell in Washington in November, 1888, and Bell contacted the Perkins Institution for the family. A little later, Captain Keller hired Anne Sullivan, a pupil of Perkins, who taught Helen. Once she overcame the behavioural obstacles, Sullivan found Helen an amazingly apt pupil. In less than three months, for example, Helen learned to spell about 400 words and to write a letter unaided. It took the child only six weeks to master braille (see Blatt, 1985).

In Canada, deaf and blind Charles Crane achieved a high level of education. The Crane Library at the University of British Columbia is named for him.

Children with multiple disabilities show evidence of independent and interdependent deficits in two or more areas of functioning. People with multiple disabilities form an extremely heterogeneous population. Innumerable combinations of impairments are possible, although some appear more often than others, and some are more difficult to cope with. Individuals may suffer multisensory impairments such as deaf-blindness, or they may have conditions that combine sensory disorders with physical, neurological, or mental handicaps. Impairments of vision or hearing occur much more frequently among children with multiple disabilities than among other children. It has been estimated that one in five can be expected to have impaired hearing and two in five impaired vision (Orelove and Sobsey, 1987).

Students with multiple disabilities usually have a range of special educational and psychosocial needs.

Children's development is integrated and organized across the various developmental domains — cognitive, language, physical, social, and emotional. Therefore, with multiple disabilities, we cannot look at the impact of a single disability in isolation, but must instead realize that the interaction of disabilities results in the appearance of unique developmental and behavioural patterns. The conditions are not additive but cumulative and present a completely unique condition that may affect all the mind/body systems in different ways and to different degrees. For example, a deaf child with severe mental retardation may have independent deficits in cognitive functioning, producing language, understanding language, and in social interaction, as well as deficits resulting from a combination of these individual impairments.

Not only do students with multiple disabilities present a range of special educational and psychosocial needs, but to an even greater degree than for children with single handicaps, each child must be considered individually. Because of their complex conditions, multiply disabled children require the services of many disciplines, most importantly, education, psychology, physiotherapy, occupational therapy, speech pathology, audiology, and medicine. As a result, a transdisciplinary approach to their treatment and education is essential.

Many of the children that we have already encountered in this text could be considered multiply disabled. The Down syndrome child with a speech disability, the deaf youngster who is also emotionally disturbed, the cerebral palsied child with language disorders, the profoundly retarded child, and the autistic child, for example, have conditions that, taken together, severely disrupt their learning. And, while multiple disabilities are usually conceptualized as severely handicapping conditions, it should be remembered that children can suffer from combinations of minor disabilities that can be devastating to their learning and behaviour. In this chapter, however, we focus on children with severe and debilitating multiple handicaps. Particular attention is paid to children who combine visual and hearing impairments.

Definitions of Multiple Disabilities

In the area of multiple disabilities, the differences among students are greater than the similarities. This makes the formulation of precise definitions a complex and virtually impossible task. The heterogeneous nature of the population and the combinations of disabilities mean that we would not have one, but dozens of definitions.

To overcome the problem, broad and encompassing generic definitions that attempt to include the entire range of possible combinations of conditions have evolved. One generic category refers to students who are severely hadicapped. These are "school-aged students who function intellectually within the lowest one percent of the particular age-groups" (Brown et al., 1983, p. 77). These students may be labelled as physically handicapped, multiply handicapped, dual sensory impaired, autistic or psychotic, and moderately, severely, or profoundly mentally retarded.

Generically, **multiple disabilities** are those in which children suffer two or more handicaps that hinder their attainment of their full potential. The category includes

> those children who, because of the intensity of their physical, mental or emotional problems, or a combination of such problems, need educational, social, psychological, and medical services which will make it possible for them to maximize their full potential for meaningful participation in society and for self-fulfillment (Thompson, 1976, p.41).

Development of the Field

From the mid-eighteenth century on, there are scattered reports of the education of children with multiple handicaps, particularly those affected by deaf-blindness. Generally, however, residential and public schools tended to exclude these students.

They were excluded from the residential schools because they had handicaps that cut across several categories of impairment. They therefore tended to fall between the cracks. For example, special services for visual impairments, hearing handicaps, and physical disabilities were not extended to children served by agencies, schools and institutions for the mentally retarded (Hammer, 1984). Public schools did not take the responsibility for providing education on the assumption that these people were uneducable, that they could not learn.

Education of children with multiple handicaps only began seriously in the 1970s, prompted by research that demonstrated conclusively that persons with severe handicaps can learn useful skills. Indeed, since the 1970s, there has been an explosion of research and demonstration projects which have shown the learning potential of children with multiple disabilities. Researchers continue to compile dramatic evidence that shows that even the most severely disabled youngsters can become productive members of society. To add to the impetus for educational intervention, parents' associations have spearheaded a social movement to extend educational and treatment services to the most severely afflicted children.

Although major advances have taken place, special education for children with multiple disabilities in Canada remains beset by unresolved problems and surrounded by controversial issues. Definitions are difficult, if not impossible, and this affects classification, prevalence figures, and identification. Some children with multiple handicaps are moving into the regular school system, but many are still accommodated in special settings. In specialized, segregated classrooms, children have few opportunities to associate with non-disabled peers. But in regular classrooms, they may not receive the special services they need to become self-sustaining adults.

This definition includes severely and profoundly retarded children, deaf-blind children, mentally retarded deaf-blind children, and physically disabled and severely emotionally disturbed children (Van Osdol and Shane, 1982). It focuses on the combinations of problems possibly present as well as the range of interventions and allied disciplines necessary if children are to achieve their potential.

Generic definitions tend to use very broad parameters which may obscure the effects of particular handicaps, making it harder to clinically interpret the needs of individual children. Moreover, generic definitions do not give rise to specific programs. For example, children with visual or hearing impairments who are enrolled in generic programs do not have access to specialist services, such as orientation and mobility training, low vision services, or communication training. Another problem is that inclusive generic definitions tend to combine multiply handicapped children with severely and profoundly retarded children, despite the fact that not all children with multiple handicaps are retarded (Rogow, 1987a).

Some educators argue that definitions should be worded in terms of children's behaviours and needs. When individuals who are multiply disabled are defined by their service needs, they are people "who require ongoing support in several major life areas in order to participate in the mainstream of community life and who are expected to require such support throughout life" (Bellamy, 1985, p. 6).

Some educators avoid generic definitions, preferring more specific definitions for particular broad groupings of individuals who are multiply disabled. **Multisensory impaired** is a term used to describe children with sight and hearing handicaps. It includes children who may also be developmentally delayed or have neurological impairments (Kysela, 1985). **Multiple dependent handicapped** refers to severely mentally handicapped children who also have sensory and/or other physical handicaps (Kysela, 1985). Children described as multiple dependent display a wide variety of visual, auditory, and physical/neurological handicaps.

Deaf-blind children are those whose disabilities are a complex of auditory, visual, communication, and language factors, often accompanied by other conditions that interfere with their learning. A deaf-blind individual is described as having

> both auditory and visual impairments, the combination of which causes severe communication and other developmental and educational problems that cannot be properly accommodated in special education programs either for the hearing handicapped child or for the visually handicapped child (Kirk and Gallagher, 1979, p.437).

This definition stresses that because deaf-blind children suffer impairments in both vision and hearing, they will not have their needs met if they are placed in special education programs for students who are only deaf or only visually impaired. Programs for students who are deaf rely heavily on the use of vision, while instruction for students with visual impairment depends on auditory instruction; but deaf-blind children suffer deficits in both these modalities.

Classification of Multiple Disabilities

The complexity and variety of multiple disabilities has not only spawned a number of definitions and descriptions but has also meant that classification systems and service delivery are beset with confusion. Generally, services have been administered on the basis of labels and discrete categories, and this tendency has resulted in the creation of a number of overlapping classification systems.

The most common way to classify multiple handicaps is in terms of primary and secondary disabilities. The major condition that causes a child to differ in learning or behaviour is referred to as the primary disability; other conditions that arise or are present are known as secondary disabilities. A child who is both visually impaired and mentally retarded may be judged to suffer visual disabilities as the primary disabling condition, with mental retardation being the secondary disability.

Problems exist with approaches that focus on presumed primary and secondary disabilities. For one thing, many children have more than one set of pertinent characteristics and the primary handicap is often impossible to identify. Blind and retarded children, for example, may be visually inattentive because they do not see or because they are intellectually unaware of the visual environment.

As well, viewing multiply handicapping conditions as primary and secondary overlooks the cumulative nature of the disabilities. Children cannot be appropriately classified under the category of a single handicap because the combination of conditions creates an entirely new disability that requires access to special services for all the child's impairments, whether sensory, physical, mental, or behavioural. Children who suffer from visual impairments as well as mentally handicapping conditions, for example, cannot be appropriately accommodated in programs for mentally handicapped children without sight problems.

Sometimes children are classified according to the agency that serves them. This also leads to problems as the same child may be identified within the service delivery system of a number of agencies. Sometimes, too, children are simply classified by the type of educational program they attend.

Children with mild physical or sensory impairments can learn well in the regular classroom provided they receive additional support.

Prevalence of Multiple Disabilities

Estimating the true incidence and prevalence of almost any handicapping condition is an onerous if not impossible task. In the case of multiple handicaps, a number of factors combine to hamper prevalence estimates. Difficulties arise for several reasons:

- Prevalence figures tend to be influenced by changes in technology, demographic trends, and social factors (Hayden and Beck, 1981).
- Interpretations of the definition of certain populations have changed dramatically. For example, the number of persons with deaf-blindness has not increased substantially since 1974. Today, however, individuals categorized as having deaf-blindness can represent those with moderate to profound auditory and visual impairments with or without other educationally disabling conditions, who need services to increase independence; those with central processing problems that result in cortical blindness or central auditory dysfunctions; or those with progressive sensory impairments such as Usher's syndrome (Michael and Paul, 1991).
- Children with combined handicaps may be registered for services with a variety of agencies so that the same multiply handicapped child might be identified within the service delivery systems of any of these agencies.
- Probably the greatest difficulty in obtaining prevalence figures arises as children are counted in terms of their primary handicap. In school districts where special programs for multiply handicapped children are unavailable, children may be entered into classes designed for mentally retarded, hearing impaired, or visually impaired children, and are then defined and counted by what is presumed to be the primary handicap.

We do know that multiple disabilities are extremely low-incidence conditions, as can be seen in Table 15-1, which indicates numbers from certain Canadian provinces. We also know that numbers of exceptional children suffer additional mild to severe handicapping conditions. As well, available prevalence figures indicate that the numbers of children with multiple handicaps are greater than previously assumed. One surveillance registry in British Columbia found an increase of 15 percent in reported cases (Hayden and Beck, 1981).

Etiology of Multiple Disabilities

The major causes of childhood disabilities that we have outlined throughout this text are also causes of multiple disabilities in children. In fact, with the exception of rubella, the etiology of multiple handicaps almost parallels that of physical handicaps. This is especially true for central nervous system damage that results in severe motor impairment.

Table 15-1

Prevalence of multiple handicaps

Province	Number of students with multiple handicaps	Percentage of total school population	Percentage of exceptional population
Newfoundland	200	0.15	1.97
Nova Scotia	149	0.08	0.79
Quebec	6821	0.72	5.39
Ontario	2839	0.16	2.08
Saskatchewan	452	0.22	7.51

Source: Canadian CEC (1989)

Rubella is the culprit in many childhood handicapping conditions. At its most devastating, rubella causes deaf-blindness and severe multiple disabilities. Studies of deaf-blind rubella children reveal great differences between this group and other deaf-blind children, primarily due to the gross effects of the rubella virus on many body parts. Most children who have combined sight and hearing problems due to rubella are neither totally blind nor profoundly deaf; however, the combination of sensory impairments creates severe learning difficulties (Van Dijk, 1982). The following profile tells of James, a child affected by rubella.

Profile

James

Mrs. J. did not know that she had contracted the rubella virus early in her third pregnancy. She felt healthy throughout the period and was not overly concerned when her infant arrived nearly a month before term. Labour was normal, lasting about fourteen hours. The infant cried lustily, and Mrs. J. readily accepted the explanation that he was in neonatal intensive care only because he was of slightly low birth-weight.

Information about the true nature of the child's condition came quickly. Within twenty-four hours, the physician explained to both parents that the child, now named James, was suffering serious defects as a result of the rubella virus. Examination had shown a defective heart and serious visual problems. The physician explained that other anomolies could emerge, possibly deafness and mental retardation, and urged the parents to think about institutional placement for James if he survived the first month.

The parents' shock was soon displaced by grief and the necessity for making decisions about care. Mr. J. urged institutionalization. Their oldest son had already been identified as learning disabled, and Mr. J. perceived a seriously handicapped infant as potentially very disruptive to the family climate. Mrs. J., on the other hand, was determined not to accept the rather hopeless prognosis of the physician. She wanted to raise the child at home, to treat him, as far as possible, like the other children, and to seek support to assist in his development.

James spent nearly three months in the neonatal unit. Once at home, he proved a fairly easy baby to handle. In fact, he was so docile and passive that this concerned his mother and spurred her to seek outside help. By the time James was nine months old, a visiting teacher was coming once a week. She worked with James on various developmental tasks, especially in the motor area. Because language was a concern, she showed Mrs. J. how to stimulate vocalizations, and gave her some tips on receptive language development.

By the time James was sixteen months old, a severe to profound hearing loss was confirmed. His vision was poor, with a restricted visual field. However, with some complaint, he accepted both a hearing aid and glasses. He also reached some major developmental milestones — he walked and began to eat solid foods.

Throughout James's preschool years, Mrs. J. behaved toward him and disciplined him just as she did the older children. She accepted his multiple disabilities but held relevant expectations for his development. He became an integral part of the family circle. Sibling resentment was not directed at any special treatment James received; it surfaced only when he got into the same type of mischief that any preschooler does. For both siblings, their proudest day was when James marched off with them to his first day at the local public school.

Chromosomal and genetic disorders account for only a tiny number of multiple disabilities. When they do appear, children often have complex multiple disorders affecting several different body systems. On the other hand, injuries to the central nervous system account for significant numbers of multiple disabilities. Neurological impairments result from damage or dysfunction of the brain and/or the spinal cord incurred before, during, or after birth. Other nervous system disorders resulting in multiple handicaps may stem from trauma, accident, or child abuse. Hydrocephalus is frequently associated with multiple disabilities. If treatment is unsuccessful or only partly successful, the child may have damage to the optic nerve as well as motor handicaps (Harley and Lawrence, 1977).

New medical technology, intensive care nurseries, and lifesaving techniques are saving many infants who would have perished just a few years ago. Children who are premature, especially those with birth-weights less than 1500 grams, are particularly vulnerable to insults of the central nervous system (Fenichel, 1980).

Meningitis contracted immediately after birth is a major cause of multiple disabilities. Fifty percent of infants who survive the disease suffer significant neurological impairments that include cerebral palsy, hydrocephalus, convulsive disorders, and hearing and visual handicaps (Fenichel, 1980).

Syndromes

Usher's syndrome is a condition of familial nerve deafness associated with pigment degeneration of the retina (Harley and Lawrence, 1977). The incidence of Usher's syndrome in the general population is no greater than one in 15 000 to 30 000 births. Nevertheless, Usher's syndrome is the most common etiology of deaf-blindness, accounting for more than half the deaf-blindness found in adults. It also accounts for 3 percent of all the profound prelingually deaf population (Miller, 1985).

Usher's syndrome is transmitted through an autosomal recessive trait. The child is born deaf and gradually loses sight due to retinitis pigmentosa. The age of onset of the visual disability ranges from early childhood to early adulthood (Harley and Lawrence, 1977). Visual problems usually begin in the early teens.

All persons with Usher's syndrome have both a hearing loss and retinitis pigmentosa. A significant number show other symptoms, such as abnormal vestibular functioning, seizures, mental retardation, abnormal EEGs, schizophrenia, and autism (Davenport et al., 1978).

Not all genetically deaf-blind individuals suffer from Usher's syndrome. The single conditions may be caused by different genes or infections. There are other syndromes, such as Refsum's and Laurence-Moon, that involve both deafness and visual impairment; however, additional pathology such as obesity, retardation, diabetes, or scaly skin clearly distinguishes them from Usher's.

Identification and Assessment

Whether diagnosis is medical or psycho-educational, the assessment of children with multiple handicaps taxes the ingenuity of clinicians. Because data generation is so difficult, a diverse range of measures are used. All attempt to assess the child's disabilities, the impact of the combination of disabilities, the possible etiology, the prognosis, and the strengths a child possesses.

Medical Assessment

A medical examination, a routine part of the diagnostic process, is undertaken with the multiply disabled child as early as possible. Several diagnostic procedures are used to determine the exact nature and sometimes the underlying causes of multiple handicaps. These include

- a careful medical history;
- psychological and psychiatric assessment;
- laboratory tests to detect metabolic disorders;
- cytogenetic studies;
- clinical neurophysiological investigation, through electroencephalogram (EEG) tests of auditory and visual potential and electromyograms to test nerve conduction;
- neuroradiology, which involves skull x-rays, echoencephalography, radio-isotope brain scans, and PET and CAT scans that can pinpoint the presence of brain lesions (Rogow, 1987a).

Assessment of Hearing

It is often difficult to distinguish whether children fail to respond to an auditory stimulus because they do not hear it or because they are simply inattentive. This is particularly true of multiply handicapped children who require a wide range of sophisticated techniques for the assessment of auditory status. For these children, audiological assessment is divided into two major methods — electrophysiological and behavioural. (See also Chapter 9.)

Electrophysiological procedures often provide the most reliable information about a child's ability to receive sound stimuli because the techniques do not rely on a child's behaviour or responses. But although these tests help to detect whether a child in fact hears sound, they do not provide information about the child's ability to interpret the auditory stimuli. Electrophysiological measures include impedance audiometry (the drum and the middle ear) and electroencephalography-evoked response audiometry. The latter refers to the measurement of various evoked electrical potentials that are responses to auditory stimuli.

Behavioural testing includes observations and play audiometry. In **behaviour observation**, a sound is presented to a child in a sound-proofed room. The tester observes any behavioural responses, such as a blink or head turning. Play audiometry involves teaching the child to respond to a sound when it is presented by performing some action, such as putting beads in a bowl. Another method used with very young and multiply handicapped children is tangible reinforcer operant conditioning audiometry which uses tactile rather than visual cues.

A primary goal in working with deaf-blind children is to teach them to communicate in the easiest way possible.

Assessment of Vision

It is often difficult to determine whether a multiply handicapped child has usable vision. This is particularly true of children with neurological handicaps who seem unable to establish normal visual contacts. A child who does not respond to conventional testing may be a candidate for several physiological tests that are administered by qualified clinical or medical personnel. Diagnosticians use electrophysiological procedures, functional tests, and behavioural measures.

Electrodiagnostic procedures assess the electrical activity of the optic pathway and occipital cortex of the brain. The presence of electrical activity indicates that an active pathway exists (Ikeda, 1976). Tests include the Visually Evoked Response (VER), also known as the Electroretinogram (ERG). This is a sophisticated technique which measures the chain of electrical nerve responses created by a flashing light and thus allows the examiner to assess the functional state of the retina. The ERG has been used extensively to determine the visual acuity of infants and children with neurological handicaps (Harley, 1983; Mohn and Van Hall-Van Duin, 1983).

The electro-oculogram, which measures the ability of visual nerve cells to respond to light, can be performed on infants and multiply handicapped children under general anaesthetic. Visual Evoked Potential (VEP) is a technique for measuring visual acuity that uses a bioelectrical signal generated in the visual cortex of the brain in response to visual stimulation. These generated bioelectrical signals are measured by recording electrodes placed over the occipital regions of the cortex (Hall, Orel-Bixler, and Haegerstrom-Portnoy, 1991). VEP can be used with anyone who can maintain fixation on a TV monitor on which black and white stripes of different widths are presented. Because the VEP technique permits the examiner to record the reception of light images by the visual cortex, it is a particularly valuable test for infants and multiply handicapped children (Ikeda, 1976). Other methods for assessing vision were discussed in Chapter 10.

Behavioural measures include field tests that use gross objects or lights. In one test, the child is held over the parent's shoulder facing the examiner while a toy or other familiar object is moved into the temporal field. The child is tested for each eye separately and for both eyes together and the child's reaction is observed (Faye, 1976).

The Bailey-Hall Cereal Test for visual acuity (Bailey and Hall, 1983) is a behavioural technique that uses picture cards including one of cereal; if the child selects the correct picture, he or she is rewarded with praise and a piece of cereal (Bailey and Hall, 1983).

For estimating the visual acuity of children with very limited cognitive abilities, diagnosticians may use the UC-Berkeley Preferential Looking Test (Bailey and Hall, 1984). This test consists of six grey rectangular cards each of which has one grey square and a second square with black and white stripes. The brightness of the grey background, the grey square, and the striped square are about equal. The procedure is based on the premise that if children see the striped square they will prefer to look at it rather than the less interesting grey square or grey background. As each square is presented, the examiner determines where the child prefers to look by observing his or her eye movements.

Functional tests assess the visual behaviour of an individual rather than just the physiological condition of the eyes. That is, they assess the ability to track objects, use visual fields, develop eye-hand co-ordination, and perform other functions that reflect visual development. The tests are portable and can be administered by trained personnel, such as teachers.

Psycho-Educational Assessment

Most students with severe and multiple disabilities do not pass through a screening process as they are obviously handicapped; the assessment begins with the diagnostic testing (Gaylord-Ross and Holveot, 1985). All assessments should be administered on a regular basis, usually once or twice a year.

The psycho-educational assessment of children who are multiply disabled has a number of separate but equally important goals which include measurement of the overall level of intellectual function and exploration of the individual child's impairments and abilities. Assessment data are used to decide on the most appropriate educational placement and to formulate an individual educational plan. Specifically, the assessment of students with multiple disabilities attempts to answer some crucial questions:

- Is the child attentive to auditory language and symbolic code systems?
- How are the child's hands used? Are they limp like wet sponges or are they actively employed for exploration and manipulation?
- How does the child respond to training?
- Does the child refuse to learn because of poor motivation or is the material too complex and confusing?
- Does the child use vision and hearing fully? (Hammer, 1984).
- Does the child indulge in stereotypic behaviours. These may serve as indicators of ability. For example, light gazing or hand flapping in front of a light indicates that the child has some vision (Ficociello, 1977).

The assessment of children who are multiply disabled is an arduous and challenging task requiring skilled practitioners, input from care providers, and many hours of observation and testing. Even so, results are always tenuous. In a comprehensive study of assessment practices of special education staff serving students with severe disabilities in five school districts, for example, researchers (Sigafoos, Cole, and McQuarter, 1987) reported that special educators lacked training in the assessment of students with severe disabilities and were limited by the unavailability of appropriate assessment tools and dependent on norm-referenced instruments. However, the standard diagnostic and evaluation tools currently utilized with mildly disabled children will generally be of little use to those involved with individuals who are severely and multiply disabled. Problems most frequently occur when a child's performance on a particular item is inappropriately influenced by the handicapping condition (Bailey and Wolery, 1989). Many of the tasks that are used in such tests must be eliminated because of motor difficulties, sensory impairments, and special problems present in the children being assessed.

Diagnosticians must devise special procedures for children

- with limited or absent expressive and/or receptive language. Children with severe communication problems may withdraw from social interaction, rendering diagnosis difficult.
- who show an inability to name letters or pictures;
- with short attention spans;
- with limited co-operation in testing situations;
- whose maximum attention is achieved when not in an upright position;
- who have limited hand use in conjunction with limited expressive language so that sign language use is affected;
- with severe cognitive delay;
- who may perform certain behaviours in one milieu but not during testing;
- who may perform tasks for a known person but not an unknown tester.

Some or all of the following adaptations enhance the assessment situation for both the child and the tester:

- A natural environment is an advantage to children. Psychological and educational assessments of children with multiple disabilities are best made in familiar surroundings using familiar tasks and materials.
- A number of adaptations to standard routines may need to be considered as we discussed in Chapter 13.
- No single assessment tool can meet all the needs of a population as diverse as that of children with multiple disabilities. Specific instruments should vary according to the needs of the individual and vary according to the areas being assessed. It is now common practice to use a combination of direct observation; informant interviews; adaptive behaviour scales; measures of prelinguistic communication behaviour and alternate methods of communication; developmental scales, observational checklists, and formal intelligence tests.
- The foundation of an accurate and appropriate assessment is the establishment of rapport with the child and the family. Having parents present may add to a child's feeling of security. Parents should also be involved during the assessment process as sources of information.
- Interdisciplinary assessments should be conducted. The size and nature of the team involved will vary according to the child's disabilities. Arena testing can be used. (See Chapter 3.)
- Findings must be frequently monitored to reflect and encourage changes in the child's competency.
- Consider other approaches to assessment besides developmental approaches using norm-referenced tools (see Bailey and Wolery, 1989; Langley, 1991).

To assess mental ability, diagnosticians usually select scales of infant development because the sensorimotor behaviours tapped are often in the repertoires of these children. Although infant scales are known to be poor predictors of later development in non-handicapped children, these measures with severely handicapped children give IQs that have proven to be good predictors of later development (Fewell and Cone, 1983). Perhaps the most widely used test of cognition for children functioning in the sensorimotor period is the Ugiris and Hunt Scale of Infant Psychological Development (1975) or its adaptations (Dunst, 1980).

Psychometric tests are not suitable for a large proportion of children who are multiply handicapped; nor are norm-referenced developmental scales that compare the exceptional child with normally developing peers in order to determine the extent of deviation from the norm. A variety of other tools are needed to measure a child's ability to perform in the areas of motor skills, language and communication, social behaviour, and self-help skills. Most instruments permit comparisons of each child's performance at a different point in time rather than trying to establish a child's relative standing on a normative scale (Liepman 1981).

The Callier-Arusa Scale (Stillman 1978), for example, is designed to assess deaf-blind and severely and profoundly handicapped children from birth to six years. It covers motor development, perceptual development, daily living-skills, communication, and social development. The scale is used in classroom settings by someone familiar with the child so that typical behaviour can be observed in natural contexts. This links assessment to curriculum so that teachers can synthesize developmentally appropriate activities for the child.

The Developmental Activities Screening Inventory 2, a screening test of functioning for children from birth to five years, has adaptations for blind and deaf children (Fewell and Langley, 1984). Motor scales include the Peabody Developmental Motor Scales and Activity Cards (Folio and Fewell, 1983).

Language assessment is both crucial and complex. Standardized measures include the Preschool Language Scale (Zimmerman, Sheener, and Pond, 1979) and the Sequenced Inventory of Communication Development (Hedrick, Pratter, and Tobin, 1975). Both provide individual scores for receptive and expressive language and both are standardized on very young children.

Children with significant disabilities meet problems in responding to interactions, in imitating, and in using basic communication. Many children are either prelinguistic or minimally linguistic. Informal language assessment for this group largely focuses on measures of prelinguistic communication behaviour. It attempts to determine a child's understanding of sounds and gestures, and includes observation of the child's response to environmental sounds, speech sounds, and response to gestures, names, and requests. It examines communication use, which includes how the child gains the attention of others; how he or she initiates play with caregivers and peers; whether the child anticipates and takes turns; and how the child interacts in routine communication events. Assessment also looks at the settings, people, and purposes for communication. Needs and interests are assessed by looking at the reasons for the child to commmunicate, the objects and activities that the child prefers, and when and with whom the most appropriate interactions occur.

Observational data and parent interviews are strong indicators of a child's level of skills and awareness. Direct observation techniques permit assessment of children's behaviour and achievements in their normal daily routine. A number of questionnaires and interview schedules have been constructed for use with parents, teachers, and other key informants which provide important information about aspects of a child's progress.

Educational assessment focuses on functional areas of competence in the domains of communication, social behaviour, self-help, and independence skills. For some children, educational assessment also measures areas of academic competence, such as reading, writing, and mathematics.

Prevention of Multiple Disabilities

Adequate prenatal care, good nutrition, and avoidance of alcohol and drugs improve the health of mothers and babies. Maternal rubella is effectively prevented by the rubella vaccine; meningitis is also prevented by immunization. Research is ongoing for ways to prevent and cure other congenital birth defects. Recent advances in genetics have increased our understanding of genetically linked disorders, and genetic counselling is available to help decrease the frequency of genetic conditions.

The most extreme consequences of severe physical, sensory, and mental handicaps can often be prevented by early intervention programs undertaken simultaneously with ongoing medical care and treatment. Some conditions of the eye and ear can be treated medically or surgically. Cosmetic or plastic surgey can, in some cases, correct skeletal anomalies that cause visual or hearing problems. Cosmetic surgery may also help the child to win social acceptance.

Developmental Consequences of Multiple Disabilities

Children with multiple disabilities are those who have two or more exceptional conditions that hinder the attainment of their full potential. The variety and combinations of disorders presented by children who are multiply disabled make generalizations about developmental consequences virtually impossible. These students may have orthopedic or health impairments, or hearing or speech disabilities. They may use unconventional behaviour to communicate a basic need or they may exhibit a combination of behaviours (Jones and Carlier, 1995).

Physical Development

Many domains of learning depend upon a child's ability to interact with the environment. As a result, many children with multiple disabilities are very late in reaching developmental milestones. Walking, using first words, and toilet training may be severely delayed.

During the period when normal children are developing most rapidly, the multiple deficits of these children prevent them from interacting with the environment in ways that are critical for the subsequent development of social, motor, cognitive, and communication skills. They are then doubly limited by their delayed physical development and by their limited ability to engage with the environment in ways that can stimulate development (Warren, Alpert, and Kaiser, 1988).

Cognitive Development

Depressed cognitive development is not a necessary concomitant of multiple disabilities. Nevertheless, the disabilities can be so severe that children function in very low ranges. Many children who are deaf and blind, for example, function in the severe to profound ranges of mental retardation as a result of their inability to perform basic skills (Orlansky, 1981).

The world is often unpredictable, irregular and full of confusion for children who are multiply handicapped. They have difficulty making sense of the confusing sounds, textures, and other stimuli that surround them. Sensory handicaps especially distort, delay, or interfere with the accuracy of perception, making it hard for children to establish the identities and relationships of people and objects. For example, a deaf-blind child or a visually impaired mentally retarded youngster may perceive only fragments of information. In their world, objects appear or disappear without any indication of where they have come from or where they have gone. These children do not see their mother place an object in their hand or watch a ball roll away. They do not know how others use the object and for what purpose it is designed (Rogow, 1987a).

Communication

Most children with multiple disabilities are deprived of orienting movements of the head and body, as well as of purposive gaze. This leaves them with no available modality through which to communicate. They are unable to clearly co-ordinate actions of looking, searching, reaching, and touching which operate as functional units of communication. Multiply disabled children find it very difficult to acquire the complex symbol system of language without enough sensory data to make language meaningful. They tend to remain at early stages of communication development for long periods of time (Rogow, 1987a).

Children lacking efficient communication are often divided into two groups. The first group comprises presymbolic children who do not use signs, words, or pictures for communication. They may not possess a recognizable communication system or may use gestures such as pointing or touching or moving objects (Owens, 1991). The second group is made up of minimally symbolic children who use some visual, verbal, or tactile symbols alone or in combinations (Owens, 1991).

Social and Emotional Development

Individuals with multiple disabilities are at a severe disadvantage in social interactions. Children find it difficult to establish spontaneous social contacts; they may feel anxious and frustrated when confronted with unfamiliar experiences and variations in their routine (Rogow, 1987a).

From the very beginning, the onset of attachment behaviours and social interactions may be severely delayed as the child's physical and behavioural deficits disrupt the natural interchange between caregiver and child that is essential to early interactions. In addition, the baby's first months may be dominated by periods of hospitalization, feeding problems, and an inability to maintain a wakeful state.

Young children may appear not to recognize other family members, or they may be obsessively engaged in such self-stimulating behaviours as light gazing or hand flapping. In older children emotional difficulties may be manifested in any or all of the following personality traits: frequent panic reactions, hyperkinesis, autism, withdrawal, and frequent tantrums (Van Dijk, 1982).

Behaviour

Problem behaviours may reflect the intense frustration caused by the child's inability to communicate. In some cases, the cause of problem behaviours is unknown, although such behaviours often seem related to the type of brain damage the child has sustained.

Academic Achievement

The learning and educational attainments of multiply handicapped children depend upon a matrix of factors; not the least of these are the quality of education, the age at which education begins, the age of onset of the conditions, the nature of the combination of handicaps, and the severity of each condition. Also important are factors such as the family's response to the child, the educational setting, the amount of integration with non-handicapped peers, the related services available for both the child and the family, and the amount of acceptance by the community.

Some children who are multiply disabled achieve well in school. For most, however, functioning is at pre-academic levels. Because their perception of events is impaired, they find it hard to develop awareness, attention, anticipation and purpose, all skills needed for efficient learning. Children with multiple disabilities must often learn the techniques for acquiring knowledge as well as the knowledge itself (Rogow, 1987a).

In teaching students with multiple disabilities, the selection of objectives should be based on their future usefulness.

Intervention with Children with Multiple Disabilities

In the past, persons with severe and multiple disabilities were excluded from educational services. Over the last forty years, the education and treatment of children who are multiply disabled has undergone considerable revision and expansion.

Treatment generally hinges on two major factors — etiology and the specific combination of disabilities. Although etiology is of less overall significance for educators, critical program modifications must be made for such secondary spin-offs as rubella-induced sensory aberrations and the psychological adjustments precipitated by Usher's syndrome.

Medical Intervention

Medical and paramedical personnel can provide information about many aspects of a child's functioning to teachers and parents. Those intervening with a multiply handicapped child require information concerning

- special arrangements that may be needed to accommodate seizure activity, medications, allergies, susceptibility to illness, poor muscle strength, and special feeding problems;
- physical deformities that may require special equipment or prosthetic devices;
- alterations that may be needed in work, play, and rest schedules;
- special positioning or handling techniques or special feeding techniques (Rogow, 1987a).

Therapy

Children with multiple disabilities require the services of a range of therapists, most specifically physical, occupational, and speech and language therapists. Physical and occupational therapists can help children to develop hand skills, body co-ordination, and other physical skills, and aid in gross motor development, muscle relaxation, and fine motor control. (See Chapter 13.)

Speech and language therapy assists the child's development of speech and language. This form of therapy may also be used with children who have difficulty in controlling the fine motor muscles needed for eating. Therapists may also develop appropriate augmentative communication for children who cannot talk.

Technical

Improved equipment and adaptive devices have developed to enrich education and improve the quality of life for individuals of all ages. (See Chapter 13.) Computer applications have been successfully used to enhance functioning and assist in the learning of a specific task. Garner and Campbell (1987), for example, used computers to develop specific cognitive skills in order to provide more opportunities for individuals to perform a wide variety of functional activities independently in integrated environments.

Technical aids continue to be developed to improve the quality of life for severely disabled children and assist in their education.

Educational Intervention

Children who are multiply handicapped take education beyond its traditional boundaries. These children may show different learning characteristics and developmental patterns. The instructional process may be hindered by maladaptive behaviour, the need to adapt technology and materials, and the difficulty in identifying appropriate reinforcers (Sisson, Van Hasselt, and Hersen, 1987).

Children's development is predicated on such factors as alteration of the physical environment, sensory stimulation, and well-planned, consistent habilitative and educational programs. Training begins with basic developmental skills and, for some, may never proceed beyond pre-academic levels. Multiple treatment modalities are employed.

Children who are multiply handicapped need an extensive network of services to enable them to thrive and learn; they also need a responsive environment capable of providing appropriate stimulation and opportunities for interaction. The difficulties and potentialities resulting from each unique combination of disabilities represents the decision point in placement and programming, so we find that students with multiple disabilities are educated in a variety of settings. Some may attend regular school or special classrooms in the local school. Others may learn in special schools, residential placements, hospitals, or clinics.

Children with mild physical or sensory impairments can learn well in the regular classroom, provided they receive additional support. These children are able to participate in academic programs, and benefit from interaction with non-disabled peers. In addition to regular instruction, they may need the services of speech therapists, physical therapists, audiologists, mobility and orientation specialists, and specialist teachers of the hearing or visually impaired.

When children with severe disabilities are placed in regular clasrooms, schools often elect one person, often a special education teacher, to act as a support facilitator. This person not only works with the severely disabled students but helps regular classroom teachers adapt instruction and aids in facilitating peer acceptance (Stainback and Stainback, 1988). A teacher's intervention is illustrated in the profile of Juanita.

If children with visual and hearing impairments see well enough to learn in classes with deaf children, they may be enrolled in special classes or schools for the hearing impaired. These children require additional help from specialist teachers of the visually impaired to develop maximum use of their remaining vision. Children with moderate to severe sensory impairments may require programs specifically designed for deaf-blind children. Some school boards in large urban areas accommodate these children within special classes in regular schools. In hospital-based day schools, children attend school in hospital classrooms, where medical treatment and physiotherapy are readily available.

Although the numbers are decreasing, some Canadian children with multiple disabilities are still educated in residential settings. Such placements have both their advocates and their opponents. Some professionals (e.g. Silverstein, 1985) feel that residential placements are appropriate not only for sensorially impaired children with severe intellectual dysfunction, but also for those with average or above average IQs. Others actively promote less restrictive environments.

With the current stress on integration and inclusion, there has been a movement away from the traditional residential model. Policy in the United States is instructive in this regard. American courts have decided that residential programming is necessary when more than six hours of instruction are required to meet the child's educational needs; when the severity of the child's language deficiency precludes meaningful benefit from peer group learning and interaction with non-handicapped peers in a mainstream setting; or when social and emotional adjustment are poor in the normal setting.

Profile

Juanita

Very early in her pregnancy, Juanita's mother contracted rubella. She was warned by medical personnel that her child might suffer some type of handicapping condition but was stunned and frightened to find that the infant was both deaf and blind and also suffered a host of other problems.

Throughout Juanita's infant and preschool years, home-visiting teachers came to show her mother a range of activities to stimulate Juanita's mobility, communication, and interpersonal interactions. Consistent medical assessment demonstrated that although the child suffered serious visual and hearing difficulties, she was not totally deaf or completely blind. Juanita had quite a lot of usable vision and, although her hearing loss was in the severe to profound range, amplification seemed to help. Not that Juanita took kindly to either a hearing aid or glasses. Despite the intensity of her handicaps, she had a mind or her own, and it took many months of perseverance on the part of her mother and the intervenors and many types of primary reinforcers before she would tolerate either appliance.

Juanita attended the local preschool classes on a part-time basis. When she was ready for school, her mother enrolled her in the neighbourhood school that had a special class for severely and multiply handicapped children. For the first little while, Juanita remained in her special class, but soon the teacher worked to integrate her into a regular classroom for short periods of the day. The teacher facilitated a "Circle of Friends" to assist Juanita's integration and worked co-operatively with the classroom teacher on planning specific activities that Juanita could accomplish in a small group setting.

Juanita is now nine years old. She still spends a great part of her time learning specific skills in the special class, but she is also comfortable and welcome in the regular classroom and has a small group of friends who share with her both in and out of school.

Educational Approaches

While the learning characteristics and needs of children who are multiply handicapped vary widely, the following components are essential to a comprehensive system of education:

- Early and continuous intervention. Early intervention can prevent the consequences of sensory deprivation and emotional withdrawal.
- Transdisciplinary models that rest on consultation and collaboration.
- Systematic instructional procedures. As students who are multiply handicapped miss so much incidental learning, they must be helped to develop a foundation for later and more complex learning.
- Appropriate curricula. Children require both educational and psychosocial development founded on a carefully task-analyzed Individual Education Plan. The more handicapped the child, the more detailed and precise the task analysis and the goals and objectives need to be. Each child's educational plan should include a range of assessment of the child's progress and a detailed evaluation of the educational program. Curriculum materials should then be developed to meet the individualized educational goals of each child.
- Critical program modifications. These must be made because children suffer from combinations of conditions that interact in such a way as to depress or block the

emergence of normal patterns of interaction with the environment (Rogow and Rodrigues, 1977). As well, accommodations provide for secondary conditions that occur on top of the original problems.

- Adjunctive services. These include the provision of medical and therapeutic services to individual children. Associated professionals may also provide specific training and instruction to parents.

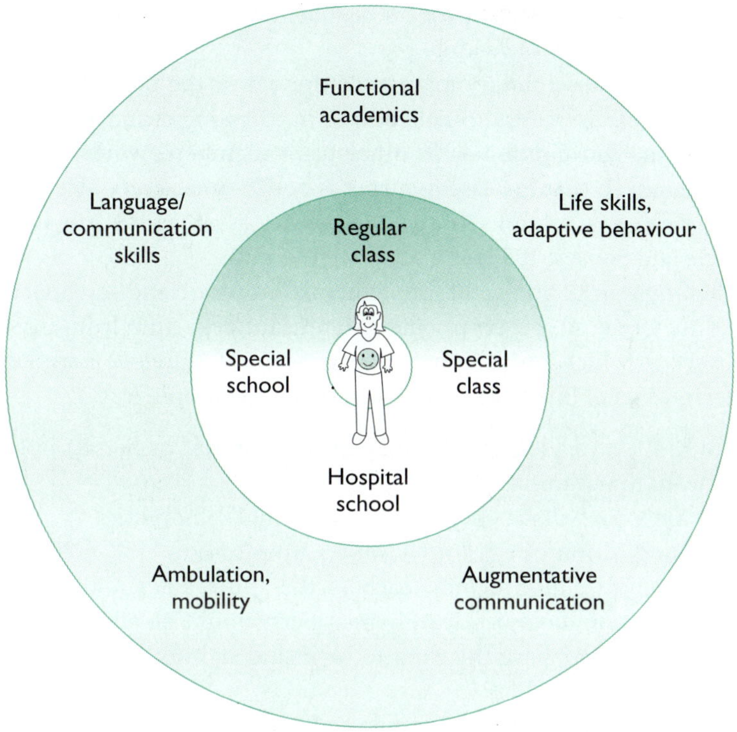

Figure 15-1
Curriculum components

Team Approaches

The training and education of children with multiple disabilities cannot rely on one person. Different disciplines bring unique skills and knowledge to intervention, and the nature of the child necessitates a partial blending of roles, skills, and knowledge across disciplines (McCollum and Thorp, 1988; Thorp and McCollum, 1988). Professionals in diverse roles will need to function co-operatively to help students achieve their goals which may be framed in the context of a transdisciplinary model.

A transdisciplinary model is a team approach in which it is assured that the team members will perform the various services together. This means that the expertise of different types of agencies serving children with disabilities can be shared so that services are enriched, expanded, and made more comprehensive. A team approach enables everyone involved to see the child as a total being rather than concentrating on one aspect of that child's development. On a team, roles and expectations are shared by more than one member and experts on the team train other members (see Landerholm, 1990).

Teamwork demands *collaboration,* which is a "generic (umbrella) term used to describe a style of interacting in which persons with diverse backgrounds voluntarily agree to work together to generate creative solutions to mutually defined problems" (CEC, 1991). Collaboration "depends inherently on the voluntary efforts of professional educators to improve their schools and their own skills through teamwork" (Smith and Scott, 1990, p. 2). In collaboration, the ownership of a problem is always shared and the consulting relationship is characterized by a sense of parity demonstrated through two-way communication and the sharing of knowledge and skills. The key hypothesis behind the process is that the group, functioning together, is greater than the sum of its individual parts.

Typically, the transdisciplinary team is composed of the family and professionals from a variety of disciplines who collaborate in assessment and program planning. One individual, in consultation with other team members, works to carry out the individual program so that the case manager is both primary provider and service coordinator. Generally, in school settings, the teacher assumes the role of service provider (Orelove and Sobsey, 1987).

Although simple in concept, the implementation of a trandisciplinary model can initially be difficult because it represents a significant departure from most models of service delivery to which professionals are accustomed (Orelove and Sobsey, 1987). Certain attributes seem important to efficient team functioning:

- Each team must have a leader who may involve himself or herself in specific tasks related to team functioning.
- The size of the team will vary according to the child's disabilities.
- While the composition of a team will differ from case to case, certain core people are usually involved. These include teachers, therapists, aides, and other paraprofessionals such as an audiologist. Family members should be encouraged to join the team; not only do they have the right to be included, but they are the people most familar with the child.
- On a team, each team member has a role and each role has a set of skills and certain expectations associated with it.
- Effective teams develop over time and they need nurturance. When the membership of the team changes frequently, implementation and maintenance of child and family goals are jeopardized.
- The way people respond to others' communication directly determines the extent to which people on the team can continue the interchanges and initiate further dialogue.
- Personal characteristics that can assist in developing good communication and collaboration on the team include being empathetic and open, being able to establish good rapport, respecting different points of view, and being positive and enthusiastic (West and Cannon, 1987).

Curricula

Curricula designed for children who are multiply handicapped must reflect all areas of development. Educational needs include language development, visual and auditory training, mobility training, and self-care skills. For deaf-blind children, stress must be placed on visual stimulation and visual perception skills as a basis for cognitive and academic tasks. The development of communication skills is a simultaneous activity. Language is the product of all aspects of development — physical, sensory, social, and neurological. Therefore, in the education of deaf-blind children, and indeed all children with multiple handicaps, no aspect of language development can be ignored. Psychosocial needs include adaptive behaviour, group activities, life skills, and a range of socialization experiences (Hammer, 1984).

For many children with multiple disabilities, training emphasizes early developmental skills usually thought of as too routine or too basic to be part of a regular instructional program. Most curricula for children with severe disorders have tended to adhere to a biological-developmental or cognitive-developmental approach. That is, developmental milestones are emphasized and skills must be developed in a specific hierarchical order regardless of the ages of the children. The developmental order of skills corresponds to what has been observed in younger children without disabilities (Bailey et al., 1983).

There are two major criticisms of the developmental approach for children with multiple disabilities. The first revolves around the contention that all children, regardless of disability, follow a logical progression of development. The second has to do with the functional value of the skills taught.

It must not be assumed that sequences of behaviour typical for non-handicapped students are relevant for the severely handicapped child; children with multiple handicaps may not develop or acquire skills in a normal sequence. When a pathology of the central nervous system exists, or when there are severe sensory losses, the organization of behaviour is disturbed and a child's early development is often uneven. Severely handicapped children may learn in a different sequence and the relationship between skills may be different (Snell, 1987). For example, a child with multiple disabilities may walk at a relatively early age, but be severely delayed in the acquisition of language.

Apart from the uneven development seen in students with multiple disabilities, a curriculum based on developmental sequences is likely to have little impact upon the ultimate attainment of self-sufficiency (Holveot et al., 1980). In teaching students with multiple disabilities, the selection of objectives should be based on their future usefulness. Skills that are useful to a student in many current and future environments are referred to as functional skills. (See Chapter 4.) Educators target those skills that have a high probability of being required at home, in school, at work, or in the community and that will increase self-sufficiency in those environments.

The functional skill approach improves the child's functioning in present environments and facilitates transition to and participation in age-appropriate future environments. For example, sorting shapes to corresponding pictures of shapes is not a skill that a child is likely to use during daily activities, whereas the child is likely to use the skill of matching various shaped lids to corresponding containers. While both skills involve matching, recognizing, and sorting shapes, the use of functional objects such as containers and lids enables the child to learn a necessary skill that will foster independence in real-life situations (Notari-Syverson and Shuster, 1995). Similarly, placing pegs in a board may aid in fine motor development but it is not really related to future needs. On the other hand, putting coins in a vending machine will develop the same motor areas and also provide a living skill.

Tips for Teachers

Tips for teachers of students with multiple disabilities

Classroom climate

- Encourage spontaneity by rewarding spontaneous behaviour.
- Co-actively imitate and play with the child.
- Model the behaviours you want the child to learn.

Instruction

- Reinforce vocalizations as consistently and frequently as possible.
- Provide vocal reinforcement for a short time after the child stops vocalizing. This offers a model dialogue and ensures that the child is not interrupted. It also reinforces turn-taking patterns.
- Vocal reinforcement should include imitation of the child's sounds, whether verbal or preverbal.
- Place your mouth on the child's neck or hand when speaking so that the child can feel your speech. Continue to hold your mouth against the child's cheek or hand between vocalizations so the child can feel the silence.
- Improve the quality of language stimulation by interspersing short bursts of speech with short periods of silence.
- Do not treat visually impaired children as if they were totally blind. However, make sure to accompany communication with rhythmic body actions, touch sensations, or actions that engage a number of senses simultaneously.
- Do not focus only on maladaptive behaviours. Use playful social routines, rhyming verses, and other communication games that are enjoyable for you and the child. For older students, try using rock and roll and other rhythmic patterns.
- Multiply handicapped children are often able to comprehend far more than they indicate; keep sentences short and use an expressive voice.
- Actively involve the child in the instruction.
- Develop short- and long-range goals that stress the child's self-help capabilities.
- Use prosthetic aids to enhance active involvement.
- Talk to the child.
- Most training efforts should be conducted in natural environments. For children with more severe deficits in speech and language, formal language training may involve lessons a few brief times daily. However, communication training with severely impaired children need not, and should not, be confined to one-to-one therapy sessions.
- Generalization of training must be carefully planned.
- Activities should contain multiple components. Multiple components provide numerous opportunities within a single activity. Painting, for example, would provide at least three opportunities for communication: obtaining access to the paint, the water, and the brush.
- Activities should lend themselves to repetitive action. If the child desires repeated actions by a caregiver, repeated opportunities exist for language use. Examples of these activities include playing catch and being pushed on a swing.

Communication Training

Of all the needs of children with multiple disabilities, the acquisition of communication skills is one of the greatest. Children require training in all aspects of understanding and expression. In language training, it is essential that the specific communication needs be identified first. These will relate to people involved as well as to the settings and purposes of communication. With these needs in mind, training may take place in one-to-one, highly structured environments, but more generally in natural contexts such as the classroom.

Children who are communicating at a level below the age of two have unique needs in language development. Often the goal of intervention is the initiation of effective communication. Two general intervention strategies are used in communication training programs for presymbolic and minimally symbolic children, often in tandem. These are presymbolic training and communication first approaches (Owens, 1991).

Presymbolic training is based on the belief that there are cognitive prerequisites for language acquisition. Teaching programs are organized around initial assessment and subsequent training related to cognitive, perceptual, social and/or communication targets identified as significant in the acquisition of symbol use in non-handicapped children. The skills that make up presymbolic training are those that are identified as characteristic of the sensorimotor stage of development. Cognitive development begins with the development of basic sensorimotor skills such as object permanence, causality, means-end behaviour, spatial relationships, schemas for relating to objects, and imitation.

A communication first approach is a functional approach to language which stresses nurturant and naturalistic language. Communication first approaches place the initial emphasis on the establishment of a communication system that can later be expanded to symbol use. The major skills taught are initial communication; turn-taking skills; generalized imitation skills; lexical growth and establishment of a basic vocabulary; early symbol communication rules; and participation in interactions that occur outside the training context (see Owens, 1991).

Alternative Methods of Communication

Relatedness to others in the environment depends on some basic communication. When speech is delayed, or when there is reason to think that it may be delayed or not develop at all (for example, when the child has multiple disabilities including a significant hearing loss), alternative means of communication are considered.

Anything that augments speech or accomplishes communication function is grouped under the term, **augmentative communication**. Augmentative communication refers to a general group of procedures designed to support, enhance, or augment the communication of non-speaking individuals or utilize and supplement whatever vocal skills an individual possesses. The various procedures that make up augmentative communication are used chiefly by individuals whose speech communication is impaired by hearing impairments; individuals with severe language deficits; individuals with severe neuromuscular or physical disabilities; and those with severe and multiple disabilities.

The selection of a communication mode and the strategies for teaching its use should be an interdisciplinary task. The choice of an adjunct to communication is ideally made in conjunction with family and therapists. Factors such as long-term linguistic needs, people with whom the child needs to communicate, and the most appropriate mode of communication must be considered. The mental ability, motivation, and voluntary movement available to the child are further considerations in selecting a mode of communication.

There are two main types of augmentation — unaided and aided approaches. Unaided approaches rely on gestural communication; aided approaches depend on a device of some kind or a pictorial or symbolic communication system.

Non-speech communication should not preclude speech therapy. A number of studies have shown an increase in speech attempts with the use of non-vocal methods of communication (Mysak, 1982).

Unaided Approaches

The major types of unaided approaches in augmentative communication are

- Signal communication, which includes the use of a simple Yes/No system and audio-signalling. Yes and no signals may be indicated by movements of head, hands, face, or eye (Mysak, 1982). A portable audio-oscillator that emits a loud tone has been used to teach four simple signals (need, help, yes, no).
- Code communication uses Morse code as a method of communication.
- Natural gestures are simple movements of one or both hands used to convey meaning to the child. For example, the word *eat* is indicated by tapping the lips with the fingertips of one hand. Although natural gestures are often used with deaf-blind children, they may also be part of communication training for multiply handicapped children who are not hearing impaired. Natural gestures may vary from child to child. If a child consistently points to the mouth to indicate hunger, then everyone working with that child should use the same gesture.
- Sign language is typically associated with deaf children; however, studies suggest that manual communication may be beneficial to a much larger population in improving communication skills (Moores, 1978). Signing uses pantomime, gesturing, and other non-verbal communication to convey ideas, language, and vocabulary to young children. Its use may potentially offer unlimited opportunities for language development and may facilitate the onset and development of spoken language in prelinguistic children (Kouri, 1989).
- Amerind is a simpler system and more suitable for low-functioning individuals for whom sign language may prove too difficult. Amerind was adapted by Madge Skelly (1979), a speech and language pathologist and full-blooded Indian, from the system she learned from her grandfather. Amerind is built on the hand signals used by Native Americans and contains about 250 hand signals that may be arranged in any combination.

Aided Approaches

- Augmentative devices are operated by the individual to communicate basic needs. They can be easily activated by movement of the head or hand, or even by an eye blink. The Vocaid is an example of an augmentative device suitable for functional needs, such as a call for assistance. Some augmentative devices make use of speech synthesis.
- Children with good intellectual ability might use a system where the child spells a message on a grid using row-column scanning with an electronic device.
- Blissymbolics has been successful with children with severe motor disabilities. Charles Bliss, a refugee from Hitler's concentration camps, went to Shanghai where he learned the Chinese writing system in which each symbol stands for an idea rather than a sound. Based on this, Bliss developed an ideographic universal writing system. It was not popular until discovered by Shirley McNaughton at the Ontario Crippled Children's Centre in Toronto. Today Blissymbolics is a complete language system. Even though it can be used for general conversation, the symbols are simple enough to be learned by children too young to read alphabetic writing (Archer, 1977). Bliss is used by 25 000 people in Canada, of whom one-quarter have cerebral palsy (Reich, 1986). Depending on a child's abilities, vocabularies of up to four hundred terms may be learned (Mysak, 1982).

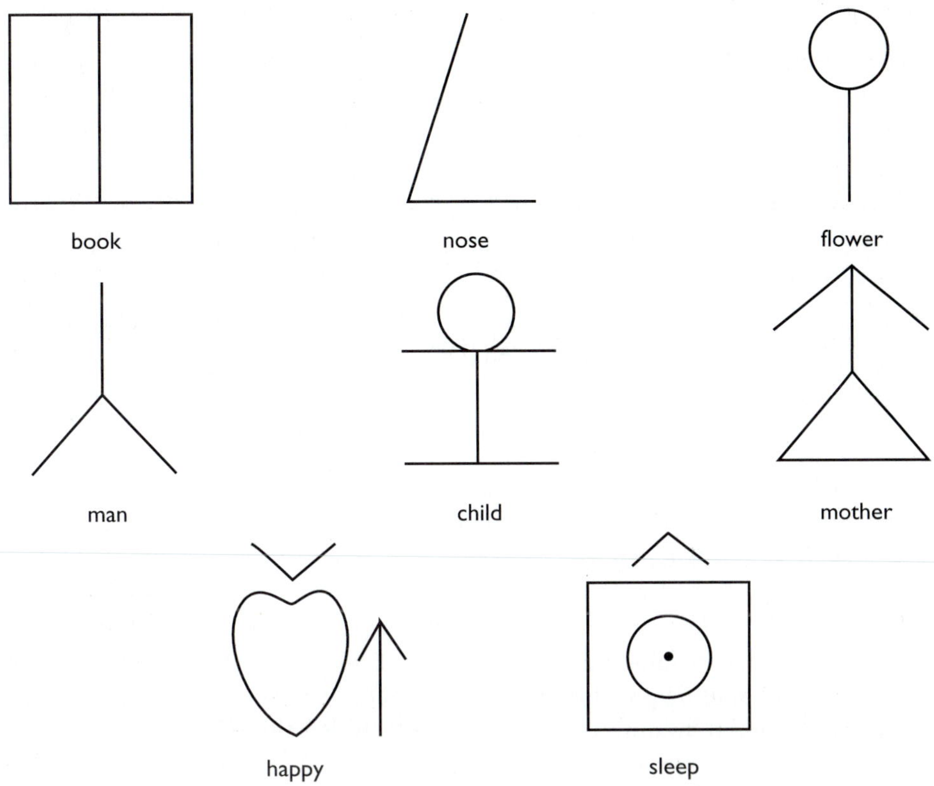

Figure 15-2
Bliss symbols

- Pictorial systems were designed to enhance oral communication among intellectually impaired non-verbal and limited-verbal individuals. They use pictures rather than the stylized symbols of Blissymbolics. For example, Pictorial Ideographic Communication (PIC) is presented on a communication board and consists of pictures and symbols that represent objects and actions.

The idea of using real pictures is based on normal child development, which demonstrates that in the typical child, representational skills emerge early in development. Children as young as twenty-four months of age recognize photographs as symbols of the objects they represent (Daehler, Perlmutter, and Myers, 1976).

Bliss or picture systems are displayed on communication boards. Picture communication boards have clear pictures or photographs depicting basic needs and activities. The board may display pictures of an item of food, a cup, a toilet or pot, a bed, and a toy. The child communicates by pointing to the appropriate pictures.

Studies have compared Blissymbolics and picture symbols (Mezriko, 1987). They report that non-handicapped preschoolers find picture symbols to be more transparent and more learnable than Blissymbolics.

Students Who are Deaf-Blind

Deprivation in one area of distance sense tends to increase reliance on the other. Deprivations in the senses of both vision and hearing place reliance on the near senses of taste, touch, and smell. Children who are deaf and blind therefore have an infinitely

Table 15-2

Alternative methods of communication

	Augmentative communication Aided	Unaided
Signal/code	**Symbol**	**Manual**
yes/no;	rebus systems;	idiosyncratic gesturing;
audio-signalling;	Blissymbolics;	Amerind;
gesturing;	Pictorial Ideographic Communication (PIC)	American Sign Language (ASL);
Morse code		school-based manual systems

more complex task in gaining information about their environments. However, approximately 94 percent of these children have either residual hearing or residual sight (Fredericks and Baldwin, 1987).

Education for deaf-blind children begins with self-care skills such as feeding, grooming, toilet-training, dressing and undressing. Associated with this is motor development, which includes body awareness, relaxation and muscle stimulation, sitting, attaining a standing position, and standing. Other areas then include movement through space, first non-ambulatory movement and then ambulation. Light stimulation, eye control and visual tracking are used for visual training. Auditory training exercises encompass vibration, music, and receptive language.

A primary goal in working with deaf-blind children is to teach them to communicate in the easiest possible way. Language is predicated on the child's ability to take in and interpret sound at some level. Children must be trained to use amplification to discriminate, understand, and remember sound. The first step in teaching expressive skills is to develop a consistent response. The child must be taught a mode of social interaction to indicate need or want. This can be a motor action, a word, or a sound. Once a child has this, he or she can experience having an effect on the environment as well as a means to initiate interactions.

For most deaf-blind children with other impairments, natural gestures offer the best foundation for communication. Natural gestures can be easily individualized. When children can consistently use a variety of gestures, they can begin to move on to more complex communication systems (Watson and Nicholas, 1978).

All children who are capable of speech should undergo intensive speech training. Many deaf-blind children have learned to perceive speech through the vibration method. With this method, the deaf blind person places a thumb on the speaker's lips, an index finger on the speaker's jaw, and three fingers on the speaker's neck. This allows the learner to manually perceive the vibrations of the speaker's voice, the tension of the speaker's face, and the shape of the speaker's lips.

A number of commercial programs have been developed for deaf-blind youngsters; for example, the Assessment-Intervention Model for Deaf-Blind Students (AIM)

(Schein et al., 1983) is a curriculum consisting of specific self-care and independence skills — drinking and pouring; dressing and undressing; using the toilet; personal care; kitchen preparation and clean up; and housekeeping. It provides very low starting points and tiny steps in the sequence of reaching behavioural objectives.

Orientation and Mobility Training Orientation and mobility training teaches individuals who have multiple disabilities that include blindness a basic knowledge of the environment and how to find their way to specific locations, such as the schoolroom or the workshop.

Although the goals of orientation and mobility training for children with multiple handicaps that include visual loss are the same as for other visually impaired children, some of the teaching techniques may differ. Multiply disabled children often need alternative methods that provide safety and information and yet are within their capabilities. Some specialists introduce cane travel before the child is technically ready in the hope of developing greater confidence. This has proved very successful with low-functioning blind children.

Summary

1. A number of useful definitions of multiple disabilities have evolved. Some attempt to offer comprehensive generic descriptions of multiple handicaps; others describe the parameters of types of disabling conditions. More specific definitions have developed to describe particular combinations of handicapping conditions.
2. Medical assessment includes auditory and visual status. A variety of clinical and functional hearing tests should be administered to children with dual sensory impairments over a period of time.
3. The assessment of multiply disabled children is difficult for even the most experienced clinicians. Because the value of IQ scores for diagnosis is relatively limited for this population, a range of assessment measures must be employed; no one measure or battery of measures is suitable for all multiply handicapped children. Assessment serves to generate data for program and placement decisions.
4. The special and diverse needs caused by the unique combinations of conditions challenge all those charged with training and educating multiply disabled children.
5. Education may take place in public schools in regular or special class settings, residential schools, or through school programs in hospitals.
6. Many students who are multiply handicapped require the expertise of specially trained staff, more intensive staffing allocations, community referenced curricula, and/or prosthetic techniques.
7. There are cognitive prerequisites for language acquisition. Some researchers suggest organizing a teaching program around the initial assessment of and subsequent training in cognitive skills. The initial emphasis is on object permanence, classification, imitation, and representational play with objects. Others stress a communication first approach.
8. Children who are unable to acquire oral language may learn other communication methods. Several systems of augmentative communication may be used in place of speech.

SECTION 7

Intervention with Infants, Preschoolers, and Young Adults

Educators are sometimes prone to think of the crucial years as those between about five and eighteen, the time when children and adolescents are students within the formal school system. As educators of students who are normally developing or those with disabilities, we cannot disregard the experiences of the preschool years or ignore the needs of young adults who are leaving the school system.

Having a child with a disability in the family has been acknowledged for many years to be a difficult situation for all family members (Widerstrom and Goodwin, 1987). Like other parents, those with children who are exceptional must learn to cope with problems in ways that will enhance rather than hinder the growth of their children. But in addition to the usual stresses and strains, parents of exceptional children face other pressures. Although families may differ greatly in structure, cultural values, and economic status, most families with a child who is disabled have to cope with additional emotional adjustments and caregiving demands.

To ameliorate the effects of a disability in a very young child and to assist the parents and family in dealing with the associated stress, early identification and early intervention are rapidly expanding and vital elements of contemporary special education. In Canada, the value of early intervention with disabled or delayed children and their families has received widespread recognition (Marfo et al., 1988). Across the country, a range of program options are available to assist young children and their families. Services may be home based, clinic based, in special settings, in regular early childhood settings, or in some combination of these. Central to this commitment to young disabled children and their families is a belief that an array of early intervention services makes possible important differences in the lives of children with disabilities and their families (Guralnick, 1988).

For students nearing the end of their school careers, interesting initiatives are being undertaken. Repeatedly, studies have shown that youths with disabling conditions are not faring well in the adult world, especially in the work force. Schools are becoming more deeply involved with assisting adolescents in negotiating the transition to independent adult living.

The concept and practice of transition is increasingly relevant in both early childhood special education and special education for older adolescents. The term and the concept were first popularized in relation to secondary school students when educators used the term to mean the movement of these older students to new environments, most often from school to work. Current conceptions of transition have taken on a broader meaning. Today, transition also refers to the movement from a home-based program to preschool, from preschool to school, elementary to junior high school, or from hospital to home.

In this section, we examine the manner in which a child with a disability impacts on the family and the influence the family has on the child's development and progress. As well, we discuss some of the types of early intervention that are available to help parents cope with and enhance prospects for optimal development for their exceptional child. Parent involvement and parent training are a major focus as research shows that early childhood special education is not as effective if parents are not involved and supported (Bricker, 1982). We also look at adolescents and the early adult years, particularly at the new initiatives in transition.

CHAPTER 16

Early Intervention

Historical Notes

There is a growing trend in North American educational systems for parents to become more involved in the educational progress of their children. This is a fairly recent phenomenon. Nineteenth-century parents had little say in their children's education; they deferred to educational experts. Schools were used to compensate for the perceived failure of parents, and communities and educators were removed from the direct influence of parents.

Parent-teacher groups sprang up in the opening decades of this century. The first parent group was the National Society for Crippled Children formed in the United States in 1921. In 1933 an Ohio group of parents of children with mental disabilities established a parents' group to advocate the legal and educational rights of disabled children. The United Cerebral Palsy Association began in 1948.

Parent groups, often in uneasy alliance with professionals, grew in the 1940s and 1950s to lobby for more effective education and more humane treatment of persons with disabilities. However, in the actual delivery of services, parents tended to be ignored; they were not invited to participate to any degree. Until the early 1970s, parents remained passive recipients of professional advice. Professionals made the major decisions about a child's needs and educational placement and then worked with the family and other agencies to attain the prescribed goals.

The traditional notion of professional expertise which denies that parents are competent to take the initiative in regard to their child began to change in the 1970s. Since then, parent organizations have had a tremendous impact on special education. Across Canada today, parent organizations exist at the local, provincial, and national level. Some of these groups are small, local, and casual; others are affiliated with professional organizations.

Parents form a strong and powerful constituency. Many parent organizations have lobbied successfully for improved educational, social, recreational, and vocational services for their children. Parent advocacy has altered the standards of treatment in institutions, the development of community-based living facilities, personnel training, and research in prevention and amelioration of disabling conditions. Parent and professional activism has also brought the plight of exceptional children to the courts. In general, parents have filed suits for two reasons. Some have objected to the lack of special education services available for their children. Others have opposed the placement of their children in special classes that they consider inappropriate.

Most professionals agree with parent advocacy. However, some warn that it can lead to adverse situations when special education policy is "formed around parent choice and parental pressure rather than any overriding educational or ethical principle" (Dessent, 1987, p. 140).

All parents want their children to be born healthy, normal, and perfect, with sturdy bones, good vision, working organs and the promise of growing into a normal, intelligent, and happy person. For most parents, the wish is fulfilled; the chances are huge that a child will be born in superlative condition.

While most children are born healthy and well formed, some parents must reduce the expectations they held for their new infant. For them, the not-so-perfect child has been born. Their children are not like other children; they have problems that potentially threaten their physical, intellectual, social, or emotional functioning. When this happens, parents face frustrations stemming from broken dreams; the goals and hopes for the child are no longer clear and the entire family functioning is affected. No family, regardless of wealth, education, religious persuasion, race, or physical and mental health, is immune. About 3 percent of newborn infants have a handicap that can be considered a developmental delay or developmental disability. Another 3 percent are born with significant conditions capable of causing medical or social handicaps (Berlin, 1983). For other children, problems appear later as a result of disease or accident.

The advent of a child with a disability brings such dramatic changes to a family's functioning that professional intervention is often necessary. For the child with a disability, early and sustained intervention increases the likelihood of attaining normal functioning. In early intervention, parents play a crucial role in facilitating and maintaining developmental gains in disabled children.

So important is work with very young children and their families that in 1986 an entirely new field, early childhood special education, was born. (See Development of the Field.)

Intervention may be seen as "care and education aimed at influencing the direction and scope of children's developmental processes" (Doxey, 1990, p. 143). Early intervention is a complex procedure and should be viewed as a means of furthering individual growth and development. **Early intervention** refers to

> a variety of educational, psychological, or therapeutic interventions provided for handicapped, at-risk, or disadvantaged infants and pre-schoolers to prevent or ameliorate developmental delays or disabilities or to provide support to children and families in cases where disabilities exist (Michael and Paul, 1991, p. 202).

Early intervention is directed toward infants, toddlers, and preschoolers. Although the National Association for the Education of Young Children defines the period of early childhood as birth to eight years, the Early Childhood Division of the Council for Exceptional Children recommends a birth-to-five-years age range for early childhood special education.

Children who can benefit from early intervention can be classified in three groups:

- medically or biologically at-risk children who have a history of health factors, such as prematurity, known to be a potential threat to development;
- disabled or developmentally delayed children who have known congenital disorders, sensory impairments, neurological dysfunctions, or significant delays in major areas of functioning;
- environmentally at-risk children who are biologically sound but whose physical or social circumstances (such as poverty, neglect, abuse) may indicate a high probability of delayed development (Dunlap, 1989; Zeitlin and Williamson, 1986).

Traditionally, early intervention was viewed as a child-centred endeavour, the major purpose of which was to enhance the developmental outcomes for young children with disabilities. Over the past five years, the focus has changed and it is now argued that the primary reason for early intervention is family support.

All families live through times of stress as well as joy. Issues such as chronic and acute stress, dual-career and single-parent homes, sexually active youngsters, and drug and alcohol abuse are all major problems that affect today's families. The discovery of a disability in a child causes great distress in many families and adds to existing tensions. However, it is only during the past few decades that professionals have begun to fully appreciate the parental pain and stress that accompany the diagnosis of a disabling condition in a child. We now realize that family problems arising from the presence of a child with a disability require as much professional attention as the educational and medical treatment of the child.

In this chapter, we present an overview of the dilemmas and stresses that may be faced by families of exceptional children. We examine a number of models used to look at families and discuss early identification and the practice of early intervention, including transition to the school system.

Development of the Field

In the very early decades of the nineteenth century, a kindergarten movement stimulated the development of programs for young children. But as educators, parents, and physicians soon came to believe that mental exertion was deleterious to the development of children, the kindergarten movement faded. Kindergarten care, together with day care and nursery education, did not become a feature of American education again until the 1880s.

Education of very young children was incompatible with the school system. Educators saw early adolescence, not early childhood, as the formative years for both normal and exceptional populations. The public schools catered to children from seven or eight years of age and up; disabled youngsters, given the perceived dangers in sending them from home and the demands of the curriculum, were admitted much later. In the schools for the blind, the limit on admittance was frequently set at ten or twelve years of age (Best, 1930). It was generally the same for deaf students; however, owing to the difference thought to exist in the development of intellect of the sexes, it was suggested that boys be admitted at twelve years of age, girls at ten.

In the belief that school was physically, psychologically, and intellectually harmful to children younger than five or six years of age, state officials, medical spokesmen, and schoolmen discouraged the attendance of very young children. Most agreed that a commitment to mental discipline was incompatible with children under the ages of six or seven (Finkelstein, 1985). "The childish brain is very vulnerable at all times," argued teachers of children with mental retardation, and "very much mental stimulus is always hurtful" (Vineland Inst., 1894, p.38).

Not all educators derided mental stimulation for young children with disabilities. Some suggested that they could be more profitably taught at home with the institutional staff acting as advisors to the mothers (Talbot, 1964). Donald Moores (1987) points out that many schools for the deaf developed instructions and procedures for parents to use with their young children and professional journals were sprinkled with suggestions for parents of young children.

In the final three decades of the nineteenth century, the view of the incapacity of young children was revised as part of the emerging child study movement. Infancy was distinguished from childhood as a discrete period of development. Educators, such as Edouard Seguin, described young children as "on the war-path of curiosity" (Thurston, 1876, p. 10) and began to suggest major changes in childhood training methods; they proposed that training ought to follow "the inherent nature of children's minds" (De Guimps, 1906). Children from birth to about six years of age were now seen to be active beings who required play rather than formal lessons, but this could be presented within the confines of educational settings.

Programs for young children with special needs were boosted early in the 1900s when Maria Montessori (1870-1962) began to work with retarded children in Italy. Montessori drew heavily on the sense training methods developed by Itard and Seguin (Lillard, 1972). She established a prepared environment in which children were free to use materials of their own choice at their own pace. Montessori wanted each of the materials to be used in a specific manner to provide a portion of the self-education that she envisoned. Her materials provided experiences with length, breadth, height, colour, texture, weight, size and form.

Montessori was instrumental in establishing educational and rehabilitation programs for retarded children. In addition, she demonstrated how these children could be helped to live fuller, more meaningful lives. Throughout this work, she insisted that mental retardation was an educational, not a medical problem (Montessori, 1912; 1917).

In the early 1960s, the impact of high-risk conditions upon children's later cognitive, linguistic, and social functioning led to the development and implementation of ameliorative programs for disadvantaged pre-schoolers across North America. One of the best known of these early intervention programs was Headstart in the United States, a compensatory program for disadvantaged children that evolved in the mid-1960s.

The late 1960s saw the beginning of what was essentially a melding of early childhood education, special education, and ameliorative programs. Since that time, early childhood special education has been accepted in the educational community as an effective intervention strategy to lessen or ameliorate the negative effects of handicapping conditions (Edmister and Ekstrand, 1987).

On August 5, 1986, the United States Congress enacted Public Law 99-457, the Handicapped Children's Protection Act, as an amendment of PL94-142. PL99-457 and IDEA of 1990 contain three sections critical to preschoolers and their families — Part H; Part B, section 619; and the Early Education Program for Children with Disabilities (EEPCD). These deal specifically with children with disabilities under the age of five and their families.

PL99-457 has been described as "the most important legislation ever enacted for developmentally vulnerable young children" (Shonkoff and Meisels, 1990, p. 19) and has intensified concerns and interest about early intervention in the United States, in Canada, and elsewhere.

In the past, public policies for families with handicapped children have been criticized for being unresponsive to family needs and unsupportive of familial care. PL99-457 relates to both families and children; its mandates explicitly assume that families with disabled children in the United States have a universal claim on public resources and that a family's service needs should be addressed in conjunction with their child's services.

Although the American federal mandates do not provide explicit instructions regarding the exact ways in which parents should be involved in early intervention planning, they do stipulate that a specific plan must be written. The purpose of the Individual Family Service Plan (IFSP) is to identify formal and informal resources and plan how they can be assembled to facilitate attainment of a family's goals for their child and themselves. The law is explicit on aspects of the IFSP'S content and process for development. Specific goals or outcomes for the family and the child must be written, along with the criteria, methods, and timing to be used to evaluate goal attainment. The services needed to achieve prescribed goals (including their frequency, intensity, and method of delivery) must be fully described, and the family's case manager, responsible for implementing the plan, must be named. The process for the development of the IFSP requires that the child's parent(s) be part of the multidisciplinary team that constructs the plan. The team's decisions must be based on a multidisciplinary assessment of the child and family.

Current early childhood special education should be thought of not as parallel care and education but as care and education that is embedded in and integral to early childhood education. Early intervention practices share a general concordance with those in early childhood education, and there are numerous areas of consistency between early childhood intervention and general educational practices.

One of the most important considerations in intervention for children with special needs in today's thinking is that it take place in programs that cater to normally developing children. In both philosophical and pragmatic terms, the most appropriate settings for young children with special needs are comprehensive programs that promote regular contact between normally developing and disabled children. Children with special needs should be placed in a centre where they can achieve at their own level, where they are challenged to develop their potential but not swamped by a program beyond their grasp, where they can receive instruction in areas of need, and where they have opportunities to interact with normally developing children. So while diverse settings and strategies are encompassed under the rubric of early childhood special education, integration with normally developing peers is now viewed as the prime way to educate most young children with exceptionalities.

Parents and Families

Parenting should be counted among the most esteemed professions. But while there are many apprenticeships available for professions and careers, none exist for that most difficult job — parenting. Few study the art — or craft — and there are no courses to teach really practical methods of child-rearing, or to teach parents how to weather the crises, frustrated ambitions, and periods of high stress that are common to most families. Nonetheless, most parents manage to raise their children remarkably well. They willingly endure many trials, problems, and moments of despair, secure in the hope that one day their children will become self-sufficient adults.

Expecting parents have great dreams for their unborn child. They hope for intelligence and physical beauty and plan ahead for later accomplishments and successes. By the time the baby is born, parents are ready to provide for the infant's physical needs and have probably consulted one of the hundreds of volumes on child care and child rearing.

Typically, the birth of a child brings joy and excitement. When a parent holds a newborn close for the first time, feelings of belonging, togetherness, and attachment are initiated. The birth ends the period of expectations about the child and brings new challenges and responsibilities for parents as they adjust to the new family member (Brooks, 1987).

The diagnosis of a disabling condition in a child shatters parental aspirations. The perfect child has died and in its place is a baby with apparent and frightening problems and unknown prospects for the future. When a disability is found, a void is created that is only bridged as the family reformulates its expectations to accommodate reality. The entire family undergoes a crisis, the resolution of which determines whether they will live together in relative peace and contentment or in frustration, anger, and guilt.

The relationship between the exceptional child and the family is reciprocal; the child deeply affects the family climate, while the family, in turn, affects the child. Families often represent the only long-term, responsible, and caring people in the life of a child with a disability. Whether the family is nuclear, single-parent, or extended, it plays a powerful role in the child's social, emotional, behavioural, and academic development and progress. The characteristics of the family — cultural back-ground, socio-economic status, size, even religion — shape its ability to cope with an exceptional child. Each family's unique combination of strengths, stressors, vulnerabilities, and coping styles come into play as the discovery of a disability in a child creates intense and conflicting feelings among the members of a family. Interaction with family members deeply influences the child's opportunities and barriers, challenges and expectations, ambitions and frustrations, and general quality of life.

Looking at Families

There are a number of ways to look at families and to conceptualize the relationship of family members, the child with a disability, the care and treatment of the disabled member, the extended family, and the wider culture. Each of the theoretical frames used to view families is a little different, although they should be seen as a continuum with a different emphasis on certain factors and components of family functioning rather than different variables. Each of these ways of looking at families is important because these frameworks undergird the manner in which professionals present early intervention programs and interact with parents.

At the outset, it should be pointed out that the research literature on families that include a member with a disability or a chronic illness is beset with a host of methodological difficulties that place severe restraints on generalizing the data. Studies conducted prior to 1975 reported four serious effects — higher divorce rates, higher incidence of depression in mothers or siblings, fathers' lack of involvement, and social isolation for the family. Recent studies do not support these stereotypes. Several factors appear to account for these different results. First, methodological problems in older studies cast doubt on the validity of the findings. Second, the mid-1970s saw a positive change in attitudes toward disabled persons in North American society that made it easier for families to keep their child at home and maintain a normal daily life. Third, the passage of PL94-142 in the United States and legislation and initiatives in Canada have resulted in more and better services for families with handicapped children (see Widerstrom and Goodwin, 1987). As well, we now have new ways of conceptualizing families and their interactions with the child, professionals, treatment regimes, and child rearing.

Stage Theories

Stage theories represent the most traditional way of examining a family that includes a member with a disability. Stage theories hold that parents pass through discrete stages before they can fully accept the child's condition (see Table 16-1). Not all parents pass through all of these stages, and each person works through them at a different rate (Eden-Piercy, Blacher, and Eyman, 1986); however, most pass through similar stages before they accept the reality of their child's condition (Chinn, Winn, and Walters, 1978).

Table 16-1

Parental reactions to the diagnosis of a disability

Acute initial reactions	Chronic adaptive reactions	Mature adaptation
shock	withdrawal and isolation	refashioning expectations
denial and disbelief	depression	coping with everyday practical problems
anger	ambivalence	maximizing the child's potential
bitterness and shame	rejection	
loss of self-esteem	overprotectiveness; self-sacrifice; defensiveness	protecting the interests of the whole family
inappropriate guilt, projection of blame	doctor "shopping"	interaction with others
disappointment, sadness, grief, and bargaining		

Acute initial (crisis) reactions accompany the diagnosis of a child's condition. These are mediated by the severity of the handicap, the parents' socio-economic status, their religious orientation, and the quality of external and intrafamily support systems (Ormerod and Huebner, 1988).

Parents are as unique as their children, and differ widely in their responses to their child's disability. The parents' history of dealing with problems will be reflected in their ability to cope with their disabled child. If past crises have tended to produce major upheavals, then the discovery of a disability in a child will only add to the existing problems. If the parents have been able to make healthy adjustments to past difficulties, they are more likely to find the route to acceptance easier. Some parents cope with steady resolve and competence; others barely manage to survive the daily routine.

When first confronted with their child's condition, most parents react with shock, often accompanied by denial and disbelief. Their expectations are violated and their hopes shattered. The period of shock is usually brief because of the necessity for making decisions regarding treatment. Parents must be concerned with the provision of daily care for their child. They may have to arrange transportation to treatment, alter methods of scheduling time, meet new financial costs, and assimilate technical information about the disability. Parents may also have to provide support for other family members (Fortier and Wanless, 1984).

In instances of clearcut organic damage or with conditions such as Down syndrome, the child will probably be diagnosed at birth or shortly afterwards and the parents will learn about the problem immediately. Other parents may discover a problem more slowly as the child matures and tends to lag behind others of the same age. When the problem is not detected at birth, parents may start to suspect some disability when their child is too slow in reaching developmental milestones.

Parents of children with severe disabilities may not deny the handicap, especially if they themselves were the first to recognize the child's disability, as in the case of deafness (Kroth, 1987). They may even respond positively when they find that they were not imagining problems. Some mothers have described feelings of relief on the confirmation of their suspicions, not defensive reactions (Faerstein, 1986). Once the problem is verbalized and labelled, some parents find that they can mobilize both the defensive and coping mechanisms available to them. For other parents, the confirmation of a diagnosis results in a compelling need for knowledge (Hobbs, Perrin, and Ireys, 1985).

In some cases, on the other hand, parents' initial grief may be more intense when the diagnosis is made well after the birth of the child. By this time, their hopes for the child have lasted longer and their bonds of affection have grown stronger (Fortier and Wanless, 1984). The period of denial may be more protracted, especially if the condition is not readily obvious to the parents. Denial may operate as a protective device, giving parents additional time to adjust to the pain and disappointment of lost expectations. Denial becomes maladaptive, however, when it results in the withholding of treatment necessary to ensure the child's optimal development. Unwittingly, family, friends, and even professionals, may support parental denial. Anxious to relieve the parents' worries, they may suggest that the child will "grow out" of the condition, and parents may delay proper treatment as a result.

Parents may also feel anger when they learn of their child's condition. In fact, anger can be the most enduring emotion among parents of handicapped children (Hall and Richmond, 1984). Some come to believe that the world is against them, as health practitioners, teachers, neighbours, and relatives confront them with the reality they do not want to accept. Initially parents may direct their anger at the child as the obvious source of frustration. When parents turn the anger inward, they can react with fear, guilt, and shame.

Fear arises when parents hold misfounded apprehensions and incorrect information about the disability, the implications, and the prognosis. Some parents worry that the handicap might be of a genetic nature and are led to worry about their future children, or sometimes to view the handicap as a defect in themselves. Many parents develop understandable apprehensions about their child's future life. Major concerns are sexual, social, and occupational exploitation of their offspring.

Parents who feel shame see their disabled child as a threat to the family's prestige. They worry about social stigma and anticipate social rejection. Some parents feel guilt because they think the condition could have been avoided if they had done something different. Others believe the disability serves as retribution for some misdeed. Parents ask, "Why us?" and seek answers in factors such as marital discord, prenuptial pregnancy, unusual sex practices, use of drugs, and unusual events during pregnancy.

Sometimes parents project guilt on others. They direct resentment and hostility at their spouses, their other children, the doctor, the counsellor, society in general, even God. Some parents question their religious beliefs; others find solace in them. Studies have found parents with a strong religious affiliation to be more accepting; their religious beliefs seem to sustain them through difficult situations in raising a child with an impairment (Erin, Rudin, and Njoroge, 1991; Zuk, 1962). For other parents, having a child with a disability destabilizes their religious beliefs; they begin to question a previously held belief in God (Erin, Rudin, and Njoroge, 1991). Preconceived notions about God, fate, a just world and their implications for personal existence, are often challenged (Chester and Barbarin, 1987).

Mourning or grief is a natural reaction to the disappointment of having a child with a disability. Like anger, denial, and guilt, grief follows the initial diagnosis and takes on different forms in different families. For some parents, grief results in withdrawal and depression. Others take recourse in bargaining — trying to make a deal with God, science, or society to cure their child. The feelings of grief may be complicated as parents mourn the lost perfect child while the child with the exceptionality is very much alive and making demands for attention and care (Trout, 1983). Grief may continue to some extent throughout the parents' life, never disappearing completely (Wikler, Wasow, and Hatfield, 1981).

With a severe disability, the family's adjustment to the idea of future dependency can be made fairly easily (Turnbull, Summers, and Brotherston, 1984). But with a milder disability, the family may find itself on a roller coaster of expectations, with hopes for the future alternately dashed and raised as the child progresses or falls back (Wadsworth and Wadsworth, 1971).

Some parents are never able to completely accept their child's condition. They may accept the diagnosis but reject the prognostic implications. Such parents are vulnerable to even the most unsubstantiated claims for cures or relief. They may embark on a trek from doctor to doctor and clinic to clinic in search of a more promising prognosis, miracle drugs, a new operation, a novel form of psychotherapy, or a radically new diet. Probably as many parents seek other opinions not because they reject or cannot handle their child but because they are simply seeking clarity about the problem (O'Hara and Levy, 1984). If a parent visits five professionals and obtains five different diagnoses, the ensuing confusion and need for clarification become obvious.

Some parents may reject the child as well as the condition. They may treat the child with open hostility, or use more subtle ploys, such as setting unrealistic goals or failing to praise positive behaviour. Other parents may develop positive and accepting attitudes, but nevertheless harbour resentment toward the child. Every parent must occasionally feel ambivalent about restricted activities, additional responsibilities, disappointments, and anxieties. If parents feel guilty about their ambivalent feelings, they may become overprotective and oversolicitous and try to compensate for their negative feelings with a life of martyrdom and self-sacrifice.

Such attitudes can foster an overdependency in the child which will eventually become circuitous. In the course of investing themselves emotionally in the child, these parents exaggerate the child's needs and promote an overly dependent attitude. Then, to prove their worth as parents, they allow their whole lives to become centred on the child. Such parents may actually resist attempts by others to ease the burden.

Most parents reach a stage of mature adaptation which is the end of the crisis period. However, acceptance does not come all at once; it begins fleetingly and goes on to fluctuate at different levels in different situations. Parental sadness may resurface at critical junctures in the life of the child and the family. A reoccurrence of sorrow and frustration may be triggered by milestones such as reaching school age, attaining puberty, and watching other children graduate from school or marry.

When parents have reached this stage, they can accept the child, the disability, and themselves. They become reconciled to the fact that their child's condition deeply affects, and will continue to affect, the entire family. As one mother explained,

> The whole process of having a handicapped child hurts. It's not the greatest thing on the face of the earth, but life throws these little curves at us and we can make our adjustments if we have good supports. Then, having a handicapped child becomes just like having any other child in the family. You deal with the problems that come along just as for any child (Wilgosh, 1990, p. 302).

Parents do not differ significantly in their level of acceptance (McLinden, 1990). Some earlier studies indicated lack of involvement with and acceptance of the child by the father (e.g., Farber and Ryckman, 1965). Investigators found that fathers, more than mothers, were affected in the social domain. Fathers had more difficulty coping with the child, were more vulnerable to social stigma, and encountered more difficulty living with the uncertainty of the child's impairment and discussing the problem with friends (Erickson, 1976). Later, Moran (1982) reported fathers to be positively involved with their handicapped children, playing with them, and helping with their daily care. Another investigator (McLinden, 1990) examined the differences between mothers and fathers in the areas of social support and family satisfaction, and in their reported frequency-of-occurrence and degree-of-problem of events and feelings related to the presence of a child with special needs. Mothers had a higher frequency of demands placed on their lives than did fathers and also experienced more negative physical and emotional states.

Life-cycle Approach

Instead of adopting a stage approach, some researchers tend to view the family and the impact of a member with a disability through a **life-cycle or lifespan approach**. A life-cycle perspective sees the family as a unit that is moving through time and experiencing a series of events, tasks, and transitions. By looking at the family life cycle, it can be seen that the impact of the disabled child on the family changes over time.

Life-cycle transitions are experienced by all families, and there seem to be specific periods which result in increased stress (Wikler, Wasow, and Hatfield, 1981). For all families with children, these are the age at which the child should begin to walk; the age at which the child should begin to talk; entry into the public school system; onset of puberty; and the twenty-first birthday. When a child with a disability is a member of the family, transitions may also include events such as first encountering the handicap; early childhood; school entry; when the development of a younger sibling surpasses that of the disabled child; when placement outside the home is considered; when a child-management crisis occurs; adolescence; beginning adult life; maintaining adult life; and when guardianship issues are discussed. These events can serve to magnify a child's special needs and create heightened stress in the family. However, each family is unique. The same event will bring different meanings and different responses from different families, so determining an individual family's responses and understanding is essential.

Systems Approach

The work of ecological theorists and of social systems theory is exerting a great deal of influence on the early intervention movement. Currently, a systems approach is seen as the most appropriate way to view families with a disabled member.

A family is more than individuals bound by a biological relationship. A **systems theory** or perspective recognizes that actions in any part of the system affect the other parts and that solutions to problems can only be found when the problem is properly defined in its larger environmental context. Under a systems model, influences are seen as multidirectional. Each adult and child influences every member of the household and each family relationship affects all the other family members. Therefore, the outcomes of any child-rearing patterns on any child depend on many factors that interact with each other. These include the child's age, sex, and temperament; the parents' personality characteristics, personal history, economic circumstances, and so on; the needs of family members; and the values of the culture.

Social Support Approach

In many ways, the social support approach overlaps the systems approach; the difference is mainly one of emphasis. Whereas a systems approach focuses chiefly on the social context of the family, a **social support approach** focuses on a family's functioning. It stresses families helping themselves and sees informal support such as the extended family and church as more important than formal support.

Family support approaches focus on the complex interactions of four family subsystems — marital, sibling, parental, and extra-familial (Carter and McGoldrick, 1980). It includes two major concepts — embededness and social networks influence. Embededness refers to the fact that a developing child is enveloped within the family system and its members, and that the family unit is embedded in broader social units consisting of relatives, friends, neighbours, church members, and so on. These people — the family's social network — directly and indirectly influence both the family and the child (Dunst et al., 1990).

The Condition

Another way to look at families is on the basis of the type of condition. This is not a theoretical model or approach as are the others mentioned, but it does recognize that the nature of a child's disability can have a substantial impact on parental stress and levels of acceptance. Researchers (Frey, Greenberg, and Fewell, 1989) have found that a child's characteristics predict the amount of stress that parents report and the amount of psychological stress reported by fathers.

Most observers conclude that raising a child with a disability is often burdensome, tiresome, and frustrating. Having a handicapped baby or toddler in the household often adds additional demands and stresses. High levels of family stress may be created by a particular child's slower progress, more difficult temperament, lack of social responsivenness, stereotypic behaviour patterns, or additional or unusual caregiving needs. Research in families with infants indicates that role confusion, social isolation, fatigue, financial worries, and lack of information on child development are cited by new mothers as primary causes of stress (Salisbury, 1987). Behaviours that parents of

Table 16-2

Looking at families

Model	Principles	Major focus
Stage theory	Parents pass through discrete stages from grief to acceptance	Parent counselling Parent therapy Parent self-help groups Information about the condition
Life-cycle theory	Families pass through cycles in which there may be crises transition points	Transition support Liaison with other agencies Family support Intervention with the child
Systems theory	The family is a system within the larger social context	Priorities set by the family Stress on all family members Functional skills for the child Improved functioning within family needs
Social support theory	Families are systems of themselves	Families helping themselves Families setting priorities Advocating for child

disabled infants have identified as most difficult, stressful, or uncomfortable are crying, resisting being held, being hard to soothe, passive non-responsiveness, tuning out, and emitting atypical motor responses.

Symptoms of stress are more evident among parents of childen with delayed rather than prompt diagnoses and with unknown rather than specified etiologies (Goldberg et al., 1986). Stress is also more evident among families when the child has a severe or profound rather than a mild or moderate condition (Frey, Greenberg, and Fewell, 1989). Studies have found greater stress reported by parents of boys and of children with limited communication skills (Frey, Greenburg, and Fewell, 1989).

Stress may occur from the outset if the attachment process between disabled infants and their parents is disrupted. Children who show disturbed interactions include preterm, Down syndrome, blind, autistic, and failure to thrive infants (Field, 1983). Some disruption may arise from the medical needs of the child. Premature and handicapped infants may be kept in neonatal intensive care for up to twelve weeks, depending on birth-weight, gestational age, physical anomalies, respiration, and weight gain. Early separation naturally affects the bonding between parent and child and may adversely affect later parent-child interactions.

Research Notes

Pre-term infants

When an infant is pre-term, many parents encounter dramatically different transitions to parenthood than they had anticipated. While the development of the premature infant is critically dependent on the parents' providing an adequate caregiving environment, social enrichment, and encouragement (Rice, 1977; Sigman et al., 1981), stressful experiences may affect the establishment of these relations.

Parents of biologically at-risk infants encounter emotional and behavioural differences in the course of early parenthood that may lead to less than optimal parent-child attachments (Easterbrooks, 1989). The early arrival of the infant can occur before the parents are psychologically and practically ready for parenthood (Levy-Shiff and Sharir, 1989). Parents must confront feelings of disappointment and failure as well as anxieties over the infant's survival, health, and development. In addition to the parent's early emotional reactions, several other factors may increase the risk of interactional difficulties among pre-term infants and their parents, including physical separation due to hospitalization and the characteristics of the infant's behaviour and appearance.

The initial stay in the hospital nursery for a prolonged period may hinder the development of attachment and certainly leaves restricted opportunities for parents and child to engage in social interactions. Lack of social interactions are often exacerbated by the effects of the surroundings (Gottfried and Wallace-Lande, 1981). The intimidating environment of the intensive care unit, the aversive medical procedures and intrusive monitoring may result in emotional withdrawal of the parents and estrangement from the infant.

In addition, the premature infant deviates from infant norms in size, weight, appearance, and pattern of crying, as well as in self-regulated behaviours and interactive skills — pre-term infants are less active, less alert, and less responsive. Low-birth-weight pre-term babies are described as less attractive, more irritating, and less likeable (Stern and Hilderbrandt, 1984), with cries that are more aversive to adults. They are less readily engaged in social play, show less positive emotion, and are more easily overstimulated and difficult to console once they become disorganized.

Early intervention is important for premature infants. The *Journal of the American Medical Association* in 1990 reported on the results of the largest study ever done of an intervention for low-birth-weight infants. After studying nearly 1000 premature infants from birth to three years of age in eight American cities, the researchers showed that outcomes for premature low-birth-weight infants known to be at risk for developmental, behavioural, and health problems can be significantly improved with early comprehensive intervention. Low-birth-weight infants in a control group who did not receive early education and developmental services were nearly three times more likely to have IQ scores in the range of mentally retarded.

Many children with disabilities are less responsive than other children and parents need to work harder to focus their attention and generate smiles and contented vocalizations. However, the stimulation threshold for handicapped children is more difficult to judge and maintain. A major problem in interactions is finding the optimal level of stimulation to elicit response from these infants. Low levels elicit few responses, whereas once an optimal level is passed the child reacts with gaze aversion or fusses and cries and is then harder to console (Field, 1983).

Children with problems such as Fetal Alcohol Syndrome, Down syndrome, and cleft palate may have feeding problems and limited abilities to suck, bite, chew, or swallow. Feeding problems are common among autistic infants, beginning with poor nursing habits and continuing through infancy and childhood. Children with chronic conditions such as cystic fibrosis require intense medical and therapeutic intervention.

Teachers and other professionals must understand parents' problems and be flexible, open, and empathetic.

The age of the child may also be related to the stress felt by the family. One mother pointed out that "the stress level of women with handicapped children increases as the child gets older" (Wilgosh, 1990, p. 302). If a severely handicapped child does not develop sufficient independence and autonomy, that child may permanently occupy the social position of the youngest in the family — the perpetual baby who never emerges from infantile status. This can easily become elevated to a source of conflict and difficulty. As well, as they grow older, children become harder to manage. At the same time, the gap between the progress of exceptional children and their peers becomes more noticeable (Bristol, 1979).

Parents with exceptional children must also take on new roles — educator, lobbyist, advocate, therapist and, of course, chauffeur. In addition, financial burdens can cause parents constant concern and frustration. The need for special equipment, special medical care, and special programs often brings financial hardship. Economic pressures can distort the family's emotional response to their child, particularly in families with limited financial resources.

The discovery that a child is intellectually disabled causes great stress for the parents and other family members. Across all socio-economic levels, mothers of mentally retarded children report depression (Breslau and Davis, 1986). Parents must eventually confront three critical issues. They must decide how to train and educate the child, accept that the child may never be self-sufficient, and decide the child's future after they die.

Parents of learning-disabled children may seem, at first glance, much more fortunate than parents of children with more severe disabilities. In fact, when a child is identified as learning disabled, parents may feel relieved at first, hoping this identification will lead to solutions that will eliminate the child's learning or behaviour problem (Bos and Vaughn, 1988). However, learning disabilities create much confusion within the family and families can be greatly affected by the presence of the child (Waggoner and Wilgosh, 1990). In particular, a lack of clear diagnosis may cause great concern and anxiety, resulting in high levels of stress for parents. Faerstein (1986), for example, found that a gap of 3.5 years elapsed between the time a learning disability was suspected and its diagnosis. This gap was not due to the mother's lack of responsibility, but more often to others who denied the child's problem and averred that he or she would outgrow it.

The receptive and expressive language problems of learning-disabled children may cause them to appear slow, confused, impulsive, inattentive, or even obstinate. Parents may react to these problems with guilt, overprotection, rejection, or concern. Some parents react by placing too much responsibility on the child; others deny the gravity of the problem. Still others place responsibility on themselves and accept failure.

Deaf children with hearing parents comprise more than 90 percent of the deaf population. Hearing parents are much more likely than deaf parents to view their child's diagnosis as a tragic crisis. Hearing parents often express feelings of incompetence, self-doubt, and sorrow. In some cases, the birth of a hearing-impaired child threatens family integration and destroys the balance of family relationships (Meadow, 1980).

Many parents of infants with severe visual impairments feel anxious and apprehensive, even grief-stricken, when they learn of their child's disability. Parents may be worried and frustrated by the infant's responses, or seeming lack of responses. Attachment behaviours between infants and parents are facilitated by the infant's ability to elicit parental responses, but very young visually impaired children do not always react to their parents in the same way that sighted children do (Ferrell, 1985). For example, blind babies do not reach out in the "Pick me up" gesture seen in sighted babies at about five months. The facial expressions of blind babies are less varied and less frequently seen; blind babies smile significantly less frequently than sighted ones, and the mother's voice does not automatically and consistently evoke smiling. As well, blind babies vocalize much less frequently than do sighted babies, and their vocalizations to initiate contact with parents appear much later, even when families encourage such interaction and reward it (Fraiberg, 1977).

Of all caretaking demands, none seems to have more impact than the demands of coping with a child who has a behavioural problem. When parents cannot handle or control the child fully, the integrity of the family is threatened. Parents can become physically and emotionally exhausted; the abusive, destructive, cantankerous behaviour of the disordered youngster causes disruption and disharmony in the home.

Parents of children with special health care needs suffer many traumas and stresses. Family reactions include depression, denial, anxiety, resentment and anger. Parents must deal with the abbreviated life expectancy of the child; some must handle the additional stress of a dying child.

When conventional medical treatment fails, parents of children with serious health disabilities sometimes hunt for miracle cures and faith healers. They may focus normal feelings of anger upon medical personnel, other family members, or any other available target. They may experience feelings of guilt, believing they should have noticed symptoms sooner or been more lenient in their discipline. Parents often transmit their anxiety to the child. They may also create conflict and jealousy among siblings by spending a disproportionate amount of time with the special child.

Raising and training a psychotic or autistic child can cause enormous stress for parents and family. Caregivers must contend with the bizarre withdrawn attitudes of autism or the clinging behaviours of schizophrenia.

Children who are autistic are likely to ignore the presence of their mother or other family members, and the parents are continually faced with their children's failure to respond to interaction. The deviant gaze pattern, known as **gaze aversion** (the failure to look directly at another individual) is a conspicuous characteristic of the autistic population and severely hinders parent-child interaction. As well, children tend to show little response to their mother's voice, do not anticipate being picked up, and do not adapt their body postures to the people holding them. These behaviours inevitably have a deep effect on parental interaction and are compounded in later years by the children's lack of verbal responsiveness and bizarre and inappropriate behaviours.

For the parents, the gifted child may be both a blessing and a burden. Although giftedness is socially acceptable, many parents of gifted children are bewildered and frustrated about issues related to both home and school. For one thing, the advent of a gifted child can alter normal parental roles. Ross (1979) hypothesized that the degree of a gifted child's impact on traditional family roles is directly related to the degree of discrepancy between the gifted child's intellectual capacity and that of other family members. Parents sometimes have difficulty clarifying the differences between parent and child roles. They wonder whether they should treat their offspring as a child or as an adult.

Gifted children are advantaged in many ways, but they may cause some disruption within the family.

A gifted child can cause parents to question their capabilities and assume an added sense of responsibility. Parents may feel pressured to develop basic parenting skills and specific strategies for encouraging learning at home. They may feel inadequate in the management of their child and unsure about how to stimulate him or her in and out of school. Parents may treat the child differently. When children are labelled as gifted, mothers clearly distinguish them from unlabelled children. Labelled children are rated higher than their siblings in academics, art, creativity, leadership, music, and social skills (Tuttle and Cornell, 1993). Then the family of a gifted child may wish to make special adaptations that can include costly and time-consuming measures, such as special schools and extra equipment. When special adaptations are made for the child, sibling competition and jealousy may result. Siblings may resent the extra money and attention spent by their parents. Cornell (1983) found that siblings of gifted children were significantly less adjusted emotionally and socially than siblings of non-gifted students. Moreover, if parents give the gifted preschooler too much attention, that child may later meet difficulties in coping with sibling and peer competition (Rimm and Lowe, 1988). Finally, parents of gifted children often have to choose between regular class placement and special programming — and even experts cannot agree on which is the best option.

Siblings

Brothers and sisters play important parts in the entire family drama, serving as a source of both nurturance and discomfort. Children share their parents' anticipation and excitement about a new addition to the family; they also share the grief, stress, and pain that accompanies the birth of a disabled brother or sister (Milstead, 1988; Seligman, 1991). While the reaction varies, the way that siblings respond invariably affects parental functioning, and vice versa.

The relationship between siblings is special and intimate, particularly during childhood when siblings serve each other as playmates, models for identification, caretakers, and socializing agents. In these roles, siblings have a profound influence on each other's social and emotional development.

Many variables affect sibling relationships. Roles are affected by family size, birth order, gender, responsibilities and roles of all family members, temperaments, feelings and perceptions of self, personalities and their match, personal values and attitudes, and style. Other variables include style and effectiveness of communication, expression or lack of expression of feelings, time management, perceived and actual favouritism, type of control exerted in the household, economic and marital status, marital harmony, competition and rivalry, outside stress and coping mechanisms, parenting and caregiving styles, and parents' attitudes toward themselves, one another, and their children (Atkins, 1987).

Sibling relationships take on special significance when one sibling is disabled. But although the points of view of parents have been investigated in depth, the possible consequences to children having a sibling with a disability have received little attention in the research literature (Edmundson, 1985), and a general picture of sibling interaction with the exceptional child has not emerged. It seems that most families function adequately and the outcomes for the other children can range from very little effect to very positive or very negative ones (Yura, 1987).

When there are concerns about siblings, they seem to fit into the following groupings:

- Role confusion. The roles a sibling normally assumes are somehow altered. A child with a disability may not function as a playmate, a caretaker, or a socializing agent for his or her siblings.

- The kind and amount of attention the disabled child requires of parents and siblings. The parents' attempts to protect the child with a disability may result in various degrees of neglect for the other children in the family and may interfere with their normal child-parent relationship, with family activity, and with social life outside the home. Researchers (Cantwell, Baker, and Rutter, 1979) found that mothers spent twice as much time in concentrated interaction with the child with a disability as they did with normally developing siblings.
- Disappointment at not having a normal sibling.
- The embarrassment of relating to the disabled sibling in the company of peers or in public.
- The heavy demands on normal siblings to care for the disabled child. In some families, the handicapped child may generate caretaking responsibilities and siblings may become overworked caretakers. Females, especially older sisters, are more likely to be adversely affected by a disabled sibling. Older sisters with mentally retarded siblings, for example, assume multiple caretaking responsibilities (Stoneman et al., 1988) and frequently assume a teacher role (Brody et al., 1991).

  When non-handicapped siblings are required to supervise, care for, defend, and protect the handicapped child, resentment often develops. Excessive responsibility for caretaking by siblings is related to anger, guilt, increased sibling conflict, decreased opportunities for peer contacts and out-of-home activities and, quite possibly, subsequent psychological damage (Seligman, 1991; Stoneman et al., 1988).
- The pressure on the normal child to "make up" for the deficits in the disabled child. Siblings may find themselves recipients of uneven expectation standards as compensation for parental disappointment. Sometimes, non-handicapped children are made to bear unrealistically high parental expectations. Or they may be expected to repress their abilities so that they do not perform better than the exceptional child.
- Some parents may develop different ways of treating the normally developing children and the child with a disability. Because parents feel uncertainty regarding the care and management of a disabled child, they may subject that child to patterns of socialization that are significantly different from those that operate in the case of the other children. They may allow two quite different disciplinary systems to run side by side — one for the non-handicapped children, and a more lenient, permissive one for the handicapped child. Some parents treat their disabled children as though they were ill; they give them fewer responsibilities, place fewer restrictions on behaviour, and are more tolerant of undesirable behaviour, often at the expense of other siblings. Two different sets of rules intensify sibling rivalry. A twelve-year-old sister of a hearing-impaired child complained, "I have to clean up my room and Mom cleans up Sherry's. That's just not fair. Her ears don't work, but her hands do" (Atkins, 1987).
- Resentment is aggravated when additional care expenses deprive the others of educational and recreational opportunities. Siblings share family resources and the sibling relationship may be negatively affected by the additional resources required by the special child (Dyson and Fewell, 1989).
- There are only a few empirical studies on the self-concept of the siblings of children with disabilities, and their results are conflicting. Some research has found that children who have siblings with disabilities scored more poorly than children with non-disabled siblings on almost every measure of internalized adjustment problems. Others have found lower than average self-concept in siblings of children with phys-

The relationship between siblings is particularly close during childhood, a time when children serve each other as playmates, role models, and caregivers.

ical handicaps (Harvey and Greenway, 1984) and with diabetes (Ferrari, 1987). In contrast, a study of 74 American and Canadian children with handicapped and non-handicapped siblings (Dyson and Fewell, 1989) showed no differences in level of self-concept. Further research has found no difference in the self-concept of siblings of chronically ill (Ferrari, 1984) and developmentally handicapped (Lobato et al., 1987) children. One study (Gayton et al., 1977) found higher than average self-concept in the siblings of children with cystic fibrosis.

The Extended Family

Children with disabilities have a considerable influence on the extended family. At the same time, the extended family may influence the development of disabled children through direct interactions and through the nature of the support provided to their parents.

There exists relatively little research on the grandparents of normal children, much less the grandparents of children with disabilities. However, in many ways, grandchildren provide a new lease on life for their grandparents (Benedek, 1970). The sense of surviving through the grandchild may help soothe the increasing infirmities of advancing age and the approaching reality of death. Grandchildren also allow grandparents to relive the joys of their own early parenthood. Playing with and caring for young grandchildren supplies grandparents with a revitalized feeling of importance and purpose in life (Gabel and Kotsch, 1981).

Like parents, grandparents hope for a healthy, normal baby. When a child is diagnosed as exceptional, they too may experience a death of expectations (Berns, 1980) that can leave them with a diminished capacity to provide support for the child's parents. Generally, more support is provided by the maternal than the paternal grandmother (Harris, Handleman, and Palmer, 1985). Such support is consistent with the maternal grandmother's understanding of her daughter's distress. On the other hand, some paternal grandmothers express their resentment toward their daughters-in-law. Pieper (1976) described how her mother-in-law lashed out in anger when presented with a disabled grandchild. The grandmother blamed the daughter-in-law for having bad blood and burdening her husband with such a child.

Early Intervention

The child with a disability has a major impact on the family. The impact, while not necessarily negative, does require modifications in family structure and roles. Parents and siblings are bound to run into problems and may need the aid of outside sources to solve them. Parents require assistance in understanding the nature and prognosis of the condition; in handling the child; in stimulating mobility, locomotion and communication; and in responding appropriately to different or unexpected behaviours.

Children who are exceptional require special assistance. This assistance may be needed for a limited time or throughout their educational careers; it should begin as early as possible, even in infancy. For the child, the chances of ever catching up are directly related to how quickly intervention begins after deficits are identified and how great the discrepancy is between the child's real and expected levels of performance (Peterson, 1987).

The term *early intervention* has a number of meanings and the meanings have changed over the past twenty years. At the present time, debate continues as to what is really encompassed by early intervention. A number of people believe that the term *early intervention* should be confined to infant and toddler programs and that *early childhood special education* or *preschool special education* should be used with three-, four-, and five-year-old children (Bricker, 1993). We use the terms *early intervention* and *early childhood special education* interchangeably. We see early childhood special education as a subset of early intervention and see the terms as applicable to all children in the early years, from infancy to kindergarten.

Early intervention cannot be separated from its natural corollary, early identification. Early identification serves no purpose if it is not followed by early intervention, and appropriate early intervention rests on accurate identification.

Early identification may be seen as the practice of screening infants and young children in an attempt to identify those likely to experience problems in learning or behaviour. The optimal time for screening is still a matter of debate, but there is increasing evidence to support preschool identification procedures. The early detection of a child's problems may prevent the development of more complex learning difficulties later in life. Following identification, early intervention activities are directed toward ameliorating problems in children with established disabilities and toward intervention with children who are at risk in order to prevent or hinder the development of conditions that impair learning or behaviour.

The current vitality of early intervention processes stem from varied sources.

- Research in child development clearly demonstrates that the early years are a time of rapid learning. Benjamin Bloom (1964), for example, summarized a plethora of studies on intellectual growth and suggested that a stimulating environment is critical to optimal cognitive growth. He proposed that intellectual development can be seen as following a negative growth curve; as the child grows older, a rich and diverse environment has a decreasingly positive effect. By the time children are six years old, almost two-thirds of their ultimate cognitive ability is formed. After the age of six, the child's potential for further intellectual growth is slowed. Thus, children at the age of three will benefit more from enrichment activities than children aged eight to ten. For this early learning, both research and experience show that young children can learn at least as well outside the home as in it.
- Early intervention can "help ensure that all young children reach their full developmental potential; that they can become valued and full participants in their families, schools and communities; and that their families benefit from consistent and supportive collaboration with service providers" (see CEC Position, 1993b).
- Early services can maximize skill development and reduce or alleviate the need for special services when a child enters school (Guralnick, 1989). Both developmental and educational intervention are likely to be more effective if they occur before the child's deficiencies become massive and are compounded by the numbing effects of extended school failure (Satz and Fletcher, 1979).
- Intervention sustains growth. Among preschoolers, for example, Down syndrome is the most frequent specific diagnosis in the population of delayed children (Lojkesek et al., 1990). For Down syndrome children, early and sustained intervention halts the decline in cognitive development that typically occurs during the first twelve to eighteen months of life (see Guralnick and Bricker, 1987) and appears to prevent further decreases throughout the remaining early childhood years. Similar outcomes have been observed for the motor development of children with cerebral palsy (Palmer et al., 1988).
- For the family, early intervention serves as a support that enhances family functioning, provides crucial information for parents, and makes parents the primary players in their child's developmental progress. Activities are designed to support families to the greatest extent possible. These family-centred activities optimally include the siblings and the extended family as well as the parents. In one study of the parents of children with disabilities (Winton and Turnbull, 1981), approximately two-thirds of the parents surveyed felt that the major value of early intervention was to provide a break from their continuous responsibility for the child.

Given the field's newness and rapid expansion, it is little wonder that the education and training of infants and preschoolers with disabilities is an area characterized by innovation and creativity. It also encompasses a variety of program models, many trends and movements, and not a little controversy. The major issues today do not revolve around the question of whether or not to provide early intervention but rather focus on the most effective and efficient type of intervention.

A Matter of Debate

Early intervention

Studies of early intervention programs cannot conclusively document positive effects for a range of problems and disability groups. Although the integration of children with exceptionalities with their normally developing peers is clearly the most appropriate option for many children, controversy and discussion still cloud the issue. However, the major issues today do not revolve around the question of whether or not to provide early intervention programs but rather focus on the most effective and efficient types of intervention.

Arguments in favour	Arguments against
For infants and toddlers with disabilities, early intervention is crucial to later educational success. In 52 reviews of early intervention efficacy studies, 92 percent of the reviews concluded that early intervention provided significant immediate effects for children who are disabled, at risk, or disadvantaged (White, Bush, and Casto, 1986). Outcomes for children are better in integrated rather than segregated programs. Children in segregated programs often miss the potential social and cognitive benefits of integration. Language abilities improve in integrated programs. Studies document substantial changes in language abilities of preschool children with autism exposed to an intensive language stimulation program (Harris et al., 1990). Segregated early intervention programs may make young children with disabilities overly dependent on adults and make their transition to school or kindergarten more difficult (Hamachek and Kauffman, 1994). The successful teaching of children with disabilities demands that trained professionals be equipped with skills for dealing with their unique characteristics and needs.	Critics of early intervention complain that too much has been claimed and too little proven concerning the efficacy of early intervention. Children in specialized settings obtain assistance for their specific disabilities. Edmister and Ekstrand (1987) point out that "generally, the only documented benefit from integration of handicapped and non-handicapped preschool-aged children seems to be in the social domain" (p. 133). Sustained social outcomes in integrated settings have been found only when interaction is frequent, planned, and carefully orchestrated by teachers. In and of itself, regular early childhood education is not designed to intervene with young children with special needs. Most teachers in general, and preschool and day-care teachers in particular, are not trained to serve children with disabilities (Rule et al., 1985). Most typical preschools do not have the rich training and staffing resources that might facilitate inclusion of children with special needs (Peck et al., 1988).

Arguments in Favour	Arguments Against
Research clearly indicates that personnel who are well trained are more effective than those who are not (Tingey-Michaelis, 1985).	Studies have failed to find adequate relationships between the intensity of intervention and the age of start and effect size. There are no conclusive data to indicate that intense and very early intervention is truly beneficial to a child.
The major difference between regular and special education deals with the extent to which a teacher directs learning activities. Children with special needs require more intentional instruction to optimize their growth and development.	Casto and Mastropieri (1986) provided no support to the principle that "earlier is better" and found that children's progress did not differ given the time that intervention was initiated.
Increased hours of programming are associated with greater gains.	
Earlier is better. That is, children seem to do better if intervention is begun before thirty-six months of age.	
When Shonkoff and Hauser-Cram (1987) studied a group of birth to three-year-old children, they indicated that more mildly handicapped children had better outcomes if they were enrolled in early intervention programs before six months of age.	

Early Identification

One of the most interesting areas of early childhood special education is that of early identification and prevention of disabilities. Studies of early intervention have provided the impetus for identifying children early. Today, assessing very young children with disabilities is a necessary and fundamental activity for teachers, therapists, and other professionals in early intervention (Bailey and Wolery, 1989). Early identification is even broader than the practices seen with school-aged children. Personnel must be acquainted with procedures for assessing infants, toddlers, and preschoolers across a variety of domains and also for assessing family functioning and the child's environment.

The early assessment of young children serves to collect data and target skills that will increase options for the child's participation in present and future environments. It is based on the assumption that early identification will lead to an individual program plan that will either prevent or diminish the effects of an inappropriate education. Lacking early assessment, a child may experience years of failure before a diagnosis is reached. There may then be the development of secondary handicapping conditions.

The identification of a child with special needs can occur at any time and involves a variety of personnel and procedures. Below we discuss the broad educational parameters of infant, preschool, and kindergarten assessment.

Infant Identification

The identification of atypical or high-risk infants and their needs is critical to the provision of appropriate early intervention. The chief purpose of infant assessment is to provide information regarding infants' strengths and weaknesses in order to plan intervention strategies.

Observation is a primary assessment strategy. A trained observer may be able to distinguish signs of sensory or neurological problems, for example. Observation also provides an assessment of the child's strengths and needs related to a particular home and/or community activity that is identified as a concern to families; for example, feeding behaviours or behaviour while shopping.

There are no tests available that adequately assess intelligence in the newborn or reliably predict later intellectual development. Measures designed to assess an infant's developmental state make use of sensorimotor tasks — gross motor behaviour, vocalization, and language behaviour. Generally, a six-month-old would be assessed on recognition of people and objects, motor co-ordination, alertness, awareness of the environment, and vocalization. Most developmental scales are not normed on handicapped children, so infant testing simply tells us whether a child is reaching the developmental milestones within normal limits in a particular domain at a particular time.

Preschool Assessment

In infants and preschoolers, screening is used to look for maturational lags and problems that can be improved through early intervention. Before examiners can assess a child, they must know what behaviours they expect to observe. To test a three-year-old, they must focus on behaviour usually exhibited by two- to four-year-olds. Such behaviours might include speaking in sentences of four to six words, building three-block pyramids, matching similiar pictures, or buttoning. Problem behaviours might include poor attention span, or failure to respond to oral language and visual symbols. A child who is out of touch with the environment, may manifest poor motor control, low body image, and poor visual and auditory discrimination.

At this age, identification is directly related to the behaviours observed by parents and preschool teachers. Observations of how a child functions in a setting such as a nursery school provides essential information about the child's progress and the effectiveness of the program. As well, it gives information to others involved with the child. An audiologist, for example, needs data on how a child is responding with specific amplification.

Together with observations, early childhood personnel may use a variety of standardized measures. Diagnosticians involved in early identification frequently use developmental checklists, rating scales, readiness measures, and basic concept inventories. They also use such scales as the Denver Developmental Screening Test (Frankenburg et al, 1994), the Boehm Test of Basic Concepts (Boehm, 1971), or the Metropolitan Readiness Test (Nurss and McGauvren, 1976).

Kindergarten Assessment

Schools assign children to a grade level based on their age, assuming that children of the same age possess the same levels of ability. This is simply not true; children reach their developmental milestones at different times, and to expect all children to be ready to learn the same things on the same schedule is clearly not reasonable. Kindergarten screening procedures may identify maturational lags and prevent children from being inappropriately labelled early in their school careers.

In kindergarten, as at the preschool level, the observation of behaviour serves as a valuable indicator of potential learning problems. Screening is used to identify children who do not possess the readiness skills needed to perform well in a structured school environment. Tests at the kindergarten level attempt to assess a child's readiness for academic learning in specific areas of school achievement as well as potential academic difficulties.

Family Needs Assessment

Family needs refers to a family's expressed desire for services to be obtained or outcomes to be achieved (Bailey and Blanco, 1990, p. 196). Family needs are determined by a needs assessment, which can be seen as a process that helps to identify and examine both values and information. A **needs assessment** evaluates current conditions and needs and provides information on what the parents' goals are for their child and for potential parent involvement in the early intervention program.

A parent interview is one mechanism used to determine family needs. In interviews, intervenors can explore child-rearing methods, discipline, the opportunities for learning in the home, and parental attitudes and perceptions about the child's behaviour and skills. Professionals and family members can then discuss questions such as: Are there specific home and/or community activities that are concerns for family members? What skills would family members like the child to learn or to do more often? What behaviours would family members like the child to do less often? Which of these concerns are priorities for family members? (Cordesco and Laus, 1993).

Formal testing can assess such variables as the parents' stress or their knowledge of infant development. However, few instruments are available to use with families of disabled children. Instruments from other fields may be applicable. One such is the Impact on Family Scale (IFS) (Stein and Riessman, 1978) developed to assess the impact of a child's illness on a family. The IFS can be used because of the similarities between parents of ill children and those of children with disabilities. The tool assesses negative effect (strain) and positive effects (coping).

Settings

All types of programs providing services for young children with disabilities and their families have grown considerably in the past few decades. Young children with disabilities may be served in the home, in clinic settings, in separate specialized programs or within the regular complex of childcare facilities. The major objective of all programs is to provide quality care and to present opportunities and encouragement for each child to develop to his or her potential.

In recent years a body of research has emerged documenting that young children with disabilities may benefit socially and educationally from being in a class with normally developing peers.

In the United States, a legal rationale — Public Law 99-457 and its amendments — underlies the rights afforded parents of preschoolers with disabilities. The reauthorization of PL 94-142 in 1986 included provisions for handicapped preschoolers and their families. With the passage of PL 99-457, a new precedent in public policy for families with a handicapped child was created in law. American legislation now mandates the full inclusion of families in any decisions relating to the preschool child or infant with a disability. All intervenors must complete and comply with an Individual Family Services Plan (IFSP).

Canada does not have comprehensive legislation on service provision for children under the age of five with special needs. In Canada, programs for preschoolers generally fall under provincial departments of social services or health and are covered by provincial legislation in these areas.

Figure 16-1
Components of an Individualized Family Service Plan

The IFSP must contain the following components:

- A statement of the infant's or toddler's present levels of development (physical, cognitive, speech/language, psychosocial, motor, and self-help).
- A statement of the family's strengths and needs related to enhancing the child's development.
- A statement of major outcomes expected to be achieved for the child and the family.
- The criteria, procedures, and timelines for determining progress.
- The specific early intervention services necessary to meet the unique needs of the child and family, including the frequency, intensity, and method of delivering services.
- The projected dates for the initiation of services and expected duration of those services.
- The name of the case manager/ service co-ordinator.
- Procedures for transition from early intervention into the preschool program.

Centre-based (or clinic-based) programs are typically specialized, serving only children with disabilities and their families. Centre-based programs designed to serve discrete disabilities exist right across the country. In centre-based programs, families bring their infant or toddler to a program or an agency setting where appropriate services are provided by professionals and paraprofessionals. Regular intervention sessions are scheduled either on an individual basis for infants or in small groups for toddlers. Most programs tend to follow developmental and therapeutic models in their curricula. A professional related to a discipline in the child's area of most significant need is the primary interventor.

While many infant programs are clinic based, educators are more often supporting the idea that early intervention for infants and toddlers takes place in the home and/or uses the home as a basis for curricular objectives. They argue that the home is the natural environment for infants and toddlers and therefore home-based programs are more normalized options. As well, methods used in restrictive clinical settings are neither as effective nor as practical as those used in the home, and the transfer and generalization of skills from a clinic setting to other situations is problematic.

Home-based programs are often referred to as **home visiting** — a process whereby a professional or paraprofessional provides help over an extended period of time to a family in its own home (Wasik, Bryant, and Lyons, 1990). In general, home-based early intervention involves a consistent contact in the client's home between the child and the family and a representative of a formal agency.

The appeal of home visiting is based on the opportunity to work with individuals within the family context. This enables professionals to learn firsthand about the conditions of life for children and parents (Powell, 1990) and means that instructional recommendations are practical and realistic because the teacher has the opportunity to observe the family's life style and available resources.

At three years of age, the child can generally be admitted to an **early childhood education program**, a program that is concerned with the development and special needs of young children and their families with particular emphasis on the preschool years (Alberta Education, 1982).

Profile

Diana

Diana is three years old and attends a preschool for hearing-impaired children five mornings a week. Diana's profound sensorineural hearing loss was diagnosed at twenty months. Since that time, she has been fitted with a hearing aid that she tolerates but does not yet appreciate.

Diana was two months premature and spent her early weeks in an incubator. Her mother suspected a hearing impairment by about eight months when Diana seemed impervious to cleaning, vacuuming, or telephone sounds. As Diana grew, she reached all the physical developmental milestones and became a sociable, gregarious child.

At two years and a half of age, Diana's expressive language was restricted to two words — *ma* for all her wants, and *moo* for a special doll. Receptively she responded consistently to her own name and *no.* Diana also began to develop her own unique set of gestures and actions to convey meaning to her listeners.

Diana's parents decided to enrol her in a total communication preschool program. This decision had more to do with geography than to adherance to any one philosophy of communication. Although the parents would desperately like Diana to speak and not sign, a total communication program was in the area. As well, the parents now realize that language acquisition is the important goal, whatever the mode.

Diana's preschool teachers have set her several long-range goals. These include the introduction of simple nouns, verbs and colour signs; some awareness of gross sounds through play activities and listening exercises; and increased vocalizations. They have also structured many activities to expose Diana to language, such as story telling, "dress up," and art and craft activities.

Diana's teachers will show her parents how to stimulate home communication and use homemaking activities to present language. Diana's parents will be encouraged to learn sign language so that they can communicate more effectively with their daughter.

Although segregated preschool programs are still to be found right across Canada, the current philosophy is that early childhood special education should generally not take place in settings separate from early childhood education. In recent years a body of research has emerged documenting that young children may benefit socially and educationally from being in a class with normally developing peers (Harris et al., 1990). The integration of children with disabilities into natural settings is predicated on the development of social interaction and friendship among children, the improvement in self-concept in children with disabilities, and observation and imitation of the language, behaviour, and skills of normally developing youngsters.

Generally the parents of young children with disabilities are enthusiastic about integration and hold positive attitudes. Parents believe that the two greatest benefits of mainstreaming are more opportunities for handicapped children to be exposed to the real world and to be accepted by their communities (Green and Stoneman, 1989).

Today, many young children with disabilities are placed in normalized preschool settings (day-care or nursery school) under naturalistic curricula. The normal developmental processes of children provide the most critical reference for teachers of preschool children with mild disabilities and the actual curriculum objectives will be the same as for normally developing children.

Children with mild disabilities need the same skills as their peers and they usually acquire the same skills in the same sequence. The regular early childhood curriculum includes communication, social and emotional development, self-care and physical development, the demands of the current environment, the skills needed in the next environment, all probably within the context of what is taught to typical children.

Very young exceptional children usually receive their education in regular classes.

Of itself, day-care is not expected to provide interventive programming. However, integration strategies will probably include early assessment, the development of an individualized program, the intervention of professionals and paraprofessionals, a range of teaching approaches and techniques, and adaptations to the environment.

Researchers have identified specific program variables likely to influence intervention outcomes significantly and positively. These include the physical and cognitive adaptation of the classroom to accommodate handicapped children; the provision of multisensory learning stimuli and experiences; incorporation of the child's strengths and weaknesses in the development of curriculum; promotion of peer tolerance; a focus on independence and exploration of the environment; and the promotion of social interaction (see Guralnick, 1988).

Parent Involvement

Parents' discovery of their child's disability brings them into the orbit of a number of professional disciplines. Learning about the exceptionality is only the first of a lifelong series of interactions; many families are plunged into the world of infant stimulation, early intervention, preschools, respite services, medical intervention, and so on.

A wide range of professionals and paraprofessionals are available to support the parents and to help the child through various stages of development. Families will interact in some way with professionals from the disciplines of education, psychology, medicine, therapy, counselling, and allied public health and social work (Bailey et al., 1990). Few exceptional children will require all, or even most, of these professional services. However, the exceptional child certainly will need some of these services at some time. A child diagnosed in infancy, for example, would encounter many of the medical personnel in hospital. Once the child is in the home, visiting personnel might provide infant stimulation, information for the parents, and the first steps for educational intervention.

Infant and toddler programs offer parents intensive participation and usually continue until the child is about three years of age. Programs try to enhance a child's development by helping the parents to become effective intervenors.

The major model in early intervention today is family centred. This model sees professionals as agents and instruments of the family who intervene in ways that maximally promote family decision-making capabilities and competencies (Dunst et al., 1991). Family-centred services are consumer driven rather than professional driven, and are competency enhancing for the consumers, generally the parents.

Family-centred models are aligned with systems theory or a social support approach and are founded on a set of discrete principles. The most important is the assumption that the developmental needs of young children with handicapping conditions can best be met by enhancing the families' effectiveness at caring for and managing these children (Mahoney, O'Sullivan, and Dennebaum, 1990). These models reflect the belief that parents must eventually learn to handle life events once professional assistance is absent or inadequate, and this means that education must enable families to become competent rather than dependent on professional helpers or systems (Dunst et al., 1991).

"Trying to educate the young child without help and support from the home is akin to trying to rake leaves in a high wind."

Within a family-centred model, families and professionals work together to implement the service delivery process. Parents are often trained to assist in program planning and/or teaching activities either at home or in a centre. Programs teach them strategies for imparting specific skills and competencies in the belief that with instruction, modelling, and reinforcement, they can become more effective teachers of their own children. Professionals assess the child to determine what skills he or she needs, help the parent plan the learning activity, and monitor parent and child progress. Some specific areas of parent training include physical management; managing self-care and daily living activities; guidance and behaviour management; understanding the nature and prognosis of the condition; handling the child; stimulating mobility, locomotion, and communication; and responding appropriately to different or unexpected behaviours.

Parent involvement does not mean that parents should do the job of professionals. Nor is parent involvement a specific set of activities such as parents' groups or teaching activities. Rather, parent involvement implies shared responsibility for a child's progress. As one worker said, "Effective parent involvement programs acknowledge the fact that parents are a child's earliest and most influential teachers. Trying to educate the young child without help and support from the home is akin to trying to rake leaves in a high wind" (Gough, 1991, p. 339).

The goal of training is to enable family members to achieve desired outcomes and to deal effectively with future concerns. For the child, the goal is optimal development in the motor, cognitive, language and communication, social, and self-help skill domains.

Depending on the special needs of a child, the treatment regime will differ somewhat. For example, parents of children with autism can learn how to manage their child and how to stimulate social, motor, and communicative development. Howlin (1981) trained parents of autistic children to use behavioural techniques to stimulate language at home and to deal with obsessions, rituals, phobias, temper tantrums, and hyperactivity. The parents also learned to teach constructive play and social skills. After a six month period, the children spoke more than previously, and used appropriate communicative language.

For a child with a hearing impairment, parents may be instructed as to the nature of hearing impairment, the stages of normal language development, the use of the hearing aid, and the various available modes of communication. Parents can be taught to reinforce their child's early vocalizations by responding with pleasure and attention through smiling, talking, and touching so that the child is encouraged to continue vocalization as a means of receiving positive reinforcement.

In the early months of the life of an infant with severe visual impairment, sound without vision does not provide adequate information. Infants with visual impairments have specific developmental needs that require the specialized services of infant/visual impairment specialists working simultaneously with the infant and the parents (Friedman, 1989).

The developmental progress of children with Down syndrome appears to be best when parents and other regular companions are persistent in their attempts to stimulate the child while providing ample emotional support (Mundy et al., 1988). With early support, children with Down syndrome can make remarkable progress. In the University of Washington Early Intervention Program for Down syndrome children, studies of experimental and control groups demonstrated that children lacking early intervention showed progressive declines in their performance compared to normally developing peers. In contrast, those children with early intervention showed positive developmental patterns. Initially they were able to perform only 62 percent of the tasks expected of their normal peers; those who participated in the program and were between three and four years of age typically performed approximately 95 percent of the tasks (Peterson, 1987).

For children with physical and health disorders, parents must be educated to promote their children's independence. This involves an acceptance of the disability as well as a recognition of the child's individual strengths and abilities. Early intervention allows treatment to begin; draws parents into the intervention process; may prevent the development of secondary conditions; and increases the chances that the child will achieve the greatest possible degree of independence.

For children with neurological disabilities, intervention must begin as early as possible in order to create opportunities and experiences necessary for the child's development. When other problems, such as sensory loss or speech disorders are also present, early intervention becomes even more vital.

For students with multiple handicaps, early intervention is crucial to later educational success (Van Dijk, 1982). The process of aiding these children's development should begin from the moment of birth. Intervention during infancy and early childhood is a potent variable in the prevention of secondary handicaps such as behavioural problems and developmental handicaps produced by experiential deprivation and understimulation. Early intervention also underlies the early acquisition of communication and language skills.

Even though parent participation is highly valued, many difficulties remain. In fact, studies (e.g. Bricker, 1986) have found that only 20 to 40 percent of parents were actively involved in their child's early intervention program. The factors that influence parent involvement are diverse and often difficult to document. Some parents simply choose not to play an active role. Sometimes, collaboration by parents is hindered by limited knowledge bases, skill deficits, lack of self-confidence, impaired objectivity, economic considerations, and the needs of other family members.

The cultural background of the family is a major factor that can alter the intervention process, the role of professionals, and the amount of active parent participation. Culturally-based beliefs affect the manner in which families adapt to the handicapped child, the family's willingness and ability to to seek help, their communication styles with professionals, the level of trust given to caregivers and caregiving agencies, the amount and type of participation, the goals and outcomes they select for the child, and the family members who will participate in intervention activities (Hansen, Lynch, and Wayman, 1990; Schorr-Ribera, 1987).

Parents and professionals are too often at odds with each other. The changing nature of today's family complicates the issue (Vincent and Salisbury, 1988). Early intervention programs must also take into consideration different family types and changing roles within families. Even though the traditional family is not as represented in today's society, infant and preschool programs are often directed toward the two-parent, one-mother, middle-class family. Some programs have assumed that mothers are the primary caregivers, that children are raised by two biological parents, and that fathers show their concern for their children through participation in organized efforts such as fund raising, meeting with legislators, and so forth. These assumptions are not based on data (Atkins, 1987). Intervention should not become the sole concern of the mother.

Difficulties can also occur when poor communication exists between the families and the professionals who serve them. A lack of language-appropriate information concerning the nature of the child's handicap and the intervention being undertaken seriously affects parents and children at every point of service delivery (Smith and Ryan, 1987). If parents and intervenors misunderstand each other, information is easily misconstrued or misinterpreted.

Even for those parents eager for involvement, the process may be neither cheap or convenient (Turnbull and Turnbull, 1986). Parents enter programs with the expectation of getting help for their child. When the assistance carries with it high explicit or implicit expectations of parent participation and time-consuming commitments by the parents, to not participate fully may make parents feel guilty. They feel that they are open to criticism for appearing not to have their child's interests at heart (Akerley, 1975).

The establishment of positive relationships between parents and professionals depends upon a number of factors. The professional must understand the parents' problems, must be flexible, and must appear open and empathetic. The professional's ability to communicate effectively with parents is of prime importance. Determining with a family their needs and the extent to which they wish or are able to be involved in case management is a critical task of family-centred early intervention services. Parents should take a major role in determining the extent and degree of their participation, allowing for differences in interest, skill, comfort, and time.

Transition

One common experience for each child and each family is the transition from a setting serving very young children to the formal school system. In early childhood special education, **transition** can be defined as the process of moving from one program to another, or from one service delivery mode to another (Chandler, 1992). When transitions are carefully planned and undertaken, transition becomes one of the processes through which we assure continuity of services for young children and their families.

Transition is more than simply transferring records or relocating a child. It is a complex process as it relates to both the family and the child. The child's transition from a preschool to a public school program is a time of change for both the child and the family. As such, it has the potential for bringing added stress as parents face changing programs, systems, and personnel.

One cause of stress is the changing roles and expectations for families that result from transitions. Preschool and public school programs differ on a number of dimensions, including location, personnel, transportation options, schedules, family support services, and methods of communication between home and teacher. Another is that the child is often labelled officially for the first time as being different. Although a mainstream placement in a regular school might clearly be in the best interests of the child, such a placement may cause problems for the parents who are faced daily with reminders of the lag between their child and other children at the school.

For the child, the goals of transition planning are to select a placement appropriate for the needs of the child and supported by the child's parents; to ensure a smooth transfer of the child; to prepare the child to function in the next environment; and to ensure a smooth and rapid adjustment to that environment.

The child's separation from a child care or preschool program may be the most abrupt and permanent break with the past that he or she experiences before leaving home as a young adult. For children, transition means severing bonds with preschool staff, making new friends, generalizing old skills to new situations, acquiring new routines, and exploring new environments. Children will be facing a group of strange people. Inevitably, they will experience separation fears. The daunting task of learning the rules and consequences of an unfamiliar environment and of learning their place in the new hierarchy will be the same as for any other child.

The factors contributing to the success or failure of transitions are multiple and complex. They involve not only the child but the quality of the sending and receiving programs, the behaviour of the teachers, families, and communities. Especially important are the preparation, implementation, and follow-up that underlie the entire transition process.

Preparing for transition involves a number of components:

- preparing children and family members for the move to a new program;
- minimizing the disruption caused by necessary changes in services;
- supporting children and family members as they adjust to the new program;
- making subsequent adjustments to new experiences for the child and the child's family;
- and providing the child with the skills to succeed in the new placement.

Preparation of the child focuses on the demands of the public school environment. These differ from those of the preschool and so do the skills that are needed for the child to function in a kindergarten program. In kindergarten classrooms, there is a predictable and consistent schedule of activities. Kindergarten teachers require children to respond to directions given once to a large group; preschool teachers often give children repeated individual directions in small groups or on a one-to-one basis. There are provisions for free play in kindergarten, but these differ from programs for younger children as does the stress on academic subjects or academic readiness. Literacy behaviour is stressed.

In a kindergarten or grade one classroom, children must learn to follow group instructions, respond to group-directed teaching activities, follow rules and routines, work and play independently in close proximity to others, work and play cooperatively with peers, take turns, share, and wait. They are expected to develop the ability to attend to tasks, to complete tasks successfully with a minimum of adult assistance, to initiate interactions appropriately, and to go along with simple classroom rules and routines. They must also understand how to ask for, offer, accept, and refuse appropriate help.

The success of transition is influenced by the skills and behaviours a child exhibits during transition and the match between the child's skills and the expectations and requirements of the receiving program. Children who make the transition to kindergarten armed with the necesary survival skills and who use those skills in appropriate contexts are more likely to succeed in the educational mainstream than peers without these skills (Fowler, Schwartz, and Atwater, 1991). However, there can never be a universal list of transition skills because classroom and teacher expectations differ too much.

The research does indicate that in kindergarten the skills most crucial for success are not naming colours or recognizing the letters of the alphabet, but social skills. These social skills are generally thought to include areas such as self-help skills, social interaction, play, and the ability to function independently. For example, the child may be required to sit quietly, work independently, and respond to group instruction.

Preparing families to be active participants in the transition process and to become informed advocates for their children is an integral component of transitional planning. Most authors acknowledge the importance of families having opportunities to be involved in, prepared for, and satisfied with the transition process. Preparation for transition must be individualized according to each family's needs, interests, and preferences (Kilgo, 1990). When families are provided with information, involved in transition planning, and encouraged to actively participate in the process, transition-related stress is likely to be reduced.

Parent Support

Before parents can effectively assist in the care and progress of their exceptional child, they need to overcome their own emotional reactions. Many parents seek counselling or join self-help groups, especially in the period immediately following the initial diagnosis.

Counselling

Many parents require counselling because they continue to experience periods of grief (Kratochvil and Devereux, 1988). While parent counselling programs offer a range of approaches, impart different information, and use different methods, their goals are essentially the same. Counselling helps parents understand the meaning of the child's diagnosis and aids them in developing realistic expectations for their child. The counselling needs of parents of mildly and moderately disabled children should focus on information about their child, the nature and degree of the handicap, educational planning, and future prognosis. Sessions provide a forum in which parents can openly express and work through their feelings of anger, fear, and anxiety; they offer coping self-help skills, group relaxation, self-praise and self-instruction, and opportunities to favourably contrast participants with each other.

The notion of therapy itself assumes the presence of pathology. Fundamental to the usual counselling approach is the common agreement that counselling is structured to facilitate changes in the client's behaviour. However, the counselling of families with disabled children is really closer to social work than to psychotherapy. Counselling is not intended to change the personalities of family members; rather, it should help the family to handle the special problems and environmental adjustments that having a child with a disability entails. The counsellor stresses immediate practical concerns and tries to develop an approach that is appropriate for the family's individual needs, life style, and culture (Hoff, 1978).

Participation in counselling may be a critical component of parent adjustment. In one study of counselling effects (Burden, 1980), parents of mentally retarded children were randomly assigned to an individual training session, ten sessions of group training, or a control group. Parents receiving individual and group training had almost identical results; both performed higher on outcome measures than the control group.

In many cases, the counselling sessions will actively involve siblings. One mother argues that any child over the age of two should be involved in solving family problems (Akerley, 1975). She urges that problems be explained simply and honestly to siblings, with a fair assessment of how the problems will affect family life. In instances where the child has a psychiatric or psychosomatic disability that appears to be maintained by the family system, intensive family therapy may be particularly valuable (Minuchin, Rosman, and Baker, 1978).

Parent Self-Help Groups

Social supports complement personal coping skills for parents. These groups promote understanding and offer parents therapeutic involvement with people with similar problems. Groups provide a forum in which parents can discuss their concerns and exchange ideas with each other. Parents can channel their frustrations and anxieties into positive action for their children while gaining more realistic hopes for the future. Groups also help parents to develop a more positive sense of their parenting roles.

Information Networks

With the enormous geographical distances in Canada, parents in rural areas may be disadvantaged in receiving services for their exceptional children. To partly overcome this difficulty, computerized information networks have evolved to provide parents and others with up-to-date information about specific conditions, additional resources, and special education programs and practices.

Summary

1. One of the major changes in early childhood education, whether it be for normally developing children or those with special needs, is a new focus on the family and the role of family members.
2. Having a handicapped child in the family has been acknowledged for many years to be a difficult situation for all family members. However, the emphasis on the family as the crucial factor in the development of a child with a disability is a fairly new thrust in early childhood special education. It is only during the past few decades that professionals have begun to fully appreciate the parental pain and stress that accompany the diagnosis of a disabling condition in a child and the degree of courage and external support that parents need to retain their equilibrium. Today there is a greater commitment to provide comprehensive, co-ordinated, and family-focused services to children with disabilities and their families.
3. The effects of stress on the families of very young handicapped or at-risk children are pervasive, multiple, and sometimes unsuspected. Families are as individual and unique as their children. With a handicapped child, some families cope effectively and adaptively others tend to feel helpless and experience less personal gratification and more child-related problems.
4. Over the years, families, family functioning, the impact of a member with a disability, and the provision of treatment and services have been looked at in different ways. Researchers examine family functioning in terms of a stage-theory approach, a life-cycle approach, a systems approach, or its first cousin, a social support approach. Each of these ways of viewing families translates into practical models for actually intervening and working with families.
5. The most common and traditional way of looking at families with a disabled member is through a stage-theory approach. This suggests that the parents of children with disabilities pass through orderly stages before they accept the reality of their child's condition. Shock, denial, blame, guilt, depression, anger, and bargaining are all responses to the disabled family member. Several authorities have questioned the validity of the stage theory in understanding parents' reactions to a child with a disability and wonder whether parents go through stages at all.
6. The life-cycle approach sees families moving through time experiencing a series of events and tasks which include transitions. The currently favoured way of viewing families is through a systems approach or perspective that sees the family as a system. A systems approach to involving families in the treatment and education of their disabled children takes into account how the family fits into the broader social context. A family support system approach stresses that the family is a system of itself and that any event involving a change in the life of a family that has a disabled child can cause stress to the whole system. Early intervention must take family dynamics into account.

7. Each parent, each sibling, and each member of the extended family may reveal different reactions to the presence of a handicapped child in the family. However, studies on sibling relationships are contradictory and inconsistent.
8. It was not until the 1980s that the term *early childhood special education* was used. Early childhood special education has its roots in early childhood education, compensatory education, and special education for school-aged children.
9. Early intervention is based on research evidence in child development, models of successful performance, the general observations of lay persons and experts, and the impetus from the American legislation, PL99-452.
10. Programs in which workers visit the home are a promising mechanism used to provide for a growing population of children under the age of three receiving special services.
11. Once it was thought beneficial to segregate children with special neeeds into programs designed to accommodate their particular problems. More recently, normal participation with everyday school and neighbourhood environments has been found to improve the functioning levels far more than placement in special settings. Children with disabilities pass through the same curriculum as do normally developing children.
12. The transition from preschool to public school programs is not only a transition for the child but also a transition for the parents. Transitions concern the transfer of skills in children as they move to new programs and settings and the ways parents cope with new routines. For the child, moving from preschool involves a movement to a larger program with more children and new expectations. Children must learn to understand co-operation, interdependence, sharing, teamwork, and group membership.
13. A number of tactics have proven useful in moving a young handicapped child from preschool to integrated settings. These include a focus on family needs and expectations; assessment of the priorities and behavioural expectations of teachers of young children in the public school setting; and direct observation of the behaviour of children judged to be successful.

CHAPTER 17

Adolescents and Young Adults

Historical Notes

For most of the nineteenth century, special education catered to discrete age groups. Schooling was not designed for young children, although a high proportion of older students were instructed within the institutional complex. Because schooling for special populations was a new enterprise, institutions in their early years were scattered with a relatively large number of adult clients. The Ontario Institution for the Deaf, for example, was established in 1870; by 1879 about 7 percent of the student population was between the ages of 21 and 40. In the schools for the blind, students were allowed to remain up to their thirtieth birthdays (Best, 1930).

Adult attendance at school was voluntary and indicated the imperative need of disabled lads — getting a job and keeping it. Some adults were early school leavers who wanted more skills for the work force; others had never before been offered the opportunity for education and training. When students were admitted for upgrading in trades they received no wages for their work but were given free room and board (Winzer, 1993).

The adult experiences of persons with disabilities have not been of great interest to historians. The formation of deaf communities is probably the most widely studied. It seems that wherever there were schools for the deaf, a community flourished with deaf adults tending to marry other deaf people, send their children to residential schools for the deaf, and confine their social relations to their community.

There are some scattered indications of blind communities in the late nineteenth century, but they seem to have been short-lived. When persons with intellectual disabilities were institutionalized, it was usually for life. However, in the early 1920s, Walter Fernald conducted a study of the later lives of persons who had left his institution at Waverley. His findings on their occupational status and independent living were generally pessimistic (see Winzer, 1993).

It is only very recently that special education has begun to focus on early childhood and late adolescence. Currently, intense research is being directed toward very young children with special needs, and interest has grown dramatically in secondary-level disabled students and the schools' responsibilities to this population. Nevertheless, there remains a relative vacuum in secondary-level programming and in information about the experiences of young adults and how the schools can assist them as they enter the work force or tertiary education.

Consistent and structured programming for adolescents with disabilities has not traditionally been a prominent feature of special education. Although the field has had access to well-articulated models of high school programs for students with mild disabilities for more than two decades, adolescents and young adults with mild disabilities have received less than their share of special education services (Halpern and Benz, 1987). While there is a far greater focus on the experiences of young adults than there was even five years ago, there continues to be limited emphasis on vocational goals or transition to postsecondary settings (Smith, 1992). As well, there is much that we still do not know about educational and counselling needs and transition planning at secondary levels and the needs of young adults with disabilities.

In concert with their non-disabled counterparts, students with disabilities experience a wide variety of post-secondary outcomes. Young people with disabilities may enroll in university or community college; they may enter competitive employment or military service; or they may be supported in more restrictive employment and sheltered workshops.

However, "the vast majority of students with disabilities never attain a satisfactory level of career development consistent with their capabilities" (Brolin and Gysbers, 1988, p. 155). When young adults with disabilities enter the work force, they find many difficulties in obtaining and retaining employment. Students with learning disabilities, intellectual disabilities, behaviour disorders, and other disabilities tend to be far less successful than their non-disabled peers. Follow-up studies have reported low levels of employment for youths exiting special education; young people in virtually all disability groups are employed at a lower rate than the general population. Moreover, these students are not as adept in general independent living skills and may show deficits in areas such as knowledge about sexual conventions and behaviour.

In one sense, adolescence officially ends at the age of eighteen or so with graduation from high school. But as educators have begun to appreciate that the needs of students with disabilities do not stop at the school door, various means of assisting young adults are being implemented. Educators stress three main areas: academic achievement, social and personal adjustment, and post-school adjustment.

In the school, counselling and sex education stand out as important elements contributing to adult life skills. There is also a greater focus on remedial education and a stress on programming designed to help students to obtain training, gain employment, and live productive, self-sufficient lives (Stodden and Boone, 1987).

All of these — counselling, sex education, and remedial programs — together with community-based programs and access to support services, can be grouped under the rubric of transition services. For adolescents at the close of their school careers, transition focuses on the school-to-community scenario. **Transition services** are intended to provide young people with disabilities access to relevant post-secondary education opportunities, employment in competititive settings, residential independence, and future self-sufficiency (Johnson et al., 1993).

In this final chapter we discuss the needs of adolescents for efficient school counselling, for transition planning, and for specific transition programming. We also mention various types of post-secondary and employment options available to persons with disabilities.

Development of the Field

As both a concept and a process, transition is relatively new in special education. It developed in recent decades in response to the poor post-school performance of many young adults with disabilities. Recently, the American government made commitments to transition services both in terms of policy and federal discretionary grants. The Education for Handicapped Children amendments (PL98-199) included a Secondary Education and Transition Services section. Section 626 authorized funds to be spent on research, training, and demonstration in the transition area (Lee and Csapo, 1989). IDEA in 1990 specified transition mandates and programming.

Most attempts to conceptualize and develop transition curricula have focused on the abrupt and often devastating transition from high school to the world of work. Essentially, transition involves finding community resources to assist students as well as the provision of school experiences that will assist in locating and maintaining employment. Transition should be seen as serving the needs of parents and students and conforming to the principles of normalization.

If normalization is to succeed, adults with disabilities must achieve independent living, occupational stability, and status within their communities. Transition programs that focus on both job finding and maintenance and self-management skills fulfill the hopes of normalization.

As students near the end of their school careers, some families feel abandoned — they realize that special education services are ending but hold little certainty that community services will begin and provide needed support. Parents are also aware that, unlike special education systems, community and work environments may not provide the support needed by the individual to ensure success. Transition should ensure access to community support and continuity of services. For the student, transition implies the maximum development of intellectual, personal, social, and vocational skills necessary for independent functioning. Programs place emphasis on the acquisition of life and vocational skills with the focus on the local community.

Transition services for young adults with disabilities are in their infancy; problems abound and there remain many barriers to the implementation of programs (Mithaug, Martin, and Agran, 1987). For one thing, in order for transition programs to succeed, greater emphasis is needed on vocational counselling and vocational training. Unfortunately, despite the fact that successful community transition depends on successful vocational experiences and the fact that vocational teachers appear willing to accept them, only low numbers of disabled students receive vocational education in high school (Sitlington and Okolo, 1987).

For another, parent involvement continues to be a major gap in successful transition services. The available evidence and collective experience of families suggest that current transition efforts are far from optimal. With a few exceptions, they are fragmented, disorganized, and largely ineffective (Johnson, Bruininks, and Thurlow, 1987).

In speaking of blind students, Houser, Moses, and Kay (1987) pointed out that families are not actively involved in the transition process; are frequently isolated from information about available resources and possibilities for employment; are frequently isolated from emotional support that other families with similar needs can supply; in many cases, are unaware of their own resources; rely on professionals to plan and implement services for them; and may not understand the differences between education and rehabilitation services.

Adolescents

The teenage years are characterized by major biological, psychological, and social changes. Adolescence is a time of confusion, uncertainty and anxiety, of rapid physiological change and acute self-awareness. It is a period of identity crisis and a period of intense peer-group relationships, a time of rebellion against established order and a time of social anxiety. Adolescent students are developing their own identities and their own expectations of the future. As they begin to think of themselves as independent individuals, not their parents' children, adolescents become less compliant with teachers and parents and prone to question and criticize more than younger children.

Every contemporary adolescent faces a daunting task in learning to become a competent adult, and the task is made more difficult if overlaid by an exceptional condition. Adolescence is a bad time to feel incompetent and unconfident. Small children can still feel comfortable being helped by adults; adults learn the limits of their abilities. But daily tests of personal competence against one's peers are the stuff of adolescence, and those who compete poorly meet a variety of problems in self-concept and interpersonal relationships.

Fulfilling the multiple tasks of adolescence is more difficult when a student has a disability; the characteristics specific to adolescents with mild disabilities exacerbate the normal difficulties of adolescence (Dossetor and Nicol, 1989). Students with intellectual disabilities, for example, do not have the cognitive ability to cope with the new developments within themselves and the new demands of the environment (Drew, Logan, and Hardman, 1988).

Academically, many senior students with disabilities do not have either the interest or the reading ability required for academic credit courses (Nesbit, 1990). Low-achieving students are frequently judged in relation to high achievers, and feelings of inferiority, lack of motivation, and interpersonal hostility often result (Levine, 1983). Students may become caught in a spiral of failure, dissatisfaction, and frustration, and lose their self-esteem and motivation.

There is more to high school success than competency in academics. Students need a plethora of survival skills that include going to class every day; arriving at school on time; bringing pencils and other supplies to class; turning in work on time; talking to teachers politely; and reading and following directions (Zigmond et al., 1984). Students with disabilities often have problems adjusting to the school, classroom routines, the pressures of daily life, peer groups, and a range of different teachers.

Peers, being popular with peers, and belonging to the right crowd become increasingly important. Between the ages of six and twelve, children spend an average of 40 percent of their waking hours in the company of peers, children of their own age and status (Cole and Cole, 1989). By adolescence, students spend far more time with friends and place special emphasis on the qualities of intimacy, mutual understanding, and loyalty. However, one report (Polloway et al., 1986) found that teacher ratings indicated that more than 20 percent of older students with mild intellectual disabilities were rejected by their peers.

For normally developing students, self-esteem increases steadily during adolescence and early adulthood; on the average, eighteen-year-olds have higher self-esteem than thirteen-year-olds. Social, physical, and cognitive deficits hinder this process in adolescents with disabilities. Physical handicaps, for example, reduce the rate of self-concept formation (Lawrence, 1991).

Of course, adolescents with disabilities share many of the same worries and anxieties as their non-disabled peers. A survey of the concerns and interests of visually impaired and sighted adolescents (Tobin and Hill, 1988), for example, found them to be similar. However, disabled teenagers often become frustrated with their lack of progress and resign themselves to a poor view of their intelligence and their ability as a whole.

For teachers at the secondary level, the world of the adolescent raises issues that are far broader than those raised by the elementary school child. These include the adolescent's emerging sexuality, vocational interests and talents, future expectations, range of leisure activities, and independent living skills (Smith, 1991). Teachers are faced with the negative attitudes toward school and academic learning that many adolescents have developed, the manifestations of disabilities, and the need for remedial programming.

Despite special education programming often offered throughout their school careers, many adolescent students with disabilities continue to function far below grade level. Adolescents do not outgrow their learning difficulties, nor is simple maturation matched with an increase in motivation and achievement. On the contrary. The gap between students with disabilities and their peers continues to widen the further they progress in school.

For example, secondary students classified as learning disabled often retain subtle manifestations of childhood traits such as lack of co-ordination and hyperactivity. While an estimated 50 percent experience a brain maturational spurt of unknown etiology and do outgrow ADHD, the other 50 percent have difficulties that persist into adulthood and cause concentration and attention problems. Lambert (1988) identified more than 100 hyperactive children in elementary school; when they were seventeen or eighteen years old, he compared them with non-hyperactive peers. He found that the hyperactive group were less likely to have graduated from high school and more likely to have run away from home or become delinquent. They were more aggressive than their peers and more likely to be receiving treatment for psychological problems. Long-term prospects for students who are both hyperactive and aggressive are even more bleak (Whalen, 1989).

Academically, adolescents with learning disabilities tend to plateau at fourth or fifth grade, a level at which basic skill instruction ceases and students move on to a new level of cognitive functioning that requires integrating and applying what is learned (Sheinker, Sheinker, and Stevens, 1984). Almost all learning-disabled adolescents lack functional proficiency in language, reading, handwriting, spelling, and arithmetic.

By secondary school, these students are characterized as passive learners, lacking in motivation, underachieving in academic skills, lacking social skills, without the ability to comprehend the varied demands of secondary school, and lacking organizational

Training in social skills is particularly important for adolescents with disabilities.

skills. Learning-disabled adolescents tend to demonstrate a high degree of anxiety, low expectations of future success, poor adaptive strategies for coping with normal stress and solving everyday personal problems, reduced motivation, and poor self-concept.

Dropouts

From a sociological perspective, high school graduation may be seen as a rite of passage marking the successful movement of an individual from adolescence into adulthood (Can. CEC, 1992b). However, 30 to 35 percent of Canadians do not make this passage; they are dropouts who fail to obtain a certificate or diploma of graduation.

Dropouts voluntarily leave the system before completing their education. A general definition used by researchers identifies a **dropout** as "any person who has left secondary school for any reason prior to graduation" (Sullivan, 1988). There is a widespread belief that many students who drop out of school are capable of graduating (Neufeld, 1992).

Factors correlated with dropping out include community type, single-parent family, attendance rate, low self-concept, low needs for self-development, pregnancy, marriage, having a job, institutionalization or incarceration, delinquency, and drug use. Poverty, membership in a dysfunctional family, and poor mental and physical health serve to further disadvantage some youth and their expectations of high school graduation (Squires, 1992).

Students themselves give varied explanations for dropping out, although three major reasons surface in the dropout literature. First is a sense of alientation on the part of dropouts, who feel that no one cares for them. Second is the belief that courses are irrelevant, which results in students being bored and unmotivated. Third is frustration born of poor academic concept, resulting in failure, grade retention, and poor self-concept (Can. CEC, 1992b).

Predicting who will drop out is not easy. Those who endeavour to do so include poor reading performance and retention in grade (Slavin et al., 1990) as factors. According to Robert Slavin and his colleagues (1990),

> Reaching the third grade on time with adequate basic skills may not provide a guarantee that a student will complete his education, but it appears that children who do not reach third grade on time with adequate skills have little chance of educational success, regardless of the remedial or special education resources invested in them later in their school careers.

Only a small amount of literature deals specifically with dropping out by students identified as candidates for special education (Lichenstein, 1989). According to Edgar (1987), "More than 30% of students enrolled in secondary special education programs drop out, and neither graduates nor dropouts find adequate employment opportunities" (p. 555). Hahn (1987) contends that many dropouts are students with undiagnosed learning disabilities or behaviour problems. It is estimated that 47 percent of adolescents with learning disabilities drop out of school by age 16 (Gartner and Lipsky, 1987). In Calgary, researchers (Watt and Roessing, 1993) tracked 388 ESL students and found a rate close to 74 percent of immigrant students dropping out of high school. Sylvia Rimm (1986) points out that "almost invariably, gifted dropouts are underachievers, talented students who are unguided, uncounseled, and unchallenged."

In the United States, the majority of special education students (60 percent) graduate from high school with a diploma or certificate of completion. Students who are visually handicapped, hard of hearing, deaf, or orthopedically impaired are the most likely to graduate with a diploma. Students who are deaf-blind, multiply handicapped, or mentally retarded are most likely to graduate with a certificate of completion (US Department of Education, 1988). In Canada, there is evidence that the majority of students in two categories of special education (gifted and physically handicapped) graduate from high school. In all other categories, non-completion rates are staggering (Can. CEC, 1992b).

Generally, high unemployment, low income, and low educational levels characterize school leavers with disabilities. The combination of disability and dropping out is even more severe for the future roles of students. When Lichenstein (1989) followed a population of students with mild handicaps beyond high school, he found that dropping out was a greater factor in unemployment than the handicap itself. Other research findings consistently suggest that young adults at greatest risk for lifelong economic and social harm are those with disabilities who also dropped out of high school. These young people are seriously at risk because of their history of inadequate educational attainment, their chronic dependence on society, and their uncertain future in the job market (Edgar, Levine, and Maddox, 1985).

Employment

Once out of school, handicapped youth experience high rates of unemployment (Hasazi, Gordon, and Roe, 1985; Mithaug, Horiuchi, and Fanning, 1985), and if they do find jobs, they often cannot keep them (see Cummings and Maddux, 1987). Secondary students with mild handicaps tend to be employed less often than their non-handicapped peers (Edgar, 1988). For disabled individuals, jobs found are often at entry level but with few employee benefits, and they are often obtained through a self-family-friend network (Lombard and Newbert, 1992). In Vermont, a study of 459 youths exiting special education (Hasazi, Gordon, and Roe, 1985) showed an employment rate of only 54 percent. In Colorado, researchers (Mithaug, Horiuchi, and Fanning, 1985) found employment rates of 69 percent, but almost half of those employed were earning less than $3 an hour.

For adolescents with disabilities, instruction should be directed toward the development of critical skills necessary for adulthood, for success in daily life and for a future career.

It is difficult to pinpoint the factors that contribute to failure for students with mild handicaps. The extent to which employment difficulties are due to conditions in the labour market, inadequate or inappropriate vocational and educational preparation, lack of transition support services, or other related factors, such as employer attitudes, is difficult to determine precisely (Rusch and Phelps, 1987).

Exactly how a disability affects an adult depends on the adult's past academic, social, and emotional experiences and the expectations of the settings in which he or she lives, works, and plays. Some adults with learning disabilities, for example, learn to compensate for their attention problems and find occupations that allow them to utilize their strengths while minimizing their shortcomings. For others, the disabling aspects of learning disabilities may become more firmly established in adulthood and actually increase as the individual experiences new social and vocational expectations (Weller and Sipherd, 1982). Many other learning-disabled adults exhibit low motivation, distractibility, self-concept problems, and lack of organization (Buchanan and Wolf, 1986). They feel frustrated, have little self-confidence, and have difficulty controlling emotions and/or temper; depression often follows (Hoffman et al., 1987). Adults with learning disabilities continue to have reading problems (Rogan and Hartman, 1990) and difficulties with written expression. In a study of adults, 74 percent indicated a need for help with math skills (Hoffman et al., 1987).

The behaviours that characterize learning disabilities in some adults contribute to the problems they experience after school. While it has been found that learning-disabled adults secure employment at nearly the same rate as their non-disabled peers, the jobs have less social status, lower wages, and fewer regular hours than those of non-disabled groups (Okolo and Sitlington, 1986). When they find jobs, students with learning disabilities often cannot keep them. It seems to be the subtle invisible aspects of learning disabilities that impede success in the work world (Hursh, 1985).

Transition from school to work is particularly difficult for behaviourally disordered adolescents. It is not surprising that these are among the students most likely to drop out of school and among the most difficult individuals to train in transition programs (Edgar, 1987; Neel et al., 1988). Many of them lack the basic skills needed for employment.

Many adults who are mildly retarded are able to merge into the community and work at a variety of semi-skilled and service positions. They have varying degrees of success in attaining and retaining employment, but most can partially or totally support themselves. However, students with intellectual disabilities do less well at getting employment than learning-disabled or emotionally disturbed subgroups (Edgar, 1988). If not underemployed or unemployed, they are often the last hired and tend to hold unskilled and semi-skilled jobs. Adults who are intellectually disabled seem to be particularly susceptible to changes in the economy.

Job success is a function of attitudes and personality, not IQ. On the job, persons with intellectual disabilities often have problems with job responsibility, task production competence, and/or social competence (Salzberg, Lignugaris-Kraft, and McCuller, 1988). Students with behaviour disorders often use inappropriate strategies to solve conflicts and cope with frustration. As well, they often behave in ways that prevent them from being accepted, liked, and helped by employers and co-workers (Hallahan and Kauffman, 1991).

In addition to problems with job finding and retention, young adults with disabilities may not possess adequate functional skills. With increasing regularity, follow-up studies of graduates of public school programs indicate that most do not utilize community services and resources effectively, and they tend to be isolated from handicapped and non-handicapped peers (see Hardman and McDonald, 1987). One study (Sitlington and Frank, 1990) found that only 54 percent of young adults with learning disabilities had achieved independent living and stable roles.

School Services

For older adolescents with disabilities, school practices attempt to establish relationships between educational variables and better employment and independent living outcomes. There are three essential components in senior programming — work preparation skills, functional academics, and life-skills training, which includes counselling and sex education.

Counselling

The needs of adolescents are quite different from those of younger children and, when the adolescent has a disability, the needs become even more intense. Both guidance and vocational counselling are important to these students.

Few adolescents, disabled or not, know about available occupations in their geographic area, the content of people's work, or their earnings. Students with congenital disabilities often have even fewer and less diverse career-related experiences and learning opportunities than do their peers without disabilities (Turner and Szymanski, 1990), and counselling assists in making appropriate career plans.

Data suggests that students are aware of their lack of preparedness. A study of 106 students with severe physical disabilities (Liebert, Lutsky, and Gottlieb, 1990), for example, found that graduates expressed a desire for more intensive guidance counselling (especially in the area of job placement), additional training in upgrading job skills, more help with transportation, and more access to social and recreational programs. In another study of students with and without learning disabilities, the learning-disabled group has a far greater desire for more information about how to find a job, keep a job, and live independently than did their non-disabled peers (Dowdy, Carter, and Smith, 1990).

For all of us, career choices are limited by such factors as individual preferences, aptitude, and temperament. Students with disabilities need to identify realistic vocational goals that match their maximum vocational potential. They will need to critically assess the competencies required in specific occupations and should be provided with astute long-term counselling. For these students, career planning and placement require careful assessment and analysis of their strengths and weaknesses, motivations and preferences, and performance in training programs (Fonosh et al., 1982).

An important goal for education is to help establish students' present levels with regard to readiness for adult settings (Smith, 1992). For those with special needs, a vocational evaluation is required (Pruitt, 1986). A **vocational evaluation** is "a comprehensive and systematic process that utilizes work (real or simulated) to asssess the vocational potential of people with disabilities. "The process incorporates data such as test scores, medical data, information on education and work experience, and the needs and interests of the disabled person in setting vocational goals and service requirements (Pruitt, 1986).

Vocational evaluation helps students identify their functional capacities and limitations, formulate realistic vocational goals, and determine their needs for rehabilitation programming (Power, 1984). Sometimes the results of a vocational evaluation will suggest that the goals of the students (and sometimes their parents) are unrealistic. At other times, job choices may be below a student's capacity.

Counsellors may use instruments such as Becker's (1981) Vocational Interest Inventory, which requires no reading. Individuals select the jobs they would prefer from 55 black and white outline drawings depicting 11 categories of unskilled, semi-skilled, and skilled jobs. Deaf students can use the Transition Competence Battery (Bullis and Reiman, 1992).

Together with vocational counselling, students with disabilities require guidance counselling. For example, children with physical disabilities reach an awareness of their disability and its implications at different ages. Generally, children move from a broad understanding of the disability at age six to a more acute realization of the implications by age eight (Dunn, McCartan, and Fugura, 1988). By the time they reach the adolescent years, students with physical handicaps hold deep concerns regarding social acceptance, sexuality, and career choices. Students may need instruction in social skills as they mature and may also have to deal with sexual needs.

By the time they reach adolescence, students with behaviour disorders show increases in antisocial and law-breaking behaviour and truancy. The emotional conflicts, personal disturbances, and learning problems characteristic of behaviour disorders suggest the need for intervention in the areas of vocation and career, sexuality, and drug abuse (Cullinan, Epstein, and Lloyd, 1983). Counselling for students with behaviour disorders must be a long-term process: it needs an extended time frame to deal with students' affect, to increase their understanding of why they behave as they do, and to explore the possibility of change (Lambert, Shapiro, and Bergin, 1986).

Learning how to dress and use make-up to improve personal appearance can prove tricky for blind students. The problem is intensified if the appearance of the eyes is abnormal, while the unattractive appearance of optical aids may cause adolescents to reject them. Students often need to be made aware of dress codes and the use of cosmetics. Personal counselling services and sex education may help them to develop greater social awareness. Career and vocational education are particularly important for visually impaired adolescents when realistic career choices are difficult.

For adolescents with hearing impairments, the problems of deciding on communication modes and on a cultural identity complicate life (Garbe and Rodda, 1988). Educators and counsellors must help hearing-impaired students adjust to the pressures of adolescence as adequately as possible. They should encourage social counselling to improve relations between hearing-impaired students and their hearing peers, and vocational training and counselling to help assess their strengths, weaknesses, and interests. Counsellors can encourage students to consider a broad array of options and to take a major role in decision making.

The needs of gifted students in the counselling process cannot be overlooked. A sympathetic school counsellor can help gifted adolescents and their parents cope with the social and emotional problems that so often arise in high school (McMillan and Loveland, 1984). When programs for the gifted have not been developed, counsellors can do a great deal to help individual students. The counsellor can plan appropriate timetables, collapse the time needed to meet core requirements, and arrange contacts in the community and post-secondary institutions. In the case of culturally different gifted students, the counsellor can help demystify the unfamiliar educational environment (McMillan and Loveland, 1984).

Multipotential can be a mixed blessing; many gifted youngsters share a feeling of ambivalence about the future and their place in it. By ages thirteen or fourteen, some gifted students are already conditioned to avoid failure at all costs. They are willing to pursue career choices far below their potential (Willings, 1983). Others cannot focus on career plans.

For average learners, career plans can change between seventeen and nineteen years of age. For the gifted, changes in career plans can occur between thirteen and fourteen, sixteen and eighteen, and twenty-one and twenty-three. A radical change in careers for the gifted develops between ages twenty-eight and thirty-two. (Talented children, on the other hand, often have fixed career goals prior to adolescence.) Gifted students need personal and career counselling, a networking system that links students to school and community resources (Clifford, Runions, and Smyth, 1986), and appropriate role models.

Sex Education

Adolescents with disabilities, particularly intellectual disabilities, are less likely to have accurate information about sex, are more subject to fears and myths, and are more likely to be sexually exploited. The need of students with intellectual disabilities for sex education that includes instruction in social behaviour and self-protection is well documented. Instruction in appropriate sexual behaviour is particularly important today, since most persons with mild and moderate retardation now live in the community and do not learn easily from non-directed observations, books, or friends.

The major goal of normalization is a normal family and community life for all individuals. Sexual activity is a normal part of human life. People with mental and physical disabilities have the same range of sexual needs and drives as everyone else. It is a myth that individuals who are physically handicapped do not have sexual needs or that persons with intellectual disabilities are asexual or over-sexed.

Persons who are intellectually disabled are just as likely to develop a strong and normal interest in the opposite sex as anyone else. But as with non-disabled people, some seem to have little need for physical contact, some express more need than the average, and the majority fall in the middle range (McClennen, 1988). If physical development is normal, sexual development follows chronological rather than cognitive development, although psychosocial development may be reached at a later chronological age (Martin and Forchuk, 1987). Because of this, some individuals who are disabled are more likely to express experimentation overtly.

To understand sexuality, an individual must be educated (Romaneck and Kuehl, 1992). Students with mental disabilities are placed at risk for developing unacceptable sexual behaviours when we do not educate them in this area and when we teach them the opposite of the behaviour we want. Adolescent students may need to be made aware that their own sexuality is acceptable and that they have the same rights to sexual expression as do their peers. Sex education programs for adolescents who are physically and mentally disabled should include explanations of bodily functions, the mechanics of reproduction, social behaviour, and preparation for marriage and family.

AIDS is also an issue for adolescents because adolescence is often a time of sexual confusion and experimentation (Sloane and Sloane, 1990). Effective AIDS education means talking about topics such as homosexuality, drugs, and condoms and this makes many parents uneasy (Kirp and Epstein, 1989).

Transition

For all students, the high school experience represents a period of transition between the security of school and the complexity associated with the opportunities and risks of adult life. For adolescents, the quality of the secondary school experience and the decisions made during this time have significant implications for the quality of life experienced after they leave school.

Transition is the movement from one service delivery system to another. Definitions of the term *transition* have in common the concept that a transition is a passage or an evolution, not simply a "here today gone tomorrow" phenomenon. In other words, transitions are not a fleeting proposition but rather represent recurrent, lifelong processes that all individuals experience (Shea and Baeur, 1991). In the previous chapter, we discussed the stress potential of transition from preschool to a public setting for young children and their parents, and emphasized the necessity for careful transition planning. The same careful planning, co-ordination, and collaboration is necessary for adolescents exiting the school system. In the transition from school to work there are two related areas which must be considered — community adjustment and employment.

Transition mandates developed as more and more data indicated that despite special education programs many students with special needs still experience major difficulties in bridging the gap from school to community work and living. Although the school experience may have been tainted with frustration and failure, it still offered some predictability. For many, the adult world does not have this predictability, and they tend to flounder in both occupations and independent living.

Upon completion of their public schooling, many young people with disabilities still need additional assistance and additional support to negotiate the transition process successfully. Edgar (1987) pointed out that "secondary special education programs appear to have little impact on students' adjustment to community life." To overcome at least some of the problems, educators are initiating programs that match the skills needed by individuals in the community and that better prepare students for post-school life.

According to the American Individuals with Disabilities Education Act (PL101-476, IDEA, 1990), transition is

> a co-ordinated set of activities for a student, designed with an outcome-oriented process, which promotes movement from school to post-school activities, including post-secondary education, vocational training, integrated employment (including supported employment), continuing and adult education, adult services, independent living, or community participation. The co-ordinated set of activities shall be based upon the individual student's preferences and interests, and shall include instruction, community experiences, and development of employment and other post-school adult living objectives, and, when appropriate, acquisition of daily living skills and functional vocational evaluation (PL101-476, Sec. 602 (a)(19)).

This definition makes a number of important points:

- The transition process is a vehicle for alleviating the problems of youth with various disabilities and need levels through integrating planning, instruction, placement, and provision of ongoing support as they leave school (Newbert, Tilson, and Ianacone, 1989).
- Initiatives at the structural level aid in enhancing the prospects for economic stability for persons who are exceptional.
- Transition is founded on the premise that all persons with disabilities can perform meaningful tasks and assume valued roles within normal community settings.
- Effective transition planning is much more than the mere physical transfer of administrative responsibility for an individual's service program from the school to adult service agencies. Successfully negotiating the transition through and out of high school is a process that requires varying degrees of assistance from family and school personnel.
- Although community employment is the goal of transition planning and secondary level vocational instruction, the placement of a graduating student into a job should not be considered an outcome in and of itself. It is also important to identify the quality of life outcomes that the student wishes to obtain through employment (Steere et al., 1990). Quality of life outcomes are the tangible and intangible results of employment that contribute to the enhancement of students' lifestyles.
- A basic objective during the transition period is to arrange for individuals with disabilities those services needed to support successful adult living. There may be many different agencies, depending on the nature and severity of the handicap.
- Transition involves collaboration and co-ordination. In order for a program to be truly successful for exceptional learners, there must be a firm alliance forged between special education, regular education, and vocational education. Co-ordination and planning are the essential underpinnings of success.
- In transition, the school has two primary roles. First, it is the school's responsibility to develop and implement an effective program that will prepare students for life in their local communities. Second, the school must take the lead in co-ordinating the transition planning process (see Figure 17-1). This involves secondary programs for transition, linkages to post-secondary environments, and post-secondary services.

For transition to succeed, the school must provide

- preparation for transitions. Preparation for transition should begin at the elementary areas. For example, students with moderate mental retardation, especially those in self-contained classes, begin to learn the rudiments of community and vocational living skills in upper elementary school (Hasazi and Clark, 1988; MacMillan, 1988).

Figure 17-1 *The transition process*

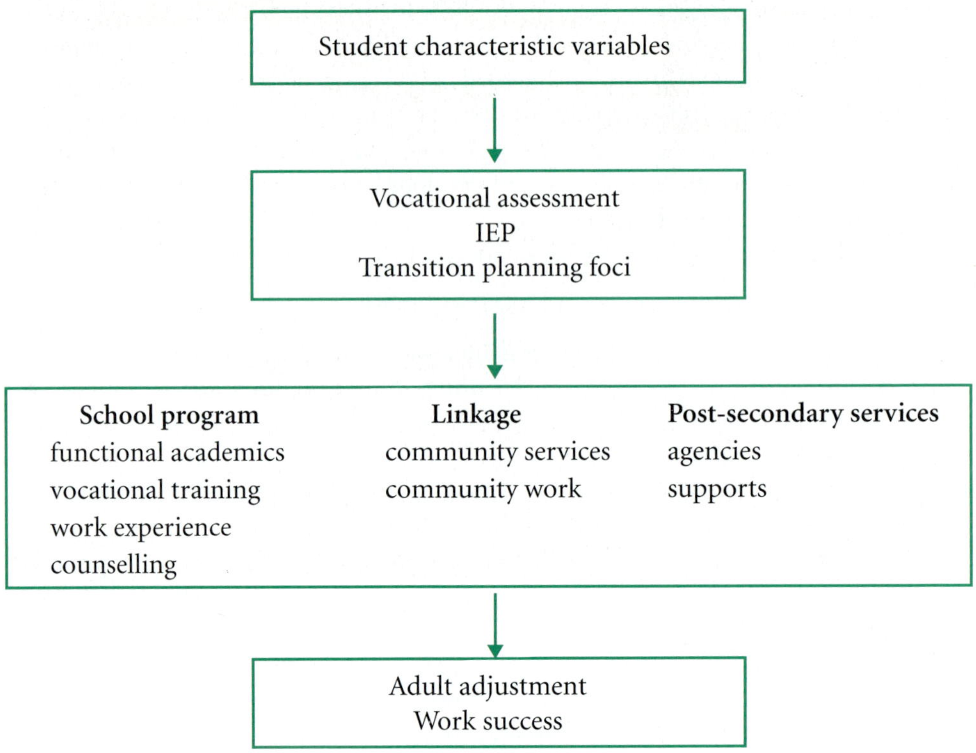

- a formal transition plan. Preparation may include an individual transition plan as part of a student's IEP. A formal transition plan will include goals and objectives, timelines, and designations of responsible persons and agencies (Moon, Diambra, and Hill, 1990). The plan will identify and teach activities that will maximize the individual's participation in community settings; identify the types of community services that will be necessary to support the individual's participation, such as personal management and work; and complete the steps required to access community services (Hardman and McDonald, 1987).
- a comprehensive curriculum that is functional in nature and that includes community-based vocational instruction (Moon, Diambra, and Hill, 1990). Curriculum should focus on vocational training, personal management, and recreation/leisure activities.
- systematic and planned opportunities for students' interactions with normal peers. There should be mainstreamed educational and vocational experiences (Hasazi, Gordon, and Roe, 1985; Pilley, 1988). In a study of 106 graduates of a school for students with severe physical disabilities, for example, investigators (Liebert, Lutsky, and Gottlieb, 1990) found that many graduates felt they would have benefited from a less sheltered environment as well as more exposure to peers without disabilities.
- vocational education and work study experiences. Transition should focus on work personality (self-concept and motivation); work competencies (habits, physical and mental skills, and interpersonal skills); and work goals (career objectives) (see Szymanski, 1994).
- real paid work experience before graduation. For disabled youth, part-time jobs during school and enrolment in vocational classes correlate with increases in

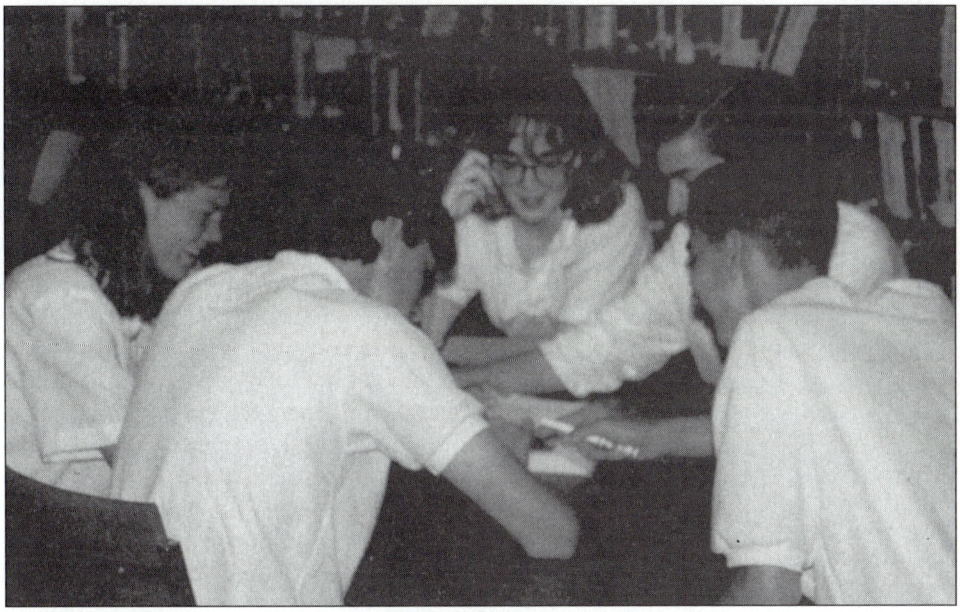

Planned and systematic opportunities to interact with non-disabled peers help prepare young people with disabilities to function independently in the general community.

employability (Siegel, Robert, and Gaylord-Ross, 1992). In fact, non-subsidized part-time or summer jobs are a better predictor of later employability than are high school vocational or work experience programs (see Edgar, 1987).

- training that facilitates students' access to and participation in the receiving environment (see O'Shea, 1994). This includes job preparation, including skills such as locating job openings in newspapers and displaying correct behaviour during a job interview.
- co-ordinated services. A transition team should include all those providing services in both school and community. That is, special educators, family members, general and vocational educators, adult service providers, employers, community leaders, and consumers (Smith, Edelen-Smith, and Stodden, 1995).
- encouragement of parent involvement. The involvement of parents in secondary programs has been traditionally underemphasized (Haring, Lovett, and Saren, 1991). For transition to be successful, parents must be involved.
- concrete outcomes, including job placements.

Settings

Adolescents with disabilities need a comprehensive curriculum that leads to successful, satisfying employment. A variety of generic curriculum domains have been proposed during recent years as important components of secondary special education. The major areas of instruction are:

- academic skills, specifically functional academics;
- remediation in deficient basic skills;
- vocational skills that include career exploration and occupational knowledge and skills, such as job finding skills, work experience, and job maintenance;
- personal management skills that include independent living knowledge and skills such as budgeting, home management, and social skills;
- leisure skills (Halpern and Benz, 1987; Wilcox and Bellamy, 1982).

Within these domains, instruction should occur throughout the school years, with the relative emphasis on the vocational domain increasing at secondary levels. Training in this area helps students to develop stronger self-concepts and to engage in self-supporting productive work.

Again and again through this text we have mentioned the dilemma of the best location in which to educate students with disabilities. Integrated settings seem natural and eminently appropriate for very young children. Younger children acclimatize more rapidly to integrated settings than older students. Integration at the secondary levels is harder to implement: not only does the mental gap between non-disabled and disabled students continually widen with age but the instructional emphasis at the secondary levels is different from that of the elementary school.

The current needs and ultimate goals of students at the end of their school careers are different from those of younger children. As Figure 17-2 shows, the needs that must be addressed by secondary programming meld into after school needs.

Figure 17-2
Needs of secondary students

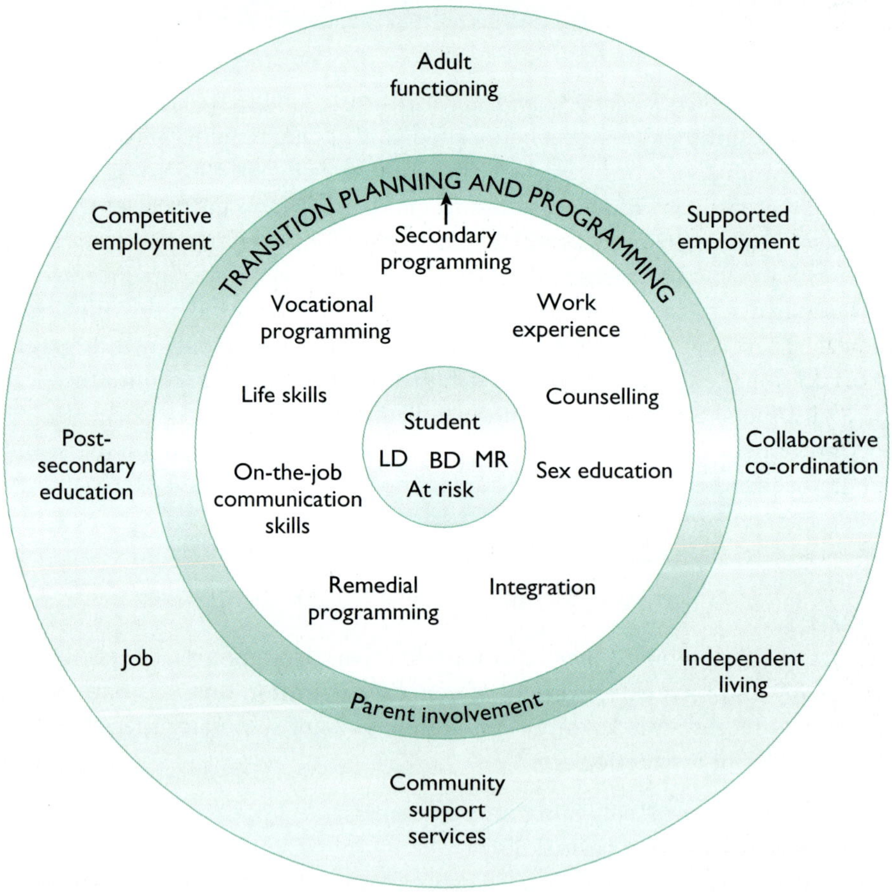

The Council for Exceptional Children (1993a) points out that

> all children, youth, and young adults with disabilities are entitled to a free and appropriate education and/or services that lead to an adult life characterized by satisfying relations with others, independent living, productive engagement in the community, and participation in society at large. To achieve such outcomes, there must exist for all children, youth, and young adults a rich variety of early intervention, educational, and vocational program options and experiences. Access to these programs and experiences should be based on individual need and desired outcomes.

Normalization and individualization therefore become paramount for adolescents with disabilities. Educators must carefully weigh the pros and cons of various settings. The preparation of special education students for productive living in the adult world is the aim, and this must be balanced against the normal high school curriculum as presented in the regular classroom.

A number of educators argue that despite the current emphasis on integration, the regular classroom may not be the most suitable setting for late-secondary students. Full academic integration may not be what is needed at the senior level, as curriculum, expectations, and outcomes may not match the needs of older disabled learners. Some go so far as to contend that at the secondary level, the full integration of all students is simply not feasible; it is an invitation to failure (Edgar, 1987; Schumaker and Deshler, 1988; Braaten et al., 1988). Some necessary skills can be taught in regular settings; some cannot. The arguments circle around three interelated themes — the characteristics of adolescent students with disabilities, the content of the regular curriculum, and the future needs of students.

Teachers of secondary students with disabilities must be concerned with targeting useful learning objectives in self-care, mobility training, communication, social interaction, health and safety, leisure time, and vocational pursuits.

Factors correlated with students with mild disabilities include physiological and neurological problems, deficits in cognitive processes such as memory and metacognitive awareness, disorders of attention, social behaviour problems, communication problems, and perceptual problems. Nevertheless, adolescents with mild disabilities who spend the majority of their school day in general education classes are expected to meet the same demands as their non-disabled peers. Students must be able to listen to lectures and take notes; complete many written assignments; read content-area information, often from poorly organized textbooks; and take tests that frequently do not facilitate students' responding.

Functioning in the regular classroom is extremely difficult; students can experience success only when the teacher is able to meet their individual learning needs through appropriate curriculum modifications (Haman, Issacson, and Powell, 1985). But curriculum adaptations are not a part of secondary classroom life. In general, regular educators teach to single large groups and incorporate little or no differentiation based on student need (Baker and Zigmond, 1990). L.S. Fuchs and colleagues (1995) found that few teachers made adaptations. When they did, it was more often than not lowering their expectations of students rather than attempting to improve their programs. Another study of sixty social studies and science teachers who were seen as effective with learning-disabled students by peers, principals, and self found that the teachers made few adapations to meet special learning needs (McIntosh et al., 1994). These and other findings suggest that teachers recognize the low achievement of learning-disabled students but do very little that is different instructionally when these students are assigned to regular-content classes. The one adjustment that is commonly made is to lower grading standards so that learning-disabled students have a good chance of passing the course (Zigmond, Levin, and Laurie, 1985).

Moreover, traditional secondary school subjects are generally not related to the future needs of students with mild disabilities, and the overall curriculum is not congruent with their present wants. Preparation for independent living requires much more than academic goals for adolescents who are disabled. Their hope is to work — not to continue schooling.

Finally, there is less likelihood that their career development needs will be met in regular classrooms (Izzo, 1987). By this stage, the major goal of education is not to compensate for intellectual and physical deficiencies per se. Rather, instruction is directed toward the development of critical skills necessary for adulthood, for success in daily life, for citizenship, and for a future career. The acquisition of requisite employment skills cannot be left to chance or viewed as a peripheral adjunct to mainstream curricula (Nesbit, 1990).

Functional Academics

Rather than focusing solely on the traditional three R's, teachers of secondary students with disabilities must be concerned with targeting useful learning objectives in self-care, mobility training, communication, social interaction, health and safety, leisure time, and vocational pursuits. The major domains that accommodate the academic needs of secondary students with disabilities are academic skills such as basic knowledge and skills in reading, computation, and study skills, and strategy training to enable older students to gain the knowledge of how to use skills to meet demands of the academic, occupational, and social environment.

In other words, students require **functional academics**, that is, academics that have meaning and are relevant to the learner soon to enter community work and life. These can be taught in integrated programs or in remedial programs. Students may also require intense remedial instruction for skill deficits. Before secondary school, learning programs are developmental in nature. At the secondary levels, basic skills remediation simply extends the elementary educational model in that students are provided individual remedial instruction for basic academic skill deficits. However, instruction assumes a more compensatory outlook. Secondary programs stress the development of basic skills or ways to compensate for their absence.

Vocational Programs

Students are given opportunities to learn a trade through high school-sponsored vocational training and on-the-job training in the context of full or part-time work/study programs. They are taught specific job skills that include understanding instruction; asking a question; asking for help; accepting criticism; ordering job responsibilities; accepting assistance; giving instruction; offering assistance; apologizing; and convincing others (Montague, 1988).

Work/study experiences are an important element of vocational programs. Persons who are intellectually disabled, for example, who have been in school work experience programs tend to respond better to occupational demands and are more employable than those not in programs (Patton et al, 1989).

Having some work experience before graduation helps adolescents with the transition to adult life.

Work/study experiences, founded on the premise that there should be a cross-co-ordination between school work and vocational experiences, play a major role in the secondary curriculum and link the preparatory employment to the receiving environment through community-based instruction. Instruction is referenced directly to activities and performance demands in the local community. Students are placed in work situations in the community, and their academic programs are oriented to supplement the work experience.

Work experiences allow individuals to try new things in an atmosphere that allows for a second chance (Nesbit, 1990). Students learn how to adapt to changes in the work environment and how to maintain acceptable levels of work performance.

Social Skills Instruction

Programs provide training in the social skills needed for job success. The existence of social skill deficits among disabled student populations has been well documented in the professional literature. Adaptive behaviour is predictive of certain aspects of future vocational performance (Harrison, 1987), and the absence of effective social skills is considered to be a major cause of the less than successful adjustment of disabled students to the regular competitive work force. Wayne Nesbit notes that when senior students finish school, their personalities must be marketable. "The reality is that they will not receive an academic high school certificate nor will they earn a university degree. It is their personality and ability to work co-operatively which determines their acceptance and success in the work world" (1990, p. 5).

In adults with intellectual disabilities, social skills that should be taught range from isolated non-verbal responses such as eye contact and gestures to complex skills involved in asking questions, expressing appreciation and praise, and carrying on a conversation (Misra, 1993). Students may also need training in aspects of speech such as loudness, intonation, and intelligibility.

Self-Management

Self-management refers to a multiplicity of skills needed for independence in the adult world. For example, students learn about apartment living, marriage, family responsibilities, budgeting, and community resources.

Students with significant disabilities need instruction in life skills, which include basic hygiene, grooming and dressing, as well as mobility, money handling, shopping, housekeeping, and leisure skills. Even for those who can never achieve full independence, life skills training contributes to feelings of confidence, self-reliance, and personal satisfaction.

Employment

Despite difficulties, many young people with disabilities move into post-secondary education or competitive employment with their non-disabled peers. At the moment, students who have suffered traumatic brain injuries represent the fastest-growing segment of the disabled population entering post-secondary institutions (Cook, 1991).

Post-Secondary Education

Students with learning disabilities can succeed in college and university if they are given reasonable accommodations. Typical approaches include modified tests, more time to complete tests, many short rather than one long examination, alternate assignments, and assistive devices such as computer access. Generally, faculty members seem willing to make accommodations (Nelson et al., 1990).

Qualified deaf students can both succeed and compete in public post-secondary institutions if provided with adequate support services such as note taking and sign language interpreting (Jones, 1986). However, full integration, especially social integration, may not occur (Brown and Foster, 1991).

Competitive Employment

Competitive employment of persons with disabilities enhances feelings of self-worth and efficacy and increases the normalization of these persons, both in self-perception and the perception of society (Scott and Sarkee, 1982; Seyfarth et al., 1985). The mere observation of disabled individuals engaging in functional, integrated, and age-appropriate activities appears to have effects on the development of a more respectful and optimistic attitude toward these individuals among the public, one factor which would contribute to employment success (Bates et al., 1984).

Supported Employment

Supported employment, sometimes referred to as sheltered workshops, offers more structure for persons with disabilities. In Canada, the term workshop is used to describe a wide variety of work situations and vocational rehabilitation programs that range from adult day programs to highly automated production factories.

In their present form, sheltered workshops are commercial-industrial models of production. They serve to assess, improve, and stabilize vocational functioning, thus assisting a disabled person to progress to employment in the competitive labour market. Within the workshop, expectations are adjusted to each individual's ability. The workers have constant input and supervision and their personal differences are tolerated.

Schools are involved in work experience in, and transition to, sheltered workshops. In a B.C. study, (Horrocks, 1991) 75 percent of the graduates labelled EMH who worked in sheltered workshop settings had been involved in work experience and summer placement at the sheltered setting. They transited immediately into the workshop. Forty-four percent of the graduates labelled TMH were involved in experiences at sheltered workshops exclusively and transited immediately into the workshop (Horrocks, 1991).

Summary

1. In recent years, special educators have examined the needs of students with disabilities as they move from the school environment to the world of employment and found that these students are in obvious need of programs and services that will enable them to make a succcessful transition from school to adult community environments.
2. Effective counselling plays an important role in guidance and career planning for students with disabilities and for gifted students. Adolescents with behaviour disorders require vocational and career guidance, instruction in matters such drug abuse, and clear information regarding human sexuality.
3. A major concern for those involved with adolescents who have intellectual or physical disabilities concerns sexual awareness.
4. Many adolescents with disabilities reach secondary school with severe deficits in the core areas of reading and math.
5. Where students should be educated is a matter of concern. Many educators contend that we may need to pay more attention to bettering the lives of students than to their school address.
6. The most critical needs area of disabled adults is in the realm of vocational competency, including the ability to find an appropriate job and the provision of rehabilitation services. A related critical need area is an individual's ability to acquire a positive self-concept, self-undertanding, and self-acceptance.
7. A new stress on transitions programs has been prompted by data that indicate that many students with disabilities are faring poorly after school. After school, disabled individuals have difficulty finding employment and, if they do find jobs, they often cannot keep them. Job success is compromised in many ways.
8. Students who are disabled need to function successfully in school, home, job, and community settings. If they are to live independently, to manage their affairs without supervision, and to be self-sufficient, they must develop marketable occupational skills.
9. It is true that most persons with disabilities can work, but what they work at and how they work is dependent upon an appropriate education. The fundamental purpose of education is to prepare students to lead productive and rewarding lives, and intervention is directed toward training pupils to eventually live and work independently in the general community. To assist students with disabilities to successfully transit to adult life, secondary programs must focus on and program for their needs.

Glossary

Acceleration: practice whereby students move faster through academic content.

Acquired aphasia: a loss in linguistic ability that occurs after language has been developed, usually as a result of brain damage caused by serious illness, trauma to the head, or stroke.

Adaptive behaviour: the extent to which a person is able to adapt to environmental demands; differs according to the individual's age group and particular situation.

Adaptive equipment: any device designed or modified to lead individuals with disabilities to independence.

Adventitious hearing impairment: a hearing impairment acquired some time after birth, through accident or disease.

Adventitious low vision: visual impairment caused by accident or disease some time after birth.

Aggression: any form of behaviour designed to harm or injure another living being who is motivated to avoid such treatment.

Albinism: a condition carried as an inherited autosomal recessive trait.

Allergy (hypersensitivity): an abnormal and varied reaction which occurs following a contact with substances or agents that normally do not cause symptoms in other individuals.

Amblyopia: visual defect, also called lazy eye blindness, resulting from strabismus. The brain, which will not tolerate double vision, eventually suppresses the image coming from the weaker eye.

Anoxia: deprivation of oxygen.

Anxiety: a fear with a future reference.

Antisocial behaviour: repeated infractions of socially prescribed behaviour patterns that violate social norms and the rights of others.

Articulation: the generation of speech sounds by modifications of the vocal tract, which consists basically of the mouth and nasal and pharyngeal cavities.

Arthritis: a common term for a variety of chronic systemic conditions involving inflammation of the joints.

Asthma: a variable, reversible obstruction of the airways characterized by the narrowing of bronchial tubes, swelling of tissues, and clogging of mucus.

Assessment: the process of gathering valid evidence to guide decisions about curriculum and instruction, and to evaluate the outcomes of instruction.

Astigmatism: a visual defect resulting from an irregularity in the curvature of the cornea or lens of the eye.

Ataxia: a type of cerebral palsy characterized by poor co-ordination of the movements associated with balance, posture, and spatial orientation.

Atrophy: a wasting away that results from neurological damage or from the weakening of muscles due to nerve degeneration.

Athetosis: a type of cerebral palsy characterized by constant, involuntary writhing movements, especially in the hands and wrists.

Atypical youngsters: those who do not reach the norm in some functional area or areas.

Audiogram: a chart used in a hearing test, on which the data for each ear are plotted.

Auditory atresia: lack of an opening in the outer auditory canal that interferes with the air conduction of sound and requires medical or surgical intervention.

Augmentative communication: a general group of procedures designed to support, enhance, or augment the communication of non-speaking individuals or to utilize and supplement whatever vocal skills an individual with severe disabilities possesses.

Autosomal (identical) chromosomal pairs: the first twenty-two chromosomal pairs which determine the thousands of traits that make up a human being.

Behaviour management: all the ways in which teachers control inappropriate and disruptive behaviour as well as ways in which children are taught discipline and to control their own behaviour.

Behaviour observation: a method of hearing assessment whereby a sound is presented to a child in a sound-proofed room and the tester observes any behavioural responses.

Bilingual: term applied to individuals who speak two languages.

Bilingual education: schooling provided fully or partly in the second language with the object of making students proficient in the second language while at the same time maintaining and developing their proficiency in the first language and fully guaranteeing their educational development.

Biological risk: a history of prenatal, perinatal, neonatal, or early developmental events resulting in biological insults to the developing nervous system of an infant or toddler.

Body image: a person's awareness of the body, its capabilities, the interrelationship of body parts, and the relationship of bodies to the environment.

Bound morphemes: sound units that are not words by themselves but units of meaning only when combined with words.

Cancer: a general term used to describe about a hundred conditions characterized by abnormal and uncontrolled cell growth.

Cataract: an opacity of the lens or its capsule which restricts the eye's ability to receive light and interferes with central and peripheral visual acuity.

Cerebral palsy: a condition characterized by damage to the brain before, during, or after birth. While chiefly a motor disorder, it is often accompanied by other disabilities.

Child abuse: any interaction or lack of interaction that results in non-accidental harm to a child's physical and/or emotional state.

Child advocacy: any social, political, or legal action that is intended to achieve a better life for children from infancy to late adolescence.

Childhood psychoses: a heterogeneous group of clinical syndromes characterized by any number of maladaptive behaviours or clusters of behaviours that affect various aspects of adaptive behaviour and the success of interpersonal relations.

Children with exceptionalities: those who have difficulty in realizing their full human potential. Their intellectual, emotional, physical, or social performance falls below or rises above that of other children. The differences may be related to physical, psychological, cognitive, emotional, or social factors, or a combination of these.

Chronic health problems: diseases or medical conditions that interfere with school attendance and learning and hinder children's ability to lead a normal life.

Classroom management: the way in which teachers manipulate the classroom environment to minimize disruptions and give all children the optimum opportunity to engage in appropriate behaviour and reach learning and social goals.

Cochlea: a tiny, snail-shaped structure in the inner ear filled with a fluid similar to cerebral spinal fluid.

Cochlear implant: device that converts sound into mild electrical currents to stimulate the cochlea and allow some recognition of sound.

Cognition: the process of recognizing, identifying, associating, and inferring meaning beyond the figural information provided by the environment that allows an understanding of a concept and application to new conditions.

Cognitive development: orderly changes that occur in the way children understand and cope with their world.

Collaboration: any mutual effort to plan, implement, or evaluate educational programs for a student or students.

Colour blindness: a sex-linked hereditary inability to differentiate among certain or all colours.

Communication: the process of exchanging information and ideas between participants.

Communication mode: the form in which the content of a message is expressed.

Communicative competence: the knowledge of how to interact, how to communicate appropriately in various situations, and how to make sense of what others say and do in communicative interactions.

Conceptual definition: a statement that describes a condition theoretically.

Conduct disorders: term used to describe the behaviour of hyperaggressive and highly disruptive children who form the major portion of those identified in the schools as behaviourally disordered.

Conductive hearing loss: hearing impairment caused by problems in the mechanical transmission of sound waves through the outer and middle ear.

Congenital amputation: term used to describe the condition of a child born with limbs or parts of limbs missing.

Congenital hearing impairment: hearing impairment that is present at birth.

Congenital low vision: visual impairments that are diagnosable at birth or shortly thereafter.

Continuum of reproductive casualty: term used in connection with established risk factors indicating that problems to be expected may range from relatively minor through to major difficulties.

Cortical blindness: blindness caused by swelling in the brain tissue due to trauma or congenital malformations. The term is sometimes used to mean simply blindness that cannot be medically explained.

Creativity: the process of bringing unusual and unexpected responses to bear on given situations; a capacity to restructure the world in unusual or useful conceptual terms.

Critical period: that part of the life cycle during which the developing organism is particularly sensitive or responsive to specific environmental forces.

Culture: the distinctive creativity of a particular group of people.

Culture-free measures: tests that purport to be free from culturally loaded content.

Culture-specific measures: tests written from the perspective of a particular minority culture or subculture.

Curriculum-based assessment (CBA): a standardized measurement system used to monitor a student's academic growth and to improve instructional programs.

Cystic fibrosis (CF): a genetically determined inborn error of metabolism characterized by pervasive dysfunction of the exocrine glands.

Deaf person: one whose hearing disability precludes successful processing of linguistic information through audition, with or without a hearing aid.

Decibel: the smallest difference in loudness intensity that can be perceived.

Delinquency: a set of antisocial behaviours acquired over time.

Delinquent behaviour: any illegal act by a juvenile, regardless of whether the perpetrators are apprehended.

Developmental delay: a condition which represents a significant delay in the process of development and the presence of which indicates that the process of development is significantly affected and that without special intervention, it is likely that educational performance at school age will be affected.

Developmentally disabled individuals: those who suffer from chronic disabilities, attributable to mental or physical impairments, or a combination of these, that are manifested before age twenty-two and that result in functional limitations in major life activities requiring special services and treatment that are of extended duration or are lifelong.

Developmental risk factors: the wide range of biological and environmental conditions that are associated with increased probability of cognitive, social, affective, and physical problems.

Diabetes mellitus: a disorder of sugar metabolism caused by a pancreatic disorder in the production of insulin, a hormone needed to metabolize glucose.

Diabetic retinopathy: a disease of the retina's blood vessels caused by diabetes.

Diagnosis: the art of identifying disease from the symptoms.

Dialects: language variations that are systematic and associated with a specific geographic, cultural, or socio-economic group.

Differential diagnosis: the precise specification that a given set of symptoms is indicative of one disorder rather than another.

Diplopia: double vision that may result from lack of co-ordination between the two eyes.

Direct audio input system: an FM system joined to the child's individual aid.

Direct instruction: activity-focused, teacher-directed classroom procedures that are systematic and usually conducted according to an individual plan.

Directionality: an awareness of left and right in the environment outside the body.

Disabilities: the consequences of impairments in terms of functional performance and activity by the individual.

Disabled children from different cultures: children who have diagnosable handicapping conditions that are recognized as such by their cultural community.

Disabled individuals: those who suffer from a disability or impairment of function in one or more areas, such as vision, hearing, or mobility.

Discipline: a form of behaviour management that teaches children to guide their own behaviour in a way that shows respect and caring for themselves, other people, and the physical environment.

Dropout: any person who has left secondary school for any reason prior to graduation.

Dyspedagogia (maleducation): poor learning brought about by inadequate teaching and other school variables.

Dysarthria: a group of speech disorders resulting from disturbed muscular control over the speech mechanisms.

Early childhood education program: a program that is concerned with the development and special needs of young children and their families with particular emphasis on the preschool years.

Early identification: the practice of screening infants and young children in an attempt to identify those likely to experience problems in learning or behaviour.

Early intervention: a variety of educational, psychological, or therapeutic interventions provided for handicapped, at-risk, or disadvantaged infants and preschoolers to prevent or ameliorate developmental delays or disabilities or to provide support to children and families in cases where disabilities exist.

Echolalia: speech that is an immediate imitation of that of some other speaker.

Elective mutism: seen in children who are emotionally disturbed who do not speak or speak only in certain circumstances.

Emotional overlay: an adverse reaction to learning problems and academic failure.

Enrichment: the provision of additional special activities in the regular classroom setting.

Environmental risk: term applied to children who are considered biologically sound but whose early life experiences (including maternal and family care, health care, nutrition, opportunities for expression of language, adaptive behaviour, and patterns of physical and social stimulation) are sufficiently limited that there is a high probability of delayed development.

Epidemiology: the study of the distribution and determinants of diseases and handicapping conditions in a population.

Established risk: a diagnosed medical disorder with a known etiology (cause) that bears relatively well-known expectancies for developmental outcomes within varying ranges of developmental disabilities.

Etiology: the process of finding causes to explain how a particular problem came into existence.

Eustachian tube: the tube that connects the middle ear to the nasopharynx.

Expressive disorders: those which affect the formulation of grammatic utterances.

External (outward) locus of control: an individual's attribution of success or failure to outside forces rather than to his or her own ability or efforts.

Extrapyramidal cerebral palsy: condition in which damage is outside the pyramidal tracts and results in abrupt involuntary movements and difficulty in maintaining posture.

Family needs: a family's expressed desire for services to be obtained or outcomes to be achieved.

Fine motor skills: those skills that involve small body movements, with particular reference to the muscles of the hand.

First trimester: opening third of pregnancy.

Flaccid paralysis: an inability to move the muscles because the neural impulses needed for muscle contractions are lacking as a result of damage to the motor cells of the spinal cord.

Fovea: the most sensitive spot of the retina.

Functional academics: academics that have meaning and are relevant to the learner soon to enter community work and life.

Functionality: the characteristics of skills needed for effective and individual coping within the daily environment.

Functional skills: those skills that help children to get along in their current and future environments.

Gaze aversion: a deviant gaze pattern in which the child fails to look directly at another individual.

General adaptation: an adaptation that does not require support or a piece of equipment but still represents a change in the basic requirements of the task or changes the utility of the skill.

Generalized seizures: seizures that are bilateral and symmetrical without local onset in the brain.

Genetic counselling: counselling that deals with the human and medical problems associated with the occurrence of risk or recurrence of a genetic disorder in the family.

Glaucoma: an eye disease characterized by increased intraocular pressure and progressive loss of vision.

Goal: a stated outcome desired as a result of some action.

Grammar: the sum total of conventions that govern the communication of meaning of a particular language.

Gross motor skills: skills that control large body movements such as running, climbing, and throwing.

Group therapy: the simultaneous treatment of several children, usually in the same age range.

Handicap: disadvantage experienced by a person with a disability as a result of environmental or functional demands related to a particular situation that are not met.

Haptic problems: problems involving touch, body movement, and position in space.

Hard-of-hearing person: one who, generally with the use of a hearing aid, has residual hearing sufficient to enable successful processing of linguistic information through audition.

Hearing impairment: a generic term indicating a hearing disability that may range in severity from mild to profound. It includes the subsets of deaf and hard-of-hearing.

Hemisphericity: a person's tendency to rely more on one cerebral hemisphere to process certain types of information.

Hereditary anomalies: genetic abnormalities present at birth.

High risk (at risk): status of children who are seen to be vulnerable to some future disabling condition.

Holophrasic speech: the child's use of a single word to express a more complex idea.

Home visiting (home-based programs): a process whereby a professional or paraprofessional provides help over an extended period of time to a family in its own home.

Hostile aggression: aggression that seems to occur for its own sake and is its own goal.

Hydrocephalus: a condition characterized by an excessive accumulation of cerebrospinal fluid in the brain due to an obstruction of its flow.

Hyperactive children: those who display rates of motor behaviour that are too high for their age groups. They indulge in excessive, non-purposeful movement.

Hyperopia: far-sightedness caused by too short an eye or too flat a corneal surface.

Idiopathic epilepsy: epilepsy of unknown origin.

Impairments: abnormalities of body structure and system function resulting from any cause.

Incidence: the number of new cases of a particular condition identified over a given period of time, usually a year.

Incus: one of the three small bones of the middle ear.

Information processing: a psychological theory which holds that humans process information in different ways and at various levels of analysis.

Instrumental aggression: aggression directed toward the achievement of a non-aggressive goal.

Intelligence quotient (IQ): the relationship between a child's mental age (MA) and chronological age (CA) as reflected by the differences between the child's performance on particular tests and the normative performance for his or her age level.

Intervention: a general term for the application of professional skills to maintain or improve a child's potential and functioning; care and education aimed at influencing the direction and scope of children's developmental processes.

Jacksonian seizure: one form of partial seizure which only occurs in cases of symptomatic epilepsy. Characterized by motor symptoms without impaired consciousness.

Labelling: the categorizing of children on the basis of their primary disability.

Labryinth: the inner ear.

Language: a system of symbols organized into conventional patterns to communicate meaning.

Language delays: significant lags in language seen in children whose language is nonetheless progressing according to the stages of normal language development.

Language disorders: impairment or deviant development of comprehension or use of a spoken, written, or other symbol system.

Language problems: a range of difficulties with the linguistic code, or with the rules and concatenations for linking the symbols and the symbol sequences.

Laterality: an internal knowledge of the difference between left and right.

Legal blindness: an acuity measure of 20/200 or less in the better eye with the best correction; or visual acuity of more than 20/200 if the widest diameter of the field of vision subtends an angle of no greater than 20 degrees.

Life-cycle (lifespan) approach: a perspective that sees the family as a unit that is moving through time and experiencing a series of events, tasks, and transitions.

Limb deficiencies: the loss or absence of limbs or parts of limbs.

Macrocephaly: an enlargement of the head.

Malleus: one of the three small bones of the middle ear.

Maturational lag: term used when a child is slow to reach some developmental milestones.

Meatus: the ear's external canal, which runs obliquely from the pinna to the ear drum.

Medically fragile children: those with special health management needs; includes children who demonstrate a wide range of chronic and progressive illnesses and severe disabilities.

Meningitis: a disease that attacks the meninges, or coverings of the brain and spinal cord.

Mental retardation: substantial limitations in personal functioning, characterized by significant subaverage intellectual functioning, existing concurrently with related limitations in adaptive skills, and manifested before age eighteen.

Metacognition: the awareness of basic learning strategies and one's own awareness of how one learns.

Microcephalus: a rare phenomenon in which brain development is impaired by an abnormally small cranium.

Minimal brain dysfunction (MBD): a diagnostic classification for children who present a diverse variety of mildly disabling symptoms.

Modulation: the ability to control the loudness of the sounds produced.

Morphology: the system of word building in the language.

Motherese: child-adult communicative interaction characterized by unique alterations in speech, meaning, form, and language usage.

Motor development: the process through which a child acquires movement patterns and skills.

Motor learning: using the body in such ways as to make the best use of what is perceived.

Motor skills: those skills related to the development and use of the muscles and limbs.

Multifactorial inheritance: inheritance that results from the interaction of many genes with other genes and/or environmental factors.

Multiple dependent handicapped: term that refers to severely handicapped children who also have sensory and/or other physical handicaps.

Multiple disabilities: those in which children suffer two or more handicaps that hinder their attainment of their full potential.

Multiple sclerosis: a progressive disease of the central nervous system characterized by patchy scarring or hardening of the myelin sheath of the nerve cells in the brain and the spinal cord.

Multisensory impaired: term used to describe children with both sight and hearing handicaps.

Muscular dystrophy: a group of inherited conditions characterized by degeneration of muscle fibres without neurological deficit.

Musculoskeletal impairments: those conditions that impede bodily movements in the absence of damage to the central nervous system.

Mutism: the total absence of speech.

Myopia: nearsightedness — the greatest single cause of defective vision in children and young adults.

Myringotomy: a puncture of the ear drum to drain off fluid.

Needs assessment: the process of identifying current conditions and needs and providing relevant information on the parents' goals for their child and potential parent involvement in the early intervention program.

Neurological impairments: those that result from damage to or dysfunction of the brain and/or the spinal cord.

Normalization: the philosophical belief that all exceptional individuals, no matter what their level and type of disability, should be provided with an education and living environment as close to normal as possible.

Normal distribution: a continuum of scores that vary from the average score by predictable amounts.

Norm-referenced test: a test designed so that an individual child's performance can be compared to that of a normative group consisting of other children of the same age.

Nystagmus: a rhythmic involuntary movement of the eyes.

Objective: a clear statement of exactly what a teacher wants a child to be able to do as a result of instruction.

Operational definitions: those that can be used in everyday situations to identify students who have certain disabilities and to guide their eligibility for the special education process.

Orthotic devices: devices that assist a limb's action.

Otitis media: a condition in which the mucosal lining of the middle ear becomes inflamed and the cavity filled with fluid.

Oval window: entrance to the inner ear.

Partial seizures: various types of seizures that begin locally, that is, in a particular area of the brain; may be characterized as simple or complex.

Pediatric AIDS: AIDS contracted by children under thirteen years of age.

Perception: the use of the senses to recognize, discriminate, and interpret stimuli.

Perseverate: to purposelessly and sometimes disadvantageously repeat an activity.

Pervasive developmental disorder: a general term used in connection with children and youth suffering from chronic and severe conditions that affect every aspect of their development.

Petit mal: absence seizure characterized by non-activity, vacant staring, and a loss or clouding of consciousness.

Phobia: an anxiety reaction that is specific to one stimulus, an intense fear with no rational basis.

Phocomelia: a congenital deformity in which parts of limbs or entire limbs are missing or very short.

Phonetics: the description of the speech sounds of a language.

Phonology: the sound system of language.

Photophobia: a condition in which very bright light decreases an individual's visual acuity.

Pinna: the cartilage structure on the side of the head that constitutes the outer ear.

Polygenic inheritance: the interaction of numerous genes.

Positioning: the way a child with physical disabilities is seated or otherwise placed.

Post-lingual deafness: deafness that occurs after the development of speech and language.

Postmature: term used for infants born two weeks or more beyond the expected due date.

Pragmatics: the ways in which we use language; the role of context in communicative interactions.

Precocity: remarkable early development.

Prelingual deafness: deafness prior to the development of speech and language.

Premature (pre-term) babies: those born before the completion of thirty-seven weeks.

Presbyopia: a condition in which the lens of the eye loses its ability to accommodate to near objects.

Prevalence: the total number of existing cases of a condition, old and new.

Preventative discipline: strategies and procedures that militate against any discipline problems arising.

Primary prevention: procedures concerned with removing the causative factors that account for the initial occurrence of a disorder or strengthening the well-being of individuals in the population as a form of inoculation against the causes of subsequent problems.

Prostheses: functional devices that substitute for missing body parts.

Prosthetic adaptation: a specific piece of equipment such as braces or a hearing aid.

Prosthetic devices: devices used to replace lost functions and/or provide support; they duplicate normal body movements as nearly as possible while restraining normal functions as little as possible.

Psycho-educational assessment: testing children across a variety of domains relevant to social and educational performance.

Psychological processing: the way an individual processes sensory information and puts it to meaningful intellectual use.

Psychomotor seizure: type of partial seizure that is most characteristically associated with lesions of the temporal lobe of the brain.

Pyramidal cerebral palsy. See *Spastic cerebral palsy.*

Receptive disorders: those that interfere with the comprehension of spoken language.

Recidivist: anyone incarcerated for new charges within two years of release from prison.

Reflexes: automatic, involuntary motor patterns that are triggered by specific stimuli.

Rehabilitation: procedures that endeavour to restore an individual to normal or optimal functioning.

Related services: those services that permit an exceptional child to benefit from special education.

Remediation: an educational term that refers to helping a child to overcome, or compensate for, specific deficits in learning and development.

Retinal detachment: condition that occurs when a hole or rip in the retina allows the inner retinal layer to separate from the back portion.

Retinitis pigmentosa: a hereditary condition that causes degeneration of retinal tissues and loss of peripheral vision.

Retinoblastoma: a condition that results from a malignant tumour on the retina and that may spread to the optic nerve and other areas.

Retinopathy of prematurity (retrolental fibroplasia): a condition occurring in premature infants treated with high levels of oxygen and affecting the retina and the vitreous humour.

Rigidity: a type of cerebral palsy that occurs when there is a low level of motor stiffness that never relaxes.

Risk factors: the causes of potential disabilities.

Special education: instruction that is specially designed to meet the unique needs of children and youth who are exceptional.

School law: the legislation, regulations, by-laws, and judicial decisions that apply primarily to all or part of the public school system.

Screening: developmental and health activities that are intended to identify those children who have a high probability of exhibiting delayed or abnormal development.

Secondary prevention: ascertaining, as early as possible, the evidence of disorders that may cause disabilities as well as allied attempts to reduce, remove, or reverse substantially complex aspects of disabilities.

Self-stimulation: a persistent, stereotypic, repetitive mannerism.

Semantics: the aspects of language concerned specifically with the meaning of words.

Sensorineural hearing impairments: impairments that interfere with the conversion of sound waves to neural impulses for the brain.

Social competence: the ability of children to successfully and appropriately select and carry out their interpersonal goals.

Socialization: the means by which individuals become reasonably acceptable and competent members of their society.

Social skills: those responses which, within a given situation, prove effective.

Social support approach: perspective that focuses on a family's functioning; stresses families helping themselves and sees informal support as more important than formal support.

Spastic cerebral palsy (pyramidal): type of cerebral palsy in which individuals have suffered damage to the motor cortex or to the pyramidal tracts of the brain.

Special education: instruction that is specially designed to meet the needs of children and youth who are exceptional.

Special needs: an educational term used to designate pupils who require special education.

Speech disorders: problems encountered in the oral production of language; impairment of verbal communication such that the intelligibility of spoken language is reduced.

Speech range: the range of pitch between 500 Hz and 2000 Hz.

Speech reading (lip reading): the skill of understanding speech through watching the lips and face.

Speech reception threshold (SRT): the level at which an individual actually understands speech.

Spina bifida: a congenital midline defect of the spinal column.

Spina bifida occulta: the mildest form of spina bifida, with few or no negative effects.

Spina bifida with meningocele: form of the condition in which the meninges protrude from the plane of the spine and form a sac containing cerebrospinal fluid.

Spina bifida with myelomeningocele: the most severe type of spina bifida, in which the protruding sac contains parts of the spinal cord as well as cerebrospinal fluid.

Stapes: one of the three small bones of the middle ear.

Strabismus: a condition that can affect one or both eyes and that results from inefficient ocular motor mobility.

Support adaptation: term used to indicate that a child must be placed in a certain position or provided with some general form of support.

Sweep test: the most common screening instrument for hearing, which uses a portable audiometer to present tones at 20 to 25 dB across a range of frequencies.

Symptomatic epilepsy: a convulsive disorder in which an individual shows strong evidence of brain damage.

Syndrome: a constellation of findings similar from patient to patient.

Symptomology: the study of symptoms and characteristics.

Syntax: the network of organizational principles underlying linguistic expression.

Systems theory: perspective which recognizes that actions in any part of a system affect the other parts, and that solutions to problems can only be found when the problem is properly defined in its larger environmental context.

Tactual map: a raised map used by blind persons as a supplemental aid for travel and navigation.

Talent: a specific dimension of a skill in areas such as music, visual arts, drama, athletics, and particular academic domains.

Task analysis: procedure that breaks a task down into its behavioural components and prerequisite skills, or a skill down into its component parts.

Teaming: the process in which two or more persons share information and expertise in order to meet a common goal.

Telegraphic speech: a stripped-down form of language that resembles a telegram in that only the essential aspects of the message, those possessing meaning, are included.

Teratogens: environmental agents that may harm the developing infant.

Teratology: the study of the agents involved in major congenital malformations.

Tertiary prevention: intervention strategies used after a negative outcome has occurred.

Tests: controlled and structured procedures that attempt to elicit particular responses that the child might not demonstrate spontaneously.

Therapy: the treatment of an illness or disabling condition.

Threshold of hearing: the level at which a person can first detect a sound.

Total communication: a system of educating hearing-impaired children that uses speech, speech reading, and amplification, along with a school-based manual system.

Toxemia: several common disorders of pregnancy.

Transition: in special education, the process of moving from one program to another, or from one service delivery mode to another.

Transition services: services intended to provide young people with disabilities access to relevant post-secondary education opportunities, employment in competitive settings, residential independence, and future self-sufficiency.

Traumatic brain injury: an insult to the brain caused by an external physical force which results in impairment of cognitive abilities or physical functioning and may result in disturbances of behaviour or emotional functioning.

Tremor: a rare type of cerebral palsy in which there is an involuntary movement in one extremity, usually a hand or arm.

Tympanic membrane: the ear drum — a tough, tightly stretched tissue that separates the outer from the middle ear.

Usher's syndrome: a condition of familial nerve deafness associated with pigment degeneration of the retina.

Vestibular mechanism: three fluid-filled semi-circular canals in the inner ear, which are the organs of balance.

Visual acuity: the measure of the smallest image distinguishable by the eye.

Visual functioning (visual efficiency): what the impaired person is doing with his or her residual vision.

Vocalization: the ability to produce sound.

Vocational evaluation: a comprehensive and systematic process that utilizes work (real or simulated) to assess the vocational potential of people with disabilities.

Zero reject: a process that prevents a child from being totally or functionally excluded from the publicly supported school system.

Bibliography

Aase, J.M. (1979) Environmental causes of birth defects. In A. Lane (Ed.) *Human growth and development of exceptional individuals.* Connecticut: Special Learning Corporation.

Abang, T.B. (1980) *Teaching visually handicapped children in Nigeria.* Ibadan, Nigeria: Cleverianum Press.

Abrami, P.C., Chambers, B., Poulsen, C., De Simone, C., d'Apollonia, S., and Howden, J. (1995) *Classroom connections: Understanding and using cooperative learning.* Toronto: Harcourt Brace.

Abroms, K.I. and Bennett, J.W. (1983) Current findings in Down's syndrome. *Exceptional Children,* 49, 449-450.

Achenbach, T.M. and Edelbrock, C. (1983) *Manual for the Child Behavior Checklist and Revised Child Behavior Profile.* Burlington, VT: University of Vermont, Department of Psychiatry.

Acredolo, L. and Goodwyn, S. (1988) Symbolic gesturing in normal infants. *Child Development, 59,* 450-466.

Adams, J.W. and Tidwell, R. (1989) An instructional guide for reducing the stress of parents of hearing impaired children. *American Annals of the Deaf, 134,* 323-328.

Adams, K. and Markham, R. (1991) Recognition of affective facial expressions by children and adolescents with and without mental retardation. *American Journal on Mental Deficiency, 96,* 21-28.

Address of Trustees of the New England Institute for the Education of the Blind to the public (1836). In C. Dunscombe, *Report upon the subject of education made to the Parliament of Upper Canada 25 February 1836, through the Commissioners, Doctors Morrison and Bruce, appointed by a resolution of the House of Assembly in 1835 to obtain information upon the subject of education, etc.* (pp. 95-109) Upper Canada: M.C. Reynolds.

Affleck. J.D., Madge, S., Adams, A., and Lowenbraum, S. (1988) Integrated classroom vs resource model: Academic viability and effectiveness. *Exceptional Children, 54,* 339-348.

Agnew, J. (1986) Tinnitis: An overview. *Volta Review, 88,* 215-221.

Akerley, M.S. (1975) Parents speak. *Journal of Autism and Childhood Schizophrenia, 5,* 373-380.

Alberta Education (1982) *Early childhood services: Philosophy, goals, and dimensions.* Edmonton: Government of Alberta.

Alberta Education Response Centre (1989-1990) *Education of the deaf and hard of hearing.* Edmonton: Author.

Alberta Education Response Centre (1989) *A teachers' guide to allergies in the classroom.* Edmonton: Alberta Education.

Alberta Teachers Association (1993) *Trying to teach.* Edmonton: Author.

Alderson, D. (1993, February) Attention Deficit Disorder. *Keeping in Touch,* p. 2.

Aleman, S.R. (1991) *CRS report for Congress: Special education for children with attention deficit disorders: Current issues.* Washington, DC: Congressional Research Services.

Algozzine, B., Morsink, C.V., and Algozzine, K.K. (1988) What's happening in self-contained special education classrooms? *Exceptional Children, 55,* 259-265.

Algozzine, B., Maheady, L., Sacca, K.C., O'Shea L., and O'Shea D. (1990) Sometimes patent medicine works: A reply to Braaten, Kauffman, Polsgrove, and Nelson. *Exceptional Children, 56,* 552-557.

Allanan, Y.O., Arajar, T., and Vitamaki, R.O. (1964) Psychoses in childhood. *Acta Psychiatrica Scandinavica,* Supp. 174.

Allen, R.E. and Wasserman G.A. (1985) Origins of language delay in abused infants. *Child Abuse and Neglect, 9,* 335-340.

Allen, R.M., Cortazzo, A.D., and Adams, C. (1970) Factors in an adaptive behavior checklist for use with retardates. *Training School Bulletin, 67,* 144-157.

Allore, R., O' Hanlon, D., Price, R., Neilson, H., Willard, H.F., Cox, D.R., Marks., A., and Dunn, R.J. (1988, March 11) Gene encoding in the B (beta) subunit of S100 protein on chromosome 21: Implications for Down syndrome. *Science,* pp.1311-1313.

Allum, N. (1975) *Spina bifida: The treatment and care of spina bifida children.* London: George Allen and Unwin.

American Association on Mental Retardation (1993) *Mental retardation: Definition, classification, and systems of support* (9th. ed.) Washington, DC: AAMR.

American Psychiatric Association, (1980/1987/1992) *Diagnostic and statistical manual of mental disorders* (3rd. ed.,3rd ed. revised, 4th. ed.). Washington, D.C.: American Psychiatric Association.

American Speech-Language-Hearing Association (1982) Definitions: Communicative disorders and variations. *ASHA, 24,* 949-959.

Anastopoulos, A.D., DuPaul, G.J., and Barkley, R.A. (1991) Stimulant medication and parent training therapies for attention deficit-hyperactivity disorder. *Journal of Learning Disabilities, 24,* 210-218.

Anderson, E.M. (1973) Cognitive defects in children with spina bifida and hydrocephalus: A review of the literature. *British Journal of Educational Psychology, 43,* 257-268.

Anderson, E. and Spain, B. (1977) *The child with spina bifida.* London: Methuen.

Anderson, H., Barr, B., and Wedenberg, E. (1970) Genetic disposition: Prerequisite for maternal rubella deafness. *Archives of Otolaryngology, 91,* 141-147.

Anderson, R.C., Hiebert, E.H., Scott, J.D., and Wilkinson, I.A.G. (1985) *Becoming a nation of readers: The report of the Commission on Reading.* Washington, DC: National Institute of Education.

Anderson, R.J. and Sisco, F.H. (1977) *Standardization of the WISC-R Performance Scale for deaf children.* Washington, DC: Gallaudet College, Office of Demographic Studies.

Anderson, R.M. and Greer, J.G. (Eds.) (1976) *Educating the severely and profoundly retarded.* Baltimore, MD: University Park Press.

Anderson-Inman, L. (1986) Bridging the gap: Student-centered strategies for promoting the transfer of learning. *Exceptional Children, 52,* 562-572.

Andrews, G.A., Craig, A., Feyer, A., Hoddinott, S., Howie, P., and Neilson, M. (1983) Stuttering: A review of research findings and theories. *Journal of Speech and Hearing Disorders, 48,* 226-246.

Andrews, J.W. and Mason, J.M. (1991) Strategy usage among deaf and hearing readers. *Exceptional Children, 57,* 536-545.

Anvar, B., Mencher, G.T., and Keet, S.J. (1984) Hearing loss and congenital rubella in Atlantic Canada. *Ear and Hearing, 5,* 346-348.

Apgar, V. and Beck, J. (1974) *Is my baby all right?* New York: Pocket Books.

Aplin, D.Y. (1987) Social and emotional adjustment of hearing-impaired children in ordinary and special schools. *Educational Research, 29,* 56-64.

Archambault, F.X. and Hallmark B.W. (1992) Regular classroom practices: Results of a national survey. In J.S. Renzulli (Chair) *Regular classroom practices with gifted students: Findings from the National Research Center on the Gifted and Talented Symposium.* Conducted at the American Educational Research Association, San Francisco.

Archer, L.A. (1977) Blissymbolics — A nonverbal communication system. *Journal of Speech and Hearing Disorders, 42,* 568-579.

Arnold, K.M. and Hornett, D. (1990) Teaching idioms to children who are deaf. *Teaching Exceptional Children, 22,* 14-17.

Arreaga-Mayer, C., Carta, J., and Tapia, Y. (1994) Ecobehavioral assessment: A new methodology for evaluating instruction for exceptional culturally and linguistically diverse students. In S.B. Garcia (Ed.) *Addressing cultural and linguistic diversity in special education: Issues and trends* (pp. 10-29). Reston, VA: CEC.

Arter, J.A. and Jenkins, J.R. (1977) Examining the benefits and prevalence of modifiabilty consideration in special education. *Journal of Special Education, 11,* 281-289.

Ashworth, M. (1975) *Immigrant children and Canadian schools.* Toronto: McClelland and Stewart.

Astin, A.W., Green, K.C., and Korn, W.S. (1989) *The American freshman: National norms for fall 1989.* Los Angeles, CA: University of California Higher Education Research Institute.

Atkins, D.V. (1987) Siblings of the hearing impaired: Perspectives for parents. *Volta Review, 89,* 32-45.

Atkinson, M.A. and MacLaren, N.K. (1990) What causes diabetes? *Scientific American,* pp. 63-71.

Audet, L.R., Burke, G.M., Hummel, L.J., Maker, S.R., and Theodore, G. (1990) *Journal of Speech and Hearing Disorders, 55,* 179-192.

Augoustinos, M (1987) Developmental effects of child abuse: Recent findings. *Child Abuse and Neglect, 11,* 15-26.

Augusto, C.R. and McGraw, J.M. (1990) Humanizing blindness through public education. *Journal of Visual Impairment and Blindness, 84,* 397-400.

Baca, L. and Amato, C. (1989) Bilingual special education: Training issues. *Exceptional Children, 56,* 168-173.

Baca, L.M. and Cervantes, H.T. (1984) *The bilingual special education interface.* St. Louis, MO: Times Mirror/ Mosby.

Baca, L. and Harris, K.C. (1988) Teaching migrant exceptional children. *Teaching Exceptional Children, 20.*

Bachor, D.G. and Crealock, C. (1986) *Instructional strategies for students with special needs.* Toronto: Prentice-Hall.

Bacon, E.H. and Schulz, J.B. (1991) A survey of mainstreaming practices. *Teacher Education and Special Education, 2,* 144-149.

Badian, N.A. (1988) The prediction of good and poor reading before kindergarten entry: A nine-year follow up. *Journal of Learning Disabilities, 21,* 98-103.

Bailey, D.B. Jr. and Blanco, P.M. (1990) Parents' perspectives of a written survey of family needs. *Journal of Early Intervention, 14,* 196-203.

Bailey, D.B. and Brochin, H.A. (1989) Tests and test development. In D.B. Bailey and M. Wolery (Eds.) *Assessing infants and preschoolers with handicaps* (pp. 22-46) Columbus, OH: Merrill.

Bailey, D.B. and Harbin, G. (1980) Nondiscriminatory evaluation. *Exceptional Children, 46,* 590-596.

Bailey, D.B., and Wolery, M. (1984) *Teaching infants and preschoolers with handicaps.* Columbus, OH: Merrill.

Bailey. D.B. and Wolery, M.(Eds.) (1989) *Assessing infants and preschoolers with handicaps.* Columbus, OH: Merrill.

Bailey, D.B. Harms, T., and Clifford, R.M. (1983) Matching changes in preschool environments to desired changes in child behavior. *Journal of the Division for Early Childhood, 7,* 61-68.

Bailey, D.B., Jens, K., and Johnson, N. (1983) Curricula for handicapped infants. In S. Garwood and R. Fewell (Eds.) *Educating handicapped infants: Issues in development and intervention.* (pp. 387-415). Rockville, MD: Aspen.

Bailey, D.B. Jr., Simeonsson, R.J., Yoder, D.E., and Huntington, G.S. (1990) Preparing professionals to serve infants and toddlers with handicaps and their families: An integrative analysis across eight disciplines. *Exceptional Children, 57,* 26-35.

Bailey, I.L. and Hall, A. (1983) *Bailey-Hall Cereal Test for the Measurement of Visual Acuity in Children.* Berkeley, CA: Multimedia Center, School of Optometry, University of California.

Bailey, I.L. and Hall, A. (1984) *U.C.-Berkeley Preferential Looking Test.* Berkeley, CA: Multimedia Center, School of Optometry, University of California.

Bain, D.A. (1980) Gifted and enriched education in Canada. In M. Csapo and L. Goguen (Eds.) *Special education across Canada: Issues and concerns for the '80s.* Vancouver: Centre for Human Development and Research.

Bak, J.J., Cooper, E.M., Dobroth, K.M., and Siperstein, G.N. (1987) Special class placements as labels: Effects on children's attitudes toward learning handicapped peers. *Exceptional Children, 54,* 151-155.

Baker, D. (1983) Justin Clark: Legal implications of the Mental Incompetency Act for "Citizens of the World." *Canadian Journal on Mental Retardation, 33,* 14-20.

Baker, J.M. and Zigmond, N. (1990) Are regular education classes equipped to accommodate students with learning disabilities? *Exceptional Children, 56,* 515-526.

Baker, L. (1982) An evaluation of the role of metacognitive deficits in learning disabilities. *Topics in Learning and Learning Difficulties, 2,* 27-35.

Baker, L. and Cantwell, D.P. (1982) Psychiatric disorders in children with different types of communication disorders. *Journal of Communication Disorders, 15,* 113-126.

Baker, L. and Cantwell, D.P. (1987) A prospective psychiatric follow-up of children with speech/language disorders. *Journal of the American Academy of Child and Adolescent Psychiatry, 26,* 546-553.

Baker, L., Cantwell, D.P., and Mathison, R.E. (1980) Behavior problems in children with pure speech disorders and in children with combined speech and language disorders. *Journal of Abnormal Child Psychology, 8,* 245-256.

Balakrishnan, T.R. and Wolf, L.C. (1976) Life expectancy of mentally retarded persons in Canadian institutions. *Journal of Abnormal Psychology, 80,* 211-224.

Ballinger, C.T., Varley, C.K., and Nolen, P.A. (1984) Effects of methylphenidate on reading in children with attention deficit disorders. *Abnormal Child Psychology, 5,* 357-369.

Balow, B. (1979) Definitional and prevalence problems in behavior disorders of children. *School Psychology Digest, 8,* 348-354.

Balow, B. and Balow, E. (1982) Education of autistic children: Philosophy and program options. In C.R. Smith, J.P. Grimes, and J.J. Frielinger (Eds.) *Autism: Programmatic considerations.* Des Moines, IO: Department of Public Instruction.

Balthazar, E.E. (1973) *The Balthazar Scales of Adaptive Behavior: Scale 2, Scales of Social Adaptation.* Palo Alto, CA: Consulting Psychologists Press.

Balthazar, E.E. (1976) *The Balthazar Scales of Adaptive Behavior: Scale 1, Scale of Functional Independence.* Palo Alto, CA: Consulting Psychologists Press.

Banbury, M.M. and Wellington, B. (1989) Designing and using peer nomination forms. *Gifted Talented Creative, 33*, 161-164.

Bank-Mikkelson, N.E. (1969) A metropolitan area in Denmark: Copenhagen. In R. Kugel and W. Wolfsenberger (Eds.) *Changing patterns in residential services for the mentally retarded.* Washington, DC: President's Committee on Mental Retardation.

Banks, J.A. (1981/1988) *Multiethnic education: Theory and practice.* Boston, MA: Allyn and Bacon.

Banks, R. (1979) "How would you like it if you were gifted?" *Special Education in Canada, 53*, 12-14.

Barden, R.C., Ford, M.E., Jensen, A.G., Rogers-Salyer, M., and Salyer, K.E. (1989) Effects of craniofacial deformity in infancy on the quality of mother-infant interactions. *Child Development, 60*, 819-824.

Barkan, J.H. and Bernal, E.M. (1991) Gifted education for bilingual and limited English proficient students. *Gifted Child Quarterly, 35*, 144-147.

Barkley, R.A. (1989) Attention deficit hyperactivity disorder. In E.J. Nash and R.A. Barkley (Eds.) *Treatment of childhood disorders* (pp. 39-72) New York: Guilford.

Barkley, R.A. (1990) Attention deficit disorders: History, definition, and diagnosis. In M.Lewis and S.M. Miller (Eds.) *Handbook of developmental psychopathology.* New York: Plenum.

Barkley, R.A., Du Paul, G., and McMurray, M. (1990) Comprehensive evaluation of attention deficit disorder with and without hyperactivity as defined by research criteria. *Journal of Consulting and Clinical Psychology, 58*, 775-789.

Barkley, R.A., Fisher, M., Newby, R., and Breen, M. (1988) Development of multi-method clinical protocol for assessing stimulant drug responses in ADHD children. *Journal of Clinical Child Psychology, 17*, 14-24.

Barnes, E. and Lehr, R. (1993) Including everyone: A model preschool program for typical and special needs children. In J. Roopnarine and J.E. Johnson (Eds.) *Approaches to early childhood education* (pp. 81-96) New York: Merrill.

Barnett, W.S. (1986) Definition and classification of mental retardation: A reply to Zigler, Balla and Hodapp. *American Journal on Mental Deficiency, 91*, 111-116.

Baron, R.A. and Byrne, D. (1981) *Social psychology: Understanding human interaction.* Boston, MA: Allyn and Bacon.

Barraga, N.C. (1976) *Increased visual behavior in low vision children.* New York: Belmont, CA: Wadsworth.

Barraga, N.C. (1977) *Teacher's guide for development of visual learning: Abilities and utilization of low vision.* Austin, TX: American Printing House for the Blind.

Barth, R. (1979) Home-based reinforcement of school behavior: A review and analysis. *Review of Educational Research, 49*, 436-458.

Barth, R.S. (1990) *Improving schools from within: Teacher, parents, and principals can make the difference.* San Francisco, CA: Jossey-Bass.

Bates, J.E. (1987) Temperament in infancy. In J.D. Osofsky (Ed.) *Handbook of infant development* (pp. 1101-1149). New York: Wiley.

Bates, P., Morrow, S.A., Pancsafar, E., and Sedlak, R. (1984) The effect of functional vs nofunctional activities on the attitudes/expectations of nonhandicapped college students: What they see is what we get. *Journal of the Association for Persons with Severe Handicaps, 9*, 73-78.

Batshaw, M.L. and Perret, Y.M. (1986) *Children with handicaps: A medical primer.* Baltimore, MD: Brookes.

Bauer, A.M. and Shea, T.M. (1989) *Teaching exceptional students in your classroom.* Toronto: Allyn and Bacon.

Baum, C. (1989) Conduct disorders. In T.H. Ollendick and M. Hersen (Eds.) *Handbook of child psychopathology.* (2nd ed.) New York: Plenum.

Baum, S. (1995) Gifted but learning disabled: A puzzling paradox. *ERIC Digest, No 479.* Reston, VA: CEC.

Baumeister, A.A., Kupstas, F., and Klindworth, L.M. (1990) New morbidity: Implications for prevention of children's disabilities. *Exceptionality, 1*, 1-16.

Bauwens, J., Hourcade, J.J., and Friend, M. (1989) Cooperative teaching: A model for general and special education integration. *Remedial and Special Education, 10*, 17-22.

Bay, E. (1975) Ontogeny of stable speech areas in the human brain. In E.H. Lenneberg and E. Lenneberg (Eds.), *Foundations of language development: A multidisciplinary approach* (vol.2). New York: Academic Press.

Beare, P.L. (1991) Philosophy, instructional methodology, training and goals of teachers of the behaviorally disordered. *Behavior Disorders, 16*, 211-218.

Becker, R. (1981) *Revised Reading-Free Inventory — Manual.* Columbus, OH: Erlbaum.

Beers, C.S. and Beers, J.W. (1980) Early identification of learning disabilities: Facts and fallacies. *Elementary School Journal, 81*, 67-76.

Belcostas, F.P. (1987) Elementary pull-out programs for the intellectually gifted — boon or bane? *Roeper Review, 9*, 41-55.

Bell, L.M. (1986) Evaluation and implementation of innovation in gifted/enrichment programs. *Gifted Education International, 4*, 120-127.

Bell, R., Fisher, M., and Rodriguez, J. (1994, Oct 30) Ritalin use sparks concern. *Calgary Sun*, pp. 3, 16-17.

Bellamy, T. (1985). Severe disability in adulthood. *Newsletter for the Association for Persons with Severe Handicaps, 11*, 1-6.

Belmont, L. and Birch, H.G. (1973) Lateral dominance, lateral awareness and reading disability. In H.A. Solan (Ed.) *The psychology of learning and reading difficulties.* New York: Simon and Schuster.

Benbow, C.P. (1991) Meeting the needs of gifted students through use of acceleration. In M.C. Wang, M.C. Reynolds, and H.J. Walberg (Eds.) *Handbook of special education*, vol. 4. (pp. 23-36). Elmsford, NY: Pergamon.

Bender, W. (1992) *Learning disabilities: Characteristics, identification, and teaching strategies.* Boston, MA: Allyn and Bacon.

Bender, W.N. and Smith, J.K. (1990) Classroom behavior of children and adolescents with learning disabilities: A meta-analysis. *Journal of Learning Disabilities, 23*, 298-305.

Benedek, T. (1970) Parenthood during the life cycle. In E.V. Anthony and T. Benedek (Eds.) *Parenthood: Its psychology and psychopathology.* Boston, MA: Little, Brown.

Benedict, H. (1979) Early lexical development: Comprehension and production. *Journal of Child Language, 6*, 183-200.

Berg, F.S. (1986) Characteristics of the target population. In F.S. Berg, J.C. Blair, S.H. Viehweg, and A. Wilson-Vlotman. *Educational audiology for the hard of hearing child* (pp. 1-24) Orlando, FL: Grune and Stratton.

Benjamin, M. (1980). Abused as a child, abusive as a parent. In R. Volpe, M. Breton, and J. Witten (Eds.) *The maltreatment of the school-aged child.* Toronto: Lexington.

Berkow, R. (Ed.) (1982) *The Merck manual of diagnosis and therapy.* Rahway, NJ: Merck, Sharp and Dohme.

Berlin, C.M. Jr. (1983) Biological causes of exceptionality. In R.M. Smith, J.T. Neisworth, and F.M. Hunt (Eds.) *The exceptional child: A functional approach.* New York: McGraw-Hill

Bernard, H. (1973) *Child development and learning.* Boston, MA: Allyn and Bacon.

Berninger, V. and Rutberg, J. (1992) Relationship of finger function to beginning writing: Application to diagnoses of writing disabilities. *Developmental Medicine and Child Neurology, 34,* 155-172.

Berns, J.H. (1980) Grandparents of handicapped children. *Social Work, 15,* 238-239.

Bernstein, D.K. and Tiegerman, E. (1989) *Language and communication disorders in children* (2nd. ed.) Columbus, OH: Merrill.

Bernthal, J. and Bankston, N. (1981) *Articulation disorders.* Englewood Cliffs, NJ: Prentice-Hall.

Berry, C.A., Shaywitz, S.E., and Shaywitz, B.A. (1985) Girls with attention deficit disorder: A silent minority? A report on behavioral and cognitive aspects. *Pediatrics, 76,* 801-809.

Bertin, O. (1988, 23 September) Computers give a technological hand to disabled kids. Toronto, *Globe and Mail,* p. B.17.

Best, H. (1930) Educational provisions for the deaf, the blind, and the feeble-minded compared. *American Annals of the Deaf, 75,* 239-240.

Betancourt, H. and Lopez, S.R. (1993) The study of culture, ethnicity, and race in American psychology. *American Psychologist, 48,* 629-637.

Betts, G.T.(1985) *Autonomous learner model for the gifted and talented.* Greeley, CO: Autonomous Learning Publications and Specialists.

Bhatara, V. (1980) Overlap of autism, mental retardation, and CNS dysfunction. *Psychiatric Annals, 10,* 298-304.

Bickel, W.E. and Bickel, D.D. (1986) Effective schools, classrooms, and instruction: Implications for special education. *Exceptional Children, 52,* 489-500.

Bierman, K.L., Miller, C.L., and Stabb, S.D. (1987) Improving the social behavior and peer acceptance of rejected boys: Effects of social skill training with instruction and prohibitions. *Journal of Consulting and Clinical Psychology, 53,* 194-200.

Bierne-Smith M. (1991) Peer tutoring in arithmetic for children with learning disabilities. *Exceptional Children, 57,* 330-337.

Bierstedt, L. (1974). *The social order* (4th. ed.) New York: McGraw-Hill.

Bigelow, A. (1987) Early words of blind children. *Journal of Child Language, 14,* 47-56.

Bigelow, A. (1991) Spatial mapping of familar locations in blind children. *Journal of Visual Impairment and Blindness, 85,* 113-117.

Bingol, N., Schuster, C., Fuchs, M., Iosub, S., et al. (1987) The influence of socioeconomic factors in the occurrence of fetal alcohol syndrome. *Advances in Alcohol and Substance Abuse, 6,* 105-118.

Binnie, C.D., Channon, S, and Marston, D. (1990) Learning disabilities in epilepsy: Neurophysiological aspects. *Epilepsia, 31* (supp. 4) 52-58.

Bishop, V. (1986) Identifying the components of success in mainstreaming. *Journal of Visual Impairment and Blindness, 80,* 939-946.

Bishop, W. (1968) Successful teachers of the gifted. *Exceptional Children, 34,* 317-325.

Blair, J.C. (1990) Front-row seating is not enough for classroom listening. In C. Flexner, D. Wray, and R. Leavitt (Eds.) *How the student with hearing loss can succeed in college: A handbook for students, families, and professionals.* Washington DC: A.G. Bell Association for the Deaf.

Blanton, R.L. (1976) Historical perspectives on classification of mental retardation. In N. Hobbs (Ed.) *Issues in the classification of children,* (vol 1). (pp. 164-193). San Francisco, CA: Jossey-Bass.

Blatt, B. (1985) Friendly letters on the correspondence of Helen Keller, Anne Sullivan, and Alexander Graham Bell. *Exceptional Children, 51,* 405-409.

Bleck, E.E. (1979) Integrating the physically handicapped child. *Journal of School Health, 49,* 141-146.

Bleck, E.L. and Nagel, D.A. (1982) *Physically handicapped children: A medical atlas for teachers.* New York: Grune and Stratton.

Block, E.L. and Goodstein, L.D. (1971). Functional speech disorders and personality: A decade of research. *Journal of Speech and Hearing Disorders, 31,* 295-314.

Block, J.H., Gersten, E., and Kromblum, S. (1980) Evaluation of a language program for young autistic children. *Journal of Speech and Hearing Disorders, 45,* 76-89.

Blomquist, H., Gustavson, K.H., Holmgren, S., Nordenson, I., and Swein, A. (1983) Fragile site x chromosomes and x-linked mental retardation in severely retarded boys in a northern Swedish county: A prevalence study. *Clinical Genetics, 21,* 209-224.

Bloodstein, O. (1975). *A handbook on stuttering* (rev. ed.) National Easter Seal Society for Crippled Children and Adults.

Bloom, B.S. (Ed.) (1956) *Taxonomy of educational objectives: Handbook 1: Cognitive domain.* New York: David McKay.

Bloom, B.S. (1964) *Stability and change in human characteristics.* New York: Wiley.

Bloom, B.S. (1974) Time and learning. *American Psychologist, 29,* 682-688.

Bloom, B.S. (1982) The role of gifts and markers in the development of talent. *Exceptional Children, 48,* 510-522.

Bloom, B.S. (1985) *Developing talent in young people.* New York: Ballantine Books.

Bloom, B.S. and Sosniak, L.A. (1981) Talent development vs schooling. *Educational Leadership, 39,* 86-94.

Bloom, B.S., Davis, A., and Hess, R. (1965) *Compensatory education for cultural deprivation.* New York: Holt, Rinehart and Winston,

Blueler, E. (1911) *Dementia praecox, or the group of schizophrenias.* Leipzig: Deutche. Trans. J. Zinkin, New York: International University Press (1950).

Bluestone, D.C. (1982) Otitis media in children: To treat or not to treat. *New England Journal of Medicine, 306,* 1399-1404.

Blumstein, A., Cohen J., and Farrington, D.P. (1988) Criminal career research: Its value for criminology. *Criminology, 26,* 1-35.

Boehm, E.A. (1971) *Boehm Test of Basic Concepts manual.* New York: Psychological Corporation.

Bomberg, D., Szurek, S., and Etemad, J. (1973) A statistical study of a group of psychotic children. In S. Szurek and I.N. Berlin (Eds.), *Clinical studies in childhood psychoses.* New York: Brunner/Mazel.

Bond, D. (1981) Aspects of behaviour and management of adolescents who are hearing impaired. *British Teacher of the Deaf, 2,* 41-48.

Bond, G.G. (1987) An assessment of cognitive abilities in hearing and hearing impaired preschool children. *Journal of Speech and Hearing Disorders, 52,* 319-323.

Bonvillian, J.D., Orlansky, M.D., and Novack, L.L. (1983) Developmental milestones: Sign language acquisition and motor development. *Child Development, 54,* 1435-1445.

Borgh, K. and Dickson, W.P. (1986) Two preschools sharing one microcomputer: Creating prosocial behavior with hardware and software. In P.F. Campbell and G.G. Fein (Eds.) *Young children and microcomputers* (pp. 37-44). Reston, VA: Reston.

Borland, J.H. (1989) *Planning and implementing programs for the gifted.* New York: Teachers College Press.

Bos, C.C. and Vaughn, S. (1988) *Strategies for teaching students with learning and behavior problems.* Boston, MA: Allyn and Bacon.

Bouchard, T.J. Jr. and McGue, M. (1981) Familial studies of intelligence: A review. *Science, 212*, 1055-1059.

Bourque, J. and Li, A. (1987) Perceived competence, social adjustment and peer relations of intellectually gifted children in segregated versus regular-classroom settings. *Canadian Journal of Special Education, 3*, 191-200.

Bower, B, (1989) Remodeling the autistic child. *Science News, 136*, 312-313

Bowley, A. and Gardner, L. (1980) *The handicapped child.* London: Churchill Livingstone.

Bowman, B. (1989) Educating language-minority children: Challenges and opportunities. *Phi Delta Kappan, 71*, 118-120.

Braaten, S., Kauffman, J.M., Braaten, B., Polsgrove, L., and Nelson C.M. (1988) The regular education initiative: Patent medicine for behavioral disorders. *Exceptional Children, 55*, 21-28.

Braden, J.P. (1987) An explanation of the superior performance IQs of deaf children of deaf parents. *American Annals of the Deaf, 132*, 263-266.

Braden, J.P. and Shaw, S.R. (1987) Computer assisted instruction with deaf children: Panacea, placebo or poison. *American Annals of the Deaf, 132*, 189-193.

Bradley, C. (1937) The behavior of children receiving Benzedrine. *American Journal of Psychiatry, 94*, 577-585.

Bradley, E. (1975) Screen them early! *Academic Therapy, 10*, 305-308.

Brady, M.P., Swank, P.R., Taylor, R.D., Frieberg, J. (1992) Teacher interactions in mainstreamed social studies and science classes. *Exceptional Children, 58*, 530-540.

Braga, L. and Braga, J. (1975) *Learning and growing: A guide to child development.* Englewood Cliffs, NJ: Prentice-Hall.

Braithwaite, J. (1981) The myth of social class and criminality reconsidered. *American Sociological Review, 46*, 36-57.

Bransford, J.D., Delchos, V.R., Vye, N.J., Burns, M.S., and Hasselbring, T.S. (1987) State of the art and future direction. In C.S. Lidz (Ed.) *Dynamic assessment: An interactional approach to evaluating learning potential* (pp. 479-496) New York: Guilford.

Bransky, T. (1987) Specific program information: A key to attitudes about the gifted education program. *Gifted Child Quarterly, 31*, 20-24.

Brantlinger, E.A. and Guskin, S.L. (1987) Ethnicultural and social psychological effects of learning characteristics of handicapped children. In M.C. Wang, H.C. Reynolds, and H.J. Walberg (Eds.) *Handbook of special education: Research and practice (vol. 1) Learner characteristics and adaptive education* (pp. 7-34) New York: Pergamon.

Bregman, S. (1984) Assertiveness training for mentally retarded adults. *Mental Retardation, 22*, 12-16.

Breslau, N. and Davis, G.C. (1986) Chronic stress and major depression. *Archives of General Psychiatry, 43*, 309-314.

Bricker, D. D. (1982) *Intervention with at-risk handicapped infants.* Baltimore, MD: University Park Press.

Bricker, D. (1986) *Early education of at-risk and handicapped infants, toddlers and preschool children.* Glenville, IL: Scott, Foresman.

Bricker, D. (1993) A rose by any other name, or is it? *Journal of Early Intervention, 17*, 89-96.

Bricker, D. and Squires, J. (1989) Low cost system using parents to monitor the development of at-risk infants. *Journal of Early Intervention, 13*, 50-60.

Brink, J.D., Imbus, C., and Woo-Sam, J. (1980) Physical recovery after closed head trauma in children and adolescents. *Journal of Pediatrics, 97*, 721-727.

Brinthaupt, G.P. (1991) Cystic fibrosis and parental adjustment. In M. Seligman (Ed.) *The family with a handicapped child* (2nd. ed.) (pp. 295-336) Boston, MA: Allyn and Bacon.

Bristol, M. (1979) Maternal coping with autistic children: Adequacy of interpersonal support and effects of child characteristics. Doctoral dissertation, University of North Carolina, Chapel Hill.

British Columbia Ministry of Education (1995) *Gifted education: A resource guide for teachers.* Victoria: Author.

British Columbia Ministry of Health, (1978) *Epilepsy: The causes, the treatment, the hope.* Victoria: B.C. Ministry of Health.

Broadhurst, D.D., Edmunds, M., and MacDicker, R.A. (1979) *Early childhood programs and the prevention and treatment of child abuse and neglect: The user manual series.* Washington, DC: U.S. Department of Health, Education and Welfare.

Brod, N. and Hamilton, D. (1973) Binocularity and reading. *Journal of Learning Disabilities, 6*, 574-576.

Broder, P.K., Dunivant, N., Smith, E.C., and Sutton, P.L. (1981) Further observation on the link between learning disabilities and juvenile delinquency. *Journal of Educational Psychology, 73*, 838-850.

Brody, G.H., Stoneman, Z., Davis, C.H., and Crapps, J.M. (1991) Observations of the role relations and behavior between older children with mental retardation and their younger siblings. *American Journal on Mental retardation, 95*, 527-536.

Brody, H. (1989) The great equalizer: PCs empower the disabled. *PC Computing, 2*, 82-93.

Brody, J. (1988, March 8) Cocaine: Litany of fetal risks grows. *New York Times.*

Brokx, J.P. (1987) The integration of hearing aid rehabilitation in the management of young hearing-impaired children. *Audiology in Practice, 4*, 7-8.

Brolin, D. and Gysbers, N. (1989) Career education for students with disabilities. *Journal of Counseling and Development, 68*, 155-159.

Brookhart, S.M. and Freeman, D.J. (1992) Characteristics of entering teacher candidates. *Review of Educational Research, 62*, 37-60.

Brooks, D.N. (1977) Auditory screening: Time for reappraisal. *Public Health, 91*, 282-288.

Brooks, J.B. (1987) *The process of parenting* (2nd. ed.) Palo Alto, CA: Mayfield Publishers.

Brosnan, F.L. (1983) Overrepresentation of low socioeconomic minority students in special education programs in California. *Learning Disability Quarterly, 6*, 517-525.

Brown, A.L. and Palinscar, A.S. (1982) Inducing strategic learning from texts by means of informed, self-control training. *Topics in Learning and Learning Disabilities, 2*, 1-17.

Brown, B.B., Clasen, D.R. and Eicher, S.A. (1986) Perceptions of peer pressure, peer conformity dispositions, and self-reported behavior among adolescents. *Developmental Psychology, 22*, 521-530.

Brown, L. (1988) Characteristics of Newfoundland dialect. St. John's: Memorial University of Newfoundland.

Brown, L., Nisbet, J., Ford, A., Sweet, M., Shirga, B., York, J., and Loomis, R. (1983) The critical need for nonschool instruction in educational programs for severely handicapped students. *Journal of The Association for the Severely Handicapped, 8*, 71-77.

Brown, P.M. and Foster, S.B. (1991) Integrating hearing and deaf students on a college campus: Successes and barriers as perceived by hearing students. *American Annals of the Deaf, 136*, 21-27.

Brown, W.T., Jenkins, E.C., Cohen I.L., et al., (1986) Fragile X and autism: A multicenter survey. *American Journal of Medical Genetics, 13*, 341-352.

Bruininks, R.H. (1977) *Manual for the Bruininks-Osteresky Test of Motor Proficiency.* Circle Pines, MI: American Guidance Service.

Bruininks, R.H. and Warfield, G. (1978) The mentally retarded. In E.L. Meyen (Ed.) *Exceptional children and youth: An introduction.* Denver, CO: Love Publishing.

Brulle, A.R., Barton, L.E., Wharton, D.L., and Brulle, C.L. (1983) A comparison of teacher time spent with physically handicapped and able-bodied students. *Exceptional Children, 49,* 543-547.

Bryan, T.H. and Pflaum, S. (1978) Social interactions of learning disabled children: A linguistic, social, and cognitive analysis. *Learning Disability Quarterly, 1,* 70-79.

Bryan, W.H. and Jeffrey, D.L. (1982) Education of visually handicapped students in the regular classroom. *Texas Teachers Journal of Education, 9,* 125-131.

Buchanan, M. and Wolf, J.S. (1986) A comprehensive study of learning disabled adults. *Journal of Learning Disabilities, 19,* 34-38.

Buescher, T.M. (1991) Gifted adolescents. In N. Colangelo and G.A. Davis (Eds.) *Handbook of gifted education* (pp. 382-401). Boston, MA: Allyn and Bacon.

Bullis, M. and Reiman, J. (1992) Development and preliminary psychometric properties of the Transition Competence Battery for deaf adolescents and young adults. *Exceptional Children, 59,* 12-26.

Burden, R.L. (1980) Measuring the effects of stress on the mothers of handicapped infants: Must depression always follow? *Child: Care, Health and Development, 6,* 111-125.

Burgio, G.R., Fraccaro, M., and Tiepolo, L. (1981) *Trisomy 21.* Berlin: Springer-Verlag.

Burgio, P. (1986) Safety consideration of cochlear implantation. *Otolaryngologic Clinics of North America, 19,* 237-247.

Burke, M. A. (1992, spring) Canada's immigrant children. *Canadian Social Trends,* pp. 15, 20.

Busse, T.V. and Mansfield, R.S. (1980) Renzulli is right. *Gifted Child Quarterly, 24,* 132.

Butts, K.R. (1980) *Breathing exercises for asthma.* Springfield, IL: Thomas.

Byrne, M. E. and Shervanian, C.C. (1977) *Introduction to communication disorders.* New York: Harper and Row.

Caccia, C.L. (1975). *Immigrant education and multiculturalism.* In A. Wolfgang (Ed.) Education of immigrant students. Toronto: OISE Press.

Caffey, J. (1946) Multiple fractures in the long bones of infants suffering from chronic subdural hematoma. *American Journal of Roentgenology, 56,* 163-173.

Cain, L.F., Levine, S., and Elzey, F.F. (1963) *Manual for the Cain-Levine Social Competency Scale.* Palo Alto, CA: Consulting Psychologists Press.

Calfee, R.C. (1977) Assessment of independent reading skills: Basic research and practical applications. In A.S. Reber and D.L. Scarborough (Eds.) *Toward a psychology of reading.* Hillsdale, NJ: Erlbaum.

Calfee, R.C. (1987) The school as a context for assessment of literacy. *The Reading Teacher, 40,* 738-743.

Calhoun, M.L. and Hawisher, M. (1979) *Teaching and learning strategies for physically handicapped students.* Baltimore, MD: University Park Press.

Callahan, C.M. (1979) The gifted and talented women. In A.H. Passow (Ed.) *The gifted and talented: Their education and development.* Chicago, Il: University of Chicago Press.

Callahan, C.M. (1981) Superior abilities. In J.M. Kauffman and D.P. Hallahan (Eds.) *Handbook of special education.* Englewood Cliffs, NJ: Prentice-Hall.

Cameron, D. R. (1979) The right to education. *Mental Retardation/Déficience Mentale, 29,* 2-5.

Camp, B. (1973) Psychiatric tests and learning tests in severely disabled readers. *Journal of Learning Disabilities, 6,* 512-517.

Campbell, M.S. Cohen S.L., and Rich, M. (1987) *Guidelines for the management of health impaired students.* ERIC No. Ed. 287 269.

Campione, J.C. (1989) Assisted assessment: A taxonomy of approaches and an outline of strengths and weaknesses. *Journal of Learning Disabilities, 22,* 151-165.

Campos, J. and Keating, R. (1988) The Carpinteria language-minority student experience: From theory, to practice, to success; In T. Skutnabb-Kargas and J. Cummins (Eds.) *Minority education: Shame to struggle* (pp. 299-307) Clevedon, England: Multilingual Matters.

Canada, Health and Welfare (1984) *Childhood hearing impairment: Report of a Task Force convened by the Health Service Directorate, Health Services and Prevention Branch.* Ottawa: Department of Health and Welfare.

Canada, *Journals,* 1858.

Canadian Association for the Mentally Retarded [1980] *Questions and answers about mental retardation.* Pamphlet, n.p., CAMR.

Canadian Council for Exceptional Children (1989) Status of education service delivery to exceptional students: A provincial survey. *Keeping in Touch.*

Canadian Council for Exceptional Children (1992a) *Equal educational opportunity for students with disabilities: Legislative action in Canada.* Montreal: Canadian CEC.

Canadian Council for Exceptional Children (1992b, March) *Monograph one: Staying in school initiatives.* Toronto: Author.

Canadian Hearing Society (1976) *Deafness: The silent epidemic.* Toronto: Canadian Hearing Society.

Canadian National Institute for the Blind (1980) Brochure. Toronto: CNIB.

Canadian Pediatric Society (1988) Hyperactivity in children. *Canadian Medical Association Journal, 139,* 211-212.

Canadian war blinded (1942) *Outlook for the blind and the Teacher's Forum, 36,* 281-286.

Cantor, S. (1988) Childhood schizophrenia. *American Journal on Mental Retardation, 94,* 688-690.

Cantor, S. (1989) *Childhood schizophrenia.* New York: Guilford Press.

Cantwell, D.P., Baker, B.L., and Rutter, M. (1979) Families of autistic and dysphonic children: Family life and interaction patterns. *Archives of General Psychiatry, 36,* 682-687.

Carbin, C. (1993/94, winter) Ontario's new ASL/LSQ law — pah! *Gallaudet Today,* pp. 15-17.

Carey, S. T. (1978) The child as word learner. In M. Halle, J. Bresnan, and G. Miller (Eds.) *Linguistic theory and psychological reality.* Cambridge, MA: MIT Press.

Carlson, N.A. (1980) General principles of learning and motivation. *Teaching Exceptional Children, 12,* 60-62.

Casto, G. and Mastropieri, M.A. (1986) The efficacy of early intervention programs: A meta-analysis. *Exceptional Children, 52,* 417-424.

Carlberg, C. and Kavale, K. (1980) The efficacy of special versus regular class placement for exceptional children: A meta-analysis. *Journal of Special Education, 14,* 295-306.

Carpenter, D. (1985) Grading handicapped pupils: Review and position statement. *Remedial and Special Education, 6,* 54-59.

Carter, D.E. and Rogers, W.T. (1989) Diagnostic and placement practice for mildly educable mentally handicapped students. *Canadian Journal of Special Education, 5*, 15-23.

Carter, E.A. and McGoldrick, M. (Eds.) (1980) *The family life cycle: A framework for family therapy.* New York: Gardner Press.

Cartledge, G. and Kleefeld, J. (1989) Teaching social communication skills to elementary shool students with handicaps. *Teaching Exceptional Children, 22*, 100-105.

Cartwright, G. P., Cartwright, C. A., and Ward, M. E. (1984) *Educating special learners* (2nd. ed.) California: Wadsworth Publishing.

Caspi, A., Elder, G.H., and Bern D.J. (1987) Moving against the world: Life-course patterns of explosive children. *Developmental Psychology, 23*, 308-313.

Casserly, P.L.(1979) Helping young women take math and science seriously in school. In N. Colangelo and R.T. Zaffran (Eds.) *New voices in counseling the gifted* (pp. 346-369). Dubuque, IA: Kendall-Hunt.

Castle, D. (1988) *Oral interpreting: Selections from papers by Kirsten Gonzales.* Washington, DC: A.G.Bell Association for the Deaf.

Cataracts: Some facts you should know. (1990) Alberta: CNIB.

Cegelka, W.J. (1978). Competencies of persons responsible for the classification of mentally retarded individuals. *Exceptional Children, 45*, 26-3l.

Center for Assessment and Demographic Studies (1991) *Stanford Achievement Test, eighth edition: Hearing-impaired norms booklet.* Washington, DC: Gallaudet University.

Chandler, L.K. (1992) Promoting young children's social competence as a strategy for transition to mainstreamed kindergarten programs. In S.L. Odon, S.R. McConnell, and M.A. McEvoy (Eds.) *Social competence of young children with disabilities* (pp. 245-276). Baltimore, MD: Brookes.

Chall, J.S. (1989) Learning to read: The great debate twenty years later — a response to "Debunking the great phonics myth." *Phi Delta Kappan, 70*, 521-538.

Chan, L.K. (1988) Comprehension monitoring in students with reading difficulties. *Australian Educational Researcher, 15*, 19-39.

Chan, L.K. and Cole, P.G. (1986) The effects of comprehension monitoring training on the reading competence of learning disabled and regular class students. *Remedial and Special Education, 7*, 33-40.

Chaney, R.H., and Eyman, R.K. (1982) Etiology of mental retardation: Clinical vs neuroavatonic diagnosis. *Mental Retardation, 20*, 123-127.

Chapman, A.H. and Cooper, E.B. (1973) Nature of stuttering in a mentally retarded population. *American Journal of Mental Deficiency, 78*, 153-157.

Chapman, L.J. and Wedell, K. (1972) Perceptual-motor disabilities and reversal errors in children's handwriting. *Journal of Learning Disabilities, 5*, 321-325.

Chasnoff, I.J. (1987, May) Prenatal effects of cocaine. *Contemporary OB/GYN*, pp. 163-179.

Chasnoff, I.J., Chisum. G., and Kaplan, W. (1988) Maternal cocaine use and genitourinary malformation. *Teratology*, 201-204.

Chasnoff, I. J. Burns, K.A., Burns, W.J., and Schnoll, S. (1988) Prenatal drug exposure: Effects on neonatal and infant growth and development. *Neurobehavioral Toxicology and Teratology, 8*, 357-362.

Cheng-Meyer, C., Seto, D., Tateno, M., and Levy J. (1988) Biological features of HIV-1 that correlate with virulence in the host. *Science, 240*, 80-82.

Chess, S. and Rosenberg, M. (1974) Clinical differentiation among children with initial language complaints. *Journal of Autism and Childhood Schizophrenia, 2*, 99-109.

Chester, M.A. and Barbarin, O.A. (1987) *Childhood cancer and the family.* New York: Brunner/Mazel.

Children should see more and more each day [1980] Toronto: National Retinitis Pigmentosa Foundation of Canada.

Children with communication disorders (1995). *ERIC Digest, H 470.* Reston, VA: CEC.

Chinn, P.C. and Hughes, S. (1987) Representation of minority students in special education classes. *Remedial and Special Education, 8*, 41-46.

Chinn, P.C., Winn, J., and Walters, R. (1978) *Two-way talking with parents of special children.* St. Louis, MO: C.V. Mosby.

Chomsky, N. (1965) *Aspects of the theory of syntax.* Cambridge, MA: MIT Press.

Chorost, S. (1988) The hearing-impaired child in the mainstream: A survey of the attitudes of regular classroom teachers. *Volta Review, 90*, 7-12.

Church, J.A., Allen, J.R., and Stiehen, E.R. (1986) New scarlet letter(s) pediatric AIDS. *Pediatrics, 77*, 423-427.

Clarizio, H.F. (1990) Assessing severity in behavior disorders: Empirically based criteria. *Psychology in the Schools, 27*, 5-15.

Clark, B. (1988) *Growing up gifted* (3rd. ed.) Columbus, OH: Merrill.

Clark, G.M. and Tong, Y.C. (1985) The engineering of future cochlear implants. In R.F. Gray (Ed.), *Cochlear implants* (pp.211-226). San Diego, CA: College-Hill Press.

Clark, G.M., Tong, Y.C., and Patrick. J.F. (Eds.) (1990) *Cochlea prothesis.* New York: Churchill Livingtone.

Clark, P.N. and Allen, A.S. (1985) *Occupational therapy for children.* St. Louis, MO: Mosby.

Clarke, B.R. and Kendall, D.C.(1976) Communication for hearing-impaired people in Canada. In H.J. Oyer (Ed.) *Communication for the hearing handicapped: An international perspective.* Baltimore, MD: University Park Press.

Clarke, B.R. and Winzer, M.A. (1983) A concise history of the education of the deaf in Canada. *The ACEHI Journal, 9*, 36-51.

Clements, D.H. (1985) *Computers in early childhood and primary education.* Englewood Cliffs, NJ: Prentice-Hall.

Clifford, J.A., Runions, T., and Smyth, E. (1986) The Learning Enrichment Service (LES): A participatory model for gifted adolescents. In J.S. Renzulli (Ed.) *Systems and models for developing programs for the gifted and talented.* Mansfield, CT: Creative Learning Press.

Coggins, T.E. and Morrison, J.A. (1981) Spontaneous imitations in Down's syndrome children: A lexical analysis. *Journal of Speech and Hearing Research, 24*, 303-308.

Cohen, I.L. (1989) A review of the association of autism and fragile x. Paper presented at the International Fragile X Conference, Denver.

Cohen, L. and Manion, L. (1983) *Multicultural classrooms: Perspectives from teachers.* London: Crook and Helm.

Colangelo, N. (1989) Moral dilemmas as formulated by gifted students. *Understanding Our Gifted, 1*, 10-12.

Colangelo, N. and Dettman, D.F. (1983) A review of research on parents and families of gifted children. *Exceptional Children, 50*, 20-27.

Colangelo, N. and Fleuridas, C. (1986) The abduction of childhood. *Journal of Counseling and Development*, 64, 561-563.

Cole, C.K., Jones, M.K., and Sadofsky, G.S. (1990) Working with children at risk due to prenatal susbstance exposure. *PRISE Reporter — Issues in the Education of Students with Handicaps, 21*, 1-6.

Cole, H. and Sarnoff, D. (1980, June) Interactive creativity: Explorations of basic meanings and their implications for teaching and counselling. Papers at the Twenty-sixth Annual Creative Problem Solving Institute, Buffalo.

Cole, K.N., Dale, P.S., Mills, P.E., and Jenkins, J.R. (1993) Interactions between early intervention curriculum and student characteristics. *Exceptional Children, 60*, 17-28.

Cole, M. and Cole, S.R. (1989) *The development of children.* San Diego, CA: Scientific American Books.

Coleman, J.M. and Minnett, A.M. (1992) Learning disabilities and social competence: A social ecological perspective. *Exceptional Children, 59*, 234-246.

Colenbrander, A. (1976) Low vision: Definition and classification. In E. Faye (Ed.) *Clinical low vision.* New York: Little, Brown.

Coles, G. (1978) The learning disabilities test battery: Empirical and social issues. *Harvard Educational Review, 48*, 313-340.

Collier, C. and Kalk, M. (1989) Bilingual special education curriculum development. In L.M. Baca and H.T. Cervantes (Eds.) *The bilingual special education interface* (2nd. ed.) (pp. 205-229) Columbus, OH: Merrill.

Conant, S. and Budoff, M. (1982) The development of sighted peoples' understanding of blindness. *Journal of Visual Impairment and Blindness, 76*, 86-90.

Conger, J.C. and Keane, S.P.(1981) Social skills intervention in the treatment of isolated or withdrawn children. *Psychological Bulletin*, 90, 478-495.

Conn-Blowers, E.A. and McLeod, H.J. (1989) Special education in Alberta. In M. Csapo and L. Goguen (Eds.) *Special education across Canada* (pp. 19-27) Vancouver: Centre For Human Development and Research.

Conners, C.K. (1969) A teacher rating scale for use in drug studies in children. *American Journal of Psychiatry, 6*, 884-888.

Conners, C.K. (1973) Rating scales for use in drug studies with children. *Psychopharmacology Bulletin, 9*, 24-81.

Conners, F.A. and Detterman, D.K. (1987) Information processing correlates of computer-assisted word learning by mentally retarded students. *American Journal of Mental Deficiency, 91*, 606-612.

Connor, F.P (1983) Improving school instruction for learning disabled children: The Teachers College Institute. *Exceptional Education Quarterly, 4*, 23-44.

Conrad, R. (1979) *The deaf school child: Language and cognitive formation.* London: Harper and Row.

Cook, J. (1991) Higher education: An attainable goal for students who have sustained head injuries. *Journal of Head Trauma Rehabilitation*, 6, 64-72.

Cooper, D.H. and Speece, D.L. (1990) Maintaining at-risk children in regular education settings: Initial effects of individual differences and classroom environment. *Exceptional Children, 57*, 117-126.

Cooper, P. and Stewart, L. (1987) *Language skills in the classroom.* Washington, DC: National Education Association.

Copeland, L., Wolraich, M., Lindgren, S., Milich, R., and Woolson, R. (1987) Pediatricians reported practices in the assessment and treatment of attention deficit disorders. *Journal of Developmental and Behavioral Pediatrics, 8*, 191-197.

Copeland, M.E. and Kimmel, J.R. (1989) *Evaluation and management of infants and young children with developmental disabilities.* Baltimore, MD: Brookes.

Cordell, A.S. and Cannon, T. (1985) Gifted kids can't always spell. *Academic Therapy, 21*, 143-152.

Cordesco, L.K. and Laus, M.K. (1993) Individualized training in behavioral strategies for parents of preschool children with disabilities. *Teaching Exceptional Children, 25*, 43-47.

Corn, A.L. (1980) Optical aids in the classroom. *Education of the Visually Handicapped, 12*, 114-121.

Cornell, D. (1983) Gifted children: The impact of positive labelling on the family system. *American Journal of Orthopsychiatry, 53*, 322-355.

Cornell, D.G. (1984) *Families of gifted children.* Ann Arbor, MI: UMI Research Press.

Cornell, D.G., Callahan, C.M., and Loyd, B.H. (1991) Socioemotional adjustments of adolescent girls enrolled in a residential acceleration program. *Gifted Child Quarterly, 35*, 58-66.

Cornett, O.R. (1984, June) Cued speech: What and why. Paper available at the A.G. Bell Conference, Portland, Oregon.

Corno, L. and Mandinach, E. (1983) The role of cognitive engagement in classroom learning and motivation. *Educational Psychologist, 18*, 88-108.

Correa, V.I. (1989) Involving culturally diverse families in the educational process. In S.H. Fradd and M.J. Weismantel (Eds.) *Meeting the needs of culturally and linguistically different students* (pp. 130-144). Boston, MA: College-Hill.

Cosden, M.A., Gerber, M.M., Semmel, D.S., Goldman, S.R., and Semmel, M.L. (1987) Microcomputer use with micro-educational environments. *Exceptional Children, 53*, 399-409.

Council for Exceptional Children (1988) *Final report: CEC and ad hoc committee on medically fragile students.* Reston, VA: CEC.

Council for Exceptional Children (1990) A brief look at the 12th. annual report to Congress. *Teaching Exceptional Children, 22*, supplement.

Council for Exceptional Children (1991) Code of ethics of the CEC. *Teaching Exceptional Children, 23*, supplement.

Council for Exceptional Children (1993a) Policy on inclusive schools and community settings. *Teaching Exceptional Children, 25*, supplement.

Council for Exceptional Children (1993b) *Position paper.* Division for Early Childhood: CEC.

Coveny, T.E. (1976) Standardized tests for visually handicapped children: A review of research. *New Outlook for the Blind*, 70, 232-236.

Cowan, W.M. (1979) *The brain.* San Francisco, CA: Freeman.

Cowen, E. (1980) The Primary Mental Health Project: A summary. *Journal of Special Education, 14*, 133-154.

Cox, B.J. (1984) Transcription of Braille textbooks by computer. *Journal of Visual Impairment and Blindness, 78*, 244-247.

Cox, C.M. (1926) *The early mental traits of three hundred genuises. Vol 2: Genetic studies of genius.* Stanford, CA: Stanford University Press.

Cox, J., Daniel, N., and Boston, B. (1985) *Educating able learners.* Austin, TX: University of Texas Press.

Craig, M. (1988) Paper presented to Ed. 3220, Memorial University of Newfoundland.

Cramer, R.L. (1978) *Children's writing and language growth.* Columbus, OH: Merrill.

Cramond, B. and Martin, C.E. (1987) Inservice and preservice teachers' attitudes toward the academically brilliant. *Gifted Child Quarterly, 31*, 15-19.

Cratty. B. (1986) *Perceptual and motor development in infants and children* (3rd. ed.) Englewood Cliffs, NJ: Prentice-Hall.

Cratty, J. (1987) Unpublished paper, Memorial University of Newfoundland.

Crawford, L.V. (Ed.) (1982) *Pediatric allergic diseases.* Garden City, NY: Medical Examination Publishing Company.

Crealock, C. (1983) Teacher and student behaviours in regular and special education settings. *B.C. Journal of Special Education, 7,* 321-330.

Crealock, C. (1986) *The learning disabilities/juvenile delinquency link: Causation or correction.* Ottawa: Ministry of the Solicitor-General.

Crealock, C. (1989) The on-task and off-task behaviour of exceptional students in segregated and mainstreamed classrooms. *Canadian Journal of Special Education, 5,* 23-32.

Crisis for the newborn [1986] Videotape, National March of Dimes Foundation.

Crockenberg, S.R. and Litman, C. (1990) Autonomy as competence in two year olds: Maternal correlates of child defiance, compliance, and self-assertion. *Developmental Psychology, 26,* 961-971.

Cruickshank, D. (1983) Human rights and charter rights in special education. *B. C. Journal of Special Education, 7,* 205-220.

Cruickshank, W.M. (Ed.) (1976) *Cerebral palsy: A developmental disability.* New York: Syracuse University Press.

Crystal, D., Fletcher, P., and Garman, M.G. (1976) *The grammatical analysis of language disability: A process for assessment and remediation.* London: Edward Arnold.

Csapo, M. (1979) Prevalence and needs assessment study of autistic children in British Columbia. *B.C. Journal of Special Education, 3,* 159-191.

Csapo, M. (1981a) *Children with behaviour and social disorders: A Canadian focus.* Vancouver: Centre for Human Development and Research.

Csapo, M. (1981b) Educational provisions for emotionally disturbed children in British Columbia: A status report. *B.C. Journal of Special Education, 5,* 357-367.

Csapo, M. (1981c) The emotionally disturbed child in Canada's schools. *Behavior Disorders, 6,* 139-149.

Csapo, M. (1983). Ethnic language schools in British Columbia. *B.C. Journal of Special Education, 7,* 351-368.

Csapo, M. (1984) Segregation, integration, and beyond: A sociological perspective of special education. *B.C. Journal of Special Education, 8,* 211-229.

Csapo, M. (1988) Sexual abuse of children. *B.C. Journal of Special Education, 12,* 121-159.

Csapo, M. and Clarke, B.R. (1984). Native Indian language programming in British Columbia. *B.C. Journal of Special Education, 8,* 125-135.

Cullen, B. and Pratt, T. (1992) Measuring and reporting student progress. In S. Stainback and W. Stainback (Eds.) *Curriculum considerations for inclusive classrooms* (pp. 171-196) Baltimore, MD: Brookes.

Cullinan, D. and Epstein, M.H. (1982) Behavior disorders. In N. Haring (Ed.), *Exceptional children and youth* (3rd. ed.) Columbus, OH: Merrill.

Cullinan, D., Epstein, M.H., and Lloyd, J. (1983) *Behavior disorders of children and adolescents.* Englewood Cliffs, NJ: Prentice-Hall.

Cullinan, D., Epstein, M.H., and Lloyd, J.W. (1991) Evaluation of conceptual models of behavior disorders. *Behavioral Disorders, 16,* 148-157.

Cummings, E.M. Ionatti, R.J., and Zahn-Waxler, C. (1989) Aggression between peers in early childhood: Individual continuity and developmental change. *Child Development, 60,* 887-895.

Cummings, J.A. and Laguene, M.C. (1990) Psychoeducational assessment research in the United States: From sociocultural context to extrapolation into the future. *McGill Journal of Education, 25,* 81-89.

Cummings, R.W. and Maddux, C.D. (1987) Holland personality types among learning disabled and non-learning disabled high school students. *Exceptional Children, 54,* 167-170.

Cummings, S.T. and Finger, D.C. (1980) Emotional disorders. In H.E. Rie and E.D. Rie (Eds.) *Handbook of minimal brain dysfunction.* New York: Wiley.

Cummins, J. (1979) Linguistic interependence and the educational development of bilingual children. *Review of Educational Research, 49,* 222-251.

Cummins, J. (1984) *Bilingualism and special education: Issues in assessment and pedagogy.* Clevedon, England: Multilingual Matters.

Cummins, J. (1985) *Disabling minority students: Power, programs, and pedagogy.* Toronto: OISE Press.

Cummins, J. (1986) Empowering minority students: A framework for intervention. *Harvard Educational Review, 56,* 18-36.

Cummins, J. (1987) Psychoeducational assessments of study related behavior. *Journal of Educational Psychology, 72,* 16-20.

Cummins, J. (1989) A theoretical framework for bilingual special education. *Exceptional Children, 56,* 111-119.

Cummins, J. (1993) The research basis for heritage language promotion. In M. Danesi, K. McLeod, and S. Morris (Eds.) *Heritage language and education: The Canadian experience* (pp. 1-22) Oakville, Ont.: Mosaic Press.

Cunningham, J.K., Eisenberg, L.S., Kirk, K.I., Luxford, W.M., and Thielmeir, M.A. (1986) Cochlear implants in children: Speech production and auditory discrimination. *Otolaryngologic Clinics of North America, 1992,* 409-421.

Curci, R.A. and Gottlieb, J. (1990) Teachers' instruction of noncategorically grouped handicapped children. *Exceptionality, 1,* 239-248.

Cutsforth, T.D. (1951) *The blind in school and society: A psychological study.* New York: American Foundation for the Blind.

Daehler, M.W., Perlmutter, M., and Myers, N.A. (1976) Equivalence of pictures and objects for very young children. *Child Development, 47,* 96-102.

Dahl, M. (1986). *The Canadian symposium on special education issues. Proceedings.* Toronto: Canadian Council for Exceptional Children.

Daiute, C. (1989) Research currents: Play and learning to write. *Language Arts, 66,* 656-664.

Dauber, S.L. and Benbow, C.P. (1990) Aspects of personality and peer relations of extremely talented adolescents. *Gifted Child Quarterly, 34,* 10-14.

Darnforth, M. (1984) Personal communication

Daurio, S.P. (1979) Educational enrichment versus acceleration: A review of the literature. In W.C. George, S.J. Cohn, and J.C. Stanley (Eds.) *Educating the gifted: Acceleration and enrichment* (pp. 13-63) Baltimore, MD: Johns Hopkins University Press.

Davenport, S.L., O'Nuallian, S., Omenn, G.S., and Wilkus, R.J. (1978) Usher's syndrome in four hard-of-hearing siblings. *British Journal of Opthalmology, 7,* 484-488.

David, C. (1987) Physically and health handicapped children. In M. Winzer, S. Rogow and C. David, *Exceptional children in Canada,* Toronto: Prentice-Hall.

Davis, G.A. and Rimm, S.B. (1985) *Education of the gifted and talented.* Englewood Cliffs. NJ: Prentice-Hall.

Davis, G.A. and Rimm, S.B. (1994) *Education of the gifted and talented* (3rd. ed.) Boston, MA: Allyn and Bacon.

Davis, H. (1978) Audiometry: Other auditory tests. In H. Davis and S.R. Silverman (Eds.), *Hearing and deafness* (4th. ed.). New York: Holt, Rinehart and Winston.

Day, C. with S. Kirk and J.J. Gallagher (1985) *Educating exceptional children* (Canadian edition.) Toronto: Nelson.

De Apodaca, R.F., Watson, J.D., Mueller, J., and Isaacson-Koiles, J. (1985) A sociometric comparison of mainstreamed orthopedically handicapped high school students and nonhandicapped classmates. *Psychology in the Schools, 22,* 95-101.

deBettencourt, L.U. (1987) Strategy training: A need for clarification. *Exceptional Children, 54,* 24-30.

De Blassie, R.R. and Franco, J.N. (1983) Psychological and educational assessment of bilingual children. In D.R. Omark and J.G. Erickson (Eds.) *The bilingual exceptional child.* San Diego, CA: College Hill.

Decker, S.N. and DeFries, J.C. (1980) Cognitive abilities in families with reading disabled children. *Journal of Learning Disabilities, 13,* 517-522.

Decker, S.N. and DeFries, J.C. (1981) Cognitive ability profiles in families of reading disabled children. *Developmental Medicine and Child Neurology, 23,* 217-227.

De Guimps, R. (1906). *Pestalozzi, his life and works.* New York: Appleton, Century, Crofts.

de l'Épee, M. C. (1860) The true method of educating the deaf and dumb, confirmed by long experience. *American Annals of the Deaf and Dumb, 12,* 1-131. First published 1784.

Delpit, L.D. (1988) The silenced dialogue: Power and pedagogy in educating other people's children. *Harvard Educational Review, 58,* 280-298.

de Mause, L. (1974) *The history of childhood.* New York: Psychohistory Press.

de Mause, L. (1975) Our forefathers made childhood a nightmare. *Psychology Today, 8,* 85-88.

De Myer, M.K. (1977) Research in infantile autism: A strategy and its results. In S. Chess and A. Thomas (Eds.), *Annual progress in child psychiatry and child development.* New York: Brunner/Mazel.

De Myer, M. (1979) *Parents and children in autism.* Washington, DC: V.H. Winston and Sons.

Deno, E. N. (1970) Special education as developmental capital. *Exceptional Children, 37,* 229-237.

Deno, S. L. (1985) Curriculum-based assessment: The emerging alternative. *Exceptional Children, 52,* 219-232.

De Pompei, R. and Blosser, J. (1987) Strategies for helping head-injured children successfully return to school. *Language Speech and Hearing Services in the Schools, 18,* 292-300

Derevensky, J. and Coleman, E. (1989) Gifted children's fears. *Gifted Child Quarterly, 33,* 65-68.

Derry, S.J. (1990) Learning strategies for acquiring useful knowledge. In B.F. Jones and L. Idol (Eds.) *Dimensions of thinking and cognitive instruction* (pp. 347-380). Hillsdale, NJ: Erlbaum.

DeRuiter, J.A. and Wansart, W. (1982) *Psychology of learning disabilities.* Rockville, MD: Aspen Systems.

Deshler, D.D. and Lenz, B.K. (1989). The strategies instructional approach. *International Journal of Learning Disability, Development and Education.*

Dessent, T. (1987) *Making the ordinary school special.* London: Falmer.

Destad, L. (1987) A personal legacy. *Phi Delta Kappan, 68,* 744-745.

Developmental delay: Questions and answers. (1991). *DEC Communicator. The Council for Exceptional Children,* 17, 1-4.

de Villiers, J.G. and de Villiers, P.A. (1978) *Language acquisition.* Cambridge, MA: Harvard University Press.

Deykin, E.Y. and MacMahon, B. (1979) The incidence of seizures among children with autistic symptoms. *American Journal of Psychiatry, 116,* 1310-1312.

Diabetic retinopathy (1990) Alberta: Canadian National Institute for the Blind.

Diamond, G.W. and Cohen, H.J. (1987, December) *AIDS and developmental disabilities: Prevention update of the National Coalition on Prevention of Mental Retardation.* Silver Spring, MD: American Association of University Affiliated Programs for Persons with Developmental Disabilities.

Dikmen, S., Matthews, C.G., and Harley, J.P. (1975) The effect of early versus late onset of major motor epilepsy upon cognition-intellectual performance. *Epilepsia, 76,* 73-81.

Directions: A report of the Canadian Organizing Committee for 1981, the International Year of Disabled Persons (1982) Ottawa: Department of Health and Welfare.

Dishart, M. (1981) Special education and personal needs of gifted and talented children. *Association of Educators of Gifted, Talented and Creative Children in B.C., 3,* 6-12.

Dodds, S.E., Volker, M., and Vivand, H.F. (1989) Educating children and youth about AIDS. In J.M. Seibert and R.A. Olson (Eds.) *Children, adolescents, and AIDS.* (chapter 5). Lincoln, NB: University of Nebraska Press.

Dodge, K.A. and Frame, C.L.(1982) Social cognitive biases and deficits in aggressive boys. *Child Development, 53,* 620-635.

Dodge, K.A., Coie, J.D., Pettit, G.S., and Price, J.M. (1990) Peer status and aggression in boys' groups: Developmental and contextual analysis. *Child Development, 61,* 1289-1309.

Dodge, K.A., Pettit, G.S., McCloskey, C.L., and Boron, M.M. (1986) Social competence in children. *Monographs of the Society for Research in Child Development, 51,* 2. Serial 213.

Dohrn, E. and Bryan, T. (1994) Attribution instruction. *Teaching Exceptional Children, 26,* 61-63.

Doig, J. (1979, January 6) From the inside out. *The Canadian, 6,* pp. 9-13.

Dokecki, F., Baumeister, A.A. and Kupstas, F.D. (1989) Biomedical and social aspects of pediatric AIDS. *Journal of Early Intervention, 13,* 99-113.

Doll, E. (1941) The essentials of an inclusive concept of mental deficiency. *American Journal of Mental Deficiency, 46,* 214-219.

Dolnick, E. (1993) Deafness as culture. *Atlantic Monthly, 272,* 37-53.

Dossetor, D.R. and Nicol, A.R. (1989) Dilemmas of adolescents with developmental retardation: A review. *Journal of Adolescence, 12,* 167-185.

Douglas, V.I., Bari, R.G., Amin, K., O'Neill, M.E., and Button, B.G. (1988) Dosage effects and individual responsivity to methylphenidate in attention deficit children. *Journal of Child Psychology and Psychiatry, 29,* 453-475.

Dowdy, C.A., Carter, J., and Smith T.E.C. (1990) Differences in transitional needs of high school students with and without learning disabilities. *Journal of Learning Disabilities, 23,* 343-348.

Downey, G. and Walker, E. (1989) Spacial cognition and adjustment in children at risk for psychopathology. *Developmental Psychology, 25,* 835-845.

Downey, J., Elkin, E.J., Ehrhardt, A.A., Meyer-Bahlberg, H., Bell, J.J., and Morishima, A. (1991) Cognitive ability and every day functioning in women with Turner's syndrome. *Journal of Learning Disabilities, 24*, 32-39.

Doxey, I.M. (1990) *Child care and education: Canadian dimensions.* Toronto: Nelson.

D'Oyley, V. (1976) Entering urban education: The case of the black student. In V. D'Oyley and M. Silverman (Eds.) *Black students in urban Canada.* Toronto: Ministry of Culture and Recreation.

Drash, P.V., Raver, S.A., Murrin, M., and Tudor, R.M. (1989) Three procedures for increasing vocal response to therapist prompt in infants and children with Down syndrome. *American Journal on Mental Retardation, 94*, 64-73.

Drew, C.J., Logan, D.R., and Hardman M.L. (1988) *Mental retardation — A life cycle approach* (4th. ed.) Columbus, OH: Merrill

Dubose, R. and Langley, (1977) *Developmental Activities Screening Inventory.*

Dudley-Marling, C. (1985) Perceptions of the usefulness of the IEP by teachers of learning disabled and emotionally disturbed children. *Psychology in the Schools, 22*, 65-67.

Dunlap, W.R. (1989) A functional classification for early childhood education. *Journal of Early Intervention, 13*, 73-99.

Dunn, L. M. (1968) Special education for the mildly retarded — Is much of it justifiable? *Exceptional Children, 35*, 5-22.

Dunn, N.L., McCartan, K.W., and Fugura, R.W. (1988) Young children with orthopedic handicaps: Self-knowledge about their disability. *Exceptional Children, 55*, 249-252.

Dunn, W. (1989) Integrated related services for preschoolers with neurological impairments. *Remedial and Special Education, 10*, 31-39.

Dunner, G.M., Connor-Kuntz, F.J., and Goodway, J.D. (1995) A physical education curriculum for all preschool students. *Teaching Exceptional Children, 27*, 28-34.

Dunscombe, C. (1836) *Report upon the subject of education made to the Parliament of Upper Canada 25 February 1836, through the Commissioners, Doctors Morrison and Bruce, appointed by a resolution of the House of Assembly in 1835 to obtain information upon the subject of education, etc.* Upper Canada: M.C. Reynolds.

Dunst, C.J. (1980) *A clinical and educational manual for use with the Uzgiris and Hunt Scales of Infant Psychological development.* Baltimore, MD: University Park Press.

Dunst, C.J., Trivette, C.M., Hamby, D., and Pollock, B. (1990) Family systems correlates of the behavior of children with handicaps. *Journal of Early Intervention, 14*, 204-218.

Dunst, C.J., Johanson, C., Trivette, C.M., and Hamby, D. (1991) Family-oriented early intervention policies and practices: Family-centered or not? *Exceptional Children, 58*, 115-126.

Dwyer, K.P. (1990). Making the least restrictive environment work for children with serious emotional disturbance: Just say NO to segregated placements. *Preventing School Failure, 34*, 14-21.

Dykens, E., Leckman, J., Paul, R., and Watson, M. (1988). Cognitive, behavioral and adaptive functioning in fragile X and non-fragile X retarded men. *Journal of Autism and Developmental Disorders,18*, 41-52.

Dyson, L. and Fewell, R.R. (1989) The self-concept of siblings of handicapped children: A comparison. *Journal of Early Intervention, 13*, 230-238.

Early, M. (1989) Using key visuals to aid ESL students' comprehension of content classroom texts. *Reading-Canada-Lecture, 7*, 202-212.

Easterbrooks, M.A. (1989) Quality of attachment to mother and to father: Effects of perinatal risk status. *Child Development, 60*, 825-830.

Eaves, L.C. (1988) Prevalence and needs survey of autistic preschool children in the lower mainland of British Columbia. *B.C. Journal of Special Education, 12*, 29-39.

Edelbrock, C. (1979) Empirical classifications of children's behavior disorders: Progress based on parent and teacher ratings. *School Psychology Digest, 8*, 355-369.

Edelbrock, C.S., and Achenbach, T.M. (1984) The teacher version of the Child Behavior Profile, 1. Boys aged 6-11. *Journal of Consulting and Clinical Psychology, 52*, 207-217.

Eden-Piercy, G.V., Blacher, J.B., and Eyman, R.K. (1986) Explaining parents' reactions to their young child with severe handicaps. *Mental Retardation, 24*, 285-291.

Edgar, E.B. (1987) Secondary programs in special education: Are many of them justifiable? *Exceptional Children, 53*, 555-561.

Edgar, E. (1988) Employment as an outcome for mildly handicapped students: Current status and future directions. *Focus on Exceptional Children, 21*, 1-8.

Edgar, E. and Hayden, A.H. (1984-85) Who are the children special education should serve and how many children are there? *The Journal of Special Education, 18*, 523-539.

Edgar, E., Levine, P., and Maddox, M. (1985) *Washingon State follow-up data of postsecondary special education students.* Seattle: Networking and Evaluation Team, University of Washington.

Edgington, D, (1976). *The physically handicapped child in your classroom.* Springfield, IL: Thomas.

Edlind, E.P. and Heansly, P.A. (1985) Gifts of mentorship. *Gifted Child Quarterly, 29*, 55-60.

Edmister, P. and Ekstrand, R.E. (1987) Preschool programming: Legal and educational issues. *Exceptional Children, 54*, 130-136.

Edmonds, C. (1985) Hearing loss with frequent diving: Deaf divers. *Undersea Biomedical Research, 12*, 315-319. In W.L. Heward and M.D. Orlansky (1992) *Exceptional children: An introductory survey of special education* (4th. ed.) Toronto: Maxwell Macmillan Canada.

Edmundson, K. (1985) The "discovery" of siblings. *Mental Retardation, 23*, 49-51.

Eichner, E.R. (1986) Sickle cell trait, exercise, and altitude. *The Physician and Sports Medicine, 14*, 144-157. In E. Miller (Ed.) *Foundations in child psychiatry.* New York: Pergamon Press.

Eisenberg, A.R. and Garvey, C. (1981) Children's use of verbal strategies in resolving conflicts. *Discourse Processes, 4*, 149-170.

Eisenson, J. (1971) Speech defects: Nature, causes, and psychological concomitants. In W. M. Cruickshank (Ed.) *Psychology of exceptional children and youth.* Englewood Cliffs, NJ: Prentice-Hall.

Eisenson, J. and Ingram, D. (1972) Childhood aphasia: An updated concept based on recent research. *Acta Symbolica, 3*, 108-116.

Eisenson, J. and Ogilvie, M. (1983) *Communicative disorders in children* (5th. ed.) New York: MacMillan.

Elias, M.J. and Taylor, M.E. (1995) Building social and academic skills via problem solving videos. *Teaching Exceptional Children, 27*, 14-18.

Ellery, W.R. and Mangubshai, F. (1983) The impact of reading in second language learning. *Reading Research Quarterly, 19*, 53-67.

Elliot, A.J. (1981) *Child language.* Cambridge: Cambridge University Press.

Elliott, L. (1993, 18 May) Mainstreaming opposed by deaf community. *ATA News*, p. 11.

Ellis, E.S. (1983) The effects of teaching learning disabled adolescents an executive strategy to facilitate self-generation of task-specific strategies. Doctoral disseration, Lawrence, KA: University of Kansas.

Elstner, W. (1983) Abnormalities in the verbal communication of visually impaired children. In A.E. Mills (Ed.) *Language acquisition in the blind child.* San Diego, CA: College Hill Press.

Englemann, S.E. (1977) Sequencing cognitive and academic tasks. In R.D. Kneedler and S.G. Tarner (Eds.) *Changing perspectives in special education.* Columbus, OH: Merrill.

Englert, C.S., Raphael, T.E., Anderson, L.M., Anthony, H., Fear, K., and Gregg, S. (1988) A case for writing intervention: Strategies for writing informational text. *Learning Disabilities Focus, 3,* 98-113.

Emery, R. (1989) Family violence. *American Psychologist, 44,* 321-328.

Epanchin, B.C. and Paul, J.L. (1986) *Emotional problems of children and adolescents. A multidisciplinary perspective.* Columbus, OH: Merrill.

Epilepsy Canada Scientific Council [1994] *Statistics.* Ottawa: Author.

Epstein, M.H., Polloway, E.A., Patton, R., and Foley, R. (1989) Mild retardation: Student characteristics and services. *Education and Training in Mental Retardation, 24,* 7-16.

Erin, J.E. (1986) Frequencies and types of questions in the language of visually impaired children. *Journal of Visual Impairment and Blindness, 80,* 670-674.

Eron, L. (1982) Parent-child interaction, television violence and aggression of children. *American Psychologist, 37,* 197-211.

Eron, L.D. and Huesmann, R.L. (1987) Television as a source of maltreatment of children. *School Psychology Review, 16,* 195-202.

Eron, L., Heusmann, L.R., Brice, P., Fisher, P., and Mermelstein, R. (1983) Age trend in the development of aggression, sex-typing, and related television habits. *Developmental Psychology, 19,* 71-77.

Erting, C. (1985) Sociocultural dimensions of deaf education: Belief systems and communicative introduction. *Sign Language Studies, 47,* 111-125.

Erickson, G. (1976) The concept of personal network in clinical practice. *Family Process, 14,* 487-498.

Erickson, J.G. and Walker, C.L. (1983). Bilingual exceptional students: What are the issues? In D.R. Omark and J.G. Erickson (Eds.) *The bilingual exceptional child.* San Diego, CA: College Hill Press.

Erin, J., Rudin, D., and Njoroge, M. (1991) Religious beliefs of parents of children with visual impairments. *Journal of Visual Impairment and Blindness, 85,* 157-162.

Esposito, B.G. and Koorland, M.A. (1989) Play behavior of hearing impaired children: Integrated and segregated settings. *Exceptional Children, 55,* 412-419.

Ewing-Cobbs, L.E., Fletcher, J.M. and Levin, H.S. (1985) Neuropsychological sequelae following pediatric head injury. In M. Ylvisaber (Ed.) *Head injury rehabilitation: Children and adolescents* (pp. 118-137). San Diego, CA: College Hill Press.

Eysenck, H.J. (1979) *The structure and measurement of intelligence.* New York: Springer-Verlag.

Faerstein, L.M. (1986) Coping and defence mechanisms of mothers of learning disabled children. *Journal of Learning Disabilities, 19,* 8-11.

Famularo, R. and Fenton, T. (1987) The effect of methylphenidate on school grades in children with attention deficit disorders without hyperactivity: A preliminary report. *Journal of Clinical Psychiatry, 48,* 112-114.

Famularo, R., Stone, K., Barnum, R., and Wharton, R. (1986) Alcoholism and severe child maltreatment. *American Journal of Orthopsychiatry, 56,* 481-485.

Farber, B. and Ryckman, D.B. (1965) Effects of severely mentally retarded children on family relationships. *Mental Retardation Abstracts, 2,* 1-17.

Farber, S. (1981) *Identical twins reared apart: A re-analysis.* New York: Basic Books.

Farkas, G.M., Sherick, R.B., Matson, J., and Loebig, M. (1981) Social skills training of a blind child through differential reinforcement. *The Behavior Therapist, 4,* 24-26.

Farrington, D.P. (1983) Offending from 10 to 25 years of age. In K.T. Van Dusen and S.A. Mednick (Eds.) *Prospective studies of crime and delinquency* (pp. 17-37). Boston, MA: Kluwer-Nijhoff.

Farrington, D.P. (1987) Early precursors of frequent offending. In J.Q. Wilson and G.C. Loury (Eds.) *From children to citizens (vol. 3) Families, schools, and delinquency prevention* (pp. 27-51) New York: Springer-Verlag.

Farrington, D.P., Gallagher, B., Morley, L., St. Ledger, R., and West, D.J. (1986) *Cambridge study in delinquent development: Long term follow-up.* Cambridge, England: Cambridge Institute of Criminology.

Fausti, S.A. (1987) Pure tone audiology and high frequencies. *Audiology in Practice, 4,* 4-6.

Fay, E.A. (1898) The eleventh census. *American Annals of the Deaf, 43,* 345-359.

Faye, E. (1976) Clinical definition and classification of the low vision patient. In E. Faye (Ed.) *Clinical low vision.* New York: Little, Brown.

Fazio, B.B. and Rieth, H.J. (1986) Characteristics of preschool handicapped children's microcomputer use during free-choice periods. *Journal of the Division for Early Childhood, 10,* 247-254.

Federal Register (1977), 41, 42. Washington, DC: US Government Printing Office.

Fehrmann, P.G., Keith, T.Z., and Reimers, T.M. (1987) Home influences on school learning: Direct and indirect effects of parental involvement in high school grades. *Journal of Educational Research, 80,* 330-337.

Feingold, B.F. (1975) Hyperkinesis and learning disabilities linked to artificial food flavors and dyes. *American Journal of Nursing, 75,* 797-803.

Feingold, B.F. (1976) Hyperkinesis and learning disabilities linked to the ingestion of artificial food colors and flavors. *Journal of Learning Disabilities, 9,* 551-559.

Feitler, F. and Tokar, E. (1982) Getting a handle on teacher stress: How bad is the problem? *Educational Leadership, 39,* 456-458.

Feldhusen, J. (1979) Student behavior problems in secondary schools. In D. L. Duke (Ed.) *Classroom management: The 78th. yearbook of the National Society for the Study of Education.* Chicago: University of Chicago Press.

Feldhusen, J.F. (1989) Synthesis of research on gifted youth. *Educational Leadership, 46,* 6-11.

Feldhusen, J.F. and Hoover, S.M. (1986) A conception of giftedness: Intelligence, self-concept and motivation. *Roeper Review, 8,* 140-143.

Feldhusen, F.F., Hoover, S.M., and Sayler, M.F. (1990) *Identification and education of gifted students at the secondary level.* New York: Trillium.

Feldhusen, J., Proctor, T.B., and Black, K.N. (1986) Guidelines for grade advancement of precocious children. *Roeper Review, 9,* 25-27.

Fencham, F.D., Hokada, A., and Sanders, R. Jr. (1989) Learned helplessness, test anxiety, and academic achievement: A longitudinal analysis. *Child Development, 60,* 138-145.

Feniak, C.A. (1988) Labelling in special education: A problematic issue in England and Wales. *International Journal of Special Education, 3,* 117-124.

Fenichel, G.H. (1980) *Neonatal neurology.* New York: Churchill Livingstone.

Fensler, M.A., Rosenberg, M.S., and Rosenberg, L.A. (1991) Concomitant learning disabilities and learning problems among students with behavioral/emotional disorders. *Behavior Disorders, 16,* 97-106.

Ferrari, M. (1984) Chronic illness: Psychological effects on siblings: 1. Chronically ill boys. *Journal of Child Psychology and Psychiatry, 25,* 459-476.

Ferrari, M. (1987) The diabetic child and well siblings: Risk to the well child's self-concept. *Children's Health Care, 15,* 141-147.

Ferrell, K.A. (1985) *Reach out and teach: Meeting the training needs of parents of visually impaired and multihandicapped children.* New York: American Foundation for the Blind.

Ferretti, R.P. and Butterfield, E.C. (1989) Intelligence as a correlate of children's problem solving. *American Journal on Mental Deficiency, 93,* 424-433.

Feshbach, S. (1970) Aggression. In P. Mussen (Ed.) *Carmicheal's manual of child psychology* (3rd. ed.) New York: Wiley.

Feuerstein, R. (1980) *Instrumental enrichment.* Baltimore, MD: University Park Press.

Feuerstein, R. (1985) The importance of the role of assessment in successful integration programmes: A dynamic alternative to traditional psychometric approaches. *Education and Child Psychology, 2,* 138-144.

Fewell, R.R. and Cone, J.D. (1983) Identification and placement of severely handicapped children. In M.Snell (Ed.) *A systematic approach for instruction of moderately, severely and profoundly handicapped children* (pp. 46-73). Columbus, OH: Merrill.

Fewell, R.R. and Langley, B. (1984) *Developmental Activities Screening Inventory, 11.* Austin, TX: Pro-Ed.

Ficociello, C. (1977) Visual stimulation for low functioning deaf-blind rubella children. In M.S. Thomas (Ed.) *Developing skills in severely and profoundly handicapped children.* Reston, VA: Council for Exceptional Children.

Fiedler, C.R. and Simpson, R.I. (1987) Modifying the attitudes of nonhandicapped high school students toward handicapped peers. *Exceptional Children, 53,* 342-349.

Field, T. (1983) High risk infants "have less fun" during early interactions. *Topics in Early Childhood Special Education, 3,* 77-87.

Figler, C.S. (1981) Peurto Rican families with and without handicapped chidren. Paper presented at CEC, New Orleans. ERIC Doc. No. 204 876.

Figueroa, R.A., Fradd, S.H., and Correa, V.I. (1989) Bilingual special education and this special issue. *Exceptional Childen, 56,* 174-178.

Fine, S. (1985, 14 September). Blacks and schools: Who fails? *Globe and Mail.*

Fine, S. (1991, 5 October) Plan would send retarded home. *Globe and Mail,* p. A8.

Fineman, C.A and Carran, D.T. (1986) An epidemiologic approach to screening gifted students utilizing WISC-R subtests. *Psychology in the Schools, 23,* 142-147.

Fink, A.H. and Janssen, K.N. (1992) The management of maltreated adolescents in school settings. *Preventing School Failure, 36,* 32-36.

Finklestein, B. (1985) Schooling and the discovery of latency in nineteenth-century America. *Journal of Psycho-History, 13,* 3-12.

Finkelstein, N.W., Gallagher, J.J., and Farran, D.C. (1980) Attentiveness and responsiveness to auditory stimuli of children at risk for mental retardation. *American Journal on Mental Deficiency, 85,* 135-144.

Finnegan, J.A. and Quarrington, B. (1979) Pre-, peri- and neonatal factors and infantile autism. *Journal of Child Psychology and Psychiatry, 20,* 119-128.

Finnegan, L.P., Reeser, P.S., and Connaughton, J.F. (1977) The effects of maternal drug dependence on neonatal mortality. *Drug and Alcohol Dependence, 3,* 131-140.

Finucane, B. (1988) *Fragile x syndrome.* Elwyn. PA: Elwyn School.

Fiore, T.S., Becker, E.A., and Nero, R.C. (1993) Educational interventions for students with attention deficit disorder. Exceptional Children, 60, 163-173.

Fish, B. and Ritvo, E. (1979) Psychoses of childhood. In W.D. Noshpitz (Ed.) *Basic handbook of child psychiatry* (vol. 2) New York: Basic Books.

Fishburne, G.J. (1989) Stimulant drug therapy and children with attention deficit disorder: An ethical issue. *McGill Journal of Education, 24,* 55-68.

Flaxbeard, R. and Toomey, W. (1987) No longer deaf to their needs. *British Journal of Special Education, 14,* 103-105.

Flenley, D.C. (1981) *Respiratory medicine.* London: Bailliere Tindall.

Flynn, G. and Kowalczyk-McPhee, B. (1989) A school system in transition. In S. Stainback, W. Stainback, and M. Forest (Eds.) *Educating all students in the mainstream of regular education* (pp. 29-41) Baltimore, MD: Brookes.

Flynn, P.T. and Byrne, M.C. (1970) Relationship between reading and selected auditory abilities of third grade children. *Journal of Speech and Hearing Research, 13,* 731-740.

Fokes, J. (1976) *Fokes Sentence Builder.* Boston, MA: Teaching Resources Corporation.

Foley, M.A., Johnson, M.K., and Raye, C.L. (1983) Age-related changes in confusion between memories for thoughts and memories in speech. *Child Development, 51,* 51-60.

Folio, M.R. and Fewell, R.R. (1983) *Peabody Developmental Motor Scale and Activity Cards.* Hingham. MA: Teaching Resources Corporation.

Folstein, S.E. and Rutter, M.L. (1988) Autism: Familial aggression and genetic implications. *Journal of Autism and Developmental Disorders, 18,* 3-29.

Fonosh, G.G., Avony, J., Lee, A., and Loving, S. (1982). Providing career planning and placement services for college students with disabilities. *Exceptional Education Quarterly, 3,* 67-74.

Fontana, V.J. and Besharov, D.R. (1979) *The maltreated child* (4th. ed.) Springfield, IL: Thomas.

Ford, A. and Davern, L. (1989) Moving forward with school integration: Strategies for involving students with severe handicaps in the life of the school. In R. Gaylord-Ross (Ed.) *Intervention strategies for students with severe handicaps* (pp. 11-32). Baltimore, MD: Brookes.

Forehand, R. and Atkeson, B.M. (1981) Behavior modification with severely disturbed children. In W.E. Craghead, A.E. Kazdin, and M.J. Mahoney (Eds.), *Behavior modification: Principles, issues, and applications.* Boston, MA: Houghton Mifflin.

Forest, M. and Lusthaus, E. (1989) Promoting educational equality for all students: Circles and maps. In S. Stainback, W. Stainback, and M. Forest (Eds.) *Educating all students in the mainstream of regular education* (pp.43-57). Baltimore, MD: Brookes.

Forness, S.R. (1985) Effects of public policy at the state level: California's impact on MR, LD, and ED categories. *Remedial and Special Education, 6,* 36-43.

Fortier, L.M. and Wanlass, R.L. (1984) Family crisis following the diagnosis of a handicapped child. *Family Relations, 33,* 13-24.

Foster, H.L. (1986) *Ribin', jiving', and playin' the dozens* (2nd. ed.) Cambridge, MA: Ballinger.

Foster, S. (1988) Life in the mainstream: Deaf college freshmen and their experiences in mainstreamed high school. *Journal of the American Deafness and Rehabilitation Association, 22,* 27-35.

Foster, S.L. and Ritchey, W.L. (1979) Issues in the assessment of social competence in children. *Journal of Applied Behavior Analysis, 12,* 625-638.

Fowler, S.A., Schwartz, I., and Atwater, J. (1991) Perspectives on the transition from preschool to kindergarten for children with disabilities and their families. *Exceptional Children, 58,* 136-145.

Fox, C.L. (1989) Peer acceptance of learning disabled children in the regular classroom. *Exceptional Children, 56,* 50-59.

Fox, C.L. and Forbing, S.E. (1991) Overlapping symptoms of substance abuse and learning handicaps: Implications for educators. *Journal of Learning Disabilities, 24,* 24-31.

Fox, L.H. (1977) Sex differences and program planning. In J.C. Stanley, W.C. George, and C.H. Solan (Eds.) *The gifted and the creative: A 50 year perspective.* Baltimore, MD: Johns Hopkins University Press.

Fradd, S.H. and Vega, J.E. (1987) Legal considerations. In S.H. Fradd and W.J. Tikunoff (Eds.) *Bilingual and bilingual special education: A guide for administrators* (pp. 45-74). Boston, MA: Little, Brown.

Fraiberg, S. (1977) *Insights from the blind.* New York: Basic Books.

Frampton, M. E. and Gall, E. D. (1955) *Special education for the exceptional, vol. 1, Introduction and problems.* Boston, MA: Porter Sargent.

Frankenberg, W.K., Dodds, J., Archer, P., Bresnick, B., Maschka, P., Edelman, N., and Shapiro, H., (1990) *Denver 11: Technical Manual.* Denver, CO: Denver Developmental Materials.

Fraser, F.C., Frecker, M., and Allderdice, P. (1986) Seasonal variation in neural tube defects in Newfoundland and elsewhere. *Teratology.*

Fraser, G.R. (1976) *The causes of profound deafness in childhood.* Baltimore, MD: John Hopkins University Press.

Fredericks, H. and Baldwin, V. (1987) Individuals with sensory impairments: Who are they? In L. Goetz, D. Guess, and K. Stremel-Campbell (Eds.) *Innovative program design for individuals with dual sensory impairments.* (pp. 3-15) Baltimore, MD: Brooks.

Freedman, R. and Doyle, G. (1974) Depression in children. *Psychology in the Schools, 11,* 19-23.

Freeman, B.J., Ritvo, E.R., Guthrie, D., Schroth, P., and Ball, J. (1978) The Behavior Observation Scale for Autism (BOS): Initial results of factor analysis. *Journal of Autism and Developmental Disorders, 10,* 343-346.

French, D.B. and MacDonnell, B.M. (1985) A survey of questions posed by regular classroom teachers integrating hearing impaired students in Nova Scotia and New Brunswick. *ACEHI Journal, 11,* 12-33.

French, R.S. (1932) *From Homer to Helen Keller: A social and educational study of the blind.* New York: American Foundation for the Blind.

Freund, J., Casey, P.H., and Bradley, R.H. (1982) A special education course with pediatric components. *Exceptional Children, 48,* 348-351.

Frey, K.S., Greenberg, M.T., and Fewell, R.R. (1989) Stress and coping among parents of handicapped children: A multidimensional approach. *American journal on Mental Retardation, 94,* 240-249.

Friedman, C. T. (1989). Integrating Infants. *Exceptional Parent,* pp. 52-57.

Friedrich-Cofer, L. and Huston, A.C. (1986) Television violence and aggression: The debate continues. *Psychological Bulletin, 100,* 364-371.

Frodi, A. M. (1981) Contributions of infant characteristics to child abuse. American Journal on Mental Deficiency, 85, 341-349.

Fuchs, D. and Fuchs, L.S. (1994) Inclusive schools movement and radicalization of special education reform. *Exceptional Children, 60,* 294-309.

Fuchs, D. and Fuchs, L.S. (1995) Counterpoint — Special education — Ineffective? Immoral? *Exceptional Children, 61,* 303-305.

Fuchs, L.S. and Deno, S.L. (1992) Effects of curriculum with curriculum-based measurement. *Exceptional Children, 58,* 232-242.

Fuchs, L.S. and Deno, S.L. (1994) Must instructionally useful performance assessment be based in the curricula? *Exceptional Children, 61,* 15-24.

Fuchs, L.S., Fuchs, D., Hamlett, C.L., and Ferguson, C. (1992) Effects of expert system, consultation within curriculum-based measurement, using a reading maze task. *Exceptional Children, 58,* 436-450.

Fuchs, L.S., Fuchs, D., Hamlett, C.L., Phillips, N.B., and Karns, K. (1995) General educators' specialized adaptations for students with learning disabilities. *Exceptional Children, 61,* 440-459.

Furth, H.G. (1966) *Thinking without language: Psychological implications of deafness.* New York: The Free Press.

Furth, H.G. (1971) Linguistic deficiency and thinking: Research with deaf subjects, 1964-1969. *Psychological Bulletin, 76,* 58-72.

Gabel, H. and Kotsch, L.S. (1981) Extended families and young handicapped children. *Topics in Early Childhood Special Education, 1,* 29-35.

Gaddes, W.H. (1981) Neuropsychology, fact or mythology, educational help or hindrance? *School Psychology Review, 10,* 322-330.

Gadow, K.D. (1979) *Children on medication: A primer for school personnel.* Reston, VA: Council for Exceptional Children.

Gadow, K. (1986) *Children on medication (vol 1.): Hyperactivity, learning disabilities, and mental retardation.* Boston, MA: College Hill.

Gage, N.L. and Berliner, D.C. (1984/1986) *Educational psychology* (3rd. ed., 4th. ed.) Boston, MA: Houghton Mifflin.

Gagné, F. (1985) Giftedness and talent: Reexamining an examination of the definitions. *Gifted Child Quarterly, 29,* 103-112.

Gagné, F. (1989) Peer nominations as a psychometric instrument: Many questions asked but few answered. *Gifted Child Quarterly, 33,* 53-58.

Gagné, F. (1991) Toward a differential model of giftedness and talent. In N. Colangelo and G.A. Davis (Eds.) *Handbook of gifted education* (pp. 65-80). Needham Heights, MA: Allyn and Bacon.

Galambos, S.J. and Goldwin-Meadow, S. (1990) The effects of learning two languages on levels of metalinguistic awareness. *Cognition, 34,* 1-56.

Gallagher, J.J. (1972) *The search for an educational system that doesn't exist.* Reston, VA: Council for Exceptional Children.

Gallagher, J.J. (1975) *The gifted child in the elementary school.* Washington, DC: American Educational Research Foundation.

Gallagher, J.J. (1984). Learning disabilities and the near future. *Journal of Learning Disabilities, 17,* 571-572.

Gallagher, J.J. (1985) *Teaching the gifted child* (3rd. ed.) Boston, MA: Allyn and Bacon.

Gallagher, J.J. (1991) Educational reform, values, and gifted students. *Gifted Child Quarterly, 35,* 12-19.

Gallagher, W.F. (1988) Categorical services in the age of integration: Paradox or contradiction. *Journal of Visual Impairment and Blindness, 82,* 226-229.

Galligan, B, (1990) Serving people who are dually diagnosed: A problem evaluation. *Mental Retardation, 28,* 353-358.

Galton, F. (1869) *Hereditary genius: An enquiry into its laws and consequences.* London, New York: Appleton (1870).

Garbe, B. and Rodda, M. (1988) Growing in silence — The deaf adolescent. *ACEHI Journal, 14,* 59-69.

Garcia, E.E. (1988) Attributes of effective schools for language minority students. *Education and Urban Society, 20,* 387-398.

Garcia, E. (1991) *Education of linguistically and culturally diverse students: Effective instructional practices.* Santa Cruz, CA: Center of Research on Cultural Diversity and Second Language Learning.

Gardner, H. (1983) *Frames of mind: The theory of multiple intelligences.* New York: Basic Books.

Garner, J.B. and Campbell, P.H. (1987) Technology for persons with severe disabilities: Practical and ethical considerations. *The Journal of Special Education, 21,* 122-132.

Garrard, S.D. and Richmond, J.B. (1975) Mental retardation: Nature and manifestations. In M.F. Reiser and S. Arieti (Eds.) *American handbook of psychiatry* (vol. 4, 2nd.ed.) New York: Basic books.

Gartner, A. and Lipsky, D.K. (1987) Beyond special education: Toward a quality system for all students. *Harvard Educational Review, 57,* 367-395.

Gartner, A. and Lipsky, D.K. (1989) *The yoke of special education: How to break it.* Rochester, NY: National Center on Education and the Economy.

Gaylord-Ross, R.J. and Holvoet, J. (1985) *Strategies for educating students with severe handicaps.* Boston, MA: Little, Brown.

Gayton, W.F., Friedman, S.B. Tavormina, J.F., and Tucker, F. (1977) Children with cystic fibrosis: 1. Psychological test findings of patients, siblings, and parents. *Pediatrics, 59,* 888-894.

Gdowski, B.S., Sanger, D.D., and Decker, T.N. (1986) Otitis media: Effect on a child's learning. *Academic Therapy, 21,* 283-291.

Gearheart, B., Weishahn, M., and Gearheart, C. (1988) *The exceptional student in the regular classroom.* (4th. ed.) Columbus, OH: Merrill.

Gearheart, B., Weishahn, M. and Gearheart, C. (1992) *Exceptional students in the regular classroom* (5th. ed.) Columbus, OH: Merrill.

Gearheart, B., Mullen, R. C., and Gearheart, C.J. (1993) *Exceptional individuals: An introduction.* Pacific Grove, CA: Brooks/Cole.

Gedye, A. (1989) Extreme self-injury attributed to frontal lobe seizure. *American Journal on Mental Retardation, 94,* 20-26.

Gelb, S.A. and Mikokawa, D.T. (1986) Special education and social structure: The commonality of "exceptionality." *American Educational Research Journal, 23,* 543-557.

Gendreau, P., Madden, P., and Leipeiger, M. (1977) *Norms and recidivism for first incarcerates: Implications for programming.* Toronto: Ontario Ministry of Correctional Services.

Gendreau, P., Madden, P., and Leipeiger, M. (1979) Norms and recidivism rates for social history and institutional experience: Implications for programming. *Canadian Journal of Criminology, 21,* 1-26.

Gerard, J. and Junkala, J. (1980) Task analysis, handwriting, and process-based instruction. *Learning Disabilities, 13,* 49-53.

Gerber, M.M. (1988) Cognitive-behavioral training in the curriculum: Time, slow learners, and basic skills. In E.L. Meyen, G.A. Vergason, and R.J. Whelan (Eds.) *Effective instructional strategies for exceptional children* (pp. 45-64). Denver, CO: Love.

Gerbner, G., Gross, L., Morgan, M., and Signorelli, N., (1980) The "mainstreaming" of America: Violence profile no. 11. *Journal of Communication, 30,* 10-29.

Gerdtz, J. and Bergman, J. (1990) *Autism: A practical guide for those who help others.* New York: Continuum.

Gersten, J.C., Langer, T.S., Eisenberg, J.B., and Simcha-Fagen, O. (1976) Stability and change in types of behavioral disturbances of children and adolescents. *Journal of Abnormal Child Psychology, 4,* 111-127.

Gersten, R. and Dimino, J. (1993) Visions and revisions: A special education perspective on the whole language controversy. *Remedial and Special Education, 14,* 5-13.

Geschwund, N. and Galaburda, A.M. (1978) *Cerebral lateralization.* Cambridge, MA: MIT Press.

Giangreco, M.F., Denis, R., Cloninger, C., Edelman, S., and Schattman, R. (1993) "I've counted Jon:" Transformational experiences of teachers educating students with disabilities. *Exceptional Children, 59,* 359-372.

Gibson, J.T. (1978) *Growing up: A study of children.* Reading, MA: Addison Wesley.

Gillberg, C. (1980). Mental age and infantile autism. *Journal of Autism and Developmental Disorders, 10,* 293-297.

Gillberg, C. and Stiffenburg, S. (1987) Outcomes and prognostic factors in infantile autism and similar conditions: A population based study of 45 cases followed through puberty. *Journal of Autism and Developmental Disorders, 17,* 273-287.

Gillberg, C., Rosenhall, U., and Johansson, E. (1983) Auditory brainstem responses in childhood psychoses. *Journal of Autism and Developmental Disorders, 13,* 181-195

Gillberg, J. and Gillberg, C. (1988) Generalized hyperkinesis: Follow-up study from age 7 to 13 years. *Journal of the American Academy of Child and Adolescent Psychiatry, 27,* 55-59.

Gilliss, G. (1990, March/April) Coming to terms with AIDS. *ATA Magazine,* pp. 6-8.

Ginsberg, H.P. (1986) The myth of the deprived child: New thoughts on poor children. In U. Neisser (Ed.). *The school achievement of minority children: New perspectives* (pp 169-189) Hillsdale, NJ: Erlbaum.

Gittelman, M. and Birch, H.G. (1967) Childhood schizophrenia: Intellectual, neurologic status, perinatal risk, prognosis, and family pathology. *Archives of General Psychiatry, 17,* 16-25.

Glatthorn, A.A. with Coble, C.R. (1993) *Learning twice: An introduction to the methods of teaching.* New York: Harper Collins.

Gleason, J.B. (1985) *The development of language.* Columbus, OH: Merrill.

Glenn, H.S. and Nelson, J. (1987) *Raising children for success.* Fair Oaks, CA: Sunrise Press.

Gogel, E.M., McCumsey, J., and Hewitt, G. (1985, Nov/Dec.) What parents are saying. *Gifted Talented Creative,* pp. 7-9.

Goguen, L. (1980) Right to education for exceptional children in Canada: A growing national concern. In M. Csapo and L. Goguen (Eds.) *Special education across Canada: Issues and concerns for the '80's.* Vancouver: Centre for Human Development and Research.

Goldberg, S., Marcovitch, S., Macgregor, D., and Lojkasek, M. (1986) Family responses to developmentally delayed preschoolers: Etiology and the father's role. *American Journal on Mental Deficiency, 90,* 610-617.

Goldstein, A.P., Sprafkin, R.P., Gershaw, N.J., and Klein, P. (1980) *Skillstreaming the adolescent: A structured training approach to teaching prosocial skills.* Champaign, IL: Research press.

Goldwin-Meadow, S. and Morford, M. (1985). Gestures in early child language: Studies of deaf and hearing children. *Merrill-Palmer Quarterly, 31,* 145-176.

Golledge, R.G. (1991) Tactual strip maps as navigational aids. *Journal of Visual Impairment and Blindness, 85,* 296-301.

Gonzales, E. (1989) Issues in the assessment of minorities. In H.L. Swanson and B.L. Watson (Eds.) *Educational and psychological assessment of exceptional children* (2nd. ed.) (pp. 383-402). Columbus, OH: Merrill.

Goodman, R. (1987) Infantile autism: A syndrome of multiple primary deficits. *Journal of Autism and Developmental Disorders, 19,* 409-424.

Goodman, G. (1990) Utilizing the paraprofessional in the mainstream. *Support for Learning, 5,* 199-204.

Goodman, K. S. (1986) *What's whole in whole language.* Richmond Hill, Ont.: Scholastic-TAB Publications.

Goodman, R. and Sevenson, J. (1989) A twin study of hyeractivity: 2, The etiological role of genes, family relationships, and perinatal adversity. *Journal of Child Psychology and Psychiatry, 30,* 691-709.

Gottesman, I.I. and Shields, J. (1976) A critical review of recent adoption, twin, and family studies of schizophrenics: Behavioral genetic perspectives. *Schizophrenia Bulletin, 2,* 360-401.

Gottfried, A.W. and Wallace-Lande, P. (1981) Physical and social environment of newborn infants in special care units. *Science, 214,* 673-679.

Gottleib, J., Leyser, Y., and Michaels, C. (1990) Parental attitudes toward mainstreaming: A new look at an old question. In R.A. Curci and J. Gottlieb (1990) Teachers' instruction of noncategorically grouped handicapped children. *Exceptionality, 1,* 239-248.

Gough, P.B. (1991) Tapping parent power. *Phi Delta Kappan, 75,* p. 339.

Gowan, J.C. (1968) How parents can foster creativity in their children, In W. Michael (Ed.) *Reaching for creative endeavour.* Bloomington, IN: Indiana University Press.

Gray, C.D. (1989) Opening comments on the conference on developmental disabilities and HIV infection. *Mental Retardation, 27,* 199-200.

Green, A.L. and Stoneman, Z. (1989) Attitudes of mothers and fathers of nonhandicapped children. *Journal of Early Intervention, 13,* 292-304.

Greenberg, M.T. and Calderon, R. (1984) Early intervention: Outcomes and issues. *Topics in Early Childhood Special Education, 3,* 1-9.

Greenwood, C.R. (1991) Longitudinal analysis of time, engagement, and achievement in at-risk versus non-risk students. *Exceptional Children, 57,* 521-535.

Greer, J.V. (1990a) The drug babies. *Exceptional Children, 56,* 382-384.

Greer, J.V. (1990b) Shattering the monolith. *Exceptional Children, 56,* 286-289.

Greer, J.V. (1992) Quality is in the eye of the beholder. *Exceptional Children, 58,* 200-201.

Gregory, J. (1986) Phrasing in the speech and reading of the hearing impaired. *Sound of Communication Disorders, 19,* 289-297.

Gresham, F.M. (1986) Conceptual and definitional issues in the assessment of children's social needs: Implications for classification and training. *Journal of Clinical Child Psychology, 15,* 3-15.

Griffin, G.W. (1987) Childhood predictive characteristics of aggressive adolescents. *Exceptional Children, 54,* 246-252.

Grossberg, I.N. and Cornell, D.G. (1988) Relationship between personality adjustment and high intelligence: Terman versus Hollingworth. *Exceptional Children, 55,* 266-272.

Grossman, H. (Ed.) (1977) *Manual on terminology and classification in mental retardation.* Washington, D.C: American Association on Mental Deficiency.

Grossman, H. (1984) *Educating Hispanic students: Cultural implications for instruction, classroom management, and assessment.* Springfield, IL: Thomas.

Grover, R., Shahidi, S., Fisher, B., Goldberg, D., and Wethers, D. (1983) Current sickle cell screening program for newborns in New York City, 1979-1980. *American Journal of Public Health, 73,* 249-252.

Groves, P.M. and Rebec, G.V. (1988) *Introduction to biological psychology* (3rd. ed.) Dubuque, IA: Brown.

Gualtieri, G.J., Koriath, U., Van Bourgondien, M., and Saleeby, N. (1983) Language disorders in children referred for psychiatric services. *Journal of the American Academy of Child Psychiatry, 22,* 165-171.

Gubbins, E.J. (1991, April) Reseach needs of gifted and talented through the year 2000. In J.. Renzulli (Chair) *The National Research Center on the Gifted and Talented: Present activities, future plans, and an invitation for input and involvement.* Conducted at the American Educational Research Association, Chicago.

Guetzloe, E. and Cline, K. (1979) The medication of children with learning and behavior disorders. In A. Lane (Ed.), *Readings in human growth and development of the exceptional individual.* Connecticut: Special Learning Corporation.

Guilford, J.P. (1967) *Way beyond the IQ.* Buffalo, NY: Creative Educational Foundation.

Guillie, D. (1817) *Essai sur l'instruction des aveugles ou exposé des procédés pour les instruire.* Paris: Imprimé par les aveugles.

Guralnick, M.J. (1981) Programmatic factors affecting child-child social interactions in mainstreamed preschool programs. *Exceptional Education Quarterly, 1,* 71-91.

Guralnick, M.J. (1986) The peer relations of young handicapped and nonhandicapped children. In P.S. Strain, M.J. Guralnick, and H.M. Walter (Eds.) *Children's social behavior: Development, assessment, and modification* (pp. 95-140). New York: Academic Press.

Guralnick, M. (1988) Efficacy research in early childhood intervention programs. In S.L. Odem and M.B. Karnes (Eds.) *Early intervention for infants and children with handicaps: An empirical base* (pp. 75-88) Baltimore, MD: Brookes.

Guralnick, M. (1989) Recent developments in early intervention efficacy research: Implications for family involvement in PL99-457. *Topics in Early Childhood Special Education, 9,* 1-17.

Guralnick, M.J. (1990) Social competence and early intervention. *Journal of Early Intervention, 14,* 3-14.

Guralnick, M.J. and Bricker, D. (1987) The effectiveness of early intevention for children wih cognitive and general developmental delays, In M.J. Guralnick and C. Bennett (Eds.) *The effectiveness of early intervention for at-risk and handicapped children* (pp. 115-173). New York: Academic Press.

Guralnick, and H.M. Walter (Eds.) *Children's social behavior: Development, assessment, and modification* (pp. 95-140). New York: Academic Press.

Gynderson, C.W., Maesch, C., and Rees, J.W. (1987) The gifted/learning disabled student. *Gifted Child Quarterly, 31,* 158-160.

Hackett, G.T. (1969) The history of public education for mentally retarded children in the Province of Ontario, 1867-1964. Ed. D. thesis, University of Toronto.

Hagerman, R.J. (1988) Fragile x syndrome: An overview. *Early Childhood Update, 4,* pp. 1, 6.

Hagerman, R.J., and Sobesky, W.E. (1989) Psychopatholgy in fragile X syndrome. *American Journal of Orthopsychiatry, 59,* 142-152.

Hagerman, R.J., Jackson, A.W., Levitas, A., Rimland, B., and Braden, M. (1986) An analysis of autism in 50 males with the fragile x syndrome. *American Journal of Medical Genetics, 23,* 359-374.

Hahn, A. (1987, December) Reaching out to America's dropouts: What to do? *Phi Delta Kappan,* pp. 256-263.

Hakuta, K. (1989) Language amd cognition in bilingual children. In A.M. Pedilla, H.H. Fairchild, and C.M. Valadez (Eds.) *Bilingual education* (pp. 47-59). Newbury Park, CA: Sage.

Hall, A., Orel-Bixler, D., and Haegerstrom-Portnoy, G. (1991) Special visual assessment techniques for multiply handicapped persons. *Journal of Visual Impairment and Blindness, 85,* 23-28.

Hall, C.W. and Richmond, B.O. (1984) Consultation with parents of handicapped children. *Exceptional Children, 31,* 185-191.

Hall, M. and Dennis, L. (1968) *Living and learning: The report of the provincial committee on aims and objectives of education in the schools of Ontario.* Toronto: Newton Publishing.

Hallahan, D.P. (1975) Comparative research studies on the psychological characteristics of learning disabled children. In W. Cruickshank and D.P. Hallahan (Eds.) *Perceptual and learning disabilities in children: Psychoeducational practices* (vol. 1) Syracuse, NY: Syracuse University Press.

Hallahan, D.P. and Kauffman, J.M. (1988, 1991) *Exceptional children: Introduction to special education* (4th ed., 5th. ed.) Englewood Cliffs, NJ: Prentice-Hall.

Hallahan, D. P., Kauffman, J. M., and Lloyd, J. W. (1985) *Introduction to learning disabilities* (2nd. ed.) Englewood Cliffs, NJ: Prentice- Hall.

Hallahan, D.P., Keller, C.E., McKinney, J.D., Lloyd, J.W., and Byron, Q. (1988) Examining the research base of the regular education initiative: Efficacy studies and the ALEM. *Journal of Learning Disabilities, 21,* 290-35.

Halpern, A.S. and Benz, M.R. (1987) A statewide examination of secondary special education for students with mild disabilities: Implications for the school curriculum. *Exceptional Children, 54,* 122-129.

Hamachek, B. and Kauffman, J. (1994) Special education in the United States. In K. Mazurek and M. Winzer (Eds.) *Comparative studies in special education.* Washington, DC: Gallaudet University Press.

Haman, T.A., Issacson, D.K., and Powell, O.H. (1985) Insuring classroom success for the learning disabled adolescent. *Academic Therapy, 20,* 517-524.

Hamayan, E.V. and Domico, J.S. (Eds.) (1991) *Limiting bias in the assessment of bilingual students.* Austin TX: Pro-Ed.

Hammer, E. (October, 1984) Quality of life for the multiply handicapped child. Paper prepared for the Helen Keller Seminar on the Multiply Handicapped, New York City.

Hammill, D.D. (1990) On defining learning disabilities: An emerging consensus. *Journal of Learning Disabilities, 23,* 74-84.

Hammill, D.D. and Larsen, S.C. (1983) *Test of Written Language.* Austin, TX: Pro-Ed.

Hamre-Nietupski, S., McDonald, J. and Nietupski, J. (1994) Enhancing participation of a student with multiple disabilities in regulr education. *Teaching Exceptional Children, 26,* 60-63.

Hamre-Nietupski, S., Nietupski, J., Bates, P., and Maurer, S. (1982) Implementing a community-based educational model for moderately, severely handicapped students: Common problems and suggested solutions. *Journal of the Association for the Severely Handicapped, 7,* 38-42.

Handel, R.D. (1983) Teachers of gifted girls: Are there differences in classroom management? *Journal for the Education of the Gifted, 6,* 86-97.

Hansen, H. (1978) Decline of Down's syndrome after abortion reform in New York State. *American Journal of Mental Deficiency, 83,* 185-188.

Hansen, M.J., Lynch, E.W., and Wayman, L.I. (1990) Honoring the cultural diversity of families when gathering data. *Topics in Early Childhood Special Education, 10,* 112-131.

Hapkewitz, W.G.(1979) Children's reactions to cartoon violence. *Journal of Clinical Psychology, 8,* 30-34.

Haqq, C. (1985, 6 February) Scientists seek MS cure. *The Stanford Daily,* section 3.

Harber, J.R. (1980) Issues in the assessment of language and reading disorders in learning disabled children. *Learning Disability Quarterly, 3,* 20-28.

Hardman, M. and McDonald, J. (1987) Implementing federal transition initiatives for youth with severe handicaps: The Utah Community-Based Transition Project. *Exceptional Children, 53,* 493-498.

Hardy, M.I., McLeod, J., Minto, H., Perkins, S.A., and Quance, W.R. (1971) *Standards for education of exceptional children in Canada: The SEECC Report.* Toronto: Leonard Crainford.

Hardy, W.G. and Bordley, J.E. (1973) Problems in diagnosis and management of multiply handicapped deaf children. *Archives of Otolaryngology, 73,* 269-274.

Hare, E.H. (1962) Masturbatory insanity: The history of an idea. *The Journal of Mental Science, 108,* 1-25.

Haring, K.A., Lovett, D.L., and Saren, D. (1991) Parent perspectives of their adult offspring with disabilities. *Teaching Exceptional Children, 23,* 6-10.

Harley, R.D. (Ed.) (1983) *Pediatric optholomolgy* (2nd. ed.) Philadelphia, PA: Saunders.

Harley, R.K. and Lawrence, G.A. (1977) *Visual impairments in the schools.* Springfield, IL: Thomas.

Harris, A.C. (1986) *Child development.* St. Paul, MI: West.

Harris, A.J. and Sipay, E. (1980) *How to increase reading ability: A guide to developmental and remedial methods* (7th. ed.) New York: Longman.

Harris, D.B. (1963) *Goodenough-Harris Drawing Test Manual.* New York: Harcourt, Brace and World.

Harris, K., Rueda, R., and Supancheck, P. (1990) A descriptive study of literacy events in secondary special education programs in linguistically diverse schools. *Remedial and Special Education, 11,* 20.

Harris, K.R. and Pressley, M. (1991) The nature of cognitive strategy instruction: Interactive strategy instruction. *Exceptional Children, 57,* 392-404.

Harris, L., Humphrey, K., Muir, D.M., and Dodwell, P.C. (1985) Use of the Canterbury child's aid in infancy and early childhood: A case study. *Journal of Visual Impairment and Blindness, 79,* 4-11.

Harris, S.L., Handleman, J.S., and Palmer, C. (1985) Parents and grandparents view the autistic child. *Journal of Autism and Developmental Disorders, 15,* 127-137.

Harris, S.L., Handleman, J.S., Kristoff, B., Bass, L., and Gordon, R. (1990) Changes in language development among autistic and peer children in segregated and integrated preschool settings. *Journal of Autism and Developmental Disorders, 20,* 23-31.

Harrison, P. (1987) Research with adaptive behavior scales. *Journal of Special Education, 21.* 37-61.

Harrison, R. (1985) How you can help the abused child. *Learning,* 74-78.

Harrison R. and Philips, B. (1971) Observations on hearing levels of preschool cleft palate children. *Journal of Speech and Hearing Disorders, 36,* 252-256.

Harrison, T. R. (1980). *Harrison's principles of internal medicine* (9th. ed.). New York: McGraw-Hill.

Harry, B. (1992) Restructuring the participation of African-American parents in special education. *Exceptional Children, 59,* 123-131.

Harry, B., Torgeson, C., Katkavich, J., and Guerrero, M. (1993) Crossing social class and cultural barriers in working with families. *Teaching Exceptional Children, 26*, 48-51.

Hart, S.N. and Brassard, M.R. (1987) A major threat to children's mental health: Psychological maltreatment. *American Psychologist, 42*, 160-165.

Harth, R. (1988) The Feuerstein perspective on the modification of cognitive performance. In E.L. Meyen, G.A. Vergason, and R.J. Whelan (Eds.) *Effective instructional strategies for exceptional children.* Denver, CO: Love.

Hartup, W.W.(1974) Aggression in childhood: Developmental perspectives. *American Psychologist, 29*, 336-341.

Harvey, D.H.P. and Greenway, A.P. (1984) The self-concept of physically handicapped children and their nonhandicapped siblings: An empirical investigation. *Journal of Child Psychology and Psychiatry, 25*, 273-284.

Hasazi, S.B. and Clark, G.M. (1988) Vocational preparation for high school students labelled as mentally retarded: Employment as a graduation goal. *Mental Retardation, 26*, 343-349.

Hasazi, S.B., Gordon, L.R., and Roe, C.A. (1985) Factors associated with the employment status of handicapped youth exiting from high school from 1979-1983. *Exceptional Children, 51*, 455-469.

Hasenstab, M.S. (1985) Reading evaluation: A psycholinguistic approach. In C.S. Simon (Ed.) *Communication skills and classroom success — Assessment.* College Hill, CA: Little Brown.

Haugen, L. (1981) The culturally different and gifted student with emphasis on the gifted Native. *Association of Educators of Gifted, Talented and Creative Children in B.C.*, 3, 70-74.

Hauser, S.L., De Long, G.R., and Rosman, N.P. (1975) Pneumographic findings in infantile autism syndrome: A correlation with temporal lobe disease. *Brain, 98*, 667-688.

Havener, W.H. (1979) *Synopsis of ophthalmology.* St Louis, MO: Moseby.

Hawkins, J.D. and Lishner, D.M. (1987) Schooling and delinquency. In E.H. Johnson (Ed.) *Handbook on crime and delinquency prevention* (pp. 179-221) New York: Greenwood.

Hay, D.F. (1984) Social conflict in early childhood. In G. Whitechurch (Ed.) *Annals of Child Development.* Greenwich, CT: JAL.

Hay, H. (1990) Allergies and the teacher. Unpublished paper, University of Lethbridge.

Hayden, A.M. and Beck, (1981) The epidemiology of high risk and handicapped infants. In C.T. Ramey and P.L. Trohanis (Eds.) *Finding and educating high-risk and handicapped infants.* Baltimore. MD: University Park Press.

Haynes, M.C. and Jenkins, J.R. (1986) Reading instruction in special education resource rooms. *American Educational Research Journal, 23*, 161-190.

Haywood Gear, G. (1976) Accuracy of teacher judgment in identifying intellectually gifted children: A review of the literature. *Gifted Child Quarterly, 20*, 478-487.

Hazel, J.S., Schumaker, J.B., Sherman, J.A., and Sheldon-Wildgen, J. (1981) *Asset.* Champaign, IL: Research Press.

Head, W.A. (1984). Historical, social and cultural factors in the adaptation of nonwhite students in Toronto schools. In R.J. Samuda, J.W. Berry, and M. Laferriere (Eds.) *Multiculturalism in Canada.* Toronto: Allyn and Bacon.

Hearing loss and surgery. (1982) *Lifeline Magazine, 4*, 8-10.

Heber, R.A. (1961) *A manual on terminology and classification in mental retardation* (Rev. ed.) American Journal on Mental Deficiency, monograph supplement.

Hedrick, D.L., Pratter, E.M., and Tobin, A.R. (1975) *Sequenced Inventory of Communication Development.* Seattle, WA: University of Washington Press.

Helfer, R.E. (1987) The developmental basis of child abuse and neglect: An epidemiological approach. In R.E. Helfer and R.S. Kempe (Eds.) *The batttered child* (4th. ed.) Chicago: University of Chicago Press.

Henderson, A. (1987) *The evidence continues to grow: Parent involvement improves school achievement.* Columbia, MD: National Committee for Citizens in Education. ERIC Doc. No.ED 315 199)

Henderson, R.A. (1989) PKU and maternal PKU: The cure and the problem. *BC Journal of Special Education, 13*, 253-257.

Henig, R.M. (1982, February 28) Saving babies before birth. *New York Times Magazine*, pp.19-22.

Henker, B. and Whalen, B. (1980) The changing faces of hyperactivity: Retrospect and prospect. In C. K. Whalen and B. Henker (Eds.) *Hyperactive children: The social ecology of identification and treatment.* New York: Academic Press.

Henker, B. and Whalen, C.K. (1989) Hyperactivity and attention deficits. *American Psychologist, 44*, 216-223.

Henry, A. (1975). Specific difficulties in reading. *Remedial Education, 10*, 81-85.

Herbst, D.S. and Baird, P.A. (1983) Non-specific mental retardation in British Columbia as ascertained through a registry. *American Journal on Mental Deficiency, 87*, 506-513.

Hersh, R. and Walker, H.M. (1983) Great expectations: Making school effective for all children. *Policy Studies Review, 2*, 147-188.

Hessler, G. and Kitchen, D. (1980) Language characteristics of a purposive sample of early elementary learning disabled students. *Learning Disability Quarterly, 3*, 36-41.

Hetherington, E.M. and Parke, R.D. (1986) *Child psychology: A contemporary viewpoint* (3rd. ed.) New York: McGraw Hill

Heward, W.L. and Orlansky, M.D. (1992) *Exceptional children: An introductory survey of special education* (4th. ed.) Toronto: Maxwell Macmillan Canada.

Hicks, L. (1987) Unpublished papers. St. John's: Memorial University of Newfoundland.

Higginbotham, D.J. and Baker, B.M. (1981). Social participation and cognitive play differences in hearing-impaired and normally hearing pre-schoolers. *Volta Review, 83*, 135-149.

Higginbotham, D.J., Baker, B.M., and Neill, R.D. (1980). Assessing the social participation and cognitive play abilities of hearing-impaired preschoolers. *Volta Review, 82*, 261-270.

Higgins, A.T. and Turnure, J.E. (1984) Distractibility and concentration of attention in children's development. *Child Development, 55*, 1799-1810.

Hill, J.L. (1988) Integration in Canada: Implications for the certification of regular education teachers (RETS) *Exceptional Children, 4*, 123-131.

Hilliard, A.G. (1980) Cultural diversity and special education. *Exceptional Children, 46*, 584-588.

Hinshelwood, J. (1917) *Congenital word blindness.* London: H.K. Lewis.

Hobbs, N., Perrin, J.M., and Ireys, H.T. (1985) *Chronically ill children and their families.* San Francisco, CA: Jossey-Bass.

Hoben, M., Lindstrom, V., Gish, S., Shapiro, S., and Chalberg, C. (1979) *Integration of vision impaired students and hearing impaired students in regular classrooms: A report of research.* Minneapolis, MN: Hennepin Technical Center.

Hobson, R.P. (1988) Beyond cognition: A theory of autism. In G. Dawson (Ed.) *Autism: New perspectives on diagnoses, nature and treatment.* New York: Guilford.

Hoff, L.A. (1978) *People in crisis: Understanding and helping.* Menlo Park, CA: Addison Wesley.

Hoff-Ginsberg, E. (1986) Function and structure in maternal speech: Their relation to the child's development of syntax. *Developmental Psychology, 22,* 155-163.

Hoffman, F.J., Shelson, K.L., Minskoff, E.M., Sautter, S.W., Steidle, E.F., Baker, D.P., Bailey, M.B., and Echols, L.D. (1987) Needs of learning disabled students. *Journal of Learning Disabilities, 20,* 43-53.

Hoge, R,D. and Andrews, D.A. (1992) Assessing conduct problems in the classroom. *Canadian Psychology Review,* 1-20.

Holahan, C. K. (1991) Lifetime achievement patterns, retirement and life satisfaction of gifted aged women. *Journal of Geretonology, 36,* 741-749.

Holder, H.B. and Kirkpatrick, S.W. (1991) Interpretation of emotion from facial expressions in children with and without learning disabilities. *Journal of Learning Disabilities, 24,* 170.

Hollinger, C.L. and Fleming, E.S. (1984) Internal barriers to the realization of potential: Correlates and interrelationships among gifted and talented female adolescents. *Gifted Child Quarterly, 28,* 135-139.

Hollinger, J.D. (1987) Social skills for behaviorally disordered children as preparation for mainstreaming: Theory, practice, and new directions. *Remedial and Special Education, 8,* 17-27.

Holsclaw, D.S. (1978) Recognition and management of patients with cystic fibrosis. *Pediatric Annals, 7,* 9-10.

Holvoet, J., Guess, D., Mulligan, M., and Brown, F. (1980) The individualized curriculum sequencing model: 2: A teaching strategy for severely handicapped students. *Journal of the Association for the Severely Handicapped, 5,* 337-351.

Hoover, M.R., Politzer, R.L., and Taylor, O. (1987, April-July) Bias in reading tests for black language speakers: A sociolinguistic perspective. *Negro Educational Review,* pp. 81-98.

Hopkins, K.M. (1989) Emerging patterns of services and case finding for children with HIV infection. *Mental Retardation, 27,* 219-222.

Hopper, D. (1975, Oct.) Deafness, the silent epidemic. *Readers Digest reprint,* p. 1.

Horowitz, E. (1981) Popularity, decentering ability, and role taking skills in learning disabled and normal children. *Learning Disability Quarterly, 4,* 23-30.

Horrocks, C. (1991) Isolation and security: Transition process and outcomes for graduates with mental handicaps. *BC Journal of Special Education, 15,* 177-198.

Houseman, J. (1972) An ecological study of interpersonal conflicts among preschool children. Doctoral dissertation, University Microfilms No. 75-12533.

Houser, L., Moses, E., and Kay J.L. (1987) A family orientation to transition. *Education of the Visually Handicapped, 19,* 109-119.

Howard, F.E. (1935) *Mental health: Its principles and practices with emphasis on the treatment of mental deviations.* New York: Harper and Brothers.

Howard, I. and Templeton, W. (1966) *Human spatial orientation.* New York: Wiley.

Howe, M. (1977) *Television and children.* London: New University Education.

Howe, M.L. and O'Sullivan, J.T. (1990) The development of strategic memory: Coordinating knowledge, metamemory, and resources. In D. F. Bjorklund (Ed.) Children's strategies: Contemporary views of cognitive development. Hillsdale, NJ: Erlbaum.

Howlin, P. (1981) The results of a home-bound language training program with autistic children. *British Journal of Disorders of Communication, 16,* 73-87.

Howse, H. (1988) Asthma in children. Unpublished paper, St. John's: Memorial University.

Hoyme, H.E., Jones, K.L., Dixon, S.D., Jewett, T., Hanson J.W., Robinson, L.K., Masall, M.E., and Allanson, J.E. (1990) Prenatal cocaine exposure and fetal vascular disruption. *Pediatrics, 85,* 743-747.

Huberty, T.J., Austin, J.K., Risinger, M.W., and McNelis, A.M. (1992) Classroom performance and adaptive skills in children with epilepsy. *Journal of School Psychology, 30,* 331-342.

Huebner, K.M. (1985) The challenges in providing appropriate educational services to rural visually impaired children and their families. *Rural Special Education Quarterly, 6,* 2-4.

Huessman, L.R., Eron, L.D., Lefkowitz, M., and Walder, L. (1984) Stability of aggression over time and generations. *Developmental Psychology, 20,* 1120-1134.

Huntze, S. (1985) A position paper for the Council for Children with Behaviour Disorders. *Behavioral Disorders, 10,* 167-174.

Hursh, N. (1985) Vocational evaluation of learning disabled adults. *Journal of Rehabilitation, 50,* 45-52.

Hynd, G.W. and Semrud-Clikeman, M. (1989) Dyselxia and neurodevelopmental pathology: Relationship to cognition, intelligence, and reading acquisition. *Journal of Learning Disabilities, 22,* 204-216.

Hylton, J.H. and Matonovitch, R.(1979) *Job satisfaction in the Regina Police Department.* Regina: Regina Police Department.

Iadorola, G. and Kerrigan, M.B. (1986) Do you hear what I hear? *AORN Journal, 43,* 478-483.

Iber, F.L. (1980) Fetal alcohol syndrome. *Nutrition Today,* pp.4-11.

Ikeda, M. (1976) Electrophysiology of the retina and visual pathway. In F. Ross (Ed.) *Medical ophthalmology.* London: Chapman and Hall.

Illebrun, D. and Leong C.K. (1981) Evaluating the effectiveness of structured language teaching with developmentally delayed children. *The Exceptional Child, 28,* 31-42.

Ilott, H.G. (1990, June) Speech and language services. Whose responsibility? When we ask the wrong question. *Keeping in Touch,* pp. 4-5.

Immen, W. (1995, April 19) The truth about selective vision. *Globe and Mail,* p. A8.

Ingham, R.J. (1990) Commentary on Perkins (1990) and Moore and Perkins (1990): On the valid role of reliability in identifying "What is stuttering?" *Journal of Speech and Hearing Disorders, 55,* 394-397.

International Association for the Evaluation of Educational Achievement (1988) *Science achievement in seventeen countries.* Oxford, UK: Pergamon.

Irvine, J.J. (1990) *Black students and school failure. Policies, practices, and prescriptions.* New York: Praeger.

Izzo, M.V. (1987) Career development of disabled youth: The parents' role. *Journal of Career Development, 13,* 47-55.

Jacob, E. and Jordan, C. (1987). Explaining the school performance of minority students. *Anthropology and Education Quarterly, 18,* special issue.

Jacobs, L. (1991) Assessment concerns: A study of cultural differences, teacher concepts, and inappropriate labelling. *Teacher Education and Special Education, 14,* 43-48.

Jacobs, P.A., Mayer, M., and Abruzzo, M.A. (1986) Studies of the fragile (x) syndrome in populations of mentally retarded individuals in Hawaii. *American Journal of Medical Genetics, 23,* 567-572.

Jacobson, T. (1974) Learning disabilities and juvenile delinquency: A demonstrated relationship. In R.E. Weber (Ed.) *Handbook on learning disabilities: A prognosis for the child, the adolescent, the adult.* Englewood Cliffs, NJ: Prentice-Hall.

Janney, R.E., Snell, M.E., Beers, M.K., and Raynes, M. (1995) Integrating students with moderate and severe disabilities into regular education classrooms. *Exceptional Children, 61,* 425-439.

Jaussi, K.R. (1991) Drawing the insiders in: Deaf students in the mainstream. *Perspectives in Education and Deafness, 9,* 12-15,

Jenkins, J.R. and Heinen, A. (1989) Students' preferences for service delivery: Pull-out, in-class, or integrated models. *Exceptional Children, 55,* 516-526.

Jenkins, J.R., Pious, C.G., and Peterson, D.L. (1988) Categorical programs for remedial and handicapped students: Issues of validity. *Exceptional Children, 55,* 147-158.

Jensema, C.J., Karchmer, M.A., and Trybus, R.J. (1978) *The rated speech intelligibility of hearing impaired children: Basic relationships and a detailed analysis.* Series R, No. 6. Washington, DC: Gallaudet College, Office of Demographic Studies.

Johnson, A.B. (1987) Attitudes toward mainstreaming: Implications for inservice training and teaching the handicapped. *Education, 107,* 229-233.

Johnson, D., Thompson, S., Sinclair, M., Krantz, G., Evelo, S., Stolte, K., and Thompson, J. (1993) Considerations and the design of follow-up and follow-along systems for improving transitional programs and services. *Career Development for Exceptional Individuals, 16,* 225-238.

Johnson, D.G. (1989) An unassisted method of psychological testing for visually impaired individuals. *Journal of Visual Impairment and Blindness, 83,* 114-118.

Johnson, D.R., Bruininks, R.H., and Thurlow, M.L. (1987) Meeting the challenge of transition services planning through improved interagency cooperation. *Exceptional Children, 53,* 522-530.

Johnson, D.W. and Johnson, R.T (1978) Cooperative, competitive, and individualistic learning. *Journal of Research and Development in Education, 12,* 3-15.

Johnston, P., Allington, R., and Afflerbach, (1985) The consequence of classroom and remedial instruction. *Elementary School Journal, 85,* 465-477.

Jones, K.N. and Bender, W.N. (1993) Utilization of paraprofessionals in special eucation: A review of the literature. *Remedial and Special Education, 14,* 7-14.

Jones, M.H. (1983) Cerebral palsy. In J. Umbriel (Ed.) *Physical disabilities and health impairments: Assessment, treatment, education.* Baltimore, MD: University Park Press.

Jones, M.M. and Carlier, L.L.(1995) Creating inclusionary opportunities for learners with multiple disabilities: A team-teaching approach. *Teaching Exceptional Children, 27,* 23-27.

Jones, R.I. (1986) Can deaf students succeed in a public university? *ACEHI Journal, 12,* 43-49.

Jordan, T.E. (1976) *The mentally retarded* (4th.ed) Columbus, OH: Merrill.

Journal of the American Medical Association (1990)

Jurgrau, A. (1990) How to spot child abuse. *Registered Nurse, 53,* 27-33.

Kagan, J. (1983) Stress and coping in early development. In N. Garmezy and M. Rutter (Eds.) *Stress, coping, and development in children.* New York: McGraw-Hill.

Kalter, H. and Warkany, J. (1983) Congenital malformations: Etiologic factors and their role in prevention. *The New England Journal of Medicine, 308,* 424-431.

Kaluger, G. and Kolson, C.J. (1978) *Reading and learning disabilities* (2nd. ed.) Columbus, OH: Merrill.

Kanner, L. (1962) Emotionally disturbed children: A historical review. *Child Development, 33,* 97-102.

Kanner, L. (1964) *A history of the care and study of the mentally retarded.* Springfield, IL: Thomas.

Kaplan, R.M. and Saccuzzo, D.P. (1993) P*sychological testing: Principles, applications, and issues* (3rd. ed.) Pacific Grove, CA: Brooks/Cole.

Karagan, N. and Zellweger, H. (1978) Early verbal disability in children with Duchenne muscular dystrophy. *Developmental Medicine and Child Neurology, 20,* 435-441.

Karnes, M.B. and Strong, P.S. (1978) *Nurturing leadership talent in early childhood.* Urbana, IL: Institute for Child Behavior and Development, University of Illinois.

Katzen, K. (1980) An open letter to CEC. *Exceptional Children, 48,* 582.

Kauffman, J.M. (1981/1985/1989) *Characteristics of childrens' behavior disorders* (2nd. ed., 3rd. ed., 4th. ed.) Columbus, OH: Merrill.

Kauffman, J.H. (1987) Strategies for the nonrecognition of social deviance. *B.C. Journal of Special Education, 11,* 201-214.

Kauffman, J.M. (1989) The regular education initiative as Reagan-Bush educational policy: A trickle-down theory of education of the hard-to-teach. *Journal of Special Education, 23,* 256-278.

Kauffman, J.M. (1991) Restructuring in sociopolitical context: Reservations about the effects of current reform proposals on students with disabilities. In J.W. Lloyd, A. C.Repp, and N.N. Singh (Eds.) *The regular education initiative: Alernative perspectives on concepts, issues, and models* (pp. 57-66) Sycamore, IL: Sycamore Publishing Co.

Kauffman, J.M. (1993) How we might achieve the radical reform of special education. *Exceptional Children, 60,* 6-16.

Kauffman, J.M. and Wong, K.L.H. (1991) Forum: Effective teachers of students with behavioral disorders: Are generic teaching skills enough? *Behavioral Disorders, 16,* 225-237.

Kaufman, A.S. and Kaufman, N.L. (1983) *Kaufman Assessment Battery for Children.* Circle Puines, MI: American Guidance Services.

Kaufman, F.A and Sexton, D. (1983, Sept.) Some implications for home-school linkages. *Roeper Review,* pp. 49-51.

Kaufman, J. and Zigler, E. (1989) The intergenerational transmission of child abuse. In D. Cicchetti and V. Carlson (Eds.) *Child maltreatment: Theory and research on the causes and consequences of child abuse and neglect* (pp. 129-151). New York: Cambridge University Press.

Kaufman, M. J., Gottlieb, J., Agard, T. A., and Kukic, A. (1975) Mainstreaming: Toward an explication of the construct. *Focus on Exceptional Children, 7,* 1-13.

Kavale, K.A. and Forness, S.R. (1987) Substance over style: Assessing the efficacy of modality testing and teaching. *Exceptional Children, 54,* 228-239.

Kay, M. (1986) Overcoming passive behavior. *Academic Therapy, 22,* 35-39.

Kaye, K., Elkind, L., Goldberg, D., and Tytum, A. (1989) Birth outcomes for infants of drug abusing mothers. *New York State Journal of Medicine, 89,* 256-261.

Kazdin, A.E. (1989) *Behavior modification in applied settings* (4th. ed.) Pacific Grove, CA: Brooks/ Cole.

Keating, D.P. (1980) Four faces of creativity: The continuing plight of the intellectually underserved. *Gifted Child Quarterly, 24,* 56-61.

Keilitz, J. and Miller, S.L. (1980) Handicapped adolescents and young adults in the justice ststem. *Special Education for Adolescents and Young Adults, 1,* 117-125.

Keilitz, L. and Dunivant, N. (1986) The relationship beween learning disabilities and juvenile delinquency: Current state of knowledge. *Remedial and Special Education, 3,* 18-26.

Kelleher, D.K. (1979) Orientation to low vision aids. *Journal of Visual Impairment and Blindness, 73.*

Keller, H. (1933) *Helen Keller in Scotland.* London: Methuen.

Kelly, T.K., Bullock, L.M., and Dykes, M.K.(1977) Behavior disorders: Teachers' perceptions. *Exceptional Children, 43,* 316-318.

Kempe, C., Silverman, F., Steele, B., Droegemueller, W., and Silver, H. (1962) The battered child syndrome. *Journal of the American Medical Association, 181,* 17-24.

Kerr, B.A. (1988) Raising career expectations of gifted girls. *Vocational Guidance Quarterly, 32,* 37-43.

Kershner, J.R. and Ledger, G. (1985) Effect of sex, intelligence, and style of thinking on creativity: A comparison of gifted and average IQ children. *Journal of Personality and Social Psychology, 48,* 1033-1040.

Kessler, J. (1977). Parenting the handicapped child. *Pediatric Annals, 6,* 654-661.

Khatena, J. (1982) *Educational psychology of the gifted.* New York: John Wiley.

Khoury, J.T. and Appel, M.A. (1979) Gifted children: Current trends and issues. In A. Lane (Ed.) *Readings in human growth and development of the exceptional individual.* Connecticut: Special Learning Corporation.

Kilgo, J. (1990) Early transitions. *DEC Communicator, 17,* 3.

King, S.M., Rosenbaum, P., Armstrong, R.W., and Milner, R. (1992) An epidemiological study of children's attitude toward disability. In S. Towson (Ed.) *Educational psychology: Readings for the Canadian context* (pp. 376-388)

Kinsbourne, M. and Hiscock, M. (1978) Cerebral lateralization and cognitive development. In J. Chall and A. Mirsky (Eds.) *Education and the brain: The 77th. Yearbook of the National Society for the Study of Education, part 2.* Chicago, IL: University of Chicago Press.

Kirk, S. (1963, April 16) Behavioral diagnosis and remediation of learning disabilities. In *Proceedings of the conference on exploration into the problems of the perceptually handicapped child: First annual meeting* (vol. 1) Chicago.

Kirk, S. and Gallagher, J.J. (1979) *Educating exceptional children.* Boston, MA: Houghton Mifflin.

Kirp, D.L. and Epstein, S. (1989) AIDS in American schoolhouses: Learning the hard lessons. *Phi Delta Kappan, 70,* 585-593.

Kittler, F.J. (1970) The effect of allergy on children with minimal brain damage. In F. Speer (Ed.) *Allergy of the nervous system.* Springfield, IL: Thomas.

Klien, R.G. and Last, C.G. (1989) *Anxiety disorders in children.* Newbury Park, CA: Sage.

Kluwin, T.N. and Moores, D.F. (1985) The effects of integration on the mathematical achievement of hearing impaired adolescents. *Exceptional Children, 52,* 153-160.

Kneedler, R., with D.P. Hallahan and J.M. Kaufmann (1984) *Special education for today.* Englewood Cliffs, NJ: Prentice-Hall.

Knoblock, P. (1987) *Understanding exceptional children and youth.* Boston, MA: Little, Brown.

Knowlson, J. (1965) The idea of gesture as a universal language in the seventeenth and eighteenth centuries. *Journal of the History of Ideas, 26,* 495-508.

Koegel, R.L., Rincover, A., and Egel, A.L. (1982) *Educating and understanding autistic children.* San Diego, CA: College-Hill Press.

Koestler, F. (1976) *The unseen minority: A social history of blindness in the United States.* New York: David McKay.

Kohlberg, L. (1969) Stage and sequence: The cognitive-developmental approach to socialization. In D.A Goslin (Ed.) *Handbook of socialization theory and research.* Chicago, Il: Rand McNally.

Kolvin, I., Ounsted, C., and Roth, M. (1971) Cerebral dysfunction and childhood psychoses. *British Journal of Psychiatry, 118,* 407-414.

Konstantareas, M.M. (1984) Sign language as a communication prosthesis with language-impaired children. *Journal of Autism and Developmental Disorders, 14,* 9-25.

Konstantareas, M.M., Webster, C.D., and Oxman, J, (1979) Manual language acquisition and its influence on other areas of functioning in autistic and autistic-like children. *Journal of Child Psychology and Psychiatry, 20,* 337-350.

Kopp, C.B. (1983) Risk factors in development. In P.H. Mussen (Series ed.), M.M. Haith, and J. Campos (vol. eds.) *Handbook of child psychology. Vol. 2. Infancy and developmental psychobiology.* (pp. 1081-1088). New York: Wiley.

Koppitz, E.M. (1980) Strategies for diagnosis and identification of children with behavior and learning problems. In *Conflict in the classroom: The education of emotionally disturbed children.* Belmont, CA: Wadsworth.

Korabek, C.A. and Cuvo, A.J. (1986) Children with spina bifida: Educational implications of their medical characteristics. *Education and Treatment of Children, 9,* 142-159.

Korbin, J.E. (1987) Child abuse and neglect: The cultural context. In R.E. Helfer and R.S. Kempe (Eds.) *The battered child* (4th. ed.) (pp. 23-41). Chicago: University of Chicago Press.

Kouri, T. (1989) How manual sign acquisition relates to the development of spoken language: A case study. *Language, Speech and Hearing Services in the Schools, 20,* 50-62.

Kovacs, M. (1989) Affective disorders in children and adolescents. *American Psychologist, 44,* 209-215.

Kozleski, E.B. and Jackson, L. (1993) Taylor's story: Full inclusion in the neighborhood elementary school. *Exceptionality, 4,* 153-175.

Kratochvil, M.S. and Devereux, S.A. (1988) Counseling needs of parents of handicapped children. *Social Casework, 69,* 42-46.

Kraus, J.F., Fife, D., and Conroy, D. (1987) Pediatric brain injury: The nature, clinical course, and early outcomes in a defined United States population. *Pediatrics, 79,* 501-507.

Kroth, R.L. (1987) Mixed or missed messages between parents and professionals. *Volta Review, 89,* 1-10.

Krug, D.A., Arick, J.R., and Almond, P.J. (1979) Autism Screening Instrument for Educational Planning: Background and development. In J. Gilliam (Ed.) *Autism: Diagnosis, instruction, management, and research.* Texas: University of Texas and Austin Press.

Krug, D.A., Arick, J.R., and Almond, P.J. (1980) Behavior checklist for identifying severely handicapped individuals with high levels of autistic behavior. *Journal of Child Psychology and Psychiatry, 21,* 221-229

Krupp, M.A. and Chatton, M.J. (1983) *Current medical diagnosis and treatment.* Los Altos, CA: Lange Medical Publications.

Kulik, J.A. (1992) *An analyis of the research on ability grouping: Historical and contemporary perspectives.* Storrs, CT: National Research Centres on the Gifted and Talented, Univeristy of Connecticut.

Kulik, J.A. and Kulik, C.L. (1984) Effects of accelerated instruction on students. *Review of Educational Reearch, 54,* 409-425.

Kulik, J.A. and Kulik, C. (1991) Research on acceleration. In N. Colangelo and G.A. Davis (Eds.) *Handbook of gifted education* (pp. 190-191) Boston, MA: Allyn and Bacon.

Kurant, J.E. and Sever, J.L.(1977) Infectious diseases. In J.G. Wilson and F.C. Fraser (Eds.) *Handbook of teratology (vol. 1) General principles of etiology.* New York: Plenum Press.

Kurzweil, R. (1990) *The age of intelligent machines.* Cambridge, MA: MIT Press.

Kusserow, R.P. (1990, Feb.) Crack babies: A report of the office of Inspector General, Department of Health and Human Services. Washington, DC: Inspector General.

Kuzemko, J.A. (1978) *Allergy in children.* Kent, England: Pittman Medical.

Kysela, G. (1985). In F.P. Orelove and D. Sobsey (1987) *Educating children with multiple disabilities: A transdisciplinary approach.* Baltimore, MD: Brookes.

Ladd, G.W., Munson, H.L., and Miller, J.K. (1984) Social interaction of deaf adolescents in secondary-level mainstreamed programs. *Exceptional Children, 50,* 420-428.

Lagercrantz, H. and Slotkin, T.A. (1986, April) The "stress" of being born. *Scientific American,* pp. 100-107.

Lahey, B. and Carlson, C. (1991) Validity of the diagnostic category of attention deficit disorder without hyperactivity: A review of the literature. *Journal of Learning Disabilities, 24,* 11-120.

Lahey, B.B. and Ciminero, A.R.(1980) *Maladaptive behavior: An introduction to abnormal psychology.* Glenview, IL: Scott Foresman.

Lahey, B.B., Hammer, D., Crumrine, P.L., and Forehand, R.L. (1980) Birth order x sex interactions in child development problems. *Developmental Psychology, 16,* 608-615.

Lahey, M. (1988) *Language disorders and language development.* New York: MacMillan.

Lall, G.R. (1977) Hyperkinetic children: A synopsis of possible causes, treatment and educational aspects. *Special Education in Canada, 52,* 21- 23.

Lamb, M. (1977, April) Influence of the child on marital quality and family interaction during the prenatal, perinatal, and infancy periods. Paper presented at the Conference for the Contribution of the Child to Marital Quality Family Interaction through the Life Year, Penn. State University.

Lambert, M.J., Shapiro, D., and Bergin, A.E. (Eds.) *Handbook of psychotherapy and behavior change* (3rd. ed.) New York: Wiley.

Lambert, N. and Windmiller, M. (1981). *AAMD Adaptive Behavior Scale — School edition.* Washington, DC: American Association on Mental Deficiency.

Lambert, N.M. (1988) Adolescent outcomes for hyperactive children: Perspectives on general and specific patterns of childhood risk for adolescents' educational, social, and mental health problems. *American Psychologist, 43,* 786-799.

Lambert, N.M., Hartsough, C.S., Sassone, D., and Sandoval, J. (1987) Persistence of hyperactivity symptoms from childhood to adolescence and associated outcomes. *American Journal of Orthopsychiatry, 57,* 22-32.

Landau, B. (1983) Blind children's language is not "meaningless." In A.E. Mills (Ed.) *Language acquisition in the blind child.* (pp. 62-76) San Diego, CA: College Hill Press.

Landerholm, E. (1990) The transdisciplinary team approach in infant intervention programs. *Teaching Exceptional Children, 22,* 66-70.

Landesman-Dwyer, S., Martin, J.C., Smith D.W., and Streissguth, A.P. (1980) Teratogenic effects of alcohol in human and laboratory animals. *Science, 209,* 353.

Lane, B. (1980) The relationship of learning disabilities to juvenile delinquency: Current status. *Journal of Learning Disabilities, 13,* 425-435.

Lane, H. and Pillard, R. (1978) *The wild boy of Burindi.* New York: Random house.

Langdon, H.W. (1989) Language disorder or difference? Assessing the language skills of Hispanic students. *Exceptional Children, 56,* 160-167.

Langley, M.B. (1991) Assessment: A multidimensional process. In M.B. Langley and L.J. Lombardino (Eds.) *Neurodevelopmental strategies for managing communication disorders in children with severe motor dysfunction* (pp. 199-250) Austin, TX: Pro-Ed.

La Pointe, L. (1982) Neurogenic disorders of speech. In G. Shames and E. Wiig (Eds.) *Human communication disorders.* Columbus, OH: Merrill.

Lapouse, R. and Monk, M. (1958) An epidemiologic study of behavioral characteristics of children. *American Journal of Public Health, 48,* 1134-1144.

Larry P. vs Wilson Riles, 1975 495F Supp. 926 (ND Cal. 1979).

Larson, K.A., and Gerber, M.M. (1987) Effects of social, metacognitive training for enhancing overt behavior in learning disabled and low achieving delinquents. *Exceptional Children, 54,* 201-211.

LaSasso, C. and Davey, B. (1987) The relationship between lexical knowledge and reading comprehension for prelingually, profoundly hearing-impaired students. *Volta Review, 89,* 211-220.

Laski, F.J. (1991) Achieving integration during the second revolution. In L.H. Meyer, C.A. Peck, and L.Brown (Eds.) *Critical issues in the lives of people with severe disabilities* (pp. 409-421) Baltimore, MD: Brookes.

Lavach, J.F. and Lanier, H.B. (1975) The motive to avoid success in 7th., 8th., 9th. and 10th. grade high-achieving girls. *Journal of Educational Research, 68,* 216-218.

Lawrence, B. (1991) Self-concept formation and physical handicap: Some educational implications for integration. *Disability, Handicap, and Society, 6,* 139-146.

Laycock, F. (1979) *Gifted children.* Glenview, IL: Scott, Foresman.

Laycock, S.R. with Findlay, J.A. (1969) *Study of educational provisions for and needs of emotionally disturbed children in the elementary and secondary schools of BC.* Vancouver: Educational Research Institute of British Columbia.

Leavitt, A. and Ioannides, A. (1993) Using character development to improve story writing. *Teaching Exceptional Children, 25,* 41-45.

Leavitt, J.M. (1974) *The battered child.* Morristown, NJ: General Learning Press.

Le Coutuer, A., Rutter, M., Lord, C., Rios, P., Robertson, S., Holdgrafer, M., and McLennon, J.D. (1989) Autism diagnostic interview: A semi-structured interview for parents and care givers of autistic persons. *Journal of Autism and Developmental Disorders, 19,* 363-387.

Leder, G.C. and Fennema, E. (1990) Gender differences in math: A sysnthesis. In E. Fennema and G.C. Leder (Eds.) *Math and gender* (pp. 188-200) New York: Teachers College Press.

Lee, M.W.Y. and Csapo, M. (1989) Vocational transition of young people with mental handicaps. *B.C. Journal of Special Education, 13,* 35-53.

Lefebrue, A. (1983) The child with physical handicaps. In P.D. Strenhauser and Z. Rae-Grant (Eds.) *Psychological problems of the child in the family* (2nd. ed.). New York: Basic Books.

Lehr, F. (1984, February) Co-operative learning. *Journal of Reading,* pp. 458-461.

Leiter, R. (1948) *The Leiter International Performance Scale.* New York: Wiley.

Lenkowsky, R.S. (1987) Bibliotherapy: A review and analysis of the literature. *Journal of Special Education, 21,* 123-132.

Leonard, L. B. (1981). Facilitating language skills in children with specific language impairment: A review. *Applied Psycholinguistics, 2,* 89-118.

Leonard, L.B. (1982) Early language development and language disorders. In G. Shames and E. Wiig (Eds.) *Human communication disorders.* Columbus, OH: Merrill.

Lepper, M.R. and Gurtner, J. (1989) Children and computers: Approaching the twenty-first century. *American Psychologist, 44,* 170-178.

Lerner, J., Mardell-Czudnowski, C. and Goldenberg, D. (1981) *Special education for the early childhood years.* Englewood Cliffs, NJ: Prentice-Hall.

Lessen, E., Dudzinski, M., Karsh, K., and Van Acker, R. (1989) A survey of ten years of academic intervenion with learning disabled students: Implications for research and practice. *Learning Disabilities Forum, 4,* 106-122.

Leuenberger, J. and Morris, M. (1990) Analysis of spelling errors by learning disabled and normal college students. *Learning Disability Focus, 5,* 103-118.

Levin, J.R. (1986). Four cognitive principles of learning-strategy instruction. *Educational Psychologist, 21,* 3-17.

Levin, M.E. and Levin, J.R. (1990) Scientific mnemonics: Methods for maximizing the memory. *American Educational Research Journal, 27,* 301-321.

Levine, E. (1981) *The ecology of early deafness: Guides to fashioning environments and psychological assessments.* New York: Columbia University Press.

Levine, J.M. (1983) Social comparisons and education. In J.M. Levine and M.C. Wang (Eds.) *Teacher and student perceptions: Implications for learning* (pp. 29-55) Hillsdale, NJ: Erlbaum.

Levine, M.D. (1982). The child with school problems: An analysis of physical participation. *Exceptional Children, 49,* 296-304.

Levitas, A., McBogg, P., and Hagerman, R. (1983) Behavioral dysfunction in the fragile X syndrome. In R. Hagerman and P. McBogg (Eds.) *The fragile X syndrome: Diagnosis, biochemistry and intervention.* Dillos, CO: Spectrum.

Levy-Shiff, R. and Sharir, H. (1989) Mother-and-father-preterm infant relationships in the hospital preterm nursery. *Child Development, 60,* 93-102.

Lewington, J. and Orpwood, G. (1993) *Overdue assignment: Taking responsibility for Canada's schools.* Toronto: Wiley.

Lewis, J. and Samuda, R.J. (1989) Non-discriminatory assessment of culturally different students. *McGill Journal of Education, 24,* 253-266.

Lewis, R.B. and Doorlag, D.H. (1991) *Teaching special students in the mainstream.* New York: Macmillan.

Lewis, T.J., Heflin, J. and DiGangi, S. (1991) *Teaching students with behavioural disorders. Basic questions and answers.* Reston, VA: CEC

Leyton, E. (1979) *The myth of delinquency: An anatomy of juvenile nihilism.* Toronto: McClelland and Stewart.

Li, A.K.F. and Adamson, G. (1992) Gifted secondary students' preferred learning style: Cooperative, competitive, or individualistic. *Journal for the Education of the Gifted, 16,* 46-54.

Lichenstein, S. (1989) Post-school employment patterns of handicapped and nonhandicapped graduates and dropouts. *International Journal of Educational Research, 15,* 501-513.

Licht, B.A. and Dweck, C.S. (1984) Determinants of academic achievement: The interaction of children's achievement orientations with skill area. *Developmental Psychology, 20,* 628-632.

Licht, B.A. and Kistner, J.A. (1986). Motivational problems of LD children. In J.K. Torgesen and B.Y.I. Wong (Eds.), *Psychological and educational perspectives on learning disabilities* (pp. 225-255). New York: Academic Press.

Lieberman, L. (1991) REI revisited ... again. *Exceptional Children, 56,* 561-526.

Liebert, D., Lutsky, L., and Gottlieb, A. (1990) Postsecondary experiences of young adults with severe physical disabilities. *Exceptional Children, 57,* 56-63.

Liepman, M.C. (1981) Test procedures and other techniques for the assessment of handicaps: Problems of method. In B. Cooper (Ed.) *Assessing the handicaps and needs of mentally retarded children.* New York: Academic Press.

Lifter, K., Sulzer-Azaroff, B., Anderson, S.R., and Cowdery, G.E. (1993) Teaching play activities to preschool children with disabilities: The importance of developmental considerations. *Journal of Early Intervention, 17,* 139-159.

Light, J.C. (1983) Language intervention programs for autistic children. *Special Education in Canada, 57,* 11-14.

Lillard, P.P. (1972) *Montessori: A modern approach.* New York: Schocken Books.

Lin, C. (1989) High risk situations: The very low birthweight fetus. In M.I. Evans, J.C. Fletcher, A.O. Dixler, and J.D. Shulman (Eds.) *Fetal diagnosis and therapy: Science, ethics, and the law.* Phladelphia, PA: Lippincott.

Lindfors, J. (1987) *Children's language and learning* (2nd. ed.) Englewood Cliffs, NJ: Prentice-Hall.

Lindsay, B. (1978) Leadership giftedness: Developing a profile. *Journal for the Education of the Gifted, 1,* 63-69.

Link, M.P. (1991) Is integration really the least restrictive environment? *Teaching Exceptional Children, 23,* 63-64.

Links, P.S., Stockwell, M., Abichandani, F., and Simeon, E. (1980) Minor physical anomalies in childhood autism. Part 2: Their relationship to maternal age. *Journal of Autism and Development Disorders, 10,* 287-292.

Linn, R.J., Algozzine, B., Mann, L., and Schwartz, S.E. (1987) Communication skills of learning disabled adolescents. *B.C. Journal of Special Education, 11,* 301-312.

Linn, S., Schoenbaum, S., Manson, R., Rosner, B., Stubblefield, R., and Ryan, K. (1982) Coffee and pregnancy. *New England Journal of Medicine, 306,* 141-145.

Lipp, M. (1988) Educating gifted students. Paper presented at Canadian Education Association Meeting, Fredericton, May.

Little, D. M. (1980) Learning disabilities and the severely learning disabled — Status quo in B.C. *B.C. Journal of Special Education, 4,* 155-163.

Lloyd, J.W. (1975) The pedagogical orientation: An argument for improving instruction. *Journal of Learning Disabilities, 8,* 74-78.

Lloyd, J.W. (1988) Direct instruction. In M.C. Wang, M.C. Reynolds, and H.J. Walberg (Eds.) *Handbook of special education (vol. 2) Mildly handicapping conditions.* New York: Pergamon.

Lloyd, J.W., Cowly, E.P., Kohler, F.W., and Strain, P.S. (1988) Redefining the applied research agenda: Cooperative learning, prereferral, teaching consultation, and peer-mediated intervention. *Journal of Learning Disabilities, 21,* 43-52.

Lobato, D., Barbour, L., Hall, L.J., and Miller, C.T. (1987) Psychosocial characteristics of preschool siblings of handicapped and nonhandicapped children. *Journal of Abnormal Child Psychology, 15,* 329-338.

Locke, J. (1894) *An essay concerning human understanding,* vol. 1. Ed. A.C. Fraser, Oxford: Oxford University Press. Original work published 1690.

Loeber, R. (1982) The stability of antisocial and delinquent child behavior: A review. *Child Development, 53,* 1431-1446.

Loeber, R. (1985) Patterns and development of antisocial child behavior. *Annals of Child Development, 2,* 77-116.

Loeber, R. (1990) Developmental and risk factors of juvenile antisocial behavior and delinquency. *Clinical Psychology Review, 10,* 1-41.

Lojkasek, M., Goldberg, S., Marcovitch, S., and MacGregor, D. (1990) Influences on maternal responsiveness to developmentally delayed preschoolers. *Journal of Early Intervention, 14,* 236-273.

Lombard, R.C. and Newbert, D. (1992) Collaborative transition planning: Federal mandates and local solutions. *International Journal of Special Education, 7,* 123-132.

Lombroso, C. (1891) *The man of genius.* New York: Walter Scott.

Lord, C. (1988) Enhancing communication in adolescents with autism. *Topics in Language Disorders, 9,* 72-81.

Lord, C., Schopler, E., and Revicki, D. (1982) Sex differences in autism. *Journal of Autism and Developmental Disorders, 12,* 317-330.

Lotter, V. (1978) Follow-up studies. In M. Rutter and E. Schopler (Eds.) *Autism: A reappraisal of concepts and treatment.* New York: Plenum Press.

Louis, B. and Lewis, M. (1992) Parental beliefs about giftedness in young children and their relationship to actual ability level. *Gifted Child Quarterly, 36.* 27-31.

Lourie, N.V. (1975) The many faces of advocacy. In I.N. Berlin (Ed.) *Advocacy for child mental health.* New York: Brunner/Mazel.

Lovaas, O.I. (1982, September) An overview of the Young Autism Project. Paper presented at the Annual convention of the American Psychological Association, Washington, DC.

Lovaas, O.I. and Favell, J.E. (1987) Protection for clients undergoing aversive/restrictive intervention. *Education and Treatment of Children, 10,* 311-325.

Lovaas, O.I. and Smith, T. (1988) Intensive behavioral treatment for young autistic children. In B.B. Lahey and A.E. Kazdin (Eds.) *Advances in clinical child psychology* (vol. 2) New York: Plenum.

Lovaas, O.I., Newsom, C., and Hickman, C. (1987) Self-stimulating behavior and perceptual reinforcement. *Journal of Applied Behavior Analysis, 20,* 45-68.

Lovaas, O.I., Schreibman, L., and Koegel, R.L. (1974) A behavior modification approach to the treatment of autistic children. *Journal of Autism and Childhood Schizophrenia, 4,* 111-129.

Lowenbraun, S. and Thompson, M.D. (1982) Hearing impairments. In N.G. Haring (Ed.) *Exceptional children and youth* (3rd. ed.) Columbus, OH: Merrill.

Lowenthal, B. (1986) Planning abilities and metacognition. *Academic Therapy, 22,* 199-203.

Lozoff, B. (1989) Nutrition and behavior. *American Psycholoigist, 44,* 231-236.

Luce, L.F. and Smith, E.C. (Eds.) (1986) *Toward internationalism: Readings in cross-cultural communication.* (2nd. ed.) Cambridge, MA: Newbury House.

Luetke-Stahlman, B. and Luckner, J. (1991) *Effectively educating students with hearing impairments.* New York: Longman.

Luftig, R.L. (1988) Assessment of the perceived school loneliness and social isolation of mentally retarded and nonretarded students. *American Journal of Mental Retardation, 92,* 472-475.

Lynch, E.W. and Stein, R. (1982) Perspectives on parent participation in special education. *Exceptional Education Quarterly, 3,* 56-63.

Lynch, E.W. and Stein, R. (1987) Parent participation by ethnicity: A comparison of Hispanic, Black, and Anglo families. *Exceptional Children, 87,* 105-111.

Lynch, M.A. and Roberts, J (1982) *Consequences of child abuse.* London: Academic Press.

Maccoby, E.E. (1980) *Social development: Psychological growth and the parent-child relationship.* New York: Harcourt Brace Jovanovich.

McBride, S.L., Brotherson, M.J., Joanning, H., Whiddon, D., and Demmitt, A. (1993) Implementation of family-centered services: Perceptions of families and professionals. *Journal of Early Intervention, 17,* 414-430.

McBurnett, K., Lahey, B.B., and Pfiffner, L.J. (1993) Diagnosis of attention deficit disorders in DSM-1V: Scientific basis and implications for education. *Exceptional Children, 60,* 108-117.

McClennen, S. (1988) Sexuality and students with mental retardation. *Teaching Exceptional Children, 20,* 58-61.

McCollum, J.A. and Thorp, E.K. (1988) Training of infant specialists: A look to the future. *Infants and Young Children, 1,* 55-65.

McConagh, T. (1988) Canada: A leader in whole-language instruction. *Phi Delta Kappan.*

McCormick, L. (1987) Comparison of the effects of a microcomputer activity and toy play on social and communication behaviors of young children. *Journal of the Division of Early Childhood, 11,* 195-205.

McDermott, P.A. (1980) Prevalence and constituency of behavioral disturbance taxonomies in the regular school population. *Journal of Abnormal Child Psychology, 8,* 523-536.

McDermott, P.A.(1981) The manifestation of problem behaviour in ten age groups of Canadian school children. *Canadian Journal of Behavioural Science, 13,* 310-319.

MacDonald, J. (1985). Language through conversation: A model for intervention with language delayed persons. In S. Warren and A. Rogers-Warren (Eds.) *Teaching functional language* (pp. 89-122) Baltimore, MD: University Park Press.

MacDonald, J.A. (1925) Our debt to the late Sir Frederick Fraser. Halifax School for the Blind, *Annual Report.*

MacDougall, J.C. (1988, August 22) Deaf education: Time for change. Toronto, *Globe and Mail,* p. A.7.

McGann, J.B. (1888) *The deaf mute schools of Canada: A history of their development with an account of the deaf mute institutions of the Dominion, and a description of all known finger and sign alphabets.* Toronto: C.J. Howe.

McGee, D. (1990) Recognising heterogeneity: Increasing educational opportunities through mainstreaming. In M. Ross (Ed.) *Hearing impaired children in the mainstream.* Parkton, MD: York Press.

McGee, L.M. and Richgels, D.J. (1990) *Literacy's beginnings — Supporting young readers and writers.* Boston, MA: Allyn and Bacon.

MacGregor, D.L. (1980) Mental retardation and medical services. *Mental Retardation/ Déficience mentale,* 30, 3-10.

MacGregor, K., Rosenbaum, S., and Skoutajan, K. (1982) *Putting the pieces together: A parent's guide to special education in Ontario.* Toronto: Association for Children with Learning Disabilities.

McGrew, K.S., Bruininks, R.H., and Thurlow, M.L. (1992) Relationhip between measures of adaptive functioning and community adjustment for adults with mental retardation. *Exceptional Children, 58,* 517-529.

McIntosh, J. (1977) The evolution of a magazine: Special Education in Canada, 1925-1964. *Special Education in Canada, 52,* 22-25.

McIntosh, K. (1984) Viral infections of the fetus and newborn. In M. Avery and H.W. Taeusch Jr. (Eds.) *Schaffer's diseases of the newborn* (5th. ed.) Philadelphia: Saunders.

McIntosh, R., Vaughn, S., Schumm, J.S., Haager, D., and Lee, O., (1994) Observations of students with learning disabilities in general education classrooms. *Exceptional Children, 60,* 249-261.

MacKay, A. W. (1986) The equality provisions of the Charter and education: A structural analysis. *CJJE, 11,* 293-312.

MacKay, A.W. (1987a) The Charter of rights and special education: Blessing or curse? *Canadian Journal for Exceptional Children, 3,* 118-127.

MacKay, A.W. (1987b) The Elwood case: Vindicating the educational rights of the disabled. *Canadian Journal of Special Education, 3,* 113-116.

McKinney, J. D. and Forman, S. G. (1982) Classroom behavior patterns of EMH, LD, and EH students. *Journal of School Psychology, 20,* 271-279.

McKinney, J.D., McLure, S., and Feagans, L. (1982) Classroom behavior of learning disabled children. *Learning Disability Quarterly, 5,* 45-51.

McKinney, J.D., Montague, M., and Hocutt, A.M. (1993) Educational assessment of students with attention deficit disorders. *Exceptional Children, 60,* 125-131.

McLaren C. (1988, December 30) Teaching immigrant children. *Toronto Globe and Mail.*

McLaren, J. and Bryson, S.E. (1987) Review of recent epidemiological studies of mental retardation: Prevalence, associated disorders, and etiology. *American Journal on Mental Retardation, 92,* 243-254.

McLeod, P. (1981) Fetal Alcohol Syndrome. *B.C. Medical Journal, 23,* 319-320.

McLeskey, J. and Pacchiano, D. (1994) Mainstreamed students with learning disabilities: Are we making progress? *Exceptional Children, 60,* 508-517.

McLinden, D.J. (1988) Spatial task performance: A metaanalysis. *Journal of Visual Impairment and Blindness, 82,* 231-236.

McLinden, S. (1990) Mothers' and fathers' reports of the effects of a young child with special needs on the family. *Journal of Early Intervention, 14,* 249-259.

McLoughlin, W.P. (1982) The deaf, the law, and higher education. *Volta Review, 84,* 275-283.

MacMillan, D.L. (1982) *Mental retardation in school and society* (2nd. ed.) Boston, MA: Little Brown.

MacMillan, D.L. (1988) Issues in mild mental retardation. *Education and Training in Mental Retardation, 23,* 273-284.

McMillan, E. and Loveland, G. (1984) Counselling for the gifted. *Special Education in Canada, 58,* 125-126.

MacNeil, B. (1990) Educational needs for multicultural hearing-impaired students in the public school system. *American Annals of the Deaf, 135,* 75-82.

McShane, D. (1982) Otitis media and American Indians: Prevalence, etiology, psychoeducational consequences, prevention, and intervention. In S. Manson (Ed.) *New directions in prevention among American Indian children and Alaska native communities.* Portland, OR: Oregon Health Sciences University.

McWilliams, B., Morris, H., and Shelton, R. (1990) Cleft palate speech (2nd. ed.) Philadelphia, PA: B.C. Decker.

Mack, C. (1988) Celebrate cultural diversity. *Teaching Exceptional Children, 21,* 40-43.

Madden, N. and Slavin, R. (1983) Mainstreaming students with mild handicaps: Academic and social outcomes. *Review of Educational Research, 53,* 519-659.

Magnusson, D. (1988) *Individual development from an international perspective: A longitudinal study.* Hillsdale, NJ: Erlbaum.

Mahendra, B. (1985) Subnormality revisited in early 19th. century France. *Journal of Mental Deficiency Research, 29,* 391-401.

Mahoney, G., O'Sullivan, P., and Dennebaum, J. (1990) Maternal perceptions of early intervention services: A scale for assessing family-focused intervention. *Topics in Early Childhood Special Education, 10,* 1-15.

Main, M. and George, C. (1985) Responses of abused and disadvantaged toddlers to distress in agemates: A study in the day care setting. *Developmental Psychology, 21,* 407-412.

Maker, C.J. (1977) *Providing programs for the gifted handicapped.* Reston, VA: Council for Exceptional Children.

Malouf, D.B. and Schiller, E.P. (1995) Practice and research in special education. *Exceptional Children, 61,* 414-424.

Manfredini, D. (1988) Down syndrome. *ERIC Digest, No. 457.* Reston, VA: CEC.

Mangold, S.S. (1982) Teaching reading in Braille. In S.S. Mangold (Ed.) *A teacher's guide to the special educational needs of blind and visually handicapped children.* New York: American Foundation for the Blind.

Manley-Casimir, M. (1987, 25 February) The new rights reality in Canadian society: The "Chartered" path. Address at the first course in Educational Leadership, St. Bride's College, Littledale.

Mann, L., Goodman, L., and Wiederholt, J. (1978) *Teaching the learning-disabled adolescent.* Boston, MA: Houghton Mifflin.

March of Dimes (1987) *Birth defects.* Public Health Education Information Sheet, Genetic Series: Author.

Marfo, K., Browne, N., Gallant, D., Smyth, R., Corbett, A., and McLennon, D. (1988) *Early intervention with developmentally delayed infants and preschool children in Newfoundland and Labrador.* St. John's: MUN.

Margolis, H., McCabe, P., and Schwartz, E. (1990) Using cooperative learning to facilitate mainstreaming in the social studies. *Social Education, 21,* 111-114.

Marland, S.P. Jr. (1972) *Education of the gifted and talented: Report to the Congress of the United States by the Commission of Education.* Washington, DC: US Government Printing Office.

Martin, F., Daly, J., and Cody, J. (1988) Classroom teachers' knowledge of hearing disorders and attitudes about mainstreaming hard-of-hearing children. *Language, Speech, and Hearing Services in the Schools, 19,* 83-95.

Martin, M.L. and Forchuk, C. (1987) Sexuality and the developmentally handicapped: Health education strategies. *Canadian Journal of Special Education, 3,* 181-189.

Martinson, R.A. (1975) *The identification of the gifted and talented.* Reston, VA: Council for Exceptional Children.

Matsuda, M.M. (1984) A comparative analysis of blind and sighted children's communication skills. *Journal of Visual Impairment and Blindness, 78,* 1-5.

Mattes, L.J. and Omark, D.R. (1984) *Speech and language assessment for the bilingual handicapped.* San Diego, CA: College Hill.

Maudsley, H. (1868) *The physiology and pathology of mind.* (2nd. ed.) London: MacMillan.

Maurer, H. and Newbrough, J. (1987) Facial expressions of mentally retarded and nonretarded children: 1: Recognition by mentally retarded and nonretarded adults. *American Journal on Mental Deficiency, 91,* 505-510.

Mayberry, R., Woodlinger, Cohen, R., and Goldwin-Meadow, S. (1987) Symbolic development in deaf children. In D. Cicchetti and M. Beeghly (Eds.) *Symbolic development in atypical children* (pp. 109-126) San Francisco, CA: Jossey-Bass.

Mazurek, K. (1987) Multiculturalism, education and the ideology of the meritocracy. In T. Wotherspoon (Ed.) *The political economy of Canadian schooling* (pp. 141-163) Toronto: Methuen.

Mazurek, K. (1991, March 1) Defining a radical social policy: The undermining of multiculturalism. In Proceedings of the Canadian Studies Conference: 20 years of multiculturalism success and failures. Winnipeg.

Mazurek, K. and Winzer, M. (1994) *Comparative studies in special education.* Washington, DC: Gallaudet University Press.

Meadow, K.P. (1980) *Deafness and child development.* Berkeley: University of California Press.

Meece, J.L., Parsons, J.E., Kaczada, C.M., Goff, S.B. and Futterman, R. (1982) Sex differences in math achievement: Toward a model of academic choice. *Psychological Bulletin, 91,* 324-348.

Meeker, M.N. (1979) *Teachers' guide to the Structure of Intellect Learning Abilities Test.* El Segundo, CA: SOI Systems.

Meents, C.K. (1989) Attention deficit disorder: A review of the literature. *Psychology in the Schools, 26,* 168-178.

Meikle, S. and Kilpatrick, D. (1971) Changes in perceptual, motor, and reading test scores in a remedial reading group. *The Canadian Psychologist, 12,* 254-269.

Meisels, S.J. (1988) Developmental screening in early childhood: The interaction of research and social policy. *Annual Review of Public Health, 9,* 527-550.

Meisels, S.J. (1989) Can developmental screening tests identify children who are developmentally at-risk: *Pediatrics, 83,* 578-585.

Meisgeier, C., Meisgeier, C., and Werble, D. (1978) Factors compounding the handicapping of some gifted children. *Gifted Child Quarterly, 22,* 325-331.

Mellor, M.C. (1981) *Aids for the 80s: What they are and what they do.* New York: American Foundation for the Blind.

Menolascino, F.J. and Stark, J.A. (1988) *Preventative and curative intervention in mental retardation.* Baltimore, MD: Brookes.

Menser, M.A., Forrest, J.M., and Bransky, R.D. (1978) Rubella infection and diabetes mellitus. *Lancet, 78,* 57-60.

Mercer, C.D. (1979) *Children and adolescents with learning disabilities.* Columbus, OH: Merrill.

Mercer, C.D. (1987) *Students with learning disabilities* (3rd. ed.) Columbus OH: Merrill.

Mercer, J.R. (1973) *Labelling the mentally retarded.* Berkeley, CA: University of California Press.

Mercer, J.R. (1989) Alternative paradigms for assesment in a pluralistic society. In J. Banks and C. Banks (Eds.) *Multicultural education: Issues and perspectives* (pp. 289-304). Boston, MA: Allyn and Bacon.

Mercer, J.R. and Lewis, J.F. (1977) *System of Multi-Cultural Pluralistic Assessment.* New York: Psychological Corporation.

Meyers, E. (1984) A study of concerns of classroom teachers regarding a resource room program for the gifted. *Roeper Review, 7,* 32-36.

Mezriko, M. (1987) Transparency and ease of learning of symbols represented by Blisssymbols, PCS and Picsyms. *Augmentative and Alternative Communication, 3,* 129-136.

Michael, M.G. and Paul, P.V. (1991) Early intervention for infants with deaf-blindness. *Exceptional Children, 57,* 200-210.

Milisen, R. (1971) The incidence of speech disorders. In L. Travis (Ed.) *Handbook of speech pathology and audiology.* New York: Appleton-Century-Crofts.

Miller, C.A. (1985) Infant mortality in the United States. *Scientific American, 235,* 31-37.

Miller, C.R. (1976) Subtypes of the PMR: Implications for placement and progress. In C.C. Cleland, J.S. Swartz, and L.W. Talkington, *The profoundly mentally retarded.* Austin, TX: Western Reserve Conference and Hogg Foundation.

Miller, R.T., (1974) Childhood schizophrenia: A review of selected literature. *International Journal of Mental Health, 3,* 3-46.

Mills, J.R. and Jackson, N.E. (1990) Predictive significance of early giftedness: The case of precocious reading. *Journal of Educational Psychology, 82,* 410-419.

Mills, P.E., Dale, P.S, Cole, K.N., and Jenkins, J.R. (1995) Follow-up of children from academic and cognitive preschool curricula at age 9. *Exceptional Children, 61,* 378-393.

Milstead, S. (1988) Siblings are people, too! *Academic Therapy, 23,* 537-540.

Milunsky, A. (1975) The causes and prevention of mental retardation. In *The prevention of genetic disease and mental retardation.* Toronto: W.B. Saunders.

Minner, S. (1989). The use of a paraprofessional to work with parents in a rural school. Rural Special Education Quarterly, 10, 38-43.

Minner, S. (1990) Teacher evaluation of case descriptions of LD gifted students. *Gifted Child Quarterly, 34,* 37-39.

Minuchin, S., Rosman, B., and Baker, L. (1978) *Psychosomatic families: Anorexia nervosa in context.* Cambridge, MA: Harvard University Press.

Mira, M. P. and Tyler, J. S. (1991) Students with Traumatic Brain Injury: Making the transition from hospital to school. *Focus on Exceptional Children, 23,* 1-6.

Misra, A. (1993) Generalization of social skills through self-monitoring by adults with mild mental retardation. *Exceptional Children, 58,* 495-507.

Mitchell, D., Fiewell, E., and Davy, P. (1983) Spina bifida. In J. Umbriel (Ed.) *Physical disabilities and health impairments: An introduction.* Columbus, OH: Merrill.

Mithaug, D.E., Horiuchi, C.N. and Fanning, P.N. (1985) A report on the Colorado statewide follow-up survey of special education students. *Exceptional Children, 51,* 397-404.

Mithaug, D.E., Martin, J.E., and Agran, M. (1987) Adaptability instruction: The goal of transitional programming. *Exceptional Children, 53,* 500-505.

Mohn, G. and Van Hol-Van-Dwin, J. (1983) Behavioral and electrophysiological measures of visual functions in children with neurological disorders. *Behavioral Brain Research, 10,* 177-187.

Montagu, A. (1977) *Life before birth.* New York: Signet Books.

Montague, M. (1988) Job-related social skills training for adolescents with handicaps. *Career Development for Exceptional Individuals, 11,* 26-41.

Montague, M. and Graves, A. (1993) Improving students' story writing. *Teaching Exceptional Children, 25,* 36-37.

Montague, M., Maddux, C.D., and Dereshiwsky, M. (1988, April) Story grammar and learning disabled students' comprehension and production of narrative prose. Paper presented at American Educational Research Association Conference, New Orleans.

Montessori, M. (1912) *The Montessori method.* A. George (trans.) New York: Stokes.

Montessori, M. (1917) *The advanced Montessori method: Scientific pedagogy as applied to the education of children from seven to eleven years.* London: Heinemann.

Montigny, G. (1990, winter) Reading skills. *Canadian social Trends*, pp. 22-24.

Montgomary, D. (1981) Do dyslexics have difficulty assessing auditory information? *Psychological Research, 43*, 235-245.

Moog, J.S. and Geers, A.E. (1991) Educational management of children with cochlear implants. *American Annals of the Deaf, 136*, 69-76.

Moon, M.S., Diambra, T., and Hill, M. (1990) An outcome-oriented vocational process. *Teaching Exceptional Children, 23*, 47-50.

Mooney, C. and Algozzine, B. (1978) A comparison of the disturbingness of behaviors relating to learning disabilities and emotional disturbance. *Journal of Abnormal Child Psychology, 6*, 401-406.

Moore, P. (1982) Voice disorders. In G. Shames and E. Wiig (Eds.) *Human communication disorders*. Columbus, OH: Merrill.

Moore, P. (1986) Voice disorders. In G. Shames and E. Wiig (Eds.) *Human communication disorders* (2nd. ed.) (pp. 183-229) Columbus, OH: Merrill.

Moore, S.E. and Perkins, W.R. (1990) Validity and reliability of judgments of authentic and simulated stuttering. *Journal of Speech and Hearing Disorders, 55*, 383-391.

Moores, D.F. (1978/1982/1987) *Educating the deaf: Psychology, principles and practices.* (2nd ed.,3rd. ed.) Boston, MA: Houghton Mifflin.

Moran, M. (1982, April) Living with a handicapped child: Findings on families and early intervention. Paper presented at CEC, Houston, Texas.

Moran, M.J. and Pintz, A.L. (1995) Helping the child with a cleft palate in your classroom. *Teaching Exceptional Children, 27*, 46-48.

More, A. T. (1984) *Okanagan-Nikola Indian Quality of Education Study.* Penticton, BC: Okanagan Indian Learning Institute.

Morris, J.B. (1983) Classroom methods and materials. In O.N. Saracho and B. Spodek (Eds.) *Understanding the multicultural experience in early childhood education* (pp. 77-90) Washington, DC: National Association for the Education of Young Children.

Morse, W.C.(1975) The education of socially maladjusted and emotionally disturbed children. In W.H. Cruickshank and G.O. Johnson (Eds.) *Education of exceptional children and youth* (3rd. ed.) Englewood Cliffs, NJ: Prentice-Hall.

Morsink, C.V., Thomas, C.C., and Correa, V.I. (1991) *Interactive teaming: Consultation and collaboration in special programs.* New York: Merrill

Mouzakitis, C. and Vachese, R. (1985) *Social work treatment with abused and neglected children.* Springfield, IL: Thomas.

Mueller, H., Mulcahy, R., Watters, B., Wilgosh, L., and Mancini, G. (1986) An analysis of WISC-R item responses with Canadian Inuit children. *Alberta Journal of Educational Research, 32*, 12-36.

Mulcahy, R., Marfo, K., Peat, D., Andrews, J., and Clifford, L. (1986) Applying cognitive psychology in the classroom: A learning/thinking strategies instructional program. *Alberta Psychology, 15*, 9-12.

Mulcahy, R., Wilgosh, L., Crawford, B., and Watters, B. (1984) Gifted education for Inuit youngsters: Problems and issues. *Special Education in Canada, 58*, 127-129.

Mulick, J.A., Jacabson, J.W., and Kobe, F.H. (1993) Anguished silence and helping hands: Autism and facilitated communication. *Skeptical Enquiries, 17*, 270-287.

Mullin, B. (May 18, 1985) *Group has uphill battle.* Winnipeg Free Press.

Mundy, P., Sigman, M., Kasari, C., and Yirmira, N. (1988) Nonverbal communication skills in Down syndrome children. *Child Development, 59*, 235-249.

Murphy, D. (1986) The prevalence of handicapping conditions among juvenile delinquents. *Remedial and Special Education, 7*, 7-17.

Murphy, J. and Slorach, N. (1983) The language development of preschool hearing children of deaf parents. *British Journal of Disorders of Communication, 18*, 118-126.

Murray, J.P. (1980) *Television and youth: 25 years of research and controversy.* Boys Town, NE: Boys Town Center for the Study of Youth Development.

Murray, J.P. (1984) Children and television violence. In J.P. Murray and G. Salomon (Eds.) *The future of children's television.* Boys Town: NB: Father Flanagan's Boys' Home.

Murray, M.E. (1981) Diagnostic psychological testing for reading/learning disorders in preschool children. *Reading Psychology, 2*, 146-157.

Musgrove, P. (1984, November 21) Struggling to survive. *Vancouver Sun*, pp.1-2.

Myers, G., Cerone, S., and Olson, A. (1981) *A guide for helping the child with spina bifida.* Springfield, IL: Thomas.

Myers, J. (1976) The efficacy of the special day school for EMR pupils. *Mental Retardation, 14*, 3-11.

Myers, J. (1987) The training of dynamic assessors. In C. Lidz (Ed.) *Dynamic assessment: An interactional approach to evaluating learning potential* (pp. 403-425). New York: Guilford.

Myers, P. and Hammill, D.D. (1990) *Learning disabilities: Basic concepts, assesment practices and instructional strategies.* (4th. ed.) Austin, TX: Pro-Ed.

Mykelbust, H.R. (1960). *The psychology of deafness.* New York: Grune and Stratton.

Mysak, E. (1976) *Pathologies of speech systems.* Baltimore, MD: Williams and Wilkins.

Mysak, E.D. (1980). *Neurospeech therapy for the cerebral palsied.* New York: Teachers College, Columbia University.

Mysak, E. (1982) Cerebral palsy. In G. Shames and E. Wiig (Eds.) *Human communication disorders.* Columbus, OH: Merrill.

Naeyaert, K.M. and Grace, G. (1990) Prevalence and causes of blindness and visual impairment in Canada. *Journal of Visual Impairment and Blindness, 84*, 361-363.

National Advisory Committee on Dyslexia and Related Reading Disorders (1969) *Reading disorders in the United States.* Washington, DC: Department of Health, Education and Welfare.

National Association (1991) *Liaison Bulletin, 17*, 2.

National Joint Committee on Learning Disabilities (1988) *Letter to NJCLD member organizations.*

National Prevention Committee, Canadian Association for the Mentally Retarded (1982) *Final Report to the Minister of National Health and Welfare on the five regional symposia on the prevention of mental retardation in Canada.* Ottawa: Health and Welfare.

Nealis, J.T. (1983) Epilepsy: In J. Umbriet (Ed.) *Physical disabilities and health impairments: An introduction* (pp. 74-85). Columbus, OH: Merrill.

Neel, R., Meadows, N., Levine. P., and Edgar, E.B. (1988) What happens after special education: A statewide follow-up study of secondary students who have behavioral disorders. *Behavioral Disorders, 13*, 209-216.

Nelkin, D., and Tancredi, L. (1989). *Dangerous diagnostics: The social power of biological information.* New York: Basic Books.

Nelson, C.M., Rutherford, R.B. Jr., Center, D.B., and Walker, H.M. (1991) Do public schools have an obligation to serve disabled children and youth? *Exceptional Children, 57*, 406-413.

Nelson, J.R. et al. (1990) Faculty willingness to accommodate students with learning disabilities: A comparison among academic divisions. *Journal of Learning Disabilities, 23*, 185-189.

Nelson, K.B. and Ellenberg, J.H. (1986) Antecedents of cerebral palsy: Multivariate analysis of risk. *New England Journal of Medicine, 315*, 81-86.

Nesbit, W. (1988). Multiculturalism in special education. Paper presented at the Conference on Multicultural Education, Edmonton.

Nesbit, W. (1990, March) The efficacy of integrated senior programs. *Keeping in Touch*, pp. 3-4.

Nessner, K. (1990, winter) Children with disabilities. *Canadian Social Trends*, pp. 18-20.

Neufeld, R. and Stevens, A. (1992) *Stay in school initiatives — Book 1: A summary of research on school dropouts and implications for special education.* Kingston, Ont: CEC.

Neufeld, R. (1992, March). In *Staying in school initiatives. Monograph 1.* Toronto: Canadian CEC.

Newbert, D.A., Tilson, G.P., and Ianacone, R.N. (1989) Postsecondary transition needs and employment patterns of individuals with mild disabilities. *Exceptional Children, 55*, 494-500..

Newborg, J., Stock, J.R., and Wnek, L. (1984) *Battelle Developmental Inventory.* Allen, TX: DLM Teaching Resources.

Newcomb, M.D. and Bentler, P.M. (1989) Substance use and abuse among children and teenagers. *American Psychologist, 44*, 242-248.

Newcomer, P.L. (1980) *Understanding and teaching emotionally disturbed children.* Boston, MA: Allyn and Bacon.

Newman, J.M. (1985) *Whole language: Theory in use.* Portsmouth, NJ: Heineman.

Nicholls, A. C. and Martin, Y. M. (1983) Judicial decisions and the public schools. *Canadian Journal of Education/ Revue canadienne de l'éducation, 8*, 97-116.

Nicolau, S. and Ramos, C.L. (1990) *Together is better: Building strong partnerships between schools and Hispanic parents.* New York: Hispanic Policy Development Project.

Nihira, K., Foster, R., Shellhaas, M., and Leland, H. (1974) *AAMD Adaptive Behavior Scale, 1974 revision.* Washington, DC: American Association on Mental Deficiency.

Nirje, B. (1979) Changing patterns in residential services for the mentally retarded. In E. L. Meyen (Ed.) *Basic readings in the study of exceptional children and youth.* Denver, CO: Love Publishing.

Nixon, M. (1989) An old problem: Will new approaches come? *ATA Magazine, 69*, 41-43.

Nixon, N. (1990) Assessment issues in relation to experience-based learing on placement with courses. In C. Bell and D. Harris (Eds.) *World yearbook of education, 1990: Assessment and evaluation* (pp. 81-111). London: Kegan Paul.

Noel, M. (1980) Referential communication abilities of learning disabled children. *Learning Disability Quarterly, 3*, 70-87.

Nolte, J. (1976) *Nearly ... everything you've always wanted to know about the gifted and talented.* Wawatosa, WI: Wisconsin Council for the Gifted and Talented.

Northern, J.L. (1980) Acoustic impedance measures in the Down's population. Seminars in Speech, Language and Hearing, 1, 81-86.

Northern, J.L. and Lemme, M. (1982) Hearing and auditory disorders. In G.H. Shames and E.H. Wiig (Eds.) *Human communication disorders: An introduction.* Columbus, OH: Merrill.

Notari-Syverson, A.R. and Shuster, S.L.(1995) Putting real-life skills into IEP? IPSPs for infants and young children. *Teaching Exceptional Children, 27*, 29-32.

Nurss, J.R. and McGauvren, M.E. (1976) *Metropolitan Readiness Tests.* New York: Harcourt Brace Jovanovich.

O'Connor, R.E., Jenkins, J.R., Cole, K.N., and Mills, P.E. (1993) Two approaches to reading instruction with children with disabilities: Does program design make a difference? *Exceptional Children, 59*, 312-323.

Odem, S.L., Kohler, F.W., and Strain, P.S. (1987) *Teaching strategies for promoting social interaction skills.* Pittsburgh, PA: The Early Childhood Research Institute, University of Pittsburgh.

Oderkirk, J. (1993, winter) Disabilities among children. *Canadian Social Trends*, pp. 22-25.

Odgen, P.W. and Lipsett, S. (1982) *The silent garden: Understanding the hearing impaired child.* New York: St. Martin's Press.

Office of Technology Assessment, US Congress (1987) *Technology dependent children: Hospital vs home care- a technical memorandum.* OTA-TM-H-38. Washington, DC: Author.

O'Hara, D.M. and Levy, S.M. (1984) Family adaptation to learning disability: A framework for understanding and treatment. *Learning Disabilities, 3*, 63-77.

Ohlsen, M.M. (1977) *Group counseling* (2nd ed.). New York: Holt, Rinehart and Winston.

Okolo, C.M. and Sitlington, P. (1986) The role of special education in LD adolescents' transition from school to work. *Learning Disability Quarterly, 9*, 141-155.

Oller, D.K. and Eilers, R.E. (1988) The role of audition in infant babbling. *Child Development, 59*, 441-449.

Olweus, D. (1979) Stability of aggressive reaction patterns in males: A review. *Psychological Bulletin, 86*, 852-875.

Olweus, D. (1980) Familial and temperamental determinants of aggressive behavior in adolescent boys: A causal analysis. *Developmental Psychology, 16*, 644-660.

Olweus, D. (1987, fall) Schoolyard bullying: Grounds for intervention. *School Safety*, pp. 4-11.

Omark, D.R. and Watson, D.L. (1983) Psychological testing and bilingual education: The need for reconceptualization. In D.R. Omark and J.G. Erickson (Eds.) *The bilingual exceptional child.* San Diego, CA: College Hill.

O'Melia, M.C., and Rosenberg, M.S. (1994) Effects of cooperative homework teams on the acquisition of mathematics skills by secondary students with mild disabilities. *Exceptional Children, 60*, 538-548.

Onslow, M., Costa, L., and Rue, S. (1990) Direct early intervention with stuttering: Some preliminary data. *Journal of Speech and Hearing Disorders, 55*, 405-416.

Ontario, Ministry of Education (1981) *Special education handbook.* Ontario: Ministry of Education.

Ontario Ministry of Health (1978) *You and your hearing.* Toronto: Ontario Ministry of Health.

Orelove, F.P. and Sobsey, D. (1987) *Educating children with multiple disabilities: A transdisciplinary approach.* Baltimore, MD: Paul Brooks.

Orlansky, M.C. (1981) The deaf-blind and the severe/profoundly handicapped: An emerging relationship. In S.R. Walsh and R. Holzberg (Eds.) *Understanding and educating the deaf-blind/severely and profoundly handicapped* (pp. 5-23) Springfield, IL: Thomas.

Ormerod, J.J. and Huebner, E.S. (1988) Crisis intervention: Facilitating the parental acceptance of a child's handicap. *Psychology in the Schools, 25*, 422-428.

Ornitz, E.M. (1973) Childhood autism: A review of the clinical and experimental literature. *California Medicine, 118*, 21-47.

Ortiz, A.A. and Yates, J.R. (1983) Incidence of exceptionality among Hispanics: Implications for manpower planning. *NABE Journal, 7*, 41-53.

Ortiz, A.A. and Wilkinson, C.Y. (1989) Adapting IEPs for limited English proficient students. *Academic Therapy, 24*, 555-568.

Orton, S. (1927) Studies in stuttering. Archives of *Neurology and Psychology, 18*, 671-672.

O'Shea, D.J. (1994) Modifying daily practices to bridge transitions. *Teaching Exceptional Children, 26*, 29-34.

Otto, W. and Smith, R. (1980) *Corrective and remedial reading* (3rd. ed.) Boston, MA: Houghton Mifflin.

O'Tuel, F.S. et al.(1983) The SOI as an identification tool for the gifted: Windfall or washout? *Gifted Child Quarterly, 27*, 126-134.

Ovanso, C.J. and Collier, V.P. (1985) *Bilingual and ESL classrooms: Teaching in multicultural contexts.* New York: McGraw Hill.

Overton, T. (1992) *Assessment in special eduation: An applied approach.* Columbus, OH: Merrill

Owens, R. E. Jr. (1988) *Language development* (2nd. ed.) Columbus, OH: Merrill.

Owens, R.J. Jr. (1991) *Language disorders: A functional approach to assessment and intervention.* New York: Merrill.

Ozanne, A.E., Kaimmer, and Murdoch, (1990). Speech and language skills in children with early treated phenylketonuria. *American Journal on Mental Retardation, 94*, 625-632.

Paciorek, K.M. and Munro, J.H. (1995) *Early childhood education: Annual editions.* Guilford, CT: Dushkin.

Paddock, H. (1988) The destruction of language in Newfoundland. St. John's: Memorial University of Newfoundland.

Palinscar, A.S. (1986) Metacognitive strategy instruction. *Exceptional Children, 53*, 118-124.

Palmer, F.B., Shapiro, B.F., Wachtel, R.C., Allen, M.C., Hiller, J.E., Harryman, S.E., Master, B.S., Meinert, C.L., and Capute, A.J. (1988) The effects of physical therapy on cerebral palsy. *New England Journal of Medicine, 318*, 803-808.

Palmer, H. (1975). *Immigration and the rise of multiculturalism.* Ontario: Copp Clark Pitman.

Parette, H.P. Jr., Hofmann, A., and Van Biervliet, (1994) The professional's role in obtaining funding for assistive technology for infants and toddlers with disabilities. *Teaching Exceptional Children, 26*, 22-28.

Paris, S.G. and Cross, D.R. (1983) Ordinary learning: Pragmatic connections among children's beliefs, motives and actions. In J. Bisanz, G. Bisanz, and R. Kail (Eds.) *Learning in children.* New York: Springer/Verlag.

Park, G.E. and Linden, J.D. (1968) The etiology of reading disabilities: A historical perspective. *Journal of Learning Disabilities, 1*, 318-331.

Parker, J.K. and Asher, S.R. (1987) Peer relations and later adjustment: Are low-accepted children "at-risk?" *Psychological Bulletin, 102*, 357-389.

Parlatto, S.J. (1977) Those other captioned films: Captioned educational films. *American Annals of the Deaf, 122*, 33-37.

Patten, B.M.(1973). Visually mediated thinking: A report of the case of Albert Einstein. *Journal of Learning Disabilities, 6*, 415-420.

Patterson, D. (1987, August) The causes of Down syndrome. *Scientific American*, pp. 52-57, 60.

Patterson, G.R. (1982) *Coercive family process.* Eugene, OR: Castalia Press.

Patterson, G.R. and Banks, L. (1989) Some amplifying mechanisms for pathological processes in families. In M.R. Gumar and E. Thalen (Eds.) *Systems and development: The Minnesota symposium on child psychology* (vol.22) (pp. 167-209) Hillsdale, NJ: Erlbaum.

Patterson, G.R., De Baryshe, B.D. and Ramsey, E. (1989) A developmental perspective on antisocial behavior. *American Psychologist, 44*, 322-335.

Patton, J.R., Cronin, M.E., Polloway, E.A., Hutchinson, D., and Robinson G.A. (1989) Curricula considerations: A life skills orientation. In G.A. Robinson, J.R. Patton, E.A. Polloway, and L.R. Sargent. *Best practices in mild mental disabilities.* Reston, VA: CEC.

Paul. J.L. (1987) Defining behavior disorders in children. In B.C. Epanchin and J.L. Paul (Eds.) *Emotional problems of childhood and adolescence* (pp. 15-29). Columbus, OH: Merrill.

Paul, J.L. and Warnock, N.J. (1980) Special education: A changing field. *The Exceptional Child, 27*, 3-28.

Paulston, C. (1980) *Bilingual education: Theories and issues.* Rowley, MA: Newbury house.

Paynter, E.J., Jordan, W.J., and French, D.L. (1990) Patient compliance with cleft palate team regimens. *Journal of Speech and Hearing Disorders, 55*, 740-752.

Pearl, R. (1987) Social cognitive factors in learning disabled children's social problems. In S.J. Ceci (Ed.) *Handbook of cognitive, social, and neurological aspects of learning disabilties* (vol. 2) Hillsdale, NJ: Erlbaum.

Pearpoint, J. and Forest, M. (1992) Foreword. In S. Stainback and W. Stainback (Eds.) *Curriculum considerations in inclusive classrooms: Facilitating learning for all students* (pp. xv-xviii) Baltimore, MD: Brookes.

Peck, C.A., Palyo, W.J., Bettencourt, B., Cooke, T.P., and Apolloni, T.(1988). An observational study of "partial integration" of handicapped students in a regular preschool. *Journal of Research and Development in Education, 21*, 4-44

Peckham, V.C. (1993) Children with cancer in the classroom. *Teaching Exceptional Children, 26*, 26-32.

Peet, H. (1855) Inaugural address. *Medico-Legal Journal, 3*, 388-389.

Perkins Institution for the Blind, *Annual Reports.* 1834, 1837, 1839.

Perkins, W.H. (1978) *Human perspectives in speech and language disorders.* St.Louis, MO: Mosby.

Perkins, W.H. (1990) What is stuttering? *Journal of Speech and Hearing Disorders, 55*, 370-382.

Perks, B. (1984) Identification of gifted children. Ed. D. thesis, University of British Columbia.

Perlmutter, B. (1986) Personality variables and peer relation of children and adolescents with learning disabilities. In S.J. Ceci (ed.) *Handbook of cognitive, social and neuropsychological aspects of learning disabilities* (vol. 1) (pp. 339-359) Hillsdale, NJ: Erlbaum.

Perry, D.G., Perry, L.C., and Boldezar, J.P. (1990) Learning of aggression. In M. Lewis and S. Miller (Eds.) *Handbook of developmental psychopathology.* New York: Plenum.

Perry, D.G., Perry, L.C., and Weiss, R.J. (1989) Sex differences in the consequences that children anticipate for aggressors. *Developmental Psychology, 25*, 312-319.

Perry, D.G., Williard, J.C., and Perry, L.C. (1990) Peers' perceptions of the consequences that victimized children provide aggressors. *Child Development, 61*, 1310-1325.

Peter, D., Allan, J., and Horvath, A. (1983) Hyperactive children's perceptions of teachers' classroom behavior. *Psychology in the Schools, 20*, 234-240.

Peterson, K.L. (1992) Helping student teachers understand conflict among preschool children. *Journal of Early Childhood Teacher Education, 13*, 15-18.

Peterson, N. L. (1987) *Early intervention for handicapped and at-risk children.* Denver, CO: Love.

Pettito, L.A. and Marenette, P.F. (1991) Babbling in the manual mode: Evidence for the ontogeny of language. *Science, 251*, 1493-1495.

Peterson, J. (1925) *Early concepts of tests of intelligence.* Chicago, IL: World Book.

Pfeffer, C.R. (1986) *The suicidal child.* New York: Guilford.

Phillips, K. (1990) Why can't a man be more like a woman — and vice versa. *Omni*, 42-48, 68.

Phipps, (1982) The learning disabled learner is often a boy — Why? *Academic Therapy, 17*, 425-430.

Piechowski, M.M. (1991) Emotional development and emotional giftedness. In N. Colangelo and G.A. Davis (Eds.) *Handbook of gifted education* (pp. 285-306). Needham Heights, MA: Allyn and Bacon.

Pieper, E. (1976) Grandparents can help. *Exceptional Parent, 6*, 7-10.

Pierce, B.A. (1990) *Family genetic sourcebook.* New York: Wiley.

Pihl, R.D. and McLarnon, L. (1984) Learning disabled children as adolescents. *Journal of Learning Disabilities, 11*, 96-100.

Piirto, J. (1994) *Talented children and adults: Their development and education.* New York: Merrill.

Pilecka, A. (1995, July) Childhood allergies. Public lecture presented at University of Lethbridge.

Pilley, J.H. (1988) Plans and outcomes: A study of the transition of the Vancouver School Board's 1987 mentally handicapped graduates. M.A. thesis, University of British Columbia.

Pintner, R. (1941) The deaf. In R. Pintner, J. Esenson, and M. Stanton (Eds.), *The psychology of the physically handicapped.* New York: Appleton-Century Crofts.

Pituch, M. and Bruggeman, J. (1982). Lungs unlimited. *Children Today, 11*, 6-10.

Piven, J., Tsai, G., Nehme, E., Coyle, J.T., Chase, G.A., and Folstein, S.E. (1991) Platelet serotonin, a possible marker for familial autism. *Journal of Autism and Developmental Disorders, 21*, 51-54.

Planta, R.C. (1990) Widening the debate on educational reform: Prevention as a viable alternative. *Exceptional Children, 56*, 306-313.

Plata, M. and Santos, S.L. (1981) Bilingual special education: A challenge for the future. *Teaching Exceptional Children, 14*, 97-100.

Pledgie, T.K. (1982) Giftedness among handicapped children: Identification and programming development. *Journal of Special Education, 16*, 221-227.

Plomin, R. (1989) Environment and genes: Determinants of behavior. *American Psychologist, 44*, 105-111.

Plomin, R., De Fries, J.C., and McClearn, G.E. (1990) *Behavioral genetics: A primer* (2nd. ed.) New York: Freeman.

Plowman, P.D. (1981) Training extraordinary leaders. *Roeper Review, 3*, 13-16.

Pogrund, R.L. and Rosen, S.J. (1989) The preschool blind child can be a cane user. *Journal of Visual Impairment, 83*, 431-439.

Poirier, D. and Goguen, L. (1986) The Canadian Charter of Rights and the right to education for exceptional children. *Canadian Journal of Education/Revue canadienne de l'éducation, 11*, 231-244.

Poirier, D., Goguen, L., and Leslie, P. (1988) *Education rights of exceptional children in Canada: A national study of multi-level commitments.* Toronto: Carswell.

Pollack, D. (1970) *Educational audiology for the limited hearing infant.* Springfield, IL: Thomas.

Pollack, D. (1980) Acoupedics: An approach to early management. In G.T. Mencher and S.E. Gerber (Eds.) *Early management of hearing loss.* New York: Grune and Stratton.

Pollack, M. and Woerner, M.G. (1966) Pre- and peri-natal complications and "childhood schizophrenia": A comparison of five controlled studies. *Journal of Child Psychology and Psychiatry, 7*, 235-242.

Pollins, L.D. (1983) The effects of acceleration on the social and emotional development of gifted students. In C. P. Benbow and J.C. Stanley (Eds.) *Academic precocity: Aspects of its development* (pp. 160-179) Baltimore: Johns Hopkins University Press.

Polloway, E.A. (1985) Identification and placement in mild retardation programs: Recommendations for professional practice. *Education and Training of the Mentally Retarded, 20*, 218-221.

Polloway, E.A. and Smith, J.E. (1982) *Teaching language skills to exceptional children.* Denver, CO: Love Publishing.

Polloway, E. A. and Smith, J. D. (1983) Changes in mild mental retardation: Population, programs and perspectives. *Exceptional Children, 50*, 149-159.

Polloway, E.A., Epstein, M.H., Patton, J.R., Cullinan, D., and Lueble, J. (1986) Demographic, social, and behavioral characteristics of students with educable mental retardation: A survey of the field. *Education and Training of the Mentally Retarded, 21*, 27-34.

Polloway, E.A., Patton, J.R., Payne, J.S., and Payne, R.A. (1989) *Strategies for teaching learners with special needs* (4th. ed.) Toronto: Merrill.

Potter, M.L. and Wamre, H.M. (1990) Curriculum-based measurement and developmental reading models: Opportunities for cross validation. *Exceptional Children, 57*, 16-25.

Pottharst, E. (1983) Literature on tape and the hearing impaired: Listening while reading with Winnie-the-Pooh and Candide. *Volta Review, 85*, 285-288.

Powell, D.R. (1990) Home visiting in the early years: Policy and program design decisions. *Young Children, 45*, 65-73.

Power, P.W. (1984) *A guide to vocational assessment.* Austin, TX: Pro-Ed.

Powers, D.P. and Franks, C.M. (1988) Behavior therapy and the education process. In J.C. Witt, S.N. Elliott, and F.M. Gresham (Eds.) *Handbook of behavior therapy in education* (pp. 3-36) New York: Plenum.

Preece, M.A., Kearney, P.J., and Marshall, W.C. (1977) Growth-hormone deficiency in congenital rubella. *Lancet, 77*, 842-844.

Pre-natal care [1987]. Pamphlet, n.p. Available at Lethbridge Health Unit.

President's message (1988, Jan. 3) *Newsletter of the Newfoundland and Labrador Association for Multicultural Education*, p. 1.

Pressley, M. (1986) The relevance of the good strategy user model to the teaching of mathematics. *Educational Psychologist, 21*, 139-161.

Pressley, N., Levin, J.R., and McDaniel, M.A. (1987) Remembering versus inferring what a word means: Mnemonic and contextual approaches. In M.G. McKeown and M.E. Curtis (Eds.) *The nature of vocabulary acquisition* (pp. 107-127) Hillsdale, NJ: Erlbaum.

Pritchard, D.G. (1963) *Education and the handicapped.* London: Routledge and Kegan Paul.

Proctor, T.B., Black, K.N., and Feldhusen, J.F. (1984) Early admission of selected children to elementary school: A review of the research literature. *Journal of Educational Research, 80*, 70-76.

Prout, J. (1981) The incidence of suspected exceptional educational needs among youth in juvenile correctional facilities. *Journal of Correctional Education, 32*, 22-34.

Pruess, J.B., Vadazy, P.F., and Fewell, R.R. (1987) Language development in children with Down syndrome: An overview of recent research. *Education and Training in Mental Retardation, 22*, 44-55.

Pruitt, W. (1986) *Vocational evaluation* (2nd. ed.) Menomonie, WI: Walt Pruitt Associates.

Pugach, M. and Lilly, M.S. (1984) Reconceptualizing support services for classroom teachers: Implications for teacher education. *Journal of Teacher Education, 35*, 48-55.

Quay, H.C. (1972) Patterns of aggression, withdrawal, and immaturity. In H.C. Quay and J.S. Werry (Eds.) *Psychopathological disorders of childhood.* New York: Wiley.

Quay, H.C. (1986) Classification. In H.C. Quay and J.S. Werry (Eds.) *Psychopathological disorders in childhood* (3rd. ed.) New York: Wiley.

Quay, H.C. and Peterson, D.R. (1987) *Manual for the Revised Behavior Problem Checklist.* Coral Gables, FL.

Quinsland, L.K. and Vanginkel, A. (1990) Cognitive processing and the development of concepts by deaf students. *American Annals of the Deaf, 135*, 280-284.

Radbill, S.X. (1974) A history of child abuse and infanticide. In R.E. Heifer and C.H. Kempe (Eds.) *The battered child* (2nd. ed.) Chicago: University of Chicago Press.

Raimondo, D. and Maxwell, M. (1987) The modes of communication used in junior and senior high school classrooms by hearing impaired students and their teachers. *Volta Review, 89*, 263-275.

Ramcharan, S. (1988) The role of education in multi-racial Canada. *Multiculturalism, 11*, 23-27.

Ramirez, A.G. and Stromquist, N.P. (1978) ESL methodology and student language learning in bilingual elementary schools. ERIC Document, ED No. 150 879.

Ramirez, B.A. (1988) Culturally and linguistically diverse children. *Teaching Exceptional Children, 20*, 45-46.

Raschke, D.B., Dedrick, C., and Hanus, K. (1991) Adaptive playgrounds for all children. *Teaching Exceptional Children, 24*, 25-28.

Rathegerber, A.J. (1981). Manitoba vision screening study. *Journal of Visual Impairment and Blindness, 75*, 239-243.

Raven, J. (1948) *Progressive matrices.* New York: Psychological Corporation.

Reagan, T. (1988) Multiculturalism and the deaf: An educational manifesto. *Journal of Research and Development in Education, 22*, 1-6.

Reardon, S.M. and Naglieri, J.A. (1992) PASS cognitive processing characteristics of normal and ADHD males. *Journal of School Psychology, 30*, 151-163.

Reich, P.A. (1986) *Language development.* Englewood Cliffs, NJ: Prentice-Hall.

Reid, R., Maag, J.W, and Vasa, S.F. (1993) Attention deficit hyperactivity disorder as a disability category: A Critique. *Exceptional Children, 60*, 198-214.

Reinert, H. (1976/1980) *Children in conflict.* St. Louis: Mosley Co.

Reinert, H.B. and Huang, A. (1987) *Children in conflict.* Columbus, OH: Merrill.

Reis, S.M. (1989) Reflections on policy affecting the education of gifted and talented students: Past and future perspectives. *American Psychologist, 44*, 399-408.

Reis, S.M. and O'Shea, A.A. (1984) An innovative enrichment program: The Enrichment Triad/Revolving Door Model. *Special Education in Canada, 58*, 135-138.

Reis, S., Levitan, G.W., and McNally, R.J. (1982) Emotionally disturbed mentally retarded people. *American Psychologist, 37*, 361-367.

Reiss, A.L. and Freund, L. (1990) Fragile X syndrome. *Biological Psychiatry, 27*, 223-240.

Reist, M. (1991, March) The Young Offenders Act and how it impacts upon educators. *Keeping in Touch*, pp. 2-3.

Renaud, V. and Badets, J. (1993, autumn) Ethnic diversity in the 1990s. *Canadian Social Trends*, 17-22.

Renzulli, J.S. (1978) What makes giftedness? Reexamining a definition. *Phi Delta Kappan, 60*, 180-184, 261.

Renzulli, J.S. (1979) *What makes giftedness?* Los Angeles: National/State Leadership Training Institute on the Gifted and Talented, Brief no. 6. Report, (1981).

Renzulli, J. S. (1980) What we don't know about programming for the gifted and talented. *Phi Delta Kappan, 61*, 601-602

Renzulli, J.S. and Reis, S.M. (1991) The schoolwide enrichment model: A comprehensive plan for the development of creative productivity. In N. Colangelo and G. Davis (Eds.) *Handbook of gifted education* (pp. 111-141) Boston, MA: Allyn and Bacon.

Renzulli, J.S. and Smith, L.H. (1984) Revolving door: A truer turn for the gifted. *Learning, 9*, 91-93.

Renzulli, J.S., Hartman, R.K.,and Callahan, C.M. (1975) Scale for Rating the Behavioral Characteristics of Superior Students. In W.B. Barbe and J.S. Renzulli (Eds.) *Psychology and education of gifted children* (2nd. ed.) New York: Irvington.

Report of the Northlands School Division Investigation Committee (1981) Edmonton: Alberta Education.

Reschly, D.J. (1988) Minority EMR overrepresentation and special education reform. *Exceptional Children, 88*, 316-323.

Reschley, D.J. (1989) Incorporating adaptive behavior deficits into instructional programs. In G.A. Robinson, J.R. Palton, E.A. Polloway, and L.R., Sargent (Eds.) *Best practices in mental retardation* (pp. 39-63). Reston, VA: Council for Exceptional Children.

Reschly, D.L. (1987) Learning characteristics of mildly handicapped students. In M.C. Wang, M.C. Reynolds, and H.J. Walberg (Eds.) *Handbook of special education: Research and pracice (vol. 1) Learner characteristics and adaptive education* (pp. 35-58) New York: Pergamon.

Rest, M.C. (1990, July) The shadow children: Preparing for the arrival of crack babies in school. *Phi Delta Kappan Research Bulletin*, pp. 1-6.

Reyes, M. de la Luz (1991) A process approach to literacy using dialogue journals and literature logs with second language leaners. *Research in the Teaching of English, 25*, 291-313.

Reynolds, M.C. (1962) A framework for considering some issues in special education. *Exceptional Children, 28*, 367-370.

Reynolds, M.C. and Birch, J.W. (1977) *Teaching exceptional children in all America's schools.* Reston, VA: Council for Exceptional Children.

Reynolds, M.C. and Birch, J.W. (1988) *Adaptive mainstreaming.* White Plains, NY: Longmans.

Reynolds, M.C., Wang, M., and Walberg, H.J. (1987) The necessary restructuring of special and regular education. *Exceptional Children, 53*, 391-398.

Rice, R. (1977) Neurophysiological development in premature infants following stimulation. *Developmental Psychology, 13*, 69-76.

Rich, L.H. (1982) *Disturbed students: Characteristics and educational strategies.* Baltimore, MD.: University Park Press.

Rich, Y. (1986) Curriculum development for co-operative learning in mixed ability classes. *Journal of Curriculum Studies, 18,* 339-341.

Richert, E.S. (1991) Rampant problems and promising practices in identification. In N. Colangelo and G.A. Davis (Eds.) *Handbook of gifted education* (pp. 81-96). Needham Heights, MA: Allyn and Bacon.

Richert, E.S., Alvino, J.J., and McDonnell, R.C. (1982) *National report on identification: Assessment and recommendations for comprehensive identification of gifted and talented youth.* Sewell, NJ: Information Resource Center.

Richey, L. and Ysseldyke, J. (1983) Teacher expectations for the younger siblings of learning disabled students. *Journal of Learning Disabilities, 16,* 610-615.

Rimland, B. (1964) *Infantile autism.* New York: Appleton-Century-Crofts.

Rimland, B. (1974) Infantile autism: Status and research. In A. Davids (Ed.) *Child personality and psychopathology: Current topics.* New York: Wiley.

Rimland, B. (1983). The Feingold diet: An assessment of the reviews by Mattes, by Kavale and Forness and others. *Journal of Learning Disabilities, 16,* 331-333.

Rimm, S.B. (1986) *Underachievement syndrome: Causes and cures.* Watertown, WI: Apple Publishers.

Rimm, S. and Davis, G.A. (1976) GIFT: An instrument for the identification of creativity. *The Journal of Creative Behavior, 10,* 178-182.

Rimm, S. and Lowe, B. (1988) Family environments of underachieving gifted students. *Gifted Child Quarterly, 32,* 353-359.

Risko, V. (1981) Oral language. In D.D. Smith (Ed.) *Teaching the learning disabled.* Englewood Cliffs, NJ: Prentice-Hall.

Rist, R. S. (1990). Variability in program design: The interaction of process with knowledge. *International Journal of Man-Machine Studies, 33,* 305-322.

Ritchey, D. (1993, June) Frustration of a parent of gifted children. *Keeping in Touch,* 3-4.

Ritter, D.R. (1989) Teachers' perceptions of problem behavior in general and special education. *Exceptional Children, 55,* 559-564.

Rittenhouse, R.K. (1987) The attitudes of teachers toward mainstreaming of hearing impaired high schoolers. *Journal of Rehabilitation of the Deaf, 20,* 11-13.

Rittenhouse, R.K., Rahn, C.H., and Morreau, L.E. (1989) Educational interpreter services for hearing-impaired students: Provider and consumer disagreements. *Journal of the American Deafness and Rehabilitation Association, 22,* 57-63.

Ritvo, E.R., Ritvo, E.C., and Brothers, A.M. (1982) Genetic and immunohematologic factors in autism. *Journal of Autism and Developmental Disorders, 12,* 109-114.

Rivers, D. (1986) Labeling and learning disabled children: The implications of variability. In T.E.C. Smith, D.M. Finn, and C.A. Dowdy (1993) *Teaching students with mild disabilities.* Fort Worth, TX: HBJ.

Robb, P. (1981). *Epilepsy: A manual for health workers.* Bethesda, MD: Department of Health and Human Services.

Roberts, C., Pratt, C., and Leach, D. (1991) Classroom and playground interactions of students with and without disabilities. *Exceptional Children, 57,* 212-224.

Roberts, C.A., and Lazure, M.D. (1970) *One million children: A national study of Canadian children with emotional and learning disorders.* Toronto: Crainford.

Roberts, J.E., Burchind, M.R., Koch, M.A., Fodto, M.M., and Henderson, F.W. (1988) Otitis media in early childhood and its relationship to later phonological development. *Journal of Speech and Hearing Disorders, 53,* 424-432.

Robins, L.N. (1979) Follow-up studies. In H.C. Quay and J.S. Werry (Eds.) *Psychopathological disorders of childhood* (2nd. ed.) New York: Wiley.

Robins, L.N. and Earls, F. (1985) A program for preventing antisocial behavior for high-risk infants and presechoolers: A research prospectus. In R.L. Hugh, P.A. Gongla, V.B. Brown, and S.E. Goldston (Eds.) *Psychiatric epidemiology and prevention: The possibilities* (pp. 73-84) Los Angeles, CA: Neuropsychiatric Institute.

Robinson, D.O., Allen, D.V., and Root, L.P. (1988) Infant tympanometry: Differential results by race. *Journal of Speech and Hearing Disorders, 53,* 341-346.

Robinson, G.A., Palton, J.R., Polloway, E.A., and Sargent, L.R. (1989) (Eds.) *Best practices in mental retardation.* Reston, VA: Council for Exceptional Children.

Robinson, H.B. and Robinson, N.M. (1976) *The mentally retarded child: A physiological approach* (2nd. ed.) New York: McGraw Hill.

Robinson, H.B., Roedell, W.C., and Jackson, N.E. (1979) Early identification and intervention. In A.H. Passow (Ed.) *The gifted and talented: Seventy-eighth yearbook of the National Society for the Study of Education.* Chicago, IL: University of Chicago Press.

Rockefeller, N.A. (1976, Oct. 16). Don't accept anyone's verdict that you are lazy, stupid or retarded. *TV Guide,* pp. 12-14.

Rodda, M., Grove, C., and Finch, B.M. (1986) Mainstreaming and the education of deaf students. *Alberta Journal of Educational Research, 32,* 140-153.

Rodger, N.W. and Hunt, J.A. (1980) *Research horizons.* Toronto: Canadian Diabetic Association.

Rodin, D. (1989) Prognosis of cognitive function in children with epilepsy. In B.P. Hermann and M. Seidenberg (Eds.) *Childhood epilepsies: Neurophysiological, psychosocial and intervention aspects* (pp. 33-50) New York: wiley.

Rodriguez, F. (1982) Introducing a multicultural concept into special education: Guidelines for teacher trainers. *Exceptional Children, 49,* 220-227.

Roedell, W.C., Jackson, N.E., and Robinson, H.B. (1980) *Gifted young children.* New York: Teachers College Press.

Rogan, L.L. and Hardman, L.D. (1990) Adult outcome of learning disabled students 10 years after initial follow-up. *Learning Disability Focus, 5,* 91-102.

Rogers, D. (1989) "Show-me bedtime reading": An unusual study of the benefits of reading to deaf children. *Perspectives for Teachers of the Hearing Impaired, 8,* 2-5.

Rogers, J. (1993, May) The inclusion revolution. *Research Bulletin of PDK,* 1-6.

Rogers, K.B. (1990, Nov.) Using effect size to make good decisions about acceleration. Paper presented at the National Association for Gifted Children, Little Rock, Arkansas. Quoted in G.A. Davis and S. Rimm (1994) *Education of the gifted and talented* (3rd. ed.) Boston, MA: Allyn and Bacon.

Rogers, S.J. (1988a) Cognitive characteristics of handicapped children's play: A review. *Journal of the Division for Early Childhood, 12,* 161-168.

Rogers, S.J. (1988b) Review of methods for assessing young children's play. *Journal of the Division for Early Childhood, 12,* 284-287.

Rogers-Warren, A.K. and Warren, S. (1984) The social basis of language and communication in severely handicapped preschoolers. *Topics in Early Childhood Special Education, 4*, 57-72.

Rogow, S. (1987a) Children with multiple handicaps. In M. Winzer, S. Rogow, and C. David. *Exceptional children in Canada.* Toronto: Prentice-Hall.

Rogow, S. (1987b) Children with visual impairments. In M. Winzer, S. Rogow, and C. David. *Exceptional children in Canada.* Toronto: Prentice-Hall.

Rogow, S. and Rodrigues, M. (1977) *Their special needs.* Ontario: Ontario Ministry of Community and Social Services.

Romaneck, G.M. and Kuehl, R. (1992) Sex education for students with high-incidence special needs. *Teaching Exceptional Children, 25*, 22-25.

Rose, D. (1980) Some functional correlates of the maturation of neural systems. In D. Caplan (Ed.) *Biological studies of mental processes* (pp. 27-43). Cambridge, MA: MIT Press

Rose, T.L., Epstein, M.H., Cullinan, D., and Lloyd, J. (1981) Academic programming for behaviorally disordered adolescents: An approach to remediation. In G. Brown, R.L. McDowell, and J.Smith (Eds.) *Educating adolescents with behavior disorders.* Columbus, OH: Merrill.

Rosenblith, J.F. and Sims-Knight, J.E. (1985) *In the beginning: Development in the first two years.* Monterey, CA: Brooks/Cole.

Ross, D.M. and Ross, S.A. (1982) *Hyperactivity: Current issues, research, and theory* (2nd. ed.) New York: Wiley.

Ross, M. (1990a) *Hearing impaired children in the mainstream.* Parkton, MD: York Press.

Ross, M. (1990b) Implications of delay in detection and management of deafness. *Volta Review, 92*, 69-79.

Ross, R. (1979) A program model for altering children's consciousness. *Gifted Child Quarterly, 23*, 109-117.

Ross, R.R. (1982) From therapy to teaching: Some reflections on effective correctional programming. *Canada's Mental Health, 30*, 2-3, 13.

Roug, L., Lundberg, I., and Lundberg, L.J. (1989) Phonetic development in early infancy: A study of four Swedish children during the first eighteen months of life. *Journal of Child Language, 16*, 19-40.

Routh, D.K. (1980) Developmental and social aspects of hyperactivity. In C.K. Whalen and B. Henker (Eds.) *Hyperactive children: The social ecology of identification and treatment.* New York: Academic Press.

Rovet, J.F., Erlich, R.M., and Hoppe, M. (1988). Specific intellectual deficits in childhood with early onset diabetes mellitus. *Child Development, 59*, 226-234.

Rueda, R. (1989) Defining mild disabilities with language-minority students. *Exceptional Children, 56*, 121-128.

Ruiz, N.T. (1989) An optimal learning environment for Rosemary. *Exceptional Children, 56*, 130-144.

Rule, G.B. and Ferguson, T.J. (1986) *The effects of media violence on attitudes, emotions, and cognitions.* Society for the Psychological Study of Social Issues.

Rule, S., Killoran, J., Stowitschek, J.J., Innocenti, M., Striefel, S., and Biswell, C. (1985) Training and support for mainstream day care staff. *Early Child Development and Care, 20*, 99-113.

Rusch, F.R. and Phelps, L.A. (1987) Secondary special education and transition from school to work: A national priority. *Exceptional Children, 53*, 487-492.

Russell, A.T., Bott, L., and Sammons, C. (1989) The phenomenology of schizophrenia occurrring in childhood. *Journal of the American Academy of Child and Adolescent Psychiatry, 28*, 399-407.

Ruttenberg, B.A., Kalish, B.I., Wenar, C., and Wolf, E.G. (1977). *Behavior Rating Instrument for Autistic and other Atypical Children* (Rev. ed.) Philadelphia, PA: Developmental Center for Autistic Children.

Rutter, M. (1974) The development of infantile autism. *Psychological Medicine, 4*, 147-163.

Rutter, M. (1983) Cognitive defects in the pathogenesis of autism. *Journal of Child Psychology and Psychiatry, 24*, 513-531.

Rutter, M. (1985) Infantile autism and other pervasive developmental disorders. In M. Rutter and L. Herson (Eds.) *Child and adolescent psychiatry: Modern approaches* (pp. 545-566) Oxford: Blackwell.

Rutter, M. (1990) Psychosocial resilience and protective mechanisms. In J. Rolf, A.S. Masten, D. Cicchetti, K.H. Neuchterlein, and S. Weintraub (Eds.) *Risk and protective factors in the development of psychopathology.* (pp. 181-214). New York: Cambridge University Press.

Rydell, P.J. and Mirenda, P. (1991) The effects of two levels of linguistic constraint on echolalia and generative language production in children with autism. *Journal of Autism and Developmental Disorders, 21.*

Sacks, O. (1990) *Seeing voices: A journey into the world of the deaf.* New York: Harper Perennial.

Safer, D.J. and Krager, J.M. (1988) A survey of medication treatment for hyperactive/inattentive students. *Journal of the American Medical Association, 260*, 2256-2258.

Safer, N.D., Morrissey, P.A, Kaufman, M.J., and Lewis, L. (1978) Implementing IEPs: New teacher roles and requisite support systems. *Focus on Exceptional Children, 10*, 1-20.

Safran, S.P. and Safran, J.S. (1984) Elementary teachers' tolerance of problem behaviors. *Elementary School Journal, 85*, 247-253.

Safran, S.P. and Safran, J.S. (1985) Classroom context and teachers' perceptions of problem behaviors. *Journal of Educational Psychology, 77*, 20-28.

Safran, S.P. and Safran, J.S. (1987) Teachers' judgment of problem behaviors. *Exceptional Children, 54*, 240-244.

Safty, A. (1988) French immersion and the making of a bilingual society: A critical review and discussion. *Canadian Journal of Education/ Revue canadienne de l'éducation, 13*, 243-262.

Sagal, R., Rosenbaum, P., Stotskopf, B., and Milner, R. (1982) Follow-up of infants 501 to 1500 gm birth weight delivered to residents of a geographically defined region with perinatal intensive care facilities. *Journal of Pediatrics, 100*, 606-613.

Sailor, W., Guess, D., Goetz, L., Schuler, A., Utley, B., and Baldwin, M. (1980) Language and severely handicapped persons: Deciding what to teach to whom. In W. Sailor, B. Wilcox, and L. Brown (Eds). *Methods of instruction for severely handicapped students.* Baltimore, MD: Brookes.

Salend, S.J., and Andress, M. (1984) Decreasing stuttering in an elementary level student. *Journal of Language, Speech and Hearing Services in the Schools, 15*, 133-140.

Salend, S.J. and Longo, M. (1994) The roles of the educational interpreter in mainsteaming. *Teaching Exceptional Children, 26*, 22-28.

Salend, S.J. and Taylor, L. (1993) Working with families: A cross-cultural perspective. *Remedial and Special Edcuation, 14*, 25-32, 39.

Salisbury, C.L. (1987) Stressors of parents with young handicapped and nonhandicapped children. *Journal of the Division for Early Childhood, 11*, 154-160.

Salisbury, C.L. (1991) Mainstreaming during the early childhood years. *Exceptional Children, 58*, 146-155.

Salisbury C.L., Palambaro, M.M., and Hollowood, T.M. (1993) On the nature and change of an inclusive elementary school. *Journal of the Association for Persons with Severe Handicaps, 18*, 75-84.

Salkind, N. (1990) *Child Development* (6th. ed.) Fort Worth, TX: Holt Reinhart and Winston.

Salt, P., Galler, J.R., and Ramsey, F.C. (1988) The influence of early malnutrition on subsequent behavioral development. *Developmental and Behavioral Pediatrics, 9*, 1-5.

Salzberg, C.L., Lignugaris-Kraft, B., and McCuller, G.L. (1988) Reasons for job loss: A review of employment termination studies of mentally retarded workers. *Research in Developmental Disabilities, 9*, 153-170.

Sameroff, A.J., Seifer, R., Zax, M., et al. (1987) Early indicators of developmental risk: Longitudinal study. *Schizophrenia Bulletin, 13*, 383-394.

Samuels, S.J. and Miller, N.L. (1985). Failure to find attention differences between learning disabled and normal children on classroom and laboratory tests. *Exceptional Children, 51*, 358-375.

Sancilio, M.F.M, Plumment, J.M., and Hartup, W.W. (1989) Friendships and aggressiveness as determiners of conflict outcomes in middle children. *Developmental Psychology, 25*, 812-819.

Sanders, D. (1971) *Aural rehabilitation*. Englewood Cliffs, NJ: Prentice-Hall.

Sandor, G. (1981) Fetal alcohol syndrome: Cardiac malformations. *B.C. Medical Journal, 23*, 326-327.

Sandoval, J. and Haapmanen, R.M. (1981). A critical commentary on neuropsychiatry in the school: Are we ready? *School Psychology and Review, 10*, 381-388.

Santos, K. E. (1992) Fragile X Syndrome: An educator's role in identification, prevention, and intervention. *Remedial and Special Education, 13*, 32-37.

Sapon-Shivin, H. (1984) The tug-of-war nobody wins: Allocations of educational resources for handicapped, gifted, and "typical" students. *Curriculum Inquiry, 14*, 57-81.

Sasso, G.M. and Rude, H.A. (1987) Unprogrammed effects of training high-status peers to interact with severely handicapped children. *Journal of Applied Behavior Analysis, 20*, 35-44.

Satz, P. and Fletcher, J.M. (1979) Early screening tests: Some uses and abuses. *Journal of Learning Disabilities, 12*, 65-69.

Satz, P., Taylor, H.G., Friel, J., and Fletcher, J.M. (1978) Some developmental and predictive precursors of reading disabilities: A six year follow-up. In A.L. Benton and D. Pearl (Eds.) *Dyslexia: An appraisal of current knowledge*. New York: Oxford University Press.

Savage, F. (1992) Dissecting the dropout dilemma. *ATA Magazine, 72*, 32.

Savage, H. (1983) The Canadian Charter and the rights of handicapped persons: The moral imperative of blood, sweat and tears. *Canadian Journal on Mental Retardation, 33*, 28-31.

Savage, R.C. (1988) Introduction to educational issues for students who have suffered traumatic brain injury. In R.C. Savage and G.F. Wolcott (Eds.) *An educators' manual: What educators need to know about students with traumatic brain injury*. Scarborough MA: National Head Injury Foundation.

Sawyer, R.J. and Zantal-Wiener, K. (1993) Emerging trends in technology for students with disabilities: Considerations for school personnel. *Teaching Exceptional Children, 26*, 70-72.

Scaldwell, W.A. and Frame, J.E. (1985) Prevalence of otitis media in Cree and Ojibway school children in six Ontario communities. *Journal of American Indian Education, 25*, 1-5.

Scarr-Salapatek, S. (1975) Genetics and the development of intelligence. In F.D. Horowitz (Ed.) *Review of child development research* (Vol. 4) Chicago, IL: University of Chicago Press.

Scheerenberger, R.C. (1964) Mental retardation: Definition, classification and prevalence. *Mental Retardation Abstracts, 1*, 432-441.

Schein, J.D. (1989) *At home among strangers: Exploring the deaf community in the United States*. Washington, DC: Gallaudet University Press.

Schein, J. (1994) Deafness in Canada and the United States. *Deaf American Monographs*, pp.93-99

Schein, J.D., Kates, L., Wolf, E.G., and Theil, L. (1983) Assessing and developing communication abilities of deaf-blind children. *Journal of Visual Impairment and Blindness, 77*, 152-157.

Schiff, N.B. and Ventry, I.M. (1976) Communication problems in hearing children of deaf parents. *Journal of Speech and Hearing Disorders, 41*, 348-358.

Schildroth, A.N., Rawlings, B.W., and Allen, T.E. (1989) Hearing-impaired children under age 6: A demographic analysis. *American Annals of the Deaf, 134*, 63-69.

Schlesinger, H.S. and Meadow, K.P. (1972) *Sound and sign: Childhood deafness and mental health*. Berkeley: University of California Press.

Schneider, B.H., Clegg, M.R., Byrne, B.M., Ledingham, J.E., and Crombie, G. (1992) Social relations of gifted children as a function of age and school program. In S. Towson (Ed.) *Educational psychology: Readings for the Canadian context*. Peterborough, Ont: Broadview.

Schneider, J.W. and Chasnoff, I.J. (1987) Cocaine abuse during pregnancy: Its effects on infant motor development — a clinical perspective. *Topics in Acute Care and Trauma Rehabilitation, 2*, 59-69.

Scholl, G.T. (1986) Multicultural considerations. In G.T. Scholl (Ed.) *Foundations of education for blind and visually handicapped children and youth* (pp. 165-182). New York: American Foundation for the Blind.

Schopler, E., Reichler, R.J., De Vellis, R.F., and Daly, K., (1980) Toward objective classification of childhood autism: Childhood Autism Rating Scale (CARS) *Journal of Autism and Developmental Disorders, 19*, 91-103.

Schorr Ribera, H.K. (1987) Ethnicity and culture as relevant rehabilitation factors in families with children with disabilities. In M. Seligman (Ed.) *The family with a handicapped child* (2nd. ed.) Boston, MA: Allyn and Bacon.

Schrader, B. and Valus A. (1990) Disabled learners as able teachers: A cross-age tutoring project. *Academic Therapy, 25*, 589-597.

Schreibman, L. and Charlop, M.H. (1989) Infantile autism. In T.H. Ollendick and M. Hersen (Eds.) *Handbook of child psychopathology* (2nd. ed.) New York: Plenum.

Schroeder, E. (1989) Literacy: The key to opportunity. *Journal of Visual Impairment and Blindness, 83*, 290-293.

Schumaker, J.B. and Deshler, D.D. (1988). Implementing the Regular Education Initiative in secondary schools: A different ball game. *Journal of Learning Disabilities, 21*, 36-42.

Schunk, D.H. (1987) Peer models and children's behavioral change. *Review of Educational Research, 57*, 149-174.

Schwartz, L.L. (1980) Advocacy for the neglected gifted: Females. *Gifted Child Quarterly, 24*, 113-117.

Schwartz M.F. (1988) *Stuttering solved*. New York: National Center for Stuttering.

Schwartz, R.H. and Yaffe, S.J. (1980) (Eds.) *Drugs and chemical risks to the fetus and newborn*. New York: Alan R. Liss.

Schwean-Kowalchuk, V.L. and Roadhouse, A.J. (1990) A school-based social cognitive intervention for aggressive boys. *B.C. Journal of Special Education, 14*, 27-37.

Scott, E.P. (1982) *Your visually impaired child: A guide for teachers*. Baltimore, MD: University Park Press.

Scott, J.L. and Sarkee, M.D. (1982) *Vocational special needs* (2nd. ed.) Alsep, IL: Technical Publishers.

Scott, R. (1969) The socialization of blind children. In D. Joslin (Ed.), *Handbook of socialization theory and research.* New York: Rand McNally.

Scruggs, T.E. and Mastropieri, M.A (1989) Reconstructive elaborations: A model for content area learning. *American Educational Research Journal, 26,* 311-327.

Scruggs, T.E. and Mastropieri, M.A. (1990) The case for mnemonic instruction: From laboratory investigations to classroom applications. *Journal of Special Education, 24,* 7-32.

Seal, B.C. (1986) Assessing the total communication skills of students in training. *American Annals of the Deaf, 131,* 33-35.

Segalowitz, N.S. (1981) Issues in the cross-cultural study of bilingual development. In H.C. Triandis and A. Heron (Eds.) *Handbook of cross-cultural psychology* (vol. 4) (pp. 55-93) Boston, MA: Allyn and Bacon.

Seguin, E. (1864) Origin of treatment and training of idiots. In M. Rosen, G.R. Clark, and M.S. Kivitz (Eds.) (1976) *The history of mental retardation* (Vol. 1) Baltimore, MD: University Park Press.

Seidel, V.P., Chadwick, O.F.D., and Rutter, M. (1975) Psychological disorders in crippled children: A comparative study with and without bone damage. *Genetic Psychology Monograph, 75,* 255-335.

Seigel, E. (1974) *The exceptional child grows up.* New York: E.P. Dutton.

Seigel, J.P. (1969) The Enlightenment and the evolution of the language of signs in France and England. *Journal of the History of Ideas, 30,* 96-115.

Seligman, M. (1991) Siblings of disabled brothers and sisters. In M. Seligman (Ed.) *The family with a handicapped child* (2nd. ed.) Boston, MA: Allyn and Bacon.

Sellin, D.F. and Birch, J.W. (1980) *Educating gifted and talented learners.* Rockville, MD: Aspen Systems Corp.

Semel, E. (1970). *Sound-Order-Sense.* Chicago, IL: Follett.

Semel, E. and Wiig, E. (1980) *Clinical Evaluation of Language Functions.* Columbus, OH: Merrill.

Senior, E.M. (1986) Learning disabled or merely mislabeled? The plight of the developmentally young child. *Childhood Education, 62,* 161-165.

Seyfarth, J., Hill, J.W., Orelone, F., McMillan, J., and Wehman, P. (1985) Factors influencing parents' vocational aspirations for their retarded children. In P. Wehman and J.W. Hill (Eds.) *Competitive employment for persons with mental retardation: From research to practice* (pp. 315-331, vol. 1) Richmond, VA: Virginia Commonwealth University.

Seyfort, B., Spreen, O., and Lahmer, V. (1980) A critical look at the WISC-R with Native Indian children. *Alberta Journal of Educational Research, 26,* 14-24.

Shaffer, D.R. (1985) *Developmental psychology: Theory, research, and applications.* Monterey, CA: Brooks/Cole.

Shah, A. and Holmes. N. (1985) Brief report: The use of the Leiter International Performance Scale with autistic children. *Journal of Autism and Developmental Disorders, 15,* 195-203.

Shah, R. (1985) Lecture presented to Ed. 416, U.B.C.

Shames, G. and Florance, C. (1982) Disorders of fluency. In G.Shames and E. Wiig (Eds.) *Human communication disorders.* Columbus, OH: Merrill.

Shames, G.H. and Wiig, E. (1982/1990) *Human communication disorders: An introduction.* Columbus, OH: Merrill.

Shank, M.S. (1990) Old enough but too young for school. *Academic Therapy, 25,* 579.

Shantz, C.U. (1987) Conflicts between children. *Child Development, 58,* 283-305.

Shaver, K., Boughman, J., and Nance, W. (1985) Congenital rubella syndrome and diabetes: A review of epidemiologic, genetic, and immunologic factors. *American Annals of the Deaf, 85,* 526-532.

Shaywitz, S.E. and Shaywitz, B.A. (1987) Attention deficit disorder: Current perspectives. Paper presented at the National Conference on Learning Disabilities. Bethesda, MD: National institute for Child Health and Human Development.

Shea, T.M. and Bauer, A.M. (1991) *Parents and teachers of children with exceptionalities: A handbook for collaboration.* (2nd. ed.) Boston, MA: Allyn and Bacon.

Sheinker, A., Sheinker, J.M., and Stevens, L.J. (1984) Cognitive strategies for teaching the mildly handicapped. *Focus on Exceptional Children, 17,* 1-15.

Shell, P.M. (1981) Straining the system: Serving low-incidence handicapped children in an urban setting. *Exceptional Education Quarterly, 2,* 1-10.

Shepard, L.A., Smith, M.L., and Viojir, (1983). Characteristics of pupils identified as learning disabled. *Journal of Special Education, 16,* 73-85.

Shinn, M.R., Tindal, G.A., and Spera, D.A. (1987) Special education referrals as an index of teacher tolerance: Are teachers imperfect tests? *Exceptional Children, 54,* 32-40.

Shinn, M.R., Ramsey, E., Walker, H.M., Steeber, S., and O'Neill, R. (1987) Antisocial behavior in school settings: Initial differences in an at-risk and normal population. *The Journal of Special Education, 21,* 69-84.

Shivers, J.S. and Fait, H.F. (1985) *Special recreational services: Therapeutic and adapted.* Philadelphia, PA: Lea and Felsiger.

Shonkoff, J.P. and Hauser-Cram, P. (1987) Early intervention for disabled infants and their families: A quantitative anaylsis. *Pediatrics, 80,* 650-658.

Shonkoff, J. and Meisels, S. (1990) Early childhood intervention. In S. Meisels and J. Shonkoff (Eds.) *Handbook of early intervention* (pp. 3-32) New York: Cambridge University Press.

Shore, B. and Dover, A.C. (1987) Metacognition, intelligence and giftedness. *Gifted Child Quarterly, 31,* 37-39.

Shore, B. and Tsiamis, A. (1986) Identification by provision: Limited field test of a radical alternative for identifying gifted children. In K. Heller and J. Feldhusen (Eds.) *Identifying and nurturing the gifted* (pp. 93-102) Toronto: Hans Huber.

Siegel, S., Robert, M., and Gaylord Ross, R. (1992) A follow-along study of participants in a longitudinal transition program for youths with mild disabilities. *Exceptional Children, 58,* 346-356.

Siegler, R.S. and Kotovsky, K. (1985) Two levels of giftedness: Shall ever the twain meet? In R.J. Sternberg and J.E. Davidson (Eds.) *Conceptions of giftedness* (pp. 417-435) New York: Cambridge University Press.

Sigafoos, J., Cole, D.A., and McQuarter, (1987) Current practices in the assessment of students with severe handicaps. *Journal of the Association for Persons with Severe Handicaps, 12,* 264-273.

Sigman, M., Cohen S., Beckwith L., and Parmalee, A.H. Jr. (1981) Social and familial influences on the development of preterm infants. *Journal of Pediatric Psychology, 6,* 1-13.

Sigelman C.K. and Shaffer, D.R. (1991) *Life-span human development.* Pacific Grove, CA: Brooks/Cole.

Silberman, R. (1981) A comparison of visual functioning in hearing-impaired children and normally hearing children. *Volta Review, 83,* 95-104.

Silva, P.A. (1980) The prevalence, stability and significance of developmental language delays in preschool children. *Developmental Medicine and Child Neurology, 22,* 768-777.

Silverman, L.K. (1989) Invisible gifts, invisible handicap. *Roeper Review, 12*, 37-42.

Silverman, S.R. (1967) Education of the deaf. In L.E. Travis (Ed.) *Handbook of speech pathology.* New York: Appleton Century-Crofts.

Silverstein, R. (1985) The legal necessity for residential schools serving deaf, blind, and multiply impaired children. *Journal of Visual Impairment and Blindness, 79*, 145-149.

Simen, R.J. and Rogers, R.C. (1989) School psychology and medical diagnosis: The fragile x syndrome. *Psychology in the Schools, 26*, 380-388.

Simner, M.L. (1995, April) Postscript to the Canadian Psychological Association position on beginning reading instruction. *Cognitions*, pp. 6-7.

Simonds, R.J. and Rogers, M.F. (1992) Epidemiology of HIV in children and other populations. In A. Crocker, H. Cohen, and T. Kastner (Eds.) *HIV infection and developmental disabilities: A resource for service providers* (pp. 3-13). Baltimore, MD: Brookes.

Sisson, L.A., Van Hasselt, V.B., and Hersen, M. (1987) Psychological approaches with deaf-blind persons: Strategies and issues in research and treatment. *Clinical Psychology Review, 7*, 303-328.

Sitlington, P.L. and Frank, A.R. (1990) Are adolescents with learning disabilities crossing the bridge into adult life. *Learning Disability Quarterly, 13*, 97-113.

Sitlington, P.L and Okolo, C.M. (1987) Statewide survey of vocational educators: Attitudes, training, and involvement with handicapped learners. *Journal of Career Development, 13*, 21- 29.

Siwolop, S. and Mohs, M. (1985, February) The war on Down syndrome. *Discover*, pp. 67-73.

Skelly, M. (1979) *Amer-Ind gestural code based on universal American Indian hand talk.* New York: Elsivien.

Slavin, R.E., Madden, N.A., Karweit, N.L., Liverman, B.J., and Dolan, L. (1990) Success for all: First-year outcomes of a comprehensive plan for reforming urban education. *American Educational Research Journal, 27*, 255-278.

Sleeter, C.E. (1986) Learning disabilities: The social construction of a special education category. *Exceptional Children, 53*, 46-54.

Sleeter, C.E and Grant, C.A. (1994) *Making choices for multicultural education: Five approaches to race, class, and gender.* New York: Merrill.

Sloane, D.C. and Sloane, B.C. (1990) AIDS in schools: A comprehensive initiative. *McGill Journal of Education, 25*, 205-228.

Smith, B. (1995, June) Implications of the Eaton case. *Alberta CEC, 5*, p. 7

Smith, C.R. (1991) *LD: The interaction of learner, task and setting* (2nd. ed.) Boston, MA: Allyn and Bacon.

Smith, D.D. and Robinson, S (1986) Educating the learning disabled. In R.J. Morris and B. Blatt (Eds.) *Special education: Research and trends* (pp. 222-248) New York: Pergamon.

Smith, G.J., Edelen-Smith, P.J., and Stodden R.A. (1995) How to avoid the seven pitfalls of systematic planning. *Teaching Exceptional Children, 27*, 42-47.

Smith, J.O. (1992) Falling through the cracks: Rehabilitation services for adults with learning disabilities. *Exceptional Children , 58*, 451-460.

Smith, M.J. and Ryan, A.S. (1987) Chinese-American families of children with developmental disabilities: An exploratory study of reactions to service providers. *Mental Retardation, 25*, 345-350.

Smith S.C. and Scott, J.J. (1990) *The collaborative school.* Oregon: ERIC/NASSP.

Smith, S.D. and Pennington, B.F. (1987) Genetic influences. In K.A. Kavale and S.R. Forness (Eds.) *Handbook of learning disabilities (vol. 1) Dimensions and diagnosis* (pp. 49-75). San Diego, CA: College-Hill.

Smith, S.P. (1978) Some (not all) facts about asthma. *Journal of School Health, 48*, 311.

Smith, S.W. (1990) Comparison of Individualized Education Programs (IEPs) of students with behavioral disorders and learning disabilities. *The Journal of Special Education, 24*, 85-100.

Snell, M.E. (1987) *Systematic instruction of persons with severe handicaps* (3rd. ed.) Columbus, OH: Merrill.

Snow, C. (1987) Relevance of the notion of a critical period of language acquisition. In M.H. Bornstein (Ed.) *Sensitive periods in development: Interdisciplinary perspectives.* Hillsdale, NJ: Erlbaum.

Soare, P.L. and Raimondi, A. (1977) Intellectual and perceptual-motor characteristics of treated myelomeningocele children. *American Journal of Diseases in Children, 131*, 199-204.

Southern, W.T., Jones, E.D., and Fiscus, E.D. (1989) Practitioner objections to the academic acceleration of gifted children. *Gifted Child Quarterly, 33*, 29-35.

Spain, B. (1972) Verbal and performance ability in pre-school spina bifida children. *Developmental Medicine and child neurology, 27*, 155.

Sparrow, S.S., Balla, D.A., and Cicchetti, D.V. (1984) *Vineland Adaptive Behavior Scale.* Circle Pines, MN: American Guidance Services.

Spradlin, J.E. and Siegel, G.M. (1982) Language training in natural and clinical environments. *Journal of Speech and Hearing Disorders, 47*, 2-6.

Sprague, R.L. and Baxley, G.B. (1978) Drugs for behavior management. In J. Wortes (Ed.) *Mental retardation and developmental disabilities* (pp. 92-129) New York: Brunner Mazel.

Spring, C. and Sandoval, J. (1976). Food additives and hyperkinesis: A critical evaluation of the evidence. *Journal of Learning Disabilities, 9*, 560-569.

Sprinthall, N.A. and Sprinthall, R.C. (1990) *Educational psychology: A developmental approach* (5th. ed.) New York: Random House.

Squires, D. (1992, June) Forum 11: An overview, *Keeping in Touch*, pp, 2-3.

Stahl, S.L. and Miller, P.D. (1989) Whole language and language experience approaches for beginning reading: A quantitative research systhesis. *Review of Educational Research, 59*, 87-116.

Stainback, W. and Stainback, S. (1984) A rationale for the merger of regular and special education. *Exceptional Children, 51*, 102-111.

Stainback, S. and Stainback, W. (1985) The merger of special and regular education: Can it be done? *Exceptional Children, 51*, 517-521.

Stainback, S. and Stainback, W. (1988) Educating students with severe disabilities. *Teaching Exceptional Children, 21*, 16-19.

Stainback, W., Stainback, S., and Wilkinson, A. (1992) Encouraging peer supports and friendships. *Teaching Exceptional Children, 24*, 6-11.

Stanley, J.C. (1979) The study and facilitation of talent for mathematics. In A.H. Passow (Ed.) *The gifted and talented: Their education and development. Seventy-eighth yearbook of the National Society for the Study of Education.* Chicago: University of Chicago Press.

Stanley, J.C. and Benbow, C.P. (1982) Educating mathematically precocious youths: Twelve policy recommendations. *Educational Researcher, 11*, 4-9.

Stanley, J.C. and Benbow, C.P. (1986) Extremely young college gaduates: Evidence of their success. *College and University, 58*, 361-371.

Statement of policy approved for bilingual/bicultural program — Ontario. *Deaf Education, 2*, 1-2.

Statistics Canada (1985) *Canada year book.* Ottawa: Ministry of Supply and Services.

Staub, D. and Hunt, P. (1993) The effects of social interaction training on high school peer tutors of schoolmates with severe disabilities. *Exceptional Children, 60*, 41-57.

Steele, B.F. (1986) Notes on the lasting effects of early child abuse throughout the life cycle. *Child Abuse and Neglect, 10*, 283-291.

Steere, D.E., Wood, R., Pancsofar, E.L., and Butterworth, J. (1990) Outcome-based school-to-work transition planning for students with severe disabilities. *Career Development for Exceptional Individuals, 13*, 57-69.

Steffenburg, S., Gillberg, C., Hellgren, L., Andersson, L., Gillberg, I.C., Jakonsson, G., and Bohman M. (1989) A twin study of autism in Denmark, Finland, Iceland, Norway, and Sweden. *Journal of Child Psychology and Psychiatry, 30*, 405-416.

Stein, R.E. and Riessman, C.K. (1978) Impact on family scale. In S.E. McLindess-Mott and T. Braeger (1988) The impact on family scale: An adaptation for families of children with handicaps. *Journal of the Division for Early Childhood, 12*, 217-223..

Stephens, B., Grube, C., and Fitzgerald, J. (1977) *Project PAVE (fiscal report)*. Washington, DC: Bureau of Education for the Handicapped, U.S. Department of H.E.W.

Stephens, O. (1989) Braille — Implications for living. *Journal of Visual Impairment and Blindness, 83*, 288-289.

Stern, D. (1977) *The first relationship: Infant and mother.* Cambridge: Cambridge University Press.

Stern, M. and Hilderbrandt, K. (1984). A prematurity stereotype: The effects of labelling on adults' perceptions of infants. *Developmental Psychology, 20*, 360-362.

Sternberg, R.J. (1987) A unified theory of intellectual exceptionality. In J.D. Day and J.G. Borkowski (Eds.) *Intelligence and exceptionality: New directions for theory, assessment and instructional practices* (pp. 135-172). Norwood, NJ: Ablex.

Sternberg, R.J. and Davidson, J.E. (1986) (Eds.) *Conceptions of giftedness.* New York: Cambridge University Press.

Sternberg, R.J. and Spear, I.C. (1985) A triarchic theory of mental retardation: In N.R. Ellis (Ed.) *International review of research in mental retardation* (pp. 301-326) (vol. 13). New York: Academic Press.

Stewart, D.A. (1984) Mainstreaming deaf children: A different perspective. *The ACHEI Journal, 10*, 91-104.

Stewart, D.A. and Ahamatsu, C.T. (1988) The coming of age of American Sign Language. *Anthropology and Education Quarterly, 19*, 235-252.

Stewart, G.A. (1994) External validity of attention deficit disorder without hyperactivity: A review of the evidence. *Canadian Journal of School Psychology, 10*, 15-25,

Stillman, R. (Ed.) (1978) *The Callier-Azusa Scale.* Dallas, TX: Callier Center for Communication Disorders, University of Texas at Dallas.

Stodden, R. and Boone, R. (1987) Assessing transition services for handicapped youth: A cooperative interagency approach. *Exceptional Children, 53*, 537-545.

Stoel-Gammon, C. and Otomo, K. (1986) Babbling development of hearing-impaired and normally hearing subjects. *Journal of Speech and Hearing Disorders, 51*, 33-41.

Stoker, R.G. (1983) On computers and the hearing impaired. *Volta Review, 85*, 364-365.

Stokoe, W.C., Jr. and Battiston, R. (1975) Sign language, mental health and satisfactory interaction. Linguistic Research Laboratory, Gallaudet College, Washington, DC.

Stone, P. and Adam, A. (1986) Is your child wearing the right hearing aid? Principles for selecting and maintaining amplification. *Volta Review, 88*, 45-54.

Stoneman, Z., Brody, G.H., Davis, C.H., and Crapps, J.M. (1988). Childcare responsibilities, peer relations, and sibling conflict: Older siblings of mentally retarded children. *American Journal of Mental Deficiency, 93*, 174-183.

Story, C.M. (1985) Facilitation of learning: A micro-ethnographic study of the teacher of the gifted. *Gifted Child Quarterly, 29*, 155-159.

Stott, D.H. (1979) The Bristol Social Adjustment Guides. *Therapeutic Education, 7*, 34-44.

Strag, G. (1972). Comparative behavior ratings of parents with severe mentally retarded, special learning disability and normal children. *Journal of Learning Disabilities, 5*, 631-635.

Strain, P.S., Sainato, D.M., and Maheady, L. (1984) Toward a functional assessment of severely handicapped learners. *Educational Psychologist, 19*, 180-187.

Streissguth, A.P., Barr, H.M., and Martin, D.C. (1983) Maternal alcohol use and neonatal habituation assessed with the Brazelton Scale. *Child Development, 54*, 1109-1118.

Streissguth, A.P., Herman, D.S., and Smith, D.W. (1978) Intelligence, behavior and dysmorphonensis in the fetal alcohol syndrome: A report on 20 patients. *Journal of Pediatrics, 92*, 363-367.

Stuckless, E.R. (1991) Reflections on bilingual, bicultural education for deaf children: Some concerns about current advocacy and trends. *American Annals of the Deaf, 136*, 270-277.

Sugai, G. and Maheady, L. (1988) Cultural diversity and individual assesment for behavior disorders. *Teaching Exceptional Children, 21*, 28-31.

Sullivan. M. (1988) *A comparative anaylsis of dropouts and non-dropouts in Ontario secondary schools.* Toronto: Ontario Ministry of Education.

Sumara, D.J. (1991, February) Whole language and reflective teaching: Saying what we mean and meaning what we say. Paper presented at Westcast, Regina.

Suran, G.B. and Rizzo, J.V. (1983) *Special children: An integrative approach* (2nd. ed.). Glenview, IL: Scott Foresman.

Swain, M. and Barik, H. (1978) Bilingual education in Canada. In B. Spolsky, B. Cooper, and R. Cooper (Eds.) *Case studies in bilingual education* (pp. 22-71) Rowley, MA: Newbury House.

Swedo, J. (1987, fall) Effective teaching strategies for handicapped limited English proficient students. *Bilingual Special Education Newsletter*, pp. 1-5.

Swiatek, M.A. and Benbow, C.P. (1991) Ten-year longitudinal follow-up of ability-matched accelerated and unaccelerated gifted students. *Journal of Educational Psychology, 83*, 528-538.

Swanson, H.L. (Ed.) (1987) *Memory and learning disabilities: Advances in learning and behavioral disabilities.* Greenwich, CT: JAI Press.

Swanson, J.M. and Kinsbourne, M. (1980) *Artificial food colourings impair the learning of hyperactive children.* Report to the Nutrition Foundation, Hospital for Sick Children, Toronto.

Sydney, J. and Minner, S. (1984) The influence of sibling information on the placement recommendations of special class teachers. *Behavior Disorders, 10*, 43-45.

Szymanski, E.M. (1994) Transition: Life-span and life-space considerations for empowerement. *Exceptional Children, 60*, 402-410.

Tager-Flusberg, H., Calkins, S., Nolin, T., Baumberger, T., Anderson, M., and Chadwick-Deas, A. (1990) A longitudinal study of language acquisition in autistic and Down syndrome children. *Journal of Autism and Developmental Disorders, 20*, 1-21.

Talbot, M.E. (1964) *Edouard Seguin: A study of an educational approach to the treatment of mentally defective children.* New York: Teachers College, Bureau of Publications.

Tannenbaum, A.J. (1962) *Adolescent attitudes toward academic brilliance.* New York: Bureau of Publications, Teachers College, Columbia University.

Tansley, P. and Panckhurst, J. (1981). *Children with specific learning difficulties.* Windsor, England: Nelson.

Tarr, J.E. and Macklin, M. (1987) Cocaine. *Pediatric Clinics of North America, 34,* 319-331.

Taylor, D.R. (1990, Nov./ Dec.) Special education: A legal quagmire. *ATA Magazine,* pp. 40-43.

Taylor, I.K. (1976) *Introduction to psycholinguistics.* New York: Holt, Rinehart and Winston.

Teale, W.H. and Sulzby, E. (1989) *Emergent literacy.* Norwood, NJ: Ablex.

Telford, C. W. and Sawrey, J. M. (1981) *The exceptional individual* (4th. ed.) Englewood Cliffs, N. J. : Prentice-Hall.

Terman, L.M. (1926) *Genetic studies of genius: Mental and physical traits of a thousand gifted children* (2nd. ed.) Stanford, CA: Stanford University Press.

Terman, L.M. and Oden, M.H. (1951) The Stanford studies of the gifted. In P. Witty (Ed.) *The gifted child.* Lexington, MA: D.C. Heath.

Terman, L. and Oden, M.H. (1959) *Genetic studies of genius: The gifted population at mid-life* (vol. 5). California: Stanford University Press.

Tew, B. and Lawrence, K. (1975) The effects of hydrocephalus on intelligence, visual perception, and school attainment. *Developmental Medicine and Neurology, 17* (supp. 35), 129-134.

Thompson, L.J. (1971). Language disabilities in men of eminence. *Journal of Learning Disabilities, 4,* 34-44.

Thompson, R. (1976) The severely handicapped: A new horizon. *Exceptional Children, 43,* 141-143.

Thompson, T., (1993, Jan.) A reign of terror: Facilitated communication. In J.M. Kauffman (1993) How we might achieve the radical reform of special education. *Exceptional Children, 60,* 6-16.

Thorp, E. K. and McCollum, J. A. (1988) Defining the infancy specialization in early childhood special education. In J. B. Jordan, J. J. Gallagher, P. L. Huntinger, and M. B. Karnes (Eds.) *Early childhood special education: Birth to three* (pp. 147-162). Reston, VA: Council for Exceptional Children.

Thousand, J. S. and Villa, R. A. (1990) Strategies for educating learners with severe disabilities within their local home schools and communities. *Focus on Exceptional Children, 23,* 2-18.

Thousand, J., Fox, T., Reid, R., Godek, J., Williams, W., and Fox, W. (1986) *The homecoming model: Educating students who present intensive educational challenges within educational environments.* Vermont: University of Vermont, Burlington.

Thurston, R.H. (1876). *Reports of the Commissions of the United States to the International Exhibition held in Vienna, 1873.* Washington: Government Printing Office.

Tingey-Michaelis, C. (1985) Early intervention: Is certification necessary? *Teacher Education and Special Education, 8,* 91-97.

Tjossem, T. (1976) *Intervention strategies for high-risk infants and young children.* Baltimore, MD: University Park Press.

Tobin, M.J. and Hill, E.W. (1988) Visually impaired teenagers: Ambitions, attitudes, and interests. *Journal of Visual Impairment and Blindness, 82,* 414-416.

Tomlinson, J.R., Acker, N., Conter, A., and Lindberg, S. (1977) Minority status and school psychological services. *Psychology in the Schools, 14,* 456-460.

Topping, K. (1989, March) Peer tutoring and paired reading: Combining two powerful techniques. *The Reading Teacher,* pp. 488-494.

Torgenson, J.K. (1988) Studies of children with learning disabilities who perform poorly on memory span task. *Journal of Learning Disabilities, 21,* 605-612.

Torrance, E.P. (1966) *The Torrance Tests of Creative Thinking: Norms and technical manual.* Princeton, NJ: Personnel Press.

Torrance, E.P. (1969) Creative positives of disadvantaged children and youth. *Gifted Child Quarterly, 13,* 71-81.

Torrance, E.P. (1980). Assessing the further reaches of creative potential. *Journal of Creative Behavior, 14,* 1-19.

Tower, C.C. (1984) *Child abuse and neglect: A teacher's handbook for detection, reporting and classroom management.* Washington, DC: National Education Association.

Trapani, C. (1990) *Transition goals for adolescents with learning disabilities.* Boston, MA: College Hill.

Tredgold, A.F. (1908). *Mental deficiency.* London: Bailliere, Tindall and Cox.

Treffert, D.A. (1970) Epidemiology of infantile autism. *Archives of General Psychiatry,* 23, 431-438.

Treffinger, D. (1986) Research on creativity. *Gifted Child Quarterly, 30,* 15-19.

Treffinger, D.J. (1991) School reform and gifted education — Opportunities and issues. *Gifted Child Quarterly, 35,* 6-25.

Trief, E., Duckman, R., Morse, A.R., and Silberman, R.K. (1989) Retinopathy of prematurity. *Journal of Visual Impairment and Blindness, 83,* 500-504.

Trifiletti, J.J., Frith, G.H., and Armstrong, S. (1984) Microcomputers versus resource rooms for LD students: A preliminary investigation of the effects on math skills, *Learning Disability Quarterly, 7,* 69-76,

Trout, W.D. (1983). Birth of a sick or handicapped infant: Impact on the family. *Child Welfare, 62,* 337-348.

Tsai, L. and Stewart, M.A. (1983) Etiological implications of maternal age and birth order in infantile autism. *Journal of Autism and Developmental Disabilities, 13,* 57-65.

Tucker, J.A. (1980) Ethnic proportions in classes for the learning disabled: Issues in nonbiased assessment. *Journal of Special Education, 14,* 93-105.

Turnbull, A.P. and Turnbull, H.R. (1986) *Families, professionals and exceptionality: A special partnership.* Columbus, OH: Merrill.

Turnbull, A.P., Summers, J.A., and Brotherston, M.J. (1984) *Working with families with disabled members: A family systems approach.* Lawrence, KA: Kansas University Affiliated Facility, University of Kansas.

Turnbull, A.P., Summers, J.A., and Brotherston, M.J. (1986) Family life cycle: Theoretical and empirical implications and future directions for families with mentally retarded members. In J.J. Gallagher and P.M. Vietze (Eds.) *Families of handicapped persons.* Baltimore, MD: Brookes.

Turner, K.D. and Szymaski, E.M. (1990) Work adjustment of people with congenital disabilities: A longitudinal perspective from birth to adulthood. *Journal of Rehabilitation, 56,* 19-24.

Tuttle, D.H. and Cornell, D.G. (1993) Maternal labelling of gifted children. Effects on the sibling relationship. *Exceptional Children, 59,* 402-410.

Tyler, J.S. and Mira, M.P. (1993) Educational modifications for students with head injuries. *Teaching Exceptional Children, 25,* 24-27.

United States, Department of Education (1988) *Tenth Annual Report to Congress on the implementation of the Education of the Handicapped Act.* Washington, DC: US Government Printing Office.

United States, Department of Education (1989) *Eleventh annual report to Congress on the implementation of the Education of the Handicapped Act.* Washington, DC: US Government Printing Office.

United States Department of Health, Education and Welfare (1977) Education of Handicapped Children: Implementation of Part B of the Education of the Handicapped Act. *Federal Register,* 42(163).

United States (1978) *Gifted and Talented Children Act: PL 95-561, sec. 902.*

Vallecorsa, A.L. and Garriss, E. (1990) Story composition skills of middle grade students with learning disabilities. *Exceptional Children, 57,* 48-54.

Vander Kolk, C.J. and Bright, B.C. (1983) Albinism: A survey of attitudes and behavior. *Journal of Visual Impairment and Blindness, 77,* 49-51.

Van Dijk, J. (1982) *Rubella handicapped children: The effects of bilateral cataract and/or hearing impairment on behavior and learning.* The Netherlands: Swets and Zeitlinger.

Van Dyke, D.C. and Fox, A.A. (1990) Fetal drug exposure and its possible implications for learning in the preschool and school age population. *Journal of Learning Disabilities, 23,* 160-163.

Van Osdol, W.R. and Shane, D.B. (1982) *An introduction to exceptional children.* Dubuque, IO: William C. Brown.

Van Riper, C. and Emerick, L. (1990) *Speech correction: An introduction to speech pathology and audiology* (8th. ed.) Englewood Cliffs, NJ: Prentice-Hall.

Van Tassel-Baska, J. (1987) The ineffectiveness of the pull-out model in gifted education: A minority perspective. *Journal for the Education of the Gifted, 10,* 255-264.

Van Tassel-Baska, J. (1989). Appropriate curriculum for gifted learners. *Educational Leadership, 4,* 13-15.

Van Tassel-Baska J., Landau, M., and Olszewski, P. (1985) Toward developing an appropriate math/science curriculum for gifted learners. *Journal for Education of the Gifted, 7,* 257-272.

Varley, C.K. (1984) Attention deficit disorder (the hyperactivity syndrome): A review of selected issues. *Developmental and Behavioral Pediatrics,* p. 256.

Veenman, S. (1984) Perceived problems of beginning teachers. *Review of Educational Research, 4,* 143-178.

Vergason, G.A. and Anderegg, M.L. (1989) Save the baby! A response to "Integrating the children of the second system." *Phi Delta Kappan, 71,* 61-63.

Vergason, G.A. and Anderegg, M.L. (1993) Rich and Ross: A mixed message. *Exceptional Children, 59,* 475-476.

Verhaaran, P. and Connor, F.P. (1981) Physical disabilities. In J.M. Kauffman and D.P. Hallahan (Eds.) *Handbook of special education* (pp. 248-289). Englewood Cliffs, NJ: Prentice-Hall.

Vernon, M. (1969) *Multiply handicapped deaf children: Medical, educational and psychological implications.* Washington, DC: Council for Exceptional Children.

Vernon, P.E., Adamson, G., and Vernon, D.F. (1977) *The psychology and education of gifted children.* London: Methuen.

Vihman, M.M. (1986) Individual differences in babbling and early speech: Predicting to age three. In B. Lindbloom and R. Zitterstrom (Eds.) *Precursors of early speech* (pp. 95-112) Basingstoke, Hampshire: MacMillan.

Villaruel, B.A., Martin, C.A., and Dickson, W.P. (1985) Using a microcomputer to create social interactions among handicapped and nonhandicapped children in a mainstream preschool. Paper presented at AAMD, Denver.

Vincent, L.J. and Salisbury, C.L. (1988) Changing economic and social influences on family involvement. *Topics in Early Childhood Special Education, 8,* 48-59.

Vineland, the Training School at Vineland. *Annual Reports,* 1894, 1896.

Vitello, S.J. and Soskin, R.M. (1985) *Mental retardation: Its social and legal context.* Englewood Cliffs, NJ: Prentice-Hall.

Voignier, R.R. and Bridgewater, S.C. (1980) Allergies in young children. *Young Children, 35,* 67-70.

Volkmar, F.R., Sparrow, S.S., Gourdeau, D., Cichetti, D.V., Paul, R., and Cohen, D.J. (1987) Social deficits in autism: An operational approach using the Vineland Adaptive Behavior Scale. *Journal of the American Academy of Child and Adult Psychiatry, 26,* 156-161.

Vorhees, C.V. and Mollnow, E. (1987) Behavioral teratogenesis: Long-term influences from early exposure to environmental agents. In J.D. Osfosky (Ed.) *Handbook of infant development* (pp. 913-972). New York: Wiley.

Wadsworth, H.G. and Wadsworth, J.B. (1971) A problem of involvement with parents of mildly retarded children. *The Family Coordinator, 28,* 141-147.

Waggoner, K. and Wilgosh, L. (1990) Concerns of families of children with learning disabilities. *Journal of Learning Disabilities, 23,* 97-98, 113.

Wahler, R. and Dumas, J.E. (1986) "A chip off the old block": Some interpersonal characteristics of coercive children across generations. In P. Strain, M. Guralanick, and H.M. Walker (Eds.) *Children's social behavior: Development, assessment and modification* (pp. 49-91) Orlando, FL: Academic Press.

Walberg, H.J. (1991) Improving school science in advanced and developed countries. *Review of Educational Research, 61,* 25-69.

Walker, D.K., Singer, J.D. Palfrey, J.S., Orza, M., Wenger, M., and Butler, J.A. (1988) Who leaves and who stays in special education: A 2 year follow-up study. *Exceptional Children, 54,* 393-402.

Walker, H. (1983) *Walker Problem Behavior Identification Checklist — Revised.* Los Angeles, CA: Western Psychological Services.

Walker, H.M. and Bullis, M. (1991) Behavior disorders and the social context of regular class integration: A conceptual dilemma? In J.W. Lloyd, N.N. Singh, and A.C Repp (Eds) *The regular education initiative: Alternative perspectives on concepts, issues, and models* (pp. 75-93) Sycamore, IL: Sycamore.

Walker, H.M., and McConnell, S.R. (1988) *Walker-McConnell Scale of Social Competence and School Adjustment.* Austin, TX: PRO-ED.

Walker, H. and Rankin, R. (1983) Assessing the behavior expectations and demands of less restrictive settings. *School Psychology Review, 12,* 274-284.

Walker, H.M., Steeber, S., and O'Neill, R.F. (1990) Middle school behavior profiles of antisocial and at risk control boys: Descriptive and predictive outcomes. *Exceptionality, 1,* 61-77.

Walker, H.M., Shinn, M.R.D., O'Neill, R.E., and Ramsey, E., (1987) A longitudinal assessment of the antisocial behavior in boys: Rationale, methodology, and first year results. *Remedial and Special Education, 8,* 7-16.

Walker, L. (1979) Newfoundland dialect interference in fourth grade spelling. *Alberta Journal of Educational Research, 25,* 221-233.

Walker, L. (1990, June) Language use in a multicultural society. Paper presented at the Language Arts Researchers of Canada Symposium, Victoria.

Walker, M.B. (1992, 1993, Dec./Jan) Helping crack-affected children succeed. *Educational Leadership,* pp. 57-60.

Wallace, G. and McLoughlin, J.A. (1979). *Learning disabilities: Concepts and characteristics* (2nd. ed.) Columbus, OH: Merrill.

Wallace, I.F., Gravel, J.S., McCartan, C.M., and Ruben, R.J. (1988) Otitis media and language develoment at 1 year of age. *Journal of Speech and Hearing Disorders, 53,* 245-251.

Wancyzki, W. (1983) The Kindergarten Early Identification component of Bill 82. *Special Education in Canada, 57,* 25-32.

Wang, M.C. and Zollers, N.J. (1990) Adaptive instruction: An alternative service delivery approach. *Remedial and Special Education, 11,* 7-21.

Wang, M.C., Reynolds, M.C., and Walberg, H.J. (1987) Repairing the second system for students with special needs. Paper presented at the Conference on the Education of Children with Special Needs.

Wang, M.C., Reynolds, M.C., and Walberg, H.J. (1989). Who benefits from segregation and murky water? *Phi Delta Kappan, 71,* 64-67.

Warren, D. (1984) *Blindness and early child development.* New York: American Foundation for the Blind.

Warren, P. (1988) *Teachers and the law.* St. John's: Memorial University.

Warren, S.F., Alpert, C.L., and Kaiser, A.P. (1988) An optimal learning environment for infants and toddlers with severe handicaps. In E.L. Meyen, G.A. Vergason, and R.D. Whelan (eds.) *Effective instructional strategies for exceptional children* (pp. 139-156). Denver, CO: Love.

Warren, W. and Hasenstab, S. (1986) Self-concept of severely to profoundly hearing-impaired children. *Volta Review, 88,* 289-295.

Wasik, B.H., Bryant, D.M., and Lyons, C.M. (1990) *Home visiting: Procedures for helping families.* Newbury Park, CA: SAge,

Watson, M. J. and Nicholas, J.L. (1978) *A practical guide to the training of low-functioning deaf-blind children.* Connecticut: Oak Hill School.

Watt, D.L.E. and Roessing, H. (1993, Oct.) Dropout — Fall out — Push out: Results from a longitudinal study of the educational progress of high school ESL students. In A.F.K. Li (1994) Equity in assessment: From the perspective of new immigrant students. *Canadian Journal of School Psychology, 10,* 131-137.

Watters, B. (1980) Special education in the Northwest Territories. In M. Csapo and L. Goguen (Eds.) *Special education across Canada: Issues and concerns for the '80s.* Vancouver: Centre for Human Development and Research.

Webb, J.T., Meckstroth, E.A., and Tolan, S.S. (1982) *Guiding the gifted child: A practical source for parents and teachers.* Columbus, OH: Ohio Psychology Publishing.

Webb, T.P., Bundey, S.E., Thake, A.I., and Todd, J. (1986) Population incidence and segregation ratios in Martin-Bell syndrome. *American Journal of Medical Genetics, 23,* 573-580.

Wechsler, D. (1974) *Wechsler Intelligence Scale for Children-Revised.* New York: Psychological Corporation.

Wechsler, D. (1990) Wechsler Intelligence Scale for Children (3rd. ed.) New York: Psychological Corporation.

Weiner, B. (1979) A theory of motivation for some classroom experiences. *Journal of Educational Psychology, 71,* 3-25.

Weiner, J. (1987) Peer status of learning disabled children and adolescents: A review of the literature. *Learning Disabilities Research, 2,* 62-79.

Weiner, J., and Harris, P.J., (1989, May 17-20) Peer relations of learning disabled children: A reciprocity model. *Canadian Forum of the International Conference on Special Education,* University of British Columbia.

Weiner, J., Harris, P.J., and Shirer, C. (1990) Achievement and social behavioral correlates of peer status in LD children. *Learning Disability Quarterly, 13,* 114-127.

Weiner, L., and Septimus, A., (1991) Psychosocial consideration and support for the child and family. In P.A. Pizzo and C.M. Wilfert (Eds.) *Pediatric AIDS: The challenge of HIV infants, children and adolescents* (pp. 577-594). Baltimore, MD: Williams and Wilkins.

Weiss, G. and Hechtman, L. (1979). The hyperactive child syndrome. *Science, 205,* 1348-1353.

Weiss, G. and Hechtman, L.T. (1986) *Hyperactive children grown up.* New York: Guilford.

Weiss, J.B. and Weiss, J. (1981) Use of the talking calculator to improve mathematical skills. *Journal of Visual Impairment and Blindness, 75,* 61-63.

Weiss, P. and Gallagher, J.J. (1982) *Report on education of the gifted* (vol. 2) Chapel Hill, NC: Frank Porter Graham Child Development Center.

Weiss, P. and Gallagher, J.J. (1986). Project TARGET: A needs assessment approach to gifted education inservice. *Gifted Child Quarterly, 30,* 114-118.

Weissberg, R.P. and Allen, J.P. (1986) Promoting children's social skills and adaptive interpersonal behavior. In B.A. Edelstein and I. Michelson (Eds.) *Handbook of prevention.* New York: Plenum.

Weller, C. and Sipherd, C. (1982). The learning disabled woman: Implications for the workforce. *Journal of Rehabilitation, 48,* 67-70.

Wepman, J.M., Cruickshank, W.M, Deutsch, C.P., Morency, A., and Strother, C.R. (1975) Learning disabilities. In N. Hobbs (Ed.) *Issues in the classification of children,* vol. 1. San Francisco, CA: Jossey Bass.

Werner, E.E. (1986) The concept of risk from a developmental perspective. In R.B. Keogh (Ed.) *Advances in special education, vol. 5: Developmental problems in infancy and the preschool years.* Greenwich, CT: JAI Press.

Werry, J.S. (1979) The child psychoses. In H.C. Quay and J.S. Werry (Eds.), *Psychopathological disorders of childhood* (2nd. ed.). New York: Wiley.

Wesanko, E. (1990, June) Long term consequences of communication disorders. *Keeping in Touch,* p.2.

West, J.F. and Cannon, G. (1987) Essential collaborative consultation competencies for regular and special educators. *Journal of Learning Disabilities, 21,* 56-63.

Westby, C.E. (1992) Whole language and learners with mild handicaps. *Focus on Exceptional Children, 24,* 3-16.

Whalen, C.K. (1989) Attention deficit and hyperactivity disorders. In T.H. Ollendick and M. Hersen (Eds.) *Handbook of child psychopathology* (2nd. ed.) (pp. 131-169). New York: Wiley.

Whalen, C.K. and Henker, B. (1976) Psychostimulants and children: A review and analysis. *Psychological Bulletin, 83,* 1113-1130.

Whalen, C.K. and Henker, B. (1991) Social impact of stimulant treatment for hyperactive children. *Journal of Learning Disabilities, 24,* 231-241.

White, K.R., Bush, D., and Casto, G. (1986) Let the past be prologue: Learning from previous reviews of early intervention efficacy research. *Journal of Special Education, 19,* 417-428.

White, L. (1974) Organic factors and psychophysiology in childhood schizophrenia. *Psychological Bulletin, 81,* 238-255.

Whitlock, M.S. and Du Cette, J.P. (1989) Outstanding and average teachers of the gifted: A comparative study. *Gifted Child Quarterly, 33,* 15-21.

Whitman, B.C., Simpson, G.B., and Compton, W.C. (1986) Relationship of otitis media and language impairment in adolescents with Down syndrome. *Mental Retardation, 24,* 353-356.

Whitman, T.L. and Scibak, J.W. (1979) Behavior modification research with the severely and profoundly retarded. In N.R. Ellis (Ed.) *Handbook of mental deficiency: Psychological theory and research* (2nd. ed.) Hillsdale, NJ: Lawrence Erlbaum.

Whitmore, J.R. (1979) The etiology of underachievement in highly gifted young children. *Journal for the Education of the Gifted, 3,* 38-51.

Whitmore, J.R. (1980) *Giftedness, conflict and underachievement.* Boston, MA: Allyn and Bacon.

Whitmore, J.R. (1981) Gifted children with handicapping conditions: A new frontier. *Exceptional Children, 48*, 106-114.

Whitmore, J. (1985, November) Creating appropriate conditions for gifted students in the regular school program. Paper presented at the British Columbia Council for Exceptional Children conference.

Whitmore, J.R. (1988) Gifted children at risk for learning difficulties. *Teaching Exceptional Children, 20*, 10-14.

Whorf, B. (1956) *Language, thought and reality.* Cambridge, MA: MIT Press.

Whyte, L.A. (1984). Characteristics of learning disabilities persisting into adolescence. *Alberta Journal of Educational Research, 30*, 14-75.

Wicks-Nelson, R. and Israel, A.C. (1991) *Behavior disorders of childhood* (2nd. ed.) Englewood Cliffs, New Jersey: Prentice-Hall.

Widerstrom, A.H. and Goodwin, L.D. (1987) Effects of an infant stimulation program on the child and the family. *Exceptional Children, 11*, 143-153.

Widom, C.S. (1989) Does violence beget violence? A critical examination of the literature. *Psychological Bulletin, 106*, 3-28.

Wiggins, S.B. and Behrmann, M.M. (1988) Increasing independence through community learning. *Teaching Exceptional Children, 21*, 20-24.

Wight-Felske, A. and Hughson, E. (1986) Disabled persons in Canada: A review of the literature on independent living. In R. I. Brown and A. Wight-Felske (1987), Rehabilitation education: An integrated approach within the province of Alberta. *Canadian Journal of Special Education, 3*, 139-151.

Wiig, E. (1982) Language disabilities in the school-aged child. In G. Shames and E. Wiig (Eds.) *Human communication disorders.* Columbus, OH: Merrill.

Wiig, E.H. and Semel, E. (1976) *Language disabilities in children and adolescents.* Columbus, OH: Merrill.

Wikler, L., Wasow, M., and Hatfield, E. (1981) Chronic sorrow revisited: Parent vs professional depiction of the adjustment of parents of mentally retarded children. *American Journal of Orthopsychiatry, 51*, 63-70.

Wilcox, B. and Bellamy, G.T. (1982) *Design of high school programs for severely handicapped students.* Baltimore MD: Brookes.

Wiley, T.L. (1980) Hearing disorders and audiometry. In T.J. Hixon, L.D. Shribard, and J.H. Saxman. *Introduction to communication disorders.* Englewood Cliffs, NJ: Prentice-Hall.

Wilgosh, L. (1990, December) Issues in education and daily living for families of children with disabilities. *Alberta Journal of Educational Research, 36*, 299-309.

Will, M. (1986) Educating students with learning problems: A shared responsibility. *Exceptional Children, 52*, 405-411.

Williams, F. (1980) *Creativity Assessment Package.* Buffalo, NY: D.O.K. Publishers.

Williams, K. (1988) The learning-disabled gifted: An unmet challenge. *Gifted Child Quarterly, 11*, 17-18.

Willig, A.C. (1985) A meta-analysis of selected studies on the effectiveness of bilingual education. *Review of Educational Research, 55*, 269-307.

Willig, A.C., Swedo, J.J., and Ortiz, A.A. (1987). *Characteristics of teaching strategies which result in high task engagement for exceptional limited English proficient Hispanic students.* Austin, TX: University of Texas, Handicapped Minority Institute on Language Proficiency.

Willings, D. (1983) Issues in career choice for gifted students. *Teaching Exceptional Children, 15*, 266-233.

Wilson, J.Q. and Herrnstein, R.J. (1985) *Crime and human nature.* New York: Simon and Schuster.

Wilson, R.C., Mulligan, M., and Turner, R.M. (1985) Early childhood intervention in an urban setting. *Teaching Exceptional Children, 17*, 134-139.

Wilson, R.J. and Humphries, T. (1986) The impact of recent legislation on the role of Canadian school psychologists. *Canadian Journal of School Psychology, 2*, 1-6.

Wilson, R.J. and Rees, R. (1990) Ecology of assessment: Evaluation in educational settings. *Canadian Journal of Education, 15*, 215-228.

Willis, A.S. (1879) *Education of the blind: Speech in the House of Representatives in the United States, January, 17, 1879.* Washington, DC: American Printing House for the Blind.

Willis, D.H. (1976). *A study of the relationship between visual acuity, reading mode, and school systems for blind students.* Louisville, KY: American Printing House for the Blind.

Winitz, H. (1975) *From syllable to conversation.* Baltimore, MD: University Park Press.

Winton, P.J. and Turnbull, A.P. (1981) Parent involvement as viewed by parents of preschool handicapped children. *Topics in Early Childhood Special Education, 1*, 11-19.

Winzer, M.A. (1989) *Closing the gap: Special learners in regular classrooms.* Toronto: Copp Clark Pitman.

Winzer, M.A. (1993.;.) *The history of special education: From isolation to integration.* Washington, DC: Gallaudet University Press.

Winzer, M.A. (1995) *Educational psychology in Canadian classrooms* (2nd. ed.) Toronto: Allyn and Bacon.

Wolf, D., Bixby, J., and Gardiner, H. (1991) To use their minds well: Investigating newer forms of student assessment. In G. Grant (Ed.) *Review of educational research* (vol. 17) (pp. 31-74) Washington, DC: American Education Research Association.

Wolf, J.S. and Stephens, T.M. (1982) Gifted and talented. In N. Haring (Ed.) *Exceptional children and youth: An introduction to special education.* Columbus, OH: Merrill.

Wolfensburger, W. (1975) *The origin and nature of institutional models.* Syracuse, NY: Human Policy Press.

Wolman, B.B. (1978) *Children's fears.* New York: Grosset and Dunlap.

Wood, D. (1985). Multiculturalism across the curriculum. *Educational Journal, 4*, 10-23.

Wood, D. (1986) Multicultural education: Questions for the late 1980s. *Multicultural Education Journal, 4*, 10-23.

Wood, F.H. (1982) Living with the emotionally distrubed: Burden or opportunity? *B.C. Journal of Special Education, 6*, 1-10.

Wood, K.D. (1987, Oct.) Fostering cooperative learning in middle and secondary level classrooms. *Journal of Reading*, pp. 10-18.

World Health Organization (1980) *International classification of impairments, disabilities and handicaps.* Geneva: World Health Organization.

Yacobacci-Tam, P. (1987) Interacting with the culturally different family. *Volta Review, 89*, 47-57.

Yarter, B.H. (1980) Speech and language programs for the Down's population. *Seminars in Speech, Language and Hearing, 1*, 49-61.

Yates, J.R. and Ortiz, A.A. (1991) Profesional development needs of teachers who serve exceptional language minorities in today's schools. *Teacher Education and Special Education, 14*, 11-18.

Yewchuk, C. (1984) Gifted education in Alberta: Current developments. *Special Education in Canada, 58*, 142-143.

Ylvisaker, M.(1986). Language and communication disorders following pediatric injury. *Journal of Head Trauma Rehabilitation, 1*, 48-56.

Yoder, P., Kaiser, A., and Alpert, C. (1991) An exploratory study of interaction between language teaching methods and child characteristics. *Journal of Speech and Hearing Research, 34*, 155-167.

York, J. and Vandecook, T. (1990) Strategies for achieving an integrated education for middle school students with severe disabilities. *Remedial and Special Education, 11*, 6-16.

York, J. and Vandercook, T. (1991) Designing an integrated program for learners with severe disabilities. *Teaching Exceptional Children, 23*, 22-25.

York, J., Vandercook, T., MacDonald, C., Herse-Neff, C., and Caughey, E. (1992) Feedback about integrating middle-school students with severe disabilities in general education classes. *Exceptional Children, 58*, 244-259.

Young, J. (1979) Multiculturalism and its implications for youth. In K. McLeod (Ed.) *Multiculturalism, bilingualism and Canadian institutions.* Toronto: Guidance Centre, University of Toronto.

Young, P. (1980) *Asthma and allergies: An optimistic future.* Washington, DC: NIH publications, No. 80-388.

Youngblade, C.M. and Bibby. J. (1989) Child maltreatment, infant-parent attachment security, and dysfunctional peer relationships in toddler-hood. *Topics in Early Childhood Special Education, 9*, 1-16.

Ysseldyke, J.E. (1987) Classification of handicapped students. In M.C. Wang, M.C Reynolds, and H.J. Walberg (Eds.) *Handbook of special edcuation: Research and practice. vol. 1: Learner characteristics and adaptive education* (pp. 253-272). New York: Pergamon.

Ysseldyke J.E. and Algozzine, B. (1990) *Introduction to special education* (2nd. ed.) Boston, MA: Allyn and Bacon.

Ysseldyke, J.E. and Christenson, S.L. (1987) Evaluating students' instructional environments. *Remedial and Special Education, 8*, 17-24.

Ysseldyke, J.E., Algozzine, B., and Thurlow, M.L. (1992) *Critical issues in special eduction.* Boston, MA: Houghton and Mifflin.

Ysseldyke, J.E., Thurlow, J., Wesson, C., Algozzine, B., and Deno, S. (1983) Generalizations from five years of research on assessment and decision making: The University of Minnesota Institute. *Exceptional Education Quarterly, 4*, 75-93.

Yu, M. (1988, June) Ethnicity and education: Perspectives on Chinese youth. Paper presented at the Canadian Asian Studies Conference, University of Windsor.

Yule, W. and Rutter, M. (1976). Epidemiology and social implications of specific retardation. In R.M. Knight and D.J. Bakker (Eds.) *The neuropsychology of learning disorders.* Baltimore, MD: University Park Press.

Yura, M. (1987) Family subsystem functions and disabled children: Some conceptual issues. *Marriage and Family Review, 11*, 135-151.

Zappia, I.A. (1989) Identification of gifted Hispanic students: A multidimensional view. In C.J. Maker and S.W. Schiever (Eds.) Critical issues in gifted education (vol. 2) *Defensible programs for cultural and ethnic minorities* (pp. 19-26). Austin, TX: Pro-Ed.

Zaragoza, N., Vaughn, S., and McIntosh, R. (1991) Social skills intervention and children with behavioral problems: A review. *Behavioural Disorders, 16*, 260-275.

Zeitlin, S. and Williamson, G.G. (1986) Early intervention of infants and toddlers. *Teaching Exceptional Children, 19*, 57-59.

Zentall, S.S. (1983) Effects of psychotropic drugs on the behavior of pre-academic children: A review. *Topics in Early Childhood Special Education, 3*, 29-39.

Zentall, S.S. (1993) Research on the educational implications of attention deficit hyperactivity disorder. *Exceptional Children, 60*, 143-153.

Zentall, S.B., Smith, Y.N., Lee, Y.B., and Wieczarek, C. (1993) Mathematical outcomes of ADHD. *Journal of Learning Disabilities, 26*, 510-519.

Zetlin, A. and Hosseini, A. (1989) Six postschool case studies of mildly learning handicapped young adults. *Exceptional Children, 55*, 405-411.

Zetlin, A. and Murtaugh, M. (1988) Friendship patterns of mentally handicapped and nonhandicapped high school students. *American Journal on Mental Retardation, 92*, 447-454.

Zetlin, A. and Murtaugh, M. (1990) Whatever happened to those with borderline IQS? *American Journal on Mental Retardation, 94*, 463-469.

Zigler, E., Balla, D., and Hodapp, R. (1984) On the definition and classification of mental retardation. *American Journal of Mental Deficiency, 89*, 215-230.

Zigler, E., Hoddap, R.M., and Edison, M.R. (1990) From theory to practice in the care and education of mentally retarded individuals. *American Journal on Mental Retardation, 95*, 1-12.

Zigmond, N., Levine, E., and Laurie, T.E. (1985) Managing the mianstream: An analysis of teachers' attitudes and student performance in mainstream high school programs. *Journal of Learning Disabilities, 18*, 535-541.

Zigmond, N., Kerr, M.M., Brown, G.M., and Harris, A.L. (1984, April) School survival skills in secondary school age special education students. Paper presented at American Educational Research Association, New Orleans.

Zimbordo, P., Pilkonis, P., and Norwood, R. (1975) The social disease called shyness. *Psychology Today*, 69-72.

Zimmerman, I., Sheener, V., and Pond, R. (1979) *The Preschool Language Scale* (Revised ed.). Columbus, OH: Merrill.

Zimmerman, J., Rich, W., and Broder, P. (1978) *Some observations on the link between learning disabilities and juvenile delinquency.* Illinois: National Center for State Courts, Northwestern University.

Zimmerman, J., Rich, E.D., Keility, I., and Broden, P.K. (1981) Some observations on the link between learning disabilities and juvenile delinquency. *Journal of Criminal Justice, 9*, 1-17.

Zirpoli, T.J. (1990) Physical abuse: Are children with disabilities at greater risk? *Intervention in School and Clinic, 26*, 6-11.

Zirpoli, T., Snell, M., and Lloyd, B. (1987) Characteristics of persons with mental retardation who have been abused by caregivers. *The Journal of Special Education, 21*, 31-41.

Zuk, G.H. (1962) The cultural dilemma and spiritual crisis of the family with a handicapped child. *Exceptional Children, 28*, 405-408.

Subject Index

Author Index

Photo Credits

Canada Wide/Barry Gray: 51 (left)

Canadian Cystic Fibrosis Foundation: 20, 435, 452

C. Cox: 490, 498

T. Gartke: 158, 479

Dick Hemingway: 51 (right)

Paul J. Hoeffler: 210, 288

K. Hranyk: 584, 593

C. Mazurek: 146, 223, 242, 246, 321, 368

Ontario Ministry of Education: 69, 76, 233, 265, 276, 288, 339, 361, 513

T. Serdel: 134, 312

Sir William Osler High School: 364, 457, 528

B. Skeoch: 597

K. Stewart: 558

T. Wilson: 45, 160, 328

M. Winzer: 1, 89, 93, 97, 190, 389, 398, 420, 477, 570